HUMAN RESOURCE MANAGEMENT

SECOND EDITION

HUMAN RESOURCE MANAGEMENT SECOND EDITION

FUNCTIONS, APPLICATIONS, & SKILL DEVELOPMENT

ROBERT N. LUSSIER

Springfield College

JOHN R. HENDON

University of Arkansas at Little Rock

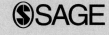

Los Angeles | London | New Delhi
Singapore | Washington DC | Boston

Los Angeles | London | New Delhi
Singapore | Washington DC | Boston

FOR INFORMATION:

SAGE Publications, Inc.
2455 Teller Road
Thousand Oaks, California 91320
E-mail: order@sagepub.com

SAGE Publications Ltd.
1 Oliver's Yard
55 City Road
London EC1Y 1SP
United Kingdom

SAGE Publications India Pvt. Ltd.
B 1/I 1 Mohan Cooperative Industrial Area
Mathura Road, New Delhi 110 044
India

SAGE Publications Asia-Pacific Pte. Ltd.
3 Church Street
#10-04 Samsung Hub
Singapore 049483

Copyright © 2016 by SAGE Publications, Inc.

Printed in Canada

Cataloging-in-publication data is available for this title from the Library of Congress.

ISBN 978-1-4522-9063-8

This book is printed on acid-free paper.

Acquisitions Editor: Maggie Stanley
Associate Editor: Abbie Rickard
Digital Content Editor: Katie Bierach
Editorial Assistant: Nicole Mangona
Production Editor: Laura Barrett
Typesetter: C&M Digitals (P) Ltd.
Proofreader: Scott Oney
Indexer: Teddy Diggs
Cover Designer: Scott Van Atta
Marketing Manager: Liz Thornton

15 16 17 18 19 10 9 8 7 6 5 4 3 2 1

··· Brief Contents

··· Detailed Contents

©iStockphoto.com/
GlobalStock

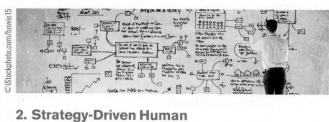
©iStockphoto.com/howie15

©iStockphoto.com/Mihej

©iStockphoto.com/AlexRathis

5. Recruiting Job Candidates 162

©iStockphoto.com/Squaredpixels

6. Selecting New Employees 192

PART III • DEVELOPING AND MANAGING 233

7. Training, Learning, Talent Management, and Development 234

8. Performance Management and Appraisal 274

©iStockphoto.com/
Neustockimages

©iStockphoto.com/-blige

PART IV • COMPENSATING   399

©iStockphoto.com/DNY59

©iStockphoto.com/
PeskyMonkey

©iStockphoto.com/KLH49

PART V • PROTECTING AND EXPANDING ORGANIZATIONAL REACH 525

©iStockphoto.com/Kickers

14. Workplace Safety, Health, and Security 526

©iStockphoto.com/
SelectStock

15. Organizational Ethics, Sustainability, and Social Responsibility 560

16. Global Issues for Human Resource Managers 590

©iStockphoto.com/Rawpixel

··· Preface

In his book *Power Tools,* John Nirenberg asks, "Why are so many well-intended students learning so much and yet able to apply so little in their personal and professional lives?" The world of business and human resource management (HRM) has changed, and so should how it is taught. Increasing numbers of students want more than lectures to gain an understanding of the concepts of HRM. They want their courses to be relevant and to apply what they learn and they want to develop skills they can use in their everyday life and at work. It's not enough to learn about HRM; they want to learn how to be HR managers. This is why we wrote the book. After reviewing and using a variety of HRM books for more than a decade, we didn't find any that (1) could be easily read and understood by students and (2) effectively taught students how to be HR managers. We wrote this text out of our desire to prepare students to be successful HR managers. As the subtitle states, this book not only presents the important HRM concepts and functions, but also takes students to the next levels by actually teaching them to apply the concepts through critical thinking and to develop HRM skills they can use in their personal and professional lives.

MARKET AND COURSE

This book is for undergraduate and graduate-level courses in human resource management (HRM) including personnel management. It is appropriate for a first course in an HRM major, as well as required and elective courses found in business schools. This textbook is also appropriate for HRM courses taught in other disciplines such as education and psychology, particularly Industrial Psychology and Organizational Psychology. The level of the text assumes no prior background in business or HRM. This book is an excellent choice for online and hybrid courses in HRM.

LEARNING BY DOING: A PRACTICAL APPROACH

I (Lussier) started writing management textbooks in 1988—prior to the calls by the Association to Advance Collegiate Schools of Business (AACSB) for skill development—to help professors teach their students how to apply concepts and develop management skills. Pfeffer and Sutton (*The Knowledge Doing Gap,* 2000) concluded that the most important insight from their research is that knowledge that is actually implemented is much more likely to be acquired from learning by doing, than from learning by reading, listening, or thinking. We designed this book to give students the opportunity to "learn by doing" with the following approaches:

- A practical **"how-to-manage"** approach which is strategy driven.
- The only HR text where every primary content area identified as *required* for undergraduate students listed in the Society of Human Resource Management **2013 Curriculum Guidebook** is specifically identified in the text where the material is covered (210 items). In addition, many of the *secondary* and *graduate students only* items are also identified as they occur in the text.
- Six types of high-quality **application materials** use the concepts to develop critical-thinking skills.

- Four types of high-quality **skill-builder exercises** help to actually develop HR management skills that can be utilized in students' professional and personal lives.
- A comprehensive **video** package reinforces HRM-related abilities and skills.
- An approach which meets the preferred learning styles of today's students.

A NEW GENERATION OF LEARNERS

Today's students, often called "Millennials," succeed when they are fully engaged in learning on multiple levels; traditional methods of teaching do not always meet their needs. Our text is flexible enough to accompany lecture-based teaching, and also offers a wide range of engaging activities which accommodate a variety of contemporary learning styles. Many of the specific learning preferences of today's students have been addressed in the book's overall approach, organization, and distinctive features:

- **Active Learning**

  A desire for **active learning** is addressed with a large variety of activities and skill-building tools.

- **Practical Approaches**

  A desire for **application and skills** in personal and professional realms is addressed by a variety of features throughout the text. **Immediate application and ongoing self-assessment** are found in the Work Application prompts and self-assessment tools. Organization tools such as **checklists, summaries, and "how to"** instructions are integrated throughout; for example, the marginal references to SHRM curriculum guidelines.

- **Accessible Content**

  Chunking of content into easily digested segments helps students to organize study time. **Visual learning** preferences are accommodated in colorful exhibits, models, and figures throughout the text, along with an ancillary package which includes visual learning options. **Internet learning** preferences are recognized in a robust web-based package which includes video and interactive features for students.

A THREE-PRONGED APPROACH

We have created a comprehensive textbook intended to develop the full range of HRM competencies. As the title of this book implies, we provide a balanced, three-pronged approach to the curriculum:

Concepts/Functions

The following features are provided to support the first step in the three-pronged approach.

HRM functions. Chapter 1 presents eight major HRM functions identified by SHRM with questions that need to be answered. The book is structured around the eight functions in five parts; see the table of contents for details. These functions are emphasized in order to show students the depth of knowledge that is required of a 21st century HR manager.

Pedagogical aids. Each chapter includes Learning Outcomes, Chapter Summary and Key Terms, and Review Questions. Marginal icons also indicate points at which

(1) International Human Resources and (2) Ethics, Sustainability and Social Responsibility are discussed in the text.

SHRM's Required Content, as well as many Secondary and Graduate-only HR Content Areas from the *SHRM Human Resource Curriculum: Guidebook and Templates for Undergraduate and Graduate Programs* (SHRM, 2013), are annotated for easy reference where they appear in each chapter of the text. A margin note identifies the Curriculum Guide topic being covered, and a reference number links to an appendix covering the entire SHRM Curriculum Guide. *Every primary Content Area and Subtopic* identified in the SHRM Curriculum Guidebook is at least introduced within the text, and most are covered in significant depth.

Applications

The following features are provided to support the second step in the three-pronged approach.

Opening Vignettes illustrate how a real-life Human Resources manager currently employed by the state of Arkansas works within the various HRM functions in her daily activities.

Organizational examples of HRM concepts and functions appear throughout the book.

Work Applications incorporate open-ended questions which require students to explain how the HRM concepts apply to their own work experience. Student experience can be present, past, summer, full-time, part-time employment, or volunteer work.

Applying the Concept features ask the student to determine the most appropriate HRM concept to be used in a specific short example.

Cases at the end of each chapter illustrate how specific organizations use the HRM functions. Critical thinking questions challenge the students to identify and apply the chapter concepts which are illustrated in each case. Several longer and more comprehensive cases are also available to the instructor on the Web site, either for testing material or to allow students to apply what they have learned over a significant part of the course.

Skill Development

The following features are provided to support the third step in the three-pronged approach.

Self-Assessments help students to gain personal knowledge of how they will complete the HRM functions in the real world. All information for completing and scoring is contained within the text.

Communication Skills at the end of each chapter include questions for class discussion, presentations, and/or written assignments to develop critical thinking communication skills; they are based on HR Content Areas.

Behavior Modeling showing step-by-step actions to follow when implementing HRM functions, such as how to conduct a job interview, performance appraisals, and coaching and disciplining, are presented throughout the text.

Skill Development Exercises develop skills that can be used in students' personal and professional lives. Many of the competitor exercises tend to be discussion-oriented exercises that don't actually develop a skill that can be used immediately on the job.

NEW TO THE SECOND EDITION

General Updates

- Two new chapters have been added: Chapter 15, Organizational Ethics, Sustainability, and Social Responsibility, and Chapter 16, Global Issues for Human Resource Managers. As a result, the Practitioner's Model has been updated to allow more in-depth discussion of ethics and globalization. The model now has a new 5th section.

- The chapters have been completely updated with nearly 80% new references in this edition to strengthen the text.

- All chapters in this 2nd edition have been updated according to the SHRM 2013 Curriculum Guidebook. The new guidebook has significantly increased the coverage of the topics of Ethics and Diversity and upgraded coverage in all "required" areas, and the chapters of this edition of HRM reflect those changes. As in the first edition, all required undergraduate guidelines are included in the text as well as many secondary and graduate guidelines.

- There are 13 new end of chapter cases and one new comprehensive case. The retained cases have been updated. All chapters now include two cases.

- There are changes to all of the Applying the Concept box questions and answers in this edition.

- Several examples using today's best companies are introduced in this new edition of the text.

Chapter 1

- The first edition Chapter 1 case has been completely revised in accordance with the latest government agency and federal court decisions.

- Chapter 1 has a new learning outcome 1-2 which increases the coverage of the four dependent variables around which 21st century HRM revolves.

- *Empathy* has been added as a new key term.

- A new section on HRM challenges has been added, with retaining and rewarding employees, the development of next generation leaders, and the use of corporate culture to attract employees at the top of the challenge list.

- The chapter also goes into more depth than in the first edition concerning employee engagement and what that engagement means to the organizational bottom-line.

- More detailed information on more of the various major HR associations has been added to this chapter.

- A second case has been added on managing HR at Zynga.

- Learning outcome 1-3 Chapter Summary now includes Appraisal and Promotion.

- Two new trends in HR have been added on creating an engaged workforce and the evidence of a potential permanent loss of middle-class jobs, to go along with the existing discussion of reverse discrimination.

Chapter 2

- Data Analytics has been added as a new key term, and Outsourcing and Sustainability have been removed.

- A new section on Data Analytics for HRM and desired outcomes has been added.

- The section on HRIS has been moved to earlier in the chapter.

- Two new trends and issues in HRM have been added on managing data for HRM decision-making and increased strategic use of social media for HRM planning.
- A second case has been added on strategy-driven HR management at Netflix.

Chapter 3

- Information on the ADA and the ADAAA Amendment has been included.
- The discussion on the EEOC has been expanded.
- Updated information on recent Affirmative Action rulings in federal courts has been added.
- A new trend in HRM has been added on federal agencies becoming more activist in pursuing discrimination claims.

Chapter 4

- An additional major option available for the job analysis process has been added: Subject matter expert panels.
- The mnemonic tool to help remember resource inputs has been updated to include Machines, added to Material, Manpower, and Money.
- There are now examples of Job analysis questionnaires included in this chapter as well.
- There is also more information about job specifications, as well as independent contractors.
- The discussion on Labor surplus as it pertains to early retirement has been expanded.
- Three new trends in HRM have been added, on O*Net as a job analysis tool, competency models in job analysis, and sustainability.
- A second case has been added on company culture at Honeywell.

Chapter 5

- Updated information on External Forces Acting on Recruiting Efforts, including the Affordable Care Act, has been added.
- There is a new section on social media recruiting.
- New issues in HRM have been added on talent wars and on-demand workforces.
- A second case has been added on recruiting and LinkedIn.

Chapter 6

- *Fitness for duty test* has been added as a new key term.
- There is now information about state laws as they pertain to job applications and preliminary screenings in this chapter.
- A new section on social media's role in job selection and web searches has been added as well.
- Exhibit 6-2 features an updated list of pre-employment inquiries.
- There is now more information on medical marijuana as it pertains to employee drug testing.
- A new discussion on Fitness-for-Duty testing as an alternative to drug testing has been added.

- There is a new section on behavior-based interview questions.
- A new trend in HRM has been added on perceived cultural fit and selection.
- A second case has been added on selecting new employees.

Chapter 7

- A greater emphasis on the need for job training and development has been incorporated into this chapter.
- Training design and delivery have been combined into a single section.
- There is a new section on measuring training success.
- New trends and issues in HRM have been added on the gamification of training and development, and social media for learning.
- A second case on Google and their Made with Code project has been added.

Chapter 8

- The chapter introduction has been revised.
- Information on the American National Standards Institute has been added.
- The section discussing the value of peer reviews has been expanded.
- There are new sections on frame-of-reference training and continuous appraisals.
- New information on Electronic Performance Monitoring (EPM) has been added as well.
- A new case on performance appraisal at Amazon has been added.

Chapter 9

- This chapter's title has been changed from Rights and Employee Development to Rights and Employee Management.
- A new learning object has been introduced: Briefly discuss the stages of the change process.
- New sections on data and device policies; coaching, counseling, and discipline; and leadership, management, and change have been added.
- A new issue in HRM has been added on Google Glass and other privacy issues.
- A second case on off-duty misconduct has been added to this chapter as well.

Chapter 10

- New research on job satisfaction has been incorporated into this chapter.
- There is new data on union membership and new information on union bargaining.
- A new trend in HRM has been added on non-union worker protection and the NLRB.
- A second case on constructive discharge and the reinstatement of strikers has been added to this chapter as well.

Chapter 11

- New research about compensation as it pertains to job satisfaction has been included in this chapter.
- New information on pay secrecy has been incorporated as well.
- There is a new discussion about Seattle's minimum wage hike.
- Exhibit 11-3 has been updated with a new list of FLSA exemptions.
- Exhibit 11-4 has been updated with new duties tests for general employee exemptions.
- A new trend in HRM on independent contractors has been added as well.
- A second case on compensation management at CVS has been added.

Chapter 12

- The section on recognition has been updated in this chapter.
- There is also new information on motivational incentives.
- A new issue for HRM has been added on the ethics of executive compensation.
- A second case on incentive pay at Barclays has been added as well.

Chapter 13

- The chapter-opening section on The Strategic Value of Benefits Programs has been updated for this edition.
- New data about the Patient Protection and Affordable Care Act has been added.
- There is a new section on the general provisions of ERISA.
- New trends and issues for HRM have been added on new information about domestic partnership and benefits, and a new section on the personalization of health care.
- A second case on employee benefits at SAS has been added as well.

Chapter 14

- New information about OSHA, including employer and employee rights and responsibilities under the Act, has been added.
- The Department of Labor posting requirements have been updated.
- There is a new section on social media for workplace safety and security.
- New trends and issues in HRM have been added on employee wellness and bullying in the workplace.
- The key term *Material Safety Data Sheets* is now *Safety Data Sheets*.
- A second case on workplace safety at Nike has been added to this chapter.

Chapter 15

A new chapter entitled Organizational Ethics, Sustainability, and Social Responsibility

Chapter 16

A new chapter entitled Global Issues for Human Resource Managers

ANCILLARIES

SAGE edge offers a robust online environment featuring an impressive array of tools and resources for review, study, and further exploration, keeping both instructors and students on the cutting edge of teaching and learning.

SAGE edge for Students provides a personalized approach to help students accomplish their coursework goals in an easy-to-use learning environment.

- Mobile-friendly **eFlashcards** strengthen understanding of key terms and concepts
- Mobile-friendly practice **quizzes** allow for independent assessment by students of their mastery of course material
- A customized online **action plan** includes tips and feedback on progress through the course and materials, which allows students to individualize their learning experience
- **Learning objectives** reinforce the most important material
- **Multimedia resources** facilitate further exploration of topics
- EXCLUSIVE! Access to full-text **SAGE journal articles** that have been carefully selected to support and expand on the concepts presented in each chapter

SAGE edge for Instructors supports teaching by making it easy to integrate quality content and create a rich learning environment for students.

- **Test banks** provide a diverse range of pre-written options as well as the opportunity to edit any question and/or insert personalized questions to effectively assess students' progress and understanding
- **Sample course syllabi** for semester and quarter courses provide suggested models for structuring one's course
- Editable, chapter-specific **PowerPoint® slides** offer complete flexibility for creating a multimedia presentation for the course
- **Chapter outlines** summarize key concepts by chapter to ease preparation for lectures and class discussions
- A **Course cartridge** provides easy LMS integration
- Cases from the book with answers to the questions assist in initiating class discussion

Access these resources online at edge.sagepub.com/lussierhrm2e

··· Acknowledgments

We would like to thank our team at SAGE Publications, which helped bring this book to fruition. Our first executive editor, Patricia Quinlin, who brought us to SAGE, and editor Lisa Cuevas Shaw have shepherded the development of *Human Resource Management* from its inception. Our current editor, Maggie Stanley, as well as Abbie Rickard, Nicole Mangona, and Katie Guarino, provided additional assistance and support. We are grateful to Scott Van Atta for a cover and interior design that sets this book apart. During the production process, Laura Barrett provided professionalism and valuable support. Liz Thornton lent her marketing experience and skills to promoting the book.

We would like to acknowledge our colleagues at SHRM who provided organizational resources to ensure that *Human Resource Management*—in particular the 2013 *SHRM Human Resource Curriculum*—is *the* textbook of choice for future HR practitioners. We would also like to recognize Cindy Wright of the Department of Human Services for Arkansas for her vital contribution of chapter opening vignettes, which feature her personal insight and experience as an HR professional. Excellent case material has been provided by Can Guler, Komal Thakker, and Herbert Sherman of the Department of Management Sciences, School of Business Brooklyn Campus, Long Island University, and by Robert Wayland, University of Arkansas at Little Rock.

Thanks to the following reviewers who participated throughout all stages of the book's development:

Carl Blencke, *University of Central Florida*

Ghadir Ishqaidef, *University of Wisconsin–Green Bay*

Kern Peng, *Santa Clara University*

Elizabeth Fair, *Georgia College & State University*

Eleanore Webster, *Santa Rosa Junior College*

Harry Whitney, *University of the Incarnate Word*

Diane Galbraith, *Slippery Rock University*

Charles Gorman, *Virginia Polytechnic Institution and State University*

Herve Queneau, *Brooklyn College-CUNY*

Jerry Sellentin, *University of Nebraska*

Susie Cox, *McNeese State University*

Suzanne Kitchen, *West Virginia University*

Jeananne Nicholls, *Slippery Rock University*

Amy Wojciechowski, *West Shore Community College*

Jonathon Halbesleben, *University of Alabama*

Kim Hester, *Arkansas State University*

Kay J. Bunch, *Georgia State University*

Donna Vassallo, *Atlantic Cape Community College*

Joann Williams, *Judson College*

Dana Cosby, *University of Louisville*

Kyra Sutton, *Miami University–Oxford*

Sheri Grotrian-Ryan, *Peru State College*

Marie Halvorsen-Ganepola, *University of Florida*

Kay Braguglia, *Hampton University*

Tracy Porter, *Cleveland State University*

··· About the Authors

Robert N. Lussier is a professor of management at Springfield College. Through teaching management courses for more than 25 years, he has developed innovative and widely adopted methods for applying concepts and developing skills that can be used both personally and professionally. A prolific writer, Dr. Lussier has more than 400 publications to his credit, including *Management* 6e (SAGE), *Human Relations* 9e (McGraw-Hill), and *Leadership* 6e (South Western/Cengage) and has published in top tier academic journals. He holds a bachelor of science in business administration from Salem State College, master's degrees in business and education from Suffolk University, and a doctorate in management from the University of New Haven. He served as founding director of Israel Programs and has taught courses in Israel.

John R. Hendon is a seven-time entrepreneur and former director of operations for a $60 million company. He brought his experience and interests to the classroom full time in 1994 and has been a Management faculty member at the University of Arkansas at Little Rock for over 17 years. An active member of the Society for Human Resource Management, he teaches in the areas of Human Resources Management, Strategy, and Organizational Management, and researches in a number of areas in the Management field, specializing in Entrepreneurial research. John is also currently the President of "The VMP Group," an Arkansas-based business consulting firm. John's company consults with a variety of businesses on human resources, family business, strategic planning, organizational design, and leadership. He has provided professional assistance in the start-up and operation of dozens of Arkansas and California-based businesses and non-profits, government agencies, and utilities. John holds an MBA degree from San Diego State University and a B.S. in Education from the University of Central Arkansas.

Part I

21st Century Human Resource Management Strategic Planning and Legal Issues

1 The New Human Resource Management Process

2 Strategy-Driven Human Resource Management

3 The Legal Environment and Diversity Management

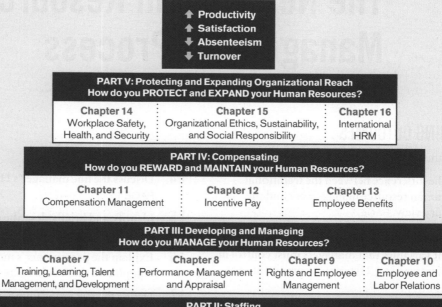

PRACTITIONER'S MODEL

⬆ Productivity
⬆ Satisfaction
⬇ Absenteeism
⬇ Turnover

PART V: Protecting and Expanding Organizational Reach
How do you PROTECT and EXPAND your Human Resources?

Chapter 14	Chapter 15	Chapter 16
Workplace Safety, Health, and Security	Organizational Ethics, Sustainability, and Social Responsibility	International HRM

PART IV: Compensating
How do you REWARD and MAINTAIN your Human Resources?

Chapter 11	Chapter 12	Chapter 13
Compensation Management	Incentive Pay	Employee Benefits

PART III: Developing and Managing
How do you MANAGE your Human Resources?

Chapter 7	Chapter 8	Chapter 9	Chapter 10
Training, Learning, Talent Management, and Development	Performance Management and Appraisal	Rights and Employee Management	Employee and Labor Relations

PART II: Staffing
What HRM Functions do you NEED for sustainability?

Chapter 4	Chapter 5	Chapter 6
Matching Employees and Jobs: Job Analysis and Design	Recruiting Job Candidates	Selecting New Employees

PART I: 21st Century Human Resource Management Strategic Planning and Legal Issues
What HRM issues are CRITICAL to your organization's long-term sustainability?

Chapter 1	Chapter 2	Chapter 3
The New Human Resource Management Process	Strategy-Driven Human Resource Management	The Legal Environment and Diversity Management

1

The New Human Resource Management Process

••• LEARNING OUTCOMES

After studying this chapter, you should be able to do the following:

1-1 Identify the difference between the traditional view of human resource management and the 21st century view. PAGE 7

1-2 Identify and briefly describe the four critical dependent variables that managers must control in order to compete in a 21st century organization. PAGE 10

1-3 Describe the major HRM skill sets. PAGE 14

1-4 Discuss the line manager's HRM responsibilities. PAGE 17

1-5 Identify and briefly describe the major HRM discipline areas. PAGE 18

1-6 Explain the practitioner's model for HRM and how it applies to this book. PAGE 26

1-7 Define the key terms found in the chapter margins and listed following the Chapter Summary. PAGE 33

Practitioner's Perspective

Cindy reflected on the current state of the HR field: Choice and change—two things you can rely on today! No longer merely concerned with hiring, firing, and record keeping, the average human resources department (HR) increasingly partners with the strategic planners in the executive suite, thanks to HR-based education and certifications. HR certification is available through HRCI with PHR, SPHR, and GPHR designations, and SHRM also offers its own program of certification with SHRM-CP and SHRM-SCP.

My professional progress began with membership in HR organizations. First, I became a SHRM student member, which provided access to SHRM's website—which was in turn valuable for research while I was a student. I still use it frequently. Next, my involvement spread to the local HR association. The chapter meetings provided excellent opportunities for education through the monthly programs, as well as for networking and swapping "best practices" with my colleagues.

SHRM HR CONTENT

See Appendix: *SHRM 2013 Curriculum Guidebook* for the complete list

A. Employee and Labor Relations (required)

   4. Employee engagement

   5. Employee involvement

   6. Employee retention

  20. Attendance

B. Employment Law (required)

  21. Professional liability

C. Ethics (required)

   8. Codes of ethics

D. HR's Role in Organizations (required)

   1. Generally . . . discuss HR's role with regard to each of the individual HR disciplines

F. Managing a Diverse Workforce (required)

   8. Reverse discrimination

J. Strategic HR (required)

   5. Sustainability/corporate social responsibility

   6. Internal consulting (required—graduate students only)

   9. Ethics (integrated)

  11. Organizational effectiveness

O. Globalization (required—graduate students only)

   7. Offshoring/outsourcing

   8. Global labor markets

Q. Organizational Development (required—graduate students only)

   5. Improving organizational effectiveness

   6. Knowledge management

   9. Ongoing performance and productivity initiatives

  10. Organizational effectiveness

My involvement inspired me to become certified as a professional. But beyond that, I have found that those who invest in certification tend to become more involved in their profession and, by extension, more successful.

I invite you to join me as we explore the field of human resource management (HRM). Chapter 1 gives an overview of HRM as a profession.

● ● ●

©Cindy Wright

Cindy Wright, PHR, came late to the Human Resources profession, and perhaps that explains some of her passion for the field. Wright graduated summa cum laude with a Business Administration degree, HR emphasis. She was recognized as "Outstanding Graduate" by the Human Resources Management department. After employment as a benefits administrator for seven thousand telecommunication's retirees, then as an HR Generalist for a gas well drilling company of 500 employees, Wright is now working in personnel management for the Department of Human Services in the Division of Behavior Health Services. Besides membership in the profession's national organization—the Society for Human Resource Management (SHRM), Wright has been active in the local affiliated chapter—the Central Arkansas Human Resources Association (CAHRA). Wright served as Vice President of Administration for the chapter's Board as well as Chair of the College Relation Committee. She was recognized by her peers with the "Rising Star" award for her work in creating a student chapter membership and was involved in the initial efforts to create satellite CAHRA chapters. Wright's mission is to provide assistance to others interested in entering into and advancing within the Human Resources profession.

● ● ● CHAPTER OUTLINE

Why Study Human Resource Management (HRM)?

HRM Past and Present

Past View of HRM

Present View of HRM

21st Century HRM

New HRM Challenges

Critical Dependent Variables

The HRM Strategic View

Technology and Knowledge

Labor Demographics

Productivity and Competitiveness Through HRM

HRM Skills

Technical Skills

Human Relations Skills

Conceptual and Design Skills

Business Skills

Line Managers' HRM Responsibilities

Line Versus Staff Management

Major HR Responsibilities of Line Management

HR Managers' Responsibilities: Disciplines Within HRM

The Legal Environment: EEO and Diversity Management

Staffing

Training and Development

Employee Relations

Labor and Industrial Relations

Compensation and Benefits

Safety and Security

Ethics and Sustainability

HRM Careers

Society for Human Resource Management (SHRM)

Other HR Organizations

Professional Liability

How to Find More Information

Practitioner's Model for HRM

The Model

Sections of the Model

Trends and Issues in HRM

Creating an Engaged Workforce

A New Normal for Individuals With Moderate Skills Doing Routine Work

Ethical Issues: Reverse Discrimination

WHY STUDY HUMAN RESOURCE MANAGEMENT (HRM)?

It's natural to think, "What can I get from this book?" or "What's in it for me?" These are important questions,[1] and the answers to them should be based on evidence.[2] Success in our professional and personal lives is about creating relationships,[3] and students generally understand the importance of relationships.[4] The better you can work with people, the more successful you will be in your personal and professional lives—whether as an employee, a line manager, or a human resource manager. And that's what this book is all about.

There is strong evidence that today's students want courses to have practical relevance.[5] Organizations also want their new managers to have the ability to apply knowledge.[6] The role of modern managers also continues to change, requiring today's organizational leaders to deal with increasingly dynamic and complex environments.[7] This brings us to the focus of this book; we designed it to be the most relevant "how to" book ever written on managing others in organizations. As indicated by the subtitle, *Functions, Applications, and Skill Development*, this book uses a three-pronged approach, with these objectives:

- To teach you the important functions and concepts of HRM
- To develop your ability to apply HRM functions and concepts through critical thinking
- To develop your HRM skills in your personal and professional lives
- To offers some unique features to further each of these three objectives, as summarized in Exhibit 1-1

Human resource issues are emerging as some of the most prominent concerns for business owners and managers.[8] You've probably heard buzzwords floating around about managers—and particularly human resource managers—needing to be more strategic, business focused, customer focused, and generally more in tune with the overall operational success of the organization.[9] So what is happening in today's business environment that might cause human resource managers to rethink their way of doing business? A key item that is causing this process of rethinking

EXHIBIT 1-1   FEATURES OF THIS BOOK'S THREE-PRONGED APPROACH

Features That Present HRM Functions and Important Concepts	Features to Apply the HRM Functions and Concepts That You Learn	Features That Foster Skill Development
• Learning Outcome statements	• Opening thoughts	• Self-Assessments
• Key terms	• Organizational examples	• Communication Skills Questions
• Step-by-step behavior models	• Work Applications	• Skill Builder Exercises
• Chapter summaries with glossaries	• Applying the Concepts	
• Review questions	• Cases	
	• Videos	

WORK
APPLICATION 1-1

How can this course help you in your personal and professional lives? What are your goals, or what do you want to get out of this course?

SHRM

SHRM Guide boxes (tied to Appendix) throughout the text will show you what SHRM says a college curriculum should teach in an HRM major.

SHRM

A:5
Employee Involvement

SHRM

A:4
Employee Engagement

Human resources (HR) The people within an organization

Employee engagement A combination of job satisfaction, ability, and a willingness to perform for the organization at a high level and over an extended period of time

management is the fact that there is much greater competition within most industries today compared to 20 or 30 years ago. That creates an absolute requirement to be more adaptable and productive as an organization.[10] As a result, human resource managers as well as operational managers have been forced to think in more strategic terms about how their organization can win against their competitors by utilizing their human resources.[11]

One simple fact is that, in the 21st century organization, **human resources (HR)**—*the people within an organization*—are one of the primary means of creating a competitive advantage for the organization, because management of human resources affects company performance.[12] This is because most organizations of comparable size and scope within the same industry generally have access to the same material and facilities-based resources that any other organization within the industry may have. This being the case, it's very difficult to create a competitive advantage based on material, facility, or other tangible or economic resources. What this frequently leaves is people as the organization's most valuable asset.[13] If the organization can manage its human resources more successfully than its competitors do, if it can get its employees involved in working toward the day-to-day success of the organization, and if it can get them to stay with the organization, then it has a much greater chance of being successful—with the term *successful* defined in this case as being more productive and more profitable than the competition.[14] Managers are responsible for getting the job done through employees,[15] so the organization's human resources are nearly always its most valuable resource. If we can get our employees fully engaged, we can make better decisions, increase employee trust and loyalty, and improve productivity.[16] (As you can see, there are SHRM Guide boxes next to this section. We will explain them in the seventh section of this chapter, "Practitioners' Model for HRM.")

While employee satisfaction (which we will talk about at length later) can be an important aspect of employee engagement, the overall concept of **employee engagement** is much larger. It is *a combination of job satisfaction, ability, and a willingness to perform for the organization at a high level and over an extended period of time.* **Google** is an example of an organization that is taking the concept of employee engagement very seriously. Google's "Project Oxygen" is one attempt to analyze what makes a better boss and use that information to train managers to be more consistent and interactive.[17] This training is designed to create greater employee satisfaction and engagement, for very practical reasons. According to *HR Magazine*, companies that fall into "the top 10% on employee engagement beat their competition by 72% in earnings per share during 2007–08."[18] A 2009 study showed that companies with high levels of satisfaction and engagement outperformed those with less engaged employees in return on investment (ROI), operating income, growth rate, and long-term company valuation.[19]

In this text, we define *engaged employees* as those who understand what they need to do to add value to the organization and are satisfied enough with the organization and their roles within it to be willing to do whatever is necessary to see to it that the organization succeeds. This book will teach you how to operate successfully within your organizations and compete productively in a 21st century organization—as an employee, HR manager, or any other type of manager—to get your employees engaged and get the results necessary to succeed against tough competitors in the new century.[20] We will focus on HR management, but the principles within this text apply to any form of management. The bottom line is that if you learn these skills and apply them successfully in your role as any type of manager, you will get your employees engaged and improve productivity. That is what will get you noticed by senior management and allow you to move up the organizational ladder. So let's get started!

HRM PAST AND PRESENT

The management of the organization's human resources has not been a static process. Let's look now at how HRM has changed over the past 40 years, taking us from the traditional view of HRM to the 21st century view.

LO 1-1

Identify the difference between the traditional view of human resource management and the 21st century view.

Past View of HRM

Back in the dark ages, around the mid-1970s—when there weren't even any computers available to most managers!—the human resource manager (we usually called them personnel managers then) was sometimes selected for the job because that person had limited skills as an operational manager. The HR manager might have less experience or be considered to be "a people person" rather than a "tough boss." In other words, this individual wasn't considered as capable of managing what were considered to be line jobs in *real* operations, so we put them in HR. This was because HRM was considered to be a bit easier than other management jobs. HR managers were only expected to be paper pushers who could keep all of the personnel files straight. They maintained organizational records on the people who worked for the company, but they had very little to do with the management of the organization's business processes. Since in most cases, all they had to do was manage paper (not people), we frequently put those with more limited skills in the personnel job.

In this environment, most HR departments provided limited services to the organization—keeping track of job applicants, maintaining employee paperwork, and filing annual performance evaluations. The line managers were the ones responsible for directly managing the people within the organization.

COST CENTERS. In these types of organizations, the human resources department was considered to be a cost center for the organization. A **cost center** *is a division or department that brings in no revenue or profit for the organization—running this function only costs the organization money.* As you can easily see, we don't want many (or any) cost centers in an organization if we can help it. We need revenue centers instead.

REVENUE CENTERS. **Revenue centers** *are divisions or departments that generate monetary returns for the organization.* Where cost centers eat up available funds, revenue centers provide funds for the organization to operate in the future. So, what's a good HR manager to do? HRM departments are not able to generate revenue *directly* because of their tasking within the organization, but they can generate significant revenue and profit in an indirect fashion.

Present View of HRM

The old workplace in which managers simply told employees what to do is gone. You will most likely work in a team and share in decision making and other management tasks. Today, people want to be involved in management,[21] and organizations expect employees to work in teams and participate in managing the firm.[22] Modern organizations also expect significantly greater productivity than occurred in their historical counterparts.

PRODUCTIVITY CENTERS. Welcome to the 21st century and the productivity center. A **productivity center** *is a revenue center that enhances the profitability of the organization through enhancing the productivity of the people within the organization.* So,

Cost center A division or department that brings in no revenue or profit for the organization—running this function only costs the organization money

Revenue centers Divisions or departments that generate monetary returns for the organization

Productivity center A revenue center that enhances the profitability of the organization through enhancing the productivity of the people within the organization

SHRM

Q:9
Ongoing Performance and
Productivity

why does a modern organization worry so much about HRM? Today's HR managers are no longer running an organizational cost center. Their function, along with all other managers within the organization, is to improve organizational revenues and profits—to be a profit center. But how does HR create revenue and profits for the organization? They do it by enhancing the productivity of the people within the organization—by being a productivity center. **Productivity** *is the amount of output that an organization gets per unit of input, with human input usually expressed in terms of units of time.* We must be more competitive in today's business environment if we are to survive for the long term. As managers of any type, we must do things that will improve the productivity of the people who work for us and our organization, so we create productivity centers.

But how can we become more productive? Productivity is the end result of two components that managers work to create and improve within the organization:

- **Effectiveness**—*a function of getting the job done whenever and however it must be done.* It answers the question, "Did we do the right things?"
- **Efficiency**—*a function of how many organizational resources we used in getting the job done.* It answers the question, "Did we do things right?"

Both of these are important, but most of the time, we are focused on efficiency. Our people allow us to be more efficient as an organization *if* they are used in the correct manner. This course is about how to make our people more efficient.

Companies around the world are taking this need for efficiency very seriously, and a few examples will quickly show how seriously. Teresa Taylor of **Qwest Communications International** (now **CenturyLink**), Lisa Brummel of **Microsoft**, and Leslie Locke of **Athenahealth** were all line managers with significant experience, but *none of them had senior HRM experience* when their organizations asked them to become HR leaders. Each of the companies was concerned about employee engagement and productivity, and especially about improving efficiency in their respective organizations,[23] so the companies put some of their best managers in the HRM job. In addition to improving efficiency, some fairly new research has shown that among Fortune 500 firms, having a senior HR manager in the "C-suite"—meaning having a chief of human resources operations (CHRO) in addition to having a chief operations officer (COO), a chief finance officer (CFO), etc.—increased profitability by 105% over peer companies that did not have a CHRO![24]

SHRM

Q:5, 10, J:11
Improving Organizational
Effectiveness; Organizational
Effectiveness

Recall that efficiency is a function of how many organizational resources we use up in order to get the job done. It doesn't matter what kind of resources we are talking about. We burn up material, monetary, and facility resources doing our jobs. But do we burn up *human* resources? Well, not literally, though we can burn them out and thus make them useless if we subject them to intolerable working conditions. But we do burn up their time. This is the value that we have in our people—their time. We physically use up monetary resources, facility resources, and material resources, but we use up the time available from our people.

HR management deals primarily with improving the efficiency of the people within our organization. If our people are inefficient, it can literally kill our organization. Our organization will fail if our people are inefficient over long periods of time. If we don't use our people efficiently, we're ultimately going to be forced out of business by somebody who is better at using those resources than we are. So the primary reason we're worried about HR management within an organization is to improve the efficiency of our human beings.

So how do we make our people more efficient? Well, the problem is that we can't really *directly* affect the performance of individuals within the organization. We can't force employees to act in a certain way all of the time within the organization, and while we have the ability to punish them when they don't do what

Productivity The amount of output that an organization gets per unit of input, with human input usually expressed in terms of units of time

Effectiveness A function of getting the job done whenever and however it must be done

Efficiency A function of how many organizational resources we used in getting the job done

we need them to do, we don't have the ability to directly control all of their actions. So as managers for the organization, we have to do things that will have an indirect effect on our people's productivity—their efficiency and effectiveness. And we do have certain things within our control as managers that can cause our people to do things that we need them to do.

21ST CENTURY HRM

Now let's look at some of the issues facing today's HR managers, including HRM challenges, the variables that we briefly mentioned above, the strategic view, and some other factors that help us affect productivity and competitiveness through HRM.

Today's technology improves the effectiveness and efficiency of HR managers, leading to higher levels of productivity throughout the organization.

New HRM Challenges

What types of issues are today's HR managers concerned with? A recent SHRM survey of HR professionals asked what challenges they think will be most significant over the next 10 years. Here is a brief review of what they said.[25]

The three biggest challenges:

1. Retaining and rewarding the best employees

2. Developing the next generation of corporate leaders

3. Creating a corporate culture that attracts the best employees

The HR competencies and subcompetencies that will be the most critical:

1. Business acumen

    a. HR metrics/analytics/business indicators

    b. Knowledge of business operations and logistics

    c. Strategic agility

2. Organizational leadership and navigation

3. Relationship management

4. Communication

Reviewing these challenges, HRM has been reasonably good at identifying and meeting some of them, while others have gone without significant attention to date in most companies. We have pursued better selection and retention strategies for a number of years, and we have recently become much better at identifying future leaders and managing organizational relationships, culture, and structure.

Where we have not done as well—at least in most organizations to this point—is in business acumen, especially in quantitative areas dealing with metrics and data analytics. This is an area that will explode in the next few years in HR departments all over the world. The ability to analyze large data sets will allow HRMs to work toward overcoming another of their challenges—creating strategic agility. We will introduce you to some of the basic HR metrics as we go through this text so that

WORK
APPLICATION 1-2

Recall your most recent job. Did you work in a traditional cost center, a revenue center, or a productivity center? Briefly describe the firm and department and what made it a cost, revenue, or productivity center.

you have a working understanding of how they might be used in each functional area of HRM.

LO 1-2

Identify and briefly describe the four critical dependent variables that managers must control in order to compete in a 21st century organization.

Critical Dependent Variables

Before we go further, let's look at some of the things that managers tell us they *must* control to compete in today's business environment but that they can't *directly* manipulate. These are called *dependent variables* because they can only be affected through indirect means. We have to control some other variable—called an *independent variable* because we can independently control it—to affect these items in any meaningful way.

Every time that we survey managers in any industry or any department about managing others, they bring up the following issues as being among the most important and most difficult things that they deal with:[26]

1. *Productivity*—defined above
2. *Job satisfaction*—a feeling of well-being and acceptance of our place in the organization
3. *Turnover*—permanent loss of workers from the organization. When people quit, it is considered voluntary turnover, while when people are fired, it is involuntary turnover.
4. *Absenteeism*—temporary absence of employees from the workplace

Note that all of these issues deal with people: not computers, not buildings, not finances—people! Also, managers have no *direct* control over these things. They only affect these items through indirect actions. In other words, we can't *force* employees to come to work and thus avoid absenteeism, nor can we force employees to be happy with their work. We have to create conditions in which employees are willing to or even want to come to work and in which they can enjoy the job. We can and should do this through employment practices that the employee perceives as fair and reasonable, such as providing acceptable pay for the tasks performed by the employee.

We have already introduced you to productivity, but what about the other three items? Why do we care about job satisfaction, turnover, and absenteeism? Let's take a moment for a more detailed look at each of them.

Job satisfaction, as noted above, *is the feeling of well-being that we experience in our jobs—it's basically whether or not we like what we do and the immediate environment surrounding us and our jobs*, or "the extent to which people like (satisfaction) or dislike (dissatisfaction) their jobs."[27] Why do we as managers worry about our employees' job satisfaction? Well, there is a wealth of research that shows that if our employees are highly dissatisfied with their jobs, they will be far more likely to voluntarily leave and create turnover.[28] They will typically also have lower than average productivity. Is the opposite true? If we have highly satisfied employees, will they necessarily have higher productivity? Not necessarily, although they could.[29] But let's leave that discussion for later. For right now, just understand that low job satisfaction typically leads to lower productivity, so we want to maintain reasonably high job satisfaction.

Turnover *is the permanent loss of workers from the organization.* Does turnover cost the organization? Absolutely![30] There is strong and "growing recognition that collective turnover can have important consequences for organizational productivity, performance, and—potentially—competitive advantage."[31] What specific issues are associated with turnover? Well, first is the cost of the paperwork associated with the departing employees, and if they left involuntarily, we may have increases in our

SHRM

A:6
Employee Retention

Job satisfaction The feeling of well-being that we experience in our jobs—basically whether or not we like what we do and the immediate environment surrounding us and our jobs

Turnover The permanent loss of workers from the organization

unemployment insurance payments and might even have some potential security issues. Next, there is finding someone else to do the job, which incurs job analysis costs, recruiting costs, and selection costs (we will talk about all of these later). Once we hire someone new, we have orientation and other training costs, costs associated with getting the new worker up to speed on their job (something we call a *learning curve*), and the costs associated with them just not knowing our way of doing business (every company has a unique culture, and not knowing how to act within that culture can cause problems). So again, because we have many costs associated with turnover in the organization, we want to minimize turnover.

How about absenteeism? **Absenteeism** *is the failure of an employee to report to the workplace as scheduled.* So what's the problem with that? If employees don't come to work, we don't have to pay them, right? Well, some of them anyway—but not when we give paid sick leave or when they are "exempt" employees (we will talk about exemptions in Chapter 11). So why do managers worry about absenteeism? Well, for one thing, it *does* cost the organization money[32]—not necessarily directly, but indirectly. On an annual basis, absenteeism costs in the United States went from an estimated $30 billion in 1984[33] to anywhere from $100 to $150 billion per year in 2011.[34,35] And even if we don't have to pay employees when they are absent from work, we still have to maintain benefits like health insurance. We also likely lose productivity in other employees because of having to do the missing employee's work and not being able to do their normal job; that costs us money, too. In addition, if some of our workers are frequently absent, it causes lower job satisfaction in others who have to continually "take up the slack" for their absent coworker. And there are other issues as well. So, we can quickly see that even though we don't have to pay some of our workers if they don't come to work, absenteeism still costs the organization money.

Note that these four issues are interrelated. Absenteeism is costly, is often due to a lack of job satisfaction, and leads to lower productivity.[36] People tend to leave their jobs (turnover) when they don't have job satisfaction, and while they are being replaced and sometimes after, productivity goes down.[37] Seeing that job satisfaction can affect absenteeism, turnover, and productivity, we will discuss job satisfaction in some more detail in Chapter 10.

So now we can see the importance of these four big issues that managers can't directly control. The bottom line is this:

As managers, we always need to be doing things that will improve productivity and job satisfaction and that will reduce absenteeism and turnover. These items are critical. Everything in HRM revolves around these four things.

The HRM Strategic View

Strategy and strategic planning deal with a process of looking at our organization and environment—both today and in the expected future—and determining what we as an organization want to do to meet the requirements of that expected future. We work to predict what this future state will look like and then plan for that eventuality.

Only in the last 30 to 40 years has HR management really gone from reactive to proactive in nature. Instead of waiting for someone to quit and then going out and finding a replacement, HR managers are now actively seeking out talent for their organizations.[38] Good HR managers are constantly looking at processes within the organization and, if there is something going wrong, figuring out how to assist the line management team in fixing the problem—whether it is a training problem, a motivation problem, or any other people-oriented problem. The function of HR has been redesigned to enhance the other (line) functions of the business.

SUSTAINABLE COMPETITIVE ADVANTAGE. Why has HR been redesigned? To make our organizations more competitive and to create sustainable competitive advantages.

SHRM

A:20
Attendance

WORK
APPLICATION 1-3

How would you rate your level of productivity, job satisfaction, turnover, and absenteeism on your current job or a past job?

Absenteeism The failure of an employee to report to the workplace as scheduled

WORK
APPLICATION 1-4

Recall your most recent job. What is the firm's competitive advantage, and how would you rate its sustainability?

This is the basis of *strategic HRM.*[39] Strategy and strategic planning deal with the concept of creating **sustainable competitive advantage,** *which is a capability that creates value for customers that rivals can't copy quickly or easily and that allows the organization to differentiate its products or services from those of competitors.*

Can we gain an advantage from our buildings, our physical facilities, or our equipment? Can we create machinery that our competitors can't create or imitate? Do we have access to computers that they don't have access to? Of course not—not in most cases anyway. It is very rare that we can create any real technological advantage over any significant period of time, even if our technology is proprietary. If we create a technological advantage in today's business environment, it's usually overcome, or at least closely matched, fairly quickly. So where within the organization can we create sustainable competitive advantage? The only place we can consistently create advantage that our rivals can't quickly match is through the successful use of our human resources—getting them to be more productive and more engaged with the organization than our rivals' human resources are.[40] If we can create an organization where people want to come to work and where they are therefore more productive, less likely to leave, less likely to be absent, and more creative and innovative—then guess who wins? We win, you lose, you die. It's that simple.

THE MAIN GOALS OF STRATEGIC HRM. So then, what are the main goals of strategic HRM? In the 21st century organization, the primary HRM function is no longer just one of ensuring that the company has (1) the correct number of employees with the levels and type of skills the organization requires and (2) control systems to make sure employees are working toward the achievement of the goals in the strategic plan. This is a control model for organizational management that doesn't work in many of today's organizations. So while we must successfully do these things sometimes, we also have to encourage our human resources to the maximum extent possible through motivation, leadership, environmental analysis, and organizational changes that lead to improved job satisfaction and employee engagement. The model for a successful HR manager has evolved to encompass the processes required to get that necessary employee engagement (and the associated increases in productivity and job satisfaction) while lowering absenteeism and turnover. That's a full plate for any manager. As a result, HR managers *have to be* part of the strategic planning team today. And this means that HR managers *have to* have strong business and strategic planning knowledge.

ANALYZE STRATEGIC DIRECTION FOR HR FIT. One of the most interesting and exciting jobs within the HRM field is being part of the strategic planning efforts for the organization. Why is it so interesting and exciting? If you play a role in creating the strategy for the organization, you have a hand in creating the organization's future. As we have already noted, HRM efforts are critical for the organization to be able to carry out plans and reach goals that have been defined by the strategic plan. While being part of the strategic planning process is not usually an option for those who are early in their HR careers, it becomes an option as you get experience in the four skill sets that we will shortly talk about in more detail—human relations skills, technical skills, conceptual and design skills, and especially business skills.

Technology and Knowledge

Why has the job of the HR manager changed so drastically? It has changed primarily because of the type of work that we do today in organizations compared to the type of work that was common in the last century. The 20th century saw the growth and decline of the Industrial Age in the United States and most other developed countries around the world. However, as we neared the end of the 20th century, we started to enter the **Information Age**—*an era that began around 1980, in which information became one of the main products used in organizations; it is characterized by exponential increases in available information in all industries.* This was when assembly

Sustainable competitive advantage A capability that creates value for customers that rivals can't copy quickly or easily and that allows the organization to differentiate its products or services from those of competitors

Information Age An era that began around 1980, in which information became one of the main products used in organizations; it is characterized by exponential increases in available information in all industries

line work began to be taken over more and more by computers, robots, and other machines, and it was when the humans in our organizations were beginning to provide more than just labor; they started to provide intelligence—or knowledge. In the Information Age, we began to see a new kind of worker.

KNOWLEDGE WORKERS AND THE KNOWLEDGE-BASED FIRM. **Knowledge workers** *are workers who "use their head more than their hands" and who gather and interpret information to improve a product or process for their organizations.* There has been a lot written in the past 20 years on knowledge workers, but we can boil it down to the fact that most workers in 21st-century organizations are not working primarily with their hands; they work with their minds. In essence, knowledge workers manage knowledge for the firm.

SHRM
Q:6
Knowledge Management

THE PACE OF TECHNOLOGICAL CHANGE. One of the most critical issues that we face in the 21st century is the fact that technology is currently outstripping our ability to use it. In other words, we are creating computers and other technological systems that we can't figure out how to use before new ones come out that make the old ones obsolete. Computers get faster and faster, but the human beings that have to use them don't. What does this mean to a business? It means that if we—the *people* in the organization—can figure out ways to take advantage of the technology better and quicker than our competitors can, then we can create a sustainable competitive advantage. Notice that we didn't say create *better technology*—that wouldn't give us a sustainable advantage since our competitors could just copy the technology and improve it once we designed it. We must continually figure out ways to *use the technology* more successfully through hiring and training better and more capable employees—our *human* resources. If we do this, then as the technology changes, our people will continually figure out ways to take advantage of it before our competitors' people do. This ability of our people is the thing that creates a continuing advantage over competitors who either don't have people with as much or varied knowledge and skill sets, or don't have people who want to assist the organization because they are not engaged and not satisfied.

Knowledge is precious in an organization. We can never have enough knowledge. There is a continuous shortage of knowledge workers for our organizations—those people with specialized sets of knowledge that they can apply to problems within our companies. They don't work with their hands—they work with their heads. In fact, "The majority of jobs being created in the United States require skills possessed by only twenty percent of the current workforce."[41] And the United States is not alone. In most countries of the world, the news is the same—too few knowledge workers and too many knowledge jobs open and waiting for them. This means that for the foreseeable future, we will have a shortage of knowledge workers on a global scale.

Note: As you go through this book the symbol above will note major global issues.

SHRM
Q:8
Global Labor Markets

What does this mean to the organization's HR manager? This means that each HR manager is going to be competing with every other HR manager in the world for that 20% of the workforce that comprises the pool of knowledge workers. If the HR manager's organization has a reputation as a difficult place to work, then will the company succeed in getting knowledge workers to come to work for the organization when they have so many other opportunities? That would be very unlikely! Only if the organization manages its human resources successfully and maintains a reasonable working environment will it have any chance of filling most of the jobs that it has available.

Labor Demographics

In addition to the issues of knowledge workers and knowledge-based organizations, we face significant demographic changes in the labor force that will be available to our companies over the next 20 years.

Knowledge workers Workers who "use their head more than their hands" and who gather and interpret information to improve a product or process for their organizations

Part of the diversity in today's workforce is people retiring later in life and working part-time.

Companies are already seeing a reduction in the number and quality of potential employees, as well as greater gender, ethnic, and age diversity than at any time in the past. The lack of skilled workers for increasingly complex jobs is considered to be a major, ongoing problem.[42,43] Partly as a result of this shortage of skilled labor, we are seeing more older employees with high-level skill sets remain in the workforce. Some agencies estimate that over 90% of the growth in the US labor force between 2006 and 2016 will be from workers ages 55 and older.[44] So as a manager in a 21st century organization, your workforce will look much older than it has historically.

Your organization will also look more culturally diverse—even compared to today. The growth in immigrant workers will be substantial. Hispanic workers (of all nationalities) alone are predicted to be approximately 24% of the workforce in 2050, but today, they only compose about 14% of the workforce. Asian workers are expected to move up from about 4% now to about 8% of the workforce in 2050. But the gender mix will stay fairly close to what it is today. The percentage of women in the workforce has stabilized at about 47% or 48%.[45]

All of this means that managers of a 21st century organization will need to be more culturally aware and able to deal with individuals with significantly different work ethics, cultural norms, and even languages.

Productivity and Competitiveness Through HRM

Remember that managing productivity is the main job of every manager in an organization. However, the only way that we can get top-notch productivity is to also manage job satisfaction, absenteeism, and turnover indirectly through the things that are within our control as managers. If we succeed in increasing productivity, we directly affect our company's competitiveness because increased productivity leads to increased profitability. And if we are more profitable, we have many options for increasing our competitiveness over the long term by creating that sustainable competitive advantage that we talked about earlier.

LO 1-3

Describe the major HRM skill sets.

HRM SKILLS

What skill sets will an HR manager need in order to succeed in their job? All managers require a mix of technical, human relations, conceptual and design, and business skills in order to successfully carry out their jobs (see Exhibit 1-2). HR managers are no different, so all leaders need management skills to improve organizational performance.[46] The set of necessary HR skills is similar to the skills needed by other managers, but of course, it emphasizes people skills more than some other management positions do.

Technical Skills

The first skill set that an HR manager must develop to be successful, and also the easiest one to develop, is the technical skill set.[47] **Technical skills** are defined as *the ability to use methods and techniques to perform a task*. Being successful as an HR manager requires many skills, including comprehensive knowledge of laws, rules, and regulations relating to HR; computer skills (because everything in HR is now computerized); interviewing skills; training knowledge and skills; understanding of

Technical skills The ability to use methods and techniques to perform a task

EXHIBIT 1-2 HRM SKILLS

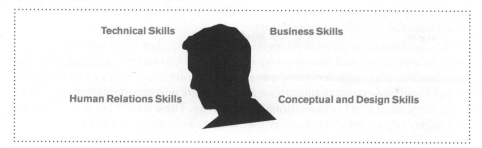

performance appraisal processes; cultural knowledge (so we don't make culture-related mistakes); and many others. We will cover many of these skills in the remaining chapters of this book.

Human Relations Skills

The second major skill set is **human relations skills**, which comprise *the ability to understand, communicate, and work well with individuals and groups through developing effective relationships.* The resources you need to get the job done are made available through relationships with people both inside the organization (i.e., coworkers and supervisors) and outside the organization (i.e., customers, suppliers, and others).[48] Organizations are seeking employees with good human relations skills,[49] and business schools are placing more emphasis on people skills.[50] We will focus on interpersonal skills throughout this book, and you will have the opportunity to develop your human relations skills through this course.

HR managers must have strong people skills. This does not mean that HR managers have to always be gullible or sympathetic to every sob story, but it does mean that they have to be *empathetic.* **Empathy** *is simply being able to put yourself in another person's place—to understand not only what that person is saying but why the individual is communicating that information to you.* Empathy involves the ability to consider what the individual is feeling while remaining emotionally detached from the situation.

Human relations skills The ability to understand, communicate, and work well with individuals and groups through developing effective relationships

Empathy The ability to put yourself in another person's place—to understand not only what that person is saying but why the individual is communicating that information to you

---

1-1 APPLYING **THE CONCEPT**

HRM Skills

Identify each activity as being one of the following types of HRM skills and write the letter corresponding to each skill before the activity or activities describing it:

a. technical
b. human relations
c. conceptual and design
d. business

_____ 1. The HR manager is working on the strategic planning process.

_____ 2. The HR manager is working on determining why more employees have been coming to work late recently.

_____ 3. The HR manager is filling out a complex government form.

_____ 4. The HR manager is talking socially with a few of her staff members.

_____ 5. The HR manager is praising a staff member for finishing a job analysis ahead of schedule.

_____ 6. The HR manager is assigning projects to various staff members.

_____ 7. The HR manager is communicating with employees throughout the company via email.

WORK
APPLICATION 1-5

Give examples of how a present or past boss of yours used each of the four HRM skills.

Human relations skills also involve the ability to work well with others in teams; to persuade others; to mediate and resolve conflicts; to gather information from others; and to jointly analyze, negotiate, and come to a collective decision. We will discuss many of these skills later in this text.

Finally, human relations skills involve the ability to relate to, as well as influence, both the employees and the executive staff of the organization. The HR manager must be able to work both sides of any issue. There are many times when they have to speak with the executive suite about issues that are uncomfortable or that, at least in the short term, affect organizational productivity. These conversations are delicate and require significant ability to sway the thoughts and opinions of others.

Conceptual and Design Skills

Conceptual and design skills are another skill set required in a successful HR manager. Such skills help in decision making. Clearly, the decisions you have made over your lifetime have affected you today. Likewise, leaders' decisions determine the success or failure of the organization.[51] So organizations are training their people to improve their decision-making skills.[52] **Conceptual and design skills** *include the ability to evaluate a situation, identify alternatives, select a reasonable alternative, and make a decision to implement a solution to a problem.*

Conceptual skills are the ability to understand what is going on in our business processes—the ability to "see the bigger picture" concerning how our department or division and the overall organization operates. These also include the ability to see if we are operating outside expected process parameters. In other words, are we doing things that we shouldn't be, or are we not successfully doing the things necessary to maintain a high level of productivity? *Design skills* are the other part of the equation. These are the part of our skill set that allows us to figure out novel or innovative solutions to problems that we have identified with our conceptual skills. So, one part of this skill set is identification of any problems that exist, and the second part is decision making to solve problems.

Business Skills

Lastly, HR managers must have strong general business skills. Like technical skills, business skills are easier to develop than human relations and conceptual and design skills. **Business skills** *are the analytical and quantitative skills—including in-depth knowledge of how the business works and its budgeting and strategic planning processes—that are necessary for a manager to understand and contribute to the profitability of the organization.* HR professionals must have knowledge of the organization and its strategies if they are to contribute strategically. This also means that they must have understanding of the financial, technological, and other facets of the industry and the organization. Finally, more and more today, HR managers must gain the capability to manipulate large amounts of data using data analytics programs and HR metrics.

Conceptual and design skills The ability to evaluate a situation, identify alternatives, select a reasonable alternative, and make a decision to implement a solution to a problem

Business skills The analytical and quantitative skills—including in-depth knowledge of how the business works and its budgeting and strategic planning processes—that are necessary for a manager to understand and contribute to the profitability of the organization.

LINE MANAGERS' HRM RESPONSIBILITIES

What if you are not planning on becoming an HR manager? Why do you need to understand the topics that we are discussing throughout this book? Well, line managers are the first point of contact with most of our employees when they have questions about human resources policies or procedures. As a result, you have to have a basic understanding of the management of your organization's human resources. You need to be able to answer employee HR questions, and if you don't follow company HR policies, you can cause legal problems for your firm, get disciplined and fired, and potentially even spend time in jail. So in this section, we explain the difference between line and staff management and line managers' major HRM responsibilities.

Line Versus Staff Management

Line managers *are the individuals who create, manage, and maintain the people and organizational processes that create whatever it is that the business sells.* Put simply, they are the people who control the actual operations of the organization. A line manager may have direct control over staff employees, but a staff manager would not generally have any direct control of line employees.

Bloomberg/Bloomberg/Getty Images

Line and staff employees can work more effectively together with today's technology.

HR managers, on the other hand, would generally be **staff managers**, *individuals who advise line managers in some field of expertise.* These managers act basically as internal consultants for the company, within their fields of specialized knowledge. As an example, a company accountant or lawyer would usually have staff authority within a manufacturing firm—they would be there to *advise* the operational managers concerning what is legal or illegal. However, in a law firm, a lawyer would usually be a line manager, because the organization's end product is knowledge and application of the law. In this case, the lawyer would have the ability to control the organization's processes to produce their output—a legal briefing, a lawsuit, or a contract agreement, for instance.

J:6
Internal Consulting   SHRM

Major HR Responsibilities of Line Management

What does a line manager need to know about HR management? A lot! Remember that every manager's primary job is to manage the resources of the organization, including the human resources. The following list shows some of the major items that line managers would need to understand in order to successfully do their job.

LO 1-4

Discuss the line manager's HRM responsibilities.

LEGAL CONSIDERATIONS. Line managers can inadvertently violate the law if they don't know what the various employment laws say and what actions are prohibited or required in dealing with employees. Laws that a line manager needs to understand include employment laws, workplace safety and health laws, labor laws, and laws dealing with compensation and benefits.

LABOR COST CONTROLS. What can and can't line managers do to minimize labor costs? All managers need to know how they can manage labor costs, both from an efficiency standpoint and from the standpoint of understanding the state and federal laws that limit our options for managing our labor resources.

WORK
APPLICATION 1-6

Give examples of line and staff positions at an organization where you work or have worked.

LEADERSHIP AND MOTIVATION. Obviously, one of the major reasons to have managers is to provide motivation and leadership to employees in our organizations. Managers are worth less than nothing if they don't improve their workers' performance and productivity through the use of motivation and leadership.

TRAINING AND DEVELOPMENT. Line managers are generally the first to see a problem with organizational processes. This is frequently an indication that some type of training is needed. Line managers are also the individuals who would debrief most employees on their annual performance appraisals. This is another situation in which a manager might recognize the need for further training of their workforce.

Line managers The individuals who create, manage, and maintain the people and organizational processes that create whatever it is that the business sells

Staff managers Individuals who advise line managers in some field of expertise

WORK
APPLICATION 1-7

Give examples of HR responsibilities performed by your present boss or a past boss.

Finally, line managers are the people responsible for making changes to organizational processes. As a result of these changes, we frequently need to train our people on the new methods of doing our work.

Line managers are also the people responsible for identifying the talented workers in the organization whom we need to develop so that they can move into higher-level positions when they are needed. The organization needs to have these people "in the pipeline" so that as others leave the company or retire, we have qualified individuals to take their place.

APPRAISAL AND PROMOTION. Line managers should almost always be responsible for the appraisal (also called evaluation) of the people who work for them as well as the process of debriefing these individuals on their annual (or more frequent) work evaluations. Line managers should also have a strong voice in who should be eligible for promotions in the organization, since these managers' job is to know their people and their capabilities and limitations.

SAFETY AND SECURITY OF EMPLOYEES. Line management has primary responsibility for maintaining the safety and security of the organization's workforce. They must know federal and state laws concerning occupational safety and health as well as procedures for securing the organization's workspaces and people from both outsiders and other employees who would want to harm them. Line managers need to monitor the areas under their physical control to minimize the hazards that can occur inside our companies.

So line managers have a lot to do with the human resources in the organization, don't they? All line managers need to know all of these things and more in order to be successful in their jobs.

LO 1-5

Identify and briefly describe the major HRM discipline areas.

SHRM

D:1
HR's Role in Organizations

HR MANAGERS' RESPONSIBILITIES: DISCIPLINES WITHIN HRM

But what if you *are* planning to become an HR manager? HR managers take the lead in the management and maintenance of the organization's people. HRM is an exciting field with many different paths that you can take over the course of your career. The field is so broad that you could do something different each year for a 40-year career and never exactly duplicate an earlier job.

So if you have decided that you would like to explore the field of HRM as a career, what kind of jobs could you expect to fill inside your organization? What are your options for a career, and what kinds of specialized training and certification are available for you in the field? Although there are many different jobs in the field, most of them fall into a few categories. Let's briefly take a look at each of these disciplines or specialties. We will provide the details in later chapters.

Most HR jobs are either *generalist* jobs, in which the HR employee works in many different areas, or *specialist* jobs, in which the employee focuses on a specific discipline of HR. What specialties are available? Below is a partial list of some of the major specialist careers that you can get into if you desire. But first, complete the self-assessment below to help you better understand your overall interest in HR and which specialties interest you more.

The Legal Environment: EEO and Diversity Management

Equal employment opportunity (EEO) and diversity management specialists are involved with the management of the organization's employee-related actions to ensure compliance with equal opportunity laws and regulations as well as organizational affirmative action plans (when such plans are required or desired). Such specialists also have responsibilities related to the management of diverse employee groups within the company. There are many management-level issues in the diversity effort, including intergroup conflict management, creating cohesiveness, combating prejudice, and others. We will discuss some of these issues later in the text.

The HR legal and regulatory environment is critical to every organization today. This is also quite likely the area that changes more than any other in HRM. Every court case that deals with the human resource environment inside any organization has the potential to affect every organization. Even if the court ruling doesn't change the way a company has to do business, if a federal or state legislature sees that ruling as unfair, then it may change the law and thus affect each organization under its jurisdiction. This is how the Lilly Ledbetter Fair Pay Act (among other laws) was created. The US Supreme Court heard a case dealing with unequal pay and made its ruling based on existing laws, and because the US Congress felt that the ruling was unfair, it enacted a new law to change certain rules on how and when an equal pay complaint can be filed. We will talk a little more about this law in Chapter 3.

So if every court case that deals with equal opportunity, compensation and benefits, harassment, or discrimination in any form has the potential to change the way in which every company does business, then you can quickly see that the HR-related legal environment is an area of critical importance to your company. Therefore, people with strong expertise in HR law are equally critical to the organization. So if you want a job where you *really* never do the same thing twice, look at becoming an HR legal specialist.

Staffing

Staffing includes all of the things that we need to do to get people interested in working for our company—going through the recruiting process, selecting the best candidates who apply, and getting them settled into their new jobs. This is likely one of the most rewarding areas in HRM. We get to hire people into the organization who want to work for us. However, it is also a highly complex job in which we have to understand the other jobs for which we are hiring, the people who apply to fill those jobs, and the legalities involved with the hiring process. This is the first line of defense for the company. This area can literally make or break the organization in its ability to be productive.[53] If we attract and hire the right types of people with the right attitudes and skills, then the organization will have a good start at being successful. If we hire the wrong types—people who don't want to work or don't have the correct skill sets—then the organization will have a very difficult time being successful in the long term.

Training and Development

Next, we have the training and development discipline. This is where the education and training function occurs in organizations. A modern organization won't get very far without constantly training its employees. Research supports the idea that employees who participate in more training and development are less likely to leave the company (i.e., less likely to cause turnover) and less likely to engage in neglectful behavior.[54] We train people for a variety of reasons, from teaching them their basic job to teaching them the things that they will need in order to move up in the organization as people above them resign or retire. If you enjoy teaching and learning, this might be an area to consider as a career field in HRM. Many HR managers stay in training and development for their entire career, because they like it. They get to interact with many different people within the organization and get to learn about many different parts of the company as they go through the training processes.

As a training and development specialist, you would have responsibility for the training processes within the organization, as well as for the development of curricula

1-1   SELF ASSESSMENT

HR Disciplines

Following are 24 HR activities that you could be involved in. Rate your interest in each specialty with a number (1–7) that represents your interest in the activity.

I'm not really interested in doing this						I'm really interested in doing this
1	2	3	4	5	6	7

1. _____ Working to make sure everyone in the firm is treated fairly
2. _____ Working against discrimination and helping minorities to get hired and promoted
3. _____ Knowing the laws, helping the firm implement laws, and reporting how the firm complies with the HR laws
4. _____ Working to get people to apply for jobs, such as writing advertisements and attending job fairs
5. _____ Interviewing job candidates
6. _____ Orienting new employees to the firm and their jobs
7. _____ Teaching employees how to do their current jobs
8. _____ Developing employees' general skills so they can progress in the firm
9. _____ Designing curricula and lesson plans for others to teach employees
10. _____ Coaching, counseling, and disciplining employees whose work quality is not up to standards
11. _____ Working with teams and helping resolve conflicts
12. _____ Working to understand and improve the level of job satisfaction throughout the firm
13. _____ Working with union employees
14. _____ Collective bargaining with unions
15. _____ Solving employee complaints
16. _____ Working to determine fair pay for different jobs, including investigating competitors' pay scales
17. _____ Creating incentives to motivate and reward productive employees
18. _____ Finding good benefits providers, such as lower-cost and higher-quality health insurance providers
19. _____ Making sure that employees don't get hurt on the job
20. _____ Working to keep employees healthy, such as developing diet and exercise programs
21. _____ Ensuring the security of the facilities and employees, issuing IDs, and keeping employee records confidential
22. _____ Ensuring that employees are ethical, such as developing and enforcing codes of ethics
23. _____ Enforcing ethical standards, such as maintaining methods for employees to confidentially report ethics violations
24. _____ Working to help the organization develop methods to improve efficiency while protecting our environment

Scoring and Interpreting Individual Discipline Results

Place your rating numbers (1–7) below and total the three scores for each discipline. Then rank your totals from 1 to 8 to determine which disciplines interest you most:

Legal Environment: EEO and Diversity Management

1 _____

2 _____

3 _____

_____ Total   (Rank this total: _____ [1–8])

Staffing

4 _____

5 _____

6 _____

_____ Total   (Rank this total: _____ [1–8])

and lesson plans and the delivery of training courses. You would also be involved with the development of talent within the company so that employees are trained and ready to move into more senior positions as those positions become vacant.

Employee Relations

This specialty covers a very wide array of items associated with management and employee relations. It involves such things as coaching, conflict resolution,

Training and Development

7 _____
8 _____
9 _____
_____ Total (Rank this total: _____ [1–8])

Compensation and Benefits

16 _____
17 _____
18 _____
_____ Total (Rank this total: _____ [1–8])

Employee Relations

10 _____
11 _____
12 _____
_____ Total (Rank this total: _____ [1–8])

Safety and Security

19 _____
20 _____
21 _____
_____ Total (Rank this total: _____ [1–8])

Labor and Industrial Relations

13 _____
14 _____
15 _____
_____ Total (Rank this total: _____ [1–8])

Ethics and Sustainability

22 _____
23 _____
24 _____
_____ Total (Rank this total: _____ [1–8])

The higher your total in each discipline, the greater your interest in that area of HR at this point in time. Of course, your interest levels can change as you learn more about each discipline. You will also be doing self-assessments in all the other chapters that relate to these eight disciplines.

Scoring and Interpreting Total Discipline Results

Now add up your grand total interest score from all 24 activities and write it here: _____ Then compare it to the continuum below to gauge your overall level of interest in working in human resources:

Low interest in HR   24   50   75   100   125   150   168   High interest in HR

The higher your score, the greater is your overall interest in HR, again at this time only.

You should realize that this self-assessment is only designed to show your current level of interest. It may not predict how much you will enjoy working in any HR discipline in the future. For example, if you get a real job in an area where you gave yourself a low score today, you could end up finding it very interesting. The self-assessments throughout this book are designed to give you a better understanding of your interest and aptitudes at the present time, and they are open to your interpretations. For example, some people tend to rate themselves much lower or higher than others even though they have the same level of interest—so don't be too concerned about your score. There are *no* correct answers or scores. Some people with lower scores may actually enjoy the course more than those with higher scores. The purpose of these self-assessments is to help you gain self-knowledge and get you thinking about how the topic of HRM relates to you.

So at this point, you should have a better idea of what the eight HR disciplines are and which areas are of more and less interest to you. But as you read the rest of this chapter and the others and learn more about each discipline, you may change your mind.

counseling, and disciplining the workforce as needed. It also involves leadership and team-building efforts within the organization. Virtually every 21st century organization operates with at least some teams as part of its structure, and teams create unique problems within the company that employee relations managers must address.

We also measure and evaluate job satisfaction and employee engagement as part of employee relations. HR managers in this function have to keep up with the many and varied laws relating to employee relations, and this specialty also involves the management of employee communication.

WORK
APPLICATION 1-8

Give brief examples of the HR disciplines performed by the HR department (or individuals responsible for HR) where you work or have worked.

Labor and Industrial Relations

The labor and industrial relations specialist works with the laws and regulations that control the organization's labor-related relationships with their workforce. This is also the area that manages any relationships the organization has with unions. HR managers who work in this area might be involved in union votes, negotiatons for union agreements, contract collective bargaining, handling grievances, and other items that affect the union/management relationship within the organization. This area also includes all labor relations activities, even in nonunion businesses. These managers have to maintain a working knowledge of all of the federal labor laws such as the National Labor Relations Act and the Taft-Hartley Act. Again, we will cover this in more detail later.

Compensation and Benefits

A compensation and benefits specialist might find jobs in compensation planning, salary surveys, benefits management, incentive programs, and more. This area deals with how we reward the people who work for us. Rewards come in many styles and types, and the compensation and benefits specialist helps decide the total compensation package that the organization will use to attract and retain the best mix of people with skills that are specifically suited to the organization. Here again, a manager will have to understand the federal and state laws that deal with compensation management within businesses, including the Fair Labor Standards Act plus EEO and discrimination laws. Compensation management also includes issues such as pay secrecy, comparable worth, and wage compression—topics that we will cover in some detail in later chapters.

In this specialty, you would have a hand in setting pay scales, managing pay of various types, and administering benefits packages. All of the processes within this discipline are designed to help the organization attract and keep the right mix of employees. You would also deal directly with all of the federal and state compensation laws to ensure compliance in organizational pay and benefits procedures.

Safety and Security

We also need to protect our human resources. In the safety and security discipline, a manager might work in the area of occupational safety and/or health to make sure we don't injure our people or cause them to become sick because of exposure to some substance they work with. This discipline also includes fields such as stress management and employee assistance programs, which help employees cope with the demands of their jobs on a daily basis. And finally, this function works to ensure that employees are secure from physical harm inflicted by other workers, outsiders, or even acts of nature. We have to protect our people if we are going to expect them to do their jobs.

As a safety and security specialist, the HR manager works to ensure that the work environment is safe for all workers so that on-the-job injuries, illnesses, and other negative events are minimized to the greatest extent possible. You also have responsibility for managing the organization's plans for securing the workforce, both from being harmed by other people and from natural disasters such as earthquakes or tornados. Maintaining the privacy of employees' confidential HR files is also part of this specialty.

ESR

As you go through this book, the symbol above will note ethics, sustainability, and social responsibility issues.

Ethics and Sustainability

In this specialty, you would bear responsibility for seeing to it that the organization acts in an ethical and socially responsible manner. You would work on codes of ethics and also make sure employees live by those codes, such as by maintaining ways in which employees can report violations of ethics (also known as *whistle-blowing*).

Environmental issues are now major social concerns,[55] and sustainable development has become one of the foremost issues facing the world.[56] *Sustainability* is meeting the needs of today without sacrificing future generations' ability to meet their needs.[57] All developed societies and a growing number of developing countries expect sustainability, and that includes wanting managers to use resources wisely and responsibly; protect the environment; minimize the amount of air, water, energy, minerals, and other materials used in the final goods we consume; recycle and reuse these goods to the extent possible rather than drawing on nature to replenish them; respect nature's calm, tranquility, and beauty; and eliminate toxins that harm people in the workplace and in communities.[58] Some companies have historically done a relatively poor job of maintaining the environment in some less developed countries in which they operated. In fact, in many cases, companies decided to operate out of a particular country to minimize their costs associated with conservation and sustainability.

Recycling contributes to our present and future sustainability.

——————— SHRM
J:5
Sustainability/Corporate Social Responsibility

——————— SHRM
J:9
Ethics (integrated)

——————— SHRM
C:8
Codes of Ethics

If you take a look at the table of contents as well as the practitioner's model below, you will realize that this book is organized to discuss the eight areas of HRM listed above. We have gone through the disciplines pretty quickly thus far, but we will deal with each in much more detail as we continue through this text. For right now, just understand that there are many different functions and areas in which an HR manager can work as part of their organization. So, it is pretty much guaranteed that you won't get bored in your role as a 21st century HR manager if you don't want to.

Next, let's take a look at some of the professional organizations that are out there to help you get where you want to go in HRM.

HRM CAREERS

If you are interested in HRM as a career, there are several professional associations and certification programs associated with HR management that will help you get into these jobs and help you advance more quickly in the future. We've listed some of them below, and there are several others within specific HR disciplines that are not discussed here.

Society for Human Resource Management (SHRM)

The **Society for Human Resource Management (SHRM)** *is the largest and most recognized of the HRM advocacy organizations in the United States.* According to its website, SHRM is "the world's largest association devoted to human resource management . . . representing more than 250,000 members in over 140 countries."[59]

What does SHRM do? Probably the biggest part of its work is dedicated to (1) advocacy for national HR laws and policies for organizations and (2) training and

Society for Human Resource Management (SHRM) The largest and most recognized of the HRM advocacy organizations in the United States

1-2 APPLYING THE CONCEPT

HRM Disciplines

Identify each HRM discipline and write the letter corresponding to it before the activity involving it:

a. Legal Environment: EEO and Diversity Management
b. Staffing
c. Training and Development
d. Employee Relations
e. Labor and Industrial Relations
f. Compensation and Benefits
g. Safety and Security
h. Ethics and Sustainability

_____ 8. The HR manager is writing an ad to recruit a job candidate.

_____ 9. The HR manager is investigating an employee complaint of racial discrimination.

_____10. The HR manager is taking a class in preparation for the exam to become certified as a Professional in Human Resources (PHR).

_____11. The HR manager is working with an insurance company to try to keep the high cost of health insurance down.

_____12. The HR manager is replacing the office copier with a more energy-efficient model.

_____13. The HR manager is having a new software program installed to protect employee records from theft.

_____14. The HR manager is working on the new collective bargaining contract with the Teamsters Union.

_____15. The HR manager is looking for potential new employees at the LinkedIn website.

_____16. The HR manager is filling out an accident report with a production worker who got hurt on the job.

_____17. The HR manager is reviewing a report that compares its wages and salaries to other businesses in the area.

_____18. The HR manager is giving priority to promoting a member of a minority group to a management position.

_____19. The HR manager is teaching the new employee how to use the HR software program.

_____20. The HR manager is referring an employee to a marriage counselor.

certification of HR professionals in a number of specialty areas. SHRM also provides its members with a place to network and learn from their peers, plus a vast library of articles and other information on HR management.

SHRM is an outstanding organization that anyone thinking about a career in human resources should consider joining. Student memberships have always been and continue to be very inexpensive, especially considering all that is available to members of the organization. If you are a college or university student, does your school have a student SHRM chapter? If it does and you are serious about a career in HR—join. If your school doesn't have a chapter, consider starting one.

SHRM interacts with the Human Resource Certification Institute (HRCI), which provides some of the most respected certifications for HR personnel anywhere in the world. The three biggest certification programs are the PHR, SPHR, and GPHR certifications. PHR stands for Professional in Human Resources, SPHR stands for Senior Professional in Human Resources, and GPHR stands for Global Professional in Human Resources. These certifications are recognized by organizations worldwide as verification of a high level of training.

SHRM also provides a curriculum guide for colleges and universities that offer HRM degree programs. The guide identifies specific areas in which SHRM feels students should gain competence as HRM majors. It breaks down curriculum areas into required, secondary, and integrated sections. Because SHRM is such a significant force in each of the HRM fields, we have decided to show you where each of the required curriculum areas is covered within this text. In each chapter, you will see notes on the side of the page when a *SHRM required* topic is discussed. These notes are alphanumerically keyed to the information in the Appendix *SHRM Curriculum Guide 2013*. You might want to pay special attention to these side notes if you have plans to become an HR manager.

If you do decide to work toward a goal of becoming an HR manager, you will need to think about taking the SHRM Assurance of Learning Exam. This exam is sort of a student version of the PHR exam noted above. According to the SHRM website, "First and foremost, passing the assessment will help students show potential employers they have acquired the minimum knowledge required to enter the HR profession at the entry level."[60] To get more information about the Assurance of Learning Exam, go to the SHRM website at http://www.shrm.org/assessment/.

WORK
APPLICATION 1-9

Are you joining or will you join a professional association, and will you seek certification? Explain why or why not.

Other HR Organizations

In addition to SHRM, there are two organizations that have certification programs that are recognized in many countries around the world. The first one is the **Association for Talent Development (ATD)**. As its name implies, ATD primarily focuses on the training and development functions of HR managers.[61] Its major certifications include the Certified Professional in Learning and Performance (CPLP) and the Human Performance Improvement (HPI) certification. According to the ATD website, CPLP certification is "a credential for training and development practitioners offered by ATD Certification Institute. It is a broad-based certification and addresses ten areas of expertise as defined by the ATD Competency Model."[62] On the other hand, becoming certified in "the art and science of Human Performance Improvement (HPI) helps organizations become better and faster at achieving their business goals."[63]

The other organization is **WorldatWork**. Certifications from this organization include Certified Compensation Professional (CCP), Certified Benefits Professional (CBP), Global Remuneration Professional (GRP), Work-Life Certified Professional (WLCP), Certified Sales Compensation Professional (CSCP), and Certified Executive Compensation Professional (CECP). As you can quickly see, WorldatWork mainly deals with compensation, benefits, and performance management programs.[64]

Both of the above certification bodies are quite high in quality within their areas of focus. Each of them has extensive websites (the primary sites are http://astd.org and http://worldatwork.org). If you are interested in these specific areas within HRM, take a look as you have time.

Professional Liability

One of the more important things that you need to understand if you are thinking about becoming an HR manager is the issue of professional (personal) liability for the actions that you take on behalf of the organization. You most likely don't know that HR managers can be held personally liable for some of the actions that they take as part of their job. For instance, two federal laws—the Fair Labor Standards Act and the Family and Medical Leave Act (which we will discuss in more detail in later chapters)—"have both been construed by courts to provide for individual liability."[65] Both the organization *and managers* who have authority to make decisions for the organization can be sued by an employee who feels that his or her rights under these laws have been violated. This is one of the many reasons why if you plan to manage people, you really want to understand all of the HRM concepts as well as possible. These are only two examples of potential professional liability that HR managers can incur if they fail to take federal and state laws into account. There are many others, so you need to be aware of the potential for personal liability, and in some cases, you may even need to consider professional liability insurance—for instance, if you are an HRM consultant to outside organizations.

SHRM

B:22
Professional Liability

How to Find More Information

HRM is one of the most constantly changing areas in business. Because of this fact, HR practitioners must continually work to stay up-to-date on news from their profession. Use the sites in this appendix to maintain your knowledge base as the HR functions you just learned about continue to adapt and change.

LO 1-6

Explain the practitioner's model for HRM and how it applies to this book.

PRACTITIONER'S MODEL FOR HRM

We have given you a (very) brief history of the HRM world and what HR management does for the organization. Now we need to get into the particulars of the matter and start talking about some of the detailed information that you will need to know in order to be a successful HR (or other) manager for your organization. How will we do that? We are going to work through what you need to know using a practitioner's model for HRM, shown in Exhibit 1-3.

The Model

The practitioner's model is designed to show you how each of the sections of HRM interact and which items you must deal with before you can go on to successfully work on the next section—kind of like building a foundation before you build a

EXHIBIT 1-3 THE PRACTITIONER'S MODEL FOR HRM

End Result = Organizational Success

⬆ Productivity
⬆ Satisfaction
⬇ Absenteeism
⬇ Turnover

PART V: Protecting and Expanding Organizational Reach
How do you PROTECT and EXPAND your Human Resources?

| Chapter 14 Workplace Safety, Health, and Security | Chapter 15 Organizational Ethics, Sustainability, and Social Responsibility | Chapter 16 Global Issues for Human Resource Managers |

PART IV: Compensating
How do you REWARD and MAINTAIN your Human Resources?

| Chapter 11 Compensation Management | Chapter 12 Incentives Pay | Chapter 13 Employee Benefits |

PART III: Developing and Managing
How do you MANAGE your Human Resources?

| Chapter 7 Training, Learning, Talent Management, and Development | Chapter 8 Performance Management and Appraisal | Chapter 9 Rights and Employee Management | Chapter 10 Employee and Labor Relations |

PART II: Staffing
What HRM Functions do you NEED for sustainability?

| Chapter 4 Matching Employees and Jobs— Job Analysis and Design | Chapter 5 Recruiting Job Candidates | Chapter 6 Selecting New Employees |

PART I: 21st Century Human Resource Management Strategic Planning and Legal Issues
What HRM issues are CRITICAL to your organization's long-term sustainability?

| Chapter 1 The New Human Resource Management Process | Chapter 2 Strategy-Driven Human Resource Management | **Chapter 3** The Legal Environment and Diversity Management |

house. The model first provides you with knowledge of which organizational functions are critical to ensure that the organization can be viable over the long term—so that it will operate legally and work toward the goals that it has identified as critical to gaining success. Second, the model helps you learn what things the organization needs to do in order *to sustain itself and its human resources* over the long term—including identifying and setting up different jobs, finding the right people, and getting them into the organization and ready to work. Next, the model discusses the critical issues in managing those human resources successfully—training, developing them for the future, evaluating and improving their performance, and maintaining a strong relationship between management and employees. Fourth, the model discusses how to *maintain your workforce* through managing the compensation and benefits provided to your people—including determining fair pay and incentives for work completed, as well as what benefits to provide to workers. Finally we look at some *special issues* that have become far more important to organizational success over the past 30 years: safety and health, ethics and social responsibility, and global issues.

Sections of the Model

Let's discuss the details of each section of the model separately.

SECTION I: 21ST CENTURY HRM, STRATEGIC PLANNING, AND HR LAWS. You have already begun Section I, where we talk about HRM in the 21st century, including the necessity of having strategy-driven HRM and a strong understanding of the basic HR legal environment. This is the basis for everything else that a 21st century HR manager will do, so it is the foundation of our diagram. These are the things that are *most critical* to the organization's basic stability and success, because if we don't get them right, we will probably not be around long enough as an organization to be successful in the sections resting on this one.

SECTION II: STAFFING. Now that we have a stable organization with some form of direction, we start to look at getting the right people into the right jobs in Section II. This section includes the items that will allow the organization to get its work done successfully over long periods of time. We first look at identifying the jobs that will need to be filled and then work through how to recruit the right numbers and types of people to fill those jobs. Finally, we find out what our options are concerning methods to select the best of those job candidates whom we have recruited. The items in Section II are absolutely necessary for long-term organizational *sustainability and success.*

EXHIBIT 1-4 PART I: PRACTITIONER'S MODEL FOR HRM

PART I: 21st Century Human Resource Management Strategic Planning and Legal Issues What HRM issues are CRITICAL to your organization's long-term sustainability?		
Chapter 1 The New Human Resource Management Process	Chapter 2 Strategy-Driven Human Resource Management	**Chapter 3** The Legal Environment and Diversity Management

EXHIBIT 1-5 PART II: PRACTITIONER'S MODEL FOR HRM

PART II: Staffing What HRM Functions do you NEED for sustainability?		
Chapter 4 Matching Employees and Jobs— Job Analysis and Design	Chapter 5 Recruiting Job Candidates	Chapter 6 Selecting New Employees

EXHIBIT 1-6 PART III: PRACTITIONER'S MODEL FOR HRM

PART III: Developing and Managing How do you MANAGE your Human Resources?			
Chapter 7 Training, Learning, Talent Management, and Development	Chapter 8 Performance Management and Appraisal	Chapter 9 Rights and Employee Management	Chapter 10 Employee and Labor Relations

SECTION III: DEVELOPING AND MANAGING. In the third section, we learn how to manage our people once they have been selected into the organization. We have to train (and retrain) our people to do jobs that are ever changing in today's organization; we have to evaluate them in some formal manner so that they know how well they are doing in the eyes of their management; and we have to develop them so that they can fill higher-level positions as we need people to step up into those positions. We sometimes have to coach, counsel, and/or discipline our employees as well, so we need to learn how to do those things so that we can improve motivation when possible, and if we can't improve motivation or overcome poor work behaviors, we will know how to correctly and humanely separate (i.e., terminate) the individual from the organization. Finally, Section III addresses the role of employee and labor relations, with emphasis on the function of unions within organizations. So Section III shows us how to *manage* our human resources *on a routine basis.*

SECTION IV: COMPENSATING. The fourth section will cover the compensation and benefits packages that we work with to keep our people satisfied (or at least not dissatisfied). Both direct compensation, in the form of base pay and incentives, and indirect pay, in the form of worker benefits, provide us with some level of control over what our employees decide to do for the organization (since we cannot directly make them more productive). Section IV shows us how to *reward and maintain* our workforce, since they are so critical to our ongoing success.

SECTION V: PROTECTING AND EXPANDING. The last section's topics include managing safety and health, providing ethical and social responsibility guidelines to members of the organization, and the globalization issues involved in working in multiple countries and cultures. The area of worker safety and health is critical because the

EXHIBIT 1-7 PART IV: PRACTITIONER'S MODEL FOR HRM

PART IV: Compensating How do you REWARD and MAINTAIN your Human Resources?		
Chapter 11 Compensation Management	Chapter 12 Incentives Pay	Chapter 13 Employee Benefits

EXHIBIT 1-8 PART V: PRACTITIONER'S MODEL FOR HRM

PART V: Protecting and Expanding Organizational Reach How do you PROTECT and EXPAND your Human Resources?		
Chapter 14 Workplace Safety, Health, and Security	Chapter 15 Organizational Ethics, Sustainability, and Social Responsibility	Chapter 16 Global Issues for Human Resource Managers

employees of a 21st century organization are almost always the basis of at least some of our competitive advantage over our rivals in any industry, so we need to keep them healthy and happy. In addition to safety and health, two areas have become far more important since the beginning of the information age in the early 1980s: ethical, sustainable, and socially responsible organizations; and the ability to operate in a global business environment.

TRENDS AND ISSUES IN HRM

In each chapter of this text, we will discuss some of the most important issues and trends in HRM today. These issues and trends will cover areas such as the use of technology in HRM, HR in small businesses, ethical issues in HR, and diversity and equal opportunity. For this chapter, we have chosen the following issues: creating an engaged workforce, a new normal for individuals with moderate skills doing routine work, and the ethical issue of reverse discrimination.

Creating an Engaged Workforce

We mentioned the concept of employee engagement earlier in this chapter, but it bears a closer look before we continue on. Remember that employee engagement is defined as a combination of job satisfaction, ability, and a willingness to perform for the organization at a high level and over an extended period of time. This combination of satisfaction, ability, and willingness is more critical today than ever before in business. Many of our employees are highly talented and extremely difficult to replace, but according to a recent Gallup report, 70% of them just aren't being made an integral part of the organization through the use of management techniques that cause them to become more interested in both their work and the work of the organization overall.[66] This same Gallup report shows that companies with the most engaged workforce had 147% higher earnings per share, better productivity and profitability, and lower absenteeism and turnover than their competitors, so there is certainly strong reason to work toward a more engaged workforce. So what is a 21st century manager to do?

Higher rates of pay are not the answer, or at least not the *complete* answer. Evidence shows that increases in pay do not provide the motivational potential that most employees and managers believe they do.[67] Many nonmonetary actions, such as workplace flexibility and more autonomy on the job, provide more return than money. However, actions by the company that increase autonomy alone are not the answer, either. Employees are people, and people need strong relationships with other people that feed their collective creativity.

So what should you do? The first and most important thing that companies must do to improve engagement is to find, hire, and *train* the right managers on how to create employee engagement. Train them to communicate, listen, and be empathetic without being dupes to outlandish employees. Train them to provide the necessary feedback to their workers so that employees know that their managers recognize good work.[68] The evidence says that poorly trained managers are likely the biggest reason for employees being actively disengaged.

The second thing is to create and adhere to company values and goals that make employees feel they are part of something that is important and much bigger than they could do on their own.[69] They will be forced to be engaged with others in order to have access to coworkers who will be available to help in reaching those goals. These corporate values and goals have to be published, they have to have *senior executive commitment*, and they have to be enforced with everyone in the organization, down to the lowest levels.

WORK
APPLICATION 1-10

Explain how technology is used where you work or have worked.

Third, you have to make the hard decision to get the actively disengaged employees out of the company. This *is* a case of "one bad apple spoiling the whole barrel." Every manager has seen one dysfunctional individual cause everyone else in a division or department to become less satisfied and less engaged with their coworkers. Actively dissatisfied employees create tension in the workplace, which converts to disengagement among other employees who were just recently excellent workers.[70] The detrimental individual has to be taken out of the equation in order to restore harmony.

We haven't said anything here that is new. We just need to understand the consequences of failure to create employee engagement. Do you want your company to be the one with 147% greater EPS and more profitability, or do you want to be part of the mass of organizations with disengaged employees and poor ROI, low creativity, and high turnover?

A New Normal for Individuals With Moderate Skills Doing Routine Work

Another trend in work that is becoming apparent is the loss of significant numbers of middle-wage jobs, especially in the United States and other developed countries. A series of reports by the various branches of the US Federal Reserve and several articles in the American Economic Review have noted that "routine" work is being displaced more and more by both automation and offshoring of these tasks.[71] Much of this routine work historically was accomplished by middle-skilled workers. This hollowing out of the middle class is being called "labor market polarization," and it is associated with job losses in a wide variety of middle-class occupations.

SHRM

0:7
Offshoring/Outsourcing

Offshoring is being fed by the ability to do routine work in remote settings—all over the world. The ability to do these jobs anywhere allows companies to trade in tasks or services of an individual instead of going the traditional route of exporting and importing of goods.[72] Companies are moving these routine tasks to lower-cost locations at an increasing rate. There has been some recent talk of "onshoring," or bringing jobs back to the United States from other countries, but as of yet, there is little evidence that this is a significant trend.[73] As a result, we have hollowed out some of those historical middle-class jobs, such as routine office management or blue-collar manufacturing jobs.

Automation is also cutting into routine jobs, in all countries. As computers become more capable of analyzing and performing routine tasks, those tasks will inevitably move from the hands of individuals to the appendages of robots or the bitstreams of computers. For instance, computers have the capability to manage routine surveillance of a call center today, where historically, several managers might be required to manage a call center of any significant size. In the same way, tasks such as metal fabrication, printing operations, and automotive diagnostics are each being accomplished, at least partially, by automation.

Finally, evidence shows that even at the low end of the job-skills spectrum, job growth in core service occupations is responsible for nearly all job growth.[74] These are jobs in such areas as restaurant servers, janitors, and child care and elder care providers. Many individuals have little desire to serve in these occupations. However, without significant skills in decision making, problem solving, data analysis, or other skill sets that allow individuals to solve nonroutine problems, a large portion of the workforce will likely be relegated to these positions.

WORK
APPLICATION 1-11

How has globalization affected where you work or have worked?

Ethical Issues: Reverse Discrimination

In 2009, a case claiming "reverse discrimination" came to the Supreme Court. *What is reverse discrimination?* It is discrimination against a majority group rather than a minority group. In general in the United States, this would be discrimination against white male employees or applicants. Is reverse discrimination wrong? We

ESR

protect many different racial, ethnic, gender and other groups within the United States, but how do we, and how should we, protect the majority group? At what point does the protection of minority groups cross over to discrimination against the majority?

The 2009 case that brought back discussions about reverse discrimination was *Ricci v. DeStefano.*[75] It renewed the discussion of race-based decision making in employment. And while there were many nuances to the case and ultimately to the Supreme Court decision, the end result was that reverse discrimination was deemed to have occurred. The basic issue was that a written promotion exam for firefighters was considered by the city of New Haven, Connecticut, to be discriminatory when no black and only one Hispanic test-taker passed the exam. As a result, the city threw the entire exam out due to disparate impact (we will discuss this term in Chapter 3) and didn't promote anyone. The firefighters who scored highest on the exam sued based on reverse discrimination. According to the local newspaper, "The justices concluded that some of the city's arguments justifying its actions to the high court 'are blatantly contradicted by the record,' and the justices found that the city 'turned a blind eye to evidence supporting the exam's validity.'"

Was the decision right or wrong? We can't make that determination here, but employment discrimination of all types continues to be something that HR managers have to be very aware of and guard against to the best of their ability. Nobody in your workforce likes feeling that they have been treated unfairly, whether they happen to be in a federal or state "protected class" or a member of the workforce majority. Fairness is one of the critical themes you will see dealt with throughout this book. The HR department is, and will continue to be, the organization's watchdog on the topic of workforce discrimination and fairness to all employees.

SHRM

F:8
Reverse Discrimination

WORK
APPLICATION 1-12

What is your opinion regarding reverse discrimination? Have you experienced or seen discrimination at work?

• • • CHAPTER SUMMARY

1-1   Identify the difference between the traditional view of HRM and the 21st century view.

The traditional view holds that human resource management is a *cost center*, meaning a department or division within an organization that uses up organizational resources but doesn't create revenues for the company. In the 21st century organization, we view HRM as a productivity center for the company. As a *productivity center*, HR fulfills a revenue-generating function by providing the organization with the right people in the right place and with the right skills so that organizational productivity can be improved.

1-2   Identify and briefly describe the four critical dependent variables that managers must control in order to compete in a 21st century organization.

The four critical variables are productivity, job satisfaction, absenteeism, and turnover.

1. *Productivity* is the amount of output that an organization gets per unit of input, with human input usually expressed in terms of units of time.

The two parts of productivity are efficiency and effectiveness.

2. *Job satisfaction* is a feeling of well-being and acceptance of our place in the organization.

3. *Turnover* is permanent loss of workers from the organization. When people quit, it is considered voluntary turnover, while when people are fired, it is involuntary turnover.

4. *Absenteeism* is temporary absence of employees from the workplace.

1-3   Describe the major HRM skill sets.

The HRM skill sets include technical skills, human relations skills, conceptual and design skills, and business skills. *Technical skills* include the ability to use methods and techniques to perform a task. *Human relations skills* provide the ability to understand, communicate, and work well with individuals and groups through developing effective relationships. *Conceptual and design skills* provide the ability to evaluate a situation, identify alternatives, select an alternative, and implement a solution to the problem.

Finally, *business skills* provide analytical and quantitative skills, including the in-depth knowledge of how the business works and of its budgeting and strategic planning processes that is necessary for a manager to understand and contribute to the profitability of the organization.

1-4   Discuss the line manager's HRM responsibilities.

Line managers require knowledge of each of the following topics:

- *Major employment laws.* Line managers must know all of the major employment laws so that they don't accidentally violate them in their daily interactions with their employees.

- *Labor cost controls.* Line managers have to understand what they are legally and ethically allowed to do to control labor costs.

- *Leadership and motivation.* Probably the most significant function of line managers is that of being leaders and motivators for the people who work for them. Managers are worth less than nothing if they don't improve employee performance.

- *Training and development.* Line managers are typically the first point of contact to determine whether or not their workforce needs training or development to perform at a high level. They are also the people responsible for making changes to organizational processes. Training in these new processes is typically required to create maximum productivity in our workforce.

- *Appraisal and promotion.* Line managers are the primary individuals who evaluate subordinates' work performance, and they should have a strong voice in who should be eligible for promotions in the organization, since their job is to know their people and each of their capabilities and limitations.

- *Employee safety and security.* Line managers have primary responsibility for the safety and security of the workers in an organization. They have to know the laws that deal with occupational safety and health as well as security procedures to protect their people from individuals who might want to do them harm.

1-5   Identify and briefly describe the major HRM discipline areas.

- *The legal environment: EEO and diversity management.* This discipline deals with equal opportunity laws and regulations as well as management of a diverse workforce.

- *Staffing.* This discipline manages the processes involved in job analysis, recruiting, and selection into the organization.

- *Training and development.* This discipline has responsibility for the training processes within the organization, for developing curricula and lesson plans, and for delivery of training courses. It is also involved with development of talent within the company to provide a group of employees who will be able to move into more senior positions that become vacant.

- *Employee relations.* This area involves the coaching, counseling, and discipline processes, along with employee communication and stress management. It is also typically responsible for the management of job satisfaction and employee engagement.

- *Labor and industrial relations.* This discipline works with the laws and regulations that control the organization's relationships with their workforce. It also works with any union-management contracts, including but not limited to union votes, grievances, contract negotiations, and bargaining with union representatives.

- *Compensation and benefits.* This discipline works with pay of various types and with benefits packages, all of which are designed to attract and keep the right mix of employees in the organization. It also deals directly with all of the federal and state compensation laws to ensure compliance.

- *Safety and security.* This discipline works to ensure that the environment on the job is safe for all workers so that on-the-job injuries and illnesses are minimized to the greatest extent possible. It also involves managing the organization's planning for securing the workforce, both from being harmed by other people and from natural disasters such as earthquakes or tornados.

- *Ethics and sustainability.* This discipline bears responsibility for seeing to it that the organization acts in an ethical and socially responsible manner, to minimize harm to the environment and its various stakeholders. It involves managing the sustainability efforts in the organization to minimize the organization's "footprint" on the environment—in other words, to minimize the depletion of worldwide resources caused by the organization's carrying out its processes.

1-6   Explain the practitioner's model for HRM and how it applies to this book.

The practitioner's model is designed to show the relationships between each of the functions and disciplines within HRM. On the first level are the items that are absolutely critical to the organization if it is going to continue to operate (and stay within federal and state laws while doing so) and be stable and successful for a significant period of time. The second level encompasses those things that are required to identify the kinds of jobs that must be filled and then recruit and select the right types of people into those jobs so the company can maximize productivity over the long term. These are the items that will allow the organization to get its work done successfully over long periods of time. As we get into the third tier, we concern ourselves with management of the human resources that we selected in the second level. We have to get them training to do their jobs and allow them to perform those jobs for a period of time. We then have to appraise their performance and, if necessary, correct their behaviors that are not allowing them to reach their maximum potential. We do the latter through the coaching, counseling, and disciplinary processes. As this is occurring,

we need to ensure that we maintain positive relationships with our employees so that they remain engaged with the organization and productive. We manage these positive relationships in many ways, from measuring and assessing job satisfaction periodically to managing relationships with union employees. Finally, in the top tier, we want to make sure that we reward and maintain our workforce to minimize unnecessary turnover and dissatisfaction. We do this through fair and reasonable compensation planning and through the maintenance of a safe and secure workplace.

1-7 Define the key terms found in the chapter margins and listed following the Chapter Summary.

Complete the Key Terms Review to test your understanding of this chapter's key terms.

• • • KEY TERMS

absenteeism	human relations skills	revenue center
business skills	human resources	Society for Human Resource
conceptual and design skills	Information Age	Management (SHRM)
cost center	job satisfaction	staff manager
effectiveness	knowledge worker	sustainable competitive
efficiency	line manager	advantage
empathy	productivity	technical skills
employee engagement	productivity center	turnover

• • • KEY TERMS REVIEW

Complete each of the following statements using one of this chapter's key terms.

1. _____ consists of the people within an organization.

2. _____ is a combination of job satisfaction, ability, and a willingness to perform for the organization at a high level and over an extended period of time.

3. _____ is a division or department within an organization that brings in no revenue or profit; in other words, it costs money for the organization to run this function.

4. _____ is a division or department that generates monetary returns for the organization.

5. _____ is a revenue center that enhances the profitability of the organization through enhancing the productivity of the people within the organization.

6. _____ is the amount of output that an organization gets per unit of input, with human input usually expressed in terms of units of time.

7. _____ answers the question "Did we do the right things?" It is a function of getting the job done whenever and however it must be done.

8. _____ is a function of how many organizational resources we used in getting the job done; it answers the question "Did we do things right?"

9. _____ is the feeling of well-being that we experience in our work—basically, whether or not we like what we do and the immediate environment surrounding us and our work.

10. _____ is the permanent loss of workers from the organization.

11. _____ is the failure of an employee to report to the workplace as scheduled.

12. _____ is a capability that creates value for customers that rivals can't copy quickly or easily and that allows the organization to differentiate its products or services from those of competitors.

13. _____ is an era that began around 1980, when information became one of the main products used in organizations; it is characterized by exponential increases in available information in all industries.

14. _____ are workers who "use their head more than their hands" to gather and interpret information to improve a product or process for their organizations.

15. _____ include the ability to use methods and techniques to perform a task.

16. _____ include the ability to understand, communicate, and work well with individuals and groups through developing effective relationships.

17. _____ is being able to put yourself in another person's place—to understand not only what they are saying but why they are communicating that information to you.

18. _____ are made up of the ability to evaluate a situation, identify alternatives, select an alternative, and make a decision to implement a solution to a problem.

19. _____ are the analytical and quantitative skills, including in-depth knowledge of how the business works and of its budgeting and strategic planning processes, that are necessary for a manager to understand and contribute to the profitability of the organization.

20. _____ create and manage the organizational processes and the people that create whatever it is that a business sells.

21. _____ are the individuals that advise line management of the firm in their area of expertise.

22. _____ is the largest and most recognized of the HRM advocacy organizations in the United States.

• • • COMMUNICATION SKILLS

The following critical-thinking questions can be used for class discussion and/or for written assignments to develop communication skills. Be sure to give complete explanations for all answers.

1. Why is it important for all business majors to take this course in HRM?

2. Are you interested in becoming an HR manager? Why or why not?

3. Do you agree with the statement "Effectively utilizing the human resources within the organization is one of the few ways to create a competitive advantage in a modern business"? Why or why not?

4. Is employee engagement possible in an age when people tend to have very little loyalty to their employers and vice versa? How would you work to increase employee engagement as a manager?

5. Can HRM really create revenue for the organization? If so, how?

6. Identify some things that could be done by a manager to increase productivity and job satisfaction and decrease absenteeism and turnover. Make a list for each item.

7. If you were the HR manager for your organization, what would you do to increase the number of applicants who apply for "knowledge worker" positions in your organization? Assume you can't pay them more.

8. Is there anything that an individual within an organization can do to help improve relations among diverse workers? If so, what?

9. Some say that for managers, hard skills (technical and business skills) are more important than soft skills (human relations and conceptual and design skills). What do you think, and why?

10. Are external certification programs (in all jobs) becoming more important? Why?

• • • CASE 1-1 BA-ZYNGA! ZYNGA FACES TROUBLE IN FARMVILLE

In late 2011, Zynga's employees were showing serious frustration with long hours, high-stress deadlines, and especially the leadership of the company. Responses to a quarterly staff satisfaction survey provided lots of criticism of both the company culture and Mr. Mark Pincus—the CEO. One individual was so disenchanted that he openly expressed his intent to "cash out" and leave after the company's initial public offering (IPO) in December 2011.

Zynga was one of the fastest growing web-based companies at that point in time. It operated with an almost military command-and-control structure, with autonomous units in charge of each game (most of you will recognize the games FarmVille and CityVille). At times, it was "a messy and ruthless war."[76] Employees worked long hours while "managers relentlessly track[ed] progress, and the weak links [were] demoted or let go."[77] The entire environment could be described as intense.

There were serious concerns about the long-term viability of this culture, though. "While some staff members thrive in this environment, others find it crushing. Several former employees describe emotionally charged encounters, including loud outbursts from Mr. Pincus, threats from senior leaders, and moments when colleagues broke down [in] tears."[78] A number of former employees spoke about how the high-pressure culture might become a major liability as the company continued to grow. The consensus of these former workers appeared to be that the company might not continue to be able to attract and retain the top engineering and programming talent that they would need going forward.

"While from the outside Zynga may have the fun and whimsy of the Willy Wonka chocolate factory, the organization thrives on numbers, relentlessly aggregating performance data, from the upper ranks to the cafeteria staff."[79] Everything was measured and mapped, and results were used to identify the top performers along with the "not-so-top" performers and their groups. (Top teams had been known to be rewarded with vacations for the entire team, with spending money provided by the company!) Mr. Pincus personally tracked large amounts of data showing performance levels for the 3,000 employees and their work teams.

It wasn't that Zynga was failing, or even that there was an open fear of failure. Zynga was one of the rare Internet start-ups that were actually making money. Zynga had garnered $828.9 million in revenue in the first nine months of 2011 and had earned $121 million since the start of 2010. However, the company culture was purely performance driven. The best employees were rewarded very well, while people who couldn't "hit the numbers" were likely to disappear.

Other local companies and their human resources managers were looking on in anticipation. They also had talent acquisition problems, but many had a much more collaborative culture than Zynga did, and they thought they would be able to use these cultural attributes to steal talent from Zynga after the IPO concluded. They knew that most of Zynga's early employees who had some type of stock or options in the company would not be likely to leave until the IPO was finalized, but that many would be looking around soon after.

Questions

1. Imagine you are the new HR director at Zynga. What do you think you might do in this situation to limit the potential loss of a large number of very talented employees?

2. Are there any benefits or incentives that you can think of that might make more people want to stay on at Zynga after the IPO is complete and they can "get their money"?

3. HR managers frequently have to teach other senior managers how to deal with their employees better. What do you think you would do about Mr. Pincus? Is there anything you *could* do? Could you coach him concerning his management style? Do you think this would be effective?

4. Do you think that big cash and stock rewards for top performers and "the boot" for poor performers is the appropriate way to manage talent in this type of high-tech business? Why or why not?

• • • CASE 1-2 WELCOME TO THE WORLD OF 21ST CENTURY HRM

Angie was standing at her (former) desk, picking up her personal items and wondering how she had gotten into this mess. At one shoulder was the head of HR, and at the other was one of the security officers. They were there to escort her out of the building as soon as she retrieved her personal items. Thinking back, the last hour or so had been a whirlwind. She had come to work like she had for the past several months, maybe a little late and a little hung over, but she was there.

Shortly after she had sat down at her desk to start making phone calls, her supervisor had called her into his office. He asked her to accompany him to the HR manager's office. Once there, she saw a printout of her (public) Facebook page and the blog that she kept on pretty much a daily basis. She was a little embarrassed by the photos on the printout, but at least they weren't as racy as some she had considered putting up. She was really glad

that when she graduated from college, she had purged her account of all of those pictures of the Florida vacations on the beach (and other places).

Angie knew, like all of the other employees, that company management had been recently going through some of the social networking sites to review potential recruits before they decided to hire them, but she didn't know anything about management reviewing current employees' personal webpages. She had, however, read (well, scanned) the company's social media policy in the employee handbook and had signed a form saying she understood the requirements. Well, she thought, my pages are pretty clean since I was warned about this by career services in college.

However, what she saw next really bothered her. There was the highlighted section of her blog from last Thursday. She had forgotten about that! In it, she noted that she had a whopping hangover because of the girls' night out on

Wednesday night, and she had said, "I think I'll call in sick because I just can't face working for that idiot with this headache." Well, they knew that she wasn't sick. How could she have been that stupid?

As she sat there, she suddenly realized that this was no normal conversation—it looked more like an inquisition. And when the HR manager informed her that the company was going to terminate her employment because she had violated the social media policy, she couldn't believe it. What had happened to freedom of speech? What had happened to a person's right to have a life outside of work? Could the company monitor her personal communications that had nothing to do with work and then use them against her? She wasn't sure, but she thought that was wrong. Nonetheless, here she was, cleaning out her desk.

A 2012 report by SilkRoad Technology declares, "75% of workers access social media on the job from their personal mobile devices at least once a day, and 60% access it multiple times." But "fewer than 10% of companies offer social media training to their employees. And only 23% have a specific policy regarding use of social media."[80]

Also, according to a recent study by Harris Interactive for Careerbuilder.com, about two out of every five employers are using social networks to screen job candidates.[81] More than 40% of employers have decided not to offer jobs to potential candidates based on content from their social networking sites, including Facebook, LinkedIn, Myspace, Twitter, and others. At the same time, 19% said they had hired individuals because of their social media activities. A *Business Insider* article identifies several recent firings because of social media. These include an employee ranting about his employer on Facebook, a breach of personal privacy when putting photos on Instagram, and using company equipment to make a video complaining about the company, among other issues.[82]

The National Labor Relations Board (NLRB) has recently jumped into the debate on social media posts, with some new policies and some mixed rulings in social media cases. The NLRB rulings generally direct that it is illegal to adopt overly broad social media policies "like bans on 'disrespectful' comments or posts that criticize the employer—if those policies discourage workers from exercising their right to communicate with one another with the aim of improving wages, benefits, or working conditions."[83] But employers have been judged to be within their rights in other cases when disciplining employees who acted alone to disparage or vilify their employer or its customers. According to a quote in *Forbes* magazine by Tony Wagner, a spokesman for the National Labor Relations Board, "The NLRA does not protect personal rants that don't pull in other employees who may be experiencing poor working conditions."[84]

Social media sites are no longer just a location where you can connect with your friends. Companies are routinely using these sites to research both recruits for employment *and* the actions of current employees. The Internet is full of references of people fired for things that they said on their personal web pages. And it doesn't necessarily matter if you set your pages to private. Your friends may still capture comments that you've made on their pages without you even knowing about it. In addition, recruiters in some states can use your "friend" list to find people to call for references, and if your friends are unaware of the purpose for the call, they might say something that you'd rather they didn't. Employers can look at who has recommended you on sites such as LinkedIn and may approach those references as well.[85]

Social media is here to stay, and companies are using it—but is Angie right? Can the company use her personal pages on social media sites against her as an employee? Should the employer be able to discipline an employee because of a personal social media page? Even if it can, is it ethical? Can employees have any expectation that their personal rants—whether against their employer, a local store, or a former boyfriend or girlfriend—are private? Isn't free speech protected by the Constitution?

Organizations (and many employees and former employees) are now struggling with these questions. We will discuss these questions as we explore the world of 21st century HRM over the next 16 chapters, but what do you think?

Questions

1. Does Angie have a right to say what she wants on her Facebook page or in her blog? Why or why not?

2. What if she harmed the company or its reputation in some way with what she posted? Would that change your answer?

3. What if she gave out confidential information about new products or services?

4. Is it legal for the company to terminate an employee because of something she did away from work?

5. If it is legal for the company to terminate an employee for something she did on her own time, in what circumstances would it be legal? For example:

   - Would it be legal for the company to terminate an employee because the employee campaigned for a politician who was writing legislation that would harm the interests of the company?

   - Would it be legal for the company to terminate someone who wrote in a blog that they had physically assaulted another person?

   - Would it be legal to terminate someone who wrote that they had carried a gun to work, even though the person really hadn't?

6. Does Angie have any legal recourse because of the company firing her over her social media posts?

$SAGE edge™

Sharpen your skills with SAGE edge at edge.sagepub.com/lussierhrm2e

SAGE edge for students provides a personalized approach to help you accomplish your coursework goals in an easy-to-use learning environment.

• • • SKILL BUILDER 1-1 GETTING TO KNOW YOU

Objectives

1. To get acquainted with some of your classmates
2. To gain a better understanding of what the course covers
3. To get to know more about your instructor

Skills

The primary skills developed through this exercise are as follows:

1. *HR management skill*—Human relations
2. *SHRM 2013 Curriculum Guidebook*—A: Employee Relations

Procedure 1 (5–8 minutes)

Break into groups of five or six, preferably with people you do not know. Have each member tell the group their name and two or three significant things about themselves. Then have all group members ask each other questions to get to know each other better.

Procedure 2 (4–8 minutes)

Can everyone in the group address every other person by name? If not, have each member repeat their name. Then each person in the group should repeat the names of all the group members until each person knows everyone's first name.

Application

What can you do to improve your ability to remember people's names?

_____
_____
_____
_____
_____

Procedure 3 (5–10 minutes)

Elect a spokesperson for your group. Look over the following categories and decide on some specific questions you would like your spokesperson to ask the instructor from one or more of the categories. The spokesperson will not identify who asked the questions. You do not have to have questions for each area.

- *Course expectations.* What do you expect to cover or hope to learn from this course?
- *Doubts or concerns.* Is there anything about the course that you don't understand?
- *Questions about the instructor.* List questions you'd like to ask the instructor to get to know them better.

Procedure 4 (10–20 minutes)

Each spokesperson asks the instructor one question at a time until all questions have been answered. Spokespeople should skip questions already asked by other groups.

Apply It

What did I learn from this experience? How will I use this knowledge in the future?

_____
_____
_____

• • • SKILL BUILDER 1-2 COMPARING HR MANAGEMENT SKILLS AND HR RESPONSIBILITIES

Objective

To better understand the importance of good HR management skills and implementing HR responsibilities effectively

Skills

The primary skills developed through this exercise are as follows:

1. *HR management skills*—Conceptual and design

2. *SHRM 2013 Curriculum Guidebook*—A: Employee Relations

Compare Your Supervisors' HR Management Skills and HR Responsibilities Effectiveness

Recall the best supervisor or boss you ever worked for and the worst one you ever worked for (preferably line managers, not HR managers). Compare these two people by writing brief notes in the following chart about each person's HR management skills and HR responsibilities.

HR Management Skills and HR Responsibilities

Best Supervisor or Boss		Worst Supervisor or Boss
	Technical	
	Human Relations	
	Conceptual and Design	
	Business Skills	
	Legal Considerations	
	Labor Cost Control	
	Leadership and Motivation	
	Training and Development	
	Appraisal and Promotion	
	Safety and Security	

Based on your own experiences with a good boss and a poor one, what do you believe are the key differences between good and poor managers?

Apply It

What did I learn from this exercise? How will I use this knowledge in the future?

_____

_____

_____

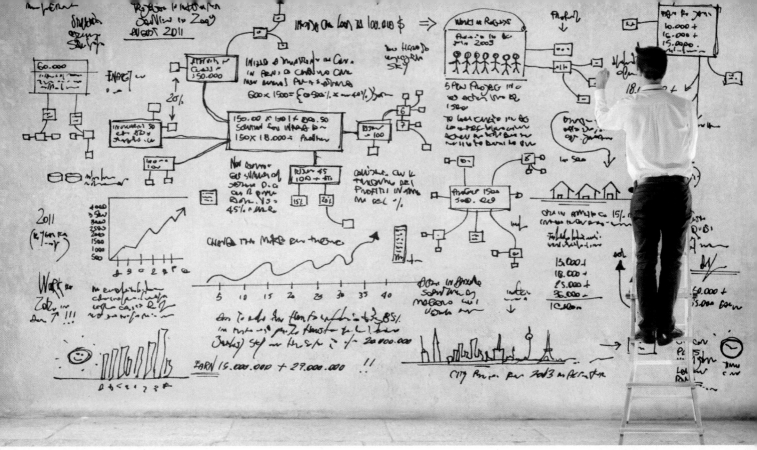

2 Strategy-Driven Human Resource Management

••• LEARNING OUTCOMES

After studying this chapter, you should be able to do the following:

2-1 Identify and explain the major components of the external environment. PAGE 43

2-2 Describe the three major organizational factors that affect our strategic options. PAGE 46

2-3 Discuss how having a vision and mission helps organizations focus their resources. PAGE 48

2-4 Identify and describe the major components of organizational structure and why it is important to understand them. PAGE 56

2-5 Describe organizational culture and how it affects the members of the organization. PAGE 59

2-6 Describe human resource information systems (HRIS) and identify how they can help HR make decisions. PAGE 65

2-7 Identify the common measurement tools for strategic human resource management (HRM). PAGE 65

2-8 Define the key terms found in the chapter margins and listed following the Chapter Summary. PAGE 72

Practitioner's Perspective

Cindy notes that one thing many family get-togethers have in common is storytelling—reminiscing about common experiences and outstanding members. These stories are part of the ties that bind and define the group, and the same is true for your work "family."

For example, take this story about Bill, an executive who started work as an emergency medical technician (EMT). One time while Bill was moving a nursing home resident, the resident's bedridden roommate feebly attempted to say good-bye. Young and impatient, Bill didn't stop to let the two talk but hurried off to the hospital with his passenger. The next time he was at that location, Bill was pulled aside by a nurse who said, "What I am about to say will break your heart, but it will make you a better man. The woman you transported died in the hospital that night. The roommate was her husband of 70 years, and you didn't give him time to say good-bye." Ever afterward in his career, Bill's motto was "Patients First," and that goal permeates his institution even today in everything it does.

What else defines company culture? Chapter 2 examines strategies, mission statements, vision, and values—all important pieces of a company's identity.

SHRM HR CONTENT

See Appendix: *SHRM 2013 Curriculum Guidebook* for the complete list

A. Employee and Labor Relations (required)

3. Managing/creating a positive organizational culture

C. Ethics (required)

3. Individual versus group behavior

E. Job Analysis/Job Design (required)

9. Organization design (missions, functions, and other aspects of work units for horizontal and vertical differentiation)

G. Outcomes: Metrics and Measurement of HR (required)

1. Economic value added
2. Balanced scorecard: HR and organization level
7. Return on investment (ROI)
8. HR scorecard
9. Organizational scorecard

J. Strategic HR (required)

1. Strategic management
2. Enhancing firm competitiveness
3. Strategy formulation
4. Strategy implementation
7. Competitive advantage
8. Competitive strategy
10. Linking HR strategy to organizational strategy
13. Mission and vision
14. Quality management

Q. Organizational Development (required—graduate students only)

12. Organizational structure and job design

STRATEGY AND STRATEGIC PLANNING IN THE 21ST CENTURY: THE ORGANIZATION AND THE ENVIRONMENT

The concepts of strategy and strategic planning were introduced briefly in Chapter 1. As indicated there, strategy and strategic planning deal with a process of looking at our organization and its environment—both today and in the expected future—and determining what we as an organization want to do to meet the requirements of that expected future (see Exhibit 2-1). This process of strategic analysis and building a coherent strategy is more critical today than it has ever been before.[1,2,3,4] This is because in most worldwide industries today, we have far more competition and capacity than ever before, making it more difficult to create the sustainable competitive advantage that we need in order to survive over the long term.

Strategic planning is about planning for the future, and to be successful, you need to plan using goals and measurable standards.[5] There is an old saying: "When you fail to plan, you plan to fail." Research supports this saying and confirms the importance of planning.[6] Some managers complain that they don't have time to plan, yet research shows that managers who plan are more effective and efficient than nonplanners. Before we get into the details of strategic planning, complete Self-Assessment 2-1 to determine your level of planning.

Our internal and external environments largely determine how we as managers must act to provide the organization with the right combination of people to help us reach our strategic goals. HRM is a critical component of meeting organizational goals, because without the right people with the right types of education, skills, and

• • • CHAPTER OUTLINE

mind-set, we cannot expect to accomplish the objectives that we set for ourselves.[7] Again, people are one of the most difficult organizational resources to imitate, and therefore, the right people give us a powerful competitive advantage over our rival firms.

In this chapter, we focus primarily on the organization's environment. The environment has two parts: internal and external. First, we briefly discuss the external environment. Then we describe in detail three key aspects of the internal environment: strategy, structure, and culture.

THE EXTERNAL ENVIRONMENT

The external environment consists of a series of influences that originate outside the organization and that the company cannot control. Each of these forces acts on the firm and causes the firm to have to change and adapt, usually in the form of strategic responses to environmental changes.[8] The nine major forces originating in the external environment are shown in Exhibit 2-2, along with an explanation of each.

©iStockphoto.com/elenaleonova

Strategic planning is a key part of the foundation of an organization's success.

LO 2-1

Identify and explain the major components of the external environment.

• *Customers*. Customers have more power today than ever before, as they have a major effect on the organization's performance through their purchase of products. Without customers, there's no need for an organization. Therefore, companies must continually improve products and services to create value for their customers.[9] This process of product improvement requires skilled employees who are willing to use their creativity to add to the organization's knowledge and thereby help create new products and services for customers. During a turnaround effort at **JC Penney**, CEO Ron Johnson attempted to bring in new customers while basically turning his

EXHIBIT 2-1   STRATEGIC CHOICE

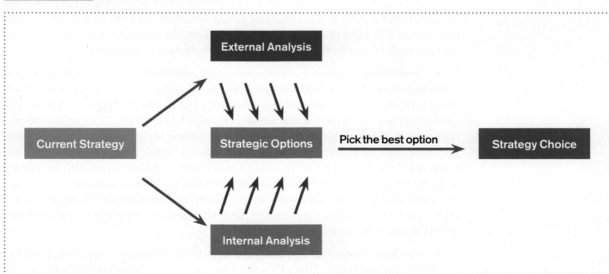

2-1 · SELF ASSESSMENT

Level of Planning

Write a number from 1 to 5 before each statement to indicate how well each statement describes your behavior.

Describes me				Does not describe me
5	4	3	2	1

_____ 1. Whenever I start a project of any kind, I have a specific end result in mind.

_____ 2. When setting objectives, I state only the end result to be accomplished; I don't specify how the result will be accomplished.

_____ 3. I have specific and measurable objectives; for example, I know the specific grade I want to earn in this course.

_____ 4. I set objectives that are difficult but achievable.

_____ 5. I set deadlines when I have something I need to accomplish, and I meet those deadlines.

_____ 6. I have a long-term goal (what I will be doing in 3–5 years) and short-term objectives that will get me there.

_____ 7. I have written objectives stating what I want to accomplish.

_____ 8. I know my strengths and weaknesses, am aware of threats, and seek opportunities.

_____ 9. I analyze a problem and consider alternative actions, rather than immediately jumping in with a solution.

_____ 10. I spend most of my day doing what I plan to do, rather than dealing with emergencies and trying to get organized.

_____ 11. I use a calendar, appointment book, or some form of to-do list.

_____ 12. I ask others for advice.

_____ 13. I follow appropriate policies, procedures, and rules.

_____ 14. I develop contingency plans in case my plans do not work out as I expect them to.

_____ 15. I implement my plans and determine if I have met my objectives.

Add up the numbers you assigned to the statements to see where you fall on the continuum below.

Planner						Nonplanner
75	65	55	45	35	25	15

Don't be too disappointed if your score isn't as high as you would like. All of these items are characteristics of effective planning. Review the items that did not describe you and consider making an effort to implement those characteristics of planning.

---

back on the company's core customer group—women over 40. As a result, he was removed as CEO less than 18 months after taking the job, and his predecessor was brought back in to reestablish relationships with those core customers.[10]

- *Competition.* Businesses must compete for customers, and their performance is not simply a function of their own actions. Each firm's performance must be understood relative to the actions of its *competitors*.[11] For example, **Apple** has historically been renowned for its continuous innovation, which provides it a competitive advantage over its rivals. But there is concern now among stakeholders that with Steve Jobs gone, the company may have lost that edge.[12] If Apple loses its innovation lead, rivals may be able to move in on Apple's customers.[13] Organizations also frequently compete for the same employees and sometimes for suppliers,[14] and almost everyone has heard of one organization stealing employees from another similar organization, especially in high-technology fields.[15] Also, changes in competitors' strategy often affect the performance of the organization.

- *Suppliers.* Organizations buy resources from suppliers. Therefore, partnerships with *suppliers* also affect firm performance.[16] The Japanese earthquake and

EXHIBIT 2-2 THE EXTERNAL ENVIRONMENT

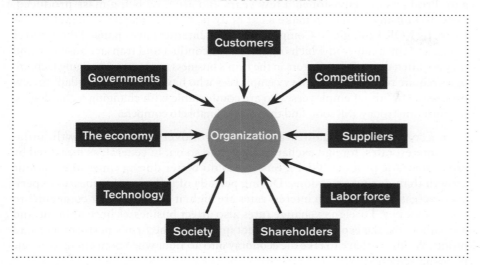

tsunami, for instance, affected virtually every company in the auto industry because electronic components made in northern Japan were unavailable for an extended period of time.[17] Therefore, it is important to develop close working relationships with your suppliers, and building close relationships requires employees who have the ability to communicate, empathize, negotiate, and come to mutually advantageous agreements.

• *Labor force.* The employees of and the talent pool available to an organization have a direct effect on the organization's performance. The US labor market has been weak over the past several years due to the recession of 2007–2008, and predictions for future labor force participation show a slower growth rate than over the past 30 years. This prediction holds in the United States and in many other industrialized countries, due to slower population growth overall.[18] Management recruits human resources from the available labor force outside the company's boundaries, so slow population growth will limit the available talent pool. Unions can provide employees for the organization, but they are considered an additional external factor because they run collective bargaining for those employees. Nevertheless, some companies are growing rapidly even in the current labor market. **Living Social** is an example of a fast-growing company that recruited thousands of new workers in 2013.[19]

• *Shareholders.* The owners of a corporation, known as shareholders, influence management. Most shareholders of large corporations are generally not involved in the day-to-day operation of the firm, but they do vote for the directors of the corporation. The board of directors is also generally not involved in the day-to-day operation of the firm, but it may hire or fire top management. The top manager reports to the board of directors, and if the organization does not perform well, the board can fire that manager and others.[20]

• *Society.* Our society, to a great extent, determines what acceptable business practices are.[21] Individuals and groups of stakeholders work to pressure businesses to make changes. For example, **Pepsi** has been pressured by Oxfam International to identify its sugar suppliers and investigate suspected land grabs made by those suppliers from poor farmers.[22] In other cases, people who live in the same area as the business do not want it to pollute the air or water or otherwise abuse natural resources.

WORK
APPLICATION 2-1

Give examples of how customers, competitors, and suppliers have affected an organization where you work or have worked.

WORK
APPLICATION 2-2

Give examples of how society and technology have affected an organization where you work or have worked.

WORK
APPLICATION 2-3

Give examples of how the economy and government have affected an organization where you work or have worked.

LO 2-2

Describe the three major organizational factors that affect our strategic options.

SHRM

J:8
Competitive Strategy

- *Technology.* Few organizations operate today as they did even a decade ago. Products not envisioned a few years ago are now being mass-produced. New 3-D printers can even make a car body from basic materials (e.g., the new Urbee by **KOR Ecologic**).[23] Computers and the Internet have changed the speed at which and the manner in which organizations conduct and transact business, and they are often determining factors in the firm's business processes. Changing technologies require technologically savvy employees who have the ability to adapt to new processes.[24] Without employees who are comfortable with changing technologies, organizations today will soon find themselves unable to compete.

- *Economic.* No organization has control over economic growth, inflation, interest rates, foreign exchange rates, and so on. In general, as measured by gross domestic product (GDP), businesses do better during times of economic growth than during recessions. During periods of inflation, businesses experience increased costs. When interest rates are high, it costs more for companies to borrow money. Foreign exchange rates also affect businesses both at home and abroad. Thus, the economy has a direct impact on the firm's performance and profits. We always have to take the economy into account when performing strategic planning activities.

- *Government.* National, state, and local governments all set laws and regulations that businesses must obey. According to a CNBC story, for small firms, the annual cost of complying with government regulations is $10,585 per employee.[25] The Occupational Safety and Health Administration (OSHA) sets safety standards, and the Environmental Protection Agency (EPA) sets pollution standards that must be met. Companies like **Pfizer, Novartis,** and **Merck** cannot market drugs without Food and Drug Administration (FDA) approval. As a result, to a large extent, business may not do whatever it wants to do; the government tells business what it can and cannot do.[26] So government matters, as it affects how business is conducted.[27] Due to the recent financial crisis, Congress decided to create new financial regulations to help prevent another crisis and recession. One was the Regulatory Flexibility Act, which lowered costs of compliance for small businesses by about $2.5 billion in 2013.[28] Federal and state governments create both opportunities and obstacles for businesses. **Allstate** insurance left the state of Massachusetts because of the unfavorable regulatory environment there. To learn more about the US federal government, visit its official web portal at http://www.usa.gov/.

In addition to our analysis of the major external environmental factors above, we need to review some internal organizational factors to decide what we want to do as an organization as we move into the future. The major factors in our analysis of our internal environment are shown in Exhibit 2-3 and are discussed in this and the next two sections.

STRATEGY

Strategy and the strategic planning process have a long history, and businesses have adapted these principles to their own use. As G. F. Keller said, "Many military historians and contemporary business students view the Chinese military strategist Sun Tzu (ca. 500 BCE) as the developer of "the Bible" of strategy . . . Sun Tzu's principles are divided into two components: 1) knowing oneself and 2) knowing the enemy."[29] To put Sun Tzu's words in a contemporary business context, one should know one's internal and external environments. But how does a modern business go about creating and implementing a strategic plan? Well, strategic planning follows a process,[30] so let's discuss that process now.

2-1 APPLYING THE CONCEPT

The External Environment

Read each statement and write in the letter corresponding to the external environmental factor it refers to.

a. customers
b. competition
c. suppliers
d. labor force
e. shareholders
f. society
g. technology
h. the economy
i. governments

_____ 1. The CEO was fired by the owners because our company is not profitable.

_____ 2. GE wanted to acquire our company, but the SEC said that would be in violation of antitrust laws, thereby preventing the deal.

_____ 3. Karen bought a new oven that will cook our pizza in half the time and make it taste even better.

_____ 4. **eHarmony** online dating service is losing some customers to other services focusing on Christian, African-American, and older people seeking matches.

_____ 5. Our purchasing agent just closed a deal that will let us buy sugar for a few cents less per pound, saving us thousands of dollars per year.

EXHIBIT 2-3   THE INTERNAL ENVIRONMENT

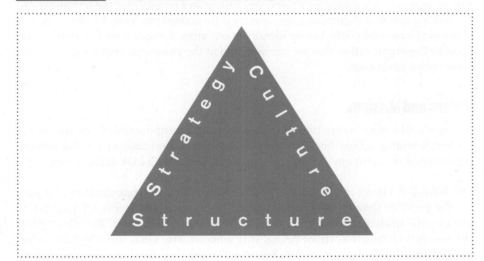

What Is Strategy?

Research has shown that HRM is an important strategic business function that influences the performance of both large and small firms.[31] But what is strategy? At its most basic level, a **strategy** is *a plan of action designed to achieve a particular set of objectives*. And what does strategy take into account? It looks at the external (industry and macro-) environment and the internal (organizational) environment in order to create strategic advantage. Strategic advantage occurs when you analyze the environment better and react to it quicker than your competitors do while using all of your internal resources efficiently, thus creating the sustainable competitive advantage that we introduced in Chapter 1.

SHRM

J:1
Strategic Management

Strategy A plan of action designed to achieve a particular set of objectives

In this section, we look at the following three major strategic questions to analyze what kind of strategic plan we need to write:[32]

1. What is our present situation (where are we now)?
2. Where do we want to go?
3. How do we plan to get there?

These questions are both very simple and very complex. On the surface, you would think that answering question 1 would be easy—but you must answer many other questions before you can confidently answer the question "Where are we now?" These other questions include "Are we making a profit?" "Do our products satisfy our customers' current needs?" "Do we have the right kind of workforce in place at this time?" "Is our technology working like it should?" "Do we have sufficient physical resources like plant, machinery and equipment, and retail locations?" "Are our advertising and marketing programs successful?" and many more. Answering these questions creates a picture of your organization at a particular point in time, and that picture has to be comprehensive so that you know what is happening, good and bad, within the organization in significant detail. If you think about each of these other questions for just a second, you will see how complex answering question 1 really becomes.

Answering questions 2 and 3 is just as complex. Question 2 is basically asking us what we plan to "look like" as an organization at a particular point in the future, meaning it's asking us what is our *vision and mission* for the organization. Answering question 3 gives us the necessary information to create the plan that will allow us to reach the goals that we identify in our answer to question 2 so that we can become the organization that we envision and at the same time create a sustainable competitive advantage.

Visions and Missions

A vision and a mission are two of the most critical components of any successful corporate strategy. Together, they provide the information necessary to focus every employee on the company's goals and objectives. Let's take a look at them now.

THE VISION. A **vision** *is what we expect to become as an organization at a particular point in time in the future.* The vision by necessity is a fuzzy thing; it is not specific in that it doesn't say *how* we're going to achieve it. But we identify the vision as a future state of being. It is who we are, what we stand for, what we believe in, and what we want to become. Despite their fuzziness, visions are very powerful when used correctly. A vision provides a *focus point* for the future; it tells the company where it is headed.[33] It allows the company leaders to look into the future and see what they want to look like as a company at that time—basically, it lets them answer the question of what they want to be when they "grow up." If everyone is focused on the same future end state, they will work toward that same end state.

So, basically the vision answers the question "What do we want to become as an organization?" But the firm is only successful when the followers share the leader's vision,[34] and HR is where many organizations perform the culture training that promotes a shared vision within the organization.

THE MISSION. In contrast, the mission is where we start to become specific. The **mission statement** *lays out our expectations of what we're going to do in order to become the organization that we have envisioned.* The mission statement is a statement of

SHRM

J:7
Competitive Advantage

LO 2-3

Discuss how having a vision and mission helps organizations focus their resources.

SHRM

J:13
Mission and Vision

Vision What we expect to become as an organization at a particular point in time in the future

Mission statement A statement laying out our expectation of what we're going to do in order to become the organization that we have envisioned

what the various organizational units will do and what they hope to accomplish, in alignment with the organizational vision. The mission is generally narrower and more specific than the vision, which means that it generally must be a bit longer-winded. The mission statement takes into account things like whom we serve (in terms of customer groups, types of products and services, technologies we use, etc.) and how we serve them. Fundamentally, it answers the question "What do we need to do in order to become what we have envisioned?"

Trader Joe's is known for its strong company vision and mission.

PUTTING THE VISION AND MISSION TOGETHER. Let's use as an example the vision and mission statements of the **College of Business of the University of Arkansas at Little Rock**. Its vision statement is as follows: "The College of Business serves as a catalyst to advance education and economic development in the State of Arkansas."[35] Notice that this vision statement does not tell you how the college will be a catalyst. It doesn't say what the college is going to *do*. All it tells you is that it expects to be a catalyst. But what is a catalyst? It's "a substance that modifies and increases the rate of a reaction without being consumed in the process."[36] So, that means the college is going to be an organization that increases the rate of change in education and economic development in its home state.

However, this vision does not tell us anything about how the college is going to do this. For that information, we look at the mission of the organization, which tells us how the organization expects to do what the vision puts forth. So let's look at the mission statement of this college of business. It says, "The mission of the College of Business is to prepare students to succeed as business professionals in a global economy and to contribute to the growth and viability of the region we serve."[37] So this means the college of business will achieve its vision by providing education that gives its students the tools they need to succeed in business and create change in the state. This, in turn, will act to improve the state's economic fortunes.

When you put the vision and mission together, the people—executives, managers, and staff—in the organization get a more complete picture of the direction in which they are expected to go. This allows all the people in the organization to focus on going in that direction, and that in turn makes it much easier for them to help the organization achieve its goals. **The fact that they create a focus is the thing that makes a vision and mission so powerful.** If everyone in the organization is focused on the same end result, it is much more likely that the organization will achieve that end result.

This focus on an end result also gives everyone a clearer picture of what is expected of them individually. Think of it as follows: If you're a bricklayer and you're laying bricks, you may not pay attention to each of the bricks you lay if you have no mental picture of the finished project. However, if you're building a beautiful art museum and you have been shown a picture of what the museum will look like when finished, you're more likely to pay close attention to each brick because you will want to be able to say that you helped create something beautiful.

WORK
APPLICATION 2-4

Identify the vision and mission of an organization where you work or have worked.

A strong vision and a good mission statement are critical parts of the strategic planning process. *Everything* else in strategic planning comes from the vision and mission.

Vision + Mission = FOCUS!

Finally, organizations go through a series of analyses of both external and internal factors to come up with the plan of action that answers question 3. Strategic planners look at each of the environmental factors that we noted above, and they analyze the company's capabilities and limitations to come up with a workable plan. We will discuss some of these factors in the following sections.

Types of Strategies

There are several generic strategy types that we are able to categorize. Some researchers break these down into just two or three categories, while others list several more. We will try to keep this as simple as possible right now, since for our purposes, we only need to know the major categories. So we will break the types of strategies down into three categories: cost leadership, differentiation, and focus or niche strategies.[38]

COST LEADERSHIP. Cost leaders do everything that they can to lower the organizational costs required to produce their products or services. However, cost leaders do not necessarily provide their products or services to the customer for a lower price. They can choose to keep their prices down and maintain the same margin as their higher-cost competitors, or they can choose to charge the same price as their competitors and thus increase their profit margin above that of their competitors on each of the goods or services they sell. **Wal-Mart** has had great success with this strategy, and during the recession and coming out of it, Wal-Mart reduced its prices even more aggressively to combat loss of business to "dollar" stores.[39] However, low-cost strategies can have a downside as well. **Tata Motors'** cheap Nano automobile at first failed because potential customers saw it as "too cheap" and therefore thought, "It must be unreliable." So, Tata is now building more expensive Nanos, hoping that they will catch on with young buyers.[40]

DIFFERENTIATION. This strategy attempts to create an impression of difference for the company's product or service in the mind of the customer. The differentiator company stresses its advantage over its competitors.[41] If the company is successful in creating this impression, it can charge a higher price for its product or service than can its competitors. Differentiation, it should be noted, is not necessarily based on real difference but on the perception of difference, which is often created through advertising.[42] **Nike, Harley Davidson, Margaritaville,** and others place their corporate name prominently on their products to differentiate those products from those of the competition. According to *Coca-Cola,* the three keys to selling consumer products are differentiation, differentiation, and differentiation, which it achieves with its scripted name logo and contour bottle.

WORK
APPLICATION 2-5

Identify the strategy of an organization where you work or have worked and explain how the organization uses the strategy against its competitors to gain customers.

FOCUS OR NICHE. With this strategy, the company focuses on a specific portion of a larger market. For instance, the company may focus on a regional market, a particular product line, or a buyer group. Within a particular target segment or market niche, the firm may use differentiation or a cost leadership strategy. Businesses can win big by thinking small.[43] It is hard to compete head-on with the big companies like **Coca-Cola** and **Pepsi,** but the much smaller **Dr Pepper Snapple Group's** two non-colas have a differentiated taste for a much smaller target market, but it is still very profitable.[44]

2-2 APPLYING THE CONCEPT

Identify which strategy is used by each brand or company listed and write the letter corresponding to the company's strategy by the company's name.

a. cost leadership
b. differentiation
c. focus or niche

____ 6. iPhone
____ 7. *Bodybuilder* magazine
____ 8. Rolex watches
____ 9. TOMS shoes
____ 10. Wal-Mart

How Strategy Affects HRM

There are several areas where the generic corporate strategy affects how we do our jobs within HR. Let's take a look at a few of the significant differences between generic strategies. A little later in this chapter, we will also review how HRM affects the ability to commit to a particular corporate strategy. We will continue to discuss these areas in greater detail as we progress through the book.

HRM AND COST LEADERSHIP. If our organization is following a generic cost leadership strategy, we are going to be most interested in minimizing all internal costs, including employee costs. So we are concerned with maximum efficiency and effectiveness.[45] Because we are concerned with maximum efficiency, we will probably create highly specialized jobs within the organization so that we have people doing the same thing repeatedly. This will generally cause employees to get much better and faster at their jobs. We will also have a specific job description for each position and job-specific training with very little, if any, cross-training. We will hire new workers based on technical skills and abilities, and we will most likely emphasize performance pay by which the employees get paid more if they perform their job faster and better. We will also provide incentives that emphasize cost controls and efficiency. Finally, it's quite likely that managers will use performance appraisals as a control mechanism to allow them to weed out less efficient and less effective employees.

HRM AND DIFFERENTIATION. On the other hand, if our organization is following a differentiator strategy, we're going to be more concerned with employees who are flexible and adaptable, who have the ability to innovate and create new processes, and who can work in uncertain environments within cross-functional teams.[46] In a differentiator organization, we will most likely have much broader job classifications, as well as broader work-planning processes. Individuals will be hired and paid based on individual knowledge and skill sets, not specifically based on skills related to the job they fill upon entering the organization. Here, our incentive programs will reward innovation and creativity. Finally, in the differentiator organization, performance appraisals will generally be used as a tool to develop the skill sets of the valuable knowledge workers within the organization, not as a tool to punish and weed out poor performers. So you can see very quickly that HRM will need to do its job in a significantly different way based on the type of generic strategy that the company decides to follow.

Strategic Analysis

There are two primary components of strategic analysis used by most organizations. The first is called five-forces analysis, and it is a tool that organizations use to analyze the external competitive environment. The second is called SWOT analysis (SWOT stands for strengths, weaknesses, opportunities, and threats), and it is used to analyze

WORK
APPLICATION 2-6

Conduct a five-forces competitive analysis for an organization where you work or have worked.

the company-specific (internal) environment. There are many other strategic-analysis tools, but let's save those for another course.

FIVE-FORCES ANALYSIS. Five-forces analysis is again brought to us by Michael Porter, who identified competition within an industry as being a composite of five competitive forces that should be considered in analyzing competitive situations.[47] See Exhibit 2-4 for a list of the five forces.

1. *Rivalry among competitors.* Porter calls this scrambling and jockeying for position.[48] Businesses do this in different ways, including competing for customers on the basis of price, quality, or speed of delivery. How much rivalry there is among competitors determines things like how competitive the industry is and which competitors are targeting the same customer groups. Rivals need to anticipate each other's moves. **Coke** and **Pepsi** are long-time rivals in the soft drink industry, while **Nissan** and **Toyota** are long-time rivals in the auto industry.

2. *Threat of substitute products and services.* Companies in other industries may try to take a company's customers away. For example, newer methods of storing and playing music and videos—like the streaming music services **iHeart-Radio** and **Pandora**—are taking significant market share from manufacturers of MP3 players, which previously took significant market share from CD and DVD manufacturers.

3. *Potential new entrants.* How difficult and costly is it for new businesses to enter the industry as competitors? Does the company need to plan for new competition? Are there significant barriers to entry that would prevent such new competition? In many industries today, all it takes to enter is the ability to create and host a website.[49] If it is easy to enter an industry and profitability is significant,

EXHIBIT 2-4   FIVE-FORCES COMPETITIVE ANALYSIS

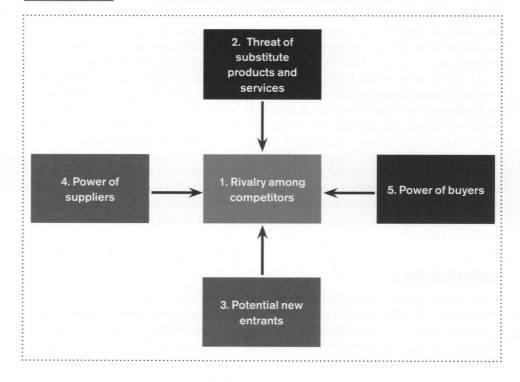

then the threat of new entrants is much higher. If it's more difficult to enter an industry, for instance because of high capital equipment costs or other barriers to entry, and profitability is lower, possibly because the product is a commodity (think about the steel manufacturing industry), then the threat of new entrants is significantly lower.

4. *Power of suppliers.* How much does our business depend on its suppliers? If the business has only one major supplier of a critical component, with no alternatives available, then the supplier has greater bargaining power over the business. However, if our business can get its major supplies from any one of many different suppliers, then the suppliers will have very little power over the business.

Wal-Mart holds power over suppliers because of the volume of goods that it buys.

5. *Power of buyers.* How much does our business depend on its buyers? If one buyer or a few large buyers purchase most of what we provide, then the buyer has significant bargaining power over our company. As an example, almost every business student has heard of the power **Wal-Mart** holds over its suppliers because of the volume of goods that it buys. However, if we provide products or services to many different buyers, none of which provides us with a major portion of our business, then the buyers may have very little bargaining power.

Companies use the five-forces analysis and other industry and competitive-situation analysis tools primarily at the corporate level to make decisions regarding which lines of business to enter and exit and how to allocate resources among existing lines of business.

SWOT ANALYSIS. While five-forces analysis is a primary tool for analyzing the external environment, SWOT analysis is a tool to analyze the organization's internal environment, meaning its specific capabilities and limitations. In the process of SWOT analysis, the organization creates a list of its strengths, weaknesses, opportunities, and threats. See Exhibit 2-5 for a format in which to list SWOTs. Once this list is created, the organization evaluates each of the sections of the list in order to decide *where it can use its resources most effectively.*

If, for example, we have an organizational strength that is critical to maintain in order to serve our most important customer groups, then we will allocate resources toward maintenance of that strength. If, however, we have strengths on our list that no longer provide us with the potential for advantage over our competitors, then we may choose not to use organizational resources to maintain those strengths. So as you can see, the process of SWOT analysis is a process of balancing our available resources in order to make the most of our strengths and opportunities and to minimize any danger to the organization from its weaknesses and threats.

Designing a Strategy

Once we have identified an organizational vision and mission, decided which generic strategic type we're going to pursue, and done some analysis of the external environment and our organizational capabilities, we're ready to start designing our organization's strategy. The next steps in our design process include setting

WORK
APPLICATION 2-7

Conduct a SWOT analysis for an organization where you work or have worked.

SHRM

J:3
Strategy Formulation

EXHIBIT 2-5   SWOT ANALYSIS

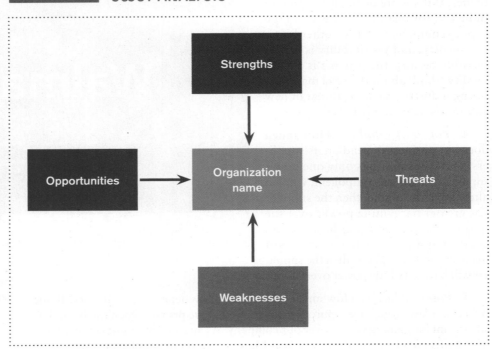

WORK
APPLICATION 2-8

Write an objective for an organization where you work or have worked that is specific, that is measurable, and that has a target date.

objectives, creating a strategic plan, implementing that plan, and monitoring and evaluating its success. Let's take a brief look at each of these steps.

SETTING OBJECTIVES. Successful strategic management requires a commitment on the part of managers to a defined set of objectives. Successful managers have a goal orientation,[50] which means they set and achieve objectives. Goal orientation can also be learned.[51]

After developing our vision and mission and completing a situation analysis, the next step is to set objectives that flow from the mission to address strategic issues and problems identified through situation analysis. **Objectives** *state what is to be accomplished in singular, specific, and measurable terms, with a target date.* The organization has to write at least one objective for every major goal that is set forth in its strategy. You must begin with the end in mind, and objectives do not state how they will be accomplished—just the end result you want to accomplish.[52]

Here is a model adapted from Max Weber to help you write effective objectives, followed by a few company examples.

To + action verb + singular, specific, measureable result + target date

Honda:[53] To + introduce + 12 new Honda models for Chinese markets + over 3 years, beginning in 2013

Nike:[54] To + increase + annual revenues to $36 billion + by 2017

Dell:[55] To + cut costs + by $4 billion + in 2011

We will talk a little more about organizational objectives a little later.

CREATE A STRATEGY. Once we've identified our set of objectives, the next step is to weave them into a cohesive organizational plan. This is the point at which we

Objectives Statements of what is to be accomplished in singular, specific, and measurable terms, with a target date

Writing Objectives

For each objective, write in the letter corresponding to which "must" criteria is not met.

a. single result
b. specific
c. measurable
d. target date

_____ 11. To start working out aerobically within a few weeks
_____ 12. To double ticket sales

_____ 13. To sell 7% more sandwiches and 15% more chips in 2016
_____ 14. To decrease the number of sales returns by year end of 2016
_____ 15. To be perceived as the best restaurant in the Boston area by 2017

determine what we're going to do to achieve the objectives that we have set. Taking into account the vision and mission that we have decided on—and having determined our environment and each of our strengths, weaknesses, opportunities, and threats— we begin to plan activities within the organization that will allow us to reach those objectives. Looking at this process, you should be able to quickly see that no organization should ever just copy another organization's strategy—even if that strategy has been successful for the company that is being copied. Why? The simple answer is that no two organizations have the same vision and mission; organizational environment; or strengths, weaknesses, opportunities, and threats and—as a result—no two organizations should have the same objectives. Therefore, no two organizations could *ever* expect to be successful by following the same strategy.

IMPLEMENTING, MONITORING, AND EVALUATING STRATEGIES. Green Bay Packers coach Vince Lombardi was known to have said, "The best game plan in the world never blocked or tackled anybody."[56] This is true, no matter the organization and the strategic plan—*execution* of the plan is the key. The last items in the strategic planning process are implementing and then monitoring and evaluating the plan's success. The goal here is to ensure that the mission and objectives of the organization are achieved. Successful implementation of strategies requires effective and efficient support systems throughout the organization. It also requires a dedication to the plan at all levels of the organization. Although strategic planning usually goes well, implementation is often a problem.[57] One reason is that strategic plans often end up getting buried in bottom drawers; all too frequently, no action is taken to implement the strategy.

As strategies are implemented, they must also be monitored and evaluated. *Controlling* is the process of establishing and implementing mechanisms to ensure that objectives are achieved. An important part of controlling is measuring progress toward the achievement of the objective and taking corrective action when needed. Another important part of controlling is staying within budgets when appropriate or changing them when necessary to meet changes in the environment.

Quality management is one example of where the controlling process allows the company to adjust its internal processes to reach a predetermined level of quality control. Quality must consistently be monitored—because while quality costs, lack of quality costs much more. So as part of strategy execution, we always need to watch quality through the controlling process.

SHRM
J:4
Strategy Implementation

SHRM
J:14
Quality Management

SHRM

J:10
Linking HR Strategy to
Organizational Strategy

SHRM

J:2
Enhancing Firm Competitiveness

How HR Promotes Strategy

So, what does HRM have to do with a particular strategy? Do HR managers need to recruit, select, train, evaluate, and interact with employees differently based on different organizational strategies? Of course they do. We showed you earlier how we might manage people differently based on different generic strategies. The same holds true when looking at different sets of objectives, different competitors, different organizational strengths and weaknesses, and many other industry and company characteristics. If the objective is to win a race, you wouldn't hire a cab driver to drive a Formula One race car! Both the cabbie and the Formula One driver can drive, but they do it differently to achieve different goals. HR managers have to evaluate all of the organizational characteristics to determine what kinds of people to bring into the organization and then how to maintain those people once they have become a part of the company. This is the reason that it's so critical for HR managers to understand organizational strategy.[58] In fact, as you go through the remainder of this book, you will see continuing references to how HRM will affect the company's ability to do its work over the long term. Everything that HR does must mesh with the chosen strategy to provide the right kinds of employees, who will learn and do the right types of jobs so that the company can achieve its goals.

LO 2-4

Identify and describe the major components of organizational structure and why it is important to understand them.

STRUCTURE

Organizational structure *refers to the way in which an organization groups its resources to accomplish its mission.* There must be a sound organizational structure if a strategy is to be successfully implemented.[59] Why do you see firms that seem to be equal in size and capability execute at different levels of efficiency? The answer lies in how their resources are differently structured and managed.[60] Thus, the selection of a proper organizational structure is critical to business success.[61]

In HRM, managers need to have an understanding of organizational structure to do their jobs correctly. An organization is a system that is typically, but not always, structured into departments such as finance, marketing, production, human resources, and so on. Each of these departments affects the organization as a whole, and each department is affected by the other departments. Organizations structure their resources to transform inputs into outputs. All of an organization's resources must be structured effectively if it is to achieve its mission.[62] As a manager in any department, you will be responsible for part of the organization's structure.

SHRM

E:9
Organizational Design

Basics of Organizational Structure

One way to look at organizational structure is to identify a series of fundamental components. Each of these components identifies part of how we divide the organization up and group its resources to make them more efficient and effective. Let's discuss complexity, formalization, and centralization as structural components.

COMPLEXITY. **Complexity,** the first major component of organizational structure, *is the degree to which three types of differentiation exist within the organization.* These three types of differentiation are vertical differentiation, horizontal differentiation, and spatial differentiation. Each of these three subcomponents demonstrates a way in which we break the organization up into smaller and more differentiated pieces. How one does this is very important. For example, **Microsoft** is currently working through how it wants to change its organizational structure under new CEO Satya Nadella because its historical structure has become too expensive.[63]

Organizational structure The way in which an organization groups its resources to accomplish its mission

Complexity Degree to which three types of differentiation exist within the organization

Vertical differentiation deals with how we break the organization up vertically, meaning how many layers there are in the organization from the top to the bottom. How many bosses are there, and whom does each one report to? Whom does the HR manager report to? You also need a clear overall boss who is accountable for results.[64] The organizational chart is typically used to show the chain of command.

Horizontal differentiation identifies how we break the organization up horizontally. We usually do this by breaking the organization up into departments. For example, HR is commonly a department within the organizational structure, advising and assisting all the other departments in the firm. But there are other ways in which we can segment the organization horizontally, including by customer type, product or process type, geographic divisions, etc. **Zappos** just recently changed to a "holacracy," meaning a structure in which there are no departments, job titles, or managers. This is a radical way to wipe out vertical *and* horizontal differentiation.[65]

Spatial differentiation deals with the physical separation of different parts of the organization. For instance, we may have headquarters in Los Angeles, California, while we may have a production plant in Indonesia. Spatial differentiation can make it much more difficult to manage the organization due to the fact that the organization is spread out among many locations. For example, **GE** operates in more than 160 countries.[66] Now that is complex!

So complexity involves the way in which we divide the organization into different segments, both physically and within artificial boundaries such as departments. Why does this matter to the organization's managers? The more the organization is broken into segments, the more difficult it becomes to manage within it. If we have many vertical layers in the organization (vertical differentiation) and many horizontal divisions of the organization (horizontal differentiation), and if the organization has many different physical locations (spatial differentiation), then it is much more difficult to conduct business than if there were fewer divisions. More complexity makes it more difficult to communicate between the different parts of the organization, makes it more difficult to make decisions within the organization, and makes it more difficult to find information that we need when it's in another part of the organization. In fact, duplication of processes is a common problem in highly complex organizations.[67] As a result of this difficulty in making decisions and communicating, the cost of managing an organization goes up as it becomes more complex and bureaucratic. As an example, in a February 2014 article, Bloomberg noted that as college and university bureaucracies in the United States get larger, the cost of college goes up for students.[68] This means that we want to minimize complexity as much as possible in order to minimize organizational costs.

FORMALIZATION. **Formalization,** the second major component of organizational structure, *is the degree to which jobs are standardized within an organization, meaning the degree to which we have created policies, procedures, and rules that "program" the jobs of the employees.* If we make things routine by creating standard operating procedures and other standard processes, we can usually increase the efficiency and effectiveness of the people within the organization, in turn making the entire organization more productive on a per-unit basis.[69] So the more that we can formalize the jobs within the organization, the easier it is to manage the people in those jobs. We also tend to see lower costs in organizations that are highly formalized, because jobs in such organizations are done in a routine, repetitive manner—at least when it is possible to do so.

As a result, we generally want to formalize all of the processes that we can within the organization, but we can't always formalize everything that we do. How much

Formalization Degree to which jobs are standardized within an organization, meaning the degree to which we have created policies, procedures, and rules that "program" the jobs of the employees

WORK
APPLICATION 2-9

Briefly describe the complexity, formalization, and centralization of the organizational structure where you work or have worked.

we're able to formalize jobs within the organization depends on what the organization is designed to do. If the organization is designed to do the same thing over and over, such as producing a low-cost commodity, then we can usually formalize many of its procedures. On the other hand, if the organization is designed to do unique and nonroutine things as a differentiator (meaning it never does the same thing twice), then we will probably not be able to formalize very much of what the organization does.[70]

CENTRALIZATION. **Centralization,** the third major component of organizational structure, *is the degree to which decision making is concentrated within the organization.* The degree of centralization in an organization has to do with dispersion of authority for decision making and delegation of authority. If we can concentrate authority in decision making with one or a few individuals, we can concentrate on hiring people who are very good at making business decisions in those few positions and not worry about the decision-making skills of the rest of our employees.[71]

Centralization of decision making tends to create greater control within the organization, because the organization's few decision makers will soon find that they make similar decisions over and over. They thereby become very good at determining the best course of action in a particular situation. In other words, there is a learning curve in decision making. The more decisions you make, the better you get at making high-quality decisions.[72]

However, there's a tradeoff to centralized decision making. As the organization gets larger, we may have to go through many layers of the organization in order to get a decision made. This can slow down the processes within the firm—in some cases, to such an extent that by the time a decision is made, it becomes irrelevant. For example, **TEPCO** was criticized for having a complex bureaucratic decision-making process that led to the meltdown of three reactors at one of its nuclear plants in Japan.[73] So we have to balance centralization and decentralization within our firms, and the current trend is toward decentralization.[74] However, we know that centralized decision making gives us greater control and thus generally tends to lower our costs for decision making. So other things being equal, we would rather have highly centralized decision making.

IS THERE ONE "BEST" STRUCTURE? No. The best structure is one that fits the firm's current competitive situation as well as its internal capabilities and that enables it to implement its strategies successfully. Warren Buffett advises businesses to keep things simple,[75] and Peter Drucker may have said it as well as anyone when he noted, "The simplest organization structure that will do the job is the best one. What makes an organization structure 'good' is the problems it does not create.... To obtain both the greatest possible simplicity and the greatest 'fit,' organization design has to start out with a clear focus on KEY ACTIVITIES needed to produce KEY RESULTS."[76]

How Does Structure Affect Employee Behavior?

We now know that structure is made up of complexity, formalization, and centralization. Does the way in which we combine these components cause employees within the organization to act in different ways? In fact, it does. Think for a second of an organization that in your mind is a bureaucracy. It might be a government agency, a corporation that you've worked for, or the college or university at which you study. Chances are that this organization is highly complex, has many standard procedures or ways of doing things (formalization), and is probably at least partially centralized (meaning only certain individuals can make major decisions). If you are part of this organization and someone asks

Centralization Degree to which decision making is concentrated within the organization you to do something that is outside the scope of your job, then you most likely would say, "That's not my job," and tell them to go to a different person to accomplish that task. You don't have the authority or the knowledge to be able to help them.

Now let's look at a different kind of organization. You have taken a job with a brand-new, entrepreneurial firm—like **Zappos**. There are no departments or standard procedures, and you were hired at least in part because of your ability to "think on your feet" and make decisions. Someone again asks you to do something that is outside the scope of your normal job. In this environment, you're much more likely to take upon yourself the task of figuring out a way to assist the other person instead of passing them to someone else. The structure of the organization has changed the way that you react to a request to do something that is outside the scope of your job. Either that, or the request becomes your job.

SHRM

C:3
Individual vs. Group Behavior

SHRM

Q:2
Organizational Structure and Job Design

How Does Structure Affect HRM?

As the HR manager, would your job change if your organization adopted the structure of one of the two companies above? In a small entrepreneurial firm, there usually is no HRM department, but someone has to perform the HR functions. Would you need to recruit and hire different types of people in a bureaucratic organization than you would in an entrepreneurial organization? Indeed, you would. In the more bureaucratic organization, you would most likely look for and hire people who had significant depth of expertise in a narrow area within their field of knowledge, so that they could apply that expertise in a highly efficient manner. That would make the organization more productive over the long term. Your training programs would also probably be more specific and geared toward particular jobs. In addition, your performance appraisal processes would be aimed at evaluating more specific tasks and functions than would be the case in the entrepreneurial organization. In fact, the organizational structure will affect virtually every function of the HR manager. So in order to be a successful HR manager, you have to understand and adapt to the particular organizational structure of your firm.

ORGANIZATIONAL CULTURE

Organizational culture is another characteristic that affects how the HR manager operates within the firm. Fostering the right organizational culture is one of the most important responsibilities of the CEO and other corporate executives.[77] Management needs to be involved in establishing shared values, beliefs, and assumptions so that employees know how to behave.[78] Every group of humans that gather together anywhere at any point in time create a unique group culture. They have their own group standards, called norms, which create pressure for the group's members to conform. Social groups have societal cultures, nations have national cultures, and organizations have their own distinct organizational cultures.

LO 2-5
Describe organizational culture and how it affects the members of the organization.

SHRM

A:3
Managing/Creating a Positive Organizational Culture

What Is Organizational Culture?

Organizational culture *consists of the values, beliefs, and assumptions about appropriate behavior that members of an organization share.* Culture describes how employees do what they do (behavior) and why they do what they do (values, profits, customers, employees, society). Every organization has a culture, and success depends on the health and strength of its culture.[79] Therefore, leaders should spend a

Organizational culture The values, beliefs, and assumptions about appropriate behavior that members of an organization share

EXHIBIT 2-6 **CULTURE ARTIFACTS AND LEVELS OF CULTURE**

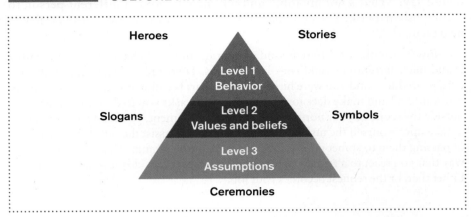

WORK
APPLICATION 2-10

Briefly describe some of the organizational culture artifacts where you work or have worked.

lot of time building the organization's culture.[80] Organizational culture is primarily learned through observing people and events in the organization.

ARTIFACTS OF ORGANIZATIONAL CULTURE. There are five artifacts of organizational culture that help employees learn the culture:

1. *Heroes,* such as founders Steve Jobs of **Apple,** Sam Walton of **Wal-Mart,** Herb Kelleher of **Southwest Airlines,** Frederick Smith of **FedEx,** and others who have made outstanding contributions to their organizations.

2. *Stories,* often about founders and others who have made extraordinary efforts. These include stories about Sam Walton visiting every Wal-Mart store yearly, or someone driving through a blizzard to deliver a product or service. Public statements and speeches can also be considered stories.

3. *Slogans,* such as **at McDonald's.** Q, S, C, V (or quality, service, cleanliness, and value)

4. *Symbols,* such as plaques, pens, jackets, or a pink Cadillac at the cosmetics firm **Mary Kay.**

5. *Ceremonies,* such as awards dinners for top achievers at **Mary Kay.**

THREE LEVELS OF CULTURE. The three levels of culture include behavior, values and beliefs, and assumptions. Exhibit 2-6 illustrates the three levels of culture.

Level 1: Behavior. Behavior includes the observable things that people do and say or the actions employees take. *Artifacts* result from behavior and include written and spoken language, dress, material objects, and the organization's physical layout. Heroes, stories, slogans, symbols, and ceremonies are all part of behavior-level culture. The behavior level is also called the *visible level.* Values, beliefs, and assumptions are considered the *invisible level,* as you cannot actually observe them.

Level 2: Values and beliefs. Values represent the way people believe they ought to behave, and beliefs represent "if, then" statements like "If I do X, then Y will happen." Values and beliefs provide the operating principles that guide decision making and shape the behaviors that result in level-1 culture. Values and beliefs cannot be observed directly; we can only infer from people's behavior what they value and believe.

Although organizations use heroes, stories, symbols, and ceremonies to convey important values and beliefs, slogans are critical to level-2 culture. A slogan expresses key values. Slogans are part of organizational mission statements, while a *philosophy* (e.g., FedEx's philosophy of people-service-profit) is a formal statement of values and beliefs.

Level 3: Assumptions. Assumptions are values and beliefs that are so deeply ingrained that they are considered unquestionably true. Because assumptions are shared, they're rarely discussed. They serve as an automatic pilot to guide behavior. In fact, people often feel threatened when assumptions are challenged. If you question employees about why they do something or suggest a change, they often respond with statements like "That's the way it's always been done." Assumptions are often the most stable and enduring part of culture and are difficult to change.

Notice that behavior is at the top of the diagram in Exhibit 2-6. Assumptions, values, and beliefs affect behavior, not the other way around; in other words, cause and effect work from the bottom up.

How Culture Controls Employee Behavior in Organizations

Because organizational culture is based at least partly on assumptions, values, and beliefs, it is a very powerful force in controlling how people act within its boundaries. For instance, if the culture says that we value hard work and productivity but an individual on one of the teams fails to do his or her part, work hard, and be productive, then the other members of the team are quite likely to pressure that individual to conform to the culture. Since assumptions, values, and beliefs are so strong, shirking individuals will most likely change their actions to conform to those that the culture values.

You may not believe that culture has the ability to cause you to change the way you act, but it does. Have you ever done something to fit in, or have you ever done something you really didn't want to do because of peer pressure? Doesn't peer pressure control most people—at least sometimes? Think about the way you act as part of your family, and then compare that to the way you act as a student at school, with

©iStockphoto.com/kupicoo

In a strong organizational culture, employees tend to dress and behave in similar ways.

WORK
APPLICATION 2-11

Give examples of how culture controls employee behavior where you work or have worked.

a group of your friends, or as an employee at work. Chances are quite high that you act differently within these different "cultures." We all act to conform, for the most part, to the culture that we happen to be in at that point in time, because the culture's values push us to act that way.

Social Media and Culture Management

Recall that there is an internal and an external environment that every organization is concerned with. See Exhibit 2-7 for a review of the components making up the environment.

Social media is one of the mechanisms that we now use to both monitor and—at least partially—control organizational environments.[81] How does social media help monitor the environment, both external and internal? You will recall the case of Angie in Chapter 1. Angie did some things she should not have done, and the company was monitoring social media and happened to find the posting that she made. This is one example of monitoring the internal environment, which gives management a feel for the culture within the organization.

Companies can also actively seek out information internally using various forms of social media[82] and can even ask company members to interact on social media platforms such as LinkedIn and Facebook. Have you ever known a friend whose organization asked employees to "like" them on Facebook? This mechanism is becoming more important every day and will continue to do so for the immediate future.

The same is true for the external environment, from following competitors on social media sites to following government Web pages and media links. Governments and other entities are even using social media to extend their reach into communities that are generally hard to reach, because they don't pay much attention to standard methods of communication like State of the Union addresses and regulatory bulletins. In the United States, President Obama's administration turned to social media to attract younger individuals (who don't tend to get as involved with government issues) to the federal health care exchanges. The administration did this because the new health care law required younger members to sign up to offset the higher cost of insuring older individuals.[83]

WORK
APPLICATION 2-12

Give examples of how you have used social media at work.

2-4   APPLYING THE CONCEPT

The Internal Environment

Identify which internal environmental factor is referred to in each statement and then write the letter corresponding to that factor before the statement.

   a.   strategy
   b.   structure
   c.   culture

_____ 16. "At **Victoria's Secret**, we focus on selling clothes and other products to women."

_____ 17. "At the SEC, we have several layers of management."

_____ 18. "At **Ford**, quality is job one."

_____ 19. "Walking around the office, I realized that I would have to wear a jacket and tie every day."

_____ 20. "I work in the production department, and she works in the marketing department."

EXHIBIT 2-7 THE INTERNAL AND EXTERNAL ENVIRONMENT

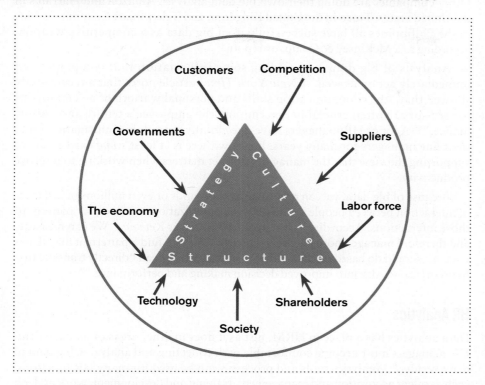

So as you can see, social media continues to become more important to even traditional businesses and governments. You can bet that governments will pay more attention to social media in the future, since many of the "Arab Spring" uprisings were coordinated via social media.[84] This is just one example of the power of social media sites.

AN INTRODUCTION TO DATA ANALYTICS FOR HRM

Data analytics *is the process of accessing large amounts of data in order to analyze those data and gain insight into significant trends or patterns within organizations or industries.* Computing power has obviously been increasing at a remarkable rate for the past 20 years, as has the ability to both create and store large amounts of data and information. This ability to create huge amounts of data has led to the concept of "big data."

Big data involves the collection of extremely large data sets—so large, in fact, that data analytics on these data sets would have been impossible until very recently, since we just did not have the computing power or the programs available. With the advent of faster computers and new analytics programs, we can now find patterns in these massive data sets that allow us to make important organizational decisions—especially strategic decisions.

A Brief on Data Analytics

Companies like **Google** grew up on data analytics and big data. Director of Research Peter Norvig said recently, "We don't have better algorithms than anyone else; we just have more data."[85] And Google analyzes *all* of that data looking for patterns that it can use. Many other companies have also jumped on this bandwagon, including

Data analytics Process of accessing large amounts of data in order to analyze those data and gain insight into significant trends or patterns within organizations or industries

some powerful outsourcers like **IBM** and **Oracle**, who are selling big data services.[86] Other companies are doing their own big data analysis. **Amazon** and **Harrah's** in the United States, **Tesco** in the United Kingdom, and **Telco Smart Communications** in the Philippines all have successfully used big data as a competitive weapon, according to a McKinsey & Company report.[87]

Analysis of big data is providing some information that companies can immediately act on as well. A *New York Times* article notes that a recent study showed that "the communication skills and personal warmth of an employee's supervisor are often crucial in determining the employee's tenure and performance."[88] A lot of HR managers have anecdotally passed this information on to their line managers for many years, but now there is at least *some* hard evidence supporting the view that the manager's skill set matters when working to improve productivity.

Because of big data, we can now analyze thousands or even millions of instances of interaction between people in and between organizations and look for patterns to those interactions. According to the *Harvard Business Review*, "We can measure, and therefore manage, more precisely than ever."[89] If we find a pattern, it may tell us what we should do based on data rather than instinct. We can "directly translate that [pattern] knowledge into improved decision making and performance."[90]

HR Analytics

Data analytics has a place in HRM, just as it does in other areas of management. HR managers must become comfortable with collecting and analyzing big data to drive results.[91] Analytics tools and processes can be used for many HR functions, such as talent acquisition and management, training and development, work and job analysis, productivity analysis, motivation, retention, and engagement.[92] However, according to a recent set of studies from Accenture and the United Kingdom's Chartered Institute of Personnel and Development (CIPD), organizational silos, skills shortages, and suspicion about reducing human beings to data points are "preventing HR departments from effectively using talent analytics."[93]

The convergence of HRM and big data is sometimes called *workforce science*. Peter Capelli, director of the Center for Human Resources at the University of Pennsylvania at Wharton, says, "This is absolutely the way forward."[94] The ability to measure actions and reactions in large numbers and find patterns in them is going to change the management of people in organizations—not just in the long term, but in the immediate future. In fact, it is already happening. Again, **Google** uses data analysis in HR just as much as it does in the marketing of products and services. Google knows, for instance, that its most innovative workers "are those who have a strong sense of mission about their work and . . . have autonomy."[95]

Desired Outcomes

Companies shouldn't do anything without good reason. What are the outcomes that we seek from big data and data analytics? A recent Boston Consulting Group (BCG) study found that "companies that are highly skilled in core HR practices experience up to 3.5 times the revenue growth and as much as 2.1 times the profit margins of less capable companies."[96] That is a shocking differential between skilled and less skilled organizations. Successful discovery and utilization of data in HR metrics is one major point of difference between top companies and others. HR managers who can use such metrics can gain their "seat at the table" when strategy is being discussed in their firms.

A study by Accenture noted that businesses are increasingly looking at internal people processes in order to predict the impact of those processes on their business results.[97] There is no doubt that data analytics is becoming a critical area of expertise for HR managers—especially at higher management levels.

A couple of quotes from a recent *Harvard Business Review* research report summarize these issues nicely: "The evidence is clear: data-driven decisions tend to be better decisions," and "Smart leaders across industries will see using big data for what it is: a management revolution."[98]

HUMAN RESOURCE INFORMATION SYSTEMS (HRIS)

Strategic planning requires the management and manipulation of large amounts of data through the use of the data analytics processes introduced above. HR serves as a broad-based organizational system using data to influence business performance.[99] As a result, most organizations today use complex computer systems to manage and manipulate those data. Human resource information systems (HRIS) are one type of system used to manage and analyze data in organizations.

What Are HRIS?

Human resource information systems (HRIS) *are interacting database systems that "aim at generating and delivering HR information and allow us to automate some human resource management functions."*[100] Some of the most common features in HRIS include modules for tracking attendance and leave, job, and pay history and logging appraisal scores and review dates. Others include modules for benefits enrollment and tracking, succession management, training management, and time logging. There are additional modules available depending on the size and type of the organization.[101]

How Do HRIS Assist in Making Decisions?

HRIS allow us to maintain control of our HR information, and they make it available for our use during the strategic planning process. Organizations can access things such as training records, job descriptions, work histories, and much more. Having this aggregate information immediately available makes the strategic planning process both quicker and smoother. If we are planning a new strategic initiative that is going to require certain training and skill sets, we can immediately search the HRIS database to see how many individuals have the requisite skills and training. We can also use the information stored in the database to make daily decisions within the HR department. For example, since training records are available in the HRIS, if we need to determine who has completed conflict management coursework for a new team being created in the company, we can quickly identify those individuals with that skill set. We can also use the same databases when considering promotions, transfers, and many other daily activities that are required inside the organization.

MEASUREMENT TOOLS FOR STRATEGIC HRM

Housed within many HRIS are statistical packages for HRM. Just as we have to quantify and measure other parts of the organization, we also have measurement tools specific to HRM. Some of the most common tools are economic value added (EVA) balanced scorecards, including organizational scorecards and HR scorecards, and return on investment (ROI). Let's take a brief look at each of these tools.

WORK APPLICATION 2-13

How does the HR department where you work or have worked use HRIS? If you don't know, ask an HR manager.

LO 2-6

Describe human resource information systems (HRIS) and identify how they can help HR make decisions.

LO 2-7

Identify the common measurement tools for strategic human resource management (HRM).

Human resource information systems (HRIS) Interacting database systems that aim at generating and delivering HR information and allow us to automate some human resource management functions

Economic Value Added (EVA)

Economic value added (EVA) is designed as a method for calculating the creation of value for the organization's shareholders. **Economic value added (EVA)** *is a measure of profits that remain after the cost of capital has been deducted from operating profits.* It provides shareholders and managers with a better understanding of how the business is performing overall. As an equation, EVA would look like this:[102]

$$EVA = \text{Net operating profit after tax} - (\text{Capital used} \times \text{Cost of capital})$$

So EVA is a measure of how much money we made through our operations minus the amount of money that we had to spend or borrow (at a particular interest rate) in order to perform those operations. For a company to grow, it must generate average returns higher than its capital costs.

Return on Investment (ROI)

The concept of ROI is, at its core, very simple. **Return on investment (ROI)** *is a measure of the financial return we receive because of something that we do to invest in our organization or its people.* ROI is most commonly used in financial analyses, but many areas of HR lend themselves to ROI calculations. These areas include training, outsourcing, benefits, diversity, and many others. In each of these areas, we can calculate the cost of the process—whether that process is training, diversity management, or anything else—and compare that to the returns we get from the process.

To calculate ROI, you need two figures: the cost of the investment and the gain that you receive from making the investment. From there, the calculation is pretty simple:

$$ROI = \frac{\text{Gain from investment} - \text{Cost of investment}}{\text{Cost of investment}}$$

Let's use a quick example to illustrate. Assume that we create a training course to improve the skills of our assembly workers, and also assume that we send those workers through that program. To send all of the workers through the training costs us $1,000,000. We know that historically, during a normal year of production, the assembly workers have been able to assemble $5,000,000 worth of our product. However, after the training is complete, we measure our assembly process over the ensuing year and find that our amount of product created that year has increased to $8,000,000. This gives us a $3,000,000 gain from the investment. We can plug these numbers into our calculation and find out the following:

$$ROI = \frac{\$3,000,000 - \$1,000,000}{\$1,000,000} = \frac{\$2,000,000}{\$1,000,000} = 2 \text{ or } 200\%$$

So in this case, our return on investment over the course of 1 year is 2 times the cost of the investment.

It is always important to calculate at least a rough ROI for any investment in organizational resources. There's a definite need to understand how much we get in return for an investment in our people. Don't just assume that the return on investment is always positive—because it's not.

Economic value added (EVA) Measure of profits that remain after the cost of capital has been deducted from operating profits

Return on investment (ROI) Measure of the financial return we receive because of something that we do to invest in our organization or its people

Balanced Scorecard (BSC)

Is your organization achieving its mission? If you don't have a quick and accurate answer, then besides financial measures, you need a BSC.[103] The BSC is one of the most highly touted management tools today.[104] The BSC concept, credited to Robert Kaplan and David Norton,[105] basically states that measurement of an organization's success using purely financial measures is not sufficient. The organization also has to take into account nonfinancial measures, like the learning and growth rate of its human resources pool, designed to help the organization compete strategically within its industry.[106]

The **balanced scorecard (BSC)** *measures financial, customer service, internal process, and learning and growth (or sustainability) measures.* All four dimensions of the scorecard are equally important, because the results in each area affect the other areas of performance.

HR Scorecard

In addition to the organization's balanced scorecard, an HR scorecard has been designed and is being used by many businesses in operation today. The **HR scorecard** *identifies HR deliverables and HR system alignment, compares HR alignment with strategy, and measures organizational gains created by HR practices.*[107] Let's explain each of these four dimensions of the HR scorecard.

1. *Identifying HR deliverables.* What functions does HR perform, and what services does HR deliver that provide value to the organization? These functions include many things we will introduce you to in this book—recruiting, selection, training, employee development, compensation and incentives, and many more.

2. *Identifying HR system alignment through the use of a high-performance work system (HPWS).* HPWS is a set of HR practices—including comprehensive employee recruitment and selection procedures, compensation and performance management systems, information sharing, and extensive employee involvement and training—that can improve the acquisition, development, and retention of a talented and motivated workforce.[108]

3. *Aligning the system with company strategy.* This is the process of comparing the HPWS with the organization's strategic plan and making sure that the HR procedures being followed match well with a strategic direction of the company. In other words, if we are a differentiated producer, we need to make sure all of the recruiting, selection, training, and other processes are aligned with that differentiation strategy.

4. *Identifying HR efficiency measures.* This is the process of measuring the returns that the organization gets from its HR management policies through the use of items such as the EVA and ROI calculations above.

TRENDS AND ISSUES IN HRM

Here we continue our discussion of some of the most important issues and trends in HRM today. In this chapter, we chose the following issues: managing data to improve structure, culture, and staffing; the increasing strategic use of social media in organizations; and the continuing globalization of business, which increases the need for strategic planning. Let's discuss each of these topics separately.

SHRM

G:2/ G:9
Balanced Scorecard/Organizational Scorecard

SHRM

G:8
HR Scorecard

WORK
APPLICATION 2-14

Which measurement tools are used where you work or have worked. If you don't know, ask a financial manager whether EVA, ROI, BSC, and/or an HR scorecard are used.

Balanced scorecard (BSC) A scorecard measuring financial, customer service, internal process, and learning and growth (or sustainability) measures

HR scorecard A score identifying HR deliverables and HR system alignment; compares HR alignment with strategy, and measures organizational gains created by HR practices

Everything Old Is New Again: Managing Data for HRM Decision Making

The first real computer revolution in business occurred in the 1980s, just after the invention of the desktop microcomputer. This was the first chance that most companies had to purchase computing systems for use in their businesses, and it was a significant boon to productivity. However, in most cases, the microcomputer didn't give us the ability to analyze massive data sets for information that would allow us to make optimal decisions. The computing and storage systems were just too limited in their capabilities.

As we noted in the section on big data, there have been new advances in both computing power and storage in the past few years, and we now have the ability to do data analysis that we could not attempt in the 1980s or before. These improvements in data capability have in turn led to improvements in virtually every area of strategic and HRM planning as a component of strategy. From talent issues to structural problems to corporate culture mismatches, data are leading us to new conclusions concerning our people and their work. For instance, when **Xerox** had problems staffing a call center, it turned to analysis of a large data set that identified successful employees and consequently indicated that the company was hiring based on the wrong characteristics.[109] Xerox had assumed that people with call center experience would do better, but it turned out that was not true. People who were more creative did better than others in Xerox's call center environment.

Data analysis is being used around the world to find the right type of workers for specific jobs, and when done correctly, it allows companies to lower turnover and manage engagement better than ever. Technology and societal changes have increased environmental complexity, and that in turn has increased the internal complexity in many of today's firms.[110] The data are there to help you make better business decisions; the challenge is to use the data to improve workplace attractiveness to employees, who can then increase the company's chances of success through increased engagement with their employer and increased belief in its mission and vision.

Increasing Strategic Use of Social Media

Social media today is everywhere you look. Nearly every person who has a smartphone uses one or more social media sites, whether for work or professional purposes (e.g., **LinkedIn**), for a combination of professional and personal use (e.g., **Twitter**), or for play (e.g., **Foursquare** and **Yelp**). Companies are increasingly using social media to both gather and provide information to their employees and customers.[111] Social features such as liking, retweeting, and sharing have become the norm on company websites, but companies are also surveying various stakeholders on these sites as well.

Collaboration at work is getting a boost from social networks as well, as are many other business functions. Some companies are using reasonably new platforms such as **Yammer, Chatter,** and **SAP Jam** to increase social collaboration at work.[112] Companies are also using social media for HR purposes such as recruiting and testing potential employees, gauging employee satisfaction and engagement,[113] and even identifying how the outside world sees the organization through monitoring of sites such as **Glassdoor.com**[114] and through stories in *Forbes* and Bloomberg's *Business Week.*

Employees—especially millennials—pay attention to the company's reputation. To these employees, the brand is almost as important as the job itself.[115] They expect the management of the company to be accessible, and they are used to having direct contact with others through social media networks. Also, they will challenge the organizational beliefs of previous generations of workers if they think that the organization is not being responsive to either their issues or those of the outside stakeholders.

However, not all is well with social media. Companies have to balance open communication with organizational constraints such as considerations for confidentiality, both in products and services and in employee confidentiality. Organizations balance these considerations daily. A white paper by SilkRoad noted these central social media issues that organizations must take into account:[116]

Going global takes effective strategic planning.

- Employees access personal social media daily from mobile devices in surprising numbers—about 75% of workers do so at least once per day.
- Blocking, restricting, or monitoring social media sites at work does not curtail employees' use of personal social media during the workday.
- Developing social media policy is a thorny and confusing issue for companies, and many still have no policy at all.
- Organizations and (particularly) HR professionals must be aware of the legal implications regarding asking employees or candidates for social media passwords.
- Organizations are asking employees to perform work far outside their formal job, and this is particularly concerning given the federal laws on "off-the-clock" work.

So you can see that social media is both a valuable tool and a potential hazard to businesses in the 21st century. HR managers will need to continue to update their knowledge of these tools so that reasonable policies can be created for their companies.

Continuing Globalization Increases the Need for Strategic and HRM Planning

As business in most industries continues to globalize, competition will continue to increase. This is primarily due to the fact that as industries globalize, competitors who used to be limited to one region, country, or group of countries gain access to many more markets. As more and more competitors gain access to more and more markets, competition is likely to increase. This increasing competition puts pressure on businesses to create a plan to overcome their competitors' advantages.

As we noted earlier in this chapter, the process of strategic planning is designed to analyze the competitive landscape that our organization faces and create a workable plan that will allow us to compete within that landscape. So as competition increases, developing a good, solid "global" strategy and implementing continuous reviews of our strategic plans become more and more significant.

Companies must become more competent global competitors. For HRM, this means that HR managers will need to become better at managing expatriate employees, paying wages across national borders, managing disparate country laws and regulations, and much more. We will discuss the globalization issues for HRM in more detail in Chapter 16.

• • • CHAPTER SUMMARY

2-1   Identify and discuss the major components of the external environment.

There are nine major external forces: customers, competition, suppliers, the labor force and unions, shareholders, society, technology, the economy, and governments. Each factor is briefly discussed below.

- *Customers*. Companies must continually improve products to create value for their customers.

- *Competition*. Organizations must compete against each other for customers, for the same employees, and sometimes for suppliers. Competitors' changing strategic moves affect the performance of the organization.

- *Suppliers*. The firm's performance is affected by its suppliers. Therefore, it is important to develop close working relationships with your suppliers, and close relationships require employees who have the ability to communicate, empathize, negotiate, and come to mutually advantageous agreements.

- *Labor force*. The recruits available to and the employees of an organization have a direct effect on its performance. Management recruits human resources from the available labor force outside the company's boundaries.

- *Shareholders*. The owners of a corporation, known as shareholders, influence management. Most shareholders of large corporations are not involved in the day-to-day operation of the firm, but they do vote for the board of directors, and the top manager reports to the board of directors.

- *Society*. Individuals and groups within society have formed to pressure business for changes. People who live in the same area with the business do not want it to pollute the air or water or otherwise abuse natural resources.

- *Technology*. Computers and the Internet have changed the speed and the manner in which organizations conduct and transact business, and they're often a major part of the firm's systems processes. Changing technologies require technologically savvy employees who have the ability to adapt to new processes.

- *Economic*. No organization has control over economic growth, inflation, interest rates, foreign exchange rates, and so on. In general, as measured by gross domestic product (GDP), businesses do better when the economy is growing than they do during recessions.

- *Governments*. National, state, and local governments all set laws and regulations that businesses must obey. Governments create both opportunities and obstacles for businesses. To a large extent, business may not do whatever it wants to do; the government tells business what it can and cannot do.

2-2   Describe the three major organizational factors that affect our strategic options.

Our strategic options are governed to a great extent by our current strategy, our organizational structure, and our culture. Strategy deals with how the organization competes within its industry. *Strategy* is just a plan of action to achieve a particular set of objectives. It looks at the external environment and the organizational environment to create strategic advantage. Strategic advantage occurs when you analyze the environment better and react quicker than your competitors do, thus creating a sustainable competitive advantage.

Organizational structure refers to the way in which an organization groups its resources to accomplish its mission. Organizations structure their resources to transform inputs and outputs. All of an organization's resources must be structured effectively to achieve its mission. As a manager in any department, you will be responsible for part of the organization's structure.

Organizational culture consists of the shared values, beliefs, and assumptions about appropriate behavior among members of an organization. Organizational culture is primarily learned through observing people and events in the organization.

2-3   Discuss how having a vision and mission helps organizations focus their resources.

The *vision* is fuzzy; it is not specific in that we don't say how we're going to do a particular thing. Instead, we identify a future state for the organization. So, the question that we answer with the vision is "What do we want to become as an organization?"

In contrast, the *mission* is more specific. It is a statement of what the various organizational units will do and what they hope to accomplish, in alignment with the organizational vision. So, the mission statement answers the question "What do we need to do in order to become what we have envisioned?"

When you put the vision and mission together, the people in the organization get a more complete picture of what direction they are expected to go in. This allows the people in the organization to focus on going in that particular direction. Once everyone is focused on going in the same direction, it becomes much easier for the organization to achieve its goals. This focus on moving in the same direction is the thing that makes a vision and mission so powerful. If everyone in the organization is focused on the same end result, it is much more likely that the organization will achieve that end result.

2-4   Identify and describe the major components of organizational structure and why it is important to understand them.

All of an organization's resources must be structured effectively if it is to achieve its mission. Structure is made up of three major components:

- *Complexity*, which is the degree to which three types of differentiation exist within the organization. These three types are vertical differentiation, horizontal differentiation, and spatial differentiation. The more the organization is divided—whether vertically, horizontally, or spatially—the more difficult it is to manage.

- *Formalization*, which is the degree to which jobs are standardized within an organization. The more we can standardize the organization and its processes, the easier it is to control those processes.

- *Centralization*, which is the degree to which decision making is concentrated within the organization at a single point—usually at the top. A highly centralized organization would have all authority concentrated at the top, while a decentralized organization would have authority spread throughout. If authority can be centralized, we can take advantage of learning curve effects that help to improve our decision making over time.

2-5   Describe organizational culture and how it affects the members of the organization.

Organizational culture consists of the values, beliefs, and assumptions about appropriate behavior that members of an organization share. Organizational culture is primarily learned through observing people and events in the organization.

Because organizational culture is based at least partly on assumptions, values, and beliefs, the culture can control how people act within its boundaries. Since assumptions, values, and beliefs are such strong influences, individuals will generally act to conform to the culture. For the most part, we all act to conform to the culture that we happen to be in at any given point in time, and that's because cultural values push us to act that way.

2-6   Describe HRIS and identify how they can help HR make decisions.

Human resource information systems (HRIS) are interacting database systems that aim to generate and deliver HR information and allow us to automate some HRM functions. They are primarily database management systems, designed especially for use in HR functions.

HRIS allow us to maintain control of our HR information and make it available for use during the strategic planning process. Having this information immediately available makes the strategic planning process both quicker and smoother. We can also use the information stored in the database to make daily decisions within the HR department, such as a decision on whom to send to a particular training class. We can also use these databases when considering promotions, transfers, team assignments, and many other daily activities that are required inside the organization.

2-7   Identify the common measurement tools for strategic HRM.

We discussed four common tools in this chapter: economic value added (EVA), return on investment (ROI), the balanced scorecard (BSC), and the HR scorecard.

EVA is a measure of profits that remain after the cost of capital has been deducted from operating profits. ROI is a measure of the financial return we receive because of something that we do to invest in our organization or its people. The BSC says that measurement of an organization's success using purely financial measures is not sufficient. The organization also has to take into account nonfinancial measures designed to help the organization compete strategically within its industry. While financial measurement is one of the four perspectives in the organization's BSC, the BSC also includes customer measures, internal process measures, and learning and growth (or sustainability) measures.

Many businesses today use the *HR scorecard*. The four dimensions of the HR scorecard are (1) identifying HR deliverables, (2) identifying HR system alignment through use of the high-performance work system, (3) aligning the system with company strategy, and (4) identifying HR efficiency measures.

2-8   Define the key terms found in the chapter margins and listed following the Chapter Summary.

Complete the Key Terms Review to test your understanding of this chapter's key terms.

• • • KEY TERMS

balanced scorecard (BSC)
centralization
complexity
data analytics
economic value added (EVA)
formalization

HR scorecard
human resource information systems
   (HRIS)
mission statement
objectives
organizational culture

organizational
   structure
return on investment (ROI)
strategy
vision

• • • KEY TERMS REVIEW

Complete each of the following statements using one of this chapter's key terms.

1. _____ is a plan of action to achieve a particular set of objectives.

2. _____ is what we expect to become as an organization at a particular future point in time.

3. _____ consist of our expectations of what we're going to do in order to become the organization that we envisioned.

4. _____ state what is to be accomplished in singular, specific, and measurable terms, with a target date.

5. _____ refers to the way in which an organization groups its resources to accomplish its mission.

6. _____ is the degree to which three types of differentiation exist within the organization.

7. _____ is the degree to which jobs are standardized within an organization.

8. _____ is the degree to which decision making is concentrated within the organization at a single point—usually at the top of the organization.

9. _____ consists of the values, beliefs, and assumptions about appropriate behavior that members of an organization share.

10. _____ is the process of accessing large amounts of data in order to analyze those data and gain insights into significant trends or patterns within organizations or industries.

11. _____ are interacting database systems that aim at generating and delivering HR information and that allow us to automate some human resource management functions.

12. _____ is a measure of profits that remain after the cost of capital has been deducted from operating profits.

13. _____ is a measure of the financial return we receive because of something that we do to invest in our organization or its people.

14. _____ measures financial, customer service, internal process, and learning and growth (sustainability).

15. _____ identifies HR deliverables, identifies HR system alignment, compares HR alignment with strategy, and measures organizational gains created by HR practices.

• • • COMMUNICATION SKILLS

The following critical-thinking questions can be used for class discussion and/or for written assignments to develop communication skills. Be sure to give complete explanations for all answers.

1. Can you name a business that you know of in which competition has increased significantly in the past few years? Why do you think competition has increased in this case?

2. What are some of the ways in which the environmental factors that we discussed in this chapter directly affect the organization?

3. Do you agree that every organization needs a strategic plan? Why or why not?

4. Think about the technological changes that have occurred since you were born. Do you think those changes have affected the strategic planning process? How?

5. What should a mission statement focus on—customers, competitors, products/services, the employee environment, or something else? Identify why you chose a particular answer.

6. We discussed the three major generic strategies in this chapter. Can you think of examples of each of the three strategies in specific businesses you know of? In your opinion, how successful have these companies been with their strategy?

7. If you were going to design the structure for a new, innovate start-up company, what kind of structure would you try to create in regard to level of complexity, formalization, and centralization? Why would you set up this type of structure?

8. Which of the five artifacts, or important ways in which employees learn about culture, do you think is most important? Why?

9. Name some situations in HRM when you would want to use either economic value added (EVA) or return on investment (ROI) as an analytical tool.

10. Do you agree that balanced scorecards are good tools for evaluating the organization's overall performance? Why or why not? What measures would you add to the scorecard to improve it?

••• CASE 2-1 BUILDING UP OUR ASSETS: DHR CONSTRUCTION

In August 2011, when the Dow Jones Industrial Average dipped under 8,000 from a high of almost 11,500, Richard Davis and Stephen Hodgetts, academics, friends, and coauthors, were lamenting their ever-shrinking retirement funds. As Hodgetts was fond of saying, "America believes in education: The average professor earns more money in a year than a professional athlete earns in a whole week."

After a long discussion, they decided that they needed to take direct control of their investments and not be prisoners to the rise and fall of the stock market. Davis had done enough preliminary research on the real estate market in their area and convinced Hodgetts that there was money to be made in property ownership and renting starter homes (three bedrooms, two baths) to individuals with poor credit who could not afford a home but who had excellent rental track records. Davis and Hodgetts formed D&H Management and found six families in three months who were happy to rent and eventually purchase homes in the $175K price range. The deal was so attractive that D&H even had a waiting list of new tenants. The six homes, though, gobbled up their initial investment and required additional capital.

The New Firm: DHR Construction, LLC

Their construction company started off as just a small capital-raising venture. Hodgetts and Davis would finish off the basements of their rental homes, get the homes reappraised, and then remortgage the properties, pulling out an additional $10K to $20K per home. These funds could then be used as down payments for future rental homes.

In chatting about this matter with some of their renters, Davis and Hodgetts were approached by one of them to perform all of the nonlicensed work (excluding electrical, plumbing, HVAC, etc.). Davis explained to the renters (Alan and Wilma Bronson) that they would have to form their own company and act as any other subcontractor. After completing a few basements, Alan and Wilma enjoyed working on these basements so much that they

approached Davis and Hodgetts about figuring out a way that Davis and Hodgetts could keep them occupied all year round. In essence, Alan would quit his job and work as a subcontractor for Davis and Hodgetts. This was not possible, though, since there was not enough work to keep Alan and Wilma busy. Yet a few days later the situation dramatically changed.

One of Davis's students, David Russ, who was designing their basements, said that he thought that Davis and Hodgetts could cut out the middleman in terms of the rental business if they built their own homes. Davis thought that Russ was crazy at the time, but they talked after class and Russ said that he would be happy to act as the general contractor and that he knew all of the subcontractors who were needed in order to construct new homes. Alan and Wilma would do all of the interior work, and Alan could hire some part-time workers to help himself out. Davis and Hodgetts could then build the rest of their homes under a different company name, sell them to themselves for a small profit, and then make a profit renting the homes.

In around nine months, the preliminary profits derived from their construction operation led Davis and Hodgetts to build homes not only to be purchased by D&H Management but also for public consumption. In May DHR Construction broke ground on their first home to be sold to the public.

In November, Davis and Hodgetts bought out David Russ's interests in DHR Construction due to differences in management and business philosophies. Davis was left to act as contractor while Hodgetts handled D&H Management. By January 2014, they had completed three homes at St. Andrews subdivision. Alan quickly took over the role of foreman/contractor when DHR shifted their building site to another location, the Florence Development, which had a much more upscale look. DHR was no longer building starter homes; they shifted into the midsize market (four bedrooms, $300K) where they could make a higher profit margin. By April, DHR had built three homes in Florence, had plans to build five more in that area, and were looking at other developments for future growth and expansion.

Branching Out: Patio Homes

In June, Davis located a brand-new development about 10 miles east of where they currently were building, in an area called Snowy Mountains. Snowy Mountains was a unique project for the area since the developers had built lakes, a golf course, and a clubhouse (including a three-star restaurant) and had very specific designs for community development. The housing currently in the development (Phase 1) ran the gamut of homes, from four-bedroom patio homes (that started around $450K) to multimillion-dollar estates on the lake.

DHR Patio Homes was formed by Davis and Hodgetts (run under the corporate label of DHR Construction), who decided to build the lower-end patio homes; these homes would yield them their highest profit margins to date. Using the same management and work crew as DHR, Davis acted as the architect and head of operations for construction while Alan acted as foreman and continued his own subcontracting work. Hodgetts remained in charge of the rental operation but served as an adviser to Davis on an "as needed" basis.

Questions

1. Describe Davis and Hodgetts's strategic planning process. What seems to be the driving force for their planning?

2. What was Davis and Hodgetts's original strategy for managing their retirement funds? How did that strategy change?

3. What type of strategy did Davis and Hodgetts first use in their business? How did that strategy change with the change in their business?

4. What HRM issues might Davis and Hodgetts have to address given their changing business strategy?

5. Describe the structure of DHR Construction.

6. In your opinion, how does this structure affect HRM?

Case created by Herbert Sherman, PhD, and Theodore Vallas, Long Island University School of Business, Brooklyn Campus

• • • CASE 2-2 STRATEGY-DRIVEN HR MANAGEMENT: NETFLIX, A BEHIND-THE-SCENES LOOK AT DELIVERING ENTERTAINMENT

Netflix is a highly successful retailer of movie rental services, with a market value of over $25 billion. It offers a subscription service that allows its members to stream shows and movies instantly over the Internet on game consoles, Blu-ray players, HDTVs, set-top boxes, home theater systems, phones, and tablets. Netflix also includes a subscription service for those who prefer to receive discs via the US mail (rather than streaming), without the hassle of due dates or late fees.

The idea of a home delivery movie service came to CEO Read Hastings when he was forced to pay $40 in overdue fines after returning a video of the movie *Apollo 13* to Blockbuster. He realized that he could capitalize on an existing distribution system (the US Post Office) that did not require renters to leave their homes. The Netflix website was launched on August 29, 1997, with only 30 employees and 925 movies available for rent. It used a traditional pay-per-rental model, charging $0.50 per rental plus US postage, and late fees applied. Netflix introduced the monthly subscription concept in September 1999, and then it dropped the single-rental model in early 2000. Since that time, the company has built its reputation on the business model of flat-fee unlimited rentals without due dates, late fees, or shipping and handling fees. In addition, its online streaming service doesn't have per-title rental fees.[117] Throughout 2014, Netflix's total sales grew by 21%, generating a net income of $112 million.[118] Subscribers increased by almost 40% that year, reaching 46 million, and the stock value tripled from 2012 to 2014. But how did they reach that point?[119]

There are many reasons why Netflix's strategy is successful, yet the numbers tell only the results and not the behind-the-scenes story. According to Read Hastings and former chief talent officer (CTO) Patty McCord, this success is not a surprise at all given Netflix's business model. But more important, they say, is Netflix's HR strategy, which is to create an environment of fully motivated employees who understand the culture of the company and perform exceptionally well within it. Hastings and McCord had the foresight to document their HR strategy via PowerPoint, and soon these slides went viral, with more than 5 million views on the Web. McCord described Netflix's HR strategy as consisting of the following steps:

1. *Selecting new employees/recruiting*. Hire employees who care about, understand, and then prioritize the company's interests. This will eliminate the need for formal regulations and policies, because these employees will strive to grow the company for their own self-satisfaction. This sets Netflix apart from the many companies that do not hire employees who would be a great fit with the company's culture and that therefore still spend great amounts of time and money on enforcing their HR policies—policies that target only 3% of their workforce.[120]

2. *Talent management/matching employees with jobs.* To avoid high employee turnover, a company must recruit talented people with the right skills, although mismatches may occur. Layoffs and firings are also inevitable given changing business cycles. In such cases, it is HR's duty to place employees in departments that match the employees' skill sets, as well as to train employees to meet changing business needs.[121]

3. *Send the right messages.* To boost overall employee morale, most HR departments throw parties or give away free items. But when stock prices are decreasing or sales numbers are not as high as predicted, what use would a company have for an office party? Netflix executives stated that they have not seen an HR initiative that truly improved morale. Instead of cheerleading, employees need to be educated about how the company earns its revenue and what behaviors will drive its success. By receiving clear messages about how employees should execute and commit to their duties, employees will be more informed about the criteria they will need to meet to receive their bonuses, and they will therefore be more apt to receive those bonuses. Knowing what to do and how to do it, employees' motivation will increase, and with increased motivation, morale and performance will improve.[122]

4. *Performance evaluation.* Netflix implemented informal 360-degree reviews after realizing that formal review sessions were not effective. These informal 360-degree sessions allowed workers to give honest opinions about themselves and colleagues—focusing on whether certain policies should stop, start, continue, or change. Instead of relying on bureaucratic measures, employees valued these conversations as an organic part of their work, and those conversations have been demonstrated to increase employee performance.[123] For example, Netflix found that when its employees perceived their bosses as less than expert in their field, employee performance dropped. Employees indicated that managers who relied on charm or IQ were not trusted and received low subordinate appraisals.

Questions

1. Netflix was a pioneer in the online video rental market, making "old-fashioned" DVD rentals a thing of the past and putting Blockbuster out of business. Using the five-forces model, describe how Netflix changed the entertainment rental industry.

2. What is Netflix's competitive strategy? What does it believe is the driving force that makes this strategy so successful? Do you agree?

3. In terms of sustaining the company's competitive advantage, what is the most important step that Netflix has taken, as noted by Hastings and McCord?

4. "Where we want to be, how to get there, and where are we now" are key points of a successful company's strategy. How do the company's HR policies support the firm's strategy?

5. How does Netflix monitor its employees' performance? Would you prefer to be evaluated this way or through a balanced scorecard (BSC) approach? Explain your position.

6. How would you create a link between customers and the way employees perform to assure that incentives are distributed evenly and equally at Netflix?

Case created by Herbert Sherman, PhD, and Theodore Vallas, Long Island University School of Business, Brooklyn Campus

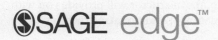

Sharpen your skills with SAGE edge at edge.sagepub.com/lussierhrm2e

SAGE edge for students provides a personalized approach to help you accomplish your coursework goals in an easy-to-use learning environment.

••• SKILL BUILDER 2-1 WRITING OBJECTIVES

For this exercise, you will first work at improving ineffective objectives. Then you will write nine objectives for yourself.

Objective

To develop your skill at writing objectives

Skills

The primary skills developed through this exercise are as follows:

1. *HR Management skills*—conceptual and design

2. *SHRM 2013 Curriculum Guidebook*—J: Strategic HR

Part 1

Indicate which of the criteria each of the following objectives fails to meet in the model and rewrite the objective so that it meets all those criteria. When writing objectives, use the following model:

To + action verb + single, specific, and measurable result + target date

1.   To improve our company image by the end of 2017

Criteria not met: _____

Improved objective: _____

_____

2.   To increase the number of customers by 10%

Criteria not met: _____

Improved objective: _____

_____

_____

To increase profits during 2017

Criteria not met:

Improved objective:

_____

_____

To sell 5% more hot dogs and 13% more soda at the baseball game on Sunday, June 14, 2016

Criteria not met:

Improved objective:

_____

_____

Part 2

Write three educational, three personal, and three career objectives you want to accomplish. These may be short-term (something you want to accomplish today), long-term (something you want to have accomplished 20 years from now), or medium-term objectives. Be sure to structure your objectives using the model and meeting the criteria for effective objectives.

Educational Objectives

1 _____

2 _____

_____

3 _____

_____

Personal Objectives

1 _____

_____

2 _____

_____

3 _____

_____

Career Objectives

1 _____

_____

2 _____

_____

3 _____

_____

Apply It

What did I learn from this experience? How will I use this knowledge in the future?

_____

_____

Your instructor may ask you to do this Skill Builder in class in a group. If so, the instructor will provide you with any necessary information or additional instructions.

● ● ● SKILL BUILDER 2-2 STRATEGIC PLANNING AT YOUR COLLEGE

This exercise enables you to apply the strategic planning process to your college or university as an individual and/or a group. Complete each step by typing or writing out your answers. You can also conduct this exercise for another organization.

Objective

To develop your strategic planning skills by analyzing the internal environment of strategy, structure, and culture

Skills

The primary skills developed through this exercise are as follows:

1. *HR Management skills*—conceptual and design
2. *SHRM 2013 Curriculum Guidebook*—J: Strategic HR

PART A: STRATEGY

Step 1: Develop a Mission

1. What is the vision and mission statement of your university/college or school/department?
2. Is the mission statement easy to understand and remember?
3. How would you improve the mission statement?

Step 2: Identify a Strategy

Which of the three generic strategies does your school or department use?

Step 3: Conduct Strategic Analysis

1. Conduct a five-forces competitive analysis, like that in Exhibit 2-4 (page 52).
2. Complete a SWOT analysis, like that in Exhibit 2-5 (page 54).
3. Determine the competitive advantage (if any) of your university/college or school/department.

Step 4: Set Objectives

What are some objectives of your university/college or school/department?

Step 5: Implement, Monitor, and Evaluate Strategies

How would you rate your university/college's or school/department's strategic planning? How could it be improved?

PART B: STRUCTURE

Describe your school or department's organizational structure in terms of its complexity, formalization, and centralization.

PART C: CULTURE

Identify artifacts in each of the categories of heroes, stories, slogans, symbols, and ceremonies.

Identify the cultural levels of the organization's behaviors, values and beliefs, and assumptions.

Apply It

What did I learn from this experience? How will I use this knowledge in the future?

_____

_____

_____

Your instructor may ask you to do this Skill Builder in class in a group. If so, the instructor will provide you with any necessary information or additional instructions.

©iStockphoto.com/Mihej

3 The Legal Environment and Diversity Management

• • • LEARNING OUTCOMES

After studying this chapter, you should be able to do the following:

3-1 Describe the OUCH test and its four components and identify when it is useful in an organizational setting. PAGE 81

3-2 Identify the major equal employment opportunity (EEO) laws and the groups of people that each law protects. PAGE 83

3-3 Describe the three main types of discrimination in the workplace. PAGE 84

3-4 Discuss the organizational defenses against accusations of discrimination. PAGE 86

3-5 Briefly discuss the two major federal immigration laws and how they affect the workplace. PAGE 94

3-6 Briefly identify and discuss the major functions of the Equal Employment Opportunity Commission (EEOC). PAGE 96

3-7 Discuss the differences among equal employment opportunity, affirmative action, and diversity. PAGE 98

3-8 Identify the two primary types of sexual harassment. PAGE 103

3-9 Define the key terms found in the chapter margins and listed following the Chapter Summary. PAGE 112

Practitioner's Perspective

Cindy says: One of the reasons some agree with the Dilbert comic strip depiction of the HR manager as devoid of feeling is due to the necessity of fair and uniform enforcement of government rules and regulations, as well as the company's own policies and procedures. Aaron—a favorite with the patients and a willing overtime worker—misread the schedule and missed a day of work at the hospital. A no-call/no-show merits a written warning, but Aaron's supervisor didn't want to administer the discipline.

"Well," I asked, "what if we were talking about another less exemplary employee? What about, oh, let's say—Sandy? What would you do if she was NC/NS?"

"Hey, no problem there—I'd write up Sandy in an instant!" replied the supervisor.

"Wait—wouldn't that be discrimination?" Different treatment of individuals who are in similar circumstances opens the door to legal liability. In Chapter 3, we'll explore why HR is required to advise and assist with compliance issues—no matter how "heartless" it may appear.

SHRM HR CONTENT

See Appendix: *SHRM 2013 Curriculum Guidebook* for the complete list

B. Employment Law (required)

1. Age Discrimination in Employment Act of 1967
2. Americans with Disabilities Act of 1990 and as amended in 2008
3. Equal Pay Act of 1963
4. Pregnancy Discrimination Act of 1978
5. Title VII of the Civil Rights Act of 1964 and 1991
6. Executive Order 11246 (1965)
10. Rehabilitation Act (1973)
15. Uniformed Services Employment and Reemployment Rights Act of 1994 (USERRA)
17. Enforcement agencies (EEOC, OFCCP)
24. Disparate impact
25. Disparate treatment
27. Unlawful harassment
    Sexual
    Religious
    Disability
    Race
    Color
    Nation of origin
28. Whistle-blowing/retaliation
29. Reasonable accommodation
    ADA
    Religious

31. Lilly Ledbetter Fair Pay Act
32. Genetic Information Nondiscrimination Act (GINA)
35. Immigration Reform and Control Act (IRCA)
38. Immigration and Nationality Act (INA)

E. Job Analysis/Job Design (required)

6. Compliance with legal requirements

   Equal employment (job-relatedness, bona fide occupational qualifications and the reasonable accommodation process)

F. Managing a Diverse Workforce (required)

1. Equal opportunity employment
2. Affirmative action
4. Individuals with disabilities
6. Racial/ethnic diversity
7. Religion
9. Sex/gender issues
12. Business case for diversity

I. Staffing: Recruitment and Selection (required)

15. Bona fide occupational qualifications (BFOQs)

WORK
APPLICATION 3-1

Give examples of how you and other employees legally discriminate at work.

Discrimination The act of making distinctions or choosing one thing over another; in HR, it is making distinctions among people

THE LEGAL ENVIRONMENT FOR HRM: PROTECTING YOUR ORGANIZATION

The HRM environment has become much more complex in the past 30 years. There were a significant number of laws enacted during and immediately prior to that period, laws that affect how organizations now must do business. In addition, we have grown to believe in the value of a diverse workforce, much more so than in the 1960s and '70s.[1] In this chapter, we will explore some of the laws that HR managers have to work with on a daily basis, and we will also look in some more depth at diversity and why it is valuable in an organization.

One of the primary jobs of an HR manager in any organization is to assist in avoiding any discriminatory employment situations that can create legal, ethical, or social problems with employees, former employees, the community, or other stakeholders.

As a result, one of the first things we need to do in this chapter is define discrimination, *which is the act of making distinctions or choosing one thing over another; in HR, it is making distinctions among people.* So you can see very quickly that we *all* discriminate, every day. If managers don't discriminate, then they're not doing their job. However, we want to avoid *illegal* discrimination based on a person's membership in a protected class (we will discuss protected classes shortly) and we want to avoid unfair treatment of any of our employees at all times. Illegal discrimination *is making distinctions that harm people and that are based on those people's membership in a protected class.* This chapter will teach you some of the tools that we can use to avoid illegal discrimination.

A USER'S GUIDE TO MANAGING PEOPLE: THE OUCH TEST

Before we start talking about equal employment opportunity and all of the forms of illegal discrimination in the workplace, let's take the opportunity to introduce you to the OUCH test.[2] The OUCH test *is a rule of thumb rule used whenever you are contemplating any employment action, to maintain fairness and equity for all of your employees or applicants.* You should use this test whenever you are contemplating any action that involves your employees. For example you should use it when hiring new people, promoting employees, deciding whether or not to give someone a raise, analyzing potential disciplinary action against an employee, or in any other job-related action.

OUCH is an acronym that stands for **O**bjective, **U**niform in application, **C**onsistent in effect, **H**as job relatedness (see Exhibit 3-1).

Objective

Is the action objective, or is it subjective? Something that is objective is based on fact, cognitive knowledge, or quantifiable evidence. Something that is subjective is based on your emotional state, your opinion, or how you feel in a certain circumstance, not on your cognitive knowledge. You should make your employment actions as objective as possible, in all cases.

Uniform in Application

Is the action being uniformly applied? In other words, if you apply an action in an employment situation, are you applying that same action in all cases of the same type? For example, if you have one applicant for a position take a written test, are you also having all the applicants for that same position take the same written test, under the same conditions, to the best of your ability? Making your actions uniform in application is more difficult than you probably think it is.

LO 3-1

Describe the OUCH test and its four components and identify when it is useful in an organizational setting.

EXHIBIT 3-1 THE OUCH TEST

Objective	Fact-based and quantifiable, not subjective or emotional
Uniform in Application	Apply the same "tests" in the same ways
Consistent in Effect	Ensure the result is not significantly different for different groups
Has Job Relatedness	Action must relate to the essential job functions

Illegal discrimination The act of making distinctions that harm people and that are based on those people's membership in a protected class

OUCH test A rule of thumb rule used whenever you are contemplating any employment action, to maintain fairness and equity for all of your employees or applicants

WORK
APPLICATION 3-2

Select an employment policy at the company where you work or at a company where you have worked. Give it the OUCH test, stating whether it does or does not meet each of the four criteria.

If you ask someone to perform a test (whether written, verbal, or physical), you need to create the exact same testing circumstances, as much as you can control them. For instance, if you asked people to take a written exam, you would need to provide the exact same type of setting for the test. If one person took the exam in a quiet room and the other in a noisy hallway, you would not be uniform in application.

Consistent in Effect

Does the action taken have a significantly different effect on one or more protected groups than it has on the majority group? Determining consistency in effect is a bit more difficult than the other three OUCH test characteristics. There are many protected groups in United States law. We have to try to make sure that we don't affect one of these protected groups disproportionately with an employment action. But how can we know?

The Department of Labor and the EEOC have given us the **Four-Fifths Rule**,[3] *which is a test used by various federal courts, the Department of Labor, and the EEOC to determine whether disparate impact exists in an employment test.* If the selection ratio for any group (e.g., Asian males) is less than four-fifths of the selection rate for the majority group (e.g., white males) in an employment action (e.g., promotions), then it constitutes evidence of potential disparate impact (we will discuss the term "disparate impact" in more detail shortly).

The best way to quickly explain the Four-Fifths Rule is to give you a simplified example. Take a look at Exhibit 3-2. Let's suppose that we live in an area that is basically evenly split between African-American and White, non-Hispanic populations. You are planning on hiring about 40 new employees for a general position in your company. You decide to give each of the potential employees a written test. If the results of the test disproportionately rule out the African-American portion of the population, then your written test is not consistent in effect. So let's use the Four-Fifths Rule to find out whether or not you were being consistent. Look at the numbers in Exhibit 3-2.

If we are out of compliance with the Four-Fifths Rule, have we automatically broken the law? No.[4] We do have to investigate why we are outside the four-fifths parameter, though. If there is a legitimate reason (we will discuss this shortly) for the discrepancy that we can prove in a court case, then we are probably OK with a selection rate that is outside the parameters. By the way, we *can* also look at six fifths to determine the possibility of reverse discrimination, so we would want to have between 16 and 24 African-American males selected in the first example, since 6/5 of 20 is 24.

Consistency in effect is by far the most complex of the four OUCH test factors. However, it is also very important for us to show consistency in our actions as managers in an organization.

Has Job Relatedness

Is the action directly related to the primary aspects of the job in question? The word "primary" will become very important later, when we discuss the Americans with Disabilities Act (ADA), which calls these factors "essential functions." For right now, just understand that our actions have to be directly job related.[5] In other words, if your job has nothing to do with making coffee for the office in the morning, I cannot base any employment action such as a hiring or firing on whether or not you can make coffee.

Four-Fifths Rule A test used by various federal courts, the Department of Labor, and the EEOC to determine whether disparate impact exists in an employment test

EXHIBIT 3-2 THE FOUR-FIFTHS RULE

Example 1: You are planning to hire about 40 new employees. The statistical information on applicants is below:

	White Males	African-American Males
Applicants	100	100
Selected	20	17
Selection rate	20% (20/100)	17% (17/100)

4/5ths = 80%, so 80% of 20 (0.80 × 0.20) = 16%.

The selection rate of 17% is greater than 16%, so the Four-Fifths Rule is met.

Example 2: What if you didn't have equal numbers of applicants in each group?

	White Males	African-American Males
Applicants	100	40
Selected	29	9
Selection rate	29%	22.5% of 40

4/5ths = 80%, so 0.80 × 0.29 = 0.232 or 23.2%

The selection rate of 22.5% is *less* than the 23.2% required, so the Four-Fifths Rule is *not* met.

You would have to hire 9.28 or more people (23.2% of 40 = 9.28) in this case to be in compliance with the Four-Fifths Rule. You can't have 28% of a person, so you need to round up to 10 to be within the requirement. Therefore, you need one more African-American male (10 − 9 selected) to meet the 4/5 ratio requirement.

In the first example, the selection rate of African-American males (the protected group in this case) was 17%, which is above the Four-Fifths Rule threshold of 16%. Therefore, we are "consistent in effect," based on the Four-Fifths Rule.

However, in the second example, the selection rate of African-American males was 22.5%, and the minimum value by the Four-Fifths Rule was 23.2%. As a result, we would be outside the boundaries of being consistent in effect in this case.

Remember that the OUCH test is a rule of thumb and does not work perfectly. It is not a legal test by itself. It is a good guide to nondiscriminatory practices, but it is only a guide.

MAJOR EMPLOYMENT LAWS

In any management position within any organization today, you need a basic understanding of the major employment laws that are currently in effect. If you don't understand what is legal and what isn't, you can inadvertently make mistakes that may cost your employer significant amounts of money and time, and if

LO 3-2

Identify the major equal employment opportunity (EEO) laws and the groups of people that each law protects.

that happens, that organization may not be your employer anymore. You don't want that to happen, so let's take a chronological look at some of the laws listed in Exhibit 3-3.

Equal Pay Act of 1963

SHRM

B:3
Equal Pay Act of 1963

The first modern equal employment opportunity (EEO) law that we will review is the Equal Pay Act. The act requires that women who do the same job as men, in the same organization, must receive the same pay. It defines *equal* in terms of "equal skill, effort, and responsibility, and . . . performed under similar working conditions."[6] However, if pay differences are the result of differences in *seniority*, *merit*, *quantity or quality of production*, *or any factor other than sex* (e.g., shift differentials and training programs), then pay differences are legally allowable.[7] This wording makes the act a weaker law than was originally intended. Even so, it was followed the next year by a law that was much tougher concerning equality and nondiscrimination.

Title VII of the Civil Rights Act of 1964 (CRA)

SHRM

B:5
Title VII of the Civil Rights Act of 1964 and 1991

This act was probably the most significant single piece of legislation regulating EEO in the history of the United States.[8] It changed the way that virtually every organization in the country did business, and it even helped change employers' attitudes about discrimination. Even in cases where the law does not directly apply to an organization, it has been used to evaluate internal policies to attempt to ensure fairness and equality for all of our workers.

The 1964 CRA states that it is illegal for an employer "(1) to fail or refuse to hire or to discharge any individual, or otherwise to discriminate against any individual with respect to his compensation, terms, conditions, or privileges of employment, because of such individual's race, color, religion, sex, or national origin; or (2) to limit, segregate, or classify his employees or applicants for employment in any way which would deprive or tend to deprive any individual of employment opportunities or otherwise adversely affect his status as an employee, because of such individual's race, color, religion, sex, or national origin."[9]

The act applies to organizations with 15 or more employees who are working 20 or more weeks a year and who are involved in interstate commerce. Why does the organization have to be involved in interstate commerce? Mainly because of the 10th Amendment to the US Constitution, which deals with states' rights. The federal government can't make any laws that apply wholly within the borders of a single state. The law also generally applies to state and local governments; educational institutions, public or private; all employment agencies; and all labor associations of any type.

Important concepts introduced by the CRA of 1964 include the following:

- Disparate treatment
- Disparate (also called adverse) impact
- Pattern or practice
- Bona fide occupational qualification (BFOQ)
- Business necessity
- Job relatedness

LO 3-3

Describe the three main types of discrimination in the workplace.

TYPES OF DISCRIMINATION. The 1964 CRA identified, really for the first time, three types of discrimination. While it didn't specifically name these types, it did describe the process of each of the three in some detail. Once this was done, court rulings

EXHIBIT 3-3 MAJOR EEO LAWS IN CHRONOLOGICAL ORDER

Law	Description
Equal Pay Act of 1963	Requires that women be paid equal to men if they are doing the same work
Title VII of the Civil Rights Act of 1964	Prohibits discrimination on the basis of race, color, religion, sex, or national origin in all areas of the employment relationship
Age Discrimination in Employment Act of 1967	Prohibits age discrimination against people 40 years of age or older and restricts mandatory retirement
Vietnam Era Veterans Readjustment Assistance Act of 1974	Prohibits discrimination against Vietnam veterans by all employers with federal contracts or subcontracts of $100,000 or more. Also requires that affirmative action be taken.
Pregnancy Discrimination Act of 1978	Prohibits discrimination against women affected by pregnancy, childbirth, or related medical conditions
Americans with Disabilities Act of 1990	Strengthened the Rehabilitation Act of 1973 to require employers to provide "reasonable accommodations" to allow disabled employees to work
Civil Rights Act of 1991	Strengthened civil rights by providing for possible compensatory and punitive damages for discrimination
Uniform Services Employment and Reemployment Rights Act (USERRA) of 1994	Ensures the civilian reemployment rights of military members who were called away from their regular (nonmilitary) jobs by US government orders
Veterans Benefits Improvement Act of 2004	Amends USERRA to extend health care coverage while away on duty, and requires employers to post a notice of benefits, duties, and rights of reemployment
Genetic Information Nondiscrimination Act of 2008	Prohibits the use of genetic information in employment, prohibits intentional acquisition of same, and imposes confidentiality requirements
Lilly Ledbetter Fair Pay Act of 2009	Amends the 1964 CRA to extend the period of time in which an employee is allowed to file a lawsuit over pay discrimination

helped to further define the three types, which we have come to call disparate treatment, disparate impact, and pattern or practice. Disparate treatment and impact are also called adverse treatment or impact.

In addition to the three types of discrimination that were more or less directly identified in the 1964 CRA, a fourth and fifth type have been determined to exist by federal courts based on the wording of the CRA. These other two types of discrimination are religious discrimination and sexual harassment.[10] But for now, let's discuss the three forms of discrimination that were directly identified in the CRA. We will save the fourth and fifth items for later in the chapter.

Disparate (Adverse) Treatment. **Disparate treatment** *exists when individuals in similar situations are intentionally treated differently and the different treatment is based on an individual's membership in a protected class.* In a court case, the plaintiff must prove that there was a discriminatory motive—that is, that the employer *intended*

SHRM

B:25
Disparate Treatment

Disparate treatment When individuals in similar situations are intentionally treated differently and the different treatment is based on an individual's membership in a protected class

ASSOCIATED PRESS/Al Behrman

Effective HRM practices can help to prevent lawsuits. Firefighter Mark Broach filed a complaint against two white captains at the Cincinnati Fire Department for discrimination.

B:24
Disparate Impact

LO 3-4

Discuss the organizational defenses against accusations of discrimination.

Disparate impact When an officially neutral employment practice disproportionately excludes the members of a protected group; it is generally considered to be unintentional, but intent is irrelevant

Pattern or practice discrimination When a person or group engages in a sequence of actions over a significant period of time that is intended to deny the rights provided by Title VII of the 1964 CRA to a member of a protected class

to discriminate—in order to prove disparate treatment.[11] Disparate treatment is generally illegal unless the employer can show that there was a "bona fide occupational qualification" (or BFOQ—we will talk about these shortly) that caused the need to intentionally disallow members of a protected group from applying for or getting the job. One place where disparate treatment still occurs with some frequency is in access to mentoring and leadership development, where women are still "substantially underrepresented."[12]

Disparate (Adverse) Impact. **Disparate impact** *occurs when an officially neutral employment practice disproportionately excludes the members of a protected group; it is generally considered to be unintentional, but intent is irrelevant.* For there to be discrimination under disparate treatment, there has to be intentional discrimination. Under disparate impact, intent does not matter.[13]

Some characteristics (e.g., height and strength) are not distributed equally across race and gender groups, and in some jobs, these characteristics may be related to successful performance in the job. Therefore, disparate impact is not *necessarily* illegal. The important question is whether the characteristic is related to successful performance on the job, meaning whether it has job relatedness. Disparate impact is generally judged by use of the Four-Fifths Rule that we discussed earlier. Both the Department of Labor (through their Uniform Guidelines on Employee Selection Procedures) and the EEOC have expressed a preference for using the Four-Fifths Rule to determine disparate impact.[14] If the four-fifths requirement is not satisfied, discrimination is considered to have occurred but *illegal* discrimination has not *necessarily* occurred.

The Four-Fifths Rule requires that if we fall outside of its boundaries, we must investigate to ensure that we haven't used an *illegal protected class characteristic* to bias an employment outcome. If our investigation shows that an employment test or measure was biased toward or against a certain group, then we have to correct the test or measure unless there was a legitimate reason to measure that particular characteristic (as discussed below). However, if our investigation shows that the test was valid and reliable and that there was some other legitimate reason why we did not meet the four-fifths standard, then illegal discrimination *may* not exist. We always need to investigate thoroughly if we fall outside the four-fifths standard.

Pattern or Practice. **Pattern or practice discrimination** *occurs when a person or group engages in a sequence of actions over a significant period of time that is intended to deny the rights provided by Title VII of the 1964 CRA to a member of a protected class.* If there is reasonable cause to believe that any organization is engaging in a pattern or practice that denies the rights provided by Title VII, the US Attorney General may bring a federal lawsuit against it.[15] In general, no individual can directly bring a pattern-or-practice lawsuit against an organization. As with the disparate treatment concept, it must be proven that the employer intended to discriminate against a particular class of individuals and did so over a protracted period of time.

See Exhibit 3-4 for types of discrimination and types of organizational defenses against illegal discrimination charges.

ORGANIZATIONAL DEFENSES AGAINST DISCRIMINATION CHARGES. The organization *does* have some ways to defend against charges of illegal discrimination. We can defend

| EXHIBIT 3-4 | ORGANIZATIONAL DEFENSES TO DISCRIMINATION CHARGES | |

Discrimination Type	Intent	Organizational Defense
Disparate Treatment	Intentional	BFOQ
Disparate Impact	Unintentional	BFOQ or business necessity and job relatedness
Pattern or Practice	Intentional	BFOQ (unlikely defense)

WORK
APPLICATION 3-3

Give examples of BFOQ for jobs at an organization where you work or have worked.

ourselves by showing either that there was a need for a particular characteristic or qualification for a specific job or that there was a *requirement* that the business do certain things in order to remain viable and profitable so that we didn't harm *all* of our employees by failing and shutting down. Let's review these defenses now.

Bona Fide Occupational Qualification (BFOQs). The first defense is a **bona fide occupational qualification (BFOQ)**, *a qualification that is absolutely required in order for an individual to be able to successfully do a particular job.* The qualification cannot just be a *desirable* quality within the job applicant—it must be *mandatory.*[16] A BFOQ would be a legitimate defense against a charge of disparate treatment. As an example, in 2012 in a case brought by the EEOC against **Exxon-Mobil**, a Texas District judge ruled that terminating pilots from corporate employment at age 60 was legal because federal aviation regulations required commercial pilots to be under 60 years old. The judge deemed that this regulation created a BFOQ of "age" for both corporate and commercial pilots, since the corporate pilots acted in the same general way as commercial pilots do, by flying passengers all over the world.[17] Another example of a BFOQ is a requirement that only persons of particular religious faith be allowed to apply for a job as a worker within a mosque, church, or synagogue. In this case, there's a reasonable expectation that people who do not share the same faith would not have the knowledge (qualifications) to be able to fill the job and would in fact almost certainly violate some of the rules of the faith if they were to be employed in such a position.

On the other hand, there was a very famous case of an employer attempting to use the BFOQ defense in response to a lawsuit. In this case, the defense was considered to be invalid. In 1971, a man named Celio Diaz sued **Pan American World Airways** in the United States for discrimination based on the fact that he had been denied the opportunity to apply for a flight attendant position with the airline. At the time, the airline required that flight attendants be female. In court, the airline defended the requirement that flight attendants be female based on the fact that passengers *expected* the role of a flight attendant to be filled by a woman. The company maintained that the passengers' expectation was tantamount to a requirement. However, the courts ruled against the airline. The reasoning of the courts was that expectation or "customer preference" does not create a requirement in the eyes of the law.[18] A BFOQ defense can be used against both disparate impact and disparate treatment allegations.

Business Necessity. **Business necessity** *exists when a particular practice is necessary for the safe and efficient operation of the business and when there is a specific business purpose for applying a particular standard that may, in fact, be discriminatory.* A business necessity defense is applied by an employer in order to show that a particular practice was necessary for the safe and efficient operation of the business and

SHRM

I:15
Bona Fide Occupational Qualifications (BFOQs)

bona fide occupational qualification (BFOQ) A qualification that is absolutely required in order for an individual to be able to successfully do a particular job

Business necessity When a particular practice is necessary for the safe and efficient operation of the business and when there is a specific business purpose for applying a particular standard that may, in fact, be discriminatory

3-1 APPLYING THE CONCEPT

BFOQ

State if each of the following would or wouldn't meet the test of a BFOQ:

    a. It is a legal BFOQ

    b. It is NOT a legal BFOQ

_____ 1. For the job of modeling women's clothing, applicants must be female.

_____ 2. For a job of loading packages onto trucks to be delivered, applicants must be able to lift 35 pounds.

_____ 3. For the job of teaching business at a Catholic college, applicants must be practicing Catholics.

_____ 4. For the job of attendant in a men's locker facility at a gym, applicants must be male.

_____ 5. For the job of a guard in a prison with male inmates, applicants must be men.

that there is a specific business purpose for applying a particular standard that may, in fact, be discriminatory.

Business necessity defenses must be combined with a test for job relatedness (discussed next). If an organization can show a legitimate business necessity for the test that they apply in an employment action, then they have a legitimate defense against charges of disparate impact. However, business necessity is specifically prohibited as a defense against disparate treatment.[19]

Job Relatedness. **Job relatedness** *exists when a test for employment is a legitimate measure of an individual's ability to do the essential functions of a job.* For job relatedness to act as a defense against a charge of discrimination, it first has to be a business necessity, and then the employer must be able to show that the test for the employment action was a legitimate measure of an individual's ability to do the job.[20] This test doesn't have to be a paper and pencil test. The federal government defines a "test for employment action" as the full range of assessment techniques, including written exams, performance tests, training programs, probationary periods, interviews, reviews of experience or education, work samples, and physical requirements.[21]

As an example of business necessity and job relatedness, the 5th Circuit Court of Appeals agreed that the **National Park Service** was allowed to transfer a park ranger out of the field due to the onset of a disability (Type I diabetes). The Park Service claimed the transfer was job related and consistent with business necessity, and the Court agreed. In the ruling, the Court noted that in the specific standards under which Atkins was transferred, the "focus on the physical consequences of uncontrolled diabetes was 'related to the specific skills and requirements' of being a park ranger and, therefore, job-related," and "the Standards also 'substantially promote[d]' [National Park Service] needs, consistent with business necessity."[22]

There is one thing that all good managers, especially HR managers, should keep in mind, though. The best way to defend against illegal discrimination charges is to avoid actions that could bring such charges about. If the company follows the laws and regulations, charges of discrimination become significantly less likely, so HR needs to ensure that we do everything possible to avoid those charges.

Age Discrimination in Employment Act of 1967 (ADEA)

The ADEA prohibits discrimination against employees age 40 or older. In this case, it applies if the organization has 20 or more workers instead of 15. The wording of this act almost exactly mirrors Title VII with the exception of the 20-worker minimum. This mirroring of the 1964 CRA is true of nearly all of the protected class discrimination laws that came about after 1964.

SHRM

B:1

Age Discrimination in Employment Act of 1967 (1967)

Job relatedness When a test for employment is a legitimate measure of an individual's ability to do the essential functions of a job

Why did Congress pass the ADEA? It was passed in response to a business practice that started to become a significant issue in the 1960s. Companies began to lay off older workers who tended to have higher salaries and then hire younger workers who would usually work for significantly less money. Congress became aware of these actions and decided that this was an unfair form of discrimination against people who had spent many years of their lives working for these same companies. The law that resulted was the ADEA.

Age discrimination complaints make up one-fifth to one-quarter of all actions filed with the EEOC, and these cases can be very costly. In a single 2013 case, **3M** agreed to pay $3 million to settle a class action ADEA lawsuit.[23]

Vietnam Era Veterans Readjustment Assistance Act of 1974 (VEVRAA)

This act again provides basically the same protection as the CRA does, but for Vietnam veterans. However, it only applies to federal contractors. Why was this law enacted? It was primarily due to the fact that after the war with Vietnam, soldiers came home to a public that was largely opposed to our participation in the war. As a result, some employers would discriminate against Vietnam veterans for taking part in a war that they personally had been opposed to. Congress decided that it was not acceptable for employers to single out veterans who had only done what the country had required of them, so they passed VEVRAA to prohibit such behaviors. The law requires that "employers with federal contracts or subcontracts of $100,000 or more provide equal opportunity *and* affirmative action for Vietnam era veterans, special disabled veterans, and veterans who served on active duty during a war or in a campaign or expedition for which a campaign badge has been authorized."[24]

Pregnancy Discrimination Act of 1978 (PDA)

The Pregnancy Discrimination Act requires that employers treat any woman who is pregnant in the same manner as they would treat any other employee with a medical condition. It prohibits discrimination against women affected by pregnancy, childbirth, or related medical conditions as unlawful sex discrimination under Title VII and requires that they be treated as all other employees for employment-related purposes, including benefits.[25]

Here, too, one wonders why this law was necessary. As insurance costs started to rise in the 1970s, companies started to look for ways to lower those costs. One way they found was to exclude pregnancy from their health insurance policies. By the mid-1970s, only a minority of employers covered pregnancy and related illnesses in their health policies, even though women made up about 45% of the workforce.[26] Finally, in 1976, a Supreme Court decision ruled that denying benefits for pregnancy-related disability was *not* discrimination based on sex.[27] This ruling outraged many women's advocacy organizations that in turn put pressure on Congress, which passed the PDA in 1978. Again, this law is mandatory for companies with 15 or more employees, including employment agencies, labor organizations, and state and local governments.

Americans With Disabilities Act of 1990 (ADA), as Amended in 2008

The first major federal law dealing with discrimination against disabled individuals was the 1973 Rehabilitation Act. This act stated that agencies of the federal government, federal contractors, and subcontractors with contracts exceeding $10,000 had to take affirmative action and could not discriminate on the basis of disabilities

SHRM

B:4
Pregnancy Discrimination Act of 1978

SHRM

B:2
Americans with Disabilities Act (ADA)

SHRM

B:10
Rehabilitation Act (1973)

in any employment actions.[28] However, this act only applied to a relatively small number of companies in the United States. Conversely, the ADA is one of the most significant employment laws ever passed in the United States. It also prohibits discrimination based on disability in all employment practices, such as job application procedures, hiring, firing, promotions, compensation, and training. However, it applies to virtually *all* employers with 15 or more employees in the same basic ways as the CRA of 1964 does.

There are many things about the ADA that make it difficult for employers to implement. The first of these is the definition of the word "disability." The ADA defines a **disability** as *a physical or mental impairment that substantially limits one or more major life activities, a record of having such an impairment, or being regarded as having such an impairment.*[29] According to rulings on the law, conditions such as obesity, substance abuse, and left-handedness are not covered disabilities (You may laugh, but it's true!), but something like obesity—if caused by a medical condition that would qualify as a disability—could be covered in some cases.

The definition of a disability is interesting because of the fact that anyone who has a record of having had an impairment covered by the ADA is considered in the same manner as someone who has a current disability. It is the same with someone who is regarded as having an impairment. How can someone be regarded as being impaired or disabled when they currently aren't? Well, as an example, if you have ever seen someone who has been severely burned on the face and hands, you may have had some questions as to whether the individual was disabled or not. Under the ADA, you must treat that person as disabled because of your concerns that the person may have a disability.

WHAT DOES THE ADA REQUIRE OF EMPLOYERS? An organization must make "reasonable accommodations" to the physical or mental limitations of an individual with a disability *who was otherwise qualified* to perform the "essential functions" of the job, unless it would impose an "undue hardship" on the organization's operation.[30]

So, what is a reasonable accommodation? A **reasonable accommodation** *is an accommodation made by an employer to allow someone who is disabled but otherwise qualified to do the essential functions of a job to be able to perform that job.* Reasonable accommodations are usually inexpensive and easy to implement. Here again, an example works best. If a job in a particular company requires that the employee use a computer keyboard and a blind individual applies for that job, the organization can make a reasonable accommodation to the individual by purchasing a Braille keyboard. In this case, Braille keyboards are inexpensive and provide the blind individual with the ability to do the job based on the reasonable accommodation provided.

In defining reasonable accommodations, it is also necessary to distinguish between "essential" and "marginal" job functions. Although essential functions are noted in the ADA, they are not defined there. Our understanding of essential functions comes mainly from court decisions concerning ADA cases. Based on these court cases, **essential functions** *are the fundamental duties of the position.* A function can generally be considered essential if it meets one of the following criteria:

1. The function is something that is done routinely and frequently in the job.

2. The function is done only on occasion, but it is an important part of the job.

3. The function may never be performed by the employee, but if it were necessary, it would be critical that it be done right.

Marginal job functions, on the other hand, *are those that may be performed on the job but need not be performed by all holders of the job.* Individuals with

---

SHRM

F:4
Individuals With Disabilities

SHRM

B:29
Reasonable Accommodation—ADA

Disability A physical or mental impairment that substantially limits one or more major life activities, a record of having such an impairment, or being regarded as having such an impairment

Reasonable accommodation An accommodation made by an employer to allow someone who is disabled but otherwise qualified to do the essential functions of a job to be able to perform that job

Essential functions The fundamental duties of the position

Marginal job functions Those functions that may be performed on the job but need not be performed by all holders of the job

disabilities *cannot* be denied employment if they cannot perform marginal job functions.[31]

What would be an example of a marginal job function? Let's say that in a clerical job, one of the job holder's duties is to file paperwork. However, the filing cabinet is a vertical five-drawer cabinet, and someone in a wheelchair would not be able to file papers in the upper drawers. The person in the job only spends about 5 minutes per day filing and only a portion of that filing in the upper two drawers of the filing cabinet. So would filing be an essential function in this job? No, it wouldn't—for a couple of reasons. First, it takes up a very small part of the day, so it is not something that the employee would do a lot. Second, in most cases, the company could buy horizontal filing cabinets that the disabled individual could reach, thus providing a reasonable accommodation to the disability. Finally, if for some reason, the company could not put horizontal filing cabinets into the area (e.g., if there were severe space limitations and no way to expand at a reasonable cost), then someone else could do the filing in the upper drawers for a couple of minutes per day. So in this case, filing would be a marginal job function.

Keith Brofsky/Photodisc/Thinkstock

HRM should focus on the ability to do the job and should not eliminate applicants based on non-job-related disabilities.

Generally, although not always, we find a list of the essential functions of the job in the organization's job descriptions and specifications (as discussed in Chapter 4). If the function is not listed as essential in the job description and specifications, we may have difficulty using it as a defense in a disability case. Therefore, we generally want to ensure that we list all of the essential functions of the job in the job description and specification documents.

So we have to make reasonable accommodations, but do employers have to take the initiative to make *every* job disability friendly? No. Under the ADA, employers are[32]

- Not required to make reasonable accommodations if the applicant or employee does not request it;
- Not required to make reasonable accommodations if applicants don't meet required qualifications for a job;
- Not required to lower quality standards or provide personal use items such as glasses or hearing aids to make reasonable accommodations; and
- Not required to make reasonable accommodations if to do so would be an undue hardship.

An **undue hardship** *exists when the level of difficulty for an organization to provide accommodations, determined by looking at the nature and cost of the accommodation and the overall financial resources of the facility, becomes a significant burden on the organization.* In general, the Department of Labor notes that most accommodations are relatively easy and inexpensive (usually costing less than $500—think of the Braille keyboard above, which costs about $25).[33] However, we must note that an undue hardship may be different for different companies. For instance, a small company with only a few million dollars in revenue per year may have an undue burden

Undue hardship When the level of difficulty for an organization to provide accommodations, determined by looking at the nature and cost of the accommodation and the overall financial resources of the facility, becomes a significant burden on the organization based on a relatively low-cost accommodation to a disabled individual, while a larger company could not claim undue hardship for the same accommodation.

An example helps here, too. If we were the owners of a small company housed on the second floor in a downtown historic-district building, and if we had an applicant for a job who was wheelchair bound, would we be required to consider that applicant for a job and accommodate that individual by rebuilding the historic building? The answer is most likely no, because of the fact that the accommodation required in one of the historic houses in such a district would require a major rebuilding effort, since stairways and doors in such houses are typically very narrow. This effort would cost a significant amount of money—an amount that would be unreasonable for the organization to pay. However, if we were faced with the same disabled individual and we were a large company headquartered in a modern building, then we would certainly be required to make the reasonable accommodations necessary to allow an individual in a wheelchair to work within the confines of our building.

The biggest problem that employers have with the ADA is the fact that it contains a number of words and phrases that can be interpreted in a wide variety of ways. Many of these were further defined in the 2008 ADA Amendments Act (ADAAA), but there still remains significant room for interpretation of many of these terms. For example, the term "reasonable accommodation" is open to broad interpretation because it is not defined very specifically in the ADA. "Essential function" is another term that can be defined in a wide variety of ways, although continuing court cases have narrowed it down some over the past 20 years. Because of these poorly defined terms, companies have had a difficult time in applying the ADA in a consistent manner, and as a result, they have quite likely been involved in more lawsuits per disabled employee than with any other protected group.[34] Companies have worked for more than 20 years to get clarification of the meaning of some of these words in the ADA, but without success to this point.

Civil Rights Act of 1991

SHRM

B:5
Title VII of the Civil Rights Act of 1991

The CRA of 1991 was enacted as an amendment designed to correct a few major omissions of the 1964 CRA as well as to overturn several US Court decisions.[35] One of the major changes in the amendment was the addition of compensatory and punitive damages in cases of intentional discrimination under Title VII and the ADA, when intentional or reckless discrimination is proven. **Compensatory damages** *are monetary damages awarded by the court that compensate the injured person for losses.* Such losses can include future pecuniary loss (potential future monetary losses like loss of earnings capacity), emotional pain, suffering, and loss of enjoyment of life. **Punitive damages** *are monetary damages awarded by the court that are designed to punish an injuring party that has intentionally inflicted harm on others.* They are meant to discourage employers from intentionally discriminating, and they do this by providing for payments to the plaintiff beyond the actual damages suffered.

Recognizing that one or a few discrimination cases could put an organization out of business, adversely affecting many innocent employees, the CRA of 1991 provides for a sliding scale of upper limits or "caps" on the combined amount of compensatory and punitive damages based on the number of employees employed by the employer. The limitations are shown in Exhibit 3-5.[36]

Another major area in which the 1991 Act changed the original CRA is in the application of quotas for protected group members. Many companies, after the 1964 CRA, created and used quotas for hiring and promotion. The quotas were made explicitly illegal by the 1991 act. In addition, the act prohibits "discriminatory use" of test scores, which is also called race norming. **Race norming** *exists when different groups of people have different scores designated as "passing" grades on a test for employment.* One group may have higher requirements for passing grades while

Compensatory damages Monetary damages awarded by the court that compensate the injured person for losses

Punitive damages Monetary damages awarded by the court that are designed to punish an injuring party that has intentionally inflicted harm on others

Race norming When different groups of people have different scores designated as "passing" grades on a test for employment

EXHIBIT 3-5 CAPS ON COMPENSATORY AND PUNITIVE DAMAGES BY EMPLOYER SIZE

Employer Size	Caps on Damages
15 to 100 employees	$ 50,000
101 to 200 employees	$100,000
201 to 500 employees	$200,000
501 employees or more	$300,000

another is allowed to pass at a lower level. The 1991 act basically equated this with quotas and, as such, made it illegal.[37]

Uniformed Services Employment and Reemployment Rights Act of 1994 (USERRA)

USERRA was passed to ensure the civilian reemployment rights of military members who were called away from their regular (nonmilitary) jobs by US government orders. Unlike other EEO laws, there is no minimum number of employees required for coverage by USERRA.[38] Per the US Department of Labor website, "USERRA is intended to minimize the disadvantages to an individual that occur when that person needs to be absent from his or her civilian employment to serve in this country's uniformed services. USERRA makes major improvements in protecting service member rights and benefits by clarifying the law and improving enforcement mechanisms."[39]

USERRA covers virtually every individual in the country who serves or has served in the uniformed services, and it applies to all employers in the public and private sectors, including federal employers. It also provides protection for disabled veterans, requiring employers to make reasonable efforts to accommodate their disabilities.[40]

SHRM

B:15
Uniformed Services Employment and Reemployment Rights Act of 1994 (USERRA)

Veterans Benefits Improvement Act of 2004 (VBIA)

The VBIA was enacted as an amendment to USERRA. It made two significant changes to USERRA: it extended the requirement for employers to maintain health care coverage for employees who were serving on active duty in the military (originally, this period was 18 months, but the VBIA changed it to 2 years), and it also required employers to post a notice of benefits, duties, and rights under USERRA/VBIA in a place where it would be visible to all employees who might be affected.[41]

Title II of the Genetic Information Nondiscrimination Act of 2008 (GINA)

Title II of the Genetic Information Nondiscrimination Act of 2008 (GINA) "prohibits the use of genetic information in employment, prohibits the intentional acquisition of genetic information about applicants and employees, and imposes strict confidentiality requirements."[42]

As with previously mentioned laws, some of you may be wondering why this law was enacted. GINA was created basically because of recent advances in genetic testing. We are now able to identify some genetic information that relates to a predisposition to contract certain diseases or disorders, such as Alzheimer's and Huntington's diseases. In order to prevent increases in medical premiums, some companies were starting to use these tests as a decision-making tool in hiring of employees, and some insurance companies were using such tests to determine health care coverage.

SHRM

B:32
Genetic Information Nondiscrimination Act (GINA)

Research has shown the benefits of having a diverse workforce.

There was some question about "preexisting conditions"—if you have the genetic marker for a disease, does that mean it is a preexisting condition and therefore not covered by some insurance policies?

Because companies were starting to use these tests to make employment and health care decisions, Congress decided to address their use. The result was GINA. The law prohibits discrimination based on genetic information and restricts acquisition and disclosure of such information. They enacted this law so that the general public would not fear adverse employment-related or health coverage–related consequences for having a genetic test or participating in research studies that examine genetic information.[43]

SHRM

B:31
Lilly Ledbetter Fair Pay Act

Lilly Ledbetter Fair Pay Act of 2009 (LLFPA)

This law amended Title VII of the 1964 CRA, as follows: "(3)(A) For purposes of this section, an unlawful employment practice occurs, with respect to discrimination in compensation in violation of this title, when a discriminatory compensation decision or other practice is adopted, when an individual becomes subject to a discriminatory compensation decision or other practice, or when an individual is affected by application of a discriminatory compensation decision or other practice, including each time wages, benefits, or other compensation is paid, resulting in whole or in part from such a decision or other practice."[44]

So, what does this mean? In practical terms, the LLFPA extends the period of time in which an employee is allowed to file a lawsuit for compensation (pay) discrimination. The 1964 CRA only allowed 180 days from the time of the discriminatory action for an individual employee to file a lawsuit. The LLFPA allows an individual to file a lawsuit within 180 days after "any application" of that discriminatory compensation decision, including every time the individual gets paid, as long as the discrimination is continuing, which would usually be for the entire period of their employment.

One of the most significant aspects of the LLFPA is that the amendments to the time allowed to file a discrimination complaint *could* also be determined by the courts to apply to other antidiscrimination laws like the Age Discrimination in Employment Act and the Americans with Disabilities Act, which borrow Title VII's limitations period.

LO 3-5

Briefly discuss the two major federal immigration laws and how they affect the workplace.

SHRM

B:38
Immigration and Nationality Act (INA)

Immigration Laws Relating to Employment and Equal Opportunity

Immigration and the employment of immigrant workers are controlled by a series of federal laws. In general, these laws are designed for two purposes: to require verification of the legal right to work within the United States and to prevent potential discrimination against immigrant workers who are legally allowed to work in the country. The two major laws in this area are the Immigration and Nationality Act of 1952 (as amended) and the Immigration Reform and Control Act of 1986. While immigration law is extremely complex, for our purposes in an introductory HR text, we will only discuss the basic employment provisions of these two laws.

IMMIGRATION AND NATIONALITY ACT OF 1952 (INA). The INA was designed to take a variety of different immigration laws and combine them into a single Act. Before

3-2 APPLYING THE CONCEPT

Employment Laws

Review the laws listed below and then write the letter corresponding to each law before the statement(s) describing a situation where that law would apply.

a. Equal Pay
b. Title VII CRA 1964
c. ADEA
d. VEVRAA
e. PDA
f. ADA
g. CRA 1991
h. USERRA
i. VBIA
j. GINA
k. LLFPA
l. Immigration laws

_____ 6. I had to take a medical test, and the company found out that I am at high risk to get cancer. So it decided not to hire me so it could save money on medical insurance.

_____ 7. Although I was the best qualified, I was intentionally not promoted because I am a woman.

_____ 8. I can't understand why this firm doesn't want to hire me just because I served my country. I didn't want to go and fight overseas, but I was drafted into the Army in 1969 and had no choice; I didn't want to go to jail for draft evasion.

_____ 9. My boss is laying me off because I serve in the National Guard and will be deployed overseas for six months. As a result, I will have to find a new job when I get back.

_____ 10. The firm is laying me off to hire some younger person to save money. Is this what I deserve for my 20 years of dedication?

_____ 11. The company I work for is in trouble with the INS because it never asked me any questions about my being legally eligible to work in America.

_____ 12. I'm being paid less than the men who do the same jobs, just because I'm a woman.

_____ 13. The firm hired this new guy and bought a special low desk because he is so short.

_____ 14. I'm suing the firm for lost wages because they intentionally discriminated against me and fired me when I complained about it.

INA, a number of federal laws governed immigration, but they were not consistent and were not organized in one location under one authority.[45] INA allows companies in the United States to employ immigrant workers in certain specialty occupations. For example, foreign workers such as engineers, teachers, computer programmers, medical doctors, and physical therapists may be employed under INA.[46] However, specific requirements apply to such employment, and there are annual limits to the number of workers who can apply for work visas in these specialty occupations.

One company recently found out how expensive it can be to try to circumvent INA. Infosys paid the largest fine in history—$35 million—to the U.S. government for visa fraud. The company intentionally used a B-1 visa, which is meant for short business visits, instead of the H1-B visa, which is the work visa that foreign individuals need in order to work legally in the United States.[47] Make sure you heed this warning not to try to play around with the work rules—no matter what country you are in or where you source your employees.

Because Congress foresaw the potential for companies to discriminate against *all* alien workers to avoid any accusation of hiring undocumented workers, INA also has a nondiscrimination requirement when dealing with alien workers who have the right to work in the United States. Such workers become another protected class for the purposes of EEO.

IMMIGRATION REFORM AND CONTROL ACT OF 1986 (IRCA). Under IRCA, employers may only hire individuals who are authorized to legally work in the United States. IRCA has a provision that prohibits employers from knowingly hiring undocumented workers, and it requires employers to verify each employee's eligibility for employment. The employer is required to verify the identity and employment eligibility

SHRM

B:35
Immigration Reform and Control Act (IRCA)

WORK
APPLICATION 3-4

Give examples of how major employment laws have affected an organization where you work or have worked, preferably as the law relates directly to you. Be sure to specify the law and what the firm does or doesn't do because of the law.

of anyone it hires, through the use of a form called the Employment Eligibility Verification Form (I-9). However, the act also provides employers complying "in good faith" with the requirements of IRCA with what is called an affirmative defense to inadvertently hiring an unauthorized alien. An *affirmative defense* means basically that if we made a legitimate and complete effort to verify a person's legal status and it turns out that person provided false documents, or that we were tricked or lied to in some other way, we won't be held liable for any potential fines that would have otherwise been assessed for hiring undocumented workers.[48]

Reminder: State and Local EEO Laws May Be Different

As with any introductory textbook, we can't tell you all of the laws that would apply in the various locations across the United States, and we certainly can't go into all the labor laws in other countries around the world. We can only cover the major laws that affect virtually everyone in each of the United States. Each state, as well as many cities, has its own equal opportunity laws that employers within that state must follow. It's up to the HR manager to keep up to date on the local and state laws and regulations concerning equal opportunity.

EQUAL EMPLOYMENT OPPORTUNITY COMMISSION (EEOC)

The various federal equal employment opportunity (EEO) laws are enforced by the Equal Employment Opportunity Commission (EEOC). The EEOC was created by the 1964 CRA as an enforcement arm for the act. It is a federal agency that has significant power over employers in the process of investigating complaints of illegal discrimination based on "race, color, religion, sex (including pregnancy), national origin, age (40 or older), disability, or genetic information."[49]

What Does the EEOC Do?

The EEOC is the federal agency primarily charged with enforcement of the federal equal employment opportunity laws. The EEOC basically has three significant responsibilities: (1) investigating and resolving discrimination complaints through either conciliation or litigation, (2) gathering and compiling statistical information on such complaints, and (3) running education and outreach programs on what constitutes illegal discrimination.[50] Additionally, every company with more than 100 employees or with more than 50 employees *and* with federal contracts totaling $50,000 or more must file an EEO-1 Report with the EEOC each year.[51] The EEO-1 identifies the company's EEO compliance data based on protected classifications within federal law.

General EEO timelines for complaints are as follows:

- Individuals must typically file a complaint within 180 days of the incident (or the last occurrence of the incident if it is ongoing).
- The complainant must give the EEOC up to 60 days to investigate the complaint.
- Generally, if the complainant is dissatisfied with the outcome, legal charges must be filed before 300 days have passed since the last incident of discrimination. If not, the case cannot go forward in court. However, recall that the LLFPA increases the length of time that complainants have to file a lawsuit in at least those cases relating to pay or other compensation.
- The complainant has sole responsibility for ensuring that deadlines are met. If the individual does not file required items by their due dates, then the case is generally not able to be taken forward.

If the EEOC determines that discrimination has taken place, it will attempt to provide reconciliation between the parties without burdening the courts. If the EEOC cannot come to an agreement with the organization, there are two options:

1. The agency may aid the alleged victim in bringing suit in federal court.
2. It can issue a "right-to-sue" letter to the alleged victim. A **right-to-sue** is a *notice from the EEOC, issued if it elects not to prosecute an individual discrimination complaint within the agency, that gives the recipient the right to go directly to the courts with the complaint.*

If the EEOC does not believe the complaint to be valid or fails to complete the investigation, the complainant still may sue in federal court on their own. However, without a right-to-sue letter, it will generally be difficult for a complainant to succeed in getting a judgment against the employer.

Employee Rights Under the EEOC

Employees have the right to bring discrimination complaints against their employer by filing a complaint with the EEOC. They also have the right to participate in an EEOC investigation, hearing, or other proceeding without threat of retaliation; rights related to the arbitration and settlement of the complaint; and the right to sue the employer directly in court over claims of illegal discrimination, even if the EEOC does not support their claim.

Employer Prohibitions

The employer has some rights as well. The employer has a right to defend the organization using the defenses noted earlier: BFOQ, business necessity, and job relatedness. However, the employer does not have a right to *retaliate* against individuals who participate in an EEOC action, either through filing charges or through participating in the above investigations, hearings, or proceedings. The employer also is prohibited from creating a work environment that would lead to charges of *constructive discharge*. Both of these items are prohibited in each employment law that deals with discrimination.

RETALIATION. In addition to providing defenses against discrimination claims, the 1964 civil rights act identifies a situation in which organizations can be held liable for harming the employee because of retaliation.[52] **Retaliation** *is a situation where the organization takes an "adverse employment action" against an employee because the employee brought discrimination charges against the organization or supported someone who brought discrimination charges against the company.* An **adverse employment action** *is any action such as firings, demotions, schedule reductions, or changes that would harm the individual employee.*

Retaliation is a form of harassment based on an individual filing a discrimination claim. Each of the EEO laws identifies retaliation as illegal harassment based on the protected class identified within that law. The EEOC is responsible for enforcing compliance with all EEO laws concerning retaliation. As stated on the EEOC website, "All of the laws we enforce make it illegal to fire, demote, harass, or otherwise "retaliate" against people (applicants or employees) because they filed a charge of discrimination, because they complained to their employer or other covered entity about discrimination on the job, or because they participated in an employment discrimination proceeding (such as an investigation or lawsuit)."[53]

There are severe penalties for engaging in retaliation against an employee or applicant for participating in protected activity. In 2013, over 40% of all EEOC complaints had a retaliation claim as at least a component of the complaint.[54] Every

SHRM

F:1
Equal Opportunity Employment

SHRM

B:27
Unlawful Harassment

SHRM

B:28
Whistle-blowing/Retaliation

Right-to-sue A notice from the EEOC, issued if it elects not to prosecute an individual discrimination complaint within the agency, that gives the recipient the right to go directly to the courts with the complaint

Retaliation A situation where the organization takes an "adverse employment action" against an employee because the employee brought discrimination charges against the organization or supported someone who brought discrimination charges against the company

Adverse employment action Any action such as firings, demotions, schedule reductions, or changes that would harm the individual employee

WORK
APPLICATION 3-5

Has an organization where you work or have worked had any potential or actual cases brought to the EEOC against it? If so, explain the complaint(s). The HR staff at your employer may not be too eager to talk about this, but you can do some research on larger corporations.

manager needs to be aware of this concept in order to avoid actions that might be construed as retaliatory.

CONSTRUCTIVE DISCHARGE. In addition to retaliation, the organization can be guilty of "constructive discharge" due to discriminatory actions on the job. Again, the EEOC would generally be the agency responsible for initially investigating claims of constructive discharge.[55]

Basically, **constructive discharge** *exists when an employee is put under such extreme pressure by management that continued employment becomes intolerable and, as a result, the employee quits, or resigns from the organization.* In a Supreme Court decision in 2004,[56] the court noted that the US Court of Appeals had identified constructive discharge as the following: "(1) he or she suffered harassment or discrimination so intolerable that a reasonable person in the same position would have felt compelled to resign . . .; and (2) the employee's reaction to the workplace situation—that is, his or her decision to resign—was reasonable given the totality of circumstances."

So if an individual can show that constructive discharge caused them to resign from the organization, then the individual would be eligible for all employee rights associated with being involuntarily terminated from the company. If, in fact, the individual suffered sexual harassment or discrimination that resulted in their constructive discharge, the organization would also suffer liability for those employment actions. The EEOC would be the agency charged with investigating and arbitrating the results of this conduct by the employer. The 2004 Supreme Court case set new standards for demonstrating constructive discharge from a company, and in so doing, it created a more difficult employment environment for employers. Every employer or manager needs to understand this concept.

LO 3-7

Discuss the differences among equal employment opportunity, affirmative action, and diversity.

EEO, AFFIRMATIVE ACTION, AND DIVERSITY: WHAT'S THE DIFFERENCE?

As a manager, you need to understand the terms *equal employment opportunity* (EEO), *affirmative action*, and *diversity*. These are significantly different concepts, but many employees and employers, and even some educators, tend to use them interchangeably. *EEO* is the term that deals with a series of laws and regulations put in place at the federal and state government level over the last 45 years. As such, EEO is very specific and narrowly defined within federal and various state laws.

On the other hand, affirmative action as a concept was created in the 1960s through a series of policies at the presidential and legislative levels in the United States. Affirmative action, except in a few circumstances, does not have the effect of law.[57] We will discuss those circumstances in the next section. Therefore, affirmative action is a much broader concept based on policies and executive orders (orders from the president); EEO is more narrowly based on law.

Finally, diversity is not law, nor *necessarily* even policy within organizations. Diversity is a very broad set of concepts that deal with the differences among people within organizations. Today's organizations view diversity as a valuable part of their human resources makeup. However, there are no specific laws that deal with requirements for diversity within organizations, beyond the EEO laws that specifically identify protected class members and require that organizations deal with those protected class members in an equal way when compared to all other members of the organization.

While this certainly creates some greater diversity in organizations, the concept of diversity goes much further than just EEO. We have already discussed many of the major equal employment opportunity laws. Now, let's take a look at affirmative action and the concept of diversity. Exhibit 3-6 provides a summary of these three concepts.

Constructive discharge When an employee is put under such extreme pressure by management that continued employment becomes intolerable and, as a result, the employee quits, or resigns from the organization

EXHIBIT 3-6 EQUAL EMPLOYMENT OPPORTUNITY, AFFIRMATIVE ACTION, AND DIVERSITY

Topic	Governance	Concept
EEO	Federal (and state) law	Narrow, specific requirements and prohibitions
Affirmative Action	Executive orders, federal court orders, or voluntary	Policies that broadly define situations in which actions should be taken to balance a workforce with its surroundings
Diversity	Organizational policies	No legal requirement; designed to better serve a more diverse customer base

Affirmative Action (AA)

Affirmative action is a series of policies, programs, and initiatives that have been instituted by various entities within both government and the private sector that are designed to prefer hiring of individuals from protected groups in certain circumstances, in an attempt to mitigate past discrimination. However, affirmative action policies and programs do not generally have the same effect as EEO laws. There are actually only two specific cases in which affirmative action can be mandated or required within an organization.[58] In all other cases today, creation of an affirmative action program is strictly voluntary. The two situations where affirmative action is mandatory are as follows:

EXECUTIVE ORDER 11246. If the company is a contractor to the federal government and receives more than $10,000 per year, they are required by presidential order (Executive Order 11246) to maintain an affirmative action program. Exemptions from this order include the following:

- The order "shall not apply to a Government contractor or subcontractor that is a religious corporation, association, educational institution, or society, with respect to the employment of individuals of a particular religion to perform work connected with the carrying on by such corporation, association, educational institution, or society of its activities. Such contractors and subcontractors are not exempted or excused from complying with the other requirements contained in this Order."[59]

- "The Secretary of Labor may also provide, by rule, regulation, or order, for the exemption of facilities of a contractor that are in all respects separate and distinct from activities of the contractor related to the performance of the contract: provided, that such an exemption will not interfere with or impede the effectuation of the purposes of this Order: and provided further, that in the absence of such an exemption all facilities shall be covered by the provisions of this Order."[60]

FEDERAL COURT ORDERS FOR AA PROGRAMS. If an organization is presented with a federal court order to create an affirmative action program to correct past discriminatory practices, it must comply. This is usually only done when there is an egregious history of past discriminatory practices in the organization.

SHRM

F:2
Affirmative Action

SHRM

B:6
Executive Order 11246 (1965)

Affirmative action A series of policies, programs, and initiatives that have been instituted by various entities within both government and the private sector that are designed to prefer hiring of individuals from protected groups in certain circumstances, in an attempt to mitigate past discrimination

WORK
APPLICATION 3-6

Has an organization where you work or have worked had an affirmative action program? If so, describe it. Also, has there been any reverse discrimination?

The following web links do an excellent job of telling you about the current body of information on the concept of affirmative action and its history to date:

http://www.infoplease.com/spot/affirmative1.html
http://plato.stanford.edu/entries/affirmative-action/

The *Bakke* decision noted in the above Stanford University link is the basis for the concept of **reverse discrimination**, *which is discrimination against members of the majority group in an organization, generally resulting from affirmative action policies within an organization.*

There have been a number of recent affirmative action rulings in federal courts that have upheld limits to affirmative action. For example, the Supreme Court ordered a lower court to reconsider a "race-conscious" admissions plan at Texas state universities,[61] and it also upheld a voter-backed affirmative action ban in Michigan's universities.[62] Additionally, other states are looking at possible partial or full bans on affirmative action. This will be an area to watch in HRM over the next few years.

The Office of Federal Contract Compliance Programs (OFCCP)

SHRM

B:17
Enforcement Agencies—OFCCP

The OFCCP is in charge of monitoring and enforcing Executive Order (EO) 11246, Section 503 of the 1973 Rehabilitation Act, and the 1974 VEVRAA.[63] We have already discussed VEVRAA above, so let's take a look at EO 11246 and the Rehabilitation Act as they relate to the OFCCP.

The OFCCP is in charge of federal contract compliance, and both EO 11246 and the Rehab Act require that federal contractors who receive more than a certain dollar value per year in contracts from the federal government provide equal opportunity and take affirmative action toward protected class individuals. In the case of EO 11246, those groups are based on race, color, religion, sex, and national origin, and in the case of the Rehab Act, the designated group is disabled individuals.

Diversity in the Workforce

Diversity *is simply the existence of differences—in HRM, it deals with different types of people in an organization.* This brings up a number of questions. Why do we want to have diversity in organizations? What are the advantages that we create by having a more diverse workforce? Are there any disadvantages to having a more diverse work group? What can we do about any disadvantages? Let's discuss diversity as it provides both opportunities and challenges.[64]

SHRM

F:6
Racial/Ethnic Diversity

DEMOGRAPHIC DIVERSITY. Is diversity really all that important? The answer is yes.[65] For one thing, there is currently a shortage of skilled workers—and there will be for the foreseeable future, so to exclude a qualified person because that individual is different in some way is counterproductive to business success. Also, as we have already discussed, discrimination is against the law.

According to the United Nations, in late 2011, the world population hit 7 billion people.[66] However, the world Caucasian population is shrinking as more whites die each year than are born. It takes about 2.1 children per woman (the fertility rate) to replace the current generation, but the estimated 2014 fertility rate in the European Union was 1.59 and in the United States it was 2.01,[67] while worldwide, it is 2.45.[68]

As of 2012, white births were also no longer a majority in the United States.[69] White women are having fewer children than nonwhites, while the growth of mixed marriages has led to more multiracial births. Among Hispanics, there are roughly nine births for every one death, compared with about a one-to-one ratio for whites.[70]

Reverse discrimination Discrimination against members of the majority group in an organization, generally resulting from affirmative action policies within an organization

Diversity The existence of differences—in HRM, it deals with different types of people in an organization

In 2010, Caucasians only composed 54% of the under-18 age-group.[71] In 2010, in 10 US states, more than 50% of the under-15 population consisted of minorities.[72]

With these statistics, it should be clear that increasing cultural diversity in the workforce poses one of the most challenging human resource and organizational issues of our time.[73]

WHY DO WE NEED DIVERSITY? Diversity is important and needed because as the white population continues to shrink and minority populations grow, selling your goods and services to a variety of groups increases sales, revenues, and profits—in other words, embracing diversity creates business opportunities.[74] Organizations today have begun to value the diversity of their workforces simply due to the fact that as they become more diverse, they can serve a larger and more diverse customer base.[75] Diverse employees allow us to see the diversity around us, in our customers and other stakeholders, much better than we would if our work groups were more homogenous.[76] As a result, we are better able to provide products and services that will appeal to the larger and more diverse groups that we come into contact with during the course of doing business.[77]

WHAT ARE THE ADVANTAGES OF A DIVERSE WORKFORCE? The primary advantages of a diverse workforce come from the ability to stimulate and provide more creative and innovative solutions to organizational problems.[78] How does a more diverse workforce add to the creativity and innovation in an organization? **Creativity** *is a basic ability to think in unique and different ways and apply those thought processes to existing problems*, and **innovation** *is the act of creating useful processes or products based on creative thought processes.*

Basically, if we look at a problem from different perspectives, we find out that there are more facets to the problem than we originally realized. Have you ever been in a situation where you just couldn't find something, you asked someone else to help you search for it, and they found it almost immediately? A diversified group looking at a problem will look at the problem from different directions and in different ways, and therefore, it will discover more of the aspects of the problem than would a single person or a more homogeneous work group.[79]

But why is creativity necessary in a business today? Simply put, it helps the organization innovate. Organizations in today's fast-moving industries have to be able to innovate and change to adapt to their external environment—their competitors, their customers, and changes in technology. If an organization is unable to rapidly innovate, it will almost certainly die in today's business world.

Also, creativity is a rare commodity in organizations. Why is it so hard to be creative? Most of us have learned not to be creative—we have been told over and over as we grow up that we should do things the way everyone else does them. In other words, we have been *trained* not to be innovative! Over time, this has the effect of causing most of us to give up on being very creative and just go along with the way that the majority of people do something. We lose the ability to think differently. This ability, called divergent thinking, is necessary in order to come up with creative solutions to a problem.[80] **Divergent thinking** *is the ability to find many possible solutions to a particular problem, including unique, untested solutions.*

By introducing diversity into our workforce, we assist the process of divergent thinking. Different people think differently because they have different backgrounds and have solved problems differently in the past. We all bring this unique set of problem-solving skills to our work. Luckily, we don't all have the same background, so this has the effect of increasing the creativity and innovation in the organization without the individual having to relearn the ability to be highly creative.

ARE THERE ANY CHALLENGES TO DIVERSITY? Of course there are. There are several things that can cause diversity to break down the organization instead of allowing it

SHRM

F:12
Business Case for Diversity

Creativity A basic ability to think in unique and different ways and apply those thought processes to existing problems

Innovation The act of creating useful processes or products based on creative thought processes

Divergent thinking The ability to find many possible solutions to a particular problem, including unique, untested solutions

WORK
APPLICATION 3-7

Discuss how demographic diversity and the need for diversity is affecting an organization you work for or have worked for. What are some of the advantages and challenges faced by the firm? Also, describe how diversity is managed at the organization.

Conflict The act of being opposed to another

Functional conflict How organizations go through the process of creating new things–the opposition itself drives the organization to change

Dysfunctional conflict When conflict gets to the point where creativity is stifled and in fact almost all work becomes difficult or impossible because of the conflict's intensity

Cohesiveness An intent and desire for group members to stick together in their actions

to become better and more creative.[81] The first issue is conflict. **Conflict** *is simply the act of being opposed to another.* Conflict occurs in all interactions between individuals. There are many reasons for conflict. However conflict is typically greater when people are significantly different from each other, which means that if we create a more diverse workforce, there's a greater likelihood for more significant conflict.

Is conflict bad? Not necessarily. Conflict can basically be broken down into functional conflict and dysfunctional conflict.[82] **Functional conflict** *is how organizations go through the process of creating new things—the opposition itself drives the organization to change.* If we don't have conflicts, the organization never changes. However, **dysfunctional conflict** *occurs when conflict gets to the point where creativity is stifled and in fact almost all work becomes difficult or impossible because of the conflict's intensity.* Dysfunctional conflict breaks down the organization, while functional conflict allows it to grow.

The second big issue is group cohesiveness. **Cohesiveness** *is an intent and desire for group members to stick together in their actions.* In organizations, we have learned that in order for a work group to become as good as it possibly can be, the group has to become cohesive. The members have to learn to *want* to be part of the group and want to interact with other members of the group in order for the group to perform at a high level. So we need cohesiveness to be high. However, the more diversity there is within the group, the more difficult it is to create the cohesiveness necessary for high performance. So, more diverse groups tend to be less cohesive—not always, but as a general rule.[83]

A third significant issue in diversity is *resistance to change.* If organizations are used to being less diverse, then diversity can be something that is scary to the people in the organization. If they are uncomfortable with the change, they *will* resist. This resistance can be taken care of through a number of methods including the creation of a more participative decision-making environment, creating cognitive dissonance, coercion, and a number of other methods.

There are several other things that make diversity a challenge. The above items are some of the most significant, but if you are interested, you can always find out more by reading a variety of organizational management, psychology, or sociology literature.

MANAGING DIVERSITY. Diversity affects bottom-line profits, but so do some of the challenges associated with diversity, like conflict and reduced cohesiveness. In other words, if all of our diverse employees don't work well together, the organization does not work well.[84] Creating a cohesive, operational, and highly successful diverse workforce doesn't just happen. Management has to work to create success with diversity. Managing diversity so that we gain the benefits available is one of the most critical jobs of a 21st century manager. Diversity can be managed successfully only in an organizational culture that values diversity.[85] While the details of a diversity management program are a topic for discussion in another course, we can briefly review what managers need to be concerned with.

Exhibit 3-7 illustrates the process of managing diversity. Successfully managing diversity requires top management support and commitment.[86] Senior managers have to "walk the talk" of the diversity program if it is going to succeed. Employees throughout an organization look to *top management* to set an example. If the management is committed to maintaining a diverse workplace characterized by dignity, others at all levels of the organization will be as well.

Managing diversity further requires leadership.[87] *Diversity leadership* refers to having top-level managers who are responsible for managing diversity. The diversity leaders must also set *policies and practices* relating to maintaining diversity.

Finally and most importantly, employees must be provided with training so that they can work together as teams despite differences in race, gender, age, ability, and

EXHIBIT 3-7 MANAGING DIVERSITY

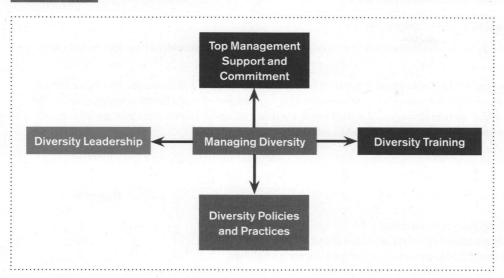

other factors.[88] Therefore, corporations are providing diversity training for their managers and employees.[89] In fact, training is one of the most common activities included in diversity initiatives.[90] The primary goal of diversity training is to remove obstacles faced by members of the organizations that might prevent their professional and personal growth.[91]

Through managing diversity, affirmative action and diversity programs have been used to help women and minorities advance in organizations. Complete Self-Assessment 3-1 to determine your attitude toward women and minorities advancing at work.

SEXUAL HARASSMENT: A SPECIAL TYPE OF DISCRIMINATION

Sexual harassment is a special type of discrimination identified as part of the 1964 CRA (the prohibition of discrimination based on sex), but it is one of the two items we mentioned earlier in the chapter that was not specifically recognized as a separate type of discrimination until federal courts started hearing cases on the act. In the case of sexual harassment, it was a Supreme Court decision in the 1980s that finally identified such harassment as specifically violating the CRA. The case was *Meritor Savings Bank v. Vinson*, and it confirmed the intent of the 1964 CRA that sexual harassment was specifically prohibited by the act. Sexual harassment is a pervasive issue in organizations, and as managers, we need to understand what it is and how to avoid creating a situation where it can occur at work.

Types of Sexual Harassment

Sexual harassment is defined by the EEOC as *"unwelcome sexual advances, requests for sexual favors, and other verbal or physical conduct of a sexual nature constitutes sexual harassment when submission to or rejection of this conduct explicitly or implicitly affects an individual's employment, unreasonably interferes with an individual's work performance or creates an intimidating, hostile or offensive work environment."*[92] There are two types of sexual harassment specifically delineated in the *Vinson* case: quid pro quo harassment and hostile work environment.[93] Both are discussed below.

LO 3-8

Identify the two primary types of sexual harassment.

SHRM

F:9
Sex/Gender Issues

Sexual harassment As defined by the EEOC, "unwelcome sexual advances, requests for sexual favors, and other verbal or physical conduct of a sexual nature constitutes sexual harassment when submission to or rejection of this conduct explicitly or implicitly affects an individual's employment, unreasonably interferes with an individual's work performance or creates an intimidating, hostile or offensive work environment"

3-1 SELF ASSESSMENT

Attitudes About Women and Minorities Advancing

Be honest in this self-assessment, as your assessment will not be accurate if you aren't. Also, you should not be asked to share your score with others.

Each question below is actually two questions. It asks you about your attitude toward women, and it also asks you about your attitude toward minorities. Therefore, you should give two answers to each question: one regarding women and the other regarding minorities. Write the number corresponding to your answer (5 = agree, 3 = don't know, 1 = disagree) about women in the Women column, and write the number corresponding to your answer about minorities in the Minorities column.

Agree				Disagree
5	4	3	2	1

Women   **Minorities**

Women		Minorities
_____	1. Women/Minorities lack motivation to get ahead.	1. ____
_____	2. Women/Minorities lack the education necessary to get ahead.	2. ____
_____	3. Women/Minorities working has caused rising unemployment among white men.	3. ____
_____	4. Women/Minorities are not strong enough or emotionally stable enough to succeed in high-pressure jobs.	4. ____
_____	5. Women/Minorities have a lower commitment to work than do white men.	5. ____
_____	6. Women/Minorities are too emotional to be effective managers.	6. ____
_____	7. Women/Minority managers have difficulty in situations calling for quick and precise decisions.	7. ____
_____	8. Women/Minorities have a higher turnover rate than do white men.	8. ____
_____	9. Women/Minorities are out of work more often than are white men.	9. ____
_____	10. Women/Minorities have less interest in advancing than do white men.	10. ____
_____ Total		Total ____

Women: To determine your attitude score toward women, add up the total of your 10 answers in the Women column and place the total on the Total line and on the following continuum. The higher your total score, the more negative your attitude.

10 _____	20 _____	30 _____	40 _____	50

Positive attitude   Negative attitude

Minorities: To determine your attitude score toward minorities, add up the total of your 10 answers from the Minorities column and place the total on the Total line and on the following continuum. The higher your total score, the more negative your attitude.

10 _____	20 _____	30 _____	40 _____	50

Positive attitude   Negative attitude

Each statement is a negative attitude about women and minorities at work. However, research has shown all of these statements to be false; they are considered myths. Such statements stereotype women and minorities unfairly and prevent them from advancing in organizations through gaining salary increases and promotions. Thus, part of managing diversity and diversity training is to help overcome these negative attitudes to provide equal opportunities for ALL.

Quid pro quo harassment Harassment that occurs when some type of benefit or punishment is made contingent upon the employee submitting to sexual advances

QUID PRO QUO HARASSMENT. Literally, quid pro quo means "This for that." Quid pro quo harassment *is harassment that occurs when some type of benefit or punishment is made contingent upon the employee submitting to sexual advances.* "If you do something for me, I will do something for you, or conversely if you refuse to do something for me, I will harm you." Quid pro quo is a direct form of harassment aimed at an individual and is most commonly seen in supervisor-subordinate relationships, although this is not always the case. It is, however, based on the power of one individual over another. If the harasser has no power to reward or punish the individual who is the object of the harassment, then it is difficult for quid pro quo harassment to exist. In the case of coworkers where one is pressuring the other concerning a relationship, the situation would more likely be considered to be a hostile work environment.

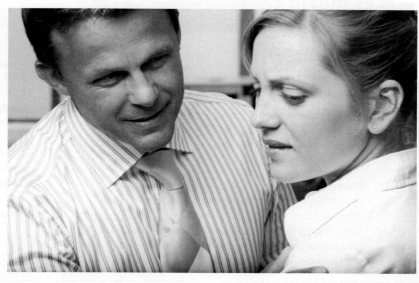

HOSTILE WORK ENVIRONMENT. Hostile work environment is a very specific legal term in HRM meaning *harassment that occurs when someone's behavior at work creates an environment that is sexual in nature and that makes it difficult for someone of a particular sex to work in that environment.* Hostile work environment sexual harassment happens when a "reasonable person" determines that the behavior in question goes beyond normal human interaction and the jokes and kidding that accompany such interaction, instead rising to a level that such a reasonable person would consider the act or acts to be both harassing and sexual in nature.[94] For the purposes of the law, a reasonable person *is the "average" person who would look at the situation and its intensity to determine whether the accused person was wrong in their actions.*

All employees should feel comfortable with coworkers on the job.

What Constitutes Sexual Harassment?

Can sexual harassment in any form occur between a female supervisor and a male subordinate? Can sexual harassment occur between two male employees or two female employees? Absolutely! Sexual harassment does not have to occur between a male supervisor and female subordinates. For example, there is a famous Supreme Court case of male-on-male harassment on an offshore oil platform. In *Oncale v. Sundowner Offshore Services*,[95] Joseph Oncale quit his job on an oil rig and filed a harassment suit against his employer. The Court ruled that he was harassed to the point that it met the standard where a reasonable person would have considered it sexual harassment.

As in other forms of illegal discrimination, the plaintiff only has to show a prima facie (literally "on the face of it," meaning it looks like harassment to our reasonable person) case that harassment has occurred. To qualify as a prima facie case of sexual harassment, the work situation must include the following characteristics:[96]

1. The plaintiff is a member of a protected class;
2. The harassment was based on sex;
3. The person was subject to unwelcome sexual advances; *or*
4. The harassment was sufficiently severe enough to alter the terms, conditions, or privileges of employment.

In order for the organization to be considered for liability, two critical conditions must exist:[97]

1. The plaintiff did not solicit or incite the advances.
2. The harassment was undesirable and severe enough to alter the terms, conditions, and privileges of employment.

Hostile work environment Harassment that occurs when someone's behavior at work creates an environment that is sexual in nature and that makes it difficult for someone of a particular sex to work in that environment

Reasonable person The "average" person who would look at the situation and its intensity to determine whether the accused person was wrong in their actions

3-3 APPLYING THE CONCEPT

Sexual Harassment

Write the letter and number codes listed below before each statement to indicate the kind of behavior it describes.

    a. sexual harassment: After the harassment letter, write in if it is (1) quid pro quo or (2) hostile work environment harassment (i.e., write a/1 or a/2).

    b. not sexual harassment

_____ 15. Karen tells her coworker Jim an explicitly sexual joke, even though twice before, Jim told her not to tell him any dirty jokes.

_____ 16. Ricky-Joe typically puts his hand on his secretary's shoulder as he talks to her, and she is comfortable with this behavior.

_____ 17. José, the supervisor, tells his secretary, Latoya, that he'd like to take her out for the first time today.

_____ 18. Cindy tells her assistant, Juan, that he will have to go to a motel with her if he wants to be recommended for a promotion.

_____ 19. Jack and Jill have each hung up pictures of nude men and women on the walls near their desks, in view of other employees who walk by.

_____ 20. As coworker Rachel talks to Carlos, he is surprised and uncomfortable because she gently rubbed his buttock.

Some cases are clearly sexual harassment on the first offense, such as requesting sex as part of the job and any unwanted sexual touching. However, some offenses are not so obvious, such as touching on an arm or shoulder or asking a person to go on a date. In these gray areas, affected employees should tell the harasser that they find the behavior offensive and will report the person for sexual harassment if the behavior is repeated.

Reducing Organizational Risk From Sexual Harassment Lawsuits

Once the plaintiff has shown a prima facie case for the accusation, and once it has been determined that the harassment was potentially severe enough to alter the terms, conditions, and privileges of work (and assuming that the organization can't show the plaintiff invited or incited the advances, as in the case of quid pro quo harassment); then the courts will determine whether the organization is liable for the actions of its employee based on the answers to two primary questions:

1. Did the employer know about, or should the employer have known about, the harassment?

2. Did the employer act to stop the behavior?

In general, if the employer knew or should have known about the harassment and did nothing to stop the behavior, then the employer can be held liable.

So how do you protect your organization from liability in case of a charge of sexual harassment, either quid pro quo or hostile work environment? Exhibit 3-8 shows five important steps to follow.[98]

In general, management in the organization should probably institute and communicate a zero-tolerance policy for sexual harassment. It should be a "one strike and you're out" offense—a major disciplinary infraction for which a person should be terminated. Why should we have zero tolerance for this type of behavior? Well, consider if you had an employee who was guilty in the past of harassing another employee. You did the investigation, found that the harassment did occur, and disciplined but did not terminate the harasser. What if, months or even years later, the same employee acted in the same manner toward another individual in your organization? You might be put in the position where you would have to go to court and defend your earlier actions.

WORK
APPLICATION 3-8

A high percentage of people, especially women, have been sexually harassed. Have you or anyone you know been sexually harassed at work? Briefly describe the situation, stating if it was quid pro quo or a hostile work environment.

EXHIBIT 3-8 LIMITING ORGANIZATIONAL LIABILITY FOR SEXUAL HARASSMENT

1. Develop a policy statement making it clear that sexual harassment will not be tolerated. You have to delineate what is acceptable and what is not. The policy should also state that anyone participating in a sexual harassment complaint or investigation should not be retaliated against.

2. Communicate the policy by training all employees to identify inappropriate workplace behavior. Make sure that everyone is aware of the policy.

3. Develop a mechanism for reporting sexual harassment that encourages people to speak out. It is critical in this case to create a mechanism outside of the normal chain of command. The typical case of harassment is between an individual and the immediate supervisor. Because of this, if the organization does not have a way to report the behavior outside the normal supervisory chain of command, the courts will consider that the company does not have a mechanism for reporting.

4. Ensure that just cause procedures (we will talk about these in Chapter 9) are followed when investigating the complaint.

5. Prepare to carry out prompt disciplinary action against those who commit sexual harassment.

In a case such as this, it would be very difficult to claim that you and the organization did not know or could not have known that more harassment might occur. The result would quite likely be that your organization would lose this case in court and might have to pay a significant settlement to the aggrieved individual. Sexual harassment should be treated very seriously, because the consequences can be grave for the organization if it doesn't do what it should to prevent the harassment.

RELIGIOUS DISCRIMINATION

As we noted earlier in this chapter, the federal courts have also determined that religious discrimination is a violation of the 1964 CRA because it identifies religion as a protected class. Because religion was specifically identified in the CRA, we can't use it as a factor in making "any employment decision" with our employees. Religion is a less obvious characteristic than gender or race, so it is usually not a characteristic on which we base decisions. However, if a person's religion requires a certain type of dress or observation of religious holidays or days of worship that is not in keeping with the normal workday practices of the organization, and if the individual requests accommodation for these religious beliefs, then we generally would need to make every reasonable effort to accommodate such requests.

Employers must provide a "reasonable accommodation" for requests that are based on "employees' sincerely held religious beliefs or practices, unless doing so would impose an 'undue hardship' on their business operations."[99] We have already defined *reasonable accommodations* and *undue hardship* earlier in this chapter, but the general result of a series of federal court rulings on religion and religious practices has been that if such practices can be accommodated by the organization without creating an excessive burden on the organization, then they must be accommodated, under penalty of law.

However, if the job description and specifications require employees to work specific days and hours of the day, and if an applicant accepts the job, then the employer

SHRM
B:29
Reasonable Accommodation–Religious

SHRM
F:7
Religion

WORK APPLICATION 3-9

Describe the sexual harassment policy where you work or have worked. If you are not sure, check the company HR handbook or talk to an HR department staff member to get the answer.

does not need to accommodate any employee requests not to work during those hours or days. For example, many health care workers are religious Christians and don't want to work on Christmas, Good Friday, Easter, and other holy days; but they do because it is part of the job. On the other hand, if a Muslim wants to take a break at a certain time of the work day to pray, that is reasonable to accommodate. Some companies have even built quiet rooms for prayer, meditation, or simple relaxation.

TRENDS AND ISSUES IN HRM

We again end this chapter with some significant trends and issues that are affecting HRM. In this section, we will cover four items that have been recent issues with employers—both large and small. These issues include religious discrimination, managing EEO as a path to organizational stability, global corporations and their susceptibility to US EEO laws, and small organizations' compliance issues under EEO.

Federal Agencies Are Becoming More Activist in Pursuing Discrimination Claims

A number of federal agencies have become much more active over the past few years in pursuing large-scale claims against U.S. businesses. Instead of waiting for an individual complaint, the EEOC, the Occupational Safety and Health Administration (OSHA), the National Labor Relations Board (NLRB), and other agencies have begun to act directly against companies in many cases without a complaint being filed by an employee or a job seeker. EEOC systemic discrimination investigations constitute one type of investigation that has increased dramatically.[100]

Systemic discrimination is defined by the EEOC as "a pattern or practice, policy, or class case where the alleged discrimination has a broad impact on an industry, profession, company, or geographic area."[101] In 2013, 23% of EEOC's active cases dealt with systemic discrimination claims.[102] In that year alone, several large cases netted the agency more than $10 million. These included cases against **Burger King** ($2.5 million), **Interstate Distributor** ($4.9 million), **Dillard's** ($2 million), **Mesa Systems** ($450,000), and **Presrite** ($700,000). And these are just the large awards. In the same year, "the EEOC's field offices completed work on 300 systemic investigations, resulting in 63 settlements or conciliation agreements, recovering approximately $40 million" in total monetary awards.[103]

What does this mean to you and your current or future company? As the HR manager, you need to know that there is no longer a minimal chance of being investigated for potential wrongdoing if there isn't an employee complaint. Federal agencies are actively seeking out evidence of "pattern or practice" forms of discrimination and then prosecuting those cases independent of an individual complainant. So you will need to be more diligent than ever in maintaining a fair workplace, free of the various forms of discrimination that we have discussed in this chapter.

Religious Discrimination

Religion-based discrimination and the ability of employers to create work rules that may affect religious freedom continue to be an issue in the workplace.[104] The issue of standards of dress in a number of religions, most notably Islam's standards for women's attire in public (including the hijab or niqab), has become a point of contention in some workplaces. However, individuals with a wide range of religious views are becoming more assertive concerning their rights at work. As an example, could a devout Christian county clerk refuse to issue a marriage license to a gay couple even though state law allows such a license?[105]

How about employers? If an employer sees the niqab as a symbol of repression, can the employer deny the right to wear such head coverings and use the antidiscrimination statutes concerning gender as justification? Can an employer require drivers that work for them to deliver alcohol to customer warehouses when the drivers may have a religious opposition to drinking alcohol?[106] There are many religious freedom questions that we are dealing with in companies today, and there are certainly no easy answers.

What should you do as the HR manager, if a manager or the president of the company comes to you wanting to ban head coverings for employees? Well, Title VII (the 1964 CRA) requires "reasonable accommodation of employees' sincerely held religious beliefs, observances, and practices when requested, unless accommodation would impose an undue hardship on business operations."[107] So in order to comply, the rules that we talked about under the 1964 CRA would apply here as well.

You have to make accommodations *if* the individual requests them and the accommodations are based on sincerely held beliefs, *unless* there is a business necessity requiring you to do something that conflicts with the religious belief or if doing so would create an undue hardship on the organization.[108] For instance, according to the EEOC, "If a security requirement [for example—wearing of a scarf covering the head] has been unilaterally imposed by the employer and is not required by law or regulation, the employer will need to decide whether it would be an undue hardship to modify or eliminate the requirement to accommodate an employee who has a religious conflict."[109]

The ADA and the ADA Amendments Act (ADAAA)

In our final trends segment for this chapter, let's take a quick look at the ADAAA and how it has affected the number and types of discrimination cases in the past few years. Claims under the ADA increased from 17,734 in 2007 to more than 25,000 in 2011, mostly due to the changes in the ADAAA.[110] This increase is at least in part due to the increase in *association discrimination* claims—claims that one has been discriminated against because one is, for example, associated with a partner who has HIV or has a family member who is disabled and needs care.[111]

Recent EEOC guidance also notes several conditions that may be episodic or in remission where the changes in the ADAAA have made it clear that those conditions are covered by the law. Among these conditions are cancer, diabetes, and epilepsy.[112] In one 2013 case filed by the EEOC, Midwest Regional Medical Center in Oklahoma was charged with firing an employee because of her ongoing cancer treatments.[113] The EEOC filed suit on behalf of the individual when she was terminated, noting that she could have returned to work after a short period of sick leave and been able to perform the essential job functions if she had been allowed to do so.

Another case against Kyklos Bearing International identifies cancer discrimination as well. The EEOC lawsuit says Kyklos terminated an employee based on her status as a cancer survivor, noting that "she had limited ability to lift (required in her job) due to medical restrictions." But the EEOC says this was not the case and that in fact the employee had provided documents from her doctor showing that she was cleared to work with no restrictions.[114]

Enforcement actions based on the ADAAA revisions will almost certainly continue to evolve for several years. As an HR manager, you will need to keep apprised of the developments in this amendment to the ADA to provide good counsel to the executives and managers in your company or other organization.

• • • CHAPTER SUMMARY

3-1   Describe the OUCH test and its four components and identify when it is useful in an organizational setting.

The OUCH Test is a rule of thumb you should use whenever you are contemplating any employment action. You use it to maintain fairness and equity for all of your employees or applicants. **OUCH** is an acronym that stands for **O**bjective, **U**niform in application, **C**onsistent in effect, and **H**as job relatedness. An employment action should generally be objective instead of subjective; we should apply all employment tests the same way, every time, with everyone, to the best of our ability; the employment action should not have an inconsistent effect on any protected groups; and the test must be directly related to the job to which we are applying it.

3-2   Identify the major equal employment opportunity (EEO) laws and the groups of people that each law protects.

The Equal Pay Act of 1963 requires that women be paid equal to men if they are doing the same work.

Title VII of the Civil Rights Act of 1964 prohibits discrimination on the basis of race, color, religion, sex, or national origin, in all areas of the employment relationship.

The Age Discrimination in Employment Act of 1967 prohibits age discrimination against people 40 years of age or older, and it restricts mandatory retirement.

The Vietnam Era Veterans Readjustment Assistance Act of 1974 prohibits discrimination against Vietnam veterans by all employers with federal contracts or subcontracts of $100,000 or more. It also requires that affirmative action be taken.

The Pregnancy Discrimination Act of 1978 prohibits discrimination against women affected by pregnancy, childbirth, or related medical conditions, and it treats such discrimination as unlawful sex discrimination.

The Americans with Disabilities Act of 1990 strengthened the Rehabilitation Act of 1973 to require employers to provide "reasonable accommodations" to allow disabled employees to work.

The Civil Rights Act of 1991 strengthened civil rights by providing for possible compensatory and punitive damages for discrimination.

The Uniform Services Employment and Reemployment Rights Act (USERRA) ensures the civilian reemployment rights of military members who were called away from their regular (nonmilitary) jobs by U.S. government orders.

The Veterans Benefits Improvement Act of 2004 amends USERRA to extend health care coverage while away on duty, and it requires employers to post a notice of benefits, duties, and rights of reemployment.

The Genetic Information Nondiscrimination Act of 2008 prohibits the use of genetic information in employment, prohibits intentional acquisition of the same, and imposes confidentiality requirements.

The Lilly Ledbetter Fair Pay Act of 2009 amends the 1964 CRA to extend the period of time in which an employee is allowed to file a lawsuit over pay discrimination.

3-3   Describe the three main types of discrimination in the workplace.

Disparate treatment exists when individuals in similar situations are intentionally treated differently and the different treatment is based on an individual's membership in a protected class.

Disparate impact occurs when an officially neutral employment practice disproportionately excludes the members of a protected group. For there to be discrimination under disparate *treatment*, there has to be intentional discrimination. Under disparate *impact*, intent does not matter.

Pattern or practice discrimination occurs when, over an extended period of time, a person or group engages in a sequence of actions that is intended to deny the rights of a member of a protected class as defined by the 1964 CRA. If there is reasonable cause to believe that an employer is engaging in a pattern or practice that denies the rights provided by Title VII, the U.S. Attorney General may bring a federal lawsuit against the employer.

3-4   Discuss the organizational defenses against accusations of discrimination.

The first defense is a bona fide occupational qualification (BFOQ)—a qualification that is absolutely required for an individual to be able to successfully do a particular job. A BFOQ cannot just be a desirable quality within the job applicant—it must be mandatory to perform the job. A BFOQ would be a legitimate defense against a charge of disparate treatment.

A *business necessity* defense exists when a particular practice is necessary for the safe and efficient operation of the business, and when there is a specific business purpose for applying a particular standard that may, in fact, be discriminatory. A business necessity defense *may* be a defense to disparate impact charges. Business necessity defenses must be combined with a test for *job relatedness*. For job relatedness to act as a defense to a discriminatory action, it has to be a business necessity, and then the employer must be able to show that the test for the employment action was a legitimate measure of an individual's ability to do the job.

3-5 Briefly discuss the two major federal immigration laws and how they affect the workplace.

In general, the federal immigration laws are designed to require verification of the legal right to work within the United States and to avoid potential discrimination against immigrant workers who are legally allowed to work in the country. The two major laws in this area are the Immigration and Nationality Act (INA) of 1952 (as amended) and the Immigration Reform and Control Act (IRCA) of 1986.

The INA allows the employment of immigrant workers in certain specialty occupations, subject to specific requirements to apply for such employment. The INA has a nondiscrimination requirement when dealing with alien workers who have the right to work in the United States.

The IRCA prohibits employers from knowingly hiring undocumented workers, and it requires employers to verify each employee's eligibility for employment through the use of a form called the Employment Eligibility Verification Form (I-9). The act also provides employers that comply "in good faith" with the requirements of IRCA with an affirmative defense to inadvertently hiring an unauthorized alien.

3-6 Briefly identify and discuss the major functions of the Equal Employment Opportunity Commission (EEOC).

The EEOC is a federal agency that investigates complaints of illegal discrimination based on race, color, religion, sex (including pregnancy), national origin, age (40 or older), disability, or genetic information.

The EEOC has three significant functions: investigating and resolving discrimination complaints through either conciliation or litigation, gathering and compiling statistical information on such complaints, and running education and outreach programs on what constitutes illegal discrimination.

3-7 Discuss the differences among equal employment opportunity, affirmative action, and diversity.

Equal employment opportunity deals with a series of laws and regulations put in place at the federal and state government levels in the last 45 years. As such, equal employment opportunity is very specific and narrowly defined within US law and various state laws.

Affirmative action, except in a few circumstances, does not have the effect of law. Therefore, affirmative action is a much broader concept based on policy than is EEO, which is more narrowly based on law.

Finally, diversity is not law, nor *necessarily* even policy within organizations. Diversity is a very broad set of concepts that deal with the differences among people within organizations. Today's organizations view diversity as a valuable part of their human resources makeup, but there are no specific laws that deal with requirements for diversity within organizations beyond the EEO laws.

3-8 Identify the two primary types of sexual harassment.

Quid pro quo harassment occurs when some type of benefit or punishment is made contingent upon the employee submitting to sexual advances. In other words, if you do something for me, I will do something for you, or conversely, if you refuse to do something for me, I will harm you.

Hostile work environment harassment occurs when someone's behavior at work creates an environment that is sexual in nature and makes it difficult for someone of a particular sex to work in that environment. Hostile environment sexual harassment happens when a "reasonable person" would determine that the environment went beyond normal human interactions and the jokes and kidding that go with those interactions and rose to the level that such a reasonable person would consider the act or acts to be both harassing and sexual in nature.

3-9 Define the key terms found in the chapter margins and listed following the Chapter Summary.

Complete the Key Terms Review to test your understanding of this chapter's key terms.

••• KEY TERMS

adverse employment action	disparate treatment	pattern or practice
affirmative action	divergent thinking	discrimination
bona fide occupational qualification (BFOQ)	diversity	punitive damages
business necessity	dysfunctional conflict	quid pro quo harassment
cohesiveness	essential functions	race norming
compensatory damages	Four-Fifths Rule	reasonable accommodation
conflict	functional conflict	reasonable person
constructive discharge	hostile work environment	retaliation
creativity	illegal discrimination	reverse discrimination
disability	innovation	right-to-sue
discrimination	job relatedness	sexual harassment
disparate impact	marginal job functions	undue hardship
	OUCH test	

••• KEY TERMS REVIEW

Complete each of the following statements using one of this chapter's key terms.

1. _____ is the act of making distinctions or choosing one thing over another—in HR, it is distinctions among people.

2. _____ is making distinctions that harm people by using a person's membership in a protected class.

3. _____ is a rule of thumb used whenever you are contemplating any employment action, to maintain fairness and equity for all of your employees or applicants.

4. _____ is a test used by various federal courts, the Department of Labor, and the EEOC to determine whether disparate impact exists in an employment test.

5. _____ exists when individuals in similar situations are intentionally treated differently and the different treatment is based on an individual's membership in a protected class.

6. _____ occurs when an officially neutral employment practice disproportionately excludes the members of a protected group; it is generally considered to be unintentional, but intent is irrelevant.

7. _____ occurs when, over a significant period of time, a person or group engages in a sequence of actions that is intended to deny the rights provided by Title VII (the 1964 CRA) to a member of a protected class.

8. _____ is a qualification that is absolutely required for an individual to successfully do a particular job.

9. _____ exists when a particular practice is necessary for the safe and efficient operation of the business, and when there is a specific business purpose for

applying a particular standard that may, in fact, be discriminatory.

10. _____ exists when a test for employment is a legitimate measure of an individual's ability to do the essential functions of a job.

11. _____ is a physical or mental impairment that substantially limits one more major life activities, a record of having such an impairment, or a condition of being regarded as having such an impairment.

12. _____ is an accommodation made by an employer to allow someone who is disabled but otherwise qualified to do the essential functions of a job to be able to perform that job.

13. _____ consist of the fundamental duties of the position.

14. _____ are those that may be performed on the job but need not be performed by all holders of the job.

15. _____ occurs when the level of difficulty for an organization to provide accommodations, determined by looking at the nature and cost of the accommodation and the overall financial resources of the facility, becomes a significant burden on the organization.

16. _____ consists of monetary damages awarded by the court that compensate the person who was injured for their losses.

17. _____ consist of monetary damages awarded by the court that are designed to punish an injuring party that intentionally inflicted harm on others.

18. _____ occurs when different groups of people have different scores designated as "passing" grades on a test for employment.

19. _____ is a notice from the EEOC, if they elect not to prosecute an individual discrimination complaint within the agency, that gives the recipient the right to go directly to the courts with a complaint.

20. _____ is a situation in which the organization takes an "adverse employment action" against an employee because the employee brought discrimination charges against the organization or supported someone who brought discrimination charges against the company.

21. _____ consist of any actions such as firings, demotions, schedule reductions, or changes that would harm the individual employee.

22. _____ exists when an employee is put under such extreme pressure by management that continued employment becomes intolerable for the employee and, as a result of the intolerable conditions, the employee resigns from the organization.

23. _____ is a series of policies, programs, and initiatives that have been instituted by various entities within both government and the private sector to create preferential hiring of individuals from protected groups in certain circumstances, in an attempt to mitigate past discrimination.

24. _____ is discrimination against members of the majority group in an organization, generally resulting from affirmative action policies within an organization.

25. _____ is the existence of differences—in HRM, it deals with different types of people in an organization.

26. _____ is a basic ability to think in unique and different ways and apply those thought processes to existing problems.

27. _____ is the act of creating useful processes or products based on creative thought processes.

28. _____ is the ability to find many possible solutions to a particular problem, including unique, untested solutions.

29. _____ is the act of being opposed to another.

30. _____ is how organizations go through the process of creating new things—the opposition itself drives the organization to change.

31. _____ occurs when conflict gets to the point where creativity is stifled and almost all work becomes difficult or impossible because of the conflict's intensity.

32. _____ is an intent and desire for group members to stick together in their actions.

33. _____ consists of unwelcome sexual advances, requests for sexual favors, and other verbal or physical conduct of a sexual nature; when submission to or rejection of this conduct explicitly or implicitly affects an individual's employment; unreasonably interferes with an individual's work performance; or creates an intimidating, hostile, or offensive work environment.

34. _____ is harassment that occurs when some type of benefit or punishment is made contingent upon the employee submitting to sexual advances.

35. _____ is harassment that occurs when someone's behavior at work creates an environment that is sexual in nature and makes it difficult for someone of a particular sex to work in that environment.

36. _____ is the "average" person who would look at the situation and its intensity to determine whether the accused person was wrong in their actions.

••• COMMUNICATION SKILLS

The following critical-thinking questions can be used for class discussion and/or for written assignments to develop communication skills. Be sure to give complete explanations for all answers.

1. Do you agree that applying the OUCH test to an employment situation will minimize illegal discrimination? Why or why not?

2. Are there any groups of people in the United States that you think should be covered by federal laws as a protected group but are not currently covered? Why or why not?

3. In your opinion, is most discrimination in the United States unintentional (disparate impact), or is most

discrimination intentional (disparate treatment)? Why do you think so?

4. What is your opinion of organizations using bona fide occupational qualifications (BFOQs) to limit who they will consider for a job?

5. Do we *really* need all of the laws that protect the equal employment opportunities of different groups (age, military veterans, pregnant women, etc.)? Why or why not?

6. Do you agree that most employers probably *want* to obey the Americans with Disabilities Act but don't know exactly what they are required to do under the law? Do you think that most employers would rather not hire disabled people? Justify your answer.

7. How would *you* define the terms "reasonable accommodation" and "undue hardship" if you were asked by one of your company managers?

8. Has affirmative action gone too far in creating a *preference* for historically underrepresented groups over other employees and applicants instead of treating everyone equally?

9. Is illegal immigration really hurting this country, when most illegal immigrants take jobs that Americans don't want to do anyway?

10. Do you think that sexual harassment in the workplace is overreported or underreported? Justify your answer.

• • • CASE 3-1 ENGLISH-ONLY: ONE HOTEL'S DILEMMA

Erica, the Human Resource Manager, was frustrated by many of her hotel staff speaking Spanish in the hallways and rooms as they were cleaning them.

The Sawmill Hotel where Erica works is situated in downtown Minneapolis, Minnesota. Its target market includes sports enthusiasts attending nearby professional (Twins, Vikings, Timberwolves, Wild) games but also business professionals and families. This four-star hotel features an indoor and outdoor swimming pool, a message center, three stores, two restaurants, and a beauty shop. Total staff includes about 10 managers, 30 cleaning assistants to take care of rooms, 10 front desk specialists, and 25 who are involved with the stores, restaurants, and beauty shop. All are required to focus on customer service as their number-one value.

Erica hires everyone in the hotel except for the Chief Executive Officer, Vice President of Finance, and Vice President of Marketing. For the rest of the managers, the 30 cleaning assistants, and the store, restaurant, and beauty shop workers, she advertises for openings with the local job service and the Minneapolis *Star Tribune* (with the associated website). A typical *Tribune* ad for a cleaning assistant reads as follows: Cleaning Assistants Wanted, Sawmill Hotel, $9–$11/hour. Prepare rooms for customers and prepare laundry. Contact: Erica Hollie, Human Resource Manager, 555-805-1234.

As a result of the advertising, Erica has been able to obtain good help through the local target market. Twenty-seven of the 30 cleaning assistants are women. Twenty of the 30 have a Hispanic background. Of the Hispanics, all can speak English at varying levels.

Rachel, the lead cleaning assistant, believes that maximizing communication among employees helps the assistants become more productive and stable within the hotel system. She uses both English and Spanish to talk to assistants under her. Spanish is useful with many assistants because they know Spanish much better than English. Spanish also is the "good friends" language that allows the Spanish speakers to freely catch up on each other's affairs and that motivates them to stay working at the hotel. The use of the Spanish language among cleaning assistants has been common practice among them for the two years since the hotel opened.

In the last few months, top management decided to have an even greater focus on customer service by ensuring customer comment cards are available in each room and at the front desk. Customers also can comment online about their stay at the hotel.

There have been several customer complaints that cleaning assistants have been laughing about them behind their back in Spanish. One customer, Kathy, thought that staffers negatively commented about her tight pink stretch pants covering her overweight legs. Other customers have complained they didn't think asking staff for help was easy given the amount of Spanish spoken. In all, about 15 out of 42 complaints in a typical month were associated with the use of the Spanish language.

Though bellhops and front desk clerks are typically the workers who handle complaints first, Erica, the Human Resource Manager, has the main responsibility to notify workers about customer complaint patterns and to set policy in dealing with the complaints. The prevalence of complaints concerning workers speaking Spanish each month led Erica to make a significant change in policy concerning the use of Spanish. In consultation with top management, Erica instituted the following employee handbook policy effective immediately:

"English is the main language spoken at the hotel. Any communication among employees shall be in English. Use of Spanish or other languages is prohibited unless specifically requested by management or the customer."

In an e-mail explanation for the new policy, Erica stated the number of complaints that had come from the use of Spanish and the need for customer courtesy and communication.

Rachel immediately responded to Erica's e-mail by stating that the new policy was too harsh on the native Spanish-speaking assistants at the hotel. She thought that a better policy is to allow her assistants to communicate with each other through Spanish but by quietly doing so away from customer earshot. If there is a general discussion in front of a customer, it is recommended to speak English. There should never be discussions in any language about customer appearances.

Though Rachel grumbled, the policy stuck because Erica and top management wanted to stop customer complaints. As a result of the policy, 10 of the 20 Spanish-speaking assistants quit within two months. These were high-quality assistants who had been with the hotel since the start. Their replacements came from a job service and have not worked out as well in their performance.

Questions

1. What law(s) do you think might apply in this case?

2. Should a complete ban of Spanish be instituted among staff of the hotel unless customers use Spanish themselves, or should the use of Spanish be completely allowed by staff among themselves as long as it is quiet (why or why not)?

3. What rules, if any, would you put into effect in this situation, knowing about the customer complaints? Explain your answer.

Case created by Gundars Kaupins of Boise State University

• • • CASE 3-2 WHEN RELIGION IS ON THE AGENDA

The Loxedose Company near Chicago transfers computer models into hard physical copies. Computer programmers design the representation, and machines sculpt the product line by line from the bottom to the top by adding levels of materials that adhere and are durable.

Two managers who founded the company celebrate individual and company successes. For example, Founders Day, August 25, features all 30 members of the company (or whoever is available) helping blow out the company birthday cake. Labor Day features a camping trip for those interested, at a manager's cabin at the largest lake in the area. Halloween features most employees wearing a costume, unless they are out on a sales or delivery run. Thanksgiving features a turkey lunch, whether vegetarians like it or not.

The managers believe that everyone should be working together and celebrating together. Accordingly, Christmas is not only a great year-end celebration but also a super holiday party. Traditionally, gifts are exchanged, Christmas carols are sung, and computer-designed trophies are given to the employees with bonus checks attached. Employees have to be present to receive the prizes made from Loxedose computer designs and materials.

This year, Loxedose hired a married couple, Omar and Judy, to be a part of the sales staff. Omar was from Saudi Arabia and also was studying in a university in Chicago. His wife was an American who was going to the same university.

Judy joined the Islamic faith when she married Omar. She was a Christian early in her life and then was unchurched through many years before she met Omar.

The upcoming Christmas party was a mandatory meeting and celebration. Employees had to be there to pick up their trophy along with the $200 bonus check. Judy was OK with going to the celebration, but Omar was not because it was a Christian celebration. Judy decided to go to the Christmas party without Omar to pick up Omar's statue along with hers.

The party started just fine with an exchange of presents, a birthday cake for Jesus, and a bunch of thank-yous from top management. When it came to giving out the celebratory statues and money, the managers stated you had to be there. Omar and Judy were mentioned together so Judy started picking up both statues when the company managers said Omar had to be there. Judy protested saying this was part of a Christmas celebration that was not part of his religion. Omar's statue and money were forced to remain.

Judy and Omar protested to management that they were discriminating based on religion because the bonus based on performance was distributed through the Christmas party and not offered if the employee didn't attend. All employees should have an equal right to get the bonus. Furthermore, not everyone will always be able to attend the parties because of illnesses, family matters, and other issues.

The managers proposed creating a new employee handbook policy associated with celebrations, awards, and religion. The following choices were suggested in a company meeting:

1. Celebrations within the company are important because they bring the employees together beyond the basic job. Employees will be required to attend Christian celebrations during work hours because that is the dominant religion.

2. Celebrations within the company are important because they bring the employees together beyond the basic job. Employees will be required to attend celebrations unless there are religious reasons or other reasons approved by management.

3. Celebrations within the company are important because they bring the employees together beyond the basic job. However, no celebrations shall be related to any, or for any, religious holiday, in order to respect the beliefs of those who do not celebrate as such. Anyone missing any party needs prior approval from management.

4. Celebrations within the company are optional. However, rewards will be provided for performance at a December party. If no reward is received at the party, it will be delivered to the employee the next day.

5. No statues or awards will be given at company celebrations. They will be mailed to employees or added to payroll automatically.

Top management strongly opposes the last two proposals because they would actually destroy the effect of providing awards in front of everyone. They prefer the second proposal because everyone would need to contact management and management would have control of who would be at the celebration. Omar and Judy do not like the fact that they would be forced (in Proposal 2) to reject the Christmas party because it is Christian. They much prefer Proposal 3 that eliminates religion-related celebrations. Top management does not like the proposal because it thinks religion-based celebrations are an important part of life.

Questions

1. Does the current policy pass the OUCH test?

2. Does management have a legal defense to discriminate by requiring attendance at religious based events? Which defense is management using for keeping the policy?

3. Which employment law or laws does this case involve? How would the law(s) that you identified apply in this case?

4. Which employee handbook proposal should the company incorporate (if any) and why?

5. How effective in the company's culture is giving out awards in front of everyone else?

6. Should religious parties be optional? Mandatory? Offered? Not offered?

Case created by Gundars Kaupins of Boise State University

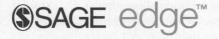

Sharpen your skills with SAGE edge at edge.sagepub.com/lussierhrm2e

SAGE edge for students provides a personalized approach to help you accomplish your coursework goals in an easy-to-use learning environment.

• • • SKILL BUILDER 3-1 THE FOUR-FIFTHS RULE

For this exercise, you will do some math.

Objective

To develop your skill at understanding and calculating the Four-Fifths Rule

Skills

The primary skills developed through this exercise are as follows:

1. *HR management skill*—Analytical and quantitative business skills

2. *SHRM 2013 Curriculum Guidebook*—G: Outcomes: Metrics and Measurement in HR

Complete the following Four-Fifths Problems

1:

	Males	Females
Applicants	100	100
Selected	50	40
Selection rate	50% (50/100)	40% (40/100)

4/5 = _____ %.

The selection rate of _____% is equal to, less than, or greater than _____% or 4/5.

Therefore, the Four-Fifths Rule is or is not met. How many total females and how many more females should be hired? _____

2:

	White	Nonwhite
Applicants	120	75
Selected	80	25
Selection rate	_____	_____

4/5 = _____ %.

The selection rate of _____% is equal to, less than, or greater than _____% or 4/5.

Therefore, the Four-Fifths Rule is or is not met. How many total and how many more nonwhites should be hired? _____

3:

	White Females	Nonwhite Females
Applicants	63	109
Selected	17	22
Selection rate	_____	_____

4/5 = _____ %.

The selection rate of _____% is equal to, less than, or greater than _____% or 4/5.

Therefore, the Four-Fifths Rule is or is not met. How many total and how many more nonwhite females should be hired? _____

• • • SKILL BUILDER 3-2 DIVERSITY TRAINING

Objective

To become more aware of and sensitive to diversity

Skills

The primary skills developed through this exercise are as follows:

1. *HR management skill*—Human relations skills
2. *SHRM 2013 Curriculum Guidebook*—L: Training and Development

Answer the following questions:

Race and Ethnicity

1. My race (ethnicity) is _____.
2. My name, _____, is significant because it means _____. [or]

   My name, _____, is significant because I was named after _____.
3. One positive thing about my racial/ethnic background is _____.
4. One difficult thing about my racial/ethnic background is _____.

Religion

5. My religion is _____.
6. One positive thing about my religious background is _____.
7. One difficult thing about my religious background is _____.

Gender

8. I am _____ (male/female).
9. One positive thing about being (male/female) is _____.
10. One difficult thing about being (male/female) is _____.

Age

11. I am _____ years old.
12. One positive thing about being this age is _____.
13. One difficult thing about being this age is _____.

Other

14. One way in which I am different from other people is _____.
15. One positive thing about being different in this way is _____.
16. One negative thing about being different in this way is _____.

Prejudice, Stereotypes, and Discrimination

17. Describe an incident in which you were prejudged, stereotyped, or discriminated against. It could be something minor, such as having a comment made to you about your wearing the wrong type of clothes/sneakers or being the last one picked when selecting teams.

Apply It

What did I learn from this experience? How will I use this knowledge in the future?

Your instructor may ask you to do this Skill Builder in class in a group. If so, the instructor will provide you with any necessary information or additional instructions.

_____

_____

_____

_____

Part II

Staffing

4 Matching Employees and Jobs: Job Analysis and Design

5 Recruiting Job Candidates

6 Selecting New Employees

PRACTITIONER'S MODEL

- ↑ **Productivity**
- ↑ **Satisfaction**
- ↓ **Absenteeism**
- ↓ **Turnover**

PART V: Protecting and Expanding Organizational Reach
How do you PROTECT and EXPAND your Human Resources?

Chapter 14	**Chapter 15**	**Chapter 16**
Workplace Safety, Health, and Security	Organizational Ethics, Sustainability, and Social Responsibility	International HRM

PART IV: Compensating
How do you REWARD and MAINTAIN your Human Resources?

Chapter 11	**Chapter 12**	**Chapter 13**
Compensation Management	Incentive Pay	Employee Benefits

PART III: Developing and Managing
How do you MANAGE your Human Resources?

Chapter 7	**Chapter 8**	**Chapter 9**	**Chapter 10**
Training, Learning, Talent Management, and Development	Performance Management and Appraisal	Rights and Employee Management	Employee and Labor Relations

PART II: Staffing
What HRM Functions do you NEED for sustainability?

Chapter 4	**Chapter 5**	**Chapter 6**
Matching Employees and Jobs: Job Analysis and Design	Recruiting Job Candidates	Selecting New Employees

PART I: 21st Century Human Resource Management Strategic Planning and Legal Issues
What HRM issues are CRITICAL to your organization's long-term sustainability?

Chapter 1	**Chapter 2**	**Chapter 3**
The New Human Resource Management Process	Strategy-Driven Human Resource Management	The Legal Environment and Diversity Management

©iStockphoto.com/TommL

4 Matching Employees and Jobs
Job Analysis and Design

Practitioner's Perspective

Cindy's day started when an executive burst into the HR office. "Hold everything!" he shouted. "Doug just announced he's retiring unexpectedly, and we've got to start advertising for someone to replace him immediately. I don't know how we can manage without him!"

"Calm down—we can do this," she replied. "Just send us your succession planning matrix and his functional job description, and we'll start the process to replace him."

"I hate to admit it, but I never completed that matrix, and I don't have an updated job description for Doug," the manager replied sheepishly. "There have been so many changes with the department reorganizations this year that we need to reconfigure everything."

While hiring someone new is the perfect time to update the job description for a position, it is not the best time to create one. Why is it important to have a current job description, and how does one go about writing one? Chapter 4 shows how to successfully identify and document motivational positions.

SHRM HR CONTENT

See Appendix: *SHRM 2013 Curriculum Guidebook* for the complete list

E. Job Analysis/Job Design (required)

1. Job/role design (roles, duties, and responsibilities)

7. HR planning (skill inventories and supply/demand forecasting)

8. Work management (work processes and outsourcing)

G. Outcomes: Metrics and Measurement of HR (required)

3. Measuring absenteeism

4. Measuring turnover

5. Trend and ratio analysis projections

10. Quantitative analysis

12. Analyzing and interpreting metrics

13. Forecasting

I. Staffing: Recruitment and Selection (required)

1. The employment relationship: Employees, contractors, temporary workers

J. Strategic HR (required)

12. Trends and forecasting in HR

M. Workforce Planning and Talent Management (required)

1. Downsizing/rightsizing (secondary)

2. Planning: Forecasting requirements and availabilities, gap analysis, action planning, core/flexible workforce

5. Retention: Measurement

6. Labor supply and demand

7. Succession planning

Q. Organization Development (required—graduate students only)

15. Succession planning

S. Downsizing/Rightsizing (secondary)

1. Employment downsizing

2. Alternatives to employment downsizing

4. Why downsizing happens

5. When downsizing is the answer

7. Alternatives to downsizing

8. Consequences of employment downsizing

9. Approaches to reducing staff size

13. Importance of focusing on individual jobs versus individual staff members

14. Layoffs

EMPLOYEE AND JOB MATCHING

Now that we have learned some of the basics concerning how to treat our human resources fairly and equitably, we need to start putting our people to work in the organization. Let's start with the realization that in order for our organization to maximize productivity, we must match the right people with the right jobs.[1] Why? Because mismatched workers tend to have low job satisfaction, leading to absenteeism, higher turnover, and lower levels of productivity than those who are matched effectively.[2] The first step to matching people to the right jobs is to determine what jobs we need to have performed and the qualifications needed to do the jobs (the job description and specifications). Then we can match employees to those jobs.

We need to start by showing how we design the flow of work and subsequently the jobs in our organizations. Workflows create the need for certain types of tasks to be performed within each part of the organization. Once we have identified those tasks, we determine how to lump those tasks into jobs—and we then design the resulting jobs in certain specific ways, depending on what our priorities are as an organization. For instance, motivational job design allows us to provide jobs that our employees will see as having more extrinsic motivating potential.[3] We can also use motivational job tools to assist us in improving job satisfaction and lowering absenteeism and turnover in at least some situations.

In the section on HR forecasting, we will also take a look at another aspect of matching people with jobs. HR forecasting tries to match the numbers and types of people that we will need with the numbers and types of jobs that we need to fill within a specific period of time. This process can tell us whether we might need to shed some types of employees from our rosters, retrain them to do other jobs, potentially hire more people with skill sets that we expect will be in short supply, or do some other things that can make employee supply match employee demand within the company.

Let's start by taking a brief look at workflow analysis.

• • • CHAPTER OUTLINE

WORKFLOW ANALYSIS

Let's imagine that we are starting up a brand-new company. The first thing we have to know is what we expect the organization to do. Do we plan to make products (e.g., to be a manufacturer of electronics like **Samsung**), or do we plan to provide services (e.g., to offer TV and movie programming services like **Netflix**)? Who is going to depend on whom, what processes are going to be accomplished in what ways, and how quickly?[4] Per our discussion of organizational structure in Chapter 2, the way in which we put the organization together will depend on what we expect it to do, and that in turn will help determine the workflow. **Workflow analysis** *is the tool that we use to identify what has to be done within the organization to produce a product or service.* For each product or service that we provide in the organization, we have to identify the work processes that create that product or service.

LO 4-1

Describe the process of workflow analysis and identify why it is important to HRM.

`SHRM`

E:8
Work Management (Work Processes and Outsourcing)

Organizational Output

Workflow analysis is a bit different from some of the other things we do—because we have to do it backward. The first thing we analyze is the end result of our processes: our expected organizational outputs, or the end state of a process.[5] In other words, we need to know what the customer wants from us.[6]

Why do we do it this way? Well, if you think about this backward method, it starts to make sense fairly quickly. As we noted in Chapter 2, How can we design the steps to do something if we don't know what it is supposed to look like when we are finished? If we decide that we are going to make desks but we don't identify what kind of desks we're going to make, then do we need skilled craftsman who can work with hardwoods and design a beautiful handmade wooden desk, or do we need metalworkers who can bend tubing and attach Formica surfaces to a metal frame to make a standard office desk? The answer is, of course, that it depends on what kind of desk we plan to make. So identifying the end result is a critical first step in identifying the workflows needed to create that result.

Tasks and Inputs

So we start our workflow analysis by looking at the end result. Once we identify the result we expect, we can then determine the steps or activities required to create the end result we've identified. Finally, based on the steps that we identify and the tasks that will have to be performed, we can identify the inputs that are going to be necessary to carry out the steps and perform the same tasks.[7]

There is a simple mnemonic (a memory tool) available to remember what resource inputs we have available. It is called the 4 Ms:[8]

1. *Machines*—resources such as tools, equipment, manufacturing machinery, and other machines that are used in completing work
2. *Material*—any physical resource (e.g., wood, metal, buildings, real estate, etc.) that we use in production
3. *Manpower*—the people that are needed in a particular production process—both quantity and types
4. *Money*—the capital that must be spent to perform our processes

These are the four large categories of resources that we in the organization use up in doing what we intend to do.[9] Whenever we look at workflow analysis, we have to identify which of the 4 Ms and how much of each we are using up in a particular process. The final result of our workflow analysis is shown in Exhibit 4-1.

Workflow analysis The tool that we use to identify what has to be done within the organization to produce a product or service

WORK
APPLICATION 4-1

Using Exhibit 4-1 as an example, identify the output and 4 Ms inputs for an organization that you work for or have worked for.

Workflow analysis almost always shows us that some steps or jobs within the organization can be combined, simplified, or even eliminated. (We will talk more about work simplification shortly.) In some cases, workflow analysis will show that certain types of groups or self-managed work teams—rather than individual workers—should be the basic building blocks of our processes.

Does HR do all of this workflow analysis? No, the organization's line management is typically responsible for mapping out workflows. However, HR managers need to understand the process so that they can assist line managers in identifying the tasks and the human inputs required to do those tasks and so that they can design appropriate organizational systems—such as training, development, and incentive compensation systems—for the human resources that will be performing the tasks. This will keep those people both motivated and efficient.

JOB ANALYSIS

Once we understand the workflows in the organization, the next thing that we need to do is figure out which parts of the workflows are done where. This is the concept of job analysis. **Job analysis** *is the process used to identify the work performed and the working conditions for each of the jobs within our organizations.* Job analysis results will include duties, responsibilities, skills, knowledge required, outcomes, conditions under which the worker must operate, and possibly other factors.[10]

EXHIBIT 4-1   WORKFLOW ANALYSIS

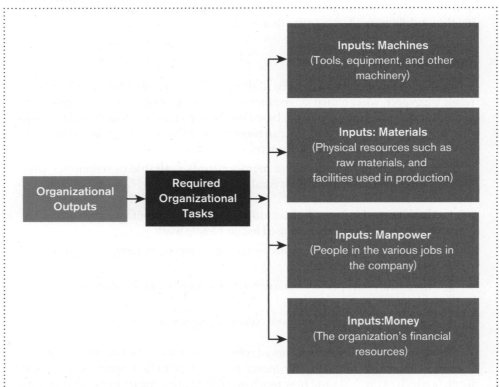

Job analysis The process used to identify the work performed and the working conditions for each of the jobs within our organizations

The two primary outcomes for most job analysis projects are the job description and the job specification. The **job description** *identifies the major tasks, duties, and responsibilities that are components of a job*, while the **job specification** *identifies the qualifications of a person who should be capable of doing the job tasks noted in the job description.*

Why Do We Need to Analyze Jobs?

Job analysis is at the core of HRM. It is the basis of just about everything that HR does.[11] If you think about it for just a minute, you will realize that we need to identify and correctly analyze the jobs in the organization in order to perform *any* of the following functions:

1. *Human resource planning.* Job analysis helps us design jobs better to get the results that we need. (We will talk about job design shortly.)
2. *Job evaluation for compensation.* If we don't know what the job consists of, how can we determine how much the job is worth to the organization so we know how much to pay the person?
3. *Staffing (recruiting and selection).* If we don't know what an employee is going to do and how much we will pay that employee, then how do we know whom to recruit and hire?
4. *Training.* If we don't know what the job consists of, how can we teach people to do the job?
5. *Performance management.* How can we evaluate performance if we don't know what the worker's job consists of?
6. *Maintain a safe work environment.* Job analysis will help us identify hazards that the job incumbent will need to understand, as well as any required personal protective equipment and training the person will need to safely carry out the job.

Other things that can be affected by job analysis include individual career planning and development, organizational strategy and structure, employee relations and legal compliance, and many other HRM tasks.

So job analysis is important to the HR department, but how does it affect other managers? Think about the following issues that *any* organizational manager may face on a routine basis:

1. Managers must have detailed information about all the jobs in their work groups so that they can understand the workflow processes.
2. Managers need to understand job requirements in their work groups so that they can make intelligent hiring, training, and promotion decisions.
3. Every manager is responsible for conducting performance evalutation to ensure that all employees are performing their jobs satisfactorily.

So we can see that job analysis is very important to both HR managers and line managers in the organization. But how do you analyze a job?

Databases

There are various databases that can be helpful to those performing job analysis. The **US Department of Labor's O*NET**[12] provides data on over 900 different job

Job description Identification of the major tasks, duties, and responsibilities that are components of a job

Job specification Identification of the qualifications of a person who should be capable of doing the job tasks noted in the job description

titles, and the list is continually updated. The information is free and open to the public (unless you are going to use it to develop other products, software, or applications). O*NET data gives you general information on these job titles, and you can then adjust that information for your company's specific circumstances. Other databases are also available commercially, and the information they provide can also help with job analysis of a large number of jobs that are common across many different companies. It can also be modified as necessary for specific organizations and jobs.

Therefore, using a database can be a good starting point for job analysis. However, each job analysis will most likely need to be customized, and if you can't find one on a database, you need to conduct your own job analysis. How to do so is our next topic.

LO 4-2

Identify the five major options available for the job analysis process.

Job Analysis Methods

Five commonly used methods of job analysis include the use of questionnaires, interviews, diaries, observation, and subject matter expert panels.[13,14] No matter how the process is completed, the result that we are looking for is a description of what work occurs in that particular job and what qualifications are needed in order for a person to be successful in the position. Let's take a closer look at the five methods.

QUESTIONNAIRES. A number of highly valid and reliable questionnaires are available for use in the job analysis process. A questionnaire can be given to many different people in order to analyze the job in question. It may be given to the current jobholder (the incumbent), the supervisor, or others who are affected by the way the job is done in the organization. Most of the questionnaires follow similar processes. Each asks questions that help to identify the functions that are a part of a particular job, and then, in most cases, it assigns a point value to that function.[15] For example, one function might be preparing and distributing budget reports using a spreadsheet, and this function may be worth 25 points in a particular questionnaire. On the other hand, the function of analyzing complex financial data for trends might be worth 65 points in such a questionnaire. The *Position Analysis Questionnaire* and the *Management Position Description Questionnaire* are two examples of this type of job analysis.[16]

Questionnaire Advantages

- Quick way to get information from large number of sources
- Usually easy to quantify
- Relatively low cost
- Generally valid and reliable instruments
- No need for a trained interviewer or observer

Questionnaire Disadvantages

- Incomplete responses (nobody is interviewing or observing actions, so there is no follow-up)
- Responses may be hard to interpret.
- Low response rates are possible if there is no supervisory follow-up.

INTERVIEWS. Another available method is the job analysis interview, in which questions are usually asked of the incumbent and the answers are compiled into a profile of the job. For the interview method, we need a trained interviewer who knows how to interpret answers and ask follow-up questions if needed. The interviewer asks job-related questions, and the incumbent describes the job based on the questions asked.

Interview Advantages

- The incumbent is most familiar with the job.
- Can include qualitative data
- Allows the interviewer to follow up confusing or incomplete answers
- Simple, quick, and more comprehensive than some other forms
- Provides an opportunity to explain the need for the analysis and answer questions

Interview Disadvantages

- Dependent on trained interviewer and well-designed questions
- Workers may exaggerate their job duties.
- Time-consuming and may not be cost efficient

DIARIES. Here the worker maintains a work log, or *diary*, in which the employee writes down the tasks accomplished while going about the job.[17] This log becomes the document from which we build the description of the job.

Diary Advantages

- Participatory form of analysis
- May collect data as it happens
- The worker knows the job and what is important.
- Useful for jobs that are difficult to observe

Diary Disadvantages

- Relies on worker writing all work down
- Worker may rely on memory of things done earlier in the day
- Information distortion
- Data is not in a standard format—makes quantifying difficult

OBSERVATION. We can also use observation of the person at work, in which an observer shadows the worker and logs tasks that the worker performs over a period of time. If observers are trained, they will usually identify tasks that workers don't even think about doing and therefore wouldn't have noted in a log or diary.

Observation Advantages

- Firsthand knowledge
- Allows the analyst to see the work environment, view the tools and equipment the worker uses, observe the worker's interrelationships with other workers, and gauge the complexity of the job
- Reduces information distortion common in some other methods
- Relatively simple to use

WORK
APPLICATION 4-2

Which of the five job analysis processes would be the most appropriate to use to write the job description and job specifications for a job you hold or have held? Explain why it has advantages over the other methods.

Observation Disadvantages

- Observer may affect the job incumbent's performance
- Inappropriate for jobs that involve significant mental effort
- May lack validity and reliability
- Time-consuming
- Requires a trained observer

SUBJECT MATTER EXPERT (SME) PANEL. In some cases, we can also call on a panel of subject matter experts.[18] Also called a "technical conference method," the use of such experts allows them to bring to the process their strong knowledge of the jobs they evaluate. It also allows them to brainstorm to identify the key factors of the job, based on their background and expertise. They also use their knowledge to identify the major tasks associated with the jobs they are tasked with analyzing.

Subject Matter Expert Advantages

- SMEs are chosen for expertise and competence.
- Data received from SMEs are generally comprehensive.
- SMEs can apply any other methods of job analysis (such as diaries or questionnaires) they think are necessary.

Subject Matter Expert Disadvantages

- SMEs may have trouble breaking work into tasks and describing work.
- Time-consuming, which means *expensive*
- SMEs need to resolve any differences of opinion to create a consensus.
- Dependent on the validity of the opinions and the judgment of the SMEs

The five methods listed above are certainly not the only methods of job analysis, and they may not even be the best options for any particular situation. There are many other options, including work sampling, videotaping of jobs, and others. However, these five types of analysis demonstrate the basic process of job analysis.

4-1 APPLYING THE CONCEPT

Job Analysis Methods

Review the following job analysis methods and then write the letter corresponding to each method before the situation in which it would be the most appropriate.

a. questionnaire
b. interview
c. diary
d. observation
e. subject matter expert (SME) panel

_____ 1. On your staff, you have an industrial engineer who is an efficiency expert. You want her to improve the productivity of your machinists.

_____ 2. You have a new job to analyze, and you would like to get help from a few other professionals who know the job much better than you do.

_____ 3. You have professionals who work independently using different methods of developing computer games.

_____ 4. In your call center, where hundreds of employees make cold calls to sell your products, there is a high turnover rate that you want to improve.

_____ 5. You have several service call employees who repair a variety of computers. You would like to have a better idea of what types of computers they are fixing.

We also need to understand that in many cases, we may want to use more than one method to analyze a particular job if one method won't provide a good analysis by itself. But remember that the more methods we use to analyze a single job, the more it costs to do the analysis, so we have to sometimes make a trade-off between a better analysis and a less expensive one.

Do We Really Have "Jobs" Anymore?

A number of researchers today are talking about the decline in the value of traditional job analysis, saying that it is static and looks at the past rather than the future.[19] Another argument against job analysis is that stable jobs don't exist in today's workplace. Stable jobs are a characteristic of what is often referred to as a *mechanistic* organization, and there are fewer mechanistic organizations today than in the past. The basis of the arguments—that job analysis is static and looks at the job from a historical perspective—is true, but the fact is that job analysis is still valid for many types of jobs in many organizations, such as **McDonald's** and **Ford**.

As with everything in management, whether job analysis is valuable depends on other factors. As a rule, job analysis is of more value to organizations making a product than to those providing a service and those in a more stable environment. Also, some parts of the firm, such as production, can be more stable than other parts, such as research and development. If jobs in the organization are stable and are going to be designed using one of the four basic job design options (we will talk about these shortly), then job analysis is still a valuable part of designing those jobs. If, on the other hand, the organizational structure is going to be highly *organic* in nature, changing rapidly, and if there are no well-defined jobs within the structure, then job analysis will be of less value in helping us identify the type of person who will need to be hired for a general job category.

Task or Competency Based?

As we go through the process of analyzing jobs, we have to make some other decisions. One decision is whether our job analysis will be task based or competency based.[20] What's the difference? In task-based job analysis, we describe the job as a function of the tasks performed within the job, while in competency-based job analysis, we look at the capabilities that an individual would need to have to succeed in the job. Task-based job analysis tends to be simpler in form and execution,

Job analysis is still relevant for companies like McDonald's.

while competency-based job analysis is more complex due to the fact that we have to think about a broader set of skills and abilities as opposed to the ability to do a set task.

So, which is better? Again, it depends on what the organization is doing as its primary function. In more stable, traditional, and bureaucratic organizations, task-based job analysis is usually the norm. We would use competency-based job analysis in organizations that are less structured and less stable in the work that they accomplish. For example, we would probably choose competency-based job analysis for an advertising agency or a research and development laboratory, while we would use task-based job analysis for a manufacturer of office furniture.

Outcomes: Job Description and Job Specification

So, you now know that job analysis is the process of determining what a position entails and the qualifications needed to staff that position. The primary outcomes that we are looking for in any job analysis are the creation of a job description and a job specification.[21] These two outcomes are routinely written into one document. As we noted earlier, the job description identifies the tasks and responsibilities of a position. Simply put, it describes the job itself, not the person who will do the job. A job specification, our other job analysis outcome, identifies the qualifications needed by the person who is to fill a position. In other words, the job specification tells us what kind of person we need to successfully do the job. We will use the job specification to go out and recruit when we have an opening for the job. The trend today is to describe jobs more broadly in order to design enriched jobs and to allow more flexibility in the work that is assigned.[22] Exhibit 4-2 shows a sample job description and specification.

At **JobDescription.com**, you can create individual, customized job descriptions that meet legal requirements. You work completely online, and it's fast and easy. The job library has more than 3,700 job descriptions that include competencies that you can customize to help define jobs, and the site helps you create and place job advertisements on the Web and generate job-specific, behavior-based interview questions. It also provides expert advice for each step.[23]

JOB DESIGN/REDESIGN

Tasks to be performed by organizations are grouped by the organization, usually into functional departments, and the tasks are further grouped into jobs for each employee, providing structures and processes. **Job design** *is the process of identifying tasks that each employee is responsible for completing, as well as identifying how those tasks will be accomplished.* Job design is crucial because it affects job satisfaction and productivity, along with a large number of other functions in HRM.[24]

Job redesign refers to changing the tasks or the way work is performed in an existing job. The nature of work has dramatically changed over the last decade.[25] Many organizations, including **Boeing** and **Amazon**, are asking employees to suggest ways to redesign their work. Job design, which includes redesign, is about working smarter, not harder, to find new ways of doing things that boost productivity.[26]

Organizational Structure and Job Design

In Chapter 2, we said that the way in which we combine the components of an organizational structure causes employees within that organization to act in different ways. This is due to the expectations that are created within the structure about how we should interact with each other. Jobs in the organization have to be designed to fit within the confines of the structure that we have designed.[27]

Job design The process of identifying tasks that each employee is responsible for completing, as well as identifying how those tasks will be accomplished

EXHIBIT 4-2 JOB DESCRIPTION—APPLE "CHANNEL COMPLIANCE REPORTING MANAGER"

Jobs at Apple

Requisition Number 4391934

Job title: Channel Compliance Reporting Manager

Location: Santa Clara Valley

Country: United States

City: Cupertino

State/Province: California

Job type: Full Time

Job description: Team up with Apple, one of the most influential technology leaders in the industry. Join the Apple Finance organization and make a positive impact on a company that is known for its impressive lineup of products, including Mac, iPod, iPhone, iTunes, and iLife. At Apple, you'll share in a commitment to excellence by partnering with world-class managers, all with one unified vision—creating innovative products that delight customers. Finance is about "fueling innovation." We do this by hiring quality individuals with integrity, personal accountability, teamwork, excellence, and proactive thinking. If you exemplify our values and want to be part of something big, contact us today.

Summary of the position: Reporting to Channel Compliance Management, this role has the responsibility for the global development, deployment and maintenance of channel member regulatory compliance training program. This individual will be a key resource to introduce and implement best practices, reusability and streamlining online and classroom compliance training for channel member employees.

Key Duties and Responsibilities:

- Responsible to develop, implement and maintain a comprehensive global compliance training program to deliver training to applicable channel member employees
- Identify the training needs based on local regulatory guidelines (Laws & Regulations), global and US regulations and Apple Policy
- Collaborate with subject matter experts to ensure the compliance training material is current and reflects changes in Regulations/Policies
- Manage the training content localization and deployment of the material
- Schedule and implement a risk based and effective training calendar
- Develop a process and system to track classroom training accomplishments
- Ensure effective document and record keeping for all Channel Compliance related training programs
- Develop and implement an effective and efficient management reporting for compliance training program
- Efficiently manage the training resources within allocated budget

Key Skills and Competencies:

- Successful implementation and management of channel member training programs in large and global distribution model
- Must have excellent project management and time management skills
- Exercise good business judgment and excellence in problem solving
- Possess strong writing, editing, communication, and negotiation skills
- Demonstrated ability to maintain and develop relationships across a large virtual team
- Experienced in managing external parties—vendors, resellers, distributors, etc.
- Strong data analysis skills and obsessive about details and accuracy
- Advanced Excel user
- BA/BS degree or higher
- 5 to 8 years in areas of Analysis & Reporting, Working cross-functionally, and Project Management.

If we have a more relaxed, flatter structure with lots of autonomy for our workers, we will need to design our jobs to take advantage of that autonomy or self-direction on the part of our employees. If, on the other hand, we have a rigid, bureaucratic organizational structure with strong centralized decision making and control (which usually makes it cheaper to run the organization), then our jobs have to be designed so that they can be readily controlled by a central authority.

4-1 SELF ASSESSMENT

Organizational Structure and Job Design Preference

Individuals differ in the type of organizations and job designs in which they prefer to work. To determine your preference, evaluate each of the following 12 statements, using the scale below. Assign each statement a number from 1 to 5, representing your level of agreement with the statement (5 = strong agreement, 3 = not sure, 1 = strong disagreement).

I agree				I disagree
5	4	3	2	1

_____ 1. I prefer having just one boss telling me what to do, rather than multiple people.

_____ 2. I prefer to just perform my job, rather than being concerned about organizational objectives and being involved in setting them.

_____ 3. I prefer knowing the reporting relationship, knowng who is whose boss, and working through proper channels—rather than just working directly with a variety of people based on the situation.

_____ 4. I prefer having a clear job description so I know just what I need to do at work, rather than having the ambiguity of not being sure and doing whatever needs to be done.

_____ 5. I prefer being a specialist doing one job really well, rather than being a generalist doing several things not as well.

_____ 6. I prefer doing my own thing that contributes to the organization, rather than coordinating the work I do with that of others in teams.

_____ 7. I prefer slow change, rather than regular fast changes.

_____ 8. I prefer routine at work, rather than being delegated new tasks to perform.

_____ 9. I prefer doing more simple tasks, rather than more complex tasks that take more time and effort.

_____ 10. I prefer that people get promoted based primarily on seniority, rather than based on performance.

_____ Total

Scoring: To determine your preference, add up the numbers you assigned to the statements (the total will be between 10 and 50) and place your total score on the continuum below:

10	15	20	25	30	35	40	45	50
Organic								Mechanistic

Recall our discussion of mechanistic and organic structures, which you will learn more about throughout this chapter. The higher your score, the more you prefer to work in a more traditional, mechanistic, stable structure and job design. The lower your score, the more you prefer to work in a more contemporary, organic, changing structure and job design.

Review your answers, knowing that the opening statement applies to mechanistic and the opposite statement (after "rather than") applies to organic organizational structure and job design. Most firms and people prefer organizations somewhere between the two extremes.

LO 4-3

Discuss the four major approaches to job design.

Mechanistic job design Designing jobs around the concepts of task specialization, skill simplification, and repetition

Approaches to Job Design and Redesign

Job design/redesign can take several forms, depending on what we are trying to accomplish in the organization. Are we trying to increase motivation levels in our workforce in a customer relations management firm or direct-marketing business? If so, we may choose a specific type of job design that will help motivate the individual worker. Are we trying to simplify the work being done in a manufacturing setting so that the workers are more efficient? If this is the case, we may want to segment the work into very simple component parts so that employees can do their work quickly and more efficiently because they are only being asked to do a few different things. There are four primary approaches to job design: mechanistic, biological, perceptual-motor, and motivational.[28]

1. **Mechanistic (vs. organic) job design** *focuses on designing jobs around the concepts of task specialization, skill simplification, and repetition.* In other words, if we are going to design a mechanistic job, we will try to make the job simple and repetitive so that the worker can get very good and very fast at doing it. This

approach is based on the old (early 1900s) concept of scientific management developed by Frederick Taylor. Here we are designing jobs to fit into a mechanistic organizational structure, rather than the opposite end of the continuum: an organic structure. An example of mechanistic job design would be a job in a manufacturing plant where the worker attaches the desktop to its base using six fasteners and then goes to the next desk to fasten another identical top to another base. As stated in the self-assessment, many firms design jobs that are in between the two extremes of mechanistic and organic. The biggest problem in mechanistic job design is that we might overspecialize the work to the point that it becomes too repetitive and thus very boring.[29] This is not the way to get the best performance from your workforce!

2. **Biological job design** *focuses on minimizing the physical strain on the worker by structuring the physical work environment around the way the body works.* Here we are trying to make the job physically easier so that workers can be more efficient and so that it is less likely that they will be injured and have to miss work when they are needed. An example of biological job design would involve installing a conveyor belt that first lifts a vacuum cleaner up to eye level so that a worker can attach wheels to the vacuum cleaner's base and then drops the vacuum cleaner down to about waist level so that another worker can attach the bag to the vacuum cleaner. This allows the workers to do their jobs with minimal physical strain. Again, though, this approach does little to make workers more motivated or satisfied with their work.

3. **Perceptual-motor job design** *focuses on designing jobs with tasks that remain within the worker's normal mental capabilities and limitations.* Instead of trying to minimize the physical strain on the workforce, the goal is to design jobs in a way that ensures they moderate the mental strain on a worker.[30] For example, we might use the perceptual-motor approach to break down an executive assistant's job into a report writer and a scheduler job, because the sets of skills needed in these two areas are significantly different. Here again, though, we may create jobs that are not very motivating. If you want to know why, look at the two-factor motivation theory developed by Fredrick Herzberg.[31]

4. **Motivational job design** *focuses on the job characteristics that affect the psychological meaning and motivational potential of the job, and it views attitudinal variables as the most important outcomes of job design.* The theory is that if workers are more motivated, they will produce more work. It is to this last approach to job design that we can apply the job characteristics model, which we will discuss next.

The Job Characteristics Model (JCM)

The **job characteristics model**, developed by Richard Hackman and Greg Oldham, *provides a conceptual framework for designing or enriching jobs based on core job characteristics.*[32] The model can be used by individual managers or by members of a team. Use of the job characteristics model improves employees' motivation and job satisfaction,[33] and it can increase performance.[34] As Exhibit 4-3 illustrates, users of the JCM focus on core job dimensions, the psychological states of employees, and the strength of employees' need for growth. Use of the job characteristics model improves employees' motivation, performance, and job satisfaction and reduces their absenteeism and job turnover. Most of these variables should look familiar to you since we introduced them in Chapter 1, where we also discussed the HRM challenges that managers tell us make their jobs more difficult and that they can't directly control.[35] Research supports the idea that use of the JCM increases performance by meeting employee needs to grow and develop on the job.[36]

In the JCM, the five core job characteristics can be fine-tuned to improve the outcomes of a job in terms of employees' productivity and their quality of working life:

WORK
APPLICATION 4-5

Which of the four approaches to job design/redesign best describes a job you hold or have held? Explain how the job incorporates the features of the approach.

SHRM

E:1
Job/Role Design (Roles, Duties, and Responsibilities)

LO 4-4

Identify and briefly describe the components of the job characteristics model (JCM).

Biological job design Designing jobs by focusing on minimizing the physical strain on the worker by structuring the physical work environment around the way the body works

Perceptual-motor job design Designing jobs with tasks that remain within the worker's normal mental capabilities and limitations

Motivational job design Designing jobs by focusing on the job characteristics that affect the psychological meaning and motivational potential of the job; this approach views attitudinal variables as the most important outcomes of job design

Job characteristics model A conceptual framework for designing or enriching jobs based on core job characteristics

4-2 APPLYING THE CONCEPT

Job Design

Review the list of job design techniques below and write the letter corresponding to each technique before the statement exemplifying that technique.

a. mechanistic
b. organic
c. biological
d. perceptual-motor
e. motivational

____ 6. We are required to wear these special belts when we unload the trucks at **Target.**

____ 7. We have added enough employees so that we are breaking the human resources function into its own department. Jack will now focus on compensation and benefits, and Jill will conduct the training. Latoya will be responsible for safety and security.

____ 8. Here at **Intel,** we are going to change your job so that you can develop new skills and complete entire jobs by yourself. We're doing this to make the job more meaningful to you and so that you can do the job the way you want to and know how you are doing.

____ 9. I just finished the Casey project. What should I do now?

____ 10. This is the 30th customer I've checked out at **Stop & Shop** supermarket today.

1. *Skill variety* is the number of diverse tasks that make up a job and the number of skills used to perform the job.

2. *Task identity* is the degree to which an employee performs a whole identifiable task. For example, does the employee put together an entire television or just place the screen in the set?

3. *Task significance* is an employee's perception of the importance of the task to others—the organization, the department, coworkers, and/or customers.

4. *Autonomy* is the degree to which the employee has discretion to make decisions in planning, organizing, and controlling the task performed.

5. *Feedback* is the extent to which employees find out how well they perform their tasks.

Note that if employees are not interested in enriching their jobs, the job characteristics model will fail.

The first three of the core job characteristics lead collectively to the psychological state (in the second column of Exhibit 4-3) of *experienced meaningfulness of work*, which means that if we provide workers with a variety of things to do (meaning they need multiple skills in order to do their job), if they can identify what it is that they are accomplishing, and if they think that their job is a significant endeavor, then they will think that their work has meaning and thus be more likely to stay in the job and do it well.

©iStockphoto.com/1001nights

Organizations need employees with different specializations and skill sets, based on the job analysis.

The core characteristic of *autonomy* lead to the psychological state of *experienced responsibility for outcomes*. If we give people the ability to make some decisions on their own, it is likely that they will feel more responsible for the outcome of the decisions that they make.

Finally, *feedback* leads to the psychological state of *knowledge of results*. However, it is not the knowledge of the result itself that matters. Remember that the second column is *psychological* states! It is the psychological feeling that we get from

EXHIBIT 4-3 THE JOB CHARACTERISTICS MODEL (JCM)

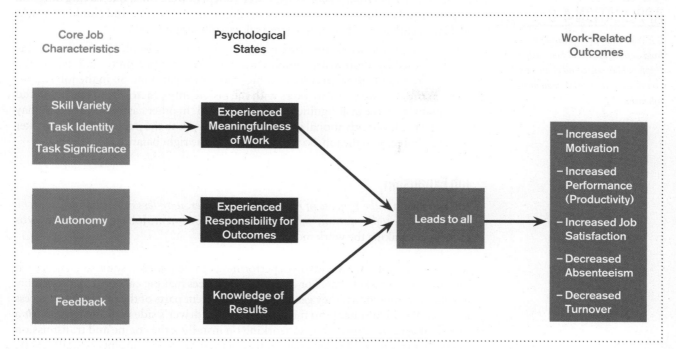

knowing the results that create the state of, for lack of a better term, satisfaction with the results of our work.

All of the psychological states *collectively* lead to all of the outcomes noted on the right side of the diagram. It is an interesting list. If the job is designed correctly, the model says that the worker will quite possibly be more motivated and more productive and have higher job satisfaction while also being less likely to be absent or leave the organization.

DESIGNING MOTIVATIONAL JOBS

A variety of different job tools can be used in different circumstances to design or redesign motivational jobs. Our tools include job simplification, job expansion, work teams, flexible work, and JCM. Each is discussed next.

Job Simplification

The best advice golfer **Tiger Woods** ever got was to simplify.[37] **Job simplification** *is the process of eliminating or combining tasks and/or changing the work sequence to improve performance.* Job simplification makes jobs more specialized. It is based on the organizing principle of division of labor plus Frederick Taylor's principles of scientific management. It's not about hustling to get more done; it's about using our brains.[38] Job simplification breaks a job down into steps using a flowchart, and then employees analyze the steps to see if they can do the following:

- *Eliminate.* Does the task, or do parts of it, have to be done at all? If not, don't waste time on it or them.
- *Combine.* Doing similar things together often saves time. Make one trip to the mailroom at the end of the day instead of several throughout the day.
- *Change sequence.* Often, a change in the order of doing things, or designing new systems, results in a lower total time spent on tasks.

LO 4-5

Describe the three major tools for motivational job design.

Job simplification The process of eliminating or combining tasks and/or changing the work sequence to improve performance

WORK
APPLICATION 4-6

Give one example of how a job you hold or have held could be simplified. Explain how one could eliminate, combine, or change the sequence of job tasks.

Intel managers decided that it was not necessary to fill out a voucher for expenses amounting to less than $100. Thus, fewer vouchers were filled out, saving time and paperwork. **GE** developed its Work Out Program to improve and eliminate work, and **Pizza Hut** credits increases in store sales to job simplification.

In some cases, work simplification may be motivational. If an individual is overwhelmed by a job, work simplification allows that person to understand the job better, and the job therefore becomes more motivational. So in the job simplification process, we assist workers with the task identity factor from the JCM, and potentially with the task significance factor as well. In other cases, however, we may make the job less motivational if we simplify the work to the point where the worker becomes bored with the job. So we have to strike the right balance.[39]

Job Expansion

Job expansion *is the process of making jobs broader, with less repetition. Jobs can be expanded through rotation, enlargement, and enrichment.* Job expansion allows us to focus on making the work more varied.[40]

JOB ROTATION. Job rotation involves performing different jobs in some sequence, each one for a set period of time. For example, employees making cars on a **GM** assembly line might rotate so that they get to work on different parts of the production process for a set period of time. John might work on the driver's side restraint system for a period of time and then move to working on installing the engine and transmission in another rotation. This can assist him even more with the concepts of skill variety, task identity, and task significance. It may also help him with the core characteristic of feedback, depending on how we rotate jobs. If John rotates to a job that is affected by his previous work, he will see how his performance in one job affects another—hence, he gets feedback on his earlier job performance. Many organizations develop conceptual skills in management trainees by rotating them through various departments. A few of the companies that have used job rotation are **Bethlehem Steel, Target, Ford, Motorola, National Steel,** and **Prudential Insurance.**

WORK
APPLICATION 4-7

Give one example of how a job you hold or have held can be enlarged. Explain how the job can use job rotation, enlargement, or enrichment.

JOB ENLARGEMENT. Job enlargement involves adding tasks—at the same level in the organization—to broaden variety. For example, we may have construction workers doing dirt work, concrete forming, and framing carpentry at different times. **AT&T, Chrysler, GM, IBM,** and **Maytag** are a few of the companies that have used job enlargement. When we broaden the number of tasks for a worker, we are affecting the core job characteristic of skill variety, and we may be helping with task identity and significance. Unfortunately, adding more similar tasks to an employee's job is often not a great motivator.

JOB ENRICHMENT. Job enrichment is the process of building motivators into the job itself to make it more interesting and challenging, frequently through increasing autonomy.[41] Job enrichment works for jobs of low motivation potential and for employees who are ready to be empowered to do meaningful work.[42] A simple way to enrich jobs is for the manager to delegate more authority to employees to make a job satisfying.[43] In this way, the employee becomes more autonomous (another core job characteristic) and can make some decisions that were reserved for management prior to the job enrichment process.[44] An enriched job may also help the employee with the characteristics of task identity and significance in some cases. **Maytag, Monsanto, Motorola,** and **Travelers Insurance** have successfully used job enrichment.

Job expansion The process of making jobs broader, with less repetition. Jobs can be expanded through rotation, enlargement, and enrichment

Work Teams

The traditional approach to job design has been to focus on individual jobs, but today, work teams are the rage—or, to be more accurate, teams are redesigning members' jobs.[45] The purpose of team-based job design is to give the team an entire piece of work. When we provide the team with an entire piece of work, it is a form of job enrichment, and as a result, autonomy, task identity, and task significance go up at a substantial rate. Teams develop innovative routines that get passed on to other teams.[46] Two common types of work teams are integrated teams and self-managed teams.

INTEGRATED WORK TEAMS. *Integrated work teams* are assigned a number of tasks by a manager, and the team in turn gives specific assignments to members and is responsible for rotating jobs. Students commonly use this approach for group projects. Each member does part of the work, and someone pulls it all together. Unlike with self-managed teams, most members have no input into each other's work.

SELF-MANAGED WORK TEAMS. Self-managed work teams are assigned a goal, and the team plans, organizes, leads, and controls to achieve the goal.[47] Usually, self-managed teams operate without a designated manager; the team is both manager and worker.[48] Teams commonly elect their own members and evaluate each other's performance. **W. L. Gore** relies on small teams throughout the organization.

Applying the Job Characteristics Model (JCM)

You should be able to see that job simplification, job expansion, and work teams can all be part of applying the JCM. The JCM helps provide a comprehensive system for designing and redesigning jobs to make them more motivational.[49] Exhibit 4-4 reviews the job design options we have discussed so far as they relate to JCM.

So let's tie things together by redesigning a job using the JCM, and let's see how we can make it more motivational. John is a worker in an automotive factory. He installs the driver's side seat. The job as it currently exists tends to be very boring, so John tends to get distracted. He ends up playing games with his tools and with coworkers, and as a result, he may not do this job very well and in fact may waste materials and supplies or possibly injure another employee.

We can look at this job and see that John does not have very much skill variety. He probably also doesn't identify very much with the end product (a car) if the only thing he does is install a seat. It is also likely that he doesn't see much significance in his work. He certainly has no autonomy and probably gets very little feedback.

WORK APPLICATION 4-8

Give one example of a work team where you work or have worked. Explain why and how it is either an integrated or self-managed work team.

4-3 | **APPLYING THE CONCEPT**

Designing Motivational Jobs

Review the following job design techniques and write the letter corresponding to each technique before the statement exemplifying it.

    a. job simplification

    b. job rotation

    c. job enlargement

    d. job enrichment

    e. work teams

_____ 11. Would you like more job variety? If so, I can add three new tasks to your job to make it less repetitive.

_____ 12. I'm going to teach you to balance the accounts so that you can do it for Carlos while he is on vacation.

_____ 13. Would you like me to delegate a new task to you to make your job more challenging?

_____ 14. **Dominic's Pizza** stopped requiring customers to sign a credit card slip for under $25.

_____ 15. I'm creating a new crew with the seven of you. There will not be a formal manager; you will share that responsibility. From now on, you don't have a manager. So share the job together.

EXHIBIT 4-4 JOB DESIGN OPTIONS, PROCESSES, AND THE JCM

Option	Process	Core Characteristics Affected (JCM)
Job simplification	Eliminate tasks	Task identity and significance
	Combine tasks	
	Change task sequence	
Job expansion	Rotate jobs	Skill variety, task identity, and significance
	Enlarge jobs	Possibly feedback
	Enrich jobs	
Work teams	Integrated	Skill variety, task identity, and significance
	Self-managed	Feedback

Now let's redesign John's job and make him the "driver's side restraint system technician." John will now put in the driver's side seat track, the driver's side seat, the seat belt, and the driver's side airbag (*job enlargement*). What will this do to the five core job characteristics? Certainly, John has more skill variety in his new job. It is likely that he'll be able to identify the end product better than he did before, because he is making a larger part of the overall product. He probably also feels that it's more significant that he do this job well, because he is responsible for the restraint system that will determine the safety of the driver. If we allow him to do these jobs in any order he sees fit, and to check his own work for errors, then he has greater autonomy (*job enrichment*).

John's supervisor came to him today and told him that one of the cars that he built last week was in an accident. The driver had run into a tree head-on, and as a result of the safety systems in the car, she had walked away without serious injuries (*feedback*).

Let's explore John's psychological state. Because of the increased skill variety, task identity, and task significance John feels that his work has greater meaning. He also feels a great sense of responsibility for the drivers of the cars that he has manufactured. And by receiving feedback, his knowledge of the results of this work shows that his work allowed this driver to survive a bad accident. What kind of outcomes do you think John has gained from this experience? John is almost certain to be more motivated to do his job, he's probably more productive, he is certainly likely to be more satisfied with his work, he is likely to be absent less, and he is not as likely to leave the organization. We have redesigned John's job to make it more motivational. That's the value of the JCM.

We, as managers, have to make decisions over time about what kind of job design process we are going to utilize. It is not always the motivational approach! Sometimes, we may need to use the mechanistic job design approach, the biological approach, the perceptual-motor approach, or a combination of those approaches. However, we need to make these decisions during the job design phase so that we understand what end result we are looking for.

Job Design for Flexibility

In addition to the primary tools for designing and redesigning specific jobs above, we have another set of tools that can be used in the workplace to improve motivation in entire groups of jobs or maybe even the entire workforce.[50] These tools include flex-time, job sharing, telecommuting, and compressed workweeks.[51]

Flextime allows us to provide workers with a flexible set of work hours. We usually create a set of *core hours* where everyone is at work, *bandwidth* or *work hours* available, and then a set of *flex hours* when people can be at work or can take time off. Individuals have the opportunity to modify their schedule within the work hours as long as they complete a set number of hours per day or week at work. Flextime has the potential to motivate workers because it allows them much greater autonomy with regard to their schedule. Take a look at Exhibit 4-5 for a sample flextime schedule.

WORK
APPLICATION 4-9

Give one example of how an organization, preferably one you work for or have worked for, uses any of the flexible job design tools. State which one is used, explain how it is implemented, and discuss how it affects employee motivation.

EXHIBIT 4-5   SAMPLE FLEXTIME WORK SCHEDULE[52]

ACMEMEGADYNE CORPORATION FLEXTIME WORK SCHEDULE
Normal operating hours: 8:30 a.m.–5:30 p.m. Monday through Friday (1 hour for lunch)
Full-time workers (40 hours per week):
Core hours: 9:00–11:00 a.m.; 1:00–3:00 p.m.
Flexible hours: 7:30–9:00 a.m.; 11:00 a.m.–1:00 p.m.; 3:00–6:30 p.m.
Work hours (bandwidth): 7:30 a.m.–6:30 p.m.
"A flextime arrangement may be suspended or cancelled at any time. Exempt employees must depart from any flextime schedule to perform their jobs. Nonexempt employees may be asked to work overtime regardless of a flextime schedule" (from SHRM flextime policy sample).

In *job sharing* (also called work sharing) we allow two (or more) people to share one whole job, including the workload and any benefits that are associated with that job. Job sharing again allows greater autonomy in the individual's job.

Telecommuting allows workers to work from a location other than the corporate office, usually from home. Telecommuting is another form of autonomy, but we need to make sure that telecommuters get opportunities to engage with coworkers and receive feedback concerning their work, since an absence of these opportunities are two of the major drawbacks to telecommuting.[53]

Finally, a *compressed workweek* means that we take the normal 5-day, 40-hour workweek and compress it down to less than 5 days. One common example would be a 4-day, 10-hour per day workweek.

Each of these additional tools allows us to design greater flexibility into our organization in one way or another. As a result, in many cases, we can improve both productivity and job satisfaction and in turn lower rates of absenteeism and turnover—a win-win for the organization and the employee within it.

Job Design Is Country Specific

One more thing that we need to make clear in this section of our text is that job design varies significantly from one country to another as well as from one company to another.[54] While job design in the United States has focused more on designing motivational jobs over the past several years, in many other countries, mechanistic job design is still the dominant method. It may come down to the primary types of work being done within different national environments. For instance, if many of the jobs in one country are basic manufacturing or routine service jobs, such as in a technical assistance call center, those jobs may be designed in a very mechanistic manner.

If, however, jobs in another country tend to be focused more on knowledge creation and innovation, those jobs would almost certainly be designed to be more organic and therefore more motivational to that particular workforce.

Alternatively, differences in job design may be associated with the cultural differences between countries. For instance, in a collectivist culture, job designs that isolate individuals and their actions (such as mechanistic designs) might not work as well as methods that encourage collaboration (like motivational designs).[55] Or differences may be due to other reasons entirely. Remember, though, that what is motivational as a job design in one country (for example personal autonomy in the United States) may be absolutely demotivational in another country like China or Slovenia (two highly collectivist cultures). Globalization also leads to more competition and the need for using the latest technology, which requires increasing skill requirements and ongoing job redesign.[56]

HR FORECASTING

SHRM

M:2
Forecasting Requirements and Availabilities, Gap Analysis, etc.

SHRM

E:7
HR Planning (Skill Inventories and Supply/Demand Forecasting)

HR forecasting and labor requirements planning are at the core of our ability to analyze future employment needs for our organizations.[57] Through the process of forecasting future labor requirements, we will make determinations—based on both quantitative and qualitative information—of what types of jobs and how many of each type we will need to fill over a particular period of time. If we fail to get it right, we won't get the right people in place at the right time when they are needed and will always be chasing voluntary and involuntary turnover, which causes lower organizational productivity. HR forecasting *identifies the estimated supply and demand for the different types of human resources in the organization over some future period, based on analysis of past and present demand.*

Before we get into the forecasting process, we need to understand a couple of terms. You always need to make sure that any analytical process you use includes valid and reliable measures. If you don't, then your results will always be suspect and will generally be of very little value. So what do these terms mean?

Reliability. Basically, reliability identifies how consistent a particular measure is. In other words, does the measure give a similar result every time it is used or when it is used by more than one person? If it does, then it is probably reliable. For instance, if I give a test of comprehension on a set of terms after teaching those terms in the same manner to several groups of third graders, and if the results in each group are similar, then the test is most likely reliable.

Validity. Validity refers to whether or not we measured what we thought we measured. It seems obvious to us what we are measuring, but we sometimes make mistakes. A good example is measuring job satisfaction. We might give our employees a survey concerning their job satisfaction and get high results. We might not, however, have done the survey anonymously. As a result of the overt nature of the survey, our workers may have all told us that they were highly satisfied because they might have thought that if we saw that they were disgruntled, we would want to fire them. In this case, our measure wasn't valid because we actually measured the level of concern our workers have for the company's honesty and the reasons for the survey when we meant to measure their real satisfaction level with their work.

Also, a measure can be reliable but not valid, but it can't be valid if it is not reliable. For example, if I step on a low-quality home scale and weigh 175, get off and on again several times, and weigh 175 every time, then the scale is reliable. However, if I go to a high-quality scale at the doctor's office and weigh 180 repeatedly, then the measurements I get from my home scale are reliable but not valid. So remember validity and reliability as you decide on the tools that you are going to use in the forecasting process.

HR forecasting Identifying the estimated supply and demand for the different types of human resources in the organization over some future period, based on analysis of past and present demand

Forecasting Methods

Forecasting labor requirements should be completed in two distinct steps. First, we complete a quantitative analysis of our workforce using one or more of several methods, and then we adjust the results of the quantitative analysis using qualitative methods. Both of these analyses have value to the organization.[58] The value of quantitative data should be obvious to you by this point in your business education, but qualitative analyses are also important. There is no match for years of expertise when analyzing situations that are unique or different from what has happened in our business environment in the past, and qualitative analysis looks at the differences between the "historical" and the "now." Let's take a little closer look at each type.

QUANTITATIVE FORECASTING. A **quantitative forecast** *utilizes mathematics to forecast future events based on historical data.* The three most common quantitative methods of forecasting labor demand are trend analysis, ratio analysis, and regression analysis.[59] Let's take a quick look at each method in Exhibit 4-6, followed by a discussion of each.

Trend analysis *is a process of reviewing historical items such as revenues and relating changes in those items to some business factor to form a predictive chart.* For example, we could look at historical revenues and relate those revenue volumes to the number of people in the organization for each year, or alternatively, we could analyze historical production levels and relate those levels to the number of people used to accomplish those levels of production. Either of these would give us a historical trend that we could then extend into the future to predict the number of people that would be required for a particular sales or production level.[60] Take a look again at the figures in Exhibit 4-6.

Ratio analysis *is the process of reviewing historical data and calculating specific proportions between a business factor (such as production) and the number of employees needed.* It generally gives us very similar results to trend analysis, but it should be a bit more precise because we are computing an exact value for the ratio. Again, take a look at Exhibit 4-6.

Regression analysis *is a statistical technique that identifies the relationship between a series of variable data points for use in forecasting future variables.* We can use statistical software to create the regression diagram (most HRIS include this capability). All we would have to do in our example from Exhibit 4-6 is provide the data points for employees and revenues for each company and each year. The software would calculate and draw the regression line for us. Then it is just a process of looking at the values along the line and applying them to your company's situation in a given year.

QUALITATIVE FORECASTING. **Qualitative forecasting** *uses nonquantitative methods to forecast the future, usually based on the knowledge of a pool of experts in a subject or an industry.* We provide our group of experts with the quantitative predictions that we have created and ask for their assessment of the data, taking into account circumstances within our industry and the general economic climate while comparing the present situation with the historical environment on which the quantitative evaluations are based. The experts will then come to a consensus about how to adjust the quantitative data for today's environment.

We need to use both quantitative and qualitative analysis to get good forecasts for the future needs of the organization and its human resources. This is because (a) quantitative analysis is based solely on historical data and not on the current business environment and (b) sometimes, situations will occur for which there is no historical precedent—for example, the massive banking and financial services failures leading to the worldwide recession of 2008 and 2009. We look at both forecasting methods and identify whether we expect to have a surplus or a shortage of people in the

SHRM
G:13
Forecasting

LO 4-6
Discuss the three most common quantitative HR forecasting methods.

SHRM
G:10
Quantitative Analysis

SHRM
J:12
Trends and Forecasting in HR

SHRM
G:5
Trend and Ratio Analysis Projections

SHRM
G:12
Analyzing and Interpreting Metrics

Quantitative forecast Utilizing mathematics to forecast future events based on historical data

Trend analysis A process of reviewing historical items such as revenues and relating changes in those items to some business factor to form a predictive chart

Ratio analysis The process of reviewing historical data and calculating specific proportions between a business factor (such as production) and the number of employees needed

Regression analysis A statistical technique that identifies the relationship between a series of variable data points for use in forecasting future variables

Qualitative forecasting The use of nonquantitative methods to forecast the future, usually based on the knowledge of a pool of experts in a subject or an industry

EXHIBIT 4-6 QUANTITATIVE FORECASTING ANALYSIS

Trend Analysis

Historical Data	2010	2011	2012	2013	2014
Revenues ($MM)	27.84	29.92	25.48	26.3	30.12
Total # of Employees	225	244	215	214	240

We then estimate the number of employees needed based on the historical trend. In this case, how many total employees would you say we need if we expect 2014 revenues to be $31.8 million? You likely said something around 250 people, because you looked at the historical trend.

Ratio Analysis

Historical Data	2010	2011	2012	2013	2014
Production Levels ($MM)	18.62	20.58	17.44	17.23	19.16
Avg. # Production Workers/Year	62	71	61	55	61
$ Production/Worker (000's)	300	290	286	313	314

The average production per worker for the 5 years listed would be just under $301,000, so $301,000:worker is our ratio. If we expect production requirements to be $20.2MM in 2015, we could divide $20,200,000 by $301,000 and get approximately 67 production workers as an expected complement for 2015. If we had 61 workers at the end of 2014, we would need to recruit 6 more for 2015—assuming no voluntary turnover during the year.

Regression Analysis

A regression diagram of all of the companies in our industry by year for the past 10 years, plotted with the number of employees on the x-axis and revenues on the y-axis, might look like this:

Based on this diagram, if we were expecting to have revenues of $29MM next year, we would need approximately 254 employees.

organization over the next few years. More likely, we will find that we will have a surplus of some types of people and a shortage of others. Regardless of the situation, once we know what to expect, we can set up procedures to correct the expected problem.

Measuring Absenteeism and Turnover

As we go through the process of forecasting HR needs for the future, we can't lose sight of the fact that we will have some voluntary turnover in addition to any changing personnel needs in the organization. No matter how satisfied our workforce is, we will have some people leave the organization voluntarily—for many different reasons. We will also have some involuntary turnover due to the fact that some people in the organization just can't seem to figure out what is necessary to be successful in their individual jobs, and we will therefore have to terminate their employment.

M:5
Retention: Measurement

G:4
Measuring Turnover

G:3
Measuring Absenteeism

We also have to account for the need for extra employees to cover for hours that are missed within the company due to absenteeism. When individuals miss work, we have to have their jobs done, somehow. We may hire temporary workers, or we may redistribute work to other individuals; we may even have an "office pool" of workers available to cover for missing employees, but no matter how we do it, we have to cover the hours missed. As a result of these voluntary absences from work (either permanent or temporary), we have to adjust employment numbers again to get valid and reliable numbers for our future workforce. See Exhibit 4-7 to learn how to calculate absenteeism and turnover.

EXHIBIT 4-7 MEASURING ABSENTEEISM AND TURNOVER

Absenteeism	
$\dfrac{\text{No. of employees absent}}{\text{Total employees}}$	Percentage or ratio of employees not at work for a specified period of time. Other workers, or temps, are often needed to do their work.
$\dfrac{3}{100} = 3\%$ or 3:100 ratio	So 1 out of every 33.3 employees is absent.
Turnover	
$\dfrac{\text{No. of employees leaving}}{\text{Total employees}}$	Percentage or ratio of employees leaving the organization during a specified period of time. They often need to be replaced with new employees.
$\dfrac{26}{100} = 26\%$ or 26:100 ratio	So just over 1 out of every 4 employees leaves the company each year.

RECONCILING INTERNAL LABOR SUPPLY AND DEMAND

After completion of the labor requirements planning process, where we create forecasts of our need for people, we end up with either a shortage or a surplus of people in each type of job in the organization. External job supply and demand affect the frequency with which people leave their jobs, and high turnover negatively affects organizational performance.[61] Therefore, balancing our supply and demand for labor affects our firm's productivity.

M:6
Labor Supply and Demand

4-4   APPLYING THE CONCEPT

Quantitative Methods

Complete each problem below:

____ 16. Turn to the Regression Analysis section of Exhibit 4-6. Assume that in 2012, you expect a recession and revenues to drop to $24MM. Around how many employees will you need?

a.   160   b.   180   c.   210   d.   230

____ 17. You have 253 employees. Over the past year, there were 26 absences. What is the approximate percentage and ratio of absenteeism?

a.   9.7%, 1–10   b.   10%, 1–10   c.   10%, 1–100

d.   12%, 1–12

____ 18. You have 1,215 employees. Over the past year, 298 left the firm. What is the approximate percentage and ratio of turnover?

a.   4%, 1–20   b.   40%, 4–10   c.   22%, 22–100

d.   25%, 1–4

____ 19. Turn to the Trend Analysis section of Exhibit 4-6. Assume that in 2012, you expect revenues to be $35MM. Around how many employees will you need?

a.   210   b. 230   c.   250   d.   270

____ 20. Turn to the Ratio Analysis section of Exhibit 4-6. Assume that in 2015, you expect the production level to increase to $22,000,000. Around how many employees will you need, and how many new workers do you need to add?

a.   72 and 11   b.   73 and 12   c.   74 and 13

d.   75 and 14

We have to figure out how to make supply match up with our expected demand. In business today, we are beginning to experience a major shortage of qualified people who are able to fill our jobs. There are many books and articles written on this subject, and they all agree that this shortage of skilled workers will get worse long before it will get better.[62] If all or most of the jobs in a particular company utilize a skilled workforce, company management needs to understand that filling existing openings will be increasingly difficult.

However, in other areas, we are experiencing a large surplus of available workers. Most of these jobs tend to require fewer skills, and many are being replaced by computer-guided equipment or other time-saving and labor-saving tools. If our business works more with less-skilled individuals, we may have a continuing surplus of workers.[63]

Regardless of whether we have a shortage or a surplus of people, we have to make an attempt to get the right numbers of people with the right skills sets into our organization at the right time. Doing otherwise is just too expensive for the organization. What are the options when faced with a shortage of personnel? What if we have a surplus? What we decide to do will have as much to do with our strategy and our business philosophy and values as it does with the facts of the situation. Some organizations will work *very* hard to avoid layoffs of any kind because they have a philosophy of caring for their employees. But in other organizations, if there is a surplus of people, the first thing that happens is a round of layoffs because that is the most expedient thing to do. What are our options, and how does each option affect the company and its workforce? Let's look at this subject next.

SHRM

S:1
Employment Downsizing

SHRM

S:5
When Downsizing Is the Answer

LO 4-7

Identify the seven major options for decreasing organizational numbers when faced with a labor surplus.

SHRM

S:9
Approaches to Reducing Staff Size

Options for a Labor Surplus

If we are predicting a surplus of people going into the future, what can we do about it? We can't usually just hang on to people that aren't needed in the organization. This is too expensive. However, we don't necessarily have to fire a large number of employees, either. How we handle the situation will depend on how soon we are able to predict that there will be a surplus, and it will also depend on our strategy, values, and philosophy, as noted above. In any situation of surplus, we need to look at how quickly we need to lower our employee numbers but also look at how any action we take will affect the remaining employees. For example, implementing a layoff is a very quick process, but it also creates a lot of engagement and satisfaction problems among the remaining employees. On the other hand, early retirement programs can actually be beneficial for the retiring employees and not harmful to the remaining workers, but the process is pretty slow. We have to understand the consequences of each option and choose wisely.

DOWNSIZING AND LAYOFFS. Our first option may be a layoff, especially if we have large numbers of surplus people. A **layoff** *is a process of terminating a group of employees, usually due to some business downturn or perhaps a technological change, with intent to improve organizational efficiency and effectiveness.* Layoffs go by many names today (downsizing, rightsizing, downscaling, cutbacks, etc.), but the result is still the same: We are terminating the employment of a reasonably large number of people. Layoffs don't occur person by person. If you are terminating one person, that is typically a disciplinary process, and you should go through the required due process steps in Chapter 9 to justify that termination. In a layoff, however, we are generally allowed to terminate the employment of a group of individuals with very little advance warning, and we usually don't have to provide any disciplinary or other justification for what we are doing. In a few situations, we will have to comply with the Worker Adjustment and Retraining Notification Act (WARN Act), which we will discuss in some detail in Chapter 10, but other than that, we have few documentation needs other than ensuring that there is no illegal discrimination in a layoff event.[64] We do have to document the method by which we determined who should be in the layoff, and it would be wise not to be arbitrary in our selection of individuals. But again, the requirements are minimal unless there is a union contract that restricts layoffs in some way. We will discuss unions and collective bargaining in Chapter 10.

What are the business advantages of a layoff? The most satisfying result for management is that the resulting savings are immediately added to bottom-line corporate performance.[65] In other words, if I lay off people whose salaries total a million dollars, then that million dollars is not spent—it becomes profit or minimized losses, assuming everything else is held constant. This is the reason that companies tend to overuse layoffs. In some cases, they are trying to dress up the financial statements for investors or the investment community to make the company look better than it really is. However, investors are starting to catch on to this type of trick, so it isn't working as well as it used to.

Although temporarily improving the financials is probably a shortsighted viewpoint, it is something that executives frequently think about when considering a layoff. Why is this view shortsighted? Layoffs create all kinds of potential problems for the organization, including lower employee morale and job satisfaction. They also foster a corporate culture of employees "lying low" or not standing out in any way, so that they don't get caught up in the next downsizing.[66] Alternatively, the remaining employees may have survivor's guilt that makes them ask things like "Why Bill? He has a family to feed." So we end up with a lot of stress issues in layoffs, and these create problems for the organization.

Historically, companies have probably been too fast to use downsizings or layoffs.[67] If you are forecasting correctly, you should not have to do layoffs very often. In most cases, you should be able to see that you are going to have a surplus in the near future and that you should use some of the other tools that cause less stress and suffering instead. So layoffs are usually performed because HR and the other management in the firm failed to do their jobs. However, unpredictable events such as recessions can be difficult to forecast.[68] It is also difficult to forecast how much your sales may drop during a recession, and projecting sales is not part of HRM.

An interesting note is in order here, though. There is some pretty good evidence that companies typically do worse financially after a large-scale layoff than they did before. Almost all of the layoff research supports this.[69] The reasons for this include

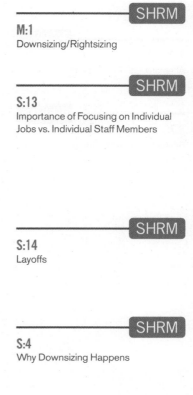

M:1
Downsizing/Rightsizing

S:13
Importance of Focusing on Individual Jobs vs. Individual Staff Members

S:14
Layoffs

S:4
Why Downsizing Happens

S:8
Consequences of Employment Downsizing

Layoff A process of terminating a group of employees, usually due to some business downturn or perhaps a technological change, with intent to improve organizational efficiency and effectiveness

losing good employees through the layoff and the fact that good employees may leave voluntarily if they fear a layoff is coming. Only the lower-quality usually can't get another job, so they will stay. The organization might also lay off too many people, or it could remove the wrong people and cause greater problems in the organization as a result. So, layoffs are not a cure-all. Sometimes they need to be used, but it will be an unusual case when a layoff is going to be valuable to the organization over the long term.

SHRM

S:2
Alternatives to Employment Downsizing

SHRM

S:7
Alternatives to Downsizing

PAY REDUCTION, WORK SHARING, NATURAL ATTRITION, HIRING FREEZES, RETRAINING, AND TRANSFERS. A second option for mitigating a labor surplus is a *pay reduction* for all or part of the workforce. In some cases, pay reductions may be a valid option for a company. Supply and demand for various types of labor drive the market value of the people who provide that labor. If there is an oversupply of people in a particular field, or if new technology has made the job easier, then those employees may not be worth as much as they were 5 or 10 years ago. In other cases, economic conditions may demand a cut in organizational expenses, and labor is the biggest organizational expense in many companies.[70] Again, this option can be accomplished fairly quickly, but it certainly is unlikely to improve employee morale or job satisfaction.

A third option for lowering labor costs without terminating employees is some form of *job- (or work-) sharing* arrangement. We may cut the hours available to each worker because fewer jobs are available in the company, but instead of cutting workers, we may split one job up among more than one worker. This way, nobody is laid off, but all of the workers suffer to some extent because of a decrease in income. Some companies would much rather go to a work-sharing arrangement than terminate employees because it seems to be fairer to all of their employees and because the companies' corporate philosophy and values may indicate that fairness is a critical concept to them.[71] Everyone in the organization suffers equally as a result of this type of policy. There is certainly still some suffering in the workforce due to a reduction in income, but nobody loses an entire paycheck. Plus, when the firm comes out of a recession, it already has enough skilled workers to meet the increase in business.

Next, we have the option in some cases to allow *natural attrition* to lower organizational numbers without the need for a layoff or pay reduction. We can just allow positions to stay unfilled as turnover occurs. This option, along with the slightly more stringent option of a *hiring freeze*, causes our number of employees to drop slowly. Therefore, it can't be used in a situation where speed in reducing expenses is critical, but if we have done our job in the forecasting process above, we may have enough time for this option to work for us without putting massive stress on our workforce.

Retraining workers and *transferring* them from one job to another may be options in some circumstances. However, this option will only work if we have too many employees in one type of job and too few in another. If there are no positions where we have a shortage, retraining workers will do no good. Here again, the process is a little slow due to the fact that the person has to be retrained in a new field. But if we have a good worker who is willing to try a new job, and if a position is available, then using this option can allow us to retain that good employee into the future.

LO 4-8

Discuss the problems that need to be considered in offering an early retirement program.

EARLY RETIREMENT. The last option that we will discuss here is *early retirement*. Early retirement can be a valuable option in some cases. However, there can be many pitfalls to using early retirement to reduce an organization's workforce.[72] In an early retirement offer, employees are given the choice of leaving the company before they would ordinarily do so (due to reaching the "normal" retirement age of 65, for instance), and in exchange for leaving, the employee will receive benefits of some type from the organization.

There are some good reasons to use early retirement as an option to reduce an employee surplus, but it is a slow method of getting rid of people, and we have to be careful in planning for and offering early retirements. Problems with early retirement include the following:[73]

- Too many people may take our early retirement offer. If we make the early retirement offer too attractive, we may have more people take it than we expected, and we may end up with a shortage of people. Then we will incur additional costs in recruiting and hiring new people because of the newly created shortage.

- Too few may take the offer, requiring us to consider offering a sweetened deal to the rest of the workforce. You really want to avoid this situation. Why? Let's look at an example. Five years ago, we offered an early retirement package to our workforce, and the first package wasn't very good, so not too many people took it. So, we decided that we needed to have more people retire. As a result, we offered a better deal, and a second group took that deal—but it was still not enough. Finally, we offered a very good deal, and enough took it that we got the number of retirees that we needed. Now we come to the present, and we have to reduce the number of people again. What is going to happen when we offer an early retirement deal this time? It's quite possible that nobody is going to take it because they "know" that a better deal is going to come after this one, since that is what happened last time. So if we made multiple offers and sweetened each offer in the past, that is what our employees will expect to happen again.

- The wrong types of people may take the early retirement deal. One of the issues with early retirements is that our best people might take the offer and then immediately go to work for a competitor. These top-notch candidates can usually find work easily. Conversely, the people who are borderline in their capabilities or motivation may be the ones who are afraid that if they take our early retirement offer, they won't be able to find another job. So we may end up losing our good people and keeping our worst performers!

- People may perceive that they are being forced out. We absolutely cannot push people to take an offer of early retirement. Generally, the individuals who would be eligible for early retirement fall within the age-group protected by the ADEA (discussed in Chapter 3): those 40 years of age and older. If there is pressure on these individuals to take the offer, we could be confronted with an EEOC lawsuit for age discrimination.

Generally if we are going to offer an early retirement option, we have to do some specific things. We have to offer it to all people in a particular employee category. For instance, we have to offer it to all people in a department that is overloaded, all nonmanagerial employees in that department, a division that is overstaffed, or a particular plant within the company. You can't select individuals who happen to be in a particular category and not offer it to other employees in the same category. If you only offer an early retirement package to select people, you might create the possibility of legal actions (such as age discrimination complaints if you pick only those older employees). So you need to allow everyone in a category the option for early retirement if you are going to offer it to any. Age *can* be a criterion, but you have to be absolutely sure that you don't push people to accept the offer if you make age a factor.

Another thing that you are required to do is allow people a "reasonable period of time" to accept or not accept the offer. What is a reasonable period of time? Generally the EEOC and court case history shows that 45 to 60 days is a reasonable period of time. Anything less is generally not enough time for employees to consider their options, and a judge might decide that you are pressuring people to act quickly without time to weigh the value of the early retirement option.

In a surplus situation, we want to use the options that we discussed in this section from the bottom up—starting with things like early retirements and attrition, because they are the least disruptive to the workforce and allow us to maintain motivation and job satisfaction levels much better than things like layoffs and pay reductions. This will provide us with the best long-term results.

LO 4-9

Identify the seven major options for overcoming a labor shortage.

Options for a Labor Shortage

What if our forecasts show an expected shortage? What we need to look at here is how fast we can solve the problem, but we also want to look at how quickly we can lower our number of employees again if we need to. In other words, how quickly can we reduce numbers in the future if we end up with too many people? The best options here are methods that are really fast in solving the shortage but that also can be reversed really quickly if a surplus of employees starts to take form.

As opposed to the surplus situation in the last section, where we ideally choose options from the bottom up, in a situation where we are facing a personnel shortage, we want to work from the first options down to the bottom. We would start with things like asking for or requiring overtime and working down the list as we have to, because again, we want the smallest possible disruption to our workforce.

OVERTIME. Our first option—the quickest and easiest way to fix a personnel shortage—is asking or requiring our employees to work *overtime*. Whoa! Can we really force you to work overtime? The answer is yes. No federal law limits the option to require you to work a "reasonable amount" of overtime if you are an employee of the organization.[74] So, overtime is a very quick method of resolving an employee shortage—we can do it immediately. It's as simple as saying, "We are behind on an order and you need to stay overtime today. Tomorrow, when we have finished the order, you can go home at the end of the workday." Overtime is our first and best option until we get to the point where we are starting to stress our people too much because the overtime becomes excessive. When stress levels get too high, the employee's work will suffer (stress is discussed in more detail in Chapter 14) and poor work quality will ensue.[75] So, if we start to see too much stress among our workforce, we need to do something else to relieve our personnel shortage. What other options do we have?

I:1
Employment Relationship: Employees, Contractors, Temporary Workers

TEMPORARY OR CONTRACT WORKERS. We can frequently use *temporary or contract workers* to overcome a short-term shortage, but we probably don't want to use temporary workers for more than a year at most, for reasons we will discuss shortly. Since the recession of 2008, many employers are reluctant to hire full-time employees, so many firms are using independent contractors who are not legally employed by the firm. At more than 7% of the workforce, contractors are an important and growing segment of the US population and are increasingly prevalent throughout the developed world.[76]

When there is too much work for the current employees, temporary and contract workers can help get the job done.

But while hiring temporary and contract workers is a quick method of overcoming a worker shortage, that only applies when you are hiring people to perform general duties. However, if you need someone with a specific high-level skill set, it might take a while to find a temp worker.

David Wooley/Photodisc/Thinkstock

For instance, if you need a temporary CEO (yes, they are available!), it might take a few months to find one. There are companies that specialize in providing temporary executive help, including CEOs. And the upside is that hiring temporary help is easy to take back. When we no longer need the temporary worker, we just release that individual back to the temp agency. If we are using contract workers, we allow the contract to lapse in order to release them.

However, there are some common problems with temporary and contract workers. First, they have little or no loyalty to you and your organization.[77] And what are they going to be doing when they are not working for you? They are working for someone else, and that someone else is frequently your competition, and the temporary or contract worker who was in your office last week may tell your competitors how you do things—which might help your competitors in some way.

Temporary and contract workers also may not know the specific jobs in your company, and they generally don't know the company as well as do your permanent workers.[78] They are also frequently not very motivated to work for you because they know that they aren't staying. There can also sometimes be a clash between temp workers and permanent employees. Why? There are a couple of reasons. One is that the permanent workers may think that the temp is trying to take their job. Another is that if we have had a layoff in the fairly recent past, the permanent worker will likely resent the temp for taking the job that a friend of the permanent worker used to have.

In addition to the basic problems of loyalty, knowledge of the company and job, and relationships with coworkers, temps can also create legal problems for the organization. If an organization classifies a worker as an "independent contractor," and if the organization exerts significant control over the actions of that worker, then the organization can be judged guilty of misclassification of the worker as an outside contractor.[79] That means the government can penalize the organization for not withholding employment taxes on the "employee" and not paying for required benefits such as workers' compensation insurance and Social Security withholding.

Along the same lines, if the company keeps temporary employees longer than a year, then those workers are probably not really temporary, and they may be eligible for full-time employment benefits. As examples, **Microsoft** had to pay almost $100 million to about 10,000 workers that it had classified as temporary, and a transportation company was charged $319 million in unpaid employment taxes and penalties in 2007 because it misclassified drivers as contract workers.[80] In 2014, several members of the **Buffalo Jills** (the cheerleading squad for the Buffalo Bills football team) even sued the team for misclassification as independent contractors due to the women having little to no control over their work and working conditions. So, you can see that it can be very expensive and can create a public relations nightmare to call someone a temporary or contract worker if that person is actually working as a regular employee of the company. These are just some of the problems with temporary and contract workers. However, both are highly revocable if we no longer need them.

RETRAINING WORKERS, OUTSOURCING, AND TURNOVER REDUCTION. The next options take a bit longer to put into effect. We can *retrain workers*, but doing so it isn't a quick response to a shortage.[81] This option is especially useful if we have a surplus of employees somewhere else. The advantage is that the retrained employees know the company and know the work procedures better than someone off the street, so retraining can be a good option in some cases. It is also moderately fast and generally easy to revoke, because the workers are still trained to do their old job.

Outsourcing may be another option. We can outsource to someone outside the organization a whole function that we currently do in-house.[82] For instance, we might outsource all of our computer-programming jobs to an outsourcing company that specializes in computer programming. This option is moderately fast, but it is not extremely fast because we have to find a company that can do the job, research

SHRM

E:8
Work Management (Work Processes and Outsourcing)

the company, negotiate with it, come up with a contract, and then finally get it to do the work. It's not going to take forever, but it will probably take a few months. It is also moderately revocable because we generally have to create a contract with a specific time period during which we are required to use the services of the outsourcer. Plus, we are now a customer, and we may not get the quick attention that we would from our own in-house employees. Nevertheless, the general sentiment in business is to do what you do best and outsource the rest.

Our next option is *turnover reduction*. If fewer people voluntarily leave the organization than we have predicted, we can reduce a projected shortage.[83] But how can we reduce turnover?

We can improve working conditions or do other things that may cause our workforce to become more satisfied. We can also shorten work hours (minimally), make benefits packages better, and maybe make work schedules a little better. As discussed, we can also use job design flexibility. Any of these things might cause turnover to go down. But this won't happen overnight because it takes some time to change people's opinions of the organization.

We will also probably have trouble if we decide we want to allow turnover to increase again later, perhaps because we are predicting a surplus of workers at that point in time. We can take back some of the above benefits that caused turnover to go down, and over time, turnover will move back up. But we don't want to (in fact, may not be able to) take these things back all at once, because we may create some severe problems in motivation and job satisfaction. So this option is very difficult to take back later.

NEW HIRES AND TECHNOLOGICAL INNOVATION. Our next option is to *hire new employees*. But this option takes a while, doesn't it? We have to go through a long process of analyzing the job and updating its description, finding out what skills are needed, and then going out and recruiting people. Once we have a pool of recruits, we can select them, train them, and get them up to speed and into the job. We can see that this is a slow method of resolving a worker shortage. It is also not easy to take back. Once we hire new employees and they are beyond their probationary period, it is hard to get rid of them other than for reasons of just cause (we will discuss this concept in Chapter 9).[84] Thus, the trend of using more temporary or contract workers continues.[84]

Finally, we may be able to overcome a shortage of personnel through *technological innovation*. In other words, we may be able to use machinery that can do the job of a human being. But again, this is a slow process, and it also cannot be revoked. We can't create or find new equipment, install it, and make it operational overnight. Also, if we create a group of robots that are capable of assembling our product, we are not going to stop using them and hire a bunch of new assembly workers again, are we? So, it is really not revocable at all once the equipment has been identified and installed.

SUCCESSION PLANNING

SHRM

M:7/Q:15
Succession Planning

Succession planning is a significant issue in many different situations.[85] Larger organizations need to plan for smooth transitions from one key employee to another in order to minimize disruption of the organization's work. Family businesses are also very concerned with the process of succession, usually from one generation of the family to the next. Even in smaller, nonfamily companies, succession helps the organization survive and succeed over the long term as the owner/founder of the business decides to retire or move on to other businesses.[86] Why are we talking about succession planning at this point? Planning for succession is just another type of forecasting. It is a problem of supply and demand. Do we expect to have a shortage or a surplus of managerial and other valuable candidates over a particular period of time? We know that managers and executives will move through the organization at a certain pace, and we have the ability to plan (at least to some extent) for that movement so that we will have the people in place to move into the vacated positions as the incumbent manager/executive moves on to other jobs or moves into retirement.

Succession planning is also critical to organizational development over time. As the organization grows and changes, we have to be able to provide the leadership to allow it to succeed. The forecasting process that we use in planning for other human resource needs can also be used to make predictions for leadership requirements over the forecasted time period. Using this forecast information allows us to either prepare new leaders within the company to take on those positions or alternatively go out and recruit the people whom we need in order to ensure smooth transitions in organizational leadership over time.

TRENDS AND ISSUES IN HRM

In this chapter's trends and issues section, we will again discuss current questions and problems in organizational HRM. First, we will review O*Net as a job analysis tool in some more detail. Next, we will explore the use of competency models in job analysis. In our third topic, we will brief you on how organizations can "think sustainability" in their workflow analysis and job design processes.

O*Net as a Tool for Job Analysis

O*Net is a service provided by the US Department of Labor Employment and Training Administration (DOLETA).[87] We briefly introduced you to the O*Net database earlier in this chapter, but let's take just a minute and go into a little more detail on how O*Net can help your organization with job analysis, job descriptions, and job specifications.

HR managers need large amounts of information to analyze the jobs in their organization. O*Net and its partner site, O*Net OnLine, provide information on nearly 1,000 jobs that are common to many different businesses and industries. Using the O*Net Toolkit (http://www.onetcenter.org/toolkit.html), managers can learn how the O*Net website works.[88] Once you have reviewed the toolkit, you might want to take a look at O*Net OnLine at http://www.onetonline.org/. This site provides a search interface with the O*Net database, using a variety of search options.[89]

HR managers can use this information to complete a job analysis and create job descriptions and specifications quickly and easily. The O*Net "Content Model"[90] identifies six categories within its occupational classification structure (see Exhibit 4-8):

- *Worker characteristics* (enduring traits that influence a person's performance on the job)—abilities, interests, work styles, and work values
- *Worker requirements* (attributes acquired through experience and/or education)—knowledge, and skills
- *Experience requirements* (training and experience needed)—job zone, education, training, and experience
- *Occupational requirements* (actual work performed on the job)—work activities
- *Workforce characteristics* (labor market–related information)—wages and employment
- *Occupation-specific information* (detailed elements of specific jobs)—tasks

EXHIBIT 4-8 O*NET CONTENT MODEL

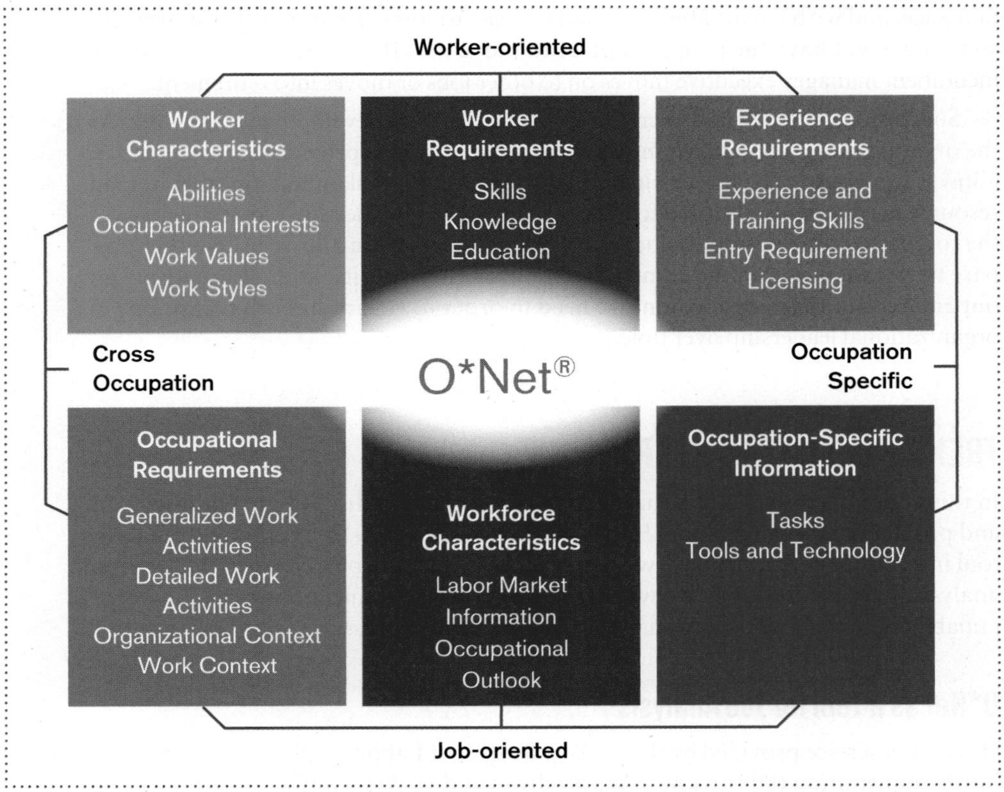

Source: O*Net, US Department of Labor Employment and Training Administration (DOLETA), http://www.onetonline.org/

Using the information from the content model, the HR manager can create custom reports on each occupation searched through O*Net. The HR manager can then use that information to design or redesign job characteristics, leading to high-quality job descriptions and specifications from which they can then go out and recruit new employees with the required skill sets for each job. In addition, the O*Net characteristics help in pricing each job in the organization to provide a competitive compensation system and lower voluntary turnover in the company (we will discuss compensation systems in Chapter 11). So O*Net is a handy free resource for job analysis, job descriptions, and job specifications.

Competency Models and Job Analysis

It has been said that traditional job analysis looks at the history of what has been done in a particular job that is being analyzed—identifying the tasks, duties, and responsibilities—while *competency modeling* looks at what will be needed in the future in order to be "competent" to do that job. This means looking at skills, attitudes, and personality attributes that will allow the person to succeed even in a changing environment. Competency modeling is designed to be a better process for jobs, organizations, and industries that are not stable over time. If the environment is rapidly changing, many experts say that competency modeling will provide the organization with a better "road map" concerning who to hire than will traditional job analysis. But what is competency modeling?

According to the US Office of Personnel Management (OPM), "a competency is a measurable pattern of knowledge, skills, abilities, behaviors, and other characteristics that an individual needs to perform work roles or occupational functions successfully."[91] So as you can see, when we use competency modeling, we spend much less time identifying the "what" (what is or has been done in a particular job) and much more time identifying the "who" (the knowledge and skills that should allow a person to succeed in that job). Looking at it another way, the emphasis in a traditional job analysis is on the resulting job description, but the emphasis in a competency model is on the job specification.

What are the major differences between job analysis and competency modeling?[92,93] The advantages of job analysis include the following:

- A more rigorous analytical method
- Easier to defend adverse employment actions such as termination in a legal setting

While the advantages of competency modeling include the following:

- Links to organizational strategy and goals
- Better identifies behaviors necessary in rapidly changing work environments
- Can help with setting work expectations and framing training and development needs

While there is no consensus on which is better in all situations, there is some agreement that job analysis and competency models can be complementary when identifying knowledge, skills, abilities, and other behaviors in today's organizations.[94] Each option has its place, and the various options are not mutually exclusive in today's HR organizations.

Workflows and Job Design for Sustainability

As in many other areas of business today, we can frequently incorporate sustainability initiatives into our work design processes to help us mitigate our effect on the environment as well as save the organization time and money. How do we do this? First, recall the workflow process. We noted early in this chapter that workflows are designed around the expected end results. Based on the end result, we design the work processes that will be performed and identify the tools, equipment, and human resources that will be used to complete the processes. If we design work processes with sustainability in mind, we can frequently identify process changes that will lower our impact on critical natural resources.[95] For example, we may be able to use less water in a cooling operation by using a more open design that allows for radiational cooling of parts being produced instead of using water to cool those same parts.

 ESR

We can also utilize some of our job design options to help with conservation of resources in our organizations. Earlier, we discussed options for work including telecommuting, compressed workweeks, and flextime opportunities. Each of these options can lower the need for our workers to commute to and from work.[96] Telecommuting may be able to completely eliminate putting another car on the road at rush hour, but compressed workweeks and flextime can both also lower the number of trips our employees have to make to and from work in a given week/month/year. Each of these options not only minimizes wasted time for the individual but also lowers the use of fuel for their cars or whatever other conveyances they would use for their commute.

In addition to designing a specific job, we may also be able to lower our effect on the environment by using a technique called hoteling.[97] *Hoteling occurs when the organization has less office space than it would have in a traditional office arrangement (where everyone has an assigned space), so it uses a software program that*

Hoteling When an organization uses a software program that allows employees to "reserve" office space for particular parts of the workweek when they will need it

allows employees to "reserve" office space for particular parts of the workweek when they will need it. At other times, that same office space will be available to other employees for their use. Hoteling can lower the total amount of office space that we need in an average business, and as a result, it can lower the usage of all of the common services that are needed for that office space—such as electricity, heating and air-conditioning, water for bathroom facilities, overall energy consumption, and other items. This in turn lowers our impact on the environment.

So if we think about the workflows and processes that have to occur in our organization, we can frequently design changes to those processes that will minimize our use of precious environmental resources. And as a bonus, we can save money for the organization because we don't use resources that were historically wasted anyway. That's a win-win situation if there ever was one!

● ● ● CHAPTER SUMMARY

4-1   Describe the process of workflow analysis and identify why it is important to HRM.

We start our workflow analysis by determining the end result. Once we identify the result we expect, we can then determine the steps or activities required to create the end result that we've identified. This is basically an analysis of the tasks that are going to have to be performed in order to create the output that we expect. Finally, we can identify the inputs that are going to be necessary to carry out the steps and perform the same tasks. The inputs are the following items, known as the 4 Ms: machines (tools, equipment, and machines), material (physical resources used in production), manpower (the people needed in a particular production process), and money (the capital that must be spent to perform our processes).

4-2   Identify the five major options available for the job analysis process.

Questionnaires ask questions that help to identify the functions that are a part of a particular job, and then, in most cases, they assign a point value to each of those functions. In the job analysis *interview*, questions are asked verbally, usually of the incumbent, and the answers are compiled into a profile of the job. *Diaries* have the workers maintain a work log, or diary, in which they write down the tasks that they accomplish as they go about their job. This log becomes the document from which we build the description of the job. We can also use *observation* of the worker at work, where an observer shadows the worker and logs tasks that are performed over a period of time. Finally, the use of *subject matter expert* (SME) panels, chosen for their knowledge of a set of jobs, helps identify the major tasks within those jobs.

4-3   Discuss the four major approaches to job design.

Mechanistic job design focuses on designing jobs around the concepts of task specialization, skill simplification, and repetition. *Biological job design* focuses on minimizing the physical strain on the worker by structuring the physical work environment around the way the body works. *Perceptual-motor job design* attempts to make sure that workers remain within their normal mental capabilities and limitations. *Motivational job design* focuses on the job characteristics that affect psychological meaning and motivational potential, and it views attitudinal variables as the most important outcomes of job design.

4-4   Identify and briefly describe the components of the job characteristics model (JCM).

The five core job characteristics include skill variety, task identity, task significance, autonomy, and feedback. The first three lead collectively to the psychological state of *experienced meaningfulness of work*, in which workers think that their work has meaning. The fourth core characteristic of autonomy leads to the psychological state of *experienced responsibility for outcomes*. Finally, feedback leads to the psychological state of *knowledge of results*—the psychological feeling that we get from knowing the results and that in turn creates *satisfaction* with the results of our work.

All of the psychological states *collectively* lead to the outcomes: motivation, performance, job satisfaction, absenteeism, and turnover. These can go up or down depending on the design of the job.

4-5   Describe the three major tools for motivational job design.

Job simplification is the process of eliminating or combining tasks and/or changing the work sequence to improve performance. It makes jobs more specialized. However, we might make the job less motivational if we simplify the work to the point where the worker gets bored. *Job expansion,* on the other hand, makes jobs less specialized. Jobs can be expanded through rotation, enlargement, and enrichment. *Team-based job design* gives the team an entire piece of work. It is a form of job enrichment that can increase autonomy, task identity, and task significance for the worker.

4-6   Discuss the three most common quantitative HR forecasting methods.

Trend analysis allows the company to look at historical trends—for instance, whether employment went up or down in a given year and how the number of employees related to revenue or productivity—and make judgments from those trends. *Ratio analysis* calculates specific values by comparing a business factor with the number of employees needed. *Regression analysis* is a statistical technique in which we use a regression diagram made from historical data points to predict future needs presented with a *y*- and *x*-axis.

4-7   Identify the seven major options for decreasing organizational numbers when faced with a labor surplus.

A *layoff* is the process of terminating a group of employees to improve organizational efficiency and effectiveness. A *pay reduction* lowers the rate of pay for groups of employees within the organization. *Work sharing* occurs when we cut the hours available to each worker on a per-week or per-month basis, because fewer hours of work are available in the company. The option to allow *natural attrition* may also occur. In this case, we lower employee numbers by not refilling jobs when turnover occurs. In a *hiring freeze,* we allow natural attrition, but in addition, we don't create any new jobs, even if they are needed. We stop all hiring—not just rehiring for existing positions. *Retraining and transferring workers* from one job to another may allow us to lower the number of workers in a particular part of our business, but it will only work if we have too many employees in one type of job and too few in

another. *Early retirement* can be a valuable option in some cases. In an early retirement offer, employees are given the choice of leaving the company before they would normally retire, and in exchange, the employee will receive some benefits from the organization.

4-8   Discuss the problems that need to be considered in offering an early retirement program.

Early retirement is a slow method of getting rid of people, and we have to be careful in planning for and offering early retirements. Problems include the following: Too many or too few people may take our early retirement offer; our best people might take the offer and then immediately go to work for a competitor while the people who are borderline or poor performers won't; people may perceive that they are being forced out, and we may be vulnerable to charges of discrimination.

4-9   Identify the seven major options for overcoming a labor shortage.

The quickest and easiest way to fix a personnel shortage is asking or requiring employees to work *overtime.* It is our best option until we get to the point where we are starting to stress our people too much because the overtime becomes excessive. Hiring *temporary workers* is another quick method of overcoming a worker shortage. Remember, though, that temporary workers create some problems for the organization. We may also be able to *retrain workers* if we have a surplus of employees in another part of the company. We might also be able to utilize *outsourcing* of some of our current in-house functions as another option. We can also attempt to *reduce turnover.* If fewer people voluntarily leave the organization than we had predicted, we can reduce a projected shortage. We can *hire new employees.* Finally, *technological innovation* may help alleviate a shortage if we can create machinery that can do the job of a human being.

4-10   Define the key terms found in the chapter margins and listed following the Chapter Summary.

Complete the Key Terms Review to test your understanding of this chapter's key terms.

••• KEY TERMS

biological job design	job expansion	perceptual-motor job design
hoteling	job simplification	qualitative forecasting
HR forecasting	job specification	quantitative forecast
job analysis	layoff	ratio analysis
job characteristics model	mechanistic vs. organic	regression analysis
job description	job design	trend analysis
job design	motivational job design	workflow analysis

• • • KEY TERMS REVIEW

Complete each of the following statements using one of this chapter's key terms.

1. _____ is the tool that we use to identify what has to be done within the organization to produce a product or service.

2. _____ is the process used to identify the work performed and the working conditions for each of the jobs within our organizations.

3. _____ identifies the major tasks, duties, and responsibilities that are components of a job.

4. _____ identifies the qualifications of a person who should be capable of doing the job tasks noted in the job description.

5. _____ is the process of identifying tasks that each employee is responsible for completing as well as how those tasks will be accomplished.

6. _____ focuses on designing jobs around the concepts of task specialization, skill simplification, and repetition.

7. _____ focuses on minimizing the physical strain on the worker by structuring the physical work environment around the way the body works.

8. _____ focuses on designing jobs in which the tasks remain within the worker's normal mental capabilities and limitations.

9. _____ focuses on the job characteristics that affect the psychological meaning and motivational potential, and it views attitudinal variables as the most important outcomes of job design.

10. _____ provides a conceptual framework for designing or enriching jobs based on core job characteristics.

11. _____ is the process of eliminating or combining tasks and/or changing the work sequence to improve performance.

12. _____ is the process of making jobs broader, with less repetition.

13. _____ identifies the estimated supply and demand for the different types of human resources in the organization over some future period, based on analysis of past and present demand.

14. _____ utilizes mathematics to forecast future events based on historical data.

15. _____ is a process of reviewing historical items such as revenues, and relating those changes to some business factor to form a predictive chart.

16. _____ is the process of reviewing historical data and calculating specific proportions between a business factor (such as production) and the number of employees needed.

17. _____ is a statistical technique that identifies the relationship between a series of variable data points for use in forecasting future variables.

18. _____ uses non-quantitative methods to forecast the future, usually based on the knowledge of a pool of experts in a subject or an industry.

19. _____ is a process of terminating a group of employees, usually due to some business downturn or perhaps a technological change, with intent to improve organizational efficiency and effectiveness.

20. _____ occurs when the organization has less office space than it would in a traditional office arrangement (where everyone has an assigned space) and uses a software program that allows employees to reserve office space for particular parts of the workweek when they will need it.

• • • COMMUNICATION SKILLS

The following critical-thinking questions can be used for class discussion and/or for written assignments to develop communication skills. Be sure to give complete explanations for all answers.

1. Do you agree that stable jobs don't exist in today's workplace and that as a result, we shouldn't worry about job analysis? Why or why not?

2. Looking at the company where you work (use a company that you know well if you are not currently working), does it appear that the organization uses task-based or competency-based job analysis? Why do you think this?

3. Can more than one of the four main approaches to job design be used at the same time to design a job? Can you provide an example of how this could work?

4. Are there any situations in which you might design a job using the JCM and yet the job would still not be motivational? What circumstances might cause this to happen?

5. Do you think that using flextime, telecommuting, job sharing, or compressed workweeks is really going to motivate employees? Why or why not?

6. Are there situations in which working in teams might be demotivating? How could this occur?

7. Have you seen job simplification, job rotation, or job expansion being used in your workplace? (if you aren't currently working, use a workplace that you are familiar with.) Did it work to motivate the employees? Why?

8. Which of the three HR forecasting methods do you think would give you the most accurate forecast? Explain your choice.

9. Is a layoff, or downsizing, ever the best option to resolve a projected surplus in an organization? Justify your answer.

10. How much overtime is reasonable in a week? How long can the company expect workers to continue to work overtime before they see employee stress levels getting significantly higher than normal?

• • • CASE 4-1 THE EXPLOSION AT DHR CONSTRUCTION

A Forced Changing of the Guard

Richard Davis, who handled the corporation's finances at DHR Construction, LLC (the same company discussed in the case in Chapter 2 and again in Chapter 8), had decided some time back that it was time to upgrade from using a part-time bookkeeper to an accountant. A two-year audit conducted by the accountant revealed that about $25,000 of expenses connected to Alan's (their foreman's) corporate credit card account were for nonbusiness items (i.e., Christmas trees), were questionable in multiple cases (i.e., filling up the company truck six times in one day), and, at times, were signed by someone other than Alan (signatures on receipts did not match Alan's signature). After a discussion with their lawyer and Alan, Hodgetts and Davis agreed to let Alan go without pressing criminal charges.

Alan's separation from the business left a wide managerial gap. So who was going to take over as foreman in the short term until they could conduct a thorough search and hire a new one? Davis and Hodgetts agreed that they needed someone immediately (tomorrow) to fill the position so they could focus on conducting their job search. There was only one likely candidate who came to mind, Davis's daughter Delores (nickname RJ). RJ had the free time, had worked in a very tough and stressful environment (a legal office and a hospital) and excelled, and seemed to have both the interest and the tenacity to try to learn the contracting portion of the business. From Richard Davis's perspective, this would provide RJ an opportunity to determine whether she would want to be the one to eventually take over the family business; she needed to learn the business from the ground up.

Richard Davis then spent a few days at the work site with RJ to introduce her to the numerous subcontractors and to spread the word that RJ was going to take over the job of foreman while the business was searching for an experienced person. Richard also gave RJ a copy of all of the building blueprints, as well as work charts showing which subcontractor had to be working at what time point in each home and what work the subcontractor would perform. RJ was a very quick learner, and after having several question and answer sessions with Davis and Hodgetts, they decided that RJ was ready to go solo on the job site.

The next day RJ was at the construction site checking in with all of the subcontractors to make sure that everyone knew what needed to be done by whom and in what order. RJ came home from the first day of the job exhausted and a bit disgruntled. At the dinner table RJ described how the electrical problems still had not been solved in one home and how the electrician guaranteed that he'd get the job done even if he had to work through the night to do it. Other problems kept creeping up, and RJ had to be "the problem solver." Many of these problems would throw the building schedule off, and RJ had to shuffle the subcontractors between building sites in order to accommodate the numerous mishaps found in each home.

A Failed Inspection and Tempers Flare

After a few days on the job, RJ felt like work was unmanageable. One home in particular was quite problematic since the electrician seemed absolutely baffled as to what the problem was with the wiring in the dining room yet did not inform RJ of this dilemma until the electrical inspector showed up for a scheduled appointment at the work site. Other problems were also evident in other homes, with at least one other home failing a framing inspection. RJ's reaction to all of this was simple. After "playing nice" with the subcontractors who were giving RJ problems, RJ decided to turn hard-hitting and give these subcontractors a tough talking to. Heated words were exchanged, and RJ and the subcontractors angrily parted company.

The Scene Is Set—Action!

That night, after the failed electrical inspection, Hodgetts was invited over to the Davis house for dinner so they could discuss the business and see how RJ's first few days on the job were working out. The dinner conversation started out in its usual jovial manner but eventually moved to a discussion of the progress being made on the construction site.

RJ gave a summary of the past few days, including the failed inspections and the tough time she was having managing the contractors. Davis and Hodgetts were absolutely silent through RJ's description of the situation, and everyone tried to keep their body language as controlled as possible. RJ finally came to an abrupt finish. This left a long pause for everyone else at the dinner table to fill with table talk or comments about the business. Before anyone could ask RJ a question about the building projects, she announced she was quitting the job. "I quit." Those two little words were dropped like an atomic bomb and seemed to burst across the dinner table at the Davis residence. RJ silenced the room, and then she quickly vacated the premises. No one uttered a sound—the devastation was complete and absolute.

Questions

1. Describe RJ's job as foreman in terms of its resource inputs. Which resource was causing her the most difficulties?

2. How would job analysis have helped RJ perform her job as foreman?

3. If Davis and Hodgetts were going to analyze the foreman's job, what method(s) should they employ?

4. If Davis and Hodgetts were going to design (or redesign) the foreman's job, what method(s) should they employ?

5. Describe how the team approach to job design might be helpful to Davis and Hodgetts when considering the foreman's position.

6. How might flexible techniques for job design help the firm better manage the subcontractors?

Case created by Herbert Sherman, PhD, and Theodore Vallas, Long Island University, Brooklyn Campus

• • • CASE 4-2 GAUGING EMPLOYMENT AT HONEYWELL

Honeywell is a diverse, differentiated industrial conglomerate with segments such as transportation systems, performance materials and technologies, aerospace, and automation and control solutions, yet the company is best known for its thermostats. According to the 2013 Fortune 500 list, Honeywell ranked 78th out of all US companies, with a revenue of $39 billion.

In 1999, Honeywell merged with AlliedSignal and Pittway but encountered problems when they realized that each company possessed its own unique corporate culture. During the next several years, Honeywell found itself addressing new challenges while trying to absorb its acquisitions. For example, environmental-related business liabilities had never been addressed and now required real attention, while managers were disinvesting in research and development because their divisions showed higher profits. New product development ceased. Honeywell also experienced high turnover in upper management, having three different CEOs in 4 years.[98]

Honeywell's main focus in the past decade has been on resolving these issues by first implementing their "One Honeywell" culture. This strategy increased overseas sales by 10% while also helping the company become more aware of and responsive to its environmental responsibilities. Investments in new products and services increased while turnover started to decrease, with employees filling more than 85% of the vacancies in top-level positions. Just as Honeywell turned the corner in 2008, the United States entered a recession and Honeywell's orders were being cancelled or postponed. No new orders were being placed, and sales were decreasing. As a result, direct costs of production were decreasing because the company simply did not need to purchase raw materials to make new products.[99]

In the manufacturing industry, the cost of people covers more than 30% of total expenses, and most firms responded to the recession by restructuring their workforce by firing thousands of employees. Cutting costs for production was not an option because a loss of customers is a major risk for the company; therefore, the only option left was cutting costs through employees. Honeywell knew that even the worst recessions usually last about 12 to 18 months, but the company wanted to be prepared when the economy started to heal.

With its new culture in place, Honeywell took a different approach than its competitors did. Honeywell projected the possible impact of economic recovery on its business, noting that it would have to rehire many of the employees it would lay off during the recession. Given this projection, Honeywell then followed a different method of restructuring and let its workers take furloughs, that is, temporary unpaid leaves of absence. Honeywell also knew that furloughs would harm the morale and loyalty of its employees. Even the employees who stayed would be distracted, thinking that their own jobs might be at stake. To benefit from furloughs, Honeywell limited their use by implementing more diligent performance reviews and avoiding hiring for new positions.

Honeywell CEO David Cote believed that most of his managers still overestimated the savings from layoffs and underestimated how disruptive layoffs would be given that the average employee received 6 months' worth of severance pay, meaning that Honeywell would only start saving money 6 months after the firm laid off an employee. However, the value of the employees' contributions was intangible since the firm might be losing its most skilled employees. The results of keeping the valuable employees were that Honeywell bounced back quicker than its competitors did after the recession and its business increased at a quicker pace.[100]

1. How does the use of HR forecasting reflect Honeywell's strategy and culture?

2. Which quantitative or qualitative manpower forecasting method do you believe Honeywell used to decide to move forward with furloughs rather than layoffs? Explain.

3. What options did Honeywell use to overcome the projected labor surplus during the recession? Were there other available options?

4. Compared to layoffs, do you expect the impact of furloughs to be higher on the turnover rate or lower? Explain your reasoning.

5. How might job analysis and job design minimize the impact of furloughs on organizational performance and productivity? How does hoteling fit into this scenario?

6. How could CEO Cote use trend/ratio/regression analysis to support his contention that most Honeywell managers overestimated their savings and underestimated how disruptive layoffs would be to the firm's operations?

Case created by Herbert Sherman, PhD, and Theodore Vallas, Long Island University, Brooklyn Campus

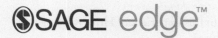

• • • SKILL BUILDER 4-1 JOB ANALYSIS

Objective

To develop your skill at completing a job analysis; to improve your ability to get ready

Skills

The primary skills developed through this exercise are as follows:

1. *HR management skills*—technical, business, and conceptual and design skills

2. *SHRM 2013 Curriculum Guidebook*—E: Job Analysis/Job Design

Overview

Your output is to arrive at school or work. Your inputs (4 Ms) are each and every task you perform until you arrive at your destination. Through your job analysis flowchart, improve the efficiency of your inputs so you can get more done in less time, with better results.

Step 1. Make a Flowchart

List step-by-step exactly what you do from the time you get up (or start your routine) until the time you start school or work. Get up or start earlier, say 15 minutes, to give you time to complete your flowchart without making you late. Be sure to number each step and list each activity separately with its M (don't just say go to the bathroom—list each activity in sequence while in there). For example:

1. Get up at 7:00—manpower
2. Go to bathroom—manpower
3. Take shower—material
4. Dry hair—material
. . .
18. Drive car—material
19. Buy coffee—money
20. Walk in to school at 8:00—manpower

Step 2. Analyze the Flowchart

Later in the day, when you have time, do a job simplification analysis of your flowchart of activities to determine if you can do the following:

— Eliminate: Are you doing anything that you don't need to do?

— Combine: Can you multitask any simple tasks, make fewer trips to the bathroom, etc.?

— Change Sequence: Will you be more efficient if you rearrange your flowchart of tasks?

3. Develop a New Flowchart

Based on your analysis, make a new flowchart that eliminates, combines, and changes the sequence of tasks you will perform to get ready more efficiently.

4. Change Your Routine

Consciously follow the steps of your new flowchart until it becomes your new habit.

Apply It

What did I learn from this experience? How will I use this knowledge in the future?

_____

_____

Your instructor may ask you to do this Skill Builder in class in a group. If so, the instructor will provide you with any necessary information or additional instructions.

● ● ● SKILL BUILDER 4-2 JOB CHARACTERISTICS MODEL (JCM)

Objective

To develop your skill at implementing the JCM

Skills

The primary skills developed through this exercise are as follows:

1. *HR management skills*—technical, business, and conceptual and design skills
2. *SHRM 2013 Curriculum Guidebook*—E: Job Analysis/Job Design

Preparation

Select a job you have now or have held in the past. Using Exhibit 4-3: The Job Characteristics Model and Exhibit 4-4: Job Design Options, Processes, and the JCM, apply these concepts to do a job analysis for your job. Be sure to use the exact terms from the text. The two exhibits provide a good summary of the process and terminology.

Apply It

What did I learn from this experience? How will I use this knowledge in the future?

_____

_____

Would you change your job to make it more motivational? If so, how and why?

Your instructor may ask you to do this Skill Builder in class in a group. If so, the instructor will provide you with any necessary information or additional instructions.

● ● ● SKILL BUILDER 4-3 O*NET

Objective

To visit O*Net and learn how to use Career Exploration Tools and/or to learn more about a job.

Skills

The primary skills developed through this exercise are as follows:

1. *HR Management skills*—technical, business, and conceptual and design skills
2. *SHRM 2013 Curriculum Guidebook*—E: Job Analysis/Job Design

Preparation

The instructor or student selects one or both options:

a. Select a job you would like to learn more about, visit http://www.onetonline.org, and search for the job. Write a brief report identifying your job search and state what you learned about the job.

b. Go to http://www.onetcenter.org. Click the "Products—Career Exploration Tools" link. From the drop-down menu, select "Computerized Interest Profile." In the overview, click either the full O*NET Interest Profiler or the Interest Profiler Short Form. Click "on the Web." Then take the Interest Profile and complete the self-assessment as instructed and get your results and print them. Write a brief report including your results and identifying what you learned about yourself.

Apply It

What did I learn from this experience? How will I use this knowledge in the future?

_____

_____

Your instructor may ask your to discuss your results in a group or as a class. If so, the instructor will provide you with any necessary information or additional instructions.

5 Recruiting Job Candidates

••• LEARNING OUTCOMES

After studying this chapter, you should be able to do the following:

5-1 Identify and discuss the primary goal of the recruiting process. PAGE 164

5-2 Briefly discuss the main external forces acting on recruiting efforts. PAGE 165

5-3 Discuss the major advantages and disadvantages of both internal and external recruiting. PAGE 169

5-4 Briefly discuss the major challenges and constraints involved in the recruiting process. PAGE 177

5-5 Discuss the value of a realistic job preview (RJP). PAGE 178

5-6 Discuss the characteristics needed in a capable recruiter. PAGE 178

5-7 Discuss the basic methods available for evaluating the recruiting process. PAGE 180

5-8 Define the key terms found in the chapter margins and listed following the Chapter Summary. PAGE 186

Practitioner's Perspective

Cindy describes the day that Angie timidly knocked at her door before she came into her office. Angie said, "I know I just started here last month, but I'm giving you my two weeks' notice. I just can't do this anymore."

"What seems to be the problem?" she asked.

"Well, when I accepted the job of quality administrative assistant, I never expected to actually have to go to the units to gather information as part of my work. Being around the patients makes me uncomfortable."

Uh-oh. Angie and Cindy just experienced the fallout from a process breakdown that apparently prevented her from getting a realistic preview of her job duties. Why does an honest exchange of information matter when you are recruiting? How does a high turnover rate impact your company? The factors you need to consider as you endeavor to attract and retain the best qualified candidates are highlighted in Chapter 5.

THE RECRUITING PROCESS

The costs associated with recruiting, selecting, and training new employees often add up to more than 100% of their annual salary.[1] Recruiting is important for many businesses,[2] but for **Zulily**, it is more difficult than for most other companies, as the company went from 329 to 1,100 employees in just 24 months.[3] In fact, in its 2013 annual SEC Form 10-K filing, Zulily noted that "We may not be able to hire new employees quickly enough to meet our needs."[4]

After we have determined our hiring needs through the forecasting process, and after we have done job analyses (providing job descriptions and job specifications), we need to recruit the correct numbers and types of people to fill our position openings. So the actual first step in matching employees and jobs is recruiting. We can't hire good employees without effectively recruiting them.[5]

But what are we attempting to do when we begin recruiting? Either we are trying to get people inside the company to apply for different job openings, or we are trying to get outsiders to join the company. In this section, you will learn about the recruiting process.

SHRM HR CONTENT

See Appendix: *SHRM 2013 Curriculum Guidebook* for the complete list

G. Outcomes: Metrics and Measurements of HR (required)
6. Calculating and interpreting yield ratios

I. Staffing: Recruitment and Selection (required)
2. External influences on staffing: Labor markets, unions, economic conditions, technology
3. External recruitment: Recruiters, open vs. targeted recruitment, recruitment sources, applicant reactions, medium (electronic, advertisement), fraud/misrepresentation
4. Internal recruitment: Timing, open/closed/targeted recruitment, bona fide seniority systems
5. Internal recruitment: Promotability ratings, managerial sponsorship, self/peer assessments, panels/review boards

So what is the goal of recruiting? Do we want to get a huge pool of people who want to join the organization, or do we want to find just a couple of skilled people who can do the job—in other words, discriminate in detail among reasonably qualified applicants? Well, it varies. At **Groupon**, they work to get the best people in the shortest time,[6] but if you think about it for just a minute, you will see that if you find too many applicants, it costs the organization too much to go through the selection process. On the other hand, if you find too few, there is no selection process, and you don't have the option to find the individual who best fits in the position and the organization.

Typically, a good rule of thumb might be to find about 15 to 25 people who want to be a part of the organization *for each opening*. That's just a rule of thumb, but it is probably going to allow an applicant pool. You can then probably cut that applicant pool to four or five pretty quickly, and that is a reasonable number of people from whom to choose a new member of the organization. You certainly don't want a massive number of recruits because it is too time-consuming and it costs the company too much to cull that number to a usable pool. However, especially when the unemployment rate is high, you may get more than 1,000 applications during the recruiting process if you don't target your recruiting correctly.

LO 5-1

Identify and discuss the primary goal of the recruiting process.

Recruiting The process of creating a reasonable pool of qualified candidates for a job opening

Defining the Process

Recruiting *is the process of creating a reasonable pool of qualified candidates for a job opening.* Notice that this definition identifies the fact that we need *qualified* applicants.[7] The process does us no good if the candidates whom we attract are not qualified to do the work. One of the most critical things that you have to do in the recruiting process is to determine very early in the process whether the individuals who are recruited are qualified. Thus, a good job analysis, including and up-to-date job description and specification, is helpful to the company and to the people looking for jobs because it helps everyone involved to know whether a given candidate is a match for a given job opening.

To fill an opening, potential job candidates must generally be made aware that the organization is seeking employees. They must then be persuaded to apply for the

• • • CHAPTER OUTLINE

jobs. In HR recruiting, we want to use a series of tools to show the candidates why they might want to become a part of the organization. We will discuss these tools as we go through the remainder of this chapter.

External Forces Acting on Recruiting Efforts

First, though, we want to identify the forces that affect our ability to successfully recruit new employees. There is a series of external forces that affect our ability to recruit individuals into our organization at a particular point in time.[8] One factor is the general shape of the national and world economies. During the 2008–2009 recession, 63% of HR executives said recruiting was cut back in their organizations.[9] In 2009, 48% of HR executives also had to manage layoffs, but by 2013, employers were becoming significantly concerned with "employee retention" and the cost of new hires.[10] Also, legal and regulatory changes such as the Affordable Care Act have had at least some effect on the hiring of part-time and temporary workers instead of full-time employees.[11] In one 2013 survey, 59% of CFOs reported that they increased the proportion of their workforce made up of temporary and part-time workers or that they shifted toward outside advisers and consultants. Among these firms shifting away from full-time employment, 38% said the shift had occurred, in part, due to implementation of the Affordable Care Act.[12]

Think about what is happening around you right now. Is the unemployment rate high or low? Are there government incentives to increase hiring of the unemployed, or is government doing very little to increase employment? Is the available supply of people with advanced skills very large, or are there not enough people with high-level skill sets available to companies? All of these things affect your ability to recruit new workers into your company.

Generally, the external forces acting on recruiting fall into two large categories: the available labor market and the social and legal environment. Let's take a quick look at each.

THE LABOR MARKET. The availability of talent to fill our needs depends on several items in the labor market.[13] The **labor market** *is the external pool of candidates from which we draw our recruits.*

Supply and demand and the unemployment rate. First, we must consider the *supply and demand* factors in a particular category of jobs. If we are in need of a mechanical engineer, how many mechanical engineers are available in the labor environment? Are there too many for the available number of jobs, or are there more jobs than engineers? If there is a large pool of engineers desiring a job in their field, then our job of recruiting one will be significantly easier than if there are very few available and lots of job openings.

This issue of supply and demand usually ties in directly with the *unemployment rate* in an area. Every business recruits primarily from an identifiable geographic area. Some will recruit locally (perhaps within a metropolitan area or a single city). Others will recruit regionally or nationally, while still others may recruit internationally. We need to identify our recruiting area and then determine what the unemployment rate is in that area. If unemployment is high, the job of recruiting is generally easier than if unemployment is very low. However, even when the unemployment rate in the United States was around 10% in 2010 and 2011 and there were thousands of people looking for jobs, there was a shortage of qualified candidates for some highly skilled jobs.[14]

Competitors. We also have to consider our *competitors* and how much they contend with us for the available talent in a particular field. If competition is very strong for available technical talent such as mechanical engineers—for instance, if there are a significant number of competitors and each competitor needs a large number of engineers—then it will be a more difficult recruiting environment.[15] Similarly, if there

LO 5-2

Briefly discuss the main external forces acting on recruiting efforts.

SHRM

I:2
External Influences on Staffing: Labor Markets, Unions, Economic Conditions, Technology

Labor market The external pool of candidates from which we draw our recruits

aren't many competitors who need a particular type of mechanical engineer and are working to attract such applicants to their business, then the recruiting environment will likely be much less difficult. So our recruiting environment depends on the labor market and on our competitors.

SOCIAL AND LEGAL ENVIRONMENT. The social environment in the country in which we are operating also affects our ability to recruit new people into our organizations.[16] Today, people put more weight on "me time" and job satisfaction than they did in past years, and as a result, workers look at the social environment in the organization to make decisions concerning whether or not to apply for a job there. In many cases, new employees also expect a high level of benefits and good opportunities for training and development.[17] As a result, the social environment drives our ability to recruit our 21st century workforce.

We also have to take into account the various laws that limit the ways in which we can recruit. First and most obviously, we have to abide by all of the EEO laws that we discussed in Chapter 3, and we must avoid any issues of discrimination in our recruiting efforts. So, this is another area in which we could apply the OUCH test to ensure fairness and equity in our processes. There are also laws in some situations that limit our ability to lure employees away from competitor firms. In other cases, labor agreements may limit our ability to recruit, or the union itself may be able to place limits on our ability to recruit from outside of the union's ranks. We may also choose to recruit more part-timers due to the costs involved with the new health care law. In addition, non-compete agreements might not allow us to recruit certain individuals who are bound by such agreements. State laws might also apply to recruiting in certain industries or to recruiting certain types of employees. HR managers must therefore be well versed in the various laws, agreements, and regulations that in any way limit their ability to recruit.

ORGANIZATIONAL RECRUITING CONSIDERATIONS

Once we become aware of the limitations that are placed on us by the labor market and the legal environment, we can start to consider the internal issues that control our recruiting processes. When should we go through the recruiting process, what alternatives do we have to recruiting (outsourcing, retraining, etc.), and should we recruit our applicants from internal sources (within the company) or external sources? We have to set policies on these topics in order to maintain consistency, and we need consistency in order to be fair and equitable and so that we can defend our processes if it becomes necessary. So, what do we have to think about, and in what level of detail?

What Policies to Set

We have to think about a lot of things as we work to allay a shortage of people within the company. We need to determine *how* we are going to go through the recruiting process before we start trying to recruit new members into our workforce. Among other things, we have to answer the following questions:

- Under what conditions will we recruit new people into the company?
- What alternatives do we have, and when will we use them?
- Should we recruit locally, regionally, nationally, or globally?
- Are we going to recruit from within our own ranks first or go outside the organization first?
- What primary recruiting sources will provide us with the best recruits for our company?

We have to make these determinations based on our particular company circumstances, taking into account all of the information from our forecasting processes. Let's discuss four of the primary items we will need to think about before the recruiting process starts.

When to Recruit

The answer seems obvious: We recruit when we need someone to fill a job. But it's not that simple. We don't necessarily have to recruit someone when we need a job filled. Remember what we said in Chapter 4. There are all kinds of ways to mitigate a worker shortage in the organization, and which one we choose depends on a bunch of different factors. Should we recruit or bring in temp workers? Should we add overtime or outsource some tasks? We need to identify the points at which we would generally go through the process of starting and carrying out a recruitment campaign, because the campaign itself is expensive. We don't want to go through a long recruiting process and then figure out that we didn't need to—if we did, we would just be wasting money.

Alternatives to Recruitment

Do we have a viable and financially feasible way to solve our shortage other than through recruitment? Is the alternative less expensive or better for our circumstances in some

Google campus and Google bikes. Google is famous for great benefits and a lively social environment for its employees.

other way? We don't want to recruit new employees into the organization if working a group of people overtime for a week or two, or even a month or two, will solve our problem. We may be prohibited from recruiting because of an attrition policy or a hiring freeze. We might be able to solve our problem with temporary employees instead of new full-time workers.

We have to weigh all of the available options, and we should generally have a policy that tells us when we would use each option. We need to know what the primary objectives of the organization are so that we can analyze the possibility of outsourcing (we don't want to outsource a critical task).[18] We also need to know how much overtime is currently being used so that we can know whether we are working our current employees to the point where their job satisfaction is likely to start going down.[19]

What kind of labor market is our industry in right now? If we are in a market where there are many people out of work, we may be able to get a much better new hire right now, so it might be best to recruit for new employees. Conversely, if we are in a tight labor market, we might waste a lot of resources trying to recruit new employees because we might end up getting no good candidates. We need to analyze each of the options for mitigating a labor shortage other than making new hires, and we need to create a policy concerning when each of these options is useful in our organization. We have to take all factors that we know into account in making our recruiting decision.

Reach of the Recruiting Effort

Next, we need to identify our effective labor market. Do we plan to recruit only from local sources? Should we consider people all over a particular region (e.g., the mid-South or New England)? Do we need to recruit globally or even internationally?[20] The answer, again, is "It depends."

What factors are involved with our decision? The first factor is simple: Can we find the right number and types of employees if we recruit locally? If so, then we may be able to work only in our local labor market. If not, we may be forced to recruit from a broader pool of talent. Secondly, can we get better talent to apply if we recruit regionally, nationally, or globally? Additionally, do we need this type of talent in order to accomplish our organizational goals? (Remember, if we are a low-cost producer, we may not want top-notch talent in all areas of our company.) Is the job that we are recruiting for so specialized that we need to recruit from all over the world? Do we want to recruit from locations far away from our organization if we don't have to? Of course not. It is time-consuming and expensive to bring people to the organization from far away. So we only expand our geographic recruiting area when we need to. However, remember that multinational corporations tend to hire locally, but many of their total employees are from other countries.

Social Media Recruiting

Many firms are now heavily using social media sites, including LinkedIn and Facebook, to assist with their recruiting efforts. These social media sites can provide recruiters with much more reach than they had in the past.[21] However, this reach also brings with it some significant issues for the business—such as having to pore over thousands of résumés in response to a job opening or being taken to court over what someone sees as a written promise that a job will have certain characteristics. *Wagner v. Home Depot* is an example of a case in which the plaintiff sued the organization for false promises of stable long-term employment.[22] So how do you get the value of social media without exacerbating the problems that the use of social media recruiting sources can cause? You have to understand social media's reach and use it selectively, whether you're a job seeker or a recruiter.

In a recruiting situation, social media provides a number of valuable services. As mentioned, it provides a reach that the company may not get with other means such as advertising in local newspapers or on radio or television. For example, at the end of 2013, **Facebook** had more than 1.23 billion monthly active users, meaning it gives recruiters a huge reach into the global labor market.[23] And especially in higher-level job recruiting, where there will be few individuals with the necessary skills, social media job sites like **LinkedIn** (225 million users in 2013), **Jobvite**, or **Monster.com** can get our message out to a much larger group of potential candidates across the country or even around the world.[24] In fact, in 2013, LinkedIn was being used by almost 90% of the Fortune 100 firms to track potential candidates. The online research and networking opportunities provided by such sites give the recruiter information on job candidates, in many cases before they are even directly contacted.

Second, social media sites like Facebook can also provide the candidate with information on our company values and culture.[25] Corporate profile information can help individuals make a better decision concerning whether or not they would be comfortable in our organization, which in turn lowers the possibility that they will take the job and then end up leaving within a few weeks or months. And even though Facebook is primarily a personal networking site, company recruiters can use new software programs like **BeKnown** that provide them with the ability to directly target and recruit new employees on Facebook.[26]

Additionally, in many cases, the recruiter or the individual candidate has connections on LinkedIn or Facebook that allow the recruiter to get information on the other party and, in some cases, get an introduction. An introduction from someone you know who also knows the person you are trying to contact is an extremely valuable tool in the matching process between candidate and company.[27] The networking opportunities on these sites should be neither ignored nor taken for granted. One seemingly innocent slip can have outsize consequences online since, as we all know by now, information on the Internet seldom if ever dies. So you have to be on guard when using social networking sites for your job search.

So are there any problems with social media recruiting? Yes, and some of them are significant dangers to the company. For instance, there is the potential for discrimination through disparate treatment of individuals because of information posted on their Facebook or LinkedIn sites or on their Twitter feed. A Carnegie Mellon University study found that candidates who identified themselves as Muslim on their Facebook profiles "were less likely to be called for interviews than [were] Christian applicants."[28] Pictures can also potentially identify individuals as members of a protected class, and those pictures may cause subconscious bias on the part of some recruiters. Any bias, whether intentional or unintentional, is a danger to the organization during the recruiting and hiring process.

Another thing that is at least anecdotally an issue is the potential for "goldplating," or creating massive and complex requirements in a job specification. Ironically, one example comes from the CEO of **LinkedIn**, Jeff Weiner. He noted that when his company first identified the need for a data center manager, its initial (large) list of criteria for acceptable candidates was analyzed and the company "found only seven identifiable people on Earth who met all of the conditions."[29] Once management relaxed the requirements by getting rid of some that were really not required, they quickly found 126 potential candidates. There is some evidence that this process of creating a massive catalog of qualifications that a firm would like to have but that is really not necessary is one reason companies believe they are experiencing a shortage of "qualified" employees. So we have to be careful to identify only necessary information and candidate characteristics when recruiting via social media to avoid unnecessary problems.

INTERNAL OR EXTERNAL RECRUITING?

What is our policy going to be concerning recruitment from our current pool of employees? We can very rarely just say that we will "promote from within" and stick to that policy. So we have to create policies concerning when and how we will recruit from our current employee pool and when we will go outside the organization. Why? Probably the biggest reason is so that our employees perceive fairness in our recruiting policies.

If we say we will recruit from within and then go outside the organization to recruit a new manager, many of our employees will begin to think that we were "just talking" when we said we would promote internally, and they might begin to show less loyalty to the organization because they feel that the organization failed to show them loyalty. However, if our policies say that we will go outside for recruits when it is unlikely that anyone in the organization would have the skill set necessary to do the job identified in our job specification, then we can provide a legitimate answer to someone who questions our recruiting process.

Additionally, we might have a policy that says that when we are instituting new processes or when we have identified significant resistance to change as an issue in a section of the organization, we will bring in new people with new ideas and different skills. We may also identify specific occupations in our organization that will typically be recruited from outside, usually due to the need for a specialized skill set (e.g., nuclear plant operator, corporate attorney, or emergency medical technician). It is unlikely that we would promote from within to these types of positions.

WORK
APPLICATION 5-3

Select a future job (preferably after graduation) and state the geographic area in which you will apply for jobs.

LO 5-3

Discuss the major advantages and disadvantages of both internal and external recruiting.

WORK
APPLICATION 5-4

Select an organization you work or have worked for and give an example of either an open, targeted, or closed recruiting method it uses. List the job(s) that method was used to recruit for.

These are just some of the things that we need to consider as we create our recruiting policies. Now, let's take a closer look at internal versus external recruiting efforts. Although we already noted that we need policies concerning these options, we need to look more closely at what the advantages and disadvantages of each approach are.

Internal Recruiting

Internal recruiting *involves filling job openings with current employees or people the employees know.* Here we will discuss internal recruiting sources, promotability ratings and managerial sponsorship, and the advantages and disadvantages of internal recruiting.

INTERNAL RECRUITING SOURCES. There are two common types of internal recruiting:

- *Promotions from within.* Many organizations post job openings on physical or electronic bulletin boards, in company newsletters, and so on. Current employees may apply or bid for the open positions. Cisco Systems works hard to promote its internal hiring practices.[30] Moves today are frequently lateral rather than in the form of promotions. Southwest Airlines has experienced a slowdown in growth and is overstaffed in some areas, and it is encouraging employees to move about in the company rather than laying them off.[31]
- *Employee referrals.* Employees may be encouraged to refer friends and relatives for positions. About 40% of new hires at **Groupon** historically come from employee referrals.[32] **Jobvite** notes that 44% of its client-company new hires are from existing employee referrals.[33] For hard-to-recruit-for jobs, some firms pay a bonus to employees when their referred applicant is hired.

SHRM

l:4

Internal Recruitment: Timing, Open/ Closed/Targeted, Bona Fide Seniority Systems

OPEN, TARGETED, OR CLOSED RECRUITING? When it comes to promotion from within as an internal recruiting method, the organization has several options. We can use open, targeted, or closed recruiting methods.[34] *Open recruiting* consists of advertising the job openly within the organization, and anyone who meets the qualifications can apply for the job opening.

Targeted recruiting is pretty much what it sounds like. We do not openly advertise the position internally. Instead, we ask managers to privately nominate workers who they feel would be able to do the job that needs to be filled. HR will then evaluate the candidates put forward by the managers and then forward the list of the best candidates to the hiring manager. We have to be more careful with targeted recruiting because it can allow or appear to allow bias in the recruiting and selection process.

Finally, *closed recruiting* occurs when hiring managers have a need to fill a position and they communicate that need to HR. HR recruiters will then search the organization's files for people who have the requisite skills and qualifications and send a list of such individuals to the hiring manager. The hiring manager can then select from the applicants identified by the HR department.

One of the difficult issues the organization may run into if it chooses an internal recruiting option is the presence of a bona fide seniority system, meaning a system that gives preference to individuals with longer tenure in the organization. If we have such a system, we may have to allow people with more seniority to apply for any internal job openings, which would limit our ability to use targeted or closed recruiting.

SHRM

l:5

Internal Recruitment: Promotability Ratings, Sponsorship, Assessments, Review Boards

Internal recruiting Filling job openings with current employees or people the employees know

PROMOTABILITY RATINGS AND MANAGERIAL SPONSORSHIP. We can do some things within the organization to make the internal recruiting process go a bit smoother in

5-1 APPLYING THE CONCEPT

Internal Recruiting

Review the following list of recruitment methods and then write the letter corresponding to each recruitment method before the situation(s) in which it was used.

    a. open

    b. targeted

    c. closed

_____ 1.   My supervisor got promoted to middle management and selected me to be his replacement.

_____ 2.   My company has a policy of posting all job openings, and we can apply for better jobs that we want.

_____ 3.   I got the job as supervisor in the other department because the VP of production recommended me for the position.

_____ 4.   My company stopped placing want ads in the newspaper, and it only posts openings online.

_____ 5.   I got the entry-level job because the HR representative sent me for an interview with the hiring manager.

---

most cases. As part of our annual appraisal process, we can include a "promotability rating" for each member of the organization.[35] This rating evaluates the individual for fitness for higher-level jobs in the organization. If we do it as part of our normal appraisal process, it adds very little to the workload of the managers in the company.

We may use some other tools to assess promotability in our efforts to find the best qualified individuals within the organization. We can have each of our employees complete a self-assessment, and we can also ask peers to assess their coworkers for promotability. We can also have people who desire to be considered for promotion put themselves before an organizational review board that will judge their qualifications and readiness for such promotion opportunities. Each of these options strengthens the ability of the organization to get the best possible candidates for internal promotion opportunities.

We can also request *managerial sponsorship* for a person to be considered for job opportunities through internal recruiting. In this case, we would ask managers to provide their sponsorship for an individual before that person would be considered for a promotion through the internal recruiting process. This sponsorship information would then be used in our internal recruiting efforts. This is a type of mentoring.

ADVANTAGES AND DISADVANTAGES OF INTERNAL RECRUITING. Is it generally a good idea to recruit from inside the organization? What are the major advantages and disadvantages of internal recruiting?

Advantages include the following:

- Possible increases in organizational commitment and job satisfaction based on the opportunity to advance in the organization with commensurate increases in pay
- The internal recruit will be able to learn more about the "big picture" in the company and become more valuable.
- The individual also has shown at least some interest in the organization, has knowledge of our operations and processes, and feels comfortable continuing employment within the company.
- The company has existing knowledge of the applicant and a record of that person's previous work.
- The organization can save money by recruiting internally, because of both lower advertisement costs and lower training costs.
- Internal recruiting is usually faster than external recruiting.

And here are some of the disadvantages:

- The pool of applicants is significantly smaller in internal recruiting.
- There will still be a job to fill—the employee will move from somewhere else in the organization into the new job, so that employee's old job will need to be filled as well.
- Success in one job doesn't necessarily mean success in a significantly different job, especially if the employee is promoted to supervise former coworkers.
- An external candidate may have better qualifications for the job opening.
- Current employees may feel that they are entitled to the job whether they are capable and qualified or not, especially if we have a strong policy of preferring internal candidates.
- And the biggest threat to the company: We may create or perpetuate a strong resistance to change or stifle creativity and innovation because everyone in the organization, even the "new hires," are part of the old organizational culture.

External Recruiting

SHRM

I:3
External Recruitment: Recruiters, Open vs. Targeted, Sources, etc.

Employees who are changing jobs influence organizational performance, and companies commonly recruit people from other firms to satisfy their HR needs.[36] *External recruiting is the process of engaging individuals from the labor market outside the firm to apply for a job.* External recruiting can also be accomplished in either an open or targeted manner, in much the same way as internal recruiting can. If we have an open recruiting effort, we will provide the job information for anyone who wishes to apply. If, however, we are using targeted recruiting (for example, through a head-hunter) we would seek out specific individuals with the necessary skills and invite them to apply for the job opening.

EXTERNAL RECRUITING SOURCES. When we decide to recruit from external sources, what options do we have? Where would you recruit? Again, the answer is "It depends." Recall that we are trying to get a reasonable pool of applicants. So which option will give you the best pool of applicants for the specific job? We have to look at the type of person that we are trying to find and then go to the source or sources that will most likely provide that type of person.

Here are our external recruiting options. They are also listed with a summary of strengths in Exhibit 5-1.

Walk-ins. Without actually being recruited, good candidates may come to an organization "cold" and ask for a job. Those seeking management-level positions generally tend to send a résumé and cover letter asking for an interview. Walk-ins may be good recruits for a couple of reasons. First, they have already selected your organization as an employment target because they took the initiative to come in and ask for a job. Second, there are no advertising costs associated with walk-ins, and you don't have to wait for résumés and applications to come in from an external advertisement. So the process can occur much more quickly than it would with other external recruiting methods.

Educational institutions. Recruiting takes place at high schools, vocational/technical schools, and colleges/universities. Many schools offer career-planning and placement services to aid students and potential employers. Educational institutions are good places to recruit people who have little or no prior experience. We might decide to recruit from educational institutions for a new external hire if we need somebody with a good general skill set, a degree, and some basic education. Such recruits will probably have a lot of specialized education in a specific field, which is always good. If you are looking for that type of person, a college/university might be a good place to go. If you are currently in school, have you visited your career services

External recruiting The process of engaging individuals from the labor market outside the firm to apply for a job

department? You don't have to wait for senior year, when you are about to graduate, to take advantage of what they have to offer.

Employment agencies. There are three major types of employment agencies:

Temporary agencies, like **Kelly Services** and **Accountemps,** provide part- or full-time help for limited periods. They are useful for replacing employees who will be out for a short period of time or for supplementing the regular workforce during busy periods. However, today, organizations are reluctant to add to their permanent workforce and instead create short- and long-term temporary positions (sometimes called *permatemps*) or contractual agreements with outside workers (i.e., independent contractors). Nearly 20% of individuals working in the United States are now working under such arrangements, and some HR experts expect that number to continue to increase.[37]

However, you should be cautioned here concerning the long-term use of temporary workers. There have been a number of lawsuits against employers in the past 10 years dealing with the hiring of "temporary" workers, when in fact those workers were permanent—just without the benefits associated with the company's full-time permanent workforce. As we briefly noted in Chapter 4, probably the most famous and one of the most expensive settlements came in the case of **Microsoft** using permatemp workers in the 1990s. A class action lawsuit was filed and was being heard in the US Ninth Circuit Court of Appeals when Microsoft agreed to settle with the permatemp workers for nearly $100 million.[38]

Public agencies are state employment services. They generally provide job candidates to employers at no cost or very low cost. One of the best and most often overlooked sources for external recruits, public employment agencies provide potential employees at all levels of the exempt and nonexempt workforce due to the fact that anyone who seeks unemployment assistance must be on the public employment agency rolls for possible employment. Too often, the public agencies get reputations as havens for the hard-core unemployed—those who do not want to work. However, they can be a strong source of good-quality employees, especially in bad economic conditions when many good workers lose their jobs. And the cost can't be beat.

Private employment agencies are privately owned and charge a fee for their services. These agencies generally do a lot of prescreening for companies searching for employees, which can mitigate some of the agency fees. These agencies are generally good for recruiting people with prior experience. There are several different types of private employment agencies:

- *General employment agencies* operate on a for-profit basis. Some of them charge job seekers for their services, and others charge the employer. These agencies usually do not specialize in a particular type of employee, but some may only operate in certain employment categories such as IT or accounting employment.

- *Contingency agencies* offer employees to the employer and are paid when the job candidate is hired by the employer. Contingency agencies frequently work with a more skilled set of clients—those with high-level manufacturing skills or mid-level management skills, for example, would be common candidates for contingency agencies.

- *Retained search firms or executive recruiters* are paid to search for a specific type of recruit for the organization and will be paid regardless of success in their recruiting efforts. Often referred to as "headhunters," they specialize in recruiting senior managers and/or those with specific high-level technical skills, like engineers and computer experts. They tend to charge the employer a large fee and will be at least partially paid whether or not there is a successful hire. Usually, the retained search firm will be paid in three installments,

Many companies now recruit candidates on social media sites, such as LinkedIn.

with the first installment being nonrefundable. The installments might be split as percentages—40/30/30—with the first installment due on signing the contract, the second due around 90 days afterward, and the third due on successful completion of the hiring process. According to CFO.com, "The cost of retaining a search firm can equal about 30 percent of a new hire's signing bonus, moving expenses, and first-year cash salary combined."[39] So if your organization is looking for a high-level manager at a salary level of about $100,000, it might cost almost that much to find a candidate using a headhunter. Therefore, retained search firms won't generally be used for anything but high-level employee searches.

Advertising. It is important to use the appropriate source to reach qualified candidates. A simple "Help Wanted" sign in the window is an advertisement. Newspapers are places to advertise positions, but advertising in professional and trade magazines may be more suitable for specific professional recruiting. There are also several online job search websites, such as Monster.com and CareerBuilder.com.

No matter which advertising option we use, however, we have to be aware of the potential for fraud and/or misrepresentation in our advertisements. As we noted earlier, if we knowingly (or in some cases, even unknowingly) provide misleading information, we can make the organization vulnerable to a lawsuit over fraud or misrepresentation. This is obviously something that we don't want to do, so we need to check our ads for factual errors and exaggeration before we put them out to the public. Once we have checked our ads to ensure accuracy, our options for advertising include the following:

Local mass media. Is the *Daily Planet* (Thanks, Superman!), Channel 5, or the oldies FM radio station a good option for your recruiting dollars? As usual, it depends on what kind of candidate you are looking for. Is advertising on local mass media a good option if you are looking for a lawyer or a nuclear physicist? Would it be the best place to spend your money? Maybe not. The cost per person reached by this form of advertising is very low, but you might not reach the people you are looking for.

What type of people would you look for through local mass media? Semiskilled or skilled line employees might be a good target for this type of advertisement, especially if you need a large number of them for a specific type of job. For example, when **Southwest Airlines** opened up a call center in Arkansas in the 1990s, it placed local newspaper, radio, and television ads for customer service representatives. Southwest wanted to find a large number of people (initially about 400 employees) with a basic skill set: the ability to interact with customers and solve their travel problems. The ads resulted in several thousand people applying for the customer service jobs that Southwest was trying to fill—a good 15-to-1 candidate pool, as we noted earlier.

Specialized publications. Publications that target specific groups of people—such as the *Wall Street Journal*, the *Financial Times*, or *APICS Magazine*—may be good sources of new recruits. There are many other examples of this type of specialty publication. Almost all of these publications have help-wanted advertisements similar to the local newspaper, but the ads tend to be targeted to a specific group of potential recruits. *APICS Magazine* would be a good source if your company was looking for a production or operations manager. The *Wall Street Journal* might be best if you were looking for someone for a senior level executive position, and the *Financial Times* could be a good source of financial managers and executives. However, if you are looking for a lower-level employee, these would probably not be the place to go. Ads in such specialty publications are more expensive and have less reach than do ads in the local mass media, but they are much more targeted toward the type of recruit that you may be looking for.

The Internet. What kind of people would you advertise for using the Internet? Should your company put every job opening up on the Internet? If you do, how many applicants are you going to get for each job opening? In many cases, companies are discovering that they may not want to advertise every job opening on the Internet because of its reach.[40] They just don't have the time to wade through thousands of applications for a single opening.

It seems that everybody is on the Internet today, but that isn't true, even in the United States. Around 85% of Americans are on the Internet,[41] but that still leaves 1 out of every 6 people whom you wouldn't reach via Internet recruitment. And in other countries, the percentage of people without access is significantly higher than in the United States, so international recruiting efforts via the Internet may not give you the results that you desire. In fact, overall Internet access worldwide is only about 40%.[42] The Internet is a good advertising medium for certain types of jobs, but not for every job.

What kinds of job openings would you want to advertise using the Internet? Jobs requiring computer or other high-level technical skills would probably have good potential for Internet recruitment, because technical people would tend to use the Internet more than people in nontechnical fields. But would you advertise for a five-star chef on the Internet? Unlikely. What about a janitor? Probably not. How is a five-star chef generally going to find a job? Most likely, a talented chef will find work through the use of recommendations and talking to people that the chef knows in the restaurant business. Word-of-mouth works well in this type of industry.

For people whom you will recruit from the local workforce and who have general skills (such as construction workers), it is unlikely that you will find them using the Internet. You have to look at what type of recruit you are looking for and ask whether the Internet is a logical place to advertise.

You might also want to use the Internet to recruit new employees using professional associations such as the Society for Human Resource Management (SHRM). SHRM puts employment advertisements on its website; go to http://www.shrm.org and take a look at SHRMs HR Jobs link. Professional associations give us the ability to reach highly specialized individuals with specific skill sets.

See Exhibit 5-1 for a review of internal and external recruiting sources.

ADVANTAGES AND DISADVANTAGES OF EXTERNAL RECRUITING. What are the advantages and disadvantages of external recruiting?

Advantages include the following:

- The first and biggest advantage is the mirror image of the biggest disadvantage in internal recruiting—we *avoid* creating or perpetuating resistance to change, allowing a foothold for innovative new ways of operating.
- We may be able to find individuals with complex skill sets who are not available internally.
- We can lower training costs for skilled positions by externally hiring someone with the requisite skills.
- External hires will frequently increase organizational diversity.

EXHIBIT 5-1 MAJOR RECRUITING SOURCES

Internal Sources	Strengths
A. Promotion from within	Provides current employees new job opportunities within the firm
B. Employee referral	Inexpensive recruiting based on employee knowledge of the candidate

External Sources	Strengths
C. Walk-ins	Inexpensive and self-selected
D. Educational institutions	Good basic skill sets; typically less expensive than others with more experience
E. Temporary agencies	Prescreened workers; useful in short-term shortage situations
F. Public agencies	At least some prescreening; public employment agencies are very inexpensive
G. Private agencies	Heavy prescreening of recruits, lowering organizational prescreening costs; typically very well targeted; good for experienced recruits
H. Local mass media	Fairly broad reach if searching for many recruits; cost per person is low; good for semiskilled or skilled line employees
I. Specialized publications	Good for targeting specific types of recruits; fairly good reach; fairly low cost per person
J. Internet	Very broad reach; beginning to be able to target to specific audiences as many professional organizations have sites

---

5-2 APPLYING THE CONCEPT

Recruiting Sources

Using Exhibit 5-1: Major Recruiting Sources, write the letter (A–J) of which recruiting source is most appropriate in each of the following recruiting situations:

____ 6. You need a CEO from outside the company.

____ 7. "We need more employees, Jean. Do you know anyone interested in working for us?"

____ 8. We need to hire a new history professor.

____ 9. We need another computer programmer.

____ 10. A worker got hurt on the job and will be out for a week.

____ 11. We need an experienced clerical worker, but we don't have any money for ads.

____ 12. We need a person to perform routine cleaning services, and experience is not necessary.

____ 13. The VP of finance needs a new administrative assistant.

____ 14. We have a supervisor retiring in a month.

____ 15. We like to hire young people without experience in order to train them to sell using a unique approach.

What about disadvantages? There are certainly potential problems in bringing outsiders into the company:

- Disruption of the work team due to introducing significantly different ways of operating

- External recruiting takes much longer, which means it costs more.
- Might adversely affect current employees' motivation and satisfaction due to the perceived inability to move up in the organization
- Likely will incur higher orientation and training costs than internal recruiting
- The candidate may look great on paper, but we have no organizational history on the individual.

CHALLENGES AND CONSTRAINTS IN RECRUITING

The process of recruiting is expensive and time-consuming. As a result, we want to pay attention to the effectiveness of our recruiting methods. Some methods can give us too many new recruits to review, costing us valuable time and money. Other options will not give us enough of a pool so that we have some flexibility in whom to choose, while still other options will cost too much for the results that we get. So the process of recruiting new employees has to be targeted a bit better than we may think.

All management functions are subject to constraints and challenges, and the recruiting function is no different. We have to live within certain rules and policies while still making it possible to bring in the right kinds of people in the right numbers. Let's discuss some of the most significant issues that we face in the recruiting function.

Budgetary Constraints

Probably the most obvious constraint is money. We have to live within our budgets in all cases, and recruiting is no exception. There are times when we would like to fly half a dozen top-notch recruits in from around the world to interview for a position, but such costs add up very quickly. We would need to look very carefully at whether or not funds were available and whether such a recruitment effort were necessary due to the key nature of the job being filled. We might agree to incur the cost if the position being filled was important enough, but we would not do so for a less significant job. Our budgets should always be created with the type of job that is being filled in mind.

Policy Constraints and Organizational Image

There are many *organizational policies* that can affect our recruiting efforts. We have to be familiar with such policies in detail to take them into account as we go through the recruiting process. Below are some of the policies that affect recruiting.

Whether we have a *promote-from-within* policy or not affects how we recruit. Our policies on *temporary-to-permanent* employees would also affect how we recruit in most cases. Do we have policies concerning *recruiting and hiring relatives* of current employees? If so, this would affect our recruiting efforts. Such a policy might significantly limit our ability to get referrals from current employees. Do we have an *affirmative action policy* in the organization? If so, it will dictate many of our recruiting procedures. We may also have a *policy on how and when we communicate with any recruits* or job applicants. If so, we need to understand and follow it.

We are also affected in our recruiting efforts by our *organizational image* in the markets from which we source our recruits.[43] You may know of a company in your local community that you would rather not work for because of its bad reputation. Conversely, you might also know of an employer that you would very much like to work for because of its stellar reputation. Organizational image can play a significant part in determining our ability to source the people we need from the communities around us. A few organizations have lists of the best places to

WORK APPLICATION 5-5

Identify the recruiting source that was used to hire you for your current job or a past job and explain how it was used.

LO 5-4

Briefly discuss the major challenges and constraints involved in the recruiting process.

WORK APPLICATION 5-6

Explain how a firm's image played a role in your applying for and accepting a job you currently hold or have held.

Job candidates need a realistic job preview to understand what the job is all about.

LO 5-5

Discuss the value of a realistic job preview (RJP).

 ESR

WORK
APPLICATION 5-7

Briefly describe the RJP you received for your present job or a past job. How could the RJP be improved?

LO 5-6

Discuss the characteristics needed in a capable recruiter.

Realistic job preview (RJP) A review of all of the tasks and requirements of the job, both good and bad

work, including *Fortune*'s "100 Best Companies to Work For." Companies listed include **Quicken Loans, USAA, Google, SAS,** and **Scripps Health.**[44] This is just one of many reasons why we want to maintain a strong reputation in the communities that we serve.

Job Characteristics and the Realistic Job Preview (RJP)

Let's face it. Not every job we need to fill is glamorous. Perhaps you have seen the show *Dirty Jobs* with Mike Rowe. Mike takes on jobs that most of us would not want to do, at least not on a routine basis. Almost all organizations have such jobs, whether they be facilities jobs such as housekeeping or nursing aide jobs where we might be emptying bedpans (or worse). Even though some of our jobs are not glamorous, we need to find and recruit people to do them. The more difficult, dangerous, or just downright nasty a job is, the more difficult it is to recruit people into it. Still, there are people out there who are willing to do each of them. We just need to do the work required to find them and get them to apply. As discussed in the last chapter, the key to success is matching the right person to the job.

Speaking of jobs that most of us would not want to do, should we hide the bad side of a job from recruits? This is really not an ethical thing to do and is not a good idea if we are looking at success in filling the job for the long term. Most companies have come to the conclusion that realistic job previews are a necessary part of the recruiting process. A **realistic job preview (RJP)** *is a review of all of the tasks and requirements of the job, both good and bad*. A good job analysis (Chapter 4) with a clear job description should provide a good RJP. We have found that "giving applicants a warts-and-all preview of what a job entails on a day-to-day basis can reduce turnover effectively by making sure the applicant is really a good fit for the job."[45]

Why would we want to tell people the bad parts of the job? Well, what do you think it would do to their job satisfaction, organizational commitment, and productivity levels if we hid the bad part of the job from them? Satisfaction and organizational commitment would almost certainly go down, and this would happen literally right after taking the job. Is this what we want to do in a recruiting situation? How likely is it that a person would quit very early on if they felt like they were lied to in order to get them to accept the job? And if they do quit, we incur all of our recruiting costs again, almost immediately. There is strong research evidence that an early turnover in a job is directly related to failure to provide an RJP for that job.[46]

The Recruiter–Candidate Interaction

Does the recruiter (or recruiters) affect the job candidates and their willingness to apply for a job in our organization? The obvious answer is yes. The recruiter is, in fact, one of the primary factors responsible for an applicant showing interest in our organization and our jobs.[47] What kind of recruiter do we need in a particular hiring situation? How does the recruiter affect the job seeker, and how can we make sure that the effect is both positive and realistic based on the RJP above?

The recruiter is the critical piece in the recruiting process. According to one report, "Recruiters with higher degrees of engagement and job fit dramatically outperform their peers who score lower in those areas. That's measured both in the quality of hires and in productivity."[48] If you think about it, how well do you do

5-1 SELF ASSESSMENT

Career Development

Indicate how accurately each statement describes you by placing a number from 1 to 7 on the line before the statement. 7 = strong agreement; 1 = strong disagreement.

Describes me   Does not describe me

7_____6_____5_____4_____3_____2_____1

____ 1. I know my strengths, and I can list several of them.

____ 2. I can list several skills that I have to offer an employer.

____ 3. I have career objectives.

____ 4. I know the type of full-time job that I want next.

____ 5. I have analyzed help-wanted ads or job descriptions, and I have determined the most important skills I will need to get the type of full-time job I want.

____ 6. I have or plan to get a part-time job, summer job, internship, or full-time job related to my career objectives.

____ 7. I know the proper terms to use on my résumé to help me get the next job I want.

____ 8. I understand how my strengths and skills are transferable, or how they can be used on jobs I apply for, and I can give examples on a résumé and in an interview.

____ 9. I can give examples (on a résumé and in an interview) of suggestions or direct contributions I made that increased performance for my employer.

____ 10. My résumé focuses on the skills I have developed and on how they relate to the job I am applying for, rather than on job titles.

____ 11. My résumé gives details of how my college education and the skills developed in college relate to the job I am applying for.

____ 12. I have a résumé that is customized to each part-time job, summer job, or internship I apply for, rather than one generic résumé.

Add up the numbers you assigned to the statements and place the total on the continuum below:

84_____74_____64_____54_____44_____34_____24_____12

Career ready   In need of career development

---

things if they don't matter to you? So if our recruiters aren't engaged, how can we expect them to perform at a high level for the organization?

In addition to their desire to perform, though, we have to ensure that our recruiters have certain skill sets. The most important of these skills is probably **active listening,** *which is the intention and ability to listen to others, use the content and context of the communication, and respond appropriately.* This means that recruiters have to want to listen and must have developed their active listening skills so that they not only hear the words that recruits are saying but also understand the context of the conversations (what the circumstances are and why the other is communicating this information) so that they can empathize with recruits and visualize why they are providing this information.[49] If recruiters can do this, they can respond accordingly and usually successfully. If they can't do this, they will generally not provide the appropriate response to the recruit, and as a result, they may lose a valuable opportunity to bring someone with a strong skill set into the organization. Empathy in this situation (putting yourself in another's position) allows the recruiter to visualize why something is being communicated and is critical if the recruiter is to respond correctly.

Besides active listening skills, recruiters have to have a strong set of communication skills. The recruiter must be able to talk with the recruits "on their level" in order to make them feel comfortable with the process. Recruiters need to learn when to ask

Active listening The intention and ability to listen to others, use the content and context of the communication, and respond appropriately

WORK
APPLICATION 5-8

Briefly describe the interaction you had with the recruiter for your current job or a past job. How could the interaction have been improved?

probing questions and when to lie back and let a recruit talk. Role-playing training for the recruiter is particularly effective in teaching this skill.[50]

The recruiter's job also includes successfully communicating with the hiring managers in the organization. The same active listening skills that serve recruiters with an applicant can allow them to more clearly define what the hiring manager wants and needs in the new organizational recruit. So we need to create strong training programs in communication with recruiters in the organization.[51]

We also have to train recruiters in the process of the RJP. They need to understand the job in detail so that they can give honest answers and an RJP of the job to the potential candidate. In many cases today, with our complex jobs, we may have a recruiting team with one person on the team having the "technical" knowledge of the job (maybe the supervisor of the job) and the other person having the HR-related knowledge that keeps us from inadvertently violating any laws, regulations, or internal policies. This helps us with the RJP because the technical person can explain details that the HR recruiter would generally not know or understand.

So our selection and training of the recruiter is a major factor in our overall recruiting success. We have to find individuals who have the ability to actively listen and empathize with job candidates, and then we have to train those individuals in the communication skills that they will need and the roles that they will play with both the hiring manager and the candidates.

LO 5-7

Discuss the basic methods available for evaluating the recruiting process.

EVALUATION OF RECRUITING PROGRAMS

We need to measure our recruiting processes the same as we measure every other process in the organization. We need to know how much the process costs, what our results from the process are, and whether or not the results are cost-effective. As we noted above, the recruitment process is expensive, and unless we identify and control those costs, the beneficial results may end up being outweighed by the costs. Remember, recruiting costs for one management position can run as much as 30% of the individual's yearly salary or more (and this doesn't include later costs for things like selection and initial training). So we need to pay attention to the cost-benefit results of our recruiting efforts.

See Exhibit 5-2 for an overview of five evaluation methods that we discuss in this section.

SHRM

G:6
Calculating and Interpreting Yield Ratios

Yield Ratio

First, we probably want to look at the yield ratio. The recruiting **yield ratio** *is a calculation of how many people make it through the recruiting step to the next step in the hiring process.* For example, we advertise for a job opening and receive 100 résumés and applications. Of these applicants, 50 are judged to have the basic qualifications for the job. As a result, our yield ratio on the advertisement would be 50% (50 of our 100 applicants made it through the first recruiting step). As with most metrics, we then compare to historical data or to other company benchmarks to see how we are doing in the process. If our historic yield ratio for advertisements is 40%, then our ad was much more effective than average.

Cost per Hire

Another measure that you probably want to use is how much it costs to get each person hired, or *cost per hire.* Cost per hire can be calculated based on this formula:[52]

Advertising + Agency fees + Employee referrals + Travel cost of applicants and staff + Relocation costs + Recruiter pay and benefits = Total cost

Total cost ÷ Number of hires = Cost per hire

Yield ratio A calculation of how many people make it through the recruiting step to the next step in the hiring process

EXHIBIT 5-2 RECRUITING EVALUATION METHODS

Generally, all recruiting evaluation methods are comparisons to historical averages to see whether the organization is improving in its recruiting efforts or is less successful than in the past.

Yield ratio:

Divide the number of qualified applicants by the number of applicants.

An advertisement yielded 40 applications, and 28 have the basic qualifications. The yield ratio is 28:40, or 70%.

Cost per hire:

Divide the total cost by the number of applicants hired.

$60,000/10 = $6,000

Time to hire:

The total time required from a position coming open until a new hire is in place.

A new opening on October 15 was filled on December 5, so our time to hire was 51 days.

New hire turnover:

Divide the number of recruits that left within a specified time frame by the number of new hires.

Last year 84 people were hired, and 13 of those left again within 3 months. Our new hire turnover would be 13/84, or 15.5%.

New hire performance:

Divide the difference in performance by new recruits into the average for all employees in the same category to determine the percentage above or below average.

The average of all new hire appraisals last year was 3.1 on a 4-point grading scale. The average of all appraisals in the organization last year was 3.2. Therefore, new recruits are 3.3% below average (3.2 − 3.1 = 0.1; 0.1/3.2 = 3.3%).

We needed several new customer service representatives. We were successful in recruiting and hiring 15 fully qualified applicants for the open positions. During the recruiting campaign, the company spent $140,000 on all of the recruiting costs combined. The cost per hire was therefore $140,000/15 = $9,333.33.

Time Required to Hire

You also may want to analyze how long it takes to get someone hired. *Time required to hire* is pretty self-explanatory. How many days/weeks/months did it take to get someone hired into an open position? If our company has a new opening on June 10 and we are able to fill the position on August 28, our time to hire was 79 days (June 30 − 10 = 20 + July 31 + August 28 = 79).

New Hire Turnover

Employee retention remains a critical issue for organizations and HR managers.[53] You would certainly want to know how often new hires turned over again in a short period of time. In measuring new-hire turnover, we need to identify a time frame. We would usually look at turnover within the first 3 to 6 months. Any longer than that and it is likely that factors other than the recruiting process

WORK
APPLICATION 5-9

Discuss how your present employer or a past employer evaluates its recruiting programs. If you don't know, contact the HR department to find out.

were responsible for the turnover. So we identify our time frame and then measure how many new recruits compared to all hires during that period chose to leave the organization.

If we had 30 new hires in the past year and two of them left again within 6 months of being hired (we are identifying our turnover window as 6 months), we can calculate the turnover percentage and then compare it to historical averages: 2/30 = 6.7% new-hire turnover rate. If our historical new-hire turnover is 10%, then we have improved, at least during this annual cycle.

New Hire Performance

You also want to know how well your newly recruited employees perform on the new job. We can analyze the performance ratings of new hires versus all employees. Since there are so many ways to evaluate employees, it is a bit difficult to give an example here, but suppose you evaluate employees on an overall 4.0 scale (as in college). Further, let's assume the average employee in the organization is judged to be a 3.0 on our 4-point scale. If we review new hires in their first year of service and they fall near the 3.0 average, then our new hires are performing at a rate roughly equal to all employees, which probably constitutes a pretty good result. If, however, our new hires are performing significantly below the average (say, at 2.4), we may want to analyze where they are not being successful and provide training opportunities to them and all new hires going forward to increase their chances for long-term success.

To make the measure more objective, we can calculate the percentage of new recruits who perform above or below average. You divide the difference in performance by new recruits compared to the average. Let's use the new recruit average of 2.4 compared to the 3.0 average: 3.0 – 2.4 = 0.6; 0.6/3.0 = 0.2 or 20% below average. Don't bother working with negative numbers. You can easily see if the new recruits are above or below average, so just subtract the smaller from the larger number.

TRENDS AND ISSUES IN HRM

In this section, the first item that we discuss is the looming worldwide talent war. Closely connected to this is the need for HR to create massively flexible on-demand workforces. Finally, we briefly discuss the process of recruiting for diversity.

5-3   APPLYING THE CONCEPT

Recruiting Evaluation Methods

Do the math.

16. Your company had a new opening on May 5 and you filled the position on June 25. Your time to hire was _____ days.

17. Your company hired 24 people last year, and 14 of those left again within 3 months. Your new hire turnover is _____.

18. The average of all new hire appraisals last year was 4.3 on a 5-point grading scale. The average of all appraisals in the organization last year was 4.1. Therefore, new recruits are _____ % above or ___ % below average.

19. An advertisement for a job opening receives 62 applications. Of these, 48 have the basic qualifications required for the job. The yield ratio would be _____.

20. You hired 7 workers and it cost you $72,000. The cost per hire is _____.

Talent Wars

In Chapter 1, we noted that there is an expectation that in the 21st century, there will be a major shortage of workers with the complex set of required skills. In a recent study, **Accenture** noted that "34 percent of employers worldwide are having difficulty filling open positions, and 73 percent cite lack of experience, skills, or knowledge as the primary obstacle to recruiting."[54] HR executives are also projecting significant worker shortages in many professions in 10 major industries by 2020 and 2030.[55]

As a result of this lack of skills and experience, a global war for talent has become a reality. With the shortage of skilled 21st century workers, the only way to have any real chance of recruiting for open knowledge-worker positions is to recruit in every corner of the globe. Even in organizations with increasingly contingent workforces, there is still a core set of employees who must take on the tasks of goal setting, product and process design, coordination, and other organizational tasks that require continuity. How do we find these highly skilled individuals and get them to apply for jobs in our organization?

First, we must understand labor regulations in each market in which we recruit for positions within our firm. Failing to know and follow national regulations is a quick way to get into legal problems with a foreign government. Labor regulations also include any immigration laws that must be followed. We also need to know how people in a particular nation's labor market go about looking for work. The rest of the world does not necessarily follow the US model when it comes to searching for jobs. How does a knowledge worker in China or South Africa look for work? If we are going to find the best talent, we need to know how workers will search for and find us.

In addition to understanding the regulations and the job search model, we have to find the right individuals. This is where HR analytics again comes to the forefront. Today's organizations have to become proactive in searching for the talent that they are going to need, based on their forecasts. This forecasting uses more robust data modeling and analytics tools than we have in the past, and we are also able to use analytical searches to find and source the types of people who have been identified through these forecasts.

So global recruiting is a potential method for winning the talent war. More and more, we are going to find that global searches are the only methods of finding those skilled workers that we need for our 21st century company.

Global Knowledge Workers as an On-Demand Workforce

Closely related to the global talent war, we will increasingly see a much larger number of contingent workers as a segment of our overall workforce. The core group of employees will do the work that requires continuity as noted above, but they will be surrounded by large groups of contractors, temporary workers, consultants, vendors on premises, outsourcing organizations, and other individuals.[56,57] HR will also need to become more adept at managing these contingent workforces.[58] Again, we need to know how to identify the needs and then how to source the individuals in the contingent workforce.

We will identify the need for contingent workforces in much the same way as we identify all talent needs—through analysis and forecasting. Here again, HR analytics and access to strategic planning are critical for HR recruiting success of contingent workers. The analysis must be driven by the organizational strategy and must lead to improved business outcomes. But how do we source these contingent individuals?

Right now, there is evidence that the contingent workforce in the United States is somewhere between 20% and 25% of all individuals doing economic work, and this percentage is even higher in some other countries.[59] This is 1 out of every 4 to

5 people working in the United States today! These workers can be available to the company on demand, through websites such as **Elance** and **Guru** (much like your movies and TV shows on **Netflix** and **Hulu**), through temporary agencies and other services, or through a company database of available individuals. When they aren't needed, they aren't on the payroll, but when they are, we have the ability to tap into that group of individuals and their unique talents.

According to Accenture, this "new extended workforce is also increasingly mobile, global, and borderless."[60] Just take a look at the bidders on **Elance**. They are also increasingly a key component of organizational success. Again, Accenture notes that contingent workers assist the organization with two critical items: agility in numbers and types of workers and access to skilled talent. Access to this talent will become a much more important part of HR recruiting in the near future. We will need to create partnerships with other organizations such as temporary agencies, schools, outsourcers, and even suppliers who can assist us with this sourcing. We will also need to become much better at matching workers with discrete tasks and following the assignments to make sure that results are satisfactory. This process of analysis, job matching, and follow-up is going to be a long-term requirement for 21st century HR departments.

Should We Recruit for Diversity?

Should you recruit to increase diversity in your organization? Well, if your company already mirrors the communities around you, then you may not need to specifically recruit for diversity. However, in the majority of organizations, this is not the case. Few businesses today actually mirror their external communities and customer bases. If this is the case, can you afford not to recruit for a more diverse workforce? What are the advantages of greater diversity in your organization?

The first, and arguably largest, advantage would be lower cost of discrimination litigation. If we discriminate over an extended period of time, it is almost guaranteed that someone will file an EEOC complaint against our company. Even if we go all the way and win a suit in court, we still face significant costs associated with defending the company. And if we lose, we face stiff fines, plus the potential of things such as a forced affirmative action plan. In addition, once a company is accused of discrimination, it is likely that it will be the target of additional legal actions in subsequent years.

If you are sued for discrimination, it is also likely that your reputation will suffer significantly. Several well-known companies are still haunted by past discrimination lawsuits. Such companies (and the losses they incurred) include **Abercrombie & Fitch** ($47 million),[61] **Shoney's** ($132.5 million),[62] and **Coca-Cola** ($192 million).[63] These are large settlements to be sure, but can you afford to alienate large numbers of potential customers through such a process, even if the organization wins the lawsuit?

Even if we disregard the issue of potential discrimination, do you serve the company well if you don't evaluate a diverse group of recruits for open positions within the company? If we limit our recruiting to certain groups, we run the risk of not finding the best qualified candidates. By limiting the recruiting pool, we unnecessarily tie our own hands with respect to finding the best talent available, and that is certainly not in the best interest of the organization over the long term.

On the other hand, if we seek out diverse individuals, we can increase innovation in the organization as well as increase the options for solutions to difficult problems, such as how to reach particular customer groups in the most efficient and effective ways. So looking at the facts, the company that limits its options in the recruiting process also limits its ability to compete with its rivals in an increasingly difficult competitive environment, where our people mark the difference between success and failure.

WORK
APPLICATION 5-11

Does your present employer's workforce or a past employer's workforce mirror the community around you? What effort, if any, is your firm making to increase diversity? If you don't know, contact the HR department to find out.

• • • CHAPTER SUMMARY

5-1 Identify and discuss the primary goal of the recruiting process.

Through the recruiting process, we are trying to get people inside the company to apply for different job openings or we are trying to get outsiders to join the company. The goal is to create a "reasonable pool" of candidates. Typically, a good pool is 15 to 25 candidates who are qualified and want to work for the organization.

5-2 Briefly discuss the main external forces acting on recruiting efforts.

The main external forces are the effective labor market and the social and legal forces that act on us as well as our potential recruits. These forces include (1) supply and demand, meaning whether there are plenty of candidates for the available jobs or whether there there are more jobs than candidates, (2) the unemployment rate in the recruiting area, (3) competitors and whether competition for available workers is strong or weak, and (4) the social and legal environments, meaning the social factors that recruits emphasize when weighing whether or not to accept employment in a particular company and what limits are placed on recruiting efforts by laws and regulations.

5-3 Discuss the major advantages and disadvantages of internal and external recruiting.

The major advantages of internal recruiting include increases in organizational commitment and job satisfaction, the ability to learn more about the "big picture" in the company, the fact that the individual feels comfortable working for the company, the fact that the company knows the individual and that person's work history, lower recruiting costs, and a relatively speedy process compared to external recruiting. Disadvantages include the facts that the pool of applicants is smaller, you will have to fill the old job of the person you hire, success in one job doesn't necessarily mean success in a different job, external candidates may be more qualified, internal candidates may feel that they are entitled to the job, and we may perpetuate resistance to change and stifle innovation and creativity.

Advantages of external recruiting are that we avoid perpetuating resistance to change and encourage innovation and creativity, we may be able to find individuals with complex skill sets who are not available internally, there will be lower training costs for complex positions, and we have the potential to increase diversity. Disadvantages include potential disruption of the work team, the fact that it takes longer than internal recruiting and costs

more, the fact that it may adversely affect current employees' motivation and satisfaction, higher orientation and training costs, and the fact that the candidate may look great on paper but may not perform after being hired.

5-4 Briefly discuss the major challenges and constraints involved in the recruiting process.

The most obvious constraint is money. We have to avoid spending too much on the recruiting process. Additionally, organizational policies also affect how we recruit. Our organization's image also plays a significant role in our ability to source the people we need from the communities around us. Next is the type of job. Not all jobs are clean or fun. Finally, our selection and training of the recruiter is a major factor in recruiting success. We have to find an individual who has the ability to actively listen and empathize with the candidate.

5-5 Discuss the value of a realistic job preview (RJP).

We have found that the RJP can reduce turnover by making sure the applicant is really a good fit for the job. In most cases, if we hide the truth about the job, satisfaction and organizational commitment will almost certainly go down, and it is highly likely that the person will quit. If the employee does quit, we will incur all of our recruiting costs again. Remember, too, that individuals can sue us in some cases for fraud or misrepresentation if we don't tell them the truth in any advertisement for the job.

5-6 Discuss the characteristics needed in a capable recruiter.

Recruiters need a high degree of *engagement and job fit* to be successful. In addition, we also have to ensure that our recruiters have *active listening skills* so that they can empathize with the other person. The recruiter also has to have a strong set of *communication skills*. Recruiters need to learn when and how to ask questions and when to lie back and let the recruit talk. A recruiter's job also includes successfully *communicating with the hiring managers* in the organization. Finally, we have to *train the recruiter in the RJP process*.

5-7 Discuss the basic methods available for evaluating the recruiting process.

The recruiting *yield ratio* calculates how many people make it through the recruiting step to the next step in the hiring process. Another measure is *cost per hire*. You also may want to analyze *time required to hire*. *New-hire turnover* is another measure of success. If we have high rates of turnover immediately after recruitment and selection, we probably need to reevaluate our recruiting and selection process. Finally, we can also analyze *new-hire performance ratings* and compare them to the organizational norms. If our new hires perform at a significantly lower level than the norm, we may want to analyze where they are not being successful and provide training opportunities to increase their chances for long-term success.

5-8   Define the key terms found in the chapter margins and listed following the Chapter Summary.

Complete the Key Terms Review to test your understanding of this chapter's key terms.

• • • KEY TERMS

active listening
external recruiting
internal recruiting

labor market
realistic job preview (RJP)

recruiting
yield ratio

• • • KEY TERMS REVIEW

Complete each of the following statements using one of this chapter's key terms.

1. _____ is the process of creating a reasonable pool of qualified candidates for a job opening.

2. _____ is the term for the external pool of candidates from which we draw our recruits.

3. _____ involves filling job openings with current employees or people they know.

4. _____ is the process of engaging individuals from the labor market outside the firm to apply for a job.

5. _____ is a review of all of the tasks and requirements of the job, both good and bad.

6. _____ is the intention and ability to listen to others, use the content and context of the communication, and respond appropriately.

7. _____ is a calculation of how many people make it through the recruiting step to the next step in the hiring process.

• • • COMMUNICATION SKILLS

The following critical-thinking questions can be used for class discussion and/or for written assignments to develop communication skills. Be sure to give complete explanations for all answers.

1. Should you "shop" for good employees who are out of work in a bad economy, and then should you terminate existing employees who aren't doing their jobs very well after finding a good replacement? What consequences of this course of action can you see?

2. If you were in charge of your company, would you rather recruit new employees, or would you rather use some of the other tools for addressing a shortage of employees that were discussed in this and the last chapter? Why?

3. In your personal experience, do you think that internal recruiting really improves organizational morale, job satisfaction, and productivity? Why or why not?

4. Do you think that targeted or closed recruiting leads to the potential for discrimination in recruiting efforts? Why or why not?

5. When would you *definitely* use the Internet as a recruiting tool, and when would you definitely *not* use the Internet to recruit? Why?

6. What could an organization do to improve its image if it has a bad reputation with recruits? Categorize your efforts into immediate-term and longer-term items.

7. If you were in charge of your company, what would you tell recruiters to do or not do to enhance their recruiting efforts? Why?

8. Do you think that you are a good "active listener"? Why or why not, and what could you do to become better?

9. What options do you see as alternatives to recruiting globally for knowledge-based jobs in the coming years?

• • • CASE 5-1 HERE A GM, THERE A GM, EVERYWHERE A GM (OR SO THEY THOUGHT!)

Hartson Printing Services, Inc.,* was a midsized company (revenues of approximately $12 million per year) serving the southern United States. The owners, a husband and wife, had personally managed the company for most of its nearly 25 years in business. However, as the company had grown, it was becoming more and more difficult to personally manage all of the details of daily operations. As a result, Angie and Joe Hartson decided to create and fill a new position as General Manager (GM) of the printing company. The GM would handle all of the day-to-day operations of the facility, leaving the owners free to make more strategic decisions as well as get some needed time off.

Once the decision to recruit a GM had been made, Angie and Joe decided that the best way to find a person for the job was to advertise. They discussed the kind of person that they were interested in hiring in some detail and then sat down and wrote out the following advertisement for the new opening:

Now Hiring: General Manager—Printing Services Industry

Looking for strong leader to aggressively manage and grow a high-quality printing business. Duties include daily management of midsized operations, including projects ranging from personal business cards to small-volume book binding. Candidates must have good leadership, management, and P&L skills and be able to manage in a fast-paced, deadline-driven environment. An Equal Opportunity Employer. Send résumé and cover letter to P.O. Box 66452, Gadsden, AL 35901.

The Hartsons sat back after looking at their work and congratulated themselves on writing their advertisement. They put it in the local newspaper and the *Birmingham News* the next day, and within two weeks had more than 145 responses—many more than they really had anticipated. However, as they started going through all of the responses, they realized that none of the applicants really fit what they needed for their print shop. They had received replies from an extremely diverse group of respondents with no real knowledge of an operation of the size of Hartson Printing. The cover letters didn't provide them with any valuable information on the skill sets of the applicants, and the résumés were "all over the map." One of the applicants was currently an Assistant Night Manager at a local fast-food restaurant, but

was convinced that she could manage their $12 million print shop. Another was the retired former president of an international multibillion-dollar firm, and neither Angie nor Joe could figure out why he would want such a small-scale job opportunity.

They decided to take some time away from the office to work their way through the other résumés. They scanned through more than 140 of them over the course of two full days and found out that none of the applicants really fit what they needed in a GM. Angie and Joe couldn't figure out what on earth the applicants were thinking! Most had no idea what kind of firm they were applying to, and the few who did didn't fit with the owners' vision of what they would need to be able to do and the background necessary for successfully filling the job. The Hartsons couldn't even find one applicant that they wanted to interview for the job. At this point, Angie suggested and Joe agreed that they might need some professional help, so they called a local consulting firm that had experience in management recruiting.

The next day, Tom, an HR Consultant, came to speak with Angie and Joe. He asked to see the advertisement and the résumés from the respondents. He took one look at the ad and thumbed through some of the résumés, and immediately saw what had happened. He quickly started working with the owners on a new advertisement that ended up looking as follows:

General Manager Wanted—Full P&L Responsibility

Starting salary $60,000+ with opportunity for performance incentives to be determined jointly with company owners.

Hartson Printing Services, a $12 million firm in Gadsden, AL, is seeking an experienced Printing Services Manager who will be responsible for all day-to-day operations for our printing firm. Please review our product and service line at www.hartsonprinting.com for details on the company.

Qualifications will include at least 15 years in printing and/or publishing industries; experience with bid and proposal processes; experience with short run and quick throughput jobs; knowledge of pre-press preparation, pressroom, and binding operations; knowledge of maintenance schedules for common printing equipment used in Hartson's offices; at least 5 years in a management role with responsibility for

---

*The name of the printing company and its location have been changed.

planning, organizing, and controlling the work of at least 5 employees; knowledge of organizational budgets and experience in a P&L role; 4-year business degree; proven skills in cost containment in a mid-sized printing firm. Relocation required.

To apply, provide a résumé and cover letter to Hartson Printing Services, 318 Main St., Gadsden, AL 35901. Hartson is proud to be an Equal Opportunity Employer.

The Hartsons reviewed the advertisement, and immediately had some questions for Tom. Once these questions had been answered, the three agreed that they would like to immediately get the ad published in order to get the process of finding a strong GM for the business back on track. The Hartsons were excited about this fresh start and beginning to look forward to the interviewing process (another significant challenge!).

Questions

1. What was wrong with the Hartsons' first recruiting advertisement?

2. What do you think happened to cause the first advertisement to be off target in reaching its intended audience?

3. What problems did this first attempt at an advertisement create for the owners?

4. What significant differences do you see between the first ad and the second ad?

5. Would you make any other changes to clarify the job? If so, what changes would you make and why? If not, why not?

6. In what external recruiting sources would you choose to publish the new advertisement? Be specific and provide your reasoning for your choice(s).

• • • CASE 5-2 LINKEDIN: HOW DOES THE WORLD'S LARGEST PROFESSIONAL NETWORK NETWORK?

In 2003, LinkedIn was launched to help those who felt a bit disconnected in the business world by creating a professional network where members could find jobs from the labor market, locate business opportunities, and connect with other professionals. Given its differentiation approach, LinkedIn became the dominant player, with over 300 million members in more than 200 countries. It has continued its growth strategy through acquisitions, such as the 2012 purchase of SlideShare—an application that allows users to share slideshow presentations—for some $119 million. In addition, the company has launched its Talent Pipeline offering, a new recruiter product. Mobile applications are another area of focus for the company; in 2011, about 15% of member visits came from mobile devices, and mobile page views were up more than 300% year over year. LinkedIn is also ramping up its international expansion activities, having experienced growth in India, Brazil, and China. About 60% of its member base comes from outside the United States, and its service is available in French, German, Italian, Portuguese, and Spanish. As a reflection of its global focus, LinkedIn recently opened offices in London, Mumbai, and Sydney in addition to its presence in Canada, Ireland, and the Netherlands.[64]

Through this giant network, members are able to find jobs from the labor market, locate business opportunities, and connect with other professionals. LinkedIn has become a powerful tool for large companies to find new talent as well. Unlike the other job-hunting search engines like **Monster** or **Indeed,** LinkedIn provides the opportunity for users and employers to network with each other. Companies like **Google** or **HP** use their own resources and their own search tools for headhunting; however, for the majority of the hiring process, LinkedIn is used to gather more information about candidates. LinkedIn can count executives from all Fortune 500 companies among its members, and it is believed that 90% of Fortune 100 companies use LinkedIn's corporate talent solutions to recruit employees.[65]

Successful growth requires hiring new employees. Ironically, to meet the increasing demand for their services, LinkedIn itself needed to hire new software engineers, salespeople, and corporate managers. LinkedIn may have a lot to teach its corporate users about how to benefit from its services, yet how does LinkedIn hire its own employees?

When LinkedIn needs an immediate hire for a vacant position, it requires its HR team to design, implement, and maintain the network configurations, but it also requires them to collaborate with business leaders to recruit applicants who meet the company's objectives. LinkedIn uses its own website along with a plan to recruit only the best for the company in the least amount of time possible. Whenever a user checks the profile of a LinkedIn employee, it is likely that the user will see an advertisement for a possible opening in the company. The goal is to reach the whole labor market about this vacancy and announce it to users familiar with the firm's services. The job seekers then realize it would be easier to "follow" LinkedIn's page to catch further openings, so it is not a surprise that LinkedIn's number of followers has multiplied by a factor of 10 during the past 3 years. LinkedIn also uses its database to generate links between local job listings and job seekers for specific industries—not only to search for talent in nearby locations or where the job turnover is high, as in New York City or Silicon Valley, but in places where labor supply/demand is more in balance, as in Washington, D.C., or Dallas.[66]

Key positions in the company, in one case a data center manager, required far more targeted recruiting given the technical nature of the jobs. Job specifications included 15+ years of managerial experience, at least 3 years in a similar job, a PhD in computer science, and proven leadership in the IT world. Knowing it could take more than a year and a half to persuade people to leave their current job and join LinkedIn, LinkedIn narrowed down its search by focusing on only current job seekers. In the end, the search result provided only seven résumés that matched the job's criteria—only seven identifiable people on the planet![67]

Questions

1. How does LinkedIn's growth strategy impact the recruitment function of its HR department?

2. One way that LinkedIn has grown is through acquisition. From a recruitment viewpoint, why use this method of growth rather than internal development?

3. Why would a firm use LinkedIn's services rather than those of a traditional headhunter or their in-house recruitment specialists?

4. What are alternative methods that firms can employ to recruit new employees besides using LinkedIn's services?

5. What is a realistic job preview, and how might LinkedIn be used by firms to provide such a preview to potential employees?

6. Evaluate LinkedIn's search for a data center manager. How might the company have handled this search differently in order to increase the number of potential applicants?

Case created by Herbert Sherman, PhD, and Theodore Vallas, Department of Management Sciences, Long Island University School of Business, Brooklyn Campus

Sharpen your skills with SAGE edge at edge.sagepub.com/lussierhrm2e

SAGE edge for students provides a personalized approach to help you accomplish your coursework goals in an easy-to-use learning environment.

••• SKILL BUILDER 5-1 ONLINE JOB SEARCH

Objectives

To develop your job search skills and to learn more about job descriptions and specifications

To get you thinking about your career

Skills

The primary skills developed through this exercise are as follows:

1. *HR management skills*—technical, business, and conceptual and design skills

2. *SHRM 2013 Curriculum Guidebook*—I: Staffing: Recruitment and Selection

Preparation

Study the steps in the job search, which is preparation for the written assignment.

Let's do an exercise related to your professional development. Employers recruit job candidates, so we focus on you.

1. Think about a job or internship you would like to have. You may also get ideas when you go to a job search website.

2. Go to a job search website of your choice. You may use http://www.collegejournal.com (jobs and tips for new college grads), http://www.collegerecruiter.com (career tests to identify possible jobs, internships, and entry-level jobs), http://www.shrm.org (HR jobs and advice), http://www.monster.com (simply a listing of all types of jobs), and http://www.careerbuilder.com (jobs and advice). You may want to search using other websites and use more than one job search engine. If you are interested in working for a specific business or nonprofit organization, you may also visit its website.

3. Read about the job, job description, and specifications.

4. Your professor may want the URLs you used in your job search.

Written Assignment Instructions

Type the answers to these three questions.

1. What job(s) where you searching for, and which website(s) did you use to search?

2. List three or four things that you learned about job searching.

3. How will you use this information to get a job?

••• SKILL BUILDER 5-2 RÉSUMÉ

Objective

To develop a résumé you can use for internships and part-time, summer, and full-time employment

Skills

The primary skills developed through this exercise are as follows:

1. *HR management skills*—technical, business, and conceptual and design skills

2. *SHRM 2013 Curriculum Guidebook*—I: Staffing: Recruitment and Selection

Preparation

Writing the résumé:

You may go to your college's Career Center and/or visit Proven Résumés at http://www.provenresumes.com for help. You should read the tips below before writing your résumé:

Type out your résumé, and keep it to one page, unless you have extensive "relevant" experience. Before finalizing your résumé, improve it by using the résumé assessment below, which may be used to grade your résumé.

Answer these résumé questions with Yes, Somewhat, or No:

- Within 10 seconds, can a recruiter understand what job you are applying for and that you have the qualifications (skills/experience and education) to get the position? You should not use the word *I* or *me* on a résumé.

Objective

- Does your résumé have an objective that clearly states the position being applied for (such as sales rep)? The job applied for affects all sections of your résumé because your résumé needs to state how you are qualified for the job. If you don't list the job you are applying for, your résumé will most likely

Apply It

What did I learn from this experience? How will I use this knowledge in the future?

_____

_____

Your instructor may ask you to do this Skill Builder in class in a group by sharing your answers. If so, the instructor will provide you with any necessary information or additional instructions.

be tossed out and you will not get a job with the firm.

Education (describe relevant courses)

- If education is your major qualification for the job, is there detail that states the skills developed and courses taken in school that qualify you for the position you're applying for?

- Be sure to state your degree, major, and minor and concentration, if you have them. Don't write Bachelor of Science or Master of Business Administration—use BS and name of degree or MBA. Be sure to list your month and year of graduation.

- Your résumé should do a good job of filling one page. If you don't have extensive experience, list relevant courses that prepared you for the job you are applying for. For relevant courses, don't just include a shopping list. Pick a few "relevant" courses and describe how each course qualifies you for the job listed in your objective. So if you want to be a sales rep, you should state that you are a marketing major (or that you pursued a marketing concentration) and that you have taken the Sales and Selling course. Describe the skills you developed in the sales and other relevant courses.

- If you list computer courses/skills, be sure to list programs such as Microsoft Word, Excel, Access, PowerPoint (it is *one* word, not two), Windows, SPSS, HTML, etc. If you've used them on the job, say so with the program you used.

Experience

- Does your résumé list experience or skills that support the fact that you can do the job stated in your objective?

- Be sure to list names and addresses of employers, with months and years on the job. If you want the company to which you are applying to contact your boss for a reference, list your boss's name and telephone number on your résumé.

- Don't just list activities, such as cutting grass. Focus on general skills that can be applied to the job you want. Try to show skills. Did you do any planning, organizing, leading (influencing others, communicating, and motivating), and controlling? Give examples of your skills.

- For the sales job example, if any of your past jobs don't include sales experience, list sales skills developed on the job. List communication skills that you used while interacting with customers stating how you used them. Also state that you enjoy meeting new people and that you have the ability to easily converse with people you don't know.

Accomplishments (NOT necessarily a separate section and heading)

- Does your résumé clearly list your accomplishments and valuable contributions you made while attaining your education and/or experience?

- If you have a high GPA, you should list it with your education.

- If you are on a college sports team, be sure to list it with any accomplishments (such as Maroon of the Week, captain, MVP, or selection to conference teams). A good place to list sports is in the education section.

- List job accomplishments like "Increased sales by 10% from May to August 2010," "Employee of the Month," and "Earned highest tips based on superior sales skills and excellent communication skills used with customers."

- Is your résumé neat, attractive, and free of errors? Have neat columns and use tables without gridlines. Use high-quality bond paper and ink colors for hard copies.

Apply It

What did I learn from this experience? How will I use this knowledge in the future?

_____

_____

Your instructor may ask you to do this Skill Builder in class in a group by showing others your résumé. If so, the instructor will provide you with any necessary information or additional instructions.

©iStockphoto.com/Squaredpixels

6

Selecting New Employees

• • • LEARNING OUTCOMES

After studying this chapter, you should be able to do the following:

6-1 Describe why the selection process is so important to the company. PAGE 195

6-2 Identify the three main types of "fit" that we look for in the selection process and why they are important. PAGE 197

6-3 Discuss the major points in the Uniform Guidelines on Employee Selection Procedures (UGESP). PAGE 198

6-4 Briefly discuss the use of applications and résumés as selection tools. PAGE 201

6-5 Briefly discuss the legal considerations in the selection process. PAGE 204

6-6 Discuss the major types of written testing available as selection tools. PAGE 205

6-7 Identify the requirements for organizational drug-testing programs. PAGE 209

6-8 Discuss the value of selection interviews, including the three primary types of interviews. PAGE 212

6-9 List and briefly describe the steps taken in conducting interviews. PAGE 216

6-10 Discuss the use of the various background checks as tests for employment. PAGE 216

6-11 Identify the common problems employers encounter during the selection process. PAGE 221

6-12 Define the key terms found in the chapter margins and listed following the Chapter Summary. PAGE 226

Practitioner's Perspective

In a discussion of hiring, Cindy notes that the process of moving a person from job candidate to employee is a matching game for both the candidate and the company. Job candidates want to emphasize their attractive qualities while minimizing any drawbacks. Sometimes, it is hard for an employer to determine if "what you see is really what you get." Is there a line that shouldn't be crossed in the attempt to gather information about a job candidate?

She says, "When Sacha, our finance manager, started talking about vetting the candidates for her open position by checking their Facebook accounts, I knew we needed to talk. 'But you find out so much about people by looking at their page—mostly whether or not they have done something that would disqualify them,' Sacha said."

Is there real potential to access via the Internet candidate information that an employer should not have prior to offering a position? What are the pitfalls to avoid and legal restrictions that must be respected during hiring? Chapter 6 covers the process one should follow to properly select employees.

SHRM HR CONTENT

See Appendix: *SHRM 2013 Curriculum Guidebook* for the complete list

B. Employment Law (required)

32. The Genetic Information Nondiscrimination Act (GINA)

36. Fair Credit Reporting Act (FCRA)

39. Negligent hiring

E. Job Analysis/Job Design (required)

3. Employment practices (recruitment, selection, and placement)

I. Staffing: Recruitment and Selection (required)

6. Initial assessment methods: Résumés, cover letters, application blanks, biographical information, reference/background checks, genetic screening, initial interviews, minimum qualifications

7. Discretionary assessment methods

8. Ability/job knowledge tests, assessment centers

9. Noncognitive assessments (e.g., personality assessments, integrity tests, situational judgment tests, interest inventories)

10. Structured interviews

11. Contingent assessment methods: Drug testing, medical exams

12. Measurement concepts: Predictors/criteria, reliability, validity

13. Selection decisions: Ranking, grouping/banding, random selection

Q. Organizational Development (required—graduate students only)

14. Social networking

X. Workplace Health, Safety, and Security (secondary)

10. Testing for substance abuse

THE SELECTION PROCESS

We learned in Chapter 5 how to go through the recruiting process to get our "reasonable pool" of job candidates. Now we need to select one person from the pool to fill our job opening. Selection is important because bad hires can be costly.[1] Firms should always seek to hire the most highly skilled employees to maximize their output,[2] but there is often a mismatch when the job and person don't fit together, and productivity suffers as a result.[3] Thus, managers focus on hiring as one of their critical tasks.[4] Remember, too, that in most organizations today, at least one of our competitive advantages will be our employees, so if we put the wrong people into the wrong jobs, we can have great difficulty in carrying out our strategic plans. So we need to focus on fit.[5]

Selection *is the process of choosing the best-qualified applicant who was recruited for a given job.* As with all other decisions that involve people in the organization, we can apply the OUCH test here to determine whether or not we should use a particular tool or measure in the selection process. Is the tool *objective*: Does it use facts and knowledge or is it based on bias and emotion? Are we being *uniform in application* of the measure: Are we using it with all of the people in the selection process? Is the tool *consistent in effect*: Does it have the same effect on everyone or does it have an inconsistent effect on one or more protected classes? And finally, does the tool or measure *have job relatedness:* Can it be shown to have a relationship with the primary (essential) factors in the job? The OUCH test will give us an initial analysis of the measure being used, and if it appears that we might not be able to apply the measure so that it meets the OUCH test requirements, we need to do some more investigation before we decide to use the measure in the selection process.

Selection The process of choosing the best-qualified applicant who was recruited for a given job

• • • CHAPTER OUTLINE

The Importance of the Selection Process

As we just noted, selection is a critical management task, but why is it so critical to the organization? The reasons have to do with the negative consequences of bad hiring decisions, which are essentially the results of mismatches between jobs and employees. Here are three of those reasons.

BAD HIRES COST TIME AND MONEY. First and probably most notably, while it is often important to fill jobs quickly, hurrying can result in a mismatch—or as the old saying goes, haste makes waste. If we hire someone who is not willing or able to do the job successfully, we will most likely have to go through the whole process again in a very short time. This will cost us more time and money for the new recruiting and selection process, so it is something that we must work very hard to avoid.

BAD HIRES RESULT IN LOWER PRODUCTIVITY. Think about your experiences in the past. Have you ever seen (or been a part of) an organization with employees who did the minimum amount of work possible, who didn't ever go out of their way to help customers in any situation, and who didn't cooperate with others in the organization? Do you think that organization started out that way, or did people start out working hard and paying attention? In such an organization, what kind of overall productivity are you going to have?

It is easier than you think to get into this type of situation. Just a few new hires who show this lack of concern for the organization and its customers can be highly contagious. Pretty soon, others in the organization may decide, "If they can do the absolute minimum and still get paid what I get paid, then why should I work so hard?" Once this occurs, morale, job satisfaction, and organizational commitment can drop very quickly. You don't want to put your organization in such a position, so you absolutely must give your full attention to the selection process to make sure you hire only people who fit the jobs.

BAD HIRES CAN BE NEGLIGENT HIRES. Another issue that makes selection critical is the potential for negligent hires. Almost every state in the United States recognizes this concept, so HR managers must understand it as well.[6] A **negligent hire** *is a legal concept that says if the organization hires someone who may pose a danger to coworkers, customers, suppliers, or other third parties, and if that person then harms someone else in the course of working for the company, then the company can be held liable for the individual's actions.*

For example, if a company hired a salesperson who had a criminal record for assault and who then assaulted a customer, the company could be held liable for the harm done to the customer who was assaulted. Many businesses focus on quick delivery, but when drivers have hurried and been negligent, they have caused accidents involving damage of property and injury to people, resulting in companies being sued for millions. So we have to make every legitimate attempt to find out if candidates have the potential to be a danger to others and weed them out during our selection process.

Steps in the Selection Process

The selection process follows a series of steps that are illustrated in Exhibit 6-1. Note that this is a general guide and that one may skip some steps in the process or perhaps not follow them in the exact sequence shown. For example, there may not be any preliminary testing or initial interviewing, and there may not be any drug or physical exam conditions.

There are many tools at our disposal during the selection process. There are written tests, physical tests, personality tests, honesty tests, drug testing, background

LO 6-1

Describe why the selection process is so important to the company.

SHRM

B:39
Negligent Hiring

WORK
APPLICATION 6-1

Select an organization you work for now or worked for in the past and give an example of how a mismatch of a job and an employee resulted in a negative outcome.

Negligent hire A legal concept that says if the organization hires someone *who may pose a danger to coworkers, customers, suppliers, or other third parties,* and if that person then harms someone else in the course of working for the company, then the company can be held liable for the individual's actions

| EXHIBIT 6-1 | STEPS IN THE SELECTION PROCESS

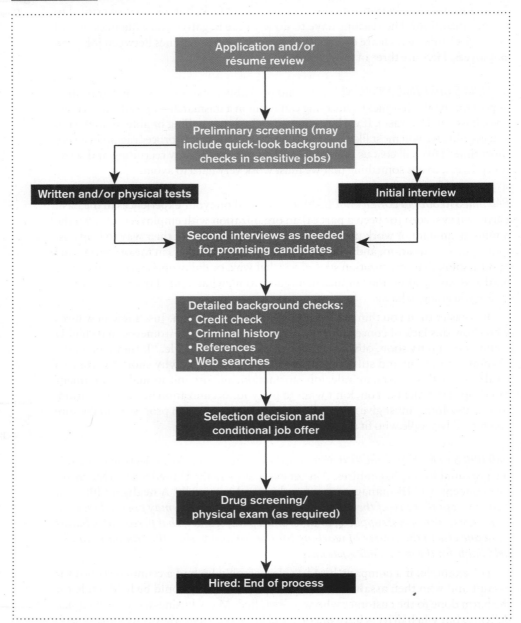

checks of various types, and more. Which tools should we use in which circumstances? Almost all of our selection devices are discretionary, or optional. We don't have to do any written or physical ability tests; we don't have to administer any cognitive ability tests; and we don't have to provide tests for stamina, honesty, or judgment.

The steps do, however, make logical sense. People apply for jobs, and then the firm screens the job candidates to narrow down the selection. This screening can include a test of some type and an initial interview for the top candidates. For lower-level jobs, it is not uncommon for the HR department to do the screening, conduct any testing and background checks, and send the best applicants to the manager the candidate will actually work for. The manager commonly conducts interviews and makes a conditional job offer that may include drug screening and/or a physical exam. The final step occurs when the applicant is hired.

In this chapter, we discuss each step in the process. But before we get into those selection steps, let's discuss the importance of selecting the applicant who best matches the job, or what we call "looking for fit." We also need to briefly discuss the federal Uniform Guidelines on Employment Selection Procedures (UGESP) that affect how we conduct each of the steps in the selection process. Once we have covered these two items, we can go into the actual steps of the selection process.

LOOKING FOR "FIT"

"We hold these truths to be self-evident, that all men are created equal."[7] Is this a true statement? It is what the US Declaration of Independence says! However, we all know that people are not equal. We also know that as managers, if we treat people equally (the same), then we really aren't doing our job. Managers are supposed to get the best productivity out of their workforce, but not everyone can do everything equally well. So we have to treat people differently *but fairly* in order to be successful in our jobs. What do we need to look for in the selection process in order to put the right person in the right job? We need to attempt to assess three things: personality-job fit, ability-job fit, and person-organization fit. Let's take a look at these items.

Personality-Job Fit

We all have unique personalities. Our personality defines to a great extent who we are and how we act and react in certain situations. Some of us are strongly extroverted and enjoy "working the crowd" in a social setting, while others may be fairly introverted and feel extremely uncomfortable in such an environment. Some of us desire to try new things constantly, while others are more comfortable with things that they know well. There are many traits that help define our personalities, but the fact remains that each of us is different.

Should you as a manager try to change the basic personality of your employees? Of course not! However, does their personality affect the things they enjoy doing and even affect the way that they work? Yes, it does. So you can't change their personality, but it affects how they work, and as a result, you have to make an attempt to identify their personality types and then put them in positions that will be enhanced by their particular personality traits. This is called *personality-job fit*.[8]

So if we need to hire an employee who will have to work the crowd in a sales job for our company, would we want to hire someone who is very uncomfortable talking with and relating to strangers? If we did hire that person, is it likely that the employee would succeed or fail in the position? Obviously, it is more likely that such a person would fail in that type of environment, so one of the things we try to determine in the selection process is the personality-job fit.

Ability-Job Fit

In addition to personality-job fit, we want to determine ability-job fit. Every individual has a certain set of physical and intellectual skills, and no two people are exactly alike. Some people are very capable at working

©iStockphoto.com/mediaphotos

To be successful, the employee must match the job and organization.

Select a present or past job of yours and explain in detail how well your personality and ability fit or did not fit the job and how well you fit the organization.

with computers, while others are more capable at physical work. Still others may be able to successfully perform both physical and computer-based tasks, but they may have difficulty with analyzing quantitative information. Each of us is more skilled at some things than others.

Managers have to analyze the set of abilities in each subordinate or new hire and understand that person's individual limitations. Using this information, the manager must hire the right people and then assign them to the types of jobs for which they are best suited. Here again, if we assign the wrong person to a job, we can easily frustrate that employee and as a result cause motivation and job satisfaction to drop, which in turn will likely cause losses in productivity. So we have to pay attention to ability-job fit.[9]

Person-Organization Fit

Finally, we have to be aware of person-organization fit when deciding on which candidate to hire.[10] There are plenty of potential employees out there who have the required skills to do the jobs that we need them to do, and they may even have the right type of personality to be comfortable in such a job. However, they just may not fit well within the organization itself. Person-organization fit deals with the cultural and structural characteristics of the organization and how well the candidate will fit within that structure and culture.[11]

If a candidate works best in a decentralized organization with strong individual reward systems, and if we are hiring people to work in a tightly controlled and centralized team-based division, then it is unlikely that the candidate will be able or willing to conform to the requirements of the company structure and culture. As a result, such candidates will likely be unhappy in this situation and will be more likely to leave as soon as they can find another opportunity that more closely matches their desires for a specific type of work environment.

LO 6-3

Discuss the major points in the Uniform Guidelines on Employee Selection Procedures (UGESP).

UNIFORM GUIDELINES ON EMPLOYEE SELECTION PROCEDURES

We are now ready to discuss a legal issue that affects each step of the selection process. The **Uniform Guidelines on Employee Selection Procedures (UGESP)** *provide information that can be used to avoid discriminatory hiring practices as well as discrimination in other employment decisions.* Most often called simply the "Uniform Guidelines," they were created to guide employers in their efforts to comply with the federal laws concerning all employment decisions, and especially the selection process.[12] Let's discuss some of the most important sections of the UGESP.

What Qualifies as an Employment Test?

The UGESP formalize and standardize the way in which the federal government identifies and deals with discriminatory employment practices. They define the concept of "tests for employment" that are used in either the selection process or other employment actions. But what is a *test for employment*? It is a pretty broad term. The guidelines define it as applying to

Uniform Guidelines on Employee Selection Procedures (UGESP) Guidelines that provide information that can be used to avoid discriminatory hiring practices as well as discrimination in other employment decisions

tests and other selection procedures which are used as a basis for any employment decision. Employment decisions include but are not limited to hiring, promotion, demotion, membership (for example, in a labor organization), referral, retention, and licensing and certification . . . Training or transfer may also be considered employment decisions if they lead to any of the decisions listed above.[13]

Although the guidelines specifically say that they "apply only to selection procedures which are used as a basis for making employment decisions,"[14] if we look closely at the definition of *employment decision* above, pretty much any selection procedure that we would use becomes a test for employment, which means that we need to follow the UGESP guidelines during every step of the selection process.

Valid and Reliable Measures

The UGESP also discusses the need for any employment test that is used by an employer to be valid and reliable. Let's discuss validity and reliability separately, and then put them together.

In simple language, **validity** *is the extent to which a test measures what it claims to measure.* The UGESP requires validity in our selection procedures. It notes that "users may rely upon criterion-related validity studies, content validity studies, or construct validity studies"[15] to validate a particular selection procedure. But what are these validity measures?

CRITERION-RELATED VALIDITY. **Criterion-related validity** *is an assessment of the ability of a test to measure some other factor related to the test.* For example, SAT scores are designed to be one of the predictors of college success. In employment, criterion-related validity occurs in selection when we can show a strong relationship between job candidates' scores on a test and on-the-job performance of those candidates after they are hired.[16] One of the issues here is that we need a fairly large number of individuals included in the analysis in order to get the statistical data necessary to show criterion-related validity.

CONTENT VALIDITY. **Content validity** *is an assessment of whether a test measures knowledge or understanding of the items it is supposed to measure.* So, in measuring content validity for selection, we have to show that "the content of a selection procedure is representative of [measures] important aspects of performance on the job."[17] "A selection procedure can be supported by a content validity strategy to the extent that it is a representative sample of the content of the job."[18] In other words, if we have good work sample tests or other tests of knowledge, skills, or abilities that are directly applicable to the job, we can probably use content validity to validate our selection procedure.

CONSTRUCT VALIDITY. **Construct validity** *measures a theoretical concept or trait that is not directly observable.* For construct validity to be applicable, we must demonstrate that "(a) a selection procedure measures a construct (something believed to be an underlying human trait or characteristic, such as honesty) and (b) the construct is important for successful job performance."[19] For example, intelligence is a construct that is measured by an IQ test, and research has supported the IQ test's validity. Intelligence is a major predictor of job performance. However, the UGESP says that this method of validation is far more difficult to demonstrate than are the other two options, so it would be best if you can show that a measure has criterion-related or content validity.

You will learn about several different types of tests that must meet criterion-related, content, and/or construct validity in the "Testing and Legal Issues" section of this chapter. But for now, let's move on to reliability, because tests also have to be reliable to be legal.

RELIABILITY. **Reliability** *is the consistency of a test measurement.* In addition to being valid, for a measure to be useful in any type of testing (including employment testing), it needs to be *reliable*.

WORK
APPLICATION 6-4

Select a present or past job of yours and explain which one of the three types of validity would be the most relevant to that job.

SHRM

I:12
Measurement Concepts: Predictors/ Criteria, Reliability, Validity

Validity The extent to which a test measures what it claims to measure

Criterion-related validity An assessment of the ability of a test to measure some other factor related to the test

Content validity An assessment of whether a test measures knowledge or understanding of the items it is supposed to measure

Construct validity An assessment that measures a theoretical concept or trait that is not directly observable

Reliability The consistency of a test measurement

6-1   APPLYING THE CONCEPT

Validity and Reliability

Write the letter corresponding to each of the following before the situation in which it is discussed.

    a. criterion-related validity

    b. content validity

    c. construct validity

    d. reliability

_____ 1.   A job candidate failed a job application test, but she claims that the test is not fair and that she can do the job. What type of evidence do you need to ensure that the test is in fact a good predictor of job performance?

_____ 2.   You are running a law firm and require all your lawyers to pass the bar exam. What does the bar exam need to do to indicate it is a good test?

_____ 3.   You have developed a new system for predicting future company sales. Your boss wants some proof that it works.

_____ 4.   An NFL team makes a recruit take an intelligence test. The recruit's score is below the acceptable level, so the team refuses to hire the player. The player complains, stating that his intelligence score has nothing to do with playing football. What evidence do you need to support not hiring the player?

_____ 5.   You decided to let the job candidate in situation 1 above take the application test again. The next day she took the test again, and the score was within a couple of points of her score on the first test. So you again decide not to hire her. What evidence do you need to support this decision?

On the face of it, what does the word *reliable* mean? It means that the measure is consistent in some way—perhaps consistent when used by two different people (called inter-rater reliability) or consistent over time (called test-retest reliability). Let's make it simple. If you go out to your car every day and it starts when you turn the ignition key, it is reliable. If it sometimes starts but sometimes doesn't, then it isn't reliable. We want our measures when we are working with people to be reliable measures, meaning they should be consistent over time and between people.[20]

THE RELATIONSHIP BETWEEN RELIABILITY AND VALIDITY. Let's put validity and reliability together by stating the obvious: If a test is not reliable, it can't be valid. For example, some jobs include a weight criterion as a job specification. If a job candidate steps on our company scale and weighs 150 pounds, then steps off and on again and weighs 155, and then does the same and weighs 153, the scale is not reliable. How much does the candidate actually weigh? If our scale is not reliable, then it can't be valid because it doesn't accurately measure what we claim it measures.

Let's make it a bit more complicated by stating that a test can be reliable but not valid, but it can't be valid without being reliable. If a job candidate steps on the company scale and weighs 150 pounds and then weighs 150 pounds three more times, our scale is reliable. However, what if we place the person on a more expensive, better scale and the person weighs 155? Then our scale is reliable but not valid because it doesn't accurately measure a person's weight.

Now that we have a general overview of the selection process and understand that we need to select for fit and follow the UGESP in every step of the selection process, we are ready to discuss the selection steps illustrated in Exhibit 6-1.

APPLICATIONS AND PRELIMINARY SCREENING

The first step in the selection process is to get job applicants to fill out an application or send in their résumé. Then we do preliminary screening that may include a quick background check, testing, and initial interviewing to narrow down the applicants to the best matches, or fit, for the job.

Because these preliminary steps may not be done or may not be done until later in the selection process, and because the process is essentially the same no matter when it is done, we will discuss testing, interviewing, and background checks in three separate sections. Here we will discuss the application and résumé and what you generally can and can't ask during the pre-employment inquiries.

Applications and Résumés

As part of the selection process, the recruited candidates are typically asked to complete an application to provide biographical data.[21] We need data to aid in selecting the best person for the job.[22] Organizations may use different application forms for different jobs. For professional jobs, a résumé may replace the application form. However, even in cases where résumés are appropriate, many companies today will request that the applicant also fill out an application.

LO 6-4

Briefly discuss the use of applications and résumés as selection tools.

Why does the company need candidates to fill out an application if it already has a résumé with the same information? There are a couple of primary reasons. First, the application gives the company information on the applicant in a standard form. This makes it easier to quickly scan and evaluate different applicants. Second, applications almost always have some legal language or "disclosures" that must be agreed to by the applicant. This information will generally include language to inform the applicant of an "employment-at-will" clause, allow the company to conduct background and reference checks with the applicant's permission, tell the applicant that the company will conduct some mandatory tests prior to final employment (e.g., drug testing), and inform the applicant that any false information provided will be grounds for immediate termination of any relationship between the company and the employee. Résumés won't have such language, so the organization will generally require that the application be completed in order to efficiently cover these items.

SHRM

I:6
Initial Assessment Methods:
Résumés, etc.

In reality, we use applications and résumés for much the same reasons. We are trying to figure out your basic skill set, background, work history, education, and other basic information. What is the major thing that we absolutely need to do with applications and résumés? We need to verify them. No one lies on a résumé, right? Well, there is anecdotal evidence from professional recruiters and background screeners that between one third and one half of all applications and résumés include significant fictitious information.[23] And companies have started to check these documents much more thoroughly because they know that many of their applicants will embellish and outright lie—and the problem has gotten worse over the years.[24]

Several organizations got have gotten burned in the last few years due to job applicants lying on their résumés. For example, basketball coach Steve Masiello was being considered for the top job as coach at the **University of South Florida** when the university found that he had not graduated from the University of Kentucky, as he had said on his résumé.[25] Also, Scott Thompson was fired after four months as the CEO of **Yahoo** when it was discovered that he did not have the college degree he had claimed on his résumé. In addition, Marilee Jones resigned from **MIT** after admitting that she had lied about having a doctorate.[26] So due to these instances and many others, companies are more concerned than ever about lies on résumés, and they therefore always want to make sure applicants have not lied on their application or résumé.[27]

One area that we absolutely want to check is education level, because this is one of the most commonly exaggerated items on a résumé or application. Does the applicant have a degree, if one is required for the job? How can we check this? If you say you are a graduate and the HR representative calls your university, will the university records office tell the HR rep whether or not you are a graduate? The answer is yes, it will. The university can and will tell the recruiter whether or not you graduated and with what degree. It typically cannot provide your transcript or GPA without your

6-2 APPLYING THE CONCEPT

Pre-employment Questions

Using Exhibit 6-2 and the general guideline not to ask any questions that are not job related unless they are BFOQs, identify whether each question can or cannot be asked on an application form or during a job interview.

    a. Legal (can ask)

    b. Illegal (cannot ask during pre-employment)

_____ 6. What languages do you speak?

_____ 7. Are you married or single?

_____ 8. How many children do you have?

_____ 9. So you want to be a truck driver. Are you a member of the Teamsters Union representing truck drivers?

_____ 10. Are you straight or a homosexual?

_____ 11. Have you ever belonged to a union?

_____ 12. What is your date of birth?

_____ 13. Have you been arrested for stealing on the job?

_____ 14. Do you own your own car?

_____ 15. Do you have any form of disability?

_____ 16. Are you a member of the Knights of Columbus?

_____ 17. Can you prove you are legally eligible to work?

_____ 18. Are you currently a member of the military reserve?

_____ 19. What is your religion?

_____ 20. How much do you weigh?

permission because of various privacy laws, but it can tell the employer whether you graduated or not.

Pre-employment Inquiries

On a job application or during an interview, no member of an organization can legally ask any questions that can be used to discriminate against an applicant, unless the questions are bona fide occupational qualifications (or BFOQs; see Chapter 3). Exhibit 6-2 lists some information on what generally can and cannot be asked during the selection process.

It may be hard to memorize the list, but to keep it simple, the two major rules of thumb are as follows:

1. Every question asked should be job related. If the question is not job related, there is a chance that it is discriminatory—so don't ask it. When developing questions, you should have a purpose for using the information. Only ask questions you plan to use in the selection process.

2. Any general question that you ask is one you should ask of all candidates.

State Laws Vary!

Whether you are reviewing an application or conducting an interview, remember that state laws may be more stringent than the existing federal laws. The way a company handles inquiries into employment of recruits is subject to the laws of that individual state, and many states have additional prohibitions in the selection process. For instance, several states—including California, Connecticut, and New York, among others—prohibit asking about arrest records that don't end in convictions.[28] So in those states, the company cannot ask in an interview or on an application about such arrest information.

Other interview or application questions that are allowed by federal law can be limited to a greater extent by state law—or even in some cases by local ordinance. One example of a specific prohibition is that in 30 states—including Nevada, Illinois, and Hawaii—you cannot ask a candidate about sexual orientation or gender identity, nor can you use that information in taking any employment-related action.[29] So you need to always be aware of state laws and how they may differ from federal laws, especially in an area such as selection applications and interviews.

WORK
APPLICATION 6-5

Have you or anyone you know ever been asked an illegal question on an application form or during a job interview? What was the question?

EXHIBIT 6-2 PRE-EMPLOYMENT INQUIRIES

Topic	Generally Acceptable	Generally Unacceptable or Risky
Name	Current legal name and whether the candidate has ever worked under a different name	Maiden name or whether the person has ever changed their name
Address	Current residence	Whether the candidate owns or rents their home
Age	Only whether the candidate's age is within a certain range (if required for a particular job); for example, an employee may need to be 21 to serve alcoholic beverages	How old are you? What is your date of birth? Can you provide a birth certificate? How much longer do you plan to work before retiring?
Sex	Candidate to indicate sex on an application only if sex is a BFOQ	Candidate's sexual preference, orientation or gender identity
Marital and Family Status	None	Specific questions about marital status or any question regarding children or other family issues
National Origin, Citizenship, or Race	Whether the candidate is legally eligible to work in the United States, and whether the candidate can provide proof of status if hired	Specific questions about national origin, citizenship, or race
Language	What languages the candidate speaks and/or writes; can ask candidate to identify specific language(s) if these are BFOQs	What language the candidate speaks when not on the job or how the candidate learned the language
Criminal Record	Whether the candidate has been convicted of a felony; if the answer is yes, can ask other information about the conviction if the conviction is job-related	Whether the candidate has ever been arrested (an arrest does not prove guilt), or charged with a crime
Height and Weight	Generally none unless a BFOQ	Candidate's height or weight if these are not BFOQs
Religion	None unless a BFOQ	Candidate's religious preference, affiliation, or denomination if not a BFOQ
Education and Work Experience	Academic degrees or other professional credentials if information is job related	For information that is not job related
References	Names of people who can verify applicant's training and experience	A reference from a religious leader
Military Record	Information about candidate's military service	Dates and conditions of discharge from the military; draft classification; National Guard or reserve unit of candidate
Organizations	About membership in job-related organizations, such as unions or professional or trade associations	About membership in any non-job-related organization
Disabilities	Are you capable of performing the essential tasks of the job with or without any accommodation?	General questions about disabilities or medical condition

LO 6-5

Briefly discuss the legal considerations in the selection process.

TESTING AND LEGAL ISSUES

As was shown in Exhibit 6-1, testing can be used during the selection process. However, as we've discussed, all tests must be valid and reliable. So obviously, the organization must ensure that it follows all applicable federal and state laws concerning employment discrimination. As we noted in Chapter 3, all of the federal EEO laws apply to "any employment action," so clearly, they apply in all selection tests. But in addition, managers must know that there are some other significant laws dealing with allowable hiring practices.

In this section, we discuss testing. We begin with a brief overview of the EEOC and testing and then move on to specific tests: polygraph testing, genetic testing, written testing, and physical testing. We then end with a discussion of whether or not to test.

The EEOC and Employment Testing

The UGESP (covered above) were created to provide a "uniform federal position in the area of prohibiting discrimination in employment practices on grounds of race, color, religion, sex, or national origin."[30] The guidelines have been formally adopted by the federal Equal Employment Opportunity Commission, the Department of Labor, the Department of Justice, and the Civil Service Commission. As such, the EEOC will use these guidelines anytime it is faced with a discrimination-in-hiring complaint, so every HR manager needs to be familiar with the UGESP and its requirements. If the EEOC investigates a complaint about employment testing being discriminatory, the company will have to show that the selection procedure that is being used is a valid measure for the job being filled. If the company can't show that the measure is valid, it is likely that the EEOC will consider the test a discriminatory hiring practice.

Polygraph Testing

Can we use a polygraph test as a selection test? Yes, but only in a few circumstances. In 1988, the Employee Polygraph Protection Act (EPPA) was passed. The act made it illegal to use a polygraph to test employees' honesty in most circumstances. However, there are two exceptions for corporations and other businesses (there are other exceptions for government and national security):[31]

(1) The use of polygraph tests on prospective employees by any private employer whose primary business purpose consists of providing armored car personnel, personnel engaged in the design, installation, and maintenance of security alarm systems, or other uniformed or plainclothes security personnel; or

(2) the use of a polygraph test by any employer authorized to manufacture, distribute, or dispense a controlled substance listed in schedule I, II, III, or IV of section 202 of the Controlled Substances Act (21 U.S.C. 812).

If you own a store and things are being stolen, can you give polygraph tests to all of your employees? No, the act says you can't. There is one other case, however, where an employer might be allowed to *request* that an employee submit to testing using a polygraph, but the use is severely restricted. This only can occur when all of the following apply:

1. There is an active investigation involving economic loss or injury to the employer's business.

2. The employee had access to the property.

3. The employer has reasonable suspicion that the employee was involved in the incident or activity under investigation.

4. The employer executes and maintains a statement of the facts for a period of 3 years and provides a copy of the statement to the employee.

However, due to the nature of this exemption for ongoing investigations and the ability of the employee to deny the request, a polygraph test is probably not generally of significant value to the average employer, and it can be the basis for a claim of discrimination. As such, the company would be advised to avoid the use of a polygraph in these situations unless there is clear and convincing evidence of the employee's involvement. Exhibit 6-3 provides a summary of exceptions to the EPPA.

EXHIBIT 6-3   EXCEPTIONS TO THE EPPA FOR POLYGRAPH TESTING

General Exception	Specific Exception—can request the employee to submit when:
1. For armored car personnel; personnel engaged in the design, installation, and maintenance of security alarm systems; or other uniformed or plainclothes security personnel	1. There is an active investigation involving economic loss or injury to the employer's business.
	2. The employee had access to the property.
2. Use by any employer authorized to manufacture, distribute, or dispense a controlled substance listed in Schedule I, II, III, or IV of Section 202 of the Controlled Substances Act	3. The employer has reasonable suspicion that the employee was involved in the incident or activity under investigation.
	4. The employer executes and maintains a statement of the facts for a period of 3 years and provides a copy of the statement to the employee.

Genetic Testing

You should recall our discussion in Chapter 3 about the Genetic Information Nondiscrimination Act (GINA). We noted that a significant number of companies at one point began to use genetic tests as a result of advances in medicine and genetic testing and analysis. The basis for this testing was an attempt to make sure that a potential employee didn't have a genetic predisposition to certain known illnesses or diseases that might adversely affect that person's ability to work. However, many individuals felt that this was a significant invasion of their privacy and as a result shouldn't be used by the potential employer. As a result of people's concerns, Congress began looking into the issue of genetic testing, and in 2008 it passed the Genetic Information Nondiscrimination Act (GINA),[32] which protects people from discrimination by health insurers and employers on the basis of their DNA information.

SHRM

B:32
The Genetic Information
Nondiscrimination Act (GINA)

Written Testing

Written tests can be used to predict job success, as long as the tests meet EEOC guidelines for validity (meaning people who score high on the test do well on the job and those who score low do not do well on the job) and reliability (meaning that if people take the same test on different days, they will get approximately the same score each time). Illegal tests can result in lawsuits. Some of the major types of written tests include skills tests, personality tests, interest tests, cognitive ability tests (tests of general intelligence or of some type of job-related aptitude), and honesty tests.

LO 6-6

Discuss the major types of written testing available as selection tools.

Today, written tests are a common part of the selection process.[33] In fact, 80% of midsize and large companies use personality and ability assessments for entry and midlevel management positions to help ensure the right fit between the job candidate and the job.[34]

SKILLS TESTS. Skills tests can be either written or done in physical form. For now, let's discuss written skills testing. A **skills test** *is simply an assessment instrument designed to determine if you have the ability to apply a particular knowledge set.* In other words, it tests whether you can actually do something that you have the knowledge to do. But how do we create written skills tests, and do they work to show a set of skills? Many of you have gone through a large number of written skills tests as you have progressed through your college courses. Have you ever taken a written test on Microsoft Word or PowerPoint? If so, you have taken a written skills test. Do these tests show us that you have a particular set of skills if you can successfully answer questions concerning those skills? In fact, they do.

When would we use skills tests? We would use them to find out how you would perform in a particular job. Can we legitimately use a written skills test? Well, let's use the OUCH test to find out. Is a skills test *objective*? Can we give you a test on Microsoft Word, for example, and then answer yes or no as to whether you know how to indent and italicize? If we can determine this, the test is objective. Is a skills test *uniform in application*? If we give the same test to everyone in the same situation, it is. Is it *consistent in effect*? In general, the answer is yes. However, we can certainly design skills tests that are not consistent in effect, whether we do so intentionally or unintentionally, so we have to validate the test. Does it *have job relatedness*—a direct relationship to the primary aspects of the job? If the answer is yes, it is a legitimate test in this case because it meets the OUCH test. **Groupon** uses skills testing that's role specific.[35] One new trend in testing is to have candidates perform a small sample of actual work for the company for free as part of the selection process.[36]

PERSONALITY AND INTEREST TESTS. **Personality tests** *measure the psychological traits or characteristics of applicants to determine suitability for performance in a specific type of job.* The Myers-Briggs Type Indicator and the Birkman Method are two common personality tests. **Interest tests** are similar, but they *measure a person's intellectual curiosity and motivation in a particular field.*

So are we allowed to use personality or interest assessments as selection tools? Who cares about your personality or personal interests, and is it legitimate for the employer to care? Sometimes, we need a certain type of personality for a job. For example, we need to ensure that a flight attendant can be trained not to panic in an emergency situation. We might also need to determine whether someone applying for a job as an outside salesperson is able to operate in unfamiliar environments with customers whom that person has never met before. An outside salesperson who is an extreme introvert or who has no personal interest in selling or motivation to sell would not work well in the job.

However, if you are an accountant, does having an introverted personality harm your ability to do the job? Not really. If you are a line assembly worker, does having an extroverted personality harm your ability to work on the line? It is unlikely. So in some cases, personality does not matter. Remember earlier in the chapter, we noted that individual personalities are part of the analysis that we may perform for job fit, but if personality or interests have nothing to do with the job, we probably don't want to do these types of testing.

However, if there is a legitimate reason for having a person with a particular type of personality or certain set of interests in a job, then we need to support the validity and reliability of the test for those personality traits or interests, because if we can't show a relationship between these items and the job, then an applicant could

SHRM

I:9
Noncognitive Assessments (e.g., Personality Assessments, etc.)

Skills test An assessment instrument designed to determine if you have the ability to apply a particular knowledge set

Personality test A test measuring the psychological traits or characteristics of applicants to determine suitability for performance in a specific type of job

Interest test A test measuring a person's intellectual curiosity and motivation in a particular field

potentially take the company to court for discriminatory hiring practices.[37] If the hiring manager is an extrovert, and if the manager uses personality testing to find other extroverted people for no other reason than enjoying being around the same type of person, then the manager has improperly used the test. It would be illegal to test personality in such a situation. So if we are going to use personality or interest tests, we have to ask if there is a potential association between the test and the job. If there is and it can be shown, then it is probably OK to use it. If not, you shouldn't use it as a selection tool. However, through an interview, you may be able to get a general idea of the applicant's personality and interest without giving a test.

COGNITIVE ABILITY TESTS. **Cognitive ability tests** *are assessments of general intelligence or of some type of aptitude for a particular job.* Here again, we need to ensure that the tests that may be used are professionally developed, reliable, and valid indicators of a particular ability or knowledge set. Otherwise, we should not use them.

There have been a large number of court cases that dealt with the ability to apply cognitive ability testing, even when such testing had a potential disparate impact, as long as the ability being tested was directly related to a business necessity and was job related.[38] In fact, the 1964 Civil Rights Act provides an exemption to "professionally developed testing":

> *Nor shall it be an unlawful employment practice for an employer to give and to act upon the results of any professionally developed ability test provided that such test, its administration or action upon the results is not designed, intended or used to discriminate because of race, color, religion, sex or national origin.*[39]

However, there has been some recent backlash against using standardized cognitive ability testing as a predictor of success—at least in some industries. Laszlo Bock of **Google** recently said, "GPA's are worthless as a criteria for hiring, and test scores are worthless—no correlation at all except for brand-new college grads, where there's a slight correlation."[40] As an HR manager, you will have to make decisions about whether or not written testing has value in your particular industry.

HONESTY OR INTEGRITY TESTS. There are actually two types of honesty tests: pen-and-paper tests and polygraph tests, also known as lie detector tests. We discussed the polygraph in the legal section earlier in this chapter, so we won't reiterate that information here.

But how good are pen-and-paper honesty or integrity tests? The employee will just tell the employer what it wants to hear, right? In reality, these tests are better than most people think.[41] There is some significant evidence that, at least in personality-based honesty or integrity tests, the applicant has trouble faking answers to the test. The tests ask questions that analyze your philosophy concerning theft or other forms of dishonesty and what you would do in certain situations. They also look for inconsistency in the answers to indicate that an applicant may be trying to give the right answers.

Honesty and integrity tests are certainly not infallible, and they can be faked in some cases. But the evidence shows that they have some value in identifying people who may be less honest and allowing the employer to weed some of these individuals out of the selection process. As such, they have value to the business.

Physical Testing

In addition to written testing, we may also want to use some form of physical testing. **Physical tests** *are designed to ensure that applicants are capable of performing on the job in ways defined by the job specification and description.* Physical testing will

WORK
APPLICATION 6-6

Have you or anyone you know taken a written test when applying for a job or on the job? If so, state the type of test and describe its content.

Cognitive ability test An assessment of general intelligence or of some type of aptitude for a particular job

Physical test A test designed to ensure that applicants are capable of performing on the job in ways defined by the job specification and description

generally be valuable where there are significant physical skills required to perform the job or where there is a significant safety risk associated with putting individuals into jobs if they have physical limitations that are not evident, if they may be under the influence of substances that could cause their work performance to suffer, and if they could create a danger for themselves or others by working in a job for which they are physically unqualified. There are many types of physical testing, but we will limit our discussion to some of the most common forms.

PHYSICAL SKILLS TESTS. We reviewed written skills tests earlier and noted that skills tests determine whether or not you have the ability to apply (use) a particular knowledge set. Physical skills tests are designed to determine whether you have the skills and abilities to perform a particular set of physical tasks. Physical skills tests may include tests of strength and/or endurance, tests of dexterity, tests of eye-hand coordination, or other physical abilities. These tests can also be conducted in several different forms, including by administering work sample tests, at assessment centers, and by using simulations.

Let's take a closer look at some of the common forms of physical testing. **Work sample** tests are basically what they sound like: *We provide a sample of the work that the candidate would perform on the job and ask the candidate to perform the tasks under some type of controlled conditions.* A simple example of a work sample test might be asking the candidate to type a particular letter and then judging the speed and accuracy of the individual's results. Another might be asking the candidate to lift a package of similar size and weight to what would have to be lifted on the job.

An assessment center is a more detailed physical testing environment. Internal and external candidates for positions are often tested through assessment centers. **Assessment centers** *are places where job applicants undergo a series of tests, interviews, and simulated experiences to determine their potential for a particular job.* For example, at **T-Mobile**, you might have to assist a fictitious customer who is mad about his bill, or you might have to provide customers with information about new company services. So an assessment center used by T-Mobile might give tests designed to make candidates demonstrate how well they can use several different computer systems designed to obtain and communicate the information that customers need. This will allow T-Mobile to evaluate those candidates more thoroughly than it could with a more simple form of testing. Some assessment center tests can go on for more than a day or even up to several days. Longer assessment center tests are more commonly used for higher-level professional and management positions.

For physical testing, we can also use **simulations**, *which allow us to put the person into a high-pressure situation but still control the environment so that we limit the danger and cost.* Simulations are very valuable in cases where a real event could be dangerous or emotionally taxing or cost a lot of money. Simulators and even virtual reality environments are beginning to be used in many situations such as military training and teaching new doctors how to perform different types of surgery.[42]

For example, commercial airline pilots are required to routinely train in flight simulators representing the type of aircraft that they fly. In this simulated environment, we can put the pilot into a situation where perhaps a control surface of the airplane jams and the pilot has to take certain actions described in the flight manual to control the aircraft and either correct the problem or figure out how to land successfully. Neither the FAA nor the airline/employer wants to actually put a pilot in an aircraft that has a major control surface failure, and it would be very dangerous and expensive if the pilot were to crash the aircraft! This is why simulators are so valuable in this type of situation.

PHYSICAL EXAMS. Physical examinations may be either desired or in some cases required for candidates for certain jobs. If the job will require heavy physical exertion, there may be a legitimate need to have individuals submit to a physical exam

SHRM

I:8

Ability/Job Knowledge Tests, Assessment Centers

SHRM

I:11

Contingent Assessment Methods: Drug Testing, Medical Exams

Work sample A test conducted by providing a sample of the work that the candidate would perform on the job and asking the candidate to perform the tasks under some type of controlled conditions

Assessment center A place where job applicants undergo a series of tests, interviews, and simulated experiences to determine their potential for a particular job

Simulation A test where a candidate is put into a high-pressure situation in a controlled environment so that the danger and cost are limited

to ensure that they are healthy enough for the stress. (Think NFL lineman!) In other cases, we may be required by the state or federal government to have individuals who work in specific fields take a physical exam before they are allowed to work in certain jobs such as driving a heavy truck (DOT physical) or flying a plane (FAA physical). Or we may just want to have our candidates take a physical exam before they start work so that we have baseline knowledge of their health at the time of hire. We can then use that baseline later to determine whether they were subjected to conditions that harmed them physically.

For instance, if we have a candidate take a physical and the physician finds out that the candidate has significant carpal tunnel syndrome in the wrists, it makes it harder for the candidate to claim after being hired that the job caused the injury. However, we have to be very aware of the potential for discrimination based on disability if we require a physical exam as a prerequisite to work in our organization. If the exam is not directly related to the essential functions of the job, it may not be advisable to require it as part of the selection process, because of the potential to illegally discriminate on the basis of disability.

DRUG TESTING. Most employers have the right to test for a wide variety of substances in the workplace.[43] While drug testing is not required by an outside authority (like the federal government) in most cases, employers can put testing programs in place. The primary reasons for drug testing will generally be workplace safety and productivity. Private sector, nonunion companies are usually allowed to require applicants and/or employees to take drug tests in most states, although some states do limit workplace drug screening. In unionized workforces, however, the implementation of testing programs must be part of contract negotiations. But all employers need to follow some guidelines to stay within the law in implementation and maintenance of any drug-testing program they choose to have. What does the company need to do?

In general, testing must be done systematically in one of two forms: either "random" or "universal." Testing can't be selective in most states. In other words, we can't decide we want to test "Amy Jones" because we just want to. Testing can be universal in some situations (e.g., after a workplace accident or on initial offer of employment) and random in others (e.g., quarterly drug testing of a sample of the workforce), but it has to be one or the other and we have to specify which option we use in each situation.

Most states now require prior authorization for drug testing. In the case of applicants, this authorization is usually part of the job application legal notices that we reviewed earlier in the chapter. For existing employees, it will usually be part of the employee handbook.

The organization also must have a drug-testing policy, which should generally contain the following information:

- Requirements for training and the frequency of training on substance abuse (generally required at least annually, but in some states semiannually)
- When individuals will be tested—for example pre-employment testing, random testing, testing after any workplace accident, or testing if there is reasonable suspicion
- Substances that will be tested for during any drug tests
- Disciplinary actions that will result from testing positive on a first test and subsequent tests if applicable
- In many states, the employer is required to "reasonably accommodate" employees who voluntarily submit to an alcohol or drug rehabilitation program. If this is the case, it needs to be noted in the policy.
- In most states, the policy is not allowed to exempt managerial employees just because they are at the managerial level.

LO 6-7

Identify the requirements for organizational drug-testing programs.

SHRM

X:10
Testing for Substance Abuse

WORK
APPLICATION 6-7

Have you or anyone you know taken a physical test when applying for a job or on the job? If so, state the type of test and describe its content.

We need to bring up one more point on workplace drug testing. There continues to be discussion of recent state laws legalizing medicinal or even recreational marijuana and how this affects company drug-testing policies. The simplest answer is that these laws do not affect company drug policies—at least not at this time. In each case where an individual has challenged a detrimental employment action (including termination for a positive drug test) in court, all the way up to the US Supreme Court (*Ashcroft v. Raich*), the decision has been that employers can "safely refuse to accept medical marijuana as a reasonable medical explanation for a positive drug test result."[44] Employers have also not been required to accommodate employee use of medical marijuana under the ADA.

Remember again, in drug testing as in all employment testing, we have to identify the relationship of the test to the job that will be done or is being done—in other words, it has to be "job related." Drug testing almost certainly meets the objective, uniform, and consistent requirements of the OUCH test, so job relatedness is the critical concern in this case. In most cases, the relationship is one of concern for safety and productivity in the workplace, but the organization has to make that determination, and if it doesn't look like drug testing will enhance safety in a particular type of job, the organization may not want to use it as a selection tool. As related to productivity, over the years, research has shown that substance abusers tend to be absent more often and more prone to having accidents on the job. This lowers their productivity. Substance abusers are also potentially negligent hires, and they cost employers millions of dollars annually. Therefore, many employers try not to hire candidates who use illegal drugs. On a personal note, if you are using illegal drugs, we suggest you get straight or be sure not to apply to organizations that test for drugs.

FITNESS-FOR-DUTY TESTING. A significant number of companies today are turning to fitness-for-duty tests in place of much more invasive drug testing. A **fitness-for-duty test** simply *identifies whether or not an employee is physically capable at a particular point in time of performing a specific type of work.*[45] For instance, some trucking firms now use fitness-for-duty testing before drivers are allowed to take an 18-wheel truck out of their terminals. Under what conditions can we generally utilize fitness-for-duty testing? Federal law notes that we can use a medical examination "if it is job related and consistent with business necessity."[46] (You should recall those terms from our discussion of employment law in Chapter 3.) A fitness-for-duty exam is just a type of medical exam.

In fact, this type of testing can be superior to drug testing for certain business purposes. For instance, if you manage a courier who drives a company vehicle and the driver is not abusing drugs but has not gotten any sleep in the past couple of days, a fitness-for-duty test would quite likely identify that the courier is unable to make quick, correct decisions, while a drug test would show that the courier is not impaired due to drug use. A common form of this type of test is based on *individual reaction time*, which slows significantly when someone is fatigued.[47] In such a case, the courier would be required to rest for a certain period of time before being allowed to drive that vehicle. Another plus for this type of testing is that it is much less invasive and much more acceptable to employees than drug testing.

To Test or Not to Test

We can choose to apply selection tests or not. A consideration is the development of the test. If you develop your own test, you have to provide support for its reliability and validity—so you have to have experts develop and test the test, which takes time and money. The other option is to use tests that have already been developed and tested for reliability and validity. The problem here is that you usually have to pay a fee for every single test that you give, not to mention the time and effort to give and assess the tests.

Fitness-for-duty test A test identifying whether or not an employee is physically capable at a particular point in time of performing a specific type of work

APPLYING THE CONCEPT

Type of Test

Write before each job situation below the letter corresponding to the type of test described.

a. genetic
b. skills
c. personality and interest
d. cognitive ability
e. honesty or integrity—polygraph
f. physical skills
g. physical exam
h. drug

_____ 21. As part of the selection process, you will have to answer questions while being monitored by this machine.

_____ 22. A paper-and-pencil test is administered so that we can determine whether you have the right characteristics to succeed on the job.

_____ 23. You have to undergo an exam by our doctor to determine whether you can handle the job.

_____ 24. To get the drywalling job, you will have to hang, tape, and paste 10 sheets while doing a quality job, all in 3 hours.

_____ 25. Part of the selection process is to take our intelligence test.

_____ 26. Part of the firefighter test is to carry this 50-pound dummy up this ladder in 2 minutes or less.

_____ 27. You have to go in the bathroom now and put a sample of your urine in this cup so we can test it.

_____ 28. You need to take a test so that we can determine if you might get any known illnesses or diseases in the future.

So testing can be time-consuming and expensive. Therefore, testing has to pay for itself through its ability to help you hire applicants who are in fact a good fit for the job and the organization. It may save you time and money by preventing you from hiring and then immediately losing employees who are a bad fit, preventing negligent hires, and improving worker productivity by maximizing the chance of hiring good-fit employees. This justifies the investment in the test.

Today, tests are common.[48] In fact, between one third and one half of all job applicants will probably have to go through some sort of pre-employment testing,[49] and almost 90% of companies who apply those tests won't hire an applicant whose test scores indicate deficiency in basic skills.[50]

Here again, the OUCH test gives us a quick guide to whether or not a particular test would be appropriate in any given situation. Let's say that we are trying to decide whether or not to use a personality test in a specific hiring situation. If we use a validated test that has proven reliable in assessing basic personality characteristics (Objective), if we give the same test to each applicant (Uniform in application), if we find that the test's effect on the various protected groups is consistent (Consistent in effect), and if we find that the test is directly applicable to a major function of the job for which we are hiring (Has job relatedness), then it would be appropriate to use such a test. If this were not the case, then we probably don't want to use a personality test. We can and should go through this thought process in determining the value of each selection tool before we decide to use it in the selection process.

Social Media's Role in Selection

You have all heard the stories about an HR manager going onto Facebook and finding out about a recruit's less-than-acceptable exploits while at college or at another time in the candidate's personal life. Is social media an acceptable tool for pre-employment screening? If so, how can it and how *should* it be used for this purpose? Or is it off-limits, especially if you have your pages set to "private"? There are many questions and issues associated with the lines between your personal life, your social media pages, and your professional life. We will talk in some detail about social media use in selection a little later in the chapter.

SELECTION INTERVIEWS

Remember that during the selection process, some of the usual steps may be skipped or completed out of sequence. While the initial interview may be skipped, rarely will a candidate get a job without being interviewed by at least one person. To review, the common role of the HR staff specialists in hiring lower-level employees is to conduct screening interviews to pick the top candidates who will continue on in the selection process. This screening step helps save the line managers time when there are large numbers of job applicants. Many organizations today are also using technology to enhance their ability to quickly complete screening interviews. Organizations including **Nike** and **PricewaterhouseCoopers** are using computers to conduct initial screening interviews. **Google** is known for having between 4 and 12 grueling screening interviews.[51]

Interviewing

To get a job, you need to be able to ace the interview,[52] but as a manager, you will need to know how to conduct a job interview. So this part of the section can help you do both well. You can practice this skill in Skill Builder 6-2.

The interview is usually the most heavily weighted and one of the last steps in the selection process.[53] The interview gives the candidate a chance to learn about the job and organization. The interview also gives a manager a chance to assess things about a candidate that can't be obtained from an application, test, or references, such as the candidate's ability to communicate and the individual's personality, interest, appearance, and motivation. Many candidates lie during a job interview,[54] so the interview is also used to check the accuracy of the application/résumé to make sure candidates did not embellish or outright lie.[55]

An important focus of the interview is to assess the applicant's personality-job fit, ability-job fit, and person-organization fit. More than half of HR professionals ranked culture fit as the most important criterion at the interview stage.[56] Because job interviewing is so important, you will learn in this subsection the basics of how to prepare for and conduct a job interview. As a manager, you will need to know how to conduct a job interview. You can practice this skill in Skill Builder 6-1.

©iStockphoto.com/Yuri

Many companies now use computers to conduct the first round of interviews.

Types of Interviews and Questions

Exhibit 6-4 shows the various types of interviews and questions, which we discuss in this section.

TYPES OF INTERVIEWS. Three basic types of interviews are based on structure. In a structured interview, all candidates are asked the same list of prepared questions. In an unstructured interview, there are no preplanned questions or sequence of topics. So, for example, at **Groupon**, there are no stock questions; interviewers are trying for a free-flowing conversation.[57] In a semistructured interview, the interviewer has a list of questions but also asks unplanned questions. The semistructured interview is generally preferred by most interviewers. It helps avoid discrimination (because the interviewer has a list of prepared questions to ask all candidates), but it also allows the interviewer to ask each candidate questions

EXHIBIT 6-4 TYPES OF INTERVIEWS AND QUESTIONS

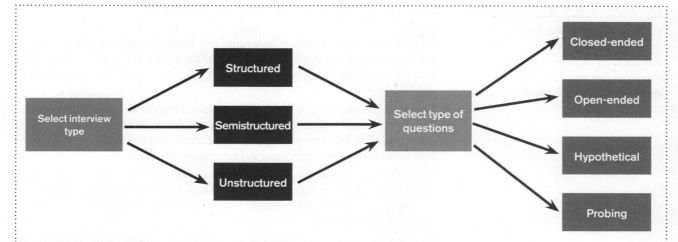

Common Interview Questions

Answering these questions prior to going to a job interview is good preparation that will help you get the job. Written answers are better preparation than verbal ones.

- How would you describe yourself?
- What two or three things are most important to you in your job and career?
- Why did you choose this job and career?
- What do you consider to be your greatest strengths and weaknesses?
- What have you learned from your mistakes?
- What would your last boss say about your work performance?
- What motivates you to go the extra mile on a project or job?
- What have you accomplished that shows your initiative and willingness to work?
- What two or three accomplishments have given you the most satisfaction? Why?
- Why should I hire you?
- What skills do you have?
- What makes you qualified for this position?
- In what ways do you think you can make a contribution to our company?
- Do you consider yourself a leader?
- How do you work under pressure?
- Why did you decide to seek a position in this company?
- What can you tell us about our company?
- What are your expectations regarding promotions and salary increases?
- Are you willing to travel and relocate?
- What are your long-range and short-range goals and objectives?
- What do you see yourself doing 5 years from now? Ten years from now?
- What do you expect to be earning in 5 years?

relating to that person's own situation. The interviewer departs from the structure when appropriate. At the same time, using a standard set of questions makes it easier to compare candidates. The amount of structure you should use depends on your experience as an interviewer. The less experience you have, the more structure you need.

TYPES OF QUESTIONS. One thing to keep in mind is the need to develop a set of consistent questions to ask all candidates so that you can objectively compare the candidates and select the most qualified.[58] The questions you ask give you control over the interview; they allow you to get the information you need to make your decision. As

WORK
APPLICATION 6-8

Select one of your jobs and identify the type of interview you had to get it. Describe how the interview went in terms of its structure.

WORK
APPLICATION 6-9

discussed in the pre-employment inquiries sections, all questions should have a purpose and should be job related.

You may use four types of questions during an interview:

1. *Closed-ended questions*, which require a limited response, often a yes or no answer, and are appropriate for dealing with fixed aspects of the job. Examples include "Do you have a class-one license?" and "Can you produce it if hired?"

2. *Open-ended questions,* which require detailed responses and are appropriate for determining candidate abilities and motivation. Examples include "Why do you want to be a computer programmer for our company?" and "What do you see as a major strength you can bring to our company?"

3. *Hypothetical questions*, which require candidates to describe what they would do and say in a given situation. These questions are appropriate for assessing capabilities. An example would be "What would the problem be if the machine made a ringing sound?"

4. *Probing questions*, which require a clarification response and are appropriate for improving the interviewer's understanding. Probing questions are not planned. They are used to clarify the candidate's response to an open-ended or hypothetical question. Examples include "What do you mean by 'it was tough'?" and "What was the dollar increase in sales you achieved?"

Today, HR interviewers prefer behavior-based questions that ask candidates to describe how they handled specific situations. Laszlo Bock, **Google**'s vice president of people operations, noted in a recent interview that "what works well are structured behavioral interviews, where you have a consistent rubric for how you assess people, rather than having each interviewer just make stuff up." One of his sample questions is "Give me an example of a time when you solved an analytically difficult problem."[59]

There are two basic types of behavior-based questions: situational questions and behavioral-descriptive questions. A *situational question* puts you in a hypothetical situation that you would likely face in the job you are applying for, and it asks, "What is your solution to this problem?" An example would be "You lead a team of marketing, operations, and engineering people working on an engineering design problem. Two of the engineers have significantly different views concerning the method of solving a problem in the design of the item. How would you interact with the two engineers to resolve the problem?" Using this question, the interviewer is trying to figure out what you would most likely do in real life to resolve a complex conflict within a team.[60]

On the other hand, a *behavioral descriptive question* asks about something specific that you have done in the past. Mr. Bock's question above—"Give me an example of a time when you solved an analytically difficult problem"—is an example of a behavioral descriptive question. It asks you to tell the interviewer what you actually did as the result of a particular situation. What's the value of this type of question? Remember that past behavior is the best predictor of future behavior. So we can find out what you have done in the past and would likely do in a future difficult analytical situation.

Preparing for the Interview

Completing the interview preparation steps shown in Model 6-1 will help you improve your interviewing skills.

Step 1: Review the job description and specifications. You cannot effectively match a candidate to a job if you do not thoroughly understand the job. Read and become familiar with the job description and job specifications. If they are outdated or do not exist, conduct a job analysis using the guidelines from Chapter 4.

Step 2: Prepare a realistic job preview. Candidates should understand what the job is and what they are expected to do. They should know the good and bad points of the job. Plan how you will present a realistic preview of the job (see Chapter 4), based on the job description. It often helps to give candidates a tour of the work area.

Step 3: Plan the type of interview. What level of structure will you use? The interview should take place in a private, quiet place, without interruptions. It may be appropriate to begin the interview in an office and then tour the facilities while asking questions. Decide when the tour will take place and what questions will be asked. Take a list with you if you intend to ask questions during the tour.

Step 4: Develop questions for all candidates. Your questions should be job related, nondiscriminatory, and, in the case of a structured interview, asked of all candidates. Use the job description and specifications to develop questions that relate to each job task and responsibility. Use a mixture of closed-ended, open-ended, and hypothetical questions. Don't be concerned about the order of questions; just write them out at this point.

Step 5: Develop a form. Once you have created a list of questions, determine the sequence. Start with the easy questions. One approach starts with closed-ended questions, moves on to open-ended questions, and then to hypothetical questions, and it uses probing questions as needed. Another approach structures the interview around the job description and specifications; each responsibility is explained, and then questions relating to each are asked.

Write out the questions in sequence, leaving space for checking off closed-ended responses, for making notes on the responses to open-ended and hypothetical questions, and for follow-up questions. Add information gained from probing questions where appropriate. Make a copy of the form to use with each candidate you will be interviewing and a few extras for future use when filling the same job or for a reference when developing forms for other jobs.

Step 6: Develop questions for each candidate. Review each candidate's application and/or résumé. You will most likely want to add specific questions to a copy of the form to verify or clarify some of the information provided; for example, ask, "I noticed that you did not list any employment during 2009; were you unemployed?" or "On the application, you stated you had computer training; what computer software were you trained to operate?" Be sure the individual questions are not discriminatory. For example, do not ask only women whether they can lift 50 pounds; ask all candidates, men and women, this question, and plan to have all candidates take this physical test if it they haven't taken it before the interview.

MODEL 6-1   INTERVIEW PREPARATION STEPS

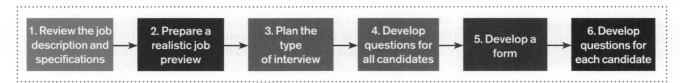

1. Review the job description and specifications → 2. Prepare a realistic job preview → 3. Plan the type of interview → 4. Develop questions for all candidates → 5. Develop a form → 6. Develop questions for each candidate

MODEL 6-2   INTERVIEWING STEPS

1. Open the interview → 2. Present the realistic job preview → 3. Ask your questions → 4. Introduce the top candidates to coworkers → 5. Close the interview

LO 6-9

List and briefly describe the steps taken in conducting interviews.

Conducting the Interview

Following the steps listed in Model 6-2 will help you do a better job of interviewing candidates.

Step 1: Open the interview. Develop rapport. Put the candidate at ease by talking about some topic not related to the job. Maintain eye contact in a way that is comfortable for you and the candidate.

Step 2: Present the realistic job preview (RJP). Be sure the candidate understands the job requirements. Answer any questions the candidate has about the job and the organization. If the job is not what the candidate expected or wants to do, allow the candidate to disqualify themselves and close the interview at that point.

Step 3: Ask your questions. Steps 2 and 3 can be combined, if you like. To get the most out of a job interview, you must take notes on responses to your questions. Tell the candidate that you have prepared a list of questions and that you plan to take notes.

During the interview, the candidate should do most of the talking. Give the candidate a chance to think and respond. If the candidate did not give you all the information you wanted, ask a probing question. However, if it is obvious that the candidate does not want to answer a question, don't force it. Go on to the next question or close the interview. End with a closing question, for example, "I'm finished with my questions. Is there anything else you want to tell me about or ask me?"

Step 4: Introduce top candidates to coworkers. Introduce top candidates to people with whom they will be working, to get a sense of the candidates' interpersonal skills and overall attitude. Introductions can also give you a sense of whether the person is a team player. It is also common to have coworkers interview the candidates and give you, the hiring manager, their assessment of the candidates.

Step 5: Close the interview. Do not lead candidates on. Be honest without making a decision during the interview. Thank candidates for their time and tell them what the next step in the selection process is, if any. Tell candidates when you will contact them. For example, say, "Thank you for coming in for this interview. I will be interviewing over the next two days and will call you with my decision by Friday of this week." After the interview, be sure to jot down general impressions not covered by specific questions.

After all interviews are completed, compare each candidate's qualifications to the job specifications to determine who would be the best fit for the job. Be sure to get coworkers' impressions of each candidate because they will have to work with the candidate. Also recall that the best fit includes fitting in with the organizational culture.[61]

©iStockphoto.com/OJO_Images

The job interview is commonly given the most weight in the selection process.

WORK
APPLICATION 6-10

Select a job interview or internship interview that you have had. Describe how each of the five steps of Model 6-2 was conducted and how it could have been improved. If any step was skipped, say so.

LO 6-10

Discuss the use of the various background checks as tests for employment.

BACKGROUND CHECKS

Background checks are needed to help prevent negligent hires.[62] During the selection process (Exhibit 6-1), in addition to verification of the information on a candidate's application form and/or résumé, several other types of background checks may or may not be appropriate. It is not unusual for the background check to be a simple

6-1 SELF ASSESSMENT

Interview Readiness

Select a professional job you would like to apply for. On a scale of 1 to 7 (1 = not confident, 7 = totally confident), indicate for each question how confident you are that you can give an answer that would make a positive impression on an interviewer.

I am confident that I have an answer   I am not confident that I have an answer

7_____6_____5_____4_____3_____2_____1

_____ 1. Why did you choose the job for which you are applying?
_____ 2. What are your long-range career goals over the next 5 to 10 years?
_____ 3. What are your short-range goals and objectives for the next 1 to 2 years?
_____ 4. How do you plan to achieve your career goals?
_____ 5. What are your strengths and weaknesses?
_____ 6. What motivates you to put forth your greatest effort? Describe a situation in which you did so.
_____ 7. What two or three accomplishments have given you the most satisfaction? Why?
_____ 8. Why do you want this job?
_____ 9. In what kind of an organizational culture do you want to work?
_____ 10. Why did you decide to apply for a position with our organization?
_____ 11. What do you know about our organization?
_____ 12. In what ways do you think you can make a contribution to our organization?
_____ 13. What two or three things would be most important to you in your job?
_____ 14. Are you willing to relocate for the job? Do you have any constraints on relocation?
_____ 15. Describe a situation in which you had to work with a difficult person (another student, a coworker, a customer, a supervisor, etc.). How did you handle the situation?
_____ Total. Add up the numbers you assigned to each question and place the total on this line and on the continuum below.

105   95   85   75   65   55   45   35   25   15

Ready for the job interview   Not ready for the job interview

These are common interview questions, so you should be prepared to give a good, confident answer to each of them. Your career services office may offer mock interviews to help you with your interview skills to help you get the job you are looking for.

pass or fail. Background checks can become rather expensive depending on which checks we do and how often we have to do them, so they are usually left until we have at least narrowed down the list of candidates to a final few, or in some cases even to the final candidate. We may then offer employment to the candidate conditioned on passing various background checks. Remember, though, that you cannot use a background check to discriminate in violation of federal or state laws.[63]

What types of background checks are available and when should we use them? The types of background checks include credit checks, criminal background checks, reference checks, and Web searches. In this section, we describe them, and we provide guidelines on when to use them.

Credit Checks

Although several states have recently put limits on its use,[64] one of the most commonly used background checks is the credit check. Credit checks are subject to the Fair Credit Reporting Act (FCRA),[65] which requires that employers disclose to the applicant that they will use credit reports for employment decisions. The act also says that if the information on the credit report results in an adverse employment action,

SHRM
B:36
Fair Credit Reporting Act (FCRA)

the employer has to give a copy of the report to the person and inform the applicant of rights under FCRA, including the right to dispute the report. FCRA lawsuits have been on the rise over the past few years, with companies such as **Disney, Domino's Pizza, Kmart,** and **Dillard's** being accused of FCRA violations in hiring.[66]

When can employers complete credit checks on applicants, and why would they do so? Credit checks will most likely be done if applicants will have access to any money or if they will work with the company's financial information. Credit checks may also be done with other employees to evaluate their personal responsibility—to see if they have a habit of being dishonest in credit transactions.

A history of not paying bills tells the organization that the person is likely to be dishonest in other ways as well. Does something like a bankruptcy on your credit report automatically knock you out of contention for a job? No. In fact, by law, the company can't refuse to hire you solely because of a bankruptcy.[67] However, again, if your credit report shows a pattern of failure to live up to your credit obligations, the company can and probably will use that information to remove you from the applicant pool, as long as the company's home state laws allow it.

Credit reports also give the employer other reference information that can be used for background checks. Your credit report generally includes historical data on your previous addresses, giving the organization information against which they can check your employment history and perform criminal background checks. If you state on your employment history that you were working at a manufacturing plant in North Carolina at a given point in time, and if you were living in Texas at that time, then there is a significant discrepancy. It may show that you are not telling the truth on your employment history. The credit report also provides information on previous employers, directly in some cases, although this information may not be complete.

Criminal Background Checks

All states allow criminal background checks in at least some cases. However, laws vary so significantly across jurisdictions that it is difficult to enumerate the circumstances in which criminal background checks are allowed. However, due to the issue of negligent hiring, most companies today will generally complete a criminal background check when it is allowed. Can or should a criminal record keep an individual from being hired? Again, it depends on what type of conviction it was, how long ago it occurred, and what type of job the individual is being considered for now.

We would have a much easier time defending the use of a criminal background check for an individual who would have access to products or funds that are easily stolen than we would in the case of someone with no access to anything of significant value in the company. Similarly, we would be more likely to be able to use a violent criminal history to rule out an applicant if the applicant would have access to children or other innocent persons who could easily be harmed by the employee. As always, we have to look at all the circumstances and make a decision based on the OUCH test and the defensibility of the selection tool that we are considering.

Reference Checks

Reference checks include not only calls to references that are provided by the applicant, but also reference letters from employers, personal letters of recommendation, and possibly cold calls to previous employers. Should the company perform a reference check on applicants? Is it going to be of any value, or are the references that the applicant provides going to say only good things about the applicant?

The basic answer is that a reference letter that is requested by the applicant is almost always going to say good things. The applicant will almost never ask anybody to provide a reference unless the applicant knows that the reference will be good. Almost! Every once in a while, you will check a reference and it will not be very good. It is rare, but it does happen, and when it happens, it is usually a good piece of information for the company. The truth is that generally, the letters don't give much information, but we want to ask for them anyway. In addition, though, we want to check references that might not have been given to us by the applicant but instead, by people such as former employers and coworkers. Does that do any good?

What is a previous employer most likely going to tell you if you call for a reference check? The most common HR answer will be in the form of "Yes, he/she worked at this company, from (date) to (date) in (job type) job." Why is this a typical response to a reference check with a former employer? This is to protect the company from being sued for providing defamatory information about the former employee, in other words, for hurting the individual's reputation unfairly. Over time, company lawyers have found that if we provide more information than noted above, we can become the target of lawsuits. So most companies won't provide more information than they have to. So if you are looking for a true reference, you are better off bypassing the HR department. Get the title and name of candidates' prior supervisors and try giving them a reference call.[68] Sometimes, the supervisor will give you the typical yes and dates of employment, but when the candidate is good, the supervisor will often say so; and when the supervisor is very vague about the former employee's performance, this may give you "the read between the lines" information that will help in the selection process.

Often, a question comes up concerning whether or not the individual is "eligible for rehire." Think about this question for a moment. As soon as a previous employer says an applicant to your company is *not* eligible for rehire, what do you think? You think that the applicant is probably not a good employee. Another comment that comes up in discussions of employer reference checks is that many states now have laws that allow a previous employer to provide an honest reference with "immunity" from legal action. Arkansas law, for instance, says,

> A current or former employer may disclose the following information about a current or former employee's employment history to a prospective employer of the current or former employee upon receipt of written consent from the current or former employee.[69]

However, the law also states,

> The immunity conferred by this section shall not apply when an employer or prospective employer discriminates or retaliates against an employee because the employee or the prospective employee has exercised or is believed to have exercised any federal or state statutory right or undertaken any action encouraged by the public policy of this state.[70]

So if the previous employer were to provide an honest reference, assuming immunity under the law, and the former employee claims that the reference was discriminatory or in retaliation for something the employer didn't like, the company can still be sued. This is why most companies still won't provide more than a basic reference on former employees.

On a personal note, if you did an internship or had a job and you know you impressed your boss, ask for a written recommendation. You can provide this letter to prospective employers. Also, for internships and jobs that you list on your résumé, if you know you will get a good recommendation, be sure to list your supervisor's name and telephone number (a direct-line number if available). Why? Because it is not unusual for a prospective employer to call your prior employer for a reference. So wouldn't you like the caller to speak directly with your boss, rather than with the HR department that will only give the standard answer listed above?

Many organizations today are doing background checks over the Internet. Some job candidates are not offered the job because of content found on the Web.

SHRM

Q:14
Social Networking

WORK
APPLICATION 6-11

Do an Internet search on yourself. Did you find any material that you or others posted that you would not want a prospective employer to find? Are your email address and telephone message professional?

Web Searches

Finally, with the ability to access very large amounts of information via the Internet, more and more organizations are using the Internet to do research on job candidates. "Googling" a candidate's name is becoming a standard practice in these organizations.[71] And it is truly amazing what the company finds in many cases.

Should social media be used as a selection device? HR departments are going to use the tools that they have available to get the best possible people, so social media will most likely continue to be one tool that is used in the recruiting and selection process. However, we need to be very careful to avoid using information that would be illegal in consideration for employment. It would be very easy to find out information on someone's religion, race, gender, or other facets of that individual's personal life—factors that would be illegal to consider in the hiring process—that might allow a company representative to make a biased and even discriminatory choice.[72] Most legal opinions seem to favor the employer in cases where there might be a question of violation of privacy if the employer is doing a check of social media to avoid negligent hires, but companies need to make sure that they are doing so in an even-handed, equitable manner, or they can be considered liable for invasions of off-duty privacy.[73]

Well then, how can a company find and use relevant employment information while still avoiding the danger of making an illegal decision? Two ways that companies have found to avoid illegal bias are to have either an outside agency do the social media search or have a company insider who has no decision authority in hiring do that same search and bring only relevant information to the person or persons doing the selection.[74] This separates the search (and any items found that would be illegal to consider) from the selection process. However, companies have to be aware that, if they use a third party (outside agency) to do a social media search, the search may then become subject to the requirements of the Fair Credit Reporting Act. Remember that this act requires the company to give prior notice to a person who is being investigated and also requires that negative information found as a result of the investigation be disclosed to unsuccessful applicants so that they can provide explanations for such information.[75]

The Stored Communications Act (SCA) may also limit employers' ability to access any websites that have some type of privacy settings—either restricted access granted by the page owner, passwords, or other protection. A prospective employer can go to Facebook and look at public pages, but if the individual has private information and the potential employer "hacks" that information on Facebook or any other site, or if the employer demands the applicant's passwords or user names, that would be a violation of the SCA.[76]

So, what should you do if you are going to use social media as one of your background checks? First, make sure that you notify the individual applicant that you will be researching open social media records for information. Second, use a separate individual or organization to do the actual review and have that entity remove any information that could cause a claim of illegal discrimination before the decision maker sees the results. Third, provide the applicant with copies of any information found that might be harmful to the application and allow the applicant to provide a written explanation of the circumstances surrounding the item. This will at least provide the company with some defense if applicants decide that they have been treated unfairly and decide to sue.

Also, on a personal note, as a potential job applicant, make sure that everything on the Web about you is information that you are comfortable with a company discovering in a Web search. You may not be putting negative things about yourself online, but you also need to make sure your friends aren't, either. Employers *will* most likely do a Web search on you as a candidate in today's world, and this goes for part-time jobs, summer jobs, and internships. Also, make sure your email address and telephone message are professional for job searching.

SELECTING THE CANDIDATE AND OFFERING THE JOB

We've made it to the last step of the selection process! You learned in previous sections that there are different tools available to employers as they go through the selection process. However, even with all of these tools, we can't find out everything about a potential job candidate. HR-savvy people who have been in recruiting and selection for any length of time know this and only try to discover a limited number of things about a candidate. You may want to just discover some basic items that tell you whether or not the individual is a *really* good fit for the job. These might include the following three things:

LO 6-11

Identify the common problems employers encounter during the selection process.

1. Does the candidate have the basic qualifications for the job—right personality, ability, and person-organization fit?
2. Does the candidate actually *want* to do the job, or does this person want just *any* job? In other words, will the candidate be satisfied with the job and stay for some time and be productive, or will the candidate be a potential negligent hire?
3. Is the candidate basically honest, and is this person telling the truth? If not, you could be looking at a problem employee.

The recruiter may know that if he can find out these three basic things, the candidate will be a valuable addition to the organization and can be trained to do any specific job that is necessary.

There are two basic methods that we use to make final selection decisions for the organization. The **multiple-hurdle selection model** *requires that each applicant must pass a particular selection test in order to go on to the next test.* If an applicant fails to pass any test in the process, that person is immediately removed from the running. On the other hand, the **compensatory selection model** *allows an individual to do poorly on one test but make up for that poor grade by doing exceptionally well on other tests.* Again, each step in the selection process (interviews and background checks) is a test. Using the compensatory model allows the employer to rank each of the candidates based on their overall score from all of the testing. The employer can also group candidates based on this same information.

SHRM

I:13
Selection Decisions: Ranking, Grouping/Banding, Random Selection

Problems to Avoid During the Selection Process

Avoid the following problems during the selection process:

- *Rushing.* Try not to be pressured into hiring just any candidate. Find the best fit or you will have turnover, productivity, and negligent hire problems.
- *Stereotyping.* Don't prejudge or leap to conclusions. Match the candidate to the job based on analysis rather than instinct.

Multiple-hurdle selection model Model requiring that each applicant must pass a particular selection test in order to go on to the next test

Compensatory selection model Model allowing an individual to do poorly on one test but make up for that poor grade by doing exceptionally well on other tests

The final step of the selection process is commonly the job offer.

- *"Like me" syndrome.* Don't look for a candidate who is your clone. People who are not like you may do an excellent job. Remember the benefits of diversity.
- *Halo and horn effects.* Do not judge a candidate on the basis of one or two favorable characteristics (the *halo effect*) or one or two unfavorable characteristics (the *horn effect*). Make the selection on the basis of the total qualifications of all candidates.
- *Premature selection.* Don't make your selection based only on a candidate's application or résumé or the fact that the candidate impressed you during the interview. Do not compare candidates after each interview. The order in which you interview applicants can influence you. Be open-minded during all interviews and make a choice only after you have finished all interviews. Compare each candidate on each job specification.

Hiring

So after all selection activities are completed, compare each candidate's qualifications to the job specifications, identify whether or not this person really wants to do the job, and analyze whether or not the individual has been basically honest during the selection process. Do all this to determine who would be the best fit for the job. Be sure to get coworkers' impressions of each candidate when appropriate because they will have to work and get along with whomever you hire (person-organization fit). Diversity should also be considered when selecting a candidate.

So to bring the selection process to an end, contact the best candidate and offer that person the job. If the candidate does not accept the job or accepts but leaves after a short period of time, you can frequently offer the next-best candidate the job.

TRENDS AND ISSUES IN HRM

In this chapter's trends and issues in HRM, we're going to take a brief look at the issue of selection with a global workforce, the effect of cultural fit on hiring decisions, and the use of HRIS in the selection process. Each of these issues has affected the process of selection in a significant way during the past decade, which in turn has caused HR managers to change the way they work.

Selection With a Global Workforce

Because we've reviewed in earlier chapters the significant coming shortage of knowledge workers worldwide, we won't go through that information again here. The shortage certainly affects our ability to select individuals for our workforce. However, we have several other issues of significance when we're dealing with selecting individuals from all over the world. The first major issue that HR managers must deal with is the process of immigration and work visas for the various countries in which the organization operates. Each country has its own requirements for immigration and for foreign workers who want to gain employment in that country. The HR manager is typically the responsible individual for identifying the requirements and making sure that the individual fulfills them.

The organization, through the HR department, is also typically responsible for assisting the individual with filling out the forms and in many cases for sponsoring the individual's work visa. The most common type of professional work visa in the United States is the H-1B visa for professional employees. Some companies might also use the L-1 for transfers to an affiliate company in the United States. The HR department also has to maintain records of the company's employees showing a legal right to work in the United States in accordance with the Immigration Reform and Control Act of 1986. The form required here is the I-9 employment eligibility verification form. As you can easily see, there is a lot of paperwork involved in moving individuals who are citizens of one country to another country in order to work for your organization—and the above paperwork is just the basics. In some circumstances, other forms are required for entry into the United States for the purpose of work.

In addition to the immigration and visa requirements, organizations that hire workers in other countries face issues with the selection process itself. How does HR select somebody who resides in another country? How difficult is it to go through the process of identification of recruits, selection testing, interviewing, and the other pieces of the selection process? In many cases, the HR representative may never even see the individual who's being hired. A large portion of the work of selection will be done virtually, typically using the Internet. This inability to interact directly with the candidate creates an entirely new set of problems for the HR representative. There may also be a language barrier between the candidate and the HR representative, and there are almost certainly cultural differences between the candidate's home country and the organization in the hiring country. Each of these barriers must be overcome, and every company handles these issues a little bit differently. However, the HR managers must understand and be able to work within the global hiring environment.

Perceived Cultural Fit and Selection

Selection based on perception of the applicant sharing, and therefore fitting into, the organization's culture is a common result of the selection process, but should we base selection on cultural fit or what we earlier called person-organization fit? We identified the "like me" error in selection earlier in the chapter. Does the evidence show that it is a significant issue? The fact is most evaluators ranked cultural fit as the *most important item* in a job interview—even above analytical thinking.[77] One of the major problems in using cultural fit as the primary criterion is that we end up not getting the best person for a particular job. Certainly, we need to analyze cultural fit as part of the selection process because the better the fit, the more likely the individual will stay on in the job for a longer period of time.[78] However, we can't use it as the sole criterion in selection.

The first rule of hiring for Jack Welch, the former CEO of **General Electric**, is "don't use your gut."[79] Don't hire people just because you're impressed with them during an interview—maybe because they share your love of bicycling or soccer. While fitting in can help with processes such as communication and teamwork, it may also harm the company's ability to maintain diversity and apply divergent thoughts to solve a problem. We may even end up with groupthink issues and an inability to adapt to external change over time.[80]

What should you do? Certainly, use cultural fit as one component of the selection process, but you have seen in this chapter how many more selection tools you have at your disposal—written tests, physical tests, background checks, and more. You need to use as many of those tools as necessary to find the right person who not only fits with the culture but also can do the job, is willing to do it, and has the intent to be a contributor to the organization over the long term.

HRIS and the Selection Process

Human resource information systems (HRIS) continue to become increasingly valuable to the organization in all HRM functions, including the selection process. The system allows the organization to automate many of the selection processes such as applications, initial screening, testing, interviewing, and corresponding with the candidate.

Modern HRIS provide organizations with the ability to automate their application process by providing a standard application to candidates by way of the Internet or company intranets. The application can even be varied for different types of jobs within the organization. The applicants identify which type of job they're interested in, and the system provides them with the online application. Virtually all of the systems are also able to accept résumé files from the applicant that can be stored in the HRIS. This can then allow automated searching of all stored résumés and applications for keywords that will provide the HR manager with a first cut of applicants for a specific job.

Once this first cut is complete, many of the systems can automatically alert each applicant to the need to log in to the company's site for any initial testing that may be required for the position. The system can be set up to score the testing and provide the HR representative with a list of the highest-scoring candidates.

Once all of the automated services are complete, HR representatives can set up and conduct interviews (which can also be graded using the HRIS) and identify any further testing necessary for the applicants. Once finalists are identified for the position, the HR representative identifies those finalists to the HRIS, and the system can create automated letters (emails) thanking the applicants for their application but letting them know that they haven't been chosen.

As you can quickly see, the HRIS can save significant amounts of money and time within the HR department. In addition, the fact that the initial application and testing are done in an automated form allows the organization to limit any human bias that might occur from face-to-face interaction between the HR representative and the candidate. This can minimize any potential for discrimination in the selection process, which is obviously something that the HR department needs to be concerned with.

• • • CHAPTER SUMMARY

6-1 Describe why the selection process is so important to the company.

Selection is important primarily because we need the best possible person in each job in order to maximize productivity. Unproductive members of the organization can cause lower motivation and job satisfaction in all of a company's employees. Second, organizations have a responsibility to avoid negligent hires—people who may pose a danger to others within the organization. The company can incur legal liability if we don't screen potential applicants carefully.

6-2 Identify the three main types of "fit" that we look for in the selection process and why they are important.

The three types of fit are personality-job fit, ability-job fit, and person-job fit. They are important because managers are supposed to get the best productivity out of their workforce. But not everyone can do everything equally well, so managers have to treat people differently, but fairly, in order to put the right person in the right job. They do this by assessing the three types of fit between the person and the company.

6-3 Discuss the major points in the Uniform Guidelines on Employee Selection Procedures (UGESP).

The UGESP provides guidelines on how to avoid discriminatory hiring practices. It identifies what the federal government considers to be an employment test and how those tests can be used in making employment decisions. The UGESP also identifies the acceptable types of validity that can be used to validate employment tests, and it notes that these tests must be reliable.

6-4 Briefly discuss the use of applications and résumés as selection tools.

Applications and résumés are used in a fairly interchangeable manner, except that the application gives the company information on the applicant that is in a standard format. This makes it easier to quickly scan and evaluate the different applicants. Applications also typically have some legal language or disclosures that must be agreed to by the applicant. Both documents should be used to review and verify both the work experience and the education of the applicant. This experience and education should always be verified, though, because evidence shows that a high percentage of people exaggerate or lie on applications and résumés.

6-5 Briefly discuss the legal considerations in the selection process.

The biggest legal considerations in the selection process are the measures that are required to ensure that we avoid illegal employment discrimination. There are also two laws that deal specifically with the ability to apply certain types of testing to employment candidates: the Employee Polygraph Protection Act of 1988 (EPPA) and the Genetic Testing Nondiscrimination Act of 2008 (GINA). The EPPA limits the use of polygraphs in normal businesses to generally two instances: when the employee will be involved in company security operations and when the employee will have access to federally identified controlled substances. GINA protects prospective employees from discrimination by health insurers and employers on the basis of their DNA information.

6-6 Discuss the major types of written testing available as selection tools.

The major types of written tests are *skills tests*, which evaluate the candidates' ability to apply their knowledge to a specific type of problem; *personality tests*, which evaluate the applicants' personal traits or characteristics so that they can be matched up with appropriate types of jobs; *interest tests*, which identify what an applicant is interested in and therefore most likely motivated to learn; *cognitive ability tests*, which are assessments of intelligence or aptitude for a specific type of work; and *honesty or integrity tests*, which evaluate the individual's philosophy concerning theft and other forms of dishonesty.

6-7 Identify the main requirements for organizational drug-testing programs.

Testing must be done in one of two forms—either random or universal. In most states, testing can't be done selectively using any other method. Most states also require prior authorization for drug testing, and the organization must have a drug-testing policy that is provided to all employees and that states the following information: the requirement for training on substance abuse, when individuals will be tested and what substances will be tested for, disciplinary action that could result from a positive test, and the reasonable accommodations that the organization will provide to employees who voluntarily submit to a substance abuse rehabilitation program. In unionized workforces, the implementation of drug-testing programs must be part of contract negotiations.

6-8 Discuss the value of selection interviews, including the three primary types of interviews.

The interview gives the manager a chance to make a face-to-face assessment of the candidate, including the person's ability to communicate and personality, appearance, and motivation. It also gives the candidate a chance to learn about the job and the organization. The three primary types of interviews are the *unstructured interview*, in which the interviewer has no preplanned questions or topics; the *semistructured interview*, where the interviewer may ask both planned and unplanned questions; and the *structured interview*, where all candidates are asked the same set of questions. Most interviewers prefer the semistructured interview.

6-9 List and briefly describe the steps taken in conducting interviews.

Step 1: Open the interview. Develop rapport and put the candidate at ease.

Step 2: Present a realistic job preview (RJP). Make sure that the candidate understands the job and what will be expected if selected for the job.

Step 3: Ask questions. Try to ensure that the candidate does most of the talking, and note their answers.

Step 4: Introduce top candidates to coworkers. Let them talk with people who they will be working with, and use that as an opportunity to judge their interpersonal skills and attitude.

Step 5: Close the interview. Thank the candidate for their time and tell them what the next step in the process will be. Tell the candidate when they will be contacted, and after the candidate leaves, make any final notes about the interview.

6-10 **Discuss the use of the various background checks as tests for employment.**

Credit checks are one of the most commonly used background checks. They should not automatically disqualify a person for a job, but if a credit report shows a pattern of dishonesty, then it can be valuable as a tool for selection. Criminal background checks may or may not be allowed by state law. Any criminal conviction should have something to do with the essential job functions, or we should not use it to disqualify an individual. Reference checks will usually not provide a lot of information, but we should complete them anyway in case they do provide valuable information. And, finally, Web searches frequently turn up information on the morals, values, or honesty of potential employees; companies use these when they are allowed under state and local laws.

6-11 **Identify the common problems employers encounter during the selection process.**

Common problems include rushing (caving in to pressure to fill a job), stereotyping (prejudging a candidate based on a perceived group to which they may belong), "like me" syndrome (liking the candidate who is most like you), halo and horn effects (making judgments based on one or two characteristics instead of evaluating the candidate's total qualifications), and premature selection (making a snap decision based on a high-quality résumé or a good interview).

6-12 **Define the key terms found in the chapter margins and listed following the Chapter Summary.**

Complete the Key Terms Review to test your understanding of this chapter's key terms.

• • • KEY TERMS

assessment center	interest test	simulation
cognitive ability test	multiple-hurdle selection model	skills test
compensatory selection model	negligent hire	Uniform Guidelines on
construct validity	personality test	Employee Selection Procedures
content validity	physical test	(UGESP)
criterion-related validity	reliability	validity
fitness-for-duty test	selection	work sample

• • • KEY TERMS REVIEW

Complete each of the following statements using one of this chapter's key terms.

1. _____ is the process of choosing the best-qualified applicant recruited for a job.

2. _____ is a legal concept that says if the organization selects someone who may pose a danger to coworkers, customers, suppliers, or other third parties, and if that person then harms someone else in the course of working for the company, then the company can be held liable for the individual's actions.

3. _____ provides information that can be used to avoid discriminatory hiring practices as well as discrimination in other employment decisions.

4. _____ is the extent to which a test measures what it claims to measure.

5. _____ is an assessment of the ability of a test to measure some other factor related to the test.

6. _____ is an assessment of whether a test measures knowledge or understanding of the items it is supposed to measure.

7. _____ measures a theoretical concept or trait that is not directly observable.

8. _____ is the consistency of a test measurement.

9. _____ is an assessment instrument designed to determine whether you have the ability to apply a particular knowledge set.

10. _____ measures the psychological traits or characteristics of applicants to determine suitability for performance in a specific type of job.

11. _____ measures a person's intellectual curiosity and motivation in a particular field.

12. _____ is an assessment of general intelligence or of some type of aptitude for a particular job.

13. _____ ensures that applicants are capable of performing on the job in ways defined by the job specification and description.

14. _____ means that we provide a sample of the work that the candidate would perform on the job and ask the candidate to perform the tasks under controlled conditions.

15. _____ are places where job applicants undergo a series of tests, interviews, and simulated experiences to determine their potential for a particular job.

16. _____ allows us to put a candidate in a high-pressure situation but still control the environment so as to limit the danger and cost.

17. _____ identifies whether or not an employee is physically capable at a particular point in time of performing a specific type of work.

18. _____ requires that each applicant must pass a particular selection test in order to go on to the next test.

19. _____ allows an individual to do poorly on one test but make up for that poor grade by doing exceptionally well on other tests.

••• COMMUNICATION SKILLS

The following critical thinking questions can be used for class discussion and/or for written assignments to develop communication skills. Be sure to give complete explanations for all answers.

1. Do you agree that selection of a top-quality candidate is a critical process in organizations, or do you think intensive training after the person is selected is more valuable? Explain your answer.

2. Should organizations be held liable by the justice system for negligent hires? Why or why not?

3. In your mind, how critical is the concept of person-organization fit? Why do you think so?

4. Are there cases other than the two instances noted in the chapter when companies should be allowed to use polygraph tests on employees? When and why?

5. Do you feel that it's OK to tell "little white lies" on résumés and applications? Why or why not?

6. Are companies overtesting applicants by using the processes that were discussed in this chapter? Explain your answer.

7. Are background checks—including credit checks, criminal history checks, and looking at a candidate's Facebook page—too invasive? Explain your answer.

8. Is the use of HRIS for narrowing down the list of candidates and sending form letters, including rejection letters, too impersonal? Why or why not?

••• CASE 6-1 WHO IS DOING THE SELLING? GERALD INTERVIEWS AT WASHINGTON HOME BUILDERS

Gerald Mahoney was working in the women's shoe department and doing the best that he could to sell a fairly expensive pair of boots to a young lady who obviously could afford to shop at a much classier store such as Nordstrom or Neiman Marcus. For some unfathomable reason, however, she decided to bestow her good graces on Macy's. After a few minutes of helping her try on several pairs of boots, Gerald was able to gently persuade Ms. Monahan to buy one of the store's most expensive boots. He rang up the sale and was complimenting himself on his persistence when out of the blue the customer said:

> Why is an obviously highly talented man like you, who has just sold me a pair of shoes I probably don't need or even want, working at a place like Macy's? My name is Ms. Monahan, and I am the Director of Recruiting and Training at Washington Home Builders, and I can tell from the way that

you have handled this sale that you would make a superb home salesperson. Here's my card. Why not call me tomorrow morning, and we can arrange a time for you to come in? Our website is also on the card, so feel free to check us out and see our job listings.

Gerald thanked Ms. Monahan for her kind words and told her he certainly would call her in the morning and arrange for an appointment.

Getting the Interview

Gerald called Ms. Monahan the next day as he had promised, and she seemed quite receptive to his call. She asked him to fax over a résumé and said that she would get back to him (or her assistant would), in order to set up an appointment for him to interview with her and some of the key salespeople in the firm. Gerald ended up faxing his résumé three days after he talked with Ms. Monahan. Her office called him back and faxed him a blank job application, which he quickly completed and mailed back. A nerve-racking week went by, and Gerald finally received an appointment for an interview for the following week.

The "Interview Process" at Washington Home Builders

Gerald thought he knew what to expect during an interview since he had been through so many—he was prepared to sell himself to Washington big-time. Usually he would meet with a store manager or the head of personnel for about an hour, and they would ask him questions about his previous employment, why he left his last job, and why he wanted to work for their firm. These were routine questions that inevitably led to a discussion of salary (if they thought he was qualified to do the job) and a job offer. Washington's interview process turned out to be far more complex.

It all started at 9 a.m. First, before he met with anyone, Gerald took a battery of exams and filled out a set of questionnaires. The exams included everything from basic math questions (which he hadn't done since his college days, nearly 30 years ago), to what seemed to be an IQ test, to questions about self-image, his honesty, and his preferences about the type of work he liked to do.

Rather than having a long break for lunch, they had a working lunch where HR went through the entire compensation package: a base salary plus commission, medical benefits, and a really good 401(k) plan where the firm contributed 5% of his salary.

His first interview that afternoon seemed to set the tone for the rest of the day. Gerald had a wonderful interview with the Sales Director, Sam Arden, and found Sam's easygoing, laid-back style a refreshing change of pace from the usual salespeople he had dealt with most of his life. Sam, after telling Gerald about the firm and the job, asked Gerald some brief standard questions about his background and sales history and what made Gerald special enough to become a Washington sales associate. Gerald expected these questions and was quite prepared.

The next series of questions, however, were very different from anything Gerald had experienced during an interview, and he found this approach very positive and exciting. Sam would tell him a little story and then ask Gerald what he would do or say if he were the manager or sales associate in the situation. No one had ever asked Gerald's opinion about anything at his prior jobs, and Gerald felt that he had finally found a firm that cared about what he thought and was willing to listen to him. Gerald thought he sailed through these scenarios with flying colors since Sam's tone was always very positive throughout the interview. It was 3 p.m. when Sam finally called an end to the session, and Gerald felt invigorated and ready for more.

Gerald was directed to a small conference room where three people who identified themselves as area managers and one person from HR asked him a series of questions about his selling approach, his work habits, and his ability to work with a sales partner. This session was repeated in another room with another three area managers and another person from personnel. Both of these sessions involved a series of follow-up questions that Gerald was happy to answer. At 5 p.m. the session ended and Sales Director Sam Arden walked in and told Gerald he would contact him in a week to let Gerald know the firm's decision. Gerald thanked Sam for the opportunity to interview for a job with Washington and said he looked forward to hearing from them.

The Letter

A week went by, and Gerald had not heard anything from Washington. Gerald finally called and was told that a letter was in the mail to him and he should await its arrival. Three days later, and with continued impatience at work and at home, Gerald received the destined letter. The first word he read, *congratulations,* sent Gerald into an ecstatic frenzy. He then read further. "Hmmm," mumbled Gerald, "this is not exactly what I was told." Their job offer was commission-based only, and, assuming that medical and dental packages ran about the same cost and that coverage was the same as his current job, Gerald would lose paid vacation time but perhaps gain in terms of contributions to a 401(k) plan. Gerald thought to himself, "Bummer! This is not the same great deal that I was told about during the interview process! Who sold who on the job?"

Questions

1. If Washington Home Builders had Gerald's résumé, why would they need him to complete a blank job application, which requests much of the same information as a résumé?

2. Once they had his job application, why do you think Washington took a week to ask Gerald to come in for an interview?

3. Gerald's morning included taking a series of exams and questionnaires. What was the purpose of the exams/questions, and what legal limitations are there to testing?

4. Analyze Gerald's interviews in light of Model 6-2, "Interviewing Steps." How well did Washington follow those steps?

5. What types of questions did it seem Washington used during the interview process?

6. In reviewing Exhibit 6-1, "Steps in the Selection Process," how successful was Washington in selecting Gerald for the job? Do you have any suggestions for improvement?

Case created by Herbert Sherman, PhD, and Theodore Vallas, Department of Management Sciences, Long Island University School of Business, Brooklyn Campus

••• CASE 6-2 NOT GETTING FACE TIME AT FACEBOOK—AND GETTING THE LAST LAUGH!

In August 2009, Facebook turned down job applicant Brian Acton, an experienced engineer who had previously worked at **Yahoo** and **Apple**. More than 4 years later, Facebook paid him $3 billion to acquire his 20% stake of **WhatsApp**, a start-up he had cofounded immediately after Facebook rejected his job application.[81] WhatsApp Messenger is a proprietary, cross-platform instant-messaging subscription service for smartphones and selected feature phones that use the Internet for communication. In addition to text messaging, users can send each other images, video, and audio media messages as well as their location using integrated mapping features.[82] How could Facebook, a highly successful firm, have made such a drastic mistake?

Back in 2009, Brian Acton was a software engineer who was out of work for what seemed like a very long time. He believed he had what it took to make a difference in the industry, but his career did not work out as planned. Even though he spent years at Apple and Yahoo, he got rejected many times by **Twitter** and Facebook.[83] Acton described the details of the interview process that he failed to do well in as follows:

> First of all, interviewing a person for a job that requires technical skills is difficult for both the interviewer and the interviewee. Facebook is a highly desirable firm to work for and requires the best skills and talents from all of their potential employees. It is therefore not surprising that the selection process rivals, if not tops, any company in the industry. The process starts with an email or a phone call from a recruiter in response to an online application or [to] a recommendation from a friend who may work for Facebook. Sometimes, in the initial chat online, timed software coding challenges are set to find the best performers. If this chat goes well, an applicant will go on to the next level—an initial in-person interview or phone screening.[84]

> In this next hurdle, the applicant will have a 45-minute chat with a fellow engineer/potential coworker, [with] whom he or she shares the same area of expertise. They will tell you about their job and what their role is in Facebook; then they ask about the applicant's résumé, motivation, and interests. Additionally, the applicant will be tested about his or her technical skills, coding exercises, and programming abilities.[85]

> If successful, the applicant will be invited for back-to-back interviews. This part of the process is very grueling and stressful since all the interviews take place throughout a single day. The candidate will also be asked to manually write a program on a whiteboard to make sure that the applicant is knowledgeable about program writing. The goal in this final step is to see how one approaches a problem and comes up with a solution [that] is simple enough to solve in 10–30 minutes and can be easily explained.[86]

> As a potential coworker, the applicant will be tested in terms of understanding and explaining complex ideas, with most tasks project related and constantly changing. This requires employees to possess a diversified set of skills. That is the reason why the applicant is not only tested in coding skills . . . but also to gauge enthusiasm and motivation. The applicant's leadership and decision-making skills are also evaluated as the company seeks to find someone who can make a large impact on the industry and make quick decisions.[87]

After going through this arduous process, Brian Acton was one of the engineers who received an email that "regretted to inform" him that he didn't get the position. Yet he stayed positive and took a different path, which led him to start his own company, WhatsApp. Teaming up with Yahoo alumni, he developed the most popular text-messaging application, and the company was sold to Facebook for a total of $19 billion in 2014.[88] This epic comeback proves how persistence and ambition play a huge role in job hunting, but it also proves how difficult it is to hire the right employee even when that person has the best skill set.[89]

Questions

1. The hiring process at Facebook consists of three steps. What are those three steps, and which type of written tests are applicable for each?

2. If you were the recruiter responsible for the preliminary screening of applicants to Facebook, how would you prepare for the interview?

3. Facebook gives a battery of tests to the applicant along several steps of the selection process. What are those tests, what are they testing for, and how might Facebook ensure the validity and reliability of those tests?

4. Psychological testing did not seem to be part of Facebook's selection process. How might it use this testing, which tests might it use, and where in the process might it use them?

5. From what you have read, what are the criteria of selection employed by Facebook? Are they valid and reliable? How might this explain why Acton was not hired?

6. Agree or disagree with this statement based upon this case: "Not hiring the right person is still better than hiring the wrong person."

Case created by Herbert Sherman, PhD, and Theodore Vallas, Department of Management Sciences, Long Island University School of Business, Brooklyn Campus

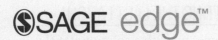

Sharpen your skills with SAGE edge at edge.sagepub.com/lussierhrm2e

SAGE edge for students provides a personalized approach to help you accomplish your coursework goals in an easy-to-use learning environment.

• • • SKILL BUILDER 6-1 INTERVIEW QUESTIONS FOR USE WHEN HIRING A PROFESSOR TO TEACH THIS COURSE

Objective

To develop your ability to develop interview questions

Skills

The primary skills developed through this exercise are as follows:

1. *HR management skills*—technical, business, and conceptual and design skills
2. *SHRM 2013 Curriculum Guidebook*—I: Staffing: Recruitment and Selection

Preparation

Assume you are the dean of your college and you need to

hire a professor to teach this course next semester. Develop a list of at least 10 questions you would ask the candidates during a job interview for the position.

Apply It

What did I learn from this experience? How will I use this knowledge in the future?

_____

_____

Your instructor may ask you to do this Skill Builder in class in a group by sharing your interview questions. If so, the instructor will provide you with any necessary information or additional instructions.

• • • SKILL BUILDER 6-2 INTERVIEWING

Objective

To develop your ability to develop interview questions
To develop your ability to interview and to be interviewed

Skills

The primary skills developed through this exercise are as follows:

1. *HR management skills*—technical, human relations, business, and conceptual and design skills
2. *SHRM 2013 Curriculum Guidebook*—I: Staffing: Recruitment and Selection

Preparation

Assume you are the HR director and you need to hire a new college grad for an entry-level HR position. Because

you are not a large company, you have a small staff and the new hire will help out in a wide variety of HR functions. Develop a list of at least 10 questions you would ask the candidates during a job interview for the position.

Apply It

What did I learn from this experience? How will I use this knowledge in the future?

_____

_____

Your instructor may ask you to do this Skill Builder in class by breaking into groups of two or three and actually conducting interviews using your questions. If so, the instructor will provide you with any necessary information or additional instructions.

Part III

Developing and Managing

7 Training, Learning, Talent Management, and Development

8 Performance Management and Appraisal

9 Rights and Employee Management

10 Employee and Labor Relations

PRACTITIONER'S MODEL

- ↑ Productivity
- ↑ Satisfaction
- ↓ Absenteeism
- ↓ Turnover

PART V: Protecting and Expanding Organizational Reach
How do you PROTECT and EXPAND your Human Resources?

Chapter 14	Chapter 15	Chapter 16
Workplace Safety, Health, and Security	Organizational Ethics, Sustainability, and Social Responsibility	International HRM

PART IV: Compensating
How do you REWARD and MAINTAIN your Human Resources?

Chapter 11	Chapter 12	Chapter 13
Compensation Management	Incentive Pay	Employee Benefits

PART III: Developing and Managing
How do you MANAGE your Human Resources

Chapter 7	Chapter 8	Chapter 9	Chapter 10
Training, Learning, Talent Management, and Development	Performance Management and Appraisal	Rights and Employee Management	Employee and Labor Relations

PART II: Staffing
What HRM Functions do you NEED for sustainability?

Chapter 4	Chapter 5	Chapter 6
Matching Employees and Jobs: Job Analysis and Design	Recruiting Job Candidates	Selecting New Employees

PART I: 21st Century Human Resource Management Strategic Planning and Legal Issues
What HRM issues are CRITICAL to your organization's long-term sustainability?

Chapter 1	Chapter 2
The New Human Resource Management Process	Strategy-Driven Human Resource Management

©iStockphoto.com/endopack

7 Training, Learning, Talent Management, and Development

• • • LEARNING OUTCOMES

After studying this chapter, you should be able to do the following:

7-1 Discuss the major difference between training and development. PAGE 237

7-2 Identify the common points in the tenure of employees within the organization where training may be needed. Briefly discuss each point. PAGE 237

7-3 Briefly discuss the steps in the training process and their interrelationship. PAGE 240

7-4 Identify the most common challenges to the training and development process. PAGE 241

7-5 Identify the three common learning theories and the type of learning that results from each theory. PAGE 244

7-6 Identify and briefly discuss the four methods for shaping behavior. PAGE 245

7-7 Identify which training methods are most commonly used with which HRM skill. PAGE 248

7-8 Discuss each of the major training delivery types. PAGE 248

7-9 Briefly discuss the Four-Level Evaluation Method for assessing training programs. PAGE 254

7-10 Discuss the term *career* and the significance of its definition in the text. PAGE 258

7-11 Briefly discuss the three common methods of employee development. PAGE 260

7-12 Briefly discuss some of the individual and organizational consequences that can occur as a result of organizational career planning processes. PAGE 261

7-13 Define the key terms found in the chapter margins and listed following the Chapter Summary. PAGE 269

Practitioner's Perspective

Cindy told the story of Jennifer, who had worked in the same position for 10 years. Jennifer had always been a valuable employee, but lately, her productivity and performance had started to decline. Her supervisor, Mandy, finally called her in to find out what was wrong.

After some hesitation, Jennifer said, "To tell the truth, I feel like I am in a rut. I just don't get the same satisfaction from doing my job that I used to get."

"I wish we'd had this talk sooner," Mandy replied, "but now that I know how you feel, there is something we can do. Let's take a look at some of the training opportunities coming up this quarter. Tell me what training classes you might be interested in taking."

What if Jennifer and Mandy never had that talk? Do you think Jennifer would have remained at her job? Chapter 7 looks at the ins and outs of managing and retaining talent through training and development.

SHRM HR CONTENT

See Appendix: *SHRM 2013 Curriculum Guidebook* for the complete list

E. Job Analysis/Job Design (required)

5. Training and development

   Vocational and career counseling

   Needs assessment

   Career pathing

L. Training and Development (required)

1. Needs assessment
2. Competency models
3. Learning theories: Behaviorism, constructivism, cognitive models, adult learning, knowledge management
4. Training evaluation: Kirkpatrick's model
5. E-learning and use of technology in training
6. On-the-job training (OJT)
7. Outsourcing (secondary)
8. Transfer of training: Design issues, facilitating transfer
9. Employee development: Formal education, experience, assessment

10. Determining return on investment (ROI)
11. The role of training in succession planning
12. Human/intellectual capital

Q. Organizational Development (required—graduate students only)

2. Developing human resources
3. Emotional intelligence
4. Equipping the organization for present and future talent needs
8. Measurement systems
11. Organizational learning
13. Outsourcing employee development
16. Training employees to meet current and future job demands

T. HR Career Planning (secondary)

1. Definition of a career
2. Balancing work and life
7. Plateauing
9. Career development

Organizational training and development is a career-long process.

THE NEED FOR TRAINING AND DEVELOPMENT

Now that we've made it through the process of selecting individuals into the organization, the next thing we need to do is train them to do their new jobs. In all cases, new employees should get at least basic training about the organization and its routine processes as well as the training for the job they are going to be filling. We can't reasonably expect them to do a job successfully unless they're trained in how to do it, and there is a relationship between training and job satisfaction.[1] Offering training and development also generally decreases expensive turnover[2] and makes it less likely that employees will engage in neglectful behavior.[3] Training is expensive, so it must be done correctly to get sufficient benefits to outweigh the cost.[4]

Effective training and development are investments, not expenses, as they pay for themselves through competitive advantage and increased performance.[5] This is why companies worldwide are investing heavily in training and long-term employee development.[6] **Hudson Trail Outfitters** even rewards employees for completing training programs.[7] As managers' skills should also be developed,[8] leadership programs and courses are currently popular.[9] This is why best-practice companies (e.g., **GE**, **IBM**, and **Johnson & Johnson**) provide leadership programs.[10]

Let's begin by discussing training and development and the difference between them, followed by when training is needed.

Training and Development

Before we get into the details of training and development, we need to understand competency models because training is based on the competencies we want employees to have. **Competency models** *identify the knowledge, skills, and abilities (known in HR as KSAs) needed to perform a particular job in the organization.* We can utilize competency models to identify what types of training a new employee or an employee changing jobs will need. We go through a process of identifying and providing the training, evaluating how well the employee has learned, and then assessing the training process itself using one of several options. We will discuss this in more detail in a little while, but for now, just remember that training is a critical piece in the education of each employee in the organization.

In this chapter, we will discuss both organizational training and the concept of employee development. The two are related but separate pieces of the organization's processes involving the management of its employees.

Training *is the process of teaching employees the skills necessary to perform a job.* We train employees to provide them with the KSAs that they will need to succeed in their work for the organization. Training is primarily intended to be put to immediate use by the individual being trained. As an example, **Amazon** focuses on customer service, so it trains its employees by drilling them in what steps to follow when they get everyday questions and when fielding more unusual requests. To make sure everyone at Amazon understands how customer service works, each employee, including the CEO, spends 2 days on the service desk every 2 years.[11]

Somewhat in contrast to the training that we do so employees can do a new job or do an existing job better is the process of employee development. Both colleges and corporations have been criticized for not doing a good job of developing our business leaders.[12] This is one of the reasons why this book focuses on developing HR *skills*, not just knowledge. **Employee development** *is ongoing education to improve knowledge and skills for present and future jobs.* So, employee development is designed to teach our workers how to move up in the organization in the future by becoming skilled at those tasks that they will need to know to move into higher level jobs. Development tends to be less technical, and it is aimed at improving human, communication, conceptual, and decision-making skills in managerial and professional employees. To remain competitive in today's dynamic environment, organizations must have employees who maintain up-to-date knowledge and skills, and development plays an important role in this effort.[13]

When Is Training Needed?

To successfully determine what kinds of training need to be carried out within the organization, HR managers should begin by completing a *needs assessment.* We will discuss needs assessments in the next section. For now, let's review some common points at which we should probably complete a needs assessment and at least consider providing training to our people.

NEW EMPLOYEE ORIENTATION. **Orientation** *is the process of introducing new employees to the organization and their jobs.* New employees are often called *newcomers* in organizational entry,[14] and newcomer socialization done effectively increases new employee job satisfaction and performance and reduces turnover rates.[15,16] Most orientations emphasize corporate values, culture, and strengths.[17] Organizations that have developed innovative orientation programs include **Rover.com, Wipro, Rackspace, Bazaarvoice,** and **Google.**[18] This socialization process is important to both newcomers and organizations, as newcomers learn the ropes and understand

LO 7-1

Discuss the major difference between training and development.

SHRM

L:2
Competency Models

SHRM

E:5
Training and Development

SHRM

Q:16
Training Employees to Meet Current and Future Job Needs

SHRM

Q:2
Developing Human Resources

LO 7-2

Identify the common points in the tenure of employees within the organization where training may be needed. Briefly discuss each point.

Competency model Model identifying the knowledge, skills, and abilities (known in HR as KSAs) needed to perform a particular job in the organization

Training The process of teaching employees the skills necessary to perform a job

Employee development Ongoing education to improve knowledge and skills for present and future jobs

Orientation The process of introducing new employees to the organization and their jobs

WORK
APPLICATION 7-1

Select a job you hold in the present or held in the past. Did you receive both training and development or just training? Explain in some detail why it was one or both.

what is expected from them in their work as they assimilate into the organization and attempt to become productive members.[19] Thus, job and career orientation have long-lasting effects on new employee job attitudes and satisfaction, behavior, work mastery, and performance.[20]

Orientation is an introduction of the person to the company. What do we need to think about when we introduce somebody to the company? We need to think about introducing the new employee to all of the things that exist within the organizational society that they are entering. The process is very similar to someone moving to a different country and having to assimilate into a new culture. What do people need to know in order to be able to go about their daily lives, do the routine things that they need to do, and provide for their own personal needs? Orientation should be designed to answer all of the questions necessary to allow new employees to integrate into the "society" that they are entering.

One of the first things an individual would need to know is what the laws, rules, and regulations are in the new society, so we need to introduce the new employee to the organization's policies and procedures, rules, and regulations. The second thing that people would probably want to know is how to act and interact with others in the new society, so in addition to introducing the employee to the job and how to perform it within the organization, we would want to talk to the individual about the underlying organizational structure, plus where to go and whom to talk to in order to get certain things done. Who should they talk to in their department if they have questions about their job or about how things are done within the department? Who should they speak with in other departments if they have questions that can't be answered within their primary workgroup, and when is it acceptable to go to individuals in other departments?

Next, they would probably want to know how they get the money that they need in order to survive in society. So we need to tell them about their pay and benefits, including whom to contact with questions. People entering this new society would also probably want to know how to stay safe as they go about their business, so we need to talk to them about safety in the organization. They would also likely need to fill out paperwork—to get a driver's license, to open a bank account, to identify who they are, and so forth. Similarly, certain paperwork is necessary for the organization to function successfully, so during orientation we ask the new employee to fill out this paperwork.

As you can see, there are many different things that we need to teach someone entering our new society, so we can't legitimately perform the orientation process in one day or a couple of hours. Effective orientation of employees also results in lower turnover rates,[21] so orientation to the firm and the new employee's job should be provided over a significant period of time, anywhere from 1 to 4 weeks or even more, depending on the complexity of the organization and the jobs. Here are a few examples of world class companies with long orientation programs: **Toyota** has a 5-week orientation, **Honda** has a 6-week orientation, and **Southwest Airlines** has a 90-day orientation.

However, in most organizations, the orientation process is significantly shorter than this, and one reason that our 21st century organizations suffer significant early turnover of new hires. If our new employee is frustrated due to not knowing how to do the job, where to locate tools, whom to go to with a problem, or how to fix an issue with pay, the likelihood of that person leaving the organization goes up drastically. Many organizations could significantly reduce new-hire turnover by modestly increasing the orientation period for new hires.

NEW JOB REQUIREMENTS OR PROCESSES. The second common point where training may be necessary occurs when jobs change in some form. Whether our employee

WORK
APPLICATION 7-2

Briefly describe the orientation you received for a job. How could it be improved?

is in the same job or is changing jobs and needs to learn new processes, if there is a significant change in any work requirements, we need to train the employee. The change may be based on discovery of new techniques or technologies to perform particular work to make the work more efficient. The organization may have changed its strategic direction, and as a result, some or all of the jobs within the organization may require new processes or procedures. In any of these cases or any similar situation where the change has significance for that job, we should go through the process of performing a training needs assessment. If the result of the needs assessment shows that training is necessary, then an appropriate training program can be designed and implemented.

REMEDIATION. The third common point at which managers need to investigate the requirement for additional training occurs when there has been some failure of an employee or some employees to perform successfully and meet organizational standards. **Remediation** *is the correction of a deficiency or failure in a process or procedure.* In remediation, we work to correct the actions of the individual or individuals responsible for the process or procedure so that they can successfully carry out the action in the future. We don't want to make a common mistake, though. Remediation is not about assigning blame for a failure. The emphasis in this case should always be on correcting the actions of the employee to better serve both the employee's and the organization's interests. Again, organizational managers act just as a good physician or mechanic would act—by diagnosing the situation first and *then* taking appropriate corrective action to solve the problem through training.

EMPLOYEE DEVELOPMENT FOR ADVANCEMENT. The next point at which to evaluate the need for training is in situations where we are working to develop current employee skills and abilities so that employees can move into higher level jobs within the organization. Offering development opportunities generally decreases turnover.[22]

L:11
The Role of Training in Succession
Planning

All organizations have a responsibility to plan for the succession of individuals in management and executive positions, and this planning is usually a function of the HR department. Providing development opportunities and succession planning is the only way the organization can be sustainable over long periods of time. To successfully carry out a succession process, people at lower levels in the organization must be trained in the knowledge and skills necessary to be able to take on higher-level duties. One area getting particular attention today is training and development in ethics and social responsibility, in part because of the litany of ethical failures in the past decade within companies in a variety of industries. While very few organizations will attempt to develop all of the employees within the firm, most organizations go through an informal or formal process of identifying high-potential individuals for development and ultimately advancement into managerial and executive slots.

Many 21st century organizations have rigorous development programs that include job rotation to various departments within the organization, classroom and on-the-job training, assigned mentors, and many other programs, all of which are designed to train employees and develop their capabilities for future use within the firm. Organizations that neglect succession processes and employee development can find themselves at a competitive disadvantage when senior personnel leave the firm through either retirement or resignation. It is critical that HR lead the process of planning for succession and employee development. Although in this chapter we will focus more on training than development (there are five major sections explaining training, followed by one section on employee development), both are important to the organization.

Remediation The correction of a deficiency or failure in a process or procedure

LO 7-3

Briefly discuss the steps in the training process and their interrelationship.

THE TRAINING PROCESS AND NEEDS ASSESSMENT

How are we going to go about training our employees? How do we know who needs what training, in what forms, and at what point? How do we determine whether or not the employee is ready and willing to participate in the training? Finally, how do we know that the training was effective? In order to answer these questions, we have to plan our training processes very carefully. We need to look at what's currently going on in the organization and how that differs from what needs to happen in the future to accomplish our strategic business goals. Once we do this, we can analyze the types of training that will be necessary to build new knowledge, skills, and abilities for our workforce.

Steps in the Training Process

This chapter is primarily organized to follow the steps in the training process. Let's take a look at how we go through the training process in Exhibit 7-1. We'll follow that up with a brief discussion of the steps and then provide more detail throughout the chapter.

Step 1: Assessing needs. We conduct a needs assessment to determine what training is necessary to improve performance. We will discuss this step in this section.

Step 2: Selecting how to shape behavior. We select a method of shaping employee behavior based on learning theories so that we can change employee behavior to improve performance. We will discuss this step in this chapter's section "Learning and Shaping Behavior."

Step 3: Designing training. We design the training and development based on the needs assessment. We must determine which training methods we will use to shape employee behavior, and we must select the delivery method. We discuss this step in this chapter's section "Design and Delivery of Training."

Step 4: Delivering training. Before we actually conduct the training and development, we must select the delivery method. We also discuss the delivery options in the section "Design and Delivery of Training."

Step 5: Assessing training. After we complete the training, our last step is to assess how effective the training was at developing the needed skills. We do this by determining our success at shaping behavior. We discuss this step in this chapter's section "Assessing Training."

Interrelationship of the Training Process Steps. Note in Exhibit 7-1 that each of steps 2-3-4-5 has a double-headed arrow; this is because all the steps are so closely related and based on each other that they are commonly planned together before actually delivering the training. In other words, you are constantly thinking ahead and behind your current step in the training process. If the assessment of the training reveals that the behavior has not been shaped (changed) as needed, we may have to go back to step 1 and start the training process again.

SHRM

Q:4
Equipping the Organization for Present and Future Talent Needs

SHRM

E:5, L:1
Needs Assessment

Needs assessment The process of analyzing the difference between what is currently occurring within a job or jobs and what is required— either now or in the future—based on the organization's operations and strategic goals

Needs Assessment

The first major step in the training process, and probably one of the most important, is the needs assessment. A **needs assessment** *is the process of analyzing the difference between what is currently occurring within a job or jobs and what is required— either now or in the future—based on the organization's operations and strategic goals.* If a needs assessment is not done correctly, a training course may be poorly designed, or it may cover the wrong information. The wrong employees may be asked to participate in the training, or they may not yet be capable of absorbing the information in the training because of a lack of a knowledge base or skill set. We may end up creating a training program that's unnecessary, or we may fail to determine

EXHIBIT 7-1   THE TRAINING PROCESS

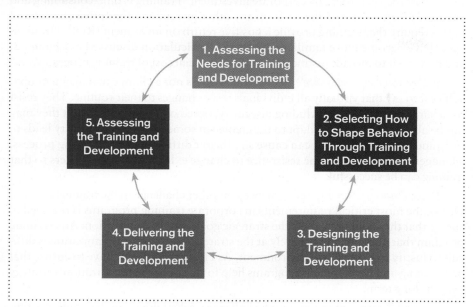

that an issue is based on poor performance rather than lack of knowledge. These are significant issues that we can avoid if we correctly go through the process of a needs assessment.

Similar to good automobile mechanics, organizational managers have to diagnose what may currently be wrong with a process so that they can successfully repair and/or tune the process up. If they don't do the diagnosis correctly—again like the mechanic working on your car—managers may create training solutions that don't solve the existing problem. So the manager has to go through a process of identifying where in a current sequence of events things are not working the way they should or how they can be done more efficiently. Only by diligently going through the process of looking at that chain of events in the status quo can a manager identify where the process can be changed to improve organizational productivity and reach the organization's goals.

Challenges to the Training Process

As part of the needs assessment, let's now discuss some common challenges to the training process. These include minimally prepared or unprepared workers, difficulty in identifying the return on investment provided from training, employee resistance to change and feelings of insecurity, matching the training to the strategic goals of the organization, and logistics issues—including scheduling and making locations available for training courses. Managers have to work through each of these challenges in order for training programs to be successful.

Unprepared Workforce. One of the most significant challenges to work process training is the fact that so many of the individuals being hired into the workforce are ill prepared in the educational basics, including reading and math skills. A recent report notes that employers hire substantial numbers of new entrants who are poorly prepared, requiring additional company investment to improve workforce readiness skills.[23] In cases where the employees don't have the basic skills necessary to succeed, the organization must train them in those basic skill sets before they can be taught the advanced skills necessary to improve organizational processes.

LO 7-4

Identify the most common challenges to the training and development process.

WORK
APPLICATION 7-3

Do a simple needs assessment for a job you have or had. Be sure to state the competency model (knowledge, skills, and abilities) it takes to do the job.

WORK
APPLICATION 7-4

Think about the people you have worked with. What is your perception of the preparation they have had for the workforce?

WORK
APPLICATION 7-5

Think about the people you have worked with. What is your perception of their resistance to changes in their work routine?

Return on Investment/Cost Justification. Businesses today are naturally concerned with the return that they get from any corporate investment. Training is time-consuming and expensive,[24] and it is no different from any other investment. Executives expect and in fact require that training provide a positive return on investment (ROI). HR managers have become more familiar with the ROI calculation discussed in Chapter 2, and they use it to provide justification for the financial cost of training programs.

Resistance to Change and Employee Insecurity. Since this is not a change management text, suffice it to say that virtually all individuals resist changes to their routine. They resist for a variety of reasons—including insecurity, based on their concern that they may not be able to successfully adapt to the change in some way. This insecurity leads to resistance to change, and it can cause significant difficulty in the training process. Management must overcome resistance to change exhibited by the workers so that training can be successful.

Strategic Congruence. Strategic congruence is another challenge to the training process. One of the most critical requirements in corporate training programs is the need to ensure that the training furthers the strategic goals of the organization. Any training program that does not aim squarely at the strategic goals of the organization is difficult to justify in a corporate environment. As HR managers, we have to ensure that our training and development programs help to carry out the organization's strategy over the long term.

Scheduling. The last of our common challenges, scheduling, involves both the timing and the location of the training. As with most things, there's never an ideal time to schedule a training course, especially if it runs for several days or even weeks. The trainees have to leave their regular jobs undone for the period of the training, and the organization has to be able to operate without those trainees performing their normal tasks. In addition, the training may require the use of physical locations that have special equipment or tools and that are only available for limited time periods during the year. These logistics issues may seem minimal, but they frequently create significant problems for the HR department in scheduling training courses.

Employee Readiness

Also, as part of our needs assessment, the manager needs to evaluate the employees who would be taking part in the training. Employees may feel insecure about their ability to learn, and they may therefore be unwilling to participate in training for new processes. We must also evaluate whether the employees are physically and mentally ready to go through the training process successfully. In other words, are they *able and willing* to learn?[25] Do they have the skills and competencies necessary to succeed in this training process?

ABILITY. We have to determine whether or not our employees feel that they are *able* to participate in the training process. They might feel that they don't have the background training necessary to succeed in training for a more complex process, meaning they may feel that their core set of skills needs to be improved before they can be successful in more intricate training. **Self-efficacy** *is whether or not a person believes that they have the capability to do something or attain a particular goal.* If the employee's self-efficacy is low, they may not believe that they have the ability to succeed in the training process. Regardless of whether or not it is true, if the employee *believes* they are unable to learn, then it is highly unlikely that they will be successful in any training process because they are unlikely to try.

If employees feel that they are unable to learn, then the job of the manager becomes one of upgrading the employees' abilities if necessary and then convincing them of their capabilities. In addition, the manager has to analyze the true abilities and limitations of each of the employees who may participate in the training

Self-efficacy Whether or not a person believes that they have the capability to do something or attain a particular goal

process. Each of us has physical abilities and intellectual abilities, but we don't all have the same physical and intellectual abilities. Again, it is management's job to diagnose and determine whether or not an individual has the abilities necessary to succeed in a training process and to not put people into situations where their lack of specific abilities condemns them to failure.

What happens when people are put into situations where they are almost certain to fail? What happens to their motivation, morale, and job satisfaction? What most likely will happen to their productivity? If we as managers put people into this type of situation, we are almost assured of lowering their performance level rather than raising it. This is certainly not the way to get maximum productivity out of our workforce, so we want to avoid putting people in training situations where they are almost certainly going to fail.

HR managers select employees who have the ability and willingness to be trained to succeed on the job.

WILLINGNESS. The second major piece in the employee readiness equation is whether or not employees are *willing* to learn what's being taught in a training program. In other words, we have to determine their motivation to learn. Why would our workers not be motivated to learn? There are several potential reasons.

First, the individual may not feel that they need to learn a new process. If they feel that the current process is sufficient and that the new process won't improve their work environment, they may be unwilling to learn. If they feel that the training process is being done solely for political reasons (e.g., many workers harbor a false belief that programs such as diversity training and sexual harassment prevention training are motivated by the perceived need of the organization to be politically correct, even though this is not true), then they may not be interested in the training. If the individual doesn't feel that the training is related to their job, they may not be motivated to learn. If the employee is concerned that their work will pile up while they're gone, they may not be motivated to train. If their coworkers or supervisors don't support the fact that the individual will have to be away from the job in order to go through a training course, and as a result put pressure on the individual, that person may not be motivated to go through the training.

A significant part of willingness to learn is based on the support the individual gets from the people around them, including coworkers, supervisors, and even family members. If one of your employees is going to be away from home for a period of several weeks and the employee's family members are opposed to this extended period of separation, it's extremely unlikely the employee is going to be willing to participate in the training. So the manager needs to make sure that the employee is willing to go through the training process.

WORK
APPLICATION 7-6

Describe your self-efficacy for a job you have or have had. How does or did your self-efficacy affect your job performance?

LEARNING AND SHAPING BEHAVIOR

Step 2 of the training process consists of selecting how to shape or change employee behavior. To do this, trainers have to understand how people learn. So in this section, we begin by explaining learning. Then we discuss three basic learning theories used to shape employee behavior. Next, we put the theories together in Exhibit 7-2 and discuss how to shape or change employee behavior, and then we end with learning styles.

WORK
APPLICATION 7-7

Do you like to learn new things? Describe your willingness to learn in college and to train on the job. Will you voluntarily sign up for company training and development programs that are not required for your job?

SHRM

Q:11
Organizational Learning

SHRM

L:3
Learning Theories: Behaviorism, etc.

LO 7-5

Identify the three common learning theories and the type of learning that results from each theory.

Learning

What is learning? Learning can be many different things, but in a business, we usually need to *know* that our employees have learned something that we are trying to train them to do. How do we know that they have learned a particular thing, then? We know because of changes in their behavior at work. So in our case, **learning** *is any relatively permanent change in behavior that occurs as a result of experience or practice*.[26] This is a good definition to use in the organizational learning process, due to the fact that it provides us with the visible evidence that individuals have learned something because they *change the way they act*.

People learn in multiple ways. We learn through trial and error, from the consequences that occur as a result of something we've done, and from the consequences of other people's actions. And what makes this process even more complex is the fact that different people prefer to learn differently. We all have preferred learning styles, and we like having the option to pick one style over another.

Learning Theories

Here we explain the three common learning theories: classical conditioning, operant conditioning, and social learning. Each of the three is useful for certain types of training.

CLASSICAL CONDITIONING. Classical conditioning was made famous by a physiologist named Ivan Pavlov. Pavlov became famous by causing dogs to salivate even when not in the presence of food. Pavlov proved that when dogs were conditioned to associate the ringing of a bell with being fed, they "learned" to salivate when the bell was rung. What does the fact that a dog would salivate on command have to do with human learning? At first glance, it looks a little silly. However, what Pavlov proved was that animals will react *involuntarily* to a stimulus in their environment if they associate that stimulus with something else. OK, but humans are not dogs, so do humans react involuntarily to a stimulus in the environment? Of course they do. Human beings react involuntarily to stimuli the same way all other animals do.

Have you ever walked down a row of restaurants in your hometown and smelled the aroma of fresh food being prepared, and did that remind you of a relative's home when they were cooking a favorite dinner of yours? This pleasant memory may change your mood, and in fact, it may change your behavior because of the feeling of well-being that it creates. Alternately, have you ever heard a sound that caused you to be afraid or to want to run away from it? Why does such as sound cause you to be afraid? If you think for a few seconds, you will probably realize that the sound indicates danger to you, whether you consciously realize it or not. You've been involuntarily conditioned to the feeling of danger associated with the sound. So, Pavlov's classical conditioning results in "direct, involuntary, learned behaviors." The behaviors are *learned* because you have changed the way you act due to some prior experience, and they are *involuntary* because you didn't intentionally learn to act in a particular way in response to the stimulus. Finally, the behaviors are *direct* because the learning occurs as a result of something happening directly to you.

OPERANT CONDITIONING. The second common learning theory is called *operant conditioning*, which is based on reinforcement. Again, most of us have heard of the individual that made this learning theory famous—B. F. Skinner. Skinner's theory of operant conditioning says that behavior is based on the consequences received from behaving in a similar way at an earlier point in time. In other words, if we acted in a certain way previously and received a reward, we will likely repeat that behavior. If, however, we acted in a particular way and received a negative consequence (punishment), then we will probably not repeat the behavior. Skinner tested his theory using

Learning Any relatively permanent change in behavior that occurs as a result of experience or practice

Learning Theories

Review the three learning theories below and write the letter corresponding to each theory before the statement(s) illustrating it:

a. classical conditioning

b. operant conditioning

c. social learning

_____ 1. My parents continuously told me how to behave properly as I was growing up. Could that be why customers comment on my good manners and social skills?

_____ 2. I got caught smoking in a no-smoking area and was given a verbal warning. I'm not doing it again because I don't want to get into more trouble and possibly end up losing my job.

_____ 3. Shelly is a very hard worker, but I've never even seen her get as much as a thank-you for her performance. So why should I work?

_____ 4. After seeing what happened to Sean, you better believe that I'm keeping my goggles on when I'm on the job.

_____ 5. I completed the project ahead of schedule and did an excellent job. As a result, my boss gave me a sincere thanks and a $100 gift certificate to Amazon.com. I learned that it is worth putting in extra effort for the boss.

---

his "Skinner box." He would put animals such as a pigeon or a rat in a box and provide a stimulus such as a light above a lever. If the animal chose the right lever, they were rewarded with food. If the animal chose the incorrect lever they would receive punishment such as a mild electrical shock.

Skinner showed that very quickly, the animals would figure out which lever to press in order to receive the reward. So, operant conditioning results in "direct, voluntary, learned behaviors." The subjects in Skinner's experiments *voluntarily* selected the lever that provided the reward, so they learned to behave in a particular way based on the *direct* consequences of their actions. So Skinner proved that animals will voluntary act in order to receive a reward and avoid acting in order to avoid receiving punishment.

SOCIAL LEARNING. Our third type of learning, social learning, is similar in form to operant conditioning. The difference here is that we are not learning from the consequences of our own actions but from the consequences of the actions of another person. Social learning is also called vicarious learning. The word *vicarious* means "experienced or realized through imaginative or sympathetic participation in the experience of another."[27] So social or vicarious learning is experienced through watching the actions of another person and witnessing the consequences of those actions. In other words, if a young boy watches his sister receive a cookie as a reward for cleaning her room and he wants a cookie too, he may determine that the best way to get a cookie is to go clean his own room. This would be an example of social learning. Again, social learning is based on *voluntary, learned* actions on the part of the individual, but it is based on *indirect* consequences of the actions of another person.

Shaping Behavior

We can use the three types of learning that we have just reviewed, especially Skinner's concept of operant conditioning, to shape the behaviors of the employees in the organization. In order to shape the behavior of our employees, we can provide reinforcement (rewards) or punishment or, as a third alternative, provide neither. Take a look at Exhibit 7-2. It shows four methods of shaping behavior. We can break these methods down into a process of applying a reward, removing a reward, applying punishment, removing punishment, or providing no response to the actions of the individual.

WORK
APPLICATION 7-8

Give examples of what you learned in an organization through classical conditioning, operant conditioning, and social learning.

LO 7-6

Identify and briefly discuss the four methods for shaping behavior.

EXHIBIT 7-2   SHAPING BEHAVIOR

(A) **Positive Reinforcement** Apply a reward	(B) **Punishment** Apply a noxious stimulus— Give bad consequence
(C) **Punishment** Remove a reward	(D) **Negative Reinforcement** Avoid or remove a noxious stimulus

Extinction (E) = The absence of a response, designed to avoid reinforcing negative behaviors
Shaping (changing) behavior:

A, D = Increasing target behaviors
B, C, E = Decreasing target behaviors

So, what's the value of understanding Exhibit 7-2 and the four methods of shaping behavior? If we understand each of the four methods, we can use them to cause workers to act in ways that are conducive to the improvement and ultimate success of the organization. Let's discuss each part of the exhibit.

Positive Reinforcement. If we *apply* a *reward* (the upper left quadrant A in the exhibit), we're using the concept of positive reinforcement. **Positive reinforcement *is providing a reward in return for a constructive action on the part of the subject.*** For example, if our employees do something that improves the safety of workers in the organization, we may give them a bonus as a reward. This would be positive reinforcement. Applying a reward to a particular behavior is likely to cause the individual to perform that behavior, or similar behaviors, again. So our employees would be likely to provide other suggestions to improve our business operations because of the past reward. We should realize that positive reinforcement is the most commonly used method of shaping employee behavior when we train new employees to do their jobs and when existing employees need to learn new job requirements and processes.

Negative Reinforcement. Our second option would be to *avoid or remove* a *noxious stimulus* (the lower right quadrant D in the exhibit), a process called negative reinforcement. **Negative reinforcement *is the withdrawal of a harmful thing from the environment in response to a positive action on the part of the subject.*** Negative reinforcement is commonly based on rules, with punishment being given for breaking the rules. A rule itself is not a punishment; it is a means of getting people to do or avoid a specific behavior, such as coming to work on time. But if the rule is broken, punishment is usually the consequence. An example of negative reinforcement working as intended would be you coming to work on time not because you want to be on time but because you want to avoid a punishment for being late. It can also be removing an employee from disciplinary probation for tardiness in response to their positive action of showing up for work on time for a period of time after being disciplined. Avoiding or taking away a negative consequence in response to a positive behavior is likely to cause the individual to perform the desired behavior again. We should realize that negative reinforcement is commonly used during the new employee orientation to make sure employees know the expected behaviors and the consequences for breaking rules. We certainly don't want to punish employees for breaking a rule that they don't know exists.

Positive reinforcement Providing a reward in return for a constructive action on the part of the subject

Negative reinforcement Withdrawal of a harmful thing from the environment in response to a positive action on the part of the subject

Punishment. In contrast to reinforcement, we may punish bad behaviors. **Punishment** *is the application of an adverse consequence, or the removal of a reward, in order to decrease an unwanted behavior.* One method of punishment would be to *remove* a *reward* (the lower left quadrant C in the exhibit) as a result of people doing something that they shouldn't have done. Think of taking away the car keys for a school-age driver who does something wrong. Or let's say that our organization has a policy of providing free parking for our workers in a crowded downtown area. We might take away the parking privileges of an individual who continually harasses other workers in the parking lot.

Alternatively, we can *apply a noxious stimulus* (the upper right quadrant B in the exhibit), which is also considered to be punishment. An example here would be suspending a worker without pay because of excessive absenteeism. By suspending the worker, we're applying a negative response. The negative response received by the worker is designed to cause a decline in the behavior that created such a response. So in other words, punishment can be the application of something bad (a noxious stimulus) or the removal of something good (a reward).

We should realize that punishment is not commonly used during training of employees; rather, it is commonly used when employees know how to do the job but just will not meet the job standards, or when employees break a rule and get disciplined for doing so. We will learn more about when and how to discipline employees in Chapter 9.

Extinction. We noted earlier in this section that there are four options for shaping behavior. What is the other option? The last option doesn't fit in the diagram itself, because it's the absence of reinforcement or punishment of any kind. **Extinction** *is the lack of response, either positive or negative, in order to avoid reinforcing an undesirable behavior.* You may have heard the phrase "Ignore it and it will go away." How does a lack of response cause behavior to be shaped in a way that we desire?

Employees will sometimes exhibit problem behavior to cause a reaction from the manager or fellow employees. The employee who exhibits the behavior may delight in causing others concern or consternation. For example, the male employee who continually asks his female manager about organizational sexual harassment policies in front of other workers to cause her discomfort as she explains the policy is most likely *intentionally* acting to cause her embarrassment. In such a case, the female manager may be able to ignore the stimulus behavior and provide no reinforcement. If the manager does so for a long enough time, the employee's behavior will most likely decline or go away completely, because it is not having the desired negative effect on the manager. We should realize that extinction is also not very commonly used because when we train employees, we don't usually ignore behavior in the hope that it will not be repeated—we correct it.

Shaping (Changing) Behavior. If you understand these methods of shaping behavior, they become powerful tools in your managerial toolbox for changing behavior to increase performance. These tools allow you to *cause* your employees to act in ways you want them to and avoid acting in ways that are detrimental to themselves, their division or department, or the organization as a whole. Now let's discuss how to increase and decrease behaviors to increase performance.

Increasing Targeted Behavior. If we want to cause the behavior to increase, then we want to use positive or negative reinforcement (quadrant A or D in Exhibit 7-2). Reinforcement, whether positive or negative, is designed to cause an increase in the targeted behavior.

Decreasing Targeted Behavior. If, on the other hand, we want to cause a particular behavior to decrease, we would use punishment (in either of its forms) or extinction (quadrant B, C, or E in Exhibit 7-2). Punishment and extinction are designed to cause a targeted behavior to decrease over time.

WORK APPLICATION 7-9

Give examples of how an organization uses positive reinforcement, punishment, negative reinforcement, and extinction to shape employee behavior.

Punishment The application of an adverse consequence, or the removal of a reward, in order to decrease an unwanted behavior

Extinction The lack of response, either positive or negative, in order to avoid reinforcing an undesirable behavior

7-2 APPLYING THE CONCEPT

Shaping Behavior

Review the following methods of shaping employee behavior and write the letter corresponding to each before the situation(s) illustrating it.

  a. positive reinforcement

  b. punishment—give bad consequence

  c. punishment—remove reward

  d. negative reinforcement

  e. extinction

____ 6. Betty used to give me that intimidating look when I assigned her a task she didn't want to do, and that behavior made me uncomfortable. So I just ignored it and didn't let her make me feel uncomfortable, and she stopped giving me the look.

____ 7. You know the rules. That behavior is going to cost you $25.

____ 8. You got that angry lady to calm down and leave the store as a happy customer. This behavior leads to keeping our customers. Thanks, keep up the good work.

____ 9. If you don't stop breaking the pricing gun, you will have to buy a new one.

____10. I know you like to get out of work for a while and get our lunches, but because you mixed up the order today, Santana will go tomorrow.

Learning Styles

As a last point in our review of the learning process, we need to briefly discuss various learning styles that people prefer to use. There are more than 70 learning style inventories available in the psychology literature and even some questionnaires that track learning style on the Internet.[28] You need to take individual learning styles into account when creating training programs and utilize teaching methods that cover each of the major learning styles to ensure the best potential outcomes. You should realize that people within your company and throughout the global village have different learning styles, so you need to be culturally sensitive in selecting the most appropriate training methods.[29]

Fleming Learning Styles. One of the common learning style inventories, by Neil Fleming, provides three primary learner options. These three options are *visual, auditory, and tactile learning.*[30] As you would think, visual learners prefer to have material provided in a visual format such as graphs and charts. Auditory learners, on the other hand, generally prefer to learn information based on hearing that information. Auditory learners tend to perform best in a historical classroom setting where the teacher stands in front of the class and teaches while the students passively listen. Finally, tactile learners prefer to learn by doing. Tactile learners want to physically perform a task in order to learn. Most of us use a mix of all three of the major learning styles. Therefore, a trainer should take each of the styles into account when creating a training program.

You should realize that we provide multiple tactile-learning application and skill-building opportunities in this book. Which of the three options do you prefer when learning something?

Kolb Learning Styles. A more complex learning style inventory was developed by David Kolb.[31] Kolb's model is probably the most accepted of the learning style models in use today.[32] To determine your preferred learning style, complete self-assessment 7-1.

LO 7-7

Identify which training methods are most commonly used with which HRM skill.

LO 7-8

Discuss each of the major training delivery types.

DESIGN AND DELIVERY OF TRAINING

Recall that back in Chapter 1, we identified four important HRM skills: technical, human relations, conceptual and design (decision making), and business skills. Essentially, all of the training methods are used to develop specific skills that can be classified into one of these four skills categories. Once we have completed our needs assessment and selected how we plan to shape behavior, we are ready to complete step 3 of the training process: designing the training by selecting training methods and then delivering the training. So in this section, we will present which training methods to use based on which types of skills we are developing. Exhibit 7-3 presents

7-1 SELF ASSESSMENT

Your Learning Style

Below are 10 statements. For each statement, distribute 5 points between the A and B alternatives. If the A statement is very characteristic of you and the B statement is not, place a 5 on the A line and a 0 on the B line. If the A statement is characteristic of you and the B statement is occasionally or somewhat characteristic of you, place a 4 on the A line and a 1 on the B line. If both statements are characteristic of you, place a 3 on the line that is more characteristic of you and a 2 on the line that is less characteristic of you. Be sure to distribute 5 points between each A and B alternative for each of the 10 statements. When distributing the 5 points, try to recall recent situations on the job or in school.

1. When learning:

_____ A. I watch and listen.

_____ B. I get involved and participate.

2. When learning:

_____ A. I rely on my hunches and feelings.

_____ B. I rely on logical and rational thinking.

3. When making decisions:

_____ A. I take my time.

_____ B. I make them quickly.

4. When making decisions:

_____ A. I rely on my gut feelings about the best alternative course of action.

_____ B. I rely on a logical analysis of the situation.

5. When doing things:

_____ A. I am careful.

_____ B. I am practical.

6. When doing things:

_____ A. I have strong feelings and reactions.

_____ B. I reason things out.

7. I would describe myself in the following way:

_____ A. I am a reflective person.

_____ B. I am an active person.

8. I would describe myself in the following way:

_____ A. I am influenced by my emotions.

_____ B. I am influenced by my thoughts.

9. When interacting in small groups:

_____ A. I listen, watch, and get involved slowly.

_____ B. I am quick to get involved.

10. When interacting in small groups:

_____ A. I express what I am feeling.

_____ B. I say what I am thinking.

Scoring: Place your answer numbers (0–5) on the lines below. Then add the numbers in each column vertically. Each of the four columns should have a total number between 0 and 25. The total of the two A and B columns should equal 25.

1. _____ A. _____ B. (5)   2. _____ A. _____ B. (5)

3. _____ A. _____ B. (5)   4. _____ A. _____ B. (5)

5. _____ A. _____ B. (5)   6. _____ A. _____ B. (5)

7. _____ A. _____ B. (5)   8. _____ A. _____ B. (5)

9. _____ A. _____ B. (5)   10. _____ A. _____ B. (5)

Totals: _____ A. _____ B. (25)   _____ A. _____ B. (25)

Style: Observing Doing   Feeling Thinking

There is no best or right learning style; each of the four learning styles has its pros and cons. The more evenly distributed your scores are between the A's and B's, the more flexible you are at changing styles. Understanding your preferred learning style can help you get the most from your learning experiences.

Determining Your Preferred Learning Style

The five odd-numbered A statements refer to your self-description as being "observing," and the five odd-numbered B statements refer to your self-description as "doing." The column with the highest number is your preferred style of learning. Write that style here:

_____

The five even-numbered A statements refer to your self-description as being a "feeling" person, and the five even-numbered B statements refer to your self-description as being a "thinking" person. The column with the highest number is your preferred style. Write that style here: _____

Putting the two preferences together gives you your preferred learning style. Check it off below:

_____ Accommodator (combines doing and feeling)

_____ Diverger (combines observing and feeling)

_____ Converger (combines doing and thinking)

_____ Assimilator (combines observing and thinking)

EXHIBIT 7-3 SKILLS AND TRAINING METHODS

Skills Developed	Methods	Description
Technical Skills	a. Written material, lectures, videotapes, question-and-answer sessions, discussions, demonstrations	Questions or problems related to previously presented material are presented to the trainee in a booklet or on a computer screen. The trainee is asked to select a response to each question or problem and is given feedback on the response.
	b. Programmed Learning	Depending on the material presented, programmed learning may also develop interpersonal and communication skills.
	c. Job Rotation	Employees are trained to perform different jobs. Job rotation also develops trainees' conceptual skills.
	d. Projects	Trainees are given special assignments, such as developing a new product or preparing a report. Certain projects may also develop trainees' interpersonal skills and conceptual skills.
Human Relations Skills	e. Role-playing	Trainees act out situations that might occur on the job, such as handling a customer complaint, to develop skill at handling such situations on the job.
	f. Behavior Modeling	Trainees observe how to perform a task correctly, by watching either a live demonstration or a videotape. Trainees role-play the observed skills and receive feedback on their performance. Trainees develop plans for using the observed skills on the job.
Conceptual and Design/ Business Skills	g. Cases	The trainee is presented with a simulated situation and asked to diagnose and solve the problems involved. Trainees usually must also answer questions about their diagnosis and solution.
	h. In-basket Exercises	The trainee is given actual or simulated letters, memos, reports, and so forth that would typically come to the person holding the job. The trainee must determine what action each item would require and must assign priorities to the actions.
	i. Management Games	Trainees work as part of a team to "manage" a simulated company over a period of several game "quarters" or "years."
	j. Interactive Videos	Trainees can view videotapes that present situations requiring conceptual skills or decision making.

WORK
APPLICATION 7-10

Identify and describe the training method(s) used to train and develop you for a job you have or have had.

the type of skills, the training methods appropriate for developing each skill, and descriptions of the training methods.

Before we actually conduct the training, in step 4, the HR department or other trainers also have to select the types of training delivery. The choice will depend to some extent on what information is being transferred, as well as on the options that are available to the particular organization. We also need to look at the best type of training to use in order to maximize transfer of knowledge while minimizing the cost of the training process. Each of the four training types has advantages and disadvantages that have to be understood to assign the correct option to a specific type of training program. In the next sections, we discuss our four options: on-the-job, classroom, distance, and simulation training.

7-3 | APPLYING THE CONCEPT

Training Methods

For each of the training situations below, identify the most appropriate training method. Use the letters a through j from Exhibit 7-3 as your answers.

_____ 11. You want your customer service staff to do a better job of handling customer complaints.

_____ 12. Your large department has a high turnover rate, and new employees need to learn several rules and regulations to perform their jobs.

_____ 13. You need your new employees to learn how to handle the typical daily problems they will face on the job.

_____ 14. You need an employee to conduct an Internet search to find out more about a new product you want to buy for the department; you want a special report.

_____ 15. You want employees to be able to do each other's job when they take vacations.

_____ 16. You want to improve your employees' ability to sell products to customers in the store so that customers don't end up leaving and buying the products online.

_____ 17. You need to prepare middle managers to advance to upper-level managers. You are considering having them run a simulated company getting quarterly results.

On-the-Job Training (OJT)

SHRM

L:6
On-the-Job Training (OJT)

On-the-job training (OJT) is done at the work site with the resources the employee uses to perform the job. The manager, or an employee selected by the manager, usually conducts the training one-on-one with the trainee. Because of its proven record of success, job instructional training (JIT)—a specific type of on-the-job training—is a popular training type used worldwide.

JOB INSTRUCTIONAL TRAINING (JIT). JIT has four steps, presented in Model 7-1 and described here.

Step 1: Preparation of the trainee. Put the trainee at ease as you create interest in the job and encourage questions. Explain the task objectives and quantity and quality requirements, and discuss their importance.

Step 2: Presentation of the task by the trainer. Perform the task yourself slowly, explaining each step several times. Once the trainee seems to have the steps memorized, have the trainee explain each step as you perform the task. Prepare a written list of the steps in complex tasks and give a copy to the trainee.

Step 3: Performance of the task by the trainee. Have the trainee perform the task slowly while explaining each step. Correct any errors and be willing to help the trainee perform any difficult steps. Continue until the employee can perform the task proficiently.

Step 4: Follow-up. Tell the trainee who is available to provide help with any questions or problems. Gradually give the trainee more autonomy. Begin by checking quality and quantity frequently; then decrease the amount of checking based on the trainee's skill level. Watch the trainee perform the task and be sure to correct any errors or faulty work procedures before they become habits. Be patient and encouraging.

MODEL 7-1 | JOB INSTRUCTIONAL TRAINING STEPS

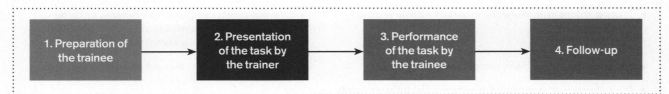

1. Preparation of the trainee → 2. Presentation of the task by the trainer → 3. Performance of the task by the trainee → 4. Follow-up

Employees are often given on-the-job training, especially in small businesses.

Stockbroker/Alamy

Even though OJT is fairly expensive on a per-person basis, many organizations still use it heavily because of the fact that it works very well. See Exhibit 7-4 for the advantages and disadvantages of OJT.

Classroom Training

Our second training option is classroom training. Classroom training is also a common form of training in organizations. To accomplish classroom training, the organization will create a training course—including content, instruction methods, lesson plans, and instructor materials—and provide all these materials to a qualified instructor who will teach the class.

Classroom training is generally very good for consistently transferring general knowledge or theories about a topic to a large number of people. It is generally not very good for teaching specific hands-on skills because of the passive nature of learning in a classroom. However, it is effective when using the same equipment that is used on the job. For example, many large banks have to train lots of tellers, and they conduct teller training in a classroom setting at headquarters, using an expert trainer so that the employees can go to the bank and actually begin work without any further training at the branch.

Let's do a quick review of some of the advantages and disadvantages of classroom training in Exhibit 7-5.

EXHIBIT 7-4   ON-THE-JOB TRAINING'S ADVANTAGES AND DISADVANTAGES

Advantages	Disadvantages
• Most people learn best by actually doing a job, in conjunction with how-to explanations.	• The one-to-one aspect of the training means that it is relatively high in cost on a per-person basis.
• The training can be immediately transferred to the job.	• Trainers may not know how to teach, may be unmotivated or unable to transfer their knowledge successfully, or may transfer their own bad habits to the trainee.
• Training occurs person to person on the actual job site and includes all of the incidental factors associated with the job.	• The training may be inconsistent unless trainers follow a standardized training plan.
• Training is done in an interactive environment, with feedback from the trainer.	• If the equipment being used is expensive, it may be dangerous to have trainees operating and potentially harming it because they are not yet skilled operators.
• The trainer is typically highly competent in doing the job.	• Training often disrupts the work environment.
• The instructor can customize the training to the trainee's needs.	

EXHIBIT 7-5 CLASSROOM TRAINING'S ADVANTAGES AND DISADVANTAGES

Advantages	Disadvantages
• Classroom training is a good method of providing consistent knowledge or information about a general topic to a fairly large number of people.	• Classroom training is often a passive environment, where the learner just absorbs the information provided.
• A significant number of students can be trained at the same time.	• The pace of the training may be too fast for some students and too slow for others, causing anxiety or boredom.
• Information provided to the trainees is typically more consistent than with OJT.	• It is more difficult to cater to different learning styles in a classroom setting than in OJT.
• Instructors are usually professional trainers.	
• Classroom training is less expensive than OJT, due to the fact that it's one-to-many training.	
• It provides a somewhat interactive environment, based on question-and-answer sessions.	
• It does not disrupt the actual work environment.	

Distance or E-Learning

Our third option is some form of distance learning—also called e-learning—in either a synchronous or an asynchronous format. *Synchronous distance learning* occurs when all of the trainees sign in to a particular website where their instructor then interacts with them and teaches the topics for the day. In contrast, *asynchronous distance learning* is a process in which the student can sign in to the training site at any point in time and materials are available for their studies. The instructor may or may not be online at the same time as the student, but there's no dedicated connection between the two for the purpose of teaching the information.

Distance learning, similar to classroom training, is also valuable for teaching basic concepts and providing general information on the topic. There's typically even less interaction between an instructor and trainees in this form than in classroom training. Let's analyze some of the advantages and disadvantages of distance learning in Exhibit 7-6.

Self-directed learning is a specific kind of distance learning. In self-directed learning, individuals go completely at their own pace, and they are able to study whatever aspects of the topic they think they need to study to be successful while leaving other parts of the training uncompleted. Self-directed training tends to have all of the potential advantages and disadvantages of other forms of distance learning. The most significant issue in self-directed learning tends to be the fact that individuals are not motivated to learn on their own, so they will be unsuccessful because nobody else is going to follow their progress and push them to complete the training.

Simulations

The trend today is toward having more active involvement of participants and offering online simulation training and development.[33] A simulation is a training method whereby we may simulate a real-life situation to teach students what actions to take in the event that they encounter the same or a similar situation on the job. Some common examples of simulations are flight simulators, driving simulators, and firefighting simulations. Simulations would typically be used in

SHRM

L:5
E-Learning and Use of Technology in Training

EXHIBIT 7-6 DISTANCE TRAINING'S ADVANTAGES AND DISADVANTAGES

Advantages	Disadvantages
• Training may be available 24/7/365.	• There is a requirement for self-discipline on the part of the trainee. The responsibility for "getting" the information shifts from the instructor to the trainee.
• Students can learn at their own pace.	• A teacher in a standardized distance learning course often lacks the ability to respond directly to student needs and questions.
• There's no requirement for a physical classroom space, or necessarily for an instructor to be available at a particular point in time. No time is lost to commuting.	• In its basic form, distance learning often lacks the functionality to provide immediate feedback to students on their success or failure.
• The option is available to provide multiple media that can enhance the learning process by matching up with different learning styles.	• Distance learning programs tend to have high initial start-up costs due to the need to create voluminous online materials.
• Distance learning is a reasonably low-cost method of training, over time. Once the course is set up, costs to train additional students are fairly minimal.	• Student dishonesty is more difficult to identify, and testing usually has to be in open-book form.
• The training does not disrupt the actual work environment.	• There is a lack of social interaction, which can inhibit learning in certain fields.

WORK
APPLICATION 7-11

Identify and describe the type(s) of training you received for a job you have or had.

SHRM

Q:8
Measurement Systems

LO 7-9

Briefly discuss the Four-Level Evaluation Method for assessing training programs.

SHRM

L:4
Training Evaluation: Kirkpatrick's Model

situations where actually performing an action or set of actions could lead to significant financial cost (because of lost equipment) or could put the trainee in significant danger of injury or death.

In these types of cases, providing simulations makes much more sense than actually performing a particular task. Asking students to perform in a simulation will also generally cause them to go through the same set of emotions that they would go through in the real-life situation being simulated. Training through the use of a simulation allows the student to experience these emotions and learn to control them in order to resolve a complex and dangerous situation. Let's review the advantages and disadvantages of simulations in Exhibit 7-7.

ASSESSING TRAINING

The fifth and last step of our training process (Exhibit 7-1) is assessment. No matter what the training covers, we always want to evaluate whether or not it achieved the shaped behavior identified through our needs assessment. Training can be designed to cause changes in a variety of employee attitudes and behaviors, and as a result, it can be assessed in a number of different ways, depending on what we were trying to accomplish. In this section, we present four assessment methods and how to choose an assessment method.

Assessment Methods

One of the most common assessment options, first identified by Donald Kirkpatrick, is called the Four-Level Evaluation Method.[34] It measures *reaction*, *learning*, *behaviors*, and *results*.

Reaction evaluations measure how the individual responds to the actual training process. Self-reporting measures are quick and common measures of training.[35] In reaction evaluations, the organization asks the participants how they feel about the training process, including the content provided, the instructors, and the knowledge that they gained by going through the process. They may also be asked about what new skills they have learned during the training process. This is the lowest level of training evaluation, and it is frequently discounted due to its subjectivity and because some people overestimate their capabilities.[36] After all, is the trainee the best person to evaluate the knowledge they've gained if that knowledge is brand new to them? Certainly, reaction evaluations are less rigorous than some other forms of evaluation, but they still provide the organization with valuable feedback concerning the learners' state of mind at the end of the training process as well as their attitude toward the process at its conclusion. Student course assessments are an example of reaction evaluations.

Organizations are now offering training and development to employees anytime, from anywhere—24/7/365.

Learning evaluations are level-two measures designed to determine what knowledge the individual gained, whether they learned any new skills because of the training, and whether the person's attitudes toward their knowledge or skill set has changed as a result of the training. Learning evaluations are easily done using quizzes, tests, and even topic-based discussions. Learning evaluations help the organization evaluate the skill of the instructor as well as the change in the knowledge set of the trainee. If the instructor is inadequate as a teacher, it should show up in a *learning evaluation* measurement. We should also be able to see whether or not the individual gained knowledge of the subject because of the training process.

Behavior evaluations are the third level of evaluating training processes. Behavior evaluations are designed to determine whether or not the trainee's on-the-job behaviors changed as a result of the training. Behavior evaluations usually take the form of observation of the individual on the job, after completion of the training process. Did the process of going through the training have a direct effect on the individual's post-training job performance? The behavior evaluation is specifically designed to identify whether or not the individual is able to transfer the knowledge gained into new skills that they then use in their work.

EXHIBIT 7-7 SIMULATION TRAINING'S ADVANTAGES AND DISADVANTAGES

Advantages	Disadvantages
• Simulation is a low-risk method of training individuals on how to react to a complex situation.	• Simulations can become "video games" to the student, and as a result, they may not be taken seriously.
• Generally, simulation is a very realistic form of training. Simulations can convincingly emulate actual physical situations.	• Simulation systems may be very expensive to create and/or maintain.
• Simulations allow the student to try out experimental solutions to a problem. If the solution fails, the simulation can just be reset.	• Complex computer-based simulations may require a very powerful and expensive processor in order to run.
• Results of the students' actions can be analyzed post hoc to determine whether or not different actions might have been more successful.	• Some processes cannot be simulated successfully due to a lack of knowledge of the details of the process.
• Simulation does not disrupt the actual work environment.	

WORK
APPLICATION 7-12

Which training assessment methods are used where you work or have worked? Give examples of the training and its assessment method.

SHRM

L:8
Transfer of Training: Design Issues, Facilitating Transfer

Results evaluation is the fourth and final level of training evaluation. In a results evaluation, we try to determine whether or not individual behavioral changes have improved organizational results. In other words, we look at the organization's bottom line to determine whether or not productivity has increased. This is the level at which ROI is measured and evaluated to see whether or not the training has paid off for the company. However, ROI is not the only thing that we measure at this level. Other results that we may measure include increased quality of work, lower absenteeism and turnover, reductions in rework and scrap, lower on-the-job accident rates, and many others. What we're looking for in a results evaluation is concrete evidence that the training resulted in organizational changes that were valuable in some form.

Choosing Assessment Methods

Why not just evaluate all of our training programs at each of the four levels? The primary reason is that it costs the organization money to go through the evaluation process. So we don't want to evaluate something unless we need to. In fact, as we go from levels one through four, the cost of evaluating the training process increases with each level. Let's identify when we might use each of the four evaluation levels.

Reaction evaluations (level 1) help us identify employee attitudes toward the training process. If, in fact, the training process has been designed to change employee *attitudes* such as motivation toward their work or satisfaction with their job, level-one evaluation may be critical. The perception of the trainee in this case may be more important in changing their level of motivation and job satisfaction than any new skills that they actually learned.

Learning evaluations (level 2) are used if there's a need to evaluate more than employee attitude. We may wish to be certain that the trainee has gained a depth of knowledge of a particular issue to ensure that they are capable of putting their knowledge to use. For instance, to comply with federal harassment statutes, all US businesses need to ensure that their employees are trained on the concept of sexual harassment and how to avoid it. If we want to be certain that our employees know what sexual harassment is, we may choose to do a learning evaluation of that particular training session through giving a test.

Behavior evaluation, level 3, is needed not only to ensure that new knowledge has been gained but also to ensure that the individual knows how to apply that knowledge by acting in a certain way. Performing a behavior evaluation is the only way that we can truly measure whether or not the individual has transferred the knowledge gained into actions that will improve their performance. An example here would be training operators for a nuclear power plant. Determining their attitude toward their work and whether or not they have the innate knowledge necessary to perform the work is insufficient in this case. It would be critical to determine whether or not they could act correctly to maintain and operate the nuclear reactor, so we would observe their actual performance on the job. You can quickly see here that we need to be absolutely certain that they'll take correct action—in other words, that they will behave in the manner necessary to correct the failure.

Measuring Training Success

One challenge in assessment is developing metrics to assess training.[37] Measurements of training have become significantly more important in the past few years. We now have the capacity to analyze large sets of data to find out how successful a particular approach is in creating a more skilled workforce. We also want to make sure we don't spend money without getting results. There are dozens of metrics for measuring training effectiveness, but let's take a look at a few of the most common measures here.

7-4 APPLYING THE CONCEPT

Training Assessment Methods

Review the following assessment methods and write the letter corresponding to each one before the situation(s) where it is most appropriate.

a. reaction evaluation
b. learning evaluation
c. behavior evaluation
d. results evaluation

____18. You are a software sales manager and you want your new sales reps to be able to demonstrate the various features of your software.

____19. You are a restaurant owner who installed a new food-ordering computer system with the objective of speeding up the time it takes to serve meals, so you need to train employees on how to use the new system.

____20. You are the HR manager and want to make sure that your staff understands what questions they can and can't legally ask during the selection process.

____21. You are the service desk manager at a retail store and need to train employees on how to effectively deal with angry customers when they return merchandise. You want the employees to remain calm and satisfy the customer.

____22. You are the HR manager responsible for diversity, and you develop a training program to help employees better understand each other and not use stereotypes so that they can work well together.

SHRM
L:10
Determining Return on Investment (ROI)

ROI (a results metric) is probably still the measure with the most meaning to those outside the HR department. Although it is sometimes hard to identify how to calculate ROI in a training situation (because of the difficulty of identifying the specific value of the gain), in at least some cases, it can be done quickly and easily. For instance, if a particular training program is designed to reduce *annual voluntary turnover rates* and it does so, the ROI measure would be as follows:

Average cost of turnover of one employee = $7,500
Annual voluntary turnover reduction after training = 8 employees
Total cost of training (course development, materials, instructor, etc.) = $25,000

$$ROI = \frac{\text{Gain from investment} - \text{Cost of investment}}{\text{Cost of investment}} = \frac{(\$7,500 \times 8) - \$25,000}{\$25,000} = \frac{\$35,000}{\$25,000} = 140\% \text{ ROI}$$

Customer satisfaction (another result) is another area where we may want to measure training results. If we perform customer service training and have baseline surveys on historical levels of customer satisfaction, we can compare those levels prior to and after the training to see whether customer satisfaction rates went up. This will not provide a direct dollar value for the training, but if the sales or marketing managers have data on "value per customer" provided to the organization and rates at which dissatisfied customers leave, and if these rates show lower *customer attrition*—then this can give us the means to do an indirect ROI calculation.

We may also want to evaluate *employee satisfaction* (reaction) levels after particular types of training—especially developmental training, which usually doesn't give us an immediate return on our investment. We will talk in detail about employee job satisfaction, and why and how we measure it, in Chapter 10. But for now, just remember that it is a predictor of absenteeism and turnover, which both cost companies lots of money. There are also strong correlations between job satisfaction and customer satisfaction as well as other positive organizational outcomes like *sales performance/revenue generation* (result), *individual productivity* (behavior), *accuracy/quality* (learning/behavior) of work, and others.

TALENT MANAGEMENT AND DEVELOPMENT

Now that you have learned about the five steps of the training process, let's discuss developing employees. We should realize, however, that development programs also follow the same five steps of the training process, as the steps listed in Exhibit 7-1 state both training and development. Remember from the beginning of the chapter that employee development deals primarily with training workers for *future* jobs, not their current position. In this section, we discuss careers, common methods of development, and a model of career development consequences.

Careers

What is a career? Is a career in the 21st century the same as a career in the 1960s or 1970s? Do individuals today go through just one or many careers throughout their work life? Half a century ago, a large percentage of people would spend their entire work life with one company. This obviously does not happen very often in modern organizations. In fact, there's much evidence that says that you will likely have several changes in career throughout your work life.

A Bureau of Labor Statistics survey that followed individuals born between 1957 and 1964 cited an average of 11 *jobs* per person in this group. The report defined a job as an uninterrupted period of work with a particular employer.[38] So, if we defined a career as we did in the 1960s and said that to have a successful career, you had to go to work after graduating from college, stay with that employer for 40 years while moving upward through a progression of jobs from lower levels to higher levels, and then retire with a pension, very few of us today would have a "successful" career. Obviously, then, the concept of career has changed.

So how do we define a career in the 21st century workforce? Douglas Hall defined career as a process where the person, not the organization, is the manager of the process. His definition states: "A **career** *is the individually perceived sequence of attitudes and behaviors associated with work-related experiences and activities over the span of the person's life.*"[39] Whew! Let's break this definition down into its subcomponents.

"Individually perceived." This definition of the term *career* relies heavily on the perception of the individual who is making the judgment concerning success or failure of the career. So, whether or not a career is defined as successful or a failure is determined within the individual's own mind. If you go through 4, or 5, or 10 different jobs in your lifetime, and if you perceive that as being successful, then you are a success. If you perceive it as a failure, then you have failed.

"Sequence of attitudes and behaviors." A career consists of both attitudes and behaviors, so it is not only *what* you do; it's also the way you *feel* about what you do and how well you think you've done over time. What is an attitude? Attitude is simply a positive or negative individual judgment about a particular situation. So your career involves not only the things that you do but also the way you think and how you feel about your progression of jobs over time.

"Associated with work-related experiences and activities over the span of the person's life." The definition of career involves not only the direct work that is done but also all work-related experiences and activities. So, even nonwork activities that are work related, such as training off-site, would be included in our definition of career. We can even extend this to the way your family and friends interact with you and your job, and we can say that any interaction of family, friends, and work could help define your career. This is one place where attitudes come into play. Your friends and family know how you feel about your job and how it allows you to interact with others or prevents you from interacting with others in different

circumstances. Using this definition of career avoids the problem of having to confront the fact that by the 1960s definition, most of us would fail to have a *successful* career, and it also allows us to take into account the significant factors of perception and attitude.

Why Career Development?

Why has career development become such a significant issue to companies, and what problems does career planning need to be designed to solve? Twenty-first century organizations need to provide our employees with reasonable career paths and career counseling so that they can achieve their personal goals over the course of their career. These services can create significant motivation in our workforce that, as we noted earlier, can lead to a major improvement in productivity and job satisfaction as well as lower absenteeism and turnover.[40]

The first factor that has caused companies to become more concerned with career development is the nature of jobs in a modern organization. Recall from Chapter 2 that many of our jobs are knowledge management jobs and that the individuals who fill these jobs have to have special skills. Because people with these special skills (human intellectual capital) are in short supply, the organization cannot afford to lose individuals with such abilities. So we spend significant amounts of time and money on developing them, which can help the organization reduce turnover of highly skilled employees.

Another issue is that the national culture of the United States has changed in the past 30 to 40 years, and the latest generation of workers—called generation Y or millennials (many of you)—have significantly different expectations of what they are going to be able to do in their careers than did their parents. Millennial workers expect to have significant freedom at work to do what they think they need to do and make the money that they expect to make. Such high expectations create difficulty for organizations. We have to create policies and procedures that will not harm these individuals' initiative to work but that will also cause them to recognize the realities of the workplace. Through the process of career development, we can show these younger workers how they can progress through the organization, be entrepreneurial, and reach their personal career goals.

The next major reason for career development is the significant continuing pressure that organizations are getting from governments to provide career paths for individuals who have historically been disadvantaged. Even though there are many different EEO laws on the books and we have had such laws for over 50 years, there's still a significant disparity between the number of Caucasian male managers and managers from all other groups.[41] Career development programs can create career paths for individuals who are members of these disadvantaged groups and who are qualified to go into management or other professional programs. This not only helps the individual employee; it also assists the organization in its diversity efforts.

Finally, good employee development and career planning programs can help the organization avoid productivity and disciplinary problems associated with employees who are stagnating in a particular job. This may be due to career plateauing. A **career plateau** *occurs when an individual feels unchallenged in their current job and has little or no chance of advancement*. If our employees feel as if their career has stagnated, they are more likely to become disciplinary problems. We may be able to avoid such problems by providing the opportunity for individuals to progress in their career over time.

There are many other reasons for career development, but these are some of the most common issues. So as you can see, there are a number of reasons why career planning has become a major issue to 21st century organizations.

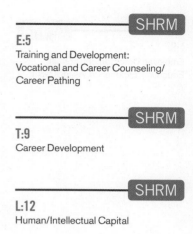

SHRM

E:5
Training and Development:
Vocational and Career Counseling/
Career Pathing

SHRM

T:9
Career Development

SHRM

L:12
Human/Intellectual Capital

SHRM

T:7
Plateauing

Career plateau When an individual feels unchallenged in their current job and has little or no chance of advancement

Briefly discuss the three common
methods of employee development.

SHRM

L:9
Employee Development: Formal
Education, Experience, Assessment

Common Methods of Employee Development

So we need to develop our employees. How do we go about doing that? There are a series of common methods that organizations use, including formal education, experience, and assessments. Let's go through a brief description of each of these options for development.

FORMAL EDUCATION. Our first method of employee development, *formal education*, provides employees the opportunity to participate in programs that will improve their general knowledge in areas such as finance, project management, or logistics. These formal education opportunities include such things as degree programs at colleges and universities, short courses of study that are available from many different sources (including private training firms and public agencies), and courses in community colleges. Such formal education courses may be held with any of the training and delivery methods discussed earlier.

The intent of formal education programs is to provide the student with a specific set of information about a particular topic. Through formal education, we can provide programs for every individual within the organization, from the executives down to the first-line supervisors. At the executive level, we might send a strong mid-level manager from the company to a university executive MBA program. In contrast, at the supervisor level, the organization would probably want new first-line supervisors to go through courses that teach supervisory skills, leadership, coaching, and basic financial analysis. Many organizations pay part or all of the cost of formal education for their employees.

EXPERIENCE. Employee development programs that use experience as a method for developing the individual would seek to put the person through a number of different types of job-related experiences over time. Such an experience-based program might include job rotation to provide them with a wide range of experiences within the company. This allows the person to see more of what goes on within the organization and how each job ties to others.

Experience-based employee development might also include the use of coaches or mentors for the individual. The coach or mentor will work with the person to identify how these different job experiences help the individual to learn and grow within the organization.[42] Development using job experience can successfully be used from the executive level all the way down to the level of work teams within the organization. In fact, there's significant evidence that career experience, team experience, and job-related skills are all related to higher levels of team performance.[43]

In today's flatter organizations, it has become more difficult to climb the old corporate ladder. Plus, younger workers become bored doing the same job. Therefore, giving employees a variety of experience through lateral jobs that provide new challenges and experience, with pay raises, may help to keep employees satisfied and with the organization.

EMPLOYEE ASSESSMENT. There are a number of different assessment tools that provide individuals with information about how they think, how they interact with others, and how they manage their own actions and emotions. These assessments provide individuals with information that allows them to understand better how they can manage others within the organization. Some of the more common measures include psychological assessments, emotional intelligence tests, and performance appraisals. Each of these assessments, if properly used, provides individuals with information that can be used to modify the way that they interact with others within the organization. We will review performance appraisals in the next chapter. However, let's take a look at the other two options now.

Psychological Assessments. These have gained significant acceptance within the workplace, and they include tests such as the Myers-Briggs Type Indicator (MBTI), the Birkman Method, and the Benchmarks Assessment tool. Each of the psychological assessment tools provides information about the person's style of thinking, interacting with others, management, and leadership.

The MBTI is probably the most common personality-type assessment used for employee development, but each of the tests has advantages and disadvantages compared to the other options. However, the validity and reliability of any of the common forms of psychological assessment has been questioned by various researchers.[44] Even with the weaknesses in validity and reliability, several of the personality assessment tools have been in use for many years and have shown legitimate real-world value in assessing the basic type of personality exhibited by individual employees within the organization.

Emotional Intelligence. **Emotional intelligence** *is the way that we identify, understand, and use our own emotions as well as the emotions of others to promote our working relationships.* It is an important part of human relations skills. Emotional intelligence is also referred to as an emotional quotient (EQ), making it similar to intelligence quotient (IQ). It is said that to be highly successful, a person needs a high IQ, a high EQ, and training on what to do to succeed.

Emotional intelligence has been described as "Our Most Versatile Tool for Success" in a 2005 SHRM white paper.[45] The Mayer-Salovey-Caruso Emotional Intelligence Test (MSCEIT) is one of the more common tools used to measure emotional intelligence. The MSCEIT consists of four pieces: perceiving emotion (the ability to identify your own and others' emotions), the use of emotion to facilitate thought (the ability to use emotions to focus attention and to think more rationally, logically, and creatively), understanding emotion (the ability to analyze and evaluate your own and others' emotions), and managing emotion (the ability to adjust emotions of yourself and others).[46]

Here again, the validity and reliability of the tests are still in some question. However, as with personality assessments, there's at least some evidence in the business arena that higher levels of emotional intelligence provide employees with a greater chance of success as they move up in the organization.[47]

A Model of Career Development Consequences

Because the organization and the individual have joint responsibility for career planning and development, both will suffer significant consequences if the planning isn't done successfully. Individual employees go through a series of career stages as they progress through their work life. Within each of these stages, the employee has different needs that the organization must meet so the relationship between the two can remain stable and the worker will continue to be motivated to produce for the organization. Organizations must respond successfully to the individual employee based on the employee's current career stage.

Let's discuss the commonly identified stages of career development first identified by Donald Super and Douglas Hall.[48] You can see them summarized in the first section of Exhibit 7-8.

Exploration. The first career development stage, called the *exploration* stage, is the period of time during which the individual is identifying the personal needs that will be satisfied by a particular type of work, the types of jobs that interest them, and the skill sets necessary to be able to accomplish those types of jobs. This stage is usually identified as being between the ages of 15 and 24.

Establishment. The second stage, called *establishment*, is the period when the individual has entered into a career and becomes concerned with building a skill set, developing work relationships, and advancing and stabilizing their career. In the

WORK
APPLICATION 7-13

State some of your career goals and the methods you will use to develop yourself to meet these goals.

SHRM

Q:3
Emotional Intelligence

LO 7-12

Briefly discuss some of the individual and organizational consequences that can occur as a result of organizational career planning processes.

Emotional intelligence The way that we identify, understand, and use our own emotions as well as the emotions of others to promote our working relationships

EXHIBIT 7-8 CAREER STAGES AND THE HIERARCHY OF NEEDS

Exploration	Establishment	Maintenance	Disengagement
Meet personal needs	Career entry	Personal satisfaction	Lower output
Identify interests	Building skills	Continue advancement	Coach/mentor as desired
Evaluate skills	Security/stabilization	Coach/mentor	Balance between work and nonwork
Tentative work choice	Work relationships	Improve policies and procedures	
	Work contributions		
	Advancement		

MASLOW'S HEIRARCHY OF NEEDS

Physiological	Safety/Security	Social	Esteem	Self-Actualization
Air, food, water, sleep, etc.	Physical shelter, physical security, financial security, stability, etc.	Friendship, love, relationships, family, belonging to social groups, etc.	Social status, recognition, self-respect, reputation, achievement, etc.	Wisdom and justice—pass knowledge to others because *you* think it is valuable.

establishment phase, we see the individual begin to make significant personal contributions to their career in the organization and begin to create relationships or alliances with coworkers that allow them to become more secure within the organization. This stage is usually identified as covering approximately age 25 through the mid-40s.

Maintenance. This is the third stage of career development. The maintenance stage covers the period from the mid-40s to age 60 years old or older. In the maintenance stage, the individual typically continues to advance but begins to seek personal satisfaction in the jobs that they perform for the organization. This is the phase where we see individual employees begin to act as mentors or trainers to their younger coworkers and to act to improve the organization and its processes and policies because they see a need to do so.

Disengagement. Finally, the fourth stage is identified as the *disengagement* stage. This stage typically shows lower levels of output and productivity as the individual prepares for life after work. During this stage, because of the desire to balance nonwork with work activities, the individual may begin to choose to work only on efforts they feel are necessary or worthy of their attention. They may continue to mentor or sponsor other individuals in the organization as those others progress through their own careers. Obviously, this stage goes from the early 60s to whatever point at which the individual finally completely disengages from the organization through retirement.

You may be wondering why these career stages matter. Let's take a look now at the second part of Exhibit 7-8. We have added Abraham Maslow's Hierarchy of Needs below each of the career stages. It's rather surprising how closely Maslow's needs hierarchy matches up with our career stages. We could accomplish a similar matching process with many other motivation theories, but this one serves to illustrate why career stages matter so much to managers in the organization, and especially to HR management.

What are people most concerned with at the earliest career stage? They are typically most concerned with physical and safety issues, right? Are they physically able to get the *basic things* that they need in order to live and work—like money for shelter, food to eat, fuel for their car? Are they getting paid enough to *survive and be safe*? Then, as they get into the establishment and maintenance stages, they become more concerned with *social interactions* and then gaining *status and recognition* as organizational leaders. Finally, as they move to the disengagement stage, they are more concerned with higher-level esteem needs such as *self-respect, achievement* of personal goals, and being able to do the *things that they think are important*. So, we see people go through these different motivational points in their life as they go through their career. It's very interesting that the career stages follow almost exactly with what the motivation theories show us.

Now that we understand a little bit about the career stages that individuals go through during their work life and how those stages identify what might motivate workers in a particular stage, let's match those up with organizational HR strategies that are available to reinforce employee behavior. This will give us a general working model of how organizational HR strategies can create either positive or negative consequences for both the individual and the organization, depending on how the HR strategies are applied in a particular situation. Take a look at Exhibit 7-9. We have individual career stages identified on the left side of the diagram. On the right side are some of the major organizational HR strategies that are available. Depending on how the HR strategies are applied, and based on the individual's career stage and motivating factors, we end up with either positive or negative consequences to both the individual and the organization.

WORK
APPLICATION 7-14

Identify the level of career development you are on. Using Exhibit 7-8, but in your own words, describe your career stage and the Maslow motivational issues you are dealing with now.

EXHIBIT 7-9 CONSEQUENCES OF CAREER PLANNING

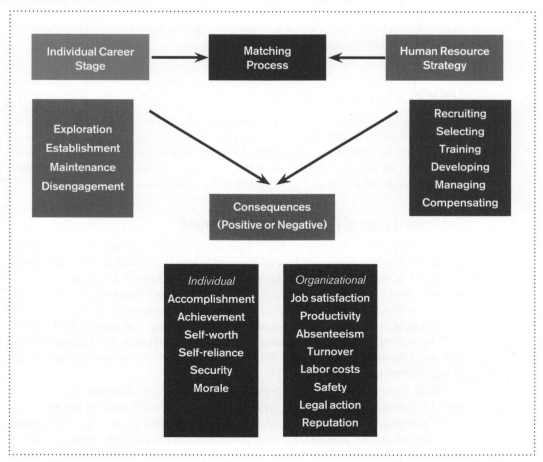

If we apply the correct HR strategy or strategies to an individual employee based on the factors that motivate the employee, we can improve each of the major organizational dependent variables that we identified in Chapter 1—job satisfaction, productivity, absenteeism, and turnover. In addition, there are several other organizational factors that can either improve or decline based on the application (or lack thereof) of the correct HR strategy. These factors include labor costs, organizational safety, employee lawsuits, and organizational reputation, among others. So as you can see, if the organization fails to apply the correct strategy to motivate the employee (based on the employee's current career stage), the consequences can be severe.

On the other side of the diagram, the consequences to the employee are equally significant. If the organization applies the correct types of HR strategies to develop the employee successfully over time, individual feelings of accomplishment and achievement increase, self-worth and self-reliance increase, the employee's sense of security increases, and their morale is likely to increase due to higher individual satisfaction levels. Again, if the strategies applied are unsuccessful, each of these individual consequences can become negative. After looking at the model, it should become obvious that successfully applying HR strategies to individual employees based on their personal motivating factors and career stage is critical to overall organizational success over time.

So now you know why it's so important to create career paths for our employees within the organization and provide employee development opportunities. If we do these things successfully, we end up with a series of positive consequences for both the organization and the individuals involved. We have better productivity, better job satisfaction and employee engagement, and lower absenteeism and turnover. However, if we fail to do these things successfully, a series of negative consequences can occur that ultimately cost both the organization and the individual time and money. Employee development is a critical piece in the organizational puzzle in order to provide long-term success.

TRENDS AND ISSUES IN HRM

Let's take a look now at some of the trends and issues in training and development. The first issue that we will discuss involves the "gamification" of training and development, and we will also briefly discuss social media's value in organizational learning. Finally, we want to briefly look at the ever-more-common trend of outsourcing training and development and other functions in organizations.

The Gamification of Training and Development

One of the trends in training and development in today's organizations is "gamification." In fact, the *Financial Post* of Toronto said it is a "revolution" in educating workers.[49] In the training world, gamification is the process of designing and utilizing video and other game technology to teach the player a business concept. Gamification is being used for such diverse topics as corporate values training, leadership development, customer service training, technical training, and more. It is also being used by a diverse group of organizations including **Deloitte**, the **Department of Defense, Microsoft, Marriott,** and **Nike,** so you can see that it isn't just useful in technology companies.[50]

What is the value gained from gamification? The major advantage that is gained through gamification of training is trainee engagement in the training process, especially with the millenial-generation employees who have grown up with gaming technologies and are comfortable with learning using this concept. However, we are finding that gamification also works with other generations of employees to more actively engage them in the training process. Other major advantages include the following:[51, 52]

- The ability to create a realistic setting and to practice an action in a "safe" setting where equipment won't be harmed and relationships with customers won't be ruined
- Immediate feedback to the player on their actions, plus rewards for success
- Less resistance to learning
- Less stress than in classroom training, with lectures and tests

What about problems with or disadvantages of gamification? One common and significant problem is in the player becoming wrapped up in playing the game, not understanding *why* a result occurs, and therefore missing the lesson to be learned. Other issues or disadvantages include the following:

- Privacy concerns about employee information exist—especially if the internet is used as the medium for the games. (Training records are employee records, after all.)[53]
- Only about 30% of employees feel that "gamification is a positive addition to recognition" programs in their companies, and they "are wary of anything that may trivialize significant work accomplishments."[54]
- Most applications (80%) fail to meet business objectives because of poor design.[55]
- Additional evidence for learning benefits is still needed.[56]

Even with these problems, one of the key challenges with training always has been to get people engaged in the process. Using gamification is proving to be one of the most important measures to get people to learn.

Social Media for Learning

Remember our earlier discussion of how people learn. One particular method of learning has particular value in social media applications: social, or vicarious, learning. People learn from each other as much as or more than they do from formal training. This is one reason why OJT is used so much. Because this type of learning works so well, and because more than *3 billion* people worldwide are members of at least one social media site, we can utilize social media as a learning tool.

Social media is all around us today. It is now easy to adapt a platform for organizational learning. According to ASTD, organizations are incorporating social media into their training in the following ways:[57]

- Using Facebook to provide advanced materials, conduct intersession activities, and build learning communities
- Using Twitter for introductions, pretraining preparation and instruction, conversations, debates, reflecting, brainstorming, and polls
- Using YouTube for training videos
- Creating blogs for additional learning information
- Creating wikis for learning resources
- Creating discussion groups around specific topics, such as onboarding for new employees
- Creating more immersive learning environments such as virtual experiences, which are particularly useful when hands-on or experiential training is required

Looking at these items, you can quickly see the value of social media as a learning device. We can discuss problems, provide video and/or audio step-by-step instructions, utilize team-based brainstorming sessions and problem analysis, and discuss complex questions with large groups of combined customers, employees, and managers. You will need to understand the applications of social media in a training and learning environment to successfully manage HR in our 21st century organizations.

Outsourcing Employee Training and Development

As we've noted earlier in the book, outsourcing has become the major topic of interest to organizations of all sizes. In fact, based on a recent survey by **ADP**, "91 percent of large companies and 80 percent of midsized companies" say that outsourcing one or more HR functions provides "real value."[58] Outsourcing of the training and development function significantly lags other functions in the HR department, though.[59] Even so, modern organizations must evaluate whether or not outsourcing of the training and development functions makes sense. If the company can reduce costs for training and development as well as improve the quality of the training function, it may make sense for the organization to consider outsourcing of these functions.

What does the organization need to consider when analyzing whether or not to outsource training and development? We need to consider basically the same things we consider when we outsource any function of the organization. Probably the most significant *strategic* issue in any outsourcing debate is whether or not the organization might lose control of key processes or functions that have historically been performed within the company. If training and development are critical functions within the organization that help us maintain or advance our competitive advantage over rivals, we can ill afford to outsource those functions.

The second likely consideration would be a *financial* analysis concerning expected cost savings from outsourcing training and development. This would depend on how efficient the organization currently is at performing the training and development function. If the organization has a well-developed training department or group and has developed detailed courses concerning the major training and development issues that face the organization, outsourcing companies may not be able to provide much cost savings. If, however, the organization doesn't perform the training function very often or very intensely, outsourcing organizations that specialize in training and development may be able to save significant amounts of money for the firm. Here again, as with so many other HR functions, the organization must evaluate the ROI expected if the process is outsourced and compare that with the internal ROI for the same function.

Finally, the organization will want to evaluate the ability to maintain or improve *service levels* to their employees if it utilizes outsourcing. If the organization is unable to provide sufficient training and development programs for its employees through outsourcing, it runs significant risks, including lower employee morale and job satisfaction, lower productivity over time, and greater absenteeism and turnover within the firm. If, however, the organization can actually increase service levels in training and development through the use of a specialty outsourcing provider, each of the above risks can turn into advantages for the firm. The organization must carefully evaluate all of the information in an analysis for potential outsourcing of the training and development function. Without this careful evaluation, significant mistakes can be made and large amounts of money may be spent without the organization receiving the requisite benefits from the process.

SHRM

L:7; Q:13
Outsourcing Employee
Development

WORK
APPLICATION 7-15

Select an organization you work for or have worked for. What, if any, training and development functions do or did it outsource—including bringing in consults to develop and conduct training and development? If you are not sure, ask the HR training specialist.

••• CHAPTER SUMMARY

7-1 **Discuss the major difference between training and development.**

Training is designed to provide employees with the knowledge, skills, and abilities (KSAs) that they need to succeed in their work for the organization. Training is primarily intended to be put to *immediate* use by the individual being trained. Employee development is designed to teach our workers how to move up in the organization in the *future* by becoming skilled at those tasks that they will need to know how to do to perform higher-level jobs.

7-2 **Identify the common points in the tenure of employees within the organization where training may be needed. Briefly discuss each point.**

The most common points at which managers should consider workforce training include new-employee *orientation,* which is used to acculturate new employees to the organization and its culture and to prepare them to do their own job within the organization; when *processes or procedures have changed;* whenever there has been some *failure to perform* successfully; or when *employee development* opportunities come up, allowing the company to develop current employees' skills and abilities so that they are able to move into higher-level jobs within the organization.

7-3 **Briefly discuss the steps in the training process and their interrelationship.**

The first step involves conducting a needs assessment to identify the type of training needed. The second step involves selecting how to shape employee behavior. The third step involves designing the training by selecting training methods. The fourth step involves selecting the delivery method and delivering the training. The last step involves assessing the training to determine if employee behavior has changed to improve performance—if not, return to step one. The steps are so closely related and based on each other that they are commonly planned together before actually delivering the training.

7-4 **Identify the most common challenges to the training and development process.**

Common challenges to the training process include unprepared workers, difficulty in identifying the ROI provided from training, employee resistance to changes in processes and procedures, matching the training to the company's strategic goals, and logistics issues—including scheduling and locations available for training courses.

7-5 **Identify the three common learning theories and the type of learning that results from each theory.**

The three common learning theories are classical conditioning, operant conditioning, and social learning theory. Classical conditioning results in *direct, involuntary, learned* behaviors. Operant conditioning results in *direct, voluntary, learned* behaviors. Social learning is experienced through watching the actions of other people and witnessing the consequences of their actions, so it is *voluntary* and *learned,* but it is based on *indirect* consequences of the actions of others.

7-6 **Identify and briefly discuss the four methods for shaping behavior.**

The four options for shaping behavior include positive reinforcement, negative reinforcement, punishment, and extinction. Positive reinforcement involves the application of a reward in response to a person's behavior in order to increase the chances that that behavior will be repeated. Negative reinforcement involves the withdrawal of a noxious stimulus, or a negative thing, in response to a person's positive behavior to increase the chances that the behavior will be repeated. Punishment occurs either when a noxious stimulus is applied or when a reward is taken away in response to a negative behavior. Extinction provides no reinforcement, either positive or negative, to the actions of the subject.

7-7 **Identify which training methods are most commonly used with which HRM skill.**

Among the most common methods used for *technical skills* training are written materials and lectures, programmed learning, projects, job rotation, discussions, and demonstrations. To train individuals in *human relations skills,* some of the most common options are role-playing and behavior modeling. Management games and cases are commonly used to develop *conceptual and design (decision making) and business skills* for managers, whereas in-baskets are more commonly used with employees, and interactive videos are used by both.

7-8 **Discuss each of the major training delivery types.**

On-the-job training (OJT) is done at the work site with the resources the employee uses to perform the job, and it is conducted one-on-one with the trainee. In *classroom training,* the organization creates a training course and provides a qualified instructor to teach the class in a single location at a specific time. *Distance learning,* also called e-learning, allows the students to sign in to the training site and provides materials to them for their studies. There's typically less interaction between an instructor and trainee than in OJT or classroom training. *Simulations* mimic a real-life situation to teach students what actions to take in the event that they encounter the same or a similar situation in their job.

7-9   Briefly discuss the Four-Level Evaluation Method for assessing training programs.

The four-level evaluation method measures *reaction*, *learning*, *behaviors*, and *results*. In *reaction evaluations*, we ask the participants how they feel about the training process, including the content provided, the instructor(s), and the knowledge that they gained. *Learning evaluations* are designed to determine what knowledge was gained by the individual, whether any new skills have been learned, and whether attitudes have changed as a result of the training. *Behavior evaluations* are designed to determine whether or not the trainee's on-the-job behaviors changed as a result of the training. In a *results evaluation*, we try to determine whether or not individual behavioral changes have improved organizational results. This is the level at which ROI will be measured and evaluated.

7-10   Discuss the term *career* and the significance of its definition in the text.

Our definition of a career is "the individually perceived sequence of attitudes and behaviors associated with work-related experiences and activities over the span of the person's life."

Individually perceived means that if you perceive your career as being successful, then you are a success. If you perceive it as a failure, then you have failed. *Sequence of attitudes and behaviors* means that your career involves not only the things that you do, but also the way you think and how you feel about your progression of jobs over time. *Associated with work-related experiences and activities over time* means that even nonwork activities that are work related would be included in our definition of career. Using this definition of career avoids the problem of having to confront the fact that by the 1960s definition, most of us would fail to have a *successful* career.

7-11   Briefly discuss the three common methods of employee development.

Formal education provides the opportunity to participate in programs that will improve general knowledge in areas such as finance, project management, or logistics. *Experience* as a method for developing the individual seeks to put the person through different types of job-related experiences over time. *Assessment* tools provide employees with information about how they think, how they interact with others, and how they manage their own actions and emotions.

7-12   Briefly discuss some of the individual and organizational consequences that can occur as a result of organizational career planning processes.

Organizational consequences include all of the major organizational dependent variables that we identified in Chapter 1: job satisfaction, productivity, absenteeism, and turnover. In addition, labor costs, organizational safety, employee lawsuits, and organizational reputation can either improve or decline based on the application (or lack thereof) of the correct HR strategy. On the employee side of the diagram, if the organization applies the correct HR strategies, individual feelings of accomplishment and achievement increase, self-worth and self-reliance increase, the employee's sense of security increases, and employee morale is likely to increase due to higher individual satisfaction levels. If the strategies are unsuccessful, each of these individual consequences can become negative.

7-13   7-13 Define the key terms found in the chapter margins and listed following the Chapter Summary.

Complete the Key Terms Review to test your understanding of this chapter's key terms.

••• KEY TERMS

career	extinction	positive reinforcement
career plateau	learning	punishment
competency model	needs assessment	remediation
emotional intelligence	negative reinforcement	self-efficacy
employee development	orientation	training

••• KEY TERMS REVIEW

Complete each of the following statements using one of this chapter's key terms.

1. _____ identifies the knowledge, skills, and abilities (KSAs) needed to perform a particular job in the organization.

2. _____ is the process of teaching employees the skills necessary to perform a job.

3. _____ is ongoing education to improve knowledge and skills for present and future jobs.

4. _____ is the process of introducing new employees to the organization and their jobs.

5. _____ is the correction of a deficiency or failure in a process or procedure.

6. _____ is the process of analyzing the difference between what is currently occurring within a job or jobs in comparison with what is required—either now or in the future—based on the organization's operations and strategic goals.

7. _____ is whether people believe that they have the capability to do something or attain a particular goal.

8. _____ is any relatively permanent change in behavior that occurs as a result of experience or practice.

9. _____ is providing a reward in return for a constructive action on the part of the subject.

10. _____ is the withdrawal of a harmful thing from the environment in response to a positive action on the part of the subject.

11. _____ is the application of an adverse consequence or removal of a reward, in order to decrease an unwanted behavior.

12. _____ is the total lack of response, either positive or negative, to avoid reinforcing an undesirable behavior.

13. _____ is the individually perceived sequence of attitudes and behaviors associated with work-related experiences and activities over the span of a person's life.

14. _____ occurs when an individual feels unchallenged in their current job and has little or no chance of advancement.

15. _____ is the way that we identify, understand, and use our own emotions as well as the emotions of others to promote our working relationships.

••• COMMUNICATION SKILLS

The following critical-thinking questions can be used for class discussion and/or for written assignments to develop communication skills. Be sure to give complete explanations for all answers.

1. Is the currently available workforce really not sufficiently trained to participate in knowledge-intensive jobs? Why or why not?

2. Think of and then list all of the items that you think should be included in a new employee orientation. Briefly justify why each item should be included.

3. What learning style is the one that you feel that you use most? Why do you think that you use this style more than the others?

4. Briefly describe a job you have or had. If you were promoted, which training method(s) would you use to train the person to do your current job?

5. Which one of the primary delivery of training types would you use to teach basic accounting to a group of employees? Justify your answer.

6. Have you ever filled out an evaluation form for an employee training class? Which type of evaluation was it? What evidence led you to think it was this type?

7. What management tools or processes would you use in order to evaluate your employees for remediation training?

8. Do you agree with the definition of a *career* presented in the text? Why or why not? How would you change it?

9. Which of the reasons for creating career development programs from the text do you feel are most valid, considering the cost of career development programs? Justify your choice.

10. Which method of development, formal education, experience, or assessment do you think is most valuable? Justify your choice.

11. Identify and discuss two or three ways in which poor application of HR strategies (Exhibit 7-9) would create negative *employee* consequences.

12. Do you think that diversity training is worth its cost to organizations? Why or why not?

13. If you were the lead trainer for your company, how would you go about trying to create an organization-wide commitment to sustainability? Why?

● ● ● CASE 7-1 WHO IS MANAGING THE MANAGER?

Gerald Mahoney, new Sales Manager and sole full-time employee of the Oreck vacuum cleaner store of Red Hook, New York, was relaxing and watching television in the back office. There were no customers in the store at the time, and Gerald was tired of repairing vacuums. There always seemed to be a million machines to repair, and the owner of the store, John Timmson, was never around to lend a hand. In fact, John would rather be out playing golf or hanging out with his girlfriend than dealing with his business. John never lent a hand with difficult customers, rarely repaired vacuums, and was always "away" when stock came in, and Gerald needed assistance to stack inventory. John refused to complete warranty reports and, most important, never, ever cleaned the store. As Gerald nestled himself into the big comfortable couch in the back office and slowly dozed off, he contemplated his 40-hour, five-day workweek and the unfairness of the situation. His last fading moments of consciousness were focused on the fact that it just didn't seem right that after four months of employment he did all of this work while John was out having a good time.

Those Happy Early Days

"I love my work, and I'm only in my first month here," Mr. Mahoney commented to his friend Stephen Hodgetts. "John is purposely never around, so I can really run the store the way I like it. I can arrange the store in a manner I think is appealing; I can sell the way that I know customers would most like to be sold, not like my old boss Mr. Paulson's hard-nosed methods. I never had a chance to do anything but sell and repair vacuums, and here I run the entire operation from purchasing to return policies. I have never had such responsibility before, but I am learning on the job and enjoying every minute of it. This is like a dream come true. As long as I continue to sell and the store makes money, what can go wrong with this deal?"

The Honeymoon Is Over

A month had passed since Gerald's conversation with Stephen, and Gerald was starting to see what could go wrong. For example, Gerald liked the store to be particularly neat and clean, and it seemed that on Gerald's days off John would let the store become disheveled. He thought, "How can I do my job to the best of my ability if John leaves me all of this extra work? For instance, my rate of completing repairs is way down, creating a backlog because of the extra time I have to spend cleaning the store. Customers are starting to complain, and I don't know what to tell them!"

John Timmson's Fateful Store Visit

It was four months into Gerald's hire, and John had regrets. John had talked with Gerald several times about the condition of the store, and all that Gerald seemed to do was grumble about the lack of support John was giving him. Gerald was sounding more and more like his last girlfriend than a manager, and John was getting fed up with Gerald's "I'm helpless, overworked, and underpaid" routine.

"Unsupportive?" John thought to himself. "As Gerald requested, I reduced his working hours from his old job with Paulson, gave him two days off, and allowed him to run the store the best way he saw fit. I gave him a chance to really be a manager, not the dumb flunky that Paulson regarded him as. And what did I get in return? I get a poorly run store, customer complaints, and reduced profits—so much for me being Mr. Nice Guy."

Gerald had let him down and just had to go, but if John fired Gerald, then John would be stuck in the store seven days a week for a while. But what else could he do? Getting an additional employee to work on weekdays was not cost-effective—the business just did not generate enough income during the week to profitably handle even a second part-time employee's salary for the days that would have to be covered when Gerald was working.

His current part-time employee did not want to work in the store full-time since this employee was semiretired and did not want to commit himself to a full-time job. Subcontracting out the repair work was also not cost-effective since many of the repairs were fairly simple and could be done in 15 minutes by a salesperson during the week, when the store was not busy.

John did not have any good answers to the problem but hoped that just maybe he and Gerald might work out something. Otherwise John's life would be ruined, at least for the next three to four months. John arrived at the store and noticed the untidiness of the store, the poor layout of the displays, and Gerald's slovenly, tired appearance. Repair work from the back office seemed to have invaded the front of the store (meaning there was an ever-growing number of machines to repair) and the tool rack was in total disarray. What a catastrophe! Gerald looked extremely nervous, like a cornered rabbit ready for the hunter to pull the trigger. He must have guessed at what was probably coming and was resigning himself to his fate.

John became furious and highly frustrated with Gerald for not taking better care of the store but decided not to vent his anger. He was the boss, and he was not going to let an employee get his goat, especially an employee who seemed short-lived at best. John also knew he had to do something in order to salvage his business, but what? John gathered himself for what was going to be a difficult discussion but a discussion that nonetheless had to occur.

Questions

1. Gerald Mahoney's attitude and performance dramatically changed after a few months on the job. What type of training should Mahoney have immediately received from John Timmson that might have avoided this?

2. Assuming Timmson keeps Mahoney as the store manager, what should be the first step he institutes in the training process?

3. Assuming that Timmson and Mahoney agree to a training program in order to solve the problem, what are some challenges Timmson might face in conducting this training?

4. According to Exhibit 7-2, there are four methods for increasing and decreasing employee behavior. What are these methods, and which one(s) do you think would work the best for changing some of Mahoney's more problematic behaviors?

5. Look at Exhibit 7-3, "Skills and Training Methods." What are some of the appropriate training techniques that Timmson might use to increase Mahoney's KSAs?

6. Mahoney jumped from being a sales associate under Mr. Paulson to a store manager under Mr. Timmson. How might career planning and development have helped him in making this transition?

Case created by Herbert Sherman, PhD, and Theodore Vallas, Department of Management Sciences, Long Island University School of Business, Brooklyn Campus

• • • CASE 7-2 GOOGLE SEARCH: BUILDING THE PROGRAM THAT WRITES THE CODE TO FIND FEMALE TALENT

Google Inc. took Web searching to a much more sophisticated level when it offered targeted search results from billions of Web pages, based on a proprietary algorithm that allowed for greater customization than did prior engines like **Web Crawler** and **Dogpile**. Employing more than 50,000 people, Google generates most of its revenue from advertising sales. In 2013, its net income was close to $13 billion, and the company showed 60% revenue growth between 2012 and 2014. Added to that, Google has been on the top of the Fortune "Best Places to Work" list since 2012.[60] Google is one of the best firms at making employees feel welcomed and supported, but being in the technology field, the company had become a "boys' club," with women constituting only 30% of its entire workforce.

Alongside Google, other Silicon Valley technology giants like **Facebook, Yahoo,** and **LinkedIn** recently disclosed their gender and racial diversity ratios in their workplaces. On average, Google's workforce consists of more than 65% males, 55% whites, and 35% Asians. The gaps between these numbers are even wider in technology-related positions. As shown in its May 2014 report, it employs only 2% blacks and 3% Hispanics. Google admitted that this problem required immediate action. Google's sharing of demographic information is a promising sign that it is willing to change, but action speaks louder than words.

Google took quick action and performed its own search. It found that women were losing interest in computer sciences as a career at an alarming rate. Only 14% of the computer science graduates were women in 2013, and surveys indicated that less than 1% of women expressed any interest in majoring in computer sciences in college.[61] Google then recognized that it could not use traditional recruitment techniques to hire women since they were just not present in the labor pool.

Google also examined its own unique hiring processes and concluded that they were both difficult and tedious—women were not emerging through these processes, and Google could not just sit back and hope to gain new female employees from a labor pool that could not supply them.[62]

Google decided to be far more proactive in the area of women employee development and committed $50 million for both research and solution strategies. Its research indicated that if women were exposed to coding at an early age, they would more likely look favorably at a career path in computer science.[63] Google's research also noted that compared to the companies led by men, tech companies led by women achieved a 35% higher return on investment and 12% higher revenue.[64]

Google understood that its answer to this labor shortage, as well as to greater profitability, was to show young girls how interesting aspects of computer science could be, as well as how lucrative, and to inspire them to pursue a career in this field. Secondly, only 10% of the schools in the United States offered computer science courses, so access to this field was a major problem. To achieve its goal of more women in the workforce, Google initiated a project called "Made With Code" (MWC) that was designed to attract women to the sciences and in the long run diminish possible gender biases in its own organization, as well as in the field.[65]

MWC was launched as an event in New York City, with the participation of teenage girls from local public schools; famous female entrepreneurs; and many professional women who utilized coding in the film, music, and fashion industries. To increase exposure and inspiration, Google is working closely with producers and writers in the **Science & Entertainment Exchange** to have more female coders in movies and television series.[66]

With the MWC program targeting the people who normally did not have the access or the opportunity to pursue a career in computer science, Google provided accelerated tech-training programs to help them succeed in high-level tech jobs. Google did this by offering free coding classes online to pull extraordinary talent from the cities surrounding Silicon Valley.[67] It also provided workshops that fostered student collaboration on simple coding projects like 3-D printed bracelets. Research has noted that women thrive in team environments, and Google wanted them to understand that teamwork is the cornerstone of software development. To this end, Google gave an additional 3 months of free access to its Code School to women.[68] Google hopes that the outcome of its programs will increase younger girls' involvement in computer science and in the long run increase women's visibility in the profession and at Google.

Questions

1. What is a needs assessment, and how might Google use this tool to increase the presence of women in its workforce?

2. Some might argue that Google's "Made With Code" program has redefined the concept of employee development. Agree or disagree and provide an explanation supporting your position.

3. Explain how Google's particular situation demonstrates the relationship between employee recruitment and employee development, given the above discussion.

4. Explain how Google's "Made With Code" has become an integral part of its career planning.

5. How might the concepts of self-efficacy and reinforcement theory help us better understand schoolgirls' relative lack of interest in computer science?

6. Assume that Google is ultimately successful and receives more female applicants, whom it then hires. What suggestions do you have for managing this new talent pool?

Case created by Herbert Sherman, PhD, and Theodore Vallas, Department of Management Sciences, Long Island University School of Business, Brooklyn Campus

Sharpen your skills with SAGE edge at edge.sagepub.com/lussierhrm2e

SAGE edge for students provides a personalized approach to help you accomplish your coursework goals in an easy-to-use learning environment.

• • • SKILL BUILDER 7-1 THE TRAINING PROCESS

Objective

To develop your ability to conduct a needs assessment, to select how to shape employee behavior, to design a training program by selecting training methods, to select a method to deliver training, and to choose an assessment method

Skills

The primary skills developed through this exercise are as follows:

1. *HR management skill*—conceptual and design skills
2. *SHRM 2013 Curriculum Guidebook*—L: Training and development

Asssignment

As an individual or group, select a job and write out your answers. Follow the steps in the training process below to train a person to do the job.

Step 1: Needs assessment. Conduct a needs assessment for the job by developing a competency model identifying the knowledge, skills, and abilities needed to do the job successfully.

Step 2: Select how you will shape behavior. Be sure to specify if you will use positive reinforcement, punishment, negative reinforcement, or extinction. State the rewards and/or punishment.

Step 3: Design the training. Select and describe in detail the training method(s) you will use to shape the behavior.

Step 4: Deliver the training. Just select one of the four methods of delivery that you will use to conduct the actual training and describe how you will deliver the training.

Step 5: Assessment of training. Just select one of the four assessment methods and describe in detail how you will determine if the training did in fact shape the behavior.

Apply It

What did I learn from this experience? How will I use this knowledge in the future?

_____

_____

Your instructor may ask you to do this Skill Builder in class by breaking into groups of four to six and doing the preparation. If so, the instructor will provide you with any necessary information or additional instructions.

• • • SKILL BUILDER 7-2 CAREER DEVELOPMENT

Objective

To begin to think about and develop your career plan

Skills

The primary skills developed through this exercise are as follows:

1. *HR management skill*—conceptual and design skills
2. *SHRM 2013 Curriculum Guidebook*—L: Training and development

Assignment

Write out your answers to the following questions.

1. Do you now, or do you want to work in HRM? Why? If not, what career do you want to pursue, and why?
2. If you want to work in HR, based on your self-assessment back in Chapter 1 or other knowledge, list

your highest levels of interest in HR disciplines. If not, what are your highest levels of interests, functions, or disciplines within your chosen career?

3. What methods of employee development (formal education, experience-internships and jobs, and assessment) are you using to prepare for your career?

Apply It

What did I learn from this exercise? How will I use this knowledge in the future?

_____

_____

Your instructor may ask you to do this Skill Builder in class by breaking into groups of two to three and discussing your career plans. If so, the instructor will provide you with any necessary information or additional instructions.

©iStockphoto.com/courtneyk

8 Performance Management and Appraisal

••• LEARNING OUTCOMES

After studying this chapter, you should be able to do the following:

Practitioner's Perspective

Cindy remarks that although performance evaluation can be uncomfortable for both managers and employees, failure to accurately and honestly evaluate performance is never a good choice. She recalls the time that a supervisor, Annette, came to see her.

"I want to fire Christine," Annette said angrily. "She entered the wrong invoice numbers again, and now I have to stay and correct her mistakes—again!"

"Is this common?" Cindy asked. "Have you expressed your concerns or initiated a performance improvement plan?"

"She does it all the time, but I usually don't catch it until after she is off for the day," Annette replied. "By morning, it doesn't seem worth my time go over it with her."

"How about her performance evaluation?" she asked next. "Have you brought Christine's poor performance to her attention at her annual evaluation?"

"Well, no, I always give all my employees a satisfactory rating—it's easier that way," answered Annette.

Without ever bringing Christine's unacceptable performance to her attention and thus giving her a chance to change, firing or otherwise severely disciplining Christine at this point would be questionable. How can this problem be avoided? In Chapter 8, you will learn how to create and utilize a performance evaluation process that works.

PERFORMANCE MANAGEMENT SYSTEMS

After we have recruited, selected, and trained employees, we must evaluate how well they perform their jobs so they know how they are doing. Therefore, performance evaluation is an important part of the jobs of managers and HRM staff.[1] We need to figure out how to manage employees' performance over time to ensure that they remain productive and

SHRM HR CONTENT

See Appendix: *SHRM 2013 Curriculum Guidebook* for the complete list

E. Job Analysis/Job Design (required)

    4. Performance management (performance criteria and appraisal)

H. Performance Management (required)

    1. Identifying and measuring employee performance

    2. Sources of information (e.g., managers, peers, clients)

    3. Rater errors in performance measurement

    4. Electronic monitoring

    5. Performance appraisals

    6. Appraisal feedback

    7. Managing performance

Q. Organization Development (required—graduate students only)

    5. Improving organizational effectiveness

    9. Ongoing performance and productivity initiatives

SHRM
Q:5
Improving Organizational
Effectiveness

hopefully become even more capable as they progress in their careers. So the primary purpose of performance appraisal should be to help employees to continuously improve their performance.[2] Remember our earlier discussion about the fact that *human* resources are typically one of the few resources we can leverage to create a sustainable competitive advantage for the firm. Based on that, we need to ensure that our human resources perform at as high a level as possible. To this end, we discuss in this section the difference between performance management and performance appraisal, and we present the performance appraisal process.

It is worth noting right at the beginning that many people in organizations do not like performance appraisal systems and do not think that these systems have the ability to improve employee performance. One study even noted that 58% of HR managers don't like their own performance review processes![3] Routinely, there are calls to do away with performance appraisal processes.[4] **Netflix** is one company that has completely stopped doing *formal* performance appraisals, even though the CEO noted that "excellent colleagues trump everything else."[5] (Netflix still does complete *informal* 360-degree appraisals. We will introduce you to these shortly.) So why does this process continue to be used by most major organizations all over the world? We will work to answer that question in this chapter, and then in the trends section, we will look at some alternatives to the historical performance appraisal process.

LO 8-1

Discuss the difference between performance management and performance appraisals.

Performance Management Versus Performance Appraisal

"In a knowledge economy, organizations rely heavily on their intangible assets to build value. Consequently, performance management at the individual employee level is essential and the business case for implementing a system to measure

Netflix is one company that has stopped doing formal performance appraisals.

and improve employee performance is strong."[6] Committing management time and effort to increase performance not only meets this goal but also decreases turnover rates.[7]

How do we manage performance within the organization? The most common part of the process, and the one with which we are most familiar, is the process of the performance appraisal, or evaluation. (In this chapter, we will use the terms *performance evaluation*, *performance appraisal*, and just *appraisal* interchangeably.) However, the performance appraisal process is not the only thing that's done in performance management. **Performance management** *is the process of identifying, measuring, managing, and developing the performance of the human resources in an organization.* Basically we are trying to figure out how well employees perform and then ultimately improve that performance level. When used correctly, performance management is a systematic analysis and measurement of worker performance (*and* communication of that assessment to the individual) that we use to improve performance over time.

Performance appraisal, on the other hand, *is the ongoing process of evaluating employee performance.* Performance appraisal should not be simply a once- or twice-a-year formal interview. As its definition states, performance appraisal is an ongoing process. Employees need regular feedback on their performance,[8] so give routine and candid assessments.[9] Performance appraisals are reviews of employee performance over time,[10] so appraisal is just one piece of performance management. Although we will spend most of the chapter discussing performance appraisals, there are several other significant pieces to performance management that we already covered in past chapters and will cover in future chapters. We already discussed "strategic planning," which provides inputs into what we want to evaluate in our performance management system, in Chapter 2. We also discussed the major method of identifying performance requirements in a particular job when we went through "job analysis and design" in Chapter 4. In Chapter 7, we discussed "training and development," which obviously plays a part in performance management. Additionally, we will discuss motivating employees, coaching and counseling, employee relations, compensation, and other pieces in Chapters 9 through 14. Now that we understand the difference between performance management and performance appraisal, let's look at the performance appraisal process.

SHRM

E:4
Performance Management
(Performance Criteria and Appraisal)

SHRM

Q:9
Ongoing Performance and
Productivity Initiatives

Performance management The process of identifying, measuring, managing, and developing the performance of the human resources in an organization

Performance appraisal The ongoing process of evaluating employee performance

WORK
APPLICATION 8-1

Select a job you have or have had. Do you or did you know the organization's mission and objectives? Briefly state the mission. If you don't know it, find out. Do you understand how your job fits or helps to meet the organization's mission and objectives? Explain in some detail.

The Performance Appraisal Process

Exhibit 8-1 illustrates the performance appraisal process. Note the connection between the organization's mission and objectives and the performance appraisal process. Here we briefly discuss each step of the process.

Step 1: Job analysis. This is logically our first step because if we don't know what a job consists of, how can we possibly evaluate an employee's performance in that job? We already learned how to do a job analysis in Chapter 4, but as shown in Exhibit 8-1, we should realize that the job must be based on the organizational mission and objectives, the department, and the job itself.

Step 2: Develop standards and measurement methods. If we don't have standards of acceptable behavior and methods of measuring performance, how can we assess that performance? We will discuss performance measurement methods in the next part of this section, and in the section "How Do We Use Appraisal Methods and Forms?" we will discuss these topics in more detail.

Step 3: Informal performance appraisal—Coaching and disciplining. Performance appraisal should not be simply a once- or twice-a-year formal interview. As its definition states, performance appraisal is an ongoing process. While a formal evaluation may only take place once or twice a year, people need regular feedback on their performance to know how they are doing.[11] We will briefly discuss coaching in the "Critical Incidents Method" subsection of "How Do We Use Appraisal Methods and Forms?" and we will discuss it in more detail in the next chapter.

Step 4: Prepare for and conduct the formal performance appraisal. The common practice is to have a formal performance review with the boss once or sometimes twice a year, using one or more of the measurement forms we will be learning about. Later in this chapter, we will discuss the steps involved in preparing for and conducting the performance appraisal.

EXHIBIT 8-1 THE PERFORMANCE APPRAISAL PROCESS

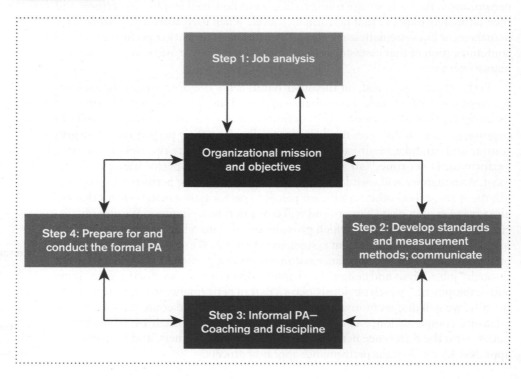

In the chapter sections to come, we discuss why we assess performance, what we assess, how we assess it, and who conducts the performance appraisal. Then we discuss performance appraisal problems and how to avoid them, and we end the performance appraisal process with the actual formal review session. But before we leave this section, we need to understand a critically important part of each step in the performance appraisal process: accurate performance measurement.

Accurate Performance Measures

To effectively assess performance, we need to have clear standards for and methods of measuring performance.[12] The **American National Standards Institute (ANSI)** has outlined the minimum required elements of a performance management system for goal setting, performance review, and performance improvement plans.[13] For details, visit the ANSI website at http://www.ansi.org. We should also accurately measure employee performance so employees will know where they can improve.[14] This in turn should lead to training employees to develop the new skills they need to improve their performance.[15]

Also, to be an accurate measure of performance, our measure must be valid, reliable, acceptable and feasible, specific, and based on the mission and objectives. Let's discuss each of those requirements here.

VALID AND RELIABLE. As in all areas of our people management process, we must do our best to make sure that all of our performance management tools are valid and reliable. Here again, we can pull out and dust off the OUCH test as a quick way to ensure fairness and equity in the performance management and appraisal process. We remember by now that OUCH stands for **O**bjective, **U**niform in application, **C**onsistent in effect, and **H**as job relatedness. However, we still need to analyze validity and reliability in some detail.

If we are not using a valid and reliable measurement, then it makes no sense to use it. If you recall, we discussed reliability and validity in Chapter 4. Recall that *valid* means that a measure is true and correct; a valid measure is a factual one that measures the process that you wanted to measure. On the other hand, *reliable* means the measure is consistent; it works in generally the same way each time we use it.[16]

ACCEPTABLE AND FEASIBLE. In addition to validity and reliability, we need to look at a couple of other characteristics of our performance measures—acceptability and feasibility.[17] *Acceptability* means that the use of the measure is satisfactory or appropriate to the people who must use it. However, in performance appraisal, this isn't enough. To be acceptable, an evaluation tool must also be feasible. Is it possible to reasonably apply the evaluation tool in a particular case, or is it too complex or lengthy to work well? As an example, if the performance evaluation form is two or three pages long and covers the major aspects of the job that is being evaluated, and if managers and employees both believe that the form truly evaluates performance measures that identify success on the job, then managers and employees are likely to feel that the tool is acceptable and feasible to use. However, if the manager must fill out a 25-page form that has very little to do with the job being evaluated, the manager may not feel that the form is acceptable or feasible, at least partially due to its length, even if the employees do.

Conversely, if the manager fills out a two-page evaluation that they feel is a true measure of performance in an employee's job, but the employee feels that the evaluation leaves out large segments of what is done in the work routine, the employee may not feel that the form is acceptable and feasible. If either management or employees feel that the form is unacceptable, it most likely will not be used correctly. (This would also mean that the person would not see the evaluation as a *valid* measure.)[18] So, we always have to evaluate the acceptability and feasibility of a measure.

LO 8-2

Identify the necessary characteristics of accurate performance management tools.

WORK
APPLICATION 8-2

SPECIFIC. Next, we want any evaluation measure to be specific enough to identify what is going well and what is not. The word *specific* means that something is explicitly identified or defined well enough that all involved completely understand the issue. In performance appraisals, a specific form provides enough information for everyone to understand what level of performance has been achieved by a particular employee within a well-identified job.

Creating specific measures is the only way to use a performance appraisal to improve the performance of our employees over time. The employees have to understand what they are and are not doing successfully. Many times, evaluation forms may be too general in nature to be of value for modifying employee behaviors because we want the form to serve for a large number of different types of jobs. This can create significant problems in the performance appraisal process.

BASED ON THE MISSION AND OBJECTIVES. Finally, you want to make sure that your performance management system leads to the accomplishment of your organizational mission and objectives. As with everything else we do in HR, we need to ensure that the performance management process guides our employees toward achievement of the company's mission and objectives over time. As managers in the organization, making sure of this connection will allow us to reinforce employee behaviors that aim at achieving organizational goals, and it will also allow us to identify for our employees things that they may be doing that actively or unintentionally harm our ability to reach those goals.

Thus, stating specific objectives saying exactly what each person in each job should achieve, or their performance outcomes, leads to accurate assessment that can increase performance. For some examples of inaccurate measures of performance, complete Applying the Concept 8-1.

LO 8-3

List and briefly discuss the purposes of performance appraisals.

WHY DO WE CONDUCT PERFORMANCE APPRAISALS?

As you can begin to see already, the appraisal process gets to be extremely complicated very quickly. And remember, anytime that a process in an organization is complicated, it is going to cost a lot of money. So why do we even do performance appraisals? What's the value provided to the organization and to the individual that makes the process of evaluating the performance of our workers so critical?

If performance appraisals are done in the correct manner, they *can* provide us with a series of valuable results. However, if not done correctly, the process of evaluating employee performance can actually lead to lower levels of job satisfaction and productivity. Let's discuss three major reasons (communicating, decision making, and motivating) why performance evaluations are completed in organizations.[19]

Communication (Informing)

The first major reason for performance appraisals is to provide an opportunity for formal communication between management and the employees concerning how the organization believes each employee is performing. All of us know intuitively that successful communication requires two-way interaction between people. "Organizations can prevent or remedy the majority of performance problems by ensuring that two-way conversation occurs between the manager and the employee, resulting in a complete understanding of what is required, when it is required, and how the employee's contribution measures up."[20]

Communication always requires that employees have the opportunity and ability to provide feedback to their bosses in order to make sure that their communication is understood. So in performance appraisals, the communication process requires that we as managers communicate with the employee to provide them with information about how we believe they're doing in their job. However, the process also requires that we provide the opportunity for the employee to speak to us concerning factors that inhibit their ability to successfully perform for the organization.

Factors in a job that management may not know about can include lack of training, poorly maintained equipment, lack of necessary tools, conflict within work groups, and many other things that management may not see on a daily basis. If the communication component of the performance appraisal process does not allow for this two-way communication, managers may not know of the obstacles that the employee has to overcome. We can only resolve problems when we know about them. So as managers, we need to communicate with our employees to find out when issues within the work environment are causing a loss of productivity so we can fix them. Thus, two-way communication is a critical component of correcting problems through the performance appraisal process.

Decision Making (Evaluating)

The second major purpose of performance appraisal is to allow management to make decisions about employees within the organization. We need to make decisions based on the information we get from our communication. Accurate information is necessary for management decision making and is absolutely critical to allow the manager to improve organizational productivity.[21] We use information from annual performance appraisals to make evaluative decisions concerning our workforce, including such things as pay raises, promotions, demotions, training and development, and termination. When we have valid and reliable information concerning each individual within our division or department, we have the ability to make decisions that can enhance productivity for the firm.

If, for instance, through the process of coaching (the third step of the performance appraisal process), we find that several machine operators are having trouble keeping their equipment in working order, then that information would quite likely lead to a *needs assessment* (as discussed in Chapter 7) to determine whether or not maintenance training is necessary for our group of operators. Without our rigorous evaluation process, we might not learn of this common problem in a timely fashion, and the result could be significant damage to very expensive equipment. This and similar types of information frequently come to the forefront as we go through the performance appraisal process. Therefore, decision making based on good communication is a very large part of why we take the time to do annual performance appraisals.

SHRM

H:7
Managing Performance

Motivation (Engaging)

The third major purpose of performance appraisals is to motivate our employees to improve the way they work, which in turn will improve organizational productivity overall.[22] But what is motivation, and are performance appraisals normally motivational? Well, from a business perspective, **motivation** can be defined as *the willingness to achieve organizational objectives*. We want to create this willingness to achieve the organization's objectives, which will in turn increase organizational productivity.

Our evaluative decisions should lead to development of employees. Returning to the above example of the machine operators having trouble keeping their equipment in working order, making the decision to train employees leads to their development, which then improves their individual performance, as well as better utilizing organizational resources.

Evaluating and Motivating = Development

An effective performance appraisal process has two parts—evaluating and motivating—and it does both parts well. Evaluating is about assessing *past* performance, and motivating is about developing employees to improve their *future* performance. But are both parts done well? Have you ever been in a position of being evaluated and debriefed as an employee? Was the process motivational? Most of us would probably reply no. Think about the appraisal process and how it was carried out. Here we discuss problems with evaluation and how to overcome them, as well as how to motivate employees. We also suggest separating formal assessment meetings designed to evaluate or motivate.

PROBLEMS IN EVALUATION. A common problem in appraisals is overpowering an employee during the evaluation debrief with large amounts of negative information that they have not heard during coaching. This tends to cause the employee to "turn off" or stop listening as the manager explains what is wrong. Employees will just "raise their shields" to ward off all of the negative information. This is a natural human trait. We are naturally suspicious of negative information for a variety of psychological reasons (i.e., defensive mechanisms), so when we are presented with a large amount of negative information, we tend to discount or even disbelieve it. Therefore, employees in such situations may consider the process unfair or one-sided and not an accurate measure of their performance, and as a result, the evaluation may become useless as a motivator that develops the employee.

AVOIDING PROBLEMS IN EVALUATION. To help overcome this problem during employee evaluations, an effective manager who is a good coach will generally never identify a weakness that the employee has not previously been made aware of during the formal appraisal interview. In other words, there are no surprises in a well-run evaluation. The evaluative part of the appraisal should only be a review of what the employee already knows and should be willing hear.

However, avoiding surprises is not enough.[23] The appraisal debrief must be a well-rounded look at the individual employee, and it should identify both positive and negative factors in the employee's behaviors and results within the job (and remember, the communication needs to be two-way). As the manager, we want to tell the employees what they did right but also where they have room for improvement. This more balanced approach to the debriefing process will minimize the risk that the employee will raise those shields and avoid listening.

MOTIVATING DEVELOPMENT. An important part of development is the need for managers to provide motivational opportunities for the employees to improve their

Motivation The willingness to achieve organizational objectives

performance over time. In other words, we need to tell them how to fix their own problems. We need to provide them with tools, training, or other methods that will allow them to improve to the point where their behavior is sufficient. Then, we must continually strive to get them to perform at an above-average level and ultimately become superior performers, helping them along the way through ongoing coaching between formal reviews.

If we provide employees with tools that allow them to improve over time, we're not focusing on negative past results but on positive future potential results.[24] If employees are given an honest opportunity to fix something that they know is a problem and are given the necessary tools or training, most will take advantage of that opportunity. So performance appraisals *can* be motivational if they are properly used and debriefed.

SEPARATING EVALUATION AND DEVELOPMENT. To improve both parts of the performance appraisal, we suggest splitting the debriefing into two separate interviews. The first meeting is to evaluate the employee's *past* performance, pointing out strengths and areas for improvement; the employee is asked to think about how to improve performance. At the second meeting, manager and employee *jointly* come up with a developmental plan that should lead to increased performance, which in turn will result in a higher future evaluative rating during the next formal appraisal. We will discuss how to conduct the two separate interviews in the "Debriefing the Appraisal" section of this chapter.

WHAT DO WE ASSESS?

Now that we know why we conduct performance appraisals, the next step is to figure out what needs to be evaluated. In other words, we have to decide what aspects of the individual and their performance we're going to measure. Discovering the best options for what to evaluate would come from analyzing the essential functions and qualifications required for a particular job, or in HR terms, our job analysis. We could then use these facts to design an appraisal instrument that uses measurable and observable factors to evaluate performance.[25] However, we can't evaluate everything that is done over the course of the year. We have to choose what we will focus on because what gets measured and evaluated gets done.[26] So, our three primary options for what to evaluate are traits, behaviors, and results.

Trait Appraisals

Traits *identify the physical or psychological characteristics of a person.* We can evaluate the traits of an individual during the performance appraisal process. Can we accurately measure traits that affect job performance, can trait measures pass the OUCH test, are traits commonly measured, and should we measure traits as part of our performance appraisal process? Here we answer these questions, and we will answer these same questions for our behavior and results options.

CAN WE ACCURATELY MEASURE TRAITS THAT AFFECT JOB PERFORMANCE? Certainly, there's some evidence that particular types of traits are valuable in jobs that require management and leadership skills. Characteristics such as inquisitiveness, conscientiousness, and general cognitive ability have been shown to have a reasonable link to job performance.[27, 28] But just how accurate is the link?

Many traits that most of us would be likely to focus on—such as physical attractiveness, height, and extroversion—actually have been shown to have very little bearing on job performance. If we're going to use traits in performance evaluation, we

WORK
APPLICATION 8-3

Assess the effectiveness of an evaluative performance appraisal you had. Did the manager present both positive and negative performance areas? Did you really listen? Were there any surprises? Explain any problems and how the evaluation could be improved.

LO 8-4

Identify and briefly discuss the options for what to evaluate in a performance appraisal.

Traits The physical or psychological characteristics of a person

must ensure that we focus on traits that have a direct relationship to the essential functions of the job being done, and they have to be accurate measures.

Is using trait-based evaluation a good method of judging work performance? How many of us would want to have judgments made about our work based on our appearance or personality? Would you consider this to be a *valid and reliable* measure of your work performance? In most cases, it's very difficult to show that personal traits are valid and reliable measures of work performance.

GIVE TRAITS THE OUCH TEST. Let's take a look at trait-based measurements using the OUCH test. Is a physical characteristic such as height or a psychological characteristic such as attitude, cheerfulness, work ethic, or enthusiasm an objective measure of an individual's work performance? We would have great difficulty in creating a quantifiable and factual link between height or enthusiasm and job performance. So when measuring traits, it's difficult to meet the *objective* requirement of the OUCH test.

If we utilized these trait-based measures in all cases in employee evaluations, we would be able to meet the *uniform in application* requirement of the OUCH test. The third test—*consistent in effect*—would likely be extremely difficult to meet due to the fact that different racial, ethnic, social, and gender groups tend to have different physical and psychological characteristics. Remember, reliability is a measure of consistency.

Could we meet the *has job relatedness* test? Is a particular trait directly related to the essential functions of the job? In a very few cases, this may be true, but in most situations, physical and personality characteristics have less to do with success in the job than certain behaviors do. So it's difficult to meet the *has job relatedness* test in most cases.

Finally, we need to ask the question of whether or not different supervisors would evaluate our traits differently, based on their traits. Would their individual biases based on their personality cause them to evaluate us differently? The answer is, of course, that different people will probably evaluate our traits differently.

ARE TRAITS COMMONLY USED TO MEASURE PERFORMANCE? Surprisingly, if you go to the local office supply store and look at standard evaluation forms that are available in preprinted pads, you will find that they usually list many traits as part of the evaluation. Why would this be the case? The simple answer is that at least some traits, both physical and psychological, are fairly easy to identify and we *assume* that they are related to how the individual will perform on the job. Many of us, individually and as managers, value certain things like enthusiasm, even if enthusiasm has very little to do with the ability to do a particular job or the actual results of job performance.

Certainly, there are some jobs where enthusiasm is critical. However, being an enthusiastic employee may have very little to do with success in the job, so if we evaluate individuals based on the characteristic of enthusiasm, we might make an error in judgment concerning their performance. And if we make errors in analyzing the performance of our employees, the appraisal form becomes much less *acceptable* to both the individual employee and management.

Finally, if our organization happened to be sued by a former employee who claimed that they were fired based on an appraisal process that was unreliable and not valid, it would be very difficult to defend trait-based evaluation forms due to their subjective nature.

SHOULD WE MEASURE TRAITS? Author Ken Blanchard said that there are too many evaluation items that can't be objectively measured—such as attitude, initiative, and promotability. Therefore, it's important to ask whether both managers and employees will agree with the measured rating as being accurate. The bottom-line test (we will call it the Blanchard test) is this: Does everyone understand why they are assessed at a specific level (evaluation) and what it takes to get a higher rating (development)?[29] We should only assess traits that meet the bottom-line test of having a direct and obvious objective relationship between the trait and success in the job.

Behavioral Appraisals

Our second option in the assessment process is to evaluate employees based on behaviors. You will recall that **behaviors** *are simply the actions taken by an individual*—the things that they do and say. Behavioral appraisals measure what individuals *do* at work, not their personal characteristics. Is this a good option to use in a performance appraisal process?

CAN WE ACCURATELY MEASURE BEHAVIORS THAT AFFECT JOB PERFORMANCE? As a general rule, it is much better to use behaviors in an appraisal than it is to use traits. While an individual supervisor or manager may make a mistake in judgment about the traits of an employee, physical actions or behaviors can be directly observed, and as a result, they are more likely to be a valid assessment of the individual's performance.

GIVE BEHAVIOR THE OUCH TEST. Let's take a look at a behavioral evaluation using the OUCH test. Would an evaluation based on actions taken by an employee be *objective*? In general, directly observing and evaluating an action is significantly more objective than making an attempt to judge a trait like individual effort. If we applied the same evaluation of behaviors to all of the individuals in the same type of job, we would have a reasonable certainty that we were being *uniform in application*. The same thing would be true here in evaluating the concept of *consistent in effect*.

So, it comes down to whether or not a behavior-based evaluation *has job relatedness*. Would a behavioral evaluation be directly related to the essential functions of a job? The answer is that it would be if we made sure that we chose behaviors that were necessarily a part of successfully accomplishing a task. For instance, if we determine that a person *acts* correctly in filling out a requisition form, putting the proper information in the correct blocks, and providing the requisition to the appropriate person who would then order the material, then we are assessing behaviors that are job related. If, however, we evaluated the action of walking to the lunchroom and walking back to one's workstation, would we be measuring a valid job-related behavior? The answer is more than likely no. Of course, this is a silly example, but it should help you understand that no matter what we do in the evaluation process, we need to ensure that our actions are job related.

OK, but would behavioral evaluations be defensible in the situation of our fired employee above? Would it be possible for us to show that our evaluation process was *valid and reliable*? If we choose to measure job-related behaviors, it becomes much easier for the organization to defend the validity and reliability of the appraisal process. Observation of actions that are directly related to a job would provide at least some presumption of validity as well as reliability, purely because the behaviors are directly job related. Again, if we chose behaviors that could not be directly associated with the job, the validity and reliability of the measures would be suspect.

SHOULD WE MEASURE BEHAVIOR? Are behaviors that measure performance more *acceptable* to the individual employee and the managers than personal traits? In fact, evidence shows that most individuals are very comfortable with the evaluation of their performance being based on "what they do," not "who they are." In general, the most useful and therefore most acceptable feedback to employees is feedback on specific job-related behaviors.[30] As managers, though, we still need to be cognizant of the fact that a behavioral evaluation can be a poor

Behaviors The actions taken by an individual

measure of work performance unless the behaviors chosen are directly applicable to being successful in the job. So as with traits, the Blanchard test asks whether employees understand why they are assessed at a specific level (evaluation) and what it takes to get a higher rating (development).[31]

Results Appraisals

Our final option is to evaluate the results, or outcomes, of the work process. **Results are simply a measure of the goals achieved through a work process.** Using results as an evaluation measure provides management with an assessment of the goals that were achieved in a particular job over time.

CAN WE ACCURATELY MEASURE RESULTS THAT AFFECT JOB PERFORMANCE? Is measuring the outcomes of a particular individual's job a valid and reliable measure of that person's performance? Well, results are certainly concrete measures of what has happened in the organization. However, could results of a job have been skewed based on factors that were outside the control of the individual who is performing that job? The answer is obviously that the results could be affected by many other factors besides the individual's performance. For example, standards could be set too low and be too easy to achieve, or they could be set too high and thus be impossible to achieve.

Even though this is true, the measurement of results is the final organizational measure of success. The results produced through organizational processes provide the company with its return on investment—in this case, its investment in the people in the organization. So, organizations really like to measure results.

GIVE RESULTS THE OUCH TEST. Let's take a look at the OUCH test concerning results-based evaluations. Is a result achieved in a particular job a concrete, factual measure that can easily be quantified? Obviously, it is a very *objective* measure of what has happened in that particular job. If we apply the same results-based measure to each similar job, then our measure is *uniform in application.* The measure of results would almost certainly be consistent across different groups of employees, so we would also meet the *consistency in effect* requirement of the OUCH test. And of course, if we are measuring the results of what happens in a job, we are certainly providing a measure that *has job relatedness.* So with a quick scan, we can see that a results-based performance appraisal meets the requirements of the OUCH test better than do either of the other two options.

SHOULD WE MEASURE RESULTS? Results-based evaluations, like behavior-based evaluations, are typically very acceptable to both the employee and the manager. Employees readily accept results-based appraisals because they feel that such appraisals are one of the fairest methods of analyzing their performance. After all, results are the most concrete measures available—either the result was achieved, or it wasn't. We can also defend this type of appraisal much more easily than we can defend the other two options, even in court. It tends to be very easy for the organization to go into a courtroom and show that an individual's results were objectively lower than those achieved by other people in the same or similar jobs, if such an action becomes necessary.

But is a performance evaluation measured on results valid and reliable? The results-based evaluation would most likely be highly valid and would usually be reliable, assuming that we were able to take into account factors outside the individual's control that nonetheless affect job performance. So as with traits and behaviors, the Blanchard test asks: Does everyone understand why they are assessed at a specific level (evaluation) and what it takes to get a higher rating (development)?[32]

Results A measure of the goals achieved through a work process

8-2 APPLYING THE CONCEPT

Assessment Options

Write the letter corresponding to each of the following assessment options for measuring performance before the situation describing it.

    a. traits

    b. behavior

    c. results

_____ 6. On the assessment form question number 7, "willingness to take responsibility," I'm giving you an average rating.

_____ 7. You have to stay calm and stop yelling at your coworkers.

_____ 8. You only sold 25 units 3 weeks in a row. You know the standard is 35, so I'm giving you a formal warning that if you don't get up to standard in 2 weeks, you will be fired.

_____ 9. When you promote one of the women, make sure she is attractive.

_____ 10. I'm pleased with your performance. It is only your second week on the job, and you are already producing the standard 10 units per day. I don't think it will be long before you exceed the standard and get bonus pay.

Which Option Is Best?

Our three options concerning what we evaluate are traits, behaviors, and results. But which option is best? The answer's not as easy as you might think. Certainly, results-based and behavior-based evaluations are more defensible due to the fact that they are more reliable and valid than trait-based evaluations. But we have to include a large number of factors in order to select which option is best in a particular situation.

For example, if we need to evaluate employees who work on the assembly line, we may need to evaluate behaviors such as punctuality. Do they show up to work on time? If we have an employee who produces at 150% of the standard when they show up, but they only show up 2 or 3 days a week, that creates a problem for the whole assembly line. In that case, we may need to evaluate attendance and punctuality (behaviors) because everyone on the assembly line depends on everyone else.

However, if we have individuals who don't do their actual work where managers can see and measure traits and behaviors—for example, people who work from home (telecommuters) and independent outside salespeople—then we need to rely on results-based measures. Other employees are often not affected by the hours that the telecommuters and salespeople work. It will not matter when they are at the office, as long as they get the job done. The firm will be concerned with how much they produced or sold. So circumstances dictate which method we will use; we cannot say one method will always be superior to the other two.

HOW DO WE USE APPRAISAL METHODS AND FORMS?

The formal performance appraisal usually involves the use of a standard form developed by the HR department to measure employee performance. Again, "If you can't measure it, you can't manage it."[33] But you must be careful how you measure success,[34] as the assessment should be as objective as possible, not subjective.[35] Employees need to know the standards and understand what good performance looks like, and they need to be able to measure their own performance. If you are stuck with a form that has subjective sections, work with your employees to develop clear, accurate standards.

Exhibit 8-2 lists the commonly used performance appraisal measurement methods and forms and displays them on a continuum based on their use in evaluative

WORK APPLICATION 8-4

Very briefly describe a job you have or had. Describe how your performance was assessed based on traits, behavior, and/or results.

LO 8-5

Briefly discuss the commonly used performance measurement methods and forms.

SHRM

H:5
Performance Appraisals

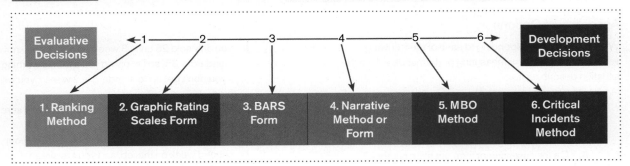

EXHIBIT 8-2 PERFORMANCE APPRAISAL MEASUREMENT METHODS AND FORMS

Critical Incidents Method

The **critical incidents method** *is a performance appraisal method in which a manager keeps a written record of the positive and negative performance of employees throughout the performance period.* There is no standard form used, so it is a method. Here, and for each of the other methods and forms, let's answer two questions: Why and when do we use the method or form, and how do we use it?

WHY AND WHEN DO WE USE THE CRITICAL INCIDENTS METHOD? Most formal reviews only take place once or twice a year. But do you want to wait for a formal review before you talk to employees about what they are doing well and when they are not performing up to expectations? No, you want to let them know how they are doing on an ongoing basis. Also, let's say you are a manager with 12 employees. Can you really remember everything each of them did well, when they messed up, and on what dates to evaluate their total performance over the past 6 to 12 months? Odds are, you can't. However, many managers don't keep a record of critical incidents, which leads to the problem of inaccurate measures during the formal review meeting.

We use critical incidents to do a good assessment of the entire review period, and we coach during the entire review period when needed for developmental decisions. We need to continually conduct informal coaching and discipline when needed as we make notes of critical incidents to use during the formal review. With clear standards and coaching, you can minimize disagreements over performance during the formal performance appraisal because employees will know what is coming.[36]

Although critical incidents are commonly used for developmental decisions, they are also used for evaluative decisions. For legal purposes, a list of documented critical incidents is especially important to have leading up the evaluative decision of firing employees. We will discuss discipline and documentation in Chapter 9.

HOW DO WE USE CRITICAL INCIDENTS? Managers commonly keep a file folder on each employee, in either hard-copy or electronic form. Critical incidents are important employee actions, not minor ones, which help or hurt performance. Every time an employee does something very well, like beating a tough deadline or keeping an angry customer from terminating a business relationship with the firm, a note goes in the employee's file. Notes also go into the file every time the employee's behavior hurts performance, such as when the employee comes to work late or doesn't meet quality standards. Each note is usually written by the manager and/or

SHRM

H:1
Identifying and Measuring Employee Performance

Critical incidents method A performance appraisal method in which a manager keeps a written record of the positive and negative performance of employees throughout the performance period is in the form of documentation, such as a warning, a performance report, or a letter from a happy customer thanking the employee for doing a great job.

Coaching is part of this ongoing process, and it involves helping employees succeed by monitoring their performance through giving feedback to praise progress and to redirect inappropriate behavior as often as needed.[37] One error managers tend to make is focusing on the negative actions of employees. Remember that a good, balanced evaluation includes both positive and negative feedback, so look for good performance, not just poor performance, and praise it when you see it.[38]

Management by Objectives (MBO) Method

The **management by objectives (MBO) method** *is a process in which managers and employees jointly set objectives for the employees, periodically evaluate performance, and reward employees according to the results.* Although there is a three-step process, there is no standard form used with MBO, so it is a method. MBO is also referred to as work planning and review, goals management, goals and controls, and management by results.

WHY AND WHEN DO WE USE THE MBO METHOD? The MBO method is one of the best methods of developing employees. As with the use of critical incidents, employees get ongoing feedback on how they are doing, usually at meetings scheduled at regular intervals. We can use the MBO method successfully with our employees if we commit to the process and truly involve employees rather than trying to make them believe that our objectives are theirs.

On an organization-wide basis, MBO is not too commonly used as the sole assessment method. It is more commonly used based on the evaluative assessment during the development part of the performance appraisal. One difficult part of MBO is that in many situations, most employees will have different goals, making MBO more difficult and time-consuming than using a standard assessment form.

HOW DO WE USE MBO? MBO is a three-step process:

Step 1: Set individual objectives and plans. The manager sets objectives jointly with each individual employee.[39] The objectives are the heart of the MBO process and should be accurate measures of performance results. To be accurate, objectives should be SMART.[40] They need to be Specific, Measurable, Attainable, Relevant, and Time based. Being specific, measurable, and time based is fairly easy to determine in a written goal, but attainable and relevant are more difficult. So we developed a model based on the work of Max E. Douglas, and we have provided two examples in Model 8-1 that we can use when setting objectives for ourselves or others.

Step 2: Give feedback and evaluate performance. Communication is the key factor in determining MBO's success or failure, and employees should continually critique their own performance.[41] Thus, the manager and employee must communicate often to

WORK
APPLICATION 8-5

Select a job you have had. Did your boss use critical incidents in your evaluations? Assess how well your boss used coaching between formal performance appraisal meetings to review your performance.

MODEL 8-1	SETTING OBJECTIVES MODEL

(1) To +   (2) Action Verb +   (3) Specific and Measurable Result +   (4) Target Date

To +   produce +   20 units + per day

To increase widget productivity 5% by December 31, 2015

Management by objectives (MBO) method A process in which managers and employees jointly set objectives for the employees, periodically evaluate performance, and reward employees according to the results

review progress.[42] The frequency of evaluations depends on the individual and the job performed. However, most managers do not conduct enough review sessions.

Step 3: Reward according to performance. Employees' performance should be measured against their objectives. Employees who meet their objectives should be rewarded through recognition, praise, pay raises, promotions, and so on.[43] Employees who do not meet their goals, so long as the reason is not out of their control, usually have rewards withheld and even punishment given when necessary.

Narrative Method or Form

The **narrative method or form** *requires a manager to write a statement about the employee's performance.* There often is no actual standard form used, but there can be a form, so it can be a method or a form.

WHY AND WHEN DO WE USE THE NARRATIVE METHOD? A narrative gives the manager the opportunity to give the evaluative assessment in a written form that can go beyond simply checking a box to describe an assessment item. The manager can also write up a developmental plan of how the employee will improve performance in the future. Narratives can be used alone, but they are often combined with another method or form. Although the narrative is ongoing, it is commonly used during the formal review.

HOW DO WE USE THE NARRATIVE METHOD OR FORM? The system can vary. Managers may be allowed to write whatever they want (i.e., use the method), or they may be required to answer questions with a written narrative about the employee's performance (i.e., use the form). Let's discuss both here.

The no-form narrative method can be the only assessment method used during the formal review process. But the narrative method, when used alone, is more commonly used with professionals and executives, not with operative employees. How we write the formal narrative assessment varies, as writing content and styles are different. A narrative based on critical incidents and MBO results is clearly the best basis for the written assessment.

The narrative is also often used as part of a form. For example, you have most likely seen an assessment form (such as a recommendation) that has a list of items to be checked off. Following the checklist, the form may ask one or more questions requiring a narrative written statement.

Graphic Rating Scale Form

The **graphic rating scale form** *is a performance appraisal checklist form on which a manager simply rates performance on a continuum such as excellent, good, average, fair, and poor.* The continuum often includes a numerical scale, for example from level 1 (lowest performance level) to 5 (highest). The self-assessment and Skill Builder exercise 8-1 uses a graphic rating scale form; it is found at the end of this chapter.

WHY AND WHEN DO WE USE THE GRAPHIC RATING SCALE FORM? The graphic rating scale form is probably the most commonly used form during the formal performance appraisal (primarily for evaluative decisions), but use of the form should lead to development decisions as well. Why the popularity? Graphic rating scales can be used for many different types of jobs, making them a kind of one-size-fits-all form that requires minimal time, effort, cost, and training. Walk into an office supply store and you can find pads of them. But on the negative side, graphic rating scales are not very accurate measures of performance because the selection of one rating over another, such as an excellent versus good rating, is very subjective.

Narrative method or form Method in which the manager is required to write a statement about the employee's performance

Graphic rating scale form A performance appraisal checklist form on which a manager simply rates performance on a continuum such as excellent, good, average, fair, and poor

For example, think about professors and how they measure performance with grades. Some give lots of work and few As, while others give less work and almost all As.

HOW DO WE USE THE GRAPHIC RATING SCALE FORM? It is very simple, and we have most likely all used one. For example, many colleges let students assess professors at the end of a course, and all the students do is check a box or fill in a circle to give their rating. One of the problems with this method is that some of us don't bother to actually read the questions. Based on our biases, some of us just go down the list, checking the same rating regardless of actual performance on the items. To be fair, this problem is not common with managers formally evaluating their employees. However, it does tend to occur when customers evaluate products and services, including when students assess professors.

To overcome this problem, we can reverse the scale from good to poor on different questions, but this is unfortunately not commonly done. Why isn't this done all the time? Some managers who make the scales do not know they should do this. Also, some who do know they should reverse the scales don't because they don't want to end up with overall ratings being pushed to the middle because people don't read the questions.

Behaviorally Anchored Rating Scale (BARS) Form

A **behaviorally anchored rating scale (BARS) form** *is a performance appraisal that provides a description of each assessment along a continuum.* As with rating scales, the continuum often includes a numerical scale that runs from low to high.

WHY AND WHEN DO WE USE THE BARS FORM? The Answers To Why And When Are The Same Here As They Are With Graphic Rating Scales, So Let's Focus On The Differences Between Graphic Rating Scales And Bars Forms. BARS forms overcome the problem of subjectivity by providing an actual description of the performance for each rating along the continuum, rather than that one simple word (*excellent*, *good*, etc.) that graphic rating scales provide. A description of each level of performance makes the assessment a more objective, accurate measure.

So if BARS forms are more accurate, why aren't they more commonly used than graphic rating scales? It's partly economics and partly expertise. Again, the graphic rating scale can be used for many different jobs, but BARS forms have to be customized to every different type of job. And developing potentially hundreds of different BARS forms takes a lot of time, money, and expertise. Even when a firm has an HR staff, the question becomes "Is developing BARS forms the most effective use of our time?" Obviously, the answer is "It depends on the types of jobs being evaluated and the resources available to complete the evaluation process."

HOW DO WE USE BARS FORMS? As with graphic rating scales, we simply select a level of performance along a continuum. College accreditation associations are requiring more measures of student outcomes as assurance of learning, and as part of that process, they want more BARS rubrics as evidence. So in college courses, especially for written assignments, professors give out rubrics that describe in some detail the difference between an excellent (A), good (B), average (C), poor (D), and not acceptable

There shouldn't be any surprises or lack of agreement on performance levels during the formal performance appraisal interview.

Behaviorally anchored rating scale (BARS) form A performance appraisal that provides a description of each assessment along a continuum

(F) grade, using multiple criteria to put together a final grade. Here is a very simple example of making a graphic rating scale item into the more objective BARS.

Attendance—excellent, good, average, fair, poor

becomes

Attendance—number of days missed 1, 2, 3–4, 5, 6 or more

Ranking Method

Ranking *is a performance appraisal method that is used to evaluate employee performance from best to worst.* There often is no actual standard form used, and we don't always have to rank all employees. This method can be contentious, as evidenced by recent announcements by Microsoft and Yahoo. In late 2013, Yahoo announced that it was adopting a ranking system,[44] but later the same day, Microsoft announced that it was dropping its forced ranking system.[45]

WHY AND WHEN DO WE USE THE RANKING FORM? Managers have to make evaluative decisions such as determining the employee of the month, who gets a raise or promotion, and who gets laid off. So when we have to make evaluative decisions, we generally have to use ranking. However, our ranking can, and when possible should, be based on other methods and forms.

Managers can also use ranking for developmental purposes by letting employees know where they stand in comparison to their peers—meaning managers can use rankings to motivate employees to improve their performance. For example, when one of the authors passes exams back to students, he places the grade distribution on the board. This does not in any way affect the current grades—but it lets students know where they stand, and he does it to motivate them to improve.

HOW DO WE USE RANKING? Under the ranking method, the manager compares an employee to other similar employees, rather than to a standard measurement. An offshoot of ranking is the forced distribution method, which is similar to grading on a curve. Predetermined percentages of employees are placed in various performance categories—for example, excellent, 5%; above average, 15%; average, 60%; below average, 15%; and poor, 5%. The employees ranked in the top group usually get the rewards (a raise, a bonus, or a promotion), those not in the top tend to have rewards withheld, and the ones in the bottom group sometimes get punished. In Skill Builder 8-1, you are asked to rank the performance of your peers.

Which Option Is Best?

While this section does not contain an exhaustive list, it provides examples of each of the major methods of performance appraisal. Which appraisal method or form is best depends on the objectives of the organization. Using a combination of the methods and forms is usually superior to using just one. For developmental objectives, the critical incidents, MBO, and narrative methods work well. For administrative decisions, a ranking method based on the evaluative methods, and especially graphic rating scales or BARS forms, works well.

Remember that the success of the performance appraisal process does not just lie in the formal method or form used once or twice a year. It depends on the manager's human relations skills in ongoing critical incidents coaching, and it also depends on effective measures of performance that are accurate enough to let everyone know why they are rated at a given level (evaluative) and how they should improve (developmental) for the next assessment.[46]

PerformanceReview.com is one website that has been designed to help managers write complete and effective performance appraisals online. The site offers practical advice to guide managers through the appraisal process.[47]

Ranking A performance appraisal method that is used to evaluate employee performance from best to worst

8-3 APPLYING THE CONCEPT

Appraisal Methods and Forms

State which of the following assessments is being described in each of the given situations, writing each assessment's corresponding letter before the situation(s) in which it is described.

a. critical incidents method
b. MBO method
c. narrative method and forms
d. BARS forms
e. graphic rating scale forms
f. ranking method

_____ 11. Hank is not doing a good job, so you decided to talk to him about it and keep track of his performance regularly.

_____ 12. Your employees perform different tasks. You want to create a system for developing each of them.

_____ 13. Sara is moving, has applied for a job at another company, and asked you for a letter of recommendation.

_____ 14. You started a new business a year ago, and you are extremely busy focusing on sales, but you want to develop a performance appraisal form you can use with all 14 of your employees, who do a variety of jobs.

_____ 15. You have been promoted, and you have been asked to select your replacement.

WHO SHOULD ASSESS PERFORMANCE?

Now that we've learned the why, what, and how of the performance appraisal process, we next need to discuss the options for choosing a rater or evaluator. There are a number of different options concerning who should evaluate the individual employee, and the decision needs to be based on a series of factors. Let's take a look at our options for deciding who should evaluate an employee.

LO 8-6
Identify and briefly discuss available options for the rater/evaluator.

Supervisor

When we ask who should evaluate an employee, the most common response is that their immediate supervisor should do it. But why would the supervisor be the best person to evaluate an employee? Well, the supervisor is supposed to know what the employee should be doing, right? Certainly, supervisors are frequently one of the best and most commonly used options as an evaluator for the employees under their control. However, this is not always the case due to problems with supervisor performance assessments.

SHRM
H:2
Sources of Information (e.g., Managers, Peers, Clients)

PROBLEMS WITH SUPERVISOR EVALUATIONS. What if the supervisor doesn't see the employee very frequently? This may not be all that uncommon in a modern organization. Many times today, supervisors may be in a different building or even a different city from that of the individuals they supervise. Virtual teams, Internet-linked offices, telecommuting, and other factors cause supervisors to not be in constant touch with their employees, unlike the situation 20 or 30 years ago.

There are other problems as well. What if there's a personality conflict? Supervisors are human, just like their employees, and they may just not relate well to some of their employees. This may cause a personal bias for or against certain employees that may invalidate the appraisal process.

What if the supervisor doesn't know what you're supposed to be doing in your job? Aren't supervisors always supposed to know every job for which they are responsible? Again, 30 years ago, this may have been true. However, in today's work environment, with the amount of information necessary to do the complex tasks that organizations must accomplish in order to compete, nobody can know every job. There's just too much information for any one individual to learn. So jobs have been segmented down into smaller and smaller areas, and the supervisor may not know each of those jobs in great detail. So there are certainly problems that can occur in the case of a supervisor being responsible for a subordinate employee's evaluation process.

AVOIDING SUPERVISOR REVIEW PROBLEMS. A simple way to overcome these problems is to have others, in addition to the supervisor, assess performance. Also, multiple measures can make a performance assessment more accurate. Using other evaluators and multiple measures can help overcome personal bias and provide information that supervisors don't always know about.

Peers

Since the supervisor is not always knowledgeable enough to make a valid assessment of employee performance, another possible option is to use coworkers or peers of the individual employee as appraisers. When would it be valuable to use peer evaluations in an organization? If the supervisor is absent or has infrequent contact with the employees, but each of the employees frequently interacts with multiple coworkers in a team or group, then peer evaluations may be valuable.[48] Peers or coworkers also often know the job of the individual employee better than the supervisor does, and they are more directly affected by the employee's actions, either positive or negative. In addition, peers can evaluate the ability of the individual to interact with others successfully in a group or team setting—something that may be very difficult for the supervisor to see unless they are intimately involved with the group.

PROBLEMS WITH PEER REVIEWS. There are certainly issues that can come up in peer evaluations that can cause the process to become less objective. In fact, research evidence regarding the validity of peer evaluations is really unclear.[49] Personality conflicts and personal biases can affect how individual employees rate their peers. Individuals within a group or team may just have significantly different personality types, and these differences can cause friction within the workgroup that may spill over when it comes time to evaluate the person that they are in conflict with.

AVOIDING PEER REVIEW PROBLEMS. Because we know that these problems can occur within a peer evaluation, the manager can take the issues into account and adjust rating values as necessary. For example, assume you are the manager of a work group of six people who, in your opinion, work very well together and provide a quality work product. When you review a set of peer evaluations from the work group, you notice that two of the group members (a young male and an older female) gave each other significantly lower than average grades. However, the other four members of the group gave both of them good marks for their contributions to the group. This quite likely is a situation where a personality conflict has occurred between the two members that caused them to lower each other's grades. Knowing that the other four members of the group evaluated these two individuals as valued members of the team, you may want to adjust the ratings from the two individuals to more closely match the overall evaluations from the team, noting that a personality conflict may have lowered their evaluations of each other. Some additional research shows that as peers evaluate each other more, their ability to provide relevant and valuable feedback increases, as does their personal confidence. So giving employees practice in peer evaluations can improve the validity and reliability of such evaluations.[50]

Even with the potential for personality conflicts and bias, peer evaluations can give us good insight into the inner workings of a group or team when the supervisor has infrequent contact with the team. In Skill Builder 8-1, you will do a performance assessment of your peers.

Subordinates

Our next available option is to have the subordinates of an individual supervisor evaluate that supervisor. We would typically only use subordinate evaluation for managerial-level employees. However, who within the firm knows, and suffers the consequences from, the actions of a supervisor more than the people who work for them? Subordinate evaluations can give us good insight into the managerial practices and potential missteps of people who control other employees in our organization. As a result, subordinate evaluations may give us valuable information that we would be unable to find out using any other means.

PROBLEMS WITH SUBORDINATE REVIEWS. Can subordinate evaluations cause problems within the department or workgroup? Is the potential for bias, especially from subordinates who have been disciplined by the supervisor, significant in this type of evaluation? Of course, the answer is yes—there is the potential for bias. Obviously, the subordinates may try to get back at their supervisor for giving them tasks that they did not want to perform or for disciplining them for failure in their jobs. There may also be a personality conflict, or some subordinates may be biased against their supervisor or manager for other reasons. So there are certainly negative aspects to subordinate evaluations. On the other end of the scale, the subordinates may inflate the capabilities of their manager, at least partly because of a lack of understanding of all the tasks and duties required of the manager. In fact, in a recent survey, about two thirds of employees rated their managers higher than the managers rated themselves.[51]

AVOIDING SUBORDINATE REVIEW PROBLEMS. In all of these problem areas, if we know that there is a potential problem, we can most likely guard against it. In many cases, as we go through a group of subordinate evaluations, we will see one or two outliers providing either very high or very low marks for the supervisor. In such a case, we should probably throw those outliers out of the calculation when determining overall marks for the supervisor. It's surprising how often these outliers are extremely easy to spot in a subordinate evaluation process.

Another significant issue in the case of subordinate evaluations is confidentiality. Subordinate evaluations *must* be confidential in nature or it is unlikely that the subordinates will provide an honest evaluation of their supervisor. Why is this the case? Obviously, if the evaluation is not confidential, the supervisor can and may exact retribution on subordinates who provide unflattering evaluations. So, if the evaluation is not anonymous, many of the subordinates will likely inflate the capabilities of the supervisor, which minimizes the value of the evaluation process itself. Even though subordinate evaluations have the potential for bias and other problems, we can help to overcome these problems, and subordinate evaluations can provide us with valuable information about the supervisor's capabilities.

Self

Self-assessment is also an option in the performance appraisal process. Virtually everyone does a self-assessment, whether they are actually formally asked to do so as part of the assessment or not. It is required with MBO. Even when they are not asked to do a self-assessment, employees will still walk into the review discussion with some informal self-assessment that they will compare to the supervisor's rating. But are self-evaluations valuable, or is the employee going to overestimate their individual capabilities and tell us that they're perfect? (As you know, every chapter of this book has one or more self-assessments, and in the one for this chapter—Skill Builder 8-1 at the end of the chapter—you will assess your performance on a group project. If you want to, you can do the self-assessment now.)

PROBLEMS WITH SELF-ASSESSMENTS. Most of the research evidence shows that self-assessments tend to overestimate the individual's ability to do a job.[52] However, some of the research says that employees either underestimate or accurately estimate their job performance over time. A significant portion of the evidence seems to show that individuals with lower overall levels of knowledge and skills tend to inflate their self-assessment of their abilities.[53] Conversely, as individuals become more knowledgeable and more skilled, the evidence tends to show that they will either accurately estimate or even underestimate their capabilities in their jobs.[54,55,56]

AVOIDING SELF-ASSESSMENT PROBLEMS. Based on the fact that most of the evidence shows that employees overestimate their ability to do their job, is self-assessment a valid performance measure? Here again, even though the measure may have validity concerns, if we know that self-evaluations tend to be skewed, we can most likely adjust for that. In addition, receiving information from the individual concerning their perception of their skill set is extremely valuable in a number of management processes—including plans for training and development opportunities, providing work assignments, and counseling and disciplinary measures. A big step in overcoming self-assessment problems, as well as other assessment problems, is the Blanchard test—which asks whether the employee understands why they are assessed at a specific level (evaluation) and what it takes to get a higher rating (development).[57]

Customers

We may also want to ask customers to evaluate individuals within the company. We use the word *customers* in a broad sense to include people outside the organization, including customers for our products and services and suppliers to the firm. Customers can also be internal, including people in other departments of the firm (for example, the print shop that makes copies for other departments and the mail room that receives mail and delivers communications and products to the rest of the firm).

When and why would we want to use customers in the evaluation process? We may want to use customers as evaluators when the individual being evaluated has frequent contact with internal or external customers. If an employee interacts routinely with internal or external customers, we need to know how those customers feel about their interactions with the employee. This particularly applies to external customers, who are the ones who ultimately pay the bills.

It does not matter what else we do successfully if our customers are uncomfortable with their interactions with our employees. If *external* customers are upset about their interactions with our employees, then they have the ability to go elsewhere with their business. And even *internal* customers can create significant problems within the firm due to conflict between departments or divisions. So we want to ask internal and external customers to evaluate the individuals with whom they come into contact.

PROBLEMS WITH CUSTOMER ASSESSMENTS. What do you think the major problem would be with customer-based evaluations? One problem is that customer assessments commonly use simple rating scales, which we discussed as being very subjective. Also, customers are usually not trained to do an accurate assessment, so bias is a problem. For these and other reasons, the popular opinion is that customer evaluations are almost always skewed to the negative. However, research shows that this is not necessarily the case.[58] In some situations, customer evaluations actually exceed internal evaluations.

AVOIDING CUSTOMER ASSESSMENT PROBLEMS. Regardless of whether or not customers will tell us when we're doing an exceptional or acceptable job, customer evaluations provide us with valuable information concerning our employees who have direct customer contact. If this is the case, can we adjust the evaluation process knowing that customer evaluations are frequently skewed either positively or negatively? Obviously, we can. One of the basic methods of adjusting the customer evaluation process is by comparing the individuals being evaluated and identifying the ratios of negative and positive comments. This allows us to identify more successful and less

WORK
APPLICATION 8-7

Select your current job or a past job. Identify who has or had input into your performance appraisal.

successful employees. Although this is an imperfect measure, it still provides value to the firm because customers' perceptions are critical to our relationships with them. So, we need to measure this relationship.

360-Degree Evaluations

In some cases, the evaluation is expanded to everyone employees come into contact with through 360-degree feedback.[59] The **360-degree evaluation** *analyzes individuals' performance from all sides—from their supervisor's viewpoint, from their subordinates' viewpoint, from their customers (if applicable), from their peers, and from their own self-evaluation.* Obviously, the 360-degree evaluation would give us the most accurate and best possible analysis of the individual and their performance within the company.

DuPont developed 360-degree reviews back in 1973, and they are still popular today.[60] With the trend of structuring work in teams, peer evaluations are now used regularly.[61] Those who fill out the appraisal form usually do so confidentially. The feedback from all these people is used to evaluate and develop the employee.

PROBLEMS WITH 360-DEGREE EVALUATIONS. If 360-degree evaluations are the best, then why don't we always use them? The simple answer is time and money. It takes a significant amount of time for a group of individuals to evaluate one person if we use a 360-degree format. Using up so much organizational time obviously also costs us a significant amount of money. If we multiply those numbers by the time it takes everyone associated with the organization to evaluate one individual, the costs can quickly become massive.

AVOIDING 360-DEGREE PROBLEMS. Unfortunately, there really is no simple way to avoid these problems besides what is commonly done—simply not using 360-degree evaluations. The 360-degree evaluation format tends to be most valuable if it is used for purposes of individual development, rather than to make administrative evaluative decisions.[62] A good 360-degree feedback system can provide specific suggestions about how to improve individual competencies."[63] It can also go a long way toward minimizing some of the most common problems with the performance appraisal process, which we will review in the next section.

Whom Do We Choose?

Now that we know our options for who should conduct an evaluation of each employee, which option should we use? Again, we need to remember that each of the options costs us money because it takes time for the individual to perform the appraisal. So, we need to determine which option or options to use. We can combine any of these methods with any other, all the way up to the point of the 360-degree evaluation. However, we only want to use a 360-degree evaluation when it's worth it. If it's not necessary, then it doesn't make a lot of sense due to the cost of this method.

For instance, is there any need to do a 360-degree evaluation of janitorial or housekeeping staff? Would this make sense? Obviously, it would not. In most cases, with low-level staff members, a supervisor's evaluation is sufficient. This is true because even though only the supervisor does the formal assessment, the supervisor often gets informal feedback on the employee's performance from customers and peers of that employee. Customers will often complain to the supervisor if the employee's service is not satisfactory, and peers will complain about a fellow employee who is not meeting standards for some reason. The supervisor's critical incident file is often written based on information received from peers and customers, and that reduces the influence of any personal bias the supervisor may have toward the employee.

LO 8-7

Briefly discuss the value and the drawbacks of a 360-degree evaluation.

360-degree evaluation An evaluation that analyzes individuals' performance from all sides—from their supervisor's viewpoint, from their subordinates' viewpoint, from their customers (if applicable), from their peers, and from their own self-evaluation

WORK
APPLICATION 8-8

What about the case of an outside salesperson? In this situation, the results tend to speak for themselves. Sales numbers are available to the salesperson and manager. If the supervisor rarely sees the individual but the customer interacts with our salesperson on a routine basis, we can ask the customer to do an evaluation of the salesperson and ask the salesperson for a self-appraisal. With the sales figures, a self-assessment, and customer feedback, we can develop a plan to increase future performance.

Finally, if we are evaluating the marketing manager for the firm, we may want to do a 360-degree evaluation because of the fact that this individual would affect all of the groups—subordinates, customers, peers, the organization, and themselves. So, we evaluate the specific situation and use the number of methods necessary to get an accurate assessment of the individual.

So once again, to get an understanding of the return on our investment, we need to do a cost-benefit analysis to determine when the benefits of increasing performance outweigh the costs of a particular person or group completing a performance appraisal. In essence, we attempt to maximize performance while minimizing the total cost of the appraisal process.

LO 8-8

Identify some of the common problems with the performance appraisal process.

PERFORMANCE APPRAISAL PROBLEMS

During the performance appraisal process, there are common problems that we face. However, knowing these common problems, we can take measures to avoid them. So in this section, we discuss the problems first with simple ways to avoid each of them as an individual. Then we discuss what the organization can do to overcome these problems on an organization-wide basis. We can actually overcome multiple problems with the same method. See Exhibit 8-3 for a list of problems and ways to avoid them.

Common Problems Within the Performance Appraisal Process

Let's briefly discuss each of the common problems during the performance appraisal process listed in Exhibit 8-3.

BIAS. **Bias** *is simply a personality-based tendency, either toward or against something.* In the case of performance assessment, bias is toward or against an individual employee. All human beings have biases, but supervisors especially cannot afford to allow their biases to enter into their evaluation of subordinates in the firm. This is very easy to say but very difficult to do. Biases make the evaluation process subjective rather than objective, and they certainly provide the opportunity for a lack of consistency in effect on different groups of employees. So to overcome the bias problem, we need to be objective and not let our feelings of liking or disliking an individual influence our assessment of that person.

STEREOTYPING. **Stereotyping** *is mentally classifying a person into an affinity group and then identifying the person as having the same assumed characteristics as the group.* Though stereotyping is almost always assumed to be negative, there are many incidents of positive stereotypes. However, regardless of whether the stereotype is positive or negative, making assumptions about individual employee characteristics based on their supposed membership in a group, rather than explicitly identifying the performance of the individual, creates the potential for significant error in evaluations. So we can avoid stereotyping by getting to know each employee as an individual and then objectively evaluating each employee based on their actual performance.

Bias A personality-based tendency, either toward or against something

Stereotyping Mentally classifying a person into an affinity group and then identifying the person as having the same assumed characteristics as the group

EXHIBIT 8-3 PERFORMANCE APPRAISAL PROBLEMS AND AVOIDING THEM

Common Problems	How to Avoid Problems
Bias	Develop asccurate performance measures
Stereotyping	Use multiple criteria
Halo error	Minimize the use of trait-based evaluations
Distributional errors	Use the OUCH and Blanchard tests
Similarity	Train your evaluators
Proximity	Use multiple raters
Recency	
Contrast	
Attribution	

HALO ERROR. Halo error occurs when the evaluator forms a *generally* positive impression of an individual and then artificially extends that general impression to many of that individual's categories of performance to create an overall evaluation of the individual that is positive.[64] (Alternatively, the evaluator can form a negative initial impression and extend it to form an overall negative evaluation—this is sometimes called the "horns error.") In other words, if an employee is judged by their supervisor to be generally a "good" employee, and if the supervisor then evaluates each of the areas of the employee's performance as good, then regardless of any behaviors or results to the contrary, the supervisor is guilty of halo error. So we can avoid halo error by remembering that employees are often strong in some areas and weaker in others, and we need to objectively evaluate each employee based on their actual performance for each and every item of assessment.

DISTRIBUTIONAL ERRORS. These errors occur in three forms: severity or strictness, central tendency, and leniency. They are based on a standard normal distribution, or the bell curve that we are all so familiar with. In *severity* or *strictness* error, the rater evaluates everyone or nearly everyone as below average. *Central tendency* error occurs when the rater evaluates everyone under their control as average—meaning nobody is rated as either really good or really bad. Finally, *leniency* error occurs when the rater evaluates everyone as above average—meaning it is basically a form of grade inflation. So we can avoid the distributional errors by giving a range of evaluations. The distribution is often based on the ranking method of evaluation and forced distribution.

SIMILARITY ERROR. This error occurs when the rater gives better evaluations to subordinates whom they consider more similar to themselves and poorer evaluations to subordinates whom they consider to be different from themselves. We all have a tendency to feel more comfortable with people who we feel are more similar to ourselves,[65] and if we are not careful, we can allow this feeling of comfort with similar individuals to be reflected in the performance appraisal process. So we can avoid similarity error by embracing diversity and objectively evaluating each employee based on their actual performance, even if they are different from us and don't do things the same way that we do.

PROXIMITY ERROR. This error states that similar marks may be given to items that are near (in other words, proximate to) each other on the performance appraisal form, regardless of differences in performance on those measures. So we can avoid the proximity error by objectively evaluating employees' actual performance on each and every item on the assessment form.

WORK
APPLICATION 8-9

Select your current job or a past job. Identify common mistakes your supervisor made when assessing your performance, during either an informal coaching or a formal appraisal review.

RECENCY ERROR. This occurs when the rater uses only the last few weeks of a rating period as evidence when putting together performance ratings. For instance, if a warehouse worker has been a strong performer for most of the appraisal period, but right before his annual evaluation, he knocked over a stack of high-cost electronic equipment while driving a forklift, he may be rated poorly due to recency error. So we can avoid recency error by evaluating the employee based on their performance during the entire assessment period, which is commonly 6 to 12 months. Using the critical incident evaluation method really helps our recall, and it helps us assess employee performance more objectively for the entire period.

CONTRAST ERROR. In contrast error, the rater compares and contrasts performance between two employees, rather than using absolute measures of performance to measure each employee. For example, the rater may contrast a good performer with an outstanding performer; then, as a result of the significant contrast, the good performer seems to be "below average." This would be a contrast error. So we can avoid contrast error by objectively evaluating the individual based on their actual performance.

ATTRIBUTION ERROR. In simplified terms, attribution is a process in which an individual makes assumptions about the reasons or motivations (such as attitudes, values, or beliefs) for an observed behavior. So, attribution error in performance appraisal might occur when the rater observes an employee action—such as an argumentative answer to a question—and assumes that the individual has a negative attitude toward their job and is a poor performer. This may not be true, and if it isn't, the rater is guilty of an attribution error.[66] So we need to avoid attribution error because it is based on our subjective conclusions. When in doubt, we shouldn't assume we know why the employee did or didn't do something. We should investigate actions so that we can objectively evaluate employees based on their actual performance.

Avoiding Performance Appraisal Process Problems

LO 8-9

Identify the major steps we can take to avoid problems with the appraisal process.

As you can see above, there are a significant number of ways that performance appraisals can fail to provide an accurate assessment of the capabilities and behaviors of individual employees. Thus far, we have only provided simple solutions to help us overcome these problems as individuals. But how can a firm avoid these problems on an organization-wide basis throughout the performance appraisal process?

Luckily, we can take a number of basic steps to minimize the negative issues that occur in the performance appraisal process. All we have to do is look at the problems noted, and we can fairly quickly come up with some possible solutions to at least the majority of those problems using the same methods. Let's discuss how the firm can limit the potential for the appraisal process to go astray by developing accurate performance measures, training evaluators, and using multiple raters.

DEVELOP ACCURATE PERFORMANCE MEASURES. As discussed earlier in this chapter, if the performance appraisal methods and forms are not accurate measures, then the entire performance appraisal process will have problems. Therefore, the organization should have its own HR specialist or hired consultants develop an objective assessment process and measures. Now, let's discuss three things HR specialists commonly do to help ensure accurate measures.

Use Multiple Criteria. One method of overcoming some of the problems with the appraisal process is to ensure that we use more than one or two criteria to evaluate an individual's performance. We should generally have at least one evaluation criterion for each major function within an individual job. As we noted earlier, behaviors and results that occur over the entire course of the evaluation period are typically

8-4 APPLYING THE CONCEPT

Avoiding Appraisal Problems

Review the list of common problems or errors and then write the letter corresponding to each one before the statement describing or involving it.

a. bias
b. stereotyping
c. halo error
d. distributional error
e. similarity error
f. proximity error
g. recency error
h. contrast error
i. attribution error

_____ 16. I got a lower rating than I deserve because I'm not afraid to speak my mind to the boss, and she doesn't like it.

_____ 17. I'm sick and tired of hearing how many units Sally produces and that I should be more like her.

_____ 18. I told my boss that I thought I deserve an excellent rating, but she said that she gives everyone a good rating.

_____ 19. I tend to take it easy during the year, but I make sure to really push and do a good job for the month of December, and that's why I got a good performance review.

_____ 20. I attended all the classes and participated in the class discussions, so the professor gave me an A even though my final average on my test scores was a B.

the best criteria to use in the process of evaluating an individual's performance, but employees behave in many different ways in different circumstances throughout the course of a year, so we shouldn't limit the appraisal process to one or two actions on the part of that individual employee. By evaluating multiple criteria, we have the ability to lower the incidence of halo, recency, contrast, and attribution errors, and we may even be able to affect bias and stereotyping because of the fact that many criteria, not just one or two, are being analyzed.

Minimize the Use of Trait-Based Evaluations. Our next method of overcoming problems within the appraisal process is to minimize the evaluation of individual traits. As we noted earlier, trait-based evaluations tend to be more subjective than behavior- or results-based evaluations, and as a result, they should generally not be used unless there is a specific reason why employees must exhibit a particular trait to be successful in a job. Only when we have a *specific reason* for trait-based evaluations should we measure those traits and evaluate them in the appraisal process.

In addition, because of their subjectivity, trait-based evaluations are much more difficult to defend in cases where the organization used the evaluation process for later disciplinary action against an individual employee. By minimizing the evaluation of traits, we lower the incidence of bias, stereotyping, similarity errors, and (potentially) attribution errors. So, minimizing trait evaluations lowers the ability of the rater to make some of the most significant mistakes that can occur in the appraisal process.

Give the Measures the OUCH and Blanchard Tests. We already stated this with each of the three types of assessment, but these two tests are so important to successful, accurate measures that they bear repeating here. With the OUCH test, is the measure objective, is it uniform in application, is it consistent in effect, and does it have job relatedness? With the Blanchard test, does everyone understand why they are assessed at a specific level (evaluation) and what it takes to get a higher rating (development)?[67]

TRAIN EVALUATORS. Once we have accurate measurement methods and forms, the next thing that we should do to help overcome some of the issues with the appraisal process is to train our evaluators to avoid the common errors and problems that occur in performance assessment and in how to use the various methods and forms.

Train Evaluators to Overcome the Common Problems of Assessment. Simply through the process of *rater error training*, we can mitigate or even eliminate many of the common problems. Once the evaluator becomes aware that the common errors occur with some regularity, the evaluator almost immediately begins to evaluate such errors and guard against them. Even bias and stereotyping errors *may* be mitigated through the rater error–training process. As we've said several times throughout this book, most of our employees want to do a good job, and once they know that an error is being committed, they will make attempts to correct that error. So, rater error training provides them with knowledge of these errors and allows them the opportunity to correct them.

A robust form of rater training is *frame-of-reference training*, which defines job performance dimensions in more concrete terms, provides samples of behaviors at each performance level, emphasizes the fact that job performance has many dimensions, and allows practice and feedback sessions. While the details of frame-of-reference training are beyond the scope of this introductory text, this method of rater training has been shown to have a significant positive effect on rater accuracy in the appraisal process.[68]

Train Evaluators to Use the Measurement Methods and Forms. Evaluators should also be trained to use the various performance assessment methods and forms. Because the critical incident method is not commonly used as a formal assessment method, evaluators should be taught to use it to help overcome recency error. Evaluators also need training to effectively use MBO and to write a good narrative. When using a rating scale, the organization should provide some training for the raters so they better understand the differences between the word descriptors along the continuum (excellent, good, etc.). BARS forms and ranking are fairly straightforward, but training can help overcome any problems encountered with them.

USE MULTIPLE RATERS. The next tool we can use to minimize errors in the evaluation process, at least in some cases, is to have multiple raters evaluate an individual. As we noted earlier, this becomes expensive very quickly, so we must decide whether or not the value inherent in using multiple evaluators overcomes the cost of the process. However, if it does, using multiple evaluators can conquer some significant problems in the appraisal process. What will the process of using multiple evaluators do to improve the appraisal process? It limits the ability of one individual appraiser to provide a biased opinion concerning an employee's performance, and it limits the potential for stereotyping in the appraisal process. In addition, halo, similarity, contrast, and attribution errors become less likely, and distributional errors tend to even out among multiple raters. It is for these reasons that 360-degree evaluations have gained favor in many organizations over the past 20 years.

DEBRIEFING THE APPRAISAL

The debriefing process is where we communicate to individuals the analysis of their performance. Earlier in the chapter, we noted that there are two major reasons for assessing performance: for evaluative decisions and for development. We also suggested breaking the formal performance appraisal debriefing into two separate interviews. In this section, we describe how to conduct both reviews.

The Evaluative Performance Appraisal Interview

Planning ahead is critical to the performance appraisal interview process. Therefore, this section is separated into preparing for and conducting the evaluative interview. Because the evaluative interview is the basis for the developmental interview, it should be conducted first.

PREPARING FOR AN EVALUATIVE INTERVIEW. When preparing for an evaluative interview, follow the steps outlined in Model 8-2. Our evaluation should be fair (meaning ethically and legally not based on any of the problems discussed).[69] If we have had

MODEL 8-2   THE EVALUATIVE PERFORMANCE APPRAISAL INTERVIEW

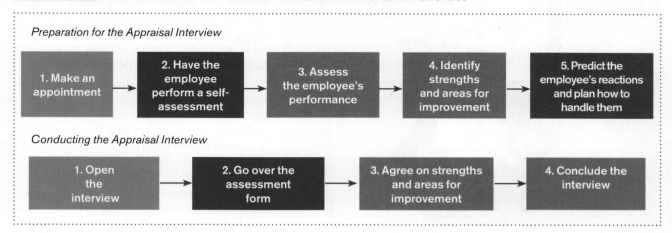

Preparation for the Appraisal Interview

1. Make an appointment → 2. Have the employee perform a self-assessment → 3. Assess the employee's performance → 4. Identify strengths and areas for improvement → 5. Predict the employee's reactions and plan how to handle them

Conducting the Appraisal Interview

1. Open the interview → 2. Go over the assessment form → 3. Agree on strengths and areas for improvement → 4. Conclude the interview

regular coaching conversations with our employees, they know where they stand,[70] and our preparation is mostly done except for filling out the form. So our relationship with the employee will directly affect the outcome.[71] Employees should also critique their own performance through a self-assessment using the form.[72]

So step 1 of Model 8-2 is to simply set up the meeting. Step 2 has the employee use the form to conduct a self-assessment, and in step 3 we, too, assess the employee's performance using the form. In keeping with the balanced evaluation, in step 4 we identify both strengths and areas for improvement that serve as the basis for the developmental interview. Finally, step 5 involves predicting employee reactions to our assessment and planning how to handle them. Using critical incidents will help support our assessment when employees disagree. And don't forget that the Blanchard test states that both you and the employee should be able to explain and agree on the employee's level of performance.

CONDUCTING AN EVALUATIVE INTERVIEW. During the interview, encourage the employee to talk and also listen to the critique of their performance.[73] Model 8-2 lists the steps for conducting an evaluative performance appraisal interview. In step 1, we open the meeting with some small talk to put the person at ease. Then in step 2, we go over our

MODEL 8-3   THE DEVELOPMENTAL PERFORMANCE APPRAISAL INTERVIEW

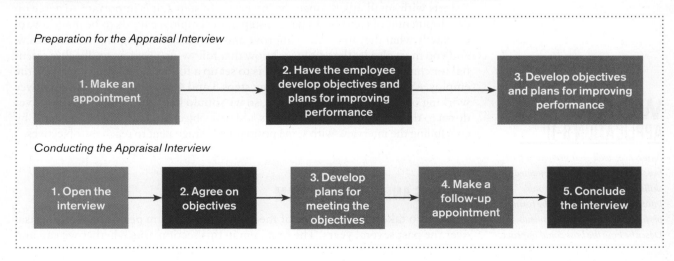

Preparation for the Appraisal Interview

1. Make an appointment → 2. Have the employee develop objectives and plans for improving performance → 3. Develop objectives and plans for improving performance

Conducting the Appraisal Interview

1. Open the interview → 2. Agree on objectives → 3. Develop plans for meeting the objectives → 4. Make a follow-up appointment → 5. Conclude the interview

A well-designed form can help managers do a good job during the formal performance appraisal.

evaluation of the items on the assessment form. In step 3, we identify the employee's strengths and weaknesses, discuss them, and agree on them. Finally, in step 4, we conclude the interview, which may involve making the appointment for the developmental interview.

During this process, employees should be open to negative feedback, even if they don't agree with it. They shouldn't make excuses or blame others. If they don't agree with the assessment, they may say something like "Thanks for the feedback, but I don't agree with it because . . ." Giving objective reasons for the disagreement is fine, as long as they do it without being argumentative and disrespectful. If there is such disagreement, we may want to schedule a follow-up meeting with the employee so that we and they may gather facts that support our or their stance on the assessment.[74]

The Developmental Performance Appraisal Interview

Again, planning ahead is critical when it comes to performance appraisal interviews. Therefore, this section is also separated into preparing for and conducting the interview.

PREPARING FOR A DEVELOPMENTAL INTERVIEW. After the employee's performance evaluation is completed, you should prepare for the developmental interview based on targeting areas for improvement. Yes, as a manager you are busy, and you may question the need for coaching and the cost of separate formal developmental interviews, but the benefit of spending time developing employees will lead to increased performance and lower turnover in your organization.[75]

To prepare for the interview, follow the steps in Model 8-3, which begins with simply setting up a time to conduct the review. As stated in step 2, have employees come up with their own objectives and strategies for improvement,[76] and also develop your own for them (step 3).

CONDUCTING A DEVELOPMENTAL INTERVIEW. The steps to follow when conducting a developmental performance appraisal interview are listed in Model 8-3. Again, step 1 starts with small talk to open the interview. In step 2, it is important to agree on developmental objectives. As part of step 3, the employee needs to be made aware of exactly what they must do to improve and increase the rating on the next review, and you must also let the employee know that follow-up progress feedback is essential for changing behavior.[77] So step 4 is to set up a follow-up meeting to review the employee's progress. When conducting steps 3 and 4, we don't want the employee working on too many things at once, so we should keep the number of objectives down to three or fewer. We can always add new objectives later. We end in step 5 by concluding the interview with some positive encouragement to reach the objectives.

WORK
APPLICATION 8-11

Assess how well your present or past boss helped develop your knowledge, skills, and competencies through informal coaching and/or the formal performance appraisal interviews. Describe how the boss could improve.

TRENDS AND ISSUES IN HRM

It's time to take a look at some of the trends and issues in performance appraisal over the past several years. The first item in this section asks whether we can and should provide employees with constant evaluations of their performance. Secondly, we take a look at electronic performance monitoring, or EPM. Does it improve performance and add value to the organization's performance appraisal process by providing results-based evidence of employee productivity? Finally, we deal with the relative merits of competency-based performance management and the more traditional task-based evaluation of performance.

Is It Time to Do Continuous Appraisals?

Samuel Culbert, a clinical psychologist at UCLA, has written a book called *Get Rid of the Performance Review!*[78] His premise is that performance appraisals are one-sided analyses by the manager that only show what the subordinate is doing wrong. He notes that if the performance review process can become two-way communication between the manager and the subordinate, then a performance review becomes a "performance preview." The boss and the subordinate "have conversations" that allow the manager to become a coach and tutor for the subordinate.

One of the more recent ideas that is gaining traction, at least in some companies, is some form of routine or continuous technology-based appraisal and feedback, rather than the traditional evaluation that Culbert and so many others are trying to toss out. For obvious reasons, this continuous appraisal seems to be more common in organizations that are less traditional and bureaucratic. Also, in organizations where results can be quantitatively measured, *results-only-work-environments* (ROWE) are beginning to be seen. About 10% of US employees are now being evaluated in a results-only manner. A results-only-work-environment is one in which employees are evaluated on outcomes only (not on behaviors or traits as in most traditional evaluation processes). Outcomes are continuously evaluated, and there is no waiting for an end-of-year performance appraisal. For a ROWE system to work, though, goals have to be quantifiable so that they can be specifically measured. The information technology company **CDW** uses a ROWE system and tracks individual employee performance electronically. If the employee doesn't complete a project on time, it is automatically logged into the performance management system.

In other organizations where results are not as easy to quantify, feedback on member behavior and outcomes can be constantly provided through technologies available to all team members. Each member is expected to provide meaningful feedback to all other members as a routine part of their work. We spoke about **Zappos'** holacracy earlier. Zappos is trying to use holistic feedback from all sides (a massive 360-degree evaluation) in order to evaluate its employees and encourage creativity and innovation.

Certainly a large number of organizations are developing many new processes to improve their performance management and appraisal process. Technology is again driving many of these processes, as it has done with many other management processes. HR managers will need to follow these discussions closely as they mature to find out over time what works and what doesn't.

Still, we have to struggle with a significant problem: Organizations legitimately use appraisals to make good decisions about their employees and employee development. If performance appraisals are not completed, the organization doesn't have valid and reliable information about its human resources, and therefore, it has no ability to make good decisions about things such as training, promotions, and pay raises. Going back to the OUCH and Blanchard tests, in *any* personnel action within the organization, we need to attempt to be as objective as possible.

Technology: Electronic Performance Monitoring

Electronic performance monitoring (EPM) *is the process of observing ongoing employee actions using computers or other nonhuman methods.* The number of

WORK
APPLICATION 8-12

Select an organization you work for or have worked for. Does it use formal evaluations? Do you believe the organization should or should not conduct formal evaluations?

SHRM

H:4
Electronic Monitoring

Electronic performance monitoring (EPM) The process of observing ongoing employee actions using computers or other nonhuman methods

WORK
APPLICATION 8-13

Select an organization you work for or have worked for. Does it use EPM? If so, describe the EPM system. Do you believe the organization should or should not use EPM?

employees monitored through EPM has increased drastically in the past 20 years. In the early 1990s, about one third of employees were being monitored electronically. By 2001, approximately 78% were being monitored electronically,[79] and that percentage has more than likely increased ever since. The reason for this steep increase is that using EPM apparently is an effective means of increasing productivity.[80] EPM allows management to know if employees are actually working or doing personal things during paid work hours. The biggest upside to EPM seems to be that it provides information for concrete, results-based performance evaluations.

Certainly, this is a valuable outcome. However, some researchers and practitioners argue against EPM because of a number of factors, including ethical questions concerning such monitoring, legal concerns over employee privacy, and potential increases in stress due to constant monitoring of performance. Stress research provides an interesting dichotomy. If the monitoring is done for employee development and involves more communication between the employee and manager, stress is generally reduced. If, however, monitoring is done as a means of giving rewards and administering punishment, stress appears to generally increase.[81] So, the questions are these: Should organizations use EPM systems? And if so, how should they use them?

There's no simple answer. Again, EPM has been shown to increase productivity, and organizations need to maximize employee productivity. However, when stress levels become too great, increased stress is known to decrease productivity. So there's an obvious tradeoff between more employee monitoring and controlling stress levels in our workforce. Management must understand this tradeoff to successfully improve productivity in the organization overall.

In addition, the ethical and legal questions noted in the previous paragraph may be significant enough in some cases to cause individual employees to leave the organization.[82] If these individuals are our more productive workers, and especially if they are knowledge workers, then what does the loss of these knowledgeable individuals do to organizational productivity? There doesn't appear to be any current research-based answer to these questions. Therefore, because these questions exist, organizations must be careful in how they implement EPM processes so that they can improve their chances of reaching the stated goal of EPM—improving organizational productivity.

Finally, as these programs are rolled out in the organization, managers must be acutely aware of the potential downside effects of increased stress levels and employees feeling that their privacy is being invaded. These could lead to decreases in productivity and higher rates of turnover.[83] In other words, management must work to overcome the potential problems and costs associated with EPM to gain the benefits.

Competency-Based Performance Management

What is competency-based performance management? Historically, the performance appraisal process evaluates specific employee skills and the employee's success in using those skills to produce products or services for the organization. Competency-based performance, on the other hand, evaluates large sets of capabilities and knowledge that, if put to good use, can improve organizational productivity to a much greater extent than just doing a job using an existing skill set. Or, using Chapter 7 terms, employee development is more effective than simply training.

Because jobs have been changing at a rapid pace over the past 20 years, competency-based performance management is becoming a more useful means of performance appraisal in some situations than the historical skill-based, transactional process. How are jobs changing? According to SHRM, the nature of work is changing: Society is moving from single-skilled to multi-skilled jobs, from repetitive tasks to problem-solving tasks, from individual work to teamwork, and from functional specialization to collaboration.[84] Taking a look at the ways in which work is changing, we can understand why it may be necessary for the organization to move from skill-based performance appraisal to evaluations based on larger-scale competencies.

Because competencies are becoming so significant in organizations, performance management systems need to be redesigned so that we can evaluate the skills and capabilities that are most important to the business. However, these types of performance management systems can present significant design challenges to the organization. To successfully use competency-based performance management, the organization has to move from an analysis and measurement of the *individual activities* within a process to a more holistic evaluation of the *ability to combine and improve activities* to create the most successful organizational outcomes.

SHRM notes that one of the problems with knowledge workers is that "performance analysts cannot directly observe much of what they do."[85] This being the case, we must design and use new competency-based evaluation methods that measure the ability to manipulate and manage information and to collaborate across many dimensions.

SHRM explains that because the most common type of historical job (the individual repetitive job) is going away, the organization has an increasing need for competency-based evaluations. SHRM also notes that doing competency-based evaluations is necessary to align performance with rewards if the organization is going to use a competency-based pay and incentives program.[86] Competency-based pay programs have been shown to align individual goals more closely with the organization's overall strategic goals. Because of all these factors, competency-based performance appraisals will likely continue to increase as a percentage of overall performance appraisal processes.

WORK APPLICATION 8-14

Select an organization you work for or have worked for. Does it use competency-based performance management? Do you believe the organization should or should not use it?

WORK APPLICATION 8-15

For a change, let's look at your college professors' grading habits. Are some professors hard graders (meaning they give few As), are others easy graders (meaning they give lots of As), or are they all consistent? Assuming there is inconsistency, should the college administration dictate a forced grade distribution?

• • • CHAPTER SUMMARY

8-1   Discuss the difference between performance management and performance appraisals.

Performance management identifies, measures, manages, and develops the performance of people in the organization. It is designed to improve worker performance over time. Performance appraisal is the part of the performance management process that identifies, measures, and evaluates the employee's performance and then discusses that performance with the individual.

8-2   Identify the necessary characteristics of accurate performance management tools.

The performance management tools and measures that we use need to be valid, reliable, acceptable/feasible, and specific. A *valid* tool measures the process that you want it to measure. A *reliable* tool works in a generally consistent way each time you use it. *Acceptability* and *feasibility* deal with the tool being satisfactory and reasonable to the people who use it and also capable of being successfully applied in a particular situation. Finally, a *specific* measure defines the performance well enough that we understand the current level of performance achieved and what, if anything, the employees need

to do to improve their performance to comply with standards.

8-3   List and briefly discuss the purposes of performance appraisals.

Communication is the first purpose. Appraisals need to provide an opportunity for formal two-way communication between management and the employee concerning how the organization feels the employee is performing. The second purpose is to gain information for evaluative decisions. We need good information on how employees are performing so that we can take fair and equitable actions with our workforce, to improve organizational productivity. Providing motivation for development is the last major purpose. Used correctly, appraisals can motivate by providing opportunities for the employees to improve their performance over time.

8-4   Identify and briefly discuss the options for what to evaluate in a performance appraisal.

Our three primary options for what to evaluate are traits, behaviors, and results. There is *some* evidence that particular types of traits are valuable in jobs that require management and leadership skills, but many traits have been shown to have very little bearing on job performance, meaning they are not valid measures of performance. We can also use behaviors to evaluate our workers. Measuring behaviors is usually a much better appraisal option because physical actions or behaviors can be directly observed, and as a result, they are more likely to be a valid assessment of the individual's performance. Finally, we can evaluate performance based on results. Results are a concrete measure of what has happened in the organization. However, results may be skewed based on factors that are outside the control of the individual who is being evaluated.

8-5   Briefly discuss the commonly used performance measurement methods and forms.

The *critical incidents* method utilizes records of major employee actions over the course of the appraisal period to complete the employee evaluation. *MBO* uses objectives jointly set by the manager and employee to gauge employee performance during the evaluation period. In the *narrative method*, the manager writes either a structured or unstructured paragraph about the employee's performance. *Graphic rating scales* provide a numerical scale so that the manager can check off where an employee falls on the continuum. *BARS* forms provide a description of the behaviors that make up acceptable performance at each level on the scale. Finally, *ranking* creates a hierarchy of employees, from best to worst.

8-6   Identify and briefly discuss available options for the rater/evaluator.

It is logical to choose *supervisors* as evaluators when they have ongoing contact with the subordinate and know the subordinate's job. When the supervisor may not spend lots of time with the individual employee, *peers* may make better evaluators because they may know the job of the individual employee better than the supervisor does and may be more directly affected by the employee's actions. *Subordinate* evaluations can give us good insight into the managers who control employees in our organization. We may want to use *customers* as evaluators when the individual being evaluated has frequent contact with those customers, because we need to know how customers feel about their interactions with our employees. *Self-evaluation* is valuable in a number of management processes, from training and development to counseling and disciplinary measures, among others.

8-7   Briefly discuss the value and the drawbacks of a 360-degree evaluation.

The 360-degree evaluation gives us the best overall analysis of any employee in the firm, because it looks at an employee's performance in the eyes of all others who are affected by that individual. The 360-degree evaluation format is more useful for individual development than it is for administrative purposes. The biggest downside is that the process takes a lot of time, which means that it also costs the company a lot of money.

8-8   Identify some of the common problems with the performance appraisal process.

Personal biases and stereotyping are two of the most significant appraisal problems. Other problems include halo error, distributional errors (either the grading is too harsh or too lenient, or everyone is judged to be average), similarity error, proximity error, recency error, contrast error, and attribution error.

8-9   Identify the major steps we can take to avoid problems with the appraisal process.

The first step would be to develop *accurate performance measures*. Accurate performance measures use *multiple criteria*, minimize *trait-based evaluations*, and can be analyzed using the OUCH test and the Blanchard test. Next, we should *train the evaluators*, because as soon as they know some of the common errors, those errors will become less pronounced. We can also *use multiple raters* to mitigate any potentially biased evaluations and minimize other errors such as similarity, contrast, and attribution errors. Finally, *don't evaluate what you don't know*. Find someone in the organization who does know the job, and have that person evaluate the individual performing the job.

8-10   Briefly discuss the differences between evaluative performance reviews and developmental performance reviews.

The *evaluative interview* is a review of the individual employee's performance over a certain period. The evaluation needs to be fair and equitable, not based on bias. The employee must be given the opportunity to talk as well as listen to the critique of their performance. The *developmental interview*, on the other hand, focuses on areas for improvement over time. You should have employees come up with their own objectives and strategies for improvement, and you should develop your own objectives for them.

8-11   8-11 Define the key terms found in the chapter margins and listed following the Chapter Summary.

Complete the Key Terms Review to test your understanding of this chapter's key terms.

••• KEY TERMS

behaviorally anchored rating
   scale (BARS) form
behaviors
bias
critical incidents method
electronic performance
   monitoring (EPM)

graphic rating scale form
management by objectives
   (MBO) method
motivation
narrative method or form
performance appraisal
performance management

ranking
results
stereotyping
360-degree evaluation
traits

••• KEY TERMS REVIEW

Complete each of the following statements using one of this chapter's key terms.

1. _____ is the process of identifying, measuring, managing, and developing the performance of the human resources in an organization.

2. _____ is the ongoing process of evaluating employee performance.

3. _____ is the willingness to achieve organizational objectives.

4. _____ identify the physical or psychological characteristics of a person.

5. _____ are the actions taken by an individual.

6. _____ is a measure of the goals achieved through a work process.

7. _____ is a performance appraisal method in which a manager keeps a written record of positive and negative performance of employees throughout the performance period.

8. _____ is a process in which managers and employees jointly set objectives for the employees, periodically evaluate performance, and give rewards according to the results.

9. _____ requires a manager to write a statement about the employee's performance.

10. _____ is a performance appraisal checklist on which a manager simply rates performance on a continuum such as excellent, good, average, fair, and poor.

11. _____ is a performance appraisal that provides a description of each assessment along a continuum.

12. _____ is a performance appraisal method that is used to evaluate employee performance from best to worst.

13. _____ analyzes individual performance from all sides—from the supervisor's viewpoint, from the subordinates' viewpoint, from customers' viewpoints (if applicable), from peers, and using the employee's own self-evaluation.

14. _____ is a personality-based tendency, either toward or against something.

15. _____ consists of mentally classifying a person into an affinity group and then identifying the person as having the same assumed characteristics as that group.

16. _____ is the process of observing ongoing employee actions using computers or other nonhuman methods.

••• COMMUNICATION SKILLS

The following critical-thinking questions can be used for class discussion and/or for written assignments to develop communication skills. Be sure to give complete explanations for all answers.

1. Other than giving an annual evaluation, what would you do to manage the performance of your employees? Explain why.

2. What would you do as the manager in order to make sure that your employees knew the standards that they would be evaluated against? Explain your answer.

3. Do you really think that it is possible for a performance appraisal to be motivational? Why or why not?

4. Can you think of a situation in which a trait-based evaluation would be necessary? Explain your answer.

5. You are in charge and you want to evaluate a group of assembly workers. Who would you choose as the evaluator(s)? What about evaluating the Director of Operations—who would you choose to do that? Explain your answer.

6. How would you minimize the chances that stereotyping could affect the evaluation process in your company?

7. Which of the solutions to performance appraisal problems would you implement first if you were in charge? Second? Why?

8. What would you do to make the performance appraisal debriefing more comfortable and less confrontational for your employees? How do you think this would help?

9. Do you agree that performance appraisals should be discontinued in companies? Defend your answer.

10. Is electronic performance monitoring ethical? Would you use it? Why or why not?

• • • CASE 8-1 BEAUTY AND THE BEASTLY SITUATION AT AEROSPACE DESIGNS' MARKETING DEPARTMENT

"Oh no! What now?" said Tom Moore, Director of Human Resources at Aerospace Designs. "Just when I thought this mess was over on how the Marketing Department does performance appraisal, we're smacked with a sexual harassment lawsuit. Well, we've got to do something about this predicament, and fast."

Aerospace Designs Background

Aerospace Designs (AD) was founded in the early 1960s. A privately held company started by two engineers, it was deliberately designed to feed off the blossoming U.S. military budget as the United States fought the Cold War. It became part of the supplier system to the massive Grumman contractor on Long Island, New York, and took on a military-like culture and structure.

Aerospace's Marketing Department

Aerospace Designs was predominantly a population of White males, and the hiring of minorities and women would assist in meeting its government-imposed affirmative action goals. The Marketing Department had never employed women. It was a very flat structure, consisting of three internal salesmen, a sales coordinator on-site, and one road salesman, who all reported directly to Frank Fasting, the Vice President of Sales and Marketing. (See the end of this case for an abbreviated organizational chart of the Sales and Marketing Department.) Aerospace Designs had hired Frank in the hope that he would be able to bring it out of its recent trend of flat growth. He was expected to grow the existing stable aerospace electronics business, and to firmly establish both a lights product line and a land-based vehicle business for military and commercial operations. The addition of new staff positions to the Marketing Department, of which the Marketing Assistant was one, was designed to help establish a web presence and improve the capabilities for print media and trade show coordination.

Enter Lola

Lola Meyer was above average in height, single, blonde, and 32 years old with lingering aspirations to be a model. Having a four-year degree, and opting out of the education field, she came over to Marketing in an attempt to find a steady job where she might be taken seriously. Although Frank had reservations regarding hiring Lola for the job given her qualifications, Sue Jones, the Human Resources Manager, eventually persuaded him to give Lola a chance. After a few months on the job, Frank approved arrangements for Lola to take courses related to the work that needed to be done, as it became apparent that she lacked some technical marketing skills necessary to be effective in her position.

Lola's Performance Evaluation

The ensuing year went by without fanfare. Lola, Frank, and the rest of the Marketing Department seemed to coexist amicably. Frank proved to be an outgoing, friendly sort, as you might expect of someone who is in Sales. His greatest weakness as a manager seemed to be his lack of administrative follow-through.

Aerospace Designs policies dictated an annual performance evaluation for every employee. This review unfortunately hadn't been done by Frank in a timely manner for Lola. By the time January rolled around, Lola's review was two months late. Frank discussed with Sue that he was not pleased with Lola's performance to date and would indicate such on her review. Sometime in April Frank became ill and needed to take time off to care for his personal health. Lola's review was written by Frank but not formally presented to Lola. Since it was now delayed nearly five months and it was apparent that Frank would be out for several more months, the decision was made to have Mark Gurello (Senior Sales Manager overseeing Marketing in Frank's absence) present Lola with the poor performance evaluation. This took place at the end of April. Lola was rated overall as "less than competent" and was not given a salary increase.

Lola's Reaction

Lola was both shocked and dismayed. In the beginning of May, she met with Sue to discuss her performance review. She handed Sue an 18-page, handwritten rebuttal of her evaluation. Her reply admitted her inability to reach designated goals, but stated that her performance was hindered due to items beyond her control. During this discussion with Sue, Lola alleged that sexual conversations and behavior had occurred in her work environment. Specifically, she cited that Frank had used highly inappropriate language, including nicknames for the President of Aerospace Designs. When she walked in on one of these conversations and was asked to comment, she abruptly left, and immediately filed her rebuttal report with HR.

Sue's Response and Lola's Bombshell

Upon reading about these incidents, Sue conducted a prompt, thorough internal investigation and determined that Lola's performance was marginal and upheld the performance review as written. She also determined that inappropriate conversations had taken place, and Frank received a written reprimand and was required to attend sexual harassment awareness training when he returned to the job. Lola's supervisor was permanently changed to Mark, and her workstation was moved to the other side of the Marketing area, away from Frank's office door. Lola was agreeable to these actions taken by the company. However, three months later Lola filed a sexual harassment lawsuit against the firm, stating that she could not get a fair evaluation given the harassing environment she was working in.

Questions

1. What evidence does this case provide for formulating and implementing a systematic approach to performance appraisal?

2. Do you believe that Lola's performance evaluation was valid and reliable? Do you feel that Frank had a bias or stereotypical mind when filling out the evaluation? Explain your answer.

3. What in the case indicates a problem with this supervisor's evaluation? Please connect examples from this case to what the chapter discusses.

4. How did Lola, her supervisor, and human resources communicate with one another? Do you feel that a performance appraisal interview should have been more formally established and conducted? Why or why not?

5. How can Lola's accusation of sexual harassment affect her personal work performance and her performance evaluation?

Case created by Herbert Sherman, PhD, and Theodore Vallas, Department of Management Sciences, School of Business Brooklyn Campus, Long Island University

Abbreviated Organizational Chart, Sales and Marketing Department, Aerospace Designs, Inc., 2001

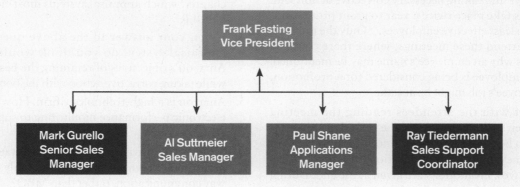

••• CASE 8-2 AMAZON.COM: SELLING EMPLOYEE PERFORMANCE WITH ORGANIZATION AND LEADERSHIP REVIEW

Amazon.com, which started as the biggest online bookstore, has become a household name by expanding rapidly in the retail market. It offers millions of movies, games, music, electronics, and other general merchandise products in several categories, including apparel and accessories, auto parts, home furnishings, health and beauty aids, toys, and groceries. Shoppers can also download e-books, games, MP3s, and films to their computers or handheld devices, including Amazon's own portable e-reader, the Kindle. Amazon also offers products and services, such as self-publishing, online advertising, an e-commerce platform, hosting, and a cobranded credit card.[87]

To keep this megastore running at a fast pace, Amazon hired 115,000 employees who generated $74 billion in 2013. **Target** and **Home Depot** made a combined income of close to $74 billion in the same year, yet they employed more than 340,000 people between them in their retail stores.[88] Why does Amazon only need one third of its competitors' labor force to produce the same revenue?

Like the other mega retailer, **Wal-Mart**, Amazon has delivered creative business solutions to their own processes to continuously increase their operating effectiveness. However, their strategy focuses on enhancing the customer shopping experience and providing excellent customer service rather than providing the lowest-priced products. To meet their customers' needs, Amazon must deliver more speed and efficiency in its giant warehouse. They use more automated work processes that reduce the company's operational costs and also increase labor efficiency and employee safety.

The quality of Amazon's warehouse labor has become the critical issue in the firm's success, and hence, hiring and retaining the best, most suitable candidates for the company's manual labor positions is a key success factor. That being said, Amazon's turnover rate at these lowest-ranked positions in the organization is high since Amazon lets go of its lowest-performing employees to make room for new, more appropriate candidates while promoting the very best. To detect the lowest- and highest-performing employees, Amazon initiated a performance evaluation system called the Organization and Leadership Review (OLR).[89]

OLR actually has two main goals: (1) finding future leaders and preparing them to be able to face the most challenging tasks presented in a fast-paced work environment; and (2) determining the 10% of employees who are the least effective and taking necessary corrective action with them. OLRs take place twice a year to grant promotions and find the least effective employees.[90] Only the top-level managers attend these meetings, where there could be two reasons why an employee's name may be mentioned. Either the employee is being considered for a promotion, or the employee's job might be at stake.

OLRs start with the attendees reading the meeting agenda. Then supervisors suggest the most deserving subordinates to be considered for promotion. All executives in the room evaluate these suggestions and then debate the alternatives. Promotions are given at the end. During the process, instead of using hard data, executives tend to evaluate employees' performance on the basis of personal, anecdotal experiences. Anyone in the meeting may deny a promotion; therefore, ambitious employees seeking a promotion should also be very friendly with their boss's peers. If an employee's supervisor cannot present that worker well enough, another's favorite subordinate will get the promotion.[91]

In terms of promotion, Amazon CEO Jeff Bezos expects the managers to set the performance bar quite high to allow only the most exceptional talent to progress.[92] Promotions are protected by well-written guidelines, which focus on delivery and impact but not on internal politics. People spend less time campaigning for their own promotions, and top performers are highly compensated based upon the quality of their work.[93] Therefore, only a few promotions are available each year, and receiving positive feedback from a supervisor is quite rare. The approval that employees get from their supervisor is not enough to earn a promotion; employees still have to "fight" for a promotion, which may not occur immediately.

Questions

1. Do you think OLRs increase employee motivation? If not, why would Amazon conduct such performance appraisals?

2. How might rater bias, stereotyping, and traits appraisal impact the accuracy of OLR? Could this be corrected? If so, how?

3. Given the differing appraisal systems described in this chapter, which appraisal systems most closely resemble OLR?

4. Given your answer to the above question, what appraisal system do you think would best meet Amazon's objectives of retaining the best employees while taking corrective action with the bottom 10%?

5. Amazon is a high-technology firm. How might it use electronic performance monitoring to supplement the OLR process?

6. What are the advantages and disadvantages of having performance reviews like OLR that only involve one-way communication, rather than MBO?

Case created by Herbert Sherman, PhD, and Theodore Vallas, Department of Management Sciences, School of Business Brooklyn Campus, Long Island University

$SAGE edge™

Sharpen your skills with SAGE edge at edge.sagepub.com/lussierhrm2e

SAGE edge for students provides a personalized approach to help you accomplish your coursework goals in an easy-to-use learning environment.

• • • SELF-ASSESSMENT AND SKILL BUILDER 8-1 PEER AND SELF-ASSESSMENTS

This exercise includes the usual self-assessment for each chapter, plus an evaluation of peers and developing measures of performance.

Objective

To develop your skill at assessing your performance and that of your peers

To develop your skill at developing measures of performance

Skills

The primary skills developed through this exercise are as follows:

1. *HR management skill*—conceptual and design skills
2. *SHRM 2013 Curriculum Guidebook*—H: Performance management

Assignment Part 1—Self-Assessment

During your college courses, you most likely had to do some form of group assignments, and you've also done group assignments in this course. Select one group you worked with, and based on your performance in that group, do a self-evaluation using the rating scale form below.

Evaluator (you) _____ (Self-Evaluation)

	A A– Always	B+ B B– Usually	C+ C C– Frequently	D+ D D– Sometimes	F Rarely
Did a "good" analysis of project					
Developed "good" questions to ask					
Actively participated (truly interested/involved)					
Made "quality" effort and contributions					
Got along well with group members					
Displayed leadership					
List at least three of your own measures of performance here					
Class attendance—number of absences	0–1	2	3	4	5+
Attendance at group meetings to prepare group project—number of absences	0	1	2	3	4+
Managed the group's time well					

This exercise can stop with just a self-assessment, or it can continue to also include peer evaluations.

Assignment Part 2—Peer Review

1. Part 2 begins by conducting a peer evaluation using the above form for each of the other members in your group, but using this heading for the form:

   Group Member _____
   (Peer Evaluation)

   Either copy the above form for each group member, do your assessment on any sheet without using the form,
   or have your instructor provide you with multiple forms that you can complete for each group member.

2. Below, rank each group member (including yourself) based on their performance. The first person you list should be the best performer, and the last person you list should be the least effective performer, based on the performance appraisal above. If members are close or equal in performance, you may assign them the same rank number, but you must list the better one first.

3. To the right of each group member (including your-self), place the overall letter grade (A–F) you would assign to that member based on the performance appraisal. You may give more than one member the same grade if those individuals deserve the same grade. You may also use plus and minus grades.

Rank	Name	Grade
_____	_____	_____
_____	_____	_____
_____	_____	_____
_____	_____	_____
_____	_____	_____

••• SKILL BUILDER 8-2 DEBRIEFING THE APPRAISAL

Note: This exercise is designed for groups that have been working together for some time as part of the course requirements. It is a continuation of Skill Builder 8-1. Based on your peer evaluations, you will conduct performance appraisals for your group members.

Objective

To develop a plan to improve your team performance, and to develop your skills in conducting performance appraisals

Skills

The primary skills developed through this exercise are as follows:

1. *HR management skill*–Conceptual and design skills
2. *SHRM 2013 Curriculum Guidebook*—H: Performance management

Assignment

You will be both the evaluator and evaluatee. Get together with group members and have each member select a letter, beginning with the letter A. Pair off as follows: A and B, C and D, E and F, etc. If the group consists of an odd number of people, each member will sit out one round. A should conduct the evaluation interview for B, C should conduct the evaluation interview for D, etc., using the form in Skill Builder 8-1. The evaluators should follow up the evaluation interview with the developmental interview to give suggestions on improving B, D, and F's performance (be sure to follow the evaluative and developmental interview steps in Models 8-1 and 8-2). Make sure you are evaluators and evaluatees; do not be peers having a discussion. When you finish, or when the instructor tells you time is up, reverse roles of evaluators and evaluatees. B, D, and F will become the new evaluators for A, C, and E.

When the instructor tells you to, or when time is up, form new groups of two and decide who will be the evaluators first. Continue changing groups of two until every group member has appraised and been appraised by every other group member.

Apply It

What did I learn from this experience? How will I improve my group performance in the course? How will I use this knowledge in the future?

_____

_____

©iStockphoto.com/Neustockimages

9 Rights and Employee Management

••• LEARNING OUTCOMES

After studying this chapter, you should be able to do the following:

9-1 Discuss the difference between a right and a privilege in a work context.

9-2 Identify the commonly accepted individual rights in the workplace.

9-3 Identify the rights that management has in modern organizations.

9-4 Briefly describe the coaching process and how it is used.

9-5 Describe the management counseling process and when it is useful.

9-6 Briefly discuss the tests for Just Cause used in disciplinary investigations.

9-7 Describe the concept of progressive discipline in the organization, including the stages of progressive discipline.

9-8 Discuss the two common situations in which an employee might be immediately discharged from the company.

9-9 Identify the factors that positive leadership takes into account to be successful.

9-10 Briefly discuss the stages of the change process.

9-11 Identify the factors that can help overcome resistance to change in organizations.

9-12 Define the key terms found in the chapter margins and listed following the Chapter Summary.

Practitioner's Perspective

Cindy says, "If it isn't documented, it didn't happen."

That's a common expression in health care settings, and it stresses the importance of record keeping for patient care. The same holds true for management of personnel issues.

"I've had it with Jeremy!" Leonard exploded when Cindy returned his phone call one morning. "I've told him a million times how to run this report, and he won't follow my instructions! If he makes one more mistake, that's it—he's out of here."

"Whoa, Leonard," Cindy soothed. "You know our policy advises progressive discipline. Are you documenting your issues with Jeremy? Have you tried nondisciplinary counseling or a written warning?"

"I don't have time for all that nonsense," scoffed Leonard. "I should be able to fire any employee I want!"

"If you haven't been keeping records to back up your management of Jeremy's performance issues, discharge is not your first option," Cindy cautioned.

For the sake of due process in disciplinary matters, supervisors must document that an employee was informed of performance issues and given an opportunity to improve. You will find helpful information on employee versus management rights and related legal requirements in Chapter 9.

SHRM HR CONTENT

See Appendix: *SHRM 2013 Curriculum Guidebook* for the complete list

A. Employee and Labor Relations (required)

1. Disciplinary actions: Demotion, disciplinary termination

7. Managing teams

22. Investigations

27. Employee records

B. Employment Law (required)

19. Employee privacy

30. Employment-at-will doctrine

C. Ethics (required)

5. Guidelines and codes

6. Behavior within ethical boundaries

H. Performance Management (required)

8. Diagnosing problems

9. Performance improvement programs

I. Staffing: Recruitment and Selection (required)

14. Job offers: Employment-at-will, contracts, authorization to work

M. Workforce Planning and Talent Management (required)

3. Retention: Involuntary turnover, outplacement counseling, alternative dispute resolution

N. Change Management (required–graduate students only)

1. Stages of change management

3. Communication

4. Building trust

6. Leading change

7. Planning change strategy

8. Implementing change

Q. Organization Development (required–graduate students only)

1. Coaching

7. Leadership development

X. Workplace Health, Safety, and Security (secondary)

12. Monitoring, surveillance, privacy

MANAGING AND LEADING YOUR WORKFORCE

To remain competitive today, organizations must continually develop and manage their employees' knowledge and skills to encourage employee engagement.[1] Effective employee engagement leads to committed, motivated employees who then increase performance.[2]

In this chapter, we follow up on the developmental interview to continuously improve individual performance through coaching, counseling, and finally to disciplining or terminating employees who cannot or will not perform to acceptable standards. In addition to individual development, we discuss team development through positive leadership, team building, and managing change.

However, before we can develop, discipline, or terminate individual employees and before we can develop high-performance teams, we need to understand employee and management rights to ensure that we don't violate those rights by disciplining employees unethically or illegally. So in this chapter we begin by discussing commonly accepted employee rights and management rights. Based on this foundation, we proceed to developing or disciplining individual employees and then to developing teams. As usual, we end with trends and issues in HRM.

COMMONLY ACCEPTED EMPLOYEE RIGHTS

In this section, we discuss six employee rights; see Exhibit 9-1 for a list.[3] However, before we discuss employee rights, we need to understand the difference between a right and a privilege.

Rights and Privileges

LO 9-1

Discuss the difference between a right and a privilege in a work context.

Individual rights are the topic of much conversation in our society today. However, how many of us actually know the difference between a right and a privilege? If we listen, we constantly hear statements such as "I have a right to drive my car the way I want," or "I have a right to go to college." Are such statements correct? In fact both of these statements describe privileges, not rights.

Privileges *are things that individuals are allowed to do based on asking permission from an authority.* In simple terms, a privilege must be *earned* because the individual does something successfully (like passing a driver's test or getting good grades in high school), while a right is provided to the individual by the society in which they are a member. We don't have a right to drive, especially not any way we want. Driving is a privilege based on the individual showing that they have knowledge of the correct way to drive so that they can avoid doing harm to others.

On the other hand, a right does not require the individual to do anything in order to gain that right *at that time in that society.* **Rights** *are things a person in a society is allowed to do without any permission required from an authority.* Rights are bestowed upon the individual based on their membership in the society.

The simple way to tell the difference between a right and a privilege in an organization is this: If the employee has to request permission to do something within the organization, then the employee is attempting to exercise a privilege. On the other hand, employees do not need permission to exercise their rights.

In general, employees have several rights. Because these are rights in the sense noted in the above paragraph, the individual employee doesn't have to do anything to gain these rights. Because the employee is a part of this society (the organization), they gain these rights. The organization has a *duty* to protect each employee's rights.

EXHIBIT 9-1   EMPLOYEE RIGHTS

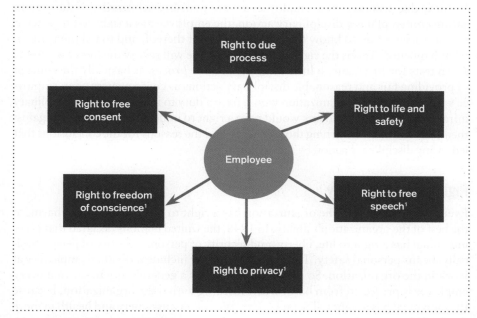

¹ Note that these three rights have limitations.

Privileges Things that individuals are allowed to do based on asking permission from an authority

Rights Things a person in a society is allowed to do without any permission required from an authority

WORK
APPLICATION 9-1

Give examples of rights and privileges where you work or have worked.

LO 9-2

Identify the commonly accepted individual rights in the workplace.

WORK
APPLICATION 9-2 AND 9-3

Give an example of how your present or past employer met your right to free consent. What did you consent to do on the job?

Have you ever not consented to do something on the job? If yes, give an example of what you refused to do.

WORK
APPLICATION 9-4

Briefly describe the due process rights where you work or have worked.

WORK
APPLICATION 9-5

Briefly describe some of the life and safety issues where you work or have worked. If applicable, give an example of how someone was hurt.

A duty, or obligation, is a societal (company) responsibility to protect the individual's (employee) rights. The individual employee *also* has a duty to avoid violating the rights of other employees in the course of exercising their own rights. So rights are always balanced by duties or responsibilities.

So what do these rights allow an individual within the organization to do, and what limitations are there on the three "limited" rights that we noted in Exhibit 9-1? Let's break down each of the six rights individually in separate sections.

Right of Free Consent

Individuals in a modern organization have the *right of free consent*, which is the right of the individual to know what they're being asked to do and the consequences of that action to the individual or others, either inside or outside the organization. People should know what they are being asked to do in their jobs, and they shouldn't be forced, manipulated, or deceived into working in situations that could cause harm. The organization's duty is to ensure that the individual *voluntarily agrees* to do a particular job or task for the organization, making them fully aware of everything involved. The organization would be violating the individual's right to free consent if it forced the person to do something against their will or manipulated them in some way to do something that they would not do if they knew all of the circumstances.

A great example of the right to free consent was shown after the Japan earthquake and ensuing tsunami in March 2011. Several nuclear reactors were damaged, and workers were needed to go into areas with significant danger.[4] The workers needed to be told about the dangers from both radiation and potentially explosive gases that they would encounter by taking on the job of working on the reactors. If the workers had not been told the extent of the danger, the company (**Tokyo Electric Power Company**) would have violated their right to free consent. For the right of free consent to be in effect, the workers would have to be given enough information so that they could understand the danger and then freely agree to do the job.

Right to Due Process

We have due process so that employees are not punished arbitrarily.[5] If the organization contemplates a disciplinary action, the employee has a right to know what they are accused of, to know the evidence or proof thereof, and to tell their side of what happened. This is the right to due process. We will review due process and the seven tests for Just Cause a little bit later, but *due process* is basically the concept of providing fair and reasonable disciplinary actions as consequences of an employee's behavior. So, the organization would have a duty to investigate any disciplinary infractions, and the employees would have a right to understand the charges against them, the evidence concerning those charges, and the reasons for the conclusions that led to any disciplinary action by the organization.

Right to Life and Safety

Every employee within the organization has a right to be protected from harm, to the best of the organization's ability. In 1948, the United Nations declared that every individual has a right to life, liberty, and security of person.[6] Security of person basically means personal safety. This would obviously include individual employees at work in the organization. So the organization has a general duty to see that every employee is protected from harm when working within the organization, because the individual has a right to life and safety. We will discuss safety and health in more detail in Chapter 14.

Right of Freedom of Conscience (Limited)

Employees generally should not be asked to do something that violates their personal values and beliefs, *as long as these beliefs generally reflect commonly accepted societal norms*. A person's conscience determines what that person considers to be right and wrong. The organization has a general duty to avoid forcing an individual to do something that they consider to be wrong, either morally or ethically, and the individual has a right to avoid doing things within the organization that would violate their personal values and beliefs.

However, this doesn't mean that a person can accept a job in, for example, a medical lab working on cancer cures, then refuse to work with living human cells because their moral convictions prohibit that, and then be free from any threat of termination of their employment. The organization would generally have the right in this case to terminate the worker for noncompliance with legitimate requirements associated with the job, since it would be almost certain that the individual would know of these requirements before accepting the job.

Right to Privacy (Limited)

This right protects people from unreasonable or unwarranted intrusions into their personal affairs. This general right to privacy would include the employee's right to have their personnel files, other employee records, and/or private areas of their workplace (such as a personal locker) kept private, *to an extent*. The organization would have a general duty to protect individual employee privacy in most cases, whether dealing with the employee's private life, personal history, or private areas in the workplace.

However, if the employer feels that there might be a hazard to others, then a locker or other personal space (e.g., a desk) could be searched. For example, if an employee reports to one of the organization's managers that another employee has a weapon in a personal space (such as their locker), then the organization probably has a right to search the individual's locker.

Another limitation on privacy is in email to and from company addresses. The employer again has a right to review any information in these types of correspondence to protect other employees and the organization.

Right to Free Speech (Limited)

The First Amendment to the US Constitution guarantees the right to freedom of speech. What most people don't understand, though, is that the First Amendment only applies to the government not being allowed to control free speech. In the workplace, individual freedom of speech is limited, based on many years of case law. Within the organization itself, individuals should be free to express concerns or discontent with organizational policies without fear of harm. Allowing such expression provides the organization an opportunity to see that problems exist, and it gives them the opportunity to correct these problems. Employees have legal protection to blow the whistle on an organization that is involved in illegal activities; in other

Organizations need to make all jobs as safe as feasibly possible.

WORK
APPLICATION 9-6

Give an example of when employees were encouraged to conduct unethical or illegal activities. Try to give an example from an organization where you work or have worked, but otherwise, give an example from another source, such as the news media.

SHRM

A:27
Employee Records

SHRM

B:19
Employee Privacy

WORK
APPLICATION 9-7

How do you feel about management going through your personal space (desk, locker, etc.) and monitoring the equipment (computer, telephone, etc.) you use to see if you are using it for personal reasons?

WORK
APPLICATION 9-8

How do you feel about employees communicating negative things about the organization to outsiders? Should management monitor employee speech and take action to stop negative speech?

LO 9-3

Identify the rights that management has in modern organizations.

words, employers can't fire or discriminate against an employee for telling others about the organization's illegal activities. (We will talk more about whistle-blowers in the next chapter.)

However, many types of speech have no protection. If the individual employee exercises the right to freedom of speech, and if, in the course of that action, the employee harms the organization or other employees, then the organization has a right to discipline the employee based on the harm that the employee did to others. For example, an organization in the private sector can discipline an employee for using demeaning language toward another employee, even though the first employee might assert the right to free speech. This is due to the requirement to maintain good order and discipline in an organization so work can be produced.

In another case, a manager might verbally and *publicly* disagree with a corporate policy. The manager certainly has a right to do so, but the organization would also have a right to discipline or even terminate the manager because of such actions, again based on maintenance of good order and discipline in the organization. In such a case, managers are generally held to a higher standard than nonmanagerial employees. You may remember the case of the president of **Chick-fil-A** saying that the company supported the "biblical definition of the family unit."[7] Or you might recall Phil Robertson of TV's **Duck Dynasty** "equating homosexuality to bestiality" in a **GQ** article.[8] These men were both criticized by politicians, news outlets, gay and lesbian organizations, and other individuals over their remarks. In fact, both were boycotted and picketed by multiple groups, and Robertson was suspended from his own show for a short period. So here again, the organization has a right to limit the rights of the individual employee (especially high-level employees) because of the harm that they could cause to others in the organization and to the organization itself.

MANAGEMENT RIGHTS

You'll notice that, for each of the rights that we've identified as limited, we've said the organization has a *right* to limit the individual employee's rights in order

---

9-1 APPLYING THE CONCEPT

Employee Rights

Review the list of rights below and write the letter corresponding to each right before the statement involving that right.

a. free consent
b. due process
c. life and safety
d. freedom of conscience
e. privacy
f. free speech

____ 1. The HR manager made me sign this form before I could start the job, stating that she had told me about the possible side effects from the lead paint removal.

____ 2. I enjoy writing negative comments online about my boss and company.

____ 3. I'm going to teach you how to use the rifle. Rule number one is to always make sure this lever is down so you don't fire the gun by accident.

____ 4. You can't discipline me for this minor safety violation. I'm going to the labor union to stop you from doing it.

____ 5. Let me keep working in security. I don't want to work in the bar, even though it pays better, because drinking is against my religion.

____ 6. Get out of my locker now. You have no right to search it without my permission.

to protect the firm. Organizations, like individuals, have rights within the larger society. Organizational rights tend to be based on the necessity for the organization to protect itself and its employees from persons that might do them harm, whether intentionally or unintentionally. While some of these rights (such as limiting certain discussions about work conditions and requiring civility in conversations between employees) have been weakened by recent labor rulings, organizations still have a set of rights that let them protect themselves and their people.

So for example, if the organization had reasonable evidence or proof that an individual had a weapon, or was harassing or bullying a coworker, or was providing organizational secrets to a competitor, we would generally have a right to investigate the individual in order to protect the organization and its other employees. Similarly, the organization has a right to determine whether or not the employee's free speech does harm to the organization or other employees that exceeds the individual's limited free speech rights. In other words, does the harm to the organization and other employees outweigh the rights of the individual to say what they want? So managers in the firm have to weigh the individual's rights against the potential harm that could be done to the organization by allowing the individual to exercise those rights.

What other rights do organizations have? In this section, we discuss six management rights; see Exhibit 9-2 for a list.

Codes of Conduct

Managers of organizations have a right to create and require compliance with a code of employee conduct. The code of conduct is the organization's mechanism for identifying the ethics and values of the firm, and it serves as a guide to individual action.[9] Research shows that making a decision without using an ethical guide leads to less ethical choices,[10] so ethical guidelines can have a positive influence.[11]

EXHIBIT 9-2   MANAGEMENT RIGHTS

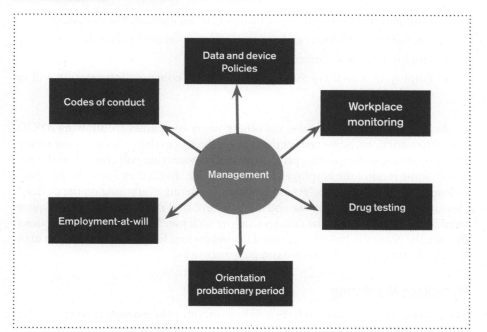

SHRM

C:5
Guidelines and Codes

SHRM

C:6
Behavior Within Ethical Boundaries

WORK
APPLICATION 9-9

Give examples of behaviors that are not acceptable in an organization where you work or have worked.

Employees are more unethical when they believe they will not get caught and punished.[12] Thus, most codes of conduct today also note the consequences that can occur if an employee does not follow the requirements in the code. A code of conduct gives an employee a practical tool for determining whether or not an action that they are contemplating is within the acceptable boundaries of conduct within their organization.

Virtually all organizations have a code of conduct. Generally, the larger the firm, the more likely the code of conduct will be in a written document or multiple documents.[13] Most large companies also have a specific section of the code of conduct, or a separate document known as the code of ethics, that spells out what is and is not ethical behavior.

Data and Device Policies

Employers have the right to create workplace policies to protect organizational data and to maintain control of their networks.[14] However, maintaining that control becomes much more difficult when many different computing devices are allowed to connect to the organization's network.

Let's take a look at one of the newest policy trends—the bring-your-own-device (BYOD) movement, which has been adopted by around 60% of US companies, including **Carfax, Kimberly-Clark, Kraft,** and **Citrix**.[15] BYOD is basically what it sounds like: The company allows employees to bring their own laptop, tablet, smartphone, etc. to work and connect that device to the company network. There are good reasons for allowing this, but there are also some problems. Reasons for allowing BYOD include the following:[16]

- It may increase productivity and employee satisfaction.
- It helps in recruiting new employees.
- It can strengthen work-life balance.
- It reduces computer hardware costs for the organization.

However, these benefits come with a host of problems, including the following:

- Multiple types of security risks, including leaks, hacking, lost devices, etc.
- The mixing of company and personal information on the same device
- Employee privacy concerns
- Employees who leave the organization with company information still on their device

As a result of the above issues and others, many companies are allowing BYOD, but with restrictions. Some restrict the types of devices to those that are more secure. Many require specific security programs on all devices that will connect to the network. Some require the employee to acknowledge that if they leave the company or lose the device, it will be "remotely wiped," deleting everything on the device.[17] Having policies covering the use and management of BYOD is an absolute requirement in any organization that decides to allow such use.[18] Regardless of the policies, though, the company has the right (*and* the obligation, for privacy reasons) to manage any device connected to secure company networks.

SHRM

X:12
Monitoring, Surveillance, Privacy

Workplace Monitoring

Managers in the organization have a right to monitor the workplace to ensure that employees are acting both legally and ethically in all of the actions that they take on behalf of the organization. One form of monitoring that we already discussed in earlier chapters is the website monitoring that companies may undertake in an attempt to ensure that employees and others don't defame the organization. Companies may also do monitoring and analysis of computer and network use within the firm, video monitoring of work spaces, and recording of phone conversations and emails. Workplace monitoring provides the organization with a mechanism to protect itself and its employees from individual actions that might harm them.

Keeping the organization's assets and employees safe takes monitoring.

Employment-at-Will

Currently, under common law, "employment relationships are presumed to be 'at will' in all US states except Montana."[19] The concept of **employment-at-will** *allows the company or the worker to break the work relationship at any point in time, with or without any particular reason, as long as in doing so, no law is violated.* This is one of management's rights in organizations, meaning the employer does not have to have *cause* (reasons) to terminate an employment relationship with an individual worker. If an organization states that employment in the firm is at-will, then it is typically presumed that the worker has no contractual rights to a continuing job with the firm.

However, employment-at-will is in reality a fairly weak law because courts in many jurisdictions in the United States have for many years ruled that employment-at-will is limited. The courts have specifically stated that there are three *standard exceptions* to employment-at-will.[20] *Public policy exceptions* to employment-at-will include such things as being terminated for filing a legitimate worker's compensation claim, refusing to lobby for a particular political candidate just because your boss likes the candidate, or refusing to violate a professional code of ethics. In other words, if the organization were violating vital public interests, and if the worker refused to participate, then the organization would not have a right to terminate the individual's employment based on employment-at-will.

The courts have also noted that frequently, there is at least some evidence of an *implied contract* between the employee and the employer. For instance, if the company were to note in its employee handbook that "our organization values hard work, and many of our employees who perform well have been with us for many years," that *might* be considered an implied contract stating, "If you work hard, we will continue to employ you." This implication of a contract could negate the employment-at-will rights of the employer.

A third case in which courts have ruled that there are exceptions to employment-at-will occurs when employers are suspected of *lack of good faith and fair dealing* in the employment relationship. In other words, if the employer does something that will benefit them significantly but will harm the individual employee, that action would create a lack of good faith and fair dealing. For instance, we might release an older employee shortly before they become eligible for a company-sponsored retirement plan in order to hire a younger (and cheaper) employee in the same position and thus not have to pay the retirement benefits. This would be lack of good faith and fair dealing, in addition to probably being against age discrimination laws.

Orientation (Probationary) Periods

Organizations have a right to set up an orientation, or introductory, period for new employees. Many of you may be familiar with the older term *probationary period*.

SHRM
B:30
Employment-at-Will Doctrine

SHRM
I:14
Job Offers: Employment-at-Will, etc.

Employment-at-will Concept allowing the company or the worker to break the work relationship at any point in time, with or without any particular reason, as long as in doing so, no law is violated

9-2 APPLYING THE CONCEPT

Management Rights

Review the list of rights below and then write the letter corresponding to each right before the statement or situation involving that right.

a. code of conduct
b. workplace monitoring
c. employment-at-will
d. orientation period
e. drug testing

_____ 7. I'm sorry, but you've been with us for a month and you haven't been able to meet the standards of your job, so we are letting you go.

_____ 8. Our records show that you have been using your computer for an average of an hour and a half per day on personal things.

_____ 9. We seem to have a personality conflict, so you're fired.

_____ 10. As part of the selection process, you will have to pass a physical exam that includes a urinalysis.

_____ 11. I found out that you paid a bribe to get that sales order with the Acamey company. Come with me to the HR department for disciplinary action.

WORK APPLICATION 9-10

How long is the typical orientation period where you work or have worked?

WORK APPLICATION 9-11

How do you feel about companies giving drug tests? Does an organization you work for or have worked for require drug tests?

This term has fallen out of favor with organizations due to the fact that courts have said that completion of a probationary period may give employees additional rights in the workplace, even if employment in the workplace is ostensibly at-will. Regardless of what it is called, the orientation period allows the organization a certain amount of time in which to assess new employees and their capabilities, before fully integrating them into the organization. The orientation period usually runs from 60 to 90 days, but it can be much longer in some organizations that provide significant training to new entrants.

Drug Testing

As we first noted in Chapter 6, "Most employers have the right to test for a wide variety of substances in the workplace.[21] While drug testing is not required in most cases, employers can put testing programs in place. The primary reason for drug testing will generally be workplace safety." So, drug testing is another major employer right. But always remember that drug testing needs to be done in either a universal or a random form.

COACHING, COUNSELING, AND DISCIPLINE

Organizations hire new employees in the hope that they will become productive workers. Ongoing employee development has three parts—coaching, counseling, and disciplining—but not all three parts are needed in all cases. As discussed in Chapter 8, managers need to continually coach virtually all employees to improve performance. Sometimes, employees will have on- or off-the-job problems and the manager should get them professional counseling through the HR department. Some employees will break the code of conduct, and the manager will need to take disciplinary action; in some cases, managers will need to terminate these employees. Also, if employees cannot meet job standards, they should be terminated. In this section, we discuss employee development through coaching, counseling, disciplining, and (if necessary) termination.

Coaching

Coaching includes a variety of behavioral techniques and methods to help improve performance.[22] Good coaching also improves communications and relationships.[23] **Coaching** *is the process of giving motivational feedback to maintain and improve*

LO 9-4

Briefly describe the coaching process and how it is used.

Coaching The process of giving motivational feedback to maintain and improve performance

performance. Coaching focuses on helping employees succeed by monitoring performance and giving feedback. Such feedback is intended to praise progress, to redirect inappropriate behavior, and to counsel employees on how to improve.[24] Employees who are given more immediate, frequent, and direct feedback perform at higher levels than those who are not given such feedback.[25]

Many people who hear the word *coaching* immediately think of athletes, but coaching is also an important management skill that is used to get the best results from each employee.[26] As implied in the definition of coaching, feedback is the central part of coaching, and the feedback should be motivational.[27] In other words, you should give more positive than negative feedback.[28]

DETERMINING CORRECTIVE COACHING ACTION. Coaching is needed when performance falls below aspirational levels.[29] When an employee is not performing up to potential, even when acceptable standards are being met, the first step is to determine why,[30] using the performance formula: Performance = Ability × Motivation × Resources. When lack of ability is holding back performance, training is needed. A good manager is also a good teacher, so when something isn't done properly, we should teach employees how to do it correctly.[31] When motivation is lacking, motivational techniques, such as coaching, may help.[32] Talk to the employee to try to determine why motivation is lacking, and develop a plan together to improve performance.[33] If motivational coaching does not work, you may have to use discipline,[34] which will be discussed later. Finally, when resources are lacking, you should work to obtain them.

THE COACHING MODEL. Coaching is a way to provide ongoing feedback to employees about their job performance.[35] However, ask managers what they tend to put off doing, and they'll likely say that they put off advising weak employees that they must improve their performance. Procrastinating managers often hope that the employees will turn around on their own, only to find—often too late—that the situation just continues to get worse. Part of the problem is that managers don't know how to coach or are not good at coaching,[36] so let's take a look at a simple coaching model that's designed to improve performance.[37] Model 9-1 presents a four-step coaching model.

Step 1: Describe current performance. Using specific examples, describe the current behavior that needs to be changed. Tell the employees exactly what they are not doing as well as they can. Notice the positive; don't tell them only what they are doing wrong.

For example, don't say, "You are picking up the box wrong." Say, "Billie, there is a more effective way of picking the box up off the floor than bending at the waist."

Step 2: Describe desired performance. Tell the employees exactly what the desired performance is, in detail. Show how they will benefit from following your advice.

If performance is *ability* related, training is needed. Good managers know that training is a large part of their job, and they constantly look at situations as training opportunities. If the employees know the proper way, then the problem is *motivational*, and training is most likely not needed. The manager may just describe the desired performance and ask the employees to state why the performance is important. So if the issue is one of ability, you might tell the employees, "If you squat down

MODEL 9-1   COACHING MODEL

1. Describe current performance → 2. Describe desired performance → 3. Get a commitment to change → 4. Follow up

WORK
APPLICATION 9-12

Assess your present or past boss's coaching skills. Did the boss follow the steps in the coaching model?

and pick up the box using your legs instead of your back, it is easier and there is less chance of injuring yourself. Let me demonstrate for you." But if the issue is one of motivation, you might ask the employees, "Why should you squat and use your legs rather than your back to pick up boxes?"

Step 3: Get a commitment to the change. When dealing with an ability issue, it is not necessary to get employees to verbally commit to the change if they seem willing to make it. However, if employees defend their way and you're sure it's not as effective as another way, explain why your proposed way is better. If you cannot get the employees to understand and agree, then get a verbal commitment. This step is also important for motivational issues, because if the employees are not willing to commit to the change, they will most likely not make the change.

So if the issue is one of ability, the employee will most likely be willing to pick up boxes correctly, and you can skip this step. But if the issue is one of motivation, then you might get a commitment from the employee by asking, "Will you squat rather than use your back from now on?"

Step 4: Follow up. Remember that some employees (those with low and moderate capability for self-control) do what managers *inspect* (imposed control), not what they *expect*. You should follow up to ensure that employees are behaving as desired.

When dealing with an *ability* issue, if the person was receptive and you skipped step 3, say nothing. However, watch to be sure that the activity is done correctly in the future. Coach again, if necessary. For a *motivation* problem, make a statement that you will follow up and that there are possible consequences for lack of progress. You may also want to set up a follow-up meeting to review progress, especially if the behavior is complex.[38]

LO 9-5

Describe the management counseling process and when it is useful.

SHRM

H:8
Diagnosing Problems

Management counseling The process of giving employees feedback (so they realize that a problem is affecting their job performance) and referring employees with problems that cannot be managed within the work structure to the organization's employee assistance program

Counseling

When you are coaching, you are fine-tuning performance. But when you are counseling and disciplining, you are dealing with an employee who is not performing to organizational standards. Good organizations realize the need to help employees with problems.[39]

When most people hear the term *counseling*, they think of psychological counseling or psychotherapy. That type of sophisticated help should not be attempted by a noncounseling professional such as a manager. Instead, **management counseling** *is the process of giving employees feedback (so they realize that a problem is affecting their job performance) and referring employees with problems that cannot be managed within the work structure to the organization's employee assistance program.*

TYPES OF PROBLEM EMPLOYEES. Problem employees have a negative effect on performance.[40] Good human resource management skills can help you avoid hiring problem employees,[41] but even so, you will most likely have to confront problem employees as a manager.[42] Problem employees display behavioral and performance-related issues. They do poor-quality work, they don't get along with coworkers, they display negative attitudes, and they frequently don't show up for work.[43]

There are four types of problem employees:

1. Employees who do not have the *ability* to meet the job performance standards. Having such employees on staff is an unfortunate situation, but if such employees cannot do a good job even after receiving extra training, they should be dismissed. Keeping an individual who cannot do a particular job not only harms the organization; it also harms the individual employee. Continued inability to perform will always lead to frustration, and frustration ultimately leads to lower job satisfaction and employee engagement.

2. Employees who do not have the *motivation* to meet job performance standards. These employees often need discipline.

3. Employees who intentionally *violate the rules or the code of conduct.* As a manager, it is your job to enforce the rules through disciplinary action when employees intentionally violate rules, regulations, or procedures.[44]

4. Employees with *problems.* These employees may have the ability to do their job, but they have a problem that affects their job performance. The problem may not be related to the job. It is common for personal problems, such as child care problems and relationship/marital problems, to affect job performance. Employees with problems should be counseled before they are disciplined.

WORK
APPLICATION 9-13

Identify a problem employee you have observed on the job. Describe how the person affected the department's performance.

Exhibit 9-3 lists some problem employees you may encounter as a manager. It is not always easy to distinguish between the types of problem employees. Therefore, it is often advisable to start with coaching/counseling and change to discipline if the problem persists.

PERSONAL PROBLEMS AND PERFORMANCE. Most managers do not like to hear the details of their employees' personal problems, in many cases because they don't know what to do about those problems. Taking action on such personal problems is not a requirement. Instead, the manager's role is to help employees realize that they have problems, to show them how those problems affect their work, and to get the employees back on track so that they can perform at an acceptable level.

The manager should not give advice on how to solve personal problems such as relationship difficulties. When professional help is needed, the manager should refer the employee to the human resources department for professional help through the employee assistance program.[45] **Employee assistance programs (EAPs)** *provide a staff of people who help employees get professional assistance in solving their problems.* Most large businesses have an EAP to help solve employees' personal problems.

EXHIBIT 9-3   PROBLEM EMPLOYEES

- The late employee
- The absent employee
- The dishonest employee
- The violent or destructive employee
- The alcoholic or drug user
- The nonconformist
- The employee with a family problem
- The insubordinate employee
- The employee who steals
- The sexual or racial harasser
- The safety violator
- The sick employee
- The employee who's often socializing or doing personal work while on the job

Employee assistance programs (EAPs) Programs providing a staff of people who help employees get professional assistance in solving their problems

To make the referral, a manager might say something like "Are you aware of our employee assistance program? Would you like me to set up an appointment with Jean in the HR department to help you get professional assistance?" However, if the employee's job performance does not return to standard, discipline is appropriate because it often makes the employee realize the seriousness of the problem and the importance of maintaining job performance. Some time off from work—with or without pay, depending on the situation—often helps the employee deal with the problem.

A manager's first obligation is to the organization's performance rather than to individual employees. Not taking action with problem employees—because you feel uncomfortable confronting them, because you feel sorry for them, or because you like them—does not help you or the employee.[46] Not only do problem employees negatively affect their own productivity, but they also cause more work for managers and other employees. Problem employees also lower morale, as others resent them for not pulling their own weight. Thus, it is critical to take quick action with problem employees.[47]

Disciplining

Coaching, which includes counseling, should generally be the first step in dealing with a problem employee. However, if an employee is unwilling or unable to change or a rule has been broken, discipline is necessary.[48] Managers can't allow employees to engage in counterproductive work behavior,[49] to be uncivil at work,[50] to be vengeful, or to show other deviant behavior. [51] Discipline can also be appropriate if an employee is guilty of doing personal tasks (many employees spend hours per day on the phone and computer for personal reasons) while on company time.[52] Many organizations have found it necessary to fire employees for inappropriate use of time and resources.[53]

Discipline *is corrective action designed to get employees to meet standards and the code of conduct.* The major objective of coaching, counseling, and disciplining is to change behavior.[54] Secondary objectives may be to let employees know that action will be taken when standing plans or performance requirements are not met, and to maintain authority when challenged. Generally, abusive supervisors[55] who yell[56] and hold grudges[57] encounter more discipline problems among their subordinates than do nonabusive supervisors.[58]

The human resources department handles many of the disciplinary details and provides written disciplinary procedures. These procedures usually outline grounds for specific sanctions and dismissal, based on the types of violations. Common offenses include theft, sexual or other types of harassment, verbal or substance abuse, and safety violations.[59] However, in unionized environments, you have to be careful because some union contracts allow employees to delay or block disciplinary action.[60]

But how do we know as managers that we are being fair in applying discipline? Let's take a look at one mechanism for determining whether or not to discipline an errant employee and what level of discipline is appropriate—Just Cause.

JUST CAUSE. **Just Cause** *is actually a set of standard tests for fairness in disciplinary actions—tests that were originally utilized in union grievance arbitrations.* However, many companies other than unionized companies have adopted tests for Just Cause in their own nonunion disciplinary processes to try to ensure *fairness* and *due process* in applying discipline with their employees. Just Cause standards try to ensure that we investigate any disciplinary infraction fully and fairly and provide disciplinary action that matches the level of the offense.

LO 9-6

Briefly discuss the tests for Just Cause used in disciplinary investigations.

Discipline Corrective action designed to get employees to meet standards and the code of conduct

Just Cause A set of standard tests for fairness in disciplinary actions—tests that were originally utilized in union grievance arbitrations

The seven tests for Just Cause are as follows:

A:22
Investigations

SHRM

1. Did the company give the employee forewarning or foreknowledge of the possible or probable disciplinary consequences of the employee's conduct?

   With this test, we basically want to determine whether or not the employee was given any knowledge beforehand that the action was prohibited. If they were told in some form, such as through the employee handbook or a posting in the workplace, then we meet this first test for Just Cause.

2. Was the company's rule or managerial order reasonably related to (a) the orderly, efficient, and safe operation of the company's business and (b) the performance that the company might properly expect of the employee?

   Here we want to find out whether the rule was reasonable. We look at orderly, efficient, and safe operations to see whether the rule or order is reasonable or not. We also look at whether or not the employee should be expected to act in a certain manner in order to follow the rule or order. If the rule was reasonable and the employee should have been expected to act a certain way, then we have met the second test.

3. Did the company, before administering discipline to an employee, make an effort to discover whether the employee did in fact violate or disobey a rule or order of management?

   Test 3 deals with investigation of the alleged infraction. The supervisor needs to investigate what happened and why it happened. If, upon investigating, the supervisor finds that there is reasonable evidence that the individual did violate the rules, then we've passed the third test.

4. Was the company's investigation conducted fairly and objectively?

   In test 4, we're looking for evidence that the investigation was conducted in the same manner as any other investigation into similar circumstances would have been. Are we utilizing facts, figures, and knowledge of the events (the OUCH test), or is the supervisor basing the investigation on some emotional reaction to the supposed infraction? If we determine that the investigation was conducted in a reasonably fair and objective manner, we meet the fourth test.

5. Upon investigation, was there substantial evidence or proof that the employee was guilty as charged?

   Test 5 asks whether or not we have substantial evidence or proof of guilt on the part of the employee. *Substantial evidence* is a large body of circumstantial information showing that the individual probably committed the offense. In a disciplinary action, we don't have to meet court standards of proof of guilt. We only have to have a substantial amount of evidence that the infraction was committed. If we have *proof*, then we meet this test, but if we have substantial evidence, we *still* meet the requirements of test 5.

6. Has the company applied its rules, orders, and penalties evenhandedly and without discrimination to all employees?

   Test 6 tries to identify whether or not the rule is applied in an equitable manner. If the company punishes one person for an infraction with a written reprimand and punishes another person for the same infraction with a disciplinary discharge, then the company may not have been evenhanded in its disciplinary action. Does this mean that we have to punish every person in the exact same way for the exact same infraction? The answer is no—and that is where we get into test 7.

WORK
APPLICATION 9-14

Assess how well your boss and the organization you work or worked for follows the Just Cause standards.

7. Was the degree of discipline administered by the company in a particular case reasonably related to (a) the seriousness of the employee's proven offense and (b) the record of the employee's service with the company?

Test 7 is where we are allowed to provide a different punishment to different people *based on past history*. It says that the discipline has to be related to the seriousness of the offense but that we also have to take into account the employee's past record. So if we have two employees who have committed the same infraction and one of the employees has never been in trouble while the other has repeatedly committed the same infraction, then we have the flexibility to provide a different punishment for the two different offenders.

GUIDELINES FOR EFFECTIVE DISCIPLINE. Exhibit 9-4 lists eight guidelines for effective discipline.

EXHIBIT 9-4   GUIDELINES FOR EFFECTIVE DISCIPLINE

A.   Clearly communicate the standards and code of conduct to all employees.
B.   Be sure that the punishment fits the crime.
C.   Follow the standing plans yourself.
D.   Take consistent, impartial action when the rules are broken.
E.   Discipline immediately, but stay calm and get all the necessary facts before you discipline.
F.   Discipline in private.
G.   Document discipline.
H.   When the discipline is over, resume normal relations with the employee.

LO 9-7

Describe the concept of progressive discipline in the organization, including the stages of progressive discipline.

WORK
APPLICATION 9-15

Assess how well your boss and the organization where you work or have worked follows the eight guidelines for effective discipline.

Progressive discipline A process in which the employer provides the employee with opportunities to correct poor behavior before terminating them

PROGRESSIVE DISCIPLINE. If discipline is deemed necessary after going through the Just Cause standards, what type of discipline is warranted? Most organizations today have a series of progressively more severe disciplinary actions that they typically use to deal with minor disciplinary infractions. **Progressive discipline** *is a process in which the employer provides the employee with opportunities to correct poor behavior before terminating them.* Progressive discipline is typically only used in cases of minor behavioral infractions such as arriving late to work or insubordination with a superior. The progressive disciplinary steps are (1) informal coaching talk, (2) oral warning, (3) written warning, (4) suspension, and (5) dismissal. In some *limited* cases, we may add a sixth option between suspension and dismissal. We will discuss this option shortly. On the other hand, suspension may not appear in the progressive discipline process—as at **Wal-Mart**, where any employee with more than three unauthorized absences in 6 months is disciplined with a warning and those with seven unauthorized absences are fired.[61] Let's briefly discuss each step in progressive discipline.

Step 1: Informal coaching talk. As we noted, the first step in progressive discipline is an *informal coaching talk*. In an informal talk, the supervisor may see an employee coming in late to work and just ask them what is going on and why they are late. Typically the manager won't even write down a recording of such conversations for their own use, although they can do so in the critical incident file (Chapter 8). They're just in an information gathering and recognition mode at this point, and they hope to avoid any further disciplinary problems.

9-3   APPLYING THE CONCEPT

Guidelines for Effective Discipline

Identify which guideline is being followed—or not being followed—in the following statements. Use the guidelines in Exhibit 9-4 as the answers, writing the letter of the guideline (A–H) on the line before the statement involving it.

_____ 12. "Are you kidding me? Can you really fire me just for being late for work once?"

_____ 13. "I didn't know that I'm not supposed to make a personal call while I'm working. Can't you let it go this one time?"

_____ 14. "Some days, my boss comments about my being late, but other days, she doesn't say anything about it."

_____ 15. "Let's get back to the way things were before I had to discipline you, OK?"

_____ 16. "Let's go to my office so that we can discuss your rule violation now."

_____ 17. "I missed it. Why was the boss yelling at Rita?"

_____ 18. "The boss comes back from break late all the time and nothing happens to him; so why do I get in trouble for being late?"

_____ 19. "When I come to work late, the manager reprimands me. But when Latoya is late, nothing is ever said."

_____ 20. "The boss gave me a written warning for being late for work and placed it in my permanent record file."

Step 2: Oral warning. In the second step, the supervisor formally tells the employee that their behavior is currently unacceptable and also tells them what they need to do to correct the behavior. In this situation, even though the supervisor does not write a report for the individual to sign, they will keep a formal record in their own files of this conversation. The oral warning is the first of our formal methods of disciplining an employee.

Step 3: Written warning. The third step is a *written warning.* In this situation, the supervisor writes up the facts of the situation (typically organizations have a standard form for documentation of written warnings). They identify the unacceptable behavior for the individual and identify ways to correct the behavior. The supervisor then speaks with the employee using the written document to assist the employee in correcting their actions. Typically here, we ask the employee to sign the written warning, acknowledging that their actions are under review and not currently acceptable. This signed paper (documentation) is then put into the employee's permanent file.[62]

Step 4: Disciplinary suspension. As a fourth step, we may move on to a *disciplinary suspension* of the employee for a period of from one day to typically a maximum of one week. Though most companies use an unpaid suspension, some companies have experimented with a paid day off to allow the employee to think of the suspension not as punishment but as time to figure out whether or not they wish to continue working for the organization. There is *some* evidence that these paid suspensions work, although the conclusions are slightly mixed.

Other Options Before Termination. Next, we have a couple of limited options we noted at the top of this section—options that would typically not be used but might be valuable in certain cases.

We can sometimes demote an individual to a lower position in the organization. In some cases, this may be valuable because the employee may be overwhelmed at the higher-level position. In general, however, demotion creates even more job dissatisfaction within the individual employee, and we may see their performance deteriorate even further.

Alternatively, we may choose in some cases to *transfer* an employee from one part of the organization to another. The only time when you should use a transfer as a progressive discipline measure would be when you know that there is a personality conflict between the employee and another employee in the unit or between the employee and their supervisor. Transfers should never be used simply to get rid of a problem employee from your department or division. If this is the reason for the transfer, the manager should not transfer the employee but should correct the problem behavior.

SHRM

A:1
Disciplinary Actions: Demotion, Disciplinary Termination

WORK
APPLICATION 9-16

Describe progressive discipline where you work or have worked.

Step 5: Termination. The last resort is *discharge*. If the employee's behavior does not improve over time as a result of verbal and written warnings, suspensions, demotions, or a transfer, we may be forced to let the employee go. However, if we followed the progressive discipline process, we will have sufficient evidence to limit the employee's opportunity to bring an unlawful termination lawsuit against us.

THE DISCIPLINE MODEL. You should follow the steps of the discipline model below each time you must discipline an employee. The five steps are presented here and summarized in Model 9-2.

MODEL 9-2   THE DISCIPLINE MODEL

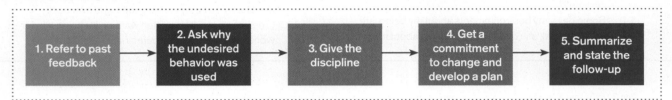

Step 1: Refer to past feedback. Begin the interview by refreshing the employee's memory. If the employee has been coached/counseled about the behavior, or if they have clearly broken a known rule, state that fact.

For example, refer to your *prior coaching* by saying, "Billie, remember my telling you about the proper way to lift boxes with your legs?" Or if there has been a *rule violation*, say, "Billie, you know the safety rule about lifting boxes with your legs."

Step 2: Ask why the undesired behavior occurred. Giving the employee a chance to explain the behavior is part of getting all the necessary facts before you administer discipline. If you used prior coaching and the employee committed to changing the behavior at that time, then ask why the behavior did not change. If the behavior had changed, discipline would not be needed. Again, be sure to describe specific critical incidents to support your contention that behavior has not changed at all or has not changed enough to be at standard.

For example, if there was *prior coaching*, say, "Two days ago, you told me that you would use your legs, rather than your back, to lift boxes. Why are you still using your back?" Or if there has been a *rule violation*, say, "Why are you breaking the safety rule and using your back, rather than your legs, to lift the box?"

Step 3: Administer the discipline. If there is no good reason for the undesirable behavior, administer the discipline. The discipline will vary with the stage in the disciplinary progression.

For example, if there has been *prior coaching*, say, "Because you have not changed your behavior, I'm giving you an oral warning." If there has been a *rule violation*, say, "Because you have violated a safety rule, I'm giving you an oral warning."

Step 4: Get a commitment to change and develop a plan. Try to get a commitment to change. If the employee will not commit, make a note of that fact in the critical incidents file or use the procedures for a written warning. If you have developed a change plan for the employee in the past, try to get the employee to commit to the plan again. Or develop a new plan, if necessary. A statement such as "Your previous attempt has not worked; there must be a better way" is often helpful. With a personal problem, offer professional help again. Offer recommendations for change and develop a plan to improve.[63]

For example, if there has been *prior coaching or a rule violation*, say, "Will you lift with your legs from now on? Is there a way to get you to remember to use your legs instead of your back when you lift?"

Step 5: Summarize and state expected follow-up. Summarize the discipline and state the follow-up disciplinary action to be taken. Part of follow-up is to document the discipline. At all stages, get the employee's signature verifying the disciplinary action taken. If necessary, take the next step in the discipline model: dismissal.

For example, if there has been prior coaching or a rule violation, say, "So you agree to use your legs instead of your back when you lift. If I catch you again, you will be given a written warning, which is followed by a suspension and dismissal if necessary."

Terminating

Unfortunately, the coaching, counseling, and disciplining process will not always work to make a problem individual into a productive employee. Because this is the case, HR managers have to understand the process of termination, which is the final disciplinary step. We do not want to terminate individuals employed by the organization because, as we noted in Chapter 1, turnover is extremely expensive for the organization. However, if an individual cannot be made into a productive member of the workforce, we have no other choice, and there is a benefit to turnover when you replace poor workers with better job matches.[64]

First, let's take a look at some of the offenses that might be cause for dismissal immediately upon completion of an investigation of the facts. Then we will discuss the dismissal process for nonmanagerial employees, managerial employees, and executives.

GROSS NEGLIGENCE AND SERIOUS MISCONDUCT. Organizations set up their own rules, listing violations that are grounds for immediate termination without progressive discipline. For example, many firms list stealing money or other assets from the organization as cause for immediate dismissal. In companies that promote open and honest communications, there might be a rule that anyone caught lying will be fired.

Two of the more common situations in which we might immediately dismiss employees would be in cases of gross negligence or serious misconduct. What constitutes gross negligence or serious misconduct? **Gross negligence** *is a serious failure to exercise care in the work environment.* It is a reckless disregard for circumstances that could cause harm to others—a lack of concern for safety or life. So if in the course of work, someone failed to exercise care in a way that would be likely to hurt or kill others, then they would be guilty of gross negligence. For example, if an employee who was an electrician left a live high-voltage electrical line dangling into a hallway, they would be guilty of gross negligence because the live electrical line could seriously injure or kill someone who happened to come by and contact it.

Serious misconduct is a little different from gross negligence. Where negligence is a failure to take care, *misconduct* is intentionally doing something that is likely to harm someone or something else. So, **serious misconduct** *is intentional behavior that has the potential to cause great harm to another or to the company.* An example of serious misconduct is bringing a weapon to work. This action has the potential to cause great harm to others. One example that resulted in termination is the case of a police officer who, while intoxicated, engaged in a conversation with a group of men in public in which he used obscenities and racial slurs, showed his badge, and told the men to "stop blowing weed in my face," all while being filmed with a smartphone.[65] These types of incidents could be cause for termination of the individual responsible—of course only after an investigation to ensure that they actually did what they are accused of.

TERMINATION OF NONMANAGERIAL EMPLOYEES. If employee offenses do not fit into the gross negligence or serious misconduct categories, should we still consider dismissal? Well, there are certainly times when we have to dismiss employees from the firm,

WORK
APPLICATION 9-17

Assess how well your present or past boss used the discipline model with employees.

SHRM

M:3
Retention: Involuntary Turnover, etc.

LO 9-8

Discuss the two common situations in which an employee might be immediately discharged from the company.

WORK
APPLICATION 9-18

Give examples of reasons why employees can be terminated where you work or have worked.

Gross negligence A serious failure to exercise care in the work environment

Serious misconduct Intentional behavior that has the potential to cause great harm to another or to the company

Losing a job is difficult, but in some cases, people go on to more satisfying jobs.

©iStockphoto.com/ClarkandCompany

such as when they fail to perform their job satisfactorily even after being thoroughly trained, or if they continually disregard rules or policies. But here, too, we have to make sure we follow the OUCH test, unlike the sheriff who terminated a deputy who attended a cookout and "liked" the sheriff's opponent in an upcoming election.[66]

Why do we need to dismiss employees who perform poorly or don't follow reasonable rules? Again, it is because these types of behavior can be contagious in the organization, especially in the lower ranks of employees, and we can't afford to have a large number of our employees failing to do their jobs correctly. In some cases, it only takes a few individuals to hurt or even destroy job satisfaction and employee engagement throughout the company. As managers in the organization, it is our job to make sure that this doesn't happen, so we sometimes have to go through a termination process.

One of the things that we have to be concerned with is the legal risk to the organization when an employee is terminated. Employment-at-will can mitigate these risks, but it doesn't completely eliminate them. As a result, we would usually want to use Just Cause procedures to analyze the situation and to make a determination concerning whether or not an employee's action was sufficiently harmful to the organization to result in termination.

Once the initial determination is made (usually by the individual's immediate supervisor), we usually want to subject the evidence to a review by another organizational manager. This individual may be the next person up the chain of command from the supervisor, it may be the company's legal counsel, or it may be an HR representative. Regardless of who it is, the second reviewer will make an attempt to ensure that the supervisors' decision was made in an objective fashion (following the OUCH test) and not based on an emotional reaction to the employee or to something they did.

MANAGERIAL OR EXECUTIVE EMPLOYEES. What if the individual to be terminated is a manager or executive in the firm? Do we need to handle this process differently than we would with a lower level employee? The answer is yes, because management in the organization typically works under different circumstances than do the lower-level employees. The basic process of analyzing the individual's actions using Just Cause procedures should still be followed. However, in many cases, managerial employees will be hired through a contractual process. If the manager has a contract with the organization, that contract will typically identify when the manager may be terminated by the firm.

However, even managerial employees who are not under contract may need to be dealt with in a slightly different manner than one would deal with a normal employee. For one thing, managerial employees are usually held to higher ethical and behavioral standards by the firm than are lower-level employees.[67] So an action that might not cause a lower-level employee to be terminated could quite possibly create a termination situation for a managerial or executive employee. As would happen in any other case, a judgment concerning the individual's actions will have to be made, and an appropriate level of reaction by the firm will be identified.

There is one more thing that makes managerial terminations different from others. In reality, in most cases when a managerial worker has failed to perform successfully or has committed a disciplinary infraction that would cause termination, they are usually given the option to resign rather than face termination by the organization. Whether this is right or wrong, it is a common practice in most industries. The only time that this would typically not happen is in a case where circumstances are so egregious that the organization is forced to terminate the individual in order to avoid other more serious consequences, such as lawsuits against the organization for the individual's behavior.

In public companies, the board of directors must agree to dismissal of executives. Another factor that must be considered is the fact that, in many cases, company executives will have a noncompete clause as part of their employment agreement. This matters because in some situations, if a noncompete case goes to court, the judge will determine whether or not the company is allowing the former executive the opportunity to make a living. If the judge feels that the noncompete clause makes it impossible for the former executive to become gainfully employed, the noncompete clause may be removed from the employment agreement. So we have to be very concerned that if we terminate a managerial-level employee, that executive will bring knowledge about our operations to a rival firm, which then will compete more effectively against our company.

One last concern in termination of managerial or executive employees is the fact that these employees typically have access to company files, records, and computers and may have broad knowledge of the firm's operations. Because of this, there's the potential for managerial or executive employees to be able to harm the organization if they know they're going to be dismissed. So, managerial and executive dismissals must include the concern that company files and records be protected to an extra degree to avoid potential sabotage or misappropriation of information.

Coaching, Counseling, and Discipline May Differ Globally

Do coaching, counseling, and discipline work the same way around the world? Not always. Much of the process of employee development will vary based on national culture, including behavioral norms. A recent article notes that "It is clear *cultural competency* will be a prerequisite for managers in the future."[68] We must keep this in mind if we wish to become successful coaches, counselors, and disciplinarians.

There are certainly cultural issues that need to be understood in global coaching and counseling sessions. For instance, in *high power-distance cultures*, it may be impossible for the manager to ask a lot of questions of the employee about what they might think of a situation. In these societies, the manager (coach) is considered to have more and better knowledge of what is necessary in an organizational context than the employee does. So if the manager asks the employee what they think should be done, the manager will quite likely lose the respect of the employee.

However, the most important thing in any successful interaction between the coach and the recipient of coaching is probably an understanding of the *individual*, not the culture that the individual comes from.[69] This is because no matter what culture a person belongs to, individual personalities may or may not adhere to cultural norms and values. Therefore, two of the most significant issues that the coach needs to attempt to determine are the individual's personality type and their motivators.[70] Once we know the individual, we can add in the cultural context to understand what is likely to happen based on a specific set of coaching actions. From these pieces of information, a good coach can design a program that will improve performance.

LEADERSHIP, MANAGEMENT, AND CHANGE

As managers, we don't need to just develop our individual employees—we need to develop them into effective teams, and this takes leadership and the ability to overcome resistance to change and to manage the change process. The three areas of

WORK
APPLICATION 9-19

Assess the leadership skills of your present or past boss. How effective was the boss at influencing employees to achieve the organization's goals?

leadership, team building, and change management are critical building blocks for 21st century organizations.[71] These are the topics of this section.

Leadership

Leadership *is the process of influencing employees to work toward the achievement of organizational objectives*. Here are a few of the thousands of statements being made about leadership today:

> "Effective global leaders are a vital asset today."[72]
>
> "Leaders have a profound impact on organizations' productivity through affecting their employee feelings, thinking, and behaving."[73]
>
> "The ability to lead is perhaps the most important skill for any manager, but many managers lack leadership skills."[74]

People tend to use the terms *manager* and *leader* interchangeably. However, managers and leaders differ.[75] Leading is just one of the five major management functions that we originally noted in Chapter 1, so management is broader in scope than leadership. A manager can have this position without being a true leader. There are managers—you may know of some—who are not leaders because they do not have the ability to influence others. There are also good leaders who are not managers. An informal leader, an employee group member, is a case in point. You may have worked in a situation (or been on a sports team) where one of your peers had more influence than the manager.

SHRM

Q:7
Leadership Development

Situational Management

Management is typically understood as taking place in a situation,[76] so leaders need to change their behavior to meet the situational characteristics.[77] This is often called *contingency leadership* or *situational leadership*.[78] Duke's basketball Coach K says you have to adjust your leadership to the composition of your team.[79]

Leaders have to take into account a variety of *contingency factors*. There are many contingency factors in modern organizations. Some of the common contingencies that we deal with in leadership include the leader's personality characteristics and style, follower ability and motivation, and the complexity of the situation, among many others.

We use models to represent the world of managers,[80] and there are many academic models of leadership.[81] But before you learn about the situational-management model and how to use it with individuals and teams, complete the self-assessment to determine your preferred management style.

According to contingency theorists, there is no best management style for all situations.[82] Instead, effective managers adapt their styles to individual capabilities or group situations.[83]

LO 9-9

Identify the factors that positive leadership takes into account to be successful.

USING THE SITUATIONAL MANAGEMENT MODEL. A leadership model is a short (one-page) summary of the theory to be used when selecting the appropriate leadership style for a given situation.[84] Now let's learn how to use the situational-management model, which promotes *positive leadership*, to select the most appropriate management style in a given situation; see Model 9-3.

Employee Capability. There are two distinct aspects of employee capability:

- *Ability*. Do employees have the knowledge, experience, education, skills, and training to do a particular task without direction?
- *Motivation*. Do the employees have the confidence to do the task? Do they want to do the task? Are they committed to performing the task? Will they perform the task without encouragement and support?

Leadership The process of influencing employees to work toward the achievement of organizational objectives

9-1   SELF ASSESSMENT

Your Preferred Management Styles

Following are 12 situations. Select the one alternative that most closely describes what you would do in each situation. Don't be concerned with trying to pick the right answer; select the course of action you would really use. Circle a, b, c, or d. (Ignore the C ____ preceding each situation and the S ____ following each answer choice; these will be explained later in Skill Building Exercise 9-3.)

C ____ 1.   Your rookie crew seems to be developing well. Their need for direction and close supervision is diminishing. What do you do?

    a.   Stop directing and overseeing performance unless there is a problem. S ____

    b.   Spend time getting to know them personally, but make sure they maintain performance levels. S ____

    c.   Make sure things keep going well; continue to direct and oversee them closely. S ____

    d.   Begin to discuss new tasks that are of interest to them. S ____

C ____ 2.   You assigned Jill a task, specifying exactly how you wanted it done. Jill deliberately ignored your directions and did it her way. The job will not meet the customer's standards. This is not the first problem you've had with Jill. What do you decide to do?

    a.   Listen to Jill's side, but be sure the job gets done right. S ____

    b.   Tell Jill to do it again the right way, and closely supervise the job. S ____

    c.   Tell her the customer will not accept the job, and let Jill handle it her way. S ____

    d.   Discuss the problem and solutions to it. S ____

C ____ 3.   Your employees work well together and are a real team; the department is the top performer in the organization. Because of traffic problems, the company president has approved staggered hours for departments. As a result, you can change your department's hours. Several of your workers are in favor of changing. What action do you take?

    a.   Allow the group to decide the new hours. S ____

    b.   Decide on new hours, explain why you chose them, and invite questions. S ____

    c.   Conduct a meeting to get the group members' ideas. Select new hours together, with your approval. S ____

    d.   Send out a memo stating the hours you want. S ____

C ____ 4.   You recently hired Bill, but he is not performing at the level expected after a month's training. Bill is trying, but he seems to be a slow learner. What do you decide to do?

    a.   Clearly explain what needs to be done and oversee his work. Discuss why the procedures are important; support and encourage him. S ____

    b.   Tell Bill that his training is over and it's time to pull his own weight. S ____

    c.   Review task procedures and supervise his work closely. S ____

    d.   Inform Bill that his training is over and that he should feel free to come to you if he has any problems. S ____

C ____ 5.   Helen has had an excellent performance record for the last 5 years. Recently, you have noticed a drop in the quality and quantity of her work. She has a family problem. What do you do?

    a.   Tell her to get back on track and closely supervise her. S ____

    b.   Discuss the problem with Helen. Help her realize that her personal problem is affecting her work. Discuss ways to improve the situation. Be supportive and encourage her. S ____

    c.   Tell Helen you're aware of her productivity slip and that you're sure she'll work it out soon. S ____

    d.   Discuss the problem and solution with Helen and supervise her closely. S ____

C ____ 6.   Your organization does not allow smoking in certain areas. You just walked by a restricted area and saw Joan smoking. She has been with the organization for 10 years and is a very productive worker. Joan has never been caught smoking before. What action do you take?

    a.   Ask her to put the cigarette out, and then leave. S ____

    b.   Discuss why she is smoking and what she intends to do about it. S ____

    c.   Give her a lecture about not smoking and check up on her in the future. S ____

    d.   Tell her to put the cigarette out, watch her do it, and tell her you will check on her in the future. S ____

(Continued)

(Continued)

C _____ 7.   Your employees usually work well together, with little direction. Recently, a conflict between Sue and Tom has caused problems. What action do you take?

    a.   Call Sue and Tom together and make them realize how this conflict is affecting the department. Discuss how to resolve it and how you will check to make sure the problem is solved. S _____

    b.   Let the group resolve the conflict. S _____

    c.   Have Sue and Tom sit down and discuss their conflict and how to resolve it. Support their efforts to implement a solution. S _____

    d.   Tell Sue and Tom how to resolve their conflict and closely supervise them. S _____

C _____ 8.   Jim usually does his share of the work with some encouragement and direction. However, he has migraine headaches occasionally and doesn't pull his weight when they happen. The others resent doing Jim's work. What do you decide to do?

    a.   Discuss his problem and help him come up with ideas for maintaining his workload; be supportive. S _____

    b.   Tell Jim to do his share of the work and closely watch his output. S _____

    c.   Inform Jim that he is creating a hardship for the others and should resolve the problem by himself. S _____

    d.   Be supportive but set minimum performance levels and ensure compliance. S _____

C _____ 9.   Barbara, your most experienced and productive worker, came to you with a detailed idea that could increase your department's productivity at a very low cost. She can do her present job plus this new assignment. You think it's an excellent idea. What do you do?

    a.   Set some goals together. Encourage and support her efforts. S _____

    b.   Set up goals for Barbara. Be sure she agrees with them and sees you as being supportive of her efforts. S _____

    c.   Tell Barbara to keep you informed and come to you if she needs any help. S _____

    d.   Have Barbara check in with you frequently so that you can direct and supervise her activities. S _____

C _____10.   Your boss asked you for a special report. Frank, a very capable worker who usually needs no direction or support, has all the necessary skills to do the job. However, Frank is reluctant because he has never done a report. What do you do?

    a.   Tell Frank he has to do it. Give him direction and supervise him closely. S _____

    b.   Describe the project to Frank and let him do it his own way. S _____

    c.   Describe the benefits to Frank. Get his ideas on how to do it and check his progress. S _____

    d.   Discuss possible ways of doing the job. Be supportive; encourage Frank. S _____

C _____11.   Jean is the top producer in your department. However, her monthly reports are constantly late and contain errors. You are puzzled because she does everything else with no direction or support. What do you decide to do?

    a.   Go over past reports, explaining to Jean exactly what is expected of her. Schedule a meeting so that you can review the next report with her. S _____

    b.   Discuss the problem with Jean and ask her what can be done about it; be supportive. S _____

    c.   Explain the importance of the report. Ask her what the problem is. Tell her that you expect the next report to be on time and error-free. S _____

    d.   Remind Jean to get the next report in on time, without errors. S _____

C _____12.   Your workers are very effective and like to participate in decision making. A consultant was hired to develop a new method for your department using the latest technology in the field. What do you do?

    a.   Explain the consultant's method and let the group decide how to implement it. S _____

    b.   Teach the workers the new method and supervise them closely as they use it. S _____

    c.   Explain to the workers the new method and the reasons it is important. Teach them the method and make sure the procedure is followed. Answer questions. S _____

    d.   Explain the new method and get the group's input on ways to improve and implement it. S _____

To determine your preferred management style, circle the letter you selected for each situation.

	Autocratic	Consultative	Participative	Empowering
1.	c	b	d	a
2.	b	a	d	c
3.	d	b	c	a
4.	c	a	d	b
5.	a	d	b	c
6.	d	c	b	a
7.	d	a	c	b
8.	b	d	a	c
9.	d	b	a	c
10.	a	c	d	b
11.	a	c	b	d
12.	b	c	d	a
Totals	_____	_____	_____	_____

Now add up the number of circled items per column. The column with the most items circled suggests your preferred management style. Is this the style you tend to use most often?

Your management style flexibility is reflected in the distribution of your answers. The more evenly distributed the numbers, the more flexible your style. A total of 1 or 0 for any column may indicate a reluctance to use that style.

Employee capability may be measured on a continuum from low to outstanding. As a manager, you assess each employee's capability level and motivation on a scale from C1 to C4; see Model 9-3.

Employees tend to start working with low capability, needing close direction. As their ability to do the job increases, managers can begin to be supportive and can probably cease close supervision. As a manager, you must gradually develop your employees from low to outstanding levels over time.

Manager/Employee Interactions. Managers' interactions with employees can be classified into two distinct categories of behavior:

- *Directive Behavior*. The manager focuses on directing and controlling behavior to ensure that tasks get done and closely oversees performance.

- *Supportive Behavior*. The manager focuses on encouraging and motivating behavior without telling the employees what to do. The manager explains things and listens to employee views, helping employees make their own decisions by building up their confidence and self-esteem.

As a manager, you can focus on directing (getting the task done), supporting (developing relationships), or both.

Management Styles. Based on the employee capability level and the type of behavior they need, we select the most appropriate management style for the situation; see Model 9-3 and the list below for a description of each of the four management styles.

MODEL 9-3   SITUATIONAL MANAGEMENT

Step 1: Determine the capability level of employees on a continuum from C1 to C4; follow the arrow from left to right.

Step 2: Match the management style (S1A, S2C, S3P, S4E) with the employee capability level; follow the arrow down from the capability level box to the management style box.

CAPABILITY LEVEL (C)
[Employee Ability and Motivation to Perform the Task]

(C1) Low Low Ability/ Low Motivation	(C2) Moderate Low Ability/ High Motivation	(C3) High High Ability/ Low Motivation	(C4) Outstanding High Ability/ High Motivation
Employees are unable to perform the task without supervision, or they lack motivation. They are unwilling to perform.	Employees have moderate ability and are motivated to do the task, with supervision.	Employees have the ability to do the task but need some motivation. They are reluctant or need their confidence built up.	Employees have the ability and motivation to perform the task without direction or support.

MANAGEMENT STYLE (S)
[Directive and Supportive Behavior That the Manager Needs to Give Employees to Perform the Task]

(S1A) Autocratic High Directive/ Low Supportive	(S2C) Consultative High Directive/ High Supportive	(S3P) Participative Low Directive/ High Supportive	(S3E) Empowerment Low Directive/ Low Supportive
Manager tells employees what to do and how to do it and closely oversees performance. Manager makes decisions without any employee input.	Manager sells employees on doing the task and oversees performance. Manager typically gets input from individual employees when making decisions.	Manager develops motivation by developing confidence. Manager typically has a group meeting to get employee input into decisions.	Manager assigns tasks and lets the employees do it on their own. Manager lets the employee or group make decisions.

- An *autocratic style* is highly directive and low in supportiveness. Using the autocratic style is appropriate when interacting with low-capability employees. Give very detailed instructions describing exactly what the task is and when, where, and how to perform it. Closely oversee performance and give some support. The majority of your time with the employees should be spent giving directions and supervising their performance. Make decisions without input from the employees.

- A *consultative style* involves highly directive and highly supportive behavior, and it is appropriate when interacting with moderately capable employees. Give specific instructions and oversee performance at all major stages of a task. At the same time, support the employees by explaining why they should perform the task as requested and answering their questions. Work on building relationships with the employees as you explain the benefits of completing the task your way. Give fairly equal amounts of time to directing and supporting employees. When making decisions, you may consult employees individually, but you must retain the final say. Once you make the decision, which can incorporate employees' ideas, you should direct and oversee employees' performance.

- A *participative style* is characterized by low directive behavior and high supportive behavior, and it is appropriate when interacting with employees with high capability. Spend a small amount of time giving general directions and a great deal of time giving encouragement. Spend limited time overseeing performance, letting employees do the task their way while focusing on the end result. Support the employees by encouraging them and building up their self-confidence. If a task needs to be done, don't tell them how to do it; ask them how they will accomplish it. Make decisions together or allow employees to make decisions subject to your guidelines and approval.

- An *empowering style* requires providing very little direction or support to employees, and it is appropriate when interacting with outstanding employees. You should let them know what needs to be done and answer their questions, but it is not necessary to oversee their performance. Such employees are highly motivated and need little, if any, support. Allow them to make their own decisions, which can be subject to your approval. Other terms for empowerment are *laissez-faire* and *hands off*. A manager who uses this style lets employees alone to do their own thing.

APPLY THE MOST APPROPRIATE MANAGEMENT STYLES. As part of Skill Builder 9-3, or on your own, return to the self-assessment, where you determined your preferred management style. Identify the employee capability level for each of the 12 items and indicate the capability level by placing a number from 1 to 4 on the line marked "C" before each item. The number 1 indicates low capability, 2 indicates moderate capability, 3 indicates high capability, and 4 indicates outstanding capability. Next, indicate the management style represented in each answer choice by placing the letter A (Autocratic), C (Consultative), P (Participative), or E (Empowering) on the line marked "S" following each answer choice. Will your preferred management style result in the optimum performance of the task?

Let's see how you did by looking back at the first situation.

C _____ 1. Your rookie crew seems to be developing well. Their need for direction and close supervision is diminishing. What do you do?

   a. Stop directing and overseeing performance unless there is a problem. S _____

   b. Spend time getting to know them personally, but make sure they maintain performance levels. S _____

   c. Make sure things keep going well; continue to direct and oversee them closely. S _____

   d. Begin to discuss new tasks that are of interest to them. S _____

- As a rookie crew, the employees' capability started at a low level, but they have now developed to the moderate level. If you put the number 2 on the C line, you were correct.

- Alternative (a) is E, the empowering style, involving low direction and support. Alternative (b) is C, the consultative style, involving both high direction and high support. Alternative (c) is A, the autocratic style, involving high direction but low support. Alternative (d) is P, the participative style, involving low direction and high support (in discussing employee interests).

- If you selected (b) as the management style that best matches the situation, you were correct. However, in the business world, there is seldom only one way to handle a situation successfully. Therefore, in this exercise, you are given points based on how successful your behavior would be in each situation. In situation 1, (b) is the most successful alternative because it involves developing the employees gradually; answer (b) is worth 3 points. Alternative (c) is the next-best alternative and is worth 2 points, while (d) is worth 1 point. That's

WORK
APPLICATION 9-20

Assess how well your present or past boss was at using the appropriate management style for your capability level and those of a couple of other employees.

SHRM

A:7
Managing Teams

because it is better to keep things the way they are now than to try to rush employee development, which would probably cause problems. Alternative (a) is the least effective and is worth 0 points. That's because choosing that option would mean you are going from one extreme of supervision to the other, and the odds are therefore great that this approach will cause problems that will diminish your management success.

The better you match your management style to your employees' capabilities, the greater are your chances of being a successful manager.

Building Effective Work Teams

Organizational leaders also have to build strong work teams in 21st century organizations. Why do we need work teams? Some US workers do not like having to work in teams due to the individualistic nature of American culture. But today, we usually don't have any choice, either as leaders or as followers, about whether or not we work in teams. The major reason is that in most cases, you can't succeed without an effective team effort, and organizations are using teams to create competitive advantage over competitors.[85]

Also, the explosion of available information continues to drive how we operate in business today. This information explosion is caused in large part by technology—computers and their storage and retrieval capabilities. Because of this vast store of information, no one individual can have a broad *and* deep amount of knowledge in any field today, so we put people together in teams so that they can share their expertise with each other.

Team building is probably the most widely used organizational development (OD) technique today, and its popularity will continue as more companies use work teams.[86] The effectiveness of each team and how the teams work together directly affect the entire organization.[87] The goals of team-building programs vary considerably, depending on the group's needs and the change agent's skills.[88] Some typical goals are as follows:

- To clarify the objectives of the team and the responsibilities of each team member
- To identify problems preventing the team from accomplishing its objectives
- To develop team problem-solving, decision-making, objective-setting, and planning skills
- To develop open, honest working relationships based on trust and an understanding of group members

Team-building programs also vary in terms of agenda and length, depending on team needs.

WORK
APPLICATION 9-21

Assess how well your present boss is or your past boss was at developing employees to perform as an effective team.

LO 9-10

Briefly discuss the stages of the change process.

SHRM

N:6
Leading Change

SHRM

N:1
Stages of Change Management

Managing the Change Process

Change happens at the individual, team, or organizational level, and it impacts all aspects of organizational life.[89] Change is critical for firm performance and survival.[90] Adapting to dynamic environments has been identified as a major element in maintaining competitiveness.[91] Research supports the idea that companies that change regularly outperform those that don't.[92] Thus, top managers are inclined to change in order to obtain a competitive advantage over competitors.[93] John Chambers, **Cisco's** CEO, said that his most important decisions are about adjusting to change.[94] So your ability to be flexible enough to change with the diversifying global environment will affect your career success.[95]

People go through four distinct stages when facing change, so we need to manage change through each stage. The four **stages of the change process** are *denial, resistance, exploration, and commitment.* They are presented in Exhibit 9-5 and are described using HP as an example below. Notice that the stages in Exhibit 9-5 are laid out in a circular formation because change is an ongoing process, not a linear one. People can regress, as the arrows show.

WORK
APPLICATION 9-22

Identify a major change. Assess how well your present or past boss was at managing change through each of the four stages of change.

EXHIBIT 9-5 STAGES OF THE CHANGE PROCESS

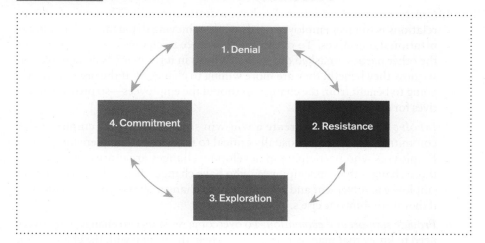

1. *Denial.* Changes are often difficult to understand or accept.[96] So when people first hear that change is coming, they may deny that it will affect them.

2. *Resistance.* Once people get over the initial shock and realize that change is going to be a reality, they often resist the change. This stage is so important that in the next subsection, we will present seven ways to help overcome resistance to change.

3. *Exploration.* When the change begins to be implemented, employees explore the change, often through training—and ideally, they begin to better understand how the change will affect them.

4. *Commitment.* Through exploration, employees determine their level of commitment to making the change a success. Commitment is necessary to implement the change, but some employees will continue to resist the change.[97]

Overcoming Resistance to Change

Some people deliberately attempt to block change efforts.[98] Most change programs fail because of employee resistance to change.[99] Because resistance to change is one of the most difficult factors in successful change implementation, let's discuss seven things we can do to overcome resistance to changes at work.

1. *Develop a positive trust climate for change.* Develop and maintain good human relations. Make employees realize you have their best interests in mind and develop mutual trust.[100] Constantly look for better ways to do things. Encouraging employees to suggest changes and implementing their ideas are important parts of continuous improvement.

2. *Plan.* Implementing changes successfully requires good planning. You need to identify the possible resistance to change and plan how to overcome it. View change from the employees' position. Set clear objectives so employees know

LO 9-11

Identify the factors that can help overcome resistance to change in organizations.

SHRM
N:8
Implementing Change

SHRM
N:4
Building Trust

Stages of the change process Denial, resistance, exploration, and commitment

exactly what the change is and how it affects them.[101] The next four steps should be part of your plan.

3. *Clearly state why the change is needed and how it will affect employees.* Employees want and need to know why the change is necessary and how it will affect them, both positively and negatively.[102] So you need to communicate clearly what you want to do.[103] Employees need to understand why the new, changed method is more legitimate than the existing method of doing things.[104] Be open and honest with employees. Giving employees the facts as far in advance as possible helps them to overcome fear of the unknown.[105]

4. *Create a win-win situation.* We have a desire to win.[106] The goal of human relations is to meet employee needs while achieving departmental and organizational objectives. To overcome resistance to change, be sure to answer the other parties' unasked question, "What's in it for me?" When people can see how they benefit, they are more willing to change.[107] If the organization is going to benefit from the change, so should the employees—so provide incentives for change.[108]

5. *Involve employees.* To create a win-win situation, involve employees. A commitment to change is usually critical to its successful implementation.[109] Employees who participate in developing changes are more committed to those changes than are employees who have changes dictated to them. To get employee involvement and commitment to change, phrase your own ideas as if they were someone else's.[110]

6. *Provide support and evaluation.* To overcome resistance to change, employees need to know that managers are there to help them cope with the changes. So, relationships matter.[111] Managers need to make the learning process as painless as possible by providing training and other support. To ensure that the change is implemented and that employees don't regress to old habits, performance appraisals (discussed in the next chapter) need to be tied to successful implementation of the change.[112]

7. *Create urgency.* When you decide on a change, you have to move fast.[113] Many people procrastinate on making changes. A feeling of urgency is the primary driver toward taking action. If something is perceived as urgent, it is given a high priority and is often done immediately.[114]

People have different attitudes toward change. Some thrive on it, some are upset by it, and many resist it at first but gradually accept it. As a manager of change, you must anticipate whether resistance will be strong, weak, or somewhere in between. Resistance will be lower if you use the seven methods for overcoming resistance to change.

TRENDS AND ISSUES IN HRM

In this chapter's trends and issues, we are first going to explore a new privacy issue in the workplace as we take a look at **Google Glass**. Next we will take a look at positive leadership and how it may minimize the need for disciplinary actions. The final issue in this chapter will discuss social media at work and the burden that such media create for the organization in controlling worker productivity.

Google Glass and Other Privacy Issues

By now, most of you have heard about Google Glass, the new wearable computer headgear from **Google**. While it is the first product of its type that has made the headlines, there are already other technology items that have the potential to upset the ability to maintain privacy and to distract their users, both in and out of the

---

SHRM

N:7
Planning Change Strategy

SHRM

N:3
Communication

WORK
APPLICATION 9-23

Assess how well your present boss or your past boss used the seven ways to overcome resistance to change.

workplace. We will continue to see smaller and more concealable products along these lines. Should companies and especially HR managers be concerned about items like Google Glass, and do we need to create policies concerning them?

The quick answers are yes and yes. Let's quickly look at why these items are concerning HR managers and others.

Security experts are worried that users of these devices can take pictures and video anywhere, without others knowing about it. In some countries and states, the recording of others without their permission is illegal, but would that stop everyone who wanted to steal information on employees, innovations, or products? HR managers have similar concerns about private employee information covered by HIPAA, FMLA (we will introduce you to these in later chapters), the ADA, employee salaries, and other private information that could be recorded.[115] Also, as with other BYOD equipment, what would happen if the user's Google Glass were stolen and the device had sensitive information stored on it?

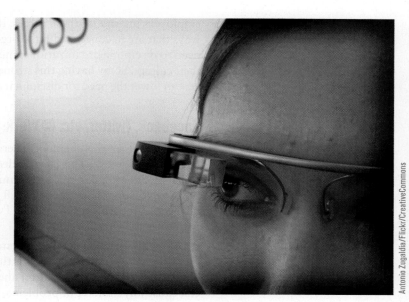

Google Glass and other like technologies create a new set of privacy concerns for HR managers.

As a result of these and other issues, HR managers are being urged to begin creating policies concerning when, where, and how to use these devices, and they are being told to start educating their employees now about these security and privacy concerns.[116] Some businesses—such as casinos, movie theaters, and bars—have simply banned the use of Google Glass on their premises due to concerns about theft, security, and privacy.[117] However, other companies should probably not completely ban the use of the devices since they provide another means of communication among employees. Companies may want to ban their use in certain areas or only allow employees to use certain functions of the equipment. Each case will likely be different, which makes creation of policies more difficult for both security and HR managers, but it is necessary that we get ahead of how employees will use these devices before it becomes a problem. If your company does not already have a policy on the use of such recording devices, you should look at the possibility of creating one in the near future.

Positive Leadership and Organizational Discipline

As we noted in this chapter's section on leadership, management and leadership are different. Many managers cannot qualify as true leaders because they do not have the ability to influence others. However, if a manager is a successful leader, can they affect and potentially lower the need for disciplinary action in the firm? A significant amount of evidence says that the answer to this question is yes. One study noted that "ethical leaders are 'courageous enough to say no to conduct that would be inconsistent with [their] values' . . . conveying information about the importance of standing up for what's right."[118] Research suggests that leaders who possess a variety of positive attributes (traits, goals, values, and character strengths) are able to positively influence followers' states, behavior, and performance.[119]

We can see from this information that when the leader stands up for the organization's core values and what is right (often called "walking the talk"), followers see these actions and will frequently act to emulate the leader. The fact is that organizational leaders have an outsized effect on organizational culture.[120] This effect on the culture causes a trickle-down of the leader's values to the individual employees. Once employees internalize these values, the organizational culture causes them to act in ways that are in concert with the organizational values. In turn, that will reduce the need to discipline organizational members for failing to live up to the standards of their culture. So by having this strong effect on organizational culture, positive leaders can lower the need for disciplinary action within the firm.

Facebook, Twitter, etc. @ Work: Are They Out of Control?

Our last issue for this chapter concerns employees' use and potential misuse of social media apps at work. This chapter deals with managing employees at work, and new social media tools can make this much more difficult than it has historically been. Nearly everyone today carries a cell phone, and most cell phones can instantly link into social media sites including Twitter, Facebook, LinkedIn, Foursquare, and many others.

How do social media tools create potential problems in the workplace? One of the issues with social media sites is the fact that they're almost instantaneous in their ability to broadcast information about the organization to the outside world. This can cause any number of problems, including the loss of trade secrets, harm to the company's reputation, the dissemination of inappropriate or unprofessional posts about the company and its policies, bullying or harassment, and public statements inconsistent with the company's public stance.[121] You may recall the Cisco recruit who said that "she would hate the job but relish the fatty paycheck." She had her employment offer rescinded when this was brought to the attention of Cisco recruiters. Or you might remember the White House staffer—Jofi Joseph, who went by @natsecwonk—who sent a slew of inappropriate tweets about his bosses and others at the White House. He was fired when it was determined that he was the source of the tweets.

A second issue is the company time that employees can waste when participating in social media interactions rather than doing their work. If left unchecked, this can cause a serious loss of productivity within the firm. So, what can we do about social media at work? According to a recent SHRM article, the organization needs to ensure that it has a strict "lack of privacy policy"[122] to let employees know that they have no expectation of privacy in social media communications in association with their workplace. You should also define the term *social media* and provide examples but also include wording that notes that the examples are not all-inclusive, since social media are still rapidly evolving. Guidelines on social media use should be put into a comprehensive policy that notes that the individual is responsible for their posts and that posts that harm other employees or the organization could result in disciplinary action. SHRM has a very good sample social media policy on its website that covers all of the major points and has been ruled as lawful by the National Labor Relations Board.[123] Social media are tools that add great value to the company, but they must be managed the same as any other business tools.

• • • CHAPTER SUMMARY

9-1 Discuss the difference between a right and a privilege in a work context.

Rights are things that an individual is allowed to do in a society—or in this case, an organization—without asking anyone's permission. Privileges, on the other hand, cannot be exercised until the individual gets permission from some authority. So, the easy way to tell the difference is this: if the employee has

to request permission to do something within the organization, that thing is a privilege. Employees would not need permission to exercise their rights.

9-2 Identify the commonly accepted individual rights in the workplace.

The commonly accepted rights of individuals within the workplace include the following:

Right of free consent—the right of the individual to know what they are being asked to do, and the consequences of doing it

Right to due process—a right to not be punished arbitrarily or without reason. Generally, we use the seven tests for Just Cause to protect this right.

Right to life and safety—the right of everyone in the organization to be protected from harm while working

Right of freedom of conscience—a general right to not be forced to violate the individual's personal values and beliefs on the job

Right to privacy—a right to protection from unreasonable searches or intrusions into their personal space at work

Right to free speech—freedom to express their opinions or concerns within the organization, without fear of harming their work relationship

9-3 **Identify the rights that management has in modern organizations.**

Management first has a right to create and enforce an employee *code of conduct*. Managers also have a right to *monitor the workplace* to protect the organization and its employees. The organization can also identify the relationship with workers as one of *employment-at-will*, which basically allows either party to break the relationship at any time, even without stating a reason. Management also has a right to set up an *orientation period* and require that new employees attend such orientation. Finally, management has a right to *test for drugs* in the workplace. In each case, these rights are offered based on the need for managers to be able to protect the organization and the employees from unnecessary danger or harm.

9-4 **Briefly describe the coaching process and how it is used.**

Coaching is designed to give employees feedback to improve their performance over time. This feedback in general should be designed to improve the employee's motivation to perform for the organization. The coaching process occurs in four basic steps:

> *Step 1: Describing the current performance*, or what is presently being done by the employee;
>
> *Step 2: Describing the desired performance*, or what the manager wants the employees to change about the way they perform;
>
> *Step 3: Getting a commitment to change*, meaning asking the employee to verbally commit to making the change the manager has asked for; and

Step 4: Following up to ensure that the employee is behaving in the desired manner.

9-5 **Describe the management counseling process and when it is useful.**

The management counseling process is designed to provide employees with feedback so that they understand that their performance is not currently at an acceptable level, and it's designed to provide them with guidance on how to improve their performance over time. The purpose of management counseling is to get employees back on track with their work so that they can perform at an acceptable or even exceptional level.

9-6 **Briefly discuss the tests for Just Cause used in disciplinary investigations.**

Just Cause is a set of standards used to test for fairness in an organizational setting in order to ensure that any disciplinary action taken has a reasonable basis. The tests attempt to ensure that the individual knew what the rules were, that there is reasonable evidence or proof that they violated or disobeyed those rules, and that if the rules were violated, the disciplinary action was appropriate and fair.

9-7 **Describe the concept of progressive discipline in the organization, including the stages of progressive discipline.**

Progressive discipline is usually used for minor disciplinary infractions within the organization. It provides progressively stronger sanctions against an employee who continues to behave in an unacceptable manner in the organization, based on rules or policies. The sequence of progressive discipline is as follows: (1) informal talk, (2) oral warning, (3) written warning, (4) suspension, (5) in *some* cases, demotion or transfer, and (6) dismissal.

9-8 **Discuss the two common situations in which an employee might be immediately discharged from the company.**

The two most common situations in which an employee might be immediately dismissed are gross negligence or serious misconduct. Gross negligence is a major failure to pay attention to the work environment that results in a dangerous situation in which the negligent individual or another employee could likely be hurt or killed. Serious misconduct is an *intentional* action by an employee that has the potential to seriously hurt or kill another person or cause great harm to the organization. Either of these situations would generally be cause for dismissal from the organization, immediately after an investigation showed that the individual did what they were accused of.

9-9 Identify the factors that positive leadership takes into account to be successful.

The first factor is *employee capability*, which consists of the *ability* and *motivation* to do the job. Next, we have to classify *manager-employee interactions* into *directive behavior*, which focuses on controlling employee behavior, and *supportive behavior*, which focuses on encouraging behavior without directly controlling that behavior. Finally, we take into account *management style*, which can be *autocratic*, *consultative*, *participative*, or *empowering*.

9-10 Briefly discuss the stages of the change process.

The four stages of the change process include denial, resistance, exploration, and commitment. Denial is frequently the first reaction when people hear that changes are going to be made in the workplace. Once employees understand that the change will affect their work, resistance to change often occurs. Next, as the change is implemented, employees may begin to explore how the change affects their work and how they can adapt to the necessary changes. Finally, through the exploration stage, the employees determine their level of commitment to the change process. Recall, however, that the change

process is ongoing, not linear. Organizations are constantly going through new change processes.

9-11 Identify the factors that can help overcome resistance to change in organizations.

There are seven major steps to overcoming resistance to change:

1. Develop a positive trust climate for change.
2. Plan the change.
3. Clearly state why the change is needed and how it will affect employees.
4. Create a win-win situation.
5. Involve employees.
6. Provide support and evaluation.
7. Create urgency.

As a manager, you must anticipate whether resistance will be strong or weak, and you should master the seven steps for overcoming resistance to change.

9-12 Define the key terms found in the chapter margins and listed following the Chapter Summary.

Complete the Key Terms Review to test your understanding of this chapter's key terms.

••• KEY TERMS

coaching
discipline
employee assistance
    programs (EAPs)
employment-at-will

gross negligence
Just Cause
leadership
management counseling
privileges

progressive discipline
rights
serious misconduct
stages of the change process

••• KEY TERMS REVIEW

Complete each of the following statements using one of this chapter's key terms.

1. _____ are things that individuals are allowed to do based on asking permission from an authority.
2. _____ are things a person in society is allowed to do without any permission required from an authority.
3. _____ allows the company or the worker to break their work relationship at any point in time, with or without any particular reason, as long as in doing so, no law is violated.
4. _____ is the process of giving motivational feedback to maintain and improve performance.
5. _____ is the process of (a) giving employees feedback so they realize that a problem is affecting their job performance and (b) referring employees

with problems that cannot be managed within the work structure to the organization's employee assistance program.

6. _____ provide a staff of people who help employees get professional assistance in solving their problems.
7. _____ is corrective action to get employees to meet standards and the code of conduct.
8. _____ is a set of standard tests for fairness in disciplinary actions; these tests were originally utilized in union grievance arbitrations.
9. _____ is a process whereby the employer provides the employee with opportunities to correct poor behavior before the individual is terminated.
10. _____ is a serious failure to exercise care in the work environment.

11. _____ is intentional employee behavior that has the potential to cause great harm to another or to the company.

12. _____ is the process of influencing employees to work toward the achievement of organizational objectives.

••• COMMUNICATION SKILLS

The following critical-thinking questions can be used for class discussion and/or for written assignments to develop communication skills. Be sure to give complete explanations for all answers.

1. Do you think that organizations should provide more rights or fewer rights to employees than those listed in the chapter? If more, what would you add? If fewer, which rights do you think are unimportant?

2. Should companies make a strong attempt to never violate the privacy rights of an employee? Why or why not?

3. Do you think an organization would be more adaptable to changes in its environment if it provided greater free speech rights to all employees? Why or why not?

4. Do you think codes of conduct have any effect on employees' activities? What would make them more or less effective in an organization?

5. Is employment-at-will fair, or should companies have to have a legitimate reason to discharge their employees? Justify your answer.

6. Should coaching, counseling, and discipline processes be utilized by the firm, or should we just terminate the employment of workers who are not doing their job? Explain your answer.

7. Is it really necessary to follow *all* of the Just Cause standards rigorously, or is it a waste of time? Explain your answer.

8. Do you feel that progressive discipline processes actually work to improve employee performance in most cases? Why or why not?

9. In your opinion, should there be any situations in which you might not immediately terminate a worker's employment as a result of gross negligence or serious misconduct? Explain why you feel this way.

10. Do you think leadership can be learned, or is it just a personal characteristic that some people have? Why do you think this way?

11. What would you do as a manager in order to create high-performing work teams in your organization? How would your actions create these high-performance teams?

12. What are some of the methods you have seen managers or others use to overcome resistance to change? Were these methods successful? Why or why not?

••• CASE 9-1 JUST ONE LITTLE SLIP

Charlene Fisher is a market analyst for the Top Cat Apparel Company, a women's boutique clothing store with shops in several southwestern states. She joined the company in early 2007 at the corporate office located in Memphis, Tennessee. Charlene previously lived in Richmond, Virginia, and worked as a market analyst for a major retailer for five years. She was looking for a better job when she found Top Cat's advertisement for a market analyst. After a telephone interview with Alan Jordan, Top Cat's Human Resource Manager, she was invited to interview with Ron McCoy, the Vice President, in Memphis. At the end of the interview, Mr. McCoy offered her the position and said that she would later receive written confirmation of the offer's terms. Within a week, Charlene received a letter of confirmation from Vice President McCoy, detailing the terms of compensation and stating that she would be offered an employment contract from year to year as long as her work performance was satisfactory. She also received a booklet containing the company's benefit plans as well as a copy of the employee handbook for all new employees. Charlene accepted the offer and moved to Memphis from Richmond, though the moving expenses cost her considerably.

As a market analyst at Top Cat, Charlene's primary function was to anticipate fashion trends and provide the shop managers with purchase recommendations about the type, brand, and quantity of clothing they should have in their store inventories. Her performance was annually rated as being very good during the first three years of her employment with the company, and therefore her contract was extended each year with a salary increase. Charlene recently made a costly forecasting error by recommending the purchase of a large number of coats that didn't sell very well in most stores. Tom Long, her manager, informed Charlene that the top management folks were very unhappy with her decision to recommend the coat purchase, and the company had decided not to renew her contract.

Charlene asked for a meeting with Mr. Long and HR Manager Alan Jordan to appeal the company's decision not to renew her employment contract, which she considered the same as a discharge for poor work performance. She claimed that her job performance should not be based upon one mistake since her performance evaluations had been consistently very good. Charlene felt that since this one error was not a typical example of her work performance throughout her employment with the company, her termination was too severe. She believed that she should have an opportunity to show that she learned from this mistake and that a similar incident would not likely occur again. Charlene pointed out a statement in the company's employee handbook that asserts employees will only be discharged for just or sufficient cause. Charlene felt that some lesser form of discipline should be considered in her case. Mr. Jordan informed her that the decision had already been made by upper management, and they were not willing to reconsider this decision. He explained that Top Cat Apparel Company is an at-will employer, and her employment can be terminated for any reason as long as the decision is not based upon some discriminatory or illegal grounds. Charlene decided to sue the company for wrongful discharge and breach of contract.

Questions

1. Does Charlene have a good argument that she is a contractual employee and that the company has a relationship with her that is controlled by either express or implied terms? Explain your answer.

2. What reasons would you expect the employer to claim in defense of their action? Thoroughly explain your answer.

3. Charlene expects the company to take a less severe and more gradual course of action. Identify and explain the steps of this process that Charlene hopes the company will follow.

4. What are the factors or questions that should be considered in order to determine if Charlene was afforded due process by the company in their decision to not continue her employment?

5. Explain how the situation may have been different if the company was located in the state of Montana.

Case created by Robert Wayland, University of Arkansas at Little Rock

● ● ● CASE 9-2 OFF-DUTY MISCONDUCT

The small Southwestern city of Happy Hollow, with a population of approximately 17,000 people, is a modern bedroom community that is located just a 15-minute drive away from a major city. Happy Hollow maintains a fire department with one fire station serving an area of 12 square miles. It is staffed with 15 full-time firefighters and 15 volunteer firefighters. The International Association of Fire Fighters (IAFF) represents all permanent, full-time employees of Happy Hollows's fire department.

Four years ago, Tim Nelson was hired as a firefighter and licensed paramedic for Happy Hollow's fire department. Previously, he worked for 3 years as a firefighter for another small city. After getting off work at 4:30 p.m. one evening, he joined a friend at a restaurant in the major city a 15- or 20-minute minute drive from where he lives and works. Nelson and his friend had dinner and several drinks at the restaurant and stayed there until after midnight, when Nelson drove the friend home and then started on the drive to his own home.

Upon receiving calls at 12:43 a.m. about someone driving erratically in a pickup truck at a high rate of speed, Happy Hollow's police department dispatched a police officer to investigate. Officer Brian Jones observed someone driving the described truck at an excessive rate of speed. He followed for approximately one-half mile while observing erratic driving before stopping the truck. Officer Jones detected a strong odor of alcohol coming from the pickup truck when he approached

it. Officer Jones then recognized the driver as firefighter Nelson, who appeared fatigued, with red, watery eyes. He noticed that Nelson had difficulty performing the simple task of retrieving his driver's license and proof of insurance coverage, and his speech was slurred. Officer Jones concluded that Nelson appeared to be intoxicated. Meanwhile, another Ford pickup truck and a second city patrol vehicle driven by Sgt. David Martinez arrived on the location. The driver and passenger in the other pickup advised the police officers that the truck driven by Nelson had sideswiped their vehicle before being stopped by Officer Jones, and they also said that Nelson had failed to stop after the accident. The collision caused damage to both trucks, ripping the mirrors from the passenger side of the truck driven by Nelson and the driver's side of the other truck.

Officer Jones determined that there was probable cause for arrest and advised Nelson that he was being arrested for driving under the influence (DUI) and leaving the scene of an accident. Upon arrival at the police station, Nelson elected to refuse to submit to a Breathalyzer test for measuring his blood alcohol. He was cited for a DUI and leaving the scene of an accident resulting in property damage to another vehicle. He was booked into jail and stayed for a few hours before he was released on bond.

Firefighter and paramedic Tim Nelson was subsequently placed on administrative leave with pay while the matter was being investigated. Following a 3-day investigation, the fire department held a predisciplinary hearing where Nelson had an opportunity to further describe his version of what had happened leading up to his early-morning arrest. Nelson described feeling a sudden jolt when his truck hit something while he was driving home, but he claimed that he did not know what he hit or if he hit anything at all. Nelson acknowledged that he had too much to drink that evening and that he should have had someone drive him home. He said that, although the incident had occurred while he was off duty, he was willing to do anything necessary to keep his job.

Fire department chief Calvin Moore pointed out that he had known that Nelson had been previously arrested for a DUI while working as a firefighter for the other small city but that he had hired Nelson as a firefighter for the Happy Hollow Fire Department anyway. Chief Moore explained that he had already given Nelson a second chance when he hired him, and he was unwilling to give Nelson a third chance. Chief Moore stated that Nelson had violated several rules and policies of the fire department and had failed in his obligation to the public as a firefighter and paramedic by not stopping to check to see if he had injured anyone in the collision that he caused that night. The incident also garnered significant media attention, including reports in Happy Hollow's local newspaper and on at least one news report from a local television station—thus potentially undermining the public's trust in the Happy Hollow fire department. For these reasons, Chief Moore informed Nelson that his employment was being terminated "for cause."

The union filed a grievance alleging that Nelson's punishment was too severe since the incident occurred while he was off duty. The union requested Nelson's reinstatement with punishment, such as a reasonable suspension without pay and a warning. The city's management responded that they had a duty to ensure the public trust in the fire department. They also said that the city's rules and policies, as written in the union-management labor agreement, stated, "Employees shall conduct themselves off duty in such a manner as to show respect as a member of the fire department. Conduct unbecoming a member of the Happy Hollow Fire Department will be subject to disciplinary action, up to and including dismissal."

Questions

1. May an employer take disciplinary action (including discharge) against an employee for illegal off-duty misconduct?

2. Which particular employee rights discussed in the chapter may be asserted by the employee and his labor union representative in this case?

3. What rights does the city management have in this case?

4. When conducting an investigation of an employee's off-duty misconduct, what are important factors for the investigator to consider before recommending disciplinary action?

5. When considering disciplinary action for an employee's off-duty misconduct, what difference would it make if an employee is or is not represented by a labor union?

Case created by Robert Wayland, University of Arkansas at Little Rock

Sharpen your skills with SAGE edge at edge.sagepub.com/lussierhrm2e

SAGE edge for students provides a personalized approach to help you accomplish your coursework goals in an easy-to-use learning environment.

• • • SKILL BUILDER 9-1 COACHING

Objective

To develop coaching skill using the coaching model

Skills

The primary skills developed through this exercise are as follows:

1. *HR management skills*—Conceptual and design

2. *SHRM 2013 Curriculum Guidebook*—L: Training and development

Procedure 1 (2–4 minutes)

Break into groups of three. Make some groups of two, if necessary. Each member selects one of the following three situations in which to be the manager and a different one in which to be the employee. In each situation, the employee knows the standing plans; the employee is not motivated to follow them. You will take turns coaching and being coached.

Three Problem Employee Situations

1. Employee 1 is a clerical worker who uses files, as do the other 10 employees in the department. The employees all know that they are supposed to return the files when they are finished so that others can find them when they need them. Employees should have only one file out at a time. The supervisor notices that Employee 1 has five files on the desk, and another employee is looking for one of them.

2. Employee 2 is a server in an ice cream shop. The employee knows that the tables should be cleaned up quickly after customers leave so that new customers do not have to sit at dirty tables. It's a busy night. The supervisor finds dirty dishes on two of this employee's occupied tables. Employee 2 is socializing with some friends at one of the tables.

3. Employee 3 is an auto technician. All employees know that they are supposed to put a paper mat on the floor of each car so that the carpets don't get dirty. When the service supervisor got into a car Employee 3 repaired, the car did not have a mat and there was grease on the carpet.

Procedure 2 (3–7 minutes)

Prepare for coaching to improve performance. Each group member writes an outline of what they will say when coaching Employee 1, 2, or 3, following the steps below:

1. Describe current performance.
2. Describe desired performance. (Don't forget to have the employee state why it is important.)
3. Get a commitment to the change.
4. Follow up.

Round 1 (5–8 minutes)

Role-playing. The manager of Employee 1, the clerical worker, coaches that employee as planned. (Use the actual name of the group member playing Employee 1.) Talk—do not read your plan. Employee 1 should put themselves in the worker's position. Both the manager and the employee will have to ad lib. The person not playing a role is the observer. This person makes notes as the observer for each step of the coaching model listed above. The manager should coach the employee and try to make positive comments and point out areas for improvement. The observer should give the manager alternative suggestions about what could have been said to improve the coaching session.

Feedback. The observer leads a discussion of how well the manager coached the employee. (This should be a discussion, not a lecture.) Focus on what the manager did well and how the manager could improve. The employee should also give feedback on how they felt and what might have been more effective in motivating change. Do not go on to the next interview until you are told to do so. If you finish early, wait for the others to finish.

Round 2 (5–8 minutes)

Same as Round 1, but change roles so that Employee 2, the server, is coached. The job is not much fun if you can't talk to your friends. As the supervisor, coach Employee 2. Again, the observer gives feedback after the coaching.

Round 3 (5–8 minutes)

Same as Rounds 1 and 2, but change roles so that Employee 3, the auto technician, is coached. As the supervisor, coach Employee 3. Again, the observer gives feedback after the coaching.

Apply It

What did I learn from this exercise? How will I use this knowledge in the future?

_____

_____

• • • SKILL BUILDER 9-2 DISCIPLINING

Objective

To develop your ability to discipline an employee using the discipline model

Skills

The primary skills developed through this exercise are as follows:

1. *HR management skills*—Conceptual and design
2. *SHRM 2013 Curriculum Guidebook*—L: Training and development

Note that this is a continuation of Skill Building Exercise 9-1. Coaching didn't work, and you have to discipline the employee.

Procedure 1 (2–4 minutes)

Break into groups of three. Make some groups of two, if necessary. Each member selects one of the three situations from Skill Builder 2. Decide who will discipline Employee 1, the clerical worker; Employee 2, the ice cream shop server; and Employee 3, the auto technician. Also select different group members to play the employee being disciplined and the observer.

Procedure 2 (3–7 minutes)

Prepare for the discipline session. Write a basic outline of what you will say to Employee 1, 2, or 3; follow the steps in the discipline model below.

1. Refer to past feedback. (Assume that you have discussed the situation before, using the coaching model.)
2. Ask why the undesired behavior occurred. (The employee should make up an excuse for not changing.)
3. Administer the discipline. (Assume that an oral warning is appropriate.)
4. Get a commitment to change, and develop a plan.
5. Summarize and state the follow-up.

Round 1 (5–8 minutes)

Role-playing. The manager of Employee 1, the clerical worker, disciplines that employee as planned. (Use the actual name of the group member playing the employee.) Talk—do not read your plan. Both the manager and the employee will need to ad lib. As the supervisor, discipline Employee 1.

The person not playing a role is the observer. This person makes notes on the five steps of the discipline model above. For each of the steps, try to make a statement about the positive aspects of the discipline and a statement about how the manager could have improved. Give alternative things the manager could have said to improve the discipline session. Remember, the objective is to change behavior.

Feedback. The observer leads a discussion of how well the manager disciplined the employee. The employee should also give feedback on how they felt and what might have been more effective in motivating change. Do not go on to the next interview until you are told to do so. If you finish early, wait until the others finish or the time is up.

Round 2 (5–8 minutes)

Same as Round 1, but change roles so that Employee 2, the ice cream server, is disciplined. As Employee 2, put yourself in the worker's position. As the supervisor, discipline Employee 2. As the observer, give feedback.

Round 3 (5–8 minutes)

Same as Rounds 1 and 2, but change roles so that Employee 3, the auto technician, is disciplined. As Employee 3, put yourself in the worker's position. As the supervisor, discipline Employee 3. As the observer, give feedback.

Apply It

What did I learn from this exercise? How will I use this knowledge in the future?

_____

_____

• • • SKILL BUILDER 9-3 SITUATIONAL MANAGEMENT

Objective

To learn how to use the situational management model to develop skill at selecting the most appropriate management style in a given situation

Skills

The primary skills developed through this exercise are as follows:

1. *HR management skills*—Conceptual and design
2. *SHRM 2013 Curriculum Guidebook*—L: Training and development

Assignment

As stated back in the chapter subsection on situational management, select the most appropriate management style for each of the 12 situations in Self-Assessment 9-1, using the situational management model. Be sure to fill in the C _____ (1-2-3-4) and S _____ (1A-2C-3P-4E) lines as instructed in the text.

Apply It

What did I learn from this exercise? How will I use this knowledge in the future?

_____

_____

Your instructor may review the situational management model, complete more of the situations in class, and/or ask you to do this Skill Builder in class by breaking into groups of two or three to select or discuss your answers. If so, the instructor will provide you with any necessary information or additional instructions.

©iStockphoto.com/-blige

10 Employee and Labor Relations

• • • LEARNING OUTCOMES

After studying this chapter, you should be able to do the following:

10-1 Briefly describe the five steps in the message-sending process. PAGE 360

10-2 Briefly describe the three steps in the message-receiving process. PAGE 362

10-3 Identify the primary reason why measuring job satisfaction is so difficult, and identify the best tool for getting employees to tell the truth about their level of satisfaction. PAGE 364

10-4 Identify the major labor relations laws in the United States and the major reasons why we have each law. PAGE 367

10-5 Briefly discuss the difference between wrongful discharge and constructive discharge. PAGE 374

10-6 Briefly discuss the NO TIPS rules for labor elections. PAGE 377

10-7 Briefly discuss what management can do to limit union organizing efforts. PAGE 379

10-8 Identify the five conflict management styles. How is each described in terms of win or lose? PAGE 381

10-9 Briefly explain the processes of mediation and arbitration and the major difference between the two processes. PAGE 388

10-10 Define the key terms found in the chapter margins and listed following the Chapter Summary. PAGE 393

Practitioner's Perspective

Cindy says: Few issues bring HR professionals out in force to voice their opinion like labor relations. The divide between management and labor may be wide, yet there is a very fine line separating management rights from unacceptable labor practices. CIndy's good friend Leah's company was facing a labor organization drive. IT reported that one of the employees had been posting complaints about her job on her Facebook page. At the weekly executive meeting, one director demanded that the employee be told to remove the offensive comments immediately or face being discharged from the company. Fortunately, Leah's boss listened to her suggestion that they consult professional legal counsel before reacting to the posts.

Why wasn't the ultimatum to the employee a good idea? Are there restrictions on the actions a company may take to counter a labor organization campaign? Chapter 10 takes on another critical legal liability portion of HR management—labor relations.

SHRM HR CONTENT

See Appendix: *SHRM 2013 Curriculum Guidebook* for the complete list

A. Employee and Labor Relations (required)

2. Alternative dispute resolution
8. Union membership
9. Union-related labor laws
10. Union/management relations
11. Union decertification and deauthorization
12. Collective bargaining issues
13. Collective bargaining process
14. Negotiation skills
15. Conflict management
16. Grievance management
17. Strikes, boycotts, and work stoppages
18. Unfair labor practices
19. Managing union organizing policies and handbooks
21. Attitude surveys

B. Employment Law (required)

11. The Labor Management Reporting and Disclosure Act of 1959 (LMRDA)
12. The National Labor Relations Act of 1935 (NLRA)
13. The Labor Management Relations Act of 1947 (LMRA)
14. The Railway Labor Act of 1926 (RLA)
16. The Worker Adjustment and Retraining Notification Act of 1988 (WARN Act)
18. Contractual and tort theories
20. Employer unfair labor practices
22. Agency relationships/quasi-contracts
23. Employment contracts
28. Whistle-blowing/retaliation

C. Ethics (required)

15. Sarbanes-Oxley Act of 2002 (SOX)
16. False Claims Act

M. Workforce Planning and Talent Management (required)

4. Retention: Voluntary turnover, job satisfaction, withdrawal, alternatives

LABOR RELATIONS:
A FUNCTION OF TRUST AND COMMUNICATION

You need strong communication skills to manage effectively.[1] No matter what else happens in an organization, managers and labor have to work together to accomplish sets of goals.[2] For this to happen successfully, people in organizations must be able to communicate with each other.[3] Both companywide and individual communications are vital.[4] Given increasing worker interdependence, many organizations need employees to engage in greater information exchange.[5] Communication allows us to control the work environment, give and receive important information, express how we feel about a set of circumstances, and motivate ourselves and others. In addition, whenever people have to communicate to accomplish a goal, the sender and receiver must establish trust to avoid creating barriers in the communication process.[6] In this section, we begin with an overview of trust and communications and then provide details of sending and receiving messages when communicating.

Trust and Communication

Trust Faith in the character and actions of another

Trust *is simply faith in the character and actions of another*. In other words, it is a belief that another person will do what they say they will do—every time. There is evidence of a "crisis of trust" in business today.[7] So how do we get others to trust us? We must do what we say we will do consistently, over a period of time. In other words, we need to "walk the talk." Jack Welch, the former CEO of **GE** and now an executive consultant, said trust "is enormously powerful in an organization and people won't do their best without it."[8] Trust is absolutely necessary to strong management-labor relations, and research shows that companies that have the trust of their employees have "lower turnover [and] higher revenue, profitability, and shareholder returns."[9]

Since a person must consistently do what they say they will over a period of time, trust isn't created immediately. But ask yourself a slightly different question: How quickly can we *lose* trust in another person? This can happen almost immediately—as soon as the other person fails to do something that we trusted them to do. So, trust takes a while to create but only takes an instant to lose.

And in the case of companies, as soon as trust goes, loyalty to the company goes with it.[10] As managers, we always have to keep this fact in mind because we need our employees to trust us when we communicate with them. In any communication, receivers take into account the trust they have in the senders, as well as the senders' credibility.[11] When receivers do not trust senders or do not believe senders know what they are talking about, then the receivers are reluctant to accept the message.[12]

So the bottom line is this: If we want to improve others' level of trust in us, we need to be open and honest with people.[13] If people catch you in a lie, they may never trust you again. To gain and maintain trust and credibility, always get the facts straight before you communicate and send clear, complete messages.[14]

Communication *is the process of transmitting information and meaning.* This meaning can be transferred verbally, nonverbally, or in writing. We are expected to work well in groups and communicate with ease.[15] Open communications are needed for the organization to be successful,[16] and good managers are good communicators.[17]

Good communication involves successfully providing information to others as a sender, as well as being a capable receiver of communications from others. Let's take a look at some tips that can help us be better communicators, as both senders and receivers.

Sending Messages

We are constantly pitching our ideas.[18] The vast majority of messages you send and receive in the workplace are simple, straightforward messages like "Please copy this document," "I'll call you when I've reviewed these specifications," and "I put the report you requested on your desk." You transmit many such messages face-to-face or in a brief memo, email, or fax. Such straightforward messages need minimal planning, because they are routine.

However, sometimes the message you need to transmit is difficult, unusual, or especially important. For example, you may have the difficult task of communicating to someone that they are to be laid off. Or perhaps you need to communicate to workers at one plant about the changes that will be occurring there as a result of closing a second plant and moving its processes to that one—an unusual situation and an important communication. So before sending a message, we should answer five basic questions: What, who, how, when, and where? What is the goal of our communication, and what is the desired end result? Who is affected by the communication? How are we sending the message—in verbal or written form? When does the message need to be sent? And where should we send it—your office, mine, or a neutral site?

Communication The process of transmitting information and meaning

| MODEL 10-1 | THE MESSAGE-SENDING PROCESS MODEL |

Briefly describe the five steps in the message-sending process.

WORK
APPLICATION 10-2

Select a present or past boss and describe how well that person sent messages. Did the boss essentially follow the steps in the message-sending process described here?

THE MESSAGE-SENDING PROCESS. Oral communication channels (channels where we *speak* to others directly) are richer than other channels, and face-to-face oral communication is the best channel to use when the message you must transmit is a difficult or complex one. When sending a face-to-face message, you can follow the steps in the message-sending process shown in Model 10-1.

Step 1: Develop rapport. Begin by putting the receiver at ease by creating a harmonious relationship. It is usually appropriate to begin communication by making a connection with the receiver through an opening conversation that's related to the message you're trying to convey.[19]

Step 2: State your communication objective. It is helpful for the receiver if you explain the objective (end result) of the communication before you explain the details.

Step 3: Transmit your message. Calmly and with respect, tell the receiver(s) whatever you want them to know. It may be helpful to also provide written directives and/or to ask the receiver to take some notes.

Step 4: Check the receiver's understanding. When giving information, ask direct questions and/or paraphrase. Simply asking, "Do you have any questions?" does not check understanding. (The next subsection describes how to check understanding.)

Step 5: Get a commitment and follow up. If the message involves assigning a task, make sure that the message recipient can do the task and have it done by a certain time or date. Finally, follow up to ensure that the necessary action has been taken.

CHECKING UNDERSTANDING: FEEDBACK. **Feedback** *is information provided by the receiver that verifies that a message was transmitted successfully.* As senders of messages, we need to get feedback from the receiver. Ask for feedback[20] because feedback increases performance.[21] Being asked for their feedback motivates employees to be creative and achieve high levels of performance.[22] The best way to make sure communication has taken place is to get feedback from the receiver about the message through questioning and paraphrasing,[23] so you should invite questions.[24]

Paraphrasing *is the process of restating a message back to the original sender in the receiver's own words.* Paraphrasing can often avoid the problem of the sender saying things like "This isn't what I asked for." So taking a minute to get feedback to ensure understanding can help ensure that the task will get done right the first time. How we ask for feedback is important because we don't want to make the receiver defensive, so we should say something like this: "Would you tell me what you are going to do so that I can be sure that I explained myself clearly?"

Receiving Messages

We need to be as effective at receiving messages as we are at sending them. Successfully receiving and interpreting messages requires concentration, and it is harder than most of us think. Here we discuss listening skills and the message-receiving process so we can round out our communication skills.

WORK
APPLICATION 10-3

Select a present or past boss and describe how effective that person is at getting feedback and paraphrasing. How often did you get the task done right the first time versus having to redo it?

Feedback Information provided by the receiver that verifies that a message was transmitted successfully

Paraphrasing The process of restating a message back to the original sender in the receiver's own words

LISTENING SKILLS. Listening is crucial for effective communication to occur.[25] If someone were to ask us if we are good listeners, most of us would say yes. However, unfortunately, a recent survey found that the number one thing lacking in new college grads is listening skills.[26] One of the biggest problems in the 21st century work environment is the fact that constant multitasking is degrading our ability to pay attention and listen for very long.[27] Multitasking can cause us to become distracted, whether we realize it or not, and to miss the message being communicated. However, there are ways to improve your skills in receiving communications. By using the message-receiving process, you can learn to become a better listener. But first, find out how good a listener you are by completing the listening skills self-assessment.

With mobile technology, employees are constantly connected and communicating.

10-1 SELF ASSESSMENT

Listening Skills

For each statement, select the response that best describes how often you actually behave in the way described. Place the letter *A, U, F, O,* or *S* on the line before each statement to indicate your response.

A = almost always   U = usually   F = frequently   O = occasionally   S = seldom

_____ 1. I like to listen to people talk. I encourage others to talk by showing interest, smiling, nodding, and so forth.
_____ 2. I pay closer attention to people who are similar to me than to people who are different from me.
_____ 3. I evaluate people's words and nonverbal communication ability as they talk.
_____ 4. I avoid distractions; if it's noisy, I suggest moving to a quiet spot.
_____ 5. When people interrupt me when I'm doing something, I put what I was doing out of my mind and give them my complete attention.
_____ 6. When people are talking, I allow them time to finish. I do not interrupt, anticipate what they are going to say, or jump to conclusions.
_____ 7. I tune out people who do not agree with my views.
_____ 8. While another person is talking or a professor is lecturing, my mind wanders to personal topics.
_____ 9. While another person is talking, I pay close attention to that person's nonverbal communication so I can fully understand what they are trying to communicate.
_____ 10. I tune out and pretend to understand when the topic is difficult for me to understand.
_____ 11. When another person is talking, I think about and prepare what I am going to say in reply.
_____ 12. When I think there is something missing from or contradictory in what someone says, I ask direct questions to get the person to explain the idea more fully.
_____ 13. When I don't understand something, I let the other person know I don't understand.
_____ 14. When listening to other people, I try to put myself in their position and see things from their perspective.
_____ 15. During conversations, I repeat back to the other person, in my own words, what the other person says; I do this to be sure I understand what has been said.

If people you talk to regularly answered these questions about you, would they have the same responses that you selected? To find out, have friends answer the questions using your name rather than "I." Then compare answers.

To determine your score, do the following:

For statements 1, 4, 5, 6, 9, 12, 13, 14, and 15, give yourself 5 points for each *A*, 4 for each *U*, 3 for each *F*, 2 for each *O*, and 1 for each *S*.

For statements 2, 3, 7, 8, 10, and 11, give yourself 5 points for each *S*, 4 for each *O*, 3 for each *F*, 2 for each *U*, and 1 for each *A*.

Write your score for each letter response on the line next to the letter. Now add up your total number of points. Your score should be between 15 and 75. Note where your score falls on the continuum below. Generally, the higher your score, the better your listening skills.

Poor Listener												Good Listener
15	20	25	30	35	40	45	50	55	60	65	70	75

LO 10-2
Briefly describe the three steps in the message-receiving process.

THE MESSAGE-RECEIVING PROCESS. The message-receiving process includes listening in a form called active listening, analyzing, and then checking for understanding. **Active listening** *is the process of paying attention to an entire message, taking into account both the content of the message and the context in which the communication is delivered.* If you apply the following tips, you can improve your listening skills. The message-receiving process is illustrated in Model 10-2.

MODEL 10-2   THE MESSAGE-RECEIVING PROCESS MODEL

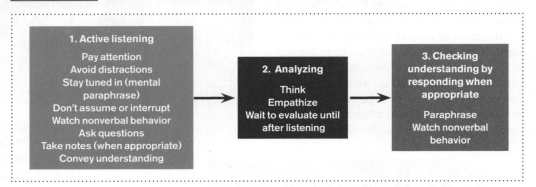

1. Active listening

Pay attention
Avoid distractions
Stay tuned in (mental paraphrase)
Don't assume or interrupt
Watch nonverbal behavior
Ask questions
Take notes (when appropriate)
Convey understanding

2. Analyzing

Think
Empathize
Wait to evaluate until after listening

3. Checking understanding by responding when appropriate

Paraphrase
Watch nonverbal behavior

Step 1: Active Listening. **Active listening** (sometimes called empathetic listening) is about giving your full attention (meaning 100% of it) to the message sender for the entire time of the message sending.[28] As the speaker sends the message, you should be doing the eight things listed in the first column of Model 10-2. If you find your mind wandering by thinking of other things (something that happens to all of us), bring it back to pay attention. One way to pay attention is to repeat in your mind what the sender is saying. Active listening is not easy, and most of us have to work hard at it to keep our minds from thinking about things besides the actual message.

Step 2: Analyzing. **Analyzing** is the process of thinking about, decoding, and evaluating the message. Poor listening is caused in part by the fact that we speak at an average rate of 120 words per minute, but we are capable of listening at a rate of 600 words per minute.[29] The ability to comprehend words more than five times faster than the speaker can talk allows our mind to wander. As the speaker sends the message, we should be doing the three things listed in the second column of Model 10-2. So while active thinking involves mental paraphrasing, empathy involves putting yourself in the other person's position to understand where they are coming from.

Step 3: Checking Understanding by Responding When Appropriate. **Checking understanding** is the process of giving feedback to the sender. Although the sender is responsible for conveying the message, it is our job to help by giving them feedback, whether they ask for it or not.

After you have listened to the message (or while listening to it, if it's a long message), check your understanding of the message by paraphrasing it. When we can repeat back a sender's message correctly, we convey that we have listened to and understood the sender.[30] Now we are ready to offer our ideas, advice, solutions, decisions, or whatever else is relevant to the sender's message. As you speak, pay attention to the other person's nonverbal communication. If the person does not seem to understand what you are talking about, clarify the message before finishing the conversation. The sender and receiver roles can continue to alternate throughout the conversation.

IMPROVING LISTENING SKILLS. Do you talk more than you listen? Ask people who will give you an honest answer—perhaps your boss, your coworkers, or your friends. Regardless of how much you listen, if you follow the guidelines discussed in this section, you

WORK
APPLICATION 10-4

Select a present or past boss and assess that person's listening skills. Be sure to give specific examples of when your boss was not listening effectively.

Active listening The process of paying attention to an entire message, taking into account both the content of the message and the context in which the communication is delivered

10-1 APPLYING THE CONCEPT

Communications

Identify whether each strategy listed below is an effective or ineffective aid to communications.

    a. effective
    b. ineffective

_____ 1. When listening to instructions, if you don't understand something being said, you should not do or say anything until you have received the entire set of instructions.

_____ 2. You should repeat back what the other person said word-for-word when you paraphrase.

_____ 3. After you finish giving instructions, you should ensure understanding by asking the person, "Do you have any questions?"

_____ 4. When giving instructions, you should tell the receiver your communication objective before giving the details of what is to be done to complete the task.

_____ 5. We should multitask while receiving messages face-to-face so that we can get more than one thing done at a time.

---

will become a better listener. Review items 1, 4, 5, 6, 9, 12, 13, 14, and 15 in Self-Assessment 10-1, which are the statements that describe good listening skills; the other numbered statements are things not to do. Select a couple of your weaker areas, the ones with lower numbers, and work to improve them.

JOB SATISFACTION

Job satisfaction, as we first noted in Chapter 1, is a feeling of well-being and acceptance of our place in the organization, and it is generally measured along a continuum from satisfied/positive/high to dissatisfied/negative/low. Remember that job satisfaction is important to us because it affects many other factors at work.[31] It can have a direct effect on all of our other dependent variables discussed in Chapter 1—productivity, absenteeism, and turnover—so high job satisfaction is beneficial for firm value.[32] Studies have also found that dissatisfied employees are more apt to break the rules and sabotage performance.[33] Unfortunately, a survey found that around 53% of Americas are unsatisfied with their jobs and only 15.4% are very satisfied.[34] So we need to know in general how satisfied our workforce is at any point in time.

Job Satisfaction/Dissatisfaction and Performance

It is very difficult to have good employee/labor relations when employees don't like their jobs, and there are many other potential consequences of poor job satisfaction, including lower levels of health and wellness, higher levels of alcohol and other substance abuse, physical or psychological withdrawal on the part of the employee, and high levels of theft and sabotage.[35] Even attempts to unionize a workforce could be the result of collective job dissatisfaction, so managers are wise to pay attention to employee satisfaction levels.

It is known that employees with the personality traits of optimism and positive self-esteem tend to have greater job satisfaction.[36] Although there has long been a debate over the expression "A happy worker is a productive worker," there is some support for the idea of a positive relationship between job satisfaction and *organizational citizenship behavior* (OCB), employee efforts that go above and beyond the call of duty,[37] which can then lead to high-level results.[38] However, even though there is no strong evidence for the notion that higher job satisfaction leads to higher productivity, there is some support for the assertion that lower job satisfaction (or higher job dissatisfaction levels) can lead to lower productivity.[39] Also, low job satisfaction is a prominent indicator of a desire to leave the firm.[40] **Google** strives to keep

WORK
APPLICATION 10-5

Review your answers to the Listening Self-Assessment. What are your two weakest areas, and how will you improve them?

SHRM

M:4
Retention: Voluntary Turnover, Job Satisfaction, Withdrawal, Alternatives

WORK
APPLICATION 10-6

Select a present or past job. Pick a person who had low job satisfaction and another that had high job satisfaction. How did their different levels of job satisfaction affect their job performance?

employees happy because it helps productivity.[41] Job satisfaction can also affect an individual's satisfaction away from the job, as people tend to take their jobs home with them.[42]

Measuring Job Satisfaction

Job satisfaction can be measured through an organizational development survey, but we have to remember that a survey is an indirect measurement. Since job satisfaction is an attitude, we can't directly see or measure it. We can only experience behaviors directly, not attitudes. We have to indirectly evaluate attitudes—we have to *ask* people about their attitudes. This is the primary reason why job satisfaction is so difficult to measure accurately. As a result of the inability to observe job satisfaction, we must rely on individuals to self-report their level of satisfaction. However, this brings up a *big* question: Will employees tell us whether or not they are satisfied with their job?

As with so many management questions, the answer is that it depends. If managers and employees trust each other, then the employees may tell their managers the truth. However, as noted earlier in this chapter, if there isn't strong trust between the two, then employees may think that if they say they are dissatisfied, their manager will get rid of them because they are "disgruntled workers."

Because of this question of trust, it's always a good idea to ensure that any job satisfaction surveys that are done within the organization remain completely *anonymous*. If the surveys are anonymous, and if the employees know that is the case, then they are much more likely to tell the truth when they take the survey.

There are two common types of job satisfaction surveys or questionnaires. Let's briefly review each of them now.

THE FACES SCALE OF JOB SATISFACTION MEASUREMENT. The first and simpler survey is called the "faces scale."[43] It's pretty much what it sounds like: a series of pictures of several faces on a sheet of paper, with the face at one end of the scale looking very happy and the face at the other end of the scale looking unhappy or angry. All that the employee is asked to do is circle the face that most closely matches their satisfaction with their job. Exhibit 10-1 shows an example of the faces scale.

EXHIBIT 10-1 FEMALE FACES SCALE

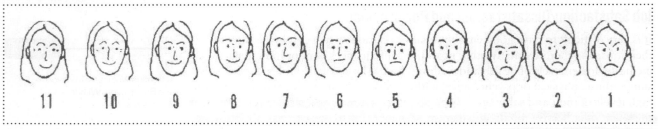

Source: "Development of a female faces scale for measuring job satisfaction" by Randall B. Dunham and Jeanne B. Herman, *Journal of Applied Psychology, 60*(5), October 1975, 629–631.

THE QUESTIONNAIRE JOB SATISFACTION MEASUREMENT. The second type of survey or questionnaire—the organizational development survey—is more complex and more comprehensive. An example of this type of survey is the Job Satisfaction Survey (JSS). Take a look at Exhibit 10-2, which shows some of the questions from the JSS.[44] There are many different surveys of this type, and this is one of only a few that have been shown to be valid and reliable when used to measure job satisfaction in a work environment.[45] The JSS includes nine factors: pay, promotion, supervision,

EXHIBIT 10-2 SAMPLE OF JOB SATISFACTION SURVEY (JSS) QUESTIONS[46]

	Disagree very much	Disagree moderately	Disagree slightly	Agree slightly	Agree moderately	Agree very much
People get ahead as fast here as they do in other places.	1	2	3	4	5	6
My supervisor shows too little interest in the feelings of subordinates.	1	2	3	4	5	6
The benefits package we have is equitable.	1	2	3	4	5	6
There are few rewards for those who work here.	1	2	3	4	5	6
I have too much to do at work.	1	2	3	4	5	6
I enjoy my coworkers.	1	2	3	4	5	6

benefits, contingent rewards, operating procedures, coworkers, nature of work, and communication.

WHICH JOB SATISFACTION MEASUREMENT SHOULD WE USE? Since there are two types of measurement options here, which one should we use? Again, it depends. If we want a quick analysis of the basic level of job satisfaction in our organization, the faces scale has been shown to be quite accurate.[47] However, if we need a more in-depth analysis of job satisfaction, including what aspects of the job our employees may be dissatisfied with, the more complex and comprehensive JSS (or another longer survey instrument) would be the appropriate choice.

Many organizations will routinely (every few months or every year) ask their employees to take the faces scale survey, and then HR will track the level of *overall* job satisfaction in the workplace. If management sees that job satisfaction is dropping, they may then utilize the JSS or another survey instrument to attempt to determine more exactly *why* the workforce is becoming dissatisfied so that they can take necessary measures to stop any slide in satisfaction. Each tool has its value, and in combination, they can help us keep track of organizational job satisfaction levels over time.

Determinants of Job Satisfaction

Although compensation (pay and benefits) is important to job satisfaction, research historically has not strongly supported the idea that pay is the primary determinant of job satisfaction, or that people in high-paying jobs are more satisfied than employees in low-paying jobs. Even though when asked, employees often reply that compensation is a primary satisfier for their work,[48] money may not necessarily make employees happy.[49] According to recent studies, the top reasons for job *dissatisfaction* are that employees don't like their boss, they feel powerless, they don't have any say in their work, and they don't feel like they get recognition for their work.[50,51]

Seven major determinants of job satisfaction are presented in Self-Assessment 10-2: Job Satisfaction. Complete it to find out what is important to you and your own level of job satisfaction. You *can* have an overall high level of job satisfaction and still not like some aspects of your job; this is common.

WORK APPLICATION 10-7

Select an organization where you work now or where you worked in the past. Does the organization measure job satisfaction? If yes, state how it is measured and the level of job satisfaction. If not, what level of satisfaction do employees feel on a scale of 1 (low) to 6 (high)?

WORK APPLICATION 10-8

Identify the three most important determinants of your job satisfaction, and explain why they are important to you.

10-2 **SELF** ASSESSMENT

Job Satisfaction

Select a present or past job. Identify your level of satisfaction with that job by placing a check at the appropriate position on the continuum for each determinant of job satisfaction.

1. Personality

I have positive self-esteem.	6 5 4 3 2 1	I have negative self-esteem.

2. Work Itself

I enjoy doing the tasks I perform.	6 5 4 3 2 1	I do *not* enjoy doing the tasks I perform.

3. Compensation

I am fairly compensated (with pay and benefits).	6 5 4 3 2 1	I am *not* fairly compensated (with pay and benefits).

4. Growth and Upward Mobility

I have the opportunity to learn new things and get promoted to better jobs.	6 5 4 3 2 1	I have *no* opportunity to learn new things and get promoted to better jobs.

5. Coworkers

I like and enjoy working with my coworkers.	6 5 4 3 2 1	I do *not* like and enjoy working with my coworkers.

6. Management

I believe that my boss and managers are doing a good job.	6 5 4 3 2 1	I do *not* believe that my boss and managers are doing a good job.

7. Communication

We have open and honest communication.	6 5 4 3 2 1	We do *not* have open and honest communication.

Overall Job Satisfaction

When determining your overall job satisfaction, you cannot simply add up a score based on the above seven determinants, because they are most likely of different importance to you. Rank your top three factors below:

1. _____

2. _____

3. _____

Now, think about your job and the above factors, and rate your overall satisfaction with your job below:

I am satisfied with my job (high level of job satisfaction).	6 5 4 3 2 1	I am dissatisfied with my job (low level of job satisfaction).

10-2 **APPLYING THE CONCEPT**

Job Satisfaction

Correctly match each statement with its determinant of job satisfaction, writing the letter corresponding to each determinant before the statement associated with it.

   a. personality

   b. work itself

   c. compensation

   d. growth

   e. coworkers

   f. management

   g. communications

_____ 6. There is a job opening in the metal fusion shop, and I am going to apply for the position.

_____ 7. I really enjoy fixing cars to help people get around.

_____ 8. I'm mad at my manager because he didn't give me the good performance review that I deserved.

_____ 9. Of course I can do that task for you.

_____ 10. The thing I like best about my job is the people I work with.

IMPROVING YOUR JOB SATISFACTION. Remember that job satisfaction is to a large extent based on personality and perception, so it can be changed. If you work at being more positive by focusing on the good parts of your job and spend less time thinking about problems, and especially complaining to others about your job, then you may increase your job satisfaction.[52] Improving your communications and human relationship skills can help you to get along better with coworkers and managers and increase your job satisfaction. It can also increase your chances for growth and your opportunities for advancement and higher compensation.

LEGAL ISSUES IN LABOR RELATIONS

As with most management processes, a number of legal issues affect labor relations. There are laws that deal with unions and unionization efforts; laws that identify what the organization has to do in the event of a significant layoff; laws that govern collective bargaining between the firm and the employees; and a series of court decisions, EEOC regulations, and other government agency rulings that limit organizational rights in managing the workforce. While each of the labor laws that we will discuss here covers many details, we will only discuss the major facets of the laws in this text—you'll get the details in your employment law class. *All* managers need to understand the constraints set by these labor laws to successfully do their job. In this section, we will introduce you to the major labor laws in the United States. See Exhibit 10-3 for a brief overview of the five major labor laws.

The Railway Labor Act (RLA) of 1926

The Railway Labor Act was originally enacted to significantly limit the potential for railroad strikes to affect interstate commerce by hindering the general public's ability to procure goods and services. Railroads were the primary means of moving goods from one state to another in 1926. Airlines were added to the act in 1936 because much of the US mail was beginning to be delivered with the help of airlines, and an airline disruption would affect the delivery of the mail. Airlines are subject to *basically* the same negotiation and mediation processes as were the railroads.[53]

The act also provides protection for workers' right to join a union,[54] and it requires that in so-called *major disputes*—disputes involving rates of pay, work rules, or working conditions—management and labor must participate in a fairly

LO 10-4

Identify the major labor relations laws in the United States and the major reasons why we have each law.

SHRM

A:9
Union-Related Labor Laws

SHRM

A:10
Union/Management Relations

SHRM

B:14
The Railway Labor Act of 1926

SHRM

A:17
Strikes, Boycotts, and Work Stoppages

EXHIBIT 10-3   MAJOR LABOR LAWS

The Railway Labor Act of 1926 (RLA)	The act was passed to significantly limit the potential for railroad strikes to affect interstate commerce; it was later expanded to include airlines. In an amendment to the law, the National Mediation Board (NMB) was established to mediate between management and labor to help them come to agreement.
National Labor Relations Act of 1935 (NLRA–Wagner Act)	The act gave employees the right to unionize without fear of prosecution, as it listed unfair employer practices. The law also established the National Labor Relations Board (NLRB) to enforce the provisions of the act and conduct elections to determine whether employees will unionize and who will be their representative in collective bargaining.
Labor Management Relations Act of 1947 (LMRA–Taft-Hartley Act)	The act was passed to offset some of the imbalance of power given to labor by previous laws. It amended the Wagner Act (NLRA) to include a list of unfair practices by unions.
Labor Management Reporting Disclosure Act of 1959 (LMRDA–Landrum-Griffin Act)	The act was passed to protect union members from corrupt or discriminatory union practices.
Worker Adjustment and Retraining Notification Act of 1988 (WARN)	The act was passed to give employees 60 days' advance notice in cases of plant closings or large-scale layoffs.

long negotiation and mediation process before a labor strike may be called. A **strike** *is a collective work stoppage by members of a union that is intended to put pressure on an employer.* This negotiation process is designed to force the two parties to come to an agreement without resorting to a strike, in almost all cases.

In 1934, the **National Mediation Board (NMB)** was created in an amendment to the RLA. If management and labor fail to negotiate a settlement to their disagreement, the NMB is tasked by the act with mediating the two parties' disagreements. The NMB can, in fact, "keep the parties in mediation indefinitely, so long as it feels there's a reasonable prospect for settlement."[55]

Even after the NMB determines that there's no reasonable prospect for settlement through mediation, it can push the two parties to submit to an arbitration process. However, both parties must consent to arbitration. Finally, if arbitration is unsuccessful or is rejected, the NMB has the authority to refer the dispute to the president of the United States, who can create a Presidential Emergency Board (PEB) as a mechanism to investigate the disagreement.

It should probably be obvious by now that the intent of the act is to draw out the bargaining process between management and labor and push the two sides to resolve a labor disagreement without having to resort to a strike. In fact, in most cases involving *minor* disputes (disputes over items *other than* collective bargaining rights such as pay, work rules, or working conditions), strikes are prohibited under this law because a disruption in railroad or airline traffic could have such a devastating effect on the general public.

The National Labor Relations Act (NLRA) of 1935 (Wagner Act)

The National Labor Relations Act (NLRA; frequently called the Wagner Act) was the first major modern law to deal with the legal issue of unions in the general

Strike A collective work stoppage by members of a union that is intended to put pressure on an employer

workforce (workers who were not covered by special laws such as the Railway Labor Act) in the United States. The act states,

> Employees shall have the right to self-organization, to form, join, or assist labor organizations, to bargain collectively through representatives of their own choosing, and to engage in other concerted activities for the purpose of collective bargaining or other mutual aid or protection, and shall also have the right to refrain from any or all such activities except to the extent that such right may be affected by an agreement requiring membership in a labor organization as a condition of employment.[56]

SHRM

B:12
The National Labor Relations Act of 1935 (NLRA)

The NLRA was considered to be very one-sided by employers because it identified five "unfair labor practices" (prohibitions) for employers but identified no unfair labor practices for employee unions or labor organizations. The act was later amended to include unfair labor practices by employees and their representatives. We will talk more about unions, other labor organizations, and their processes shortly.

The *employer* unfair labor practices identified by the NLRA include the following:

SHRM

A:18, B:20
Employer Unfair Labor Practices

1. Interfering with, restraining, or coercing employees in the exercise of the rights guaranteed in the NLRA
2. Dominating or interfering with the formation or administration of any labor organization, or contributing financial or other support to it
3. Discriminating in regard to hiring or tenure of employment or any term or condition of employment to encourage or discourage membership in any labor organization (with some specific exceptions)
4. Discharging or otherwise discriminating (retaliating) against an employee because that person has filed charges or given testimony under the NLRA
5. Refusing to bargain collectively with the legitimate representatives of employees

The NLRA is enforced by the **National Labor Relations Board** (**NLRB**), which was created by the act. According to its website, the NLRB has five primary functions: conducting elections, investigating charges, seeking resolution, deciding cases, and enforcing orders.[57] The NLRB has authority over all elections to either certify or decertify unions within a particular employer's workforce. It is also tasked with investigating any unfair labor practice charges and resolving those charges. In addition, when complaints of unfair labor practices cannot be settled, the case will typically be heard by an NLRB administrative law judge, whose ruling is subject to review by the NLRB itself. Board decisions may be appealed to a US Court of Appeals and, ultimately, to the US Supreme Court if the parties are still unsatisfied. The last of the NLRB's tasks is enforcing orders. When a circuit court, an appeals court, or the US Supreme Court issues a decision in a labor relations case, the NLRB is the enforcement arm of the US government. For more information about the NLRB, visit its website at http://www.nlrb.gov.

The Labor Management Relations Act (LMRA) of 1947 (Taft-Hartley Act)

The Labor Management Relations Act (LMRA), also called the Taft-Hartley Act, was passed by Congress as an amendment to the 1935 NLRA. Whereas the NLRA identified a series of employee rights and employer unfair labor practices, the LMRA attempted to rebalance employer and employee rights.

SHRM

B:13
The Labor Management Relations Act of 1947 (LMRA)

The LMRA included a number of new provisions that limited union and labor rights in the United States. It outlawed several types of union actions that had been used since passage of the Wagner Act. These included *jurisdictional strikes*,[58] which union members used to push companies to provide them with certain types of jobs;

wildcat strikes,[59] where individual union members participated in strikes that were not authorized by the union; *secondary boycotts,*[60] in which a union participating in a strike against a company would pressure other unions to boycott organizations that did business with that company; and *closed shops,* which provided for "the hiring and employment of union members only."[61] In addition, the law limited *union shops,*[62] where every employee was required to become a member of the union within a certain time period. Finally, the LMRA provided that supervisors had no right to be protected if they chose to participate in union activities, so if a supervisor participated in unionizing activities, the company was allowed to terminate them.

The LMRA, as noted in the beginning of this section, also created a set of unfair labor practices for unions and labor. Unfair *union/labor* practices include the following:[63]

- Restraining or coercing (a) employees in the exercise of their rights guaranteed in the NLRA or (b) an employer in the selection of his representatives for negotiations
- Causing or attempting to cause an employer to discriminate against an employee who is not a union member
- Refusing to bargain collectively with an employer, provided the union is the elected representative of its employees
- Engaging in or encouraging any individual to engage in a secondary boycott of an employer
- Requiring dues that the NLRB finds excessive or discriminatory
- Causing or attempting to cause an employer to pay for more workers than necessary or pay for services that are not performed (this is called *featherbedding*)
- Picketing or threatening to picket an employer for the purpose of forcing the employer to bargain with the labor organization, unless the labor organization is certified as the employees' representative

In addition to the limitations on unions and labor, the LMRA created mechanisms for decertifying unions through an election process, and it allowed the states to pass a right-to-work law. *Right-to-work laws* work directly against union shops by declaring that every employee in a company has a right to work, even if they choose not to join the union representing the shop.[64] Union shops cannot be set up in states that pass right-to-work laws.

The Labor Management Reporting and Disclosure Act of 1959 (Landrum-Griffin Act or LMRDA)

SHRM

B:11
The Labor Management Reporting and Disclosure Act of 1959 (LMRDA)

The LMRDA came about as the result of a congressional investigation in the 1950s that linked organized crime with some national labor unions. The act required specific disclosures by union officials and provided certain rights to union members.

Among the important provisions of the law were these:[65]

- A statement of worker rights for union members as well as all other workers in organizations whose members are represented by a union agreement
- The right of all organization members (not just union members) to receive and evaluate collective bargaining agreements
- Freedom of speech when it comes to union activities
- Requirements for periodic secret ballot elections of union officers
- Requirements for unions to file copies of their constitution, bylaws, and annual financial reports with the federal government

- Requirements that any officers of the union who receive loans or other benefits from union funds, who have financial interests in employers whose members the union represents, or who deal with the union must file declaration forms stating such facts

- A prohibition against using union funds to support any specific candidate for union elections

- A declaration that union officers have a duty to manage funds and property of the union solely for the benefit of the members. If union officials fail in this fiduciary duty, they've committed a federal crime that can be punished with a fine of up to $250,000.

The Worker Adjustment and Retraining Notification Act of 1988 (WARN Act)

The last of the major federal labor laws that we will discuss here is the Worker Adjustment and Retraining Notification Act. The WARN Act was designed to protect workers in the case of a plant closing or large-scale layoff. The act says that management has to give employees notice of a plant closing or layoff at least 60 days ahead of time if more than 50 people will be laid off and if there are more than 100 full-time employees at the workplace. All workers are entitled to notice under WARN, including hourly and salaried workers as well as managers.[66]

If we don't give our workers notice of a layoff or plant closing, can we still lay them off? In fact, we can do that by accepting the penalty provided in the law. The penalty provision says that an employer who fails to provide notice "is liable to each aggrieved employee for an amount including back pay and benefits for the period of violation, up to 60 days," plus a fine of up to $500 per day of violation.[67] What this means is if we lay people off with less than 60 days' notice, we have to pay them as if they were still employed for the 60 days anyway.

Why would we consider releasing employees but still paying them for 60 days? Well, some workers might have the ability to sabotage the organization, and therefore, we need to get them out of the company before they have a chance to hurt it. If we were to give them 60 days to stay and they had the ability to harm the organization, some of them might take advantage of that because they felt betrayed by the company. For example, if we were going to lay off a group of computer programmers, should we allow them to have access to the company computer system, knowing that they are going to lose their jobs in 60 days? Someone may potentially sabotage the system because they are mad at the company. So in some cases, we will say, "OK, I know that I am going to have to pay you anyway, but I am going to lay you off today even though I am required to give you 60 days' notice." However, if your employees are not likely to do harm to the organization in their last 60 days, you need to give them notice in accordance with the WARN Act, because that is just the right thing and a "fair and reasonable thing" to do.

Other Legal Issues in Labor Relations

In addition to the major labor laws, we need to do a quick review of some of the other issues in labor relations. There are several organizational issues that have become items of concern to companies either because of years of common law decisions or because they are associated with other federal laws that limit businesses in their ability to manage their workforce. Some of the more common issues that you might run into in your company include corporate whistle-blowers, wrongful discharge, constructive discharge, express contracts, implied contracts, and quasi-contracts.

SHRM

B:16
The Worker Adjustment and Retraining Notification Act of 1988 (WARN Act)

WORK APPLICATION 10-9

Select an organization you work or have worked for and explain how the five major labor laws apply to that firm. What can and can't the firm do under each law?

10-3 APPLYING THE CONCEPT

Labor Laws

Identify each statement by the law it is discussing, writing the letter corresponding to each law before the statement discussing it.

- a. RLA of 1926
- b. NLRA of 1935
- c. LMRA of 1947
- d. LMRDA of 1959
- e. WARN of 1988

_____ 11. Featherbedding is illegal. The union can't put in the contract that we have to pay for services that we really don't get. We should call in the National Labor Relations Board to investigate.

_____ 12. The union president is afraid that I will speak up at the discussion to vote on the contract and influence the members to vote it down. So I think he had a few of his boys warn me to keep my mouth shut.

_____ 13. I think we should call in the National Labor Relations Board to investigate the action that management is taking to stop us from unionizing.

_____ 14. The company can't give us a notice today, with our paychecks, that our factory is being closed next week and all 500 of us will be without a job.

_____ 15. As pilots, we shouldn't go on strike. Let's get the National Mediation Board to help us.

SHRM

B:28
Whistle-blowing/Retaliation

SHRM

C:15
Sarbanes-Oxley Act of 2002

SHRM

C:16
False Claims Act

Whistle-blower An individual who tells an authoritative organization (such as a TV station or a government agency) outside the individual's own company about actions within the company that the individual believes to be illegal

CORPORATE WHISTLE-BLOWERS AND THE LAW. **A whistle-blower** *is an individual who tells an authoritative organization (such as a TV station or a government agency) outside the individual's own company about actions within the company that the individual believes to be illegal.* Among the many laws that deal with protection for whistle-blowers who expose fraud are the federal False Claims Act, the Sarbanes-Oxley Act, and, most recently, the Dodd-Frank Act. In 2013, the US Department of Justice collected $3.8 billion in settlements and judgments from companies under the federal False Claims Act. Over $2.9 billion of the $3.8 billion was recovered with the help of whistle-blowers.[68] This shows the magnitude of the potential loss to organizations from whistle-blowers.

Because there are incentives for whistle-blowing in many federal and state laws, organizations need to devise policies and create cultures that encourage employees to bring complaints of fraud or other illegal activities to the attention of the organization's management. Research shows that about 90% of individuals who ultimately acted as whistle-blowers and reported company wrongdoing outside the firm first reported the illegal actions internally.[69]

So, what can the organization do to limit the potential for whistle-blowing? Here are six things that can encourage internal reporting and, as a result, limit outside reports of wrongdoing by the firm:[70]

1. Create and maintain a company culture that values reporting of unethical and illegal activities. If potential whistle-blowers feel that the company listens, they are less likely to take action outside the company.

2. Have a written policy on actions to be taken by the organization when reports of illegal or unethical activities occur. This policy should include information on avoiding adverse employment actions and should specifically address retaliation, a direct violation of many of the whistle-blower laws.

3. Routinely train all employees, especially managers and supervisors, on the contents of organizational policies concerning the reporting of illegal and unethical activities.

4. Provide multiple ways to report suspected illegal or unethical activities. As with sexual harassment, an individual's supervisor may be the person suspected of illegal activity, and therefore, the supervisor should not be the only person designated to take reports of such activities. There needs to be a

mechanism to allow the individual to avoid directly confronting the supervisor in such a case.

5. Create and follow clear guidelines for investigation of reports and keep the whistle-blower informed of the progress in the investigation. The Just Cause procedures provided in Chapter 9 can be used in this situation to ensure that a fair investigation is conducted.

6. Maintain confidentiality if at all possible during and after the investigation. In some cases, the individual reporting the suspicious activity may have to be identified in the course of a thorough investigation or in the case of a criminal complaint, but unless it is absolutely necessary, the whistle-blower's identity should be protected.

EXPRESS CONTRACTS, IMPLIED CONTRACTS, AND QUASI-CONTRACTS. Good labor relations also require an understanding of the concepts of both formal and informal agreements, so let's briefly discuss the concepts of express contracts, implied contracts, and quasi-contracts. Each of these legal concepts means something slightly different, and all of them can affect employment contracts. Let's take a quick look at the differences between the terms.

An **express contract** *is a transaction in which the agreement between two parties is specifically stated,*[71] whether orally or in writing. Generally, in employment and labor relations, any express contracts should probably be in writing due to the complex nature of the relationships between individuals. An **implied contract** *exists when "the parties form an agreement from their actions rather than from a specific oral or written agreement."*[72] Every manager needs to understand the concept of an implied contract. Nothing has to be written down; the parties don't have to sign an agreement. All that has to happen is that the two parties act in a way that creates an agreement. In many cases, managers and supervisors don't even realize that they have created an implied contract with their employees but in fact have done so and as a result cost the company significant amounts of money.

For instance, if by words and actions a supervisor lets an employee know that if they perform well, they will be promoted, the supervisor may have entered into an implied contract that the employee can then require to be enforced. If it is not enforced by the supervisor and the organization, the employee may then resort to the courts. As managers, we need to be aware of the concept of an implied contract and avoid situations that would create an organizational obligation to our employees.

Finally, a quasi-contract is a contract that doesn't really exist, but a court may create it to avoid an unfair situation. A **quasi-contract** *is a court-ordered implied agreement to prevent one party in an action from benefiting at the expense of another party.* Why would a judge or a court create an implied contract when one doesn't exist? The answer basically comes down to a question of fairness regarding goods or services provided by one party to another. One of the more common examples of a quasi-contract in HR law would be an agency relationship. Agents are individuals who act on behalf of an organization. An agent may act on behalf of the organization in a way where a quasi-contract might be judged to exist. For example, assume that our organization has a relationship with an employment firm that frequently provides us with new employees with specific computer talents. Assume further that one of our managers saw the owner of the employment agency at the grocery store two weeks ago, on Sunday. During their conversation, our manager mentioned the need for a systems analyst to help with an ongoing project. The employment agency owner thought that he was being asked to find a systems analyst, and as a result, he started a search. The employment agency spent significant time finding a systems analyst and presented our manager with a candidate's information this morning. Our manager protested that she hadn't asked the employment agency to find this individual, but our manager also had knowledge of the historical

B:18 Contractual and Tort Theories

B:23 Employment Contracts

B:22 Agency Relationships/Quasi-Contracts

Express contract A transaction in which the agreement between two parties is specifically stated

Implied contract A contract in which the parties form an agreement from their actions rather than from a specific oral or written agreement

Quasi-contract A court-ordered implied agreement to prevent one party in an action from benefiting at the expense of another party

WORK
APPLICATION 10-10

Select an organization you work for or have worked for and give an example of an express, implied, and quasi-contract that may have existed there (between you and the firm or between the firm and others).

informal relationship between the employment agency and our firm, and she should have known that such a conversation would result in the employment agency owner's beginning a search. In this case, a judge might determine that a quasi-contract existed and cause our company to pay for the search undertaken by the employment agency.

Organizational managers, and certainly HR managers, must be aware of the concepts of express contracts, implied contracts, and quasi-contracts. Obviously, managers can obligate the firm to pay significant expenses by not knowing these terms. We always have to be careful of the way in which we phrase communications with others to avoid creating a contractual liability when none is intended.

10-4 APPLYING THE CONCEPT

Labor Contracts

Identify each statement by the type of contract being discussed, writing the contract type's letter before the statement(s) describing the contract type.

  a. express contract
  b. implied contract
  c. quasi-contract

_____ 16. You must sign the standard 1-year contract if you take the job. You can join the union if you want to, but it is not a requirement to get the job.

_____ 17. If you can get the task done today, I will let you leave an hour early tomorrow.

_____ 18. Neal, you have been doing a good job. Keep it up and I will give you a raise during your next performance review.

_____ 19. After 3 months of negotiations, the union president and CEO have signed the new collective bargaining agreement.

_____ 20. I know I told you we are changing our health insurance carrier and that you have our business. Sorry, but I changed my mind—plus, we never signed anything.

LO 10-5

Briefly discuss the difference between wrongful discharge and constructive discharge.

Wrongful discharge Terminating an individual employee for an illegal reason, either in violation of a contract or in violation of state or federal law

Constructive discharge When an employee is forced to quit their job because of severe and/or pervasive harassment or intolerable working conditions

WRONGFUL DISCHARGE AND CONSTRUCTIVE DISCHARGE. The last of our legal issues concerns employee termination or discharge. There are two specific issues that we have to be concerned with to maintain good labor relations—wrongful discharge and constructive discharge. **Wrongful discharge** *is simply terminating an individual employee for an illegal reason, either in violation of a contract or in violation of state or federal law.* Even in situations where employment is at-will, employers can't violate laws or contracts to terminate employees. Many labor contracts have clauses concerning actions that constitute wrongful discharge. Employers must understand the terms of such clauses in order to avoid a contract violation.

Constructive discharge, on the other hand, is not really a direct corporate termination of employment at all. **Constructive discharge** *occurs when an employee is forced to quit their job because of severe and/or pervasive harassment or intolerable working conditions.* In this case, other members of the organization may put significant enough pressure on an individual or make it so difficult for the individual to continue normal work activities that the employee quits. This type of pressure generally occurs in retaliation for some action from the individual that harmed the employees and/or the organization.

For instance, if the individual acted as a whistle-blower and reported the company to government authorities, then managers or supervisors in the organization might retaliate by making it virtually impossible for the individual to do their assigned work. Examples of such retaliation could include constantly interrupting the individual's work efforts and then reporting poor productivity, failing to provide necessary tools and equipment, or continually harassing the individual. If pressure from the other members of the organization is of such duration and/or intensity (severe and pervasive) that the individual could no longer reasonably do their job, then constructive discharge has probably occurred. Because such actions frequently occur as a result of retaliation against the individual for some legally protected action, constructive discharge is a serious offense that company managers need to be aware of. As HR managers, we must guard against constructive discharge.

UNIONS AND LABOR RIGHTS

The United States has a fairly strong history of unions and labor rights. Workers in the United States enjoy more rights and freedoms than do workers in many other countries, including the right to form and become members of unions. However, over the past 40 years, union membership has declined, and it continues to do so.[73] In 2012, only 11.3% of American workers (approximately 14.4 million) were union members.[74] Therefore, most businesses do not have labor relations as part of their HR process.

People join unions for a variety of reasons, including increasing pay and benefits, especially good health care coverage and retirement plans. There are certainly both good and bad components to unions and unionization of organizational workforces. On the positive side, unions are tasked with providing their members with jobs in which they are provided fair wages and good benefits, as well as protecting them from arbitrary disciplinary or other actions by employers. On the negative side, unions frequently drive up employer costs, protect subpar employees, and may disrupt organizational work through strikes and other work stoppages. Let's take a look at unions and their impact on organizations.

Union Organizing

The most prominent unions are those whose members are public sector employees such as teachers and police officers.[75] Labor union membership in the private sector has decreased dramatically in the past 40 years in the United States, to the point where only about 6.7% of the private sector US workforce belongs to unions.[76] Public sector unions have also been on the decline, with legal changes in some states having significantly cut their membership. When Wisconsin passed a law in 2012 making public sector union membership optional, membership in AFSCME (one of the largest public sector unions) in the state dropped by 45%.[77] However, some experts believe that union organizing is beginning to increase.

Members of a union may go on strike to put pressure on an employer to improve working conditions.

If employees decide they want to join a union, what steps do they take? Usually, the employees will go through a union organizing process (Exhibit 10-4). In this process, employees will generally select a union to represent them and then ask for a vote of employees concerning whether or not they desire to be represented by the union. The primary method for union elections is a secret ballot. The NLRA (discussed earlier in the chapter) gives employees the right to bargain collectively with their employer and to choose a union as their representative.[78] The NLRA is the primary federal law governing union organizing and elections in private firms.

An election is authorized if at least 30% of the employees in an appropriate bargaining unit sign authorization cards allowing a union to negotiate employment

EXHIBIT 10-4   THE UNION ORGANIZING PROCESS

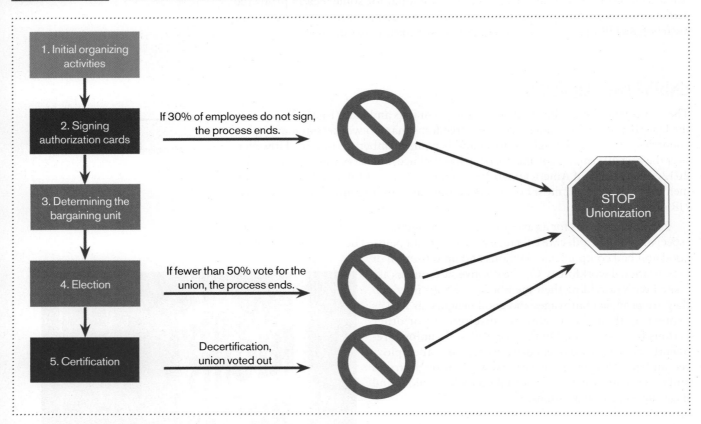

terms and conditions on the employees' behalf. The union then presents these cards to the NLRB as an election petition. Once this happens, "the NLRB sharply limits what management can say and do. Violating the rules is an unfair labor practice, and the union is likely to complain to the NLRB about any such violations and use them against the employer in the union organizing campaign."[79]

A combination of strongly pro-labor NLRB rulings and mandates has recently made it much easier to organize new bargaining units. One decision that has caused significant concern for companies is the *micro-bargaining unit* decision in *Specialty Healthcare and Rehabilitation Center of Mobile v. NLRB*, in which the 6th US Circuit Court allowed a small part of the employer's workforce to constitute a bargaining unit. The NLRB had noted that these units would be "presumptively appropriate" unless other employees share an "overwhelming community of interests."[80] There is some evidence that union organizers win more often with smaller groups of employees voting, so this ruling could lead to stronger unionization efforts of small groups. The concern is that this micro-unit bargaining could lead to companies having to deal with *several different union contracts* within one company. This could create an untenable situation due to the time cost of bargaining with multiple unions each year.

The NLRB is also, as of this writing, trying to push through a "quickie election" rule that would allow votes within 10 to 21 days of the date of the petition for election. This is about half of the current average time between petition and election vote.[81] What this does is limit the company's ability to provide employees with information that would be favorable to the organization before the vote is held. This proposed rule is sometimes referred to as the "ambush election" rule because employers feel like they are being ambushed without the opportunity to defend their current employment arrangement.

One recent NLRB effort that failed was the requirement for companies to post an 11- by 17-inch poster identifying employee rights to organize and participate in a union, as required under the NLRA. The Board lost two appeals court decisions that held that it had overstepped its authority in mandating the posters.[82] After the losses, the Board decided not to appeal the rulings to the US Supreme Court in January of 2014. It is generally expected that the NLRB will continue for at least the next few years to be much more activist in making rulings that favor labor over management, and as a result many HR managers who have historically not had to worry much about organized labor and unionizing efforts will now have to become much more aware of the procedures that are required in such situations.[83]

THE NO TIPS RULES. What practices are prohibited from the point of providing the authorization cards to the NLRB? A lot of organizations use the acronym NO TIPS to identify what the company and its managers can't do. NO TIPS stands for no *T*hreats, no *I*nterrogations, no *P*romises, and no *S*pying.[84] An example of each of these factors will help you understand what management can and can't do under the NO TIPS rules:

WORK
APPLICATION 10-11

Describe your experience with a union. If you have no experience, interview someone who has union experience to find out their views of the union. What do they like and dislike about the union?

LO 10-6

Briefly discuss the NO TIPS rules for labor elections.

- *No Threats.* Managers in the firm can't threaten employees by telling them that the company will shut down a facility that votes for unionization and send the work elsewhere, maybe overseas.
- *No Interrogations.* The manager is prohibited from calling individual employees into the manager's office and asking them about union organizing activities on the part of others in the workforce.
- *No Promises.* Management cannot promise employees that if they vote against union authorization, they will receive raises or changes in their benefits package.
- *No Spying.* Management is prohibited from planting individuals in union organizing meetings or other activities so that those individuals can report back to management on what is being discussed or who attends the meetings.

Remember, however, that these are just examples of things that are prohibited by the NLRA.

There is also one final limitation on actions by the organization and its managers in the last 24 hours prior to the union authorization election. Management is prohibited from holding group meetings with employees who will vote on unionization during this 24-hour period.

Once the election is held, a simple majority of those voting determines the success or failure of the campaign. In other words, if only 51 workers in a bargaining unit of 200 vote, and if 26 of the voters desire union membership, then membership in the union will be authorized.

Labor Relations and Collective Bargaining

Labor relations are the interactions between management and unionized employees. Labor relations are also called *union-management relations* and *industrial relations*. Since there are many more nonunionized than unionized employees, most organizations don't have to deal with labor relations as part of their human resources systems.

Collective bargaining is the negotiation process resulting in a contract between union employees and management that covers employment conditions. The most common employment conditions covered in contracts are compensation, hours, and working conditions, but a contract can include almost any condition that both sides agree to. Job security continues to be a major bargaining issue for many unions.[85]

SHRM
A:12
Collective Bargaining Issues

SHRM
A:13
Collective Bargaining Process

Labor relations The interactions between management and unionized employees

Collective bargaining The negotiation process resulting in a contract between union employees and management that covers employment conditions

MODEL 10-3   THE EMPLOYEE COMPLAINT RESOLUTION MODEL

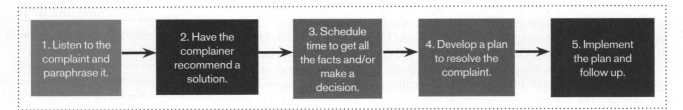

1. Listen to the complaint and paraphrase it. → 2. Have the complainer recommend a solution. → 3. Schedule time to get all the facts and/or make a decision. → 4. Develop a plan to resolve the complaint. → 5. Implement the plan and follow up.

SHRM

A:16
Grievance Management

WORK
APPLICATION 10-12

Describe a complaint that you brought to your supervisor and how it was handled. If you have never had a complaint, interview someone who has and describe the complaint and how it was handled.

Grievances

As stipulated in a union contract, a **grievance** *is a formal complaint concerning pay, working conditions, or violation of some other factor in a collective bargaining agreement.* Grievance procedures help protect employees against arbitrary decisions by management regarding discipline, discharge, promotions, or benefits. They also provide labor unions and employers with a formal process for enforcing the provisions of their contracts. Grievance procedures provide a mechanism to allow an individual to bring up a complaint and have the company resolve the complaint in a timely manner.

Providing a grievance mechanism will generally encourage employees to raise concerns about fairness, working conditions, or contract provisions directly with management, which in turn allows managers to resolve such problems quickly and efficiently. Do you remember earlier, in Chapter 9, when we discussed tests for Just Cause? Those procedures are used if a grievance involves questions of fairness in disciplinary actions.

As part of a labor contract, a formal grievance process will usually provide a mechanism to escalate discussion of the issue through successively higher layers of organizational management until the problem is resolved. It begins with an employee making a complaint to the supervisor in accordance with the labor contract provisions. The supervisor has a limited amount of time in which to investigate and respond to the complaint or to send it further up the management chain. If the complaint cannot be resolved quickly to the satisfaction of the employee, a union representative (usually the shop steward) will become the representative of the employee in further negotiations to resolve the issue. The grievance can continue up the chain until it reaches the head of the firm or the local plant manager. If it still can't be resolved, there is frequently an arbitration clause in the union contract that requires both sides to submit the grievance to an arbitrator. The arbitrator's decision on the matter is generally final—the parties cannot dispute it legally.

As a manager, when you have an employee come to you with a complaint, you can follow the steps in Model 10-3: The Employee Complaint Resolution Model. Note that in step 2, you don't have to agree and implement the recommendation, and in steps 4 and 5, unless the employee is totally wrong in the complaint, you should try to resolve the complaint.

MANAGEMENT RIGHTS AND DECERTIFICATION ELECTIONS

Of course, management also has some rights concerning union organizing and labor relations. As in all areas of business, managers have to deal with the protection of the firm and *all* of its stakeholders when union and labor issues arise. What tools do managers have at their disposal to manage their interaction with unions and labor? Let's find out in this section.

Grievance A formal complaint concerning pay, working conditions, or violation of some other factor in a collective bargaining agreement

Limiting Union Organizing Efforts

Management has some rights in limiting union organizing activities in the workplace. Let's take a look at what company managers can do to limit union organizing efforts.

NO UNIONIZATION ON COMPANY TIME. The first thing management can do is limit the ability of union organizers to solicit employees during working hours and on company time. The organization is within its rights to prevent solicitation of employees as long as it is consistent with company solicitation policies and the company handbook. So for example, the company cannot limit union organizers' rights to solicit employees but then later allow a charitable organization to solicit employees for donations. In 1992, a famous case involving **Lechmere Inc.** went all the way to the Supreme Court. The court verified the company's right to limit solicitations on company property as long as the company's policies were consistent with all solicitors.[86] However, the company *cannot limit* the rights of employees or union organizers to discuss unionization efforts *outside of normal work hours*, such as during lunch breaks and before or after work.

MANAGEMENT'S POSITION ON UNIONIZATION. Management of the firm can identify the costs associated with union membership (such as dues), as well as limits that may be imposed on promotions or compensation increases based on merit if the employees choose to unionize. Management can meet with employees to explain the company's position on unionizing efforts and to tell employees the truth about what might happen to the company and its employees as a result of a successful organizing effort. Remember, though, that the company cannot threaten that the facility will close or that massive layoffs will occur or make any other threat to try to stop employees from voting for unionization (per the No Threats part of NO TIPS). These types of communications are not protected by the NLRA and LMRA.

CHANGE AGREEMENTS AND USE OF NONUNION EMPLOYEE REPRESENTATION. Management also has a right to change working agreements, even during a period when union organizers are soliciting their workforce, to show that they are responsive to their employees' needs. This can include something called nonunion employee representation (NER), in which management gives employee representatives a voice in such things as working conditions, pay and benefits, job security policies, promotion, and grievance resolution.[87] NER policies can sometimes effectively gut a unionization effort since the areas covered by NER are the most common areas of concern that lead to unionization of the workforce in any organization.

Lockouts and Replacement Workers

Unions have the potential to strike against an employer if collective bargaining efforts have failed, but management also has a right to prevent employees from working in certain cases. Two significant tools in management's arsenal are lockouts and replacement workers.[88]

A **lockout** *occurs when management stops all work and physically prevents workers from entering the workplace.* Lockouts can put economic pressure on members of the union due to the fact that employees may not be paid during the period of a lockout.[89] If management and union representatives have made a legitimate attempt to come to an agreement on a contract but have reached an impasse in their collective bargaining process, then management is allowed to use a lockout. If negotiations have *not* reached a stalemate, a lockout is likely to be illegal.[90] A good example of a lockout occurred in a dispute between the **National Football League** and the unionized **NFL Officials**. You may remember that a blown call in a

LO 10-7
Briefly discuss what management can do to limit union organizing efforts.

SHRM
A:19
Managing Union Organizing Policies and Handbooks

WORK APPLICATION 10-13
Describe any management attempts to stop unionization that you are aware of from any source.

Lockout When management stops all work and physically prevents workers from entering the workplace

September 2012 game between Seattle and Green Bay put pressure on the NFL to settle the lockout.[91]

Another tool that management may employ in the case of a strike is the hiring of replacement workers. This action is generally legal. However, whether or not striking employees have to be offered their jobs back depends on the type of strike action undertaken by the union and its members. An economic strike *is a work stoppage over authorized collective bargaining issues such as pay or working conditions*. In the case of an economic strike, "an employer may not discriminate against a striker, but the employer is not obligated to lay off a replacement worker to give a striker his job back."[92] Alternately, a strike may be called because an employer engages in unfair labor practices as defined under the NLRA. In the case of an *unfair labor practices strike*, the employees are protected from being permanently replaced and must be offered their jobs back when the strike concludes.

Decertification Elections

SHRM

A:11
Union Decertification and
Deauthorization

Decertification elections can be held to remove a union as the representative of company workers. This cannot happen within a year of a previous failed attempt at decertification, though, and management of the company can't bring a decertification petition up on its own. Management cannot even directly encourage this action on the part of the employees, but it can provide information to employees regarding decertification processes if they request it, "as long as the company does so without threatening its employees or promising them benefits."[93]

Employees or other groups such as another union or labor organization must bring decertification petitions forward. "Any impetus for decertification must come from the workers rather than the employer."[94] In general, if there is an existing labor contract in effect and the duration of that contract is 3 years or less, a petition can't be brought to the NLRB until a window between 60 and 90 days before the end of the contract.[95]

What happens in a decertification process? First, 30% of covered employees must sign a petition for decertification of the union. Once this happens, the election process proceeds in pretty much the same way as the process *for* voting for union representation. The petition will be provided to the NLRB, which will then call an election. If a majority of the employees vote to decertify the union, then the union will no longer be authorized to bargain collectively for that employee group. In addition, if the election results in a tie, the union will be decertified because it received less than a majority of the votes. Remember, though, that the employer cannot directly or indirectly encourage the decertification process. To avoid *any* implications of influence over the process, companies need to require that signatures on the decertification petition be collected in the same manner as are signatures for a certification petition—on nonwork time and in nonwork areas.

MANAGING CONFLICT

You are in conflict when someone does something that bothers you, so conflict is part of everyday life.[96] With globalization and increasingly team-based structures, the frequency and intensity of conflict will only continue to increase.[97] Therefore, to have good human relations, you need strong conflict resolution skills.[98] Thus, no chapter on labor relations would be complete without a discussion of conflict and negotiation.

Certainly, labor and management don't intentionally create conflict, but the chance of conflict occurring is significant when two parties have to work in concert in any circumstance but each party has its own set of opposing goals. As a result of

Economic strike A work stoppage over authorized collective bargaining issues such as pay or working conditions

the potential for conflict, we as managers have to understand it and be able to work our way through conflicting goals. So let's discuss conflict and conflict management styles (including negotiation) in this section, and let's discuss negotiation in more detail in the next section.

Conflict

A **conflict** *exists whenever people are in disagreement and opposition.* Conflicts are inevitable,[99] and the chance of conflict occurring is significant when two parties have to work together in any circumstance but each party has its own set of goals. Incompatible activities occur[100] because management wants to keep costs down and employees want to maintain and improve their standard of living. Thus, you need strong conflict resolution skills to be successful in any job.[101]

©iStockphoto.com/EyeJoy

Hostess went bankrupt after failing to resolve disputes between management and labor unions.

On a personal level, in any relationship, we have expectations of what we will do and what the other party will do. As long as people meet our expectations, everything is fine. We are in conflict when people don't meet our expectations, and this happens for three major reasons. First, we fail to let others know our own expectations and we don't ask others for their expectations. Second, we assume that others have the same expectations that we have. Last, sometimes we don't know our expectations until people do things in opposition to us. Thus, it is important to share information and communicate expectations.

FUNCTIONAL VERSUS DYSFUNCTIONAL CONFLICT. People often think of conflict as "fighting" and view it as disruptive. However, conflict can frequently be beneficial,[102] or *functional*, when it helps the organization meet its goals of increasing performance.[103] On the other hand, conflict that prevents the achievement of individual and organizational objectives is called *dysfunctional* conflict.[104] Conflict between management and labor often degrades into dysfunctional conflict, because of significantly different objectives. This can produce severe negative consequences for individuals and organizations.[105] Dysfunctional conflict is often personal and can bring about many negative outcomes within an organization, including damaged relationships, decreased productivity, revenge, avoidance, and aggression.[106] Many of you lost your favorite **Hostess** CupCakes or Twinkies, and more than 18,000 people lost their jobs, when Hostess management and labor unions were unable to overcome their conflict over wage concessions and the company went bankrupt.[107] Conflict within or between groups can also impede group effectiveness. However, use of conflict management skills can lead to resolving conflicts and maintaining relationships before they become dysfunctional.[108]

Conflict Management Styles

Confronting problems helps to resolve them.[109] When we are faced with conflict, we have five basic conflict management styles to choose from. The five styles are based on two dimensions of concern: concern for others' needs and concern for our own needs, and being cooperative or not. Various levels of concern and cooperation result in three types of behavior: *passive* (taking no action or permissively giving in to others), *assertive* (defending our position while considering others' needs), and *aggressive* (fighting for what we want without considering others' needs, or taking advantage of others).

WORK
APPLICATION 10-14

Give an example of when you were in conflict at work. Describe how expectations were not met.

LO 10-8

Identify the five conflict management styles. How is each described in terms of win or lose?

Conflict Whenever people are in disagreement and opposition

EXHIBIT 10-5 CONFLICT MANAGEMENT STYLES

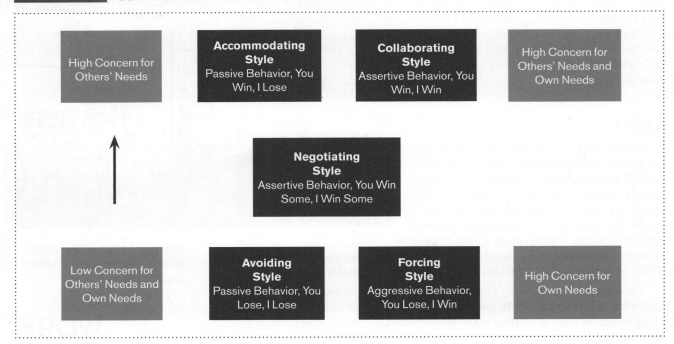

SHRM

A:15
Conflict Management

Each conflict management style results in a different win-loss pattern. The five styles are presented in Exhibit 10-5. Note that there is no right or wrong style. Each style has its advantages and disadvantages and is appropriate to use in different situations. However, collaborating is the ideal situation.

AVOIDING. The user of an *avoiding conflict style* attempts to passively ignore the conflict rather than resolve it. When we avoid a conflict, we are being passive and generally uncooperative. We avoid conflict when we refuse to take a stance, when we mentally withdraw, or when we physically leave. A "lose-lose" situation results because the conflict is not resolved.

ACCOMMODATING. The user of an *accommodating conflict style* attempts to resolve conflict by passively giving in to the opposing side. When we use the accommodating style, we are being passive but cooperative. We attempt to satisfy the needs of others but neglect our own needs by letting others get their own way. We create a "lose-win" situation—we lose and allow the other party to win.

AVOIDING VERSUS ACCOMMODATING. A difference between the two styles is this: When we avoid, we just don't say or do anything. How many times have you heard someone say something dumb and you just ignored it, rather than get into an argument? When we accommodate, we do something we don't really want to do. For example, if you and another person are working on a project together and you go along with that person's way of doing a particular task, even though you disagree with it, then you are using the accommodating style.

FORCING. Users of a *forcing conflict style* attempt to resolve conflict by using aggressive behavior to get their own way. When we use the forcing style, we are aggressive and uncooperative; we do whatever it takes to satisfy our own needs at the expense of others. Forcers use authority, threaten, intimidate, and call for majority rule when they know they will win.

Forcers commonly enjoy dealing with avoiders and accommodators. If we try to get others to change without being willing to change ourselves, regardless of the means, then we use the forcing style and create a "win-lose" situation in which we win but everyone else loses. Being in a position of authority, some managers tend to use this style frequently to get their way quickly.

NEGOTIATING. The user of the *negotiating conflict style*, also called the *compromising style*, attempts to resolve conflict through assertive give-and-take. When we use the negotiating style, we are moderate in assertiveness and cooperation, and we create a situation in which each side achieves a partial victory through compromise. This is a "win-some, lose-some" form of conflict resolution. Negotiation is how collective bargaining works, and we will discuss it in more detail in the next major section.

COLLABORATING. The user of a *collaborative conflict style*, also called the *problem-solving style*, assertively attempts to resolve conflict by working together with the other person to find an acceptable solution. When we use the collaborative approach, we are being highly assertive and cooperative. Whereas avoiders and accommodators are concerned about others' needs and forcers are concerned about their own needs, the collaborators are concerned about finding the best solution that is satisfactory to all. Unlike the forcer, the collaborator is willing to change if a better solution is presented. While negotiating is often based on secret information, collaboration is based on open and honest communication. This is the only style that creates a true "win-win" situation.

NEGOTIATING VERSUS COLLABORATING. A difference between these two options lies in the solution each option leads to. Again, suppose you and another person are working on a project and she wants to do a task in a way that you disagree with. With the negotiating style, you might do this task her way and the next task your way; you each win some and lose some. With the collaborating style, you work to develop an approach to the task that you can both agree on. The key to collaboration is agreeing that the solution picked is the best possible one. Thus, you create a win-win situation. Unfortunately, we can't always collaborate.

WORK
APPLICATION 10-15

Select a present or past boss and identify which conflict management style the boss uses most often when in conflict with employees. Give a typical example conflict and how the style is used.

WORK
APPLICATION 10-16

Which one of the five conflict management styles do you tend to use most often? Should you be using another style more often? Why or why not?

10-5 APPLYING THE CONCEPT

Conflict Management Styles

Identify the most appropriate conflict management style to use in each situation, writing the letter corresponding to each style before the situation(s) where it is appropriate.

    a. avoiding style
    b. accommodating style
    c. forcing style
    d. negotiating style
    e. collaborating style

_____ 21. As you leave your office, you see at the other end of the work area your employee Ricky, who is goofing off instead of working. You're on your way to an important meeting and running late.

_____ 22. You're overbudget for labor this month. The work load is light, so you ask Terri, a part-time employee, to leave work early. Terri says she doesn't want to go because she needs the money.

_____ 23. You have joined a committee to make contacts. You have little interest in what the committee actually does. At a meeting, you make a recommendation that is opposed by Jim. You realize that you have the better idea, but Jim is using a forcing style.

_____ 24. You are on a task force that has to select a new computer cloud service. The three alternatives will all do the job, but team members disagree about the company, price, and service they need.

_____ 25. As the sales manager, one of your competent salespeople, Anna, is trying to close a big sale. The two of you are discussing the sales call she will make. You disagree on the strategy to use to close the sale.

USING THE MOST APPROPRIATE STYLES. Again, there is no one best style for resolving all conflicts. A person's preferred style tends to meet their needs. Some people enjoy forcing; others prefer to avoid conflict. Managerial and personal success lies in one's ability to use the appropriate style to meet the situation. For most people, the two most difficult styles to develop are the negotiating and collaborating styles. Thus, we discuss these two skills in more detail next and in the next major section.

Initiating Conflict Resolution

Conflict management skills are important, so managers are often trained to use effective conflict resolution strategies. Conflict resolution models have also been shown to be effective in managing conflict, so when initiating a conflict resolution process, you may want to use the collaborative conflict resolution model. Research suggests that collaborative conflict resolution skills can be developed. The steps of the model are illustrated in Model 10-4.

MODEL 10-4   INITIATING CONFLICT RESOLUTION MODEL

1. State the problem in terms of behavior, consequences, and feelings (i.e., make a BCF statement).	2. Allow another person to respond to your BCF statement and acknowledge the problem or conflict.	3. Ask for and/or present alternative resolutions to the conflict.	4. Come to an agreement. Determine specific actions to be taken by each person.

Consider an example: Suppose that you don't smoke and are in fact allergic to cigarette smoke. Some of your coworkers do smoke, and although they are allowed to do so in the employees' lounge, most of them avoid smoking when you are in the lounge. One coworker, however, persists in smoking in your presence. This is a problem—you can't always avoid going into the lounge during breaks or lunch. You decide to initiate a collaborative solution to this problem. You begin by asking the smoker to help you solve your problem. This approach reduces defensiveness and establishes an atmosphere that will help maintain a good relationship.

Step 1. The first step in the collaborative conflict resolution model is to express the problem in a BCF statement—that is, a statement that describes a conflict in terms of behaviors (B), consequences (C), and feelings (F)—in a way that maintains ownership of the problem.

There are three things you should not do in the BCF statement:

1. Don't make judgments. This can make the person defensive.
2. Don't make threats. This can make the person defensive.
3. Don't give solutions. This is done in step 3.

Regarding the smoker, we should make statements like "When you smoke around me (B), I have trouble breathing and become nauseous (C), and I feel ill and stressed (F)." We don't want to make statements like "You are inconsiderate of others, you shouldn't smoke, and you are going to get cancer. So just quit smoking."

Note that you can vary the sequence if a situation warrants it. For example, you can say, "I fear (F) that some viewers will respond negatively to this advertisement (B) and we will lose money by running it (C)."

Now, what exactly does "maintaining ownership of the problem" mean? Think about it—is it you or the smoker who has the problem? Since the smoker is allowed to smoke in the lounge, the problem is yours. Maintaining ownership of the problem means expressing it without assigning blame or making assumptions about who is right or wrong. Fixing blame only makes people defensive, which is counterproductive in conflict resolution. Your BCF statement should be descriptive, not evaluative, and it should deal with a single issue.

Before confronting the other person, practice your BCF statement. Also, think of some possible solutions you might suggest. But be sure your ideas take into consideration the other person's point of view, not just your own. Remember to practice empathy—try to put yourself in the other person's position. If you were that person, would you like the solutions you have thought of?

Step 2. You cannot resolve a conflict if the other person does not even acknowledge that it exists. After stating the problem, let the other person respond. Your coworker might say, "Oh, I didn't realize you reacted so strongly to cigarette smoke," or "Well, that explains why everybody puts out their cigarettes when you're around." On the other hand, the coworker could say, "What's the big deal? You can just stay away from the lounge if smoke bothers you." If the other person doesn't understand or acknowledge the problem, you'll need to be persistent. Repeat your statement in different terms, if necessary.

Step 3. Once the other person acknowledges the problem, ask them how the conflict might be resolved. Perhaps the person will suggest something that you can agree to; if so, you're well on your way to a resolution of the conflict. If not, be prepared with your own suggestions. However, remember that you are collaborating, not simply trying to change the other person. If they acknowledge the problem but seem unwilling to resolve it, appeal to common goals. Try to make the other person realize how they might also benefit from a solution to this conflict.

Step 4. The final step in the collaborative conflict resolution model is to come to an agreement. Determine what specific actions you will each take to resolve the conflict. Perhaps your coworker will agree not to smoke in your presence, now that he knows how it affects you. Perhaps you'll suggest changing your lunch hour, so you don't run into each other in the lounge. Clearly state whatever actions you each agree to.

NEGOTIATIONS

In this section, we discuss the negotiation process so you will know how to negotiate effectively in your personal and professional lives. There are times when negotiations are appropriate and maybe even necessary, such as in management–union collective bargaining, when buying and selling goods and services, and when discussing a job compensation offer.[110] Thus, negotiating is an essential career skill.[111]

The Negotiation Process

Negotiating *is a process in which two or more parties in conflict attempt to come to an agreement.* If there is a set "take it or leave it" deal, there is no negotiation, so good managers generally want to try to avoid making such statements.[112] Also, not all negotiations end with an agreement.

Negotiation is often a *zero-sum game* in which one party's gain is the other party's loss. For example, every dollar less that you pay for a car is your gain and the seller's loss. Ideally, however, negotiation should be viewed by all parties as "I win some and you win some," rather than a win-lose situation; all parties should believe they got a good deal.[113] If union employees believe that they lost and management won,

SHRM

A:14
Negotiation Skills

Negotiating A process in which two or more parties in conflict attempt to come to an agreement they may become dissatisfied with their jobs, which could result in lower performance in the long run. You can develop your negotiation skills by implementing the negotiation process below.

THE NEGOTIATION PROCESS MODEL. Negotiation is a process.[114] The negotiation process has three and possibly four parts. These steps are summarized in Model 10-5 and discussed throughout this section. We discuss the process in two parts to reflect the planning and actual negotiation in which you may or may not postpone or agree to make a deal. In the course of actual negotiations, you may have to make slight adjustments to the steps in the process.

MODEL 10-5   THE NEGOTIATION PROCESS

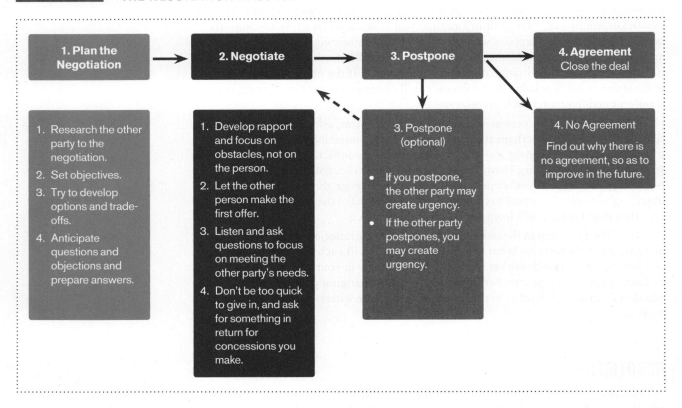

Planning the Negotiation

Success or failure in negotiating is usually based on preparation.[115] Planning has four steps:

Step 1: Research the other parties to the negotiation. Do your homework.[116] Know the key power players and make sure you are dealing with the right people.[117] Try to find out what the other parties want and what they will and will not be willing to give up before you negotiate.[118] Find out, through your networking grapevine, their personality traits and negotiation style. You can also **Google, Facebook**, etc. the people for information.[119] The more you know about those with whom you will be negotiating, the better your chances are of reaching an agreement. If you have worked with some of the people before, think about what worked and what did not work in the past. Doing your homework can result in realizing whether or not it's worth the time and effort negotiating.[120]

Step 2: Set objectives. In some negotiations, your objective will be to change someone's behavior; at other times, you may be negotiating salary or benefits or a better price from a supplier. Know what you want to get out of the deal.[121] Be clear about what it is you are negotiating. Is it price, options, delivery time, sales quantity, or something else entirely? Set limits—what price and other key terms do you need to make a deal?[122] In any case, you want to set three objectives:

- A specific lower limit that you are unwilling to give up (say, a certain behavior on the part of your peer in the department or a minimum price from your supplier). You must be willing to walk away from negotiations if this lower limit is not agreed to.[123]
- A target objective that represents what you believe is fair
- An opening objective that is more than you actually expect but that you may achieve

Remember that the other person or party is probably also setting these kinds of objectives. The key to successful negotiation is for each person or party to achieve something between their minimum objective and their target objective—that is, to win some and lose some.

Step 3: Try to develop options and trade-offs. In some negotiating situations, you may find that you are in a position of power to achieve your target objective. For example, when negotiating prices with a supplier or applying for jobs, you may be able to quote other prices or salary offers and get the other person to beat them. If you have to give up something or cannot get exactly what you want, be prepared to ask for something in return. When **GM, Eastern Airlines,** and others were having financial difficulties, the company asked employees to take a pay cut. Rather than simply accept a cut, the employees asked for company stock in a trade-off. Based on your research, you should be able to anticipate the kinds of trade-offs you might expect from the other person.

Step 4: Anticipate questions and objections and prepare answers. Very likely, the other party to negotiations wants an answer to the unasked question "What's in it for me?" Focus on how the negotiations will benefit the other person.[124] Speak in terms of "you" and "we" rather than "I."

There is a good chance that the other person will raise objections. Unfortunately, not everyone will be open about their real objections. Thus, you need to listen and ask questions to find out what is preventing an agreement. It will also help to project an attitude of enthusiasm and confidence. If the other person does not trust you, you will not reach an agreement.

Negotiate

After you have planned, you are ready to negotiate the deal. Face-to-face negotiations are generally preferred because you can see the other person's nonverbal behavior and better understand objections. However, negotiations by telephone and written negotiations (email) work, too.

It will help to keep the following in mind as you negotiate:

Step 1: Develop rapport and focus on obstacles, not on the person. Use the other person's name as you greet them. Relationships are always wrapped up in underlying influences,[125] so it is appropriate to open with small talk and develop a relationship.[126] How long you wait before getting down to negotiations will depend on the particular situation and the other person's style.

Never attack the other person's personality or use negative statements such as "You always bad-mouth me to the boss" or "You're being unfair to ask for such a price cut." Statements like these will make the other person defensive, which will make it harder to reach an agreement. During negotiations, people look for four things: inclusion, control, safety, and respect. If people perceive that you are

©iStockphoto.com/GlobalStock

Negotiations are common, making good negotiation skills important for personal and professional success.

WORK
APPLICATION 10-17

Assess how well you plan for and run a negotiation. Which steps do and don't you follow? How can you improve your negotiating skills?

LO 10-9

Briefly explain the processes of mediation and arbitration and the major difference between the two processes.

SHRM

A:2
Alternative Dispute Resolution

Mediator A neutral third party who helps resolve a conflict but has no authority to impose a solution to the conflict

pushing them into something, threatening them, or belittling them, they will not trust you and will be unlikely to come to an agreement with you.

Step 2: Let the other party make the first offer. Of course, the other party may pressure *you* to make the first offer; for example, the person may say, "Give us your best price, and we'll decide whether to take it." If so, you can counter with a question such as "What do you expect to pay?" You should let the other party go first so that if you get a better offer than you expected, you can take it and get more than your target. If the offer is lower than your target, you can negotiate to get more.

Step 3: Listen and ask questions to focus on meeting the other party's needs. Create an opportunity for the other person to disclose reservations and objections. Focus on how your deal will benefit the other party.[127] When you ask questions and listen, you gather information that will help you overcome the other party's objections. Determining whether the objection is a "want" criterion or a "must" criterion will help you decide how to proceed.

Step 4: Don't be too quick to give in, and remember to ask for something in return. Those who ask for more often get more.[128] But many people—especially many women—are reluctant to ask for what they deserve.[129] You want to satisfy the other party without giving up too much yourself; remember not to go below your minimum objective and be prepared to walk away if that minimum can't be met.[130] When you are not getting what you want, having other options can help give you bargaining power.

Though you don't want to be quick to give in, you might want to be the first to make a concession, particularly when you are negotiating complex deals. A concession makes the other party feel obligated, which gives you negotiating power. However, before making a concession, it's essential to know what all of the other party's demands are. And avoid unilateral concessions.

Be reluctant to lower your price.[131] If you have to, ask for something in return, which means giving something and getting something else. For example, if you are offered a job at $30,000 but your target is higher and the other side will or cannot come up, ask for more vacation days, more retirement, or more benefits. If you are buying a car and the sales rep will not come down in price, ask for an extended warranty, new tires, etc.

Alternative Dispute Resolution: Mediation and Arbitration

Labor and management are required by law to bargain with each other in good faith, and companies need to maintain effective employee relations—but when in conflict, we cannot always resolve our dispute alone. In these cases, we can use something called alternative dispute resolution. Alternative dispute resolution includes a series of tools, most commonly either mediation or arbitration, which parties in conflict can use to resolve their disagreements without going through the process of litigation. The US government's **Federal Mediation & Conciliation Service (FMCS)** is often used as an alternative dispute resolution resource. For more information about the FMCS, visit its website at http://www.fmcs.gov. At this point, let's take a little more detailed look at both mediation and arbitration.

In many cases in an organization where conflicts occur, a mediator may be used. A **mediator** *is a neutral third party who helps resolve a conflict but has no authority to impose a solution to the conflict.* As a manager, you may often be called upon to serve as a mediator between two employees. In this case, remember that you should be a mediator, not a judge. Your task is to get the employees to resolve the conflict themselves, if possible. You will need to work diligently to remain impartial, unless one party is violating company policies.

When bringing employees who are in conflict together, focus on how the conflict is affecting their work. Discuss the issues by addressing specific behavior that bothers the other person and not discussing personalities.[132] If a person says, "We cannot work together because of a personality conflict," ask the person to identify the specific behavior that is the root of the conflict. The discussion should make the parties aware of their behavior and of how its consequences are causing the conflict. What expectations are not being met?

In the mediation process, the purpose of the mediator is to assist the parties in overcoming barriers to communication as well as other barriers that are keeping the parties from resolving their differences. *Facilitation* is one of the major tools available to the mediator. When people act as facilitators, their primary purpose is to help individuals or groups who are in conflict to overcome hurdles that are keeping the conflict from being resolved.

As in most cases, an example will help you understand how a mediator might act in the role of facilitator. Let's assume that an individual employee and their supervisor are in conflict over how to resolve a grievance concerning unsafe tools in the workspace. The employee, in fact, filed a grievance based on a concern for their own safety and the safety of others, while the supervisor is under the impression that the employee just wants newer and nicer tools. The employee's grievance was initially denied by the supervisor, and the contract with the labor union allows a mediation process between the direct supervisor and the employee prior to going up the chain of command to higher-level managers.

In this case, the mediator could step in and assist by acting as a facilitator of communication between the two parties. While the employee is concerned with safety, the supervisor is concerned with the overall cost of buying new tools or equipment. Part of the supervisor's job is to control costs in the work area, and the tools that would have to be replaced are very expensive. However, the supervisor did not initially know the details concerning how the existing tools were unsafe, and the employee had not successfully explained the nature of the problem in the initial grievance. The mediator helps the two parties communicate with each other about their concerns—the mediator helps the supervisor relay their concern for cost controls while also providing the employee with assistance in identifying the specific problem with the tools that makes them unsafe. The result might be that both parties successfully communicate their concerns, but the supervisor realizes that the issue of safety is much more significant than the issue of cost and therefore agrees to buy the new tools that the employee has requested.

If the conflict cannot be resolved by mediation, an arbitrator may be used as a follow-up. An **arbitrator** *is a neutral third party who resolves a conflict by making a binding decision.* Many business contracts require the use of an arbitrator rather than seeking relief by way of the court system. An arbitrator basically acts like a judge in a civil hearing. The arbitrator will hear arguments from both parties in a conflict, may ask questions of each of the parties in order to clarify issues, and will then make a decision on which party will "win" the case.

The most significant difference between the processes of mediation and arbitration is that the result of an arbitration process is binding on the parties who are in conflict. Mediation, on the other hand, is merely a process designed to assist the parties in coming to an agreement on their own. The mediator has no authority to impose a solution on the two parties in conflict. Because of this difference, the use of arbitration should be kept to a minimum because it is not a collaborative process.

WORK
APPLICATION 10-18

Describe a conflict that you could not resolve on your own and that a neutral third party (a teacher, coach, or boss) got involved in to help you resolve. Assess how helpful the mediator or arbitrator was.

Arbitrator A neutral third party who resolves a conflict by making a binding decision

TRENDS AND ISSUES IN HRM

It's time to take a look at this chapter's trends and issues. Because there have been several significant NLRB rulings on labor relations issues in the past few years, we are going to focus on a couple of these issues in this Trends and Issues section.

Nonunion Worker Protection and the NLRB

Earlier in this chapter, we noted a couple of the issues that have been pushed by the NLRB in the past several years—quickie elections in union certification and certification of micro-bargaining units. Let's take a look now at how the NLRB is trying to become more relevant in nonunion work environments. For example, the Board recently got involved with the issue of **Wal-Mart** employees who walked off their jobs in states around the country in late 2012.[133] The NLRB says that these workers had a right to engage in "protected concerted activities" in the form of a short strike during the busy period leading up to the Christmas holidays. However, Wal-Mart says that the employees violated company rules by not showing up for work and that the unions behind the strikes have repeatedly violated federal law. Several of the striking employees were fired for failing to follow company rules, and now the NLRB is taking up the case through the use of an administrative law judge. The NLRB charged Wal-Mart with retaliating against employees who exercised their rights under the NLRA.[134] The Board noted that workers have a right to strike, but Wal-Mart said the intermittent nature of the employees' actions made it impossible to tell a strike from just being absent without notice.

Strikes historically occur when management and labor have a specific set of disagreements, and they generally continue until those disagreements are resolved. However, the strike against Wal-Mart and several other actions against nonunion employers around the country have not been continuing actions. They have been very short-term actions—sometimes as short as part of an employee's shift for one day—after which the workers go back to their jobs. According to the *Wall Street Journal*, labor "lawyers say it isn't clear when these strikes deserve protection under federal labor laws, and workers could lose their legal protection depending on their intentions and conduct."[135]

Wal-Mart says that the strikes are intended to interfere with its business and its customers and that the unions backing the short strikes are prohibited from taking such actions by federal law (the LMRA).[136] In some recent cases, state courts have agreed. Texas courts ruled that the labor unions and "OUR Walmart" members funded by the unions could not trespass on company property and would have to face court-ordered penalties for violating those requirements. Courts in California and Arkansas have also issued injunctions against the UFCW and OUR Walmart to stop those organizations from taking actions that disrupt the company's operations.[137] Other state courts have shown similar intent to restrain some of the union tactics, but the NLRB continues to push the issue of workers' rights to strike with the company. We will have to see how this issue will be resolved over the next few months or years, but labor rights could be significantly expanded or significantly limited based on the decisions of the administrative law judge from the NLRB and ultimately by decisions from the federal courts.

Is a Union Suppression Policy Ethical?

 ESR

Union suppression is a company using all the tactics available to prevent the unionization of the company's workforce. This is much like what Wal-Mart is doing in its current conflict with the NLRB and the unions. These tactics can include such things as spreading rumors about potential job losses, hiring consultants who specialize in union avoidance tactics, hiring labor lawyers who know the limits to what the company can do to avoid unionization, closing facilities that vote for unionization, bringing in disgruntled current members of the union to talk to your workforce, and many other tactics.

Is this process of union suppression ethical or unethical? Again, it depends. If the organization remains within the law and the NO TIPS guidelines, is it ethical for company management to engage in union suppression? Even here, you need to look at fair, reasonable, and equitable treatment of employees in the organization and not just at whether or not the company is following the letter of the law.

We have discussed the issue of ethics in several chapters of this text, and we've noted that just because something is legal, it doesn't mean that it is necessarily ethical. Staying within the letter of the law may not provide the company with the kind of workforce that it needs in order to compete with other firms in the 21st century. Here again, we return to the question of whether or not actions on the part of management will increase the satisfaction and engagement levels of the employees or cause them to decrease.

Union suppression tactics that employ actions such as the nonunion employee representation (NER) that we discussed earlier in the chapter can certainly be ethical methods of suppressing unions, in some cases. Using these representatives can also increase employee satisfaction and engagement in the organization. So this tactic and other similar tactics would be considered ethical by most.

On the flip side, planting rumors, whether true or not, concerning the potential closing of facilities if workers were to vote to unionize would probably be unethical and could even violate the rule of "no threats" in a unionization campaign. Each situation has to be looked at individually, and management needs to decide which suppression tactics are ethical and legal and which tactics might not be.

• • • CHAPTER SUMMARY

10-1 **Briefly describe the five steps in the message-sending process.**

The five steps are as follows:

1. Develop rapport—put the receiver at ease;

2. State the communication objective—the end result you want to achieve;

3. Transmit the message—tell the receivers what you want them to know;

4. Check for understanding—ask questions and/or paraphrase;

5. Get a commitment and follow up—make sure the receiver can do what is required, and check to make sure action was taken.

10-2 **Briefly describe the three steps in the message-receiving process.**

The steps are as follows:

1. Active listening—paying attention to the whole message, avoiding distractions, taking notes if necessary, and conveying understanding;

2. Analyzing—thinking, empathizing, and waiting to evaluate until after listening is complete;

3. Checking for understanding—paraphrasing back to the sender, watching nonverbal behavior, and (if appropriate) responding to the sender.

10-3 **Identify the primary reason why measuring job satisfaction is so difficult, and identify the best tool for getting employees to tell the truth about their level of satisfaction.**

Job satisfaction is an attitude, not a behavior. We can experience behaviors directly, while we can measure attitudes only indirectly. Because of this, we must use some form of survey and ask the employees about their job satisfaction level. When using job satisfaction surveys, we have to ensure that they are anonymous, or employees will most likely not tell the truth about their satisfaction levels.

10-4 **Identify the major labor relations laws in the United States and the major reasons why we have each law.**

1. The Railway Labor Act of 1926 was enacted to force negotiation between labor and management, first in railroads and later in the airlines, to prevent shutdown of these critical services.

2. The National Labor Relations Act of 1935 was the first major law to deal with the rights of labor to form unions in the general workforce and collectively bargain with employers. It identified unfair labor practices for management in negotiating with labor organizations.

3. The Labor Management Relations Act of 1947 was an amendment to the NLRA that focused on unfair labor practices on the part of unions and other labor organizations. It outlawed or restricted a variety of strikes and boycotts, and it also allowed the states to pass right-to-work laws.

4. The Labor Management Reporting and Disclosure Act of 1959 was passed as a result of congressional investigations linking organized crime with labor unions. The LMRDA required a series of reports from labor unions and created restrictions on their activities.

5. The Worker Adjustment and Retraining Notification Act of 1988 required that organizations with certain qualifying characteristics should provide 60 days' notice when laying off more than 50 people or closing a plant.

10-5 Briefly discuss the difference between wrongful discharge and constructive discharge.

Wrongful discharge is the process of terminating an individual from employment for an illegal reason. Even when employment is at-will, employers can't break the law or violate a contract to terminate employees. Constructive discharge is actually not discharge at all. In constructive discharge, an employee quits a job because of severe harassment or intolerable working conditions.

10-6 Briefly discuss the NO TIPS rules for labor elections.

NO TIPS is an acronym that stands for No Threats, No Interrogations, No Promises, and No Spying. This means first that employers cannot threaten to terminate employees from their jobs, threaten to close the plant, or threaten employees in any other manner during the period prior to a labor election. Secondly, employers cannot call the individual employees in question about union organizing activities on either their part or the part of others within the organization. Third, management cannot promise that if employees vote against unionization, the organization will provide them with benefits because of their votes. Finally, management cannot spy on individual employees taking part in union organizing events, either through planting individuals in such meetings or through electronic or other means.

10-7 Briefly discuss what management can do to limit union organizing efforts.

Management can prevent union organizers from soliciting employees on company property during working hours, as long as such prohibitions are consistent with the company's general solicitation policies. Management can also identify costs that would be associated with union membership and can provide truthful information concerning how unionization will affect relationships between individual employees and management. These relationships can include things such as performance-based promotions, merit-based raises, and training opportunities.

10-8 Identify the five conflict management styles. How is each described in terms of win or lose?

The first conflict management style is called avoiding. Avoiding is unassertive and uncooperative, leading to a "lose-lose" situation. The second style is accommodating. In accommodation, the individual is unassertive but cooperative, leading to a "lose-win" situation—the individual loses and the other party wins. The third option is forcing. Forcers are assertive but uncooperative, meaning they create a "win-lose" situation. Some managers will use this style to get things done quickly because they have legitimate authority over others. The fourth style is negotiating, which creates a "win-some, lose-some" situation. Each side gets some of what it wants through compromise, but not everything it wants. The final style is collaborating, which create a true "win-win" situation. Both sides worked together to create a solution that meets all of their needs.

10-9 Briefly explain the processes of mediation and arbitration and the major difference between the two processes.

Mediation and arbitration both deal with inserting a third party as an intermediary into a dispute between two other individuals or groups. However, they differ in how much power the third party has in the process. Mediators enter into a conflict to assist the two conflicting parties in coming to a resolution and to act as a facilitator in their negotiations, but the mediator has no authority to force a solution on the opposing parties. In contrast, arbitrators also assist the two parties in attempting to work out a solution to their conflict, but arbitrators have the ability to enforce decisions they make on both of the conflicting parties. Such decisions are called binding decisions.

10-10 Define the key terms found in the chapter margins and listed following the Chapter Summary.

Complete the Key Terms Review to test your understanding of this chapter's key terms.

••• KEY TERMS

active listening
arbitrator
collective bargaining
communication
conflict
constructive discharge
economic strike

express contract
feedback
grievance
implied contract
labor relations
lockout
mediator

negotiating
paraphrasing
quasi-contract
strike
trust
whistle-blower
wrongful discharge

••• KEY TERMS REVIEW

Complete each of the following statements using one of this chapter's key terms.

1. _____ is faith in the character and actions of another.

2. _____ is the process of transmitting information and meaning.

3. _____ is information provided by the receiver that verifies that a message was transmitted successfully.

4. _____ is the process of restating a message back to the original sender in the receiver's own words.

5. _____ is the process of paying attention to an entire message, taking into account both the content of the message and the context in which the communication is delivered.

6. _____ is a collective work stoppage, staged by members of a union, that is intended to put pressure on an employer.

7. _____ is an individual who tells an authoritative organization outside the company about actions within the company that the individual believes to be illegal.

8. _____ is a transaction in which the agreement between two parties is specifically stated.

9. _____ occurs when the parties form an agreement from their actions rather than from a specific oral or written agreement.

10. _____ is a court-ordered implied agreement to prevent one party in an action from benefiting at the expense of another party.

11. _____ consists of terminating an individual employee for an illegal reason, either in violation of a contract or because of violation of a state or federal law.

12. _____ occurs when an employee is forced to quit a job because of severe and/or pervasive harassment or intolerable working conditions.

13. _____ consists of the interactions between management and unionized employees.

14. _____ is the negotiation process resulting in a contract between union employees and management that covers employment conditions.

15. _____ is a formal complaint concerning pay, working conditions, or violation of some other factor in a collective bargaining agreement.

16. _____ occurs when management stops work and physically prevents workers from entering the workplace.

17. _____ is a work stoppage over authorized collective bargaining issues such as pay or working conditions.

18. _____ exists whenever people are in disagreement and opposition.

19. _____ is a process in which two or more parties in conflict attempt to come to an agreement.

20. _____ is a neutral third party who helps resolve a conflict but who has no authority to impose a solution to the conflict.

21. _____ is a neutral third party who resolves a conflict by making a binding decision.

••• COMMUNICATION SKILLS

The following critical-thinking questions can be used for class discussion and/or for written assignments to develop communication skills. Be sure to give complete explanations for all answers.

1. What causes you to trust or distrust someone else? Using this answer, what would you do as a manager to cause your employees to trust you?

2. Good communication skills are critical to a manager. Which do you think is more important: learning to communicate specifically as a sender, or learning to listen well as a receiver? Why?

3. What *specific* things would you think about if you were trying to empathize with employees telling you about a problem in their work group?

4. What actions would you consider taking, other than increasing pay, if job satisfaction survey data showed that your employees' satisfaction level was dropping significantly?

5. Which side do you think has an easier job when a labor organization is trying to unionize the company's employees—management or the union organizers? Why?

6. Do you think it is ever OK for employees to strike against an employer? If so, in what circumstances? If not, why not?

7. After reviewing the unfair labor practices that apply to both management and labor, do you feel that the listed practices are fairly well balanced, or do you feel that they are skewed toward either management or labor? Explain your answer.

8. What actions would you take if a potential whistle-blower told you she had evidence that an executive-level manager in your company was doing something illegal? Explain your answer in some detail.

9. Looking at the concept of constructive discharge, is it ever really possible that an employee could be harassed so severely as to be forced to quit? Can you give an example of a situation that you feel would meet this level of harassment?

10. Assume that you are a fairly high-level manager in your company and that one of your employees comes to you to tell you that other employees are attempting to unionize the company. What would your initial actions be, and why?

11. An employee who works for you confronts you with a formal grievance concerning another employee being promoted over him. What initial actions will you take in order to address this grievance?

12. If you had authority to make decisions for your organization, would you ever use a lockout to prevent workers from entering your business, even after good-faith bargaining efforts had failed? Why or why not?

13. Can opponents in a conflict ever really come to a collaborative conclusion, or is our best option a negotiation in which each party wins some of what it wants and loses other things that it desires? Explain your answer.

14. Would you personally rather have a conflict between you and another person handled by an arbitrator, or would you rather go to court and have a judge make a decision? Explain your answer.

15. Describe an example of conflict between people in an organization. How would you as a facilitator assist the people in conflict to resolve their differences?

••• CASE 10-1 DECKER DEALS WITH THE UNIONS

Tom Decker is Plant Manager of a large fruit and vegetable canning plant owned by a national grocery chain. The plant has 200 full-time production employees staffing three 8-hour shifts. Tom has just recently become aware of an attempt by the United Food and Grocery Workers Union (UFGWU) to organize the production workers in the plant. He is somewhat surprised by the union organizing campaign since he feels that employee relations have always been very good in the plant. Tom believes that employees are somewhat satisfied with the amount of compensation provided, but he thinks that it may be time to consider making some improvements. He intends to meet with management in the corporate office to convince them that improving employee wages and benefits shows that the company will take care of them and that they don't need union representation. Tom plans to hold meetings with small groups of employees in an effort to persuade them that a union is unnecessary and that having a union represent them will not necessarily help them gain better wages or benefits.

Tom asked his shift supervisors to keep their eyes and ears open in order to learn which employees are supportive of the union's organizing attempt. A few days later, the shift supervisors furnished Tom a list of all employees who they believe have signed union authorization cards. Tom's cousin, who also works in the plant, is attending union organizing meetings and is keeping management informed on the meetings. Lew Spencer, the evening shift supervisor, informed Tom that two employees working on his shift appear to be the plant leaders of a group of union sympathizers because they have been "talking up" the union to all the other employees in the plant. One of the employees, Bill Vance, has only been with the company for two years. A review of his personnel file shows that he has received reprimands for poor attendance and unsatisfactory job performance. The other employee, Jason Higgins, has been with the company for 23 years. A review of his personnel file indicates that he has always performed his job satisfactorily. He has never received any formal disciplinary action; however, Supervisor Lew

Spencer stated that he can be a hothead and occasionally tends to be very vocal and argumentative about any changes in working conditions at the plant. Tom wonders why these two employees have not been fired since they do not appear to be good employees. Corporate management has been considering reducing the workforce through an economic layoff since the plant is currently not operating at full capacity. Tom thinks that this would be an opportunity to get rid of some employees who are union sympathizers including Bill Vance and Jason Higgins.

Questions

1. Why should management personnel be careful regarding comments made to employees during a union organizing campaign? What should managers not say and what could they say to employees during a union organizing attempt?

2. If Tom Decker is correct in his assessment that the production employees are satisfied with their wages and benefits, what other factors may be motivating employees' interest in organizing with the union?

3. Should management take some employment action against any employees during this organizing campaign? Explain your answer.

4. Should management make changes in wages, benefits, and other conditions of employment during a union organizing campaign? Explain your answer.

5. What is meant by the term *exclusive bargaining agent*? What would it take for the UFGWU to become the exclusive bargaining agent if an election is held?

6. What could be a possible outcome concerning the union organizing campaign if the union files an unfair labor practice against the company with the National Labor Relations Board (NLRB)?

Case created by Robert Wayland, University of Arkansas at Little Rock

• • • CASE 10-2 CONSTRUCTIVE DISCHARGE AND REINSTATEMENT OF STRIKERS

Pearl Refining Company operates a facility in Sunflower, Arkansas, where it is engaged in the refining, sale, and distribution of petroleum products. The International Refinery Workers Union conducted an organizing drive recently at this facility, but it failed to obtain majority support in an election conducted by the NLRB. Chief Operator Gene Roberts has worked at Pearl's Sunflower refinery for about 16 years. Roberts works all three shifts on a rotating basis, earning $24 per hour. Roberts attended one union organizing meeting and voted during the union organizing election, but he didn't discuss with anyone how he voted.

Pearl Refining Company also operates a crude oil storage facility located in northern Louisiana, about 4 hours' drive from the refinery. The refinery manager, Dusty Conway, was notified by Vice-President of Refining George Letterman that the crude oil storage facility in Louisiana had recently been experiencing substantial shortages in deliveries of crude oil. Crude oil delivery receipts kept at the refinery did not correspond to the crude oil reportedly delivered by truck from independent producers to the Louisiana storage facility. It was suspected that a large portion of this shortage was due to the delivery of water rather than oil to the storage facility. To correct this problem, it was necessary to send someone to the storage facility to double-check the truck drivers' deliveries and the accuracy of their delivery reports. Refinery Manager Conway decided to send Gene Roberts to the Louisiana crude oil storage facility, thinking that he was very dependable and had the experience to do the best job of detecting who might be delivering water instead of crude oil.

Conway called Roberts to his office on Monday and instructed him not to report for the night shift, as originally scheduled, but to report to the crude oil storage facility on Wednesday morning to accept a 2-week assignment there, helping the gauging employees at the facility. Roberts said that he didn't want the assignment and that he wanted to keep his regular job as operator. Conway said, "No, Gene. Let's just think about it. You go home and think about it and come back in the morning." The next morning, Roberts told Conway that he wanted to continue working in his current job in the plant and that the Louisiana assignment might result in some conflict. Conway said, "Well, Gene, that's all there is for you, that's it, and that's all." Roberts, thinking that he had no choice in the matter, laid his hard hat on the desk, walked out of Conway's office, and left the refinery. As Roberts was walking out of the refinery, Manager Conway confronted him, stating that he was considering this a resignation and that his employment would be terminated.

The following morning, six of Roberts's fellow employees met with Conway in his office and asked that Roberts be reinstated. Conway informed them that he had no intention of rehiring Roberts. The six employees then informed Conway that if Roberts was not going to be rehired, they were going out on strike. The employees then left the refinery and started picketing.

Subsequently, Roberts filed a complaint with the National Labor Relations Board (NLRB), stating that he had been constructively discharged. In addition, the six employees on strike complained to the NLRB that they were participating in an unfair labor strike and requested that they be reinstated to their jobs and made whole. The employees were told by Refinery Manager Conway that their jobs had already been filled and that they therefore could not get their old jobs back.

Questions

1. What are the differences between "constructive discharge" and "wrongful discharge"?

2. What factors would the NLRB most likely consider in its investigation of whether or not Roberts's termination was a constructive discharge?

3. What elements should be proven to show that Roberts was "constructively discharged"?

4. What is the difference between economic strikes and unfair labor practice strikes?

5. What rights do economic strikers and unfair labor practice strikers have to reinstatement?

Case created by Robert Wayland, University of Arkansas at Little Rock

Sharpen your skills with SAGE edge at edge.sagepub.com/lussierhrm2e

SAGE edge for students provides a personalized approach to help you accomplish your coursework goals in an easy-to-use learning environment.

• • • SKILL BUILDER 10-1 CONFLICT RESOLUTION

Objective

To develop conflict resolution skills using the Initiating Conflict Resolution Model

Skills

The primary skills developed through this exercise are as follows:

1. *HR management skill*—Human relations

2. *SHRM 2013 Curriculum Guidebook*—A: Employee and labor relations

During this exercise, you will be given the opportunity to role-play a conflict (one you are facing now or have faced in the past) to develop your conflict resolution skills. Students and workers have reported that this exercise helped prepare them for successful initiation of conflict resolution with roommates or coworkers.

First, list the other party or parties in the conflict situation (you may use fictitious names):

_____

_____

_____

Describe the conflict situation:

_____

_____

_____

List pertinent information about the other party or parties (i.e., their relationship to you and their knowledge of the situation, age, and background):

_____

_____

_____

Identify the other party or parties' possible reaction to your confrontation. How receptive will they be to collaborating? What might they say or do during the discussion to resist change?

_____

_____

_____

How will you overcome the resistance to change?

Following the steps in the collaborative conflict resolution model, write out your BCF statement.

_____

_____

_____

Apply It

Your instructor may allow you to role-play the conflict in class, or you may role-play with someone outside of class, or you may just initiate the conflict resolution in your personal or professional life. If you role-play in class, the instructor will provide directions.

What did I learn from this experience? How will I use this knowledge in the future?

••• SKILL BUILDER 10-2 NEGOTIATING

Objective

To develop negotiating skills using the Negotiation Process Model

Skills

The primary skills developed through this exercise are as follows:

1. *HR management skill*—Human relations
2. *SHRM 2013 Curriculum Guidebook*—A: Employee and labor relations

You will role-play being the buyer or seller of a used car.

Procedure 1 (1–2 minutes)

Pair off and sit facing your partner so that you cannot read each other's confidential sheet. Pairs should be as far apart as possible so they cannot overhear other pairs' conversations. If there is an odd number of students in the class, one student will be an observer or will work with the instructor. Decide who will be the buyer and who will be the seller of the used car.

Procedure 2 (1–2 minutes)

The instructor will give a confidential sheet to each buyer and seller. (These do not appear in this book.)

Procedure 3 (5–6 minutes)

Buyers and sellers read their confidential sheets and jot down some plans, including what their basic approach will be and what they will say in the negotiation.

Procedure 4 (3–7 minutes)

Negotiate the sale of the car. You do not have to buy or sell the car. After you make the sale or decide not to sell, read your partner's confidential sheet and discuss the experience.

Integration (3–7 minutes)

Planning the Negotiation

Step 1. Research the other party. Did you at least consider the car to be an antique?

Step 2. Set objectives. Did you set a lower limit, target, and opening price?

Step 3. Did you develop options and/or develop trade-offs?

Step 4. Did you anticipate questions and objections and prepare answers?

Negotiating

Step 1. Did you develop rapport and focus on obstacles, not on the person?

Step 2. Did you let the other party make the first offer?

Step 3. Did you listen and ask questions to focus on meeting the other party's needs?

Step 4. Were you quick to settle for less than your target price and/or ask for something in return for giving concessions?

Did you postpone? If you did reach a sales agreement, which price did you receive? $_____

Apply It

What did I learn from this experience? How will I use this knowledge in the future?

_____

_____

Part IV

Compensating

11 Compensation Management

12 Incentive Pay

13 Employee Benefits

PRACTITIONER'S MODEL

↑ **Productivity**
↑ **Satisfaction**
↓ **Absenteeism**
↓ **Turnover**

PART V: Protecting and Expanding Organizational Reach
How do you PROTECT and EXPAND your Human Resources?

| **Chapter 14** | **Chapter 15** | **Chapter 16** |
| Workplace Safety, Health, and Security | Organizational Ethics, Sustainability, and Social Responsibility | International HRM |

PART IV: Compensating
How do you REWARD and MAINTAIN your Human Resources?

| **Chapter 11** | **Chapter 12** | **Chapter 13** |
| Compensation Management | Incentive Pay | Employee Benefits |

PART III: Developing and Managing
How do you MANAGE your Human Resources?

| **Chapter 7** | **Chapter 8** | **Chapter 9** | **Chapter 10** |
| Training, Learning, Talent Management, and Development | Performance Management and Appraisal | Rights and Employee Management | Employee and Labor Relations |

PART II: Staffing
What HRM Functions do you NEED for sustainability?

| **Chapter 4** | **Chapter 5** | **Chapter 6** |
| Matching Employees and Jobs: Job Analysis and Design | Recruiting Job Candidates | Selecting New Employees |

PART I: 21st Century Human Resource Management Strategic Planning and Legal Issues
What HRM issues are CRITICAL to your organization's long-term sustainability?

| **Chapter 1** | **Chapter 2** | **Chapter 3** |
| The New Human Resource Management Process | Strategy-Driven Human Resource Management | The Legal Environment and Diversity Management |

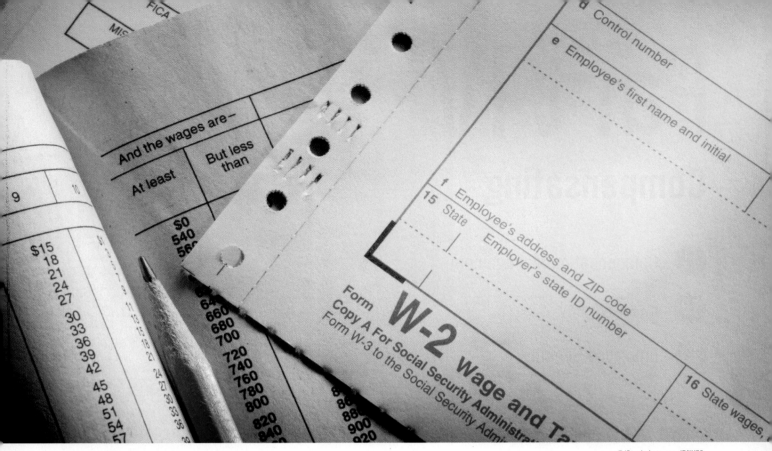

©iStockphoto.com/DNY59

11 Compensation Management

• • • LEARNING OUTCOMES

After studying this chapter, you should be able to do the following:

Practitioner's Perspective

Cindy tells the story of when Drew walked dejectedly into her office and flopped down in the nearest chair.

"I hear they hired a new payroll clerk—the same job I've been doing for five years—and this new person is going to be paid more than I make! I've been a loyal employee for years and haven't had a real raise since I started. Is that fair?"

Cindy couldn't fault Drew for his feelings, and she knew it was past time the company examined its compensation guidelines.

Once you have an established pay scale, is it really important to reexamine your compensation levels? What is the solution when the going market rate for a position outdistances your set pay scale? Chapter 11 answers these questions and more as it demonstrates the reasons why compensation management is so vital to attracting and retaining your best employees.

SHRM HR CONTENT

See Appendix: *SHRM 2013 Curriculum Guidebook* for the complete list

K. Total Rewards (required)

A. Compensation

1. Development of a base pay system

2. Developing pay levels

3. Determining pay increases

4. Role of job analysis/job design/job descriptions in determining compensation

6. Compensation of special groups (e.g., executives, sales, contingent workers, management)

7. Internal alignment strategies

8. External competitiveness strategies

9. Legal constraints on pay issues

10. Monitoring compensation costs

11. Union role in wage and salary administration

12. Minimum wage/overtime

13. Pay discrimination and dissimilar jobs

14. Prevailing wage

15. Motivation theories: Equity theory, reinforcement theory, agency theory

B. Employment Law (required)

8. The Fair Labor Standards Act of 1938 (FLSA)

E. Job Analysis/Job Design (required)

2. Job evaluation and compensation (grades, pay surveys, and pay setting)

6. Compliance with legal requirements

Equal pay (skill, effort, responsibility, and working conditions) and comparable worth

Overtime eligibility (exempt vs. nonexempt work)

G. Outcomes: Metrics and Measurement of HR (required)

11. Benchmarking

I. Staffing: Recruitment and Selection (required)

16. Employment brand

COMPENSATION MANAGEMENT

Compensation costs are frequently the largest part of total production costs at today's firms. Compensation costs are also rising as people go back to work after the latest recession.[1] According to the US Bureau of Labor Statistics, average compensation costs rose nearly a dollar per hour from March 2013 to March 2014.[2]

Compensation *is the total of an employee's pay and benefits.* The HR department generally develops pay systems, makes pay determinations, and keeps records in compliance with wage and hour laws.[3] A business designs and implements a compensation system to focus worker attention on the specific efforts the organization considers necessary to achieve its desired goals.[4] However, if rewards are to be useful in stimulating desired behavior, they must also meet the demands of employees whose behavior they're intended to influence.[5] Thus, poor compensation management practices can have negative effects on performance.[6]

Compensation affects the process of both attracting and retaining employees.[7] A recent survey revealed that for the first time in several years, pay is now the top reason for job satisfaction, overtaking job security as the top driver of satisfaction in 2013. In fact, pay is currently either first or second in importance to all four major generations of employees currently in the workforce—veterans, baby boomers, generation X, and millennials—so HR must pay attention to fair and equitable compensation for company employees.[8]

The Compensation System

The compensation system of an organization includes *anything that an employee may value and desire and that the employer is willing and able to offer in exchange.* This includes the following:

Compensation The total of an employee's pay and benefits

Compensation system Anything that an employee may value and desire and that the employer is willing and able to offer in exchange

1. *Compensation components.* All rewards that can be classified as monetary payments and in-kind payments constitute the compensation component.

2. *Noncompensation components.* All rewards other than monetary and in-kind payments (e.g., company cafeterias and gyms) constitute the noncompensation component.

TYPES OF COMPENSATION. There are four basic parts of a compensation system:

1. *Base pay.* This is typically a flat rate, either as an hourly wage or salary. Many employees consider this to be the most important part of the compensation program, and it is therefore a major factor in their decision to accept or decline the job.
   Wages vs. salary. Wages are paid on an hourly basis. *Salary* is based on time—a week, a month, or a year. A salary is paid regardless of the number of hours worked. Wages are common for blue-collar workers, and salaries are common for white-collar professionals and managers. A salary, however, does *not* make an employee "exempt"; we will cover this in detail shortly.

2. *Wage and salary add-ons.* This includes overtime pay, shift differential, premium pay for working weekends and holidays, and other add-ons.

3. *Incentive pay.* Also called variable pay, *incentive pay* is pay for performance, and it commonly includes items such as piece work in production and commissioned sales. Pay for performance, especially in the form of short-term incentive pay, continues to increase as a percentage of employee compensation due to the ability of the employer to shift risk from the company to the individual employee.[9] We will discuss incentives in detail in Chapter 12.

4. *Benefits.* This is indirect compensation that provides something of value to the employee. You need to include benefits in your system, because they cost the company a lot of money even though they aren't direct compensation to the employee. Benefits may include health insurance; payments to employees if they are unable to work because of sickness or accident; retirement pay contributions; and provision of a wide variety of desired goods and services such as cafeteria service, tuition reimbursement, and many other items. We will discuss benefits in detail in Chapter 13.

Direct Versus Indirect Compensation. The first three compensation components—base pay, any add-ons, and incentive pay—are known as *direct compensation.* These

LO 11-1

Identify the components of a compensation system.

WORK
APPLICATION 11-1

Select a job. Identify the compensation you received there in detail.

11-1 APPLYING THE CONCEPT

Types of Compensation

Review the types of compensation and then write the letter corresponding to each one before the statement(s) describing it.

a. base pay
b. wage and salary add-ons
c. incentive pay
d. benefits

_____ 1. I'd like to work for a firm that will help pay for me to get my master's of business administration (MBA) degree.

_____ 2. I only get paid $11 an hour, so I'm looking for a better job.

_____ 3. I like getting paid the same each week. It helps me to budget my expenses.

_____ 4. I like being paid for every sale I make, but my pay does vary from week to week.

_____ 5. I like working nights because it pays more.

Salespeople are often given incentive pay to motivate them to sell more.

©iStockphoto.com/kali9

SHRM

K:A15
Motivation Theories: Equity, Reinforcement, Agency Theories

LO 11-2

Briefly describe expectancy theory as it applies to compensation.

Expectancy theory A theory proposing that employees are motivated when they believe they can accomplish a task and that the rewards for doing so are worth the effort

forms of compensation go directly to the employees as part of their paycheck. Benefits are *indirect compensation*. The employees don't directly get any funds from a benefits program. Benefits are usually paid for by the company, and the employees never see those funds.

In for-profit businesses, we want to design the mix of compensation and noncompensation components that provide us with the best productivity return for the money spent. However, to do that, we need to understand something about the motivational value of our compensation system. Let's take a look at a few theories that help us understand better how compensation systems can motivate our workers to learn and act in the way we need them to act.

Motivation and Compensation Planning

When we look at designing compensation programs, we need to remember that we are trying to motivate the employee to do the things that we need them to do, consistently, over a period of time. Probably the most significant theories that help in compensation planning are expectancy theory and equity theory, which are both process theories of motivation.[10] However, we also need to look at how our employees learn and carry out their jobs in the organization, so we need to remember what we discussed in Chapter 7 about learning theories. But let's get started with motivation and how it affects the design of our compensation system.

EXPECTANCY THEORY. We said in the introduction to this section that expectancy theory is a *process theory* of motivation. This basically means that we, as human beings, go through a cognitive process to evaluate something, and if we evaluate the process positively, we will likely continue to be motivated to do the same thing. Alternately, if we evaluate the process negatively, we will be disinclined to do the same thing in the future. **Expectancy theory** *proposes that employees are motivated when they believe they can accomplish a task and that the rewards for doing so are worth the effort.* Expectancy theory is based on Victor Vroom's formula: Motivation = Expectancy × Instrumentality × Valence.[11]

For compensation purposes, we have intentionally simplified the theory to show how it affects a person's motivation to perform. *Expectancy* is the person's perception of their ability to accomplish or probability of accomplishing an objective. Generally, the higher one's expectancy, the better the chance for motivation. *Instrumentality* is the perception that a particular level of performance is likely to provide the individual with a desired reward. *Valence* refers to the value a person places on the outcome or reward, because not all people value the same reward. Again, generally, the higher the valence (meaning the importance to the individual) of the outcome or reward, the better the chance of motivation. One thing that we need to remember here is that the three components of the theory—valence, instrumentality, and expectancy—are multiplicative. This means that if any one of the three is near zero, the motivating potential is also near zero, and the individual has almost no motivation to perform![12]

How does this theory affect the compensation of our workforce? The simple way to answer is to show expectancy in action (see Exhibit 11-1). An employee will have an expectation to put forth some form of effort at work. This effort is expected to result in some level of performance, and higher effort should result in higher performance levels. (This is expectancy.) The performance level is expected to result in some type of desired reward (this is instrumentality), and if it does, the employee expects to put out more effort. (Obviously, compensation in some form is at least part of the reward expected by the employee.) The reward must be significant to the individual (this is valence), and if it is, the motivation to put forth effort should continue. As long as the process continues unbroken, the employee will continue to put out effort. In other words, as HR managers, if we help employees get what they want, they will give us the work we want to help meet the organizational goals.[13]

WORK
APPLICATION 11-2

Give an example of how expectancy theory has affected your motivation or that of someone you work with or have worked with. Be sure to specify the expectancy and valence.

EXHIBIT 11-1 EXPECTANCY THEORY AND COMPENSATION

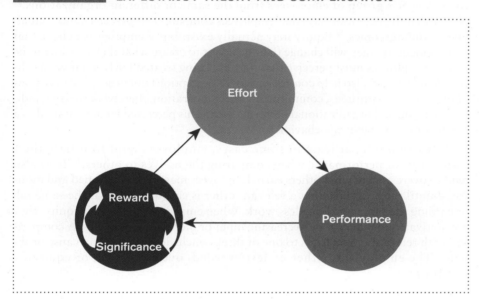

So the result of expectancy theory is that our employees will either be motivated by their outcomes, including compensation, or be demotivated by them. Knowing how people internally evaluate their outcomes using the cognitive process of expectancy theory helps us when we are structuring the compensation plan.

Motivating Employees With Expectancy Theory. Here are some keys to using expectancy theory successfully:

1. Clearly define objectives and the performance needed to achieve them. In other words, goal setting is part of expectancy theory.
2. Tie performance to rewards. High performance should be rewarded. When one employee works harder to produce more than other employees and is not rewarded, that employee may slow down.
3. Be sure rewards have value to employees. What motivates one employee may not motivate other employees, so managers should get to know employees as individuals.[14]
4. Make sure employees believe that management will do what it says it will. For example, employees must believe that management will give them a merit raise if they meet their performance goals. And, as noted in Chapter 10, management must do so to earn employees' trust.

LO 11-3

Briefly describe equity theory as it applies to compensation.

SHRM

K:A7
Internal Alignment Strategies

SHRM

K:A8
External Competitiveness Strategies

EQUITY THEORY. Equity theory is another concept that affects people in our organizations. People in companies apply equity theory constantly—we all do.[15] Equity theory, particularly the version developed by J. Stacy Adams, proposes that people are motivated to seek social equity in the rewards they receive (outcomes) for their performance (input).[16] So in general, **equity theory** *proposes that employees are motivated when the ratio of their perceived outcomes to inputs is at least roughly equal to that of other referent individuals.* Employees are more motivated to achieve organizational objectives when they believe they are being treated fairly,[17] especially regarding pay equity.[18] Equity theory is still popular today.[19]

According to equity theory, people compare their inputs (effort, loyalty, hard work, commitment, skills, ability, experience, seniority, trust, support of colleagues, and so forth), financial rewards (pay, benefits, and perks), and intangible outcomes (praise, recognition, status, job security, sense of advancement and achievement, etc.) to those of relevant others.[20] A *relevant other* could be a coworker or a group of employees from the same or different organizations.[21] Notice that the definition says that employees compare their *perceived* (not actual) inputs and outcomes.[22] Equity may actually exist, but if employees believe that there is inequity, they will change their behavior to create what they consider to be equity. Employees must perceive that they are being treated fairly, relative to others. Managers can also help control employee perceptions of fairness.[23] Perceptions of inequity hurt attitudes, commitment, and cooperation, thereby decreasing individual, team, and organizational performance.[24] This perceived inequity is used as a justification for unethical behavior.[25]

Unfortunately, at least in some cases, employees tend to inflate their own efforts or performance when comparing themselves to others.[26] They also tend to overestimate what others earn. Employees may be very satisfied and motivated until they perceive that a relevant other is earning more for the same job or earning the same for doing less work. When employees perceive inequity, they are motivated to reduce it by decreasing input or increasing outcomes. A comparison with relevant others leads to one of three conclusions, which can cause problems. The employee is either underrewarded, overrewarded, or equitably rewarded.[27]

1. *Underrewarded.* When employees perceive that they are underrewarded, they may try to reduce the inequity by increasing outcomes (e.g., requesting a raise or committing theft), decreasing inputs (doing less work, being absent, taking long breaks, etc.), rationalizing (finding a logical explanation for the inequity), changing others' inputs or outcomes (getting them to do more or receive less), leaving the situation (getting transferred or taking a better job), or changing the object of comparison. There is strong evidence that perceptions of being underrewarded can lead to some very negative consequences for the organization, including theft and sabotage, so we have to take perceptions of being underrewarded seriously.[28]

2. *Overrewarded.* Being overrewarded does not disturb most employees. People tend to tolerate overrewarded situations to a much greater extent than they do underrewarded situations. However, research suggests that if employees feel significantly overrewarded, they may reduce perceived inequity by increasing input (working harder or longer), decreasing outcomes (taking a pay cut), rationalizing ("I'm worth it"), or trying to increase others' outcomes.

3. *Equitably rewarded.* When inputs and outcomes are perceived as being equal, the theory says that employees will be motivated to continue to put forth effort for the organization so long as they are content that inputs and outcomes are in balance.[29]

Equity theory Theory that employees are motivated when the ratio of their perceived outcomes to inputs is at least roughly equal to that of other referent indivdiuals

Motivating Employees With Equity Theory. Using equity theory in practice can be difficult, because you don't know employees' reference groups and their views of inputs and outcomes. However, the theory does offer some useful general recommendations:

1. Managers should be aware that equity is based on perception, which may not be correct. Possibly, managers can create equity or inequity, so the manager's role is to be the arbiter of equity.[30] If employees believe they are not being treated fairly, there should be procedures in place to resolve the issue or complaint.[31] A good performance appraisal system (as discussed in Chapter 8) can help.

2. Rewards should actually be equitable. When employees perceive that they are not treated fairly, morale suffers and performance problems occur. Employees producing at the same level should be given equivalent rewards.

3. High performance should be rewarded, but employees must understand the inputs needed to attain certain outcomes. When using incentive pay, managers should clearly specify the exact requirements to achieve the incentive. As discussed in Chapter 8, a manager should be able to state objectively why one person got a higher merit raise than another did.

As HR managers, we need to understand that people will be demotivated if they feel (perceive) that they are not fairly compensated.[32] As a result, we have to use this information when we begin to structure our compensation plan. We need to "build in" equity to minimize the problems associated with equity theory.

LEARNING THEORIES. We talked about learning at length in Chapter 7, so we want to do just a brief review of those theories here. Remember that learning theories are about changing behaviors of people in the organization. We especially need to remember how *reinforcement* and *social learning* work, because compensation is designed at least partly to reinforce learned behaviors at work.[33] People respond to consequences and will behave as you want them to if you find the right incentives.[34]

B. F. Skinner said that if we give employees something that they want in return for doing what we need them to do, they are more likely to continue to do the same work successfully in the future, because their behavior got *positive reinforcement*. Positive reinforcement generally works better than punishment,[35] especially when training employees.[36] In the same way, if an employee sees another get positive reinforcement for doing something, Skinner said that the person observing this action is more likely to imitate the rewarded behavior, because of *social learning*, in order to get a similar reward.

We can also use *negative reinforcement* because, you will remember, it also causes a person to repeat a desired action. If employees are less motivated because they have to work too much overtime, we can take the overtime away. Because we take away something that the employees don't want, they are inclined to be more motivated. The whole point of compensation is to motivate employees, so we don't want to demotivate them because we are working them too hard.

We also set work standards to ensure that employees do a reasonable amount of work for their compensation. (This is called *avoidance reinforcement.*) If not, we use punishment, such as pay cuts, demotions, and (when necessary) firings.

ORGANIZATIONAL PHILOSOPHY

In addition to understanding our compensation options and how they motivate employees, we need to identify what our compensation philosophy will be. We need to ask ourselves (and get honest answers to) a series of questions concerning the

WORK
APPLICATION 11-3

Give an example of how equity theory has affected your motivation or that of someone you work with or have worked with. Be sure to specify if you were underrewarded, overrewarded, or equitably rewarded.

WORK
APPLICATION 11-4

Give an example of the types of reinforcement used on a present or past job.

LO 11-4

Identify the seven basic issues that make up the organizational philosophy on compensation.

WORK
APPLICATION 11-5

Assess the ability to pay of an organization you work or worked for. Explain how you came up with your answer.

SHRM

K:A10
Monitoring Compensation Costs

compensation system that we need to design. How much can we afford to pay? What are we willing to pay for? How will we structure our compensation system, and why? Will our pay structure be higher or lower than that of our competitors, and why? Let's discuss some of these major organizational issues that we will need to understand and make decisions about before we can set up our system.

Ability to Pay

Probably the first thing we need is an honest assessment of how much we can afford or are willing to afford to pay our employees. This of course means we need to complete an assessment of estimated revenues from our business operations and determine what percentage of revenues can or should realistically go toward compensation costs. There are a number of ways of figuring this out, such as building pro forma financial analyses, but these are beyond the scope of this text.

In our analysis, we want to calculate the total amount of annual organizational revenue that we expect to be available for all compensation components—wages, incentive payments, and benefits. One of the worst possible situations a company can find itself in is to have promised a particular level of compensation and then not be able to provide what was agreed upon because the funds are not available. This is especially true in the case of incentive payments. Making incentive promises at the beginning of a year and then reneging on them at the end of the year will almost always cause intense demotivation and potentially high rates of turnover among our workers.[37]

What Types of Compensation?

Once we identify how much revenue is available for compensation, the next thing we need to do is determine how to break the compensation structure down. We noted earlier in the chapter that we have four basic components to compensation—base pay, wage add-ons, incentives, and benefits. We will need to determine how to divide the funds available between each of the components.

There are some legal requirements for certain benefits such as Social Security (we will discuss these in Chapter 13), so these legal requirements have to be dealt with "off the top"—they have to be subtracted from the available funds. Once we subtract the amount necessary to provide the benefits that are legally mandated by state and federal requirements, we need to determine how much direct compensation will be in the form of base pay and how much will be incentive pay. We will have to ensure that the direct compensation that we provide will allow us to be competitive in the labor markets from which we must draw our employees. Otherwise, we may not be able to get recruits to select jobs with our firm.[38] We'll talk more about how we determine what a competitive amount of compensation will be when we get to pay structures later in this chapter.

The last type of compensation that we will consider is voluntary benefits. Here again, we need to analyze competition within the labor market and what benefits each of our close competitors provides. We will most likely have to approximately match the benefits that are provided by our main competitors.[39] In addition, we may determine that other benefits provide us with leverage that allows us to get better employees to commit to work for our firm, and such benefits may also help us keep the workers who are already part of the organization more satisfied and less likely to quit.[40]

Pay for Performance or Pay for Longevity?

In breaking down base pay versus incentives, we will need to look at whether our organization is going to have a *performance philosophy* or a *longevity philosophy*. What do we mean by performance and longevity? Some companies pay people more for *longevity* or *seniority*, meaning accumulating years of service with the firm. If we work for this type of organization, we will likely get promotions and raises over time (assuming that we meet minimal organizational standards) regardless of performance because we have been a loyal member of the organization. Other companies, however, pay more for *performance*—for completing certain tasks or doing certain things faster or better than average, not just for being there and being loyal to the firm.[41]

Why would anyone pay people just for being in the company for a long time? We may be in an industry where customers have strong relationships with their contact within the firm and don't feel comfortable when they don't have that contact available anymore. In this case, we might need to reward service because it gives us stability and our customers rely on this stability. A common example of an industry where at least part of direct compensation is based on longevity is the insurance industry. Customers create a relationship with their insurance agent, sometimes over long periods of time, and they may not feel comfortable changing to a new agent every few months. In this type of company, base pay would probably be the largest component of direct compensation. Educators are also commonly paid based on longevity, and all teachers may get a raise regardless of performance.

There certainly may be problems with longevity philosophies. Some of our employees may think, "As long as I am here, regardless of my performance, I will get more compensation over time." So entitlement-style pay philosophies don't motivate us much. They may cause us to continue to work, but they probably won't make us want to perform better over time.

However, if we are in an industry that focuses on performance and where customers want the best possible product or service, then we probably have to lean toward a performance orientation rather than a longevity-based philosophy.[42] Such industries include those where competition is intense or where products or services are constantly developing and changing. They might need to base at least a significant portion of their pay on performance. An example here might be a company such as **Samsung** or **Apple**, which is continuously developing new microcircuit-based electronic products. In these firms, speed to market is a critical component of overall strategy, so major parts of their compensation strategy may be based on worker performance. In companies such as these, incentive pay will likely be a very large component compared to base pay.

One caution here, though: Pay for performance is on the rise, but there is a potential dark side to individual incentives, as linking pay and performance is difficult in many jobs and employees frequently don't think the system is fair.[43] For example, was one of your professors (or physicians) better or worse than others? Why? And would all professors and students (or doctors and patients) agree and think it is fair to pay such a person differently based on performance? Also, many people believe in the egalitarian approach that we are all in this together, we are all equal, it is not fair to treat people differently, and we deserve the same compensation.[44] This is the common mentality of most unions (e.g., teachers' unions) that fight merit pay. So the challenging part is to design compensation programs that are perceived as fair to everyone.[45]

Skill-Based or Competency-Based Pay?

The next item that we may consider is whether or not we want to utilize *competency-based* or *skill-based pay*. Both fall within the incentive component of compensation. While Chapter 12 is the primary chapter covering incentive pay, we need to consider whether or not we're going to use this type of incentive pay before we create the company's pay structure.

If we decide to use skill-based or competency-based pay, we will pay members of the workforce for individual skills or competencies that they bring to work, whether

Organizations commonly pay based on the skills and competencies needed to do the job.

or not those skills are necessary for the individuals to do their current job. *Competencies* involve the individual's level of knowledge in a particular area, while *skills* involve the ability to apply that knowledge set in that field. Examples of competencies include such things as an understanding of negotiation and collaboration, an understanding of the basic principles of physics, or problem-solving and decision-making expertise. Examples of skills related to these competencies would include the ability to actually negotiate contract agreements, apply principles of physics to a new equipment design, or make a high-quality decision based on good analysis of a situation.

Should we use competency-based or skill-based pay? Again, it depends.[46] Probably the most important thing that we need to consider is our generic strategy. As we noted in Chapter 2, if our generic strategy is low cost, we probably want to hire and train people for specific jobs and will not generally pay them for knowledge and skills outside of that narrow job description. If, however, our strategy says that we're going to act as a differentiator, then we may gain significant value from paying individuals extra for bringing to the workplace skills or competencies that can allow them to think, analyze a situation, and come up with good solutions to organizational problems.

However, we are paying our employees for knowledge, skills, and abilities that they may not necessarily ever use in the organization. This obviously drives up our overall costs for compensation. So we have to ask whether it is valuable to have somebody who is well rounded or whether we just need someone who is specifically trained for a job. Thus, skills-based pay is commonly measured based on the number of actual jobs the person can perform. For example, on an assembly line, a person who can only work on one part of production will be paid less than a person who can work on two or three parts. People who can perform multiple jobs are more valuable because they can help out wherever they are needed at any particular time.

At, Above, or Below the Market?

The next item we must determine is whether we will pay *above market, at market,* or *below market.* Are we willing to pay more than necessary to hire individuals? Can we pay less than average and still get people to apply for jobs in our company? What are the advantages and disadvantages of each option?

Why would we ever want to pay above the market? The simple answer is to attract better workers and enhance our employment brand. We want good employees to have a strong incentive to work for us, and one way to enhance our employment brand is to pay above the market rate.[47] We also want better productivity out of our workforce if we pay more for employees.

Do better workers generally have higher levels of productivity? In fact, there is some evidence that says that this is the case. *Efficiency wage theory* says that if a company pays higher wages, it can generally hire better people who will in turn be more productive.[48] Because we have higher-quality employees, we get a productivity increase that more than offsets the higher cost of employing them.[49]

Based on efficiency wage theory, would we necessarily get lower productivity from our workforce if we paid below the market? In general, yes, but not always. If our firm is in an industry where unemployment is high, it is easy to find replacement workers, and if most positions require a low-level skill set, we may be able to get away with paying less than average. But is this a good idea? What will likely happen if the labor market gets tighter and there are fewer unemployed workers with the skills that we require? It will become easier for an employee with such skills to quit our company and go to work for another, and we will likely start to lose at least some of our more skilled employees because of job dissatisfaction and a lack of organizational commitment.[50] So if you pay too little and the skill set you need is in high demand, it will be hard to find people.

So we have to think about our overall pay levels. Are they going to be at the market average, above it, or below it? We can't pay higher than average if we can't afford to, but HRM professionals consistently conduct research to find out what the average compensation is so they know where they stand. In the end, most of them select the average option.

Wal-Mart, with its Sam's Club subsidiary, is known as a low-paying firm with limited benefits. It has been estimated that it costs $2,500 to recruit and train each of its employees. On the other hand, **Costco Wholesale Corporation** pays significantly more in wages than Wal-Mart does, with more generous benefits, but it has a lower turnover rate, saving it money. Wal-Mart is clearly a successful company with low pay, but most of the World's Most Admired Companies listed by *Fortune* magazine compensate their employees well and are reluctant to lay them off.[51]

Wage Compression

Wage compression is another concern in setting up a pay structure. **Wage compression** *occurs when new employees require higher starting pay than the historical norm, causing narrowing of the pay gap between experienced and new employees.*[52] It generally occurs over a significant period of time. We bring workers into the organization in both good economic times and bad. When the economy is doing poorly and overall wages are depressed, people will generally accept jobs for less than they would if the economy were doing well and higher-wage jobs were available. Since raises are frequently based on an employee's initial salary or pay rate, those who start at lower pay than others may stay that way over time, and pay inequality for the same work may increase over time as well.

Because we have to pay more to attract new employees when the overall economy is doing well or when their skills are in high demand, we may create a situation where workers with less time on the job might be paid nearly as much as, or more than, employees who have worked for us for many years but who came into the organization under other circumstances. For example, the supply of accounting professors with PhDs and CPA certifications is far lower than the demand. So some universities end up hiring such professors who don't have any full-time academic experience and pay them more than some tenured full professors in other areas, such as organizational behavior.

This wage compression can weaken the desired link between pay and performance, creating significant dissatisfaction on the part of long-term employees because of the pay differential.[53] Employers are usually unaware that pay compression exists until problems surface. Most companies and organizations don't set out to do this—they just fall into it.[54] If we understand wage compression when creating a pay structure for the organization, we can avoid at least some of the dissatisfaction associated with the pay differentials between short-term and long-term employees.

Pay Secrecy

As managers we know that based on equity theory, our employees will review both internal and external equity, meaning they will compare themselves to other people both inside the firm and in other companies. Because our employees do this, we also

WORK
APPLICATION 11-7

Select a job you have or have had. Did the firm provide above-average, average, or below-average compensation? Explain how you came up with your answer, using comparisons to competitors.

Wage compression When new employees require higher starting pay than the historical norm, causing narrowing of the pay gap between experienced and new employees

have to pay attention to both types of pay equity. Sometimes we actually do a worse job with internal equity than we do with external equity. We have some knowledge of what a job is worth in other companies or on the open market through the use of pay survey data. However, we can have people working next to each other who have significant differences in salary, possibly because of wage compression or possibly from other factors such as personal productivity. When workers talk to each other and find out that they are getting significantly different pay, they might get upset.

One of the solutions some companies use to deal with this issue is *pay secrecy*, which means requiring employees to not disclose their pay to anyone else. But is it legal to tell employees that they can't discuss their pay with anyone else? Why would we want to force employees to keep quiet about their pay, and how do you think employees would generally respond to a pay secrecy clause in their employment contract?

First, let's do a quick review of some of the recent rulings on pay secrecy in the United States. Over the past several years, the NLRB has consistently ruled that companies may not discipline workers who reveal information about their pay and other work conditions as long as the workers are participating in "protected, concerted activity." As a result of these rulings, any company that continues to function with pay secrecy rules and that uses those rules to discipline employees in any way may be charged by the NLRB with violating the NLRA. In addition, President Obama signed an Executive Order in 2014 (EO 13665) prohibiting pay secrecy policies in federal government contractors, with potential loss of government contracts as punishment for failure to comply. So, enforcing pay secrecy clauses is becoming more dangerous to companies.

However, there may be legitimate concerns about pay secrecy within companies. We may want to keep employees from discussing their pay because if we have two people working next to each other and doing the same basic job, and if there are big pay differences between them, then there could be a problem—even if the two individuals have significantly different performance histories. We think we may be able to avoid the problem by not letting them talk about it, but can we really avoid the problem? As a general rule, we can't.

If you're an employee who is required to sign a contract with a pay secrecy clause, what is one of the first things that pops into your head? You immediately begin to believe that we must be paying somebody else more than you. So, one of the issues here is that we almost immediately create a motivation and job satisfaction problem because of your perception of inequity (remember, *perception* is the key to equity).[55]

So there is a perception problem associated with pay secrecy, even if pay secrecy is deemed to be legal in some cases. Employees may assume the employer is unfair and biased against them, whether it is the truth or not. Therefore, they may try to balance the equation in a different way. There are also potential legal questions that the employer may be trying to avoid—potential age, race, and gender discrimination or other issues. For example, companies might have pay secrecy rules because they have older employees making less than younger employees. This may be because of the wage compression that we discussed in the last section, or it may be because the older workers have fewer current skills than someone who is just out of school. When you get out of college, you should have fairly up-to-date skills, but older employees may not even want to learn those new skill sets. In that kind of situation, the younger person may be worth more to the company, but the older person doesn't feel like that's true. So there is some potential for discrimination lawsuits.

So there are some reasons why companies might want to apply a pay secrecy clause. But will this really keep everyone from talking about their pay? Of course not—at least some people will talk. So one thing that we create by putting a pay secrecy clause into employment contracts is a whole bunch of rule breakers. This is never a good idea. Well, will it cause people to be more satisfied with their pay, since they don't *know* that anyone else is getting paid more than they are? We have already dispelled that assumption, because of perception. All right, won't we have to answer a lot of questions about why someone is getting paid more than someone else in a similar job? Yes, we might, but isn't this something that you should do proactively if you are doing your job and you know that the differential exists because of performance, knowledge, or skills? If we can explain the reason for inequity successfully, we change the equity theory equation. Finally, we have to remember that most of the recent rulings have been anti–pay secrecy. So if we look at all the evidence, there usually are no defensible reasons for pay secrecy.

Open companies, where large amounts of corporate information are available to everyone in the organization, are starting to take hold in some locations and industries. **SumAll** is one company where every employee can review "company financials, performance appraisals, hiring decisions, and employee pay, along with each worker's equity and bonuses."[56] This open-company policy removes all of the doubt that leads to perceptions of inequity among company employees. Everyone has the ability to do a direct equity comparison with others whom they choose as reference individuals. According to Ed Lawler of the University of Southern California, in the future, companies may not have a choice to remain secretive because of the nature of work in the new economy. However, this will put more pressure on management to be able to explain differences in pay when questioned.[57]

WORK
APPLICATION 11-8

Select a job you have or have had. Did people know how much other employees made, or was there pay secrecy?

LEGAL AND FAIRNESS ISSUES IN COMPENSATION

In Chapter 3, we discussed the Equal Pay Act and how it specifically deals with paying women and men equally when all other factors are the same. We also just mentioned the new EO 13665, which deals with pay openness and equity for federal contractors. We have to provide equal pay for equal work unless there is a difference in productivity, seniority, merit, or other factors "other than sex." There are also a number of federal and state laws that directly or indirectly affect pay and compensation systems. Virtually every equal employment opportunity (EEO) law identifies compensation as one of the employment actions where discrimination is prohibited if it is based on a protected characteristic. So we have to keep these laws in mind as we set up our pay system. See Exhibit 11-2 for a list of some of the major EEO laws and legal concepts that cover compensation.

EXHIBIT 11-2 MAJOR EEO LAWS AND LEGAL CONCEPTS

Antidiscrimination legislation:
1. Equal Pay Act of 1963 (EPA)
2. Title VII of the Civil Rights Act of 1964 (CRA)
3. Age Discrimination in Employment Act of 1967 (ADEA)
4. Vietnam Era Veteran's Readjustment Act of 1974
5. Americans with Disabilities Act of 1990 (ADA)
6. CRA of 1991
7. Lilly Ledbetter Fair Pay Act of 2009 (LLFPA)
Legal concepts linking employment discrimination and pay discrimination:
1. Disparate impact
2. Disparate treatment
3. Bona fide occupational qualification (BFOQ)

Employee Exemptions

Identify each job as generally being considered exempt or not from minimum wage or overtime pay (write *a* or *b* before each job type).

a. exempt

b. nonexempt

____ 6. Auto mechanic

____ 7. Fruit picker

____ 8. Worker on a foreign-flag cruise ship

____ 9. Librarian

____ 10. Taxi driver

____ 11. Real estate agent

____ 12. Bellperson at a hotel

____ 13. Computer programmer (paid more than $27.63 per hour)

____ 14. Hairdresser

____ 15. Bank teller

LO 11-5

Discuss the three major provisions of the FLSA.

SHRM

B:8

The Fair Labor Standards Act of 1938 (FLSA)

SHRM

K:A12

Minimum Wage/Overtime

WORK
APPLICATION 11-9

Select a job you have or have had. What is the minimum wage in your state? Does the firm pay its lowest-level employees below, at, or above the state minimum wage?

Minimum wage The lowest hourly rate of pay generally permissible by federal law

Fair Labor Standards Act of 1938 (Amended)

Besides the Equal Pay Act and the other EEO laws, there are some laws that deal specifically with compensation issues. The grandfather of these laws is the Fair Labor Standards Act (FLSA). We must really understand the FLSA well in order to create a pay system. The law's major provisions cover minimum wage, overtime issues, and child labor rules for most US-based businesses.[58] Let's complete a quick review of the major provisions of the FLSA.

THE MINIMUM WAGE. The first major provision of the FLSA concerns the federal minimum wage. The **minimum wage** *is the lowest hourly rate of pay generally permissible by federal law.* The current federal minimum wage for most employees in the United States is $7.25 per hour.[59] This is adjusted periodically by Congress, but the FLSA applies the minimum wage provision. It doesn't matter how the employer pays employees—the net value paid per hour can't generally fall below the minimum wage. In other words, we can compensate employees based on a "piece-rate" payment; on commission; or by use of a straight hourly wage, salary, or other common form—but the amount has to equal $7.25 per hour or more for the hours worked.[60] Some states and even cities have set the minimum wage higher than the federal rate. You may have noted that Seattle, Washington, recently set the city's minimum wage at $15 per hour! This wage has been challenged in court by a business group, but as of the time of this writing, the law had passed a city council vote.[61] In addition, as of this writing, the Secretary of Labor had proposed a rule to raise the minimum wage for federal contract workers to $10.10 per hour.[62]

Does everyone get paid at least the minimum wage for their area? Not exactly. There are some exemptions to the rules.[63] If someone is *exempt*, by the definitions in the FLSA, they are exempt from the minimum wage requirement, overtime provisions, or child labor rules or possibly all three. People not meeting any of the requirements for an exemption are called *nonexempt* and must be paid minimum wage, overtime, etc.

As an example, workers who most people know are commonly exempt include restaurant waitstaff. The current minimum wage for servers is $2.13 per hour.[64] Why should servers be paid less than $7.25? The obvious answer is that they are in a "tipped" position. Servers would normally expect to get a large portion of their wages in tips. The FLSA says that we can pay servers a minimum of $2.13 per hour as long as their tips make up the difference. If somebody in a restaurant works 20 hours in 1 week and does not make an average of $5.12 an hour in tips, it is illegal to pay that person $2.13. So just because there is an exemption, it does not mean that we can pay our servers $2.13 per hour, no matter the circumstances. This is

EXHIBIT 11-3 COMMON EXEMPTIONS

Major exemption categories:
Executive
Professional
Administrative
Outside sales
Computer employee

Some other common FLSA exemptions:[66]

(MW = minimum wage, OT = overtime, and CL = child labor)

- Airline employees–OT
- Babysitters (on a casual basis)–MW & OT
- Boat salespeople–OT
- Companions for the elderly–MW and OT
- Workers with disabilities–MW
- Domestic employees who are live-in–OT
- Federal criminal investigators–MW and OT
- Firefighters working in small (with fewer than five firefighters) public fire departments–OT
- Fishing–MW and OT
- Forestry employees of small (with fewer than nine employees) firms–OT
- Fruit and vegetable transportation employees–OT
- Homeworkers making wreaths–MW, OT, and CL
- Houseparents in nonprofit educational institutions–OT
- Livestock auction workers–OT
- Local delivery drivers and driver's helpers–OT
- Lumber operations employees of small (with fewer than nine employees) firms–OT

- Motion picture theater employees–OT
- Newspaper delivery people–MW, OT, and CL
- Newspaper employees (of limited-circulation newspapers)–MW and OT
- Police officers working in small (with fewer than five officers) public police departments–OT
- Radio station employees in small markets–OT
- Railroad employees–OT
- Seamen on US vessels–OT
- Seamen on other than US vessels–MW and OT
- Sugar-processing employees–OT
- Switchboard operators–MW and OT
- Taxicab drivers–OT
- Television station employees in small markets–OT
- Truck and trailer salespeople–OT
- Youth employed as actors or performers–CL
- Youth employed by their parents–CL

why workers at the local **McDonald's** or **Taco Bell** are not paid $2.13 an hour: Most workers at fast-food restaurants don't get tipped. For food service workers, average tips must make up the difference between the wage paid and the minimum wage, and in these businesses, tips will not do so.[65] There are also other exemptions for individuals who are live-in child care providers, newspaper carriers, seasonal workers, etc. In fact, there are hundreds of exemptions (see Exhibit 11-3 for examples).

However, there is a set of quick guidelines concerning exempt and nonexempt persons at work. If you make under $23,660, you are pretty much guaranteed to be nonexempt under the current provisions of the FLSA.[67] "Highly compensated employees" paid $100,000 or more (*and* at least $455 per week) are pretty much automatically exempt from the minimum wage and overtime rules if they regularly perform at least one of the duties of an exempt executive, administrative employee, or professional employee identified in the standard tests for exemption.[68] If an individual is paid more than $23,660 but less than $100,000, then the employee usually must meet a set of specific "duties tests" in order to fall within an exemption category (see Exhibit 11-4).

OVERTIME. **Overtime** *is a higher than minimum, federally mandated wage, required for nonexempt employees if they work more than a certain number of hours in a week.* Overtime is currently set by the FLSA as "time-and-a-half," or 150% of the individual's normal wages. If somebody is not an exempt employee and works more than 40 hours a week, do we have to pay that employee overtime? Yes, in almost all

WORK
APPLICATION 11-10

Give examples of jobs that are exempt and nonexempt. Be sure to state why they are classified as such.

SHRM

K:A6
Compensation of Special Groups (e.g., Executives, Sales, etc.)

Overtime A higher than minimum, federally mandated wage, required for nonexempt employees if they work more than a certain number of hours in a week

EXHIBIT 11-4 DUTIES TESTS FOR GENERAL EMPLOYEE EXEMPTIONS

Executive Exemption

To qualify for the *executive employee* exemption, the employee must meet all of the following criteria:

- The employee must be compensated on a salary basis (as defined in the regulations) at a rate of not less than $455 per week;

- The employee's primary duty must be managing the enterprise or managing a customarily recognized department or subdivision of the enterprise;

- The employee must customarily and regularly direct the work of at least two or more other full-time employees or their equivalent; and

- The employee must have the authority to hire or fire other employees; or the employee's suggestions and recommendations as to the hiring, firing, advancement, promotion, or any other change of status of other employees must be given particular weight.

Professional Exemption—Learned or Creative

To qualify for the *learned professional employee* exemption, the employee must meet all of the following criteria:

- The employee must be compensated on a salary or fee basis (as defined in the regulations) at a rate not less than $455 per week;

- The employee's primary duty must be the performance of work requiring advanced knowledge, defined as work that is predominantly intellectual in character and that requires the consistent exercise of discretion and judgment;

- The employee's advanced knowledge must be in a field of science or learning; and

- The employee's advanced knowledge must be customarily acquired by a prolonged course of specialized intellectual instruction.

To qualify for the *creative professional* employee exemption, the employee must meet all of the following criteria:

- The employee must be compensated on a salary or fee basis (as defined in the regulations) at a rate not less than $455 per week;

- The employee's primary duty must be the performance of work requiring invention, imagination, originality, or talent in a recognized field of artistic or creative endeavor.

Administrative Exemption

To qualify for the *administrative employee* exemption, the employee must meet all of the following criteria:

- The employee must be compensated on a salary or fee basis (as defined in the regulations) at a rate not less than $455 per week;

- The employee's primary duty must be the performance of office or nonmanual work directly related to the management or general business operations of the employer or the employer's customers; and

- The employee's primary duties must include the exercise of discretion and independent judgment with respect to matters of significance.

Outside Sales Exemption

To qualify for the *outside sales employee* exemption, the employee must meet all of the following criteria:

- The employee's primary duty must be making sales (as defined in the FLSA) or obtaining orders or contracts for services or for the use of facilities for which a consideration will be paid by the client or customer; and

- The employee must be customarily and regularly engaged away from the employer's place or places of business.

The salary requirements of the regulation do not apply to the outside sales exemption.

Computer Employee Exemption

To qualify for the *computer employee* exemption, the employee must meet all of the following criteria:

- The employee must be compensated either on a salary or fee basis at a rate of not less than $455 per week or, if compensated on an hourly basis, at a rate of not less than $27.63 an hour;

- The employee must be employed as a computer systems analyst, computer programmer, software engineer, or other similarly skilled worker in the computer field performing the duties described in the next bullet point;

- The employee's primary duty must consist of one of the following:

  1. The application of systems analysis techniques and procedures, including consulting with users to determine hardware, software, or system functional specifications;

  2. The design, development, documentation, analysis, creation, testing, or modification of computer systems or programs (including prototypes), based on and related to user or system design specifications;

  3. The design, documentation, testing, creation, or modification of computer programs related to machine operating systems; or

  4. A combination of the aforementioned duties, the performance of which requires the same level of skills.

The computer employee exemption does not include employees engaged in the manufacture or repair of computer hardware and related equipment.

Source: US Department of Labor, retrieved July 6, 2014[69]

cases. But what if the person works more than 8 hours a day? No, there is no limit to the number of hours per day for calculation of overtime. With very few exceptions, if a nonexempt employee works more than 40 hours in a week, that employee is eligible for overtime.

In a few cases, the organization may be allowed to average an employee's work hours over 2 weeks in order to determine whether the individual is eligible for overtime—but this is an exception, not the rule! One type of work for which this may be allowed is shift work for firefighters, police officers, or medical personnel who may work 12- or 24-hour shifts. This is because they may work 48 hours one week and 24 the next, so we can calculate their overtime based on a 2-week average rather than a 1-week average. Remember, though, that these situations are fairly rare and are explicitly identified in the FLSA.

What about double time? If an employee works more than 60 hours in a week, do we have to pay that person double time? In fact, we don't. The FLSA has no requirement for paying anything more than time-and-a-half for any overtime work.[70] Employers are also not required to provide paid holidays, vacation, or extra pay for working on weekends or on holidays. Many do this, though, because of the issue of job satisfaction and organizational commitment.

CHILD LABOR. The FLSA also has some rules on the use of *child labor*, meaning workers under 18 years old. If individuals are 18 or older, we can use them in any normal employment situation. However, we can only employ 16- and 17-year-olds in *nonhazardous* jobs, although their work hours are unrestricted. Finally, there are significantly different rules for 14- and 15-year-olds.

Minors age 14 and 15 may work outside school hours for no more than "three hours on a school day, 18 hours in a school week, eight hours on a non-school day, and 40 hours in a non-school week."[71] They can't start work before 7:00 a.m. or work after 7:00 p.m., except from June 1 through Labor Day, when they can work until 9:00 p.m. Jobs they can work are limited to retail, food service, and gasoline service at establishments specifically listed in the FLSA regulations. Employees 14 and 15 years old may not work overtime. While there are some exceptions to these rules for businesses such as family businesses or family farms, these are the general guidelines for child labor.

EMPLOYEE MISCLASSIFICATION UNDER THE FLSA. Misclassification of employees as exempt from minimum wage or overtime is one area where companies can get into

SHRM

E:6
Compliance With Legal Requirements: Overtime Eligibility

WORK APPLICATION 11-11

Select a job you have or have had. Who gets paid overtime, why, and how much?

WORK APPLICATION 11-12

Select a job you have or have had. Does the organization hire child labor? If so, why, and what do the child laborers do?

LO 11-6

Describe the penalties in the FLSA for misclassification of nonexempt employees.

serious trouble. In a news release in May of 2012, the Department of Labor noted the recovery of $4.83 million in back wages and nearly a half million dollars in penalties from **Wal-Mart** stores for misclassification of more than 4,500 employees.[72] What is interesting here is that the investigation was most likely initiated by the complaint of one or a few workers. So how would 4,500 people end up getting back wage settlements when perhaps only one made a complaint?

Once a complaint is filed, the Department of Labor's Wage and Hour Division (see the website at http://dol.gov/whd/), the enforcement arm for wage complaints, will investigate the situation. If it finds evidence of minimum wage or overtime violations with the complainant, it will typically investigate every employee record at the company (at least in that employee class). In Wal-Mart's case, the Department of Labor investigated various managers and coordinators who had been labeled as exempt by the company. These individuals did not meet the duties tests that we discussed earlier, and as a result, Wal-Mart agreed to pay back wages and penalties for the misclassification.

In 2013, Department of Labor regulators collected approximately $150 million in back wages from US businesses for violations of the FLSA.[73] So why does misclassification occur? Obviously, companies want to save money. Many employers think that if they put you on salary, they don't have to pay overtime—so they put you on a salary and work you 70 hours per week. Another company might say, "All my people are professionals, so they are all exempt." But this is rarely possible in reality, if you look at the FLSA rules for exemption.

So what happens if we exempt someone who is not legitimately in an exempt category? We could end up being investigated by the Wage and Hour Division of the DOL. And what are the penalties for misclassifying employees? The employer can personally be criminally prosecuted and fined up to $10,000 per infraction. That can add up real fast! Also, there is no limit to the fines in this law—a fact that most managers don't realize. A second conviction could result in imprisonment, and in addition, employers who willfully or repeatedly violate the exemption rules may be assessed civil penalties of up to $1,100 per violation. It's also worse for child labor violations. Here, the civil penalty can be up to $11,000 per worker for each violation. And this can go to as much as $50,000 or even $100,000 if the violation causes the death or serious injury of an employee less than 18 years of age.[74]

So what do we need to do as HR managers? We must try to impress on our company leadership that misclassifying employees as exempt to save a few dollars is not the smart thing to do. Would you rather pay a few extra dollars a week or have a multimillion-dollar liability because of multiple fines?

Finally, states can't allow a lower minimum wage than the federal guidelines of $7.25, but they can require a higher wage. Therefore, we need to remember that many states have a state minimum wage that is higher than the federal minimum wage.[75] About 20 states currently have their own minimums that are higher than the federal minimum wage. So we need to make sure that we know our state's laws concerning minimum wage and overtime. Note that this can be complicated for firms with employees in several states, and even more so with international business operations.

LO 11-7

Briefly describe the concept of comparable worth and how it compares with equal pay.

Pay Equity and Comparable Worth

One of the more controversial issues in compensation is comparable worth. *Comparable worth* is the principle that when jobs are distinctly different but entail similar levels of ability, responsibility, skills, and working conditions, they are of equal value and should have the same pay scale. Comparable worth legislation has been proposed as a solution to the problem of persistent gender inequity in pay. According to the EEOC, women earn an average of 77 cents for every dollar that men earn.[76] This is one of the major reasons that comparable worth continues to be an issue in both business and government. While equal pay for equal work is the law (EPA of 1963), comparable worth is not currently federal law except in some very limited cases.

What is the concept of comparable worth? It is simply "similar pay for similar work." While this sounds almost like the equal pay for equal work stipulated by the Equal Pay Act, the doctrine of comparable worth says that if we can compare your job with that of another person, and if the two jobs are *similar but not the same*, then we should pay you a similar wage but not necessarily exactly the same wage. So this concept is much broader than equal pay.

If comparable worth were federal law, companies would be required to pay people who are in similar jobs similarly, which leads to a whole bunch of questions: What is similar work? Who determines what work is comparable? How do we take market supply and demand for labor into account? And what is comparable pay?

Let's look at an example to see what comparable worth is all about. Say that Amanda and Kenny—an engineer and a nurse, respectively—both work for Baptist Medical Center. Amanda has a graduate degree in mechanical engineering. She started working at Baptist about 5 years ago as the head of heating/ventilation/air-conditioning services. Amanda is paid $85,000 a year. Her primary job is maintaining the HVAC system and reengineering it as necessary when the hospital changes its facilities in any way. Kenny, on the other hand, is a registered nurse (RN), and he also has a master's degree (in nursing). He has been at Baptist for about 5 years, too. Kenny's primary job is to work as an RN in one of the intensive care units (ICUs). He is responsible for maintaining the health of the patients in the ICU, and his job frequently involves life-and-death situations. However, Kenny only gets paid $60,000 a year. He may feel like Amanda's job doesn't involve life and death as his job does, although it might in some ways if she were to do a poor job of engineering something at the hospital and thus caused an accident. How might Kenny feel about the pay differential if he knew about it? He might feel like he is not getting paid enough, right? Kenny would therefore be using the equity equation that we talked about earlier in the chapter to determine that he is underpaid, and that is exactly what comparable worth legislation would do.

OK, so how much *should* Kenny be paid relative to Amanda?

There is no simple answer to this question, and it would be very difficult to apply comparable worth to determine a dollar value for Kenny's job. Why? It is too hard to classify these jobs and determine what is comparable, because there are too many variables. These jobs are certainly comparable in such things as education (both have graduate degrees), tenure on the job (both about 5 years), and classification (both are considered professional occupations). But are there other factors? Of course there are, including thousands of details within each job plus the supply and demand for nurses and mechanical engineers. So who should get paid more if there are too many nurses and not enough engineers? It would be very difficult to deal with the market value factor of a job within a federal law. This is probably the main reason why Congress has not been able to pass a comparable worth law, at least not one that covers most businesses. Almost every year since the mid-1990s, at least some members of Congress have tried to bring up and pass a comparable worth law. Recent proposed legislation includes the Paycheck Fairness Act and the Fair Pay Act, neither of which has passed in Congress, at least as this text goes to press, even after being brought up in every Congress for more than 20 years.[77] Attempts to pass such laws have so far failed mainly because of the issue of market forces and the difficulty of enforcing the laws.

As we noted, though, there are a few exceptions where comparable worth is law. Some states have passed comparable worth legislation that applies to state, county, and city agencies. If individuals are employed by the state or another government agency, they are subject to comparable worth assessment to determine

SHRM

K:A13
Pay Discrimination and Dissimilar Jobs

SHRM

E:6
Compliance With Legal Requirements: Equal Pay and Comparable Worth

WORK
APPLICATION 11-13

Select an organization you work at or have worked at. Could comparable worth work at that organization? Why or why not?

their pay levels. Some states such as Washington and California have also attempted to pass comparable worth laws for businesses, but they have not succeeded yet, at least partially because of the market value factor for jobs. Market value simply cannot be estimated completely, so we can't successfully define comparability—yet.

Other Legal Issues

SHRM

K:A9
Legal Constraints on Pay Issues

SHRM

K:A11
Union Role in Wage and Salary Administration

A number of other federal laws place controls on pay and benefits. Recall from Chapter 10 that the National Labor Relations Act (NLRA) allows collective bargaining on the part of workers who join a union. Since the NLRA allows employees to bargain collectively with their employers for wages, benefits, and working conditions, in limited cases, the workers can agree to a workweek that is longer than 40 hours. The wages paid must be significantly higher than the minimum wage, and other conditions apply, but it is possible for the collective bargaining unit to agree to more than a 40-hour workweek.[78]

Mandatory employee *pension and benefits legislation* also includes the following:

- Social Security
- Workers' compensation
- Unemployment insurance
- Family and Medical Leave Act (FMLA)
- Patient Protection and Affordable Care Act (PPACA)
- Employee Retirement Income Security Act (ERISA—mandatory for employers who offer pension plans)
- Health Insurance Portability and Accountability Act (HIPAA—mandatory for employers who offer health insurance)

We will discuss each of these laws further in Chapter 13.

LO 11-8

Identify the three types of job evaluation discussed in the text and discuss whether they are more objective or subjective in form.

SHRM

E:2
Job Evaluation and Compensation (Grades, Pay Surveys, and Pay Setting)

SHRM

K:A4
Role of Job Analysis/Job Design/ Job Descriptions in Determining Compensation

Job evaluation The process of determining the worth of each position relative to the other positions within the organization

JOB EVALUATION

Deciding how much to pay each employee in a company is difficult. There are two approaches to this—internal and external—though they may be used together. An *external approach* involves finding out what other organizations pay for the same or similar jobs through available pay surveys, and it sets pay levels based on market pricing. The vast majority of firms use this external approach to identifying pay levels. In a recent survey, more than two thirds of companies used pay survey data or other external information to determine market pricing for their jobs.[79] On the other hand, an *internal approach* uses job evaluation. **Job evaluation** *is the process of determining the worth of each position relative to the other positions within the organization.* The most common form of internal job evaluation, the point-factor method, was only used in about one sixth of the companies surveyed.[80] Organizations commonly group jobs into pay levels or grades, and the higher the grade of the job, the higher the pay. A common example of this type of grouping is the federal government's GS ratings.

How do we accomplish a job evaluation? There are several ways, but the methods usually involve assigning points to activities that occur within a job and totaling the points for the job. Once this is done, we can place the job in a hierarchy and create our pay grades. Let's discuss some of the more popular job evaluation methods.

Job Ranking Method

Job ranking is simply the process of putting jobs in order from lowest to highest or vice versa, in terms of value to the company. This is the easiest and fastest method of job evaluation, but it has limited usefulness because it is subjective.

When doing job ranking, we utilize the job descriptions that we discussed in Chapter 4 to identify the factors in each job and then rank those jobs based on their content and complexity. We usually do job ranking without assigning points to different jobs. So we might start at the top of the organization with the CEO as the highest-ranking person and then work all the way down to the lowest-skilled housekeeping job.

But if you look at this method for a second, you will see that somebody has to decide the value of each job and do so without any quantitative factors. Therefore, this determination requires judgment and is highly subjective. This means it is difficult to defend if we have to do so.

Generally, the higher a person is in the organization, the more compensation that employee is given.

Point-Factor Method

A second type of job evaluation is the point-factor method. The *Hay Guide* is the most well-known point-factor method, but there are many others.[81] Point-factor methods attempt to be completely objective in form. They break a job down into components like particular skills or abilities, and then they assign a number of points to each component based on its difficulty. These components are usually referred to as *compensable factors*.

Essential functions, as defined in the ADA, would certainly be compensable factors to which points would be assigned when evaluating a job. Many of the compensable factors will be common among a number of different jobs, so once we have identified the number of points the factor is worth, we can then transfer that same value to all other jobs where the factor is present. The value of the point-factor job evaluation method is that we can differentiate jobs based on the difficulty or intensity of each factor, so it becomes easier to determine the total value of the job in a quantitative form.

Factor Comparison Method

The factor comparison method combines the job ranking and point-factor methods to provide a more thorough form of job evaluation.[82] This model is somewhat similar to the point-factor method in that it assigns points to compensable factors. However, the factor comparison method first identifies a group of benchmark jobs—positions that are identified and evaluated in a large number of organizations and that can generally be found in most pay surveys. Examples of benchmark jobs include "Training Specialist I," "Accountant II," "Lending Officer I," or "Hotel Registration Clerk." These benchmark jobs are then analyzed in some detail based on their compensable factors. We then rank the benchmark jobs in order, and we finally compare all other jobs in the organization to the benchmark jobs to determine where each one fits in the rankings. Here again, the primary method of determining the monetary value of a job is through the analysis of the compensable factors.

WORK
APPLICATION 11-14

Select an organization. Identify and describe which of the four job evaluation methods are used in that organization to determine pay.

11-3 # APPLYING THE CONCEPT

Job Evaluation

Review the list of job evaluation methods and then write the letter corresponding to each method before each statement below.

    a. external
    b. job ranking
    c. point-factor
    d. factor comparison

_____ 16. I use two methods together to determine how much to pay each position because I'm an HR professional.

_____ 17. I look at the job and determine the specific skills needed to do the job, and then I add up the total point value of the skills to set the pay.

_____ 18. To figure out how much to pay the data entry person, I'm checking the SHRM data.

_____ 19. I placed all the jobs in rank order, from the one that was worth the most to the one that was worth the least, in order to determine how much to pay for each position.

_____ 20. All of the companies in our industry pay essentially the same hourly wage.

The factor comparison method is more complex and time-consuming than the ranking or point factor methods, mainly because it is customized to the individual organization and to the jobs within the organization.[83] Because the factor comparison method uses both point factors and ranking, it has both objective and subjective components.

SHRM

K:A1
Development of a Base Pay System

DEVELOPING A PAY SYSTEM

Well, we have finally gotten to the point where we can start to develop our new pay structure. Remember, though, all of the things that we had to review and decide on first. We had to review motivational theories that show us how compensation motivates our workers, and why. We also looked at how much revenue we expect to be available for compensation purposes. Then we reviewed each of our *pay policies* to make sure they were fresh in our minds so that we could maintain consistency in our compensation system.

We also reviewed each of the major *federal laws* concerning compensation and equity, and we went through the process of ensuring that our *job analysis* files were up-to-date. From these, were able to complete *job evaluations* of each of the jobs in the organization. We also most likely researched external equity using one or more industry-specific *pay surveys*.

Take a look now at Exhibit 11-5 to see how each of these items comes together to allow us to create a *pay structure* and *individual pay rates* for each job.

LO 11-9

Briefly describe the concepts of job structure and pay levels.

Job Structure and Pay Levels

A **pay structure** *is a hierarchy of jobs and their rates of pay within the organization.*[84] It allows us to identify what the pay range is for each job. Once we have completed the process of creating a pay structure, we will have the pay range for every job in the hierarchy. From that, managers can determine individual compensation levels based on the employee's performance, seniority, skills, and any other significant contingency factors.

A pay structure is composed of both a job structure and pay levels.[85] The *job structure* is what gives us our job hierarchy. As we noted in the job evaluation section of this chapter, the job structure is the stacking up of the jobs in the organization, from the lowest to the highest level. Each of the jobs within the job structure will end up at a particular pay level. On the other hand, a *pay level* (frequently called a pay

Pay structure A hierarchy of jobs and their rates of pay within the organization

EXHIBIT 11-5	CREATION OF A PAY STRUCTURE AND INDIVIDUAL PAY RATES

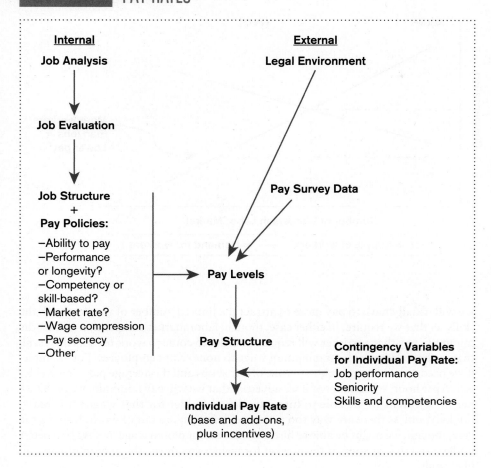

grade) is made up of many different jobs, and each pay level has a maximum pay rate and a minimum pay rate.

CREATION OF PAY LEVELS. To establish pay levels and determine the maximum and minimum pay rates for particular jobs, we have to look at some market factors. We must look at market pricing because if we don't pay attention to external equity or fairness, we are going to have trouble filling many of our jobs.

PRODUCT MARKET COMPETITION AND LABOR MARKET COMPETITION. To set the minimum value for a particular pay level, we have to look at the applicable *labor market competition*, meaning labor supply versus demand for labor. If we graph compensation for a given type of work versus the number of workers in the labor market who can do that type of work, the place where the two lines cross is the average pay for that work. Per Exhibit 11-6, when the supply of labor equals the demand for that labor in the workforce, we have equilibrium. The market will pay about what the workers demand to be paid, or workers who have the necessary skills won't be willing to fill the job.

What happens when there are more workers available than jobs? The market can get some of them to work for less than the normal rate (where the lines cross) because those workers need to work and earn a living. So the average compensation will most likely go down because we will have an oversupply situation. Conversely, what if we have more jobs available than we have workers with the requisite skills? In this case,

LO 11-10

Discuss the concepts of product market competition and labor market competition.

EXHIBIT 11-6 SUPPLY AND DEMAND CURVE

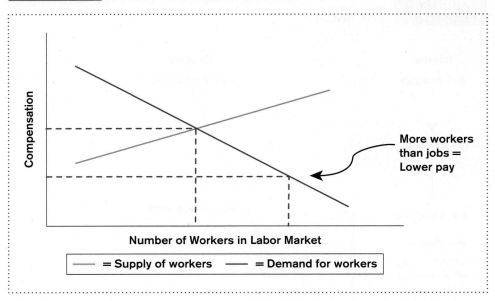

we will usually have to pay more to attract the limited number of workers with the skills set that we require. In either case, though, labor market competition will set the minimum pay that a worker will require in order to come to work for us. Also recall that we have to pay at least minimum wage to nonexempt employees. For example, if we need to hire an arc welder for one of our shops and the average pay for a welder is $16 per hour, what happens if we advertise that we will pay minimum wage ($7.25 per hour)? Will we be able to hire a qualified welder for that wage? It is really unlikely, unless there are way too many welders who are out of work. If that's the case, though, we might be able to hire a welder for minimum wage, but we had better understand that as soon as the market for welders recovers, the new employee will likely quit.

What happens if, instead of there being too many welders available, there are too few? If the average pay for a welder is $16 per hour and we advertise that we will pay $16 per hour for a welder, will we be able to hire one? We will probably have to raise the minimum amount that we are willing to pay in order to get someone to take the job. If our pay rate is too low in either situation, we won't get anybody. That's why we have a base wage—the bottom of our pay level. We have to compete for people who are willing to do the job, and labor market competition sets the minimum amount for any pay level—but it can be a moving target that we have to track.

On the other hand, how do we determine the top of the pay level? We have to look at something called *product market competition*. This is basically a function of the value of the product or service that we sell to the customer.[86] Again, an example will help make it clear.

Let's say we manufacture utility trailers (see Exhibit 11-7). The public will pay about $500 for our 5- by 8-foot utility trailers. To make the problem simple, we will pretend that we only have a couple of components that go into making that trailer: labor (our welder can also assemble other parts of the trailer) and materials (all of the pieces that go into the making of the trailer). Let's assume that all of the materials are going to cost $250 (we might need bolts, axles, angle iron for the basic frame, welding rods, etc.).

What do we have left for labor? Do we have $250? No! We also have some other indirect costs, don't we? And we would like to make a profit, right? So if we estimate all of our other costs at $50, we now have $200 left. We can pay labor $200 if we

EXHIBIT 11-7 · PRODUCT MARKET COMPETITION LIMITS

Utility Trailer Manufacturing

$500   Sale price

$$\frac{-\ \$250\quad \text{Material costs}}{\$250 = \text{Remainder}}$$

$$\frac{-\ \$50\quad \text{Overhead costs}}{\$200 = \text{Remainder}}$$

$$\frac{-\ \$160\quad \text{Labor (maximum cost of labor)}}{\$40\ =\ \text{Before-tax profit (8\%)}}$$

only want to break even. However, if we want to make any money, we have to pay less than $200 for labor. Assume again that our welder makes $20 per hour (because this employee is a good welder and has worked for us for a long time) and it takes the welder 8 hours to build a trailer—$160 for the 8 hours of labor costs. So we have a $40 profit left, or about 8% profit.

Now, our welder comes to you and says, "Boss, I need more money—I need a raise." What do you just about have to tell the employee? "We can't pay you more." The trailer can only sell for a certain amount of money. If our trailer is $800 and a competitor's trailer is $500, almost everyone will buy the competitor's trailer. We can't charge much more than the normal rate for a product or service. The labor is only worth so much money, because the sale price of the good or service has to cover the cost of the labor.

Something you always need to keep in mind in HR and as a manager is how much you can pay for labor, meaning what the job is worth. We do not price the value of a *person* when we create a pay scale—we price the value of a *job*. You need to understand that you can't pay more than the value added to the product or service by the labor. The biggest reason that you need to understand this is so that you can explain it to your employees. The decision of whether or not to pay someone more for a particular job is not a function of liking or disliking the employee; it is a function of only being able to pay a certain amount because of the product's market value. So, *product market competition* sets the top of the pay level for most types of jobs in the company.

Exhibit 11-8 shows that we have a maximum and a minimum level of pay for a particular class of jobs. So labor market competition sets the bottom of the range and

SHRM

K:A2
Developing Pay Levels

EXHIBIT 11-8 · PAY LEVELS

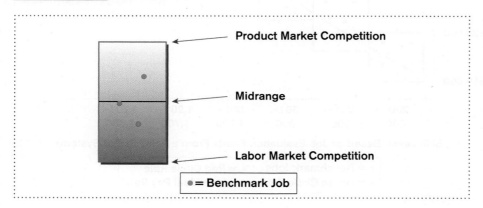

- Product Market Competition
- Midrange
- Labor Market Competition
- ● = Benchmark Job

product market competition sets the top of the range. Remember, though, that this is a simplified example—there may be other factors involved as well.

BENCHMARKING PAY SURVEY DATA. Next, we look at benchmarks from the pay survey data that we reviewed earlier and put those benchmark jobs into the pay level where they belong (the green dots in Exhibit 11-8). Once we place some benchmark jobs in a plot of our pay levels, we can get a *market pay line* (sometimes called a pay curve)—a line that shows the average pay at different levels in a particular industry (see Exhibit 11-9). We use the benchmarks to see whether or not what we are doing is OK. If the range is correct, we have successfully created a pay level; if not, we have to figure out what is wrong with our range.

After going through this process for a particular pay level, we end up with a rate range, *which provides the maximum, minimum, and midpoint of pay for a certain group of jobs.* Once the range is created, we can go in and add to the range any other jobs that are at approximately the same level based on our earlier job evaluations.

Pay Structure

All right! Now we have our first pay level. So what do we do now? We start to lay pay levels out next to each other, creating a pay dispersion.[87] Again, look at Exhibit 11-9. We take our first pay level and put it down: bottom, midpoint, and top. The bottom of the range for the first level will probably be near minimum wage in most cases. Then our second tier will start, and beyond that will be the third and the fourth, etc.

SHRM

G:11
Benchmarking

SHRM

K:A14
Prevailing Wage

LO 11-11

Briefly describe the concept of a pay structure.

Rate range The maximum, minimum, and midpoint of pay for a certain group of jobs

---

EXHIBIT 11-9 PAY STRUCTURE

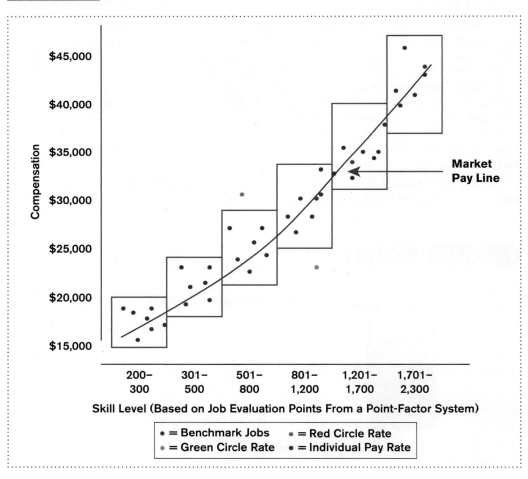

Notice that the ranges overlap each other in Exhibit 11-9. Why do they overlap? What would happen if each pay level started with its minimum pay rate at the maximum rate of the previous level? Would we have any room to pay people differentially in a particular level? Take a look at the market pay line. It would have to go exactly through the corners of each pay level if the levels didn't overlap. That doesn't give us much wiggle room on which to base people's pay rates, does it? So the major reason for the overlap is to give the company some flexibility in each person's pay within a particular pay level.

Once we set up our pay levels, we can actually plot the real pay levels for people in the organization. These are indicated in Exhibit 11-9 as black dots. We identify where people fall within the pay structure, and we will sometimes see that we have someone plotted outside our pay level ranges—either too high or too low. Individual pay rates that fall outside our pay range on the high side are called *red-circle rates* (red dots in Exhibit 11-9), and those that are lower than the bottom of the pay range are *green-circle rates* (green dots in Exhibit 11-9). If we find a green-circle rate for an individual, the correct thing to do is to raise the individual's pay to at least the minimum for that pay level, because we are not paying them fairly for their skill set.[88]

But what should we do about a red-circle rate? We probably won't cut someone's pay, but we will not be able to pay them any more unless they move up to a higher skill level, and therefore a higher pay level. For instance, if our welder is making $24 per hour, the maximum for his pay level is $20, but he wants a pay raise and hasn't had a one in several years, we may have to tell him no. However, we can also tell him that if he is willing to become a supervisor over other welders, he can get the chance to raise his pay rate because the skill level for a supervisor is higher than that of a welder.

Understanding pay levels and our pay structure allows us to provide good answers to our employees about why their pay is set at a certain level. If a worker decides to become a supervisor, that employee is worth more and we can pay more. So we are able to tell the employee, "*The job* isn't worth any more than what you are being paid," instead of saying, "You are not worth any more than that." It also gives us leverage to get good workers to consider becoming supervisors or managers if we tell them, "If you want a pay raise, become a supervisor."

DELAYERING AND BROADBANDING. A trend over many years now has been to lower the number of pay levels using one of two options—either delayering or broadbanding. **Delayering** *is the process of changing the company structure to get rid of some of the vertical hierarchy (reporting levels) in an organization.* On the other hand, **broadbanding** *is accomplished by combining multiple pay levels into one.*[89] What is the benefit of combining levels either vertically or horizontally in this way? Is it that we can make bigger groups, and bigger is always better? Well, bigger isn't always better, but in this case it can be. When we lower the number of pay levels that we have to deal with, we make the process simpler. It takes a long time to create, maintain, and evaluate 20 pay levels, when instead we can have just 5 broadbands. It also allows us more capacity to reward outstanding performers. Because we have taller and wider levels, we can move them up way more while staying within the boundaries of the pay level.

Take a look at what happens to our pay structure in Exhibit 11-10 when we convert it into a broadband pay structure. The new broadband pay structure combines the first two pay levels, the third and fourth level, and finally the fifth and sixth, making three levels instead of six. This causes our red- and green-circle rates to disappear. It also gives us greater ability to adjust the pay of people based on their performance and ability. Finally, it lowers the administrative burden of maintaining the compensation system. For these reasons, a lot of companies have broadened the pay levels that they use. It is fairly easy to see why it would be easier to work with just 5 pay levels rather than 20. It just takes much more management time to administer the larger number of levels.

WORK
APPLICATION 11-15

Select an organization. Identify the rate range for a category of jobs.

SHRM

K:A3
Determining Pay Increases

LO 11-12

Briefly discuss the value of broadbanding to the organization.

Delayering The process of changing the company structure to get rid of some of the vertical hierarchy (reporting levels) in an organization.

Broadbanding Combining multiple pay levels into one

EXHIBIT 11-10   BROADBANDING OF MULTIPLE PAY LEVELS

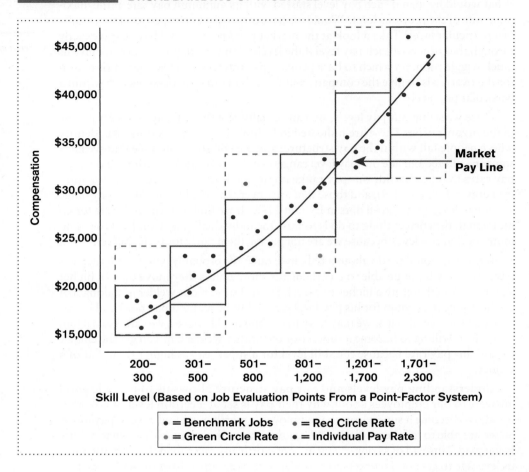

So when we are done with our pay structure, we will have created that hierarchy of jobs that we mentioned earlier—from lowest to highest. And as you have probably already guessed, much of this work is now done using computers. Once the HRIS have the necessary data, we can create most of our pay structure using existing company information. The computer models will identify the outliers for us. In many cases, the HRIS can identify the market pay line and provide other compensation information, too. We can see very quickly if we have a whole bunch of employees in level 3 and also see that they are all getting almost the highest possible pay for that level. From this information, we can analyze why this may be happening and figure out whether the pay scale needs to be changed in some manner. HRIS are very valuable tools for job structure analysis.

TRENDS AND ISSUES IN HRM

What trends are we seeing in the compensation of our 21st century workforce? One trend is toward classifying individuals as independent contractors instead of as employees. There also seems to be a strong shift from base pay to variable pay components. Finally, technology is allowing us to keep better track of our compensation programs.

Independent Contractor or Dependent Employee?

One of the most common and potentially troubling trends today is toward companies creating more contract labor (independent contractor) relationships and fewer

Compensation Management Satisfaction

This exercise is also a good review of the chapter, as it uses most of the important concepts. Select an organization that you work or have worked for and select your level of satisfaction with each of the following parts of the compensation management system, on a scale of 1 to 5.

1	2	3	4	5
Not satisfied				Satisfied

_____ 1. Base pay
_____ 2. Wage and salary add-ons
_____ 3. Incentive pay
_____ 4. Benefits
_____ 5. Meeting expectancy theory
_____ 6. Meeting equity theory
_____ 7. What the firm actually pays based on its ability to pay
_____ 8. Pay for performance vs. longevity
_____ 9. What the firm pays based on being below, at, or above market-level pay
_____ 10. Wage compression
_____ 11. Pay secrecy
_____ 12. Meeting the Fair Labor Standards Act
_____ 13. Pay equity and comparable worth
_____ 14. The system used for job evaluation
_____ 15. Job structure
_____ 16. Pay levels
_____ 17. Benchmarking
_____ 18. Pay structure
_____ 19. Pay raises
_____ 20. Benefit increases
_____ Total the points and place the score on the continuum below.

20	30	40	50	60	70	80	90	100
Not satisfied								Satisfied

The higher the score, the greater your level of satisfaction with the compensation management system of the organization. However, to most employees, what really matters most is answers to questions regarding their own pay and benefits (compensation), and we all are more satisfied when these increase.

Think about the people you worked with as a group. You can select the group's level of satisfaction with each question. Would their answers vary from yours? Would the satisfaction level vary by the level in the organization—among executives versus nonmanagers, by department, or among other groupings?

employer-employee relationships. While some of these contract relationships are absolutely legitimate, many have been set up to intentionally avoid an employee relationship and all of the associated record-keeping and legal issues. This is simply another form of intentional misclassification of employees, similar to calling an individual exempt under the FLSA when that worker is nonexempt by current laws. It is unethical *and* illegal to intentionally misclassify individuals to avoid paying them what would reasonably and ordinarily be due them in their relationship with the company.

Compensation of an independent contractor is much simpler than compensation of employees. In the contract relationship, the company pays the agreed-upon amount on the contract, and there is no need to calculate hours, minimum wage,

Truck drivers from Long Beach, California, went on strike to protest alleged labor violations.

overtime, benefits costs, health care insurance eligibility, or any other compensation factors. All of those requirements fall to the contractor to manage.

However, as we briefly mentioned in Chapter 4, independent contractors must be truly independent of the company's control. According to the IRS website, "The general rule is that an individual is an independent contractor if the payer has the right to control or direct *only the result of the work* and not what will be done and how it will be done" [emphasis added].[90] (You can go to this site if you would like more information on the rules for independent contractors: http://www.irs .gov/Businesses/Small-Businesses-&-Self- Employed/Independent-Contractor-Self- Employed-or-Employee/). A recent news item that illustrates this issue is a strike by truck drivers in the southern California ports of Los Angeles and Long Beach. The drivers are classified as independent contractors, but some experts say that the truckers should be classified as employees. One driver, Dennis Martinez, noted that "his bosses tell him where he has to go, when, and what he'll get paid."[91] If we look at the IRS note above, we will quickly see that if this is true, then Martinez does not have an independent contractor relationship with his employer.

HR managers need to be particularly aware of these quasi-independent contractor relationships, due to the fact that the president and the US Department of Labor have significantly increased funding for the DOL Wage and Hour Division (WHD) to police employment relationships. In the 2015 budget request, the DOL again asked for an 18% increase in funding for the WHD and noted that it "would be used to continue WHD's focus on independent contractor investigations," among other enforcement actions.[92] It is likely that these focused investigations will continue over the next several years at least. The HR manager has a duty to analyze any independent contractor relationships and determine whether or not they fall within the guidelines of the IRS and DOL and, if they don't, to advise executives of the dangers of such misclassification of employees.

A Shift From Base Pay to Variable Pay

As we noted earlier in this chapter, there appears to be a shift away from all or the majority of an individual's income being provided in the form of base pay and toward a larger percentage of that income being provided in variable forms. We also noted that there is a potential dark side to individual incentives, as linking pay and performance is difficult in many jobs and employees frequently don't think the system is fair. With this being the case, what reasons do companies have for the shift toward incentive compensation? One of the biggest reasons is to lower the risk to the company when markets fail or economies go into recession.

How does incentive compensation do this? If a large percentage of an employee's pay comes from incentives for productivity, then when downturns occur, the company will not have to pay out as much in overall compensation as is necessary in better economic conditions since the company won't be producing as much during the recession. An illustration of this fact is the recent recession in the United States (and most of the rest of the world). In a 2010 salary survey, it was noted that "spending on variable pay as a percentage of payroll for salaried exempt workers was 11.3 percent, down from a record high of 12.0 percent in 2009." However, according to a

2013 **Aon Hewitt** report, as the economy recovered, "Ninety percent of companies offer a broad-based variable play plan and expect to spend 12.0 percent of payroll on variable pay for salaried exempt employees in 2014. This is up significantly from a decade ago, when just 78 percent of companies offered a variable pay program, with an average increase of 9.5 percent of payroll."[93]

This provides evidence that when companies were suffering from recession, paid-out incentives dropped, and as the economy recovered, incentives increased. So when organizational output (productivity) is high, the company can afford to pay out more in overall compensation costs (through incentives), and when organizational output is lower, the company has the ability to cut overall compensation costs if a large percentage of compensation comes from performance incentives. Therefore, the employees, instead of employers, bear the risk of variable compensation based on changing business conditions.

The Technology of Compensation

Since compensation is typically one of the largest costs in most organizations, management needs to be mindful of what it gets for its money. As labor costs increase and technology costs decrease, replacing people with technology becomes more cost-effective. For a simple example, is it quick and easy to call most large businesses today and actually talk to a person?

As with so many other HR practices, we need to look at things like return on investment (ROI) from our compensation programs. New analytical programs, many within our HRIS, allow us to analyze compensation programs in more detail than has historically been possible. These programs and systems can take data from multiple sources—including external pay surveys, benchmark jobs, government databases, and company sources—and provide us with the ability to measure and monitor organizational costs and benefits.

HRIS analytical programs allow us to measure the effectiveness of incentives and compare our compensation information with industry metrics. They also help ensure compliance with various state and federal labor laws and with regulations on compensation, benefits, and medical leave. They can lower administrative costs of managing and maintaining compensation programs and can also help create higher organizational productivity, which can in turn improve employee satisfaction levels, especially when incentive programs are in place to reward productivity increases.

So given all of the capabilities of HRIS programs in compensation management, companies have to look very hard at the costs and benefits of these systems. More and more, it is becoming critical to have these tools available for our use in order to ensure compliance and improve performance.

• • • CHAPTER SUMMARY

11-1   Identify the components of a compensation system.

1. *Base pay, either an hourly wage or salary.* Base pay is frequently a major decision factor for most employees in deciding to accept the job.

2. *Wage and salary add-ons.* These include overtime pay, shift differential, premium pay for working weekends and holidays, and other add-ons.

3. *Incentive pay for performance.* Incentives give workers strong reasons to perform above the standard.

4. *Benefits.* This is indirect compensation that provides something of value to the employee. Benefits cost the company money even though they aren't direct compensation.

11-2   Briefly describe expectancy theory as it applies to compensation.

Employees *expect* to put forth some form of *effort* at work. This effort is *expected* to result in some level of *performance*. The performance level is then *expected* to result in some type of *reward*, and if it does, the employee *expects* to put out more effort. The reward has to be *significant* to the individual, and as long as it is, the employee will continue to put out effort. So employees will either be motivated by their outcomes, including compensation, or be demotivated by them.

11-3   Briefly describe equity theory as it applies to compensation.

According to equity theory, people compare their inputs (the things they *do* in the organization) and outcomes (the things that they *receive* from the organization) to those of relevant others. But it's their and others' *perceived* inputs and outcomes that employees compare, not necessarily actual inputs and outcomes. If employees believe that there is inequity, they will change their work behavior to create equity. Employees must perceive that they are being treated fairly, relative to others. Compensation is obviously a large part of the perceived outcomes.

11-4   Identify the seven basic issues that make up the organizational philosophy on compensation.

1. *Ability to pay.* This is an honest assessment of how much we can afford, or are willing to afford, in order to compensate our employees.

2. *Types of compensation.* This refers to the mix of the four basic components of compensation—base pay, wage add-ons, incentives, and benefits—that we employ. We must divide available funds among the components.

3. *Pay for performance or longevity.* Will we pay people based on organizational loyalty/tenure, or will we pay based on performance in their jobs?

4. *Skill or competency-based pay.*

5. *At, above, or below the market.* What will our general pay structure look like, and why?

6. *Wage compression.* This lowers the pay differential between long-term and newly hired employees.

7. *Pay secrecy.* Will we utilize pay secrecy clauses in employment contracts? Pay secrecy may allow us to hide actual wage inequities from employees, but it has the potential to create dissatisfaction and demotivation.

11-5   Discuss the three major provisions of the FLSA.

1. Minimum wage rates identify the lowest hourly rate of pay generally allowed under the FLSA. There are many exemptions, but if a person is *nonexempt*, minimum wage will apply.

2. Overtime rates are also required for persons who are nonexempt. However, there are different exemptions for overtime than there are for minimum wage, so HR managers must check the law to determine who will have to be paid overtime.

3. Child labor requirements within the FLSA identify the jobs and allowable working hours for individuals between 14 and 18 years old. Sixteen- and 17-year-olds can only be employed in nonhazardous jobs, but their work hours are unrestricted. However, 14- and 15-year-olds can only work outside school hours, and the jobs that they are allowed to do are limited to retail and other service positions. They may not work overtime.

11-6   Describe the penalties in the FLSA for misclassification of nonexempt employees.

The employer can personally be criminally prosecuted and fined up to $10,000 per infraction. There is no maximum limit to the allowable fines, so fines in the millions of dollars have been assessed in the past. A second conviction can result in imprisonment. Employers who willfully or repeatedly violate the exemption rules may be assessed civil penalties of up to $1,100 *per violation*. For child labor violations, the civil penalty can be up to $11,000 per worker *for each violation* and can go to as much as $50,000 or even $100,000 if the violation causes the serious injury or death of an employee less than 18 years old.

11-7   Briefly describe the concept of comparable worth and how it compares with equal pay.

Comparable worth is similar pay for similar work, which is different from equal pay for equal work. The concept of comparable worth holds that if we can compare your job with that of another person and they are *similar*, we should pay you a similar wage, which makes this concept much broader than equal pay. The biggest problem with comparable worth from a legal standpoint is how to legislate the value of a job while taking supply and demand into account.

11-8   Identify the three types of job evaluation discussed in the text and discuss whether they are more objective or subjective in form.

1. The job ranking method is simply the process of putting jobs in order from lowest to highest or vice versa, in terms of value to the company. However, it has limited usefulness because it is subjective.

2. Point-factor methods, on the other hand, attempt to be completely objective in form. They break a job down into component skills or abilities, known as factors, and then apply points to each factor based on its difficulty.

3. The factor comparison method combines the ranking and point-factor methods to provide a more thorough form of job evaluation. It identifies benchmark jobs and then analyzes and rank-orders them. We then compare all other jobs in the organization to the benchmark jobs to determine where each one fits in the rankings.

11-9   Briefly describe the concepts of job structure and pay levels.

The *job structure* is what gives us a job hierarchy. The *job hierarchy* is the stacking of the jobs in the organization from the lowest (simplest) to the highest (most complex) levels. A *pay level* (frequently called a pay grade) will be made up of several different jobs. Pay levels provide a framework for the minimum and maximum pay for a particular group of jobs in the organization. Pay levels are then laid out one next to another in order to create the entire pay structure for the company.

11-10   Discuss the concepts of product market competition and labor market competition. What are they used for?

Labor market competition sets the bottom of a pay level. We have to compete with other companies to attract labor, and if we don't pay enough, we will be unable to attract the workers we need. So we compete in the labor market for available workers. *Product market competition* sets the top of a pay level. We can only pay someone as much as we can recover from a customer when we sell our goods or services. We can't pay more than the value added to the product or service by the labor. Together, product market and labor market competition identify the maximum and minimum rates of pay for a particular group of jobs in a pay level.

11-11   Briefly describe the concept of a pay structure.

A *pay structure* is created by laying out our pay levels, one next to the other. The entire group of pay levels creates the pay structure. Benchmark jobs can be plotted on the pay structure to get a *market pay line*—a line that shows the average pay at different levels in a particular industry. Once pay levels are set, we can actually plot employee rates of pay on the pay structure to see if any are plotted outside our pay level ranges, either high or low. Individuals who fall outside our pay range to the high side are paid *red-circle rates*, and those who fall outside low are paid *green-circle rates*. Each of these rates should be reviewed and corrected if necessary.

11-12   Briefly discuss the value of broadbanding to the organization.

Broadbanding lowers the number of pay levels that a company administers by combining multiple pay levels into one. Lowering the number of pay levels makes the process simpler. It takes a long time to create, maintain, and evaluate many pay levels, but instead, we can have just a few broadbands. Because pay bands are wider and taller under broadbanding, the company also has more flexibility in pay rates for individuals who are overperforming or underperforming. Broadbanding may also cause most red- and green-circle rates to disappear. Lowering the administrative burden of maintaining the compensation system can significantly lower the person hours required to manage it and thus lessen the overall cost of the system.

11-13   Define the key terms found in the chapter margins and listed following the Chapter Summary.

Complete the Key Terms Review to test your understanding of this chapter's key terms.

• • • KEY TERMS

broadbanding	equity theory	overtime
compensation	expectancy theory	pay structure
compensation system	job evaluation	rate range
delayering	minimum wage	wage compression

• • • KEY TERMS REVIEW

Complete each of the following statements using one of this chapter's key terms.

1. _____ is the total of an employee's pay and benefits.

2. _____ includes anything that an employee may value and desire and that the employer is willing and able to offer in exchange.

3. _____ proposes that employees are motivated when they believe they can accomplish a task and the rewards for doing so are worth the effort.

4. _____ proposes that employees are motivated when the ratio of their perceived outcomes to inputs is at least roughly equal to that of other referent individuals.

5. _____ occurs when new employees require higher starting pay than the historical norm, causing narrowing of the pay gap between experienced and new employees.

6. _____ is the lowest hourly rate of pay generally permissible by federal law.

7. _____ is a higher than minimum, federally mandated wage, required for nonexempt employees if they work more than a certain number of hours in a week.

8. _____ is the process of determining the worth of each position relative to the other positions within the organization.

9. _____ is a hierarchy of jobs and their rates of pay within the organization.

10. _____ provides the maximum, minimum, and midpoint of pay for a certain group of jobs.

11. _____ is the process of changing the company structure to get rid of some of the vertical hierarchy (reporting levels) in an organization.

12. _____ is accomplished by combining multiple pay levels into one.

• • • COMMUNICATION SKILLS

The following critical-thinking questions can be used for class discussion and/or for written assignments to develop communication skills. Be sure to give complete explanations for all answers.

1. Do you believe it is always necessary to provide incentives as part of a pay structure? Why or why not?

2. As the HR manager, would you pay more attention to expectancy theory or equity theory in designing your compensation system? Why?

3. If your company had promised an incentive program right before the recession of 2007–2008, and if the recession made it impossible for the company to pay employees what they had been promised, then how would you explain this to your workforce to keep them motivated?

4. Would you rather have higher pay or better benefits? Why?

5. Would you ever consider paying below the market rate for employees if you had control of wages? Why or why not?

6. Do you believe that pay secrecy can ever really work in a business? Why or why not?

7. How would you approach a CEO or company president who insisted on classifying nonexempt workers as exempt? What would you say to get the CEO to stop this practice?

8. Do you think that comparable worth should be made federal law? Why or why not?

9. If you were the lead HR manager in your company, would you ever consider setting pay levels by just using external pay surveys and no internal analysis? What are the advantages and disadvantages of this?

10. As the head of HR, would you rather change narrow pay levels into broadbands? Can you think of any disadvantages to doing so?

• • • CASE 11-1 SELLING THE SALES FORCE ON COMMISSION COMPENSATION

Laughter could be heard from the back office as the sales associate and his part-time assistant were jokingly discussing the last sale. "Then the woman said to me, 'Do you absolutely guarantee that your product won't scratch my wood floors and won't mark my kitchen linoleum?' 'Guarantee,' I repeated. 'We not only guarantee that our product won't scuff or muff your wood or vinyl surfaces, but the Oreck vacuum has been scientifically designed with a floating head system that will adjust itself to any surface.' I then demonstrated how the vacuum easily glides from our carpeted portion of the store to the wooden area by the register. I immediately handed her the vacuum and asked her to try it herself. She vacuumed half the store just to test it out.

"She bought the best upright vacuum in the store including extra bags and a room deodorizer. Let's see if you can do any better with your next customer!"

Sales Training

The local Oreck vacuum store was owned by Mr. Paulson, who classified himself as a super salesman and took great pains in training his sales force on how to close a deal. The store was always staffed by two employees: one full-timer with one part-timer to cover Paulson's two days off. The training consisted of On-the-Job Training (usually watching Mr. Paulson go through several Oreck vacuum presentations) coupled with take-home material including a sales script and product information. Inventory was computerized, and therefore it was easy for a trainee to check his or her price knowledge using the computer. After several observations of Mr. Paulson's sales techniques, the trainee was then allowed to make a sales presentation on his or her own, with assistance provided by Mr. Paulson as needed. The trainee was then debriefed by Mr. Paulson and asked to make changes in the presentation as needed in order to better close the customer. The full-time employee worked six days, 48 hours per week (including Saturdays and Sundays), with the part-time employee working only on the weekend.

Sales and Service Revenues

There were two distinct revenue streams: sales, which accounted for 90% of the revenues (predominantly of vacuum cleaners), and repair work. In terms of sales, by far the best moving item was the Oreck XL followed by vacuum bags (which were carried for all makes and models) and cleaning accessories. The markup on vacuums and other cleaning equipment was 100% while the markup on cleaning products and ancillary items was 200%. Repair work was priced at 200% over parts costs plus a $29.95 flat labor fee.

Price Flexibility

Unlike most other retail operations, Mr. Paulson allowed his employees some price flexibility on big-ticket items including the Oreck XL. These items did not have prices listed on them, and the sales personnel were instructed not to divulge the price until their sales presentations were completed. Sales personnel were given the option of either dropping the price (e.g., a $499 machine could be lowered to $449) or offering the customer an additional incentive for purchasing the machine (e.g., extra bags, upgrade in the vacuum cleaner). Customers could also receive a trade-in allowance (e.g., $25 for a machine in any condition) at the time of the sale. Mr. Paulson preferred that his sales force drop the price rather than let a customer walk out of the store empty-handed, although he always cautioned his sales force not to drop the price too early in the sale.

Employee Compensation

The average wage earned by employees at the store was considered fairly low for the region. Full-time employees received a straight salary of $500 a week plus benefits (complete medical and dental coverage, two weeks' paid vacation, no sick or personal days, unpaid holidays when available) and earned a commission of 2.5% of gross store sales over $7,000 a week. Part-time employees received $65 a day plus a commission of 2.5% of gross store sales over $1,000 per day they worked, and they received no benefits. Store revenue generally ran about $6,500 for the week with a 20% net profit margin.

Third-party exit interviews with several of the ex-employees indicated that the owner put inordinate pressure on them to sell products and services to the customers. "I felt like I always had to sell the customer something whether they needed it or not. Paulson felt that you could always find a way to overcome customers' objections, even if it meant using pressure sales tactics. I wanted to build up customer loyalty for the store over the long run, but you can't do that by browbeating consumers into sales just to try to make commission. A straight weekly salary would have remedied that problem." Other complaints included tying the commission into total store sales (rather than individual sales), working weekends without a pay differential, working six days a week, and the fact that the commission base was set higher than the store weekly average sales.

The owner indicated that many of the employees who left the job just did not seem to have the selling instinct needed for his sales force, and high turnover was therefore not only expected but desired in order to get the best salespeople. When questioned about the compensation package, Paulson replied, "This scheme is used to motivate my sales force. I want hungry employees who want to sell. If they do a good job in selling, they get rewarded—if they don't sell, they have a base salary to get by on. Many of my employees leave because they cannot sell enough to earn a commission. I know that it's hard to live on $500 a week, but I do not want to have employees who just sit around and collect a paycheck."

Questions

1. What is the compensation package for the full-time sales force at the store? Classify by kind of compensation.

2. Explain Paulson's rationale for the current compensation system using expectancy theory. Why might his ex-employees have disagreed with his rationale?

3. Using equity theory, explain why Paulson's compensation system may be deemed inequitable by his former employees.

4. Describe Paulson's current compensation philosophy.

5. Do you think this compensation philosophy is an effective one?

6. Construct a new compensation system for Paulson's full-time employees. Make sure to address all four basic kinds of compensation.

Case created by Herbert Sherman, PhD, and Theodore Vallas, Department of Management Sciences, School of Business Brooklyn Campus, Long Island University

• • • CASE 11-2 EMPLOYEE RED-LINING AT CVS: THE HAVE AND THE HAVE NOT

CVS Caremark is the second-largest drugstore chain in the United States (just behind **Wal-Mart**). It employs 286,000 people in 45 states under the CVS logo, and it operates more than 7,600 drugstores. In 2013, CVS's sales exceeded $126 billion, but its net income was only around $4.6 billion, for about a 3.6% profit—about the median profit for the industry.[94]

As would any other public corporation, CVS wanted to increase its profitability for stockholders and regain its position as the industry leader. One method of increasing profits is cutting operational costs, and CVS decided to do just that. It adjusted employee annual pay raises by placing an earnings ceiling on salaries, and any employees earning the highest hourly wage in their job classification became ineligible for a raise.

Besides the obvious cost savings, why put a "red line" on wages? The main goal was to adjust the highest-paid employees' compensation to the job market average and, with these savings, provide raises to the employees who were paid below that average. The philosophy was that as a CVS employee, one should expect lower raises (or none at all) if one is earning much more than one's colleagues. So once an employee reached the red line, that person received no additional compensation.

CVS executives knew that the new compensation policy would negatively impact some of their most loyal employees, yet the executives felt that they needed to draw a line on salaries in order to make the most of limited compensation dollars. What they did not figure was that the policy mostly hurt the employees who had been working there the longest. Worse, these same employees feared retaliation if they publicly criticized the new policy. How would it look to the other lower-paid employees (and worse, the public at large) if the highest-paid employees complained about their lack of raises?

Nationwide, the minimum wage is set at $7.25 per hour, but the wage management guidelines of CVS are different in most regions depending on the minimum wage in each state. Lowest-ranked employees with exceptional skills would receive a 4.75% raise on an annual basis if they were making minimum wage. However, if an employee with exceptional skills in the same position was already earning $12.50 an hour, that person would not receive a raise, having already crossed the red line.[95] With employment at will, the possibility of being laid off, and a tough job market, where would these employees get such high-paying jobs in the retail and service industries? It was better for them to keep quiet about their pay and stay in a company that they were comfortable with.[96]

Wage rates depend on employees' rank, and it is no secret that the CEO is going to be paid much more than the company's average worker. This is because the CEO job requires a more demanding set of skills compared to the average store job, and the workload of a CEO is much more demanding. But if the range of compensation is so great, it may discourage employees who are paid less.[97]

Some ethical and legal concerns arose when these same red-lined employees found out that this new compensation policy did not seem to apply to the top-level executives. The CEO of CVS was paid a total of $23 million in 2013, including bonuses and additional perks. He earned a 26% raise from the previous year, and that was almost 800 times more than the median income of a CVS employee. The red-lined employees saw an inequitable pay situation, with the rich getting richer because they were allowed a raise while the in-store employees had a cap on their income. The CEO's salary package was tied to the company's performance, and according to CVS spokesperson Carolyn Castel, "Last year, CVS Caremark had an outstanding year and continued to deliver strong financial results and enhanced returns to shareholders in a challenging economic environment, performing favorably against our peer group in several key areas."[98]

Questions

1. Describe the pay structure and compensation system for a CVS store employee. How might this pay structure be different from that of the CEO of the firm?

2. Define the rate range of CVS employees. How would you change the pay structure to encourage performance, especially for red-lined employees?

3. In terms of expectancy and equity theories, describe how the red-line policy will affect the motivation of employees.

4. In light of the red-line policy, what was CVS's philosophy toward employee performance, compensation, and longevity?

5. If you were CVS's CEO, knowing that you have to reduce costs and balance employee wages, what other measures would you take besides freezing raises for the highest-paid employees?

6. Why would the firm implement an HR policy that it knew would negatively affect its highest-paid employees? Did it perhaps have a hidden agenda?

Case created by Herbert Sherman, PhD, and Theodore Vallas, Department of Management Sciences, School of Business Brooklyn Campus, Long Island University

$SAGE edge™

••• SKILL BUILDER 11-1 JOB EVALUATION

Objective

To develop a better understanding of the job evaluation process

Skills

The primary skills developed through this exercise are as follows:

1. *HR management skills*—Technical, conceptual and design, and business skills
2. *SHRM 2013 Curriculum Guidebook*—K: Total rewards

Assignment

Step 1. You decided to open a restaurant and pub, and you have five job categories:

- *Owner/manager:* You are the owner, performing all the management functions and also greeting and seating people as you oversee all activities.
- *Wait staff:* They take food orders and bring food to customers.
- *Cook:* They prepare the food.
- *Helpers:* They bus tables, wash dishes, help in food preparation, and bring food to some customers.
- *Bartenders:* They make the drinks for both the dining and bar areas.

Rank the jobs from 1 to 5, with 5 being the highest-ranking job and 1 being the lowest.

Step 2. Using the table below, rank each job for each of the five factors commonly used in job evaluations.

Job	Mental Requirements (education, intelligence, and specialized knowledge)	Physical Requirements (effort such as standing, walking, and lifting)	Skill Requirements (specific job knowledge/ training to do work)	Responsibilities (for equipment, money, public contact, and supervision)	Working Conditions (safety, heat, ventilation, and coworkers)
Manager					
Wait Staff					
Cook					
Helper					
Bartender					
Factor Rank (1–5) Weight (100%)					

Step 3. The five factors are commonly weighted since some are more important than others.

(A) In the above table in the bottom row—Factor Rank—now rank the five factors from 1 to 5, with 5 being the most important and 1 being the least important.

(B) The five factors can also be weighted as percentages. For example, based on a total of 100%, the highest-rated factor could be weighted at 40%, then the next-highest could be rated at 30%, followed by 20%, and the other two at 5% each. So also include your percentage-based weights for each factor, like in the example.

People generally will not agree on all the rankings, and that is a major reason why there is virtually always a committee that conducts job evaluations.

Step 4 (optional due to difficulty). Assign pay values to each of the five factors and weight them to determine pay levels for each job.

Apply It

What did I learn from this experience? How will I use this knowledge in the future?

_____

_____

• • • SKILL BUILDER 11-2 PRODUCT MARKET COMPETITION LIMITS

Objective

To develop a better understanding of product market competition limits

Skills

The primary skills developed through this exercise are as follows:

1. *HR management skills*—Technical and business skills
2. *SHRM 2013 Curriculum Guidebook*—K: Total rewards

Assignment

Complete the math problems below:

_____ 1. Your product sells for $1,000. Materials cost $300, labor costs $300, and overhead costs $200. What is your profit in dollars and as a percentage?

_____ 2. Your product sells for $750. Materials cost $250, labor costs $300, and overhead costs $150. What is the profit in dollars and as a percentage?

_____ 3. Your product sells for $1,000. Materials cost $300 and overhead costs $200. What is the maximum amount you can pay labor to make a $100 profit with a 10% return?

_____ 4. Your product sells for $750. Materials cost $250 and overhead costs $150. What is the maximum amount you can pay labor to make a 10% profit return on the sales price?

_____ 5. Your product sells for $800. Materials cost $300 and overhead costs $200. What is the maximum amount you can pay labor to make a 15% profit return on the sales price?

©iStockphoto.com/PeskyMonkey

12 Incentive Pay

• • • LEARNING OUTCOMES

After studying this chapter, you should be able to do the following:

12-1 Discuss the major reasons why companies use incentive pay. PAGE 442

12-2 Identify the advantages and disadvantages of individual incentives. PAGE 443

12-3 Identify the advantages and disadvantages of group incentives. PAGE 445

12-4 Briefly discuss options for individual incentives. PAGE 447

12-5 Briefly discuss options for group-based incentives. PAGE 456

12-6 Discuss the major reasons why incentive plans fail. PAGE 460

12-7 Discuss the challenges associated with incentive systems. PAGE 461

12-8 Identify the guidelines for creating motivational incentive systems. PAGE 462

12-9 Discuss the issue of whether or not executive compensation is too high. PAGE 467

12-10 Identify the major provisions of the Dodd-Frank Act that affect executive compensation. PAGE 468

12-11 Define the key terms found in the chapter margins and listed following the Chapter Summary. PAGE 475

Practitioner's Perspective

Cindy reflects: Whether the economy is up or down, your star employees can always find another job. This keeps HR departments looking for ways to keep their best employees motivated and engaged in their positions.

One of Cindy's colleagues, Terry, is a big advocate of incentive pay. "We need to look at ways to reward our exceptional employees now without expanding our base labor costs into future years," Terry said at one of their strategy meetings. "I've seen evidence to support the case that employees work harder if they know they have a fair chance of being rewarded for that extra effort."

"Well, I've heard lots of complaints against incentive pay," says Bill, another member of their department. "I'm not sure we want to open our compensation program to those issues."

Is incentive pay a good idea? The pros and cons plus the methods of implementation are detailed for your consideration in Chapter 12.

SHRM HR CONTENT

See Appendix: *SHRM 2013 Curriculum Guidebook* for the complete list

A. Employee and Labor Relations

24. Promotion

25. Recognition

26. Service awards

K. Total Rewards

A. Compensation

5. Pay programs: Merit pay, pay-for-performance, incentives/bonuses, profit sharing, group incentives/gainsharing, balanced scorecard

15. Motivation theories: Equity theory, reinforcement theory, agency theory

B. Employee Benefits

18. Financial benefits (gainsharing, group incentives, team awards, merit pay/bonuses)

LO 12-1

Discuss the major reasons why companies use incentive pay.

A:24
Promotion

Variable pay Compensation that depends on some measure of individual or group performance or results in order to be awarded

WHY DO WE USE INCENTIVE PAY?

Chapter 11 provided an overview of compensation planning, so we know that the HR department typically develops pay systems[1] and that compensation is an important part of the HRM process.[2] One component of our compensation system is variable pay, also known as incentives. People respond to incentives,[3] and rewards and recognition are motivational incentives,[4] so they are also called *incentive systems*. **Variable pay** *is compensation that depends on some measure of individual or group performance or results in order to be awarded.* But why do we need variable pay? Isn't it enough that our employees get a set amount of money each week or month in a paycheck from the organization? Not always. So to answer employees' often unasked question *What's in it for me?* companies develop incentive systems.[5] While we briefly discussed incentive pay in the last chapter, let's now get into some more detail on why we use incentives, what they are, their advantages and disadvantages, and why they might be successful in motivating our workforce.

In Chapter 11, we identified which employees fit into which pay levels. We noted, though, that individual effort and performance levels can vary. That is why we have pay ranges in each level. We want to be able to reward our best employees so that they feel that they are being recognized.[6] Recognition is a highly motivational tool that we will discuss in some detail shortly.[7] But pay levels only have so much flexibility built into them, so we would sometimes like to have a tool that will allow us to provide greater rewards to the best people in our organization. This is why we create incentives.[8]

What are we attempting to do when we provide employees with incentives? We are rewarding them for their past performance, but we are doing it in the hope that they will want similar rewards in the future and therefore will repeat the desired behaviors.[9] It is simply a reinforcement process like the one we discussed when we covered learning theories in Chapter 7.

There is a second reason why we use variable pay in organizations. Variable pay moves some of the risk associated with having employees (and the associated payroll

• • • CHAPTER OUTLINE

costs) from the firm to the individual. If the employee has variable pay that is tied to organizational productivity as part of their annual compensation, and the company (and therefore the employee) doesn't do well in that year, the individual loses part of their pay. The company does not have to pay out as much in compensation when the organization's performance in a given year is lower than expected. This effectively moves the risk associated with the incentive payment from the organization to the employee. If all annual compensation was provided in the form of base pay, we would still have to provide it to each employee, no matter how well the company did in a particular year. But if we have part of the annual compensation budget applied to variable pay, we don't have to pay out as much in lean years.

Our final reason for incentive pay ties into company strategy. We noted in Chapter 2 that "HRM is a critical component of meeting organizational goals, because without the right people with the right types of education, skills, and *mindset*, we cannot expect to accomplish the objectives that we set for ourselves." However, we can't get the right people to accomplish organizational objectives without providing some incentives to do so.[10] Incentive pay has to aim at the strategic goals of the organization in order to make any sense. Remember that people will not focus on attaining goals that we don't emphasize as important, and we emphasize what is important by attaching incentives to the achievement of the goal. People respond to incentives and can nearly always be guided toward goals if we find the right incentives.[11] Incentives are so important that they are one of the most written about topics in management.[12]

INDIVIDUAL OR GROUP-BASED INCENTIVES?

LO 12-2

Identify the advantages and disadvantages of individual incentives.

There are two basic choices in incentive pay—individual or group-based incentives. Groups can be small (a work cell of three people who assemble a computer) or large (an entire manufacturing plant or a call center), but all of these divisions are a bit artificial when it comes to incentive pay and, in fact, even the individual and group categories may cross. So in this text we will just divide incentives into individual or group options. You will see as we go through our incentive pay options that a lot of incentives can work in either an individual or a group setting. For example, bonuses have historically been provided as an individual incentive, but they can, and are, being used as group incentives as well.[13] Let's take a look at the advantages and disadvantages of each and when each option tends to work best.

Individual Incentives

Individual incentives *reinforce performance of a single person with a reward that is significant to that person.* What are some of the more common advantages and disadvantages of individual incentive plans for the organization? Let's take a look at Exhibit 12-1 for a brief list.

ADVANTAGES OF INDIVIDUAL INCENTIVES

- *Makes it easy to evaluate individual employees.* Individual incentive programs, if done correctly, make it easier to identify individual efforts. This is because performance goals will be set at the personal level, not the group or organizational level. If goals are reached, it will be due to individual efforts, not those of a larger organizational group.

- *Offers the ability to match rewards to employee desires.* Recall that expectancy theory (Chapter 11) shows the need to reinforce individual performance levels with rewards that are *significant to the individual.* Individualized incentives allow us to do this to a much greater degree than group incentives.

Individual incentives Incentives that reinforce performance of a single person with a reward that is significant to that person

EXHIBIT 12-1   INDIVIDUAL INCENTIVE PLAN ADVANTAGES AND DISADVANTAGES

Advantages	Disadvantages
Makes it easy to evaluate individual employees	Many jobs have no direct output
Offers the ability to match rewards to employee desires	May motivate undesirable employee behaviors
Promotes the link between performance and results	Record-keeping burden is high
May motivate less productive employees to work harder	May not fit organizational culture

- *Promotes the link between performance and results.* Individual incentives provide a direct link between performance levels and the rewards received—pay for performance.[14] A side benefit to this link is that we get equitable (fair) distribution of incentives; higher incentive payments go to those who perform at a higher level.

- *May motivate less productive employees to work harder.* Recall social learning theory: People learn by watching the consequences of others' behavior (Chapter 7). Less productive employees who see others getting valued rewards for performance may be convinced to increase their own performance levels in order to get similar rewards.

DISADVANTAGES OF INDIVIDUAL INCENTIVES

- *Many jobs have no direct output.* We don't have any way to directly measure results of some jobs in organizations. We discussed this in Chapter 8 when we discussed results-based performance appraisals. What is a measurable result on which we can base an incentive for most managers? How about equipment maintenance personnel or health care providers? It may be very difficult or even impossible in some jobs to identify individual output on which we can base an incentive.

- *May motivate undesirable employee behaviors.* If rewards are distributed based on personal performance levels, a perception of favoritism may be created. Jealousy can occur because of this perception. Jealousy can then cause other problems, such as dysfunctional conflict or competition—and even sabotage if it is significant enough. Another problem is that even top performers may focus only on the items that are being measured for incentive payments. So we end up with a situation where only the things that are rewarded get done. Everything else may be allowed to lag.

- *Record-keeping burden is high.* Individual incentive plans require that we keep track of individual efforts. Supervisors must develop and maintain comprehensive records to manage the program. This makes individual incentive programs much more time-intensive than group incentives.

- *May not fit organizational culture.* Individual incentives may not be acceptable in team-oriented organizations or in societies where the culture is highly collectivist. For example, in some Central and South American countries and in many countries in Southeast Asia, the national cultures do not condone the rewarding of individual efforts. In these societies, the team or group is what is valued, and therefore the team or group should be rewarded as a whole.

In these situations, individual reward systems go against the norms of the employees and will likely cause significant backlash if implemented.

CRITERIA FOR INDIVIDUAL INCENTIVES. Individual incentive plans work best in the following circumstances:[15]

- *When there are distinct, measurable outcomes for individual efforts.* If we can isolate individual results, individual incentives can work. If not, they won't be very effective at motivating employees.

- *When individual jobs require autonomy.* In some jobs, autonomy is a necessary condition, because a group effort may just cause confusion or unnecessary conflict. Individual effort is almost always necessary in one-to-one sales situations, for instance. Or think about your professor. Is at least *some* part of teaching an individual effort on the part of the professor?

Group Incentives

Individual incentive programs obviously work well in some cases. However, group incentives tend to work better in a number of other situations. CEO Alan Mulally said, "We're aligning compensation with the success of **Ford**."[16] **Group incentives** *provide reinforcement for actions of more than one individual within the organization.* What are the advantages and disadvantages of group incentive plans? See Exhibit 12-2 for a list.

ADVANTAGES OF GROUP INCENTIVES

- *Promotes better teamwork.* Group incentives, to no one's surprise, tend to encourage higher levels of teamwork and group cohesiveness. They can foster loyalty and trust between group members. Rewarding members for successfully working within the group creates an enticement to perform in ways that improve group outcomes, not just individual outcomes.

WORK
APPLICATION 12-1

Select a job. Assess the advantages and disadvantages of offering incentives for your job and whether the criteria are met for individual incentives to be effective at motivating employees.

LO 12-3

Identify the advantages and disadvantages of group incentives.

Group incentives Incentives that provide reinforcement for actions of more than one individual within the organization

---

12-1 APPLYING THE CONCEPT

Individual Incentives

Identify each statement by placing the letter of its advantage or disadvantage on the line next to it.

Advantages

a. Easy to evaluate individual employees

b. Ability to match rewards to employee desires

c. Promotes the link between performance and results

d. May motivate less productive employees to work harder

Disadvantages

e. Many jobs have no direct output

f. May motivate undesirable employee behaviors

g. Record-keeping burden is high

h. May not fit organizational culture

____ 1. The HR staff offered me a few different gifts for my top performance, but I took the cash.

____ 2. The old compensation system without incentives was easier. Now I have to keep track of everyone's performance.

____ 3. The new incentive system will be easy for me because all my employees are sales reps and we already keep track of each sale.

____ 4. I just do the minimum required for my job. If I want more compensation, I will just have to produce more to earn more.

____ 5. I'm a new high school teacher, and I'm very concerned about how the administration will assess my teaching in order to award tenure.

EXHIBIT 12-2	GROUP INCENTIVE PLAN ADVANTAGES AND DISADVANTAGES

Advantages	Disadvantages
Promotes better teamwork	Social loafing can occur
Broadens individual outlook	Individual output may be discounted
Requires less supervision	Outstanding performers may slacken efforts
Is easier to develop than individual incentive programs	Group infighting may arise

- *Broadens individual outlook.* Recall the discussion of the job characteristics model in Chapter 4. When we broaden the individual's job by giving them more and different things to do, we can ultimately increase motivation and productivity. By allowing employees to see how their actions affect others, we create positive psychological states that improve performance. Group incentives encourage this type of understanding because the employee has to know what others are doing and how one's individual efforts affect each of the members of the group.

- *Requires less supervision.* Group incentives, at least in some cases, tend to require less supervision. This is due to the tendency for the group to police its own members when they are not performing as well as they can. The "social loafers" in the group will feel pressure to improve their efforts from others in the group who are performing up to standards.

- *Is easier to develop than individual incentive programs.* Developing incentive programs for groups is less difficult than creating separate incentives for each individual in the organization. We can cover entire segments of the workforce with one set of incentives in many cases, and we may be able to design just a few different incentive program options that will motivate most of our employees.

DISADVANTAGES OF GROUP INCENTIVES

- *Social loafing can occur.* Social loafers (or free riders) may be able to stay hidden within the group while allowing others to do the majority of the group work. **Social loafers** *avoid providing their maximum effort in group settings because it is difficult to pick out individual performance.* This social loafing, if left uncorrected, can cause group morale and ultimately motivation and performance to drop significantly. If you want to learn more about social loafing, search the Internet for the "Ringelmann effect."

- *Individual output may be discounted.* Individual effort and results may get "lost" in the group. Some individuals may feel as if they are providing most of the group's effort, while others take a "free ride." Therefore, they may hold back their efforts and commitment,[17] especially when the relationship with other group members is not good.[18]

- *Outstanding performers may slacken efforts.* If the group is highly cohesive and has low performance norms, individual high-level performers may be pressured to lower their output to conform to group norms. Peer pressure can operate on the individual member to force them to stay within the performance boundaries of the rest of the group.

Social loafers Individuals who avoid providing their maximum effort in group settings because it is difficult to pick out individual performance

12-2 APPLYING THE CONCEPT

Group Incentives

Identify each statement by its group advantage or disadvantage.

Advantages

a. Promotes better teamwork

b. Broadens individual outlook

c. Requires less supervision

d. Is easier to develop than individual incentive programs

Disadvantages

e. Social loafing can occur

f. Individual output may be discounted

g. Outstanding performers may slacken efforts

h. Group infighting may arise

____ 6. What happened? Latoya and Katie used to get along so well. Now they are constantly bickering.

____ 7. Katrina, you are not being fair to the rest of us by not doing your fair share of the work.

____ 8. Now that we use a team-based process, the manager doesn't check up on us like she used to.

____ 9. By assembling the product as a team, we actually increased production by 20%.

____ 10. I know I'm the best, but none of the department members work very hard, so why should I?

- *Group infighting may arise.* There might be a breakdown of communication and/or cooperation among individuals within the group, and they might begin to compete with each other instead of cooperating. High-performance group members may even sanction or coerce low-performance group members to provide greater effort.

CRITERIA FOR GROUP INCENTIVES. Group incentive plans work best in the following circumstances:[19]

- *When we need people to cooperate.* When a group effort is necessary in order to optimize an outcome or to produce organizational goods or services, group incentives are far more powerful than individual incentives.

- *When individual contributions are difficult to identify.* When an activity requires the work of many individuals, all doing their part of the job, it may be difficult or impossible to identify how important one individual's contribution is compared to that of others in the group. Think about a team designing software: Did the interface engineer do more than the programmer, or vice versa? It may be impossible to tell.

- *When group members possess either similar or complementary skills.* If group members all have similar skill levels (think about comparable worth from Chapter 11), it may be difficult to determine whose efforts are more significant in creating the desired results. Similarly, if group members complement each other's skill sets, it may be impossible to say that one set of skills was more important than others.

OPTIONS FOR INDIVIDUAL INCENTIVES

Many different potential incentive programs can be flexible in their use to meet the award needs of every individual.[20] Remember, each person has to consider the

WORK
APPLICATION 12-2

Select a job. Assess the advantages and disadvantages of offering incentives for your work group and whether the criteria are met for group incentives to be effective at motivating employees.

LO 12-4

Briefly discuss options for individual incentives.

incentive to be significant or it won't act as a mechanism to motivate that individual to increase their performance. Because of this, sometimes the best thing to do is ask the members of the organization what they want.[21] However, some rewards have become commonplace partially because we as managers believe that they work, at least in some cases. Exhibit 12-3 summarizes some of the more common incentive options. In this section we discuss the individual option, while group incentives are presented in the next section.

We noted earlier that individual incentives work best when we can isolate individual efforts and when jobs require autonomy. There are six common options for individual incentive programs that are used in a wide variety of companies. Let's take a brief look at each of these six incentives used to reward individual employee performance.

Bonus

A **bonus** *is a lump sum payment, typically given to an individual at the end of a time period.*[22] A bonus does not carry over from one period to the next. Over what type of period do we usually provide bonuses? Generally they will be provided annually. Many companies will call them a "seasonal bonus," "holiday bonus," or "year-end bonus" or something similar. How would a bonus program have to be designed in order to motivate increased performance? We would need to identify specific and measurable goals that the individual could affect and a bonus that would cause the individual (assuming we are making this an individual incentive program) to change something that they are doing to perform at a higher level.[23] If they then reached the measurable goal, they would receive the bonus. Bonuses can also be used at the group level but are generally considered an individual incentive.

INEFFECTIVE BONUS IMPLEMENTATION. Let's look at how motivational the "year-end bonus" is *in most companies*—remember that we are talking about things that are supposed to be incentives to perform at a higher level! Three years ago, because the company was doing well, senior management decided to provide a bonus at the end of the year to all employees. Joanna received a $3,000 bonus based on her pay level at the time. Two years ago, she again received $3,000 at the end of the year (because the company was doing well). The same thing happened last year, but then this year she received no bonus. Management explained that the recession had hurt company performance and, as a result, there would be no bonuses provided at the end of the year. But Joanna had worked hard all year *expecting* to receive her bonus at year end. How do you think Joanna feels? Is she frustrated and demotivated? Wasn't a

EXHIBIT 12-3   INDIVIDUAL AND GROUP INCENTIVE OPTIONS

Individual	Group
Bonus	Profit sharing
Commissions	Gainsharing
Merit pay	Employee stock ownership plan (ESOP)
Piecework	Stock options
Standard hour	Stock purchasing
Nonmonetary awards	
Praise	

Bonus A lump sum payment, typically given to an individual at the end of a time period

bonus supposed to do the opposite—make her feel like she wanted to perform better? What happened?

What did management do wrong? First, they provided the bonus based on a period of time, not based on meeting a performance goal. Reinforcement theory says that variable reinforcement works much better than fixed reinforcement.[24] The end of each year is a fixed reinforcement period. That is one error on the part of the managers. What else did they do wrong? What individual goal did they base the bonus on? They didn't base it on individual results but on company performance, so the employees most likely did nothing different than they had done in the past. In addition, the individual employees most likely have no idea how to affect the overall performance of the company. Third, because the bonus had been provided on the fixed schedule, as soon as management provided it to the employees twice, the employees started to expect it. It became an *entitlement*, or something that they felt the company owed them because it had been provided in the past. As soon as the bonus became an entitlement (you *owe* me), it ceased to motivate any additional performance on the part of employees. This is historically how most companies use a bonus payment. And if we use it this way, it just becomes an expected part of your pay.

EFFECTIVE BONUS IMPLEMENTATION. However, to use a bonus as it was originally designed and should be used, what should we do? We create a specific, measurable, and attainable goal that the individual has control over and communicate that goal to the employee. The goal is continuously measured during the performance period. When the individual meets the goal, the bonus payment is provided—immediately, not at the end of the year.[25] The reward is applied for doing more than was required—it was a bonus! Now, the bonus can act as an incentive to perform. So the biggest problem with a bonus as an incentive is in allowing it to become a time-based entitlement instead of a performance incentive.

In the global competitive environment, many businesses are giving bonuses effectively to keep valuable employees from leaving for other companies. Bonuses are typically paid out over several years based on performance goals. Technology companies are closely looking at their top 10% of performers and asking themselves, *Are they locked in? What can we do to keep them?* **Google** awarded a $5 million bonus package to a top engineer to keep him from leaving for a job with a start-up firm.[26]

Commissions

Commissions are well-known incentive tools for sales professionals. A **commission** *is a payment typically provided to a salesperson for selling an item to a customer* and is usually paid as a percentage of the price of an item that is sold. If you sell a $100 product and you are on a 10% commission, you would receive $10 for that sale. Salespeople sometimes work on straight commission, where they only get paid when they sell an item, or they can be paid a salary plus commission, where they receive a lower salary and it is supplemented by commissions on sales. Commissions can also be used at the group level in some cases. In general, commissions are good individual incentives to sell.[27]

INEFFECTIVE COMMISSION IMPLEMENTATION. Are commissions sometimes ineffective as individual incentives? If not implemented correctly, they can certainly be unproductive. The salesperson may ignore the customer's needs or desires in order to sell something that makes the salesperson more money. If the salesperson gets the customer to buy something they didn't really want, it may harm the long-term relationship between the company and the customer. The company can also create too much competition within the sales force if the commission structure isn't set up right. We may create dysfunctional conflict among members of the sales force or even motivate one salesperson to sabotage another in order to make the sale themselves.[28] Overall,

WORK
APPLICATION 12-3

Select a job. Does the organization offer bonuses? If not, how could it offer bonuses to effectively motivate employees? Assess the advantages and disadvantages of offering bonuses at your organization. Should it offer bonuses?

Commission A payment typically provided to a salesperson for selling an item to a customer

Selling products over the phone and online is challenging, and it takes the right type of employee to be successful on commission pay.

WORK
APPLICATION 12-4

Select a job. Does the organization offer commissions? If not, how could it offer commissions to effectively motivate employees? Assess the advantages and disadvantages of offering commissions at your organization. Should it offer commissions?

however, commissions are a strong incentive to perform well in a sales role.

EFFECTIVE COMMISSION IMPLEMENTATION. In order for a commission incentive program to work, it must provide a significant return to the salesperson who is successful in selling to the customer, but it also has to provide a disincentive to harm the customer to make a "quick sale." You may have noticed that more automobile dealerships are now using customer satisfaction surveys after a customer buys a vehicle.[29] What they are trying to do is determine whether or not the salesperson may have done anything to damage the long-term relationship between the customer and the company. In some cases, dealers are even making customer complaints part of their commission structure so that if a salesperson gets too many complaints, part of their commissions will have to be reimbursed to the dealership.

Merit Pay

The next incentive option is called merit pay. **Merit pay** *is a program to reward top performers with increases in their annual wage that carry over from year to year.* Merit pay is different from most other individual incentives in that if an individual gets merit pay increases consistently over time, their annual pay can become significantly greater than that of others who do not consistently get merit increases.[30]

Merit pay works as follows: The company announces a "merit pool" available for pay increases in a given period, usually annually. The merit raises will be given to the top performers in the company based on performance evaluations. Frequently, individuals who receive either outstanding or excellent marks will get merit increases above the average, while average performers will get a lower raise and those who receive below-average marks will get no raise at all.

INEFFECTIVE MERIT PAY IMPLEMENTATION. There are some significant potential problems in using merit pay as an incentive. The first issue is that merit pay is typically a very small percentage of the individual's total pay, which makes it very difficult to use it as a motivator to perform. Remember that people need to feel that the reward is "significant" to them in order for it to motivate. In many cases, merit raises may amount to only an extra 1% of pay in any given year. Many employees won't consider this significant.

Another major issue is inflation of the performance appraisal process. If the company does not set limits on how many employees can be judged as outstanding or excellent, and supervisors know that a pay increase is attached to the individual's performance rating, nearly everyone tends to become outstanding or excellent.[31] While we know this is not true, the supervisor doesn't want to be the person to keep someone in their department from getting a pay raise. Also, when you limit the number of people who can get a merit raise in any given year, sometimes the manager rotates who will get merit pay, rather than rewarding the best performers, to keep the majority happy.

In order for merit pay to be valuable as an incentive, it must be significant, which means it must be more than 1% of the employee's pay. However, there is another problem here. Remember that merit pay increases the individual's pay from one year to the next and it carries forward, so if merit pay is 5% to 10% instead of 1% to 2%, we

Merit pay A program to reward top performers with increases in their annual wage that carry over from year to year can end up with employees who break right through our maximum wage for a specific pay level very quickly. If we had a pay level (from Chapter 11) that began at $12 per hour and went to $16 and an employee was hired with a base pay of $12, they could "max out," or reach $16 per hour, in only 3 years if they received a merit raise of 10% each year. So merit pay is difficult to use as an incentive to perform at a higher level.

EFFECTIVE MERIT PAY IMPLEMENTATION. Merit pay is one of the most frequently used individual incentive programs in companies, and it *can* be used in some team-based situations as well.[32] It requires that we pay attention to some details though. The first and probably most important item that HR needs to develop for a merit pay program is material that communicates the value of merit pay over time. We need to communicate that even what would normally be considered a small incentive can become a significant boost to an individual's pay when they are judged to have merit over several years. For instance, if we have a merit raise each year of only 2%, because of compounding, this becomes an additional *permanent increase* in the pay of an individual employee of nearly 10.5% above cost-of-living increases if received for 5 years. Over the employee's entire work life, this will make a huge difference in total wages earned. So HR needs to communicate the value of merit pay better than has historically been the case.

Secondly, we only want to reward true top performers with merit pay. If we do so, this means that those who are rewarded are truly recognized as having exceptional ability, and it also means that limited amounts of merit pay cash can provide a larger merit increase to those who deserve it. Alternately, if we provide all employees with merit raises, the pool of funds must be spread out among everyone, and the small amount of the supposed "merit" increase doesn't amount to much. Let's look at a quick example.

If your company has 1,000 employees and the annual payroll is $60 million, and the leadership decides to provide a 2% merit pool for the coming year, that is $1.2 million in available dollars for merit increases. If we spread that money evenly over all 1,000 employees, each employee receives an increase in pay of about $100 per month. However, if we truly identify the individuals who are meritorious and limit our payout to the top 30% of the employee group, each individual receives an average merit raise of about $350 per month. Most of us would consider an extra $350 per month to be significant, while $100 is probably not significant to many of us. So if we give "all As" to our employees and say that everyone is meritorious, our actual top performers are demotivated because their efforts aren't being recognized, *and* nobody in the employee group considers the reward to be significant because it is too small to make much difference in their lives.

Piecework Plans

Piecework or piece-rate plans are one of the simplest forms of compensation, and they can act as an incentive to produce at a higher level because the more workers produce, the more they get paid. In a "straight piece-rate" compensation system, the employee gets paid for every "piece" that they complete. If they are faster than the average, they can make more money than other employees.[33] A "differential piece-rate" system (sometimes called a Taylor plan after Frederick Taylor of Scientific Management fame) provides the employee with a base wage to complete a certain amount of work, and if they produce more than the standard, a differential wage is paid for the extra pieces produced. In either case, the employee is being paid for increased speed. Take a look at Exhibit 12-4 for an example of a piece-rate system.

INEFFECTIVE PIECEWORK IMPLEMENTATION. Are there any problems associated with a piecework incentive program? There is an obvious one—quality.[34] If we pay

WORK
APPLICATION 12-5

Select a job. Does the organization offer merit pay? If not, how could it offer merit pay to effectively motivate employees? Assess the advantages and disadvantages of offering merit pay at your organization. Should it offer merit pay?

EXHIBIT 12-4 PIECE-RATE PLANS

Straight Piece-Rate

Anji Presser is paid to iron and package new dress shirts in special decorative packaging. She is paid on a basic piece-rate system at $0.65 per shirt ironed and packaged. Anji works 40 hours per week, and the company estimates the value of the job at $13 per hour. Anji's production last week was as follows:

	Number of Shirts
Monday	182
Tuesday	165
Wednesday	188
Thursday	179
Friday	163
Total	877 × $0.65 = **$570.05** instead of $13.00 × 40 = **$520.00**.

Anji made an additional $50.05, a 9.6% premium, because of being efficient in her job.

Differential Piece-Rate

Bob Rivette works in a factory assembling folding chairs from parts. He is paid using a differential piece-rate. If he assembles 480 chairs or fewer in a day, he is paid $15 per hour (he works 8 hours per day). For every additional chair over 480 per day, he is paid an additional $0.25. Last week his statistics were as follows:

Monday	450—less than 480, so $15 × 8 hours =	$120
Tuesday	520—40 more than production requirement: 40 × $0.25 = $10 + $120 =	$130
Wednesday	540—60 more than production requirement: 60 × $0.25 = $15 + $120 =	$135
Thursday	532—52 more than production requirement: 52 × $0.25 = $13 + $120 =	$133
Friday	460—less than 480, so $15 × 8 hours =	$120
Total		$638

Bob made **$638** this week instead of **$600**. This additional $38 is a 6.33% premium in Bob's pay.

employees "by the piece," they may make lots of pieces with lots of quality problems because they are trying to work too fast and not paying attention to how well they are doing the work. So quality is an issue in a piece-rate system. There may also be a problem in determining where the standard is going to be set for a differential piece-rate system, and there are other potential problems.

EFFECTIVE PIECEWORK IMPLEMENTATION. However, in some situations, a piecework plan can be an incentive to produce at a faster rate. The obvious answer to potential quality problems is to set clear standards that each piece must meet to be accepted and paid for. Thus, if the employees don't do a quality job, they don't get paid. Clear standards tell the employee what they need to do in order to benefit from the piecework pay schedule. If they will not be given credit for items that don't meet quality standards, they need to know this up front. If they will have to rework any items that aren't correct, they need to know this, too. They also know that they don't have to "hit a moving target" if the standards are clear from the beginning—that the company isn't going to just lower the amount paid per piece in order to pay the employees what they have always been paid.

The other key to effective piecework plans is feedback. Employees need to know how they are doing as they go through the workweek. In some cases, they may see that they are not meeting their own goals of performance and pick up the pace, and in others, they may see that their performance is producing a desired result. Many people expect that once the employee reaches a level of production that provides them with an acceptable wage, they will slow down, but there is very little evidence that this occurs in more than isolated cases. Feedback gives the employees information about the "significant reward" that they seek and can motivate continued performance—just as expectancy theory shows.

Standard Hour Plans

Standard hour plans are used quite a bit in some types of service work. In a standard hour plan, each task is assigned a "standard" amount of work time for completion.[35] Generally, this time will be shown in a *standard-hour manual*. The individual doing the job will get paid based on the standard time to complete the job, but good workers can frequently complete the work in less than the standard amount of time. If they do, they can get paid for an hour of work while working less than an hour of time. Take a quick look at Exhibit 12-5 for two examples of a standard hour plan. In many cases, good service employees can do better than the standard most of the time, so they get an incentive to work faster.

INEFFECTIVE AND EFFECTIVE STANDARD HOUR IMPLEMENTATION. Like the piecework plan, standard hour incentives can cause quality problems. So most standard hour plans also require that if there are any quality problems, the job has to be redone; the worker must do the rework for no additional pay. This is one way to make sure that speed doesn't create poor quality. Standard hour plans, like most individual incentive programs, can be used for groups if the group is responsible for completion of the work.

Standard hour plans are used heavily in automotive and heavy equipment repair and in other areas, like heating and air-conditioning services. The biggest challenge with standard hour plans is creating the manuals showing the allowable time for a job. We have to have a large baseline measuring the amount of time necessary to perform specific tasks in order to figure out the average time needed to do a particular job. We can only do this in jobs where the same task is done many times in a year. We also need to keep an ongoing record of the actual times to do the jobs so we can adjust the standards accordingly and not over- or underpay for each job.

Giving Praise and Other Nonmonetary Incentives

People work for money, so financial rewards are critical, but just as important is recognition for the work we do.[36] Employee recognition leads to profits.[37] So both financial and nonfinancial rewards and recognition are important to motivate employees to meet objectives and put their ideas into practice.[38] We also have a nonmonetary option as an individual incentive. Nonmonetary recognition can come in many forms (e.g., service awards), but evidence says that honest praise is one of the most effective motivational tools that management has at its disposal.[39]

INEFFECTIVE RECOGNITION IMPLEMENTATION. Wait just a minute! Service awards—things like Employee of the Month—are motivators? How often is an award such as *employee of the month* just rotated among the employees? In such a case, is it a motivator, or is it a joke? It is a joke if not used correctly, because everyone knows that

WORK APPLICATION 12-6

Select a job. Does the organization offer piecework? If not, how could it offer piecework to effectively motivate employees? Assess the advantages and disadvantages of offering piecework at your organization. Should it offer piecework?

WORK APPLICATION 12-7

Select a job. Does the organization offer a standard hour plan? If not, how could it offer a standard hour plan to effectively motivate employees? Assess the advantages and disadvantages of offering a standard hour plan at your organization. Should it offer a standard hour plan?

EXHIBIT 12-5 STANDARD HOUR PLAN

Brant Wrenchright is a master mechanic at the local Honda dealership. He works on a standard hour plan. Brant is paid $32 per standard hour and works 40 hours per week. His last week's work (in standard hours billed) is shown below:

Monday	8.3
Tuesday	9.2
Wednesday	8.1
Thursday	8.8
Friday	8.7
Total	43.1

Even though Brant only worked 40 hours, he completed 43.1 *standard hours* of work. His pay is based on standard hours, so 43.1 × $32 = $1,379.20. If Brant were paid only for his actual hours, he would have been paid 40 × $32 = $1,280. Brant made an additional $99.20 because of his standard hour completion rates—or a 7.75% premium.

On the other hand, Willy Lugnutty is a young mechanic who is paid $20 per standard hour for his work. He, like Brant, worked 40 hours last week, and his standard hours are shown below:

Monday	7.3
Tuesday	8.2
Wednesday	7.1
Thursday	7.8
Friday	6.7
Total	37.1

Since Willy completed only 37.1 hours of work in a 40-hour week, he is paid $742 (37.1 × $20). If he had been paid on an hourly basis, he would have made $800. So, Willy actually lost $58, or 7.25% of his pay, because of working more slowly than the standard hour plan dictated.

SHRM

A:26
Service Awards

there are no criteria that the employee must meet in order to become "employee of the month." So how do we make an employee of the month award a valuable incentive?

EFFECTIVE RECOGNITION IMPLEMENTATION. Remember that recognition *is* a powerful incentive, so we need to use it effectively to motivate our employees. In order for this type of recognition to mean something, there has to be a specific set of criteria that must be met in order to receive the recognition. The employee has to *do something extra*, above what others do, in order to be recognized.[40]

How many of you have seen a military awards ceremony where service members receive meritorious awards? Why do military services all over the world perform these ceremonies? It takes a lot of time and manhours to do so. The ceremonies are carried out to recognize special efforts by service members, because the officers in charge know that other service members will see such ceremonies and (through social learning!) determine that they can perform at a higher level in order to also receive an award.

If service awards have strong requirements for eligibility, they can become a powerful motivational factor in any workforce. So if our company has an employee of the month or year program, it needs specific and measurable criteria, clearly communicated to the workforce, that require performance above the company's standards in order to be eligible for the award. If this is done, these awards can become excellent motivators.

PRAISE AS RECOGNITION. Empirical research studies have found that feedback and social reinforcers (praise) may have as strong an impact on performance as pay. Praise actually works by boosting levels of dopamine in the brain, a chemical linked to joy. In the 1940s, a survey revealed that what employees want most from a job is full appreciation for work done. Similar studies have been performed over the years with little change in results. Employees want to know that their organization values their contributions and cares about their well-being.[41] Giving praise is simply complimenting the achievements of others,[42] and this recognition increases performance.[43] It costs you nothing to give praise,[44] involves very little effort, and produces a lot in return.[45] It is probably the most powerful, simplest, least costly, and yet most underused motivational incentive there is.

SHRM

A:25
Recognition

Ken Blanchard and Spencer Johnson popularized giving praise back in the 1980s through their best-selling book *The One-Minute Manager*. They developed a technique that involves giving 1 minute of positive feedback. Model 12-1: The Giving Praise Model, is an adaptation. Blanchard called it "one-minute praise" because it should not take more than 1 minute to carry out. It is not necessary for the employee to say anything. The four steps are described and illustrated in Model 12-1.

MODEL 12-1 THE GIVING PRAISE MODEL

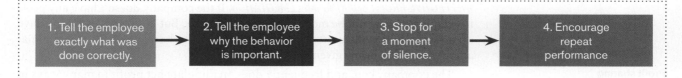

1. Tell the employee exactly what was done correctly. → 2. Tell the employee why the behavior is important. → 3. Stop for a moment of silence. → 4. Encourage repeat performance

Step 1: Tell the employee exactly what was done correctly. When giving praise, look the person in the eye. Eye contact shows sincerity and concern. It is important to be very specific and descriptive.[46] General statements, like "You're a good worker," are not as effective. On the other hand, don't talk for too long or the praise loses its effectiveness.

Step 2: Tell the employee why the behavior is important. Briefly state how the organization and/or person benefits from the action. It is also helpful to tell the employee how you feel about the behavior. Be specific and descriptive.

Step 3: Stop for a moment of silence. Being silent is tough for many managers. The rationale for the silence is to give the employee the chance to "feel" the impact of the praise. It's like "the pause that refreshes." When you are thirsty and take the first sip or gulp of a refreshing drink, it's not until you stop and maybe say "Ah" that you feel your thirst quenched.

Step 4: Encourage repeat performance. This is the reinforcement that motivates the employee to continue the desired behavior.[47] Blanchard recommended touching the employee because it has a powerful impact. However, he recommends doing this only if both parties feel comfortable. Others recommend that you don't touch employees, as physical contact could lead to a sexual harassment charge.

As you can see, giving praise is easy, and it doesn't cost a penny. Managers trained to give praise say it works wonders. It's a much better motivator than giving a raise or other monetary rewards.[48]

WORK
APPLICATION 12-8

Select a job. Does the organization offer a recognition plan? If not, how could it offer a recognition plan to effectively motivate employees? Assess the advantages and disadvantages of offering a recognition plan at your organization. Should it offer a recognition plan?

WORK
APPLICATION 12-9

Select a job. How often does your boss criticize your work? How often does your boss praise your work? What is the last thing you did that deserved praise? How often do you criticize and praise others at work? Will you now give more praise, knowing how it affects others?

Other nonmonetary recognition, besides praise, also increases motivation if the individual considers it to be significant.[49] Some of the more common forms are extra time off, ability to choose tasks or jobs, flexible hours, or extra training in a particular area of interest to the employee. Younger workers, especially, often want more flexible hours and working conditions.[50]

LO 12-5

Briefly discuss options for group-based incentives.

OPTIONS FOR GROUP INCENTIVES

Individual incentives can work well, but what can we use to motivate higher levels of performance from groups? After all, in most of our 21st century companies, groups and teams are the norm. Let's take a look at some of the more common group incentive options.

Profit Sharing Plans

Profit sharing programs *provide a portion of company proceeds over a specific period of time* (usually either quarterly or annually) *to the employees of the firm through a bonus payment.* The programs are designed to cause everyone in the company to focus on total organizational profitability.[51] This sounds like a good opportunity for the employee to get a share of the returns that the company receives from their work, right? But how well does it work? What if the company does not have any profit during a particular period? If this is the case, then there is no profit to be shared.

INEFFECTIVE PROFIT SHARING IMPLEMENTATION. If the company doesn't have any profits, employees may not be motivated to work harder. But how can a company have no profit? It is actually pretty easy for the company to have no profit, or a minimal amount of profit, in any given year.

The company can, and frequently does, manipulate net profit in many ways in order to pay less in tax on corporate profits at the end of the year, and in some cases to minimize profit sharing. Management might put profits back into the company by buying new equipment or other assets. It can decide to pay management an unscheduled bonus, acquire another business, or increase finished goods inventory. However, if the company is manipulating expenses or other cost factors to decrease

SHRM

K:B18
Financial Benefits (Gainsharing, Group Incentives, etc.)

Profit sharing programs Programs that provide a portion of company proceeds over a specific period of time (usually either quarterly or annually) to the employees of the firm through a bonus payment

12-3 APPLYING THE CONCEPT

Individual Incentive Options

Place the letter of the individual incentive on the line next to the scenario illustrating it.

a. bonus
b. commissions
c. merit pay
d. piecework
e. standard hour
f. nonmonetary awards
g. praise

_____ 11. I'm an auto mechanic at a dealership, and we have a set amount of time to complete each type of repair work. I complete a job before a stated time so that I can go on to the next car and get paid extra for being faster than the average guy.

_____ 12. I just sold that top-of-the-line BMW M3. I can't wait to get my pay this week.

_____ 13. I'm the top producer in the entire department, so I will get an extra raise for high performance this year.

_____ 14. The boss had me come to the front of the room at the annual meeting to get a plaque for five years of service to the company. She listed some of my major accomplishments.

_____ 15. The boss just thanked me for getting a shipment that was behind schedule out on time today.

profit sharing and employees find out, the plan will certainly not be a performance motivator and most likely will cause other problems.

Another issue with profit sharing as a motivator is that it is focused on total organizational profitability. How can the average employee affect company-wide profitability? If the employee doesn't know what to do in order to increase profits, what will they do differently in their job? The answer is "absolutely nothing." Remember that we need to be able to personally affect the desired result in order to be motivated to do anything different. So profit sharing in many cases does not provide the company with the expected boost in productivity.[52]

EFFECTIVE PROFIT SHARING IMPLEMENTATION. To motivate employees, we need to be sure that management is not manipulating factors to minimize profits so it doesn't have to pay much in profit sharing. The second thing is to be sure to train all employees on how to increase revenues and decrease cost in their job areas so that they can affect the bottom line and increase their profit share. In addition, a running record of organizational revenues and profitability should be maintained and updated on at least a weekly basis. This record should be posted where everyone can see it and keep track of company performance—some companies post it in the lunch/break room. This allows the employees to see how their efforts are affecting profitability of the firm overall. It can also allow interim payments of incentives, which can assist the company in maintaining high worker efficiency over longer periods of time.

Gainsharing Plans

An alternative to profit sharing is a gainsharing program. Gainsharing is similar to profit sharing because in each case, the gain (in either profit or some other factor) is shared with the employees who helped to create the gain. Gainsharing is a bit broader than profit sharing though. Gainsharing can be accomplished using any organizational factor that costs the company money and that can be analyzed and modified for performance improvement.[53] Originally, gainsharing usually used corporate revenue, but today, many gainsharing options exist. Some of the more common gainsharing options are increased revenues, increased labor productivity or lower labor costs, improved safety (fewer lost-time accidents), return on assets or investment, and increased customer satisfaction.

INEFFECTIVE AND EFFECTIVE GAINSHARING IMPLEMENTATION. Being somewhat similar to profit sharing, gainsharing has the same potential problems. Here, as with profit sharing, we have to show employees how they can affect the desired outcome in order for them to be motivated to change the way they work.[54] However, different from profit sharing, many of the options for gainsharing are more difficult for management to manipulate, so workers feel that they have more control over their results. It is tougher for management to modify total revenue or days lost to accidents, for instance, than it is to modify net profit. So gainsharing sometimes initiates a stronger reaction and more motivation from the workforce than profit sharing.

How do we incorporate gainsharing effectively in the organization? It's pretty straightforward, but easier said than done. Here is the process. We establish the objective(s), identify the performance measure (usually as a per unit value), determine how to split the gain between the organization and the employees, and then provide the payout when earned.

Employee Stock Ownership Plan (ESOP)

An employee stock ownership plan (ESOP) ultimately allows at least part of the stock in the company to be given to the employees over a period of time based on

WORK
APPLICATION 12-10

Select a job at a for-profit company. Does the organization offer profit sharing? If not, how could it offer a profit sharing plan to effectively motivate employees? Assess the advantages and disadvantages of offering profit sharing at your company. Should it offer a profit sharing plan?

WORK
APPLICATION 12-11

Select a job. Does the organization offer gainsharing? If not, how could it offer gainsharing to effectively motivate employees? Assess the advantages and disadvantages of offering gainsharing at your firm. Should it offer a gainsharing plan?

12-4 APPLYING THE CONCEPT

Group Incentive Options

Place the letter of the group incentive option on the line next to the matching description.

a. profit sharing
b. gainsharing
c. ESOP
d. stock options
e. stock purchasing

_____ 16. Our group incentive option gives us a bonus at the end of the year based on how profitable we were for the year.

_____ 17. Our group incentive option plan allows me to get stock and put it in my retirement account without paying anything for it.

_____ 18. Our group incentive option plan worked like this. The manager told us that if we could cut cost in our department by 5%, as a group we would get 5% of the savings to the company distributed evenly among us.

_____ 19. Our group incentive option allows me to buy company stock for 10% less than the market value.

_____ 20. Our group incentive option plan allows me to buy $50 shares of the company stock for only $13 apiece next year.

WORK APPLICATION 12-12

Select a job at a for-profit company. Does the organization offer ESOPs? If not, how could it offer an ESOP to effectively motivate employees? Assess the advantages and disadvantages of offering ESOPs at your company. Should it offer an ESOP?

some formula.[55] For example, if you work for the company for a year, you might get 10 shares of stock, and for every additional year of employment, you would receive 10% more than the year before. An ESOP is actually a retirement benefits plan because the company puts the tax-deferred stock in a trust for eventual use by employees who retire. But it also has the potential to be an incentive to the company's employees, because they become part owners of the firm.

Why would the current owners of the firm give away stock in the company? Well, there are a couple of major reasons. Because an ESOP is basically a "qualified" retirement benefits plan, it has some significant tax advantages to both the firm and the employee in most cases.[56] This means that owners can give their employees part of the company and receive a tax break for doing so. A second major reason for giving employees stock in the company is to cause them to act more like owners. It is thought that this will motivate employees to do such things as reduce scrap, increase quality, improve customer service, and pay attention to many other things that cost the company money over the course of a year.

INEFFECTIVE AND EFFECTIVE ESOP IMPLEMENTATION. But does an ESOP always work as intended? Of course not. Because an ESOP is like the other two group incentives, it is subject to the same potential problems and needs the same lack of manipulation and employee training.

Stock does, however, have a unique potential problem. The entire company typically has to improve in order for the value of its stock to increase. But even if the employees are highly motivated and work really hard, the value of the stock can actually go down for many reasons that are outside the control of the individual and groups. For example, the stock market may enter a bear market, and your company's stock price can go down along with the overall market. Or a recession may hit and sales and profits may go down, as well as the price of your stock. Competition can take some or all of your business away, as **Netflix** did to **Blockbuster**, or the company can go bankrupt as **Hostess** did, and you can lose it all.

Stock Options and Stock Purchasing Plans

There are two other common stock plans used by companies as incentives. The first is a stock option plan, and the second is direct stock ownership.

STOCK OPTIONS. Stock options are usually offered to an individual employee to allow them to buy a certain number of shares of stock in the company at a specified point in the future, but at a price that is set when the option is offered. [57] Options can be provided to either executives or to nonexecutive employees.[58] So, we might offer our employees the option to buy stock in the company in a year at today's stock price.

The intent here is to motivate the employees to work to improve the value of the company so that when the option to buy the stock comes up in a year, the price of the stock has increased, giving the employee more value than what they paid for. For example, we may offer our employees the option to buy 100 shares of our stock in 1 year at today's price of $10. If the company's value increases so that at the end of the year, a share of stock is worth $20, the employee can buy $2,000 worth of company stock for $1,000. However, if the value of the stock doesn't go up in a year, the option isn't worth anything.

STOCK PURCHASING. These plans are similar to stock options, but instead of giving you the option to buy stock in the future, they let qualifying employees buy the stock essentially anytime, usually at a discount. ESOPs, stock options, and stock purchasing give employees ownership in the company, but the big difference is that with an ESOP, the employees are given the stock over time, whereas with stock options or purchases, employees have to buy the stock.

WORK
APPLICATION 12-13

Select a job at a for-profit company. Does the organization offer stock options and/or stock ownership? If not, how could it offer one or the other to effectively motivate employees? Assess the advantages and disadvantages of offering stock options and stock ownership at your company. Should it offer stock options and/or a stock ownership plan?

12-1 SELF ASSESSMENT

Compensation Options

Answer each question based on how well it describes you:

1	2	3	4	5
Not like me				Describes me

_____ 1. I enjoy competing and winning.

_____ 2. I usually work faster than others.

_____ 3. I like working alone more than being part of a group.

_____ 4. I don't need to have approximately the same pay every week; varying income is fine.

_____ 5. I enjoy meeting new people and can strike up a conversation with most people.

_____ 6. I take risks.

_____ 7. I would prefer to get a large sum of money all at once, rather many smaller payments.

_____ 8. I'm thinking long term for my retirement.

_____ 9. I like working toward a set of goals and being rewarded for achieving them.

_____ 10. I like knowing that I am one of the best at what I do (merit pay and praise).

There is no simple sum to add up here. Although we would all love to have a high wage or salary with lots of incentive pay on top of it, this is not the reality in most jobs today. In general, the higher your number of "describes me" statements, the more open you are to incentives versus wages/salaries. Below is an explanation of each statement.

Item 1: If you don't like competing and winning, you may be more comfortable in a job with a wage or salary; you usually have to compete for incentives like merit raises. Item 2: If you are not faster than others, piecework and standard hour incentives may not be your best option. Item 3: Commissions, piecework, and standard hours are often based on individual performance. Item 4: Wages and salaries give you a fixed income, whereas incentives provide a variable income. Item 5 is characteristic of commission salespeople. Item 6: If you don't like risk, incentives can be risky. Item 7: Getting a large sum at once tends to involve a bonus, profit sharing, or gainsharing incentives. Item 8: ESOPs are retirement plans, and stock purchases can be, too. Item 9 reflects gainsharing and bonuses. Item 10 reflects merit pay and praise.

INEFFECTIVE AND EFFECTIVE STOCK OPTIONS AND PURCHASING IMPLEMENTATION. Stock options and stock purchasing don't always work as intended for essentially the same reasons as ESOPs. The hope is that if you are an owner, you will think more about the long-term value of the company and work to improve its performance. But with stock options, there is a unique potential problem. The employee can simply buy the stock and then quickly sell it for a profit so that they are no longer an owner of the company. The same problem can occur with stock purchases, depending on the arrangement; there can be restrictions on the sale of the stock, and if it is part of a qualified retirement plan, there are penalties for selling before retiring.

FAILURE, CHALLENGES, AND GUIDELINES IN CREATING INCENTIVE PAY SYSTEMS

Now that we know a little about the various types of incentives available to the company, let's discuss some of the issues that we will have to deal with in creating an incentive program that works.

LO 12-6

Discuss the major reasons why incentive plans fail.

Why Do Incentive Pay Systems Fail?

Too often, incentive systems are poorly designed and badly implemented.[59] If we are not going to carefully manage a system, then we shouldn't even create it. It is worse than no system at all. There are many reasons why incentive plans might fail to motivate the workforce, but let's take a look at some of the more common ones.

POOR MANAGEMENT. Even the best incentive plan won't work with bad management. Managers are the core of any incentive program, because they have to keep track of individual and group performance in order to reward those who perform the best. Management also has to monitor the program and adjust things as necessary when the environment or the organizational tasks change.

COMPLICATED PROGRAMS. If the employees can't figure out what they need to do in order to receive the incentives, they won't do anything different. Complex programs will almost always lead to failure of an incentive program because the workers don't know how to reach the goals or, in many cases, even what the true goals are.[60] In addition, failure to successfully communicate the plan to employees creates the same problem—the employee won't know how to reach the goals.

THE PLAN DOESN'T REALLY INCREASE REWARDS, OR IT PROVIDES INSIGNIFICANT REWARDS. If a plan takes away from base pay in order to add incentive pay, the employee isn't really gaining anything. The net result is the same, and employees will see right through such a "rewards" program. Even if there is a minimal increase in pay, often employees will figure that the extra effort required is not worth the return—again, we see expectancy theory in action.[61] We have to tailor the incentive program to the things that matter to each specific employee.[62]

EMPLOYEES CAN'T AFFECT THE DESIRED OUTCOMES. Frequently, we create rewards programs that promise a return to the employee, but we base the promised reward on something the employee can't do anything about. Think about company profit—what can the housekeeping staff (and many others in the organization) do about company profit? So if the desired outcome is increased profit, the employee doesn't know what to do to affect profitability.

EMPLOYEES DON'T KNOW HOW THEY ARE DOING. In order for an incentive plan to motivate, the employee has to know how they are doing compared to the desired outcomes.[63] If you know that you have to reach a certain production goal by the end of next week in order to get a desired reward and you are currently behind schedule, you will likely work harder to reach the goal. However, if you don't know where you stand, you may feel that everything is going well and won't increase your efforts. People have to know how they are doing compared to the program goals.

Challenges to Incentive Pay Systems

There are obviously going to be challenges associated with incentive systems. Employees do respond to incentives, but unfortunately, they don't always respond to incentives in the way we expect them to.[64] Questions covered in this section will discuss four of the major challenges: Do incentives work? Do incentives become entitlements? Will employees only do what they get paid for? And do extrinsic rewards decrease intrinsic motivation?

DO INCENTIVES REALLY WORK? The answer here is "It depends on who you ask." If you ask the CEO of a company that does incentive planning for other firms, they work great. If you ask some company leaders who have tried them, they don't work at all. For others, they work some of the time, but not always.[65] One of the things that we have found out over the past 20 years or so is that incentives don't work as well as we might have thought they would in at least some cases.[66]

There is some recent evidence that *group incentives* work significantly better than *individual incentives* when people in the organization *have to cooperate* or coordinate with one another in completing a set of tasks.[67] However, there is little clear evidence that supports *company-wide* applications of group incentives. One *HR Magazine* article noted that "company incentives do little to drive performance. They're the least effective motivational tool."[68] This is primarily because of the difficulty in establishing a link between the individual employee's actions and the success of the entire firm.

Does this mean companies shouldn't use incentives? No, but managers need to make sure that employees understand how their actions connect to the needed results. We have to help our people figure out how they can help the group or organization gain. If we can create the connection between how the employee acts and how they gain from it, we can create strong performance incentives. If not, the incentives will not work.

INCENTIVE TO ENTITLEMENT—AN EASY STEP. Remember from our discussion of bonuses that in order for an incentive to continue to motivate, it can't be considered an entitlement. An **entitlement** *is something that the employee feels they have a right to receive from the company.* A common example of an entitlement would be a weekly paycheck. Most employees feel that if they show up to work, the company *owes* them a paycheck. In academia, some students feel they deserve

Goodshoot RF/Goodshoot/Thinkstock

HR needs to create the right incentives to motivate employees to work hard.

WORK
APPLICATION 12-14

Select an organization that you know or work for. Assess how likely the factors that lead to failed incentives are to occur in the organization.

LO 12-7

Discuss the challenges associated with incentive systems.

Entitlement Something that the employee feels they have a right to receive from the company

WORK
APPLICATION 12-15

Select an organization that you know or work for. Do incentives really work at your organization, or would they if the firm offered them?

WORK
APPLICATION 12-16

Select an organization that you know or work for. Do employees in general have a sense of entitlement about pay and/or incentives? Is there a difference in feelings of entitlement between the younger and older workers?

WORK
APPLICATION 12-17

Select an organization that you know or work for. Do employees only do what they get paid for?

Extrinsic rewards Valued returns (such as incentive pay for performance) to the individual in exchange for doing something that the organization desires of the employee

LO 12-8

Identify the guidelines for creating motivational incentive systems.

a B for showing up. It doesn't matter whether they *did* anything or not! So we have the same challenge with regular pay and incentive compensation. However, an effective incentive makes the employees actually earn the reward based on their performance—it is not automatic like a salary. The current group of younger employees entering the workforce has been called *the entitlement generation* because of the expectation that they are entitled to certain perquisites just for becoming an employee.[69]

Consultants are seeing that in many cases, "what was intended to be 'pay for performance' in many organizations deteriorated into a bland set of rewards based on an entitlement mindset."[70] As soon as this happens, our incentive program ceases to motivate higher levels of performance. Incentive pay of any kind is going to be a significant portion of overall compensation costs in companies where it is used. In fact, it will almost always be at least a few percent of base pay and in some situations can go up to 100% of base pay or even more, so we have to ensure that we get something in return for the cost.

"DO ONLY WHAT GETS PAID FOR" SYNDROME. Another of the challenges associated with incentive programs is the tendency of people to only do what is measured and is paid for. In other words, our people will pay attention to the work that will get them the rewards that they desire. There is a lot of anecdotal evidence that this occurs. However, there is not much empirical evidence that incentive pay fails because of this syndrome. Besides, we have the same challenge with regular compensation. Remember, reinforcement theory notes that if we reward an individual for doing something, they are likely to continue to do that thing in the expectation that they will continue to receive a desired reward.

However, assuming that this might be a problem in some cases, one way to combat it is to make the incentive specific but make overall job performance a part of any variable pay program. The incentive causes the employees to focus on the specific goals that we need accomplished, but the performance component lets everyone know that they still have to do all of the other things that make the organization successful over the long term.

EXTRINSIC REWARDS MAY DECREASE INTRINSIC MOTIVATION. **Extrinsic rewards** *are valued returns (such as incentive pay for performance) to the individual in exchange for doing something that the organization desires of the employee.* Intrinsic motivation means that a person does something because they like it, it is interesting and personally satisfying, and they want to do it. More than 100 studies over many years have shown that there is a relationship between the application of extrinsic rewards and a decrease in intrinsic motivation.[71] In other words, when we get an external reward for doing something that we enjoy, the enjoyment level will go down. Some evidence says that this is due to the fact that we may feel like we are being *controlled* externally and then rebel against that control.

However, there is also evidence that in at least some cases, we can increase internalization of extrinsic motivators (cause the individual to believe that the rewards are for the "right" things), which lowers resistance to the external rewards.[72] We always need to be on the lookout for ways to show that the external motivators that we provide are good things for both the employee being rewarded and others who depend on the actions of the employee being rewarded, to increase this internalization process.

Guidelines for Creating Motivational Incentive Systems

So we now know that we have a number of factors that make incentive programs more or less successful. Anytime we are developing a variable pay plan, we have to consider what we need to do to make it work. What will make the system motivational to the workforce while also improving organization success overall? Exhibit 12-6 lists some guidelines that researchers have come up with over many years of analyzing incentive programs that can significantly increase the chances of success. Let's discuss our guidelines for creation of an effective incentive plan in a little more detail in this section.

WORK
APPLICATION 12-18

Select an organization that you know or work for. Do incentives decrease intrinsic motivation, or would they if the firm offered them?

EXHIBIT 12-6 GUIDELINES FOR CREATING MOTIVATIONAL INCENTIVE SYSTEMS

a. Base the system on organizational strategy and culture.
b. Provide incentives for all—managerial and nonmanagerial employees.
c. Make it understandable and clearly communicate the program and expected results.
d. Base the incentive on factors the individual or group can affect.
e. Make sure that you have SMART goals.
f. Clearly separate incentives from base pay.
g. Make the reward a significant piece of overall compensation.
h. Take great care in creating and administering the program.
i. Promptly provide any incentive awards.
j. Don't forget nonmonetary rewards.
k. Don't reward nonperformers.
l. Make the incentive program part of a comprehensive approach to managing people.

BASED ON ORGANIZATIONAL STRATEGY AND CULTURE. The incentive program must be based on the goals in the strategic plan—the direction of the organization.[73] Think back to when we discussed strategic HR in Chapter 2. We talked about how HR can drive people to do things for the organization that it needs to have done in order to reach its goals. One thing we can use to avoid creating the entitlement mentality that we just discussed is to avoid basing our reinforcement on a fixed period of time or a fixed number of actions by the employee. We need to base the reward on achieving specific and measurable goals and provide at least some reinforcement as soon

12-5 APPLYING **THE CONCEPT**

Effective Incentives

Identify each statement by the guideline it is violating using the letters (a) to (l) in Exhibit 12-6. You should read the explanations of each guideline before completing this application.

_____ 21. I went to the meeting to find out about the new incentive system, but I didn't understand what they were talking about.

_____ 22. I understand that if the price of the stock goes up next year, I can buy stock at today's lower price. But I don't see how my delivering mail can make any difference in the price of the stock.

_____ 23. What's the incentive for me? Management gets great bonuses every year and we do all the work and they don't give us anything.

_____ 24. How can we know if we are the best company in the sporting goods industry?

_____ 25. This system isn't fair to me. I was the top performer but Sam, who didn't even meet his quota, got the same bonus.

after the goal is achieved as is feasible. If the incentives are not driving our employees to work toward organizational goals, we won't reach those goals. One of the most common problems in incentive systems is picking an expedient goal that is easy to measure but doesn't aim at the strategic goals of the company.

Another thing that we need to keep in mind is to create both short-term and long-term goals for *all* organization members. Both short- and long-term incentives should be provided based on those goals at each level in the firm. This will both mix up the timing of the rewards provided to the employee and provide them with incentives to improve company performance over the long term.

We also need to make sure that the incentive program is consistent with the organizational culture.[74] A lot of organizational cultures are egalitarian—everyone expects that they will be compensated equally with others in similar positions. Many others are collectivist, meaning the group has a strong desire to work together. In an egalitarian culture, it will be difficult or impossible to provide different rewards to individuals, even if rewards are based on performance differences. In collectivist cultures, the group won't accept incentives that focus on the individual. So, culture must be taken into account in designing incentive systems.[75]

INCENTIVES FOR ALL. Any incentive program needs to provide performance incentives to all individuals involved in the process that is being targeted.[76] We can't just provide incentives to management, because management will attempt to force lower-level employees to perform so that the manager can get rewarded. This is a recipe for frustration and resistance by the line employees. But what if we only provide incentives for the line workers and not management? Management's job (at least a significant part of it) is to get obstacles out of the way so that line employees can do *their* jobs. If the manager has no incentive to move quickly to get obstacles out of the way, we just end up with frustrated employees who can't meet their incentive goals.

Can the incentive apply differentially? Yes, if one group's job is more important to reaching the goal, then it is OK to give them a differential incentive. However, everyone needs to be rewarded so that they have an incentive to work together.

UNDERSTANDABLE AND CLEARLY COMMUNICATED. Complexity is a part of many organizational environments in today's businesses. However, our incentive programs have to be set up in such a way that employees at every level of the firm can understand them. If people can't understand what is expected of them, there is no way that they will reach the goals that we set. In addition, even if the program is understandable, it has to be accurately communicated to everyone in the organization.[77] All of our employees need to know about the program: how to participate, what their goals are, any assistance that is available to help them meet those goals, how their performance ties in with that of others in the company, and any other pertinent information. Good incentive programs must be clearly and completely communicated to all the personnel affected by the program.[78]

BASED ON FACTORS THE TARGET CAN AFFECT. The incentive offered should be based on factors that the individual or group, whichever is the target of the incentive, can affect.[79] If it is an individual incentive, the individual employee should be able to modify their behavior to affect the outcome of the process, and the same goes for a group of employees. If the individual or group can see no connection between what they do and reaching the goal, they will most likely do nothing different than before the incentive was instituted.

SMART GOALS. Remember in Chapter 8 where we talked about goals having to be SMART—Specific, Measurable, Attainable, Relevant, and Time-based? SMART goals provide a clear link between performance and payout.[80] Here again, as with any valuable organizational goal, we have to ensure that our incentive program identifies the goals of the plan in SMART fashion. This is the only way that we can then accurately measure and reward our employees for goal attainment. So remember to use our *setting objectives* model: To + action verb + specific and measurable outcome + target date.

CLEARLY SEPARATE FROM BASE PAY. Base pay is almost always considered an entitlement by the employees in an organization. We utilize base pay to allow our workforce to meet their basic needs (Maslow's physiological, safety, and social needs). This base pay very rarely motivates additional actions on the part of our employees. Incentives need to be clearly separated from base pay to avoid creating the impression that they, too, are an entitlement. Employees need to understand that they only receive incentive rewards if they do something extraordinary.

A SIGNIFICANT PIECE OF OVERALL COMPENSATION. What is a "significant piece" of compensation? Compensation studies will tell you different things about what is considered significant.[81] A good recommendation would be at least 10% of overall pay and, in some cases, 20% or more. Why? Let's take a look at an example.

You work for XYZ Co. and are getting paid $40,000 a year. Your manager decides to give you a 2% bonus if you reach your goals this year, or $800. You reach your incentive goals at the end of the year, and it is now time to pay you. If we pay you a lump sum at the end of the year, we generally have to take out 25% for federal withholding taxes and may have to take out state tax as well, so your $800 just dropped to between $500 and $600. At a salary of $40,000 per year, if you are paid twice monthly, you would normally receive about $1,350 or so per paycheck, depending on the state in which you reside. How many of you would work really hard next year if you got a whopping $500, a little more than one third of 1 month's pay, as a bonus for meeting your goals the year before? To most of us, that would be an insignificant reward for meeting our goals for an entire year. Remember what we said when discussing merit pay earlier in the chapter: Merit pay is typically a very small percentage of the individual's total pay, which makes using it as a motivator for performance very difficult.

Alternatively, if we make your base pay $36,000 and provide a 10% incentive for reaching certain goals, you will receive around $2,600 after taxes—a sum that most people making $36,000 per year would consider significant. People need to feel that the reward is "significant" to them in order for it to motivate them.

TAKE GREAT CARE IN ADMINISTERING THE PROGRAM. Meticulously measure performance using multiple metrics and vigilantly calculate the rewards to be provided to persons who reach their incentive goals.[82] If the company owes an individual or group an incentive award based on reaching their goals, then we must make sure that it is paid. Set attainable standards and then measure them fairly, when and how they are supposed to be measured. Once performance is measured, reward those who attain the goals as soon as possible. If individuals or groups did not meet their goals, communicate that to them so that they know why they didn't get a reward.

Again, an example helps in understanding what might happen if we fail to be meticulous in our measuring and administration duties. Let's say we have 600 employees in our company and set some ambitious goals at the beginning of the year for the company and for each individual employee. As a company, we met our goals for the year, and we calculated whether or not each individual employee met their personal goals. But we miscalculated with one person. How fast will the word likely get around the company that we "cheated" that one employee? Via the employee grapevine, it will probably be known throughout the company in 2 days—possibly 1. This employee starts telling their friends that "the company cheated me and lied to me." And what will happen as soon as one person starts to complain? As soon as one person makes that claim, others will start to wonder whether or not they were treated fairly—*even though we were correct in calculating their individual payments*! Pretty soon, what was supposed to be a motivational program becomes a massive demotivator due to the fact that people begin to *perceive* that they may not have been treated fairly. We have to be meticulous in our management of any incentive program.

PROMPTLY APPLY ANY INCENTIVE AWARD. "Keep the time between the performance and reward as short as possible."[83] If the incentive is based on an annual goal, and we use a calendar year as our organizational fiscal year, our year ends in December and we should provide any incentive awards on the first payday in January, or even on December 31 if we already have results calculated. If incentives are calculated monthly, pay them at the end of the month. Why? We provide the reward to *reinforce* the employee's efforts that led to desired results. If you receive a reward 6 months after you do something, you don't really see the connection. If you don't see the connection, it does not reinforce your earlier actions.

DON'T FORGET NONMONETARY REWARDS. Remember from our discussion about praise and other nonmonetary recognition that not everyone is motivated by cash.[84] Nonmonetary rewards often work better than monetary rewards. Having a bit of time off to play with the company's resources, like **3M Company** provides, can be a huge incentive. 3M gives 15% of work time to employees to use the company's resources and labs and to just tinker around and see what they can come up with.[85] Post-it notes were created in just this way in 1974. A 3M employee was tired of bookmarks falling out of his books, so he used an adhesive that had been invented at 3M earlier (but considered a failure) and applied it to small pieces of paper. The incentive was in being *allowed* to be creative and avoid being bored. Incentives can include providing the ability to choose between work assignments, providing training and learning opportunities, allowing flexible schedules, providing extra paid time off, recognition at an awards ceremony, offers to present results to top management, having greater input into future incentive goals, and many others. We can use an on-site child care center, or a gym or lounge, as an incentive—for example, "If we reach a certain set of organizational goals by the end of the year, we will be able to build the child care center." To many people in today's workforce, this would be a significant incentive. However, to others, it may not be a reward at all. Remember that according to expectancy theory, we have to pay attention to significance.

DON'T REWARD NONPERFORMERS. When goals are not met, do not apply rewards.[86] It seems silly to have to say this, but in many cases, you will *want* to reward your employees, even when they don't quite meet the goals that were set. Why would this happen? Let's look at an example that will explain it.

Andy works for you and didn't quite meet the goals set for the incentive program at the end of the year. You are a good manager, and you saw Andy consistently come to work and work hard, but he just wasn't able to reach his goal. At the end of the year, you see that he didn't make it, but you know that Andy is a hard worker. So, you sit down and look at everyone in your department, and everyone except Andy met their goals. Then you think about how hard Andy tries and you say, "I know I saw him working all the time. I am just going to give the incentive payment to him anyway because I know that he works hard." Here again, how quickly will the word get around about Andy getting the reward even though he didn't meet his goals? Again, the communication grapevine will start working, and within 1 or 2 days everyone will know, because Andy is going to tell them.

Well, what will happen next time incentives are being calculated? Next time, maybe several workers miss their goals, and they tell you, "Boss, I worked my tail off, but I just couldn't reach my goals. But you gave Andy his incentive last time even though he missed his goal. You can go ahead and give it to me too, right?" You have succeeded in destroying your incentive program because you rewarded a nonperformer. Rewarding nonperformers just cannot be allowed if we want the incentive program to continue to work in the future.

There is, however, a way that we may be able to reward Andy, at least partially, but we have to identify it at the beginning of the program. We can create a series of progressively more difficult goals in our incentive program. This allows us to provide a minimal incentive for meeting goals that are just above a baseline and provide progressively more significant awards for meeting more difficult goals. This will let us reward Andy for going above the standard but not quite meeting an aggressive incentive goal. So, progressive or stair-step goals can help us to avoid rewarding people who don't meet the top-level, or most difficult, goals.

MAKE THE INCENTIVE PROGRAM PART OF A COMPREHENSIVE APPROACH TO MANAGING. Remember that incentives can create a "just do what you get paid for" mentality. So, as we noted earlier in this chapter, we "make the incentive specific but make overall job performance a part of any variable pay program." We can't create an incentive for every aspect of every job in most organizations, so we have to continue to evaluate and reward overall performance so that our employees know that they have to do all tasks successfully, even though only some have incentives directly attached to their performance. One easy way to do this is to provide a caveat in the incentive program that receipt of an overall performance appraisal of "Meets Expectations" or higher is required in order to be eligible for incentive rewards.

WORK
APPLICATION 12-19

Select an organization that you know or work for. In which two or three incentive pay guidelines is your organization strongest and weakest at following to ensure it effectively motivates employees?

EXECUTIVE COMPENSATION

No modern discussion of compensation is complete without at least touching on the topic of executive compensation practices. Executives drive organizational performance more than any other employees. The great debate over how much chief executive officers (CEOs) matter rages on.[87] CEOs like the late Steve Jobs of **Apple** have the power to make or break a company.[88] When he retired in August of 2011 and died shortly thereafter, Apple stock lost nearly a third of its market value (about $120 billion!) in a year.[89] Research clearly links managerial leadership to positive consequences for both the individual and organizations, including financial performance. Also, substantial evidence demonstrates that sound managerial leadership practice is critical to creating effective organizations.[90] So it makes sense that executives are well paid for their managerial and decision-making skills. But has executive pay gotten out of line? Let's take a brief look at executive compensation today.

LO 12-9

Discuss the issue of whether or not executive compensation is too high.

Too Much or Just Enough?

Charif Souki of **Cheniere Energy**—$142 million[91]

Larry Ellison of **Oracle**—$78 million[92]

Robert Iger of **Disney**—$37 million[93]

Rupert Murdoch of **21st Century Fox** and **News Corp.**—$26 million[94]

There are many cries in the business world today that executives are getting paid too much. In at least some cases, that certainly appears to be true based on the performance of their companies. But are executives generally paid too much, too little, or about right? In order to even attempt to answer such a question, we need to look at what executives are paid to do. If we were to ask you if anyone in a company *physically* produces enough products or services to make $1,000,000 or more in any given year, most of you would answer absolutely not. However, executives

There is an ongoing debate as to whether or not executives are overpaid.

 ESR

WORK
APPLICATION 12-20

Would you say the CEO of an organization you work(ed) for is overpaid, underpaid, or paid fairly for the contribution made to the firm?

LO 12-10

Identify the major provisions of the Dodd-Frank Act that affect executive compensation.

Golden parachutes Provision for executives who are dismissed from a merged or acquired firm of typically large lump sum payments on dismissal

are not paid to be production employees; they are paid to make decisions for the organization and to guide it toward its goals. In addition, the decisions that executives are paid to make are not easy decisions. Successful executive leadership requires a high level of inherent intelligence, knowledge, and skills to analyze so much information and significant experience in making decisions of similar types and consequences.

While many of us think that we could run a billion-dollar company, the reality is that very few individuals have the required skills and abilities to do so. Since labor is always at least partly priced based on supply and demand, and there are very few executives with the high-level skills necessary to run large firms, these individuals are always going to be worth quite a bit of money to the firm. And how about professional athletes' pay? Some of them make more for sitting on the bench than some CEOs, especially of smaller firms.

Think of it this way. If you were the owner of a company and had hired somebody to lead the company throughout the year, and at the end of the year this person had made you $10 billion (that's 10,000 times a million!) in profit, would you be willing to pay them $10 million (0.1% of the profit)? Most of us would have no problem paying someone this much money if they made us $10 billion. They deserve a piece of the pie they helped create.[95]

However, this is not to say that there have not been some serious excesses in executive pay in the past several years, especially when CEO pay has increased while employees were taking pay cuts and getting laid off.[96] The company is not acting ethically or in a socially responsible manner in this situation because it is harming a large number of stakeholders (including employees and shareholders and maybe others) in order to reward a single stakeholder, or a few, in the executive suites. Actions such as this are certain to affect the market value of the firm as soon as they become publicly known. One result of excessive executive compensation is recent federal legislation on executive compensation—the Dodd-Frank Wall Street Reform and Consumer Protection Act.

The Dodd-Frank Wall Street Reform and Consumer Protection Act of 2010

One of the outcomes of both perceived and actual excesses in executive pay was the Dodd-Frank Wall Street Reform and Consumer Protection Act (Dodd-Frank Act). The Dodd-Frank Act placed some significant limits on executive pay in public corporations and also added some new requirements for both reporting of compensation and shareholder involvement with executive compensation.[97]

SHAREHOLDER "SAY ON PAY" AND "GOLDEN PARACHUTE" VOTES. Among the most significant provisions of the act is that shareholders must be allowed to vote on compensation packages for their executive officers at least once every 3 years. This provision is called "say on pay." While the vote is nonbinding, it can still put pressure on executives to maintain compensation in line with organizational performance.

Shareholders also have a vote on what's called a "golden parachute" for executives. **Golden parachutes** *provide executives who are dismissed from a merged or acquired firm with typically large lump sum payments on dismissal.* This tool is typically used to discourage a takeover of the firm, because the cost of the takeover becomes much higher due to the high payout to these executives.

EXECUTIVE COMPENSATION RATIOS. Other provisions in Dodd-Frank include a requirement that every public company disclose the total compensation of the CEO and the total median compensation of all employees and provide a ratio of these two figures.[98] A 2013 survey on CEO pay found that in S&P 500 firms, the CEO–to–median employee pay ratio was 204 to 1, up 20% since 2009.[99] It would be very easy to argue that this pay ratio is significantly out of line with performance, though even the smallest of these firms have a market capitalization of about $2.5 to $3 billion.[100] However, we should also note that research shows that the *average* CEO pay in *all* public and private companies was only 5.4 times that of the average employee in the United States in 2010.[101]

Another provision of Dodd-Frank is that all public firms will be required to provide information on the relationship between executive compensation and the *total shareholder return* of the company each year. This will allow shareholders to more easily evaluate the performance of firms in which they hold stock. The act also requires that public companies establish policies to "claw back" incentives in certain cases if the company has to restate financial information that is detrimental to the firm's value.[102] In other words, if the company paid out an executive incentive based on its financial statements and then had to disclose later that those statements were not accurate, company policy would require that any incentives paid out to the executives be given back to the company.

Executive pay is obviously not a simple issue. However, there is significant evidence that at least in some industries, executive pay has gotten out of line with organizational performance.[103] As a result of this realization, and also due to new legislation placing limits on organizational compensation for executives, companies have to be more diligent both in creating and in managing their executive compensation packages.

Executive Incentives

As with any other type of incentive, executive incentives are supposed to create motivation to perform for the organization in certain ways. Executive incentives should be designed to cause the executive receiving them to make decisions that will benefit the organization over both the short and the long term. We need the executive to act as an impartial "agent" for the organization.[104] An agent is someone who acts on the owners' (shareholders) behalf. *Agency theory* says that agents will act in the way that provides the most benefit to them and not the owners, unless we provide the agent with incentives to act in ways that help the owners of the firm. The way to do this is to align the benefits that go to the agent with benefits that accrue to the firm. This is what executive incentives should be designed to do.

What are some of the common incentives that are used to create this alignment? The first and probably most common is the stock incentive.[105] We noted earlier that various types of stock incentives are available as group incentives. These same incentives—primarily stock grants and stock options—are used in executive compensation for basically the same reason. They are supposed to cause the executive to act to increase the value of the company over time, because if this is done, the executive's stock becomes more valuable.

Long-term bonuses attached to company performance goals are another popular incentive for executives.[106] These also help to focus the "agent" executive on goals that will improve the value of the company over several years. In addition to stock awards, executives may be paid retention bonuses for each year they continue in their positions, and they are often paid bonuses tied to either short- or long-term company performance.

In addition to incentive packages, executives generally receive compensation in the form of perquisites or "perks." **Perquisites** *are extra financial benefits usually provided to top employees in many businesses.* While perks are not technically

WORK APPLICATION 12-21

Would you say the Dodd-Frank Act will help, hurt, or have no effect on an organization you work or have worked for?

SHRM

K:A15
Motivation Theories: Equity, Reinforcement, Agency Theories

Perquisites Extra financial benefits usually provided to top employees in many businesses

incentive pay (they are generally classed as benefits), they do serve to entice top-level executives to consider accepting jobs within an organization in some cases. Common perks include such things as vehicle allowances, memberships in various clubs, the use of company aircraft, tax assistance in various forms, home-buying or selling assistance, security systems, and many others.[107] While the prevalence of perks continues to decline according to Hay Group research, you need to be aware of executive perks and understand that they are still a common component of executive compensation systems.

Short-term Versus Long-term

For many years now, executive incentives have been moving toward more long-term options and fewer short-term payments in order to force the executives to look at the health of the firm over many years.[108] In 2013, long-term incentives made up about one third of all executive compensation. Even though this is the case, there are still many short-term incentives being used by firms.

Most short-term incentives are in the form of bonuses for one or a combination of several company performance measures. These bonuses are (or *should* be) designed to focus executive behavior on managing performance measures that need immediate managerial attention. For example, if company labor costs are out of line with industry competitors, we could provide 10% of CEO base pay as a bonus for lowering per unit labor costs by 7% over 1 year. If workers' compensation premiums have tripled in the past 3 years due to increases in lost-time accidents, we might offer a 12% bonus for improving workplace safety (as measured by OSHA reports of lost-time accidents) by 3%. These bonuses would be designed to focus the CEO's attention on specific problems.

In contrast to short-term incentives, most long-term incentives are made in the form of stock awards or options.[109] Of course, there are other long-term incentives, such as the excess contributions to retirement plans and longevity bonuses mentioned above, but in general, at least for publicly traded companies, long-term incentives tend to be stock based. And there is a relatively new practice with long-term incentives in many companies—the "claw back" provision. The Dodd-Frank Act required this in some cases, but companies are extending the claw back to instances that are not subject to the law's provisions. Long-term incentives are designed to cause the executive to pay attention to how their decisions will affect the company and its profitability over the course of multiple years, not over the course of a single year.

The Goal of Executive Compensation

So what is the overall goal of executive compensation? Remember that we want to create a system that aligns the behavior of the executive (agent) with the interests of the owners of the firm. The best way to do this is to use a combination approach of short- and long-term incentives to focus on both the immediate future and long-term success of the organization.

One way companies are making the attempt to better align executive compensation with organizational performance is through the use of performance "scorecards."[110] The use of performance scorecards came about partly as the result of the 2008–2009 bank crisis in the United States. At least part of the crisis was blamed on CEOs who were being rewarded for short-term organizational performance. In a 2010 survey, 68% of the companies that responded had created performance scorecards that measured success of the firm in both financial and nonfinancial terms and rewarded senior executives based on this scorecard.[111] While it is still too early to tell whether this approach will work, it is at least an attempt to put a longer-term focus on executive compensation.

TRENDS AND ISSUES IN HRM

In this chapter's trends and issues section, we are going to explore the ethical questions surrounding executive compensation, the heavy reliance on incentives to perform in entrepreneurial organizations, and how incentive pay can cause unethical actions on the part of managers and employees.

Ethics of Executive Compensation

There is a lot in the news about out-of-control executive pay, and the US Congress and the president have even weighed in on the issue in various forms. Congress has passed a series of bills, including the Dodd-Frank Wall Street Reform and Consumer Protection Act (mentioned in the body of the chapter), and the president has used time in a number of speeches to discuss the creation of government limits on executive pay, specifically in government contractors. Some people are recommending a statutory limit on executive pay based on either median firm compensation or lowest-paid-employee compensation. Let's take a look at some of the issues.

The first thing that we need to remember is our review in Chapter 11 of how the bottom is set for a pay level—*labor-market competition*. We have to set the bottom of the level at a point where the available labor supply will be willing to take the job. What is the available labor supply for CEOs who can manage a multi-billion dollar company? In fact, there are fewer than 2,000 firms in the world with more than a billion dollars in sales in 2013.[112] This means that there are around 2,000 people out of 7 billion on Earth who are currently billion-dollar CEOs, a 1:3.5 million ratio. Even if we assume there are at least as many who *could* do the job (which is unlikely), we would still have a ratio of well over 1 in a million. So the labor pool is extremely small.

Second, we want to look at what billion-dollar CEOs make in a year. The arguable king of compensation in 2013 was Larry Ellison of **Oracle**. Mr. Ellison received direct compensation (not including previously awarded stock options) of $78.4 million.[113] Oracle's revenue was $37.9 billion and its profit was $11.1 billion.[114] So Mr. Ellison received compensation of 0.2% of revenue or 0.7% of company profit. This means that the shareholders received benefits in the form of 99.3% of company profits, or $11 billion (rounded). Looking at the absolute compensation of Mr. Ellison, most people would say it is out of reason. However, looking at it in light of the money he made for shareholders, would you consider this to be an ethical use of company funds, or would you be opposed to his compensation if you owned stock in the company?

Should government legislate levels of compensation in companies? After all, this is still $78 million that could have gone to other employees or shareholders. Some have tried, with limited results. California introduced legislation that would penalize companies with "excessive" executive compensation by taxing the company at a higher rate. Under the proposal, Oracle's state income tax would have increased from 8.84% in 2013 to 13%. Since the company made $11.1 billion in taxable profit, this would have added about $460 million to its state tax bill for that year. Rhode Island has taken a different tack, proposing differential treatment of companies who are vying for state contracts based on their pay structure. The state would give preference to companies who had a maximum ratio between the pay of their highest-paid employees and their lowest-paid employees of 32. For example, if the lowest-paid worker made $10 per hour, the highest-paid could make a maximum of about $700,000 annually, or the company would be penalized in contracting with the state.[115]

In other cases, such as in New York, courts have struck down state regulations that limited executive pay.[116] At the federal level, a 2013 attempt by the president and his cabinet to limit executive pay in Department of Defense contracts was excluded from final legislation introduced in Congress by the House Armed Services Committee.[117]

So, *should* governments intercede in the market for compensation of highly skilled executives? That depends on the philosophy of the person answering the question. However, government has an extremely weak record trying to change market forces in the past—from alcohol prohibition to gun sales. Here too, government has intervened in the past only to see unintended consequences. For instance, in the wake of the 2007–08 recession, the Treasury Department set a cap on cash bonuses and certain incentive pay at financial institutions that had received Troubled Asset Relief Program (TARP) funds. The result? *The next year*, base pay in the form of salaries went up by as much as 500% to compensate for lost bonuses.[118]

Entrepreneurial Organizations Rely on Incentives to Perform

Why do good, talented individuals choose to work for entrepreneurial organizations instead of established companies? By doing so, the individual increases their personal financial risk but, in turn, expects to have the *opportunity* for greater rewards. It appears that they make a conscious decision to trade security for a significant potential payoff. Most top performers who leave big companies for new start-up tech companies are typically taking a 20% to 40% cut in their base salary in hopes of securing a big payday later, usually through ESOP and/or stock options.[119]

Entrepreneurial start-ups have always had fewer slack resources than larger firms. As a result, most entrepreneurial firms tend to have their employees carry out a much broader set of duties within the company, and they need their employees to be talented in multiple areas and driven to perform. In this situation, it makes sense that entrepreneurial firms would need to provide strong incentive pay in order to get strong performance on the part of their employees, and this seems to be the case.

The preferred method of incentive compensation for people who are willing to take a risk with entrepreneurial firms appears to be equity-based incentives in the form of ESOPs or stock options. And entrepreneurs should take note that research shows a relationship between equity incentives and performance of the start-up firm.[120] Equity incentives in the form of stock in a new venture have the same advantages that they do in more established firms, plus they have additional value.

Remember that in large businesses, the individual employee may have difficulty figuring out how their work affects the firm overall. But in new and smaller firms, it is generally easier to see how one person's actions can affect the results of the organization. This allows us to provide the desired link between what the individual employee does and the results (and rewards) that they desire. So entrepreneurs need to understand the value of incentive rewards in start-up organizations and learn to use them to their advantage.

Incentives to Act Unethically?

How did we get into this mess? What caused the greatest recession of the last 80 years? That is what a lot of people were asking when the financial crisis hit home in the United States in 2008–2009. Well, at least part of it was caused by incentive programs. Recall that any incentive program is designed to cause people to be motivated to act in a certain way because they want a desired reward. So, how did incentive pay contribute to the financial crisis in the first decade of the 21st century?

Mortgage incentives both to individuals looking to buy homes and to banks and other financial firms created a "housing bubble" around 2005–2006. Mortgage brokers encouraged, and in some cases even coached, individuals to apply for loans that were of greater than normal risk because of historically low interest rates and because the brokers received incentive bonuses for providing the loans.[121] Financial firms have always used large incentive awards to encourage their employees to act in ways that create large commissions and cause higher levels of financial assets to come under their control.

This was the case in many large banks, and as a result, they made riskier and riskier loans to individual mortgage applicants. This was assisted by relaxation of documentation requirements at the federal level, but it was driven primarily by the bonus payments attached to "writing" the mortgages. Many executives in the large international banks also had their annual incentive bonuses based on assets under their control instead of based on long-term increases in the value of the firm. This put further pressure on employees to write loans that increased the value of the assets under the bank's control.

While this is certainly not the only reason for the financial problems that most of the world faced at the end of the first decade of the 21st century, it is without a doubt one of the contributing factors to the meltdown. Bonus payments created a situation where rational individuals acted unethically because of the incentives they received for taking such actions. Incentive payments have the potential to lead to such unethical actions, so we always have to guard against them when we design our incentive programs.

• • • CHAPTER SUMMARY

12-1 Discuss the major reasons why companies use incentive pay.

Incentives are necessary because they give us the opportunity to recognize our best people and provide us with flexibility to give them greater rewards than average or low performers. Variable pay systems also shift some of the company risk to the employee when economic downturns affect our businesses. Companies don't have to pay out some incentives if they are tied to organizational performance and the organization underperforms because of problems in the economy. Finally, incentive pay helps us achieve strategic goals, assuming that our incentives are aimed at accomplishing these objectives.

12-2 Identify the advantages and disadvantages of individual incentives.

Individual incentives make it easy to evaluate each individual employee; they provide the ability to choose rewards that match employee desires; they promote a link between performance and results; and they may motivate less productive workers to work harder. Disadvantages include the fact that many jobs have no direct outputs, making it hard to identify individual objectives; we may motivate undesirable behaviors; there is a higher record-keeping burden than in group incentives; and individual rewards may not fit in the organizational culture.

12-3 Identify the advantages and disadvantages of group incentives.

Group incentives help foster more teamwork; they broaden the individual's outlook by letting them

see how they affect others. They also require less supervision and are easier to develop than individual incentives. Disadvantages include the potential for social loafing; the possibility that we will discount individual efforts and output; the fact that outstanding performers may lessen their efforts; and the potential for group infighting.

12-4 Briefly discuss options for individual incentives.

Individual incentives can come in many forms. The first form that we discussed was bonus payments, lump sum payments for reaching a goal that don't change base pay. Commissions can also be used as incentives for sales. Commissions also only occur based on certain actions on the part of the employee—they don't add to base pay. Merit pay is different. Merit pay is based on past performance (appraisals) and *does* change base pay in future pay periods. However, merit pay is frequently too small to be considered a significant reward. Piecework and standard hour plans also work as incentives for speed of production. Under piecework, the employee gets paid for each item produced, and under a standard hour plan, they are paid based on a standard time allowed to perform an action. Both plans may give rise to quality issues if not monitored. Finally, there are recognition and other nonmonetary rewards, which are very powerful incentives if used in the right ways.

12-5 Briefly discuss options for group-based incentives.

Group incentives are mostly based on organizational gains of some kind or on gaining an ownership stake in the company. First, there is profit sharing, where if the company's profits increase over the course of a year, the employees share in those increased profits. However, in some cases, gainsharing may be better because profit can be easily manipulated. Gainsharing is based on other organizational gains that are more difficult to manipulate, such as revenue changes, lost-time accidents, or lower per-unit labor costs. If the company gains in these areas, it saves money, and some of the savings is shared with employees. ESOPs are the first stock (ownership) option, where at least part of the company's stock is provided to the employees over time. Other stock incentives are stock ownership awards or stock options, where employees earn stock by meeting goals.

12-6 **Discuss the major reasons why incentive plans fail.**

Incentive plans usually fail for one or more of five reasons. The first is bad management—managers have to manage the incentive program, and if they fail to do so, employees won't trust the program. Second, programs may be so complex that people can't figure them out, so they don't change their behavior. Third, plans may not really increase the potential rewards available or the rewards may not appear significant to the employees. The fourth problem is that in a lot of cases, employees can't affect the desired outcomes by their actions. Finally, in many "reward" programs, employees never know how they are doing, so they don't know whether or not to modify their behavior to change their output.

12-7 **Discuss the challenges associated with incentive systems.**

There is still some concern that, at least in some cases, incentives don't work. The evidence shows that group incentives do work better than individual incentives when cooperation is required in a work group, but in general it is difficult to tie employee actions to company success. If we fail to do that, incentives will not work. There is also an issue of incentives becoming an expected part of employee compensation—an entitlement. If this occurs, the incentive no longer motivates changed behaviors, which defeats the purpose of the incentive. Third, external incentives may act to lower a person's internal motivation to do something because they "like it." This may mean that we actually lower their performance instead of raising it when we apply incentives. Finally, there is the problem of people only focusing on what they are receiving incentive pay to do. They may neglect the rest of their job.

12-8 **Identify the guidelines for creating motivational incentive systems.**

1. Base all incentive programs on the company strategy and culture.

2. Make sure that the incentive program has some rewards for everyone—nobody should be left out.

3. Make the incentive program easy to understand and clearly communicate it to all involved.

4. Base the incentive on factors that the individual or group can affect.

5. Use SMART goals—Specific, Measurable, Attainable, Relevant, and Time-based.

6. Clearly separate incentives from base pay to avoid the question of entitlement.

7. Make the reward a significant piece of overall compensation.

8. Take great care in program administration to provide rewards in the amount owed, when they are owed.

9. Promptly apply any incentive award—immediate reinforcement works much better than delayed reinforcement.

10. Don't forget to use nonmonetary rewards too—not everyone is motivated by cash.

11. Don't reward nonperformers or you risk ruining the incentive system.

12. Make the incentive program part of a comprehensive approach to managing—pay attention to the entire performance of employees, not just specific behaviors tied to incentive payments.

12-9 **Discuss the issue of whether or not executive compensation is too high.**

There is no doubt that in some cases, executive compensation has gotten out of control. There is evidence that at the highest levels, it can be more than 200 times the average employee's pay. However, research shows that overall executive pay only runs about 5.4 times the pay of an average employee in most firms, which means that as a general rule, executive pay is probably not out of line, considering the pressure on executives to perform at the highest level all the time.

12-10 **Identify the major provisions of the Dodd-Frank Act that affect executive compensation.**

Dodd-Frank requires that shareholders be allowed a "say on pay," where they vote on executive compensation packages at least once every 3 years. Shareholders also have a vote on "golden parachute" payments to executives who are forced out of the company because of a merger or acquisition. In addition, every public company is required to disclose the total compensation of the CEO and provide a ratio of CEO pay to the average pay in the company. Finally, all public companies are required to provide information on executive compensation compared to the company's total shareholder returns every year to allow shareholders to evaluate the performance of companies in which they own stock.

12-11 Define the key terms found in the chapter margins and listed following the Chapter Summary.

Complete the Key Terms Review to test your understanding of this chapter's key terms.

• • • KEY TERMS

bonus	golden parachutes	perquisites
commission	group incentives	profit sharing programs
entitlement	individual incentives	social loafers
extrinsic rewards	merit pay	variable pay

• • • KEY TERMS REVIEW

Complete each of the following statements using one of this chapter's key terms.

1. _____ is compensation that depends on some measure of individual performance or results in order to be awarded.

2. _____ reinforce performance of a single person with a reward that is significant to that person.

3. _____ provide reinforcement for actions of more than one individual within the organization.

4. _____ avoid providing their maximum effort in group settings because it is difficult to pick out individual performance.

5. _____ is a lump sum payment, typically given to an individual at the end of a period.

6. _____ is a payment typically provided to a salesperson for selling an item to a customer.

7. _____ is a program to reward top performers with increases in their annual wage that carry over from year to year.

8. _____ provide a portion of company proceeds over a specific period of time (usually either quarterly or annually) to the employees of the firm through a bonus payment.

9. _____ is something that the employee feels they have a right to receive from the company.

10. _____ are valued returns (such as incentive pay for performance) to the individual in exchange for doing something that the organization desires of the employee.

11. _____ provide executives who are dismissed from a merged or acquired firm with typically large lump sum payments on dismissal.

12. _____ are extra financial benefits usually provided to top employees in many businesses.

• • • COMMUNICATION SKILLS

The following critical-thinking questions can be used for class discussion and/or for written assignments to develop communication skills. Be sure to give complete explanations for all answers.

1. Do you think that incentive programs can really work to align the company's goals with the employees' goals? Why or why not?

2. Would you rather be given the opportunity to receive incentives based on individual performance or group performance? Does it depend on the situation? Why?

3. As a manager, would you rather judge your employees' performance on an individual basis or as part of a group? Why?

4. Have you ever been a "social loafer" in a group? If so, why did you not put out your best effort? What could the group or the company have done to limit your social loafing?

5. Have you ever seen an incentive program that didn't work because management didn't monitor and adjust the program? What could have been done differently?

6. What level of base pay do you think is really necessary in order for people to pay attention to an incentive program—5%? 10%? More than that? Why did you choose your answer?

7. Do you feel that merit pay programs would cause you to work hard, knowing that the average merit award is only between 1% and 2%? If not, how big would they need to be to cause you to pay attention?

8. Would you rather work on a commission basis if you were in sales, or would you rather have a salary—or a combination of both? Why?

9. How would you monitor quality in a piece-rate program to assemble AM-FM radios from components?

10. Do nonmonetary rewards ever motivate you? Why do you think you answered the way that you did?

11. Would you personally rather participate in a profit sharing plan or a gainsharing plan? Why?

12. Do you think incentive programs in general really work? Why or why not?

13. Which of the 12 guidelines for creating incentive systems is the most important in your mind? Why did you choose this one?

14. If you were a compensation consultant to a company, how would you recommend it provide incentives to the CEO and other executives? Why?

15. Is the Dodd-Frank Act a good or bad idea? Why?

• • • CASE 12-1 REALTOR REWARD PLANS GONE HAYWIRE

Frank is the lead broker at the real estate firm that is located in one large city. The company has a nationally known real estate training program that costs $2,000 to attend. The program motivates real estate agents to sell more, gives tips on how to get leads, and recruits more agents to Frank's brokerage firm.

Each real estate agent in his firm grosses a 3% commission with each transaction involved with buying or selling a house. After the broker's cut, most agents net a commission of 2.1% with each transaction.

Frank's motivation is to build his training program and the size of his brokerage firm by adding real estate agents. To do so, he decided to provide his real estate agents with some incentives.

At noon on the first Monday of each month, agents sign up for four hours of floor time for the month via computer. Floor time at the downtown office allows each agent to be the sole person to accept phone calls, answer emails, or visit with walk-ins to get possible listings and generate more business. Floor time occurs from 6 a.m. to 10 p.m. each day. Agents love floor time so much that by noon each Monday sign-up day, all floor times for the month are taken.

There are other ways to get real estate leads such as contacting people who have de-listed their houses or are showing "For Sale by Owner" signs in front of their houses. But floor time in this firm accounts for a third of all leads.

Here is the new incentive policy:

Realtors can receive up to four hours of floor time per month if they have had a transaction in the last three months.

Realtors receive one additional hour of floor time per month for exceeding three transactions in a three-month period. If there are four transactions in a three-month period, Realtors receive one additional hour. If there are five transactions, Realtors receive two additional hours. Six transactions lead to three hours and so on.

Realtors receive one additional hour of floor time per month for referring one person to Frank's training program. They receive two hours for two people, three hours for three people, and so on.

The system worked well for two months after initiation of the program. On the third month, floor time ran out. Agents who had rights to floor time but could not get it were promised extra floor time the next month. The real estate firm added 16 real estate agents (while losing only two) and brought in 18 agents to the training program due to referrals from other agents. The superstar real estate agent Trina was involved with nine real estate transactions during the three-month period.

Frank decided to change the standard one week before Realtors could sign up for the next floor time. Realtors can now receive up to four hours of floor time per month if they have had a transaction in the last two months (effective next sign-up). All other aspects of the incentive program will continue.

Stacey has been a Realtor with Frank's brokerage firm for the last 15 years. She had been on vacation in February and was gone in late March, so she did not get the email on the new incentive policy. She thought she could sign up for floor time because she had a transaction in the last three months. She went on the computer to sign up for floor time as usual on Monday, April 3, at noon. She was locked out. The computer said she had insufficient transactions over the last two months.

Stacey immediately called Frank at 12:05 complaining that she couldn't sign up for floor time. Frank said that she should have been keeping up with all email correspondence from the firm. She said it wouldn't have made a difference. "I went on vacation knowing I was safe for floor time. Now you surprised me. The firm is going to get bigger and bigger, and it is only going to get tougher to get floor time."

She was disgusted by the fact that her friend Trina received 20 hours of floor time in April. The incentive plan was also unfair to newcomers who get no floor time. Stacey said, "Trina is a machine. She has a staff that helps her get sales. She even hired a person to find Realtors to go to your training seminars. How can I compete against Trina who will capture all the floor time in the firm?"

Stacey also wondered about the training seminars. She got into the business of real estate to sell houses, not seminars.

Frank stated that he wants to give the spoils to those in the firm who produce the most. Trina happens to be one of the most productive Realtors in the city and state. Trina also nets 2.5% with each transaction because she passes the magical $3 million threshold each year. Besides, said Frank, floor time is only a small piece of the pie.

Questions

1. What were Frank's strategic purposes for the incentive plan? Did the incentive plan accomplish his purposes? Why or why not?

2. Which incentive option is Frank choosing?

3. Do you think that high-level performers should get the bulk of the rewards in an organization, or should the rewards be meted out in a more egalitarian fashion?

4. Let's say Stacey represents most of the Realtors of the firm. How could Frank have improved the cooperative development of incentives with Stacey prior to incentive initiation?

5. Given Frank's strategic purposes, what alternative incentive plans would be appropriate for this real estate firm? Consider incentive plans mentioned in the chapter.

Case created by Gundars Kaupins, Boise State University

• • • CASE 12-2 BARCLAYS BONUS BANK: ROBBING PETER TO PAY PAUL

Barclays is a London-based multinational banking company that employs 140,000 employees. The company's revenue drastically decreased in 2012 ($53 billion), with a year-end deficit of $1.7 million. Later in 2012, Anthony Jenkins was appointed the new CEO in order to turn things around so as to regain the trust of investors and therein increase the profitability of the firm. In 2013, Barclays did achieve a positive net income of $890 million with sales growth of over 9%, yet stockholders demanded far greater results.[122] Why did the bank experience so huge a downturn, and what did Jenkins do to try to turn the bank around quickly?

One way a bank can boost profits is by selling more financial products and services, including new bank accounts, credit cards, life insurance, financial advising services, or mortgages to existing customers—in other words, cross-selling. In order to cross-sell these products and services, banks require employees with skills in promotion and direct marketing. Banks, not unlike other firms, use individual performance-based bonuses and commissions to reinforce customer cross-selling. This type of incentive pay increases employee motivation and positively impacts sales performance.[123]

Historically Barclays was productive in cross-selling its products to its customers until the firm initiated employee pay cuts in 2012 in order to generate more short-term profit. In return, Barclays started losing its most valuable employees, even at senior-level positions. Newly appointed CEO Jenkins decided to increase sales force salaries in 2013, but the plan failed to increase profits to desired levels. These actions came on the heels of government investigations of the bank's possible manipulation of interest and foreign exchange rates.[124]

Watching the most skilled employees leave was no longer acceptable to Jenkins. In response to low profits and returns, Jenkins felt the need to take more radical actions in the first quarter of 2014 while bearing in mind the long-term interests of the shareholders. In order to increase performance and keep the best employees, compensation had increased to more competitive levels. In early 2014, the median amount of granted incentives was around $30,000 for its 130,000 employees,[125] funded by a 10% increase in the bonus bank. The pool of funds reached $4 billion by the end of 2014.[126]

These increased incentives did not come without a price tag. In order to generate sustainable returns to shareholders and satisfy the board of directors, Jenkins decided he had to lay off employees—perhaps the hardest decision he ever had to make. More than 10,000 employees were going to be laid off to fund the bonus pool. The British government was quite concerned about such massive layoffs and suggested that the situation could be better managed by deferring the bonuses. Jenkins rejected the proposed deferral plan since employees would not receive their bonus for another 10 years, a ludicrous amount of time to ask employees to wait. Timely bonuses and incentives were essential to motivate cross-selling products for Barclays, and as long as Barclays properly motivated its sales force, the firm would generate higher profits—profits it could later use to rehire some of its former employees.[127]

Time will tell whether Jenkins's decision to fund the bonus pool rather than keep 10,000 employees was the right one.[128] Jenkins, in light of all of the firings, declined his own bonus from the board of directors in 2013, just as he did in 2012. Some might argue it was a noble gesture to refuse a bonus of $4.4 million, although it would not have had a noticeable impact on Barclays's bottom line.

Questions

1. The British government took the position that saving 10,000 jobs and deferring employee incentive pay was more important than immediate extrinsic reinforcement of sales force performance. How do the notions of entitlement and social loafing possibly explain the government's position?

2. Individual performance-based bonuses and commissions are one form of incentive pay. Might group and/or organizational incentive pay systems have achieved similar results for Barclays?

3. What other forms of individual incentive pay might Barclays have utilized? Which one of these plans might have saved the jobs lost to fund the bonus bank?

4. Develop a preliminary individual performance-based incentive plan that you think best suits cross-selling. Why?

5. Given your answer to question 4, develop a preliminary appraisal system for product cross-selling. How might this system be different if the incentive plan included group and organizational incentives?

6. Although Jenkins refused his bonuses in 2012 and 2013, as the CEO, he would have a comprehensive compensation package. What other incentives might Jenkins be entitled to beyond his annual bonus?

Case created by Herbert Sherman, PhD and Theodore Vallas, Department of Management Sciences, Long Island University School of Business, Brooklyn Campus

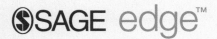

Sharpen your skills with SAGE edge at edge.sagepub.com/lussierhrm2e

SAGE edge for students provides a personalized approach to help you accomplish your coursework goals in an easy-to-use learning environment.

••• SKILL BUILDER 12-1 CALCULATING INDIVIDUAL INCENTIVES

Objective

To develop your skill at calculating incentive pay

Skills

The primary skills developed through this exercise are as follows:

1. *HR management skills*—Technical and business skills

2. *SHRM 2013 Curriculum Guidebook*—K: Total rewards

Assignment

Complete the math for the following six incentive programs.

1. **Bonus.** You have a salary of $46,000 per year, and you get a 7% bonus at year end. (1) How much is your bonus, and (2) what is the premium percentage on your annual salary?

2. **Commission.** You are an independent real estate agent in a rural area in the South, and you get a 5% commission on every house you sell. Your monthly expenses are around $10,000. This month you sold two houses: one for $168,000 and the other for $116,000. (1) How much revenue did you earn this month? (2) What was your profit for the month? (3) If this was an average month, what would be your profit for the year?

3. **Merit Pay.** You are the top performer in your department, so you are getting a 2% merit raise over the 2% that everyone else will get. (1) How much is your merit pay if your current salary is $35,000? (2) What is the merit pay premium percentage on your annual salary of $35,000? (3) What will your total pay be for next year? (4) What is the total pay premium percentage for next year?

4. **Straight Piece-Rate.** You make car parts. You get paid $1.10 for every part you make. This week you made 423 parts. (1) What is your pay for the week? (2) The estimated average pay is $450, so how much more or less than average did you make? (3) What is the premium percentage?

5. **Differential Piece-Rate.** You sell cell phones and phone service contracts in a small rural town. You are paid a salary of $7.50 per hour for a 40-hour week—$300 or $1,350 for the (180-hour) month. You also get paid $8 for every phone you sell in excess of 5 for the month. This month you sold 15. (1) What is your total pay for the month? (2) What is your premium if the average pay is $1,400 per month? (3) What is your premium percentage over the average?

6. **Standard Hour.** You rebuild transmissions. The standard rate is 6 hours each. You are paid $25 per standard hour. During this 40-hour week, you rebuilt 8 transmissions. (1) What is your pay for the week? (2) What is your premium for the week, and (3) what is your premium over the standard as a percentage?

• • • SKILL BUILDER 12-2 DEVELOPING A COMPENSATION PLAN WITH AN INCENTIVE

Objective

To develop a better understanding of creating motivational incentives

Skills

The primary skills developed through this exercise are as follows:

1. *HR management skills*—Technical, conceptual and design, and business skills
2. *SHRM 2013 Curriculum Guidebook*—K: Total rewards

After a few years of selling new cars, you managed to get the funding to start your own small new car dealership as a sole proprietorship. Your starting staff of 10 employees will be as follows:

- **You** are the **owner manager** and will oversee everything. You will also be the **sales manager** and do some selling.
- **Sales staff.** Three salespeople report directly to you.

- **Service and parts manager.** You will have one person supervise the mechanics and detailer.
- **Mechanics.** Three mechanics will work on the cars.
- **Detailer.** One person will clean the cars, help out the mechanics, and work in parts.
- **Office staff.** Two people will answer phones, greet customers, make up the bills and collect money from sales and service, and do other paperwork including bookkeeping. They will report to you.

Preparing for Exercise 12—Develop an incentive system

1. What type of compensation will each classification of employee receive for their work? Will you give them a wage, salary, or incentive pay (commissions, piecework, or standard hour)?
2. Will you give incentives (recognition and other nonmonetary incentives, merit pay, bonuses, profit sharing, gainsharing, ESOPs, stock option and/or stock purchase plans)?
3. As the only executive, what will your compensation package include?

• • • SKILL BUILDER 12-3 GIVING PRAISE

Objective

To develop your skill at giving praise

Skills

The primary skills developed through this exercise are as follows:

1. *HR management skills*—Human relations skills
2. *SHRM 2013 Curriculum Guidebook*—K: Total rewards, and L: Training and development

Assignment

Think of a job situation in which you did something well-deserving of praise and recognition. For example, you may have saved the company some money, you may have turned a dissatisfied customer into a happy one, and so forth. If you have never worked or can't think of a situation like this, interview someone who has. Put yourself in a management position and write out the praise you would give to an employee for doing what you did.

1. Briefly describe the situation in writing.
2. Write out the four steps of the giving praise model and what you would say to the person for steps 1, 2, and 4.

In-Class Role-Play

You will give and receive praise.

Procedure (10–15 minutes)

Break into groups of four to six. One at a time, give the praise you prepared.

1. Explain the situation.
2. Select a group member to receive the praise.
3. Give the praise. (Talk—don't read it off the paper.) Try to select the position you would use if you were actually giving the praise on the job (both standing, both sitting, etc.).
4. Integration. The group gives the praise giver feedback on how they did:

Step 1. Was the praise very specific and descriptive? Did the giver look the employee in the eye?

Step 2. Was the importance of the behavior clearly stated?

Step 3. Did the giver stop for a moment of silence?

Step 4. Did the giver encourage repeat performance? Did the giver of praise touch the receiver (optional)?

Overall. Did the praise take less than 1 minute? Was the praise sincere?

©iStockphoto.com/KLH49

13 Employee Benefits

••• LEARNING OUTCOMES

After studying this chapter, you should be able to do the following:

Practitioner's Perspective

Cindy says that as a benefits administrator for several years, she is a firm believer in the value of health and welfare benefits as part of an attractive total compensation package. But she asks: "Do all employees value all benefits equally?"

The first ever employee benefits survey at one company revealed real differences between different ages and classifications of employees. Older workers valued employer contributions to the 401(k) plan; younger workers wanted more paid time off. Floor workers were concerned about affordable health care premiums while the supervisors were interested in vision insurance. Management wisely proved to their employees that their opinion counted—an increase was made in the employer 401(k) contribution, vision insurance was added with the total cost of the payroll-deducted premium paid by the employee (employees still regarded it as a desirable benefit), and the firm adopted a paid-time-off plan that allowed the largely male workforce some flexible time off to attend to family responsibilities.

How do we create benefit packages that provide the greatest value to employees at a price employers can afford? Chapter 13 provides insight into voluntary and involuntary benefits and company benefit plans.

SHRM HR CONTENT

See Appendix: *SHRM 2013 Curriculum Guidebook* for the complete list

B. Employment Law (required)

7. Employer Retirement Income Security Act of 1974 (ERISA)

9. Family and Medical Leave Act of 1993 (FMLA)

33. COBRA: Consolidated Omnibus Budget Reconciliation Act of 1985

34. American Recovery and Reinvestment Act of 2009 (ARRA)

37. Health Insurance Portability and Accountability Act (HIPAA) of 1996

K. Total Rewards (required)

B. Employee Benefits

1. Statutory vs. voluntary benefits

2. Types of retirement plans (defined benefit, defined contribution, hybrid plans)

3. Regulation of retirement plans (FLSA, ERISA, Pension Protection Act of 2006)

4. Types of health care plans (multiple payer/single payer, universal health care systems, HMOs, PPOs, fee-for-service, consumer-directed)

5. Regulation of health insurance programs (COBRA, HIPAA, Health Maintenance Organization Act of 1973)

6. Federal insurance programs (Old-Age, Survivor, and Disability Insurance [OASDI], Medicare)

7. Disability insurance

8. Educational benefits

10. Family-oriented benefits

12. Life insurance

13. Nonqualified plans for highly paid and executive employees

15. Time off and other benefits

16. Unemployment Insurance

19. Managing employee benefits (cost control, monitoring future obligations, action planning, strategic planning)

20. Domestic partner benefits

21. Paid leave plans

22. Workers' compensation

THE STRATEGIC VALUE OF BENEFITS PROGRAMS

The last of our chapters on compensation deals with benefits—indirect compensation that provides something of value to the employee. Some benefits are mandatory, due to federal and state statutes, and some are optional, based on the desires of the firm. In addition, we need to understand that if we *choose* to provide some benefits to our employees, there are mandatory laws that we have to follow as well. We will get into all of these shortly. First, though, we want to discuss the cost of benefits programs to the company.

How much would you think that companies spend on benefits packages—5% of direct wages? 10%? more? According to the US Bureau of Labor Statistics (BLS), benefits average roughly 31% of total employee compensation cost.[1] Looking at it another way, benefit costs equaled about a 45.4% premium on top of direct wage costs in March 2014. This means that for every $100 that goes into employee paychecks, another $45.40 is spent on benefits. So, if you get a full-time job with average benefits and your salary is $40,000, you would be getting around $17,600 in benefits, or have a total compensation cost (to the firm) of around $58,160.

If you became the HR manager for an organization and you were spending nearly one third of your total compensation dollars on employee benefits, would you want to manage those costs as closely as possible? It makes sense that you would. Luckily, we have *some* control over benefits costs, and as HR managers we want to make sure that we get the best return possible—in loyalty, job satisfaction, and employee engagement—for our money.

The costs of benefits programs are staggering to most people. Of course, the BLS numbers are just an average cost to companies, but that means that for some employers, the costs are even higher than those noted above. Because benefits cost our companies so much, we need to plan our benefits programs to add value for our employees and their families as well as provide a strategic advantage to the company.[2] How do benefits programs provide strategic value to the firm? As we noted in Chapter 1 of this text, our *human* resources are one of the few potential sources for competitive advantage in a modern, 21st century organization. What keeps these employees happy and engaged and willing to create a competitive advantage for our firm? The totality of their compensation—including their benefits packages—is one major factor.[3] While we are all aware that most employees take a job because of the advertised level of pay, many stay with a job because of the benefits package associated with it.[4]

Today, workers are demanding more benefits and an improved mix of choices and flexibility to better fit with their lifestyle and that of their family.[5] This phenomenon has made it more difficult for the firm to keep track of and control benefits costs. Because people demand more and better benefits, companies add new benefits to what they have historically offered.[6] This requires HR to spend more time monitoring the cost as well as the value provided by different types of benefits. But this practice also provides an incentive to our employees to continue working for us due to the fact that they feel as if they are being cared for by the company.[7] We increase job satisfaction and engagement because when employees are taken care of, they work harder and take good care of our customers and the organization.[8]

Why Are Benefits Growing as a Portion of Overall Compensation?

Growth in the cost of providing employee benefits has occurred for a number of reasons. Let's take a quick look at some of the biggest reasons for growth in benefits programs in the United States and worldwide.

TAX ADVANTAGES. One reason benefits are growing is that there are federal and sometimes state tax advantages for companies that provide them. If the company provides its employees with a benefit, the firm can write off all or part of the cost of providing the benefit. Sometimes the company can get benefits pretax for employees as well. As an example, most health insurance premiums are tax deductible for employers and are not taxable as income (pretax) for employees. So providing some benefits can reduce the tax burden on both the company and the individual. Take a look at the table on benefits taxation that is reproduced from IRS Publication 15B in Exhibit 13-1.

STATUTORY REQUIREMENTS. Federal (and state) statutes require companies to provide certain benefits. In 1935, Social Security laws were passed that required companies to provide employees with old-age, survivor, and disability benefits. Over the ensuing years, Congress has added other mandatory benefits such as unemployment, workers' compensation, family and medical leave, and the new health care law called the Affordable Care Act or ACA (we will discuss each of these shortly). Each time Congress requires employers to provide a new benefit, the cost to employers for providing benefits goes up.

INFLUENCE OF ORGANIZED LABOR. We talked about the National Labor Relations Act in Chapter 9 and noted then that the act allows employees to "bargain collectively" with their employers. This is another reason that benefit costs have grown for companies over the years. A large part of collective bargaining is usually focused on employee benefits (for a variety of reasons), and once union members gain such benefits, employees in other competing companies use this as leverage to have the same benefits added to their workplace, even if the company is not unionized. Unions also use the tax-favored status of many benefits to make them more palatable to the company during negotiations, and organizations may prefer benefits concessions to wage concessions because of the tax advantages. So unions have also driven up the cost and variety of benefits.

BUYING IN BULK. Virtually everyone now knows that if you buy things in larger quantities, you get them cheaper (think **Sam's Club** or **Costco**). Buying benefits in bulk works the same way. If companies buy benefits in bulk for employees, it is cheaper than if they buy the same benefits individually.

As you can see, there are a variety of reasons why the costs of benefits have grown in the last 80 years. And once a benefit becomes part of the employee's compensation package, it is very hard to delete that benefit in the future. We consider

EXHIBIT 13-1   SPECIAL RULES FOR VARIOUS TYPES OF FRINGE BENEFITS

Type of Fringe Benefit	Treatment Under Employment Taxes		
	Income Tax Withholding	Social Security and Medicare	Federal Unemployment (FUTA)
Accident and health benefits	Exempt,[1,2] except for long-term care benefits provided through a flexible spending or similar arrangement.	Exempt, except for certain payments to S corporation employees who are 2% shareholders.	Exempt
Achievement awards	Exempt[1] up to $1,600 for qualified plan awards ($400 for nonqualified awards).		
Adoption assistance	Exempt[1,3]	Taxable	Taxable
Athletic facilities	Exempt if substantially all use during the calendar year is by employees, their spouses, and their dependent children and the facility is operated by the employer on premises owned or leased by the employer.		
De minimis (minimal) benefits	Exempt	Exempt	Exempt
Dependent care assistance	Exempt[3] up to certain limits, $5,000 ($2,500 for married employee filing separate return).		
Educational assistance	Exempt up to $5,250 of benefits each year. (See Educational Assistance, later.)		
Employee discounts	Exempt[3] up to certain limits. (See Employee Discounts, later.)		
Employee stock options	See Employee Stock Options, later.		
Group-term life insurance coverage	Exempt	Exempt[1,4] up to cost of $50,000 of coverage. (Special rules apply to former employees.)	Exempt
Health savings accounts (HSAs)	Exempt for qualified individuals up to the HSA contribution limits. (See Health Savings Accounts, later.)		
Lodging on your business premises	Exempt[1] if furnished for your convenience as a condition of employment.		
Meals	Exempt if furnished on your business premises for your convenience. Exempt if de minimis.		
Moving expense reimbursements	Exempt[1] if expenses would be deductible if the employee had paid them.		
No-additional-cost services	Exempt[3]	Exempt[3]	Exempt[3]
Retirement planning services	Exempt[5]	Exempt[5]	Exempt[5]
Transportation (commuting) benefits	Exempt[1] up to certain limits if for rides in a commuter highway vehicle and/or transit passes ($120, but see the Caution on page 1), qualified parking ($230), or qualified bicycle commuting reimbursement[6] ($20). (See Transportation, later.) Exempt if de minimis.		
Tuition reduction	Exempt[3] if for undergraduate education (or graduate education if the employee performs teaching or research activities).		
Volunteer firefighter and emergency medical responder benefits	Exempt	Exempt	Exempt
Working condition benefits	Exempt	Exempt	Exempt

Source: IRS Publication 15B Fully or Partially Tax Exempt Benefits

Notes: [1] Exemption does not apply to S corporation employees who are 2% shareholders; [2] Exemption does not apply to certain highly compensated employees under a self-insured plan that favors those employees; [3] Exemption does not apply to certain highly compensated employees under a program that favors those employees; [4] Exemption does not apply to certain key employees under a plan that favors those employees; [5] Exemption does not apply to services for tax preparation, accounting, legal, or brokerage services; [6] If the employee receives a qualified bicycle commuting reimbursement in a qualified bicycle commuting month, the employee cannot receive commuter highway vehicle, transit pass, or qualified parking benefits in that same month

them an entitlement (Chapter 12)—we feel that the company owes us this benefit.[9] So the cost of providing benefits almost never goes down; it just keeps going up. However, some companies are considering dropping health care as a result of the detailed requirements in the ACA, and this could cause the cost of certain benefits programs to go down significantly.

Considerations in Providing Benefits Programs

How do we create and then administer a benefits program for our workforce? We need to understand several things before creating the program so that we create a system that is both valuable to the employees and affordable for the organization. Remember that our goal is to have a program that increases employee motivation and engagement and helps create a competitive advantage.

AMOUNTS. The first issue that we need to understand is how much money the company is willing to spend to provide an employee benefits program. Many companies will calculate this as a percentage of direct compensation. We may analyze the current situation and come to the conclusion that we are able to provide a 40% premium to direct compensation for the cost of benefits. We have to be very careful in our consideration of the amounts available for employee benefit programs. As with other types of compensation, if we tell our employees that we will provide a benefit that they value and then fail to follow through for any reason, it is just as damaging to motivation and engagement as any other type of management action that breaks the equity theory process discussed in Chapter 11. We need to make absolutely sure that we will have the funds available if we commit to providing the benefit.

MIX. Once we know how much money is available, we need to decide what types of benefits we will offer. Here again, the number of different types of benefits has exploded over the past 40 years. In the 1960s and 1970s, most companies had limited benefit programs. They might have offered their employees a retirement benefit, health insurance, life and disability insurance, and possibly dental care, but nobody ever thought about providing "doggy day care" like **Facebook**[10] or a "nap room energy pod" like **Google**[11] (two modern-day benefits in some companies)! Today, the number and type of benefits available in some company programs is limited only by the imagination of the employees of the firm.

As an example, companies today may provide a transportation subsidy such as a vehicle allowance, a public transportation voucher, free parking near the office or a parking voucher, alternative vehicle allowances (for buying "green" vehicles), allowances for bicycles and places for bike parking, a van or shuttle service to take employees to work and back home . . . and this is just benefits associated with transporting the worker to and from work. The company can provide on-site wellness centers and child care,[12] child care vouchers, sick child care, paid child care leave, elder care, and/or pet care. **Google** is known for its crazy-free perks like free meals and comfortable places to take breaks and relax.[13] **ConocoPhillips** offers the best retirement plan.[14] **BMW** in Greer, South Carolina, has an on-site health clinic.[15] So we can quickly see how large the pool of potential employee benefits can become. We have to decide which of the options is going to provide our workforce with the best benefits package for the money spent.

Riding a bike to work provides exercise was well as transportation.

WORK
APPLICATION 13-2

How important is benefits flexibility to you? How does benefits flexibility affect employment where you work or have worked?

LO 13-4

Identify and summarize the major statutory benefits required by federal law.

SHRM

K:B6
Federal Insurance Programs
(OASDI, Medicare)

FLEXIBILITY. Finally, we need to consider how much flexibility we are willing to build into our benefits program because flexible options are very important to today's employees. Flexible benefit programs allow employees to pick from a set of benefits in some way. The employee can, at least for a portion of their benefit package, choose one type of benefit over another in flexible benefit plans.

We will get into the reasons behind these issues later in the chapter. Right now let's get into a review of the mandatory and voluntary benefits available in 21st century companies.

STATUTORY BENEFITS

Statutory benefits are benefits that are required by law. A number of benefits are required by federal laws in the United States and in many other countries. There are also laws that apply if the company chooses certain optional, or nonmandatory, benefits in certain cases. Let's now review the major mandatory benefits that are generally required in US firms.

Social Security and Medicare

By far the largest of the statutory programs, in both size and cost to employers (and employees), are Social Security and Medicare. The combined cost of the Old-Age, Survivors, and Disability Insurance (OASDI) and Medicare programs was over $1.3 trillion in 2014.[16] To put that in perspective, the total federal revenue collected in 2014 was expected to be about $2.78 trillion.[17] This means that this one group of programs cost almost 47% *of all money the federal government received* in 2014.

Employers *and* employees are required to provide funds for Social Security benefits. The program was created with the passage of the Social Security Act of 1935. The act created a series of programs for the social welfare of the population of the United States, including OASDI, Medicare for elderly and disabled individuals, and several other lesser-known programs. Since these programs are so complex, and this is an introductory overview of the field of HRM, the best that we can do in this text is to provide some general information on the programs.

How much money does the employee's Social Security benefit cost, and who pays for it? The employer and employee jointly pay into Social Security through withholdings from the employee's paycheck and a mandatory employer payment. Each of them pays 6.2% of the employee's total pay per pay period into OASDI and 1.45% of the employee's pay into the Medicare fund. The 6.2% contribution is only withheld on the first $117,000 the employee earns during the year (in 2014),[18] and then it stops, but the 1.45% tax for Medicare is paid on all income, no matter how much is earned. So the combined amount sent to the federal government is 15.3% of the employee's income, half from the employer and half from the employee.

How does an employee become eligible for OASDI benefits? As a general rule, the individual must receive 40 "credits" in their lifetime in order to become eligible for Social Security *retirement*. They must earn $1,200 in one quarter (in 2014) in order to receive 1 credit. The amount of earnings required to receive 1 credit rises each year as average earnings rise. The 40 credits do not have to be in consecutive quarters—the individual does not have to work for 10 years without a break in employment—and more than 1 credit can be earned in a quarter (if a person made $2,400 in a quarter, they would earn 2 credits), but a person can only earn 4 credits per year.[19] However, the 40-credit rule does not necessarily apply to *disability or survivor* benefits. While we would normally need 40 credits in order to be eligible for disability payments, if we were disabled before we could reasonably earn the 40 credits, we might become eligible earlier. For example, if disabled before age 24, you could qualify for disability benefits with as few as 6 credits earned in the 3 years prior to becoming disabled.[20]

RETIREMENT. Once an employee becomes eligible through earning 40 credits and meeting the retirement age requirements, they can receive a monthly check, but is that monthly check supposed to help the employee maintain the lifestyle that they had before retirement? What percentage of preretirement pay was Social Security originally designed to provide upon retirement? It was only designed to pay about 30% of preretirement income. Social Security was never supposed to replace 100% of preretirement income. However, many employees plan on it as their only retirement. As HR managers, part of your job will be to make employees aware that they need to also *save* for retirement. The savings rate in the United States compared to that in many other developed countries is low. In 1990 the US savings rate was around 7%, but by 2005 it had dropped to less than 1.5% and in 2012 had recovered to about 5%.[21] This compares with savings rates in excess of 10% in Germany, Sweden, and Belgium. The common recommendation is to start when you get your first full-time job by putting 10% of your income into a retirement fund every month, no matter how low or high your income is, and always take advantage of matching benefits from your employer.[22]

WORK APPLICATION 13-3

Look at your last pay stub. How much was taken out for Social Security tax and Medicare tax? How much did your employer pay?

The key to having money at retirement is to start saving at a young age to take advantage of compound interest.

At what age are we eligible for Social Security retirement? If you were born in 1937 or earlier, you are eligible for retirement at age 65. If you were born in 1960 or later, your retirement age is 67. For those born between 1937 and 1960, it is based on a sliding scale. Take a look at Exhibit 13-2. If you were born in 1956, you are eligible for full retirement benefits from Social Security at age 66 and 4 months.

One of the most important things to look at is how many people lived to be age 65 when the Social Security law originally passed and how many it supports now. In 1935 approximately 6% of the population was age 65 or older, but in the year 2000 that number was about 12.4%, in 2009 approximately 12.9%,[24] and in 2013 it was estimated at 14.1%.[25] The Social Security program was designed around a retiree population of 6%, but that has more than doubled, and it will continue to rise for many years to come. This is one of the issues with the way Social Security is set up today and one of the reasons that the program constantly has to be reevaluated. The changes in life span and changes in income that have occurred over the past 70 years have made the program unsustainable in its current form.

Another major issue with Social Security is the large number of baby boomers who are starting to retire, with fewer younger workers paying into the Social Security system. The Social Security Board of Governors has noted that "neither Medicare nor Social Security can sustain projected long-run programs in full under currently scheduled financing, and legislative changes are necessary to avoid disruptive consequences for beneficiaries and taxpayers."[26] The Board estimates that the OASI component of Social Security will have greater outflows of funds than it takes in beginning in 2022 and will exhaust its funds in 2035 (1 year earlier than previously projected) if legislative corrections are not undertaken. The Disability portion of OASDI is expected to be depleted as early as 2016.[27]

What about early retirement? Can a person retire earlier than age 65–67? Yes, but their benefits will be *permanently* reduced. For example, if an employee was eligible for retirement at age 65, they could take early retirement and get an 80% benefit

EXHIBIT 13-2 FULL SOCIAL SECURITY RETIREMENT AGE[23]

Age to Receive Full Social Security Benefits	
Year of Birth	Full Retirement Age
1937 or earlier	65
1938	65 and 2 months
1939	65 and 4 months
1940	65 and 6 months
1941	65 and 8 months
1942	65 and 10 months
1943–1954	66
1955	66 and 2 months
1956	66 and 4 months
1957	66 and 6 months
1958	66 and 8 months
1959	66 and 10 months
1960 and later	67

Source: US Social Security Administration

at age 62. That 20% reduction is forever, not just until they reach age 65. If an individual is not eligible for full retirement benefits until age 67 (they were born after 1960), the reduction is 30% at age 62—again for the life of the retirement benefit.

DISABILITY AND SURVIVOR BENEFITS. These components are really basically the same benefit. If an employee becomes disabled or dies and is otherwise eligible, the disability or survivor benefit will apply in most cases. The employee, or their survivors, will get payments each month roughly equal to what the employee would have gotten in retirement based on their historical earnings. If the employee is disabled for at least 5 months and is expected to be disabled for at least 12 months, Social Security disability will be allowed. The disability must last at least 12 months or be expected to ultimately cause the covered person's death.

Survivor benefits can go to a widow/widower over age 60, any child or grandchild who is a dependent of the deceased and is under age 18, or any dependent parent over 62. If an individual has survivors in multiple categories, then the survivor benefit gets split among eligible survivors.[28]

MEDICARE. Finally, there is the Medicare component. Individuals become eligible for Medicare at the same time as their eligibility for Social Security retirement begins. There are currently four parts to Medicare:[29]

- *Part A* is Hospital Insurance (HI). Hospitalization covers the inpatient care of a retiree in a hospital, skilled nursing facility, or hospice. Again, according to the Social Security Board of Governors: "The HI fund again fails the test of short-range financial adequacy, as its trust fund ratio is already below 100% and is expected to decline continuously until reserve depletion in 2026."[30]
- *Part B* covers non-hospital-related (outpatient) Medical Services Insurance (MSI).
- *Part C* Medicare recipients can also now choose this option, called Medicare Advantage plans, instead of Part A and Part B. Option C combines Part A (HI) and Part B (MSI) coverage in a plan similar to an HMO or PPO (we

WORK
APPLICATION 13-4

Using Exhibit 13-2, at what age can you expect to collect full Social Security?

will talk about these in detail shortly). Private insurance companies approved by Medicare provide this coverage. Costs may be lower than in the original Medicare Part A and B plans, and the insured may get extra benefits.

- *Part D* is a prescription drug benefit. Part A and B are basically automatic upon the individual's retirement. The retiree has to elect to participate in Part C and/or D.

Medicare is not completely free to the retiree. The covered person has to pay copayments and deductibles of various types, the details of which are beyond the scope of this text. But understand that there are out-of-pocket costs involved with Medicare. There are also limitations on what is covered. So Medicare provides basic medical benefits, but it is not a full-coverage program by any means.

Workers' Compensation

The next statutory benefit is workers' compensation. **Workers' compensation** *is an insurance program designed to provide medical treatment and temporary payments to employees who cannot work because of an employment-related injury or illness.* "Employment-related" means that the illness or injury had to do with the worker's actions for the company, although the injury or illness didn't have to happen while the person was actually at work. For instance, if an employee were traveling through an airport as part of their job and picked up their suitcase, injuring their back, this would be an "employment-related" injury.

The workers' compensation program is paid for by employers—employees pay none of the cost of workers' compensation insurance. Workers' compensation payments to sick or injured employees are not permanent in most cases. The program was created to provide workers with *short-term* relief because of work-related injuries or illnesses. Social Security disability, on the other hand, generally provides long-term relief in the form of disability payments. Workers' compensation does, however, pay a survivor benefit in the case of death of the employee.

Workers' compensation is a type of "no-fault" insurance, which means that no matter which party—the employer or the employee—was at fault in an accident- or illness-related situation, the insurance will be paid out to the party harmed. Why is no-fault such an issue? The main reason is the problems that would arise if the employee had to sue in court. First, there would almost certainly be animosity between the employer and employee if the employer were to be sued. It would also take significant time to get the case settled and for the injured party (if the decision went in their favor) to receive compensation. The employer's maximum liability is also limited by workers' compensation. Without it, the employer could potentially be bankrupted by a single employment accident or incident, especially if an employee were killed. In all but situations of *gross negligence* or *intent to harm* (willful misconduct), neither party can take the other to court over compensation for such an injury or illness because of the no-fault nature of the insurance. So the ability to provide no-fault insurance in this circumstance is valuable to both parties.

Workers' compensation is mandatory in 48 of the 50 United States, and it is governed by different laws in each state. It is elective in Texas and recently became optional in Oklahoma.[31] In the states where it is mandatory, employers must purchase workers' compensation insurance in order to operate their business. In Texas and Oklahoma, companies can choose not to purchase insurance, but in fact many still do. Why would they buy this insurance if it is not mandatory? The simple answer is that it is cheaper than losing a court case concerning an employee injury. Here again, if there isn't an insurance policy in place, the employee can, and likely will, sue the company because they are unable to work. As most of you have seen in the newspaper, these types of court cases may provide very large awards to injured parties. It is likely that workers' compensation insurance is a very low-cost method to insure

SHRM

K:B22
Workers' Compensation

Workers' compensation An insurance program designed to provide medical treatment and temporary payments to employees who cannot work because of an employment-related injury or illness against a very large potential jury award. Of course, the company can get a blanket liability policy that would cover on-the-job injuries, but it might be much more expensive than workers' compensation insurance, and the company could still be bankrupted by a lawsuit if the liability policy limits were exceeded.

Just how expensive is workers' compensation insurance? It varies, but *as an average* it generally costs between 1.2% and 2% of payroll for most companies.[32] It can go much higher than this though, in some cases. Rates are primarily determined by three factors:

1. *Occupations.* Within a company, what are the risks of injury associated with each job? Some occupations are much more risky than others. For instance, it costs a lot more to insure firefighters, police officers, or construction workers than it does to cover office workers, sales clerks in a mall, or a librarian.

2. *Experience ratings.* An **experience rating** *is a measure of how often claims are made against an insurance policy.* A company's workers' compensation experience rating is basically calculated on the frequency and severity of injuries that occur within that company. There are companies that are in dangerous industries, but they have very few on-the-job injuries because they have very strong safety programs, while other companies in the same industry might have really high injury rates because they don't pay as much attention to safety. Experience ratings can significantly affect a company's workers' compensation costs.

3. *Level of benefits payable.* Injured workers will get compensated based on their particular state's workers' compensation rating manual. This manual provides the required payout rates for various types of injuries. For instance, an amputation of a finger other than the index finger or thumb might provide the employee with a small, one-time payment, but amputation of an arm below the elbow would cost much more. Individual states can set the rates for injuries within the state's boundaries, and these rates affect the cost of workers' compensation insurance.

If you read the previous paragraph closely, you will notice that the company has some control over their workers' compensation rates. The experience rating figures heavily into the company's cost of providing this insurance, so if we can lower our experience rating, we can lower our insurance cost as well. And the savings associated with a low experience rating aren't just one-time savings; our costs continue to be lower for as long as we maintain a safer-than-average work environment (we will discuss safety further in the next chapter). This is an area that HR managers need to understand so that they can lower company costs for workers' compensation insurance.

Who manages and monitors the workers' compensation programs? State governments have the primary authority for managing their state's program. However, the insurance doesn't come from the state itself. The insurance is almost always provided by a private insurance company that provides workers' compensation insurance in that state. Each state has an insurance commission that authorizes insurance firms to operate in that state, and if insurance companies choose to offer workers' compensation insurance in a particular state, they have to follow that state's guidelines. The company approaches a private insurer for workers' compensation insurance and purchases a policy from whichever state-licensed insurer that they choose.

What if the company has a poor experience rating because of excessive accidents? In such a case, the insurers may choose not to provide insurance to the company because the risk to the insurance firm is too great. In this situation, the company that has been denied insurance can go to the state workers' compensation commission and ask to be covered in the workers' compensation pool. The pool is made up of insurers who provide workers' compensation policies in the

Experience rating A measure of how often claims are made against an insurance policy

state. Each insurer that is licensed to provide such insurance has to be part of the pool. The state commission will then assign the company requesting coverage to one of the insurers, and the insurer will have to write the policy for the company that was previously denied coverage.

The pool assignments are usually based on the percent share of each insurer's policies within the state. For instance, if one insurer writes workers' compensation policies that cover 13% of all employees in the state of Arkansas, that insurer would be asked to cover about 13% of the employees whose companies have to resort to the state pool for coverage. While this is a simplified example, it gives you an idea of how companies can get insured, even if no insurance company is willing to cover the risks associated with such an employer with a poor experience rating. Remember though that the cost associated with being in the state pool is significantly more in most cases than it is if the company can get insurance coverage without becoming part of the pool.

Because of their industry and their experience rating, there are cases where companies are spending significant amounts of money on worker's compensation. In some cases, as much as 25% of a company's total personnel costs can come from workers' compensation costs if they are in a high-risk business and their experience rating is also high. Obviously, it can be different from company to company. But again, we can actually lower our experience rating by providing safety training as discussed in Chapter 14.

Unemployment Insurance

The third statutory benefit is Unemployment Insurance. **Unemployment Insurance (UI)** *provides workers who lose their jobs with continuing subsistence payments from their state for a specified period of time.* It is a federally mandated program but is managed and administered separately by each of the states. UI originated under the Social Security Act of 1935 and is applied as a tax on the *employers*—"Only Alaska, New Jersey, and Pennsylvania levy UI taxes on workers."[33] The basic federal tax rate is set at 6.2% of wages earned (in 2011) for the first $7,000 in individual wages, but this rate can be (and generally is) reduced by up to 5.4% if the employer pays state unemployment taxes on time and avoids tax delinquencies. A minimum of 5.4% of the first $7,000 paid to each employee goes to the state unemployment fund, and 0.8% goes to the federal government.

In addition to the federal minimum of 6.2%, states can vary the tax rate and effective wage rate within their borders. Here again, as in workers' compensation, the tax rate is also affected by the company's "experience rating." Employers who tend to terminate more employees who are eligible for UI benefits have a higher experience rating and, as a result, a higher UI tax rate.[34] So, within the same state, some employers will pay much more in UI taxes than other employers will.

What is the logic behind UI? It is there to allow people to continue to have at least some purchasing power even when they are unemployed. If UI was not available, when the country experienced a recession, many individuals and families would stop spending as much as they possibly could. This could cause the recession to deepen even more and make it more difficult for the economy to recover, because consumer spending is the largest input into the national economy. If, however, unemployed individuals are provided with some funds, the overall economy is not harmed as much as it would otherwise be. In ordinary times, when unemployment rates are not very high, unemployment payments are capped at 26 weeks per recipient in most states. However, in times of high unemployment, this can be (and usually is) extended. In the most recent US recession, some states with very high unemployment rates were allowed to extend unemployment benefits to as long as 99 weeks—nearly 2 years![35]

WORK APPLICATION 13-5

How would you rate the risk of occupational injury or illness where you work or at an organization where you have worked? Is it high, moderate, or low? Why?

SHRM

K:B16
Unemployment Insurance

Unemployment Insurance (UI)
Insurance that provides workers who lose their jobs with continuing subsistence payments from their state for a specified period of time

How does an individual become eligible for UI? What has to happen? They have to be terminated from employment—either through downsizing, layoff, or other processes—and in most cases must have worked in four of the last five quarters and met minimum income guidelines in each of those quarters. What makes them *ineligible*? A series of things can occur that make the individual ineligible:

- The individual quit voluntarily.
- They fail to look for work.
- They were terminated "for cause" (because they did something wrong).
- They refuse suitable work (work comparable to what they were doing prior to being terminated).
- They, as a member of a union, participate in a strike against the company (in most states).
- They become self-employed.
- They fail to disclose any monies earned in a period of unemployment.

What does the individual receive in the way of UI benefits? Generally the weekly benefit is about 60% of what the person was making when they were employed, but this also varies some by state, and there is a cap on the amount that will be paid out in unemployment benefits. So if the individual was highly paid, in some states they may only receive 25% (or even less) of their prior weekly pay because of the cap.

Family and Medical Leave Act of 1993 (FMLA)

SHRM

B:9
Family and Medical Leave Act of
1993 (FMLA)

The next mandatory benefit is Family and Medical Act leave, more commonly known as FMLA leave. FMLA requires that the employer provide unpaid leave for an "eligible employee" when they are faced with any of the following situations:[36]

- *Leave of 12 workweeks in a 12-month period for . . .*
  - The birth of a child and to care for the newborn child within 1 year of birth
  - The placement with the employee of a child for adoption or foster care and to care for the newly placed child within 1 year of placement
  - To care for the employee's spouse, child, or parent who has a serious health condition
  - A serious health condition that makes the employee unable to perform the essential functions of their job
  - Any qualifying exigency arising out of the fact that the employee's spouse, son, daughter, or parent is a covered military member on "covered active duty"

or . . .

- *Leave of 26 workweeks during a single 12-month period* to care for a covered service member with a serious injury or illness if the eligible employee is the spouse, son, daughter, parent, or next of kin to the employee (military caregiver leave)

In addition, upon the employee's return from FMLA leave, they must be restored to their original job or one that is equivalent in pay, benefits, and other terms and conditions of employment.

Any private sector employer is covered under the act if they have 50 or more employees who worked at least 20 weeks during the year, working within a 75-mile radius of a central location.

Eligible employees must

- work for a covered employer;
- have worked for the employer for a total of 12 months (not necessarily consecutive); or
- have worked at least 1,250 hours over the previous 12 months.

The act also exempts some eligible employees. "A salaried eligible employee who is among the highest paid 10% of the employees employed by the employer within 75 miles of the facility at which the employee is employed"[37] is exempted from FMLA leave and can be denied restoration of their job if they utilize their "eligible employee" status to take such leave.

Reasons to deny restoration to a job include the following:[38]

- Such denial is necessary to prevent substantial and grievous economic injury to the operations of the employer.
- The employer notifies the employee of the intent of the employer to deny restoration on such basis at the time the employer determines that such injury would occur.
- In any case in which the leave has commenced, the employee elects not to return to employment after receiving such notice.

One of the problems that employers run into with FMLA is the definition of "serious health condition." Under FMLA, a **serious health condition** *means an illness, injury, impairment, or physical or mental condition that involves either inpatient care or continuing care for at least 3 consecutive days*, but there is strong evidence that FMLA leave is heavily abused. In a 2013 article, SHRM notes that 70% of employers surveyed had concerns about abuse of FMLA leave by employees.[39] All an employee needs in order to be able to claim FMLA leave is a document from a health care provider that says that they have such a serious health condition. When President Bill Clinton pushed the law through during his first term, the intent of the law was noble. However, the execution left something to be desired for businesses dealing with abuse of this benefit.

Why are there problems with the law? The employer has little leeway when an employee requests FMLA leave and has documentation of a serious health condition. The employer has to cover the costs of not having the employee at work (we talked about the costs of absenteeism in Chapter 1). The law also says that we have to give at least 90% (remember, we can exempt the top 10%) of our employees up to 12 weeks of FMLA leave per year and then have to give them their job back, or a comparable job. So if we have 50 employees who work within 75 miles of a central location, we would have to allow up to 45 of those employees to miss up to a quarter of the work year, every year. This puts a huge burden on both HR and operational managers, and it can easily affect morale of the other employees who have to take up the slack for the employee who is on FMLA leave. And remember when we discussed the issue of bad employees in Chapter 9, we noted that one bad employee can affect everyone's productivity. In fact, there is evidence that one person who games the company for unfair time off can bring performance of the entire organization down by 30% to 40%.[40]

Because of the burden that FMLA can create, employers want to make sure to the best of their ability that employees are not abusing FMLA. One thing that the employer can do to lower abuse is to enforce the requirement that employees give 30 days' advance notice of intent to use FMLA leave if they know that it will be

Serious health condition An illness, injury, impairment, or physical or mental condition that involves either inpatient care or continuing care for at least 3 consecutive days

Many employees want to have time to spend with their family, which is made possible through FLMA leave.

needed. The law also says that if an employee cannot foresee the need 30 days ahead of time, they must provide notice to the company as soon as practicable. Usually this is within 1 day of learning of the need for FMLA leave, or if the need is emergent (for example, an employee is hurt in a car accident), they must notify the employer as soon as possible. Employers also have the right to require that the reason behind a request for FMLA leave be documented by a health care provider, at the employee's expense. The employer can also require a second or even third opinion on such reasons for FMLA leave (at the *employer's* expense), as well as requiring periodic certification of the continuing need for FMLA leave when the condition lasts for an extended period of time. Employers should typically get a second certification when it is suspected that an employee is abusing FMLA.

Companies can additionally require that employees substitute paid leave and completely use such leave up before taking unpaid FMLA leave as long as that is the employer's normal policy. And they can recover health care premiums that were paid to an employee on FMLA leave if the employee doesn't return to work.

Additional employer requirements include the requirement to post notice of FMLA benefits prominently in the workplace and to include this notice in either an employee handbook or other written guidance to employees when they are hired. Employers must also maintain health insurance coverage for the employee on FMLA leave if such health benefits are normally provided, again adding to the employer's costs.

All in all, even though FMLA requires only *unpaid* leave, the costs to the company are significant. It puts a significant strain on businesses, especially small businesses. The HR department usually bears a large part of the burden of monitoring and curbing abuses of FMLA leave, and HR managers must be aware of the rules and regulations in order to apply the law correctly.

The Patient Protection and Affordable Care Act of 2010 (ACA)

The last mandatory benefit is the Patient Protection and Affordable Care Act of 2010. This act mandated that all employers with more than 50 employees provide their *full-time employees* with health care coverage or face penalties for failing to do so.[41] A **MetLife** study found that 60% of employees are concerned about having access to affordable health insurance and worry about how they will pay for the out-of-pocket medical costs. Employers are concerned about the rising cost of health care and how the ACA will affect their health care benefits as it is implemented over the next few years.[42] The major provisions of the law are presented in Exhibit 13-3, by the year in which they are to become effective.

The "pay or play" penalty noted in Exhibit 13-3 under 2015 applies to *full-time equivalent (FTE) employees*. Full-time equivalents are workers putting in 30 or more hours per week plus the number of hours worked by part-time employees per month divided by 120. For example, if a company has 42 employees who work 40 or more hours per week, 22 employees who work fewer than 40 hours per week but more than 30, and 25 employees who work fewer than 30 hours per week and worked a

EXHIBIT 13-3 AFFORDABLE CARE ACT

2010 (Immediately)

- Children can stay on parents' health care insurance until age 26.
- Insurance companies are banned from rescinding coverage when the covered individual gets sick and from imposing lifetime caps on benefits.
- Children with preexisting conditions can't be excluded from health care coverage.

2011

- Employers have to disclose the value of employee health insurance on IRS form W-2.
- Flexible spending accounts (FSA—we will talk about these later in the chapter) no longer allow nonprescription medicines to be reimbursed.
- Medicaid begins providing preventive care services to beneficiaries with no out-of-pocket cost.

2013

- FSA contributions are limited to $2,500 per year.
- High wage earners have an additional 0.9% Medicare tax on earnings in excess of the current limit. This additional tax starts at $200,000 for individual earnings or $250,000 for joint returns.
- Employers are required to notify employees of state health insurance exchanges.

2014

- Most individual taxpayers are required to have health coverage or pay a tax penalty at year end.
- Employer health plans may not impose more than 90-day waiting periods for new employee coverage.
- State health insurance exchanges must be open.
- State health insurance exchanges must be operational.
- Insurers will be banned from restricting coverage or providing differential premiums based on health of the covered individual.

2015

- Employers with 100 or more employees will be required to offer health benefits to employees or face penalties—this is called "pay or play."
  - o Businesses with fewer than 50 full-time equivalent employees (FTEs) are not penalized for failing to carry employer health coverage.
  - o Businesses with 100 or more FTEs will be fined $2,000 per full-time equivalent minus the first 30 FTEs.

2016

- Employers with more than 50 but fewer than 100 employees will be required to offer health benefits to employees or face penalties.
  - o Businesses with 50 or more FTEs will be fined $2,000 per full-time equivalent minus the first 30 FTEs.

Source: Affordable Care Act of 2010

total of 1,500 hours per month (an average of about 15 hours per person per week), the calculation of FTEs would be as follows:

40-hour employees (42)	30-hour+ employees (22)	1,500 hours (from employees working fewer than 30 hours per week)
Traditional full-time employees	All employees working more than 30 hours are considered full-time	The number of part-time hours divided by 120: 1,500/120 = 12.5.
42 +	22 +	12.5 = 76.5 FTE (round up to 77)

If this company chose not to provide health insurance, they would have to pay a fine of $94,000: 77 FTEs – 30 FTEs = 47, 47 × $2,000 = $94,000.

Another provision of the law is that employees not covered by a health care plan at work are *required* to go to the state health exchange where they can purchase individual coverage. Individuals who fail to gain coverage will also be fined, although the minimum fine in the first year (2014) was very low ($95 per person). But this amount is indexed based on the individual's earnings, so it can be much higher in later years. In 2015 the minimum individual cost is $325, and the penalty goes to a minimum of $695 in 2016 and is indexed for inflation after that. The total amount of the penalty for a family will not exceed $2,250.

A recent national survey from Highroads, a benefits management firm, identifies one of the most significant questions associated with the ACA: Will employers just choose to pay the fine rather than provide health insurance, because the fine is less expensive? Their survey shows that up to 85% of companies are considering moving their employees to health care exchanges within the next 5 years due to the continuing complexity and costs associated with the ACA.[43] The average cost for employer coverage of a full-time worker in 2014 was nearly $6,000,[44] and that is just the direct cost of the insurance; it doesn't include the costs of managing the program requirements created by the ACA. So a $2,000 penalty may be the lesser of two evils for companies that are struggling with profitability.

Another concern associated with the ACA is that the company only has to provide insurance to full-time employees, even though part-time employees are part of the calculation of firm size under the law. This has caused a significant number of businesses to shift at least a portion of their workforce from full-time to part-time.[45] There is concern that especially where it is not difficult to have part-time employees (such as in the fast-food industry), this shift will intensify as companies try to adjust to the new law.[46]

"Qualified" plans (plans that meet the guidelines of the law) will have to pay at least 60% of allowed charges and meet some minimum benefit standards. The plan must also be "affordable," which means it will not exceed 9.5% of the employee's household income. If an employer offers a plan that is not "qualified and affordable," they will be fined $3,000 annually for each employee who goes to the health care exchange for coverage. So, for an employer, offering *no* plan is cheaper than offering a plan that isn't qualified and affordable—it costs $2,000 per employee to have no coverage but $3,000 to have nonqualifying coverage.

LO 13-5

Identify the main statutory requirements that must be followed *if* organizations choose to provide health care or retirement plans for their employees.

Statutory Requirements When Providing Certain Voluntary Benefits

Let's take a look now at some legal requirements if we choose to provide certain benefits to our employees. These requirements don't apply unless we make the choice to provide our employees with health insurance or company-sponsored retirement plans.

CONSOLIDATED OMNIBUS BUDGET RECONCILIATION ACT OF 1985 (COBRA). If employers choose to provide health insurance, we have to abide by the Consolidated Omnibus Budget Reconciliation Act (COBRA) law. **COBRA** *is a law that requires employers to offer to maintain health insurance on individuals who leave their employment (for a period of time).* The individual former employee has to pay for the insurance, but the employer is required to keep the former employee on their group insurance policy.

Why would a former employee want to remain on the company's health insurance policy? Primarily because buying an individual health insurance policy is much more expensive than buying insurance for a group of people. According to *Smart Money,*

> Buying individual health insurance isn't as easy as having a clean bill of health and enough cash. . . . Should an insurer agree to provide coverage, it will almost certainly be costly and confusing. The average out-of-pocket costs for people insured individually is almost double what people covered by an employer pay.[47]

So this option will save people money over buying health insurance on their own. Another reason is that in most cases, people don't leave one job and start another on the same day, so they will have a gap in their health coverage if they don't utilize COBRA coverage. COBRA allows coverage after termination of employment for at least 18 months and for as many as 36 months in some limited cases. This period is usually sufficient to allow an individual to leave one job, gain employment elsewhere, and switch to the new employer's health care plan without losing health coverage for themselves and their family.

COBRA applies to companies with 20 or more full-time equivalent employees. It is required to be offered to both terminated employees and those who voluntarily quit, in most cases. An interesting thing about this law is that it doesn't make failure to comply illegal. It instead denies a tax deduction that employers could otherwise take if they fail to comply with the COBRA regulations, and the law has been amended to charge an excise tax on employers who are not in compliance. So the employer's effective tax rate goes up significantly if they fail to comply with COBRA rules.[48]

The employee, as noted earlier, has to pay the premium for health insurance continuation. The company can also charge the former employee a fee of up to 2% above the premium cost for administration costs. But even at 102% of the basic premium cost, COBRA coverage is almost always a good deal for the former employee, again because of the power of buying in bulk.

Why don't more former employees choose to continue their insurance under COBRA? In most cases it is because of the cost of paying the premium, especially if they will be out of work for a period of time. However, as HR managers we need to remember that federal law requires that we offer COBRA to individuals who leave our employment.

The American Recovery and Reinvestment Act of 2009 (ARRA) also added a new requirement to the COBRA rules that employers need to be aware of: Companies will be required to "front" a 65% subsidy of the COBRA cost of health continuation coverage for qualified employees who lost their jobs between September 2008 and December 2009. This means that the employer must pay this cost and then file for a reimbursement of the cost on their quarterly payroll tax deposits. This is significantly different from providing COBRA coverage for individuals who lost their jobs outside of this period.

HEALTH INSURANCE PORTABILITY AND ACCOUNTABILITY ACT OF 1996 (HIPAA). The Health Insurance Portability and Accountability Act (HIPAA) is another health insurance

SHRM
K:B5
Regulation of Health Insurance Programs (COBRA, HIPAA, HMO Act of 1973)

SHRM
B:33
COBRA

SHRM
B:34
American Recovery and Reinvestment Act of 2009 (ARRA)

SHRM
B:37
HIPAA

COBRA A law that requires employers to offer to maintain health insurance on individuals who leave their employment (for a period of time)

mandate from the federal government that applies *if* the company provides health insurance to its employees. Only part of the HIPAA law applies directly to all employers. What are the general provisions of HIPAA that all employers need to understand?

First, HIPAA requires that our health insurance is *"portable."* This means that if we had group health insurance at our previous employer and *if* our new employer has health care coverage for their employees, the new employer is required to provide us with the opportunity to participate in their health insurance plan. Why wouldn't the new company want us to participate in their plan? Well, if we had a preexisting condition that required a lot of health care expense, the new employer's premiums might go up.

The second issue that is mandatory for all employers under HIPAA is the *privacy* and *security* requirements for medical information on employees. This is the *accountability* part of HIPAA. HIPAA protects "the privacy of individually identifiable health information" from being disclosed to unauthorized individuals.[49] It also provides that employers must take action to ensure the security of personal health information. The *privacy* rule requires that covered firms take "reasonable steps to limit the use or disclosure of, and requests for, protected health information." The *security* rule requires covered firms to have "appropriate administrative, technical, and physical safeguards to protect the privacy of protected health information" for individual employees.[50] So COBRA and HIPAA are mandatory if we as an employer offer health insurance to our employees.

In addition to its effects on COBRA, the American Recovery and Reinvestment Act of 2009 (ARRA) also created new HIPAA privacy and security requirements for companies with group health plans. Most privacy and security rules originally created by HIPAA were limited to the covered entities, including group health benefit plans. ARRA "has extended HIPAA's privacy and security rules to business associates and other vendors directly, and has enhanced HIPAA's civil and criminal penalties."[51] New "notice requirements" for an inadvertent release of protected health information (PHI) are also included under ARRA.

SHRM

B:7
ERISA

EMPLOYEE RETIREMENT INCOME SECURITY ACT OF 1974 (ERISA). The first two government mandates that we discussed were contingent on company actions in companies that choose to provide *group health insurance* to their employees. However, the last one that we will discuss covers employers who provide a *group retirement plan and/or group health insurance*. Employee Retirement Income Security Act (ERISA) guidance must be followed in either of these cases. Let's take a look at the main provisions of ERISA.

SHRM

K:B3
Regulation of Retirement Plans
(FLSA, ERISA, etc.)

General provisions. Any organization that provides retirement or health insurance plans must provide a document called a Summary Plan Description (SPD) telling beneficiaries about the plan and how it works—in plain language that the average employee can understand. The organization also has to provide similar information whenever the plan changes significantly and send an annual report to members, as well as meet some other requirements.

Eligibility. Another major provision of ERISA is guidance on retirement (pension) plan eligibility. If the company provides employees with a retirement plan, the guidelines in ERISA say that the plan has to be available to all employees over 21 years of age who have worked in the company for 1 year. This brings up a common question about such laws. Can the company offer retirement options to employees who are not yet 21 or who haven't worked there for a year? The answer is yes. The company can *relax* the requirements of ERISA, but it cannot be more restrictive than the law allows. This is the case in many similar laws and federal regulations.

Vesting. A second major provision of ERISA is the vesting rules. **Vesting** *provides for a maximum amount of time beyond which the employee will have unfettered access to their retirement funds, both employee contributions and employer contributions*.

Vesting A maximum amount of time beyond which the employee will have unfettered access to their retirement funds, both employee contributions and employer contributions

Most retirement plans today take in contributions from both the employer and the employee. Of course, the employee's money is available to the employee at pretty much any time. There are rules about how the employee can remove money from a "qualified retirement account" (an account that has federal and sometimes state tax advantages associated with it), including the requirement that they reinvest it into another qualified retirement fund within a certain time period, but the money they contribute can be removed from the account when they leave the employer, or even before as long as they follow some IRS rules. ERISA identifies the maximum amount of time that the company can retain company contributions to the employee's retirement account. The rules in ERISA say that the employer must vest the employee in all employer contributions based on one of two options:

- 100% of employer contributions at the end of 5 years of contributions to the plan; or
- 20% of employer contributions from the end of year 3 through the end of year 7.

So if an employer and employee have been contributing to the employee's retirement fund for 5 years and the employer has provided $1,000 per year to the account, the employee can take that $5,000 employer contribution out of the retirement fund and move it to any other retirement fund that they choose. Alternately, under the 20% per year option, the employee might only be allowed to have access to 20% of $3,000 at the end of year 3, 40% of $4,000 at the end of year 4, 60% of $5,000 at the end of year 5, up until the end of year 7, when they would have access to all of the employer's contributions to their retirement fund.

Can the company allow the employee to be vested earlier? Of course it can. In some cases, companies will immediately vest employees in their own retirement funds as a recruiting incentive. This can be a significant advantage over having to wait 5 years to have access to employer-provided funds. If the company doesn't vest us in our retirement fund for 5 years, then if we leave the company for a better job after 4 years and 10 months, we forfeit all of the employer contributions to the fund (in this case about $4,850).

Employers have to be aware that a number of factors may cause retirement plans (as well as other benefits) to be nonqualified. Executive compensation in the form of a deferred contribution to the executive's retirement accounts is one of the most common forms of nonqualified retirement funds. If the benefit doesn't meet the requirements of IRS rules governing qualified retirement plans, the company must treat the contributions to the account as taxable.

Portability. The third major issue that ERISA addresses is portability of retirement accounts. The portability rule allows us to take our retirement fund and move it from our employer to another qualified fund. The employer cannot require that we keep the funds with them, or under their control. Once the vesting requirements have been met, the employee has the ability to move funds from the employer's control into another qualified retirement account.

Fiduciaries. The next provision of ERISA is the responsibility of individuals acting as fiduciaries for company retirement funds. A fiduciary is a person who has authority over how retirement funds are managed but also has financial responsibilities associated with that authority. ERISA notes that fiduciaries have the requirement to act under a concept called the "prudent man." This includes requirements that the fiduciary will act to benefit the fund's participants, minimize unnecessary expenses to the fund, and use "care, skill, prudence, and diligence" in managing the funds entrusted to them.

But what is prudence? Is it prudent to put the bulk of retirement investments into dot-com stocks, as many investment managers did prior to the year 2000? What

SHRM

K:B13
Nonqualified Plans for Highly Paid and Executive Employees

13-1 APPLYING THE CONCEPT

Statutory Benefit Laws

Place the letter of the relevant statutory benefit law on the line next to the statement below.

    a. FMLA

    b. ACA

    c. COBRA

    d. HIPAA

    e. ERISA

_____ 1. I don't trust my company's financial future, so I like this law because it will allow me to move my funds out of my company fund to a new account with the stockbroker of my choice.

_____ 2. I like this law because it will allow me to take time off from work to take care of my sick mother.

_____ 3. I'm going quit and look for a new job, so I like this law because I need to continue to have health insurance while I search for a new job.

_____ 4. I currently have health insurance and medical problems, but when I change jobs, the new company can't refuse to give me insurance based on any medical problems I have when I join the firm.

_____ 5. I'm out of school and almost 25, so I like this law that allows me to continue on my parents' insurance plan.

WORK APPLICATION 13-6

Which, if any, statutory requirements governing certain voluntary benefits would be mandatory where you work or have worked?

---

about putting large portions of the fund into financial firm stocks, as many did up until 2007–2008? While in hindsight these were probably not good investments, they would have probably passed the "prudent man" standard, so prudence is a pretty minimal standard of diligence for the managers of retirement funds.

PBGC. The last big provision of ERISA is the creation of the Pension Benefit Guarantee Corporation (PBGC). The **PBGC** *is a governmental corporation established within the Department of Labor whose purpose is to insure retirement funds from failure.* Its main function is to act as an insurer for the benefits promised to employees whose employers go bankrupt or are for other reasons not able to provide the promised retirement benefits to their employees. It covers only "defined benefit" retirement plans (which we will cover shortly)—plans that have specified benefits that will be paid out to the individual employee on their retirement. The PBGC may not fund 100% of what was promised in the specific retirement plan, but it "guarantees 'basic benefits' earned before the plan's termination date" or the employer's date of bankruptcy.[52] There are also caps on coverage of pensions, which are determined by ERISA.

Who provides funds for the PBGC? In this case, even though PBGC is a federal government entity, the funds for the program come from employer payments into the program. If an employer chooses to provide "defined benefit" retirement accounts for their employees, they are required to pay into the PBGC. These funds are then used to provide benefits to workers whose employers are unable to pay the promised benefits. So PBGC acts as a guarantor of these retirement plans.

LO 13-6

Briefly describe the main categories of voluntary benefits available to organizations.

PBGC A governmental corporation established within the Department of Labor whose purpose is to insure retirement funds from failure

VOLUNTARY BENEFITS

In addition to mandatory benefits, almost all employers provide some group of voluntary benefits to their employees. These can range from a narrow group of commonly provided benefits such as retirement accounts, life insurance, and vacation time to a very broad group including company nap rooms, sick-child care services, and personal valets. How do companies determine what voluntary benefits they are going to provide? They look at their workforce and the funds available to the company and choose the package that will best allow them to maintain a satisfied and engaged workforce. Let's discuss some of the more common voluntary benefits, including paid time off, group health insurance, retirement, and employee insurance.

Paid Time Off

Paid time off (PTO) benefits include a group of options such as vacation time/annual leave, severance pay, personal time off, sick days, and holidays. Some companies provide an all-encompassing PTO plan that allows the employee to use their paid time off in any way they wish, whether for sick days or vacation, holidays, or for any other purpose. Others apportion the available days for vacation, sick time, holidays, and others.[53] These benefits contribute approximately 7% of the average employer's total cost of wages and benefits, or 10% of direct wages.[54] Another way to look at this is that the *average cost of paid time off is $1 for every $10 in direct wages*. None of the listed PTO benefits is mandatory in the United States at this point, yet most employers provide at least some holidays off and some vacation and/or sick time. In addition, you need to be aware that some states have already passed, or are currently attempting to pass, mandatory sick leave and even in some cases annual leave laws. Paid time off is commonly viewed as an entitlement (Chapter 12). Let's do a quick review of the most common types of PTO.

VACATION OR ANNUAL LEAVE. Although federal law does not currently require any paid vacation time, the majority of US firms provide paid vacations to their employees, according to the US Bureau of Labor Statistics. In fact, about 93% of employers provide paid vacation in some form—either as a stand-alone benefit or as part of a PTO plan—to their full-time workforce.[55] The average time provided was about 10 days after 1 year of service in 2012, while workers with 10 years of service averaged 17 days.[56] Why do companies provide this time off? The simple answer is that it refreshes the employee so that they can come back to work and be more productive. Many studies show that when we leave a stressful situation for a period of time, we lower our stress level, which in turn raises our ability to be productive.[57] Good employers know this and, as a result, provide time off to allow their employees to relax.

SICK LEAVE. The next most popular PTO is sick leave. Approximately 86% of employers in the United States provide sick leave of some type to their employees, whether in an all-encompassing PTO plan or specifically designated as "sick days."[58] Paid sick leave can offer employees relief from loss of income associated with having to miss work due to an illness. However, there is significant evidence that sick leave is abused by employees, especially in the case of a "use it or lose it" sick leave policy. With the entitlement mentality, some employees take every sick day off even though they are not sick. This is one of the reasons why more companies are moving to the total PTO concept instead of designating a specific number of days as sick leave.

Family vacations help employees maintain work and family balance.

HOLIDAY PAY. Nearly all employers provide for at least some paid holidays with their work-force. In 2014, the US government identified 10 federal holidays, and many companies also observe some local, state, and religious holidays as well. Here again, companies can be subject to problems or even charges of discrimination if there is cultural or religious diversity in the firm. Because of these issues, some companies provide "floating" holidays so that the employee can pick which days they will observe as holidays during the work year. Between one third and one half of companies in the United States currently provide floating holidays.

SHRM

K:B15
Time Off and Other Benefits

SHRM

K:B21
Paid Leave Plans

Kei Uesugi/Photodisc/Thinkstock

WORK
APPLICATION 13-7

Identify the paid time off benefits offered where you work or have worked.

LO 13-7

Describe the differences between traditional health care plans, HMOs, PPOs, and HSA/MSA plans.

K:B4
Types of Health Care Plans

Traditional health care plans Plans that cover a set percentage of fees for medical services—for either doctors or in-patient care

In addition, some firms allow employees to swap holidays to observe a holiday of their choice that would normally be unpaid, for instance swapping Christmas Day for Yom Kippur.

PAID PERSONAL LEAVE. Finally, many companies today provide time off for a wide variety of personal needs. Many firms allow employees to use such leave to visit their child at school or accompany them on a field trip. Other options might include funeral leave, family leave that would not be covered under the FMLA, time off on their birthday, and "mental health" days among others. One company, **Netflix**, has even gone as far as saying that workers can take whatever vacation time they think is appropriate![59] Personal leave is an effort on the part of the organization to maintain or improve job satisfaction and organizational commitment on the part of their employees.

Group Health Insurance

As we have already noted, if a company chooses to provide health care to employees, they have to follow the COBRA, HIPAA, and ERISA rules. Companies also have to look at the rising cost of providing such care. In 1980 health care services accounted for less than 10% of gross domestic product (GDP), in 2000 that figure was 13.8%, and in 2012 (the latest government figures) these services accounted for 17.2% of GDP.[60]

A survey by the Bureau of Labor Statistics reported that 68% of private-industry workers receive medical care benefits and that employers offering health insurance paid an average of 81% of the cost of premiums for single coverage and 69% of the cost for family coverage in 2013.[61] Thus, companies that do provide health care have to be concerned with the costs. And remember that the ACA is going to require many companies to provide health insurance beginning in 2015, thereby increasing their overall costs of doing business. **Costco** offers its workers higher-than-average wages and better benefits. In 2013, 85% of its US employees, including part-time workers, received health care and other benefits (compared to less than 50% at **Walmart** and **Target**) prior to the implementation of the Affordable Care Act (ACA).[62] One of the ways that companies can control costs is to understand what coverage they are buying for what price. Let's look at the major types of group health insurance currently available to companies.

TRADITIONAL PLANS (ALSO CALLED FEE-FOR-SERVICE). **Traditional health care plans** *typically cover a set percentage of fees for medical services—for either doctors or in-patient care.* The most common percentage split between the insurance plan and the individual is 80/20. In other words, if the employee has to go to the hospital and is charged $10,000 for services, the insurance would pay $8,000 and the individual would be responsible for the other $2,000. There are, of course, some variations on these plans, but this is basically how they work. One of the issues with traditional fee-for-service plans is that they typically do not cover preventive care, such as an annual physical exam. They do, however, cover most but not all of the costs to treat medical conditions covered by the policy.

One of the biggest advantages of traditional plans is that they allow employees to go to any doctor or provider they want without a referral to see specialists. Also, if the employee has traditional health insurance, they can live anywhere. With some *managed care* health insurance (we will talk about this next), employees are limited to living within a certain range of the network controlled by the insurance company. However, the big problem with such insurance is the high overall cost of medical care today. If a patient went to the hospital for a serious medical problem, such as cancer, it would be very easy to incur bills in excess of $1 million. In such a case, the individual would be responsible for $200,000 of the total charges, unless they had separate gap coverage or other major medical insurance. So traditional plans have somewhat fallen out of favor. Traditional plans do give the employee a lot of choice, but there are some serious issues with potential out-of-pocket costs.

HEALTH MAINTENANCE ORGANIZATIONS (HMOs). HMOs are a *managed care* program. An **HMO** *is a health care plan that provides both health maintenance services and medical care as part of the plan.* This is health care that provides the patient with routine preventive care, but in the case of nonpreventive care it requires that a review of specific circumstances concerning the individual and their health condition be completed *before* any significant medical testing, medical procedures, or hospital care is approved. Managed care plans generally require that the employee and their family use doctors and facilities that are in the managed care network. In some cases, the managed care plan will allow the insured person to go outside the network, but if this is done, the cost of care is usually significantly higher. This allows the managed care company to attempt to ensure that unnecessary tests and procedures are not done, thereby saving both the insured and the insurance company money.

In the HMO form of managed care, the insured person will generally be required to use doctors and facilities in the network. The employee (and their family, if covered) will choose a primary care physician (PCP). The **primary care physician (PCP)** *will be the first point of contact for all preventive care and in any routine medical situation, except emergencies.* The PCP will see the patient and, if they feel the need for a specialist to be involved with the case, will refer the patient to that specialist. The specialists also usually have to be part of the network in order to accept referral patients from the HMO.

In the HMO form of managed care, the patient pays a copayment each time they visit their PCP and will generally also pay a copayment if they see a specialist after a referral. Once the copayment is paid, all other billable costs for the physician visit will generally be paid by the insurer. In addition, there will almost always be an annual deductible, an amount that the patient will be required to cover for any care beyond physician office visits (such as an outpatient procedure to have a child's tonsils removed) before the remainder of such costs will be paid by the insurer.

In an HMO plan, the PCP physicians are generally paid a flat fee per patient to take care of that patient for the year. This fee is provided to the physician to be the gatekeeper for any other medical services that the employee or their family may need during that year. The PCP will get the same amount of money no matter how many times a patient visits them during the year. Why is this significant? If the physician happens to be selected as the PCP by patients who don't use medical services at the average rate of the overall population, the HMO knows this (because they do a utilization analysis) and will cut payments to the physician next year because the PCP isn't using up as much time as the average physician.

The company should always do a similar utilization analysis on its employees. If the HMO can cut payments to the physicians that serve our company, we should share in the cost reduction. If the company fails to complete the utilization analysis itself, the HMO will be happy to keep all of the savings, but if the company is doing a utilization analysis, it can demand some share of the cash saved. This is another place where good HRM can save the company money.

HMOs have some very good characteristics and some bad ones. Preventive care is covered, and there are maximum out-of-pocket costs to the employee in any given year (at least for covered illnesses and injuries). However, the employee may be required to live in certain areas (because of the network of physicians and medical facilities) so that they can be safely covered without having to go long distances in an emergency. There may also be limits to the number and types of procedures that will be covered by the HMO; the employee does not have free choice in doctors, clinics, and hospitals for their care; and various copayments and deductibles are the employee's responsibility before the HMO covers the rest of the costs.

HMO A health care plan that provides both health maintenance services and medical care as part of the plan

Primary care physician (PCP) The first point of contact for all preventive care and in any routine medical situation, except emergencies

PREFERRED PROVIDER ORGANIZATIONS (PPO). **Preferred provider organizations (PPOs)** *are a kind of hybrid between traditional fee-for-service plans and HMOs.* They have some of the advantages and disadvantages as well as some of the requirements of both. PPOs have networks of physicians and medical facilities, just like HMOs. PPOs act like HMOs in that they *prefer* (but do not require) that you have a PCP within their medical network and that you go to that PCP before going elsewhere for medical care. They also provide preventive care services to their insured members, similar to HMOs, and have similar copayments and annual deductibles.

However, PPOs do not require that you have a referral from the PCP to see a specialist. In this way, they are more similar to a traditional health care plan. They will also allow you to see any provider of care either in or outside the network, although you may be required to pay a larger percentage of the cost of care if you choose to go beyond the network of physicians and facilities.

So if we compare PPOs with HMOs, we see that the advantages of PPOs include the ability to see any physician and use any medical facilities (as with a traditional plan), which in turn relieves the individual insured by the PPO of the necessity to live within certain geographical boundaries. The member can live anywhere they want because they can use any medical facilities they choose. In addition, similar to HMOs, PPOs cover preventive care. However, unlike with HMOs, the cost of care can be significantly higher if the individual chooses to go outside the preferred providers that are identified as PPO participants. So, PPOs prefer that we use physicians and facilities within their network, but we have a choice to go outside the network and pay at a higher rate if desired.

HEALTH OR MEDICAL SAVINGS ACCOUNTS (HSA/MSA). HSAs and MSAs are two very similar savings accounts for health care services. MSAs are medical savings accounts available to self-employed persons and small businesses with fewer than 50 employees. HSAs are available to employees of larger businesses who choose to provide these accounts. An **HSA or MSA** *allows the employer and employee to fund a medical savings account from which the employee can pay medical expenses each year with pretax dollars.* The money in this account is then used to pay for medical services for the employee (and their family, if desired) over the course of that year. One of the big advantages of HSAs and MSAs is that money remaining in the account at the end of the year can be rolled over to future years without paying a tax penalty as a general rule.[63]

For example, assume that our employer provides an HSA and shares equally in funding our account at the maximum amount allowed for an individual for the year 2013—$3,050. The employer puts in $1,525, and we put in $1,525 (deducted from our pay over the entire year). In February of that year, we go to our physician for our annual physical. The cost of the physical including tests is $465. Our HSA provided us with a debit card for medical expenses at the beginning of the year, so we provide the debit card to our physician and they bill $465 to our card.

The remaining balance on our card will be $2,585. Our physician reports that it appears that we have a small cancerous growth on our skin that needs to be removed in an outpatient surgery. We go to the outpatient surgery center where they remove the cancer and charge us $1,842, which we pay with our debit card, leaving a balance of $743. The only other medical service that we have that year is a physician's office visit and antibiotics for a sinus infection. We are billed for the full cost of the office visit at $80 and for the full cost of the antibiotics at $34. This would leave a balance of $629 in our HSA. At the end of the year, this $629 will roll over to next year's HSA account and be added to the new contribution of $3,050.

As you can see, in an HSA you pay the full cost of each of the medical services used in a plan year from the HSA account. There are no copayments; there are no deductibles. However, if you don't use the full value of the services, the remaining dollar amounts can be rolled over to future years, so you don't lose that money.

Preferred provider organizations (PPOs) A kind of hybrid between traditional fee-for-service plans and HMOs

HSA or MSA A plan allowing the employer and employee to fund a medical savings account from which the employee can pay medical expenses each year with pretax dollars

HSAs are also portable, so we can take our HSA balance with us if we change employers. One of the benefits to companies using an HSA or MSA is that it causes the employee to understand the full cost of providing health care for the year. If the full cost of health care is coming out of the employee's pocket through the use of the HSA debit card, it is thought that they might pay more attention to unnecessary medical expenses, including such things as going to the doctor's office when they have a cold or if they sprain a finger. The assumption is that if the employees pay more attention to the overall cost of health care, we can lower that cost.

High-deductible health plan (HDHP). One of the problems that we can quickly see within HSA is that our medical services in a particular year could cost us much more than $3,050, especially if we had to have a surgery. However, federal rules on HSAs and MSAs require that employees who have these accounts also participate in something called a HDHP. A **high-deductible health plan (HDHP)** *is a "major medical" insurance plan that protects against catastrophic health care costs and in most cases is paid for by the employer.* A very common HDHP would pay for medical costs in any given year that total more than $10,000. So if an individual exceeded the $3,050 in their HSA, they would be responsible for out-of-pocket costs of a maximum of $6,950, at which time the HDHP would take over and pay the remaining costs of the individual's health care for the year.

At first glance, this looks like a large out-of-pocket expense for the individual employee. However, in other forms of health care, the employee generally has copayments, deductibles, and prescription copayments that come out of their own pocket during the course of the year. Annual deductibles can frequently be as high as $2,000 to $4,000, while each PCP visit can cost between $20 and $40, each specialist's office visit costs $40 to $50, and prescription copayments typically cost from $25 to $40, or more. So if an individual had large-scale medical costs in any given year, they would most likely have at least as much in out-of-pocket costs as they would under the HSA plan.

One of the big advantages of HSAs and MSAs is that the individual can go to any physician or medical facility. There is no HMO network and no preferred providers. If the employee wants to go to the top specialist in their field and is willing to pay the extra cost of the office visit for such a specialist, they have the ability to go. In this way, HSAs and MSAs are much more like traditional fee-for-service plans than HMOs and PPOs. However, they are much more like HMOs and PPOs in the fact that there are maximum out-of-pocket costs per year before the HDHP takes over and pays all other medical expenses.

Because HSAs and MSAs cause the individual employee to see the total cost of their health care, and might cause these employees to use such care at a lower level because it is a direct cost to the employee, about 42% of employers now offer these accounts to employees in an attempt to control ever-rising health care costs.[64] The HSA can cause people to realize that medical care costs a lot more than their copayments. If the employee only pays $20 to go to the doctor, they will go whenever they feel the slightest problem coming on, but if they have to pay the entire $125 for the cost of the office visit, they may think much harder before they spend that money to go to the doctor to remove a splinter. Because of the fact that it makes employees aware of the entire cost of health care, it is expected that HSAs and MSA accounts will continue to become a more significant proportion of the health care plans provided by employers over at least the next several years.

UTILIZATION ANALYSIS. We briefly mentioned utilization analyses earlier. Let's take another look at them now. A **utilization analysis** *is a review of the cost of a program and comparison of program costs with the rate of the program's usage by the members of the company.* In other words, is the company getting a valuable benefit out of the program, or could the same money be spent in a different way to get better returns on money spent?

WORK
APPLICATION 13-8

Select a company that offers health insurance and identify the type of insurance it offers.

High-deductible health plan (HDHP) A "major medical" insurance plan that protects against catastrophic health care costs and in most cases is paid for by the employer

Utilization analysis A review of the cost of a program and comparison of program costs with the rate of the program's usage by the members of the company

13-2 APPLYING THE CONCEPT

Group Health Insurance

Place the letter of each type of health insurance option offered on the line next to the statement describing it.

a. Traditional
b. HMO
c. PPO
d. HSA
e. MSA

_____ 6. I don't like the new insurance plan because I can only go to doctors and hospitals that are approved by the plan. I have to stop seeing my doctor and start with a new one that I'm assigned to.

_____ 7. I have expensive health problems, and my insurance plan requires me to pay 20% of my health care costs, making it very expensive for me.

_____ 8. I like my insurance plan because I'm healthy and pay the full cost, but I don't use it all every year and it has accumulated in case I need it someday.

_____ 9. I have the same insurance deal that you have (#8), but my company only has 25 employees.

_____ 10. I do have copays and deductibles, but at least I can go to any doctor or hospital I want too at an extra cost.

If, for instance, our average employee is healthier that the national average employee, we might use fewer medical services over time than other companies of similar size in the same industry. But our premiums for health insurance will (at least initially) be based on the "average" employee in our industry. If we investigate and find that our employees do, in fact, use fewer medical services each year than the average, we can ask the insurer to lower our insurance rates to match our utilization rates. Health insurance is one of the easiest things for us to do a utilization analysis on because we are provided information on the services that our employees use by the insurance company. If we have a strong case, we need to go to the insurance company and request that they lower our rates to match our utilization of services.

Retirement Benefits

According the Bureau of Labor Statistics, employer-provided retirement plans are available to 74% of all full-time workers and 37% of part-time workers in private industry.[65] They are not mandatory, but if we provide them we have to comply with ERISA. As with health insurance, companies provide retirement benefits to motivate employees. However, as discussed in Chapter 12, employees may view them as simply an entitlement.[66] Retirement benefits are categorized into two types. Let's discuss both followed by five options for defined contribution plans.

LO 13-8

Discuss the difference between defined benefit and defined contribution retirement plans and the reasons for the shift from defined benefit to defined contribution plans.

Defined benefit plan A plan providing the retiree with a specific amount and type of benefits that will be available when the individual retires

DEFINED BENEFIT VERSUS DEFINED CONTRIBUTION PLANS. A **defined benefit plan** *provides the retiree with a specific amount and type of benefits that will be available when the individual retires.* The retiree knows exactly what they are going to receive in benefits when they retire. For instance, a simple defined benefit plan might provide that employees who work in the company for 25 years will get 60% of the average of their two highest years of pay. In addition, they will receive 1% more for every additional year that they work. So if the same employee worked for 35 years, they would receive 70% of the average of their two highest years of pay. If such an employee made $64,238 in their highest paid year and $63,724 in their second highest paid year, their two highest years' average pay would equal $63,981. If this individual retired with 25 years of service, they would receive $38,388.60 per year in retirement. If they instead retired after 35 years of service, they would receive $44,786.70 per year in retirement. Because it is a defined benefit retirement plan, the employee knows exactly what their retirement will be.

Defined contribution plan. Unlike with a defined benefit plan, under a defined contribution plan the employee does not know what their retirement benefit will be. **Defined contribution plans** *identify only the amount of funds that will go into a retirement account, not what the employee will receive upon retirement.* The employee only knows what their contribution to the retirement fund consists of. What will the employee who contributes to a defined contribution plan receive upon retirement? The answer to this question will depend on the success of the investment of their retirement funds over the years between the contribution of the funds and the employee's ultimate retirement. If the retirement funds are invested successfully, growing significantly over time, the individual's retirement account will be able to pay much higher benefits than if the funds are not invested successfully and don't grow very much.

Shift from defined benefit to defined contribution plans. Defined benefit plans used to be the most common type of retirement plan, but they have been overtaken by defined contribution plans—some would say for legitimate business reasons. In 2013 **Chrysler** announced that they would freeze their US pension plan for about 8,000 workers and transfer them to a defined contribution plan in 2014.[67] Providing a defined contribution retirement plan to employees shifts the investment risk from the company to the individual employee. Under a defined benefit plan the employer puts money into retirement accounts and expects that money to grow at a certain rate over time. But if the funds do not grow at the expected rate, the employer is left with a shortage in the retirement accounts and must add money to those accounts in order to be able to pay the promised benefit to retired workers. This happened in the US auto industry as large numbers of retiring employees combined with lower sales and a period of no profits and layoffs, which left fewer employees to cover the cost of those retirees. So the cost of adding funds to the defined benefit plans for their retirees contributed to a cost advantage for foreign automakers, and (when the 2007–08 recession occurred) to the US government bailout of **General Motors** and **Chrysler**.

In the case of a defined contribution plan, the risk of slow growth of the investment shifts to the employee. The company has no obligation to pay a specific amount to the employee, so if the fund doesn't grow at the expected rate, the employer is not required to add money to that fund. However, the employee may not be able to draw as much in benefits as they had anticipated if the account hasn't earned interest or grown at the rate that was expected over time.

There are a number of different defined contribution plans that meet federal and state guidelines for favorable tax treatment and therefore have added value to both employers and employees. Let's take a look at some of the most common types of defined contribution plans now.

401(K) AND 403(B) PLANS. The most well-known retirement plan in US companies today is the 401(k). 401(k) accounts are available to nearly all employees of corporations as well as most self-employed persons. A *401(k) retirement plan* is a savings investment account for individual employees of corporations. A *403(b) retirement plan* is a very similar plan to the 401(k) with the exception that it is used for non-profit entities.

Both the employee and the employer are allowed to contribute funds each year to the employee's 401(k) or 403(b) account, with the *employee* allowed to contribute up to a maximum of $17,500 (for an employee under 50 years of age in 2014).[68] Contributions to these accounts are made on a "pretax basis." This means that when funds are put into the account, they do not count as taxable income for the individual. Once the individual retires and begins to remove funds from the account, they pay income taxes on the distributions at their current tax rate, which tends to be lower at retirement. The earliest point at which the contributor can withdraw money without incurring a penalty from a 401(k) or 403(b) account is at age 59½.

SHRM

K:B2
Types of Retirement Plans

LO 13-9
Discuss the major retirement plan options.

Defined contribution plan A plan providing only the amount of funds that will go into a retirement account, not what the employee will receive upon retirement

Matching contributions. Many employers that offer a 401(k) or 403(b) provide a matching contribution up to a set maximum. For example, an employer might allow a 100% match of employee contributions up to a $2,000 maximum. So if the employee put $2,000 of their salary into the retirement account over the course of the year, this plus the employer's matching funds would add $4,000 a year to the individual's retirement account. Among the 250 largest companies, **ConocoPhillips** offers the largest potential match at 9%; companies at a 6% match include **Boston Scientific, Caterpillar, DuPont**, and **Visa**.[69] Because of the tax deferral associated with a 401(k), the individual's taxable income is lowered by the amount of the contribution, so take-home pay is not decreased by the full amount that the employee actually put into their retirement account.

On a personal note, never refuse free money. "If your employer offers a 401(k) plan, embrace it. . . . Whatever the match is, put as much into the plan as you need to get it."[70] You would be amazed at how many people refuse the retirement match. Taking the full match as early as you can is one of the most important tips in this book. With a $2,000 matching plan, if you start young enough, with good investing, you can retire as a millionaire. Remember the general guide to put 10% of your income every month into your retirement account, no matter how low your income is.[71]

IRAS AND ROTH IRAS. An IRA is an Individual Retirement Account. Under US law, any person who pays taxes can have and contribute to an IRA, and the contributions are tax-free (subject to a maximum annual income limit). In other words, they reduce your taxable income by the full amount of the contribution in the year in which they are contributed to the account. Both IRAs and Roth IRAs can supplement the amount that an individual is contributing to a company-sponsored 401(k) account, because we are allowed to contribute to both. An individual can contribute a maximum of 100% of their income up to $5,500 per year (in 2014) into a standard, or Roth, IRA.[72]

The Roth IRA is basically the same type of account as a regular IRA with the exception that the Roth IRA "front-loads," or requires that we pay the taxes immediately for funds put into the retirement account. If we put $4,000 into a Roth IRA in 2014 and were in the 25% federal tax bracket, we would pay $1,000 in tax for 2014, but when we withdrew these funds upon retirement, they would be tax-free. With the standard IRA, you pay no tax on the funds when you contribute them, but you pay taxes at your current tax rate when those funds are withdrawn.

What is the advantage to paying the taxes up front on a Roth IRA? If you expect to be in a much higher tax bracket later in life, it makes sense to pay the taxes at your lower (current) tax rate instead of paying a higher tax rate later. Assume that you are currently in the 15% tax bracket, but your income triples over the next 40 years and you expect that (based on current tax rates) you will be in a 38% tax bracket later. You can pay $750 on a $5,000 Roth IRA contribution today, but might have to pay $1,900 on that same $5,000 contribution (plus any interest earned) when you withdraw it in 40 years. So if you expect your tax bracket to go up over time, a Roth IRA may be advantageous.

SIMPLIFIED EMPLOYEE PENSION (SEP) PLANS. The last common retirement plan that we will discuss here is the SEP. SEPs are primarily used for self-employed individuals and members of small companies. According to the US Department of Labor, "Under a SEP, an employer contributes directly to traditional individual retirement accounts (SEP-IRAs) for all employees (including the employer). A SEP . . . allows for a contribution of up to 25% of each employee's pay" up to a maximum of $52,000 (in 2014) into the person's IRA each year.[73] Because the owner is not an employee with pay, the self-employed person can tax defer a set percentage of the company profits.

APPLYING THE CONCEPT

Retirement Plans

Recommend the appropriate retirement plan based on the person's situation.

    a. 401(k)

    b. 403(b)

    c. IRA

    d. Roth IRA

    e. SEP

_____ 11. I work for a church, but we do have a retirement account.

_____ 12. My company doesn't offer any retirement benefits for part-time employees, so how should I save for retirement?

_____ 13. I work for a major corporation, and it offers the standard retirement plan with a 5% match.

_____ 14. I already have a retirement plan at work and put in the maximum tax-deferred contribution. What other options do I have to save even more for my retirement?

_____ 15. I started my own business and want to save for retirement. What retirement plan should I use?

A SEP can also be used by a person who has a job that has retirement benefits and who is also self-employed to defer taxes and save more for retirement.

What makes a SEP retirement plan valuable to small business is the lower paperwork burden compared to a 401(k) or 403(b) retirement account. The contributions follow the same basic tax rules as a 401(k): Contributions are not taxed when made, but the individual pays taxes on the money when it is withdrawn during retirement. For self-employed proprietorships without any employees getting SEP retirement benefits, the only records needed are the individual tax return 1040 with a Schedule C for self-employed income showing the SEP deduction from profits going into the SEP, and the SEP account records verifying that the money was actually put into the SEP.

Employee Insurance Coverage

The next major category of voluntary benefits is insurance. There are a number of different types of insurance that are provided as common voluntary benefits to our employees. The largest of these is life insurance, but disability policies (both short- and long-term), supplemental unemployment policies, income continuation (also called supplemental health) policies, travel accident insurance, individual cancer and genetic disease policies, and other insurance options are also available and are part of some companies' voluntary benefit programs. Let's review some of the major employee insurance options.

LIFE INSURANCE. Many firms will provide group term life (GTL) insurance policies to provide for survivors of an employee who dies while employed by the company. In 2013, about 72% of employers provided this service to their full-time employees.[74] GTL provides for a survivor payment to occur only if the employee dies during the term that is covered by the insurance policy. It is also a valuable benefit to the employer because it is eligible for an employer tax deduction for up to $50,000 in coverage if it complies with IRS regulations.[75] A fairly standard benefit here would be 1 to 2 times the individual's annual compensation. So if an employee dies, on or off the job for most causes of death, the beneficiary would get 1 to 2 years' salary. Many companies will allow the employee to add to this coverage at the group rates, which is generally a very good deal for the employee. Generally, once the employee leaves the company, the term insurance policy will be discontinued.

In addition to GTL, employers can provide permanent, or whole, life insurance. Unlike term life policies, this life insurance benefit has no termination or end date. It

WORK
APPLICATION 13-9

Select a company that offers retirement benefits and state the type of plan it offers. If it is a defined benefit, describe the plan. If it is a defined contribution, identify the option selected and if the employer offers any matching contributions, what they are.

SHRM

K:B12
Life Insurance

continues for the life of the individual as long as premiums continue to be paid. Whole life policies can also be used for retirement. However, they are not commonly offered.

DISABILITY INSURANCE. The other large-scale insurance benefit in many companies is disability insurance. This insurance can be either short- or long-term in nature, and some companies offer both options.

K:B7
Disability Insurance

Short-term disability is insurance against being unable to perform the essential functions expected of the employee at work for up to 6 months due to illness or injury—*not necessarily a work-related illness or injury.* This is valuable because most *long*-term disability policies do not provide replacement income until the employee completes a 180-day "elimination period" (a period during which they are unable to work). Short-term coverage closes this 6-month gap. Because 71% of Americans say that it would be difficult to pay their bills if their paycheck were delayed for more than a week, waiting 6 months would likely create a massive hardship for the disabled worker.[76] Remember, too, that Social Security Disability doesn't apply unless the employee is going to be disabled *for at least 5 months*, so short-term disability can bridge this gap in income.

Long-term disability policies cover employees who are unable to work for more than 6 months due to illness or injury—again, *not necessarily a work-related illness or injury.* Long-term disability is designed to replace a portion of the disabled employee's income (*typically 50%–60%*) for extended periods of time, or even permanently.[77] This is a supplemental benefit to Social Security Disability payments because, remember, Social Security payments are not designed to replace 100% of an employee's preretirement (or predisability) income. Long-term benefits most often begin once the employee has exhausted their short-term disability benefits. Benefits from *group* long-term policies will generally continue until the employee reaches their eligible retirement age under Social Security, or until they are able to return to work.[78]

OTHER COMMON INSURANCE BENEFITS. In addition to standard life and disability insurance, there are a number of other insurance benefits provided by at least some employers. These can be loosely grouped into two categories: *life and health* and *other insurance.* Among the *life and health* benefits, we might see (percentage of firms utilizing coverage is in parentheses) vision (53%) and dental (48%) insurance; long-term care (51%); cancer insurance (4%); critical illness insurance (7%); accident insurance (49%); and supplemental insurance policies such as **AFLAC**, which pay for routine expenses (like car payments) not generally covered by health or disability insurance.[79, 80, 81]

In the *other insurance* category, we may provide many types of additional insurance to employees. Some common examples are employer-sponsored automobile (32%) insurance, homeowners and renters insurance (29%), identity theft insurance (22%), and pet insurance (19%).[82]

Employee Services

K:B8
Educational Benefits

In addition to other voluntary benefits, companies may provide a wide variety of employee services as benefits for their workforce. *Educational (or tuition) assistance* is one common benefit in this group. In 2013, roughly 60% of all companies provided some form of educational assistance to their employees.[83] Unfortunately, with the rising cost of benefits, this benefit has been cut back at many firms.

Other common employee services include on-site child care or child care vouchers; elder care assistance; company-provided gyms and fitness facilities or vouchers for memberships outside the business; organization-sponsored sports teams; services to mitigate commuting costs including work shuttles, company-provided or paid parking, "green" vehicle allowances, or public or private transportation vouchers; cafeterias or meal vouchers; plus too many others to name.

Employee services are provided in order to minimize disruptions to the employee's work life. If the employee isn't worried about their children (because the company has a day care facility on site), they can concentrate on work. If they don't have to deal with figuring out where they can park downtown, they are less stressed when they start their day. If they need 15 minutes' rest, they can take a nap, and if they want to work out to relieve some stress, they can go to the company gym. Companies don't provide these services because they like to throw money away. They provide employee services to lower stress and allow employees to concentrate on the job. Any service that takes the employee away from being able to focus on work is a legitimate target for an employee service benefit, and more and more companies are paying attention to such services.

Before we go on to discuss how to administer and communicate benefits, let's review the list of benefits discussed so far in Exhibit 13-4. Note that there are an unlimited number of voluntary benefits, but only the major ones discussed are listed here.

WORK
APPLICATION 13-10

Select a company that offers voluntary benefits. Besides paid time off, retirement, and health and employee insurance, what other benefits does it offer?

ADMINISTRATION AND COMMUNICATION OF BENEFITS

LO 13-10

Discuss the organization's options when providing flexible benefit plans to employees.

Because of their significant cost to the company, HR managers must pay close attention to the administration of benefit programs in order to get the most return for the money spent. In almost all cases today, benefit programs are not "one size fits all"—they are flexible because that is what employees want.[84] And because they are flexible for the employees, they take more management time. Let's briefly discuss the management of flexible benefits programs now, followed by how to communicate value to employees.

Flexible Benefit (Cafeteria) Plans

In a survey, 87% of respondents said that flexibility in the offered benefits package would be extremely or very important in deciding whether to take a new job or not.[85] Because the mix of workers is so broad, we need to allow at least some flexibility in

EXHIBIT 13-4 EMPLOYEE BENEFITS

Statutory Benefits	Voluntary Benefits

• Social Security and Medicare
• Workers' compensation
• Unemployment Insurance
• Family and Medical Leave Act (FMLA)
• The Patient Protection and Affordable Care Act (ACA)
• Statutory requirements when providing certain voluntary benefits
 	
  o Consolidated Omnibus Budget Reconciliation Act (COBRA)
  o Health Insurance Portability and Accountability Act (HIPAA)
  o Employee Retirement Income Security Act (ERISA)
	• Paid time off
	• Group health insurance
	• Retirement benefits
	• Employee insurance coverage
	• Employee services
	
	  o Educational (or tuition) assistance
	  o On-site child care or child care vouchers
	  o Elder care assistance
	  o Company-provided fitness facilities or vouchers for memberships
	  o Organization-sponsored sports teams
	  o Services to mitigate commuting costs including work shuttles, company-provided or paid parking, "green" vehicle allowances, public or private transportation vouchers
	  o Free or low-cost meals

13-1 SELF ASSESSMENT

Selecting Employee Benefits

Assume you are graduating with your college degree and getting your first or a new full-time job. The organization gives you the list below and asks you to rank order the list of employee benefits from 1 (the most important to you) to 11 (the least important to you).

_____   Paid time off (vacations, sick and personal days, holidays)
_____   Health insurance (traditional, HMO, PPO, HSA/MSA)
_____   Retirement benefits (401[k] or 403[b], IRA or Roth IRA, SEP)
_____   Employee insurance coverage (life, disability, others)
_____   Educational (or tuition) assistance (getting your MBA or other degree or some type of certification or license like the PHR and SPHR, CPA, or FICF)
_____   Child care (on-site or vouchers)
_____   Elder care (on-site or vouchers)
_____   Fitness (organization-provided fitness facilities or vouchers for memberships)
_____   Organization-sponsored sports teams (softball, basketball, bowling, golf, etc.)
_____   Commuting (work shuttles, company-provided or paid parking, "green" vehicle allowances, public or private transportation vouchers)
_____   Meals (free or low-cost meals on site or meal vouchers)

There is no scoring as this is a personal choice. Think about your selection today. Will your priority ranking change in 5, 10, 15, or 20 years?

our benefits system so that it can be partially tailored to the needs of the worker. We need to be careful, though. If an unlimited amount of flexibility is allowed in the benefits program, some bad consequences can occur. We will discuss this issue shortly when we cover *full-choice* plans.

What is a flexible benefits plan, commonly known as a *cafeteria* plan? Cafeteria plans are called that because they are similar to a cafeteria restaurant or college dining hall. You get to pick what you want—at least as far as what is available. You may decide that you want more paid time off and less insurance, or that you want medical coverage for you and your family, or you may choose to put more money into retirement accounts. Most cafeteria plans fall into one of three categories—each with its own advantages and disadvantages.

MODULAR PLANS. Modular plans are pretty much what they sound like. The employee has several basic modules from which they can choose to provide a set of benefits that match their life and family circumstances. Each module has a different mix of insurance, employee services, and retirement options. The employee chooses a module that most closely meets their needs. There may be a module for young single employees that maximizes work flexibility with more time off for personal activities, but has minimal or no benefits in areas such as family health plans, child care, or dental. Another module designed for families with children might have much more emphasis on family health, retirement planning, and more life insurance in case the employee were to die and leave the family without income. And still a third module might be designed for workers whose children are grown.

Modular plans are much easier for HR to manage than other types of flexible benefit plans, because there are a limited number of modules to keep track of. Because they are easier to manage, they are cheaper. We also have the advantage of having more people using the same set of benefits, so utilization analyses are a bit easier in this case. However, since there is no flexibility within each module (you get the exact set of benefits specified within the module), the employee may not be able to get the coverage and options that they want or need.

CORE-PLUS PLANS. In a *core-plus plan*, we have a base set of benefits, called the *core*, that are provided to everyone, and then employees are allowed to choose other options to meet personal needs and desires. The core benefits are there to provide basic protection for all of the company's employees in areas such as health and life insurance, and maybe a minimum amount of retirement funding. The remaining benefits are available for the employee to pick and choose other options that match their personal needs.

If the employee has a family and wants to provide them with coverage, they can choose family health coverage. If they are getting older and didn't save for retirement earlier in their work life, they can put more funds into their retirement account. The limiting factor is that each employee is provided with a benefits account and once that account is empty, they can't pick any additional benefits for their personal plan.

The biggest advantage of core-plus plans to the employee is, of course, the ability to partially tailor the plan to their individual circumstances while providing a minimum level of health and wellness benefits. The plan is also cheaper than a full-choice plan to administer. HRM personnel can still analyze the benefit options and complete utilization analyses on core-plus plans, but it is more difficult than in modular plans.

FULL-CHOICE PLANS. The full-choice plans provide complete flexibility to the organizational member. Each employee can choose exactly the set of benefits that they desire, within specified monetary limitations. If a member chooses to have no health care coverage, they can use the money saved for whatever other available benefit that they want. This is truly a cafeteria plan in that employees can choose any offered benefit they want without a modular or core set of benefits.

Probably the biggest advantage in a full-choice plan is that it is easy for the employee to understand. However, there are some significant problems with full-choice plans for both the individual and the organization. One of the problems, "moral hazard," may occur because the employee doesn't fully identify the consequences of their selection. Moral hazard problems can occur when the individual makes bad choices and will be forced to live with those choices in the future. For instance, we may have an employee that decides that they don't need a retirement account because they are going to "work until I die anyway." A few years down the line, this same person may be getting tired of working or may even be unable to continue to work in the same field because of illness or injuries and want to retire, but is unable to because of the choices made in previous years.

A second disadvantage to full-choice plans comes from the problem of "adverse selection." For example, most company plans allow changes to the employee's benefits during an open enrollment period at the end of the year. Suppose an employee knows that they have a physical problem that will likely result in the need for surgery in the coming year and they therefore choose to increase their health care insurance to pay for more of the cost of the upcoming surgery. The next year, with the surgery over and knowing that they have children who are going to need braces, they choose to increase their dental coverage and lower their health care insurance coverage. Through this manipulation of the benefits system, the overall cost to the organization for providing these benefits can go up significantly over time. So this problem of adverse selection is an issue of selecting only the benefits that we think will immediately benefit us and then dropping those benefits once we feel that we don't need them. This can cause the utilization rates for the organization to significantly increase over time, which in turn causes an increase in the cost to the organization of providing those benefits.

13-4 APPLYING THE CONCEPT

Flexible Benefit Plans

Place the letter of the type of flexible plan on the line next to statement that describes it.

    a. modular
    b. core-plus
    c. full-choice

_____ 16. I don't think our benefit plan is fair because I use my spouse's health insurance plan and I just lose the benefit. To be fair, I should be able to use the money for other benefits I want.

_____ 17. I sure wish we got more of our compensation in benefits, but at least with my benefit package, I can choose any benefit I want to every year.

_____ 18. My benefit plan has five packages, and I get to pick any one of them that I want every year. But it's difficult to select one.

_____ 19. I definitely want to get health care and retirement benefits, and it's nice to have the option of selecting a few other benefits with a set dollar value.

_____ 20. The hard part about my benefit plan is that there are so many options to choose from that I have a hard time selecting the ones I may really need.

WORK
APPLICATION 13-11

Select a company that offers a flexible benefit plan. Identify its type and describe the major benefit options within that category of flexibility.

LO 13-11

Discuss the need for benefit plans to be communicated to employees.

The third big issue with full-choice plans is the cost associated with administration of the plans. It is not too difficult to manage the paperwork of a modular plan—HRM just figures out the number of employees choosing each module and then calculates the total usage for each benefit based on the modules. In full-choice plans, every employee can change their plan (in its entirety) every year. This is much more difficult to manage and creates a much larger paperwork burden for HRM.

The bottom line is that flexible plans are really gaining ground because our workforce is much more diverse than it used to be. Benefits need to match the needs of our workers, but we have to remember that the more flexible the plan, the more expensive it is.

Communicate Value to Employees

In addition to administration of benefit programs, HR is spending significantly more time than in past years to educate their employees and communicate the value of company benefits to all workers.[86] Many of us may work for a company that provides a summary of benefits and the value of each of them on some routine basis, usually at the end of the year. The basic reason for doing so is that most of us don't understand the true cost and value of the benefits that our organizations provide. And if we don't understand the cost and the return of our benefits programs, we don't *perceive* the value that we get from having the organization provide us with these benefits.

All we really need in order to communicate the value of benefit programs is a basic, ongoing communication process. We provide information through multiple communication channels and should provide it more often than just once per year during open enrollment. There are a number of methods that have achieved acceptability in HR departments around the world and can reach at least part of our workforce.

We may want to use more than one method because of the multigenerational nature of today's workforce. For older baby boomers, *standard mailings* to the employees' homes may be a good method, but for generation X and Y employees, *searchable knowledge bases* and *email reminders* may work better, while finally with net-gen employees, *social media* may take the lead. We have to consider the makeup of our workforce and use methods that will be appropriate in reaching each of the groups within it. Finally, if we aren't sure of the best way to communicate with our employees, we should ask them. On a global basis, the channels of communication may be very different. For example, in underdeveloped countries, many employees will not have a home computer to receive the communications in an email or through a social network. Value communication is one of the most important jobs within HR in the 21st century workplace. We have to try to help all employees understand their benefit packages, which in turn makes the package more valuable to the individual employee. If they understand the total value of their benefits, we end up with a more loyal and more satisfied workforce. The effort is absolutely worth it.

WORK
APPLICATION 13-12

Does any company you know of offer domestic partner benefits? Do you believe these benefits should or should not be offered by a specific organization you work or have worked for? Why or why not?

TRENDS AND ISSUES IN HRM

The first trend that we will discuss is the question of providing benefits for "domestic partners" who are not spouses of our employees.

Benefits for "Domestic Partners"

One of the more significant recent issues in benefits management has been the question of providing benefits for domestic partners. Sometimes called "significant others," **domestic partners** *are individuals who are not legally married but who are in a one-to-one living arrangement similar to marriage*, whether that arrangement is same-sex or opposite-sex. Should we treat such domestic partners the same as spouses for the purpose of providing company benefits?

SHRM

K:B20
Domestic Partner Benefits

Our purpose here is not to discuss the validity of domestic partner arrangements and whether or not they are morally right or wrong. That is up to the organization and the state and country in which they operate. Our analysis has to look at the costs as well as any organizational advantage that might be gained by providing domestic partner coverage. Organizations may choose to provide domestic partner benefits in order to support a more diverse workforce, to recruit the best talent possible, or just to provide equity to all of their employees.

Benefits that are affected by the employee's marital status include Social Security survivor benefits, workers' compensation survivor payments, access to FMLA, and coverage under COBRA and ERISA. Each of these laws has at least some language that provides for benefits only to legal spouses of employees, not to domestic partners. In some cases, federal law requires the employer to tax any benefits provided to an employee's unmarried domestic partner, because the tax code says that to receive favorable tax treatment for benefits, such as a health savings account, the coverage has to go to the employee and their immediate family members, not to domestic partners. Employers have to be aware of the language of the laws so that they don't unintentionally violate such laws. One significant recent change in many states has been the recognition of same-sex marriage, which is different in the eyes of the law from domestic partnerships. The Treasury Department and the IRS have now ruled that legally married same-sex couples will be treated the same as other married couples for federal tax purposes.[87]

In addition, companies have to be aware that providing domestic partner benefits may cost them significant amounts of money. Allowing domestic partners to be covered under company insurance and other benefit policies will almost always add to the cost of the benefits program. We must weigh the value of the loyalty and satisfaction gained by such actions against the direct monetary cost of this type of coverage. Companies are taking a hard look at the cost of domestic partner benefits and, in some cases at least, deciding that the cost is too high to cover the added value to their employee base.

Domestic partners Individuals who are not legally married but who are in a one-to-one living arrangement similar to marriage

Personalization of Health Care

"The health care system in the United States will change more in the next five to seven years than it has in the last 50," according to Jeff Bauer, a "health futurist."[88] By all available evidence, he is correct. Individuals will continue to gain more control over their own health and their health care planning over the next several years. From apps to health services shopping, and finally to managing ongoing health care costs, the individual will continue to gain power as they become closer to the health care provider by using technology.

Smartphone apps continue to evolve as a mechanism for managing personal health care. We now have apps for checking symptoms (**WebMD** and **MayoClinic**); apps for checking and tracking heart rate, blood pressure, and other vital information (**Cardiio** and **HealthKit**); apps to interface directly with medical service providers without going into a doctor's office (**eDocAmerica**); and many others that help us manage our health—and the number and types of these tools continues to grow at a rapid rate.[89]

Shopping for the best plans for you as an individual will also continue to get easier as the state, federal, and even some private insurance exchanges become more readily available online. The new ACA law requires that the prices for insurance on these exchanges be public information, so it is pretty easy to compare coverage, which is a significant change from in the past when it was very difficult to compare policies.

Managing cost will also become easier as more of us move to HSA/MSA and HDHPs, where we directly control medical expenditures. The monies in an HSA/MSA are controlled by the insured individual[90]—again a change from what has been the case in HMO/PPO organizations. The insured person decides when, where, and how to spend their HSA/MSA funds, which gives them direct control over their health care dollars.

This trend toward individualization of health care will only continue to expand in the future. There doesn't appear to be any evidence that we are going to go back to the days when your health care decisions were made completely by other people. So company employees will need to become more knowledgeable about their health care options, which means HR will have to educate them.

● ● ● CHAPTER SUMMARY

13-1 Discuss the strategic value of benefits programs.

Human resources are one of the few potential sources for competitive advantage in a modern, 21st century organization. The totality of their compensation—including their benefits packages—is one major factor in keeping employees happy and engaged and willing to create a competitive advantage for our company. Today's workers demand more benefits and a better mix to fit their lifestyles. Because people demand it, companies add new benefits. This allows companies to increase job satisfaction and engagement because when we take care of our employees, they work harder and take better care of our customers and organization, which in turn allows us to create a competitive advantage based on our people.

13-2 Identify the major reasons for the growth of benefits as a proportion of overall compensation.

There are four major reasons for benefits growth. First, there are tax advantages to providing employee benefits to both employers and employees. Second, federal laws are requiring companies to provide more benefits than ever before. Third, organized labor has historically bargained for benefits for their workers, and benefits earned in these negotiations carry over to nonunion companies. Finally, buying in bulk can save significant amounts of money, so if companies buy many insurance plans, each plan costs less than if the individual bought the same insurance.

13-3 Briefly discuss the major considerations in providing benefits programs.

The three major considerations in providing benefits are amounts, mix, and flexibility. *Amount* is a function of how much the company is willing to spend on its employees. Many companies will calculate this as a percentage of direct compensation. *Mix* deals with the types of benefits that will be offered to employees. In many cases today, the number and type of benefits available is limited only by the imagination of the employees of the firm. Finally, we need to consider how much *flexibility* we are willing to build into our benefits program because flexible options are very important to today's employees. Can different employees choose different benefits from the mix available, or will they all have to get the same benefits?

13-4 Identify and summarize the major statutory benefits required by federal law.

Social Security and Medicare—Social Security is composed of Old-Age, Survivors, and Disability Insurance (OASDI) programs, and Medicare is the national health care program for the elderly or disabled.

Workers' compensation is a program to provide medical treatment and temporary payments to employees who are injured on the job or become ill because of their job.

Unemployment Insurance is a federal program managed by each state to provide payments for a fixed period of time to workers who lose their jobs.

FMLA is leave that must be provided by the employer to eligible employees when they or their immediate family members are faced with various medical issues. The leave is unpaid, but the employer must maintain health coverage for the employee while they are on leave.

ACA requires that all employers with more than 50 employees provide health insurance for their full-time employees or face significant penalties levied by the federal government.

13-5 Identify the main statutory requirements that must be followed *if* organizations choose to provide health care or retirement plans for their employees.

COBRA is a law that requires employers to offer continuation of health insurance on individuals who leave their employment for up to 18 to 36 months, if the employee is willing to pay the premium cost of the insurance policy.

HIPAA requires that, if the employee had health insurance at their old job and the new company provides health insurance as a benefit, it must be offered to the employee. In other words, the individual's health insurance is "portable." HIPAA also requires that companies take care to protect the health information of employees from unauthorized individuals.

ERISA lays out requirements that must be followed if the employer provides a retirement or health care plan. ERISA determines who is eligible to participate and when they are eligible, it provides rules for "vesting" of the employee's retirement funds, it requires portability of those funds, and it requires that the funds are managed "prudently" by the fiduciary that maintains them.

13-6 Briefly describe the main categories of voluntary benefits available to organizations.

Major voluntary benefits include paid time off, group health insurance, retirement plans, other insurance coverage, and employee services. Paid time off comes in various forms, such as sick leave, vacation time, holidays, and personal days. Group health insurance provides employees with health care coverage, and retirement plans allow them to save for their own retirement, sometimes with some help from the organization. Other insurance includes a wide variety of options including group term life insurance, short- and long-term disability policies, dental and vision insurance, group automobile and homeowners insurance, and many more. Finally, employee services can include a massive range of options from educational assistance to child or adult day care, gyms, cafeterias, transportation and parking assistance, and too many others to list.

13-7 Describe the differences between traditional health care plans, HMOs, PPOs, and HSA/MSA plans.

Traditional health care plans usually cover a percentage of fees (historically 80%) for all medical services. The covered individual can live anywhere and go to any doctor that they choose. Traditional plans do not generally cover preventive care, such as an annual physical exam.

HMOs provide routine preventive care, but in the case of nonpreventive care require that a review of specific circumstances concerning the individual and their health condition be completed *before* any significant medical testing, medical procedures, or hospital care is approved. There may be limits to where the covered employee can live, and there are limits to which doctors and facilities they can use.

PPOs are kind of a hybrid between HMOs and traditional plans. The PPO prefers that you see doctors and use facilities in the network, but you can go outside the network if you are willing to pay a higher percentage of the cost of care.

HSA/MSA accounts allow the employer and employee to fund a medical savings account from which the employee can pay medical expenses each year with pretax dollars. When the money runs out, the individual becomes responsible for all medical costs until they reach a large deductible. Once this deductible is reached, an HDHP takes over and pays the remaining costs for the year.

13-8 Discuss the difference between defined benefit and defined contribution retirement plans and the reasons for the shift from defined benefit to defined contribution plans.

Under a *defined benefit* retirement plan, the retiree knows exactly what benefits they will receive when they retire. *Defined contribution* plans only identify what is going to go into the retirement fund, not what will be received from it upon retirement. If the retirement funds are invested successfully, the individual's retirement account will be able to pay much higher benefits than if the funds are not invested successfully and don't grow very much.

Companies are shifting to defined contribution plans to shift the risk related to the investment of the retirement funds from the company to the individual. Under a defined benefit plan, if the funds do not grow at the expected rate, the employer must add money to retirement accounts to make the promised retirement payments. In a defined contribution plan, the risk of slow growth of the investment shifts to the employee.

13-9 Discuss the major retirement plan options.

401(k) or 403(b) plans—In a 401(k) (or 403[b] for nonprofits), the employee and the employer are allowed to contribute funds to the account up to a maximum amount. Contributions are made on a "pretax basis," which means that when funds are put into the account, they do not count as taxable income for the individual. Once the individual retires and begins to withdraw their funds, they pay income taxes on the money received.

IRAs and Roth IRAs—IRA contributions reduce the employee's taxable income in the year in which they are contributed to the account. When the person withdraws the money in retirement, they pay taxes on it at that time. A Roth IRA works in the opposite way: The employee pays the tax when they contribute the money to the account but doesn't have to pay taxes when the money is withdrawn.

Simplified Employee Pensions (SEPs)—These are primarily for self-employed persons or owners of small companies. The *employer* contributes directly to traditional individual retirement accounts (SEP-IRAs) for all employees.

13-10 Discuss the organization's options when providing flexible benefit plans to employees.

Companies can choose modular plans, core-plus plans, or full-choice plans. Modular plans provide several basic modules from which each employee chooses. There is no other option outside one of the modules. Core-plus plans provide a base set of benefits to all employees (the core) and then other options that the employee can choose from freely to meet their personal desires and needs. Full-choice plans allow the employee complete freedom of choice, but they come with some potential problems such as "moral hazard," "adverse selection," and high management costs.

13-11 Discuss the need for benefit plans to be communicated to employees.

Most employees don't understand the true cost and value of the benefits that organizations provide and, as a result, don't perceive the value that they get from having the organization provide their benefits. There are many indications that employees who are satisfied with their benefits are more satisfied with their jobs and their companies. Providing employees with knowledge concerning their benefit package will help to create and maintain trust in the organization as well as improve job satisfaction on the part of those employees.

13-12 Define the key terms found in the chapter margins and listed following the Chapter Summary.

Complete the Key Terms Review to test your understanding of this chapter's key terms.

••• KEY TERMS

COBRA	HMO	traditional health care plans
defined benefit plan	HSA or MSA	Unemployment Insurance
defined contribution plan	PBGC	utilization analysis
domestic partners	preferred provider organizations (PPOs)	vesting
experience rating	primary care physician (PCP)	workers' compensation
high-deductible health plan (HDHP)	serious health condition	

••• KEY TERMS REVIEW

Complete each of the following statements using one of this chapter's key terms:

1. _____ is an insurance program designed to provide medical treatment and temporary payments to employees who cannot work because of an employment related injury or illness.

2. _____ is a measure of how often claims are made against an insurance policy.

3. _____ provides workers who lose their jobs with continuing subsistence payments from their state for a specified period of time.

4. _____ is an illness, injury, impairment, or physical or mental condition that involves either inpatient care or continuing care for at least 3 consecutive days.

5. _____ is a law that requires employers to offer to maintain health insurance on individuals who leave their employment (for a period of time).

6. _____ provides for a maximum amount of time beyond which the employee will have unfettered access to their retirement funds, both employee contributions and employer contributions.

7. _____ is a governmental corporation established within the Department of Labor whose purpose is to insure retirement funds from failure.

8. _____ typically cover a set percentage of fees for medical services—for either doctors or in-patient care.

9. _____ is a health care plan that provides both health maintenance services and medical care as part of the plan.

10. _____ will be the first point of contact for all preventive care and in any routine medical situation, except emergencies.

11. _____ are a kind of hybrid between traditional fee-for-service plans and HMOs.

12. _____ allows the employer and employee to fund a medical savings account from which the employee can pay medical expenses each year with pretax dollars.

13. _____ is a "major medical" insurance plan that protects against catastrophic health care costs and in most cases is paid for by the employer.

14. _____ is a review of the cost of a program and comparison of program costs with the rate of the program's usage by the members of the company.

15. _____ provide the retiree with a specific amount and type of benefits that will be available when the individual retires.

16. _____ identify only the amount of funds that will go into a retirement account, not what the employee will receive upon retirement.

17. _____ are individuals who are not legally married but who are in a one-to-one living arrangement similar to marriage.

••• COMMUNICATION SKILLS

The following critical-thinking questions can be used for class discussion and/or for written assignments to develop communication skills. Be sure to give complete explanations for all answers.

1. Would you rather have better benefits and a modest salary or a high salary and lower levels of benefits? Why?

2. Based on the high cost of the average benefits package, what would you do if you were the manager in charge of figuring out how to cut benefit costs in your company? Remember that you want to meet the company's strategic goals.

3. How would you "fix" Social Security to allow it to continue as a viable retirement program? Would you raise the retirement age? Would you lower the benefit level? Are there any other options to make the program solvent long-term?

4. Should workers' compensation insurance continue to be "no-fault"? Why or why not?

5. How would you lower your company's experience rating in the areas of workers' compensation and Unemployment Insurance if you were the HR manager?

6. What would you do to minimize the abuse of FMLA leave if you became the HR manager in a company where abuse was rampant? Explain how your answer would help overcome the problem.

7. Based on what is in the chapter, should the ACA federal health care legislation remain in its current form, or should we rescind the requirement that employers and/or employees have to pay a fine if the employee is not covered by a health care plan? Explain your answer.

8. Is the vesting requirement in ERISA too long, too short, or just about right? Why did you answer the way that you did?

9. Should the United States mandate a certain amount of paid time off per year as many other countries currently do? Why or why not?

10. If you were the head of HR, would you argue for a company-sponsored retirement plan for your employees? What are the pros and cons to such an argument?

11. What employee services can you think of that were not mentioned in the text but would likely be highly valued by the employees where you work (or have worked)?

12. Do you think that in today's workforce it is becoming necessary to have a "full-choice" flexible benefits plan? Why or why not?

● ● ● CASE 13-1 DEFINED BENEFIT RETIREMENT FADES AWAY

Defined benefit retirement plans appear to be going the way of the dinosaurs. According to the Bureau of Labor Statistics, in 2011 only 20% of all private employees had access to defined benefit retirement plans while 58% had access to defined contribution plans.[91] This shift is also apparent in the amount of money being managed in each type of retirement plan. In 1985, approximately 65% of all retirement savings were held in defined benefit accounts, and only 35% were in defined contribution accounts. In 2005 the percentage had almost reversed to 60% in defined contribution accounts and only 40% in defined benefit plans.[92] And this phenomenon is not only part of the business landscape in the United States. Companies around the world continue to shift from defined benefit to defined contribution plans. According to the Canadian Press, the Royal Bank of Canada "is just the latest Canadian company" to end its defined benefit plan for new employees.[93] In the past 10 years, defined benefit plans also fell from about 97% to 60% of all pension funds in Britain, with defined contribution plans taking up the slack.

There appear to be several reasons for this shift. Among them is the fact that defined contribution plans shift the financial risk associated with funding employee retirement from the employer to the employee. The amount paid in retirement is based on the performance of the invested funds over the period of investment instead of being a fixed dollar amount. In addition, moving a defined benefit retirement account from one employer to another is virtually impossible, but defined contribution plans are basically designed for portability.

Companies, of course, are touting the value of defined contribution plans to their employees. They tell employees about defined contribution plans being more portable than defined benefit plans, so for those who will change jobs a number of times in their careers, a defined contribution plan is better. The risk of the employer underfunding the plan also disappears with a defined contribution plan, because the plan is funded directly over time in an account set up for each individual employee. Companies remind employees that defined benefit plans that are underfunded might not be there when the employee actually retires, and the Pension Benefit Guaranty Corporation only guarantees a basic retirement benefit—not 100% of what was promised by the employer. Defined contribution plans also typically have much more flexibility in how the money is invested and managed over the life of the fund, and the individual has direct control over this investment process, unlike defined benefit funds.

On the other hand, many employee associations, unions, and even some academics say that companies have been allowed to pull funding from their defined benefit plans that they knew would eventually be needed to fund employee retirements and that this is the reason that defined benefit plans are having difficulties. Ellen Smith, a Wall Street Journal reporter, says that employers have "plundered the nest eggs of American workers" by using their retirement funds as corporate piggy banks.[94] Olivia Mitchell of the Wharton School at the University of Pennsylvania says that companies pulled funds out of their retirement programs in the mid-1980s because of the significant increase in the stock market during that period.[95] When stocks started to take hits to their value several years later, the companies didn't refund their retirement plans, which left them in serious danger of being underfunded when needed.

Opponents to defined contribution plans strongly argue that defined benefit plans are more valuable to the worker because of the guaranteed benefit upon retirement. Since these plans provide a guaranteed income to the worker, it is easier for the employee to plan for their eventual retirement. The employee groups point to the fact that most defined contribution plans have not gained any significant value over the past several years because of the stagnant stock markets worldwide. As a result, employees who put money into such accounts expecting the historical average return on their investment of about 7% have seen virtually no growth in their retirement accounts, and in some cases significant declines in the invested monies. Defined contribution accounts may also be subject to inflation risks, which can reduce the actual amounts available in retirement. Finally, many employees choose not to participate in defined contribution plans, and for the ones who do, most are not capable of directly managing their funds with as much success as professional investment managers.

Questions

1. Which side are you on in the debate—should companies be allowed to discontinue existing defined benefit plans or not? Explain your answer.

2. If you were the benefits manager for a large national bank, which defined contribution plan(s) identified in the text would you consider as options for your workforce? Explain your answer.

3. As the benefits manager, what would you need to do to ensure that the retirement plan you chose would have value to both the company and the employees?

• • • CASE 13-2 GOOGLE SEARCHES SAS FOR THE BUSINESS SOLUTION TO HOW TO CREATE AN AWARD-WINNING CULTURE

Statistical Analysis System Institute Inc. (SAS) is a privately held company that develops software to provide business solutions for their clients. As of 2013, they employed more than 14,000 people and reported revenues of $3 billion. Founded in 1976, they have maintained high profits during the five recessions since then. They have also maintained a growth rate of more than 10% per year from 1980 to 2000.[96] Besides posting impressive growth, SAS has made it onto the Fortune "Best Companies to Work For" list for almost two decades. Google has made it to the top of this list for the past 3 years, but they do not hesitate to confess that they implemented SAS's model in their HR practices. Yet why would Google, a very successful firm in its own right, copy SAS?[97]

Perhaps Google mimics SAS because the company's achievements are built upon a culture that keeps their employees satisfied and motivated. Feeling ecstatic about the company's cultural environment, SAS employees are highly motivated, intensely loyal, and very dedicated to delivering only the highest performance results. Why? According to the CEO/cofounder, James Goodnight, SAS functions like a triangle where happy employees are essential for great customer service and great customer service is the key to a successful business. Employees know that SAS will provide anything that will increase productivity or inspire their imagination. For example, more than 3,000 pieces of art are displayed throughout its premises, and two full-time artists are employed to keep the environment updated.[98] By testing their perks, SAS realized that these types of benefits are key factors to their highly profitable business.

One advantage of running a private business is that CEO James Goodnight does not have the obligation to answer to shareholders, a board of directors, or anyone on Wall Street and therefore can take some calculated risks when it comes to building that cutting-edge culture, a culture that focuses on creating an environment that fosters originality and innovation and keeps employees' minds sharp. Software development is a mentally challenging business, and therefore the proper environment is needed to foster creativity and thinking outside the box. The goal of SAS is to create a stress-free environment for their employees so they enjoy being at work, and SAS does this by providing a work environment with as much comfort and convenience as possible.[99] What are the foundations of a stress-free environment?

SAS provides their employees competitive pay, discretionary bonuses, medical care, retirement plans (401[k]), profit sharing, and disability benefits. SAS also provides a vast amount of what are called "convenience benefits," which are very appealing to job applicants. These new benefits began with free M&Ms every Wednesday and later included a no dress code policy and no specific working hours when employees have to clock in or clock out.[100]

In addition, the main headquarters in North Carolina provides employees with an on-site, state-of-the-art fitness center, a swimming pool, tennis courts, and even a golf course. The following no-cost amenities are also available: dry-cleaning, car detailing, day care programs for employees' children, and a cafeteria that serves 2,500 meals per lunch with no reserved room for executives. In SAS there is a work/life center that provides care for the elderly, helps manage financial debts, and handles personal problems like divorce. SAS provides in-house health benefits and amenities free to all their employees. They only require an employee to pay 20% of the bill when seeing an outside specialist.

SAS's culture and benefits programs have led to a remarkably low employee turnover rate of 3%.[101] But good luck landing a job there: They receive more than 15,000 applications per year![102]

Questions

1. What are the statutory benefits SAS must offer every employee? What defined benefits do they offer beyond those requirements?

2. SAS offers an array of employee benefits, especially at their main headquarters. What might be their rationale for providing such services to their employees?

3. What would you suggest if utilization analysis indicated that only a few employees used those additional benefits, such as the work/life center?

4. What seems to be the weakest part of SAS's benefits package? What would you do instead of offering that particular benefit?

5. What additional amenities might SAS offer their employees? Why?

6. How does their 3% turnover rate impact training and recruiting expenses?

Case created by Herbert Sherman, PhD, and Theodore Vallas, Department of Management Sciences, School of Business Brooklyn Campus, Long Island University

$SAGE edge™

Sharpen your skills with SAGE edge at edge.sagepub.com/lussierhrm2e

SAGE edge for students provides a personalized approach to help you accomplish your coursework goals in an easy-to-use learning environment.

••• SKILL BUILDER 13-1 DEVELOPING FLEXIBLE EMPLOYEE BENEFIT PLANS

Objective

To develop your skill at designing flexible benefits

Skills

The primary skills developed through this exercise are as follows:

1. *HR management skills*—Technical, conceptual and design, and business skills

2. *SHRM 2013 Curriculum Guidebook*—K: Total rewards—Employee benefits

Assignment

1. Using the "Voluntary Benefits" column of Exhibit 13-4: Employee Benefits, as the HR benefits manager select the benefits to be offered in three different modular plans. Be sure to identify the target group for each of the three modules.

2. Again using Exhibit 13-4, as the HR benefits manager, develop a core-plus benefits plan.

••• SKILL BUILDER 13-2 SELECTING FLEXIBLE EMPLOYEE BENEFIT PLANS

Objective

To develop your skill at selecting flexible benefits

Skills

The primary skills developed through this exercise are as follows:

1. *HR management skills*—Technical, conceptual and design, and business skills

2. *SHRM 2013 Curriculum Guidebook*—K: Total rewards—Employee benefits

Assignment

As an employee, rank order the voluntary benefits listed in Self-Assessment Exercise 13-1 from 1 being most important to 9 being the least important to you. In class, break into groups of four to six and discuss your rankings. (For online classes, use your discussion system.) What similarities and differences emerge in the discussion of your rankings?

ICATION FOR
LTH BENEFITS

	(First)			(Middle Initial)
	(City)		(State)	(Zip)

ssed? Yes No

Part V
Protecting and Expanding Organizational Reach

14 Workplace Safety, Health, and Security

15 Organizational Ethics, Sustainability, and Social Responsibility

16 International HRM

PRACTITIONER'S MODEL

| ↑ Productivity |
| ↑ Satisfaction |
| ↓ Absenteeism |
| ↓ Turnover |

PART V: Protecting and Expanding Organizational Reach		
How do you **PROTECT** and **EXPAND** your Human Resources?		
Chapter 14 Workplace Safety, Health, and Security	**Chapter 15** Organizational Ethics, Sustainability, and Social Responsibility	**Chapter 16** International HRM

PART IV: Compensating		
How do you **REWARD** and **MAINTAIN** your Human Resources?		
Chapter 11 Compensation Management	**Chapter 12** Incentives Pay	**Chapter 13** Employee Benefits

PART III: Developing and Managing			
How do you **MANAGE** your Human Resources?			
Chapter 7 Training, Learning, Talent Management, and Development	**Chapter 8** Performance Management and Appraisal	**Chapter 9** Rights and Employee Management	**Chapter 10** Employee and Labor Relations

PART II: Staffing		
What HRM Functions do you **NEED** for sustainability?		
Chapter 4 Matching Employees and Jobs: Job Analysis and Design	**Chapter 5** Recruiting Job Candidates	**Chapter 6** Selecting New Employees

PART I: 21st Century Human Resource Management Strategic Planning and Legal Issues		
What HRM issues are **CRITICAL** to your organization's long-term sustainability?		
Chapter 1 The New Human Resource Management Process	**Chapter 2** Strategy-Driven Human Resource Management	**Chapter 3** The Legal Environment and Diversity Management

©iStockphoto.com/kickers

14 Workplace Safety, Health, and Security

••• LEARNING OUTCOMES

After studying this chapter, you should be able to do the following:

14-1 Identify the responsibilities of both employers and employees under the general duties clause of the OSH Act. PAGE 528

14-2 Briefly describe what OSHA does in a worksite inspection. PAGE 529

14-3 Discuss employer rights during an OSHA inspection. PAGE 530

14-4 Identify the types of violations that OSHA looks for in inspections. PAGE 532

14-5 Discuss the primary job of NIOSH as it applies to workplace safety and health. PAGE 533

14-6 Briefly discuss EAPs and EWPs and what their value is to companies and employees. PAGE 538

14-7 Discuss the concept of ergonomics. Identify OSHA's function in ergonomics in the workplace. PAGE 539

14-8 Briefly discuss the causes of stress and how it can be managed. PAGE 540

14-9 Identify the top concerns for security in the workplace today. PAGE 545

14-10 Define the key terms found in the chapter margins and listed following the Chapter Summary. PAGE 555

Practitioner's Perspective

Describing her workplace, Cindy says: We believe a safe and healthy workplace is a right—whether you work in a factory or an office. Is it also an employer's responsibility to provide for their employees' mental health? Not everyone may see it as an obligation, but there is great benefit in assisting an employee whose personal issues may be impacting their job performance.

"I think I am going to have to take time off," Nancy confessed the other day. "I just can't seem to manage everything going on in my life, and I can't concentrate at work."

"I know things are tough with the divorce—but can you really afford to miss work right now?" her coworker Chloe queried. "Have you seen the information HR posted about the Employee Assistance Program? Let's get the contact information. It's completely confidential and available to you and your family. Perhaps they can help. In the meantime, you can talk to your supervisor about the new flexible work hours until things are better."

Could this level of support "save" a good employee? Learn more about the issues and ethics behind workplace health, safety, and security in Chapter 14.

See Appendix: *SHRM 2013 Curriculum Guidebook* for the complete list

A. Employee and Labor Relations (required)

23. Posting requirements

B. Employment Law (required)

26. The Occupational Safety and Health Act of 1970 (OSHA)

C. Ethics (required)

6. Behavior within ethical boundaries

14. Abusive behavior—Workplace bullying

E. Job Analysis/Job Design (required)

6. Compliance with legal requirements

   Ergonomics and workplace safety (work hazards and mitigation)

K. Total Rewards (required)

B. Employee Benefits

9. Employee assistance/wellness programs

17. Wellness programs

T. HR Career Planning (secondary)

4. Company policies to accommodate work and nonwork activities

X. Workplace Health, Safety, and Security (secondary)

1. OSHA citations and penalties (required)

2. Disaster preparation, continuity, and recovery planning

3. Employee health

4. Inspection

5. Protection from retaliation

6. Safety management

7. Security concerns at work

8. Communicable diseases

9. Data security

11. Ergonomics

WORKPLACE SAFETY AND OSHA

We now have a workforce that is reasonably compensated, well trained, and productive. The next major management concern is to keep them safe and healthy so that they can continue to perform at high levels. This chapter will first focus on federal workplace safety laws and regulations as well as the governing agencies for industrial safety and health. Later in the chapter, we will cover employee health issues—including the need for work-life balance for our employees, employee assistance and employee wellness programs, and stress—and how they affect our employees. Finally, we will take a look at the increasingly important topic of workplace security from the organizational perspective, so let's get started.

LO 14-1

Identify the responsibilities of both employers and employees under the general duties clause of the OSH Act.

The Occupational Safety and Health Act (OSH Act)

Safety affects recruitment and retention,[1] and it is a major problem globally as hundreds of employees die on the job each year.[2] To help protect employees, the Occupational Safety and Health Act (OSH Act) of 1970 requires employers to pursue workplace safety. **Workplace safety** *deals with the physical protection of people from injury or illness while on the job.* Employers must meet all Occupational Safety and Health Administration (OSHA) safety standards, maintain records of injuries and deaths due to workplace accidents, and submit to on-site inspections when notified. Those who do not comply are subject to citations and penalties, usually in the form of fines.[3] **BP** had to pay $50.6 million for safety violations found by OSHA regulators at one of its refineries.[4]

Many of you know that OSHA is a US safety and health regulator, but did you know that employers can go to prison for willfully failing to maintain safe work environments? You may have heard that the walls of a building that was being demolished in Philadelphia in 2013 caved in on a Salvation Army store, killing six people. The company in that case, **Campbell Construction**, has been cited for *willful violations* (we will discuss this term shortly) of the OSH Act, and the general contractor, Griffin Campbell, has personally been charged with third-degree murder in that case and could be jailed for failing to follow a series of safety procedures. In addition, the crane operator subcontractor who was working on the building when it collapsed

Workplace safety The physical protection of people from injury or illness while on the job

was charged with involuntary manslaughter.[5] In another recent case, the owner of **MR Asphalt** in Montana could go to prison and have to personally pay a fine, and his company may have to pay $500,000 if he is convicted of violating federal safety standards and causing an employee's death.[6] Willful violations of the OSH Act that cause a death are punishable with a fine of up to $500,000 for the organization and $250,000 and up to 6 months in prison for an individual who is found culpable.

Today, the HR department commonly has responsibility for ensuring the health and safety of employees. HRM works closely with other departments and maintains health and safety records along with managing safety training programs. As an HR manager, it will be absolutely critical that you know the safety rules, be sure your employees know them, and enforce them to prevent accidents. In addition to many specific requirements in the act, the *general duties clause* in OSHA that *covers all employers* states that each employer[7]

1. shall furnish a place of employment that is free from recognized hazards that are causing or are likely to cause death or serious physical harm to employees;
2. shall comply with occupational safety and health standards and all rules, regulations, and orders issued pursuant to this Act which are applicable to his own actions and conduct.

The general duties clause also states that *each employee* has a *duty to comply* with occupational safety standards, rules, and regulations.

In 1970, the year that OSHA was passed, job-related accidents accounted for more than 14,000 worker deaths in the United States.[8] The good news is that the rate of fatal work injuries has fallen, but the bad news is that in 2012 (the last year of available Bureau of Labor Statistics information), there were still 4,628 fatalities[9] and almost 3 million injuries or illnesses, half of which required time away from work.[10] This is a rate of almost 3.4 per 100 equivalent full-time workers. Recall from Chapter 1 that absenteeism is one of the major concerns of all managers, and by allowing injuries and occupational illnesses to occur, we are contributing to that absenteeism. So, losing this many workdays, as well as more than 4,600 lives, has to be a concern for HRM as well as other managers.

The Occupational Safety and Health Administration (OSHA)

OSHA is the division within the Department of Labor that is charged with overseeing the OSH Act. It was created to "assure safe and healthful working conditions for working men and women by setting and enforcing standards and by providing training, outreach, education and assistance."[11] OSHA has broad authority to investigate complaints and impose citations and penalties on employers who violate the OSH Act.

WHAT DOES OSHA DO? OSHA is responsible for setting federal safety and health standards and promulgating those standards to employers. OSHA is also the responsible agency of the federal government for occupational safety and health inspections. Inspections are made *without any advance notice* to the employer and are done based on the following issues (in priority order):[12]

- Imminent danger
- Catastrophes (fatalities or hospitalizations of more than three employees)
- Worker complaints and referrals
- Targeted inspections (such as companies with high injury rates)
- Follow-up inspections

Inspectors must identify themselves and tell the employer the reason for the inspection upon arrival at the worksite. The employer *can* decide not to allow the

LO 14-2

Briefly describe what OSHA does in a worksite inspection.

WORK
APPLICATION 14-1

Identify any unsafe or unhealthy working conditions that you have observed in any organization (business, sports, school, etc.).

LO 14-3

Discuss employer rights during an OSHA inspection.

SHRM

X:4
Inspection

inspection without an *inspection warrant* (a court order establishing OSHA's probable cause for the inspection), but this is generally not a very good idea on a number of levels. Besides making it look like the company might have something to hide, it wastes time, and the inspector will be less likely to be disposed to assist the employer in immediately correcting discrepancies that might be found during the inspection—*which will ultimately occur anyway* after the warrant is provided. In general, it makes more sense to allow the inspection to go on, in accordance with OSHA rules.[13]

EMPLOYER AND EMPLOYEE RIGHTS AND RESPONSIBILITIES UNDER OSHA. General rights of employers and employees are shown in Exhibit 14-1. We want to make sure that company management always stays within their rights in interactions with OSHA.

Employer Rights. Employer rights *during an inspection* are a bit more specific. The employer has a right to get the inspector's credentials, including their name and badge number, and to receive information on the reason for the inspection—either the employee complaint or the program inspection information. The employer also has the right to refuse to allow the inspection without a warrant being provided (which we have already said is generally a bad idea).

EXHIBIT 14-1 EMPLOYER AND EMPLOYEE RIGHTS AND RESPONSIBILITIES UNDER OSHA

Employer Rights[14]	Employee Rights[15]
OSHA inspections should be conducted "reasonably"	Working conditions free from unnecessary hazards
Have an opening conference/know the reason for inspection visits	Receipt of information and training on workplace hazards
Accompany inspectors when on site	File a complaint about hazardous working conditions and request an inspection
Contest OSHA citations	Maintain anonymity when filing a complaint
Know the names of employees interviewed in an inspection	Use their rights without fear of retaliation or discrimination
Take notes on what is inspected and any discrepancies	Object to the time frame for correction of discrepancies
Employer Responsibilities	**Employee Responsibilities**
General Duty Clause	Follow employer safety and health rules and keep the workplace free from hazards
Find and correct safety/health hazards	Comply with OSHA standards and regulations
Inform and train employees about existing hazards in the workplace	Report hazardous conditions to their supervisor
Notify OSHA within 8 hours if a fatality occurs or if 3 or more workers are hospitalized	Report job-related injuries or illnesses to their supervisor
Provide personal protective equipment necessary to do the job at no cost to workers	Tell the truth if interviewed by an OSHA inspector
Keep accurate records of work-related injuries or illnesses	
Avoid retaliation against workers who exercise their rights under the OSH Act	

Source: OSHA

So assuming that the inspection is allowed, we need to be aware of some things that we have a right to and should do during the inspection.

- If the inspection is being conducted due to a worker complaint, we have the right to get a copy of the complaint (without the employee's name), and we want to do so because we want to know what is being alleged.
- Secondly, we have a right to have a company representative accompany inspectors as they go through their site visit, and we, as the HR representative, want to accompany them.

There are a few reasons to accompany the inspector. First, we want to understand any violations that the inspector finds and notes because sometimes, no matter how hard a person tries to describe a problem, it will sometimes be unclear unless we see it ourselves. Secondly, in many cases we can immediately fix a discrepancy such as loose lines or hoses strung across a workspace. Although the discrepancy will almost surely still be noted, the inspector will see that we are willing to comply with the law and OSHA regulations quickly and to the best of our ability. This willingness can keep minor infractions from becoming major infractions. Third, we want to make sure that the inspection stays within the scope noted in the complaint or the program inspection guidelines. We don't really want the OSHA representative wandering all over the worksite, and we have a right to limit their movements to only cover the inspection scope.

An employer representative also has a right to be present when the inspector is interviewing employees (unless the interview is private by request of the employee being interviewed) and the right to stop interviews that are becoming confrontational or disturbing the work environment.

The employer also has a right to inform the employees of their rights during the inspection. The inspector will provide the employer with a list of discrepancies upon completion of their inspection. After an inspection, employers have a right to contest any citations that they receive through OSHA.

Employee Rights. Employee rights during inspections include the right to refuse to be interviewed, or if an employee agrees to an interview, they can request that an employer representative be present *or* that the interview be held in private. The employee also has the right to legal representation during the interview if they request it, and they can end the interview at any point in time just by requesting that the interview be discontinued. Finally, employees have a right against company retaliation for taking part in an interview with the inspector and telling the truth.

SHRM

X:5
Protection From Retaliation

14-2 APPLYING THE CONCEPT

Employee Rights and Responsibilities Under OSHA

Respond yes or no to each questions regarding employee rights and responsibilities.

    a. Yes
    b. No

_____ 8. Is it OK to object to the time frame for correction of discrepancies of OSHA standards?

_____ 9. Can OSHA make my employer maintain working conditions free from any hazards?

_____ 10. If I see hazardous conditions, does OSHA state that I have to tell my supervisor?

_____ 11. Do I have to wear this back brace? It is heavy and uncomfortable, and I can't move as well with it on.

_____ 12. If I report hazardous conditions to HR, do I have to tell them who I am?

_____ 13. If an OSHA inspector interviews me, can I cover up for the company and say we followed OSHA guidelines so we don't get into trouble?

_____ 14. Do I have to tell my supervisor I just got hurt? I don't want him to be mad at me for making him do all the paperwork.

HAZARD COMMUNICATION STANDARDS. OSHA requires that all employers maintain information at each work site that describes any chemical hazards that may be present on-site. A new set of Hazard Communication Standards (HCS) was promulgated in 2012 and can be found on the OSHA website (http://www.osha.gov). Under federal law, "All employers with hazardous chemicals in their workplaces are required to have a hazard communication program, including container labels, safety data sheets, and employee training."[16] **Safety Data Sheets** (SDS) *are documents that provide information on a hazardous chemical and its characteristics.* The OSHA-required SDS format is provided in Exhibit 14-2. The SDS provides employees with a quick reference to the hazards of working with a particular chemical compound. Electronic versions of SDS are acceptable, as long as there are no barriers to immediate access at the worksite.

LO 14-4

Identify the types of violations that OSHA looks for in inspections.

SHRM

X:1
OSHA Citations and Penalties

VIOLATIONS, CITATIONS, AND PENALTIES. OSHA violations include the following:[18]

- *Willful*—a violation in which the employer knew that a hazardous condition existed but made no effort to eliminate the hazard

- *Serious*—a violation where the hazard could cause injury or illness that would most likely result in death or significant physical harm

- *Other than serious*—a violation where any illness or injury likely to result from the hazard is unlikely to cause death or serious physical harm, but the violation does have a direct impact on employees' safety and health

- *De minimis*—violations that have no direct or immediate safety or health danger. This does not result in citations or penalties.

- *Failure to abate*—violations where the employer has not corrected a previous violation for which a citation was issued and the settlement date has passed

- *Repeated*—violations where the employer has been previously cited for the same type of violation within the previous 5 years

Safety Data Sheets
Documents that provide information on a hazardous chemical and its characteristics

Willful and repeated violations can bring the employer up to a $70,000 fine for each violation. *Failure to abate* violations can cost the employer as much as $7,000 per day while the violation continues to exist, and *serious* violations can also cost the employer a $7,000 fine.

EXHIBIT 14-2 SAFETY DATA SHEETS (SDS) FORMAT[17]

WORK
APPLICATION 14-2

Identify any organization (business, sports, school, etc.) that was cited and/ or penalized for not meeting OSHA standards. Be sure to provide details of the situation.

OSHA now requires that Hazard Communication SDS follow the following 16-section format.

Section 1, Identification includes product identifier; manufacturer or distributor name, address, phone number; emergency phone number; recommended use; restrictions on use.

Section 2, Hazard(s) identification includes all hazards regarding the chemical.

Section 3, Composition/information on ingredients includes information on chemical ingredients.

Section 4, First-aid measures includes important symptoms/effects (acute, delayed) and required treatment.

Section 5, Fire-fighting measures lists suitable extinguishing techniques, equipment; chemical hazards from fire.

Section 6, Accidental release measures lists emergency procedures; protective equipment; proper methods of containment and cleanup.

Section 7, Handling and storage lists precautions for safe handling and storage.

Section 8, Exposure controls/personal protection lists OSHA's Permissible Exposure Limits (PELs); Threshold Limit Values (TLVs); appropriate engineering controls; personal protective equipment (PPE).

Section 9, Physical and chemical properties lists the chemical's characteristics.

Section 10, Stability and reactivity lists chemical stability and possibility of hazardous reactions.

Section 11, Toxicological information includes routes of exposure; related symptoms, acute and chronic effects.

Section 12, Ecological information includes ecotoxicity (aquatic and terrestrial); persistence and degradability; bioaccumulative potential; mobility in soil.

Section 13, Disposal considerations includes description of waste residues and information on their safe handling and methods of disposal.

Section 14, Transport information includes transport hazard class(es); environmental hazards; special precautions which a user needs to be aware of, or needs to comply with, in connection with transport.

Section 15, Regulatory information includes safety, health, and environmental regulations specific for the product in question.

Section 16, Other information, includes the date of preparation or last revision.

Source: OSHA

National Institute of Occupational Safety and Health (NIOSH)

NIOSH works under the umbrella of the Centers for Disease Control and Prevention (CDC). NIOSH was also created as part of the 1970 OSH Act, and its mission is global in scope. "[NIOSH] is the federal agency that conducts research and makes

LO 14-5

Discuss the primary job of NIOSH as it applies to workplace safety and health.

Some jobs require safety equipment.

SHRM

X:8
Communicable Diseases

SHRM

A:23
Posting Requirements

WORK
APPLICATION 14-3

Identify safety and health posters you have seen displayed at any organization (business, sports, school, etc.).

recommendations to prevent worker injury and illness."[19] NIOSH notes three major goals in its strategic plan:[20]

- Conduct research to reduce work-related illnesses and injuries.
- Promote safe and healthy workplaces through interventions, recommendations, and capacity building.
- Enhance international workplace safety and health through global collaborations.

NIOSH routinely works with worldwide government health laboratories and other member nations in the World Health Organization (WHO) to identify workplace issues that can cause illness or injury and to create standards for the WHO member countries. NIOSH also works hand in hand with OSHA to identify workplace illnesses and to track diseases that can be passed from one person to another in the work environment. It does research on occupational safety and health topics from ergonomics (we will discuss this shortly) to MRSA (methicillin-resistant *Staphylococcus aureus*) infections and workplace violence. NIOSH research frequently provides the data that OSHA uses to create new workplace standards and regulations.

One of the most significant areas of research at NIOSH is communicable disease research. Again, in conjunction with other countries in the WHO, NIOSH has done research on a number of respiratory diseases that can be passed from one person to another, including tuberculosis and various strains of flu virus. NIOSH research attempts to identify methods of transmission and then provide guidelines for minimizing danger of transmission of dangerous diseases that may exist in the workplace. The entire intent of NIOSH research is to make the workplace safer for all employees.

Federal Notice Posting Requirements

There are a number of notices that employers are required to post in a convenient location frequented by employees during normal working hours. The notices or posters contain important information about employee rights and company responsibilities under federal law. OSHA's Job Safety and Health Protection poster is one of these, but there are also other posting requirements. Take a look at the following information for general federally mandated posting requirements.

The Department of Labor provides a number of posting requirements on its website (http://www.dol.gov), and we have reproduced some of the major ones in an abridged version in Exhibit 14-3.

Besides the requirements identified by the Department of Labor, SHRM has identified a series of other required postings, depending on the nature of the employer. We have reproduced part of the SHRM[21] list in Exhibit 14-4.

In addition to all of the other requirements, each state has its own posting requirements. Most states have requirements to at least post information on workers' compensation, unemployment insurance, and state minimum wage laws, while many states have a large number of other requirements as well. We need to become

EXHIBIT 14-3	DEPARTMENT OF LABOR POSTING REQUIREMENTS FOR BUSINESSES AND OTHER EMPLOYERS

Poster	Who Must Post	Citations/ Penalty	Other Information
JOB SAFETY AND HEALTH PROTECTION Occupational Safety and Health Administration 29 USC 657(c), 29 CFR 1903.2	Private employers engaged in a business affecting commerce. Does not apply to federal, state, or political subdivisions of states.	Any covered employer failing to post the poster may be subject to citation and penalty.	Employers in states operating OSHA-approved state plans should obtain and post the state's equivalent poster. For more information about Job Safety and Health, please visit http://www.osha.gov/Publications/poster.html.
EQUAL EMPLOYMENT OPPORTUNITY IS THE LAW Office of Federal Contract Compliance Programs Executive Order 11246, as amended; Section 503 of the Rehabilitation Act of 1973, as amended; 38 U.S.C. 4212 of the Vietnam Era Veterans' Readjustment Assistance Act of 1974, as amended; 41 CFR Chapter 60-I.42; 41 C.F.R. 60-250.4(k); 4 1 C.F.R. 60-74 1.5(a)4	Entities holding federal contracts or subcontracts or federally assisted construction contracts of $10,000 or more; financial institutions that are issuing and paying agents for US savings bonds and savings notes; depositories of federal funds or entities having government bills of lading	Appropriate contract sanctions may be imposed for uncorrected violations.	Post copies of the poster in conspicuous places available to employees, applicants for employment, and representatives of labor organizations with which there is a collective bargaining agreement. Also, nonconstruction contractors or subcontractors with 50 or more employees and a contract of $50,000 or more [otherwise required by 41 CFR 60-2.1(a)] should develop an equal opportunity policy as part of an affirmative action plan and post the policy on company bulletin boards. 41 CFR 60-2.2 1 (a)(9).
Fair Labor Standards Act (FLSA) Minimum wage poster Wage and Hour Division	Every private, federal, state, and local government employer employing any employee subject to the Fair Labor Standards Act, 29 USC 211, 29 CFR 516.4 posting of notices	No citations or penalties for failure to post	Any employer of employees to whom sec. 7 of the Fair Labor Standards Act does not apply may alter or modify the poster legibly to show that the overtime provisions do not apply. For information on how to order a poster, please visit http://www.dol.gov/whd/publications/.
YOUR RIGHTS UNDER THE FAMILY AND MEDICAL LEAVE ACT Wage and Hour Division 29 CFR 825.300, .402	Public agencies (including state, local, and federal employers), public and private elementary and secondary schools, as well as private sector employers who employ 50 or more employees in 20 or more workweeks and who are engaged in commerce or in any industry or activity affecting commerce, including joint employers and successors of covered employers	Willful refusal to post may result in a civil money penalty by the Wage and Hour Division not to exceed $100 for each separate offense.	Where an employer's workforce is not proficient in English, the employer must provide the notice in the language the employee speaks. The poster must be posted prominently where it can be readily seen by employees and applicants for employment. For information on how to order a poster, please visit http://www.dol.gov/whd/publications/.
Uniformed Services Employment and Reemployment Rights Act (Notice for use by all employers.)	The full text of the notice must be provided by each employer to persons entitled to rights and benefits under USERRA.	No citations or penalties for failure to notify. An individual could ask USDOL to investigate and seek	Employers may provide the notice by posting it where employee notices are customarily placed. However, employers are free to provide the notice in other ways that will minimize costs while

(Continued)

EXHIBIT 14-3 (CONTINUED)

Poster	Who Must Post	Citations/ Penalty	Other Information
Veterans' Employment and Training Service 38 U.S.C. 4334, 20 CFR 1002.		compliance, or file a private enforcement action to require the employer to provide the notice to employees.	ensuring that the full text of the notice is provided (e.g., by distributing the notice by direct handling, mailing, or via electronic mail). For more information about USERRA, please visit http://www.dol.gov/vets/programs/userra/.
NOTICE: EMPLOYEE POLYGRAPH PROTECTION ACT Wage and Hour Division 29 CFR 801.6	Any employer engaged in or affecting commerce or in the production of goods for commerce. Does not apply to federal, state, and local governments or to circumstances covered by the national defense and security exemption.	The Secretary of Labor can bring court actions and assess civil penalties for failing to post.	The act extends to all employees or prospective employees regardless of their citizenship status. Foreign corporations operating in the United States must comply or will result in penalties for failing to post. The poster must be displayed where employees and applicants for employment can readily observe it. For information on how to order a poster, please visit http://www.dol.gov/whd/publications/.
NOTIFICATION OF EMPLOYEE RIGHTS UNDER FEDERAL LABOR LAWS Office of Labor-Management Standards Executive Order 13496; 29 CFR Part 471	Federal contractors and subcontractors must post the employee notice conspicuously in and around their plants and offices so that it is prominent and readily seen by employees. In particular, contractors and subcontractors must post the notice where other notices to employees about their jobs are posted. Additionally, federal contractors and subcontractors who post notices to employees electronically must also post the required notice electronically via a link to the OLMS website.	The sanctions, penalties, and remedies for noncompliance with the notice requirements include the suspension or cancellation of the contract and the debarring of federal contractors from future federal contracts.	The notice, prescribed in the Department of Labor's regulations, informs employees of federal contractors and subcontractors of their rights under the NLRA to organize and bargain collectively with their employers and to engage in other protected concerted activity. Additionally, the notice provides examples of illegal conduct by employers and unions, and it provides contact information to the National Labor Relations Board (http://www.nlrb.gov), the agency responsible for enforcing the NLRA. For more information about OLMS Federal Labor Laws, please visit http://www.dol.gov/olms/regs/compliance/EO13496.htm.

Source: US Department of Labor

aware of and maintain knowledge of our state's requirements. Finally, employers must make certain that they also notify new hires of the above information.

EMPLOYEE HEALTH

Employee health The state of physical and psychological wellness in the workforce

Meeting OSHA requirements is necessary, but there are many other aspects to maintaining good employee health. **Employee health** *is the state of physical and psychological wellness in the workforce.* We have to consider both physical *and* psychological health in order to have a strong workforce. We need to provide our

EXHIBIT 14-4 OTHER REQUIRED POSTINGS

Federal Posting Requirements

Employers engaged in interstate commerce; state and local governments, federal employees, employment agencies, and labor organizations **with 20 or more members**:

- Consolidated Omnibus Protection Act (COBRA) Job Loss Poster *(This notice is optional but recommended)*

Employers engaged in interstate commerce; state and local governments, federal employees, employment agencies, and labor organizations **with 15 or more members**:

- Consolidated EEO "Equal Employment Opportunity Is the Law poster" "EEO Is the Law Poster Supplement"
- Title VII of the Civil Rights Act of 1964
- The Americans With Disabilities Act of 1990
- The Age Discrimination in Employment Act of 1967
- The Equal Pay Act of 1963
- The Genetic Information Nondiscrimination Act of 2008

E-Verify Participation Posters must be displayed by participating employers to inform their current and prospective employees of their legal rights and protections.

Federal government contractors and subcontractors:

- Rehabilitation Act (private employers with federal contracts or subcontracts of $10,000 or more)
- Executive Order 11246 (federal government contractors, subcontractors and contractors working on federally assisted construction contracts)
- Executive Order 13201—Beck Notice (federal contractors and subcontractors with 15 or more employees)
- McNamara-O'Hara Service Contract Act (private employers with government agency service contracts in excess of $2,500)
- Vietnam-Era Veterans' Readjustment Assistance Act (employers with federal contracts of $100,000 or more)
- Davis-Bacon Act (employers working on public construction projects in excess of $2,000)
- Walsh-Healey Act (employers with federal contracts or subcontracts worth $10,000 or more)

Farm labor contractors, agricultural employers, and agricultural associations:

- Migrant and Seasonal Agricultural Worker Protection Act Poster

Source: Society of Human Resource Management (SHRM)

employees with the ability to maintain both. In this section, we are going to complete a quick review of some of the other physical and psychological issues in today's workplace.

SHRM
X:3
Employee Health

Work-Life Balance

With mobile technology, the boundary between work and nonwork hours becomes fuzzy,[22] as employees even check in at work during their vacation and weekends, increasing the likelihood of work-family spillover. Spillover is the effect of work and family on one another that generates similarities between the two domains.[23] People are seeking work-life balance,[24] and many individuals are even taking classes to learn how to better balance the two.[25] In fact, recent research shows that work-life balance now ranks second only to compensation as the most important driver of employee attraction, commitment, and retention.[26] Balance between work and home lives is sought but rarely happens for long because of work-family conflict. This conflict is also linked with some other bad consequences such as stress; absenteeism; burnout; and dissatisfaction with job, family, and life—all of which can lead to excessive job turnover and the breakup of families.[27]

To help employees maintain a better work-life balance, the trend is for firms to offer more work-family benefits.[28] For example, employers are offering flexible work

SHRM
T:4
Company Policies to Accommodate Work and Nonwork Activities

WORK
APPLICATION 14-4

Assess your work-life and/or school-life balance? What percentage of your waking hours are typically devoted to work, school, and personal life? How can you improve the balance?

LO 14-6

Briefly discuss EAPs and EWPs and what their value is to companies and employees.

SHRM

K:B9
Employee Assistance/Wellness Programs

SHRM

K:B17
Wellness Programs

WORK
APPLICATION 14-5

Select an organization that offers an Employee Assistance Program (EAP) and Employee Wellness Program (EWP). Describe the program offerings.

EAP A set of counseling and other services provided to employees that help them to resolve personal issues that may affect their work

EWPs Plans designed to cater to the employee's physical, instead of psychological, welfare through education and training programs

Ergonomics According to OSHA, "the science of fitting workplace conditions and job demands to the capabilities of the working population"

schedules so that employees can start and end work around the times that help them balance work and family, and they also allow their people flexible time off to attend family activities such as parent-teacher meetings and sporting events. Many more firms are offering child care and elder care on or near their place of work than in the past, and they are providing the flexibility for their employees to select this as a standard benefit. Some organizations are offering courses on how to better balance work and life. Others provide counseling benefits to help improve family life so that it doesn't have a negative impact on work. Such counseling is commonly offered through the EAP, our next topic.

Employee Assistance Programs (EAP) and Employee Wellness Programs (EWP)

Two significant employee services that can assist with work-life balance and other aspects of employee mental and physical health are Employee Assistance Programs (EAPs) and Employee Wellness Programs (EWPs), also known as Workplace Wellness Programs (WWPs). EAPs and EWPs continue to grow in popularity in the United States and other countries around the world, most likely because companies are seeing results from the use of such programs.[29]

EAPS. An **EAP** *is a set of counseling and other services provided to employees that help them to resolve personal issues that may affect their work.* More than half of private sector workers have access to an employee assistance plan (EAP).[30] An EAP is designed to assist employees in confronting and overcoming problems in their personal life such as marital problems or divorce, financial problems, substance addictions, emotional problems, and many other issues. Why do half of all employers pay for these services? The simple answer is that such services can save valuable employees and, as a result, save the company money if they are available to the employee when they are needed.[31,32]

EAPs are confidential services provided to the employee. The employee can contact the company EAP and receive counseling and/or treatment for emotional or other personal issues as necessary. In some cases, EAPs may be regulated by federal laws, including the requirements of ERISA and COBRA, so company HR personnel need to be aware of this fact.

EWPS. **EWPs** *are designed to cater to the employee's physical, instead of psychological, welfare through education and training programs.* Wellness programs offer health education, training and fitness, weight and lifestyle management, and health risk assessment services to employees. The obvious goal is improving the health of our workforce, but why? Companies like **Johnson & Johnson** claim EWPs have succeeded in slowing health care cost increases.[33] EWPs can return from $2 to $6 in lower health care and lost productivity costs for every dollar spent.[34] Another interesting effect of EWPs appears to be lower turnover: "Healthy employees stay with your company. . . . [O]rganizations with highly effective wellness programs report significantly lower voluntary attrition than do those whose programs have low effectiveness (9% vs. 15%)."[35] So wellness programs provide employers with high return on investment and help with productivity, absenteeism, and turnover. No wonder companies continue to institute these programs.

Ergonomics and Musculoskeletal Disorders (MSDs)

According to OSHA, "Ergonomics *is the science of fitting workplace conditions and job demands to the capabilities of the working population.*"[36] The CDC identifies the goal of ergonomics as being to "reduce stress and eliminate injuries and disorders associated with the overuse of muscles, bad posture, and repeated tasks."[37]

Workplace ergonomics focuses on design of jobs and workspaces to limit the repetitive stresses that employees face in doing their daily work. OSHA provides employers with a set of voluntary guidelines on ergonomics in the workplace. These voluntary guidelines took the place of an earlier set of more rigid rules from OSHA on ergonomics that were rescinded by Congress in 2001.[38]

Several industries, including shipyards, poultry processors, retail stores, and nursing homes, among others, have specific sets of guidelines provided by OSHA. Other industries have the general set of voluntary guidelines published by OSHA.[39] It is wise for the organization to know OSHA's voluntary guidelines for their industry even though the earlier ergonomics rule was rescinded, because the OSHA website notes that "under the OSH Act's General Duty Clause, employers must keep their workplaces free from recognized serious hazards, including ergonomic hazards. This requirement exists whether or not there are voluntary guidelines."[40]

In addition to the potential for enforcement actions on the part of OSHA, it just makes sense to pay attention to ergonomics. Musculoskeletal disorders (MSDs) "affect the body's muscles, joints, tendons, ligaments and nerves" and can occur in many different work environments. They can take a toll on employee productivity when workers suffer from these issues. MSDs include a commonly known *repetitive stress injury (RSI)* called *carpal tunnel syndrome* where the nerves in the wrist become inflamed and painful, making movement difficult. But a large number of other problems fall under the MSD category, including other RSIs like rotator cuff syndrome, tennis elbow, carpet layer's knee, and many others.[41] All of these problems have the potential to cost the organization money in the form of lost productivity as well as workers' compensation claims. So paying attention to ergonomics at work can both improve productivity and save the company money.

Cornell University has an ergonomics program called **CUErgo** that has a large number of tools to help design jobs that are less stressful on employees; for a listing, go to its website at http://ergo.human.cornell.edu. It provides information from research by the Cornell Human Factors and Ergonomics Research Group (CHFERG).[42] It also provides information on everything from hospital work environments to general workstation design in offices and is a great help in identifying potential ergonomic issues in the workplace.

Safety and Health Management and Training

HR managers need to understand OSHA rules and standards in order to be able to make the workplace as safe as possible, and offering EAPs and EWPs and stress management training (our next section) is part of safety and health management.

By keeping the number of accidents and incidents low, we lower absenteeism plus increase job satisfaction. Nobody wants to work in an unsafe environment. Because we improve two of our four most important variables at work—absenteeism and job satisfaction—we are almost assured of increasing productivity over time. This is yet another way that HRM can assist in reaching organizational goals while using the least amount of organizational resources possible.

STRESS

People often have internal reactions to external environmental stimuli. **Stress** *is the body's reaction to environmental demands.* This reaction can be emotional and/or physical. According to *Forbes*, 35% of Americans have thought about leaving a job because of stress at work, and 42% have *actually done so!*[43] As stated in Chapter 1, absenteeism is costly, and there is a relationship between absenteeism and workplace stress.[44] In this section, we discuss functional and dysfunctional stress, the causes of stress, how to manage it, and the stress tug-of-war.

LO 14-7
Discuss the concept of ergonomics. Identify OSHA's function in ergonomics in the workplace.

SHRM
E:6
Compliance With Legal Requirements: Ergonomics and Workplace Safety

SHRM
X:11
Ergonomics

WORK APPLICATION 14-6
Identify potential ergonomics and musculoskeletal disorders (MSDs) in an industry that you work in or want to work in.

SHRM
X:6
Safety Management

WORK APPLICATION 14-7
Describe any safety, health, and stress training offered by an organization, preferably one you work or have worked for.

Stress The body's reaction to environmental demands

WORK
APPLICATION 14-8

Assess your ability to deal with stress. Identify when you tend to get stressed and the negative consequences you experience from dysfunctional stress.

Functional and Dysfunctional Stress

Let's begin by describing the difference between functional and dysfunctional stress and the consequences of dysfunctional stress.

FUNCTIONAL STRESS. Stress is *functional* (also called acute stress) when it helps improve performance by challenging and motivating people to meet objectives. People perform best under some pressure. Stress is an asset that stretches capacity and fuels creativity. When deadlines are approaching, adrenaline flows and people rise to the occasion. Stress actually provides greater strength and focus than we think we are capable of—so long as we are in control of it.[45]

DYSFUNCTIONAL STRESS. On the other hand, too much stress is dysfunctional because it decreases performance. **Stressors** *are factors that may, if extreme, cause people to feel overwhelmed by anxiety, tension, and/or pressure.* Stress that is constant, chronic, and severe can lead to burnout over a period of time.[46] **Burnout** *is a constant lack of interest and motivation to perform one's job.* Burnout results from too much stress. Stress that is severe enough to lead to burnout is dysfunctional stress.[47] But stress is an individual matter. Some people are better at handling stress than others.[48]

NEGATIVE CONSEQUENCES OF DYSFUNCTIONAL STRESS. Some readers may wonder why individual stress is a topic in an HRM text. The fact is that stress has some significant organizational consequences due to its effects on individual employees, so HR managers need to understand and be able to recognize the symptoms of stress, and especially dysfunctional stress because it causes mental and physical health problems.[49] More than 80% of Americans said they were less productive at work because of stress. Stress costs an estimated $300 billion a year in absenteeism; decreased productivity; employee turnover; accidents; and medical, legal, and insurance fees.[50] Stress causes headaches, depression, and illness.[51] Here are some other things dysfunctional stress does to us: It weakens our immune system, it makes us sick more often, it ages us so we look older, it makes us fatter, it decreases our sex drive, it ruins our sleep, and it can even kill us.[52] Stress, like perception, is an individual matter. In the same situation, one person may be very comfortable and stress-free, while another feels stressed to the point of burnout.

LO 14-8

Briefly discuss the causes of stress and how it can be managed.

Causes of Job Stress

There are five common contributors to job stress: personality type, organizational culture and change, management behavior, type of work, and interpersonal relations.

PERSONALITY TYPE. The *Type A personality* is characterized as fast-moving, hard-driving, time-conscious, competitive, impatient, and preoccupied with work. The Type B personality is pretty much the opposite of Type A. In general, people with Type A personalities experience more stress than people with Type B personalities. If you have a Type A personality, you could end up with some of the problems associated with dysfunctional stress. Complete Self-Assessment 14-1 to determine your personality type as it relates to stress.

ORGANIZATIONAL CULTURE AND CHANGE. The amount of cooperation and motivation that a person experiences and the level of organizational morale both affect stress levels. The more positive the organizational culture, the less stress there is. Organizations that push employees to high levels of performance but do little to ensure a positive work climate create a stressful situation. A climate with fear of layoffs can also be extremely stressful. Plus, change is stressful to many people, so cultures that continually make major changes can be stressful.[53]

Stressors Factors that may, if extreme, cause people to feel overwhelmed by anxiety, tension, and/or pressure

Burnout Constant lack of interest and motivation to perform one's job

14-1 SELF ASSESSMENT

Personality Type A or B and Stress

Identify how frequently each item applies to you at work or school. Place a number from 1 to 5 on the line before each statement.

5 = usually   4 = often   3 = occasionally   2 = seldom   1 = rarely

_____ 1. I enjoy competition, and I work/play to win.
_____ 2. I skip meals or eat fast when there is a lot of work to do.
_____ 3. I'm in a hurry.
_____ 4. I do more than one thing at a time.
_____ 5. I'm aggravated and upset.
_____ 6. I get irritated or anxious when I have to wait.
_____ 7. I measure progress in terms of time and performance.
_____ 8. I push myself to work to the point of getting tired.
_____ 9. I work on days off.
_____ 10. I set short deadlines for myself.
_____ 11. I'm not satisfied with my accomplishments for very long.
_____ 12. I try to outperform others.
_____ 13. I get upset when my schedule has to be changed.
_____ 14. I consistently try to get more done in less time.
_____ 15. I take on more work when I already have plenty to do.
_____ 16. I enjoy work/school more than other activities.
_____ 17. I talk and walk fast.
_____ 18. I set high standards for myself and work hard to meet them.
_____ 19. I'm considered a hard worker by others.
_____ 20. I work at a fast pace.
_____ Total. Add up the numbers you assigned to all 20 items. Your score will range from 20 to 100. Indicate where your score falls on the continuum below.

Type A   Type B
100_____90_____80_____70_____60_____50_____40_____30_____20

The higher your score, the more characteristic you are of the Type A personality. The lower your score, the more characteristic you are of the Type B personality.

MANAGEMENT BEHAVIOR. The better managers are at supervising employees, the less stress there is.[54] Lack of control tends to induce stress. Calm, participative management styles are less stressful. Bad bosses cause employee stress. Workers with bad bosses are more likely to report the stress-related problems that we discussed earlier.

TYPE OF WORK. Some types of work are more stressful than others.[55] People who have jobs that they enjoy derive more satisfaction from their work and handle stress better than those who do not. In some cases, changing to a job with more enjoyable work is a wise move that can lower stress levels. This is one major reason that people decide to make career changes.

INTERPERSONAL RELATIONS. Conflicts among people who do not get along can be very stressful. People who don't really like the work they must perform, but who do like the people they work with, can feel less stress and experience higher job satisfaction.

Stress Management

When we continually feel pressured and fear that we will miss deadlines or fail, we are experiencing stress. People watch TV or movies, drink, take drugs, eat, or sleep

How we manage stress affects our job performance and health.

more than usual to escape stress. But for the most part, these activities don't work in the long run because they are used mostly to escape stress, rather than deal directly with the stress.

We can limit job stress,[56] so many firms are making wellness a top priority through training employees in stress management.[57] EWPs (mentioned earlier in this chapter) frequently provide stress management programs for employees. Stress management is about taking control of stress and making it functional.[58] We can reduce stress with stress management interventions by better recognizing and managing stress symptoms as they occur.[59] *Stress management* is the process of reducing stress and making it functional. Here are *six stress management techniques*. We don't need to use them all because little changes can make big differences, so just implement the techniques that interest you.[60]

TIME MANAGEMENT. Generally, people with good time management skills experience less job stress. Vince Lombardi, the famous football coach, said, "Plan your work and work your plan." Remember that procrastinating gives us more time to think about what we have to do and to get stressed before starting. It's a huge relief when we finish the task.[61] If we are perfectionists, we may do a high-quality job, but perfectionism stresses us as we perform the work, so sometimes it's OK to define what is "good enough" and stop there.

RELAXATION. Relaxation is an excellent stress management technique, and we should relax both on and off the job. *Laughter* releases stress-reducing endorphins that lower blood pressure, relax muscles, stimulate our brain, improve our mood, and increase our oxygen intake—so laugh it up.[62] In addition, understand that each of us has their own way of relaxing. Some will read a book; others will lie in the sun; still others will play a game. It doesn't matter *how* you relax, as long as you relax in a way that is soothing to you.

Relaxation on the Job. Use relaxation on the job, and off, when feeling stress coming on by meditating, deep breathing, and/or muscle relaxation exercises.[63]

- *Meditation.* This can be simple. When we feel stress, we can close our eyes and think happy thoughts to calm ourselves: for example, picture ourselves doing something we enjoy or visualize the ocean with waves crashing down. Meditation works well with deep breathing.

- *Deep breathing.* When feeling stress, simply take five slow deep breaths, preferably through the nose. Hold each breath (about 5 seconds), then let it out slowly (about 7 seconds), preferably through lightly closed lips. To breathe deeply, we must inhale by expanding the stomach, not the chest. Think of the stomach as a balloon; slowly fill and then empty it. We can also breathe deeply while performing relaxation exercises.

- *Muscle relaxation exercises.* When feeling stress, we can also perform relaxation exercises. If we feel tension in one muscle, we may do a specific relaxation exercise. We may relax our entire body going from head to toe, or vice versa. Exhibit 14-5 lists relaxation exercises that we can do almost anywhere.

EXHIBIT 14-5 RELAXATION EXERCISES

Forehead: Wrinkle forehead by trying to make eyebrows touch hairline; hold for 5 seconds.

Eyes, nose: Close eyes tightly for 5 seconds.

Lips, cheeks, jaw: Draw corners of the mouth back tightly in a grimace; hold for 5 seconds.

Neck: Drop chin to chest, slowly rotate head without tilting it back.

Shoulders: Lift shoulders up to the ears and tighten for 5 seconds.

Upper arms: Bend elbows and tighten upper arm muscles for 5 seconds.

Forearms: Extend arms out against an invisible wall and push forward with hands for 5 seconds.

Hands: Extend arms to front; clench fists tightly for 5 seconds.

Stomach: Suck in and tighten stomach muscles for 5 seconds.

Back: Lie on back on the floor or a bed and arch back up off the floor, while keeping shoulders and buttocks on the floor; tighten for 5 seconds.

Hips, buttocks: Tighten buttocks for 5 seconds.

Thighs: Press thighs together and tighten for 5 seconds.

Feet, ankles: Flex feet with toes pointing up as far as possible and hold position for 5 seconds; then point feet down and hold for 5 seconds.

Toes: Curl toes under and tighten for 5 seconds; then wiggle toes to relax them.

Relaxation off the Job. We need to relax off the job. Try to leave work behind—don't do any work while away, and don't even think about it. If you have a Type A personality, slow down and enjoy yourself. Cultivate interests that do not relate to the job.

- *Activities.* Take time for yourself and do things you enjoy to relax and get away from work. What do you enjoy doing?

- *Sleep.* For most people, there is nothing more rejuvenating than a solid 7 or 8 hours of sleep, and fewer than 6 hours make most people more susceptible to the negative effects of stress.[64] But Americans are sleeping less on average today than in the past.[65] If we wake up tired and/or are tired throughout the day, maybe we need more or better sleep. Do you get enough quality deep sleep?

- *Sleeping tips.* Stress can delay sleep or reduce deep sleep. Working, using the Internet, cellphones, text messages, and caffeine close to bedtime can delay sleep and increase alertness. Doing a relaxing activity, like reading, before going to bed helps us sleep. We should shut off the TV, computer, and cell phone because the flickering lights from these devices overstimulate our brain and hurt the quality of our sleep.[66] Alcohol *can* promote sleep initially, but it can contribute to wakefulness later.[67]

NUTRITION. Good health is essential to everyone's performance, and nutrition is a major factor in health. Underlying stress can lead to overeating and compulsive dieting, and being overweight is stressful on the body. Unfortunately, around 34% of Americans are obese, while another 32% are overweight.[68] Men with a waist over 40 inches, and women over 35 inches, are twice as likely to die a premature death.[69] Obesity costs US businesses about $45 billion a year in medical expenses and lost productivity.[70] Are you overweight? Do you need to change your eating habits?

WORK
APPLICATION 14-9

Identify your major causes of stress; then select stress management techniques you will use to help overcome the causes of your stress.

We should watch our intake of junk foods, which contain fat (fried meat and vegetables, including French fries and chips), sugar (pastry, candy, fruit drinks, and soda), caffeine (coffee, tea, soda), and salt. Eat more fruits and vegetables and whole grains, and drink pure juices. Realize that poor nutrition; overeating; and the use of tobacco, alcohol, and drugs to reduce stress often create other stressful problems over a period of time.

When we eat, we should take our time and relax, because rushing is stressful and can cause an upset stomach and weight gain. Also, when people eat more slowly, they tend to eat less. Taking a break generates energy and makes us more productive. So we should avoid eating at our work area.

Breakfast is considered the most important meal of the day for good reason. Getting up and going to work just drinking coffee or soda without eating until lunch is stressful on the body. A good breakfast increases our ability to resist stress.

EXERCISE. Contrary to the belief of many, proper exercise increases our energy level rather than depleting it. If we are stressed for any reason, the fastest way to tame our anxiety can be physical activity. In fact, exercise is usually more effective than antidepressants in making moderate depression disappear.[71]

Aerobic exercise, in which we increase the heart rate and maintain it for 30 minutes, is generally considered the most beneficial type of exercise for stress reduction. Fast walking or jogging, biking, swimming, and aerobic dance or exercise fall into this category. Playing sports and weight lifting are also beneficial and can be aerobic if we don't take many breaks and we cross-train by mixing weights with other aerobic exercises.

Before starting an exercise program, check with a doctor to make sure you are able to do so safely. Always remember that the objective is to relax and reduce stress. The "no pain, no gain" mentality applies to competitive athletes, not to stress management.

If we don't enjoy the workout, we most likely will not stick with it anyway, so pick something fun or at least enjoyable, like playing a sport. Having an exercise partner really makes exercise more enjoyable, and it helps motivate us to show up and exercise when we'd rather not. We may also find out that we get in a great workout when we think we were too tired to exercise.

POSITIVE THINKING. People with an optimistic personality and attitude generally have less stress than pessimists because thoughts of gloom and doom (which are often distorted anyway) lead to stress.[72] Once we start having doubts about our ability to do what we have to do, we become stressed. Make statements to yourself in the affirmative, such as "This is easy," and "I will do it." Repeating positive statements while doing deep breathing helps us relax and increase performance.

SUPPORT NETWORK. Reaching out to supportive family, friends, and colleagues in our network can help reduce stress.[73] So we can find a confidant at work, or people outside of the workplace, and talk things through.[74] Venting to people we trust and hearing their support of our abilities relieves stress. Being out of work-life balance is stressful, so cultivate a supportive network of family, friends, and colleagues to help maintain that critical work-life balance.[75]

The Stress Tug-of-War

Think of stress as a tug-of-war with you in the center, as illustrated in Exhibit 14-6. On the left are causes of stress trying to pull you toward burnout. On the right are stress management techniques you use to keep you in the center. If the stress becomes too powerful, it will pull us off center to the left, and we may suffer burnout

EXHIBIT 14-6 THE STRESS TUG-OF-WAR

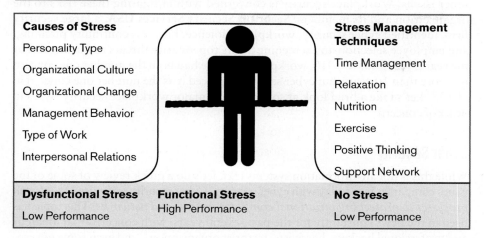

Causes of Stress		Stress Management Techniques
Personality Type		Time Management
Organizational Culture		Relaxation
Organizational Change		Nutrition
Management Behavior		Exercise
Type of Work		Positive Thinking
Interpersonal Relations		Support Network

Dysfunctional Stress	Functional Stress	No Stress
Low Performance	High Performance	Low Performance

and dysfunctional stress with low performance. If there is no stress, we tend to move to the right and just take it easy and perform at low levels. The stress tug-of-war is an ongoing game. Our main objective is to stay in the center with functional stress, which leads to high levels of performance.[76]

If we try stress management but still experience long-term burnout, we should seriously consider getting out of the situation. Ask yourself two questions: Is my long-term health important? Is this situation worth hurting my health for? If you answer yes and no respectively, a change of situations may be advisable. Career changes are often made for this reason.

WORKPLACE SECURITY

Workplace security *is the management of personnel, equipment, and facilities in order to protect them.* While workplace safety deals with the issue of minimizing occupational illness and injury, workplace security covers topics such as violence in the workplace (including bullying), bomb threats, management of natural and

LO 14-9

Identify the top concerns for security in the workplace today.

Workplace security The management of personnel, equipment, and facilities in order to protect them

---

14-3 APPLYING **THE CONCEPT**

Stress Management Techniques

Put the letter of the technique being used on the line next to the corresponding statement.

a. time management
b. relaxation
c. nutrition
d. exercise
e. positive thinking
f. support network

_____ 15. "I've been stressed out, so I have been praying more lately."

_____ 16. "I've been working on positive affirmations, so I have been repeating to myself that 'I can meet the deadline.'"

_____ 17. "I'm not too organized, so I've started using a to-do list."

_____ 18. "I've been taking a walk at lunchtime with Latoya."

_____ 19 "I've been getting up earlier and eating a healthy breakfast."

_____ 20. "I have a bad boss, so I've been talking to my colleague Tom about her."

SHRM

X:7
Security Concerns at Work

man-made disasters, risk to company computer systems and intranets, and many other issues. Workplace security is concerned with mitigating these risks to the organization and its members. **Securitas Security Services USA**, a large security firm, identified cyber security, workplace violence, business continuity planning, and employee selection and screening as the top security threats to businesses for the year 2012. Prior to 2010, workplace violence had been the number one concern for more than 10 years, but cyber security replaced it as the number one concern in 2010.[77] Let's take a brief look at some of these major workplace security issues in order of concern.

Cyber Security

While this is not an information systems text, let's do a quick review of some of the issues companies face today with cyber security. **Cyber security** *is the use of tools and processes to protect organizational computer systems and networks.* This topic has been in the news constantly for the past several years, with concerns that amateur and professional hackers, hactivists, terrorist organizations, and even some governments are working to break into company computer systems for a variety of purposes. The US attorney general recently accused hackers working for the Chinese government of hacking US companies, including **Westinghouse, Alcoa,** and the **United Steel Workers Union.**[78] Every company has to be concerned with this issue and do what they can to prevent becoming a victim.

SHRM

X:9
Data Security

HRM is especially concerned with outsiders penetrating company computer systems that have sensitive employee information on them, such as information on medical records, payroll and banking data, and other personal data. HR managers must work with company security managers to put up strong roadblocks to outsiders who seek to enter systems with this type of data. In 2013, **AvMed** left two unsecured laptops with private employee data on them in an unlocked conference room, and they were stolen. The company ultimately agreed to pay a $3 million settlement to the employees for failure to safeguard information in accordance with HIPAA.[79] While there is no foolproof way to harden company computer systems, we have to do the best that we can to make it as hard as possible for hackers or other unauthorized users to find and exploit employee data. Obviously, the HR manager won't be the person to research and implement this type of computer security, but we do need to know that it is an issue. We will work with our company's computer security managers to make it as hard as possible to get access if a person is not an authorized user. One simple tool is to encrypt any company computers with sensitive data on their hard drives. This makes it much more difficult to gain access to such information.

Workplace Violence

Now, let's focus on anger that can lead to violence and how to prevent it. Human resource managers have reported increased violence between employees, stating it can happen anywhere. And don't think that this is just an issue of men harming women. Women commit nearly a quarter of all threats or attacks. There has also been an increase in violence between outsiders and employees, such as customers shooting employees and other customers. A psychiatrist at **Mercy Fitzgerald Hospital** outside Philadelphia was forced to shoot and kill a patient after he in turn had killed a case worker in 2014, and this is just one of thousands of incidents that occur in the United States alone each year. In some years, more than 1,000 workers have been killed. The key to preventing workplace violence is to recognize and handle suspicious behavior before it turns violent;[80] that's what this subsection is all about.

CAUSES OF ANGER AND VIOLENCE . Anger can lead to violence. You have most likely heard of road rage. In business we have *desk rage,* which can take the form of yelling, verbal abuse, and physical violence. Frustration, stress, and fear also bring out

Cyber security The use of tools and processes to protect organizational computer systems and networks

anger.[81] Unresolved *inter*personal conflicts make people angry.[82] In fact, violence is almost always prompted by unresolved conflict, and the violence often takes the form of sabotage against other employees (backstabbing, spreading false rumors) or the organization (damage to property) to get even.[83]

The physical work environment (such as space to work, noise, odors, temperature [hot], ventilation, and color) contributes to making people angry. A bad work environment (called *toxicity*) leads to violence. People also tend to copy, or model, others' behavior. For example, children who have been abused (emotionally and/or physically) are more likely, as parents, to abuse their children. If employees see others being violent, especially managers, and nothing is done about it, they are more apt to also use violent behavior at work. Violence in the community surrounding an organization, including family violence, may be brought into the workplace. Some but not all experts also report that drugs contribute to violence.[84]

Security is of concern to organizations today.

DEALING WITH ANGER

Your Anger and Emotional Control. A secondary feeling of anger follows many of our feelings. Your boss may surprise you with extra work, which makes you angry. Disappointment often leads to anger. Your coworkers don't do their share of the work, so you get mad at them. Buddha said, "You will not be punished FOR your anger; you will be punished BY your anger." Anger can lead to perception problems and poor decisions and hostility, which are stressful and can harm your health.[85]

It is natural to get angry sometimes, as we cannot control the feeling of anger. However, we can control our behavior, and we can learn to deal with anger in more positive ways to get rid of it. Letting anger build up often leads initially to passively not doing or saying anything, but then later blowing up at another person. Here are some tips for effectively getting rid of our anger:

- Use objective, rational thinking. For example, when dealing with customers, tell yourself, "Their anger is to be expected. It's part of my job to stay calm."

- Look for positives. In many bad situations, there is some good.

- Look for the humor in the situation to help defuse the anger. Finding appropriate humor can help keep us from moping and getting angry.

- Develop a positive attitude about how to deal with anger. Develop positive affirmations such as "I stay calm when in traffic" (not "I must stop getting mad in traffic") and "I get along well with Joe" (not "I must stop letting Joe get me angry").

- Use an anger journal. A first step to emotional control of anger is self-awareness. Answer these questions. How often do you get irritated/angry each day? What makes you irritated/angry? How upset do you get? What feelings do you have when you are angry? What behavior (yell, say specific words, pound desk, do and say nothing, accommodate) do you use when you are angry? Are you good at dealing with your irritations/anger? One good way to improve your ability to control your anger is to write the answers to these questions in an anger journal. It is a method of letting out the anger in an effective way. People who use a journal often change their behavior without even trying.

Anger of Others and Emotional Control. Here are some tips from the Crisis Prevention Institute and the National Institute for Occupational Safety & Health (NIOSH) to help us deal with the anger of others through our emotional control to prevent violence. These tips can be very valuable to us as managers:

- Never make any type of putdown statement, as it can make the person angrier. As stated above, you may use appropriate humor to cut the tension, but be careful that it is not viewed as a sarcastic putdown. Such behavior can lead to violence.

- Don't respond to anger and threats with the same behavior. This is the key to success in maintaining your emotional control.

- Don't give orders or ultimatums. This can increase anger and push the person to violence.

- Watch your nonverbal communications to show concern and to avoid appearing aggressive. Use eye contact to show concern, but be aware that staring or glaring can make you appear aggressive. Maintain a calm, soothing tone to defuse anger and frustration. Talking loudly and with frustration, anger, or annoyance in your tone of voice will convey aggression. Don't move rapidly, point at the person, get too close (stay 2–5 feet apart), or touch.

- Realize that anger is natural and encourage people to vent in appropriate ways. With the aggressor, the problem is usually to keep the behavior acceptable. With the passive person, you may need to ask probing questions to get them to vent, such as "What is making you angry? What did I do to make you mad?"

- Acknowledge the person's feelings. Using reflective responses by paraphrasing the way the person appears to be feeling shows that we care and helps calm the person so they can get back in control of their emotions.

- Get away from the person if necessary. If possible, call in a third party to deal with the person and leave.

SIGNS OF POTENTIAL VIOLENCE. Workplace violence is rarely spontaneous; it is more commonly passive-aggressive behavior in rising steps, related to an unresolved conflict. Employees do give warning signs that violence is possible, so it can be prevented if we look for these signs and take action to defuse the anger before it becomes violent.[86]

- Take verbal threats seriously. Most violent people do make a threat of some kind before they act. If we hear a threat, or hear about a threat from someone else, talk to the person who made the threat and try to resolve the issue.

- Watch nonverbal communication. Behavior such as yelling, gestures, or other body language that conveys anger can also indicate a threat of violence. Talk to the person to find out what's going on.

- Watch for stalking and harassment. It usually starts small, but it can lead to violence. Put a stop to it.

- Watch for damage to property. If an employee kicks a desk, punches a wall, and so on, talk to the person to get to the reason for the behavior. People who damage property can become violent to coworkers.

- Watch for indications of alcohol and drug use. People can be violent under their influence. Get them out of the workplace and get them professional help from the EAP, if it's a recurring problem.

- Include the isolated employee. It is common for violent people to be employees who don't fit in, especially if they are picked on or harassed by coworkers. Reach out to this employee and help them fit in or get them to a place where they do.

- Look for the presence of weapons or objects that might be used as weapons. You may try talking to the person if you feel safe, but get security involved if you feel the least bit unsafe.

ORGANIZATIONAL PREVENTION OF VIOLENCE. The number one preventive method is to train all employees to deal with anger and prevent violence,[87] which is what you are learning now. However, the starting place is with a written policy addressing workplace violence, and a zero-tolerance policy is the best preventive policy. From the HR manager's perspective, it is very important to take quick disciplinary action against employees who are violent at work. Otherwise, aggression will spread in the organization, and it will be more difficult to stop. Managers especially need to avoid using aggression at work because employees more readily copy managers' behavior than other employees.

As discussed in Chapter 10, the organization should have a system for dealing with grievances, and it should also track incidents of violence as part of its policy. Organizations can also screen job applicants for past or potential violence so that they are not hired. They should also develop a good work environment addressing the issues listed above as causes of violence. Demotions, firing, and layoffs should be handled in a humane way following the guidelines to deal with anger, and outplacement services to help employees find new jobs can help cut down on violence.

INDIVIDUAL PREVENTION OF VIOLENCE. One thing you should realize is that the police department will not help prevent personal or workplace violence. Police only get involved after violence takes place. We have already given you most of the tips above. But here are a few more tips.[88] Keep in mind that there is always potential violence, and look for escalating frustration and anger to defuse it before it becomes violence. Never be alone with a potentially violent person or stand between the person and the exit. Know when to get away from the person, and utilize the organization policy of calling in security help if you are concerned. Report any troubling incidents to security staff.

Social Media for Workplace Safety and Security

We have discussed a number of areas of HRM that have been enhanced through the use of social media. This is another case where social media tools can assist companies in dealing with a situation where employees may need information quickly and accurately. Organizations around the world are establishing security alert systems to be used in the case of a company emergency of any type, including a violent individual or group on organization property. The systems use existing technology like **Twitter** and text messaging to provide immediate warnings to all persons who are signed up to receive alerts, and they can even give them information on what steps to take to remain safe in such situations. These systems have already undoubtedly saved lives in violent incidents in many companies, and any company without such a system should probably look at installing the capability as soon as feasible.

Employee Selection and Screening

We discussed tools concerning employee selection and screening in Chapter 6, but we need to be reminded of some of them again here, because of their importance to company security. The first tool that we want to make sure that we use in employee screening is background checks. Recall that we can be held liable for monetary damages if we are guilty of a "negligent hire." One way to guard against such a hire is through the consistent use of criminal background checks that specifically look for a history of violent actions or threats of violence on the part of an applicant or employee.

WORK
APPLICATION 14-10

Recall a situation in which someone was angry with you, preferably at work. What was the cause of the anger? Did the person display any signs of potential violence? If so, what were they? How well did the person deal with their anger? Give specific tips the person did and did not follow.

WORK
APPLICATION 14-11

Recall a situation in which you were angry with someone, preferably at work. What was the cause of your anger? Did you display any signs of potential violence? If so, what were they? How well did you deal with your anger? Give specific tips you did and did not follow.

Other background checks can also help with organizational security. Web searches can sometimes turn up negative information on an applicant that may show that they are a potential security risk, even when criminal checks do not. In addition, credit checks might show evidence of a history of unethical behavior that would make it more likely that an applicant might be unscrupulous, and might even intentionally harm other employees if hired. So we do have some tools available in background checks to mitigate the risk of hiring the wrong type of person.

In addition to background checks, substance abuse testing can provide us with a tool to minimize the security dangers in your company. As we noted in Chapter 6, "Most employers have the right to test for a wide variety of substances in the workplace,"[89] and the former head of the White House Office of National Drug Control Policy has said that the "issue of drugs in the workplace is an understated crisis that results in $200 billion in lost productivity annually."[90] According to SHRM, "Substance abuse prevention is an essential element of an effective workplace safety and security program. Properly implemented preventive programs—including drug and alcohol testing—protect the business from liability."[91] The US Department of Justice noted that "the link between drug use and crime has been well-documented in recent years."[92] Screening out substance abusers in the applicant stage can minimize security threats to the organization because there is strong evidence that at least some substance abusers will commit crimes, including violent crimes at work in many cases.

SHRM
X:2
Disaster Preparation, Continuity, and Recovery Planning

General Security Policies, Including Business Continuity and Recovery

Common disasters and emergencies might include such events as fires, floods, earthquakes, severe weather, tsunamis, terrorist attacks, bomb threats, and many others. Some are dependent on the company's geographic location, while others are universal possibilities. One thing is sure, though—disasters and emergencies happen without warning, creating a situation in which the normal organizational services can become overwhelmed or even disappear. You may remember the nuclear crisis in Fukushima, Japan, when a tsunami wiped out electrical power to a nuclear plant and then, because there was no power to pump water, several of the reactors melted down. During such a crisis, companies require a set of processes that address the needs of emergency response and recovery operations. The power company, **TEPCO**, did not have a sufficient process for such a disaster. To address these types of emergencies, the company should establish an emergency response plan, which provides guidelines for immediate actions and operations required to respond to an emergency or disaster, and these guidelines need to take into consideration *everything* that a company can think of in order to provide the appropriate plan.

The overall *priorities* of any plan in any emergency or disaster should be these:

- Protect human life; prevent/minimize personal injury.
- Preserve physical assets.
- Protect the environment.
- Restore programs and return operations to normal.

The overall *objective* is to respond to the emergency and manage the process of restoring the organization, as well as its associated programs and services.

But what part does the HRM professional play in this planning process? HRM should be part of the management team that determines the goals of the plan. Once the goals are determined, HR can again help operational management to staff the various key positions in the disaster recovery teams by understanding the types of people that are necessary to do these jobs under crisis circumstances.

Additionally, HR is typically responsible for the training function in the company, and everyone in the organization needs to be trained on the plan and its processes. The training should also become part of the new employee orientation (Chapter 7) so that all personnel are aware of the correct responses to potential emergencies. There are many examples of good emergency response and business recovery plans out there on the Internet for free. All the company needs to do is find a good sample and modify it for their particular circumstances and the likely disasters that would occur based on their geographic locations. A company in Arkansas probably doesn't need a plan for tsunami recovery, while a company on the coast of California is unlikely to need tornado or hurricane sheltering plans.

One final thing that HRM needs to determine is where extra assistance might come from if needed because of a disaster or emergency. For instance, if severe weather were to kill and injure a number of company employees, grief counseling services might become necessary. Most companies don't routinely have grief counselors on hand, but in this type of situation may need access to such counselors very quickly. HRM can think of likely situations and their aftermaths and determine where these types of services might be procured if the need presented itself. One potential provider in at least some cases might be the vendor that services the company EAP. Recall that EAPs are services for the psychological well-being of our employees. Therefore, they may have the needed personnel to handle the psychological aftermath of a disaster.

TRENDS AND ISSUES IN HRM

What are some of the significant trends and issues in workplace safety and health? First, we are going to explore employee wellness in a bit more detail. The second item we will look at is the trend toward government safety agencies becoming significantly more activist under the Obama administration. Third, we will take a look at one program that uses the Internet to promote workplace health—a trend that is occurring with greater frequency in today's 21st century workplaces, so let's get started.

Employee Wellness in a WALL-E World

You might remember the movie about a robot, Wall-E, who helped the obese inhabitants of a spaceship reclaim Earth. Unfortunately, this picture of a society where machines do everything for people is not too far removed from reality today. There is strong evidence that Americans (and people in most other countries) do not exercise enough. More than a third of Americans are obese, with many more overweight.[93] Obesity and excess weight create all kinds of health problems, and we are seeing the effects of overweight employees at work. Many employees have health problems such as diabetes, high blood pressure, and heart disease that are brought on by excess weight. Employee wellness programs (EWPs) work to help our employees become more healthy and fit and to lower the incidence of these types of health problems.

So what are companies doing in these EWPs, and are the results worth the effort? The answer is that companies are doing anything that they can figure out that gets employees up and off of their duff! Any exercise is better than none. In a recent *Harvard Business Review* article, a Harvard lecturer said that "sitting is the smoking of our generation."[94] A research study by the **National Institutes of Health** says that "sitting for prolonged periods can compromise metabolic health," and that "too much sitting is distinct from too little exercise."[95] Getting people up and moving is valuable to organizations. The **City of Charlotte**, North Carolina, has had some success using games and competitions between groups of employees. **Tokyo Electron** bought **Fitbit** fitness trackers for all of their employees to encourage them to get up and move.

However, not all is rosy in the wellness business. **PepsiCo** runs a Healthy Living wellness program for more than 67,000 employees that has, according to the company, produced "a substantial return on investment" [96] through managing existing diseases, *but no benefit from lifestyle management programs.*[97] The **RAND Corporation** has done several recent studies on wellness programs in which they note that "effects of wellness program effects on health care cost are lower than most results reported in [previous] literature" but also note that their research isolates measurements of the effects of *lifestyle management programs* specifically. The **Institute of Medicine** also claims that at least part of $210 billion in *unnecessary* annual health care costs are due to corporate wellness programs.[98] However, even with this information, companies should consider wellness programs for their workforce—even if the cost-benefit relationship is basically 1:1. The peripheral benefits of lower absenteeism and higher productivity and job satisfaction will likely lead to at least an indirect benefit from such programs, even if we do not directly save money on health premiums for our employees. Another indirect benefit of these programs comes from the recent Affordable Care Act, which allows an incentive for participation in wellness programs of up to 30% of an employee's total health care premium, up from a 20% premium prior to the law's passage.

Bullying in the Workplace

SHRM

C:6
Behavior Within Ethical Boundaries

Have you ever been the victim of a bully—on the school playground or at work? The year 2013 was an eye-opening year for both employers and employees who are concerned with, or have been victims of, bullying. You may remember that **Rutgers University** fired their head basketball coach, Mike Rice, after a video showing him bullying and verbally abusing his players came to light.[99] Also, a **Miami Dolphins** player, Richie Incognito, was terminated from the team due to a series of bullying incidents both inside and outside the locker room that led another player, Jonathan Martin, to quit the team.[100] These high-profile incidents have brought the subject of workplace bullying to the forefront of the minds of HR managers around the world once again. Information on bullying has come up in past years, but this was nationally, even internationally, newsworthy bullying behavior!

SHRM

C:14
Abusive Behavior—Workplace Bullying

Managers do not want their company put into the news spotlight as these coaches and teams were. Bullying behaviors have been found to be four times more common than sexual harassment,[101] but there are still no laws at the *national level* in the United States that deal *directly* with bullying as an offense.[102] There are certainly ways in which managers can use existing laws when bullying behaviors are based on protected class characteristics (e.g., race, religion, disability, etc.) or other illegal actions such as assault or sexual harassment, but there is no federal law directly associated with workplace bullying. There is, however, an excellent website run by the US Department of Health and Human Services that addresses the issue and provides a state-by-state review of bullying laws (http://www.stopbullying.gov). The site is primarily aimed at youth, but the principles of action to stop bullying can also apply to the workplace.

HR managers need to know the state and local laws that can be used for bullying behaviors, but they also need to address the issue in company handbooks and provide training on processes that should be used if someone suspects bullying behaviors or are themselves a victim of such behavior. What policies can the company put into place to combat these behaviors? Here is a basic set of steps (you may notice that they are very similar to the steps the company should take to avoid sexual harassment) that we need to put into place in order to stop bullying in our company:

1. Develop a policy on bullying, defining the concept and making it clear that bullying behavior will not be tolerated.
2. Train all employees on the policy on a routine basis—typically at least once per year and upon hiring of new employees.

3. Develop mechanisms for reporting bullying behaviors that are outside the normal chain of command, since bullying frequently occurs with supervisors who have control over other employees.

4. Investigate all reported incidents of bullying using the Just Cause procedures that we discussed in Chapter 9.

5. Take prompt, fair disciplinary action with those individuals who have been found to be guilty of bullying behaviors, whether senior members of the organization or subordinate individuals.

HR managers should expect that some type of federal law will come out within the next year or two and be cognizant of the need to train all employees on this deleterious issue that costs companies due to lower job satisfaction; lower productivity; higher absenteeism, turnover, and sick days; and many other problems.

eDocAmerica—Health and Wellness Online

One example of a new kind of online provider of occupational and employee health-related services is **eDocAmerica**, found at http://www.edocamerica.com. eDocAmerica is a health care service provider that "gives individuals and their family members unlimited email access to board certified physicians, psychologists, pharmacists, dentists, dietitians and fitness experts who provide personal answers to all health-related questions."[103] eDocAmerica was started by a physician at the University of Arkansas for Medical Sciences to provide outreach services to employees of client businesses.

The services of eDocAmerica, and other similar providers, make it much easier and quicker for employees of client firms to get answers to most of their routine health questions. This has two major benefits. First, it allows the employee to take more control of their personal and family health, and secondly, it takes some pressure off of the larger health care system because employees are not running to the doctor's office every time they need a simple question answered.

As a side benefit for the organization, it appears that companies may save money on their group health insurance plans because of the lower utilization rates made possible by quick and easy email access to expertise. eDocAmerica has so far been quite successful in creating a more open and accessible health care system with their client company employees. This is just one of the new breed of web-based providers of safety and health services to companies and employees. We will likely continue to see more companies with similar services come online in the near future.

• • • CHAPTER SUMMARY

14-1 Identify the responsibilities of both employers and employees under the general duties clause of the OSH Act.

Employers have to provide employees with a place of employment free from recognized hazards that are causing or are likely to cause death or serious physical harm and are required to comply with occupational safety and health standards identified in the act.

Employees also have a duty to comply with occupational safety standards, rules, and regulations in all cases while at work.

14-2 Briefly describe what OSHA does in a worksite inspection.

OSHA can inspect a worksite without advance notice. The inspector will identify themselves and provide the reason for the inspection when they arrive. Once the employer provides access to the worksite, the inspector will do an inspection. The inspector has the right to interview employees during the inspection and may do so unless the interview becomes confrontational or disruptive of the work environment. The inspector will provide the employer with a list of discrepancies upon completion of the inspection.

14-3 Discuss employer rights during an OSHA inspection.

The employer has a right to ask for positive identification from the OSHA inspector, including their badge number. The employer also has a right to know the reason for the inspection. Employers can refuse to allow the inspector into the worksite, unless they have a court order, but this is usually not a very good idea. The employer also has a right to have a representative accompany the inspector while they are on the worksite and has the right to tell employees their rights in the inspection process. The employer can also have a representative in any interviews unless the employee specifically requests that the interview be private, and the employer can stop interviews if they become disruptive. Finally, the employer has the right to contest any citations that they receive.

14-4   Identify the types of violations that OSHA looks for in inspections.

Violations include the following:

Willful—where the employer knew that a hazardous condition existed but made no effort to eliminate the hazard

Serious—where the hazard could cause injury or illness that would most likely result in death or significant physical harm

Other than serious—where any illness or injury incurred is unlikely to cause death or serious physical harm, but the violation does have a direct impact on safety and health

De minimis—violations that have no direct or immediate safety or health danger

Failure to abate—where the employer has not corrected a previous violation for which a citation was issued and the settlement date has passed

Repeated—the employer has been cited for the same type of violation within 5 years

14-5   Discuss the primary job of NIOSH as it applies to workplace safety and health.

The primary job of NIOSH is to provide research, information, education, and training in the field of occupational safety and health. NIOSH notes three major goals in its strategic plan:

- Conduct research to reduce work-related illnesses and injuries.

- Promote safe and healthy workplaces through interventions, recommendations, and capacity building.

- Enhance international workplace safety and health through global collaborations.

14-6   Briefly discuss EAPs and EWPs and what their value is to companies and employees.

EAPs and EWPs both help employees with their work-life balance. EAPs provide confidential counseling and other personal services to employees to help them cope with stress created by personal issues related to either work or home life. EWPs help employees with their physical wellness. They provide programs to employees such as health education, training and fitness programs, weight management, and health risk assessments.

14-7   Discuss the concept of ergonomics. Identify OSHA's function in ergonomics in the workplace.

Ergonomics is the science of fitting workplace conditions and job demands to the capabilities of the working population. The goal of ergonomics is to reduce stress and limit injuries due to overuse of muscles, bad posture, and repetitive tasks. OSHA provides guidelines on ergonomics in the workplace that are voluntary but that can be assessed during an inspection based on the general duties clause of the OSH Act. OSHA also has specific ergonomic guidelines for a number of different industries, so HR representatives should check to make sure that they are following OSHA guidelines based on the industry that they are a part of.

14-8   Briefly discuss the causes of stress and how it can be managed.

The major causes of stress include personality type, organizational culture and change, management behavior, type of work, and interpersonal issues. Type A personalities, weak organizational cultures and rapidly changing organizations, bad management, jobs that employees don't enjoy, and poor interpersonal relations all make stress more prevalent in the workplace. Stress management techniques include good time management skills, the ability to relax once in a while (in whatever form you choose), good nutrition, moderate amounts of exercise, positive thinking skills, and a strong personal support network. All of these tools help us cope with stress successfully.

14-9   Identify the top concerns for security in the workplace today.

The four biggest concerns of employers today are cyber security, workplace violence, business continuity planning, and employee selection and screening. Cyber security deals with the company's computer and network security. Workplace violence is another major issue because of the continuing rise in incidents of workplace violence. Third, business continuity planning has become a much more significant issue to most employers in the past 10 years, partly because of terrorism threats but also because of a number of large-scale environmental and natural disasters worldwide. Finally, employee selection and screening have become more of an issue because of the problem of negligent hires and the possibility for increased workplace violence if we allow individuals who have a history of violence into our organization.

14-10 Define the key terms found in the chapter margins and listed following the Chapter Summary.

Complete the Key Terms Review to test your understanding of this chapter's key terms.

• • • KEY TERMS

burnout	ergonomics	stressors
cyber security	EWPs	workplace safety
EAP	Safety Data Sheets	workplace security
employee health	stress	

• • • KEY TERMS REVIEW

Complete each of the following statements using one of this chapter's key terms.

1. _____ is the physical protection of people from injury or illness while on the job.

2. _____ are documents that provide information on a hazardous chemical and its characteristics.

3. _____ is the state of physical and psychological wellness in the workforce.

4. _____ is a set of counseling and other services provided to employees that help them to resolve personal issues that may affect their work.

5. _____ are designed to cater to the employee's physical, instead of psychological, welfare through education and training programs.

6. _____ is the science of fitting workplace conditions and job demands to the capabilities of the working population.

7. _____ is the body's reaction to environmental demands.

8. _____ are factors that may, if extreme, cause people to feel overwhelmed by anxiety, tension, and/or pressure.

9. _____ is a constant lack of interest and motivation to perform one's job.

10. _____ is the management of personnel, equipment, and facilities in order to protect them.

11. _____ is the use of tools and processes to protect organizational computer systems and networks.

• • • COMMUNICATION SKILLS

The following critical-thinking questions can be used for class discussion and/or for written assignments to develop communication skills. Be sure to give complete explanations for all answers.

1. Are some number of occupational illnesses and injuries an acceptable part of doing business? Why or why not? Explain your answers.

2. Do you foresee a situation in which you would ever refuse to allow an OSHA inspector on your worksite? Why or why not?

3. What actions would you take if you were the company representative accompanying an OSHA inspector who found a serious violation in your company? Explain your answer.

4. Is there ever a reason why a company should be charged with a failure to abate a hazard in the workplace? Can you think of any situations that might cause such a charge that would be outside the employer's control?

5. Do you think the OSHA and NIOSH occupational safety and health requirements generally make sense? Why or why not?

6. If you were in charge, would you put an EAP into place at your company? How about an EWP? Why or why not?

7. Can you think of some things that you might be able to institute at work for very little or no cost in order to improve work-life balance for your employees? Be specific in your answers.

8. Have you ever suffered from a MSD injury? Were you able to recover from it? What did you do to help you recover or mitigate the problem associated with the MSD injury?

9. Do you think that you suffer from too much stress? Name a few things that you could do to minimize the dysfunctional stress in your life.

10. Go through the process of how you would train your employees on a new business continuity and disaster

recovery plan. What do you think the most important part of the training would be? Why?

11. Should smoking be banned in all buildings where smokers and nonsmokers have to work together? Why or why not?

12. What programs would you put into effect as a leader in order to make your employees understand that occupational safety and health are critical to a modern company?

• • • CASE 14-1 HANDLING THE UNHEALTHY EMPLOYEE

Bill is an award-winning newspaper reporter for the city news who can crank out twice as many feature articles as anyone else. To keep relevant in a period of downsizing in the newspaper industry, Bill also maintains the newspaper blog and social network pages. Over time, his work hours grew. He often chain-smoked his way to three hours of sleep or less. He gained weight and started to develop a considerable waist. He always had snacks by his desk because he had little time to go out to a restaurant or make a home-cooked meal.

Bill was known to be irritable and often yelled at his colleagues for not getting information he needed for articles. "Time is important. The second reporter to the story might as well be the last reporter to the story." His colleagues thought he was too pushy and often yelled back at him.

One morning he collapsed at his office desk. He was rushed to the hospital via ambulance. Doctors found that he had a retinal stroke with loss of significant vision in his right eye. Doctors said he would be fine as long as he would lose weight and take better care of himself.

Diane is the owner/manager of the newspaper and is concerned about Bill's condition along with the other overworked reporters and editors who have been survivors of the many downsizings over the years. She has decided to implement several stress and health management policies to help maintain productivity while keeping the employees healthy. In an employee meeting, she mentioned several new initiatives as follows:

First, in the past, smoking has been limited to offices. Now smoking will be banned from the building. If you want to smoke, there will be a designated smoking area in back of the building.

Second, in the past, vending machines have had junk food. Now the machines have been eliminated. Fresh fruits and vegetables will be provided for free in the cafeteria.

Third, periodically, courses on healthy eating and exercise will be provided by experts. These courses will be regarded as important as mandatory staff meetings. The courses will last for approximately one hour and may involve minor physical activity.

Fourth, health checks by a nearby medical service will be available for free twice a year. This will be totally paid for by our organization.

Finally, if management feels that you are overworked or overstressed, we would like to sit down with you and talk to see what is happening.

Bill was aghast at this new policy. In discussions with a colleague, Bill said the following:

"Diane is trying to impose her will and culture upon me. Smoking relaxes me. I write better when I smoke. Now that there is a no-smoking policy in the office, this is the one thing that would increase my blood pressure through the roof."

"The vending machines were a convenient way to get food. I am a carnivore, and I like my occasional beef jerky. I like my chips. Granola is for the birds."

"The mandatory classes concerning nutrition and exercise are a waste of time for the staff. If there is a great story out there, it is more important to get the story in the middle of the day than waste time on Diane's religion. The newspaper provides significant financial incentives for each feature that is published every week. I write the most features because I am good at it, I write fast, and I need the money. My wife's sick in the hospital, and I've got two teenagers to feed. I might lose my house."

"The 'free' medical service and management visits about health are basically nosy efforts by management to pry into personal business. It is none of management's business to intervene in my personal affairs."

There are several other reporters in the office who feel the same way as Bill and have threatened to resign if Diane's initiatives go through. The reporters offered a very simple alternative of having the newspaper add three days of sick leave benefits per year. They feel that Diane has no right to impose her lifestyle and her culture on them. Diane especially has no right to monitor the lifestyle and personal habits of employees that do not affect work.

Diane counters the group by saying that lifestyle and culture can affect work. "If you are not healthy, in the long term, you will not be productive. I want you around for a long time."

Questions

1. What are the causes of stress in Bill's organization?

2. Has Diane gone too far in imposing a smoking policy, removing junk food from the vending machines, and offering free medical service and management visits?

3. Diane has selected several ways to reduce the stress and improve the health of her employees. What other ways did the chapter mention she could also use to reduce stress and improve employee health?

4. What do you think about the reporters' sick leave proposal?

Case created by Gundars Kaupins, Boise State University

• • • CASE 14-2 NIKE: TAKING A RUN AT FIXING OUTSOURCED WORKER SAFETY

During the past two decades, manufacturing companies have relied more than ever on low-wage workers in the Far East as an alternative to high US labor costs in order to remain competitive in world markets. However, these multinational companies have been criticized for their insensitivity toward their subcontracted employees' working conditions. A Bangladeshi minimum wage of about $38 a month is appealing to major corporations as it helps them expand internationally at low cost; they spent about $1 trillion on outsourcing there in 2014. However, Bangladesh's worker safety record poses a big threat to the reputations of the companies that conduct business in this country. Even the companies that effectively made efforts toward improving safety conditions are now at risk, as the problems in Bangladesh are widespread and rising throughout the garment industry—a case in point being the footwear giant Nike.[104]

In 2014 Nike was worth $66 billion and manufactured goods in more than 740 factories worldwide with sales of $24 billion.[105] Founded in 1971, Nike became the industry leader in designing and manufacturing shoes, apparel, equipment, and accessories because they manufactured high-quality, high-priced goods with low manufacturing costs. These costs were kept low by contracting overseas low-cost labor, an idea that the cofounder and chairman of the company, Phillip H. Knight, came up with when he was pursuing his MBA. Nike set the industry trend for outsourcing manufacturing; back in 1971, 4% of US footwear was made overseas, but as of 2014, that had risen to 98%.[106]

Nike grew rapidly in the '70s with their strength in high-quality, low-cost products, but soon the company became a target for protestors. In the 1990s, many consumers rallied against Nike's horrendous overseas factory work conditions. As reported by the press, Nike took no responsibility for these factory employees' work surroundings, stating that since their manufacturing was outsourced and they did not own these factories, they therefore could not be held accountable for the safety problems or labor conditions there.[107]

Mere protests that began with Nike's sweatshops in the early 1990s continued up until the two fatal incidents that took place in Bangladesh. In November 2012, 112 workers were killed by a fire in a Nike-contracted factory because they were trapped behind locked doors. Then in April 2013, another 1,129 deaths occurred after an outsourced factory collapsed on top of its workers due to an unstable infrastructure. Companies who outsourced production overseas to these factories did not accept responsibility for their actions (except for **Walt Disney Co.**); these firms claimed that they were in fact surprised to see that their branded apparel was found in the factory rubble. These calamities epitomized the worst characteristics of subcontracting and indicated the need for a thorough overhaul of the entire industry, including factory owners, labor unions, and related government agencies.[108] The Bangladeshi garment association met with the representatives of these firms to discuss a solution strategy; however, only two major brands were willing to sign any agreement. The rest of the companies found it too costly to implement the suggested changes and decided to fix the problems on their own.[109]

Nike fortunately implemented their own work-safety program, Project Rewire, even before the incidents had occurred. This program gave Nike control over their subcontracted employees' work environments. Initially, Nike started by removing hazardous materials, such as toxic solvents and molecular gases, from their products, thereby reducing possible exposure health issues. This also targeted their concern about global warming and the environment. They then examined their supply chain in order to minimize worker safety issues. They eliminated excessive overtime for factory workers, increased the hours of safety training, and reevaluated their contracts with the factories, continuing to do business only with those firms that were committed to worker safety and the environment.[110]

Nike isn't "doing it" just yet. The Worker Rights Consortium, a nonprofit group partially funded by universities that monitors factories producing college athletic gear, has published reports on 16 of Nike's suppliers since 2006 alleging violations of overtime and worker abuse. In August of 2013, the Consortium sent an email to Nike asking why it didn't take action after it was told one of its suppliers in Bangalore, India, hadn't raised wages for its 10,000 workers after a government-mandated increase. A Nike spokesperson confirmed the factory had failed to comply with wage rules and said workers were compensated later.[111]

Questions

1. Nike products are made by over 1,000,000 workers in 744 factories worldwide. How can the company

monitor worker safety and health issues at all of these locations?

2. If Nike was manufacturing their products in the United States in the same way they were being made in overseas factories, which OSHA laws would have been violated?

3. In terms of Employee Wellness Programs, how did Nike improve working conditions for overseas employees?

4. What ergonomic principles might be applied to factory working conditions to improve operational settings and reduce employee stress?

5. Project Rewire represents a major commitment by Nike to improve outsourced employee working conditions. What more should the company do, in your opinion, to increase workplace safety for these factory workers?

6. For many firms, "the bottom line" is the driving force behind many strategic decisions. How does being a "differentiator" help Nike determine how much they should spend on overseas worker safety?

Case created by Herbert Sherman, PhD, and Theodore Vallas, Department of Management Sciences, School of Business Brooklyn Campus, Long Island University

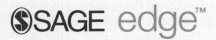

Sharpen your skills with SAGE edge at edge.sagepub.com/lussierhrm2e

SAGE edge for students provides a personalized approach to help you accomplish your coursework goals in an easy-to-use learning environment.

••• SKILL BUILDER 14-1 DEVELOPING A STRESS MANAGEMENT PLAN

Objective

To develop your skill at managing stress

Skills

The primary skills developed through this exercise are as follows:

1. *HR management skills*—Conceptual and design
2. *SHRM 2013 Curriculum Guidebook*—X: Workplace health, safety, and security

Assignment

Write out the answers to these questions:

1. Identify your major causes of stress.
2. How do you currently manage stress?
3. Select stress management techniques you will use to help overcome the causes of your stress.

••• SKILL BUILDER 14-2 THE MOST IMPORTANT THINGS I GOT FROM THIS COURSE

Objective

To review your course learning, critical-thinking application, and skill development

Skills

The primary skills developed through this exercise are as follows:

1. *HR management skills*—Conceptual and design

2. *SHRM 2013 Curriculum Guidebook*—L: Training and development

Assignment

Think about and write/type the three or four most important things you learned or skills you developed through this course and how they are helping you or will help you in your personal and/or professional life.

©iStockphoto.com/SelectStock

15 Organizational Ethics, Sustainability, and Social Responsibility

Practitioner's Perspective

Reflecting on ethics, Cindy says: There are many definitions of *ethics* and many shades of gray in their interpretations. Some decisions may be legal but not "fair," justifiable but not "correct," and sometimes it is hard to determine who should even be setting the standards. I prefer to compare ethical behavior to behaving with integrity. My definition is C. S. Lewis's observation: "Integrity is doing the right thing, even when no one is watching." Business does not always behave with integrity, as we know from scandals since the turn of the century. In 2002, a lack of integrity was exemplified by Enron and its accounting misrepresentations; in 2007, it was the banking industry and the subprime mortgage morass. Each time new rules and regulations are put into place to prevent such ethical abuses from ever happening again. But it takes more than reactive rules and regulations. To really make a difference in business behavior, we need to begin with ourselves—we can chart the course for a better future. Chapter 15 takes an in-depth look at what you need to know about business ethics.

SHRM HR CONTENT

See Appendix: *SHRM 2013 Curriculum Guidebook* for the complete list

C. Ethics (required)

1. Rules of conduct
2. Moral principles
4. Organizational values
7. Facing and solving ethical dilemmas
9. Compliance and laws
10. Confidential and proprietary information
11. Conflicts of interest
12. Use of company assets
13. Acceptance or providing of gifts, gratuities, and entertainment

F. Managing a Diverse Workforce (required)

3. Aging workforce
10. Gay, lesbian, bisexual, transgender (GLBT)/sexual orientation issues
11. Glass ceiling

R. Corporate/Social Responsibility and Sustainability (secondary)

2. Ethics
8. Community/employee engagement
10. The business case for CSR

WORK
APPLICATION 15-1

Thinking of business leaders, preferably where you work or have worked, do you trust them to act ethically? Why or why not?

ETHICAL ORGANIZATIONS

Some people ask, *Does it pay to be ethical?* The simple answer is yes. Research studies have reported a positive relationship between ethical behavior and leadership effectiveness.[1] Most highly successful people are ethical.[2] Being ethical may be difficult, but it has its rewards.[3] It actually makes you feel better.[4] Honest people have fewer mental health and physical complaints, like anxiety and back pain, and better social interactions.[5] Mahatma Gandhi called business without morality a sin. On the reverse side, unethical behavior is costly, as it contributed to the 2008 financial crisis that resulted in the world economies going into recession.[6] This unethical behavior is costly to society as well, since people lose money. It has long-term negative consequences for companies, including hurt reputation, legal fees, and fines.[7] Also, sales declines, increasing cost of capital, market share deterioration, and network partner loss can all be the result of unethical corporate behavior.[8] Some companies have even gone out of business. Due to ethical scandals, the loss of public trust threatens the integrity of business.[9]

Thus, there have been strong and recurring calls for more ethical business practices globally. To improve ethics, business schools doubled the number of ethics-related courses to help students prepare to face ethical dilemmas during their careers.[10] We constantly have to make decisions that are ethical or unethical.[11] But what is ethics, and what business practices are, or should be, considered "ethical"? Let's take a look at some information on ethics and ethical organizations.

LO 15-1

Discuss the term *ethics*, including common elements of the definition.

Ethics Defined

Before we define ethics, complete Self-Assessment 15-1 to determine how ethical your behavior is.

Ethics has been defined in many books and articles. Let's do a quick review here of some of the common definitions of *ethics* and then see if we can apply those definitions to business ethics.

- "Ethics is a reflection on morality, that is, a reflection on what constitutes right or wrong behavior."[12]
- "[Ethics is] the principles, values and beliefs that define right and wrong decisions and behavior."[13]
- "Ethics is a set of moral principles or values which is concerned with the righteousness or wrongness of human behavior and which guides your conduct in relation to others."[14]

• • • CHAPTER OUTLINE

SELF ASSESSMENT

How Ethical Is Your Behavior?

For this exercise, you will respond to the same set of statements twice. The first time you read them, focus on your own behavior and the frequency with which you behave in certain ways. On the line before each statement number, place a number from 1 to 4 that represents how often you do that behavior (or how likely you would be to do it) according to the following scale:

Frequently			Never
1	2	3	4

The numbers allow you to determine your level of ethics. You can be honest, as you will not tell others in class your score. *Sharing ethics scores is not part of the exercise.*

Next, go through the list of statements a second time, focusing on other people in an organization that you work for now or one you have worked for. Place an *O* on the line after the number of each statement if you have observed someone doing this behavior; place an *R* on the line if you reported this behavior within the organization or externally: *O* = observed, *R* = reported.

In College

_____ 1. _____ Cheating on homework assignments
_____ 2. _____ Cheating on exams
_____ 3. _____ Submitting as your own work papers that were completed by someone else

On the Job

_____ 4. _____ Lying to others to get what you want or to stay out of trouble
_____ 5. _____ Coming to work late, leaving work early, taking long breaks/lunches and getting paid for them
_____ 6. _____ Socializing, goofing off, or doing personal work rather than doing the work that you are getting paid to do
_____ 7. _____ Calling in sick to get a day off when you are not sick
_____ 8. _____ Using an organization's phone, computer, Internet access, copier, mail, or car for personal use
_____ 9. _____ Taking home company tools or equipment without permission for personal use
_____10. _____ Taking home organizational supplies or merchandise
_____11. _____ Giving company supplies or merchandise to friends or allowing friends to take them without saying anything
_____12. _____ Applying for reimbursement for expenses for meals, travel, or other expenses that weren't actually incurred
_____13. _____ Taking a spouse or friends out to eat or on business trips and charging their expenses to the organizational account
_____14. _____ Accepting gifts from customers/suppliers in exchange for giving them business
_____15. _____ Cheating on your taxes
_____16. _____ Misleading a customer to make a sale, such as promising rapid delivery dates
_____17. _____ Misleading competitors to get information to use to compete against them, such as pretending to be a customer/supplier
_____18. _____ Taking credit for another employee's accomplishments
_____19. _____ Selling more of a product than the customer needs in order to get the commission
_____20. _____ Spreading rumors about coworkers or competitors to make yourself look better, so as to advance professionally or to make more sales
_____21. _____ Lying for your boss when asked or told to do so
_____22. _____ Deleting information that makes you look bad or changing information to make yourself look better
_____23. _____ Allowing yourself to be pressured, or pressuring others, to sign off on documents that contain false information
_____24. _____ Allowing yourself to be pressured, or pressuring others, to sign off on documents you haven't read, knowing they may contain information or describe decisions that might be considered inappropriate
_____25. _____ If you were to give this assessment to a coworker with whom you do not get along, would she or he agree with your answers? If your answer is yes, write a 4 on the line before the statement number; if your answer is no, write a 1 on the line.

After completing the second phase of the exercise (indicating whether you have observed or reported any of the behaviors), list any other unethical behaviors you have observed. Indicate if you reported the behavior, using *R*.

26. _____
27. _____
28. _____

(Continued)

(Continued)

Note: This self-assessment is not meant to be a precise measure of your ethical behavior. It is designed to get you thinking about ethics and about your behavior and that of others from an ethical perspective. All of these actions are considered unethical behavior in most organizations.

Another ethical aspect of this exercise is your honesty when rating your behavior. How honest were you?

Scoring: To determine your ethics score, add up the numbers for all 25 statements. Your total will be between 25 and 100. Place the number that represents your score on the continuum below. The higher your score, the more ethical your behavior.

```
  25      30      40      50      60      70      80      90      100
Unethical                                                      Ethical
```

SHRM

R:2
Ethics

You might notice that these definitions all have some common elements: morals, values, beliefs, principles of conduct. So for our purposes, ethics *is the application of a set of values and principles in order to make the right, or good, choice.* It is not a long leap to then note that ethics also must include personal integrity and trust in the character and behavior of others. *Integrity* means being honest; lying, cheating, and stealing are unethical. If we do not think that an individual can be trusted and that they have integrity, we will not believe that they will make ethical choices if there is an opportunity to enrich their personal situation even to the detriment of the organization. If you are not honest, the truth will eventually catch up with you.[15] And when it does, you will lose the trust of people and hurt your relationships for a very long time before you will be able to earn their trust back—if you ever can.[16] Remember the common elements above as we review some factors contributing to unethical behavior and learn about a few ethical approaches.

Contributing Factors to Unethical Behavior

Let's discuss some of the reasons why unethical behavior occurs—or why do good people do bad things?

PERSONALITY TRAITS AND ATTITUDES. You probably already realize that because of their personalities, some people have a higher level of ethics than others, as integrity is considered a personality trait. Unfortunately, a culture of lying and dishonesty is infecting American business and society as these behaviors have become more common and accepted.[17] Some people lie deliberately, based on the attitude that lying is no big deal; some people don't even realize that they are liars.[18]

MORAL DEVELOPMENT. A second factor affecting ethical behavior is *moral development*, which refers to distinguishing right from wrong and choosing to do the right thing.[19] People's ability to make ethical choices is related to their level of moral development.[20] There are three levels of personal moral development. At the first level, the *preconventional* level, a person chooses right and wrong behavior based on self-interest and the likely consequences of the behavior (reward or punishment). This preconventional level is typical of a young child. Those whose ethical reasoning has advanced to the second, *conventional* level seek to maintain expected standards and live up to the expectations of others. Most people are on this level and do as the others in their group do—they easily give in to peer pressure to act ethically or unethically. Those at the third level, the *postconventional* level, make an effort to define moral principles for themselves; regardless of leaders' or the group's ethics, they do the right thing. People can be on different levels for different issues and situations.[21]

Ethics The application of a set of values and principles in order to make the right, or good, choice

15-1 APPLYING THE CONCEPT

Level of Moral Development

Place the letter of the level of moral development on the line next to the statement that illustrates it.

    a. preconventional level

    b. conventional level

    c. postconventional level

_____ 1. I lie to customers to sell more products because the others sales reps do it, too.

_____ 2. I lie to customers so that I can sell more products and get larger commission checks.

_____ 3. I don't lie to customers because it is unethical to lie.

_____ 4. Carl says to John, "You're not selling as much as the rest of us. You really should lie to customers like we do. If the boss asks why you aren't selling as much as the rest of us, you'd better not tell him we lie, or you will be sorry."

_____ 5. Karen says to John, "Telling lies to customers is no big deal—we're helping them buy a good product."

THE SITUATION. A third factor affecting ethical behavior is the situation. In certain situations, it can be tempting to be unethical,[22] such as when you are negotiating.[23] Unsupervised people in highly competitive situations are more likely to engage in unethical behavior. Unethical behavior occurs more often when there is no formal ethics policy or code of ethics and when unethical behavior is not punished. In other words, people are more unethical when they believe they will not get caught.[24] Unethical behavior is also more likely when performance falls below aspiration levels.

People are also less likely to report unethical behavior (blow the whistle) when they perceive the violation as not being serious or when they are friends of the offender. It takes high moral responsibility to be a *whistle-blower*.

JUSTIFICATION OF UNETHICAL BEHAVIOR. Most people understand right and wrong behavior and have a conscience. So why do good people do bad things? Most often, when people behave unethically, it is not because they have some type of character flaw or were born bad. Most people aren't simply good or bad. Just about everyone has the capacity to be dishonest.[25] One percent of people will always be honest, 1% will always be dishonest, and 98% will be unethical at times, but just a little.[26] We respond to "incentives" and can usually be manipulated to behave ethically or unethically, if you find the right incentives.[27] The incentive can be personal gain or to avoid getting into trouble.[28]

Few people see themselves as unethical. We all want to view ourselves in a positive manner. Therefore, when we do behave unethically, we often justify the behavior to protect our *self-concept* so that we don't have to feel bad.[29] If we only cheat a little, we can still feel good about our sense of integrity.[30] Take a look at some common justifications for our unethical behavior:

- Everyone else does it—we all pad the expense account.
- I did it for the good of others or the company—I cooked the books so the company looks good.
- I was only following orders—my boss made me do it.
- I'm not as bad as the others—I only call in sick when I'm not sick once in a while.
- Disregard or distortion of consequences—No one will be hurt if I inflate the figures, and I will not get caught. And if I do, I'll just get a slap on the wrist anyway.

WORK
APPLICATION 15-2

Give an example of unethical business behavior from your personal experience or the news and the reason given to justify it.

15-2 APPLYING THE CONCEPT

Justifying Unethical Behavior

Place the letter of the justification given for engaging in unethical behavior on the line next to the statement exemplifying it.

a. Everyone else does it.

b. I did it for the good of others or the company.

c. I was only following orders.

d. I'm not as bad as the others.

e. Disregard or distortion of consequences.

_____ 6. Don't blame me. It was the boss's idea to do it. I just went along with it.

_____ 7. It's no big deal that I lie to customers because no one gets hurt. In fact, I'm helping them buy a good product.

_____ 8. I changed the numbers so the department will look good on our quarterly report to top management.

_____ 9. Yes. I do lie to customers, but it's the way we do business here.

_____ 10. I do take some of the company product home, but I take a lot less than the others.

LO 15-2

Briefly discuss each of the identified ethical approaches.

SHRM

C:7
Facing and Solving Ethical Dilemmas

Ethical Approaches

Several common ethical approaches, or guidelines, exist to help you make ethical choices. Understanding some of the common approaches will help you resolve ethical dilemmas that you will certainly face at work. What common approaches exist? Let's discuss three guides to ethical behavior below and codes of ethics in the next section.

GOLDEN RULE. Do you know the Golden Rule? "Do unto others as you would have them do unto you," or "Don't do anything to anyone that you would not want someone to do to you." It is a lesson that our body knows, and when we follow it, we feel an immediate reward.[31] Most successful people live by the Golden Rule.[32] This is a moral principle in virtually every religious text in the world. Following the golden rule will help you to be ethical.

FOUR-WAY TEST. Rotary International uses a four-way test to determine ethical behavior:[33] (1) Is it the truth? (2) Is it fair to all concerned? (3) Will it build goodwill and better friendship? (4) Will it be beneficial to all concerned? If the answers are yes, then the action is probably ethical.

STAKEHOLDERS' APPROACH TO ETHICS. The stakeholders' approach tries to create win-win results for all stakeholders affected by the decision. This is the approach put forth by Warren Buffett at Berkshire Hathaway, known as one of the most ethical organizations in business today. Exhibit 15-1 gives the statement taken from Berkshire's Code of Business Conduct and Ethics.

EXHIBIT 15-1   BERKSHIRE HATHAWAY CODE OF BUSINESS CONDUCT AND ETHICS[34]

When in doubt, remember Warren Buffett's rule of thumb:
"I want employees to ask themselves whether they are willing to have any contemplated act appear the next day on the front page of their local paper—to be read by their spouses, children and friends—with the reporting done by an informed and critical reporter."

So, if you are comfortable telling people who are affected by your decision what you have decided, it is probably ethical. But if you keep rationalizing the decision and try to hide it from others, it is quite likely unethical—at least to some of the affected stakeholders. You can't always create a win for everyone, but you can try.

DISCERNMENT AND ADVICE. Research shows that making a decision without using an ethical guide leads to less ethical choices.[35] Using ethical guides at the point of making a decision helps keep you honest.[36] If you are unsure whether a decision is ethical, talk to your boss, higher-level managers, and other people with high ethical standards. If you are reluctant to ask others for advice on an ethical decision because you may not like their answers, the decision may not be ethical.

Each of these approaches should cue you to think about some concepts that we have previously discussed in this text—trust, integrity, and consistency. If you recall our conversation about trust in Chapter 10, you will remember that trust is "faith in the character and actions of another." Does that sound familiar when you take a look at the definitions of *ethics* above? Without trust, we cannot successfully manage in the organization for very long, so we have to do what we said we would do *consistently* over time in order to get our stakeholders to trust us.

So integrity (honestly doing what you say you will do) and trust (the expectation that you will continue to do so) are important to managers in the firm because research shows that companies who have the trust of employees have lower turnover and higher revenue, profitability, and shareholder returns. But how do we get others to be trustworthy and make decisions based on principles, values, beliefs, and character? Most organizations (like Buffet's **Berkshire Hathaway**) today use a *code of ethics*, sometimes called a code of conduct, to project the values and beliefs of the organization to their employees.

Codes of Ethics

Every culture endorses an ethical way to live.[37] Following the code of ethics is actually an ethical approach. The *Houston Chronicle* provides a good template on their http://chron.com website for an organizational code of ethics that includes the following factors:[38]

VALUES. **Values** are *our basic concepts of good and bad, or right and wrong*. Values come from our society and culture. Every culture has concepts of right and wrong, although these values do vary some from culture to culture (we will discuss this further in Chapter 16). The *Chronicle* article notes that "a primary objective of the code of ethics is to define what the company is about and make it clear that the company is based on honesty and fairness."

PRINCIPLES. **Principles** are *a basic application of our values*. We *apply* principles to specific situations in order to come up with a set of actions that we consider to be ethical. An example of an ethical principle would be to *maintain personal integrity*. This is obviously based on the application of the values of honesty and integrity. Another example would be the principle to *treat all employees fairly*, which would match up with the value of equality.

MANAGEMENT SUPPORT. Managerial support, and especially top management support, is absolutely critical to a successful code of ethics. Remember what Jack Welch of GE said: "We need to walk the talk." If senior managers pay no attention to the code of ethics, subordinate managers and employees will pay no attention as well. In addition, we need to encourage reporting of unethical behavior to management. In the *Chronicle* article, they note that open-door policies and processes that allow the anonymous reporting of ethics issues should be included in the code. These processes help management maintain and uphold the code across the organization.

WORK
APPLICATION 15-3

Describe any guidelines you use, or will use in the future, to help you make ethical decisions.

LO 15-3

Briefly discuss each factor required in a good code of ethics.

SHRM

C:4
Organizational Values

SHRM

C:2
Moral Principles

SHRM

C:1
Rules of Conduct

Values Our basic concepts of good and bad, or right and wrong

Principles Basic application of our values

WORK
APPLICATION 15-4

Describe a code of ethics, preferably where you work or have worked. Provide a copy if possible.

LO 15-4

Discuss the terms *authority*, *responsibility,* and *accountability* and how they relate to ethical behavior.

SHRM

C:11
Conflicts of Interest

Authority The right to give orders, enforce obedience, make decisions, and commit resources toward completing organizational goals

Responsibility The obligation to answer for something/someone—the duty to carry out an assignment to a satisfactory conclusion

PERSONAL RESPONSIBILITY. This is the concept that everyone in the organization is responsible for the ethical conduct of business, not just "the boss." Personal responsibility also refers to accountability for one's own actions, so we need to identify the consequences to an employee if they violate the code of ethics. The *Chronicle* article also notes that people have a personal responsibility to report others' violations of the code to the appropriate authority.

COMPLIANCE. The compliance factor can identify applicable laws or industry regulations that must be adhered to as part of the code of ethics. Certainly, the OSH Act, the Sarbanes-Oxley Act, and the Dodd-Frank Act would apply to pretty much all public companies, but other laws and regulations apply to certain industries and groups, so we need to note them in the code as well. This is just another reinforcement of the annual training that we have to do regarding each law or regulation that covers our business and industry.

Remember that the code of ethics is important because a culture of misconduct can result in higher turnover and lower productivity and profitability.[39] Management always has to take the lead in being ethical, or employees will not perform.

Creating and Maintaining Ethical Organizations

The code of ethics is a first strong step in maintaining an ethical organization, but as already noted, managers must lead ethically. However, is the right (ethical) choice always the obvious choice? Unfortunately, it is not that easy. People that we interact with continuously give us the opportunity to be unethical by providing us with personal advantages that help us but do not help the organization—for instance, by offering us gifts. What is the right thing to do when we have the opportunity to improve our own personal situation, but must do it at the expense of the company that we work for? In order to understand what managers should do, we need to look at what they can do, based on authority, responsibility, and accountability. Let's look at these concepts in an organizational setting.

AUTHORITY. **Authority** *is the right to give orders, enforce obedience, make decisions, and commit resources toward completing organizational goals* (this will be important shortly). So authority allows managers to tell people who work for them what to do and to use organizational resources in the course of their work.

RESPONSIBILITY. **Responsibility** *is the obligation to answer for something/someone—the duty to carry out an assignment to a satisfactory conclusion.* So responsibility means that, when we are given authority, we have to accept a position-based

15-3 APPLYING THE CONCEPT

Ethical Approach

Place the letter of the approach to making ethical decisions on the line next to the statement that illustrates it.

a. Golden Rule
b. Four-way test
c. Stakeholders' approach
d. Discernment and advice
e. Code of ethics

____ 11. I'm a member of Rotary International, and I use its approach when I make decisions.

____ 12. When I make decisions, I follow the guidelines the company gave all of us to use to make sure I'm doing the right thing.

____ 13. I try to make sure that everyone affected by my decisions gets a fair deal.

____ 14. I try to treat people the way I want them to treat me.

____ 15. Hi, Latoya. What do you think of my decision about how to handle this customer's complaint?

obligation to the organization to use those resources that we are given to help the organization meet its goals.

ACCOUNTABILITY. **Accountability** *is the personal duty to someone else (a higher-level manager or the organization itself) for the effective use of resources to complete an assignment.* In other words, the manager can be held *personally liable* for failing to use resources in the way that they should to help the organization. Unethical behavior often has personal negative consequences,[40] such as getting into trouble at work, being fired, and even going to jail. If you get away with unethical behavior, it can be contagious and lead to more and larger transgressions.[41] It's the lies and cover-up, not the initial unethical behavior, that take people down.[42]

Establishing a code of ethics helps ensure employees know what is and is not ethical behavior.

So why do you need to understand these concepts, and what is the difference between responsibility and accountability? First let's look at authority and responsibility. Henri Fayol, in his 14 principles of organizing, noted that authority and responsibility are linked and that they have to be balanced. Note that authority is a *right* to give orders, and responsibility is an *obligation* to answer for those orders. This means at its core that authority can be granted by the organization but responsibility has to be accepted by the party. Peter Drucker, the noted management author, also said, "Whoever claims authority thereby assumes responsibility."[43] In order to be *allowed to use* the authority given, the person must *accept*, or assume responsibility. Both of these concepts are tied to the *position* of the manager in the organization. In other words, if you have the position of HR manager, you may be given some types of authority (for instance, authority to require annual EEO and sexual harassment training programs). However, you have to accept the responsibility to carry out these training programs—the buck stops here, with you. If you do not accept the responsibility for doing so, then the authority needs to be rescinded (you need to be taken out of the position of HR manager).

Authority and responsibility always need to be balanced. This is one of the most common failures in organizations. An example would be a CEO who requires subordinate managers to take responsibility for their department's expenditures but doesn't give them authority to veto purchases. This is requiring the subordinate to accept responsibility without commensurate authority. Or consider the sales manager who uses their authority to require subordinates to complete minor tasks that take up large amounts of time and then provides these subordinates with a poor evaluation for failure to sell. This is using positional authority without taking responsibility. So we have to try to make sure that these factors are balanced and that the person accepts their responsibilities.

If you accept responsibility, at that point you become accountable (personally liable) for the effective completion of the action. In the case above of the HR manager and training, you would have *personal accountability* even if someone else who works for you actually does the training. Accountability goes beyond an obligation to do something for the organization. It now requires that the person be held to account for their actions—that they give reasons why they did or did not do a certain thing and justify how their actions helped the organization reach its goals. So authority and responsibility give the manager rights and obligations based on their job in the company, but accountability concerns when they can be punished—in some cases even go to prison—if they do not exercise their authority in a responsible manner.

DOING THE RIGHT THING. So we can now look at how understanding authority, responsibility, and accountability can help us with ethical issues. As we noted

Accountability The personal duty to someone else (a higher-level manager or the organization itself) for the effective use of resources to complete an assignment

SHRM

C:10
Confidential and Proprietary
Information

above, we constantly have the opportunity to make decisions that will benefit us as an individual but do harm to the organization or our subordinates. Think about the ability that you have as a manager to use your employees' time to benefit you but not the organization. For instance, you could use employee time to complete a task that makes you look good to your boss but that costs the employee the ability to do their own job. If you apply the concept of responsibility to the situation (an obligation to use those resources to benefit the organization), then it is easy to see that you are being unethical. If you then continue anyway, the consequences of your actions might cause you to be held accountable by the organization and potentially disciplined or even fired if you misuse resources to a great extent.

Another way in which we may enrich ourselves at the expense of the organization and others would be the misuse of confidential company information, as we noted in the very first case study in Chapter 1. What is the right thing to do when we have the opportunity to improve our own personal situation, but must do it at the expense of others and the company that we work for?

LO 15-5

Identify some of the common ethical issues that managers face in business.

SHRM

C:13
Acceptance or Providing of Gifts, Gratuities, and Entertainment

SHRM

C:12
Use of Company Assets

Just Because It's Legal, Doesn't Mean It's Ethical!

You are the manager in charge of purchasing products used in the daily operations of your company. The salesperson for a chemical company that has been trying to become your main chemical supplier just happens to have tickets to the concert that—you checked last week—is sold out, and your spouse really wants to go. The salesperson gives them to you after hearing that your spouse loves the band. There are no strings attached . . . or are there? Is this an ethical thing to do based on your position in the company? Even if the salesperson does not specifically ask for favorable treatment in return, can you be objective in your interactions in the future? Whether the tickets are worth $1,000 or $10, they still may cause you to fail to act in an ethical, responsible manner, and since you have purchasing authority, this can put you in a bad spot.

Managers face both simple and complex ethical questions almost on a daily basis. Should you choose a favorite employee to do overtime work instead of the employee who is best for the job because you know your favorite needs extra money? Should you tell the manager of another department a small lie because you haven't completed a project yet? Should you accept the concert tickets from the salesperson who wants your business? We have to learn to apply the concepts of authority, responsibility, and accountability constantly in order to avoid unethical actions, and in doing so, we gain the trust of others in the organization. We have to know the appropriate use of company assets and what constitutes misuse of those assets as well. What are some of the most *common ethical issues* that both managers and their companies have to deal with on an ongoing basis?

BRIBERY. A bribe is a payment meant to cause someone to make decisions that may help a person or an organization but do significant harm to other organizations or other stakeholders in the decision. (We will discuss how companies are able to do this even though a US law prohibits it in Chapter 16.) In a recent case where a US company *was* determined to be acting illegally, clothing company **Ralph Lauren** recently agreed to pay a $1.6 million fine for bribing Argentinian officials from 2005 to 2009.[44]

CORRUPT PAYMENTS TO GOVERNMENT OFFICIALS. This type of payment is designed to allow the company to avoid scrutiny of their actions by government agencies or to facilitate a desired company action, such as building a new factory in an environmentally sensitive area. Corruption at the highest government levels was common for many years under the regime of President Suharto of Indonesia; if you were going to do business in Indonesia, you had to pay bribes to government officials and members of the Suharto family. But it has since been cleaned up to a significant extent by the leaders that have followed him.

EMPLOYMENT AND PERSONNEL ISSUES. Who to fire or hire, promotions, and changes in compensation and working conditions all can be affected by managerial decisions, which in turn will affect productivity, absenteeism, and turnover in the company. **Walmart** is a good example of a company that has been identified as having managers that use bias in making personnel decisions.[45] In addition, in many countries, practices such as the use of child labor and forced labor by convicts are common, and many other discriminatory labor practices occur, but many of these practices are not only unethical but illegal in US firms.

MARKETING PRACTICES. Dishonest marketing practices can ruin corporate reputations and even cause them to fail.[46] Remember the ignition switch issue in some **General Motors (GM)** cars that was hidden from customers and regulators for several years and that was connected to a number of deaths.[47] The effects on GM sales are yet to be assessed in this case. However, **Countrywide Financial** is an excellent example of a company that made billions of dollars by unethical marketing of low-documenation and no-documentation loans to individuals during the housing boom of the early 2000s, and it was still in danger of bankruptcy, even after being purchased by **Bank of America** as late as 2013.[48]

IMPACT ON THE ECONOMY AND ENVIRONMENT. Unethical practices on the part of many financial firms (including Countrywide) are thought to be the main cause of the massive recession that started in late 2007. In addition, past practices in many industries have had a long-lasting (if not permanent) effect on the environment around the world. Examples include the use of asbestos long after we knew the health hazards, strip-mining leading to massive flooding in many countries, or recent concerns that some pesticide producers are possibly creating "superbugs" that will be pesticide resistant.[49]

EMPLOYEE AND CUSTOMER PRIVACY. Due to advancements in technology, the ability to gather and maintain large amounts of personal data has become common in organizations. Use of such data must be for legitimate business purposes only. You may recall that **Facebook** recently received a huge number of complaints when they decided to experiment on their users by showing them happier or sadder newsfeeds on their personal pages.[50] Many of these customers felt as though this was not done for a legitimate business purpose. There are also many companies who now monitor all employee communication on company computers and other devices. Is this universal monitoring ethical, or is it an invasion of employee privacy?

Of course, all of the information that we have discussed does no good unless and until the manager makes the choice to do the right thing—makes the ethical decision. And this is not always easy. In many cases, there is no single right or wrong decision—it is *shades of gray*. One decision may be more ethical, but it still harms some stakeholders, while the other decision harms more people and has fewer beneficiaries. In other cases, the ethical decision may be bad for us personally because it exposes the fact that we may have made a previous decision that was wrong—for instance, we may have lied on a report to the federal government because our boss pressured us to, and now we have to verify that lie because evidence has been found that refutes it.

Here is the simplest takeaway that we can provide you: If you don't think about making the ethical decision *before* a situation arises that requires you to have integrity, you will probably make the expedient decision (the decision that does you the least personal harm) and not the ethical decision, and you will *know* this because you will not be willing to tell others what is going on and what decision you have made. So following the ethical approaches including the code of ethics does help us make ethical decisions.

CORPORATE SOCIAL RESPONSIBILITY (CSR)

Ethics and corporate social responsibility (CSR) are closely related, as being socially responsible means going beyond legal and economic obligations to do the right things by acting in ways that benefit society. CSR is an umbrella term for exploring the responsibilities of business and its role in society.[51] CSR has been in the news constantly for the past several years. Many of the business problems that have occurred—from the early-2000s financial crisis to **Walmart**'s recent bribery scandal[52] to the **Lululemon** founder blaming women with big thighs for his too-sheer yoga pants[53]—have been caused at least in part by a lack of corporate social responsibility. Let's review this concept and then take a look at some of the stakeholders that are affected by CSR.

CSR Defined

LO 15-6

Briefly discuss the "business case" for corporate social responsibility (CSR).

What is corporate social responsibility, and what do managers need to know about it? The concept is based on the belief that "companies have some responsibilities to society beyond that of making profits for the shareholders."[54] So **corporate social responsibility** *is the concept that organizations have a duty to all societal stakeholders to operate in a manner that takes each of their needs into account.* In other words, companies need to look at their effects on society and all corporate stakeholders, not just shareholders. They must provide *employees* with safe working conditions and with adequate pay and benefits. Companies must provide safe products and services to *customers.* For *society,* the company should improve the quality of life, or at least not destroy the *environment.* The company must compete fairly with *competitors* and work with *suppliers* in a cooperative manner. It must abide by the laws and regulations of *government.* At the same time, the company must provide *shareholders* with a reasonable profit.

THE BUSINESS CASE FOR CSR. A "business case" is simply a justification for an organizational action. In other words, does it pay to be socially responsible? The answer is yes. If it didn't, why would virtually all of the Fortune 500 companies have formal CSR programs?[55] CSR can improve stock returns.[56] With a choice of two products of similar price and quality, 80% of surveyed customers said they are willing to buy the more sustainable option.[57] Being socially irresponsible has negative consequences, as it gives the company a negative reputation that leads to more difficulty in attracting customers, investors, and employees and it can lead to costly lawsuits.[58] Money can be made again, but a negative reputation can take years to improve, and a good reputation may be lost forever.[59] If you are attending a nonprofit college or university, the odds are that it receives money or other resources from companies as part of its CSR. Visit your favorite large corporation's website and you will most likely find a link stating how the firm engages in CSR; it is even included in most companies' annual reports, where it is often called a *social audit* because it is a measure of social behavior.

SHRM

R:10
The Business Case for CSR

If we were to look only at shareholders, the business case would always be based on whether or not an action made the shareholders wealthier. However, we cannot ignore other stakeholders—especially in today's business world where other stakeholders can create very difficult situations for the company. For instance, you might have read about the short strikes that have occurred with some frequency at fastfood businesses across the country.[60] Workers at these businesses want better wages and have set out to publicize the fact that they are paid rather poorly. These employee stakeholders have caused a lot of bad publicity for restaurants in the industry. In other cases, customer stakeholders have forced companies to stop using sweatshop labor in their manufacturing. Government stakeholders have limited the ability of companies to merge (for example, the merger between **Time Warner** and **Comcast**) or to spin off parts of the company if the government thought that it would cause competition problems.

Corporate social responsibility The concept that organizations have a duty to all societal stakeholders to operate in a manner that takes each of their needs into account

So the business case for CSR is based on the ability of the organization to help or harm various stakeholder groups and the ability of all stakeholder groups to help or harm the company. Each stakeholder group has different—and sometimes competing—interests, but the organization must balance these "social responsibilities" among all of the groups. If we help shareholders make more money to the detriment of society, government stakeholders will step in and sanction the company. If we help customers by sourcing items from questionable suppliers, the community may get angry with us and put pressure on customers to stop doing business with us. Each stakeholder group has to be balanced against the others and managed for maximum engagement with the organization. Every group has to be thought of in a modern company, much more so than ever in history.

A concept called the social contract model, which discusses the need for the company to take society into account while doing business, has been around for a number of years now.[61] This contract says that all organizations have an implied contract with society as a whole (remember our discussion of implied contracts in Chapter 10). A productive organization should enhance the welfare of, and minimize the drawbacks to, employees, consumers, and other stakeholders in any society in which the organization operates. A social contract should also avoid violating the rights of individuals in the society in which it operates. We discussed employee rights in Chapter 9, and we can extend those rights and other societal rights to all organizational stakeholders.

R:8
Community/Employee Engagement

Recall, too, that when we discussed those employee rights, we also said that the organization has a contrasting obligation to allow and protect those rights. It is the same with other stakeholder members of the society where the organization operates. The organization has a specific duty[62]

1. not to actively deprive persons of their rights;
2. to help protect people from deprivation of their basic set of rights; and
3. to aid those who are deprived.

So the organization has to take the interests of all stakeholders into account.

Finally, for those of you who are considering "whether or not all of this CSR is really necessary," remember that it is "hard to hide" now with the immediate availability of mountains of information. If you try to bury information inside the organization, it is quite likely to get out because of the power of the Web and its ability to connect people who may be interested in what your company is doing. Again, we can note the **Facebook** privacy breaches and **GM** ignition switch failures, both of which were at least partially revealed in Web posts at first. Think about how rapidly **Twitter** forwards information to users and how comprehensive **LinkedIn** is when it covers company issues. So if you think the information won't get out, you may want to think again.

SOCIAL ENTREPRENEURS. There is growth in the number of *social entrepreneurs* that combine their concern for social issues with their desire for financial rewards.[63] Blake Mycoskie founded his fourth business, **TOMS,** at age 29 to make money and help solve the social problem of children having no shoes to wear, which resulted in blisters, sores, and infections. His business model is "With every pair you purchase, TOMS will give a pair of new shoes to a child in need. One for One." He wrote *Start Something That Matters* to guide others in helping society.[64] With a social mission, TOMS received lots of free publicity and sales have increased, resulting in Mycoskie making lots of money for being socially responsible.

Stakeholders and CSR

In addition to being good public practice, CSR is also being codified more often in law in the United States and in other countries. There are a number of corporate

SHRM
C:9
Compliance and Laws

compliance laws written by state and federal government stakeholders, many of which we have already discussed. The Dodd-Frank Wall Street Reform and Consumer Protection Act (Chapter 12), the Sarbanes-Oxley Act (Chapter 10), the OSH Act (Chapter 14), the Fair Labor Standards Act (Chapter 11), and many others have already been covered, and we will briefly review another significant compliance law in Chapter 16 called the US Foreign Corrupt Practices Act. You will have to become familiar with each of the major compliance laws as well as those other compliance regulations in your state or country as you begin your career as a manager.

Many employee stakeholder subgroups are also beginning to receive much more attention than has historically been the case. Among these groups are older workers, women in management and the executive suite, gay/lesbian/bi/transgender employees, and a more racially and ethnically diverse employee pool. Public pressure has contributed to the interests of these and other groups in organizations, and therefore companies are having to figure out how to meet the needs of these stakeholders in the organization. Let's quickly review some of the major issues that the organization has to take into account with each.

F:3
Aging Workforce
`SHRM`

OLDER WORKERS. The evidence speaks for itself. Americans and workers in many other countries are working much later in life than they historically have. A record number of Americans over the age of 65 are continuing to work. In fact, the number of workers over the age of 75 has increased by more than 75% in the last 20 years.[65] While there are many reasons for this, the reasons don't matter as much to the HR manager as the fact that we have these workers available in our organizations. However, we also have to be careful to not run afoul of the various age-related laws, including the ADEA, as we manage these individuals at work.

F:11
Glass Ceiling
`SHRM`

WOMEN EXECUTIVES. Women in the executive suite have been getting a lot of attention since the book *Lean In* by Sheryl Sandberg of **Facebook**. The book encourages women to seek executive careers and break the "glass ceiling" that still exists today, even though women have been in the workforce in large numbers since the 1970s. The **glass ceiling** *is the thought that there are invisible barriers to advancement in business to women as well as minority employees.* The truth is that women still only fill about 16% of the board seats at large public companies and are only 4% of CEOs in S&P 500 firms, despite the fact that 57% of bachelor's degrees in the United States are held by women.[66] Part of CSR is providing appropriate opportunities to women and minority employees in the firm to change this ratio.

F:10
GLBT/Sexual Orientation Issues
`SHRM`

LESBIAN/GAY/BI/TRANSGENDER (LGBT) EMPLOYEES. Several recent state laws and executive orders at the federal level have brought the topic of LGBT individuals to the forefront of attention in many businesses. While there is no federal law that currently prohibits workplace discrimination on the basis of sexual orientation, there have been a number of recent changes in state laws and regulation of government contractors.[67] A presidential amendment to Executive Orders 11246 and 11478 did, however, recently make it illegal for *federal agencies* and *federal contractors* to discriminate based on sexual orientation or gender identity.[68] It should be expected that the law concerning this employee group will continue to change over the next few years, including the possibility that a new federal law may be passed concerning nondiscrimination against individuals because of sexual orientation or gender identity.

INCREASING DIVERSITY. It is now true: The majority group in the United States is a minority in at least one area. The birthrate of Caucasian children is now less than 50% of the total birthrate.[69] In 10 states, white children are a minority, and in 23 states, minorities now make up more than 40% of the child population.[70] One in 12 children (8%) born in America are offspring of illegal immigrants, and those children are US citizens.[71] The total Caucasian population throughout the world, including America, is decreasing as there are more deaths than births,[72] and the percentage of the population that is Caucasian is decreasing.[73] By around 2040, less than one

Glass ceiling The thought that there are invisible barriers to advancement in business to women as well as minority employees

half of the total US population will be Caucasian.[74] By 2060, it is estimated that Caucasians will be 43% of the US population and 1 in 3 people will be Hispanic.[75] What does this shift mean to the organization? It means that employee diversity will continue to grow and we will have to become better at managing that diversity than we have been in the past. Recall what we said back in Chapter 3 about workforce diversity: "There is currently a shortage of skilled workers—and there will be for the foreseeable future, so to exclude a qualified person because that individual is different in some way is counterproductive to business success." Managing diversity is becoming critical in all organizations and in all industries. We have to continue to get better at this HRM task in order to engage *all* of our future employees.

WORK
APPLICATION 15-5

Select a business, preferably one you work or have worked for, and identify how it is socially responsible on a specific issue.

Levels of Corporate Social Responsibility

Clearly, in today's society, the question is not whether business should be socially responsible. Instead, the question is, *At what level of CSR should the business operate?* Businesses do vary greatly in their social responsibility activities, based on the overall level of CSR at which they decide to operate.[76] Managers can choose to operate the business at one of three levels of CSR. The levels of corporate social responsibility are *legal, ethical,* or *benevolent.* However, a firm can be between levels or be on different levels for different issues. See Exhibit 15-2 for an illustration of the three levels.

1. *Legal CSR* focuses on maximizing profits while obeying the law; it focuses on increasing sales and cutting costs to maximize returns to stockholders. In dealings with market stakeholders, these firms meet all of their legal responsibilities, such as fulfilling contract obligations and providing legally safe products while honoring guarantees and warranties. They do what it takes to beat the competition legally. In dealing with nonmarket stakeholders (society and government), they obey all the laws and regulations, such as not polluting more than the legal limits and meeting all OSHA standards. Some firms have been criticized for their behavior at this legal level. **Philip Morris (PM)** and others sell cigarettes that are not illegal, but some question the ethics of a business that causes health problems.

2. *Ethical CSR* focuses on profitability and doing what is right, just, and fair. Providing ethical leadership and avoiding questionable practices mean doing more than is required in dealing with market stakeholders, such as treating employees right and paying them fair wages, providing safer products, not squeezing suppliers, and competing to win business ethically. These companies meet reasonable societal expectations and exceed government laws and regulations to be just and fair to stakeholders. Many companies, including **Costco** and **Dick's Sporting Goods**, have return policies that allow customers to get refunds or exchanges without good reason, exceeding legal requirements.

3. *Benevolent CSR* focuses on profitability and helping society through philanthropy. This highest level of CSR is also called "good corporate citizenship."

EXHIBIT 15-2 LEVELS OF CORPORATE SOCIAL RESPONSIBILITY

3. **Benevolent CSR**. Focus on profitability and helping society through philanthropy.

2. **Ethical CSR**. Focus on profitability and going beyond the law to do what is right, just, and fair.

1. **Legal CSR**. Focus on maximizing profits while obeying the law.

Volunteering during work hours is part of CSR.

Benevolent firms are *philanthropic*, giving gifts of money, or other resources, to charitable causes. Employees are expected, encouraged, and rewarded for being active volunteers in the community, often on company time. **Apple** under CEO Steve Jobs operated at the ethical level, as Jobs did not believe in corporate philanthropy. However, under its current CEO, Tim Cook, Apple now operates at the benevolent level. For example, Cook implemented a matching program to supplement employee donations to nonprofits that Jobs long resisted.[77]

In addition to giving corporate money, many rich entrepreneurs set up foundations and give their own money (e.g., **Carnegie Foundation**, **Ford Foundation**, and **Bill & Melinda Gates Foundation**). Billionaire Bill Gates (cofounder of **Microsoft**) pledged to give away 95% of the Gateses' wealth, only giving a fraction—a mere few million—to his three children. Warren Buffet teamed up with the Gates family, giving billions to the foundation. So far the foundation has given away more than $26 billion.[78]

AN OVERALL APPROACH TO CSR. Let's be clear about the difference between an overall and a situational approach to CSR. Top corporate managers decide on the firm's overall commitment, or level, of CSR. The board of directors and managers often make corporate policies to guide employee actions in dealing with stakeholders, and some have CSR mission statements. Some companies even have separate departments and executive titles for CSR.

A SITUATIONAL APPROACH TO CSR. Although firms have an overall guiding commitment to CSR, the level of CSR can and does vary based on individual issues. CSR has been called *enlightened self-interest* because firms will be motivated to engage in CSR activities when the benefits outweigh the costs, as there is a link between single stakeholder-related issues and CSR and financial performance.[79] However, determining the appropriate level of CSR to meet the business's and stakeholders' self-interests is not quick and easy. Each issue requires analysis, risk-reward considerations, and determining how stakeholder relations affect the overall health of the corporation.[80]

Where You Stand Depends on Where You Sit!

You can see from our discussion that ethics and CSR are not concrete subjects—especially when you look at what is acceptable in the eyes of each stakeholder group. It is always a balancing act to make good decisions concerning the ethical path of the organization. However, we have to keep all of these groups in mind as we make managerial decisions if we want to continue in business for very long. Nobody said being a manager was easy. If it were, people would not be paid so well to be a manager. Remember: If you don't think about making the ethical decision using an ethical approach *before* a situation arises, you will probably make the expedient decision (the decision that does you the least personal harm) and not the ethical decision that is socially responsible to stakeholders.

SUSTAINABILITY

Sustainability practices are part of CSR. As with ethics and CSR, it pays to implement sustainability practices. **Sustainability** *involves meeting the needs of the current*

WORK
APPLICATION 15-6

Select a business, preferably one you work or have worked for, and identify its level of corporate social responsibility. Be sure to explain your answer with examples of specific things it does.

LO 15-7

Briefly describe the concept of sustainability in a business context.

Sustainability Meeting the needs of the current generation without compromising the ability of future generations to meet their needs

©iStockphoto.com/asiseeit

generation without compromising the ability of future generations to meet their needs.[81] It is the process of accessing how to design products that will take advantage of the current environmental situation and enhancing how well a company's products perform with renewable resources. *Sustainability* is now a business buzzword,[82] and based on the gravity of environmental problems, it is an important topic for all countries.[83] Countries and businesses are realizing that economic growth and environmental sustainability can work together.[84] Some people refer to the triple bottom line: concern for profit, society, and the environment.

Society expects sustainability and for managers to use resources wisely and responsibly; protect the environment; minimize the amount of air, water, energy, minerals, and other materials found in the final goods we consume; recycle and reuse these goods to the extent possible rather than drawing on nature to replenish them; respect nature's calm, tranquility, and beauty; and eliminate toxins that harm people in the workplace and communities.[85] Thus, including sustainability in managing the business is being socially responsible.

What does business need to do in order to be considered sustainable? Organizations use up resources in the course of their operations. Any resource that is used must be replenished or it disappears forever. In years past, it was thought that resources were so abundant that we could never use them up, but we now know better. There are already shortages of some critical items necessary for the survival of humans, and other species, over the long term—shortages of good drinking water in some areas, for instance. As this is written, the state of California is suffering from a severe drought, and it is becoming more difficult to get water resources into the hands of the state's population of more than 39 million people, or about one eighth of the entire US population.

HR and Organizational Sustainability

Organizations have to practice sustainability in today's business environment. We cannot afford to waste resources that are difficult to replace.

SUSTAINABILITY PRACTICES AND GREEN COMPANIES. Sustainability issues influence activities in the business world.[86] A *green company* acts in a way that minimizes damage to the environment. With the current worldwide environmental problems, many new ventures have been created in green management.[87] Social entrepreneurs are taking advantage of sustainability. For example, Bob Shallenberger and John Cavanaugh launched **Highland Homes** in St. Louis to build environmentally friendly condos and houses.[88]

Large corporations are engaging in sustainability practices in a big way. A new corporate title has emerged—chief sustainability officer (CSO). CSOs are in charge of the corporation's environmental programs. Nearly all of the 150 world's largest companies have a sustainability officer with the rank of vice president or higher.[89] Some examples of organizations that have CSOs include **AT&T, DuPont, Google,** and **Sun Microsystems.** Many companies, including **Intel,** are giving annual sustainability reports.[90]

Johnson & Johnson and **Weyerhaeuser** now have dedicated sustainability programs.[91] **Starbucks** encourages sustainable farming for its coffee growers. **Google** has a zero-carbon quest and has a goal of becoming the world's most energy-efficient

Conserving our natural resources is part of sustainability.

WORK
APPLICATION 15-7

Select an organization, preferably one you work or have worked for. Describe its sustainability practice efforts.

company.[92] **Amazon** is also a green company that has reduced packaging and makes sure packaging is made from recycled materials that can be recycled again. Also, its headquarters was built to have eco-friendly buildings with **LEED** (Leadership in Energy and Environmental Design) certified interiors and exteriors.

Walmart is a leader in sustainability. Back in 2010, it stated that it would cut some 20 million metric tons of greenhouse gas emissions from its supply chain by the end of 2015.[93] Walmart's requirements of reduced waste from packaging have created industry-wide reforms.[94] It essentially pressures all of its thousands of suppliers to meet its sustainability standards. Even the greenest companies tout their close ties to Walmart in their promotional materials.[95] Walmart is also working with truck manufacturers to build energy-efficient trucks.

At a lower level, many businesses are at least recycling. However, many companies are not yet doing what they should in terms of sustainable business practices.[96]

THE NEED FOR MANAGEMENT COMMITMENT. Sustainable practices require a strong commitment by companies in order to create the necessary follow-through at all levels of the company. As with any other ethical issue, we have to get the most senior level of management to commit to sustainability and walk the talk. The process of sustainable design requires that everyone think about what resources are being used in every action that the company takes.

Sustainability goals and objectives tied to the company strategy are an essential part of the efforts to "green the company," and HR must play its part in these efforts. *Performance evaluations* of all managers should contain items relating to their sustainability efforts, and in many cases part of their *incentive compensation* may be tied to those efforts. HR may even decide to source some employees locally in some cases, instead of from a wider recruiting pool, in order to minimize impact on the environment. While this is only possible in some limited circumstances, management—including HR management—needs to think about every way in which they can minimize the company's ecological impact. It takes tenacity to make any program take hold in an organization, and the effort to become sustainable is no different than with any other program. HR managers also need to implement *sustainability training* to inform and guide all employees in their sustainability efforts. Let's take a look at sustainability training now.

 ESR

Sustainability Training

Look back just a few years and you would probably find that there were very few sustainability training programs in major corporations. Fortunately for all of us, this is no longer the case. While a very small number of organizations have been concerned with social responsibility and sustainability for many years (for example **Ben and Jerry's Ice Cream,** founded in 1978), most larger businesses didn't become concerned with sustainability programs until about the turn of the 21st century. However, the concept of sustainability is increasingly viewed as providing value to "the so called triple bottom line of economic, social, and environmental performance."[97]

Organizations with sustainability programs tend to gain the trust of their customers and surrounding communities. By doing so, these organizations may gain great competitive advantage over their rivals who are less oriented to the sustainability of the community in the environment. Because a sustainable organization embodies the values of its customers and community, those customers and community members become willing to provide reciprocal concern for the organization. This can create significant loyalty to the organization and its brands.

However, as we just noted, it can be extremely difficult for organizations to embed the concept of social responsibility and sustainability throughout the firm. A sustainability mind-set must be incorporated into the corporate culture, and that can only typically happen from the top of the organization down.[98] So any organizational sustainability training program must begin at the top and change the culture of the executives and managers. Strong organizational cultures that have sustainability as one of their core concepts can begin to create a collective commitment to social responsibility and sustainability within the entire workforce. But how do corporations disseminate this culture of sustainability down into the employee ranks?

Certainly, training that involves identification of the concept of sustainability and how the organization can affect its environment plays a large part in disseminating this information. In addition, the organization may choose to provide all employees with information in the company code of conduct or code of ethics that identifies sustainability as one of the core principles of the firm.

In conjunction with the training and code of conduct, the organization must measure the impact of their sustainability programs to allow modifications to those programs if necessary. Changes in company policies and procedures, as well as organizational structure, may also assist in improving sustainability within the organization. Again though, *training* on the changes in policies, procedures, and structure must occur in order to modify those employees' behaviors.

Several challenges have been identified to teaching employees about sustainability issues.[99] The first challenge concerns organizational resources. All organizations have limited resources and as a result must make choices concerning which stakeholder issues to address. Overcoming resistance to addressing environmental issues is one of the main challenges to training for sustainability.

Second, raising awareness of sustainability issues may engender optimism concerning the company's ability to "solve the problem." Organizations conducting sustainability training must ensure that the employees understand that there are limits to what the firm can accomplish on its own.

Third, solutions to some sustainability problems may lie beyond the knowledge and skills of the organization and its members. If the knowledge and skills necessary to solve a problem involve bringing in personnel from outside the firm, the organization may revert to the first challenge above and claim that limited resources prevent it from resolving the issue.

The fourth issue concerns employee willingness to learn and commit to change actions to improve organizational sustainability. At this point, the change in culture at the top of the organization can assist in pushing culture change at lower levels. If successful, the culture change that values sustainability will, over time, lower employees' levels of resistance to change.

So, as you can see from these challenges, organizational training must provide information on both the concept of sustainability and the impact of the organization on the sustainability of its environment, as well as provide training to modify the organizational culture to place greater value on organizational social responsibility and environmental sustainability. If the organization succeeds in these training efforts, corporate sustainability efforts will be likely to significantly improve over time.

The Sustainable 21st Century Organization

There is evidence that more than 4 out of 5 customers are concerned with sustainability and that more of them today are willing to avoid doing business with companies who do not pay attention to their social responsibility and sustainability. So what will our sustainable 21st century company look like? What do organizational leaders need to know? Unfortunately, there is no single answer to this question. However, we do know some of the things that companies need to think about in their quest to become more sustainable.

MIT Sloan Management Review and The Boston Consulting Group research business sustainability on an annual basis. According to this research, 86% of companies

WORK APPLICATION 15-8

Select an organization, preferably one you work or have worked for. Describe how it is using training and development to meet the challenges of sustainability.

say that sustainability initiatives are necessary in order to be competitive in today's markets.[100] Other articles note that "the concept of sustainability is moving from 'nice to have' to 'need to have,'"[101] and that "there is an entire ecosystem of stakeholders who care. Governments care. Investors care. Employees care."[102] Evidence shows that companies are going to have to become more transparent in their efforts to create sustainable products, because social media, and especially Web-based social media, is going to cause those companies to be held more responsible and accountable for their decisions that affect the environment.

Leading companies are already starting to put their sustainability efforts out in full view of their customers as well as their detractors to show what they are doing. In some cases, they are even asking, "What else can we do?" **Patagonia** is doing this through "The Footprint Chronicles," which, according to their website, "examines Patagonia's life and habits as a company. The goal is to use transparency about our supply chain to help us reduce our adverse social and environmental impacts."[103] **Chipotle Mexican Grill** has an entire section on its website on "Food With Integrity" that discusses its environmentally friendly policies and sustainability initiatives.[104] Many other companies around the world have similar initiatives. But what can your company do if it has not yet jumped on the transparency bandwagon?

The World Business Council for Sustainable Development (WBCSD) provides a reasonably compact set of takeaways in its "Action 2020" document:[105]

1. Get business to buy into long-term goals for sustainability.
2. Change the nature of the debate from attacks and counterattacks on company sustainability initiatives to the science behind the need for sustainable business practices.
3. Speak the right language—the language of business. This means putting the information into the business cycle of "plan, do, check, act."
4. Work toward building partnerships and collaboration, because that is the only way to have a large-scale effect on the environment.
5. Make solutions "open source" and allow all entities who can benefit from them to use them.

Companies in every industry are beginning to be affected by the issue of sustainable supplies along with the sustainability of their own products and/or services. The need to act is not only created because of the ability of the Internet to make business practices transparent. The need to act is driven by business necessity. If we do nothing, supplies in many global industries will eventually run out, and we will have no ability to recover them. The fact is, the earlier that companies decide to take action, the less severe the operational changes and adaptations will need to be.

Where can you go for more information? There are many good sources for data and information on corporate environmental impact and sustainability. Exhibit 15-3 provides you with information on some of the major sites hosting this information.

Now that you have some working knowledge of ethics, CSR, and sustainability and where to find more information, let's move on to this chapter's trends and issues.

TRENDS AND ISSUES IN HRM

For this chapter's trends and issues, we are going to take a look at some sustainability-based benefits available in organizations today, followed by a look at the value of diversity training.

| EXHIBIT 15-3 | INTERNET RESOURCES FOR CORPORATE SUSTAINABILITY |

World Business Council for Sustainable Development (WBCSD): http://www.wbcsd.org

Provides a platform for business collaboration around the "Vision to Action" model for sustainable business.

International Organization for Standardization (ISO): http://www.iso.org

The ISO 14000 series of standards address environmental management in organizations, providing "practical tools for companies . . . looking to identify and control their environmental impact."[106]

International Institute for Sustainable Development (IISD): http://www.iisd.org

The IISD champions sustainability development around the world through innovation, partnerships, research, and communications.

United Nations Global Compact: http://www.unglobalcompact.org

Provides "supply chain sustainability" information based on 10 principles that drive the Global Compact efforts.[107]

International Organization for Sustainable Development (IOSD): http://www.iosd.org

A United Nations registered site, IOSD provides a number of white papers on sustainability issues around the world.

World Economic Forum (WEF): http://www.weforum.org

"The World Economic Forum is an international institution committed to improving the state of the world through public-private cooperation."[108] They provide sustainability information on everything from climate to food insecurity at http://www.weforum.org/issues/sustainability/.

National Association of Environmental Managers (NAEM): http://www.naem.org

NAEM is a membership organization that focuses on environmental health and safety, including sustainability as part of its environmental health mission.

Corporate Social Responsibility Newswire (CSRwire): http://www.csrwire.com

CSR Wire is a newswire service that provides "the latest news, views and reports in corporate social responsibility (CSR) and sustainability."[109] This is a very good site that gathers news and information on CSR and sustainability issues.

Sustainability-Based Benefits

 ESR

One area that has seen recent interest is sustainability-based benefit programs. A number of companies are looking at options for providing benefits to their employees that assist with improving environmental stability and sustainability over the long term. It is not only politically correct; it is an additional way to show the corporation's true concern for the environment as well as their concern for their employees. These programs can range from providing "credits" to employees for riding bicycles or public transportation to work all the way to sharing the costs of cars or home appliances that lower energy usage.

Benefits that will lower the employee's individual "carbon footprint" help the environment and help the employee because such benefits almost always lower the employee's cost of living. An example is a program called HEAL Arkansas. This program was started by the **Addison Shoe Factory** when they learned that many of their employees spent *up to half of their income* on energy bills.[110] The HEAL program is now offered through the state of Arkansas to selected businesses and provides "facility audits and zero interest retrofit financing of energy efficiency improvements for their facilities."[111] The companies in turn must use part of their energy savings to help employees with home audits and retrofitting of appliances, windows, and other energy-saving items by providing the employees with zero-interest loans for such improvements.

Companies may also provide a variety of other "green" subsidies so that employees can help the environment. These might include assistance to employees with purchasing renewable energy options for their homes such as solar cells or hybrid, electric, or alternative fuel vehicles. **Clif Bar and Company** in Berkeley, California, "provides points to employees for selecting alternate modes of transportation to work, such as walking, biking, carpooling, or mass transit."[112] Even telecommuting can be a sustainability benefit because it lowers the number of employees commuting to work. So employers just need to use a bit of imagination and a good search engine to find ways in which they can encourage sustainable practices on the part of their employees as well as practices that they can put into effect within the company.

Does Diversity Training Work?

Competitive organizations always need to work to maximize the talent pool from which they can draw recruits. If, in fact, the organization arbitrarily limits the number and types of recruits through artificial limits on organizational diversity, it restricts its ability to draw on the best talent available from the at-large workforce. However, most organizations today accept the fact that *unmanaged* diversity can decrease employee commitment and engagement, lower job satisfaction, increase turnover, and increase conflict. Organizations must create a *cultural change* in order for diversity training to be successful. But since cultural change is very difficult, many organizations try to shortcut the process and as a result end up with failed programs.[113]

How can organizations create and deliver a diversity training process that has a chance of being successful? Common diversity initiatives include such things as diversity recruitment, diversity training, and formal mentoring programs. However, plugging these programs into organizational training without providing a process by which they can be integrated into the daily activities of the members of the organization will likely lead to minimal if any success. Let's take a quick look at the history of diversity training and its effectiveness.

Diversity training has been around in some form since the 1960s. In its earlier days, diversity training primarily focused on organizational *compliance* with equal opportunity laws. Later on, diversity training moved through a sequence of options—from attempting to *assimilate* different individuals into an organizational culture; through attempting to make employees sensitive to others and their differences; and more recently to trying to create *inclusion* of all individuals, from all backgrounds, into the organization.[114]

In each of the phases of diversity training, there appeared to be significant pushback on the part of one or more groups involved in the training. Whether the pushback was from the white male majority, feeling that they were being persecuted, or from females or minority individuals, feeling that they had to conform to the organization and its practices, each of the phases had significant hurdles to overcome in order to move the organization forward. Today, organizations are attempting to integrate diversity more directly into the business and its strategies. Companies that lead the diversity initiative are becoming much more involved at all levels of the organization, from the executive suite to the shop floor.

Throughout each phase of diversity training's existence, its effectiveness has been questioned by many organizations and researchers. Evidence appears to be growing that diversity training in its present form does add value to the organization, both sociologically and economically.[115,116] In addition, when diversity training focuses on the *similarities* between individuals rather than their *differences*, trainees appear to become more capable of resolving conflict that may occur as a result of individual diversity.[117] Finally, the bottom line is that most major corporations believe that diversity adds significant value to their organizations, both from the perspective of providing different viewpoints and solutions to problems and from the perspective of providing the organization with a larger talent pool in a period when qualified applicants are becoming less and less available in the at-large workforce.

WORK
APPLICATION 15-10

Select an organization, preferably one you work or have worked for. Describe how it is using training and development to meet the challenges of an increasingly diversified world.

• • • CHAPTER SUMMARY

15-1 **Discuss the term *ethics*, including common elements of the definition.**

There are many definitions of *ethics*, but they all have some common elements. The common elements include the concepts of morals, values, beliefs, and principles. These in turn lead to the need for personal integrity and trust in the character of another, or we won't believe that they will act ethically if they have an opportunity for self-enrichment at the expense of others.

15-2 **Briefly discuss each of the identified ethical approaches.**

The Golden Rule is one approach that says to basically treat others as you would want to be treated. The Rotary's four-way test asks four questions: (1) Is it the truth? (2) Is it fair to all concerned? (3) Will it build goodwill and better friendship? (4) Will it be beneficial to all concerned? If the answers are yes, then the action is probably ethical. The stakeholder approach says that if you are willing to have your decisions written about on the front page of the newspaper, then you can probably feel comfortable that your decision was ethical.

15-3 **Briefly discuss each factor required in a good code of ethics.**

Values are the first factor. They "define what the company is about and make it clear that the company is based on honesty and fairness." *Principles* apply our values to specific situations to identify actions that we consider ethical. *Management support* is critical because if senior managers do not pay attention to the code, others will not either. *Personal responsibility* identifies the fact that everyone is personally accountable for their own behavior and is expected to act ethically. Finally, *compliance* identifies applicable laws and regulations that guide ethical behavior in specific industries.

15-4 **Discuss the terms *authority*, *responsibility*, and *accountability* and how they relate to ethical behavior.**

Authority is a *positional right* within the organization that allows the person to give orders to others in order to accomplish organizational goals. Responsibility requires the individual to accept their positional obligation to use the company's resources effectively to help reach the organization's goals. Accountability is the personal duty to use organizational resources correctly, and if we do not do so, we can be held personally liable for that misuse.

15-5 **Identify some of the common ethical issues that managers face in business.**

Bribery—Payments are made to others to cause decisions that are favorable to the person providing the bribe.

Corrupt payments—These are made to allow the company to avoid scrutiny of their actions by government agencies.

Employment and personnel issues—Bias, child labor, forced labor, and other discriminatory labor practices all create the danger of unethical decisions.

Marketing practices—Dishonesty in marketing and the hiding of safety and quality defects may be tempting because of the cost of being honest.

Impact on the economy and environment—Unethical activity on the part of financial institutions can create terrible economic consequences, and other organizational actions that don't take the consequences of those actions into account can cause irreversible harm to the environment.

Employee and customer privacy—Personal privacy can be harmed by unethical actions on the part of company employees, especially the use of databases with large amounts of personal information for unauthorized purposes.

15-6 **Briefly discuss the "business case" for CSR.**

CSR says that organizations have a duty to all stakeholders to operate in a manner that takes each of their needs into account. All stakeholders means *all*—not just shareholders or executives. The business case for CSR is based on the ability of the organization to help or harm various stakeholder groups and of those stakeholder groups in turn to help or harm the company. Each stakeholder group has different—and sometimes competing—interests, but the organization must balance these "social responsibilities" among all of the groups in order to succeed.

15-7 Briefly describe the concept of sustainability in a business context.

Sustainability means meeting the needs of the current generation without compromising the ability of future generations to meet their own needs.

Business must practice sustainability today because so many resources are being overused to the point where they cannot be replenished and will ultimately disappear unless we quickly change our practices. Sustainability goals must be created and managed like any other organizational goal in order to improve business sustainability.

15-8 Define the key terms found in the chapter margins and listed following the Chapter Summary.

Complete the Key Terms Review to test your understanding of this chapter's key terms.

● ● ● KEY TERMS

accountability
authority
corporate social responsibility

ethics
glass ceiling
principles

responsibility
sustainability
values

● ● ● KEY TERMS REVIEW

Complete each of the following statements using one of this chapter's key terms.

1. _____ is the application of a set of values and principles in order to make the right, or good, choice.

2. _____ are our basic concepts of good and bad, or right and wrong.

3. _____ are a basic application of our values.

4. _____ is the right to give orders, enforce obedience, make decisions, and commit resources toward completing organizational goals.

5. _____ is the obligation to answer for something/someone or the duty to carry out an assignment to a satisfactory conclusion.

6. _____ is the personal duty to someone else for the effective use of resources to complete an assignment.

7. _____ is the concept that organizations have a duty to all societal stakeholders to operate in a manner that takes each of their needs into account.

8. _____ is the thought that there are invisible barriers to advancement in business for women as well as other minority employees.

9. _____ involves meeting the needs of the current generation without compromising the ability of future generations to meet their needs.

● ● ● COMMUNICATION SKILLS

The following critical-thinking questions can be used for class discussion and/or for written assignments to develop communication skills. Be sure to give complete explanations for all answers.

1. Do you think the term *ethics* is overused in today's business environment? Justify your answer.

2. Will applying the Golden Rule always result in a decision that you can defend as "ethical"? Why or why not?

3. Can you think of situations where someone might violate the code of ethics in a company but should not be punished for it? Give examples.

4. As the HR manager, how would you go about getting the senior executives of the company to buy into adhering to the code of ethics?

5. Using the concepts of authority, responsibility, and accountability, can you explain what should happen to an individual who misuses company resources for personal gain? Provide an example.

6. Give two examples of decisions that could be made in a company that are legal but are still unethical.

7. Do you agree that companies have a duty to stakeholders other than their shareholders? If so, justify who else they are obligated to and why.

8. Can you identify one case where you think the government (state or federal) is the most important stakeholder of a firm (do not use the government as a customer but as another external stakeholder)? Explain your answer.

9. In your opinion, do companies have a "social contract" with society? Why or why not?

10. If you were in charge, what would you do to help some disadvantaged employee groups gain equality in your company?

11. Is sustainability just a marketing tool to get people to "think green," or is it a necessary business tool? Defend your answer.

12. How would you motivate people in your organization to practice sustainability? Be specific with the managerial tools that you would use.

• • • CASE 15-1 TAKE THE MONEY AND RUN: WHITE-COLLAR CRIME AT DHR CONSTRUCTION

"Jim!" Richard Davis, managing partner of DHR, shouted in disbelief. "Are you trying to tell me that over the past two years my right-hand man, Alan Thompson, has embezzled nearly $25,000?"

"Figures don't lie, but liars figure," retorted James J. Carroll, CPA, the accountant for the firm. "I've just finished auditing your firm's financials and found that purchases have been charged to Thompson's corporate credit card that either have nothing to do with the business or seem far-fetched, like buying gasoline six times in the same day for the same vehicle. Worse, I've noticed that for several procurements, the signatures on the receipts do not even come close to matching the signature on the back of the corporate credit card. I think someone who is not authorized has used his card—that's not only embezzlement, my friend, that's credit card fraud and forgery!"

The Way Things Were

Alan and Wilma Thompson were tenants as well as the construction managers of DHR Construction and seemed to flourish under Davis's leadership style. Alan was a soft-spoken individual who had really never been given the opportunity to work the way he wanted to work. Davis gave Alan the autonomy to purchase tools and other building materials as needed, allowed him to use the business truck as his own vehicle, and gave Alan the authority to deal directly with subcontractors. Alan was therefore the point man for the building operation and focused on providing quality workmanship by building a solid network of subcontractors.

Davis's trust in Alan and Wilma seemed to be reciprocated by their devotion to the business. Alan and Wilma stuck with Davis through the business's tough times, and they developed what Davis thought were strong social bonds. When Alan's brother Marvin came on board, all social events included Marvin and his family as well. This cemented the familial bonds within the business. All seemed to be well from Davis's standpoint, and the business seemed in solid hands with Alan and family.

Exit Bookkeeper, Enter Accountant

Davis employed Wilma's cousin, Sally Stone, as the firm's bookkeeper after meeting her at one of the business's summer barbeques. Sally would take all of the monthly receipts, deposits, and bills; record them in the firm's journal; and write out any checks for outstanding bills. As the operation grew and became more complex, however, Sally realized that she was getting in way over her head and that the services of an accountant were needed. With a heavy heart, Sally informed Davis that she could no longer properly service the firm and that she would reconcile the books at the end of the fiscal year and then depart.

After chatting with several of the other small local builders, Davis made several phone calls to prospective accountants. They all seemed very competent, but one in particular, James J. Carroll, CPA, not only understood the business but also owned rental property. Davis met with Carroll and hit it off quite well with him and immediately turned over a copy of the books.

A few days later, after digging into the books, Mr. Carroll noticed numerous strange credit card charges to the same credit card: a Christmas tree and gifts from Home Depot, over $200 of food purchased at Walmart, and 15 to 20 specialty tools purchased over and over again in a span of just a few weeks. Carroll, having worked with several other small businesses, knew that some small business owners would charge family expenses to their corporate credit cards. He hoped that this was not the case since Mr. Carroll would not service any client who mixed personal expenses in with business expenses. He decided that before discussing the ramifications of this behavior with Davis, he'd better do more digging. Perhaps he could discern a pattern that would explain such behavior.

The Search and the Findings

Carroll plodded through all of the receipts, checks, and journal entries and hoped that perhaps these personal charges were at best accidental personal charges that might be considered "loans" that would be paid back to the businesses. Carroll quickly noticed that the personal incidentals all seemed to be made on only one person's credit card, that of Alan Thompson. Carroll tabulated these expenses, along with expenses he thought were perhaps frivolous or questionable, and found about $25,000 of these types of expenditures over a 2-year period. Mr. Carroll also checked the signature of Thompson's card and noticed that on several occasions, the signature was different on the signed credit card receipt than on the actual credit card. He took his findings to Richard Davis, who at first was totally incredulous. However, after examining all of the evidence, Davis knew that he had a real problem—a problem with really appalling ramifications. The question is, now what should he do about it?

Questions

1. Given the textbook's definition of ethics, what are the ethical issues in this case?

2. What human resource management practices of DHR might have led to the alleged unethical behavior?

3. How might having a code of ethics have clarified the ethical values of the firm?

4. Who are the key stakeholders in this case? Why?

5. Assuming that Thompson is accused of misappropriating DHR funds, what do you believe is Davis's social responsibility in this matter? To which stakeholders?

6. Assume that Thompson is terminated over this incident. If you were Davis, how would you handle this termination? Why?

Case created by Herbert Sherman, PhD, and Theodore Vallas, Department of Management Sciences, School of Business Brooklyn Campus, Long Island University

• • • CASE 15-2 MICROSOFT, NOKIA, AND THE FINNISH GOVERNMENT: A PROMISE MADE, A PROMISE BROKEN?

At the turn of the 21st century, Microsoft seemed invincible as both a firm and an operating system, and controlled the tech industry by completely overshadowing its nemesis, Apple. After launching successful operating systems like Windows XP and 2000, the company gained wealth, recognition, and power by creating a near monopoly over personal computing devices.[118] Although they were not the pioneers of user-friendly operating systems (accolades to Apple for developing the first mass merchandised system), they were enjoying a 97% market share. In 2000, personal computers were the only available noncommercial computing devices and Microsoft dominated them all.[119]

As of 2005, the demand for smartphones started to increase and the market increased opportunities for new entrants. Microsoft's decline started in 2007 after Apple introduced the first iPhone. The market was moving away from Microsoft's products; compared to Apple's Mac operating system, Windows Vista was barely holding up and was considered inferior to its predecessor, Windows XP. Apple showed tremendous growth over the next decade and Wall Street announced that Apple was valued higher than Microsoft in 2010. Google then introduced its Android system to compete with Apple's iPhone OS. This new system was adopted by the other half of the smartphone industry. As a late entrant, Microsoft introduced their first Windows Phone in 2010 and the next year, they announced their commitment to Finnish expertise in the telecommunications sector by partnering with Nokia and functioning as one team. This arrangement permitted all Nokia devices to use Microsoft operating systems, which reintroduced Microsoft to the smartphone market.[120]

By 2013, there were approximately 2.5 billion computing devices, including tablets, that were dominated by three companies: Microsoft, Google, and Apple. The total number of personal computer sales had yet to reach 500 million, but smartphones had already sold more than 1.5 billion units over a decade.[121] Smart phones had dominated the tech industry as the major item in the personal computer market. Apple's iPhone was a huge success, which created billions of dollars' worth of supplementary revenue from mobile applications. In this respect, Apple's iTunes and Samsung's alignment with Google enhanced user experiences with smartphones. Microsoft, on the other hand, was not prepared for the sudden shift in the market, and although still a tech giant, they were clearly caught off guard.

With its market cap at 20%, Microsoft desperately wanted to regain market share. They installed a new CEO who was tasked with realigning the company under the "One Microsoft" vision. The company was ready to change its business model, to increase the speed of innovation, increase efficiency, and rebuild the company culture. To that end they announced Office 2013, a new operating system called Windows 8.1, and Xbox One, their new gaming console.[122]

In 2013, the agreement between Microsoft and Nokia became more than a partnership as Microsoft bid to acquire Nokia in a $7.2 billion deal. Founded in 1865, Nokia is a Finnish telecommunications and technology company that engaged more than 90,000 employees and reported around $12 billion in annual revenues. This was a big move for Microsoft since Nokia had experienced its own declines as indicated by its stocks dropping by 80% in the prior few years. Both companies had ignored the winds of change and both paid the price for letting their competitors slide past them.[123]

The acquisition of Nokia, however, was delayed by numerous legal issues with the Finnish government, who approved the deal with the understanding that layoffs would not be forthcoming. The purchase was finally approved by the numerous international governmental regulatory agencies in the first quarter of 2014. With purchase in hand, Microsoft felt they now had good access to the mobile phone industry with $50 billion in annual sales. Three months after the deal was inked, Microsoft's first major action was to lay off 18,000 people in their work force. This was the largest layoff in the tech industry, but it helped Microsoft save about $600 million a year.[124]

Finnish Prime Minister Alexander Stubb received a call in July 2014 from Stephen Elop, the head of Microsoft Corp.'s device business and a former Nokia Corp. chief executive. Elop alerted him that Microsoft would cut 1,100 of the 4,700 jobs in Finland that came with its purchase of Nokia's mobile phone operations. Mr. Stubb called the layoffs "extremely regrettable" and said the government would do all it could to cushion the blow to those affected. Finnish politicians issued statements calling on Microsoft to show social responsibility and offer retraining and generous severance packages to the people it was dismissing, something that Nokia has done in the past in Finland and abroad. Some went further and accused Microsoft of reneging on the promises it

supposedly made about job security and Finland's place in its strategy. "You can say we were betrayed," said Finland's newly minted minister of finance, Antti Rinne, a Social Democrat.[125]

Questions

1. Who are Microsoft's key stakeholders in this case? Why?

2. Using the five forces model from Chapter 2, describe how the changes in the computer technology industry impacted Microsoft's ability to compete. Which force most negatively impacted Microsoft? Why?

3. What seems to be Microsoft's ethical approach? How does this approach seem to impact their human resource management decisions?

4. Describe the conflict between stakeholders' interests and the Finnish government's perception of Microsoft's lack of social responsibility to Nokia's employees. Whom do you side with and why?

5. Instead of layoffs, what if Microsoft decided to decrease the total compensation to Nokia employees. What part of that package would you decrease and why?

6. Besides changing the compensation package, what other human resource management options might IBM consider rather than layoffs?

Case created by Herbert Sherman, PhD, and Theodore Vallas, Department of Management Sciences, School of Business Brooklyn Campus, Long Island University

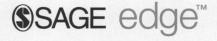

Sharpen your skills with SAGE edge at edge.sagepub.com/lussierhrm2e

SAGE edge for students provides a personalized approach to help you accomplish your coursework goals in an easy-to-use learning environment.

• • • SKILL BUILDER 15-1 ETHICS AND WHISTLE-BLOWING

Objective

To determine your level of ethics

Skills

The primary skills developed through this exercise are as follows:

1. *HR management skills*—Conceptual and design skills
2. *SHRM 2013 Competencies*—C: Ethics

Assignment

For this exercise, first complete Self-Assessment 15-1 in the chapter (page 563).

Discussion Questions

1. Who is harmed and who benefits from the unethical behaviors in items 1 through 3?

2. For items 4 to 24, select the three (circle their numbers) you consider the most unethical. Who is harmed by and who benefits from these unethical behaviors?

3. If you observed unethical behavior but didn't report it, why didn't you report the behavior? If you did blow the whistle, what motivated you to do so? What was the result?

4. As a manager, it is your responsibility to uphold ethical behavior. If you know employees are doing any

of these unethical behaviors, will you take action to enforce compliance with ethical standards?

5. What can you do to prevent unethical behavior?

6. As part of the class discussion, share any of the other unethical behaviors you observed and listed.

You may be asked to present your answers to the class or share them in small groups in class or online.

••• SKILL BUILDER 15-2 CODE OF ETHICS AND CORPORATE SOCIAL RESPONSIBILITY

Objective

To better understand a business's ethics and CSR

Skills

The primary skills developed through this exercise are as follows:

1. *HR management skills*—Conceptual and design skills

2. *SHRM 2013 Competencies*—C: Ethics

Assignment

Select a specific business. It can be one you work for or, better yet, one you would like to work for in the future.

Make sure the company you select meets the following criteria: It must have a written code of ethics and operate at the benevolent level of CSR.

Go online to the company's website and get a copy of its code of ethics and its report on its corporate social responsibility programs. Be sure to identify any of its sustainability practices—this information may be at a separate link.

Be prepared to make a report on your company's code of ethics and CSR to the entire class or in a small group.

©iStockphoto.com/Rawpixel

16 Global Issues for Human Resource Managers

••• LEARNING OUTCOMES

After studying this chapter, you should be able to do the following:

Practitioner's Perspective

Cindy says: One of the biggest changes in business has been the explosion of the global marketplace. Business doesn't compete across the country, but around the world. Americans tend to be Eurocentric (the viewpoint that Western civilization is superior). We must recognize that foreign cultures deserve to be valued in the same manner as a diverse workforce is valued, and that what is acceptable behavior in the United States can be anything but in another country.

Zac is an assistant manager for *Kawasaki Heavy Industries*, a global company with US manufacturing plants. After escorting US employees to company meetings in Japan, Zac has some amusing stories to tell. His favorite is about the fellow who went around waving and saying "Hi" to everyone. *Hi* in Japanese means yes, so imagine how strange this literal "*yes*-man" appeared. Another interesting difference is giving and receiving business cards. In the United States, one would usually put a business card away after receiving it, but in Japan, that would be considered extremely rude. There one must leave the card lying on the table until all business is concluded.

What will you discover about global issues in Chapter 16?

SHRM HR CONTENT

See Appendix: *SHRM 2013 Curriculum Guidebook* for the complete list

C. Ethics (required)

   3. Individual versus group behavior

  17. Foreign Corrupt Practices Act

F. Managing a Diverse Workforce (required)

   5. Language issues

  13. Cultural competence

K. Total Rewards (required)

  B. Employee Benefits

    11. Global employee benefits

    14. Outsourcing (secondary)

O. Globalization (required–graduate students only)

  1. Global business environment

  2. Managing expatriates in global markets

  3. Cross-border HR management

  4. Repatriating employees post international assignment

  6. Inshoring

  7. Offshoring/outsourcing

  9. Cross-cultural effectiveness

GLOBALIZATION OF BUSINESS AND HRM

We live in a world that is dynamically globally interconnected.[1] The major factor increasing the complexity of the environment is the globalization of markets[2]—the buying and selling of goods and services worldwide. Think about the complexity of **FedEx**'s environment, delivering to more than 220 countries and territories.[3] Therefore, it has to follow the rules and regulations of different governments in countries with different economies, labor forces, societies, and so on. Refer back to Chapter 2, Exhibit 2-5, for a review of analysis of the environment. Clearly, to be successful, companies need global leaders.[4] For example, Carlos Ghosn is the CEO of two companies, **Renault** (France) and **Nissan** (Japan), on two different continents conducting business globally. Today's managers—and students of management—cannot afford to underestimate the importance of the global environment to business.[5]

Even if your company does not face direct competition from global competitors, you will still be affected by global suppliers, partners, or customers for your products and services. Capital and goods flow easily between countries. Because of the ability to communicate instantly, services can generally be performed in the location where they have the lowest cost for the most efficient (*not* necessarily the *best*, but the most efficient!) service quality. One model identifies four types of capital that flow between countries:[6]

SHRM

0:1
Global Business Environment

- *Natural capital.* Natural resources such as timber, water, and minerals are "components of nature that can be linked with *human welfare.*"
- *Social capital.* This "consists of the *social networks* that support an efficient, cohesive society, and facilitate social and intellectual interactions among its members. Social capital refers to those stocks of social trust, norms and networks that people can draw upon to solve common problems and create social cohesion."
- *Manufactured capital.* This is *human-made* capital like machines, tools, buildings, and other infrastructure that are used to produce other assets.
- *Human capital.* This "generally refers to the health, well-being and productive potential of individual *people.*"

If you take another look at these types of capital, there appears to be a theme throughout—humans, people, us! Because every form of capital that is exchanged between countries is controlled in some way by people, we have to figure out how to manage those individuals in order to maximize organizational returns.

However, there are significant cultural differences between countries and regions. In fact, in many cases, there are multiple cultures in a single country. All of this makes global business more challenging. Let's take a look at how HRM has to be managed differently in global firms.

Reasons for Business Globalization

LO 16-1

Identify and discuss the reasons for increasing business globalization.

The world was simpler when it was difficult to move goods across borders or oceans and it was just as difficult to move people between countries. A business could work in its local environment, taking only its local customers into account as it produced the goods and services that those customers wanted. However, our environment has conspired to make it easier to move both goods and people, along with abstract ideas and concrete knowledge, across borders and around the world. In turn, business must adapt to this new environment as surely as having to adapt to a climate change or a threat of disease. What has happened that created this environment?

There are many reasons why business continues to globalize on a scale never seen before. One is to increase business. Another reason businesses have reached beyond their own borders is the rise of the "global village," with associated declining barriers to trade in goods, investment, travel, and communication. Declining barriers of distance and culture, international normative agreements on trade between countries, the rise of trade blocs, and uneven competition between domestic and international firms are other reasons why companies are expanding beyond their own countries' borders.

INCREASE BUSINESS. Let's face it: Most large corporations want to continue to grow. If you are a major corporation like **Coca-Cola**, is there anyplace in America to expand? No, the market is saturated. Also, the US population is only 318.74 million, a small fraction of the world's population of 7.19 billion.[7] So if large corporations want to grow, they have to go overseas. However, businesses of all sizes, regardless of how saturated the US market is, also have billions of other potential customers if they go global. The other reasons for the globalization of business apply regardless of the size of the business.

THE GLOBAL VILLAGE. The global village concept has become—in many ways—a reality. Essentially the entire world can see and interact with goods and services that were only available to others in "the village" a hundred years ago. Ideas, goods, and services move easily across borders and around the world. This free flow of ideas, information, and knowledge through the use of the Internet and other media has reshaped the way people see their world. It has also allowed connections between people with shared interests in a much more intimate manner than was ever possible before. All of this serves to, among other things, bring vendor and customer closer together, creating global demand for products that the customer would not have even been aware of 25 years ago.

DECLINING TRADE BARRIERS, GATT, AND THE WTO. Another impetus for increasing globalization over the past 50 years was the changing disposition toward the use of tariffs and other trade barriers by country governments. During the 1920s and 1930s, many countries erected barriers to international trade in the form of tariffs—taxes that a government imposes on imported goods. The aim of tariffs is to protect domestic industries and jobs from foreign competition. However, as often happens when one entity makes a move to give it a competitive advantage but has no way

Growth in international business will continue.

to defend that advantage (no ability to protect the advantage or make it hard to copy), if one country imposed tariffs on goods coming in, other countries immediately retaliated with the same types of trade barriers to goods from the first country's market. So retaliation became the norm when tariffs were imposed. In fact, there is at least some evidence that the Great Depression of 1929 was in part caused by these tariff and trade wars.[8]

Shortly after World War II, an agreement framework called the *General Agreement on Tariffs and Trade*, or GATT, originally signed by 23 member countries, was negotiated.[9] It was the basis for an era in which tariffs and other trade barriers were significantly reduced in much of the world. Ultimately in the 1990s, the GATT agreements were formalized into the World Trade Organization (WTO), with a mission to be "the international organization whose primary purpose is to open trade for the benefit of all."[10] The WTO monitors and arbitrates trade disputes among its more than 160 member countries. Because the WTO and its predecessors have been so effective at lowering trade barriers, international trade has opened up to businesses that would not have been able to compete internationally before these organizations and agreements existed.

DECLINING BARRIERS OF DISTANCE AND CULTURE. In the 1950s, it was difficult to transport goods across country borders and over oceans. It was also difficult to communicate between one location and another. Think about it: If you wanted to call up a friend in central China in 1955, would you have been able to do so? It's highly unlikely that you would. Along the same lines, would you be able to manage a production facility in Shanghai if you were in New York? You couldn't easily call from one facility to the other; you certainly couldn't just hop on an intercontinental jet and fly to Shanghai; you couldn't contact the plant via Skype, or even email. International business was a very difficult thing to manage. That is why most businesses did not have international operations. Both communication and transportation were difficult things to accomplish in an international business.

But—things have changed! Communication to most parts of the world is nearly instantaneous. You can dial up your friend in China, or get on the Internet and use a webcam to see exactly what is wrong with your production equipment in Shanghai, and provide instructions on how to fix it in a few minutes. If you need to send experts to the plant, they can be anywhere in the world in about a day (in the 1950s, it would have taken about three weeks!). And as soon as it became possible to operate a business globally, managers were figuring out how to create a strategy to build a sustainable competitive advantage by doing so.

Trade blocs Groups of countries who form an association for the purpose of facilitating movement of goods across national borders

THE RISE OF TRADE BLOCS. Around the early to mid-1990s we started seeing countries forming reasonably large trade blocs to encourage trade between member countries but discourage trade from outside the trade blocs through trade barriers, again including at least some tariffs. **Trade blocs** *are groups of countries who form an association for the purpose of facilitating movement of goods across national borders.* One of the early trade blocs was NAFTA—the North American Free Trade Agreement among Canada, the United States, and Mexico. Others include the European Economic Community (EEC—which later became the European Union [EU]), the Association of Southeast Asian Nations (ASEAN), and the Central American Free Trade Agreement (CAFTA), plus several others. These trade blocs allow free, or

Digital Vision/Photodisc/Thinkstock

low-cost, passage of goods among member nations to encourage companies to specialize in certain types of goods to become more efficient and therefore lower the cost of those goods to all member countries.

However, if you are not part of the bloc, trade barriers tend to be significant, and they will raise your cost of doing business with the countries in the bloc. One method of getting around the barriers is to become part of the bloc. This is usually accomplished by having business operations in at least one country within the bloc, which will make your company a de facto member of the bloc and reduce or eliminate this barrier. So companies will now frequently build factories, design facilities, component plants, or other facilities within the bloc in order to overcome the trade barrier associated with that trade bloc.

TO REMAIN COMPETITIVE! The last reason for business globalization is simple:

Global corporations vs. Domestic organizations = One-sided competition

In many cases, if a domestic firm is competing head-to-head with a global firm, the competition is seriously one-sided. The global firm will source all of its capital resources from wherever they are the most efficient. If the global company sources raw materials from one country for half the cost, component production in another country for 75% of the cost, and labor from a third country for 25% of the cost of the domestic competitor, who is going to win the battle for the customers? The customer *will not* pay double the price for the same good of the same quality, no matter where it is made! The domestic firm is at an absolute cost disadvantage versus the global firm.

Ethnocentrism Is Out and "Made in America" Is Blurred

Parochialism means having a narrow focus, or seeing things solely from one's own perspective. *Ethnocentrism* is regarding one's own ethnic group or culture as superior to that of others. Thus, a parochial view, which we will discuss again later, is part of ethnocentrism. Successful managers of large companies headquartered in the United States (including **Coca-Cola, FedEx, GE,** and **3M,** to name just a few) are not ethnocentric; they don't view their firms simply as American companies but rather as companies conducting business in a global village. If they can buy or make better or cheaper materials, parts, or products and make a profit in another country, they do so. **British Petroleum (BP)** has been doing business in the United States for more than 100 years and employs close to 250,000 workers across America.[11]

Many consumers subscribe to the idea behind "Buy American," but few know the country of origin of the products they regularly buy. Look at the labels in your clothes and you will realize that most clothing is not made in America; 76.5% are made in Asia, with close to 40% coming from China.[12] Did you know that although **Nike** is an American company, its clothes and sneakers are not made in the United States? Some **GM** cars are made in America but with more than 60% of the parts coming from foreign companies. **Toyota** makes some cars in America with around 25% of the parts coming from foreign companies. So what's *really* made in America? The **Made in America** store has a challenge stocking the store with fashionable only-American merchandise and hasn't been able to find any electric or electronic products because they are all made abroad.[13]

In addition to not knowing products are foreign, some people don't care where the products they buy come from; price is more important to them. Plus, some people prefer products, such as cars, made by foreign companies. Test your global knowledge of companies' and products' country of ownership by completing Self-Assessment 3-1.

WORK
APPLICATION 16-1

Identify a global business, one you have worked for if possible. Discuss the reasons it went global.

WORK
APPLICATION 16-2

Do you believe in buying American products? Do you try to buy only American products, and should you?

16-1 SELF ASSESSMENT

Products by Country of Origin

For each item, determine the country of origin. If your answer is the United States, place a check in the left-hand column. If it's another country, write the name of the country in the right-hand column.

	Product	United States	Other (list country)
1.	Shell gasoline	_____	_____
2.	Nestlé hot cocoa	_____	_____
3.	Unilever Dove soap	_____	_____
4.	Nokia cell phones	_____	_____
5.	L'Oreal cosmetics	_____	_____
6.	Johnson & Johnson baby powder	_____	_____
7.	Burger King fast food	_____	_____
8.	Samsung televisions	_____	_____
9.	Bayer aspirin	_____	_____
10.	Anheuser-Busch beer	_____	_____
11.	Volvo cars	_____	_____
12.	AMC theaters	_____	_____

1. Shell is owned by Royal Dutch Shell of the Netherlands. 2. Nestlé is headquartered in Switzerland. 3. Unilever is British. 4. Nokia was a Finnish company but was acquired by US Microsoft in September 2013. 5. L'Oreal is French. 6, Johnson & Johnson is a US company. 7. Burger King is Brazilian owned. 8. Samsung is South Korean. 9. Bayer is German. 10. Anheuser-Busch InBev is Belgian owned. 11. Volvo and 12. AMC are both Chinese owned.

How many did you get correct?

LO 16-2

Discuss the stages of corporate globalization through which companies move from local to global operations.

Stages of Corporate Globalization

Marshall McLuhan's "global village," whether you like it or not, is a reality! In many ways, people around the world are becoming more similar in what they want, especially as consumers.[14] The Internet and other forms of instant communication have changed the way people around the world think, act, and react. These individuals— whether in the United States, India, Russia, or Peru—desire many of the same consumer goods and services and want the same employment opportunities. So business has to expand to where the customers are and to where capable recruits are ready to go to work. But how does a business expand from being a local producer to an international firm? There are several different models of international expansion, but for our purposes, we can take a look at just one that helps to identify how companies expand globally. Nancy Adler has been studying global businesses for more than 30 years. She has noted four stages in the evolution of a company from local producer to global firm: domestic, international, multinational, and transnational.[15] Take a look at the different phases in Exhibit 16-1.

As you can quickly see in the exhibit, the HRM function becomes more complex as we move further down the stages of globalization of the firm. As we move to the transnational firm, we have to develop transnational HR systems that take into account the culture and business practices of every country in which we operate.

So, if going global complicates the management of the organization, why expand operations to other countries? Let's take a look at some reasons for globalization and also some problems that we are sure to encounter if we decide to continue with our international expansion.

EXHIBIT 16-1   STAGES IN CORPORATE GLOBALIZATION

Domestic:	Firms have a one-country market and serve primarily one set of customers. The firm does not develop products for other countries' markets, and management does not have to be culturally sensitive, other than to local customers and employees.
International:	New firms enter the company's markets, causing the firm to also search for new markets. Generally, the company will enter only a few other countries' markets in this stage—initially by exporting goods or services from the home-country location and at some point expanding production to those secondary countries. Units in each country tend to be managed independently in an international division, so divisional managers must have some cultural sensitivity but other managers do not.
Multinational:	As country competition gets more intense, firms need to become more efficient and lower product/service costs. The multinational company (MNC) usually has partial or full ownership of the operations in another country—a separate independent business facility (factories or offices). They begin to source the various types of capital resources from wherever they are the lowest cost to the firm. They also tend to standardize more of their processes, also to increase efficiency. Operations across countries become more integrated—again lowering overall costs. Management has to begin to understand the cultural issues in all countries in which they operate and act in accordance with those local cultures.
Transnational:	Transnationals are a type of MNC that eliminates artificial geographical barriers without having a real single national headquarters. **IBM** changed its structure from country-based to industry groups to transcend boundaries. Competition continues to increase across country markets, and product life cycles shorten to the point where the company needs continual innovation. At this point, the company has to begin competing on a global scale, sourcing every input in a lowest-cost environment and providing "state of the art, top quality products and services."[16] In this stage, we need "transnationally competent managers," which Adler identified as managers who are culturally sensitive; they have "the ability to work with people of other cultures as equals."

Source: Adler, N. J., & Bartholomew, S. (1992). Managing globally competent people. *The Executive, 6*(3), 52–65.

WORK APPLICATION 16-3

Select a business, preferably one you work or have worked for, and describe its stage of globalization.

16-1   APPLYING THE CONCEPT

Stages in Corporate Globalization

Place the letter of the state of corporate globalization on the line next to the corresponding description of each firm.

a. domestic
b. international
c. multinational
d. transnational

____ 1. Our company exports our books to other countries through our website in America.

____ 2. Our company opened its third factory overseas to better serve our customers in those countries.

____ 3. Just because we only do business in one country doesn't mean we don't compete with global companies.

____ 4. Our company prides itself on not having any geographical boundaries or barriers, as we conduct business globally.

____ 5. We import tires from Japan and sell them in America.

Is HRM Different in Global Firms?

As you can see, the more a business moves toward corporate globalization, the more complex are its HRM needs. "To function effectively in a multicultural global business environment, individuals and organizations must be capable of adapting smoothly and successfully across cultural boundaries."[17] This means that as the organization expands beyond its original borders, employees need to learn to change their personal perceptions from a local focus toward a broader concept of society. They need to become capable cultural chameleons—able to change on the fly as necessary in order to interact with other employees, customers, vendors, and any other stakeholders—to manage the business. Yet, the evidence shows that this is one of the most significant weaknesses of individuals who have graduated with a business degree but have little work experience.[18]

Companies nearly always start out small and local—they have one shop or store in one town in a single country. If you remember back to Chapter 2 where we talked about organizational structure, when managing this "simple" organization structure, the complexity is minimal. Generally, all decisions are made by the boss. As we get larger and more complex, management in the organization has to change and adapt to that complexity by loosening up on centralized authority so that things can get done in a reasonable time frame.

Ultimately, in many industries at least, the company will consider international operations of some type to gain a competitive advantage over its competitors. And along with the creation of an international presence, the complexity of the firm goes up even more. This is the point at which HR must become a different and more complex department. International operations require us to rethink every major function in HRM. For example:

- *Staffing.* Home-country, host-country, and third-party employees all require different sourcing, training, disciplinary actions, and compensation and may require many other differences in management.
- *Training.* From orientation to culture and religion, to language problems and managing infrastructure, training will need to be modified. For instance, safety training will need to be provided in multiple languages in many cases, and it will have to be accomplished so as to comply with multiple country laws and regulations.
- *Employee and labor relations.* Different countries' laws concerning employee relations require HR to become competent in legal issues where the company operates. Many countries' labor laws are strongly oriented toward protection of the individual employee—much more so than in the United States—and the HR manager must become competent in all of these legal differences. In addition, cultural attitudes and national laws also affect when and how employees are disciplined.
- *Compensation.* Should the company pay local average wages, home-country average wages, or other wage levels? How do incentives work with employees from different cultures?

These are just a few of the many issues that must be taken into account as we move from a single-country business to a global firm. Throughout the rest of this chapter, you will learn more about global HRM functions.

LEGAL, ETHICAL, AND CULTURAL ISSUES

"If you see in any given situation only what everybody else can see, you can be said to be so much a representative of your culture that you are a victim of it."

—*US Senator S. I. Hayakawa*

Legal, ethical, and especially cultural issues also have to be examined by companies considering global operations. The HR department has responsibility for many of these issues, including international labor laws, organizational ethics policies, communication training, and cultural training—for both national culture adaptation and corporate culture orientation.

International Laws

As the company begins to operate in more than one country's market, the managers, including HR managers, have to ensure that the company complies with each country's legal requirements. In what areas does HRM need to adapt as we move more toward a multinational or transnational firm? The major HR laws tend to be in the areas of staffing, labor relations, and disciplinary action/termination. Let's look at a few examples that allow us to see the types of complexity involved in global operations.

CHINA[19,20,21]

- "Dispatch" workers (temporary or contract workers) are capped at 10% of total employment.

- Employers can include a noncompete clause in employment contracts but must pay the worker who leaves the company during the noncompete period.

- Government constrains both hiring and firing practices to a great extent. Employees can only be terminated for one of the identified statutory reasons (including criminal conduct, violation of company rules, corruption, etc.) or at the end of their employment contract. There is no employment-at-will.

- Severance must be paid to terminated employees in nearly all cases.

BRAZIL[22,23]

- Most labor relations are regulated by national laws; there is no employment-at-will.

- Employees have a right to 30 days of vacation per year.

- Overtime is required for more than 8 hours per day *or* 44 hours per week.

- A bonus is typically paid to all workers at the end of the year.

- Temporary workers can only be used as a general rule in two situations: to substitute for a regular employee on leave or during an extraordinary increase in workload. They can generally only be used for a maximum of 3 months.

GERMANY[24,25]

- Although negotiations for a minimum wage beginning in 2015 are currently occurring, wages are controlled for most workers by employee unions' collective bargaining agreements.

- "Temporary" workers must actually be temporary. The general limit is no more than 18 months.

- In terms of age discrimination, companies are allowed to use the fact that a worker is vested in their state pension to justify dismissal.

- Workers generally have protection against dismissal except in three cases: personal capability or health, misconduct, or redundancy (downsizing).

- "Works councils" elected by and acting on behalf of employees in nonunion environments negotiate various working conditions with employers.

As you can see from just these examples, employment and labor law in different countries is highly complex. Your organization will need to do significant research before moving operations into another country to avoid violating that country's labor laws.

US Law

You know that most organizations within the United States are subject to a variety of EEO laws. But are employees of foreign companies working in the United States subject to the same laws, and are employees of US companies operating in other countries subject to these laws? Again, the EEOC gives us guidance on these situations.

According to the EEOC,

> All employees who work in the U.S. or its territories . . . are protected by EEO laws, regardless of their citizenship or work authorization status. Employees who work in the U.S. or its territories are protected whether they work for a U.S. or foreign employer.[26]

So if you are in the United States or a US territory, you are covered by US EEO laws.

But what about Americans working outside the United States? According to the EEOC, "U.S. citizens who are employed outside the U.S. by a U.S. employer—or a foreign company controlled by a U.S. employer—are protected by Title VII, the ADEA, and the ADA." However, "U.S. employers are not required to comply with the requirements of Title VII, the ADEA, or the ADA if adherence to that requirement would violate a law of the country where the workplace is located."[27] Finally, if you are employed by a foreign company in a country other than the United States, the laws of that country would apply, so you would not have the protection of US EEO laws in such a case.

The United States also has a law specifically addressing corruption and bribery by US national companies while operating in other countries. The **Foreign Corrupt Practices Act** (FCPA) *bars US-based or US-listed companies from bribing foreign officials in exchange for business.* The FCPA also requires companies to keep accurate books and records concerning their foreign operations. However, it is sometimes hard to tell the difference between a legitimate business expense and a bribe.[28] So global companies need to clarify the difference in their code of ethics, top managers must set a good example, and penalties for unethical and illegal behavior must be enforced.

Remember that different countries have different employment laws that must be obeyed. So think about the complexity facing the HR executive working for a multinational company doing business in more than 100 countries! Thus, multinationals need HR legal specialists in each country.

SHRM

C:17
Foreign Corrupt Practices Act

International Ethics

Recall our discussion of ethics in Chapter 15 where we noted that ethics are based on societal values, principles, and beliefs. This creates some issues for businesses operating in multiple countries. Different countries' cultures have different values and beliefs and therefore will have different ethics—at least to some extent—as what is considered ethical in one country may not be considered ethical in another country. Whose ethical perception should be followed in situations where the values in one country conflict with those in another? How do employees know how they are expected to act?

The answer to the above question should be found in the company code of ethics. Remember that this code is the document that is used "to project the values and

Foreign Corrupt Practices Act Law barring US-based or US-listed companies from bribing foreign officials in exchange for business

beliefs of the organization to their employees." So, even though the company culture may not exactly match the culture of a country where they are doing business, the company has laid out a set of principles that employees can apply to a situation to determine whether they are acting ethically according to the organization's desires. But how does that word *culture* affect the employees in the company? Let's take a look.

National Culture

Recall that we discussed organizational culture in Chapter 2. All of that information also applies to national culture, but national culture is even more powerful in many cases. It is what people have known their entire lives, and like the old adage about a fish in water not knowing that there *is* any other possible environment, people who have lived their lives in one culture many times don't even realize that there *are* other options for values, beliefs, and culture. This view of the world is called **parochialism**—*a narrow-minded view of the world with an inability to recognize individual differences.* Managers in global organizations cannot survive with a parochial view of the world.

To be successful internationally, we must be sensitive to cultural differences.

SHRM

F:13
Cultural Competence

Differences in national culture influence the effectiveness of different managerial behaviors, so if you are going to have to manage in an international setting, you will need to understand the cultures that you are dealing with. For instance, singling out and praising an individual worker in Japan is tantamount to yelling at an American employee on the shop floor and telling them that the report they wrote looked like it was written by a third-grader. Japan, as a highly collectivist culture (we will discuss this momentarily), does not single out the individual for either praise or discipline in a public setting.

HOFSTEDE'S MODEL OF NATIONAL CULTURE. Let's look at the first way that we can classify country cultures in order to determine how to train managers to successfully work with employees in that culture—*Hofstede's model of national culture.*

LO 16-3

Identify and discuss the five dimensions of Hofstede's model of culture.

Geert Hofstede is a trained psychologist who was hired in the 1960s by IBM (at the time, one of the few really global companies in the world with about 100,000 employees in more than 70 countries) to help them identify cultural differences within countries where they operated.[29] His data allowed him to develop a model of national culture that is still widely used today. He identified five dimensions—each of which allows a country culture to be plotted along a continuum. Each dimension was measured on a scale of 0 to 100, with 100 being the highest exhibition of that dimension. (More countries were added to Hofstede's model in later years, resulting in some scores moving above 100.) Let's look at the dimensions of the model in Exhibit 16-2.

After reading through the exhibit, you are probably saying to yourself, "So what?" What is the value in knowing that Russian culture is oriented toward the short term, Japan is highly masculine, and India is moderately collectivist? The *value* in the model is in knowing how significant the differences are between two countries' cultures. The greater the difference in the two cultures on each of the dimensions, the more difficult it is to bring employees from one culture into the other. For instance, if you compare China and the United States, you will find that

SHRM

C:3
Individual Versus Group Behavior

Parochialism A narrow-minded view of the world with an inability to recognize individual differences

EXHIBIT 16-2   HOFSTEDE'S MODEL OF NATIONAL CULTURE[30]

1. *Power-Distance (low vs. high)*—The degree to which societies accept that inequalities in power and well-being among members of the society are the result of differences in their individual abilities, both physical and intellectual, and their social status. In societies where these inequalities are allowed to continue or even grow, we consider the society to be a high power-distance culture. In societies where the differential value of rich and poor, intelligent and less intelligent, manager and employee, is not an accepted part of the culture, we say that they exhibit low power-distance.

2. *Individualism (vs. Collectivism)*—The basis of this dimension is the degree to which individuals are integrated into groups. Individualist cultures value individual freedom and self-expression and believe that people should be judged on their personal achievements. Collectivist cultures believe that the group is the primary unit of value, and the individual only has value insofar as he or she assists the group in reaching its overall goals.

3. *Masculinity (vs. Femininity) or Assertiveness (vs. Nurturing)*—Hofstede used the terms *masculinity* versus *femininity* back in the 1960s. However, for political correctness, these terms have been changed to *assertiveness* versus *nurturing*. Masculine or assertive societies value performance/winning, assertiveness, competition, and success. Masculine societies value heroes and material rewards. Feminine or nurturing cultures, on the other hand, value relationships with others, interaction over winning, quality of life, and concern for others. So in a masculine society, you might see a sign saying "He who dies with the most toys wins," but a feminine option might be "The best things in life are free."

4. *Uncertainty Avoidance (high vs. low)*—Societies, like individuals, differ in their tolerance of risk. The uncertainty avoidance dimension "expresses the degree to which the members of a society feel uncomfortable with uncertainty and ambiguity." Societies that are high in uncertainty avoidance will make attempts to avoid uncertainty—at least as much as possible. Cultures with low uncertainty avoidance can tolerate significant risk within their society and will not spend as much societal effort to protect their citizens.

5. *Long-Term Orientation (vs. Short-Term Orientation)*—This dimension was not part of the original Hofstede model, but he added it after it became apparent that different cultures had differing concepts of past, present, and future. Cultures with a long-term orientation value saving, thrift, and persistence in working toward and reaching future goals. In cultures with a short-term orientation, we will see little intent to save for the future and a focus on immediate, or at least relatively quick, results.

Hofstede's dimensions with country examples:[31]

Low Power-Distance ← → **High Power-Distance**

Denmark (18)	Italy (50)	Panama (95)

Collectivist ← → **Individualist**

Colombia (13)	India (48)	USA (91)

Feminine/Nurturing ← → **Masculine/Assertiveness**

Sweden (5)	Turkey (45)	Japan (95)

Low Uncertainty Avoidance ← → **High Uncertainty Avoidance**

Jamaica (13)	Philippines (44)	Belgium (94)

Short-Term ← → **Long-Term**

Russia (10)	Singapore (48)	Hong Kong (91)

Source: The Hofstede Centre

China has high power-distance, low individualism, and a fairly low level of uncertainty avoidance and is long-term oriented. The United States is moderately low in power-distance and very high in individualism, has a moderate level of uncertainty avoidance, and is reasonably short-term oriented. This means that a manager coming from China to run a facility in the United States is going have some difficulty adjusting to the culture (unless they have previously been exposed to it) without significant culture-adaptation training by the organization. Similarly, putting employees from these two cultures together to accomplish any task is likely to fail unless they are given cultural training before working together. The HR department is typically charged with cross-cultural training of employees who will be working outside their native culture. (On a side note: If you ever get bored and want to watch a pretty good movie about extreme culture clash, watch a film from the 1980s called *Gung-Ho* with Michael Keaton. You will quickly see why cultural differences matter in business.)

GLOBE. As Hosftede's research became dated, Project GLOBE confirmed his dimensions are still valid today and extended and expanded his five dimensions into nine. The project includes hundreds of companies and includes more countries. GLOBE stands for *Global Leadership and Organizational Behavior Effectiveness*, and it is an ongoing cross-cultural investigation of leadership and national culture. The GLOBE research team uses data from hundreds of organizations in more than 62 countries to identify nine dimensions in which national cultures are diverse. See Exhibit 16-3 for a list of the dimensions with examples of country ratings.[32] Notice that some of the GLOBE dimensions have the same or similar names as Hofstede's five dimensions.

WORK APPLICATION 16-4

Give an example of cultural diversity you have encountered, preferably at work.

EXHIBIT 16-3 *GLOBE DIMENSIONS*

Dimension	LOW	MODERATE	HIGH
Assertiveness People are tough, confrontational, and competitive.	Switzerland New Zealand	Ireland Philippines	Spain United States
Future Orientation People plan, delaying to invest in the future.	Russia Argentina	Slovenia India United States	Netherlands Canada
Gender Differences People have great gender role differences.	Sweden Denmark United States	Brazil Italy	Egypt China
Uncertainty Avoidance People are uncomfortable with the unknown/ambiguity.	Bolivia Hungary	Mexico United States	Austria Germany
Power Distance People accept power inequality differences.	South Africa Netherlands United States	England France	Spain Thailand
Societal Collectivism Teamwork is encouraged (vs. individualism).	Greece Germany	Hong Kong United States	Japan Singapore
In-Group Collectivism People take pride in membership (family, team, organization).	Denmark New Zealand	Israel Japan United States	China Morocco
Performance Orientation People strive for improvement and excellence.	Russia Venezuela	England Sweden	Taiwan United States
Humane Orientation People are fair, caring, and kind to others.	Singapore Spain	United States Hong Kong	Indonesia Iceland

Source: Adapted from M. Javidon and R. J. House, "Cultural acumen for the global manager: Lessons from Project GLOBE." *Organizational Dynamics 29* (2001), 289–305.

16-2 APPLYING THE CONCEPT

GLOBE Dimensions

Place the letter of the dimension of cultural diversity on the line next to the statement exemplifying it.

    a. assertiveness

    b. future orientation

    c. gender differences

    d. uncertainty avoidance

    e. power distance

    f. societal collectivism

    g. in-group collectivism

    h. performance orientation

    i. humane orientation

_____ 6. The people seem to prefer sports like soccer and basketball to sports like golf and track-and-field.

_____ 7. Managers place great importance on status symbols such as the executive dining room, reserved parking spaces, and big offices.

_____ 8. Managers provide poor working conditions.

_____ 9. Employees get nervous and stressed when changes are made.

_____ 10. Incentives motivate employees to achieve high levels of success.

GLOBAL STAFFING

As you can see, operating a business on a global scale requires some complex sets of skills. How are we going to staff the organization with people who have both the ability and the desire to work in this type of environment? We will need to recruit people with a specific set of skills. We will also have to make some choices about what types of employees we are going to recruit, and from which countries. Then we will have to determine what training is necessary for them to be successful. These choices by the HRM can determine the success or failure of our global organization.

LO 16-4

Briefly discuss the Big Five personality traits in relation to international assignments.

Skills and Traits for Global Managers

Going back to Chapter 1, you probably remember that we identified four skill sets that managers need to have in various measures in order to be successful in their particular jobs. We noted that all "managers require a mix of technical, human relations, conceptual and design, and business skills in order to successfully carry out their jobs." In international assignments, all of these skill sets can differ from what a manager or employee would typically learn in order to do their job. The way work is carried out—for instance in a high power-distance culture where employees expect to receive and carry out orders without question—may affect the way a manager does their job, so an American manager going into a high power-distance culture would need different technical skills than normal. Certainly with multiple cultures, probably speaking multiple languages, in one location, managers will need very strong human relations skills, and even conceptual and design skills may need to vary from what the manager would consider "normal" in different cultures. And finally, as we have already noted, business skills can be significantly different due to the variance in laws, regulations, and business structures in different countries (think of the *keiretsu* and *chaebol* partnerships in some Asian countries).

But what else do we need to take into account before sending someone to another country to work with or manage others? Companies may want *previous international experience* in the employees that they are considering sending on assignments outside of their home country. The feeling is that people who have made the adjustment before will have an easier time adjusting to yet another environment. This is not always true, but it can help to have a history of living in different cultures. Culture shock (we will discuss this shortly) is thought to decrease as people are exposed to, and live in, multiple different cultures. This can be advantageous to both the individual and the organization because the individual can settle in and become more productive sooner if they do not have to learn how to behave within the culture.

We noted in Chapter 8 that it is sometimes necessary to evaluate *individual traits* when evaluating our employees. This is one of those cases where it is indeed necessary. "Personality traits have been widely regarded as among the most important potential factors leading to expatriate adjustment,"[33] so a global assignment is one situation in which we will need to attempt to assess the traits of the people we are considering sending to another country to live. Some very strong evidence says that expatriates will fit into a culture better if their personality traits match up well with the culture's most significant characteristics.[34]

Let's take a look at some of the information that we can get from the Big Five personality characteristics about ability to adapt to a different culture:[35,36]

- *Extroversion.* Some evidence shows that extroverts will have an easier time adjusting to a different culture. However, little evidence shows that extroverts are more effective in their work relationships. Extroverts are also less likely to terminate an international assignment early—which costs the organization a significant amount of time and money.
- *Openness to experience.* In most cases, people with high openness to experience will be able to adjust better to a foreign culture than those who are low on this scale.
- *Conscientiousness.* Conscientiousness apparently has little effect on a person's overall ability to tolerate international work assignments.
- *Agreeableness.* Agreeable individuals also tend to adjust to a new culture well. Again, people who are higher in this trait are less likely to terminate their assignment early.
- *Neuroticism (negative affectivity).* People high on this characteristic tend to have more trouble adjusting to living conditions that are different from home and, as a result, may have a stronger negative reaction to taking on an international assignment. Higher neuroticism is correlated with a higher likelihood of terminating the assignment early.

So you can quickly see that this is one case where we do need to take a person's personality traits into account because they have a direct impact on their ability to do the job.

Secondary only to the individual employee's traits are the personalities and *suitability of immediate family* who will accompany the employee. We have to consider the entire family when making an international assignment unless the assignment will be "unaccompanied," which means the family will not move with the employee. If they do accompany the employee, they will need to be assessed for suitability and disposition as well as being trained right along with the employee.

All of the assessment that we will accomplish prior to sending an individual on an international assignment is designed to identify the "fit" of the individual with the assignment. Remember that we also discussed *personality-job fit* and *person-organization fit* along with ability-job fit in Chapter 6. Personality-job fit and person-organization fit will need to be measured and analyzed in conjunction with a potential international assignment just as if we were hiring the person into the organization from the outside world. They will have to adapt to the organization and the job in a very different environment from the one that they are coming from, and there is a high risk of failure in the job if we don't do the analysis successfully.

Finally, *language ability* is something that may need to be taken into consideration. This will depend on the assignment, the difficulty of learning the language, the

WORK
APPLICATION 16-5

How would you assess your personality fit, family situation, and language ability in terms of an overseas assignment? Are you interested in working in another country? If so, in which country(ies) would you like to work?

SHRM

F:5
Language Issues

benefits of language training, and other considerations, but we do have to at least identify the possible need for the employee to speak the native language of the people in the assignment location.

Staffing Choice: Home-, Host-, or Third-Country Employees

Our next consideration is where we will source the individual from for an international assignment. We have three generic options, each of which may be the best in some circumstances:

LO 16-5

Briefly identify the advantages and disadvantages of parent-country, host-country, and third-country nationals for international assignments.

- *Parent- (home-) country nationals*—People who work for the organization in the country where the organization is headquartered
- *Host-country nationals*—People who live in a different country where a work assignment will take place
- *Third-country nationals*—People who happen to have a skill set needed for an international assignment but who are not citizens of either the home or host country

Which one we choose is probably driven by the general approach that we choose in managing the organization. These approaches are (1) ethnocentric, (2) geocentric, or (3) polycentric.[37] *Ethnocentric* organizations tend to believe that their values and culture are superior to others, and they will therefore frequently choose to staff international facilities with home-country managers. *Polycentric* firms will generally emphasize adapting to local culture and practices and will generally choose to use host-country employees. Finally, *geocentric* businesses believe in managing globally, using the best people no matter where they are located, and therefore will usually choose to mix in third-country nationals along with parent- and host-country employees.

Each of the three staffing options has advantages and disadvantages.[38] Let's identify what you might need to know in order to consider each option in Exhibit 16-4.

Outsourcing as an Alternative to International Expansion

As an alternative to expanding the home organization, outsourcing is one way in which organizations can manage work without creating a direct international subsidiary. **Outsourcing** *is the process of hiring another organization to do work that was previously done within the host organization*. In quite a few cases, the organization to which we outsource a particular process will be located in another country. In

Outsourcing The process of hiring another organization to do work that was previously done within the host organization

---

16-3 APPLYING THE CONCEPT

Global Staffing

Place the letter of the type of staffing on the line next to each example statement.

   a. ethnocentric
   b. polycentric
   c. geocentric

_____ 11. I work for the American company **GM**, but I live in China and have been promoted to a management position.

_____ 12. I work for the Japanese company **Toyota**, and they are sending me to America to fill a high-level management position.

_____ 13. I'm French, but I work for American **IBM** in England, and they are sending me to work in Germany.

_____ 14. I'm American and work for US **Google**, and I've already worked in two different European countries, and now they are sending me to China.

_____ 15. I'm Australian and work for an Australian company, but I am looking forward to my transfer to work in America.

	EXHIBIT 16-4 ADVANTAGES AND DISADVANTAGES OF PARENT, HOST, AND THIRD-COUNTRY NATIONALS		

	Parent-country	Host-country	Third-country
Advantages	– Generally have a better understanding of the organization, strategy, structure, and culture of the business – Allows managers to gain international experience – More effective communication with parent-country management	– Minimizes language and culture problems – Compensation is generally easier and is based on local pay scale – Less expensive than moving someone to the country – Better understanding of local business laws, culture, and customs	– Can hire the best talent from wherever they are located – May be less expensive than either parent- or host-country managers – May be more advantageous than parent-country managers due to similar culture and/or language with host
Disadvantages	– Language differences may be a problem – Compensation may be more of a problem than with host-country nationals – Country culture may create barriers to success for employee and family – Income and other tax rules can be complex	– Company culture and ways of doing business may create problems – May create more problems communicating with the parent office – Loyalty to the country may outweigh loyalty to the company	– Still may have company culture and business process issues – Host-country government may create barriers to third-party managers – Income and other tax rules can be complex

Source: Dörrenbächer, C., Gammelgaard, J., McDonald, F., Stephan, A., & Tüselmann, H. (2013). Staffing foreign subsidiaries with parent country nationals or host country nationals? Insights from European subsidiaries (No. 74). Working Papers of the Institute of Management Berlin at the Berlin School of Economics and Law (HWR Berlin).

this case, the outsourcing is often referred to as *offshoring*. This can have the effect of lowering the number of employees in the home-country organization and as a result lowering the cost of managing the human resources within that company. **Nike** doesn't own any manufacturing facilities—all its manufacturing is outsourced.

On the other hand, in the United States and many other developed countries, there has been a recent governmental push to return jobs that have been offshored to the home country. This is called onshoring (you may also see the terms *inshoring* and *reshoring*). **Onshoring** *is the process of shuttering operations in other countries and bringing work back to the home country* to increase employment there. In some cases this onshoring makes sense, but in others it may not. However, it is also an ethical question in the minds of a significant number of home-country citizens.

The ethical question in each of these cases first involves the potential for job loss or gain within the home organization because of shipping jobs overseas. In the case of offshoring, the organization may cut entire divisions' worth of employees and send that work to the offshore organization. Many US firms did this with customer service operations in the early 2000s, but you may also recall that several high-profile failures occurred in offshoring, such as Dell moving several thousand jobs back to the United States in 2003 after significant customer complaints about support. Secondarily, companies have to be concerned with doing what is best for their shareholders and in fact have a fiduciary responsibility to do so. As a result, even when there is pressure from governments to reshore jobs, companies have to consider this option very carefully before taking that step. Most **Apple** products are made in China, but Apple has agreed to make some of its products in the United States.

SHRM
K:B14
Outsourcing

SHRM
0:7
Offshoring/Outsourcing

SHRM
0:6
Inshoring

Onshoring The process of shuttering operations in other countries and bringing work back to the home country

SHRM

0:3
Cross-Border HR Management

DEVELOPING AND MANAGING GLOBAL HUMAN RESOURCES

Once we have determined that we are going to expand internationally, we need to ensure that our employees will be able to successfully integrate into another country culture and complete their assignments. We need to select the right types of individuals, train them appropriately, and support them during their international assignments. Finally, we will have to make sure that they reintegrate into the home-country operations once they return from the assignment. Let's look at some details on how we can do that.

Recruiting and Selection

We mentioned the problems companies are currently facing with finding knowledge workers in Chapter 1. This continuing issue is causing more and more companies to source employees, including managers from wherever they can find them. If they have to build a facility in another country to find enough of these workers, then that is what they will do. Historically, advanced companies operated out of advanced economies—what we generally call the developed countries. Talented people from these advanced companies were called on to leave their home country in order to establish, or work in, a plant in another country where less expensive but less skilled labor was available. However, in today's world economy, where those low-skilled jobs are going away and we are constantly searching for knowledge workers, we have seen a shift to sourcing skilled employees from any country where they can be found and moving them to the locations where they are most needed. Many of the "lesser-developed economies," such as the *BRIC economies* (Brazil, Russia, India, and China), are now developing at a rapid rate and have become *sources* of talented knowledge workers, where 10 years ago they were importing skilled talent to these countries.[39]

So, companies are now sourcing managerial and technical talent from offshore.[40] Social media tools are one method that we are now using to reach these knowledge workers worldwide. LinkedIn may very well be the leading source for such talent searches. But what processes are we using to recruit and select this talent? Both recruiting and selection follow the same basic steps that we outlined for you in Chapters 5 and 6, but we have to take particular care in a few areas. Let's take a quick look at *negotiating the assignment*, including *individual tax issues* and *relocation costs*.

- *Negotiating the assignment.* This is a bit more complex in an international recruiting and selection process. We need to make the offer in the same way we discussed in Chapter 6, but we also have to negotiate compensation differently than we ordinarily would (we will discuss this in the next major section), the length of the assignment and repatriation (we will also discuss this shortly), allowances for relocation to and from the assignment, housing arrangements, family accompaniment, income and other individual tax issues, and potentially several other items. So the negotiation process will necessarily be longer and more detailed.

- *Tax issues.* Taxes are one of the more complex parts of international assignments. Where will the employee pay taxes—in their home country or in the country where they are assigned? This isn't an individual choice. It is set by the laws of the country where the individual works, as well as sometimes by laws in their home country. So to avoid unnecessary harm to the employee, we have to assist them in developing a tax strategy for the duration of the assignment.

- *Relocation costs.* Relocation costs including housing can also be difficult when moving to certain locations. There may not be enough housing, or it may be prohibitively expensive (think of the cost of living in Hong Kong, where a one-bedroom apartment runs $2,000+, or Singapore, where a similar apartment would cost $2,900).[41] Housing may also be substandard in some areas unless a premium price is paid. So we may have to have company housing or have contracts with local firms that will house employees for a set fee. The key is that these issues must be negotiated up front. Now let's see what we need to do to prepare our employee for the move.

Expatriate Training and Preparation

Carlos Ghosn, the CEO of **Renault-Nissan Alliance**, said in a recent interview:

> You have to know how to motivate people who speak different languages, who have different cultural contexts, who have different sensitivities and habits. You have to get prepared to deal with teams who are multicultural, to work with people who do not all think the same way as you do.[42]

An *expatriate is an employee who leaves their home country to go work in another country.* As discussed, they can be home-, host-, or third-country employees. The cost of expatriates is very high, so we have to carefully select and develop these human resources.[43]

CULTURAL TRAINING. So global competencies are becoming necessary for expatriates in the workplace, and as demand for these competencies increases, companies have to create and apply a set of tools to help prepare their employees for international assignments. Preparing employees for expatriate assignments will primarily be a training process, and the biggest training issue will usually be cross-cultural training. Why is cross-cultural training necessary? *Culture shock* can occur when we move from one culture to another. This culture shock can cause significant problems for the expatriate employee, and in fact there is evidence that up to 50% of employees fail to complete their international assignment, with the major reason being an inability (on the part of the employee or family members) to adapt to cultural differences.[44] This inability to adapt may be because the parent company does not support the employee and family members in learning the culture that they will have to live in for an extended period of time.[45] Alternately, it may be due to a bad selection process, as we noted above in the section on personality traits.[46] Regardless, culture shock is one of the main reasons for early termination of an international assignment. But what is culture shock? Let's look at a diagram in Exhibit 16-5 to help explain.

If you take a look at the diagram, you will see that at about 4 to 6 months into an international assignment, many people actually become depressed because they don't understand the culture that they have been forced to live in. This leads to hostility toward the culture, which can also cause significant behavioral changes in the employee and may make it difficult or impossible for them to interact with others in order to do their job successfully. As a result, we may have to end up bringing the employee home before the end of their assignment. This problem of serious culture shock can be mitigated, though, through cross-cultural training before the assignment begins. If people know what to expect and have some training in how to adapt, the problems associated with hostility and depression can be lessened. They will *not* go away, but they can be lessened, and this lessening may be enough to allow employees to ultimately adapt and be able to finish their assignment. "Effective pre-departure training is essential to support the employee to adapt to a new culture and country—as well as a new job."[47]

COMMUNICATION TRAINING. A second type of training that is frequently required is communication training. Both language training and other communication training (verbal, nonverbal, and symbolic) may be needed before sending an employee on

SHRM

0:2
Managing Expatriates in Global Markets

LO 16-6

Explain the potential effects of culture shock on the expatriate employee.

SHRM

0:9
Cross-cultural Effectiveness

Expatriate An employee who leaves their home country to go work in another country

EXHIBIT 16-5 CULTURE SHOCK

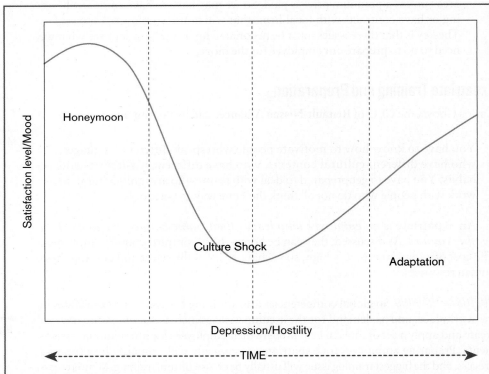

Honeymoon phase (approximately the first 1–3 weeks). Everything is interesting and new. It is exciting to be in a new country, and you feel like you are on an adventure.

Culture shock (month 1–3, or longer). The initially interesting and new things that you recently saw are now annoying. Why can't they do things the same way as they are done at home? You are frustrated by simple everyday things like going to the store or the bank, driving or commuting rules and procedures—and *what's that smell?*

Depression or hostility (month 4–7+). You are frustrated constantly with how different things are. You may even be depressed and not want to go outside and interact with people. You may avoid doing anything that requires that you involve yourself in the culture of the country.

Adaptation (month 7+). You start to accept the cultural norms and can interact with others successfully. You are now accustomed to the way things are done and the normal way to act in common situations. You feel "normal" in your everyday activities.

assignment. As we noted in Chapter 10, communication is sometimes difficult even when everyone is speaking the same language. It becomes much more difficult when there is more than one language being spoken and also when you have different nonverbal and symbolic cues based on two different cultures. Verbal communication is obviously the language being used, and nonverbal communication includes things such as hand gestures, facial expressions, and other forms of body language, all of which vary based on culture. So individuals need to be trained on how to manage their body language and other nonverbal cues.

But what is symbolic communication? It is communication using items that we surround ourselves with. It can be a type of clothing or hat; it can be a crucifix necklace; it can be jewelry or body piercings, or even the type of vehicle that you drive. Everything that we surround ourselves with that then conveys meaning to others is part of symbolic communication, and it can have very different meanings in different cultures. You would not want to have a visible crucifix in many Muslim countries. If you drive a large SUV in other countries, you may be considered to be a drug dealer or worse. So our employees need training on the various forms of communication.

OTHER EXPATRIATE ISSUES. Other key problems associated with expatriate employees include the following:

- *Reporting structure.* Who will the employee report to in both the host country and at home?
- *Performance management process.* Will host-country or home-country managers complete the performance appraisal and manage the employee's performance during the assignment?
- *Mentoring.* Will they have a host-country mentor to assist with cultural adaptation?
- *Other support.* What other support will be available during the assignment?
- *Repatriation.* What assistance will be provided upon completion of the assignment and repatriation to the home country?

This last question is our next topic.

Repatriation After Foreign Assignments

Would you care to guess what is likely to happen after a lengthy international assignment when an individual (and possibly their family, too) returns to their home country? You probably guessed right. They are going to go through another culture shock. The same adjustment will be necessary as they return home, because they have adapted to another culture and other ways of doing everyday things. So reacculturation training will most likely be necessary.

Repatriation generally should include a series of steps that need to occur in order to get the employee back into the home-country work routine. These items include the following:[48, 49]

- Reentry training, including cultural training (things change in several years—even if you are moving back to your home culture!)
- Job placement into a position commensurate with the employee's level of expertise and that will use their knowledge, skills, and abilities developed during their assignment in the host country
- Possibly mentoring assistance and other support to help the returning employee reintegrate quicker and more successfully
- A show of appreciation for the employee's international service and facilitation of knowledge transfer to others who may benefit from a better understanding of the host country and its culture

Repatriation is a critical activity because there is strong evidence that there are high levels of voluntary turnover of repatriates once they complete their international assignments and return to the home office. Because the process of preparing expatriates and sending them to another country is a significant expense for the organization, we need to improve the odds that our newly returned employees will stay with the firm once they do return.

SHRM

0:4
Repatriating Employees Post International Assignment

Foreign assignments help develop international business skills.

Jupiterimages/Goodshoot/Thinkstock

16-4 APPLYING THE CONCEPT

Global Compensation

Place the letter of the type of compensation on the line next to the corresponding example.

a. balance sheet
b. split-pay
c. negotiation
d. localization
e. lump sum

_____ 16. I'm going overseas for a 6-month assignment, and they are giving half the money in US dollars and half in euros.

_____ 17. I'm going overseas for a 6-month assignment, and they are paying me in the other country's currency, the euro.

_____ 18. I'm going overseas for a 6-month assignment, and they are continuing to pay me in euros, but they are also giving me a US dollar allowance for the higher cost of living in New York.

_____ 19. I'm going overseas for a 6-month assignment, and we are having a meeting to discuss my compensation for while I'm away.

_____ 20. I'm going overseas for a 6-month assignment, and they are giving me one check to pay for the entire time I'm away.

LO 16-7

Briefly define the options for compensation of expatriate workers.

WORK
APPLICATION 16-7

Assume you were going to become an expatriate. What questions would you have about your pay, and which pay method would you want to have?

COMPENSATING YOUR GLOBAL WORKFORCE

The obvious first question about compensation in a global environment is whether compensation in various countries needs to be different and, if so, why and how do we compensate a global workforce fairly. In this section, let's discuss the components of a compensation system we discussed in Chapters 11 to 13 (pay, incentives, and benefits) as they relate to a global workforce.

Pay

Do we need to compensate differently globally? The answer is "Of course," and the reason is that each country has a different standard and cost of living. Therefore, if we want to keep high-quality managers and workers in our organization while asking them to work in various countries around the world, we need to compensate them fairly. But what is fair? Is it fair to take a manager from a high-cost country and send them to a location that has a lower cost of living (United States to China), and once there lower their pay to match the local norm? If you were the manager, would you accept this?

Conversely, if we bring a manager from a low-cost economy to a higher-cost environment, we probably need to increase their pay to match the country or region in which they will be working. However, if we return them to their home country or location, should we lower their pay back to the original rate? Another question concerns the currency in which the employee will be paid. Should we pay our employees in their home currency, or should we pay them in the local currency where they are assigned?

As you can see, compensation of a global workforce becomes pretty complex very quickly. Let's discuss some options for paying expatriates.

BALANCE SHEET APPROACH. One of the common methods to manage expatriate compensation is called the *balance sheet approach.* Using the balance sheet approach, the organization continues to pay the individual at a rate equivalent to their home-country salary while providing allowances during an overseas assignment to enable that employee to maintain their normal standard of living. Obviously, this is only necessary when an individual is moving to a higher-cost environment and out of their home country.

SPLIT-PAY APPROACH. A variant on the balance sheet approach is to use *split pay*.[50] In fact, about half the organizations in a recent survey said that they use split pay as part of their compensation strategy.[51] Split pay is a process where the organization pays the individual partly in home-country currency and partly in the currency of their work location. This allows the individual to lower currency exchange rate risks in moving money from one location to another and to pay obligations in both their home location and their work location much easier than if all their pay were in one currency.

Compensating the global workforce makes the HRM process more complex.

OTHER APPROACHS. Other options for compensating employees on international assignments include a *negotiation approach*, where the employer and employee mutually agree on a compensation package; a *localization approach*, where the expatriate's compensation is based on local (host-country) norms; and a *lump sum option*, which pays the expatriate a lump sum of money to use on items such as taxes, vehicles, housing, and similar items during their assignment.[52]

Compensation in an environment where workers are operating all over the world is a very difficult process. However, HR must play a part in the analysis and implementation of a compensation system that will allow the company to attract and retain high-quality managers and employees for their facilities. The only way to do this, based on our discussions of operant conditioning and reinforcement as well as equity and expectancy theories, is to provide reasonable and fair returns to those employees for the job that they do.

Incentives in Global Firms

Effective global leaders are a vital asset that can offer a competitive advantage within organizations today.[53] Former CEO Mike Duke of **Walmart** said that his biggest challenge was to continue to develop the leadership talent to grow the company around the world.[54] But do incentive programs work the same worldwide? The answer, briefly, is "No, but they are becoming more similar over time." In fact, in some emerging-market countries, variable pay is a higher proportion of overall compensation than in most developed markets.[55] However, in other countries, variable pay still has negative connotations, especially as an *individual* incentive. Many countries' cultures do not mesh well with individual incentive programs, and some do not readily accept even group incentive programs.[56]

One study of two cultures notes that "many multinational companies have 'exported' their human resource practices overseas," but some studies "have revealed that people in different cultures prefer different means of reward distribution." This study analyzed the United States (an individualistic society) compared to Hong Kong (a collectivist culture) and determined that "people in a collective culture more readily relate individual contributions to group performance and they also appreciate linking rewards with group performance."[57] There are many other studies that relate similar information concerning the effectiveness of incentive pay across the globe. The main thing that compensation professionals need to understand is that we cannot provide the same types of incentives to employees regardless of the organizational and country culture and structure. We have to understand the function of "significance" in expectancy theory and always make sure that our system rewards are significant and acceptable to our employees.

WORK
APPLICATION 16-8

Assume you were going to become an expatriate. Would you prefer straight salary or to have incentives? What type of incentive would entice you to take an overseas assignment?

SHRM

K:B11
Global Employee Benefits

Benefit Programs Around the World

If we just think about it, benefit programs must adapt to the part of the world in which our employees work and live. For one thing, some countries mandate certain benefits that are not required in other countries, and we have no choice but to offer them. In other cases, the living conditions may be such that different benefit packages just make sense. Let's take a look at some examples of differences that we might see in benefit programs in other parts of the world.

Due to government laws, companies in many of the European Union countries have to provide more benefits than in the United States. One of the most significant factors in international benefits management has been the worldwide recession that put pressure on both governments and companies to reduce their expenses. Because of these cost pressures, governments started looking at reducing the benefits that they provided to workers in their countries, especially for retirement programs and health care. Companies also felt the same cost crunch around the world and are constantly looking at ways to cut their expenses while still providing the benefits necessary to attract and retain top-quality employees.

Retirement benefits vary among countries, with some governments providing a strong centralized retirement system (Australia is a good example) and others providing very little in the way of centralized retirement planning and savings. Even in countries where there is a strong central government plan, most employees are concerned that they have not saved enough for retirement. In a survey that included employees in five countries—Australia, Brazil, India, Mexico, and the United Kingdom—in every country "outliving retirement money" was one of the top three worker concerns.[58] One reason for this is that people are living longer today than ever before—all across the globe. Another issue is that in most countries, the population is planning on retiring at an earlier age than has historically been the case. In most cases, workers plan to retire in their 60s or earlier.[59] This combination of living longer and retiring earlier is creating the potential for a gap in retirement plan funding. More and more companies are working with employees to narrow this gap through a series of options. Some are providing financial counseling to show workers how much they need to be saving for retirement, and others are providing additional voluntary benefit programs where the employee can fund additional retirement accounts that will help fill the gap in their current retirement plans.

A significant trend is the move by companies toward offering more, and a larger variety of, voluntary benefits that are fully paid by the employee, instead of the employer providing at least part of the money to cover the cost of such benefits. In Brazil, for example, almost a third of female employees expressed interest in accident and pension funds for which they would pay 100% of the cost. Likewise, in Mexico, 56% of workers said that they would like a wider choice of voluntary benefits, and about one fourth said that would pay the *full cost* for life, disability, and health insurance.[60]

Even if there are some significant differences in benefit plans around the world due to differing government policies, the consensus is that a good benefit package is a powerful force in employee satisfaction and retention—and employees globally like flexible benefits so that they can choose the benefits they want and need the most. Employers worldwide would be well served to start formal communications with their employees to find out what types of benefits will best serve to improve satisfaction and retention in their organizations.

TRENDS AND ISSUES IN HRM

In our last "Trends and Issues" section, we will take a look at a couple of globalization issues. The first issue is whether or not globalization is a fading trend and what managers need to do about it. The second is how labor organizations are increasingly affecting employee relations in the global environment. So let's get to it.

Globalization of Business *Is* a Trend!

We have been talking about the effect of globalization on HRM for an entire chapter now, but is it really all that important to the companies that *you* will be working for? The evidence says that it is. *Forbes* magazine noted that "the major cause of [business model] disruption is the rapid advancement of technology and globalization, which allows new business models to be introduced at an ever-increasing rate and with rapidly declining costs."[61] A recent Deloitte Consulting report also notes that the BRIC economies "collectively quadrupled their GDP" in the first decade of the 21st century, compared to an 18% increase in the United States and the United Kingdom and an increase of less than 10% in Germany and Japan.[62] So globalization of production of both goods and services is increasing at a massive rate.

At the same time, though, evidence is also pretty strong that some developed countries are retrenching a bit when it comes to international operations. Governments are putting pressure on business to reshore some of their operations after the recession of 2007–2008, and global trade has actually shrunk to just over half of what it was as a percentage of global GDP before the recession occurred.[63] In fact, in a 2013 survey, a majority of large manufacturers said that they are planning to reshore at least some production jobs back to the United States.[64] At the same time, instability of some countries has made doing business in those locations much more risky, so there is evidence of some companies pulling back here as well. But don't think global business is going to go away anytime soon. Even with retrenchment of businesses in the developed economies after the recent recession, 59% of 1,200 CEOs in another survey said that they plan to increase the number of their international assignments as part of their HR strategy.[65]

So the bottom line is that while companies may retrench some jobs back to their home countries, it appears that some production and service jobs will continue to be moved out of home countries to other locations around the world to take advantage of capital cost savings. This means that managers, including HR managers, are going to have to continue getting more capable in training and preparing employees for international assignments.

The Worldwide Labor Environment

In the global village, developing-country unionization is just beginning, and it is expanding quickly. For example, in China angry migrant workers have used the Internet to organize. China has 348 million users, which is more than the total population of the United States at around 309 million,[66] and it has 787 million mobile phones available to help workers organize. Workers at **Honda** plants went on strike and won big increases in compensation. Compensation has increased to the point where the United States and other countries, and even Chinese manufacturers, are outsourcing some production to other countries.[67] Let's take a quick look at a few countries around the world and how unions can affect work processes.

BRAZIL. As with many other South and Central American countries (as well as other countries all over the world), Brazil's labor regulations tend to favor the employee over the employer and provide strong protection for unions. This is in part a function of the history of the country, where privileged employers treated their workers unfairly for many years before a military intervention created the impetus for major changes in the labor laws in the country. In addition to labor laws favoring the employee, Brazil has also seen a significant increase in unionized workers in the past several years. The number of unionized workers stood at 18.35% in 2005, up from

16.73% in 2001.[68] Labor is also guaranteed the right to strike in the constitution, and labor agreements can either be in writing "or may be implied from the relationship between an individual and the company."[69] Labor laws in Brazil also require any disputes between management and workers "to be settled in labor tribunals rather than in the companies involved, so little space is left for direct negotiations between employers and employees."[70]

SOUTH KOREA. South Korea's basic laws concerning labor relations are similar to those in the United States. The South Korean Trade Union Act allows workers to organize, collectively bargain, and act in concert to achieve labor goals. However, for many years the government had direct control of the major labor union in the country. This is not so any longer, and as a matter of fact, South Korea recently passed legislation that allows multiple unions to represent different workers within the same organization. South Korean employers are concerned that relations with employees will deteriorate due to this multiple unions system.[71] About 10% of South Korea's workforce is currently unionized, but employers are worried that this will increase with the new law allowing multiple union representation.[72]

CZECH REPUBLIC. While the numbers of employees who are members of trade unions in the Czech Republic are high compared to most other countries, this number has been steadily declining since the early 1990s. In 1990, more than 80% of workers in the Czech Republic were trade union members. In 2004, the number had decreased to 22%.[73] Part of this decrease is probably due to the continuing transformation of the economy of the Czech Republic from a state-controlled economy (as part of the Soviet bloc) to an open economy vying for its place in world markets. Unions are fighting back, trying to recruit new members from the ranks of workers, but have so far had limited success. The country's trade unions are also currently fighting amendments to the labor code, which could weaken the unions' position as negotiators for workers in the country.[74]

FRANCE. While in many countries labor unions focus on worker rights and fair pay, French unions have historically played an active part in the political system of the country. Labor unions in France routinely directly advocate for candidates who are friendly to labor issues. At least partly because of this political activity, unions in France have been able to control the work environment in the areas of pay and benefits as well as work-life balance. Even though only about 5% of French workers are in trade unions, the unions and their supporters have been able to get laws passed at the national level that limit the organization's ability to vary such things as workload, working hours, part-time employment, and compensation.[75] Also, throughout the EU, labor has won greater benefits, including more paid vacation, than most employees get in the United States.

As we can quickly see from the sample of countries above, union influence affects relationships between labor and management in significantly different ways in different countries. For those working in a business that operates in multiple countries, these differences in labor laws will be significant. You may have to become well informed on the differing laws concerning labor relations and union representation in each of the countries in which your firm works.

••• CHAPTER SUMMARY

16-1 Identify and discuss the reasons for increasing business globalization.

The main reason is to increase business, which is aided by the world becoming a global village where goods, ideas, services, and knowledge flow freely across national borders, creating greater demand for products. Barriers to trade have been minimized compared to historical norms, even though there is a series of trade blocs that operate in multiple countries. Barriers to transportation, communication, and culture have also lessened. But the biggest reason for globalization is to remain competitive.

16-2   Discuss the stages of corporate globalization through which companies move from local to global operations.

The stages are domestic, international, multinational, and transnational. Domestic firms generally operate in one country's market. International firms operate in a few, typically similar countries' markets, primarily through importing and exporting. Multinational businesses start to source capital resources from wherever they are lowest cost, own operating facilities in multiple countries, and integrate their various country operations. Transnational firms compete on a global scale without boundaries or barriers, strongly integrating their operations to improve efficiencies and lower costs. They are also culturally sensitive.

16-3   Identify and discuss the five dimensions of Hofstede's model of culture.

Power-distance is the degree to which societies accept that people will have different power because of their abilities and social status. Individualist cultures believe in the value of the individual and judge the individual, while collectivist cultures believe that the group is the unit of value in society, not the individual. Masculine societies value performance, winning, competition, and success, while feminine societies value relationships between members and quality of life more than winning. High-uncertainty avoidance cultures will do whatever they can to minimize risks to members of the society, and low-uncertainty avoidance cultures will not try to mitigate these risks nearly as much. Finally, short-term societies focus on immediate or short-term outcomes, while long-term societies focus on saving for the future, thrift, and persistence.

16-4   Briefly discuss the Big Five personality traits in relation to international assignments.

Evidence shows that *extroversion* makes it somewhat easier to adapt to a new culture, and extroverts are therefore less likely to terminate an expatriate assignment early. People high on the *openness to experience* scale also adjust better to a foreign culture. There isn't much effect on ability to enter a different culture from being highly *conscientious*, but *agreeable* individuals do adjust to a new culture well and are less likely to terminate an assignment early. Finally, people high on the *neuroticism* scale tend to have trouble adjusting to a new culture and are more likely to terminate an international assignment early.

16-5   Briefly identify the advantages and disadvantages of parent-country, host-country, and third-country nationals for international assignments.

Parent-country members usually know the organization better, know the strategy and structure, and communicate better. However, language, compensation issues, cultural barriers, and national laws on income may be disadvantages. Host-country nationals present advantages with respect to the language, culture, compensation issues, and local laws and regulations, but they may not have the company knowledge that is needed, may be less loyal to the firm, and could have problems communicating with the home office. Third-country nationals allow us to hire the best person for a job and may be less expensive in some cases. They may also share a language or similar culture with the host-country office. Disadvantages include host-country laws concerning third-party employees, income and other tax rules, and potential lack of knowledge of company procedures and culture.

16-6   Explain the potential effects of culture shock on the expatriate employee.

People who suffer from culture shock go through four phases:

Honeymoon phase. Everything is new and interesting, and the job is an adventure.

Culture shock. Things start to bother the employee. They are more frustrated with everyday things like going to the store.

Depression or hostility. Constant frustration leads to anger and potentially depression, so the employee doesn't want to interact with local nationals and participate in the culture.

Adaptation. The individual starts to understand and accept the way things are done in this culture and feels reasonably normal acting the same way as the local citizens.

16-7   Briefly define the options for compensation of expatriate workers.

The *balance sheet* approach is one of the most common methods. This is where the employee is paid their home salary, but allowances are provided to "balance" the different costs associated with the overseas assignment. Another option is *split-pay*, where part of the compensation is paid based on the home-country norm and part is paid in the assignment-country currency to minimize exchange rate risk. We can also use a straight *negotiation* approach, where the compensation package is agreed to upfront; a *localization* approach, where compensation is based on the host-country standards; or a *lump sum* approach, where a set amount of money is given to the employee to use on unique expenses associated with an assignment to a particular country.

16-8   **Define the key terms found in the chapter margins and listed following the Chapter Summary.**

••• KEY TERMS

expatriate	onshoring	parochialism
Foreign Corrupt Practices Act	outsourcing	trade blocs

••• KEY TERMS REVIEW

Complete each of the following statements using one of this chapter's key terms:

1. _____ are groups of countries who form an association for the purpose of facilitating movement of goods across national borders.

2. _____ bars US-based or US-listed companies from bribing foreign officials in exchange for business.

3. _____ is a narrow-minded view of the world with an inability to recognize individual differences.

4. _____ is hiring another organization to do work that was previously done within the host organization.

5. _____ is the process of shuttering operations in other countries and bringing work back to the home country.

6. _____ is an employee who leaves their home country to go work in another country.

••• COMMUNICATION SKILLS

The following critical-thinking questions can be used for class discussion and/or for written assignments to develop communication skills. Be sure to give complete explanations for all answers.

1. Do you expect that globalization of business will continue to expand? Why or why not?

2. Is it fair to utilize the least expensive "capital resources," no matter where they come from? Why?

3. Is the use of a trade bloc simply another form of trade barrier that we shouldn't use? Explain your answer.

4. How should countries manage transnational firms that have no real home country, including with tax policies and employment laws?

5. How would you as the HR manager prepare another employee for managing the workforce in a transnational firm?

6. Do you agree or disagree that people all over the world are getting more similar in their desire for certain products and services? Is this a good or a bad thing?

7. Should tariffs and other trade barriers be increased in order to protect jobs in the home country? Why or why not?

Complete the Key Terms Review to test your understanding of this chapter's key terms.

8. The United States is one of only a few countries that has a law like the Foreign Corrupt Practices Act. Does it put us at a disadvantage as compared to other countries' businesses? If so, should it be repealed? Why?

9. Do you believe that Hofstede's culture model is accurate? If not, what would you change to make it more useful in training people to work in a different culture?

10. Is knowing the local language always necessary when working internationally? Why?

11. Who would you rather assign to manage a foreign office of *your* business? Would you rather have a home-country, host-country, or third-country national? Why?

12. Should companies reshore more jobs that have been moved overseas? What are the pros and cons of doing so?

13. Would you ever consider sending someone to work in another country without cultural training if you were the HR manager? If so, in what circumstances?

14. Have you ever spent more than 6 months in a foreign country? Did you feel culture shock? If so, what did you do to get over it?

15. Can you think of some instances where symbolic communication might be critical? Give examples.

16. Which option for compensation would you want if you were assigned by your company to work in another country? Why?

• • • CASE 16-1 IBM (I'VE BEEN MOVED) AT HSBC: KEEPING COMPENSATION COMPETITIVE WITH ECA INTERNATIONAL

HSBC is one of the world's largest banking groups by assets (and the leader in customer deposits, with more than $1 trillion), with HSBC Holdings owning subsidiaries throughout Europe, Hong Kong, and the rest of the Asia/Pacific region, the Middle East and Africa, and the Americas. All told, the company has some 7,200 locations in more than 80 countries. Its activities include consumer and commercial banking, credit cards, private banking, investment banking, and leasing. Its North American operations include HSBC USA, HSBC Bank Canada, HSBC Bank Bermuda, and Grupo Financiero HSBC in Mexico.[76]

With around 9,500 offices in 85 countries and territories, employee work and life balance satisfaction is an international enterprise and requires constant vigilance. Employees at HSBC are extremely consistent in highlighting the enormous benefits that the company's HR policies and work experiences bring to their careers. They indicate that the global nature of the bank brings tremendous international exposure to the role of employees at the bank, right from the start. "The makeup and strategy of the bank allows you to have constant exposure to interesting and complex international operations," explains one employee. "The best thing about this job is seeing how intrinsically linked the global economy is to everything that we do here at HSBC," says another. This also allows for endless international travel opportunities, with HSBC employees wayfaring to almost anywhere in the globe; they should expect to relocate at least twice in their career if they wish to climb the corporate ladder.[77]

Job mobility is an integral part of HSBC's operations, and tracking employee salaries is a key factor in their HRM success formula. HSBC typically pays its employees 5% above market value, with competitive firms such as JP Morgan Chase and Citibank paying only 3% above market.[78] Benefits include health insurance (medical, dental, vision), life insurance, retirement and savings programs including a 401(k) match, and other employee services including adoption assistance, time-off programs, and concierge services.[79] The challenge for HSBC then was how to ensure that they would continue to pay their employees a premium salary and benefits package worldwide, especially when employees are constantly being switched from one location to another where salaries and benefits may vary drastically.

HSBC quickly realized that such a large operation required expert advice and counsel. HSBC contracted with ECA International to design and implement a new assignment salary and benefits management system to help them with their 1,400 long-term assignees in 50 locations.[80] ECA is one of the world's leaders in the development and provision of solutions for the management and assignment of employees around the world. Their highly skilled teams help to ensure that businesses' international assignments operate efficiently and cost-effectively. Delivering data, expertise, systems, and support in formats that suit its clients, ECA's offer includes a complete "outsource" package of calculations, advice, and services for companies with little international assignment management experience or resource; subscriptions to comprehensive online information and software systems for companies with larger requirements; and custom policy and system development projects for companies that manage thousands of international assignees around the world.[81]

The key objectives of the project was to improve efficiency, accuracy, consistency, and transparency of calculation and data storage of salary and benefits information while reducing operational costs and allowing HSBC to react quickly to international opportunities. The new system needed to be able to incorporate all elements of HSBC's HR policies for consistency of application while accommodating the inevitable policy deviations experienced country by country, and it had to be accessible from HSBC's three regional hubs and be completely secure.

ECA's software team prototyped a new solution for HSBC based on ECAEnterprise, a comprehensive, data-populated, web-enabled salary and benefits calculator and database, and then developed the prototype in close collaboration with HSBC through a shared website. HSBC worked with both ECA's client services and software experts, who advised on both policy and technical matters, ensuring the system fulfilled HSBC's policy objectives and user needs.

On time and on budget, the customized, hosted version allowed for a seamless transition between the old and the new operating systems. At the time the new web-enabled tool became operational, users in all three of HSBC's hubs had been trained on-site by ECA staff.

Harry Lister, senior manager of benefits and international mobility, is pleased with the new system.

"HSBCEnterprise fulfills all of the business goals we set out to achieve," Lister says. "We can now calculate and store salary and benefits packages for all of the Group's international assignees efficiently and with a transparency that our previous legacy systems did not allow."[82]

Questions

1. Describe some of the ethical and legal issues HSBC should be cognizant of given the breadth of their international operation. What might be some key HR issues for this firm?

2. HSBC has numerous office locations and subsidiaries. What seems to be the firm's generic business strategy?

3. Given your answer to question 1, how does the firm's policy regarding employee travel, job mobility, and relocation support HSBC's generic strategy? Why?

4. HSBC is a global firm with nearly 9,500 offices in 85 countries. In such a large international operation, why would tracking employee salaries and benefits be such a key factor in the HRM success formula? How does this formula support the firm's generic strategy?

5. ECA develops and implements solutions for the management and assignment of employees around the world for global firms. What other HRM functions might be included in those services? Why?

6. HSBC has offices in the Middle East. What HR concerns might HSBC have regarding employees working in that particular region, especially expatriates?

Case created by Herbert Sherman, PhD, and Theodore Vallas, Department of Management Sciences, School of Business Brooklyn Campus, Long Island University

• • • CASE 16-2 THE GREAT SINGAPORE SALE AT JURONG POINT: FINDING AND RETAINING BARGAIN EMPLOYEES

Singapore is an island of 646 square kilometers, about the size of Chicago. It is located at one of the crossroads of the world. Singapore's strategic position has helped it grow into a major center for trade, communications, and tourism. In just 150 years, Singapore has grown into a thriving center of commerce and industry.[83] Shopping is second to eating as a national pastime in Singapore. The island has an outstanding range of products that are available in shopping malls, department stores, boutiques, and bargain stores. Avid shoppers love the annual Great Singapore Sale, which usually falls in June to July. It has become a legendary annual event for both Singaporeans and visitors alike. Wide ranges of goods, including designer products, are marked down to present a mighty shopping extravaganza. The bargains are genuine and definitely give value for money. Shoppers can also expect private events that are hosted by the distinguished Sotheby's, Christie's, Tresors, and Glerums & Bonhams and feature exclusive items, such as works of art and jewelry. Antique rugs and carpets can also be bought at a cheaper price during the Great Singapore Sale.[84]

Jurong Point Shopping Centre ("Jurong Point") is a leading suburban retail mall situated in the western part of Singapore. Strategically located next to Boon Lay MRT Station and Bus Interchange, Jurong Point serves as the gateway to the Jurong West industrial estate, Singapore's key educational institutions, and the residential population in the west. Jurong Point in 2014 is the largest suburban mall in Singapore, housing about 450 retailers and showcasing their products and services to 6 million visitors a month. The revamped Jurong Point houses a range of retail zones— expanded and revamped Ginza Delights, Mongkok, Rackets & Track, Korean Street, Malaysia Boleh, Takeaway Alley, Gourmet Garden, and many more. In addition, there are also a 67-bay air-conditioned bus interchange, 11 civic community tenants, and to top it all off, a 610-unit condominium nestled above the retail podium.

Jointly owned by Guthrie GTS Limited and Lee Kim Tah Limited, Jurong Point is poised to take a leap forward to be the "heart of a vibrant community, abuzz with activity and a passion for life, offering WOW experiences for one and all."[85] Jurong Point Shopping Centre has an HR staff of 3 employees who oversee 160 in-house staff with an additional 2,500 employees working for the mall's tenants. Singapore is seeing a growing number of mall projects as more foreign retailers enter the local market, with 13 new malls in the works and scheduled to open between 2014 and 2017. As competition heats up, existing retailers are seeking new and innovative ways to engage and retain their employees.[86]

HR at Jurong Point has launched a number of initiatives to attract the right talent into its fold. One of the most effective means has been the organization's in-house staff referral program, shares Sally Yap, senior HR and administration manager at Jurong Point Shopping Centre. "They receive cash incentives if the employee is confirmed after three months." Recruitment efforts do not stop at in-house and operational roles but extend to the tenants. The mall launched its own job portal in 2012 to help its tenants look for staff. It also runs regular recruitment fairs to attract suitable candidates. This additional help is especially valued by the mall's smaller shops that have resource constraints, shares Yap.

Jurong Point has also beefed up its service levels to keep its customers coming for more. One of the ways it achieves this is by conducting training programs for its tenants. Employees from the mall's various outlets are taken through bite-sized modules that focus on areas such as how to serve people better, personal grooming, and basic conversational English. The latter can be a barrier for some staff, so courses like these help them perform their daily tasks better, says Yap. "We treat our tenants like family. We won't be strong if they are not strong." The mall is also partnering with Singapore Polytechnic (SP) to offer a service training program for its retail and food-and-beverage staff. In this program, employees undergo 30 hours of training focusing on areas such as retail strategies and operations, visual merchandising, restaurant management and challenges, and menu design and pricing. Upon completion, course participants receive a joint certificate from SP and Jurong Point. "It's a sweetener that will encourage them to stay at Jurong Point," Yap says. "It adds value and enhances their employability."

Jurong Point is fully absorbing the cost of training and hopes to put 500 to 700 service staff through the program's 2-year pilot phase. It plans to extend it to the mall's full staff within the next 5 years. According to Yap, the customized training will focus on improving the productivity, emotional intelligence, and entrepreneurial mind-set of in-house and tenant staff.

Once employees are recruited and trained, an employee empowerment program sets the culture for the firm. A bottom-up team approach gives employees the freedom to work out the operational details with their teams. This makes decisions less hierarchical, and employees are also happier as they are not micromanaged, says Yap. Employees are not limited to the roles that they initially signed up for. If an employee in the operations department is interested in a marketing role, they can get a transfer when the right opportunity arises. This flexibility is appreciated by the organization's younger employees in particular. "They are more restless and don't want to be stuck at the computer doing mundane things. We are very open to doing things differently," says Yap.

The HR team at Jurong Point follows this ethos and takes a nontraditional approach to its role. It works very closely with other departments to push out new ideas and programs. It also serves as the umbrella HR organization for the mall's tenants and is actively involved in ensuring a consistent culture across the property. Interaction between departments is also encouraged through activities such as overseas trips. "Every department is represented by a team member, and it allows employees to bond outside of work," says Yap. Quarterly buffet lunches are organized to encourage employees to eat and mingle together while exchanging updates on the latest happenings. "We don't work in silos and like to come together to support each other," says Yap.[87]

Questions

1. Taubman Centers Inc. (TCO) is the owner, manager, and/or lessor of regional, super-regional, and outlet shopping centers in the United States and Asia. They are looking to extend their expertise to booming markets in China and South Korea. Assuming they wanted to break into the Singapore market, what international expansion strategies might they have relative to Jurong Point?

2. Assuming Taubman was to purchase Jurong Point, what legal and cultural issues must they address in order to facilitate a smooth ownership transition?

3. Given your answer to question 2, what global staffing issues would Taubman have to immediately address? Longer-term issues?

4. Human resources play a critical role in Jurong Point's competitive strategy. What HR functions does the small HR staff focus on? Why?

5. Jurong Point's HR staff outsources some of its functions to its tenants. What are those functions, and how does this HR strategy fit Jurong Point's generic strategy?

6. Organizational culture seems to be a distinctive competency for Jurong Point. What is their culture, and what HR policies nurture that culture? How might this culture change if Jurong Point were acquired by Taubman?

Case created by Herbert Sherman, PhD, and Theodore Vallas, Department of Management Sciences, School of Business Brooklyn Campus, Long Island University

Sharpen your skills with SAGE edge at edge.sagepub.com/lussierhrm2e

SAGE edge for students provides a personalized approach to help you accomplish your coursework goals in an easy-to-use learning environment.

• • • SKILL BUILDER 16-1 THE GLOBAL HRM ENVIRONMENT

Objective

To develop your global HRM awareness

Skills

The primary skills developed through this exercise are as follows:

1. HR *management skills*—Conceptual and design, and business skills

2. *SHRM 2013 Curriculum Guidebook*—Parts of multiple guides including Question 3—B: Employment Law, Question 4—F: Managing a Diverse Workforce, Question 5—I. Staffing: Recruitment and Selection,

Question 6—L: Training and Development, Questions 7 and 8—K: Total Reward, Question 9—C: Ethics

Assignment

For this exercise, select a company that conducts business as an MNC or a transnational global corporation, preferably one you work or would like to work for. You will most likely need to conduct some research to get the answers to the questions below, such as visiting the company's website and talking to HR professionals.

1. Explain the stage of corporate globalization.

2. List at least five countries it conducts business in and the trade agreements these countries participate in.

3. Identify some of the key differences in laws among the five countries.

4. Compare the company's nine GLOBE dimensions for the five countries it does business in. Make a chart similar to Exhibit 16-3: GLOBE Dimensions.

5. Explain how it recruits and selects expatriate employees.

6. Describe how it trains its expatriates and families.

7. Discuss the method(s) of compensation for its expatriates.

8. Compare the compensation (pay, incentives, and benefits) among the five countries.

9. Does the company have any specific code of ethics for conducting business in other countries, and if so, describe the code.

Your professor may or may not require you to answer all nine questions. You may be asked to pass in this assignment, present your answers to the class, and/or discuss your answers in small groups or online.

• • • SKILL BUILDER 16-2 CULTURAL DIVERSITY AWARENESS

Objective

To develop your global cultural awareness

Skills

The primary skills developed through this exercise are as follows:

1. *HR management skills*—Human relations skills

2. *SHRM 2013 Curriculum Guidebook*—F: Managing a Diverse Workforce

Assignment

Procedure 1 (4–6 minutes)

You and your classmates will share your international experience and nationalities. Start with people who have lived in another country, then move to those who have visited another country, and follow with discussion of nationality (e.g., "I am half French and half Irish but have never been to either country"). The instructor or a recorder will write the countries on the board until several countries/nationalities are listed or the time is up.

Procedure 2 (10–30 minutes)

You and your classmates will share your knowledge of cultural differences between the country in which the course is being taught and those listed on the board. This is a good opportunity for international students and those who have visited other countries to share their experiences. You may also discuss cultural differences within the country.

• • • SKILL BUILDER 16-3 THE MOST IMPORTANT THINGS I GOT FROM THIS COURSE

Objective

To review your course learning, critical thinking, and skill development

Skills

The primary skills developed through this exercise are as follows:

1. *HR management skills*—Conceptual and design

2. *SHRM 2013 Curriculum Guidebook*—The guide will vary with student answers

Assignment

Think about and write/type the three or four most important things you learned or skills you developed through this course and how they are helping or will help you in your personal and/or professional life.

You may be asked to pass in this assignment, present your answers to the class, and/or discuss your answers in small groups or online.

··· Appendix

SHRM 2013 CURRICULUM GUIDEBOOK

Required and Secondary HR Content Areas
(Reordered and numbered for reference)

The Society for Human Resources Management (SHRM), the world's largest Human Resource Management association, periodically puts out guidance on college and university curricula for human resource management (HRM) programs (what they think we need to teach you). The latest version of their guidebook is provided below for your information and use. This guidance provides information on what SHRM considers to be critical in the study of HRM. If you choose to pursue human resource management as a career choice, this information will help you with the process of certification through the Human Resource Certification Institute (HRCI) or through SHRM's new internal accreditation program. Even if you don't decide to pursue HRM as a career, this is the information that will be most pertinent to your success as a manager in any field of business.

It makes sense that an introductory textbook would introduce you to each of the areas that are critical in that field of study. As a result, in this textbook we've chosen to discuss all *"Required Content" for undergraduate HR programs* from the most recent version (2013) of the *Curriculum Guide*. As far as we know, no other introductory HRM textbook does this. This has been done to introduce you to each of the topics that SHRM considers to be critical. We have reordered the information from the SHRM curriculum guide to emphasize the required content first, and then the secondary and graduate content areas, but the content itself is identical to the guidelines from SHRM. You can call up the guide itself at http://www.shrm.org/Education/hreducation/Documents/2013_SHRM%20HR%20Curriculum%20Guidelines%20and%20Templates_View%20Only_FINAL.pdf.

This appendix is designed to link back to each of the chapters and identify where each of the required content areas is discussed within the textbook. When you see a box in the chapter titled *SHRM Guide*, it will have an alphanumeric reference. That alphanumeric reference ties to this appendix by Section (the capital letter) and Subtopic (the numeral). For example, if you see the box in the margin here, it would lead you to Section A (Employee and Labor Relations), Subtopic 5 (Employee Involvement). Next to each of the subtopics is the page number on which the topic is discussed. This should help if you are looking for information on a particular topic within the chapters.

━━━━━━ SHRM

A:5
Employee Involvement

REQUIRED CONTENT: UNDERGRADUATE CURRICULUM

A. Employee and Labor Relations

1. Disciplinary actions: Demotion, disciplinary termination [Chapter 9, p. 333]

2. Alternative dispute resolution [Chapter 10, p. 388]

3. Managing/creating a positive organizational culture [Chapter 2, p. 59]

4. Employee engagement [Chapter 1, p. 6]

5. Employee involvement [Chapter 1, p. 6]

6. Employee retention [Chapter 1, p. 10]

7. Managing teams [Chapter 9, p. 344]

8. Union membership [Chapter 10, p. 375]

9. Union-related labor laws [Chapter 10, p. 367]

10. Union/management relations [Chapter 10, p. 367]

11. Union decertification and deauthorization [Chapter 10, p. 380]

12. Collective bargaining issues [Chapter 10, p. 377]

13. Collective bargaining process [Chapter 10, p. 377]

14. Negotiation skills [Chapter 10, p. 385]

   Interdependence

   Mutual adjustment

   Cognitive biases

   Communication

   Conflict

   Value claiming

   Value creation

   Distributive bargaining

   Alternative dispute resolution: Negotiation, mediation, and arbitration

   Contract negotiation

   Framing

   Integrative negotiation

   International negotiation

15. Conflict management [Chapter 10, p. 382]

16. Grievance management [Chapter 10, p. 378]

17. Strikes, boycotts, and work stoppages [Chapter 10, p. 367]

18. Unfair labor practices [Chapter 10, p. 369]

19. Managing union organizing policies and handbooks [Chapter 10, p. 379]

20. Attendance [Chapter 1, p. 11]

21. Attitude surveys [Chapter 10, p. 364]

22. Investigations [Chapter 9, p. 331]

23. Posting requirements [Chapter 14, p. 534]

24. Promotion [Chapter 12, p. 442]

25. Recognition [Chapter 12, p. 455]

26. Service awards [Chapter 12, p. 454]

27. Employee records [Chapter 9, p. 321]

B. Employment Law

1. Age Discrimination in Employment Act of 1967 [Chapter 3, p. 88]

2. Americans with Disabilities Act of 1990 and as amended in 2008 [Chapter 3, p. 89]

3. Equal Pay Act of 1963 [Chapter 3, p. 84]

4. Pregnancy Discrimination Act of 1978 [Chapter 3, p. 89]

5. Title VII of the Civil Rights Act of 1964 and 1991 [Chapter 3, pp. 84, 92]

6. Executive Order 11246 (1965) [Chapter 3, p. 99]

7. Employer Retirement Income Security Act of 1974 (ERISA) [Chapter 13, p. 498]

8. Fair Labor Standards Act of 1938 (FLSA) [Chapter 11, p. 414]

9. Family and Medical Leave Act of 1993 (FMLA) [Chapter 13, p. 492]

10. Rehabilitation Act (1973) [Chapter 3, p. 89]

11. Labor Management Reporting and Disclosure Act of 1959 (LMRDA) [Chapter 10, p. 370]

12. National Labor Relations Act of 1935 (NLRA) [Chapter 10, p. 369]

C. Ethics

9. Compliance and laws [Chapter 15, p. 573]

10. Confidential and proprietary information [Chapter 15, p. 570]

11. Conflicts of interest [Chapter 15, p. 568]

12. Use of company assets [Chapter 15, p. 570]

13. Acceptance or providing of gifts, gratuities, and entertainment [Chapter 15, p. 570]

14. Abusive behavior [Chapter 14, p. 552]

    Workplace bullying

15. Sarbanes-Oxley Act of 2002 (SOX) [Chapter 10, p. 372]

    Whistle-blowers

    Fraud

16. False Claims Act [Chapter 10, p. 372]

17. Foreign Corrupt Practices Act [Chapter 16, p. 600]

D. HR's Role in Organizations

1. It is generally expected that faculty will discuss HR's role with regard to each of the individual HR disciplines whenever an individual discipline is taught. This may take the form of describing HR's role in developing human capital, its effect on the organization's success, or the interplay among the various disciplines—meaning how decisions in one HR discipline affect other HR disciplines. [Chapter 1, p. 18]

E. Job Analysis/Job Design

1. Job/role design (roles, duties, and responsibilities) [Chapter 4, p. 133]

2. Job evaluation and compensation (grades, pay surveys, and pay setting) [Chapter 11, p. 420]

3. Employment practices (recruitment, selection, and placement) [Chapter 6, p. 197]

4. Performance management (performance criteria and appraisal) [Chapter 8, p. 277]

5. Training and development [Chapter 7, p. 237]

    Vocational and career counseling

    Needs assessment

    Career pathing

6. Compliance with legal requirements [Chapter 3, p. 96; Chapter 11, pp. 417, 419; Chapter 14, p. 539]

    Equal employment (job-related-ness, bona fide occupational qualifications, and the reasonable accommodation process)

    Equal pay (skill, effort, responsibility, and working conditions) and comparable worth

    Overtime eligibility (exempt vs. nonexempt work)

    Ergonomics and workplace safety (work hazards and mitigation)

7. HR planning (skill inventories and supply/demand forecasting) [Chapter 4, p. 140]

8. Work management (work processes and outsourcing) [Chapter 4, pp. 123, 149]

9. Organization design (missions, functions, and other aspects of work units for horizontal and vertical differentiation) [Chapter 2, p. 56]

F. Managing a Diverse Workforce

1. Equal employment opportunity (EEO) [Chapter 3, p. 97]

2. Affirmative action (AA) [Chapter 3, p. 99]

3. Aging workforce [Chapter 15, p. 574]

4. Individuals with disabilities [Chapter 3, p. 90]

5. Language issues [Chapter 16, p. 605]

6. Racial/ethnic diversity [Chapter 3, p. 100]

7. Religion [Chapter 3, p. 107]

8. Reverse discrimination [Chapter 1, p. 31]

9. Sex/gender issues [Chapter 3, p. 103]

10. Gay, lesbian, bisexual, transgender (GLBT)/sexual orientation issues [Chapter 15, p. 574]

11. Glass ceiling [Chapter 15, p. 574]

12. Business case for diversity [Chapter 3, p. 101]

13. Cultural competence [Chapter 16, p. 601]

G. Outcomes: Metrics and Measurement of HR

1. Economic value added [Chapter 2, p. 66]

2. Balanced scorecard: HR and organization level [Chapter 2, p. 67]

3. Measuring absenteeism [Chapter 4, p. 143]

4. Measuring turnover [Chapter 4, p. 143]

5. Trend and ratio analysis projections [Chapter 4, p. 141]

6. Calculating and interpreting yield ratios [Chapter 5, p. 180]

7. Return on investment (ROI) [Chapter 2, p. 66]

8. HR scorecard [Chapter 2, p. 67]

9. Organizational scorecard [Chapter 2, p. 67]

10. Quantitative analysis [Chapter 4, p. 141]

11. Benchmarking [Chapter 11, p. 426]

12. Analyzing and interpreting metrics [Chapter 4, p. 141]

13. Forecasting [Chapter 4, p. 141]

H. Performance Management

1. Identifying and measuring employee performance [Chapter 8, p. 288]

2. Sources of information (e.g., managers, peers, clients) [Chapter 8, p. 293]

3. Rater errors in performance measurement [Chapter 8, p. 298]

4. Electronic monitoring [Chapter 8, p. 305]

5. Performance appraisals [Chapter 8, p. 287]

6. Appraisal feedback [Chapter 8, p. 302]

7. Managing performance [Chapter 8, p. 282]

8. Diagnosing problems [Chapter 9, p. 328]

9. Performance improvement programs [Chapter 9, p. 327]

I. Staffing: Recruitment and Selection

1. Employment relationship: Employees, contractors, temporary workers [Chapter 4, p. 148]

2. External influences on staffing: Labor markets, unions, economic conditions, technology [Chapter 5, p. 165]

3. External recruitment: Recruiters, open vs. targeted recruitment, recruitment sources, applicant reactions, medium (electronic, advertisement), fraud/misrepresentation [Chapter 5, p. 172]

4. Internal recruitment: Timing, open/closed/targeted recruitment, bona fide seniority systems [Chapter 5, p. 170]

5. Internal recruitment: Promotability ratings, managerial sponsorship, self/peer assessments, panels/review boards [Chapter 5, p. 170]

6. Initial assessment methods: Résumés, cover letters, application blanks, biographical information, reference/background checks, genetic screening, initial interviews, minimum qualifications [Chapter 6, p. 201]

7. Discretionary assessment methods [Chapter 6, p. 196]

8. Ability/job knowledge tests, assessment centers [Chapter 6, p. 208]

9. Noncognitive assessments (e.g., personality assessments, integrity tests, situational judgment tests, interest inventories) [Chapter 6, p. 206]

10. Structured interviews [Chapter 6, p. 212]

11. Contingent assessment methods: Drug testing, medical exams [Chapter 6, p. 208]

12. Measurement concepts: Predictors/criteria, reliability, validity [Chapter 6, p. 199]

13. Selection decisions: Ranking, grouping/banding, random selection [Chapter 6, p. 221]

14. Job offers: Employment-at-will, contracts, authorization to work [Chapter 9, p. 325]

15. Bona fide occupational qualifications (BFOQs) [Chapter 3, p. 87]

16. Employment brand [Chapter 11, p. 410]

J. Strategic HR

1. Strategic management [Chapter 2, p. 47]

2. Enhancing firm competitiveness [Chapter 2, p. 56]

3. Strategy formulation [Chapter 2, p. 53]

4. Strategy implementation [Chapter 2, p. 55]

5. Sustainability/corporate social responsibility [Chapter 1, p. 23]

6. Internal consulting (required for graduate students only) [Chapter 1, p. 17]

7. Competitive advantage [Chapter 2, p. 48]

8. Competitive strategy [Chapter 2, p. 46]

9. Ethics [Chapter 1, p. 23]

10. Linking HR strategy to organizational strategy [Chapter 2, p. 56]

11. Organizational effectiveness [Chapter 1, p. 8]

12. Trends and forecasting in HR [Chapter 4, p. 141]

13. Mission and vision [Chapter 2, p. 48]

14. Quality management [Chapter 2, p. 55]

K. Total Rewards

A. Compensation

1. Development of a base pay system [Chapter 11, p. 422]

2. Developing pay levels [Chapter 11, p. 425]

3. Determining pay increases [Chapter 11, p. 427]

4. Role of job analysis/job design/job descriptions in determining compensation [Chapter 11, p. 420]

5. Pay programs: Merit pay, pay-for-performance, incentives/bonuses, profit sharing, group incentives/gainsharing, balanced scorecard [Chapter 12, p. 448]

6. Compensation of special groups (e.g., executives, sales, contingent workers, management) [Chapter 11, p. 415]

7. Internal alignment strategies [Chapter 11, p. 406]

8. External competitiveness strategies [Chapter 11, p. 406]

9. Legal constraints on pay issues [Chapter 11, p. 420]

10. Monitoring compensation costs [Chapter 11, p. 408]

11. Union role in wage and salary administration [Chapter 11, p. 420]

12. Minimum wage/overtime [Chapter 11, p. 414]

13. Pay discrimination and dissimilar jobs [Chapter 11, p. 419]

14. Prevailing wage [Chapter 11, p. 426]

15. Motivation theories: Equity theory, reinforcement theory, agency theory [Chapter 11, p. 404; Chapter 12, p. 469]

B. Employee Benefits

1. Statutory vs. voluntary benefits [Chapter 13, p. 482]

2. Types of retirement plans (defined benefit, defined contribution, hybrid plans) [Chapter 13, p. 507]

3. Regulation of retirement plans (FLSA, ERISA, Pension Protection Act of 2006) [Chapter 13, p. 498]

4. Types of health care plans (multiple-payer/single-payer, universal health care systems, HMOs, PPOs, fee-for-service, consumer-directed) [Chapter 13, p. 502]

5. Regulation of health insurance programs (COBRA, HIPAA, Health Maintenance Organization Act of 1973) [Chapter 13, p. 497]

6. Federal insurance programs (Old-Age, Survivor, and Disability Insurance [OASDI], Medicare) [Chapter 13, p. 486]

7. Disability insurance [Chapter 13, p. 510]

8. Educational benefits [Chapter 13, p. 510]

9. Employee assistance/wellness programs [Chapter 14, p. 538]

10. Family-oriented benefits [Chapter 13, p. 482]

11. Global employee benefits [Chapter 16, p. 614]

12. Life insurance [Chapter 13, p. 509]

13. Nonqualified plans for highly paid and executive employees [Chapter 13, p. 499]

14. Outsourcing (secondary) [Chapter 16, p. 607]

15. Time off and other benefits [Chapter 13, p. 501]

16. Unemployment Insurance [Chapter 13, p. 491]

17. Wellness programs [Chapter 14, p. 538]

18. Financial benefits (gainsharing, group incentives, team awards, merit pay/bonuses) [Chapter 12, p. 456]

19. Managing employee benefits (cost control, monitoring future obligations, action planning, strategic planning) [Chapter 13, p. 482]

20. Domestic partner benefits [Chapter 13, p. 515]

21. Paid leave plans [Chapter 13, p. 501]

22. Workers' compensation [Chapter 13, p. 489]

L. Training and Development

1. Needs assessment [Chapter 7, p. 240]

2. Competency models [Chapter 7, p. 237]

3. Learning theories: Behaviorism, constructivism, cognitive models, adult learning, knowledge management [Chapter 7, p. 244]

4. Training evaluation: Kirkpatrick's model [Chapter 7, p. 254]

5. E-learning and use of technology in training [Chapter 7, p. 253]

6. On-the-job training (OJT) [Chapter 7, p. 251]

7. Outsourcing (secondary) [Chapter 7, p. 266]

8. Transfer of training: Design issues, facilitating transfer [Chapter 7, p. 256]

9. Employee development: Formal education, experience, assessment [Chapter 7, p. 260]

10. Determining return on investment (ROI) [Chapter 7, p. 257]

11. The role of training in succession planning [Chapter 7, p. 239]

12. Human/intellectual capital [Chapter 7, p. 259]

M. Workforce Planning and Talent Management

1. Downsizing/rightsizing (secondary) [Chapter 4, p. 145]

2. Planning: Forecasting requirements and availabilities, gap analysis, action planning, core/flexible workforce [Chapter 4, p. 140]

3. Retention: Involuntary turnover, outplacement counseling, alternative dispute resolution [Chapter 9, p. 335]

4. Retention: Voluntary turnover, job satisfaction, withdrawal, alternatives [Chapter 10, p. 363]

5. Retention: Measurement [Chapter 4, p. 143]

6. Labor supply and demand [Chapter 4, p. 143]

7. Succession planning [Chapter 4, p. 150]

REQUIRED CONTENT: GRADUATE CURRICULUM

N. Change Management

1. Stages of change management
   Indifference
   Rejection
   Doubt
   Neutrality
   Experimentation
   Commitment

2. Dimensions of change
   Culture
   Coaching
   Direction
   Communication
   Accountability
   Resilience

   Skills and knowledge
   Recognition
   Managing projects
   Involvement

3. Communication

4. Building trust

5. Creating a foundation for problem solving

6. Leading change

7. Planning change strategy

8. Implementing change

9. Coping strategies for employees

10. Adjusting to change within the organization

O. Globalization

1. Global business environment

2. Managing expatriates in global markets

3. Cross-border HR management

4. Repatriating employees post international assignment

5. Global security and terrorism

6. Inshoring

7. Offshoring/outsourcing

8. Global labor markets

9. Cross-cultural effectiveness

P. Internal Consulting

1. Assess customers' needs

2. Influence cross-departmentally

3. Identify areas for HR intervention and design intervention

4. Advise management and colleagues cross-divisionally

5. Analyze and recommend solutions to business problems

6. Analyze data and prepare reports to inform business decisions

7. Recommend changes for process improvement

8. Conduct periodic audits

9. Lead special and cross-functional project teams

Q. Organizational Development

1. Coaching

2. Developing human resources

3. Emotional intelligence

4. Equipping the organization for present and future talent needs

5. Improving organizational effectiveness

6. Knowledge management

7. Leadership development

8. Measurement systems

9. Ongoing performance and productivity initiatives

10. Organizational effectiveness

11. Organizational learning

12. Organizational structure and job design

13. Outsourcing employee development

14. Social networking

15. Succession planning

16. Training employees to meet current and future job demands

SECONDARY CONTENT

R. Corporate/Social Responsibility and Sustainability

1. Corporate philanthropy

2. Ethics

3. Diversity

4. Financial transparency

5. Employee relations and employment practices
   Participative decision making

6. Supply chain management

7. Governance

8. Community/employee engagement

9. Green management

10. The business case for CSR

11. Reputation and brand enhancement

12. Accountability and transparency

13. Risk management

14. Linking organizational culture and corporate values

S. Downsizing/Rightsizing

1. Employment downsizing

2. Alternatives to employment downsizing

3. Strategies for long-term success

4. Why downsizing happens

5. When downsizing is the answer

6. Effectively managing a downsizing effort

7. Alternatives to downsizing

8. Consequences of employment downsizing

9. Approaches to reducing staff size

10. Identifying and eliminating unnecessary work

11. Prioritizing jobs for combining, streamlining, or eliminating

12. Identifying selection criteria for making downsizing/rightsizing decisions

13. Importance of focusing on individual jobs vs. individual staff members

14. Layoffs

15. Reductions in force

T. HR Career Planning

1. Definition of a career
2. Balancing work and life
3. Career management systems
4. Company policies to accommodate work and nonwork activities
5. Coping with job loss
6. Developing leader skills
   Authentic leadership
   Contingency theory
   Ethical decision making
   Leader-member exchange theory
   Path-goal theory
   Situational approach
   Skills approach
   Style approach
   Team leadership
   Trait approach
   Transformational leadership
7. Plateauing
8. Skills obsolescence
9. Career development

U. HR Information Systems

1. Conducting systems needs assessments
2. Determining system specifications
3. Selecting an HR information system
4. Using HR data for enterprise management
5. Issues to consider when selecting HRIS software

V. Mergers and Acquisitions

1. Conducting HR due diligence
2. Integrating HR systems
3. Assimilating work cultures
4. Integrating compensation and benefits structures
5. Merging workplace cultures
6. Integrating performance management systems
7. Cultural compatibility
   Address cultural differences
   Degree of internal integration
   Autonomy
   Adaptability
   Employee trust
   Diversity
8. Integration
   Communication
   Employee anxiety
   Rumors
   Redundancy
   Downsizing
   Morale

W. Outsourcing

1. Creating an outsourcing strategy
2. Preparing a request for information (RFI) or request for proposal (RFP)
3. Identifying third-party providers (contractors)
4. Evaluating proposals from contractors
5. Conducting cost-benefit analyses
6. Negotiating contract terms
7. Retaining management rights
8. Importance of legal review of contracts
9. Managing vendor/staff relationships
10. Managing a vendor's performance under the contract terms
11. Managing communications and deliverables
12. Evaluating effectiveness of outsourcing efforts

X. Workplace Health, Safety, and Security

1. OSHA citations and penalties (required)
2. Disaster preparation, continuity, and recovery planning
3. Employee health
4. Inspection
5. Protection from retaliation
6. Safety management
7. Security concerns at work
8. Communicable diseases
9. Data security
10. Testing for substance abuse
11. Ergonomics
12. Monitoring, surveillance, privacy

··· Notes

CHAPTER 1

1. J. Welch, S. Welch, "How Not to Succeed in Business," *Businessweek* (March 2, 2009), p. 74.

2. P. Bansal, S. Bertels, T. Ewart, P. MacConnachie, J. O'Brien, "Bridging the Research-Practice Gap," *Academy of Management Perspectives* (2012), 26(1), pp. 73–92. doi:10.5465/amp.2011.0140

3. A.C. Cosper, "How to Be Great," *Entrepreneur* (March 2010), p. 12.

4. J.C. Santora, "Quality Management and Manufacturing Performance: Does Success Depend on Firm Culture?" *Academy of Management Perspective* (2009), 23(2), pp. 103–105.

5. R. Rubin, E. Dierdorff, "Building a Better MBA: From a Decade of Critique Toward a Decennium of Creation," *Academy of Management Learning and Education* (2013), 12(1), pp. 125–141.

6. T.T. Baldwin, J.R. Pierce, R.C. Joines, S. Farouk, "The Elusiveness of Applied Management Knowledge: A Critical Challenge for Management Educators," *Academy of Management Learning & Education* (2011), 10(4), pp. 583–605. doi:10.5465/amle.2010.0045

7. R. Grossman, E. Salas, D. Pavlas, M.A. Rosen, "Using Instructional Features to Enhance Demonstration-Based Training in Management Education," *Academy of Management Learning & Education* (2013), 12(2), 219–243. doi:10.5465/amle .2011.0527

8. R. Mitchell, S. Obeidat, M. Bray, "The Effect of Strategic Human Resource Management on Organizational Performance: The Mediating Role of High-Performance Human Resource Practices," *Human Resource Management* (2013), 52(6), pp. 899–921.

9. I.R. Gellatly, K.H. Hunter, L.G. Currie, P.G. Irving, "HRM Practices and Organizational Commitment Profiles," *International Journal of Human Resource Management* (April 2009), p. 869–884.

10. http://www.mckinsey.com/insights/ organization/organizational_health_the_ulti mate_competitive_advantage (retrieved December 30, 2013).

11. C. Brewster, P.J. Gollan, P.M. Wright, "Guest Editors' Note: Human Resource Management and the Line," *Human Resource Management* (2013), 52(6), pp. 829–838.

12. R.S. Rubin, E.C. Dierdorff, "On the Road to Abilene: Time to Manage Agreement About MBA Curricular Relevance," *Academy of Management Learning & Education* (2011), 10(1), pp. 148–161.

13. G. Colvin, "Ignore These Insights at Your Peril", *Fortune* (October 28, 2013), p. 85.

14. B.A. Campbell, R. Coff, D. Kryscynski, "Rethinking Sustained Competitive Advantage From Human Capital," *Academy of Management Review* (2012), 37(3), pp. 376–395.

15. I.S. Fulmer, R.E. Ployhart, "Our Most Important Asset: A Multidisciplinary/ Multilevel Review of Human Capital Valuation for Research and Practice," *Journal of Management* (2014), 40(1), pp. 161–192.

16. D.M. Rousseau, S. McCarthy, "Educating Managers From an Evidence-Based Perspective," *Academy of Management Learning & Education* (2007), 6(1), pp. 84–101. doi:10.5465/AMLE.2007.244 01705

17. A. Bryant, "Google's Quest to Build a Better Boss," *The New York Times* (March 13, 2011), p. BU-1.

18. A. Fox, "Raising Engagement," *HR Magazine* (May 2010), p. 36.

19. A. Edmans, "Does the Stock Market Fully Value Intangibles? Employee Satisfaction and Equity Prices," *Journal of Financial Economics* (September 2009), 101(3), pp. 621–640.

20. K.W. Mossholder, H.A. Richardson, R.P. Settoon, "Human Resource Systems and Helping in Organizations: A Relational Perspective," *Academy of Management Review* (2011), 36(1), pp. 33–52.

21. K. Blanchard, D. Hutson, E. Wills, *The One-Minute Entrepreneur* (New York, NY: Currency, 2008).

22. H.H. McIntyre, R.J. Foti, "The Impact of Shared Leadership on Teamwork: Mental Models and Performance in Self-Directed Teams," *Group Processes & Intergroup Relations* (2013), 16(1), pp. 46–57.

23. "HR Departments Get New Star Power at Some Firms," *The Wall Street Journal*, http://online.wsj.com/news/articles/ SB121417392782995251 (retrieved December 26, 2013).

24. http://www.successfactors.com/ en_us/company/press-releases/2013/ companies-with-chief-hr-officers-consistent ly-outperform-peers.html (retrieved January 20, 2014).

25. http://www.shrm.org/Research/ SurveyFindings/Articles/Documents/SHRM-Challenges-Facing-HR-Future-2022-FINAL .pptx (retrieved December 26, 2013).

26. J.G. Proudfoot, P.J. Corr, D.E. Guest, G. Dunn, "Cognitive-Behavioural Training to Change Attributional Style Improves Employee Well-being, Job Satisfaction, Productivity, and Turnover," *Personality and Individual Differences* (2009), 46(2), pp. 147–153.

27. P.E. Spector, *Job Satisfaction: Application, Assessment, Causes and Consequences* (London, UK: Blackwell, 1997).

28. http://www.shrm.org/hrdisciplines/ staffingmanagement/Articles/Pages/More-Voluntary-Exits (retrieved January 20, 2014).

29. R. Dalal, M. Baysinger, B. Brummel, J. LeBreton, "The Relative Importance of Employee Engagement, Other Job Attitudes, and Trait Affect as Predictors of Job Performance," *Journal of Applied Social Psychology* (2012), 42, pp. 295–325.

30. R.S. Rubin, E.C. Dierdorff, "On the Road to Abilene: Time to Manage Agreement About MBA Curricular Relevance," *Academy of Management Learning & Education* (2011), 10(1), 148–161.

31. A.J. Nyberg, R.E. Ployhart, "Context-Emergent Turnover (CED) Theory: A Theory of Collective Turnover." *Academy of Management Review* (2013), 38(1), pp. 109–131. doi:10.5465/amr.2011.0201

32. H. Nguyen, M. Groth, A. Johnson, "When the Going Gets Tough, the Tough Keep Working: Impact of Emotional Labor on Absenteeism," *Journal of Management* (2013), published online. doi:10.1177/0149206313490026

33. M.S. Christian, A.J. Ellis, "Examining the Effects of Sleep Deprivation on Workplace Deviance: A Self-Regulatory Perspective," *Academy of Management Journal* (2011), 54(5), pp. 913–934. doi:10.5465/amj.2010.0179

34. https://www.shrm.org/Publications/ hrmagazine/EditorialContent/2011/0911/ Pages/0911grossman.aspx (retrieved January 20, 2014).

35. http://www.gallup.com/poll/150026/unhealthy-workers-absenteeism-costs-153-billion.aspx (retrieved January 20, 2014).

36. H. Nguyen, M. Groth, A. Johnson, "When the Going Gets Tough, the Tough Keep Working: Impact of Emotional Labor on Absenteeism," *Journal of Management* (2013), published online. doi:10.1177/0149206313490026

37. R. Rubin, E. Dierdorff, "On the Road to Abilene: Time to Manage Agreement About MBA Curricular Relevance," *Academy of Management Learning & Education* (2011), 10(1), pp. 148–161.

38. http://www.forbes.com/sites/joshbersin/2013/04/05/can-hr-managers-think-like-economists (retrieved December 30, 2013).

39. P. Buller, G. McEvoy, "Strategy, Human Resource Management and Performance: Sharpening Line of Sight," *Human Resource Management Review* (2012), 22(1), pp. 43–56.

40. P. Patel, J. Messersmith, D. Lepak, "Walking the Tightrope: An Assessment of the Relationship Between High-Performance Work Systems and Organizational Ambidexterity," *Academy of Management Journal* (2013), 56(5), pp. 1420–1442.

41. E.E. Gordon, *The 2010 Meltdown: Solving the Impending Jobs Crisis* (Westport, CT: Praeger, 2005).

42. B. Eversole, D. Venneberg, C. Crowder, "Creating a Flexible Organizational Culture to Attract and Retain Talented Workers Across Generations," *Advances in Developing Human Resources* (2012), 14(4), pp. 607–625.

43. S.A. Mohrman, E.E. Lawler I, "Generating Knowledge That Drives Change," *Academy of Management Perspectives* (2012), 26(1), pp. 41–51. doi:10.5465/amp.2011.0141

44. C. Phillipson, "Commentary: The Future of Work and Retirement," *Human Relations* (January 2013), 66, pp.143–153.

45. http://www.bls.gov/opub/ted/2012/ted_20120501.htm (retrieved January 24, 2014).

46. R.S. Rubin, E.C. Dierdorff, "On the Road to Abilene: Time to Manage Agreement About MBA Curricular Relevance," *Academy of Management Learning & Education* (2011), 10(1), pp. 148–161.

47. D.R. Laker, J.L. Powell, "The Differences Between Hard and Soft Skills and Their Relative Impact on Training Transfer," *Human Resource Development Quarterly* (2011), 22(1), pp. 111–122.

48. A.C. Cosper, "How to Be Great," *Entrepreneur* (March 2010), p. 12.

49. http://blogs.wsj.com/moneybeat/2013/11/11/investment-banks-seek-arts-graduates-people-skills-in-demand (retrieved December 30, 2013).

50. L. Dragoni, P.E. Tesluk, J.E.A. Russell, I. Oh, "Understanding Managerial Development: Integrating Developmental Assignments, Learning Orientation, and Access to Developmental Opportunities in Predicting Managerial Competencies," *Academy of Management Journal* (2009), 52(4), pp. 731–742.

51. E.M. Wong, M.E. Ormiston, P.E. Tetlock, "The Effects of Top Management Team Integrative Complexity and Decentralized Decision Making on Corporate Social Performance," *Academy of Management Journal* (2011), 54(6), pp. 1207–1228.

52. R.S. Rubin, E.C. Dierdorff, "How Relevant Is the MBA? Assessing the Alignment of Required Curricula and Required Managerial Competencies," *Academy of Management Learning & Education* (2009), 8(5), pp. 208–224.

53. H.J. Walker, T. Bauer, M. Cole, J. Bernerth, H. Feild, J. Short, "Is This How I Will Be Treated? Reducing Uncertainty Through Recruitment Interactions," *Academy of Management Journal* (2013), 56(5), pp. 1325–1347.

54. K. Pajo, A. Coetzer, N. Guenole, "Formal Development Opportunities and Withdrawal Behavior by Employees in Small and Medium-Sized Enterprises," *Journal of Small Business Management* (2010), 48(3), pp. 281–301.

55. S. Elliot, "A Transdisciplinary Exploratory Model of Corporate Responses to the Challenges of Environmental Sustainability," *Business Strategy and the Environment* (2013), 22(4), pp. 269–282.

56. A. Gunasekaran, A. Spalanzani, "Sustainability of Manufacturing and Services: Investigations for Research and Application," *International Journal of Production Economics* (2012), 140(1), pp. 35–47.

57. Definition developed by the Brundtland Commission. Cited from Colvin Interview of Linda Fisher, *Fortune* (November 23, 2009), pp. 45–50.

58. A.A. Marcus, A.R. Fremeth, "Green Management Matters Regardless," *Academy of Management Perspectives* (2009), 23(3), pp. 17–26.

59. http://www.shrm.org/about/pages/default.aspx (retrieved December 30, 2013).

60. http://www.shrm.org/about/pressroom/PressReleases/Pages/AssuranceofLearningAssessment.aspx (retrieved December 30, 2013).

61. Association for Talent Development, http://www.astd.org (retrieved December 30, 2013).

62. http://www.astd.org/Certification/For-Candidates/FAQs (retrieved December 27, 2013).

63. http://www.astd.org/Education/Programs/Human-Performance-Improvement-Programs (retrieved December 27, 2013).

64. WorldatWork, www.worldatwork.org (retrieved May 28, 2010).

65. G.E. Calvasina, E.J. Calvasina, R.V. Calvasina, "Personal Liability and Human Resource Decision Making," *Journal of Management and Marketing Research* (2006), 18(4), pp. 21–39.

66. http://www.gallup.com/strategicconsulting/163007/state-american-workplace.aspx (retrieved January 20, 2014).

67. S. Abraham, "Job Satisfaction as an Antecedent to Employee Engagement," *SIES Journal of Management* (2012), 8(2), pp. 27–36.

68. http://go.globoforce.com/rs/globoforce/images/WP_Engagement_Globoforce.pdf (retrieved January 21, 2014).

69. http://go.globoforce.com/rs/globoforce/images/WP_Engagement_Globoforce.pdf (retrieved January 21, 2014).

70. K. Wollard, "'Quiet Desperation': Another Perspective on Employee Engagement," *Advances in Developing Human Resources* (2011), 13(4), pp. 526–537.

71. D. Autor, D. Dorn, "The Growth of Low-Skill Service Jobs and the Polarization of the U.S. Labor Market," *American Economic Review* (2013), 103(5), pp. 1553–1597.

72. G. Grossman, R. Rossi-Hansberg, "Trading Tasks: A Simple Theory of Offshoring," *American Economic Review* (2008), 98(5), pp. 1978–1997.

73. L. Fratocchi, P. Barbieri, C. Di Mauro, G. Nassimbeni, M. Vignoli, "Manufacturing Back-Reshoring: An Exploratory Approach for Hypotheses Development" *XXIV Riunione Scientifica Annuale Associazione Italiana di Ingegneria Gestionale, "Entrepreneurship, Innovation and the Engine of Growth"* (Milano, Italy: Politecnico di Milano, 2013), pp. 17–18.

74. F. Mandelman, "The Asymmetric Impact of Offshoring and Low-Skill Immigration on Employment and Wages," *Federal Reserve Bank of Atlanta, Center for Human Capital Studies* (2013), white paper.

75. R. Berger Levinson, "Gender-Based Affirmative Action and Reverse Gender Bias: Beyond Gratz, Parents Involved, and Ricci," *Harvard Journal of Law and Gender* (2010), 34.

76. E. Rusli, "Zynga's Tough Culture Risks a Talent Drain," *The New York Times*, http://dealbook.nytimes.com/2011/11/27/zyngas-tough-culture-risks-a-talent-drain/?_r=0 (retrieved December 29, 2013).

77. Ibid.

78. Ibid.

79. Ibid.

80. http://pages.silkroad.com/rs/silkroad/images/Social-Media-Workplace-Collaboration-SilkRoad-TalentTalk-Report.pdf (retrieved December 29, 2013).

81. http://thehiringsite.careerbuilder.com/2013/07/01/two-in-five-employers-use-social-media-to-screen-candidates (retrieved December 29, 2013).

82. http://www.businessinsider.com/6-reasons-social-media-got-people-fired-2013-7 (retrieved December 29, 2013).

83. http://www.nytimes.com/2013/01/22/technology/employers-social-media-policies-come-under-regulatory-scrutiny.html?pagewanted=all (retrieved December 29, 2013).

84. http://www.forbes.com/sites/susanadams/2013/01/22/when-is-it-ok-to-diss-your-boss-online (retrieved December 29, 2013).

85. http://bits.blogs.nytimes.com/2009/08/20/more-employers-use-social-networks-to-check-out-applicants (retrieved July 16, 2010).

CHAPTER 2

1. P. Ghemawat, "Finding Your Strategy in the New Landscape," *Harvard Business Review* (2010), 88(3), pp. 54–60.

2. H. Steenhuis, E. De Bruijn, H. Heerkens, "New Entrants and Overcapacity: Lessons From Regional Aircraft Manufacturing," *International Journal of Technology Transfer and Commercialisation* (2010), 9(4), pp. 342–372. doi:10.1504/IJTTC.2010.0354

3. Institute for Energy Research, "Overcapacity Plagues Solar Industry" (January 3, 2012), http://www.instituteforenergyresearch.org/2012/01/03/overcapacity-plagues-solar-industry (retrieved September 23, 2014).

4. J. Hökerberg, "China Infected With Overcapacity" (July 26, 2013), http://brightmarketinsight.com/headlines/china-infected-with-overcapacity (retrieved September 23, 2014).

5. K. Blanchard, D. Hutson, E. Wills, *The One-Minute Entrepreneur* (New York, NY: Currency, 2008).

6. C. Dibrell, J. Craig, D. Neubaum, "Linking the Formal Strategic Planning Process, Planning Flexibility, and Innovativeness to Firm Performance," *Journal of Business Research* (2014), 67, http://www.academia.edu/7908997/Linking_the_formal_strategic_planning_process_planning_flexibility_and_innovativeness_to_firm_performance (retreived September 23, 2014). doi:10.1016/j.jbusres.2013.10.011

7. W. Zheng, B. Yang, G. McLean, "Linking Organizational Culture, Structure, Strategy, and Organizational Effectiveness: Mediating Role of Knowledge Management," *Journal of Business Research* (2010), 63(7), pp. 763–771. doi:10.1016/j.jbusres.2009.06.005

8. J. Shin, M. S. Taylor, M.G. Seo, "Resources for Change: The Relationships of Organizational Inducements and Psychological Resilience to Employees' Attitudes and Behaviors Toward Organizational Change," *Academy of Management Journal* (2012), 55(3), pp. 727–748.

9. M. Kibbeling, H. van der Bij, A. van Weele, "Market Orientation and Innovativeness in Supply Chains: Supplier's Impact on Customer Satisfaction," *Journal of Product Innovation Management* (2013), 30(3), pp. 500–515.

10. B. Thau, "JC Penney Shoppers React to CEO Ouster," *Forbes* (April 11, 2013).

11. S. Droege, M. Lane, M. Casile, "A Tumultuous Decade in Thailand: Competitive Dynamics Among Domestic Banks and Multi-national Entrants in an Emerging Market," *International Journal of Business and Emerging Markets* (2013), 5(4), pp. 371–387. doi:10.1504/IJBEM.2013.056814

12. E. de Oliveira Teixeira, W. B. Werther Jr., "Resilience: Continuous Renewal of Competitive Advantages," *Business Horizons* (2013), 56(3), pp. 333–342. doi:10.1016/j.bushor.2013.01.009

13. J. O'Mahony, "Apple Losing Innovative Edge, Three in Four Investors Say," *The Telegraph* (May 17, 2013).

14. R. King, "War for Tech Talent Heats Up," *The Wall Street Journal* blog (July 23, 2012), http://blogs.wsj.com/cio/2012/07/23/war-for-tech-talent-heats-up/.

15. http://www.businessinsider.com/as-war-for-talent-heats-up-so-does-employee-poaching-2011-3 (retrieved January 24, 2014).

16. K.D. Dea Roglio, G. Light, "Executive MBA Programs: The Development of the Reflective Executive," *Academy of Management Learning & Education* (2009), 8(2), pp. 156–173.

17. H.R. Huhman, "As War for Talent Heats Up, So Does Employee Poaching," *Business Insider* (March 11, 2011).

18. M. Toossi, "Labor Force Projections to 2020: A More Slowly Growing Workforce," *Monthly Labor Review* (2012), 135(1), p. 43.

19. Inc., "LivingSocial" [company profile], http://www.inc.com/profile/livingsocial/ (retrieved February 28, 2014).

20. M.J. Canyan, "Executive Compensation and Incentives," *Academy of Management Perspectives* (2006), 20(1), pp. 25–44.

21. E.M. Wong, M.E. Ormiston, P.E. Tetlock, "The Effects of Top Management Team Integrative Complexity and Decentralized Decision Making on Corporate Social Performance," *Academy of Management Journal* (2011), 54(6), pp. 1207–1228.

22. D. Charles, "Pepsi Pressured to Fight Big Sugar's 'Land Grab,'" NPR blog (November 23, 2013), http://www.npr.org/blogs/thesalt/2013/11/23/246753281/pepsi-pressured-to-fight-big-sugar-s-land-grab/.

23. Stratasys, "Urbee: Stratasys 3D Printers Build Urbee, First Prototype Car to Have Entire Body Created With an Additive Process," http://www.stratasys.com/resources/case-studies/automotive/urbee/ (retrieved February 28, 2014).

24. L.F. Katz, R.A. Margo, "Technical Change and the Relative Demand for Skilled Labor: The United States in Historical Perspective," NBER Working Paper 18752 (February 2013), http://www.nber.org/papers/w18752/.

25. S. Graves, "Stop Government Abuse: We Need Common Sense for Federal Regulations," *CNBC* (February 25, 2014), http://www.cnbc.com/id/101443196/.

26. A. McWilliams, D. Siegel, "Corporate Social Responsibility: A Theory of the Firm Perspective," *Academy of Management Review* (2001), (26)1, pp. 117–127.

27. P.M. Vaaler, "How Do MNCs Vote in Developing Country Elections?" *Academy of Management Journal* (2008), 51(1), pp. 21–43.

28. Small Business Administration, "Report on the Regulatory Flexibility Act, FY 2013," *Small Business Research Summary* (February 2014), 421, http://www.sba.gov/sites/default/files/rs421_0.pdf.

29. G.F. Keller, "The Influence of Military Strategies on Business Planning," *International Journal of Business and Management* (May 2008), p. 129.

30. C. Wolf, S. Floyd, "Strategic Planning Research: Toward a Theory-Driven Agenda," *Journal of Management*, published online (March 26, 2013), doi:10.1177/0149206313478185

31. P.M. Wright, G.C. McMahan, "Exploring Human Capital: Putting 'Human' Back Into Strategic Human Resource Management," *Human Resource Management Journal* (2011), 21(2), pp. 93–104.

32. I. Ugboro, K. Obeng, O. Spann, "Strategic Planning as an Effective Tool of Strategic Management in Public Sector Organizations: Evidence From Public Transit Organizations," *Administration and Society* (2011), 43(1), pp. 87–123.

33. J. Welch, S. Welch, "Inventing the Future Now," *Businessweek* (May 11, 2009), p. 76.

34. W. Bennis, "Acting the Part of a Leader," *Businessweek* (September 14, 2009), p. 80.

35. University of Arkansas Little Rock, http://http://ualr.edu/cob/about-us/mission/ (retrieved March 1, 2014).

36. *The American Heritage College Dictionary* (New York: Houghton Mifflin, 1993).

37. University of Arkansas Little Rock, http://ualr.edu/cob/about-us/mission/ (retrieved March 1, 2014).

38. M. Porter, *Competitive Strategy: Techniques for Analyzing Industries and Competitors* (New York, NY: Free Press, 1980), p. 15.

39. G. Anderson, "Can Walmart Beat Dollar Stores on Their Own Turf?" Forbes blog (May 14, 2013), http://www.forbes.com/sites/retailwire/2013/05/14/can-walmart-beat-dollar-stores-on-their-own-turf/.

40. D. Buss, "Tata Builds Upgrade After Cheap Nano Falls Flat in India," *BrandChannel,* (October 15, 2013), http://www.brandchannel.com/home/post/Tata-Nano-Overhaul-101513.aspx.

41. H.L. Smith, R. Discenza, K.G. Baker, "Building Sustainable Success in Art Galleries: An Exploratory Study of Adaptive Strategies," *Journal of Small Business Strategy* (2005/2006), 16(2), pp. 29–41.

42. J. Cazier, B. Shao, R. St. Louis, "E-Business Differentiation Through Value-Based Trust," *Information and Management* (September 2006), 43(6), pp. 718–727.

43. E.K. Clemons, P.F. Nunes, M. Reilly, "Six Strategies for Successful Niche Marketing," *The Wall Street Journal* (May 24, 2010), p. R6.

44. N. Byrnes, "Why Dr. Pepper Is in the Pink of Health," *Businessweek* (October 26, 2009), p. 59.

45. Y.H. Hsieh, H.M. Chen, "Strategic Fit Among Business Competitive Strategy, Human Resource Strategy, and Reward System," *Academy of Strategic Management Journal* (2011), 10(2).

46. Ibid.

47. M. Porter, "How Competitive Forces Shape Strategy," *Harvard Business Review* (1979), 57(2), pp. 137–145.

48. M.E. Porter, *Competitive Strategy: Techniques for Analysing Industries and Competitors* (New York, NY: Free Press, 1980).

49. I. Jacobs, J. Jaffe, P.L. Hegaret, "How the Open Web Platform Is Transforming Industry," *IEEE Internet Computing*, 16(6).

50. G. Hirst, D. Van Knippenberg, J. Zhou, "A Cross-Level Perspective on Employee Creativity: Goal Orientation, Team Learning Behavior, and Individual Creativity," *Academy of Management Journal* (2009), 52(2), pp. 280–293.

51. L. Dragoni, P.E. Tesluk, J.E.A. Russell, I. Oh, "Understanding Managerial Development: Integrating Developmental Assignments, Learning Orientation, and Access to Developmental Opportunities in Predicting Managerial Competencies," *Academy of Management Journal* (2009), 52(4), pp. 731–742.

52. S. Covey, "Time Management," *Fortune* (September 19, 2009), pp. 28–29.

53. T. Ito, "CEO Message" (June 19, 2013), http://world.honda.com/investors/policy/ceo/.

54. Nike, Inc., "Nike, Inc. Announces Target for FY17 Revenues of $36 billion" [press release] (October 9, 2013), http://nikeinc.com/news/nike-inc-announces-target-for-fy17-revenues-of-36-billion-2nd-release/.

55. "Dell," *The Wall Street Journal* (February 27, 2009), p. A1.

56. S.H. Appelbaum, J. Gallagher, "The Competitive Advantage of Organizational Learning," *Journal of Workplace Learning*, 12(2), pp. 40–56.

57. M. Pirtea, C. Nicolescu, C. Botoc, "The Role of Strategic Planning in Modern Organizations," *Annales Universitatis Apulensis Series Oeconomica* (2009), 11(2), pp. 953–957.

58. J.H. Marler, "Strategic Human Resource Management in Context: A Historical and Global Perspective," *The Academy of Management Perspectives* (2012), 26(2), pp. 6–11.

59. P. Jarzabkowski, "Shaping Strategy as a Structuration Process," *Academy of Management Journal* (2008), 51(4), pp. 621–650.

60. S. Postrel, "Multitasking Teams With Variable Complementarily: Challenges for Capability Management," *Academy of Management Review* (2009), 34(2), pp. 273–296.

61. M.S. Wood, "Does One Size Fit All? The Multiple Organizational Forms Leading to Successful Academic Entrepreneurship," *Entrepreneurship Theory and Practice* (2009), 33(4), pp. 929–947.

62. P. Fiss, E. Zajac, "The Symbolic Management of Strategic Change: Sensegiving via Framing and Decoupling," *Academy of Management Journal* (2006), 49(6), pp. 1173–1193.

63. R. Adhikari, "Nadella Begins Microsoft Leadership Transformation," *E-Commerce Times* (March 3, 2014), http://www.ecommercetimes.com/story/80075.html.

64. M. Rhee, "An Educated Work Force," *The Wall Street Journal* (January 23, 2009), p. R3.

65. P. Hutton, "Learning From Zappos: Why Every School Needs an Organizational Mindset," *The Huffington Post* (February 19, 2014), http://www.huffingtonpost.com/peter-hutton/learning-from-zappos_b_4817430.html.

66. GE, "Fact Sheet," http://www.ge.com/about-us/fact-sheet/ (retrieved March 6, 2014).

67. F.A.A. Rub, A.A. Issa, "A Business Process Modeling-Based Approach to Investigate Complex Processes: Software Development Case Study," *Business Process Management Journal* (2012), 18(1), pp. 122–137.

68. R.K. Vedder, "As Tuition Increases, So Do College Bureaucracies," *Bloomberg View* (February 3, 2014), http://www.bloombergview.com/articles/2014-02-03/how-many-provosts-do-colleges-need/.

69. M.K. Fiegener, Matching Business-Level Strategic Controls to Strategy: Impact on Control System Effectiveness, *Journal of Applied Business Research (JABR)* (2011), 10(1), pp. 25–34.

70. Ibid.

71. M. Guadalupe, H. Li, J. Wulf, "Who Lives in the C-Suite? Organizational Structure and the Division of Labor in Top Management," *Management Science* (2013).

72. A. Aïte, G. Borst, S. Moutier, I. Varescon, I. Brown, O. Houdé, M. Cassotti, "Impact of Emotional Context Congruency on Decision Making Under Ambiguity," *Emotion* (2013), 13(2), pp. 177–182.

73. P.M. Figueroa, "Risk Communication Surrounding the Fukushima Nuclear Disaster: An Anthropological Approach," *Asia Europe Journal* (2013), 11(1), pp. 53–64.

74. Ibid.

75. B. Gates, "The Best Advice I Ever Got," *Fortune* (July 6, 2009), p. 43.

76. P. Drucker, *Management: Tasks, Responsibilities, Practices* (Oxford, UK: Butterworth-Heinemann, 1999), p. 546.

77. A. Lashinsky, "Microsoft Culture Must Change, Chairman Says," *Fortune* (February 27, 2014), http://tech.fortune.cnn.com/2014/02/27/microsoft-culture-must-change-chairman-says/.

78. L.Z. Wu, H.K. Kwan, F.H.K. Yim, R. Chiu, X. He, "CEO Ethical Leadership and Corporate Social Responsibility: A Moderated Mediation Model," *Journal of Business Ethics* (February 2014), published online.

79. D. West, lecture at Springfield College (November 23, 2009).

80. P. Bolton, M.K. Brennermeier, L. Veldkamp, "Leadership, Coordination, and Corporate Culture," *Review of Economic Studies* (2013), 80(2), pp. 512–537.

81. M.J. Culnan, P.J. McHugh, J.I. Zubillaga, "How Large U.S. Companies Can

Use Twitter and Other Social Media to Gain Business Value," *MIS Quarterly Executive* (2010), 9(4), pp. 243–259.

82. M.W. DiStaso, T. McCorkindale, D.K. Wright, "How Public Relations Executives Perceive and Measure the Impact of Social Media in Their Organizations," *Public Relations Review* (2011), 37(3), pp. 325–328.

83. K. Steinmetz, "Obama Asks Celebs to Tweet About ObamaCare," *Time* (October 2, 2013), http://swampland.time.com/2013/10/02/obama-asks-celebs-to-tweet-about-obamacare/.

84. M. Lim, "Clicks, Cabs, and Coffee Houses: Social Media and Oppositional Movements in Egypt, 2004–2011," *Journal of Communication* (2012), 62(2), pp. 231–248.

85. S. Cleland, "Google's 'Infringenovation' Secrets," *Forbes* (October 3, 2011), http://www.forbes.com/sites/scottcleland/2011/10/03/googles-infringenovation-secrets/.

86. S. Lohr, "Big Data, Trying to Build Better Workers," *The New York Times* (April 21, 2013), p. BU4.

87. "Big Data: The Next Frontier for Innovation, Competition, and Productivity," *McKinsey Global Institute* (June 2011), p. 23.

88. S. Lohr, "Big Data, Trying to Build Better Workers," *The New York Times* (April 21, 2013), p. BU4.

89. A. McAfee, E. Brynjolfsson, "Big Data: The Management Revolution," *Harvard Business Review* (October 2012), p. 4.

90. Ibid.

91. J. Schramm, "Future Focus: The Trouble With Algorithms," *HR Magazine* (November 2013), 58(11), p. 80.

92. M. L. Brosnan, C. S. Farley, D. Gartside, H. Tambe, "How Well Do You Know Your Workforce?" Accenture (October 2013), http://www.accenture.com/us-en/outlook/Pages/outlook-journal-2013-how-well-do-you-know-your-workforce-analytics.aspx.

93. Chartered Institute of Personnel and Development, *Talent Analytics and Big Data—The Challenge for HR* (London, UK: CIPD, 2013), p. 2, http://www.oracle.com/us/products/applications/human-capital-management/talent-analytics-and-big-data-2063584.pdf.

94. S. Lohr, "Big Data, Trying to Build Better Workers," *The New York Times* (April 21, 2013), p. BU4.

95. Ibid.

96. Boston Consulting Group, "People Management Translates Into Superior Economic Performance," [press release] (August 2, 2012), http://www.bcg.com/media/PressReleaseDetails.aspx?id=tcm:12-110525/.

97. http://www.shrm.org/hrdisciplines/staffingmanagement/articles/pages/tapping-talent-analytics-potential.aspx retrieved March 15, 2014

98. A. McAfee, E. Brynjolfsson, "Big Data: The Management Revolution," *Harvard Business Review* (October 2012), pp. 4, 9.

99. K.W. Mossholder, H.A. Richardson, R.P. Settoon, "Human Resource Systems and Helping in Organizations: A Relational Perspective," *Academy of Management Review* (2011), 36(1), pp. 33–52.

100. D. Mueller, S. Strohmeier, C. Gasper, "HRIS Design Characteristics: Towards a General Research Framework," *3rd European Academic Workshop on Electronic Human Resource Management* (May 2010).

101. S. Pande, P. Khanna, "Leveraging Human Resource Information Systems: Alignment of Business With Technology," *International Journal of Computer Applications* (2012), p. 56.

102. Society for Human Resource Management, http://www.shrm.org/Publications/hrmagazine/EditorialContent/Pages/0808hrsolutions.aspx (retrieved, July 7, 2010).

103. A. Gumbus, R.N. Lussier, "Entrepreneurs Use a Balanced Scorecard to Translate Strategy Into Performance Measures," *Journal of Small Business Management* (2006), 44(3), pp. 407–425.

104. A. Gumbus, R.N. Lussier, "Developing and Using a Balanced Scorecard," *Clinical Leadership & Management Review* (2003), 17(2), pp. 69–74.

105. R. Kaplan, D. Norton, *Alignment* (Boston, MA: Harvard Business School, 2006).

106. Society for Human Resource Management, http://www.shrm.org/TemplatesTools/hrqa/Pages/WhatisaBalancedScorecard.aspx.

107. Ibid.

108. National Centre for Partnership and Performance, the Equality Authority, *New Models of High-Performance Work Systems: The Business Case for Strategic HRM, Partnership and Diversity and Equality Systems* (Dublin, Ireland: NCPP, 2008), p. 46.

109. J. Walker, "Companies Trade in Hunch-Based Hiring for Computer Modeling," *The New York Times* (September 20, 2012), p. B1.

110. S. Mohrman, E. Lawler, "Generating Knowledge That Drives Change," *Academy of Management Perspectives* (2012), 26(1), pp. 41–51.

111. A.D. Wright, "Making Social Media Work—at Work" (March 3, 2014), http://www.shrm.org/hrdisciplines/technology/articles/pages/social-media-at-work.aspx?latestnews/.

112. Ibid.

113. Ibid.

114. Ibid.

115. Ibid.

116. SilkRoad Resource Center, *Social Media and Workplace Collaboration: 2012 Latest Practices, Key Findings, Hottest Topics* (2012), http://pages.silkroad.com/rs/silkroad/images/Social-Media-Workplace-Collaboration-SilkRoad-TalentTalk-Report.pdf.

117. Wikipedia. (2014). Netflix. Retrieved June 15, 2014 from http://en.wikipedia.org/wiki/Netflix.

118. P. McCord, "How Netflix Reinvented HR, "*Harvard Business Review* 92(1/2), pp. 70–76.

119. P. Sikka, Netflix Will Raise Its Prices After Better-Than-Expected Earnings, *MarketRealist.com*. Retrieved from http://marketrealist.com/2014/04/netflix-will-raise-prices-better-expected-earnings/.

120. P. McCord, "How Netflix Reinvented HR," *Harvard Business Review*, 92(1/2), pp. 70–76.

121. Ibid.

122. Ibid.

123. Ibid.

CHAPTER 3

1. S. Nkomo, J. Hoobler, "A Historical Perspective on Diversity Ideologies in the United States: Reflections on Human Resource Management Research and Practice," *Human Resource Management Review* (April 2014), p. 24. doi:10.1016/j.hrmr.2014.03.006

2. J. Hendon, "Hiring and the OUCH Test," *Arkansas Business* (May 3, 2010).

3. http://www.eeoc.gov/policy/docs/qanda_clarify_procedures.html (retrieved May 24, 2014).

4. http://uniformguidelines.com/uniformguidelines.html#18/ (retrieved May 24, 2014).

5. http://www.eeoc.gov/policy/docs/factemployment_procedures.html (retrieved May 24, 2014).

6. http://www.eeoc.gov/laws/statutes/epa.cfm (retrieved July 20, 2010).

7. Ibid.

8. http://www.cnn.com/2014/04/10/politics/civil-rights-act-interesting-facts/ (retrieved May 24, 2014).

9. http://www.eeoc.gov/laws/statutes/titlevii.cfm (retrieved May 24, 2014).

10. http://www.justice.gov/crt/about/edu/types.php (retrieved May 24, 2014).

11. http://www.eeoc.gov/policy/docs/factemployment_procedures.html (retrieved May 24, 2014).

12. M.L. McDonald, J.D. Westphal, "Access Denied: Low Mentoring of Women and Minority First-Time Directors and Its Negative Effects on Appointments to Additional Boards," *Academy of Management Journal* (2013), 56(4), pp. 1169–1198.

13. http://www.eeoc.gov/policy/docs/factemployment_procedures.html (retrieved May 24, 2014).

14. http://www.eeoc.gov/policy/docs/qanda_clarify_procedures.html (retrieved May 24, 2014).

15. http://www.eeoc.gov/laws/statutes/titlevii.cfm (retrieved July 21, 2010).

16. http://www3.ce9.uscourts.gov/jury-instructions/node/182/ (retrieved May 24, 2014).

17. http?//www.ca5.uscourts.gov/opinions%5Cunpub%5C13/13-10164.0.pdf (retrieved May 21, 2014).

18. 442 F2d 385, *Diaz v. Pan American World Airways Inc.*

19. http://www.eeoc.gov/laws/statutes/titlevii.cfm (retrieved May 24, 2014).

20. http://www.eeoc.gov/laws/statutes/titlevii.cfm (retrieved May 24, 2014).

21. http://www.eeoc.gov/policy/docs/factemployment_procedures.html (retrieved May 24, 2014).

22. http://caselaw.findlaw.com/us-5th-circuit/1598962.html (retrieved May 21, 2014).

23. http://www.natlawreview.com/article/3m-to-pay-3-million-to-settle-eeoc-age-discrimination-suit/ (retrieved May 21, 2014).

24. http://www.dol.gov/compliance/laws/comp-vevraa.htm (retrieved May 24, 2014).

25. http://www.eeoc.gov/facts/fs-preg.html (retrieved May 24, 2014).

26. http://www.answers.com/topic/pregnancy-discrimination-act/ (retrieved May 24, 2014).

27. "All Things Being Equal . . . General Electric Co. v. Gilbert: An Analysis," *Journal of Law and Education* (1978), 7(1), pp. 21–30.

28. http://www.dol.gov/compliance/laws/comp-rehab.htm (retrieved May 24, 2014).

29. http://www.ada.gov/pubs/adastatute08.htm (retrieved May 24, 2014).

30. Ibid.

31. http://www.ada.gov/employmt.htm (retrieved May 24, 2014).

32. http://www.ada.gov/pubs/adastatute08.htm (retrieved May 24, 2014).

33. http://www.dol.gov/odep/pubs/fact/diverse.htm (retrieved May 24, 2014).

34. http://www.eeoc.gov/eeoc/statistics/enforcement/charges.cfm (retrieved May 24, 2014).

35. Civil Rights Act of 1991–Public Law 102-166.

36. http://www.eeoc.gov/employers/remedies.cfm (retrieved May 24, 2014).

37. http://www.eeoc.gov/eeoc/history/35th/thelaw/cra_1991.html (retrieved May 24, 2014).

38. http://www.dol.gov/vets/usc/vpl/usc38.htm#4301/ (retrieved May 24, 2014).

39. http://www.dol.gov/elaws/vets/userra/userra.asp (retrieved May 24, 2014).

40. http://www.dol.gov/vets/usc/vpl/usc38.htm#4301/ (retrieved May 24, 2014).

41. http://www.dol.gov/vets/regs/fedreg/final/2005023960.htm#regs/ (retrieved May 24, 2014).

42. http://www.eeoc.gov/laws/statutes/gina.cfm (retrieved May 24, 2014).

43. http://www.eeoc.gov/laws/statutes/gina.cfm (retrieved May 24, 2014).

44. http://www.gpo.gov/fdsys/pkg/BILLS-111s181es/html/BILLS-111s181es.htm (retrieved May 24, 2014).

45. http://www.dol.gov/compliance/guide/h1b.htm (retrieved May 24, 2014).

46. http://www.dol.gov/compliance/guide/h1b.htm (retrieved May 24, 2014).

47. http://online.wsj.com/news/articles/SB10001424052702304200804579163604195741612/ (retrieved May 25, 2014).

48. http://www.eeoc.gov/eeoc/history/35th/thelaw/irca.html (retrieved May 24, 2014).

49. http://eeoc.gov/eeoc/ (retrieved May 24, 2014).

50. http://eeoc.gov/eeoc/ (retrieved May 24, 2014).

51. http://www.eeoc.gov/employers/eeo1survey/faq.cfm (retrieved May 21, 2014).

52. http://www.eeoc.gov/laws/statutes/titlevii.cfm (retrieved May 24, 2014).

53. http://www.eeoc.gov/laws/types/retaliation.cfm (retrieved May 24, 2014).

54. http://eeoc.gov/eeoc/statistics/enforcement/charges.cfm (retrieved May 21, 2014).

55. http://www.eeoc.gov/laws/practices/index.cfm (retrieved May 24, 2014).

56. *Pennsylvania State Police v. Suders* (03-95), 542 U.S. 129 (2004), 325 F.3d 432.

57. http://ecfr.gpoaccess.gov/cgi/t/text/text-idx?c=ecfr&tpl=/ecfrbrowse/Title29/29cfr1608_main_02.tpl (retrieved July 21, 2010).

58. http://www.shrm.org/templatestools/hrqa/pages/whenisanaapneeded.aspx (retrieved May 24, 2014).

59. 41 CFR Part 60-1.

60. Ibid.

61. http://www.supremecourt.gov/opinions/12pdf/11-345_l5gm.pdf (retrieved May 25, 2014).

62. http://www.nytimes.com/2014/04/23/us/supreme-court-michigan-affirmative-action-ban.html?_r=0 (retrieved May 25, 2014).

63. http://www.dol.gov/ofccp/aboutof.html (retrieved May 24, 2014).

64. Z.T. Kalinoski, D. Steele-Johnson, E.J. Peyton, K.A. Leas, J. Steinke, N.A. Bowling, "A Meta-Analytic Evaluation of Diversity Training Outcomes," *Journal of Organizational Behavior* (2013), 34(8), pp. 1076–1104.

65. A. Joshi, H. Roh, "The Role of Context in Work Team Diversity Research: A Meta-Analytic Review," *Academy of Management Journal* (2009), 52(3), pp. 599–627.

66. http://www.un.org/apps/news/story.asp?NewsID=40257#.U35knCiF8ws (retrieved May 22, 2014).

67. https://www.cia.gov/library/publications/the-world-factbook/fields/2127.html (retrieved May 22, 2014).

68. https://www.cia.gov/library/publications/the-world-factbook/geos/xx.html (retrieved May 22, 2014).

69. http://www.infoplease.com/us/statistics/population-majority-no-more.html (retrieved May 22, 2014).

70. C. Dougherty, "U.S. Nears Racial Milestone," *The Wall Street Journal* (June 11, 2010), p. A3.

71. "What the Next Census Will Tell Marketers," *Businessweek* (November 9, 2009), p. 8.

72. C. Dougherty, "U.S. Nears Racial Milestone," *The Wall Street Journal* (June 11, 2010), p. A3.

73. E. Kearney, D. Gebert, S.C. Voelpel, "When and How Diversity Benefits Teams: The Importance of Team Members' Need for Cognition," *Academy of Management Journal* (2009), 52(3), pp. 581–598.

74. C.L. Holladay, M.A. Quiñones, "The Influence of Training Focus and Trainer Characteristics on Diversity Training Effectiveness," *Academy of Management Learning & Education* (2008), 7(3), pp. 343–354.

75. C.T. Kulik, L. Roberson, "Common Goals and Golden Opportunities: Evaluation of Diversity Education in Academic and Organizational Settings," *Academy of Management Learning & Education* (2008), 7(3), pp. 309–331.

76. S.D. Sidle, "Building a Committed Global Workforce: Does What Employees Want Depend on Culture?" *Academy of Management Perspectives* (2009), 23(1), pp. 79–80.

77. S. Bell et al., "Getting Specific About Demographic Diversity Variable and Team Performance Relationships: A Meta-Analysis," *Journal of Management* (2011), 37(3), pp. 709–743.

78. A.N. Pieterse, D. van Knippenberg, D. van Dierendonck, "Cultural Diversity and

Team Performance: The Role of Team Member Goal Orientation," *Academy of Management Journal* (2013), 56(3), pp. 782–804.

79. M. Mayfield, J. Mayfield, "Developing a Scale to Measure the Creative Environment Perceptions: A Questionnaire for Investigating Garden Variety Creativity," *Creativity Research Journal* (2010), 22(2), pp. 162–169.

80. M.A. Runco, S. Acar, "Divergent Thinking as an Indicator of Creative Potential," *Creativity Research Journal* (2012), 24(1), pp. 66–75.

81. F. Stevens, V. Plaut, J. Sanchez-Burks, "Unlocking the Benefits of Diversity," *Journal of Applied Behavioral Science* (2008), 44(1), pp. 116–133.

82. F.R. de Wit, L.L. Greer, K.A. Jehn, "The Paradox of Intragroup Conflict: A Meta-Analysis," *Journal of Applied Psychology* (2012), 97(2), p. 360.

83. S. Benard, L. Doan, "The Conflict-Cohesion Hypothesis: Past, Present, and Possible Futures," *Advances in Group Processes* (2011), 28, pp. 189–225.

84. E.A. Okoro, M.C. Washington, "Workforce Diversity and Organizational Communication: Analysis of Human Capital Performance and Productivity," *Journal of Diversity Management* (2012), 7(1), pp. 57–62.

85. S.D. Sidle, "Building a Committed Global Workforce: Does What Employees Want Depend on Culture?" *Academy of Management Perspectives* (2009), 23(1), pp. 79–80.

86. Y. Yang, A.M. Konrad, "Understanding Diversity Management Practices: Implications of Institutional Theory and Resource-Based Theory," *Group & Organization Management* (2011), 36(1), pp. 6–38.

87. K.Y. Ng, L. Van Dyne, S. Ang, "From Experience to Experiential Learning: Cultural Intelligence as a Learning Capability for Global Leader Development," *Academy of Management Learning & Education* (2009), 8(4), pp. 511–526.

88. Y. Yang, A.M. Konrad, "Understanding Diversity Management Practices: Implications of Institutional Theory and Resource-Based Theory. *Group & Organization Management* (2011), 36(1), pp. 6–38.

89. Y. Yang, A.M. Konrad, "Understanding Diversity Management Practices: Implications of Institutional Theory and Resource-Based Theory," *Group & Organization Management* (2011), 36(1), pp. 6–38.

90. C.T. Kulik, L. Roberson, "Common Goals and Golden Opportunities: Evaluation of Diversity Education in Academic and Organizational Settings," *Academy of Management Learning & Education* (2008), 7(3), pp. 309–331.

91. Y. Yang, A.M. Konrad, "Understanding Diversity Management Practices: Implications of Institutional Theory and Resource-Based Theory," *Group & Organization Management* (2011), 36(1), pp. 6–38.

92. http://www.eeoc.gov/facts/fs-sex .html (retrieved May 24, 2014).

93. http://caselaw.lp.findlaw.com/ scripts/getcase.pl?court=US&vol=477 &invol=57 (retrieved May 24, 2014).

94. http://www.eeoc.gov/policy/ docs/currentissues.html (retrieved May 24, 2014).

95. http://www.law.cornell.edu/ supct/html/96-568.ZO.html (retrieved May 24, 2014).

96. Ibid.

97. Ibid.

98. Ibid.

99. http://www.shrm.org/ TemplatesTools/Samples/PowerPoints/ Documents/2008 Religion in the Workplace .ppt (retrieved May 25, 2014).

100. http://www.eeoc.gov/eeoc/ newsroom/release/4-4-06.cfm (retrieved May 24, 2014).

101. http://www.eeoc.gov/eeoc/ systemic/ (retrieved May 24, 2014).

102. http://www.eeoc.gov/eeoc/ plan/2013parhigh_discussion.cfm (retrieved May 24, 2014).

103. Ibid.

104. http://www.shrm.org/legalissues/ federalresources/pages/headscarf-accommodation-muslim-applicant.aspx (retrieved May 23, 2014).

105. M. Trottman, "Religious-Discrimination Claims on the Rise," *The Wall Street Journal* (October, 28, 2013), p. B-1.

106. Ibid.

107. http://www.eeoc.gov/laws/ statutes/titlevii.cfm (retrieved July 22, 2010).

108. http://www.shrm.org/legalissues/ federalresources/pages/headscarf-accommodation-muslim-applicant.aspx (retrieved May 23, 2014).

109. http://www.eeoc.gov/policy/ docs/religion.html (retrieved July 22, 2010).

110. http://www.insidecounsel .com/2012/02/06/labor-increased-litigation-under-the-adaaa/ (retrieved May 23, 2014).

111. Ibid.

112. http://www1.eeoc.gov/eeoc/ newsroom/release/5-15-13.cfm (retrieved May 23, 2014).

113. http://www.eeoc.gov/eeoc/ newsroom/release/7-30-13a.cfm (retrieved May 23, 2014).

114. http://www.eeoc.gov/eeoc/ newsroom/release/8-1-13.cfm (retrieved May 23, 2014).

CHAPTER 4

1. A.L. Kallenbert, "The Mismatched Worker: When People Don't Fit Their Jobs," *Academy of Management Perspectives* (2008), 22(1), pp. 24–40.

2. T. Barmby, A. Bryson, B. Eberth, "Human Capital, Matching and Job Satisfaction," *Economics Letters* (2012), 117(3), pp. 548–551.

3. M. White, A. Bryson, "Positive Employee Attitudes: How Much Human Resource Management Do You Need?" *Human Relations* (2013), 66(3), pp. 385–406.

4. J. Eder, E. Panagos, M. Rabinovich, "Time Constraints in Workflow Systems," *Lecture Notes in Computer Science* (2010), 1626, pp. 286–300.

5. G. Cravo, "Applications of Propositional Logic to Workflow Analysis," *Applied Mathematics Letters*, 23(3), pp. 272–276.

6. H.C.W. Lau, G.T.S. Ho, K.F. Chu, W. Ho, C.K.M. Lee, "Development of an Intelligent Quality Management System Using Fuzzy Association Rules," *Expert Systems With Applications* (2009), 36(2), pp. 1801–1815.

7. Y. Gil, V. Ratnakar, J. Kim, P.A. González-Calero, P. Groth, J. Moody, E. Deelman, "Wings: Intelligent Workflow-Based Design of Computational Experiments," *IEEE Intelligent Systems* (2011), 26(1), pp. 62–72.

8. A.H. Memon, I.A. Rahman, A.A. Aziz, K. Ravish, N.M. Hanas, "Identifying Construction Resource Factors Affecting Construction Cost: Case of Johor," in *Malaysian Technical Universities International Conference on Engineering & Technology* (2011).

9. O. Henry, "Organisational Conflict and Its Effects on Organisational Performance," *Research Journal of Business Management* (2009), 2(1), pp. 16–24.

10. P. Singh, "Job Analysis for a Changing Workplace," *Human Resource Management Review* (2008), 18(2), pp. 87–89.

11. J.I. Sanchez, E.L. Levine, "The Rise and Fall of Job Analysis and the Future of Work Analysis," *Annual Review of Psychology* (2012), 63, pp. 397–425.

12. http://www.onetcenter.org/ overview.html (retrieved August 22, 2010).

13. M. Robinson, "Work Sampling: Methodological Advances and New Applications," *Human Factors and Ergonomics in Manufacturing & Service Industries* (2010), 20(1), pp. 42–60.

14. S.G. Gibson, "Generalized Work Dimension Analysis," in *The Handbook of Work Analysis: Methods, Systems, Applications and Science of Work Measurement in Organizations*," edited by

M.A. Wilson, W. Bennett, S.G. Gibson, G.M. Alliger (New York, NY: Taylor & Francis, 2012), pp. 215–230.

15. J. Kilgour, "Job Evaluation Revisited: The Point Factor Method; The Point Factor Method of Job Evaluation Consists of a Large Number of Discretionary Decisions That Result in Something That Appears to Be Entirely Objective and, Even, Scientific," *Compensation & Benefits Review* (July/August 2008), 40, pp. 37–46.

16. S.G. Gibson, "Generalized Work Dimension Analysis," in *The Handbook of Work Analysis: Methods, Systems, Applications and Science of Work Measurement in Organizations*," edited by M.A. Wilson, W. Bennett, S.G. Gibson, G.M. Alliger (New York, NY: Taylor & Francis, 2012), pp. 215–230.

17. M. Robinson, "Work Sampling: Methodological Advances and New Applications," *Human Factors and Ergonomics in Manufacturing & Service Industries* (2010), 20(1), pp. 42–60.

18. S.G. Gibson, "Generalized Work Dimension Analysis," in *The Handbook of Work Analysis: Methods, Systems, Applications and Science of Work Measurement in Organizations*," edited by M.A. Wilson, W. Bennett, S.G. Gibson, G.M. Alliger (New York, NY: Taylor & Francis, 2012), pp. 215–230.

19. J.I. Sanchez, E.L. Levine, "The Rise and Fall of Job Analysis and the Future of Work Analysis," *Annual Review of Psychology* (2012), 63, pp. 397–425.

20. K. Soderquist, A. Papalexandris, G. Ioannou, G. Prastacos, "From Task-Based to Competency-Based: A Typology and Process Supporting a Critical HRM Transition," *Personnel Review* (2010), 39(3), pp. 325–346.

21. S.H. Yun, "Enterprise Human Resource Matching Model Based on Job Analysis and Quality Assessment," in *The 19th International Conference on Industrial Engineering and Engineering Management* (Heidelberg, Germany: Springer, 2013), pp. 761–771.

22. Society for Human Resource Management, "Job Descriptions Remain a Weak Link in Hiring Process," http://www.shrm.org/hrdisciplines/staffingmanagement/articles/pages/weak-job-descriptions.aspx (retrieved May 28, 2014).

23. JobDescription.com, "Insperity," http://www.jobdescription.com (retrieved June 29, 2010).

24. A.C. Keller, N.K. Semmer, "Changes in Situational and Dispositional Factors as Predictors of Job Satisfaction," *Journal of Vocational Behavior* (2013), 83(1), pp. 88–98.

25. S.K. Parker, A. Johnson, C. Collins, H. Nguyen, "Making the Most of Structural Support: Moderating Influence of Employees' Clarity and Negative Affect," *Academy of Management Journal*, 56(3), pp. 867–892.

26. J. Lahart, "Moment of Truth for Productivity Boom," *The Wall Street Journal* (May 6, 2010), pp. A1, A16.

27. G.R. Oldham, J.R. Hackman, "Not What It Was and Not What It Will Be: The Future of Job Design Research," *Journal of Organizational Behavior* (2010), 31(2–3), pp. 463–479.

28. F.P. Morgeson, G.J. Medsker, M.A. Campion, "Job and Team Design," in *Handbook of Human Factors and Ergonomics* (2012), edited by Gabriel Salvendy (Hoboken, NJ: Wiley, 2006), pp. 428–457.

29. G.P. McClelland, D.J. Leach, C.W. Clegg, I. McGowan, "Collaborative Crafting in Call Centre Teams," *Journal of Occupational and Organizational Psychology* (2014).

30. R.W. Proctor, K.P.L. Vu, "Cumulative Knowledge and Progress in Human Factors, *Annual Review of Psychology* (2010), 61, pp. 623–651.

31. M.E. Malik, B. Naeem, "Towards Understanding Controversy on Herzberg Theory of Motivation," *World Applied Sciences Journal* (2013), 24(8).

32. J.H. Batchelor, K.A. Abston, K. Lawlor, G.F. Burch, "The Job Characteristics Model: An Extension to Entrepreneurial Motivation," *Small Business Institute® Journal* (2014), 10(1), pp. 1–10.

33. D. Liu, T.R. Mitchell, T.W. Lee, B.C. Holtom, TR. Hinkin, "How Employees Are Out of Step With Coworkers: How Job Satisfaction Trajectory and Dispersion Influence Individual- and Unit-Level Voluntary Turnover," *Academy of Management Journal* (2012), 55(6), pp. 1360–1380.

34. A.M. Grant, "Giving Time, Time After Time: Work Design and Sustained Employee Participation in Corporate Volunteering," *Academy of Management Review* (2012), 37(4), pp. 589–615.

35. J.G. Proudfoot, P.J. Corr, D.E. Guest, G. Dunn, "Cognitive-Behavioural Training to Change Attributional Style Improves Employee Well-Being, Job Satisfaction, Productivity, and Turnover," *Personality and Individual Differences* (2009), 46(2), pp. 147–153.

36. S.K. Parker, "Beyond Motivation: Job and Work Design for Development, Health, Ambidexterity, and More," *Annual Review of Psychology* (2014), 65, pp. 661–691.

37. T. Woods, "The Best Advice I Ever Got," *Fortune* (July 6, 2009), p. 43.

38. J. Lahart, "Moment of Truth for Productivity Boom," *The Wall Street Journal* (May 6, 2010), pp. A1, A16.

39. A. Jagoda, "Deskilling as the Dark Side of the Work Specialization," *International Journal of Academic Research* (2013), 5(3).

40. K. Swisher, "A Question of Management," *The Wall Street Journal* (June 2, 2009), p. R4.

41. A.M. Grant, "Giving Time, Time After Time: Work Design and Sustained Employee Participation in Corporate Volunteering," *Academy of Management Review* (2012), 37(4), pp. 589–615.

42. E. Gibson, "The Stop-Managing Guide to Management," *Businessweek* (June 15, 2009), p. 73.

43. C. Tuna, "Micromanagers Miss Bull's-Eye," *The Wall Street Journal* (November 3, 2008), p. B4.

44. M.R. Barrick, M.K. Mount, N. Li, "The Theory of Purposeful Work Behavior: The Role of Personality, Higher-Order Goals, and Job Characteristics," *Academy of Management Review* (2013), 38(1), pp. 132–153.

45. J. Hu, R.C. Liden, "Antecedents of Team Potency and Team Effectiveness: An Examination of Goal and Process Clarity and Servant Leadership," *Journal of Applied Psychology* (2011), 96(4), p. 851.

46. H. Bresman, "Changing Routines: A Process Model of Vicarious Group Learning in Pharmaceutical R&D," *Academy of Management Journal* (2013), 56(1), pp. 35–61.

47. J.R. Hollenbeck, B. Beersma, M.E. Schouten, "Beyond Team Types and Taxonomies: A Dimensional Scaling Conceptualization for Team Descriptions," *Academy of Management Review* (2013), 37(1), pp. 82–106.

48. N.B. Moe, T. Dingsøyr, T. Dybå, "A Teamwork Model for Understanding an Agile Team: A Case Study of a Scrum Project," *Information and Software Technology* (2010), 52(5), pp. 480–491.

49. M.R. Barrick, M.K. Mount, N. Li, "The Theory of Purposeful Work Behavior: The Role of Personality, Higher-Order Goals, and Job Characteristics," *Academy of Management Review* (2013), 38(1), pp. 132–153.

50. L. McNall, A. Masuda, J. Nicklin, "Flexible Work Arrangements, Job Satisfaction, and Turnover Intentions: The Mediating Role of Work-to-Family Enrichment," *The Journal of Psychology: Interdisciplinary and Applied Issue* (2010), 144(1), pp. 61–81.

51. A.D. Masuda, S.A. Poelmans, T.D. Allen, P.E. Spector, L.M. Lapierre, C.L. Cooper, . . . I. Moreno-Velazquez, "Flexible Work Arrangements Availability and Their Relationship With Work-to-Family Conflict,

Job Satisfaction, and Turnover Intentions: A Comparison of Three Country Clusters," *Applied Psychology* (2012), 61(1), pp. 1–29.

52. Society for Human Resource Management, "Sample Policy: Flextime," http://www.shrm.org/templatestools/samples/policies/pages/cms_007473.aspx (retrieved May 27, 2014).

53. US Office of Personnel Management, "Performance Management: Performance Management Cycle," http://www.opm.gov/perform/articles/2001/win01-1.asp (retrieved August 21, 2010).

54. M. Erez, "Culture and Job Design," *Journal of Organizational Behavior* (2010), 31(2–3), pp. 389–400.

55. L.Q. Yang, P.E. Spector, J.I. Sanchez, T.D. Allen, S. Poelmans, C.L. Cooper, . . . J.M. Woo, "Individualism-Collectivism as a Moderator of the Work Demands–Strains Relationship: A Cross-Level and Cross-National Examination," *Journal of International Business Studies* (2012), 43(4), pp. 424–443.

56. A.M. Grant, Y. Fried, S.K. Parker, M. Frese, "Putting Job Design in Context: Introduction to the Special Issue," *Journal of Organizational Behavior* (2010), 31(2–3), pp. 145–157.

57. S. Mayer, "Strategic Human Resource Management Practices of High Performance Organizations," http://www.innovativehumandynamics.com [newsletter (2008)], pp. 1–4.

58. J. Wong, A. Chan, Y.H. Chiang, "A Critical Review of Forecasting Models to Predict Manpower Demand," *Australasian Journal of Construction Economics and Building* (2012), 4(2), pp. 43–56.

59. http://www.referenceforbusiness.com/management/Gr-Int/Human-Resource-Information-Systems.html (retrieved August 22, 2010).

60. S. Strohmeier, F. Piazza, "Domain Driven Data Mining in Human Resource Management: A Review of Current Research," *Expert Systems With Applications* (2013), 40(7), pp. 2410–2420.

61. J.I. Hancock, D.G. Allen, F.A. Bosco, K.R. McDaniel, C.A. Pierce, "Meta-Analytic Review of Employee Turnover as a Predictor of Firm Performance," *Journal of Management* (2013), 39(3), pp. 573–603.

62. A. Cancino, "Shortage of Skilled Workers Leaves 10 Million Jobs Unfilled, Report Says," *Chicago Tribune* (April 24, 2012), http://articles.chicagotribune.com/2012-04-24/business/ct-biz-0425-global-manufacturing--20120424_1_skilled-workers-skills-gap-manufacturing-jobs/.

63. J. Mauldin, "A Bubble in Complacency," *Forbes* (May 25, 2014), http://www.forbes.com/sites/johnmauldin/2014/05/25/a-bubble-in-complacency/.

64. M. Levinson, "Nine Things Managers and Employees Need to Know About Layoffs," *CIO* (March 18, 2008), http://www.cio.com/article/198702/Nine_Things_Managers_and_Employees_Need_to_Know_About_Layoffs/.

65. F. Gandolfi, "HR Strategies That Can Take the Sting out of Downsizing-Related Layoffs," *Ivey Business Journal* (July/August 2008), http://iveybusinessjournal.com/topics/strategy/hr-strategies-that-can-take-the-sting-out-of-downsizing-related-layoffs#.U4oRwygkTv4/.

66. Ibid.

67. J. Pfeffer, "Layoff the Layoffs," *Newsweek* (Feb. 15, 2010) pp. 34–37.

68. A. Alesina, "Fiscal Policy After the Great Recession," *Atlantic Economic Journal* (2012), 40(4), pp. 429–435.

69. K. Mellahi, A. Wilkinson, "Slash and Burn or Nip and Tuck? Downsizing, Innovation and Human Resources," *The International Journal of Human Resource Management* (2010), 21(13), pp. 2291–2305.

70. F. Gandolfi, "HR Strategies That Can Take the Sting out of Downsizing-Related Layoffs," *Ivey Business Journal* (July/August 2008), http://iveybusinessjournal.com/topics/strategy/hr-strategies-that-can-take-the-sting-out-of-downsizing-related-layoffs#.U4oRwygkTv4/.

71. R. Zeidner, "Cutting Hours Without Increasing Risk," *HR Magazine* (April, 2009), pp. 44–48.

72. K.M. Day, A.A. Armenakis, H.S. Feild, D.R. Norris, "Other Organizations Are Doing It, Why Shouldn't We? A Look at Downsizing and Organizational Identity Through an Institutional Theory Lens," *Journal of Change Management* (2012), 12(2), pp. 165–188.

73. E. Krell, "Make It Easier to Say Goodbye," *HR Magazine* (2012), 57(10), pp. 40–44.

74. US Department of Labor, Wage and Overtime Division, "Overtime Pay," http://www.dol.gov/whd/overtime_pay.htm (retrieved August 22, 2014).

75. M.A. Tipgoes, J.P. Trebby, "Job-Related Stresses and Strains in Management Accounting," *Journal of Applied Business Research* (2011), 3(3), pp. 8–14.

76. M.J. Bidwell, F. Briscoe, "Who Contracts? Determinants of the Decision to Work as an Independent Contractor Among Information Technology Workers," *Academy of Management Journal* (2009), 52(6), pp. 1148–1166.

77. M.E. Lapalme, G. Simard, M. Tremblay, "The Influence of Psychological Contract Breach on Temporary Workers' Commitment and Behaviors: A Multiple Agency Perspective," *Journal of Business and Psychology* (2011), 26(3), pp. 311–324.

78. M.J. Chambel, F. Sobral, "Training Is an Investment With Return in Temporary Workers: A Social Exchange Perspective," *Career Development International* (2011), 16(2), pp. 161–177.

79. R.W. Wood, "New Crackdown on Using Independent Contractors," *Forbes* (November 15, 2012), http://www.forbes.com/sites/robertwood/2012/11/15/new-crackdown-on-using-independent-contractors/.

80. Microsoft had to pay almost $100 million to about 10,000 workers whom it had classified as temporary, and a transportation company was charged $319 million in unpaid employment taxes and penalties in 2007 because it misclassified drivers as contract workers.

81. G. Jericho, "Alleviating Skills Shortages Takes Time (and Lots of It)," *The Drum* (June 6, 2012), http://www.abc.net.au/unleashed/4053438.html.

82. M.C. Davidson, Y. Wang, "Sustainable Labor Practices? Hotel Human Resource Managers' Views on Turnover and Skill Shortages," *Journal of Human Resources in Hospitality & Tourism* (2011), 10(3), pp. 235–253.

83. J.I. Hancock, D.G. Allen, F.A. Bosco, K.R. McDaniel, C.A. Pierce, "Meta-Analytic Review of Employee Turnover as a Predictor of Firm Performance," *Journal of Management* (2013), 39(3), pp. 573–603.

84. M.J. Bidwell, F. Briscoe, "Who Contracts? Determinants of the Decision to Work as an Independent Contractor Among Information Technology Workers," *Academy of Management Journal* (2009), 52(6), pp. 1148–1166.

85. SHRM, "Succession Planning With Your Board," http://www.shrm.org/communities/volunteerresources/pages/succplg.aspx (retrieved May 30, 2014).

86. S.J. Kowalewski, L. Moretti, D. McGee, "Succession Planning: Evidence from Best Companies in New York," *International Journal of Management & Marketing Research* (2011), 4(2).

87. O*Net Resource Center, "About O*Net," http://www.onetcenter.org/overview.html (retrieved May 30, 2014).

88. O*Net Resource Center, "O*Net Toolkit for Business," http://www.onetcenter.org/toolkit.html (retrieved May 30, 2014).

89. O*Net Resource Center, http://www.onetonline.org (retrieved May 30, 2014).

90. O*Net Resource Center, "The O*Net Content Model," http://www.onetcenter.org/content.html (retrieved May 30, 2014).

91. US Office of Personnel Management, "Assessment & Selection: Competencies," http://www.opm.gov/policy-data-oversight/assessment-and-selection/competencies/ (retrieved May 30, 2014).

92. J.I. Sanchez, E.L. Levine, "The Rise and Fall of Job Analysis and the Future of Work Analysis," *Annual Review of Psychology* (2012), 63, pp. 397–425.

93. R.L. Fraser, M. Montgomery, "Navigating the Competency Modeling Maze," http://ipacweb.org/Resources/Documents/conf12/fraser.pdf (retrieved May 30, 2014).

94. E.L. Levine, J.I. Sanchez, "Evaluating Work Analysis in the 21st Century," in *The Handbook of Work Analysis: Methods, Systems, Applications and Science of Work Measurement in Organizations*, edited by Mark A. Wilson (New York, NY: Routledge, 2012), p. 127.

95. J.H. Spangenberg, A. Fuad-Luke, K. Blincoe, "Design for Sustainability (DfS): The Interface of Sustainable Production and Consumption," *Journal of Cleaner Production* (2010), 18(15), pp. 1485–1493.

96. N. Landrum, S. Edwards, *Sustainable Business, An Executive's Primer* (New York, NY: Business Expert Press, 2009).

97. Ibid.

98. Cote, D. M. (2013, June). Honeywell's CEO on how he avoided layoffs. *Harvard Business Review*. Retrieved from http://hbr.org/2013/06/honeywells-ceo-on-how-he-avoided-layoffs/.

99. Hoover's Inc. (2014). *Honeywell International, Inc.* [Hoover's Company Records: In-Depth Records]. Retrieved July 3, 2014, from Long Island University Academic Database.

100. Cote, D. M. (2013, June). Honeywell's CEO on how he avoided layoffs. *Harvard Business Review*. Retrieved from http://hbr.org/2013/06/honeywells-ceo-on-how-he-avoided-layoffs/.

CHAPTER 5

1. D.G. Allen, P.C. Bryant, J.M. Vardaman, "Retaining Talent: Replacing Misconceptions With Evidence-Based Strategies," *Academy of Management Perspectives* (2010), 24(2), 2010, pp. 48–64.

2. H.J. Walker, T.N. Bauer, M.S. Cole, J.B. Bernerth, H.S. Feild, J.C. Short, "Is This How I Will Be Treated? Reducing Uncertainty Through Recruitment Interactions," *Academy of Management Journal* (2013), 56(5), pp. 1325–1347.

3. J. Cook, "Zulily to Spend Heavily to Fill Mid-level Management Gap, Sparked by Insane Growth Rate," *GeekWire* (March 1, 2014), http://www.geekwire.com/2014/zulily-spend-heavily-fill-mid-level-manager-gap-sparked-insane-growth-rate/.

4. Zulily Inc., "US Securities and Exchange Commission Form 10-K for the Fiscal Year Ended December 29, 2013," http://www.sec.gov/Archives/edgar/data/1478484/000144530514000741/zu-12292013x10k.htm.

5. R.E. Ployhart, J.A. Weekley, J. Ramsey, "The Consequences of Human Resource Stocks and Flow: A Longitudinal Examination of Unit Service Orientation and Unit Effectiveness," *Academy of Management Journal* (2009), 52(5), pp. 996–1015.

6. V. Elmer, "Hiring Without a Net: Groupon's Recruiter Speaks," *Fortune* (July 25, 2011), p. 34.

7. S.D. Maurer, D.P. Cook, "Using Company Web Sites to E-Recruit Qualified Applicants: A Job Marketing–Based Review of Theory-Based Research," *Computers in Human Behavior* (2011), 27(1), pp. 106–117.

8. M. Guthridge, A. Komm, E. Lawson, "Making Talent a Strategic Priority," *The McKinsey Quarterly* (January 2008), http://www.dnlglobal.com/includes/repository/newsitem/TheMcKinseyQuarterly01_08.pdf (retrieved September 20, 2010).

9. *Bloomberg Businessweek*, "New Priorities for Employers," http://images.businessweek.com/mz/10/38/1038taunemployed54.pdf (retrieved June 2, 2014).

10. J. Bersin, "Employee Retention Now a Big Issue: Why the Tide Has Turned," [LinkedIn post, August 16, 2013], https://www.linkedin.com/today/post/article/20130816200159-131079-employee-retention-now-a-big-issue-why-the-tide-has-turned/.

11. Y. Noguchi, "As Health Law Changes Loom, a Shift to Part-Time Workers," NPR (April 29, 2013) http://www.npr.org/2013/04/29/179864601/as-health-law-changes-loom-a-shift-to-part-time-workers/.

12. The Fuqua School of Business, Duke University, "Survey: CFOs Weigh In on Affordable Care Act, Interest Rates, Stock Market Overheating" (September 11, 2013), http://www.fuqua.duke.edu/news_events/news-releases/cfo-survey-results-2013-q3/#.U4zUAygkTv4/.

13. D. Autor, L. Katz, M. Kearney, "Trends in U.S. Wage Inequality: Revising the Revisionists," *The Review of Economics and Statistics* (2008), 90(2), pp. 300–323.

14. D. Dahl, "A Sea of Job Seekers, but Some Companies Aren't Getting Any Bites," *The New York Times* (June 28, 2012), p. B-7.

15. E. Glazer, "Problems and Solutions—We Asked HR Executives: What's Your Biggest Challenge?" *The Wall Street Journal* (October 24, 2011), p. R-2.

16. S. Sorenson, J. Mattingly, F. Lee, "Decoding the Signal Effects of Job Candidate Attraction to Corporate Social Practices," *Business and Society Review* (2010), 115(2), pp. 173–204.

17. J. M. Henderson, "Job Stability vs. Job Satisfaction? Millennials May Have to Settle for Neither," *Forbes* blog (December 22, 2012), http://www.forbes.com/sites/jmaureenhenderson/2012/12/22/job-stability-vs-job-satisfaction-millennials-may-have-to-settle-for-neither/.

18. M.J. Mol, M. Kotabe, "Overcoming Inertia: Drivers of the Outsourcing Process," *Long Range Planning* (2011), 44(3), pp. 160–178.

19. S.G. Toh, E. Ang, M.K. Devi, "Systematic Review on the Relationship Between the Nursing Shortage and Job Satisfaction, Stress and Burnout Levels Among Nurses in Oncology/Haematology Settings," *International Journal of Evidence-Based Healthcare* (2012), 10(2), pp. 126–141.

20. K. Lundby (Ed.), *Going Global: Practical Applications and Recommendation for HR and OD Professionals in the Global Workplace* (San Francisco, CA: Jossey Bass, 2010), pp. 114–115.

21. S. Raice, "Friend—and Possible Employee," *The Wall Street Journal* (October 24, 2011), p. A-2.

22. *Wagner v. The Home Depot USA, Inc.*, US District Court Oregon (Portland), Civil Case No. 10-901-KI, November 9, 2010, http://law.justia.com/cases/federal/district-courts/oregon/ordce/3:2010cv00901/98822/13/.

23. Facebook, "Facebook Reports Fourth Quarter and Full Year 2013 Results," [press release], January 29, 2014, http://www.prnewswire.com/news-releases/facebook-reports-fourth-quarter-and-full-year-2013-results-242637731.html.

24. J. Hempel, "LinkedIn: How It's Changing Business," *Fortune* (July 1, 2013), p. 70.

25. J. Barrett-Poindexter, "How to Find Out What a Company's Culture Is Really Like," *Glassdoor* blog (July 22, 2013), http://www.glassdoor.com/blog/find-companys-culture/.

26. "Global Economics: It's Not What Grads Know, It's Who They Know," *Bloomberg Businessweek* (June 18–24, 2012), pp. 9–10.

27. G. Segal, "The Real Way to Build a Network," *Fortune* (February 6, 2013), pp. 23–32.

28. J. Valentino-Devries, "Social Media and Bias in Hiring," *The Wall Street Journal*, (November 21, 2013), p. B-4.

29. G. Anders, "Insider Trading for Talent," *Forbes* (November 18, 2013), 192(7), p. 1-1.

30. R.E. Silverman, "It Pays to Promote From Within: Here's How," *The Wall Street Journal* blog (May 30, 2013), http://blogs .wsj.com/atwork/2012/05/30/it-pays-to-promote-from-within-heres-how-to-do-it/ (retrieved June 4, 2014).

31. G. Kelly, "A View From the Top," *Fortune* (March 16, 2009), p. 107.

32. V. Elmer, "Hiring Without a Net: Groupon's Recruiter Speaks," *Fortune* (July 25, 2011), p. 34.

33. Jobvite, "Jobvite Declares May National Employee Referral Month," [press release] (May 1, 2012), http://recruiting .jobvite.com/company/press-releases/2012/jobvite-declares-may-national-employee-referral-month/.

34. Society for Human Resource Management, *SHRM Human Resource Curriculum: An Integrated Approach to HR Education* (Alexandria, VA: SHRM, 2013), http://www.shrm.org/Education/hreducation/Documents/2013_SHRM%20HR%20Curriculum%20Guidelines%20and%20Templates_View%20Only_FINAL.pdf.

35. S.C. Paustian-Underdahl, J.R. Halbesleben, D.S. Carlson, K.M. Kacmar, "The Work–Family Interface and Promotability Boundary Integration as a Double-Edged Sword," *Journal of Management* (2013).

36. J.I. Hancock, D.G. Allen, F.A. Bosco, K.R. McDaniel, C.A. Pierce, "Meta-Analytic Review of Employee Turnover as a Predictor of Firm Performance," *Journal of Management* (2013), 39(3), pp. 573–603.

37. R. Bonet, P. Cappelli, M. Hamori, "Labor Market Intermediaries and the New Paradigm for Human Resources," *The Academy of Management Annals* (2013), 7(1), pp. 341–392.

38. K.H. Wears, S.L. Fisher, "Who Is an Employer in the Triangular Employment Relationship? Sorting Through the Definitional Confusion," *Employee Responsibilities and Rights Journal* (2012), 24(3), pp. 159–176.

39. L. Yoon, "How to Hunt for a Headhunter," *CFO.com* (September 16, 2005), http://www.cfo.com/article .cfm/4288677/.

40. E. Parry, S. Tyson, "An Analysis of the Use and Success of Online Recruitment Methods in the UK," *Human Resource Management Journal* (2008), 18(3), pp. 257–274.

41. Internet Live Stats, "Internet Users by Country (2014)," http://www .internetlivestats.com/internet-users-by-country/ (retrieved June 4, 2014).

42. Internet Live Stats, "Internet Users," http://www.internetlivestats.com/internet-users/ (retrieved June 4, 2014).

43. W-C. Tsai, I. W-F. Yang, "Does Image Matter to Different Job Applicants? The Influences of Corporate Image and Applicant Individual Differences on Organizational Attractiveness," *International Journal of Selection and Assessment* (2010), 18(1), pp. 48–63.

44. *Fortune,* "Best Companies 2014: Google," from http://fortune.com/best-companies/google-1/ (retrieved June 4, 2014).

45. D.R. Earnest, D.G. Allen, R.S. Landis, "Mechanisms Linking Realistic Job Previews With Turnover: A Meta-Analytic Path Analysis," *Personnel Psychology* (2011), 64(4), pp. 865–897.

46. Ibid.

47. C.C. Chen, C.S. Hsu, P.S. Tsai, "The Process Mechanisms Linking Recruiter Positive Moods and Organizational Attraction," *International Journal of Selection and Assessment* (2013), 21(4), pp. 376–387.

48. S. Overman, "Help Recruiters Vault Ahead," *Staffing Management Magazine* (2006), 2(2), pp. 32–35.

49. H. Weger Jr, G. Castle Bell, E.M. Minei, M.C. Robinson, "The Relative Effectiveness of Active Listening in Initial Interactions," *International Journal of Listening* (2014), 28(1), pp. 13–31.

50. C.B. Felsen, E.K. Shaw, J.M. Ferrante, L.J. Lacroix, B.F. Crabtree, "Strategies for In-Person Recruitment: Lessons Learned From a New Jersey Primary Care Research Network (NJPCRN) Study," *The Journal of the American Board of Family Medicine* (2010), 23(4), pp. 523–533.

51. C.C. Chen, C.S. Hsu, P.S. Tsai, "The Process Mechanisms Linking Recruiter Positive Moods and Organizational Attraction," *International Journal of Selection and Assessment* (2013), 21(4), pp. 376–387.

52. Society for Human Resource Management, "Cost per Hire" [spreadsheet template], http://www.shrm.org/templatestools/samples/metrics/documents/cost%20per%20hire.xls. (retrieved June 10, 2014).

53. D.G. Allen, P.C. Bryant, J.M. Vardaman, "Retaining Talent: Replacing Misconceptions With Evidence-Based Strategies," *Academy of Management Perspectives* (2010), 24(2), pp. 48–64.

54. D. De Leon, K. LaVelle, S. Cantrell, "Trends Reshaping the Future of HR: Tapping Skills Anywhere, Anytime," *Accenture* (January 22, 2013), p. 3.

55. HR executives are also projecting significant worker shortages in many professions in ten major industries by 2020 and 2030.

56. P. Cappelli, J.R. Keller, "Classifying Work in the New Economy," *Academy of Management Review* (2013), 38(4), pp. 575–596.

57. D. Gartside et al., "Trends Reshaping the Future of HR: The Rise of the Extended Workforce," *Accenture* (January 22, 2013), p. 3.

58. D. De Leon, K. LaVelle, S. Cantrell, "Trends Reshaping the Future of HR: Tapping Skills Anywhere, Anytime," *Accenture* (January 22, 2013), p. 5.

59. P. Cappelli, J.R. Keller, "Classifying Work in the New Economy," *Academy of Management Review* (2013), 38(4), pp. 575–596.

60. D. Gartside et al., "Trends Reshaping the Future of HR: The Rise of the Extended Workforce," *Accenture* (January 22, 2013), p. 4.

61. US Equal Employment Opportunity Commission, "EEOC Agrees to Landmark Resolution of Discrimination Case Against Abercrombie & Fitch," [press release] (November 18, 2004), http://www.eeoc.gov/eeoc/newsroom/release/11-18-04.cfm.

62. R. Austin, "'Bad for Business': Contextual Analysis, Race Discrimination, and Fast Food," *John Marshall Law Review* (Fall 2000), pp. 207–244.

63. "Coca-Cola Settles Race Suit," *CNN Money* (November 16, 2000), http://money.cnn.com/2000/11/16/companies/coke/.

64. Hoover's Inc. (2014). *LinkedIn* [Hoover's Company Records: In-Depth Records]. Retrieved July 17, 2014, from Long Island University Academic Database.

65. Anders, G. (2013, November 18). Insider trading for talent. *Forbes,* 192(7), 1-1.

66. Linkedin Corporation. (2014). *About LinkedIn.* Retrieved June 3, 2014, from http://press.linkedin.com/about/.

67. Ibid.

CHAPTER 6

1. CareerBuilder, "Bad Hires Can Be Costly," *HR Magazine* (February 2013), p. 18.

2. Z. Syed, W. Jamal, "Universalistic Perspective of HRM and Organisational Performance: Meta-Analytical Study," *International Bulletin of Business Administration ISSN* (2012).

3. P. Moen, J. Lam, S. Ammons, E.L. Kelly, "Time Work by Overworked Professionals Strategies in Response to the Stress of Higher Status," *Work and Occupations* (2013), 40(2), pp. 79–114.

4. M. Nemko, "Hiring Wisely: The Art of Selection," *US News & World Report* (July 1, 2013), http://money.usnews.com/money/blogs/outside-voices-careers/2013/07/01/hiring-wisely-the-art-of-selection/.

5. V. Elmer, "Hiring Without a Net: Groupon's Recruiter Speaks," *Fortune* (July 25, 2011), p. 34.

6. L.B. Hollinshead, "Social-Media Privacy and Protection Laws," *Employment Relations Today* (2013), 40(3), pp. 73–82.

7. T. Jefferson, *The Declaration of Independence*, http://www.archives.gov/exhibits/charters/declaration_transcript.html.

8. M.T. Iqbal, W. Latif, W. Naseer, "The Impact of Person Job Fit on Job Satisfaction and Its Subsequent Impact on Employees' Performance," *Mediterranean Journal of Social Sciences* (2012), 3(2), pp. 523–530.

9. J.L. Burnette, J.M. Pollack, "Implicit Theories of Work and Job Fit: Implications for Job and Life Satisfaction," *Basic and Applied Social Psychology* (2013), 35(4), pp. 360–372.

10. D.G. Allen, P.C. Bryant, J.M. Vardaman, "Retaining Talent: Replacing Misconceptions With Evidence-Based Strategies," *Academy of Management Perspectives* (2010), 24(2), pp. 48–64.

11. E.M. Nolan, M.J. Morley, "A Test of the Relationship Between Person-Environment Fit and Cross-Cultural Adjustment Among Self-Initiated Expatriates," *The International Journal of Human Resource Management* (2014), 25(11), published online.

12. US Equal Employment Opportunity Commission, "Employment Tests and Selection Procedures (September 23, 2010), http://www.eeoc.gov/policy/docs/factemployment_procedures.html (retrieved June 9, 2014).

13. US Office of Personnel Management, "Frequently Asked Questions: Assessment Policy," https://www.opm.gov/FAQs/QA.aspx?fid=a6da6 c2e-e1cb-4841-b72d-53eb4adf1ab1&pid=402c2b0c-bb5c-44e9-acbc-39cc6149ad36 (retrieved June 9, 2014).

14. US Code of Federal Regulations, "Title 29: Labor, Part 1607: Uniform Guidelines on Employee Selection Procedures (1978)," http://www.gpo.gov/fdsys/pkg/CFR-2011-title29-vol4/xml/CFR-2011-title29-vol4-part1607.xml (retrieved June 9, 2014).

15. Ibid.

16. "Title 29: Labor," http://www.gpo.gov/fdsys/pkg/CFR-2011-title29-vol4/xml/CFR-2011-title29-vol4-part1607.xml (retrieved June 9, 2014).

17. Uniform Guidelines on Employee Selection Procedures, "III. General Questions Concerning Validity and the Use of Selection Procedures" (2013), http://www.uniformguidelines.com/questionandanswers.html#3 (retrieved June 9, 2014).

18. US Office of Personnel Management, "Frequently Asked Questions: Assessment Policy," https://www.opm.gov/FAQs/QA.aspx?fid=a6da6c2e-e1cb-4841-b72d-53eb4adf1ab1&pid=402c2b0c-bb5c-44e9-acbc-39cc6149ad36 (retrieved June 9, 2014).

19. Uniform Guidelines on Employee Selection Procedures, "III. General Questions Concerning Validity and the Use of Selection Procedures" (2013), http://www.uniformguidelines.com/questionandanswers.html#3 (retrieved June 9, 2014).

20. US Equal Employment Opportunity Commission, http://www.eeoc.gov (retrieved July 9, 2013).

21. D.G. Allen, P.C. Bryant, J.M. Vardaman, "Retaining Talent: Replacing Misconceptions With Evidence-Based Strategies," *Academy of Management Perspectives* (2010), 24(2), pp. 48–64.

22. V. Elmer, "Hiring Without a Net: Groupon's Recruiter Speaks," *Fortune* (July 25, 2011), p. 34.

23. K. Connell, "AccuScreen CEO Will Discuss Résumé Lying on Fox 13 News Tampa Bay" (January 14, 2009), http://www.accuscreen.com/index.php?s=lying+on+resumes/.

24. M. Henricks, "Interview for Integrity," *Entrepreneur* (April 2009), p. 22.

25. B. McMurphy, "UK: Steve Masiello Didn't Graduate," *ESPN.com* (March 26, 2014), http://espn.go.com/mens-college-basketball/story/_/id/10675532/south-florida-bulls-kill-coaching-deal-steve-masiello-lying-resume/.

26. M. Mackey, "Ex-Yahoo CEO Scott Thompson and Seven Other Cases of Résumé Fraud," *The Huffington Post* (May 15, 2012), http://www.huffingtonpost.com/2012/05/15/yahoo-ceo-scott-thompsons-resume-fraud_n_1516061.html.

27. K. Rogers, "Why Lying on Your Résumé Is Never a Good Idea," *Fox Business* (September 13, 2013), http://www.foxbusiness.com/personal-finance/2013/09/13/why-should-never-lie-on-your-resume/.

28. EmploymentLawFirms.com, "Illegal Employment Interview Questions, http://www.employmentlawfirms.com/resources/employment/hiring-process/illegal-employment-interview-questions/ (retrieved June 6, 2014).

29. ACLU, "Non-discrimination Laws: State-by-State Information—Map." https://www.aclu.org/maps/non-discrimination-laws-state-state-information-map/ (retrieved June 6, 2014).

30. Uniform Guidelines on Employee Selection Procedures, "IV.A. Criterion-Related Validity" (2013), http://www.uniformguidelines.com/questionandanswers.html#5 (retrieved June 10, 2014).

31. US Department of Labor, "Employee Polygraph Protection Act of 1988." (Pub. L. 100-347, July 27, 1988), http://www.dol.gov/whd/regs/statutes/poly01.pdf.

32. National Human Genome Research Institute, "Genetic Information Nondiscrimination Act of 2008," http://www.genome.gov/10002328/ (retrieved January 27, 2014).

33. M.Y. Alsabbah, H.I. Ibrahim, "Recruitment and Selection Process and Employee Competence Outcome: An Important Area for Future Research," *Human Resource Management Research* (2013), 3(3), pp. 82–90.

34. http://smallbusiness.foxbusiness.com/biz-on-main/2011/03/04/businesses-hire-based-personality/ (retrieved June 10, 2014).

35. V. Elmer, "Hiring Without a Net: Groupon's Recruiter Speaks," *Fortune* (July 25, 2011), p. 34.

36. J. Alsever, "How to Get a Job: Show, Don't Tell," *Fortune* (March 19, 2012), pp. 29–31.

37. J.M. McCarthy, C.H. Van Iddekinge, F. Lievens, M.C. Kung, E.F. Sinar, M.A. Campion, "Do Candidate Reactions Relate to Job Performance or Affect Criterion-Related Validity? A Multistudy Investigation of Relations Among Reactions, Selection Test Scores, and Job Performance," *Journal of Applied Psychology* (2013), 98(5), p. 701.

38. *Watson v. Fort Worth Bank & Trust*, 487 US 977 (1988), http://supreme.justia.com/cases/federal/us/487/977/case.html.

39. US Equal Employment Opportunity Commission, "Title VII of the Civil Rights Act of 1964 (Pub. L. 88-352)," http://www.eeoc.gov/laws/statutes/titlevii.cfm (retrieved June 10, 2014).

40. A. Bryant, "In Head-Hunting, Big Data May Not Be Such a Big Deal," *The New York Times* (June 20, 2013), p. F6.

41. D.S. Ones, C. Viswesvaran, F.L. Schmidt, "Integrity Tests Predict Counterproductive Work Behaviors and Job Performance Well: Comment on Van Iddekinge, Roth, Raymark, and Odle-Dusseau," *Journal of Applied Psychology* (2012), 97(3), pp. 537–542.

42. Science Clarified, "Chapter 3: The Virtual Classroom; Virtual Reality in Training and Education," in *Virtual Reality,* http://www.scienceclarified.com/scitech/Virtual-Reality/The-Virtual-Classroom-Virtual-Reality-in-Training-and-Education.html (retrieved October 10, 2010).

43. US Department of Labor, "Drug-Free Workplace Policy Builder: Section 7–Drug Testing," http://www.dol.gov/elaws/asp/drugfree/drugs/screen92.asp (retrieved June 10, 2014).

44. J.E. Kenney, S. Hoffman, "Substance Abuse Program Administrators Association (SAPAA) Position Paper on Medical Marijuana" (September 4, 2013), http://www.sapaa.com/resource/resmgr/sapaa_med_marijuana_white_p.docx.

45. C. Sargent, D. Darwent, S.A. Ferguson, G.D. Roach, "Can a Simple Balance Task Be Used to Assess Fitness for Duty?" *Accident Analysis & Prevention* (2012), 45, pp. 74–79.

46. US Equal Opportunity Commission, "ADA: FMLA; Reasonable Accommodation–Leave; Medical Exams and Inquiries," http://www.eeoc.gov/eeoc/foia/letters/2008/ada_fmla_reasonableaccommodation_leave.html.

47. M. Basner, J. Rubinstein, "Fitness for Duty: A 3-Minute Version of the Psychomotor Vigilance Test Predicts Fatigue-Related Declines in Luggage Screening Performance," *Journal of Occupational and Environmental Medicine/American College of Occupational and Environmental Medicine* (2011), 53(10), p. 1146.

48. D. Potosky, "A Conceptual Framework for the Role of the Administration Medium in the Personnel Assessment Process," *Academy of Management Review* (2008), 33(3), pp. 629–648.

49. S. Halzack, "Online Tests Are the Latest Gateway to Landing a New Job," *The Washington Post* (May 8, 2014), http://www.washingtonpost.com/business/capitalbusiness/online-tests-are-the-latest-gateway-to-landing-a-new-job/2014/05/08/c5eebc6a-cb2d-11e3-95f7-7ecdde72d2ea_story.html.

50. L. Quast, "Pre-employment Testing: A Helpful Way for Companies to Screen Applicants," *Forbes* (September 13, 2011), http://www.forbes.com/sites/lisaquast/2011/09/13/pre-employment-testing-a-helpful-way-for-companies-to-screen-applicants/.

51. A. Lashinsky, "Larry Page Interview," *Fortune* (February 6, 2012), pp. 98–99.

52. J. Alsever, "How to Get a Job: Show, Don't Tell," *Fortune* (March 19, 2012), pp. 29–31.

53. H. Ismail, S. Karkoulian, "Interviewers' Characteristics and Post-hire Attitudes and Performance," *Contemporary Management Research* (2013), 9(4).

54. D.M. Cable, V.S. Kay, "Striving for Self-Verification During Organizational Entry," *Academy of Management Journal* (2012), 55(2), pp. 360–380.

55. M. Henricks, "Interview for Integrity," *Entrepreneur* (April 2009), p. 22.

56. D. Meinert, "Cultural Similarities Influence Hiring Decisions," *HR Magazine* (February 2013), p. 18.

57. V. Elmer, "Hiring Without a Net: Groupon's Recruiter Speaks," *Fortune* (July 25, 2011), p. 34.

58. T. Lytle, "Streamline Hiring," *HR Magazine* (April 2013), pp. 63–65.

59. A. Bryant, "In Head-Hunting, Big Data May Not Be Such a Big Deal," *The New York Times* (June 19, 2013), http://www.nytimes.com/2013/06/20/business/in-head-hunting-big-data-may-not-be-such-a-big-deal.html.

60. http://www.shrm.org/templatestools/samples/interviewquestions/pages/competenciesksa%E2%80%99s.aspx (retrieved June 7, 2014).

61. D. Meinert, "Cultural Similarities Influence Hiring Decisions," *HR Magazine* (February 2013), p. 18.

62. M. Henricks, "Interview for Integrity," *Entrepreneur* (April 2009), p. 22.

63. US Equal Employment Opportunity Commission and Federal Trade Commission, "Background Checks: What Employers Need to Know," http://www.eeoc.gov/eeoc/publications/background_checks_employers.cfm (June 8, 2014).

64. D.B. Weisenfeld, "Colorado Becomes 9th State to Limit Employer Credit Checks" (April 30, 2013), http://www.xperthr.com/news/colorado-becomes-9th-state-to-limit-employer-credit-checks/9819/.

65. Federal Trade Commission, "Employment Background Checks" (February 2013), http://www.consumer.ftc.gov/articles/0157-employment-background-checks/.

66. A. Preston, "Disney Sued for Misusing Background Checks" (November 20, 2013), http://www.shrm.org/hrdisciplines/safetysecurity/articles/pages/disney-sued-background-checks.aspx.

67. "11 U.S. Code § 525: Protection Against Discriminatory Treatment," http://www.law.cornell.edu/uscode/text/11/525/ (retrieved June 10, 2014).

68. M. Henricks, "Interview for Integrity," *Entrepreneur* (April 2009), p. 22.

69. "Arkansas SB 843," ftp://www.arkleg.state.ar.us/acts/2013/Public/ACT1039.pdf (retrieved June 10, 2014).

70. "2010 Arkansas Code Title 11: Labor and Industrial Relations, Chapter 3: Labor Relations and Practices, Subchapter 2: Hiring Practices, § 11-3-204: Providing references to prospective employers," http://law.justia.com/codes/arkansas/2010/title-11/chapter-3/subchapter-2/11-3-204/ (retrieved June 10, 2014).

71. B. Yuille, "Four New Job-Search Trends," *Forbes* (February 23, 2010), http://www.forbes.com/2010/02/23/job-search-trends-personal-finance-resume.html.

72. R. McHale, "Using Facebook to Screen Potential Hires Can Get You Sued," *Fast Company* (July 20, 2012), http://www.fastcompany.com/1843142/using-facebook-screen-potential-hires-can-get-you-sued/.

73. K. Schoening, K. Kleisinger, "Off-Duty Privacy: How Far Can Employers Go?" *Northern Kentucky Law Review* (2010), 37, p. 287.

74. G.M. Saylin, T.C. Horrocks, "The Risks of Pre-employment Social Media Screening" (July 18, 2013), http://www.shrm.org/hrdisciplines/staffingmanagement/articles/pages/preemployment-social-media-screening.aspx.

75. M.C. Hershiser, "The Latest Frontier for Pre-employment Screening," http://www.koleyjessen.com/resources/the-latest-frontier-for-pre-employment-screening/ (retrieved June 7, 2014).

76. R. Bentz, "Pre-employment Screening: The Next Generation," from http://www.workplacemagazine.com/Ezine/FullStory.aspx?EzineDataID=1296 (retrieved June 7, 2014).

77. D. Meinert, "Cultural Similarities Influence Hiring Decisions," *HR Magazine* (February 2013), p. 18.

78. L.A. Rivera, "Hiring as Cultural Matching the Case of Elite Professional Service Firms," *American Sociological Review* (2012), 77(6), pp. 999–1022.

79. J. Welch, "Avoid These 3 Hiring Mistakes," [LinkedIn post, June 4, 2013], https://www.linkedin.com/today/post/article/20130604104616-86541065-avoid-these-3-hiring-mistakes/.

80. L. Hill, "Only BFFs Need Apply," *Bloomberg Businessweek* (January 7, 2013), pp. 63–65.

81. *Forbes.* (n.d.). *The World's Billionaires: #596 Brian Anton.* Retrieved July 17, 2014, from http://www.forbes.com/profile/brian-acton/.

82. Wikipedia. (2014). WhatsApp. Retrieved July 17, 2014, from http://en.wikipedia.org/wiki/WhatsApp.

83. Anders, G. (2014, February 19). He wanted a Job; Facebook said "no"–in a $3 billion mistake. *Forbes.* Retrieved http://www.forbes.com/sites/georgeanders/2014/02/19/he-wanted-a-job-facebook-said-no-in-a-3-billion-mistake/.

84. Gordon, C. (2012, October 5). Getting a job at Facebook: Inside the "Meritocratic" hiring process. Retrieved from the AOL website at http://jobs.aol.com/articles/2012/10/05/want-to-get-a-job-at-facebook-weve-demystified-the-hiring-proc/.

85. Bueno, C. (2012, July 20). Get that job at Facebook. Retrieved from the Facebook Engineering page at https://www.facebook.com/notes/facebook-engineering/

get-that-job-at-facebook/101509
64382448920/.

86. Ibid.

87. Ibid.

88. *Forbes.* (n.d.). *The World's Billionaires: #596 Brian Anton.* Retrieved July 17, 2014, from http://www.forbes.com/profile/brian-acton/.

89. Wikipedia. (2014). WhatsApp. Retrieved July 17, 2014, from http://en.wikipedia.org/wiki/WhatsApp.

CHAPTER 7

1. R.C. Rose, N. Kumar, O.B. Pak, "The Effect of Organizational Learning on Organizational Commitment, Job Satisfaction and Work Performance, *Journal of Applied Business Research* (2011), 25(6).

2. D.G. Allen, P.C. Bryant, J.M. Vardaman, "Retaining Talent: Replacing Misconceptions With Evidence-Based Strategies," *Academy of Management Perspectives* 24(2), 2010, pp. 48–64.

3. K. Pajo, A. Coetzer, N. Guenole, "Formal Development Opportunities and Withdrawal Behavior by Employees in Small and Medium-Sized Enterprises," *Journal of Small Business Management* (2010), 48(3), pp. 281–301.

4. M. Ali, A.A. Shaikh, M. Karamat, N. Ali, "Comparative Analysis of Cost and Benefits of Training," *International Journal of Basic and Applied Sciences* (2012), 1(4), pp. 627–636.

5. S.K. Johnson, L.O. Garrison, G.H. Broome, J.W. Fleenor, J.L. Steed, "Go for the Goals: Relationships Between Goal Setting and Transfer of Training Following Leadership Development," *Academy of Management Learning & Education* (2012), 11(4), pp. 555–569.

6. M. Festing, "Strategic Human Resource Management in Germany," *Academy of Management Perspectives* (2012), 26(2), pp. 37–54.

7. E. Krell, "Get Sold on Training Incentives," *HR Magazine* (February 2013), pp. 57–60.

8. A. Fox, "Help Managers Shine," *HR Magazine* (February 2013), pp. 43–46.

9. B. Schyns, T. Kiefer, R. Kerschreiter, A. Tymon, "Teaching Implicit Leadership Theories to Develop Leaders and Leadership: How and Why It Can Make a Difference," *Academy of Management Learning & Education* (2011), 10(3), pp. 397–408.

10. S.K. Johnson, L.O. Garrison, G.H. Broome, J.W. Fleenor, J.L. Steed, "Go for the Goals: Relationships Between Goal Setting and Transfer of Training Following

Leadership Development, *Academy of Management Learning & Education* (2012), 11(4), pp. 555–569.

11. H. Green, "How Amazon Aims to Keep You Clicking," *Businessweek* (March 2, 2009), pp. 34–40.

12. http://www.entrepreneur.com/article/224440/ (retrieved June 14, 2014).

13. T. Sitzmann, K. Ely, K.G. Brown, K.N. Bauer, "Self-Assessment of Knowledge: A Cognitive Learning or Affective Measure?" *Academy of Management Learning & Education* (2010), (9)2, pp. 169–191.

14. D.M. Cable, V.S. Kay, "Striving for Self-Verification During Organizational Entry," *Academy of Management Journal* (2012), 55(2), pp. 360–380.

15. D.G. Allen, P.C. Bryant, J.M. Vardaman, "Retaining Talent: Replacing Misconceptions With Evidence-Based Strategies," *Academy of Management Perspectives* (2010), 24(2), pp. 48–64.

16. D.M. Sluss, R.E. Ployhart, M.G. Cobb, B.E. Ashforth, "Generalizing Newcomers' Relational and Organizational Identifications: Process and Prototypicality," *Academy of Management Journal* (2012), 55(4), pp. 949–975.

17. R.E. Silverman, "First Day on Job: Not Just Paperwork," *The Wall Street Journal* (May 28, 2013), p. D1.

18. Ibid.

19. D.G. Allen, L.R. Shanock, "Perceived Organizational Support and Embeddedness as Key Mechanisms Connecting Socialization Tactics to Commitment and Turnover Among New Employees," *Journal of Organizational Behavior* (2013), 34(3), pp. 350–369.

20. C. Tschopp, G. Grote, M. Gerber, "How Career Orientation Shapes the Job Satisfaction–Turnover Intention Link," *Journal of Organizational Behavior* (2014), 35(2), pp. 151–171.

21. D.G. Allen, P.C. Bryant, and J.M. Vardaman, "Retaining Talent: Replacing Misconceptions With Evidence-Based Strategies," *Academy of Management Perspectives* (2010), 24(2), pp. 48–64.

22. Ibid.

23. http://www.forbes.com/sites/kathycaprino/2014/02/22/how-millennials-can-better-prepare-for-todays-workforce-10-critical-steps/ (retrieved June 14, 2014).

24. J.C. Percival, B.P. Cozzarin, S.D. Formaneck, "Return on Investment for Workplace Training: The Canadian Experience," *International Journal of Training and Development* (2013), 17(1), pp. 20–32.

25. C.B. Cox, M.F. Beier, "Too Old to Train or Reprimand: The Role of Intergroup Attribution Bias in Evaluating Older Workers," *Journal of Business and Psychology* (2013), pp. 1–10.

26. S. Robbins, M. Coulter, *Management* (Saddle River, NJ: Pearson Education, 2014), p. 466.

27. http://mw1.merriam-webster.com/dictionary/vicarious/ (retrieved December 19, 2010).

28. F. Coffield, D. Moseley, E. Hall, K. Ecclestone, *Learning Styles and Pedagogy in Post-16 Learning: A Systematic and Critical Review* (London, UK: Learning Skills and Research Centre, 2004).

29. M. Li, W.H. Mobley, A. Kelly, "When Do Global Leaders Learn Best to Develop Cultural Intelligence? An Investigation of the Moderating Role of Experiential Learning Styles," *Academy of Management Education & Learning* (2013), 12(1), pp. 32–50.

30. W. Leite, M. Svinicki, Y. Shi, "Attempted Validation of the Scores of the VARK: Learning Styles Inventory With Multitrait-Multimethod Confirmatory Factor Analysis Models," *Educational and Psychological Measurement* (2009), 70(2), pp. 323–339.

31. The material in this section is adapted from David Kolb Learning Style Inventory, which is sold through the Hay Group. For more information, visit www.haygroup.com.

32. C. Manolis, D.J. Burns, R. Assudani, R. Chinta, "Assessing Experiential Learning Styles: A Methodological Reconstruction and Validation of the Kolb Learning Style Inventory," *Learning and Individual Differences* (2013), 23, pp. 44–52.

33. M. Magni, C. Paolino, R. Cappetta, L. Proserpio, "Diving Too Deep: How Cognitive Absorption and Group Learning Behavior Affect Individual Learning," *Academy of Management Learning & Education* (2013), 12(1), pp. 51–69.

34. P.E. Kennedy, S.Y. Chyung, D.J. Winiecki, R.O. Brinkerhoff, "Training Professionals' Usage and Understanding of Kirkpatrick's Level 3 and Level 4 Evaluations," *International Journal of Training and Development* (2014), 18(1), pp. 1–21.

35. D.S. Chiaburu, J.L. Huang, H.M. Hutchins, R.G. Gardner, "Trainees' Perceived Knowledge Gain Unrelated to the Training Domain: The Joint Action of Impression Management and Motives," *International Journal of Training and Development* (2014), 18(1), pp. 37–52.

36. Ibid.

37. T. Sitzmann, K. Ely, K.G. Brown, K.N. Bauer, "Self-Assessment of Knowledge: A Cognitive Learning or Affective Measure?" *Academy of Management Learning & Education* (2010), 9(2), pp. 169–191.

38. http://www.bls.gov/news.release/pdf/nlsoy.pdf (retrieved June 14, 2014).

39. D.T. Hall, *Careers in and out of Organizations* (Thousand Oaks, CA: SAGE, 2002).

40. D.G. Allen, P.C. Bryant, J.M. Vardaman, "Retaining Talent: Replacing Misconceptions With Evidence-Based Strategies," *Academy of Management Perspectives* (2010), 24(2), pp. 48–64.

41. http://www1.eeoc.gov/eeoc/statistics/employment/jobpat-eeo1/2012/index.cfm#select_label (retrieved June 14, 2014).

42. C. Hu, S. Wang, C.C. Yang, T.Y. Wu, "When Mentors Feel Supported: Relationships With Mentoring Functions and Protégés' Perceived Organizational Support," *Journal of Organizational Behavior* (2014), 35(1), pp. 22–37.

43. S. Humphrey, F. Morgeson, M. Mannor, "Developing a Theory of the Strategic Core of Teams: A Role Composition Model of Team Performance," *Journal of Applied Psychology* (2009), (94)1, pp. 48–61.

44. E.N. Carlson, "Overcoming the Barriers to Self-Knowledge: Mindfulness as a Path to Seeing Yourself as You Really Are," *Perspectives on Psychological Science* (2013), 8(2), pp. 173–186.

45. E. Guss, "Emotional Intelligence: Our Most Versatile Tool for Success" [SHRM white paper], http://www.shrm.org/Research/Articles/Articles/Pages/CMS_014158.aspx (retrieved December 27, 2010).

46. A. Maul, "The Validity of the Mayer-Salovey-Caruso Emotional Intelligence Test (MSCEIT) as a Measure of Emotional Intelligence," *Emotion Review* (2012), 4(4), pp. 394–402.

47. Ibid.

48. D. Super, D. Hall, "Career Development: Exploration and Planning," *Annual Review of Psychology* (1978), 29, pp. 333–372.

49. http://business.financialpost.com/2014/01/09/gamification-newest-tool-in-corporate-training-arsenal/ (retrieved June 11, 2014).

50. http://www.forbes.com/sites/jeannemeister/2012/05/21/gamification-three-ways-to-use-gaming-for-recruiting-training-and-health-amp-wellness/ (retrieved June 13, 2014).

51. http://www.astd.org/Publications/Magazines/TD/TD-Archive/2013/12/Webex-7-Trends-Shaping-E-Learning (retrieved June 13, 2014).

52. https://www.trainingindustry.com/wiki/entries/gamification.aspx (retrieved June 13, 2014).

53. F. Groh, "Gamification: State of the art definition and utilization," in *Proceedings of the 4th Seminar on Research Trends in Media Informatics* (Ulm, Germany: Institute of Media Informatics, Ulm University), pp. 39–46.

54. http://www.shrm.org/hrdisciplines/employeerelations/articles/pages/gamification-doesn%27t-motivate.aspx (retrieved June 14, 2014).

55. http://www.gartner.com/newsroom/id/2251015 (retrieved June 14, 2014).

56. R.N. Landers, R.C. Callan, "Casual Social Games as Serious Games: The Psychology of Gamification in Undergraduate Education and Employee Training," in *Serious Games and Edutainment Applications*, edited by M. Ma, A. Oikonomou, L.C. Jain (London, UK: Springer, 2011) pp. 399–423.

57. http://www.astd.org/Publications/Magazines/TD/TD-Archive/2013/12/Webex-7-Trends-Shaping-E-Learning (retrieved June 14, 2014).

58. ADP (Ed.), "Outsourcing and the Future of HR," *ADP* (2012), p. 3.

59. Jon Hay (Ed.), "HR Outsourcing Trends and Insights 2009," *Hewitt Associates* (2009), p. 10.

60. Hoover's Inc. (2014). Google Inc. [Hoover's Company Records: In-Depth Records]. Retrieved July 19, 2014, from Long Island University Academic Database.

61. Lapowsky, I. (2014, July 1). Google and Square recruit girls early to tackle tech's gender problem. *Wired.com*. Retrieved from http://www.wired.com/2014/07/girls-coding/.

62. Warnes, S. (2014, July 1). 70% male, 50% white: Why Silicon Valley needs to diversify. *Mirror*. Retrieved from http://ampp3d.mirror.co.uk/2014/07/01/70-male-50-white-why-silicon-valley-needs-to-diversify/.

63. Mejia, P. (2014, July 11). Codes, not bros: Google pledges $50 million to ladies in tech. *Newsweek*. Retrieved from http://www.newsweek.com/codes-not-bros-google-pledges-50-million-ladies-tech-258298/.

64. Warnes, S. (2014, July 1). 70% male, 50% white: Why Silicon Valley needs to diversify. *Mirror*. Retrieved from http://ampp3d.mirror.co.uk/2014/07/01/70-male-50-white-why-silicon-valley-needs-to-diversify/.

65. Mejia, P. (2014, July 11). Codes, not bros: Google pledges $50 million to ladies in tech. *Newsweek*. Retrieved from http://www.newsweek.com/codes-not-bros-google-pledges-50-million-ladies-tech-258298/.

66. Ibid.

67. Jones, V. (2014, July 8). How to hook up tech sector with talent. *CNN.com*. Retrieved from http://www.cnn.com/2014/07/08/opinion/jones-tech-minorities/.

68. Mejia, P. (2014, July 11). Codes, not bros: Google pledges $50 million to ladies in tech. *Newsweek*. Retrieved from http://www.newsweek.com/codes-not-bros-google-pledges-50-million-ladies-tech-258298/.

CHAPTER 8

1. J. Welch, S. Welch, "Dealing With the Morning-After Syndrome at Facebook," *Fortune* (March 19, 2012), p. 92.

2. M.K. Duffy, K.L. Scott, J.D. Shaw, B.J. Tepper, K. Aquino, "A Social Context Model of Envy and Social Undermining," *Academy of Management Journal* (2012), 55(3), pp. 643–666.

3. C. Suddath, "You Get a D+ in Teamwork," *Bloomberg Businessweek* (November 7, 2013), p. 91.

4. A.S. DeNisi, "Managing Performance to Change Behavior," *Journal of Organizational Behavior Management* (2011), 31(4), pp. 262–276.

5. P. McCord, "How Netflix Reinvented HR," *Harvard Business Review* (2014), p. 1.

6. http://www.shrm.org/templatestools/toolkits/pages/managingemployeeperformance.aspx (retrieved June 20, 2014).

7. D.G. Allen, P.C. Bryant, J.M. Vardaman, "Retaining Talent: Replacing Misconceptions With Evidence-Based Strategies," *Academy of Management Perspectives* (2010), 24(2), pp. 48–64.

8. S.K. Johnson, L.O. Garrison, G.H. Broome, J.W. Fleenor, J.L. Steed, "Go for the Goals: Relationships Between Goal Setting and Transfer of Training Following Leadership Development," *Academy of Management Learning & Education* (2012), 11(4), pp. 555–569.

9. "Master Class," *Businessweek* (May 6–12, 2013), p. 83.

10. http://www.shrm.org/Education/hreducation/Documents/Performance_Management_PPT_SL_Edit_BS.ppt (retrieved June 20, 2014).

11. C.O. Longenecker, "How the Best Motivate Workers," *Industrial Management* (2011), 53(1), pp. 8–13.

12. K. Gurchiek, "New HR Standard on Performance Management," *HR Magazine* (April 2013), p. 74.

13. http://www.ansi.org (retrieved July 10, 2013).

14. S.A. Culbert, "Get Rid of the Performance Review," *The Wall Street Journal* (October 20, 2008), p. R4.

15. D.G. Allen, P.C. Bryant, and J.M. Vardaman, "Retaining Talent: Replacing Misconceptions With Evidence-Based

Strategies," *Academy of Management Perspectives* (2010), 24(2), pp. 48–64.

16. A.S. DeNisi, "Managing Performance to Change Behavior," *Journal of Organizational Behavior Management* (2011), 31(4), pp. 262–276.

17. I.A. Scott, G. Phelps, C. Brand, "Assessing Individual Clinical Performance: A Primer for Physicians," *Internal Medicine Journal* (2011), 41(2), pp. 144–155.

18. A.S. DeNisi, "Managing Performance to Change Behavior," *Journal of Organizational Behavior Management* (2011), 31(4), pp. 262–276.

19. Ibid.

20. http://www.shrm.org/ templatestools/toolkits/pages/ managingemployeeperformance.aspx (retrieved June 20, 2014).

21. Society for Human Resource Management, *Performance Management Survey* (2000), http://www.shrm.org/ Research/SurveyFindings/Documents/ Performance%20Management%20Survey .pdf, p. 7.

22. http://www.shrm.org/hrdisciplines/ employeerelations/articles/Pages/ UsedtoMotivateWeedOut.aspx (retrieved June 20, 2014).

23. A.S. DeNisi, "Managing Performance to Change Behavior," *Journal of Organizational Behavior Management* (2011), 31(4), pp. 262–276.

24. Ibid.

25. P.F. Buller, G.M. McEvoy, "Strategy, Human Resource Management and Performance: Sharpening Line of Sight," *Human Resource Management Review* (2012), 22(1), pp. 43–56.

26. K. Blanchard, D. Hudson, E. Wills, *The One Minute Entrepreneur* (New York, NY: Currency, 2008).

27. G. Blickle, J.A. Meurs, A. Wihler, C. Ewen, A. Plies, S. Günther, "The Interactive Effects of Conscientiousness, Openness to Experience, and Political Skill on Job Performance in Complex Jobs: The Importance of Context," *Journal of Organizational Behavior* (2013), 34(8), pp. 1145–1164.

28. P. Mussel, "Introducing the Construct Curiosity for Predicting Job Performance," *Journal of Organizational Behavior* (2013), 34(4), pp. 453–472.

29. K. Blanchard, D. Hudson, E. Wills, *The One Minute Entrepreneur* (New York, NY: Currency, 2008).

30. J. Goodale, "Behaviorally-Based Rating Scales: Toward an Integrated Approach to Performance Appraisal," *Contemporary Problems in Personnel* (Chicago, IL: St. Clair Press, 1977), p. 247.

31. K. Blanchard, D. Hutson, E. Wills, *The One Minute Entrepreneur* (New York, NY: Currency, 2008).

32. Ibid.

33. Ibid.

34. R. Youngjohns, "How Can I Keep My Sales Team Productive in a Recession?" *Fortune* (March 2, 2009), p. 22.

35. S.A. Culbert, "Get Rid of the Performance Review," *The Wall Street Journal* (October 20, 2008), p. R4.

36. K. Blanchard, D. Hutson, E. Wills, *The One Minute Entrepreneur* (New York, NY: Currency, 2008).

37. Ibid.

38. D.G. Allen, P.C. Bryant, J.M. Vardaman, "Retaining Talent: Replacing Misconceptions With Evidence-Based Strategies," *Academy of Management Perspectives* (2010), 24(2), pp. 48–64.

39. H.K. Fulk, R.L. Bell, N. Bodie, "Team Management by Objectives: Enhancing Developing Teams' Performance," *Journal of Management Policy and Practice* (2011), 12(3), pp. 17–26.

40. Wikipedia.com (retrieved January 17, 2011). The first known uses of the term SMART goals occur in the November 1981 issue of *Management Review* by George T. Doran.

41. E. Gibson, "The Stop-Managing Guide to Management," *Businessweek* (June 15, 2009), p. 73.

42. H.K. Fulk, R.L. Bell, N. Bodie, "Team Management by Objectives: Enhancing Developing Teams' Performance," *Journal of Management Policy and Practice* (2011), 12(3), pp. 17–26.

43. S. McCartney, "How US Airways Vaulted to First Place," *The Wall Street Journal* (July 22, 2009), p. D3.

44. http://www.shrm.org/publications/ hrnews/pages/announcements-on-stack-rankings-touch-off-debate.aspx (retrieved June 22, 2014).

45. S. Ovide, "Microsoft Abandons Dreaded Stack," *The Wall Street Journal* (November 13, 2013), p. B1.

46. K. Blanchard, D. Hutson, E. Wills, *The One Minute Entrepreneur* (New York, NY: Currency, 2008).

47. https://www.performancereview .com/pfasp/main.asp (retrieved June 20, 2014).

48. M. Ohland, M. Loughry, D. Woehr, C. Finelli, L. Bullard, R. Felder, . . . D. Schmucker, "The Comprehensive Assessment of Team Member Effectiveness: Development of a Behaviorally Anchored Rating Scale for Self and Peer Evaluation," *Academy of Management Learning & Education* (2012).

49. A. Sudarsan, "Concurrent Validity of Peer Appraisal of Group Work for Administrative Purposes," *The IUP Journal of Organizational Behavior* (2010), 9(1 & 2), pp. 73–86.

50. S. Brutus, M. Donia, S. Ronen, "Can Business Students Learn to Evaluate Better? Evidence From Repeated Exposure to a Peer Evaluation Process," *Academy of Management Learning & Education* (2012).

51. http://www.shrm.org/hrdisciplines/ employeerelations/articles/Pages/ ManagerEmployeePerceptions.aspx (retrieved June 20, 2014).

52. J. Breidert, J. Fite, "Self Assessment: Review and Implications for Training," *U.S. Army Research Institute for the Behavioral and Social Sciences Research Report 1900* (June 2009).

53. N. Castle, H. Garton, G. Kenward, "Confidence vs. Competence: Basic Life Support Skills of Health Professionals," *British Journal of Nursing* (2007), 16, pp. 664–666.

54. M. Matthews, S. Beal, "Assessing Situation Awareness in Field Training Exercises," *U.S. Army Research Institute for the Behavioral and Social Sciences Research Report 1795* (2002).

55. K. Sullivan, C. Hall, "Introducing Students to Self-Assessment," *Assessment & Evaluation in Higher Education* (1997), 22, pp. 289–305.

56. B. McKinstry, H. Peacock, D. Blaney, "Can Trainers Accurately Assess Their Training Skills Using a Detailed Checklist? A Questionnaire-Based Comparison of Trainer Self-Assessment and Registrar Assessment of Trainers' Learning Needs," *Education for Primary Care* (2003), 14, pp. 426–430.

57. K. Blanchard, D. Hutson, E. Wills, *The One Minute Entrepreneur* (New York, NY: Currency, 2008).

58. H. Han, S.S. Hyun, "Image Congruence and Relationship Quality in Predicting Switching Intention Conspicuousness of Product Use as a Moderator Variable," *Journal of Hospitality & Tourism Research* (2013), 37(3), pp. 303–329.

59. R.J. Ely, H. Ibarra, D.M. Kolb, "Taking Gender Into Account: Theory and Design for Women's Leadership Development Programs," *Academy of Management Learning & Education* (2011), 10(3), p. 474.

60. J. McGregor, "There Is No More Normal," *Businessweek* (March 23 & 30, 2009), pp. 30–34.

61. M. Gordon, C. Musso, E. Rebentisch, N. Gupta, "The Path to Developing Successful New Products," *The Wall Street Journal* (November 30, 2009), p. R5.

62. E.M. Mone, M. London, *Employee Engagement Through Effective Performance Management: A Practical Guide for Managers* (New York, NY: Routledge/Taylor & Francis, 2011).

63. H. Aguinas, *Performance Management* (Upper Saddle River, NJ: Pearson Education, 2007), p. 184.

64. A. Thomas, J. Palmer, J. Feldman, "Examination and Measurement of Halo via Curvilinear Regression: A New Approach to Halo," *Journal of Applied Social Psychology* (February 2009), 39(2), pp. 350–358.

65. A.N. Esfahani, M. Abzari, S. Dezianian, "Analyzing the Effect of Performance Appraisal Errors on Perceived Organizational Justice," *International Journal of Academic Research in Accounting, Finance and Management Sciences* (2014), 4(1), pp. 36–40.

66. P.J. Rosopa, A.N. Schroeder, A.L. Hulett, "Helping Yourself by Helping Others: Examining Personality Perceptions, *Journal of Managerial Psychology* (2013), 28(2), pp. 147–163.

67. K. Blanchard, D. Hutson, E. Wills, *The One Minute Entrepreneur* (New York, NY: Currency, 2008).

68. S.G. Roch, D.J. Woehr, V. Mishra, U. Kieszczynska, "Rater Training Revisited: An Updated Meta-Analytic Review of Frame-of-Reference Training," *Journal of Occupational and Organizational Psychology* (2012), 85(2), pp. 370–395.

69. C. Dusterhoff, J.B. Cunningham, J.N. MacGregor, "The Effects of Performance Rating, Leader-Member Exchange, Perceived Utility, and Organizational Justice on Performance Appraisal Satisfaction: Applying a Moral Judgment Perspective," *Journal of Business Ethics* (2014), 119(2), pp. 265–273.

70. J. McGregor, "Job Review in 140 Keystrokes," *Businessweek* (March 23 & 30, 2009), p. 58.

71. D.G. Allen, P.C. Bryant, and J.M. Vardaman, "Retaining Talent: Replacing Misconceptions With Evidence-Based Strategies," *Academy of Management Perspectives* (2010), 24(2), pp. 48–64.

72. E. Gibson, "The Stop-Managing Guide to Management," *Businessweek* (June 15, 2009), p. 73.

73. Ibid.

74. T. Gutner, "Ways to Make the Most of a Negative Job Review," *The Wall Street Journal* (January 13, 2009), p. D4.

75. D.G. Allen, P.C. Bryant, J.M. Vardaman, "Retaining Talent: Replacing Misconceptions With Evidence-Based Strategies," *Academy of Management Perspectives* (2010), 24(2), pp. 48–64.

76. E. Gibson, "The Stop-Managing Guide to Management," *Businessweek* (June 15, 2009), p. 73.

77. T. Gutner, "Ways to Make the Most of a Negative Job Review," *The Wall Street Journal* (January 13, 2009), p. D4.

78. S.A. Culbert, *"Get Rid of the Performance Review! How Companies Can Stop Intimidating, Start Managing—and Focus on What Really Matters"* (New York, NY: Business Plus, 2010).

79. W. Carroll, "The Effects of Electronic Performance Monitoring on Performance Outcomes: A Review and Meta-Analysis," *Employment Rights & Employment Policy Journal* (2008), 29, pp. 29–47.

80. Ibid.

81. D. Perkins, "Electronic Performance Monitoring in Call Centers: An Ethical Decision Model," *EJBO: Electronic Journal of Business Ethics and Organization Studies* (2013), 18(1), pp. 4–14.

82. S. Sarpong, D. Rees, "Assessing the Effects of 'Big Brother' in a Workplace: The Case of WAST," *European Management Journal* (2014), 32(2), pp. 216–222.

83. D.G. Allen, P.C. Bryant, J.M. Vardaman, "Retaining Talent: Replacing Misconceptions With Evidence-Based Strategies," *Academy of Management Perspectives* (2010), 24(2), pp. 48–64.

84. http://www.shrm.org/Research/Articles/Articles/Pages/Competency_20Models_20Series_20Part_20III_20Competency-Based_20Performance_20Management.aspx (retrieved June 20, 2014).

85. Ibid.

86. Ibid.

87. Hoover's Inc. (2014). *Amazon.com, Inc.* [Hoover's Company Records—Competitive Landscape/In-Depth Records]. Retrieved July 13, 2014, from Long Island University Academic Database.

88. Ibid.

89. B. Stone, Why It's So Difficult to Climb Amazon's Corporate Ladder," *Bloomberg BusinessWeek* (October 15, 2013). Retrieved from http://www.businessweek.com/articles/2013-10-15/careers-at-amazon-why-its-so-hard-to-climb-jeff-bezoss-corporate-ladder/.

90. Ibid.

91. Ibid.

92. Ibid.

93. T. Soper. Here's What Employees Love and Hate About Working at Amazon, Microsoft," *Geek Wire* (December 13, 2012). Retrieved from http://www.geekwire.com/2012/employees-love-hate-working-amazon-microsoft/.

CHAPTER 9

1. T. Sitzmann, K. Ely, K.G. Brown, K.N. Bauer, "Self-Assessment of Knowledge: A Cognitive Learning or Affective Measure?" *Academy of Management Learning & Education* (2010), 9(2), pp. 169–191.

2. B. Shuck, "Four Emerging Perspectives of Employee Engagement: An Integrative Literature Review," *Human Resource Development Review* (2011), published online.

3. G.F. Cavanagh, D.J. Moberg, M. Velasquez, "The Ethics of Organizational Politics," *Academy of Management Review* (1981), 6(3), pp. 363–374.

4. http://www.neimagazine.com/news/newswho-report-cancer-risk-from-fukushima-is-low (retrieved June 23, 2014).

5. J. Hughes, C. Babcock, F. Bass, "Your Fired, Now Get Back to Work," *Businessweek* (August 1–7, 2011), pp. 31–32.

6. United Nations, *Universal Declaration of Human Rights* (adopted by the General Assembly December 10, 1948), UN Doc. GA/RES/217 A (III).

7. http://www.vanderbiltlawreview.org/content/articles/2014/01/Sinclair-67-Vand.-L.-Rev.-239.pdf (retrieved June 23, 2014).

8. http://www.gq.com/entertainment/television/201401/duck-dynasty-phil-robertson (retrieved June 23, 2014).

9. S.S. Wiltermuth, F.J. Flynn, "Power, Moral Clarity, and Punishment in the Workplace," *Academy of Management Journal* (2013), 56(4), pp. 1002–1023.

10. B.C. Gunia, L. Wang, L. Huang, J. Wang, J.K. Murnighan, "Contemplation and Conversation: Subtle Influences on Moral Decision Making, *Academy of Management Journal* (2012), 55(1), pp. 13–33.

11. Ibid.

12. D. Ariely, "Why We Lie," *The Wall Street Journal* (May 26–27, 2012), pp. C1–C2.

13. S.S. Wiltermuth, F.J. Flynn, "Power, Moral Clarity, and Punishment in the Workplace," *Academy of Management Journal* (2013), 56(4), pp. 1002–1023.

14. http://www.washingtonpost.com/pb/business/on-small-business/how-employers-can-keep-their-it-systems-safe-in-this-byod-era/2012/01/25/gIQAllfkQQ_story.html (retrieved June 22, 2014).

15. http://www.businessweek.com/articles/2012-10-02/the-risks-and-rewards-of-personal-electronics-in-the-workplace (retrieved June 22, 2014).

16. http://www.shrm.org/publications/hrmagazine/editorialcontent/2012/0212/pages/0212tech.aspx (retrieved June 22, 2014).

17. R. Cheng, "So You Want to Use Your iPhone for Work? Uh-oh," *The Wall Street Journal* (April 25, 2011), p. R1

18. http://www.shrm.org/hrdisciplines/technology/articles/pages/rethinking-mobile-security.aspx (retrieved June 22, 2014).

19. http://www.sba.gov/community/blogs/community-blogs/business-law-advisor/how-fire-employee-and-stay-within-law retrieved (June 23, 2014).

20. C.J. Muhl, "Employment-at-Will Doctrine: Three Major Exceptions," *The Monthly Labor Review*, 124(3), pp. 3–11.

21. http://www.dol.gov/elaws/asp/drugfree/drugs/screen92.asp (retrieved June 23, 2014).

22. J. Segers, D. Vloeberghs, E. Henderickx, I. Inceoglu, "Structuring and Understanding the Coaching Industry: The Coaching Cube," *Academy of Management Learning & Education* (2011), 2(2), pp. 204–221.

23. "Need Coaching?" *HR Magazine* (February 2013), p. 66.

24. S.K. Johnson, L.O. Garrison, G.H. Broome, J.W. Fleenor, J.L. Steed, "Go for the Goals: Relationships Between Goal Setting and Transfer of Training Following Leadership Development," *Academy of Management Learning & Education* (2012), 11(4), pp. 555–569.

25. B. Menguc, S. Auh, M. Fisher, A. Haddad, "To Be Engaged or Not to Be Engaged: The Antecedents and Consequences of Service Employee Engagement," *Journal of Business Research* (2013), 66(11), pp. 2163–2170.

26. A.D. Ellinger, "Supportive Supervisors and Managerial Coaching: Exploring Their Intersections," *Journal of Occupational and Organizational Psychology* (2013), 86(3), pp. 310–316.

27. T. Gutner, "Ways to Make the Most of a Negative Job Review," *The Wall Street Journal* (January 13, 2009), p. D4.

28. K. Blanchard, D. Hutson, E. Wills, *The One Minute Entrepreneur* (New York, NY: Currency, 2008).

29. R.J. Jones, S.A. Woods, Y. Guillaume, "A Meta-Analysis of the Effectiveness of Executive Coaching at Improving Work-Based Performance and Moderators of Coaching Effectiveness," in *British Psychological Society Annual Division of Occupational Psychology Conference, 06/01/14–08/01/14* Brighton, UK: British Psychological Society, 2014.

30. A.H. Jordan, P.G. Audia, "Self-Enhancement and Learning From Performance Feedback," *Academy of Management Review* (2012), 37(2), pp. 211–231.

31. J. Sinegal, "Show Don't Tell," *Fortune* (July 6, 2009), p. 44.

32. K.W. Mossholder, H.A. Richardson, R.P. Settoon, "Human Resource Systems and Helping in Organizations: A Relational Perspective," *Academy of Management Review* (2011), 36(1), pp. 33–52.

33. A.D. Ellinger, "Supportive Supervisors and Managerial Coaching: Exploring Their Intersections," *Journal of Occupational and Organizational Psychology*, 86(3), pp. 310–316.

34. C.N. Thoroughgood, S.T. Hunter, K.B. Sawyer, "Bad Apples, Bad Barrels, and Broken Followers? An Empirical Examination of Contextual Influences on Follower Perceptions and Reactions to Aversive Leadership," *Journal of Business Ethics* (2011), 100(4), pp. 647–672.

35. G. Colvin, "Why Talent Is Over Rated," *Fortune* (October 27, 2008), pp. 138–147.

36. J. Segers, D. Vloeberghs, E. Henderickx, I. Inceoglu, "Structuring and Understanding the Coaching Industry: The Coaching Cube," *Academy of Management Learning & Education* (2011), 2(2), pp. 204–221.

37. E. De Haan, C. Bertie, A. Day, C. Sills, "Clients' Critical Moments of Coaching: Toward a 'Client Model' of Executive Coaching," *Academy of Management Learning & Education* (2010), 9(4), pp. 607–621.

38. T. Gutner, "Ways to Make the Most of a Negative Job Review," *The Wall Street Journal* (January 13, 2009), p. D4.

39. N. Tocher, M.W. Rutherford, "Perceived Acute Human Resource Management Problems in Small and Medium Firms: An Empirical Examination," *Entrepreneurship Theory and Practice* (2009), 33(2), pp. 455–479.

40. S. Shellenbarger, "Meet the Meeting Killers," *The Wall Street Journal* (May 16, 2012), pp. D1, D3.

41. CareerBuilder, "Bad Hires Can Be Costly," *HR Magazine* (February 2013), p. 18.

42. J.R. Detert, A.C. Edmondson, "Implicit Voice Theories: Taken-for-Granted Rules of Self-Censorship at Work," *Academy of Management Journal* (2011), 54(3), pp. 461–488.

43. CareerBuilder, "Bad Hires Can Be Costly," *HR Magazine* (February 2013), p. 18.

44. A. Hopkins, "Risk Management and Rule Compliance: Decision Making in Hazardous Industries," *Safety Science* (2011), 49(2), pp. 110–120.

45. J.M. Jacobson, P. Sacco, "Employee Assistance Program Services for Alcohol and Other Drug Problems: Implications for Increased Identification and Engagement in Treatment," *The American Journal on Addictions* (2012), 21(5), pp. 468–475.

46. M. Voronov, R. Vince, "Integrating Emotions Into the Analysis of Institutional Work," *Academy of Management Review* (2012), 37(1), pp. 58–81.

47. CareerBuilder, "Bad Hires Can Be Costly," *HR Magazine* (February 2013), p. 18.

48. R.E. Kidwell, "A Strategic Deviance Perspective on the Franchise Form of Organizing," *Entrepreneurship Theory and Practice* (2011), 35(3), pp. 467–482.

49. R.S. Dalal, H. Lam, H.M. Weiss, E.R. Welch, C.L. Hulin, "A Within-Person Approach to Work Behavior and Performance: Concurrent and Lagged Citizenship-Counterproductivity Associations and Dynamic Relationships With Affect and Overall Job Performance," *Academy of Management Journal* (2009), 52(5), pp. 1051–1066.

50. S.D. Sidle, "Workplace Incivility: How Should Employees and Managers Respond?" *Academy of Management Perspective* (2009), 23(4), pp. 88–89.

51. R.E. Kidwell, "A Strategic Deviance Perspective on the Franchise Form of Organizing," *Entrepreneurship Theory and Practice* (2011), 35(3), pp. 467–482.

52. C. Matsuda, "Hello? You've Got a Job to Do," *Entrepreneur* (March 2010), p. 73.

53. W.P. Smith, F. Tabak, "Monitoring Employee E-mail: Is There Any Room for Privacy?" *Academy of Management Perspectives* (2009), 23(4), pp. 33–48.

54. M. Goldsmith, "What Got You Here Won't Get You There: How Successful People Became Even More Successful," *Academy of Management Perspective* (2009), 23(3), pp. 103–105.

55. D. Liu, H. Liao, R. Loi, "The Dark Side of Leadership: A Three-Level Investigation of the Cascading Effect of Abusive Supervision on Employee Creativity," *Academy of Management Journal* (2011), 55(5), pp. 1187–1212.

56. S. Shellenbarger, "When the Boss Is a Screamer," *The Wall Street Journal* (August 15, 2012), pp. D1, D2.

57. T. Lenski, "Talk It Out," *Businessweek* (December 10–16, 2012), p. 85.

58. E.R. Burris, "The Risk and Rewards of Speaking Up: Managerial Responses to Employee Voice," *Academy of Management Journal* (2012), 55(4), pp. 851–875.

59. M.S. Christian, A.P. Ellis, "Examining the Effects of Sleep Deprivation on Workplace Deviance: A Self-Regulatory Perspective," *Academy of Management Journal* (2011), 54(5), pp. 913–934.

60. J. Hughes, C. Babcock, F. Bass, "Your Fired, Now Get Back to Work," *Businessweek* (August 1–7, 2011), pp. 31–32.

61. K. Hudson, K. Maher, "Wal-Mart Adjusts Attendance Policy," *The Wall Street Journal* (October 14, 2006), p. A3.

62. A.R. Gardner, "No Finding of Race Discrimination in Failure-to-Promote Case," *HR Magazine* (April 2013), p. 74.

63. T. Gutner, "Ways to Make the Most of a Negative Job Review," *The Wall Street Journal* (January 13, 2009), p. D4.

64. R. Batt, A.J. Colvin, "An Employment Systems Approach to Turnover: Human Resources Practices, Quits, Dismissals, and Performance," *Academy of Management Journal* (2011), 54(4), pp. 695–717.

65. http://newsone.com/2723745/jigaboo-david-edgmon/ (retrieved June 22, 2014).

66. http://www.shrm.org/legalissues/federalresources/pages/cookout-facebook.aspx (retrieved June 22, 2014).

67. S. Wiltermuth, F. Flynn, "Power, Moral Clarity, and Punishment in the Workplace," *Academy of Management Journal* (2012).

68. M. Moral, P. Warnock, "Coaching and Culture: Toward the Global Coach," in M. Goldsmith & L. Lyons (Eds.), *Coaching for Leadership: The Practice of Leadership Coaching From the World's Greatest Coaches* (2nd ed.) (San Diego, CA: Pfeiffer, 2006), pp. 126–135.

69. D. Peterson, "Executive Coaching in a Cross-Cultural Context," *Consulting Psychology Journal: Practice and Research* (2007), 59(4), pp. 261–272.

70. S.D. Sidle, "Personality Disorders and Dysfunctional Employee Behavior: How Can Managers Cope?" *Academy of Management Perspective* (2009), 25(2), pp. 76–77.

71. D.S. DeRue, S.B. Sitkin, J.M. Podolny, "Call for Papers—Teaching Leadership," *Academy of Management Journal* (2010), 33(4), pp. 922–923.

72. K.Y. Ng, L. Van Dyne, S. Ang, "From Experience to Experiential Learning: Cultural Intelligence as a Learning Capability for Global Leader Development," *Academy of Management Learning & Education* (2009), 8(4), pp. 511–526.

73. G.A. Van Kleef, A.C. Homan, B. Beersma, D. Van Knippenberg, F. Damen, "Searing Sentiment or Cold Calculation? The Effects of Leader Emotional Displays on Team Performance Depend on Follower Epistemic Motivation," *Academy of Management Journal* (2009), 52(3), pp. 562–580.

74. "Leaders of Tomorrow," *Fortune* (November 24, 2008), p. 27.

75. S. McVanel, "Review Subject: How to Grow Leaders; The Seven Key Principles of Effective Leadership Development," *Leadership & Organization Development Journal*, 31(1), pp. 98–99.

76. M.A. Hogg, D. Van Knippenberg, D.E. Rast, "Intergroup Leadership in Organizations: Leading Across Group and Organizational Boundaries," *Academy of Management Review* (2012), 37(2), pp. 232–255.

77. H.R. Greve, "Microfoundations of Management: Behavioral Strategies and Levels of Rationality in Organizational Action," *Academy of Management Perspectives* (2013), 27(2), pp. 103–119.

78. A.M. Grant, S.V. Patil, "Challenging the Norm of Self-Interest: Minority Influence and Transitions to Helping Norms in Work Units," *Academy of Management Review* (2012), 37(4), pp. 547–568.

79. S.B. Sitkin, J.R. Hackman, "Developing Team Leadership: An Interview With Coach Mike Krzyzewski," *Academy of Management Learning & Education* (2011), 10(3), pp. 494–501.

80. J.D. Harris, S.G. Sounder, "Model-Theoretic Knowledge Accumulation: The Case of Agency Theory and Incentive Alignment," *Academy of Management Review* (2013), 38(3), pp. 442–454.

81. B. Benjamin, C. O'Reilly, "Becoming a Leader: Early Career Challenges Faced by MBA Graduates," *Academy of Management Learning & Education* (2011), 10(3), pp. 452–472.

82. M. Farjoun. "Beyond Dualism: Stability and Change as a Duality," *Academy of Management Review* (2010), 35(2), pp. 202–225.

83. R. Greenwood, D. Miller, "Tackling Design Anew: Getting Back to the Heart of Organizational Theory," *Academy of Management Perspectives* (2010), 24(4), pp. 78–84.

84. B.P. Owens, D.R. Hekman, "Modeling How to Grow: An Inductive Examination of Humble Leader Behaviors, Contingencies, and Outcomes," *Academy of Management Journal* (2012), 55(4), pp. 787–818.

85. R. Greenwood, D. Miller, "Tackling Design Anew: Getting Back to the Heart of Organizational Theory," *Academy of Management Perspectives* (2010), 24(4), pp. 78–84.

86. P. Navarro, "The MBA Core Curricular of Top-Ranked U.S. Business Schools: A Study of Failure?" *Academy of Management Learning & Education* (2008), 7(1), pp. 108–123.

87. E. Kearney, D. Gebert, S.C. Voelpel, "When and How Diversity Benefits Teams: The Importance of Team Members' Need for Cognition," *Academy of Management Journal* (2009), 52(3), pp. 581–598.

88. J.D. Ford, L.W. Ford, A. D'Amelio, "Resistance to Change: The Rest of the Story," *Academy of Management Review* (2008), 33(2), pp. 362–377.

89. J.K. Summers, S.E. Humphrey, G.R. Ferris, "Team Member Change, Flux in Coordination, and Performance: Effects of Strategic Core Roles, Information Transfer, and Cognitive Ability," *Academy of Management Journal* (2012), 55(2), pp. 314–338.

90. S.J. Shin, T.Y. Kim, J.Y. Lee, L. Bian, "Cognitive Team Diversity and Individual Team Member Creativity: A Cross-Level Interaction," *Academy of Management Journal* (2012), 55(1), pp. 195–212.

91. P. Klarner, S. Raisch, "Move to the Beat: Rhythms of Change and Firm Performance," *Academy of Management Journal* (2013), 56(1), pp. 160–184.

92. Ibid.

93. Z. Tang, C. Hull, "An Investigation of Entrepreneurial Orientation, Perceived Environmental Hostility, and Strategy Application Among Chinese SMEs," *Journal of Small Business Management* (2012), 50(1), pp. 132–158.

94. D. Brady, J. Chambers, *Businessweek* (August 27–September 2, 2012), p. 76.

95. W.M. Murphy, "From E-Mentoring to Blended Mentoring: Increasing Students' Developmental Initiation and Mentors' Satisfaction," *Academy of Management Education & Learning* (2011), 10(4), pp. 606–622.

96. P. Monin, N. Noorderhaven, E. Vaara, D. Kroon, "Giving Sense to and Making Sense of Justice in Postmerger Integration," *Academy of Management Journal* (2013), 56(1), pp. 256–284.

97. J. Shin, M.S. Taylor, M.G. Seo, "Resources for Change: The Relationships of Organizational Inducements and Psychological Resilience to Employees' Attitudes and Behaviors Toward Organizational Change," *Academy of Management Journal* (2012), 55(3), pp. 727–748.

98. J.L. Petriglieri, "Under Threat: Responses to and the Consequences of Threats to Individuals' Identities," *Academy of Management Review* (2011), 36(4), pp. 641–662.

99. J. Shin, M.S. Taylor, M.G. Seo, "Resources for Change: The Relationships of Organizational Inducements and Psychological Resilience to Employees' Attitudes and Behaviors Toward Organizational Change," *Academy of Management Journal* (2012), 55(3), pp. 727–748.

100. M. Goldsmith, "What Got You Here Won't Get You There: How Successful People Became Even More Successful," *Academy of Management Perspective* (2009), 23(3), pp. 103–105.

101. S.K. Johnson, L.O. Garrison, G.H. Broome, J.W. Fleenor, J.L. Steed, "Go for the Goals: Relationships Between Goal Setting and Transfer of Training Following Leadership Development," *Academy of Management Learning & Education* (2012), 11(4), pp. 555–569.

102. P. Monin, N. Noorderhaven, E. Vaara, D. Kroon, "Giving Sense to and Making Sense of Justice in Postmerger Integration," *Academy of Management Journal* (2013), 56(1), pp. 256–284.

103. R. Karlgaard, "Energy in 2050: Shell's Peter Voser," *Forbes* (April 23, 2012), p. 34.

104. L.P. Tost, "An Integrative Model of Legitimacy Judgments," *Academy of Management Review* (2011), 36(4), pp. 686–710.

105. W.J. Henisz, "Leveraging the Financial Crisis to Fulfill the Promise of Progressive Management," *Academy of Management Learning & Education* (2011), 10(2), pp. 298–321.

106. M. Cuban, "Motivate Yourself," *Businessweek* (April 11, 2013), online.

107. J. Welch, S. Welch, "How Not to Succeed in Business," *Businessweek* (March 2, 2009), p. 74.

108. S.S. Chakravorty, "Where Process-Improvement Projects Go Wrong," *The Wall Street Journal* (January 25, 2010), p. R6.

109. J. Shin, M.S. Taylor, M.G. Seo, "Resources for Change: The Relationships of Organizational Inducements and Psychological Resilience to Employees' Attitudes and Behaviors Toward Organizational Change," *Academy of Management Journal* (2012), 55(3), pp. 727–748.

110. M. Selman, "Manipulate Creative People," *Businessweek* (April 11, 2013), p. 92.

111. J.D. Ford, L.W. Ford, A. D'Amelio, "Resistance to Change: The Rest of the Story," *Academy of Management Review* (2008), 33(2), pp. 362–377.

112. S.S. Chakravorty, "Where Process Improvement Projects Go Wrong," *The Wall Street Journal* (January 25, 2010), p. R6.

113. R. Karlgaard, "Energy in 2050: Shell's Peter Voser," *Forbes* (April 23, 2012), p. 34.

114. B. Farber, "Close the Deal With Urgency," *Entrepreneur* (May 2009), p. 60.

115. https://www.americanexpress.com/us/small-business/openforum/articles/google-glass-in-the-workplace-cool-benefits-and-surprising-dangers/ (retrieved June 23, 2014).

116. http://www.shrm.org/hrdisciplines/technology/articles/pages/why-google-glass-could-shatter-workplace-policies.aspx (retrieved June 23, 2014).

117. http://www.cio.com/article/743958/Does_Google_Glass_Pose_Safety_Health_and_Security_Risks_/ (retrieved June 23, 2014).

118. L. Treviño, M. Brown, L. Pincus Hartman, "A Qualitative Investigation of Perceived Executive Ethical Leadership: Perceptions From Inside and Outside the Executive Suite," *Human Relations* (2003), 56(5), pp. 5–37.

119. F. Walumbwa, S. Peterson, B. Avolio, C. Hartnell, "An Investigation of the Relationships Among Leader and Follower Psychological Capital, Service Climate, and Job Performance," *Personnel Psychology* (2010), 63, pp. 937–963.

120. G. Yukl, "How Leaders Influence Organizational Effectiveness," *The Leadership Quarterly* (Yearly Review of Leadership, December 2008), 19(6), pp. 708–722.

121. S. Sobell, "Social Networking @ Work," *The Costco Connection* (June 2011), p. 21.

122. J. Deschenaux, "Employee Use of Social Media: Laws Fail to Keep Pace With Technology," http://www.shrm.org/LegalIssues/FederalResources/Pages/EmployeeUseofSocialMedia.aspx (retrieved March 20, 2011).

123. http://www.shrm.org/templatestools/samples/policies/pages/socialmediapolicy.aspx (retrieved June 23, 2014).

CHAPTER 10

1. A. Konrad, "Virtual-Workforce Manager," *Fortune* (July 23, 2012), p. 32.

2. N. Saif, N. Razzaq, S.U. Rehman, A. Javed, U. Ahmad, "The Role of Workplace Partnership Strategies in Employee Management Relations," *Information and Knowledge Management* (2013), 3(6), pp. 34–39.

3. M.W. Kramer, R.J. Meisenbach, G.J. Hansen, "Communication, Uncertainty, and Volunteer Membership," *Journal of Applied Communication Research* (2013), 41(1), pp. 18–39.

4. A. Fox, "Put Plans into Action," *HR Magazine* (April 2013), pp. 27–31.

5. H.A. Richardson, S.G. Taylor, "Understanding Input Events: A Model of Employees' Responses to Requests for Their Input," *Academy of Management Review* (2012), 37(3), pp. 471–491.

6. D.B. Arnett, C.M. Wittmann, "Improving Marketing Success: The Role of Tacit Knowledge Exchange Between Sales and Marketing," *Journal of Business Research* (2014), 67(3), pp. 324–331.

7. R. Hurley, "Trust Me," *The Wall Street Journal* (October 24, 2011), p. R4.

8. "Jack Welch's Lessons for Success," *Fortune* (1993), 127(2), pp. 86–93.

9. R. Hurley, "Trust Me," *The Wall Street Journal* (October 24, 2011), p. R4.

10. Knowledge @ Wharton (Ed.), (2012). "Declining Employee Loyalty: A Casualty of the New Workplace," https://knowledge.wharton.upenn.edu/article/declining-employee-loyalty-a-casualty-of-the-new-workplace/ (retrieved June 25, 2014).

11. B. Jullien, I.U. Park, "New, Like New, or Very Good? Reputation and Credibility," *The Review of Economic Studies* (2014).

12. E.C. Tomlinson, R.C. Mayer, "The Role of Causal Attribution Dimensions in Trust Repair," *Academy of Management Review* (2009), 34(1), pp. 85–104.

13. D. Dowell, T. Heffernan, M. Morrison, "Trust Formation at the Growth Stage of a Business-to-Business Relationship: A Qualitative Investigation," *Qualitative Market Research: An International Journal* (2013), 16(4), pp. 436–451.

14. P.H. Kim, K. Dirks, C.D. Cooper, "The Repair of Trust: A Dynamic Bilateral Perspective and Multilevel Conceptualization," *Academy of Management Review* (2009), 34(3), pp. 401–422.

15. J. Paskin, "Finding the 'I' in Team," *Businessweek* (February 18–24, 2013), p. 78.

16. Dreamworks, http://www.dreamworksstudios.com (retrieved May 16, 2011).

17. J. Birkinshaw, "Why Good Management Is So Difficult," *Strategic HR Review* (2014), 13(2).

18. R. McCammon, "Cool Rules," *Entrepreneur* (May 2012), pp. 22–23.

19. R. McCammon, "Accentuate the Negative," *Entrepreneur* (October 2012), pp. 18–19.

20. C.A. Rusnak, "Are You Confusing People With Your Leadership Style?" *Costco Connection* (March 2012), p. 11.

21. A.H. Jordan, P.G. Audia, "Self-Enhancement and Learning From Performance Feedback," *Academy of Management Review* (2012), 37(2), pp. 211–231.

22. C.H. Wu, S.K. Parker, J.P. de Jong, "Feedback Seeking From Peers: A Positive Strategy for Insecurely Attached Team Workers," *Human Relations*, published online.

23. E. Bernstein, "The Hidden Benefits of Chitchat," *The Wall Street Journal* (August 13, 2013), pp. D1–D2.

24. "Master Class," *Businessweek* (April 29–May 5, 2013), p. 71.

25. E. Bernstein, "The Hidden Benefits of Chitchat, *The Wall Street Journal* (August 13, 2013), pp. D1–D2.

26. Public Radio News Broadcast, WFCR 88.5 (May 28, 2010).

27. J. Robinson, "E-mail Is Making You Stupid?" *Entrepreneur* (March 2010), pp. 61–63.

28. R. Charan, "The Discipline of Listening," *Harvard Business Review* blog (2012), http://blogs.hbr.org/cs/2012/06/the_discipline_of_listening.html.

29. D. Gladstone, L. Gladstone, *Venture Capital Investing: The Complete Handbook for Investing in Private Businesses for Outstanding Profits* (Upper Saddle River, NJ: FT/Prentice Hall, 2004).

30. E. Bernstein, "Putting the Honey Back in 'Honey, I'm Home,'" *The Wall Street Journal* (October 4, 2011), p. D4.

31. L.E. Sears, Y. Shi, C.R. Coberley, J.E. Pope, "Overall Well-Being as a Predictor of Health Care, Productivity, and Retention Outcomes in a Large Employer," *Population Health Management* (2013), 16(6), pp. 397–405.

32. A. Edmans, "The Link Between Job Satisfaction and Firm Value, With Implications for Corporate Social Responsibility," *Academy of Management Perspectives* (2012), 26(4), pp. 1–19.

33. B.A. Scott, C.M. Barnes, D.T. Wagner, "Chameleonic or Consistent? A Multilevel Investigation of Emotional Labor Variability and Self-Monitoring," *Academy of Management Journal* (2012), 55(4), pp. 905–926.

34. K. Hannon, "It's Never Too Late to Love Your Job," *AARP Magazine* (May 2013), pp. 44–45.

35. M. Mount, R. Ilies, E. Johnson, "Relationship of Personality Traits and Counterproductive Work Behaviors: The Mediating Effects of Job Satisfaction," *Personnel Psychology* (2006), 59, pp. 591–622.

36. N.A. Bowling, K.J. Eschleman, Q. Wang, C. Kirkendall, G. Alarcon, "A Meta-Analysis of the Predictors and Consequences of Organization-Based Self-Esteem," *Journal of Occupational and Organizational Psychology* (2010), 83(3), pp. 601–626.

37. S. Swaminathan, P.D. Jawahar, "Job Satisfaction as a Predictor of Organizational Citizenship Behavior: An Empirical Study," *Global Journal of Business Research* (2013), 7(1), pp. 71–80.

38. D. Strigl, "Management Tools: Results Drive Happiness; Focus on Getting Results From Your People, and That Will Make Them Happy," *HR Magazine-Alexandria* (2011), 56(10), p. 113.

39. H.C. Wan, L.A. Downey, C. Stough, "Understanding Non-Work Presenteeism: Relationships Between Emotional Intelligence, Boredom, Procrastination and Job Stress," Personality and Individual Differences, 65, pp. 86–90.

40. M.S. Direnzo, J. H. Greenhaus, "Job Search and Voluntary Turnover in a Boundaryless World: A Control Theory Perspective," *Academy of Management Review* (2011), 36(3), pp. 567–589.

41. A. Lashinsky, Larry Page Interview, *Fortune* (February 6, 2012), pp. 98–99.

42. C.H. Chang, C.C. Rosen, P.E. Levy, "The Relationship Between Perceptions of Organizational Politics and Employee Attitudes, Strain and Behavior: A Meta-Analytic Examination," *Academy of Management Journal* (2009), 52(4), pp. 779–801.

43. R. Dunham, J. Herman, "Development of a Female Faces Scale for Measuring Job Satisfaction," *Journal of Applied Psychology* (1975), 60(5), pp. 629–631.

44. P. Spector, "Measurement of Human Service Staff Satisfaction: Development of the Job Satisfaction Survey," *American Journal of Community Psychology* (1985), 13(6), pp. 693–713.

45. C. Ai-Hong, J.S. Nafisah, M.N.A. Rahim, "Comparison of Job Satisfaction Among Eight Health Care Professions in Private (Non-government) Settings," *The Malaysian Journal of Medical Sciences* (2012), 19(2), p. 19.

46. P. Spector, "Measurement of Human Service Staff Satisfaction: Development of the Job Satisfaction Survey," *American Journal of Community Psychology* (1985), 13(6), pp. 693–713.

47. C. Fisher, "Mood and Emotions While Working: Missing Pieces of Job Satisfaction," *Journal of Organizational Behavior* (2000), 21(2), pp. 185–202.

48. J. Schramm, "Happy Workers," *HR Magazine—Alexandria* (2014), 59(4), p. 96.

49. D.C. Wyld, "Does More Money Buy More Happiness on the Job?" *Academy of Management Perspective* (2011), 25(1), pp. 101–102.

50. http://www.shrm.org/hrdisciplines/employeerelations/articles/pages/miserable-workers.aspx (retrieved June 25, 2014).

51. T. Lytle, "Employee Relations: Give Employees a Say; How to Encourage Ideas From Employees—and Pick the Best Ones to Act on," *HR Magazine—Alexandria* (2011), 56(10), p. 68.

52. G. Alessandri, L. Borgogni, W. Schaufeli, G.V. Caprara, C. Consiglio, "From Positive Orientation to Job Performance: The Role of Work Engagement and Self-Efficacy Beliefs," *Journal of Happiness Studies* (2014), pp. 1–22.

53. Ibid.

54. http://www.nmb.gov/resources/docs/the-railway-labor-act/ (retrieved June 28, 2014).

55. http://www.fra.dot.gov/Elib/Document/1647/ (retrieved June 28, 2014).

56. http://www.nlrb.gov/national-labor-relations-act/ (retrieved June 28, 2014).

57. http://www.nlrb.gov/what-we-do/ (retrieved June 28, 2014).

58. http://law.justia.com/cases/california/cal2d/49/625.html (retrieved June 28, 2014).

59. http://www.perb.ca.gov/csmcs/glossary.pdf (retrieved June 28, 2014).

60. http://www.dol.gov/oasam/programs/history/glossary.htm (retrieved April 9, 2011).

61. Ibid.

62. Ibid.

63. http://www.nlrb.gov/resources/national-labor-relations-act/ (retrieved June 28, 2014).

64. Collins, B. *Right to Work Laws: Legislative Background and Empirical Research* (Washington, DC: Congressional Research Service, 2012), http://fas.org/sgp/crs/misc/R42575.pdf.

65. http://www.shrm.org/LegalIssues/FederalResources/FederalStatutes RegulationsandGuidanc/Pages/Labor-ManagementReportingandDisclosure Act%28LMRDA%29.aspx (retrieved June 28, 2014).

66. http://doleta.gov/programs/factsht/warn.htm (retrieved June 26, 2014).

67. http://doleta.gov/programs/factsht/warn.htm (retrieved June 26, 2014).

68. http://www.justice.gov/opa/pr/2013/December/13-civ-1352.html (retrieved June 25, 2014).

69. http://www.whistleblowers.org/storage/whistleblowers/documents/DoddFrank/nwcreporttosecfinal.pdf (retrieved April 16, 2011).

70. D. Meinert, "Whistle-Blowers: Threat or Asset?" *HR Magazine* (April 2011), 56(4), pp. 27–32.

71. A. Goldman, W. Sigismond, *Business Law: Principles and Practices* (Mason, OH: Cengage Learning, 2011), p. 124.

72. Ibid.

73. http://www.bls.gov/news.release/union2.nr0.htm (retrieved June 25, 2014).

74. http://www.bls.gov (retrieved July 11, 2013).

75. http://www.bls.gov/news.release/union2.nr0.htm (retrieved June 25, 2014).

76. Ibid.

77. K. Maher, "Labor Faces New Challenge," *The Wall Street Journal* (2012), 259(132), p. 1.

78. http://www.nlrb.gov/resources/national-labor-relations-act/ (retrieved June 25, 2014).

79. http://www.velaw.com/uploadedFiles/VEsite/Resources/UnionOrganizationProcess(5-501-0280).pdf (retrieved June 25, 2014).

80. http://online.wsj.com/public/resources/documents/NLRB.pdf (retrieved June 25, 2014).

81. http://www.shrm.org/legalissues/federalresources/pages/new-organizing-rules.aspx (retrieved June 25, 2014).

82. http://www.shrm.org/legalissues/federalresources/pages/nlrb-poster

.aspx?latestnews (retrieved June 25, 2014).

83. http://www.tlnt.com/2012/07/11/is-it-time-that-we-finally-part-ways-with-the-nlra/ (retrieved June 25, 2014).

84. http://www.velaw.com/uploadedFiles/VEsite/Resources/UnionOrganizationProcess(5-501-0280).pdf (retrieved June 25, 2014).

85. M. Valdez, "Boeing Machinists OK Contract Tied to 777x," Associated Press (January 4, 2014).

86. http://caselaw.lp.findlaw.com/scripts/getcase.pl?court=us&vol=502&invol=527 (retrieved June 25, 2014).

87. N. Cullinane, J. Donaghey, T. Dundon, E. Hickland, T. Dobbins, "Regulating for Mutual Gains? Non-Union Employee Representation and the Information and Consultation Directive," The International Journal of Human Resource Management, 25(6), pp. 810–828.

88. S. Greenhouse, "More Lockouts as Companies Battle Unions," The New York Times (2012), p. 22.

89. S. Greenhouse, "Labor Battle at Kellogg Plant in Memphis Drags On," The New York Times (2014), p. B1.

90. J. Beatty, S. Samuelson, Introduction to Business Law, 3rd ed. (Mason, OH: Cengage Learning, 2009), p. 320.

91. "A Blown Call Draws Heat," Bloomberg Businessweek (October 1–7, 2012), p. 33.

92. J. Beatty, S. Samuelson, Introduction to Business Law, 3rd ed. (Mason, OH: Cengage Learning, 2009), p. 320.

93. http://www.shrm.org/TemplatesTools/hrqa/Pages/decertifyaunion.aspx (retrieved June 25, 2014).

94. http://www.shrm.org/TemplatesTools/hrqa/Pages/decertifyaunion.aspx (retrieved June 25, 2014).

95. Ibid.

96. T. Lenski, "Talk It Out," Businessweek (December 10–16, 2012), p. 85.

97. R. Fehr, M.J. Gelfand, "The Forgiving Organization: A Multilevel Model of Forgiveness at Work," Academy of Management Review (2012), 37(4), pp. 664–688.

98. A.M. Grant, S.V. Patil, "Challenging the Norm of Self-Interest: Minority Influence and Transitions to Helping Norms in Work Units," Academy of Management Review (2012), 37(4), pp. 547–568.

99. E. Gibson, "The Stop-Managing Guide to Management," Businessweek (June 15, 2009), p. 73.

100. H. Ren, B. Gray, "Repairing Relationship Conflict: How Violation Types and Culture Influence the Effectiveness of Restoration Rituals," Academy of Management Review (2009), 34(1), pp. 105–126.

101. H.G. Barkema, M. Schijven, "Toward Unlocking the Full Potential of Acquisitions: The Role of Organizational Restructuring," Academy of Management Journal (2008), 51(4), pp. 696–722.

102. T. Lenski, "Talk It Out," Businessweek (December 10–16, 2012), p. 85.

103. K.A. Eddleston, R.F. Otondo, F.W. Kellermanns, "Conflict, Participative Decision Making, and Generational Ownership Dispersion: A Multilevel Analysis," Journal of Small Business Management (2008), pp. 456–464.

104. E.B. King, J.F. Dawson, M.A. West, V.L. Gilrane, L. Bustin, "Why Organizational and Community Diversity Matters: Representativeness and the Emergence of Incivility and Organizational Performance," Academy of Management Journal (2011), 54(6), pp. 1103–1116.

105. H. Ren, B. Gray, "Repairing Relationship Conflict: How Violation Types and Culture Influence the Effectiveness of Restoration Rituals," Academy of Management Review (2009), 34(1), pp. 105–126.

106. R. Fehr, M.J. Gelfand, "The Forgiving Organization: A Multilevel Model of Forgiveness at Work," Academy of Management Review (2012), 37(4), pp. 664–688.

107. R. Feintzeig, M. Spector, J. Jargon, "Twinkie Maker Hostess to Close," The Wall Street Journal (November 17, 2012), p. A1.

108. R.S. Rubin, E.C. Dierdorff, "How Relevant Is the MBA? Assessing the Alignment of Required Curricula and Required Managerial Competencies," Academy of Management Learning & Education (2009), 8(5), pp. 208–224.

109. J.R, Detert, A.C. Edmondson, "Implicit Voice Theories: Taken-for-Granted Rules of Self-Censorship at Work," Academy of Management Journal (2011), 54(3), pp. 461–488.

110. C. Suddath, "The Art of Haggling," Businessweek (November 26–December 2, 2012), p. 98.

111. W.M. Murphy, "From E-Mentoring to Blended Mentoring: Increasing Students' Developmental Initiation and Mentors Satisfaction," Academy of Management Education & Learning (2011), 10(4), pp. 606–622.

112. S. Wilson, "Think Like a Negotiator," Entrepreneur (May 2009), p. 28.

113. V. Harnish, "Five Ways to Close Big Deals Now," Fortune (February 4, 2013), p. 32.

114. M. Cording, P. Christmann, D.R. King, "Reducing Causal Ambiguity in Acquisition Integration: Intermediate Goals as Mediators of Integration Decisions and Acquisition Performance," Academy of Management Journal (2008), 51(4), pp. 744–767.

115. S. Boras, "Be Effective, Not Popular," Fortune (July 6, 2009), p. 46.

116. M. Port, "Know Who You Want to Know," Entrepreneur (April 2010), p. 48.

117. S. Waterhous, "How Can I Keep My Sales Team Productive in a Recession?" Fortune (March 2, 2009), p. 22.

118. C. Suddath, "The Art of Haggling," Businessweek (November 26–December 2, 2012), p. 98.

119. M. Port, "Know Who You Want to Know," Entrepreneur (April 2010), p. 48.

120. B. Farber, "It's Always Your Lucky Day," Entrepreneur (July 2008), p. 71.

121. S. Wilson, "Think Like a Negotiator," Entrepreneur (May 2009), p. 28.

122. W. Ross, "Good Execution Beats a Bad Idea," Fortune (November 23, 2009), p. 42.

123. B. Farber, "It's Always Your Lucky Day," Entrepreneur (July 2008), p. 71.

124. V. Barret, "Silicon Valley Cinderella," Forbes (April 9, 2012), pp. 98–102.

125. M. Port, "Know Who You Want to Know," Entrepreneur (April 2010), p. 48.

126. B. Farber, "Be All You Can Be," Entrepreneur (August 2008), p. 69.

127. S. Wilson, "Think Like a Negotiator," Entrepreneur (May 2009), p. 28.

128. C. Suddath, "The Art of Haggling," Businessweek (November 26–December 2, 2012), p. 98.

129. M. Buckingham, "How Women Handle Success," Businessweek (November 2, 2009), pp. 70–71.

130. B. Farber, "Constructive Criticism," Entrepreneur (November 2008), p. 73.

131. S. Waterhous, "How Can I Keep My Sales Team Productive in a Recession?" Fortune (March 2, 2009), p. 22.

132. E. Berstein, "Honey, Do You Have to . . ." The Wall Street Journal (April 20, 2010), p. D1.

133. http://www.reuters.com/article/2014/01/17/us-walmart-labor-analysis-idUSBREA0G05F20140117/ (retrieved June 28, 2014).

134. M. Trottman, "U.S. Admonishes Wal-Mart," The Wall Street Journal (November 19, 2013), p. B2.

135. http://online.wsj.com/news/articles/SB10001424052702304851104579359042604153758/ (retrieved June 28, 2014).

136. http://thehill.com/blogs/congress-blog/labor/208512-courts-agree-

unions-latest-tactics-are-illegal/ (retrieved June 28, 2014).

137. http://www.employerlaborrelati ons.com/2014/04/08/complaint-issues-against-ufcw-for-unlawful-coercion-of-wal-mart-employees/ (retrieved June 28, 2014).

CHAPTER 11

1. M. Philips, "Wage Growth May Signal Inflation Ahead," *Bloomberg Businessweek* (January 21–27, 2013), pp. 13–15.

2. http://www.bls.gov/news.release/pdf/ecec.pdf (retrieved July 5, 2014).

3. D. Zielinski, "Tech Support," *HR Magazine* (February 2013), pp. 34–38.

4. J. DeVaro, "A Theoretical Analysis of Relational Job Design and Compensation," *Journal of Organizational Behavior* (2010), 31(2–3), pp. 279–301.

5. R. E. Johnson, C.D. Chang, L.O. Yang, "Commitment and Motivation at Work: The Relevance of Employee Identity and Regulatory Focus," *Academy of Management Review* (2010), 35(2), pp. 226–245.

6. R.S. Rubin, E.C. Dierdorff, "On the Road to Abilene: Time to Manage Agreement About MBA Curricular Relevance," *Academy of Management Learning & Education* (2011), 10(1), pp. 148–161.

7. G.O. Trevor, G. Reilly, B. Gerhart, "Reconsidering Pay Dispersion's Effect on the Performance of Interdependent Work: Reconciling Sorting and Pay Inequality," *Academy of Management Journal* (2012), 55(3), pp. 585–610.

8. http://www.shrm.org/research/surveyfindings/documents/14-0028%20 JobSatEngage_Report_FULL_FNL.pdf (retrieved July 5, 2014).

9. http://www.worldatwork.org/waw/adimLink?id=74763 (retrieved July 5, 2014).

10. J. DeVaro, "A Theoretical Analysis of Relational Job Design and Compensation," *Journal of Organizational Behavior* (2010), 31(2–3), pp. 279–301.

11. V. Vroom, *Work and Motivation* (New York: John Wiley & Sons, 1964).

12. M. Renko, K.G. Kroeck, A. Bullough, "Expectancy Theory and Nascent Entrepreneurship," *Small Business Economics* (2012), 39(3), pp. 667–684.

13. R.L. Purvis, T.J. Zagenczyk, G.E. McCray, "What's in It for Me? Using Expectancy Theory and Climate to Explain Stakeholder Participation, Its Direction and Intensity," *International Journal of Project Management* (2014).

14. Ibid.

15. http://knowledge.wharton.upenn .edu/article/balancing-the-pay-scale-fair-vs-unfair/ (retrieved July 5, 2014).

16. J. S. Adams, "Toward an Understanding of Inequity," *Journal of Abnormal and Social Psychology* (1963), 67, pp. 422–436.

17. C.P. Long, C. Bendersky, C. Morrill, "Fairness Monitoring: Linking Managerial Controls and Fairness Judgments in Organizations," *Academy of Management Journal* (2011), 54(5), pp. 1045–1068.

18. A. Edmans, "The Link Between Job Satisfaction and Firm Value, With Implications for Corporate Social Responsibility, *Academy of Management Perspectives* (2012), 26(4), pp. 1–19.

19. P. Monin, N. Noorderhaven, E. Vaara, D. Kroon, "Giving Sense to and Making Sense of Justice in Post-Merger Integration," *Academy of Management Journal* (2013), 56(1), pp. 256–284.

20. http://www.mindtools.com/pages/article/newLDR_96.htm (retrieved July 9, 2014).

21. M.K. Duffy, K.L. Scott, J.D. Shaw, B.J. Tepper, K. Aquino, "A Social Context Model of Envy and Social Undermining," *Academy of Management Journal* (2012), 55(3), pp. 643–666.

22. S.A. Samaha, R.W. Palmatier, R.P. Dant, "Poisoning Relationships: Perceived Unfairness in Channels of Distribution," *Journal of Marketing* (2011), 75(3), pp. 99–117.

23. C.P. Long, C. Bendersky, C. Morrill, "Fairness Monitoring: Linking Managerial Controls and Fairness Judgments in Organizations," *Academy of Management Journal* (2011), 54(5), pp. 1045–1068.

24. G.O. Trevor, G. Reilly, B. Gerhart, "Reconsidering Pay Dispersion's Effect on the Performance of Interdependent Work: Reconciling Sorting and Pay Inequality," *Academy of Management Journal* (2012), 55(3), pp. 585–610.

25. K. Leavitt, S.J. Reynolds, C.M. Barnes, P. Schilpzan, S.T. Hannah, "Different Hats, Different Obligations: Plural Occupational Identities and Situated Moral Judgments," *Academy of Management Journal* (2012), 55(6), pp. 1316–1333.

26. O. Janssen, G.S. van der Vegt, "Positivity Bias in Employees' Self-Ratings of Performance Relative to Supervisor Ratings: The Roles of Performance Type, Performance-Approach Goal Orientation, and Perceived Influence," *European Journal of Work and Organizational Psychology* (2011), 20(4), pp. 524–552.

27. R.L. Bell, J.S. Martin, "The Relevance of Scientific Management and Equity Theory in Everyday Managerial Communication Situations," *Journal of Management Policy and Practice* (2012), 13(3), pp. 106–115.

28. L.K. John, G. Loewenstein, S.I. Rick, "Cheating More for Less: Upward Social Comparisons Motivate the Poorly Compensated to Cheat," *Organizational Behavior and Human Decision Processes* (2014), 123(2), pp. 101–109.

29. http://www.mindtools.com/pages/article/newLDR_96.htm (retrieved July 9, 2014).

30. J. Welch, S. Welch, "Layoffs: HR's Moment of Truth," *Businessweek* (March 23 & 30, 2009), p. 104.

31. J.C. Polster, "Workplace Grievance Procedures: Signaling Fairness but Escalating Commitment," *NYUL Review* (2011), 86, p. 638.

32. C.O. Trevor, G. Reilly, B. Gerhart, "Reconsidering Pay Dispersion's Effect on the Performance of Interdependent Work: Reconciling Sorting and Pay Inequality," *Academy of Management Journal* (2012), 55(3), pp. 585–610.

33. R.R. Kehoe, P.M. Wright, "The Impact of High-Performance Human Resource Practices on Employees' Attitudes and Behaviors," *Journal of Management* (2013), 39(2), pp. 366–391.

34. S.D. Levitt, S.J. Dubner, "SuperFreakonomics," *Academy of Management Perspectives* (2011), 25(2), pp. 86–87.

35. R. McCammon, "Approval Ratings," *Entrepreneur* (February 2012), pp. 16–17.

36. "Master Class," *Businessweek* (April 29–May 5, 2013), p. 71.

37. H. Yang, "Efficiency Wages and Subjective Performance Pay," *Economic Inquiry* (2008), 46(2), pp. 179–196.

38. http://handle.dtic.mil/100.2/ADA499480 (retrieved July 9, 2014).

39. http://blog.roberthalf.com/are-you-staying-competitive-with-employment-benefits (retrieved July 9, 2014).

40. B.E. Baran, L.R. Shanock, L.R. Miller, "Advancing Organizational Support Theory Into the Twenty-First Century World of Work," *Journal of Business and Psychology* (2012), 27(2), pp. 123–147.

41. P. M. Madhani, "Rebalancing Fixed and Variable Pay in a Sales Organization: A Business Cycle Perspective," *Compensation Benefits Review* (2010), 42(3), p. 179–189.

42. F. Ederer, G. Manso, "Is Pay for Performance Detrimental to Innovation?" *Management Science* (2013), 59(7), pp. 1496–1513.

43. S.A. Culbert, *Get Rid of the Performance Review! How Companies Can Stop Intimidating, Start Managing–and*

Focus on What Really Matters, with L. Rout (New York, NY: Business Plus, 2010).

44. M. Conlin, "The Case for Unequal Perks," *Businessweek* (March 23 & 30, 2009), pp. 54–55.

45. L. Bareket-Bojmel, G. Hochman, D. Ariely, "It's (Not) All About the Jacksons Testing Different Types of Short-Term Bonuses in the Field," *Journal of Management* (2014), published online.

46. Y-C. Wei, T-S. Han, I-C. Hsu, "High-Performance HR Practices and OCB: A Cross-Level Investigation of a Causal Path," *The International Journal of Human Resource Management* (2010), 21(10), pp. 1631–1648.

47. J. Helyar, D. MacMillan, "In Tech, Poaching Is the Sincerest Form of Flattery," *Businessweek* (March 7–13, 2011), pp. 17–18.

48. G.N. Stock, C. McDermott, M. McDermott, "The Effects of Capital and Human Resource Investments on Hospital Performance," *Hospital Topics* (2014), 92(1), pp. 14–19.

49. C.N. Halaby, "Supervision, Pay, and Effort," *Social Forces* (2014), 92(3), pp. 1135–1158.

50. K. Evans, "A Nation of Quitters? Could Be a Good Sign," *The Wall Street Journal* (February 8, 2011), p. C1.

51. G. Colvin, "How Are Most Admired Companies Different? They Invest in People and Keep Them Employed—Even in a Downturn," *Fortune* (March 22, 2010), p. 82.

52. D.H. Bradley, *The Federal Minimum Wage: In Brief* (Washington, DC: Congressional Research Service, 2013), http://fas.org/sgp/crs/misc/R43089.pdf.

53. B. Bartling, F.A. von Siemens, "The Intensity of Incentives in Firms and Markets: Moral Hazard With Envious Agents," *Labour Economics* (2010), 17(3), pp. 598–607.

54. http://www.shrm.org/hrdisciplines/compensation/articles/pages/salary-compression-lid.aspx (retrieved July 6, 2014).

55. E. Belogolovsky, P. Bamberger, "Signaling in Secret: Pay for Performance and the Incentive and Sorting Effects of Pay Secrecy," *Academy of Management Journal* (2014).

56. E. Silverman, "Psst . . . This Is What Your Co-worker Is Paid," *The Wall Street Journal* (January 30, 2013), p. B6

57. Ibid.

58. http://www.dol.gov/whd/regs/statutes/0002.fair.pdf (retrieved July 9, 2014).

59. http://www.dol.gov/compliance/guide/minwage.htm (retrieved July 9, 2014).

60. http://www.dol.gov/whd/regs/compliance/whdfs23.pdf (retrieved July 9, 2014).

61. http://www.usatoday.com/story/news/nation/2014/06/11/seattle-minimum-wage-15-challenge/10344443/ (retrieved July 6, 2014).

62. http://www.dol.gov/opa/media/press/whd/WHD20141131.htm (retrieved July 7, 2014).

63. http://www.dol.gov/compliance/guide/minwage.htm (retrieved July 9, 2014).

64. Ibid.

65. http://www.dol.gov/whd/regs/compliance/whdfs15.pdf (retrieved July 9, 2014).

66. http://www.dol.gov/elaws/esa/flsa/screen75.asp (retrieved July 6, 2014).

67. http://www.dol.gov/whd/regs/compliance/fairpay/fs17g_salary.htm (retrieved July 6, 2014).

68. http://www.dol.gov/whd/regs/compliance/fairpay/fs17h_highly_comp.pdf (retrieved July 6, 2014).

69. http://www.dol.gov/whd/regs/compliance/fairpay/fs17g_salary.htm (retrieved July 6, 2014).

70. http://www.dol.gov/elaws/faq/esa/flsa/016.htm (retrieved July 9, 2014).

71. http://www.dol.gov/compliance/guide/childlbr.htm (retrieved July 9, 2014).

72. http://www.dol.gov/opa/media/press/whd/WHD20120801.htm (retrieved July 7, 2014).

73. http://ogesdw.dol.gov/views/data_summary.php (retrieved July 7, 2014).

74. http://www.dol.gov/compliance/guide/minwage.htm#Penalites (retrieved July 7, 2014).

75. http://www.dol.gov/whd/minwage/america.htm (retrieved July 9, 2014).

76. http://www.eeoc.gov/eeoc/newsroom/equal_pay_day_2014.cfm (retrieved July 7, 2014).

77. B. Collins, J. Feder, *Pay Equity: Legislative and Legal Developments* (Washington, DC: Congressional Research Service, 2013).

78. http://www.dol.gov/oasam/programs/history/flsa1938.htm (retrieved July 9, 2014).

79. http://www.worldatwork.org/adimLink?id=74254 (retrieved July 8, 2014).

80. Ibid.

81. http://www.haygroup.com/ww/services/index.aspx?id=1529 (retrieved July 9, 2014).

82. http://www.shrm.org/Research/Articles/Articles/Pages/Compensation_20Series_20Part_20II__20Job_20Evaluation.aspx (retrieved July 9, 2014).

83. Ibid.

84. http://www.shrm.org/Education/hreducation/Pages/Designinga Pay StructureACaseStudyandIntegrated Exercises.aspx (retrieved July 9, 2014).

85. http://www.shrm.org/Education/hreducation/Pages/DesigningaPay StructureACaseStudyandIntegrated Exercises.aspx (retrieved July 9, 2014).

86. M. Guadalupe, J. Wulf, "The Flattening Firm and Product Market Competition: The Effect of Trade Liberalization on Corporate Hierarchies," *American Economic Journal: Applied Economics* (2010), 2(4), pp. 105–127.

87. G.O. Trevor, G. Reilly, B. Gerhart, "Reconsidering Pay Dispersion's Effect on the Performance of Interdependent Work: Reconciling Sorting and Pay Inequality," *Academy of Management Journal* (2012), 55(3), pp. 585–610.

88. http://www.shrm.org/TemplatesTools/HowtoGuides/Pages/HowtoEstablishSalaryRanges.aspx (retrieved July 9, 2014).

89. http://www.shrm.org/hrdisciplines/compensation/Articles/Pages/CMS_000067.aspx (retrieved July 9, 2014).

90. http://www.irs.gov/Businesses/Small-Businesses-&-Self-Employed/Independent-Contractor-Defined (retrieved July 9, 2014).

91. http://money.cnn.com/2014/02/19/news/economy/port-truck-drivers-wages/?iid=EL (retrieved July 9, 2014).

92. http://www.wagehourlitigation.com/dol-compliancerule-making/keeping-the-pressure-on-employers/ (retrieved July 9, 2014).

93. http://aon.mediaroom.com/2013-08-29-Aon-Hewitt-Survey-Shows-2014-Salary-Increases-to-Reach-Highest-Levels-Since-2008 (retrieved July 9, 2014).

94. 94. Hoover's Inc. (2014). *CVS Caremark Corporation* [Hoover's Company Records: In-Depth Records]. Retrieved July 12, 2014, from Long Island University Academic Database.

95. D. Lazarus. "At CVS, Only the Very Rich Get Much Richer," *Los Angeles Times,* http://www.latimes.com/business/la-fi-lazarus-20140627-column.html (June 26, 2014).

96. Ibid.

97. Ibid.

98. J. Kell. "CVS Caremark CEO's Pay Jumps 44%," *Wall Street Journal*, http://online.wsj.com/news/articles/SB10001424127887323501004578390383929384430 (March 29, 2013).

CHAPTER 12

1. D. Zielinski, "Tech Support," *HR Magazine* (February 2013), pp. 34–38.

2. G.O. Trevor, G. Reilly, B. Gerhart, "Reconsidering Pay Dispersion's Effect on the Performance of Interdependent Work: Reconciling Sorting and Pay Inequality," *Academy of Management Journal* (2012), 55(3), pp. 585–610.

3. S.D. Levitt, S.J. Dubner, "SuperFreakonomics," *Academy of Management Perspectives* (2011), 25(2), pp. 86–87.

4. M. Pennington, "The 99% Movement Scorns American Creativity," *Forbes* (June 4, 2012), p. 30.

5. F. Bridoux, R. Coeurderoy, R. Durand, "Heterogeneous Motives and the Collective Creation of Value," *Academy of Management Review* (2011), 36(4), pp. 711–730.

6. R. E. Johnson, C.D. Chang, L.O. Yang, "Commitment and Motivation at Work: The Relevance of Employee Identity and Regulatory Focus," *Academy of Management Review* (2010), 35(2), pp. 226–245.

7. D. Hantula, "What Performance Management Needs Is a Good Theory: A Behavioral Perspective," *Industrial & Organizational Psychology* (2011), 4(2), pp. 194–197.

8. http://www.sibson.com/publications/surveysandstudies/P4P.pdf (retrieved July 14, 2014).

9. R. Gray, "The Return on Incentives," *Human Resources* (October 2010), pp. 49–50, 52.

10. http://www.haygroup.com/downloads/ww/misc/cfr_global_report.pdf (retrieved July 14, 2014).

11. R. Pinheiro, "SuperFreakonomics: Global Cooling, Patriotic Prostitutes, and Why Suicide Bombers Should Buy Life Insurance," *Academy of Management Perspectives* (2011), 25(25), pp. 86–87.

12. E. Morrison, "From the Editors," *Academy of Management Journal* (2010), 53(5), pp. 932–936.

13. J. Kragl, "Group vs. Individual Performance Pay in Relational Employment Contracts When Workers Are Envious," *European Business School Research Paper No. 09-09* (January 13, 2010).

14. A.K. Jha, "Time to Get Serious About Pay for Performance," *JAMA* (2013), 309(4), pp. 347–348.

15. J.J. Martocchio, *Strategic Compensation: A Human Resource Management Approach* (Upper Saddle River, NJ: Prentice Hall, 2015), pp. 80–84.

16. C. Rose, "Charlie Rose Talks to Alan Mulally," *Businessweek* (August 1–7, 2011), p. 27.

17. R. E. Johnson, C.D. Chang, L.O. Yang, "Commitment and Motivation at Work: The Relevance of Employee Identity and Regulatory Focus," *Academy of Management Review* (2010), 35(2), pp. 226–245.

18. S. Anand, P.R. Vidyarthi, R.C. Linden, D.M. Rousseau, "Good Citizens in Poor-Quality Relationships: Idiosyncratic Deals as a Substitute for Relationship Quality," *Academy of Management Journal* (2010), 53(5), pp. 970–988.

19. J.J. Martocchio, *Strategic Compensation: A Human Resource Management Approach*, (Upper Saddle River, NJ: Prentice Hall, 2015), pp. 84–85.

20. S. Anand, P.R. Vidyarthi, R.C. Linden, D.M. Rousseau, "Good Citizens in Poor-Quality Relationships: Idiosyncratic Deals as a Substitute for Relationship Quality," *Academy of Management Journal* (2010), 53(5), pp. 970–988.

21. B. Nelson, *1501 Ways to Reward Employees* (New York, NY: Workman, 2012).

22. J.J. Martocchio, *Strategic Compensation: A Human Resource Management Approach* (Upper Saddle River, NJ: Prentice Hall, 2015), p. 86.

23. C.S. Jung, "Extending the Theory of Goal Ambiguity to Programs: Examining the Relationship Between Goal Ambiguity and Performance," *Public Administration Review* (2014), 74(2), pp. 205–219.

24. J.M. MacDonald, W.H. Ahearn, D. Parry-Cruwys, S. Bancroft, W.V. Dube, "Persistence During Extinction: Examining the Effects of Continuous and Intermittent Reinforcement on Problem Behavior," *Journal of Applied Behavior Analysis* (2013), 46(1), pp. 333–338.

25. Ibid.

26. J. Helyar, D. MacMillan, "In Tech, Poaching Is the Sincerest Form of Flattery," *Businessweek* (March 7–13, 2011), pp. 17–18.

27. A.A. Zoltners, P. Sinha, S.E. Lorimer, "Breaking the Sales Force Incentive Addiction: A Balanced Approach to Sales Force Effectiveness," *Journal of Personal Selling & Sales Management* (2012), 32(2), pp. 171–186.

28. J. Yoo, G.L. Frankwick, "Exploring the Impact of Social Undermining on Salesperson Deviance: An Integrated Model," *Journal of Personal Selling and Sales Management* (2013), 33(1), pp. 79–90.

29. http://edweb.sdsu.edu/people/ARossett/pie/Interventions/od_1.htm (retrieved July 14, 2014).

30. A.J. Nyberg, J.R. Pieper, C.O. Trevor, "Pay-for-Performance's Effect on Future Employee Performance: Integrating Psychological and Economic Principles Toward a Contingency Perspective, *Journal of Management* (2013), published online.

31. F. Christensen, J. Manley, L. Laurence, "The Allocation of Merit Pay in Academia," *Economics Bulletin* (2011), 31(2), pp. 1548–1562.

32. F. Meng, J. Wu, "Merit Pay Fairness, Leader-Member Exchange, and Job Engagement: Evidence From Mainland China," *Review of Public Personnel Administration* (2012), published online.

33. L.A. Myers Jr., "One Hundred Years Later: What Would Frederick W. Taylor Say?" *International Journal of Business and Social Science* (2011), 2(20), pp. 8–11.

34. J. S. Heywood, S. Siebert, X. Wei, "Unintended Consequences of a Piece Rate? Evidence From a Field Experiment" (2013), http://www.birmingham.ac.uk/Documents/college-social-sciences/business/events/beyond-wages/stansiebert/9weiheywoodsiebertexperiment.pdf.

35. H. Young Shin, W. Lee, "How Can We Introduce the Most Effective Incentive Plan for Non-exempt Employees?" (2013), http://digitalcommons.ilr.cornell.edu/student/18/.

36. A. Edmans, "The Link Between Job Satisfaction and Firm Value, With Implications for Corporate Social Responsibility, *Academy of Management Perspectives* (2012), 26(4), pp. 1–19.

37. R. McCammon, "Approval Ratings," *Entrepreneur* (February 2012), pp. 16–17.

38. M. Baer, "Putting Creativity to Work: The Implementation of Creative Ideas in Organizations," *Academy of Management Journal* (2012), 55(5), pp. 1102–1119.

39. J. Paterson, "Breeding Loyalty," *Employee Benefits* (February 2011), pp. 27–28.

40. R. E. Johnson, C.D. Chang, L.O. Yang, "Commitment and Motivation at Work: The Relevance of Employee Identity and Regulatory Focus," *Academy of Management Review* (2010), 35(2), pp. 226–245.

41. D.R. Hekman, G.A. Bigley, H.K. Steensma, J.F. Hereford, "Combined Effects of Organizational and Professional Identification on the Reciprocity Dynamic for Professional Employees," *Academy of Management Journal* (2009), 52(3), pp. 506–526.

42. V. Barret, "Silicon Valley Cinderella," *Forbes* (April 9, 2012), pp. 98–102.

43. National Public Radio (April 30, 2013).

44. M. Selman, "Manipulate Creative People," *Businessweek* (April 11, 2013), p. 92.

45. R. McCammon, "Approval Ratings," *Entrepreneur* (February 2012), pp. 16–17.

46. Ibid.

47. "Master Class," *Businessweek* (April 29–May 5, 2013), p. 71.

48. Based on one of the authors' consulting experiences.

49. B. Nelson, *1501 Ways to Reward Employees* (New York, NY: Workman, 2012).

50. D. Gursoy, C.G.Q. Chi, E. Karadag, "Generational Differences in Work Values and Attitudes Among Frontline and Service

Contact Employees," *International Journal of Hospitality Management* (2013), 32, pp. 40–48.

51. J.J. Martocchio, *Strategic Compensation: A Human Resource Management Approach* (Upper Saddle River, NJ: Prentice Hall, 2015), p. 92.

52. Ibid., p. 86.

53. D. Kruse, R.B. Freeman, *J.R. Blasi, Shared Capitalism at Work: Employee Ownership, Profit and Gain Sharing, and Broad-Based Stock Options* (Chicago, IL: University of Chicago Press, 2010).

54. Ibid.

55. J. Blasi, D. Kruse, D. Weltmann, "Firm Survival and Performance in Privately Held ESOP Companies," *Advances in the Economic Analysis of Participatory & Labor-Managed Firms* (2013), 14, pp. 109–124.

56. http://www.nceo.org/main/article.php/id/30/ (retrieved July 14, 2014).

57. D.C. Wyld, "Do Employees View Stock Options the Same Way as Their Bosses Do?" *Academy of Management Perspectives* (2011), 25(4), pp. 91–92.

58. Y. Hochberg, L. Lindsey, "Incentives, Targeting, and Firm Performance: An Analysis of Non-executive Stock Options," *The Review of Financial Studies* (2010), 23(11), pp. 4148–4186.

59. D. Finn, "Outsourcing Employment Programmes: Contract Design and Differential Prices," *European Journal of Social Security* (2010), 12, p. 289.

60. A.K. Jha, "Time to Get Serious About Pay for Performance," *JAMA* (2013), 309(4), pp. 347–348.

61. Ibid.

62. J. Paterson, "Breeding Loyalty," *Employee Benefits* (Feb 2011), pp. 27–28.

63. J. Moniz, "The Basics for Building and Maintaining Incentive Plans at Smaller Firms," *Compensation Benefits Review* (July/August 2010), 42(4), p. 256–264.

64. R. Pinheiro, "SuperFreakonomics: Global Cooling, Patriotic Prostitutes, and Why Suicide Bombers Should Buy Life Insurance," *Academy of Management Perspectives* (2011), 25(25), pp. 86–87.

65. M. Kroumova, M. Lazarova, "Broad-Based Incentive Plans, HR Practices and Company Performance," *Human Resource Management Journal* (2009), 19(4), pp. 355–374.

66. http://www.shrm.org/hrdisciplines/compensation/Articles/Pages/EntitlementPay.aspx (retrieved July 14, 2014).

67. T. Libby, L. Thorne, "The Influence of Incentive Structure on Group Performance in Assembly Lines and Teams," *Behavioral Research in Accounting* (2009), 21(2), pp. 57–72.

68. D. Cardrain, "Put Success in Sight," *HR Magazine* (May 2003), 48(5), p. 84.

69. J. Stein, "Millennials: The Me Me Me Generation," *TIME Magazine* (2013), cover.

70. http://www.shrm.org/hrdisciplines/compensation/Articles/Pages/Entitlement Pay.aspx (retrieved July 14, 2014).

71. Q. Ma, J. Jin, L. Meng, Q. Shen, "The Dark Side of Monetary Incentive: How Does Extrinsic Reward Crowd Out Intrinsic Motivation," *Neuroreport* (2014), 25(3), pp. 194–198.

72. Ibid.

73. "The Changing Face of Reward," *Global Management Consultancy Hay Group* (2010).

74. http://www.sibson.com/publications/surveysandstudies/P4P.pdf (retrieved July 15, 2014).

75. D. Naranjo-Gil, G. Cuevas-Rodríguez, Á. López-Cabrales, J.M. Sánchez, "The Effects of Incentive System and Cognitive Orientation on Teams' Performance," *Behavioral Research in Accounting* (2012), 24(2), pp. 177–191.

76. A. Thompson Jr., J. Gamble, A. Strickland III, *Crafting and Executing Strategy,* 19th ed. (New York, NY: McGraw-Hill Irwin, 2013).

77. J. Sammer, "Weighing Pay Incentives," *HR Magazine* (June 2007), 52(6), pp. 64–68.

78. http://www.sibson.com/publications/surveysandstudies/P4P.pdf (retrieved July 14, 2014).

79. M. Rosenthal, R. Adams Dudley, "Pay for Performance: Will the Latest Payment Trend Improve Care?" *Journal of the American Medical Association* (2007), 297(7), pp. 740–744.

80. J. Sammer, "Weighing Pay Incentives," *HR Magazine* (June 2007), 52(6), pp. 64–68.

81. Ibid.

82. http://www.sibson.com/publications/surveysandstudies/P4P.pdf (retrieved July 14, 2014).

83. A. Thompson Jr., J. Gamble, A. Strickland III, *Crafting and Executing Strategy,* 19th ed. (New York, NY: McGraw-Hill Irwin, 2013).

84. http://www.shrm.org/hrdisciplines/compensation/Articles/Pages/PinkMoney.aspx (retrieved July 14, 2014).

85. http://www.fastcodesign.com/1663137/3ms-key-to-innovation-give-everyone-the-day-off/ (retrieved July 14, 2014).

86. A. Thompson Jr., J. Gamble, A. Strickland III, *Crafting and Executing Strategy,* 19th ed. (New York, NY: McGraw-Hill Irwin, 2013).

87. "The CEO Conundrum," *Businessweek* (June 15, 2009), p. 12.

88. S. Gustin, "Two Years After Steve Jobs' Death, Is Apple a Different Company?" *TIME Magazine* (October 4, 2013).

89. http://ycharts.com/companies/AAPL/market_cap/ (retrieved July 13, 2014).

90. R.S. Rubin, E.C. Dierdorff, "On the Road to Abilene: Time to Manage Agreement About MBA Curricular Relevance," *Academy of Management Learning & Education* (2011), 10(1), pp. 148–161.

91. http://www.bloomberg.com/news/2014-04-29/cheniere-s-souki-becomes-top-paid-ceo-with-142-million.html (retrieved July 13, 2014).

92. http://www.nytimes.com/2014/04/13/business/still-no-1-and-doing-what-he-wants.html (retrieved July 13, 2014).

93. http://www.usatoday.com/story/money/business/2014/04/03/2013-ceo-pay/7200481/ (retrieved July 13, 2014).

94. http://www.nytimes.com/2014/04/13/business/executive-pay-invasion-of-the-supersalaries.html?_r=0 (retrieved July 13, 2014).

95. http://www.cornellhrreview.org/throwing-out-the-baby-and-weighing-the-bathwater-the-nonsense-of-executive-compensation-oversight/ (retrieved July 14, 2014).

96. M. Krantz, B. Hansen, "CEO Pay Soars While Worker's Pay Stalls," *USA Today* (April 1, 2011), pp. B1–B2.

97. Executive Compensation Group Advisory, *Vedder Price P.C.* (July 2010)

98. http://www.bloomberg.com/news/2013-09-17/ceo-to-worker-pay-ratio-disclosure-proposal-to-be-issued-by-sec.html (retrieved July 13, 2014).

99. Ibid.

100. http://www.fool.com/investing/general/2013/11/02/will-jc-penney-jds-uniphase-and-us-steel-leave-the.aspx (retrieved July 13, 2014).

101. http://www.ft.com/intl/cms/s/0/304564c4-531d-11e0-86e6-00144feab49a.html#axzz1PB0uFmWB (retrieved July 15, 2014).

102. "Executive Compensation Group Advisory," *Vedder Price P.C.* (July 2010).

103. http://www.businesswire.com/news/home/20110203006706/en/Companies-Set-Failing-Grades-Pay-Performance-Test/ (retrieved July 15, 2014).

104. M. Friedman, "The Social Responsibility of Business Is to Increase Profits," *Corporate Ethics and Corporate Governance* (2007), Part IV, pp. 173–178.

105. http://www.shrm.org/hrdisciplines/compensation/Articles/Pages/CMS_014050.aspx (retrieved July 15, 2014).

106. Ibid.

107. http://www.salary.com/advice/layouthtmls/advl_display_nocat_Ser300_Par454.html (retrieved July 15, 2014).

108. http://www.shrm.org/hrdisciplines/compensation/Articles/Pages/PerformTies.aspx (retrieved July 15, 2014).

109. Ibid.

110. http://www.shrm.org/hrdisciplines/compensation/Articles/Pages/Financial Firms.aspx (retrieved July 15, 2014).

111. Ibid.

112. http://www.forbes.com/global2000/list/#page:20_sort:3_direction:desc_search:_filter:All%20industries_filter:All%20countries_filter:All%20states (retrieved July 14, 2014).

113. http://blogs.reuters.com/great-debate/2014/04/30/supersize-salaries-how-much-is-that-ceo-worth/ (retrieved July 14, 2014).

114. http://www.forbes.com/global2000/list/#page:20_sort:3_direction:desc_search:_filter:All%20industries_filter:All%20countries_filter:All%20states (retrieved July 14, 2014).

115. http://fortune.com/2014/06/24/rhode-island-ceo-pay/ (retrieved July 14, 2014).

116. http://www.governmentcontractorcomplianceupdate.com/2014/05/06/new-york-court-strikes-down-regulations-limiting-executive-compensation-and-administrative-expenses/ (retrieved July 14, 2014).

117. http://www.execcomp.org/News/NewsStories/obama-cap-on-federal-contractor-pay-rejected-by-house-defense-panel/ (retrieved July 14, 2014).

118. http://fortune.com/2014/06/24/rhode-island-ceo-pay/ (retrieved July 14, 2014).

119. J. Helyar, D. MacMillan, "In Tech, Poaching Is the Sincerest Form of Flattery," Businessweek (March 7–13, 2011), pp. 17–18.

120. J. Arbaugh, L. Cox, S. M. Camp, "Employee Equity, Incentive Compensation, and Growth in Entrepreneurial Firms," New England Journal of Entrepreneurship (2004), 7(1), pp. 15–25.

121. http://graphics8.nytimes.com/packages/pdf/business/20110428-docs/allstate.pdf (retrieved July 15, 2014).

122. Hoover's Inc. (2014). Barclays PLC [Hoover's Company Records: In-Depth Records]. Retrieved July 15, 2014, from Long Island University Academic Database.

123. Accenture.com. (2011, August), Smarter on-boarding: The key to higher client retention and cross-sell. Retrieved from the Accenture website at http://www.accenture.com/us-en/Pages/insight-smarter-on-boarding-key-higher-client-retention-cross-sell.aspx.

124. J. Anderson. Barclays chief defends contentious increase in bonus pay. DealBook [blog of the New York Times]. Retrieved from http://dealbook.nytimes.com/2014/03/05/barclays-chief-defends-contentious-increase-in-bonus-pay/ (March 5, 2014).

125. S. Slater, M. Scuffham, "Barclays to cut 12,000 jobs, pays bigger bonuses." Reuters." Retrieved from http://www.reuters.com/article/2014/02/11/us-barclays-earnings-idUSBREA190ES20140211/ (February 11, 2014).

126. G. Jozwiak. "Barclays raises bonuses by 10%," HR Magazine. Retrieved from http://www.hrmagazine.co.uk/hro/news/1142131/barclays-raises-bonuses/ (February 12, 2014).

127. Ibid.

128. S. Slater. "Barclays CEO turns down bonus for 2013." Reuters. Retrieved from http://uk.reuters.com/article/2014/02/03/uk-barclays-ceo-bonus-idUKBREA1216E20140203/ February 3, 2014).

CHAPTER 13

1. http://data.bls.gov/cgi-bin/print.pl/news.release/ecec.t01.htm (retrieved July 22, 2014).

2. D.B. Montgomery, C.A. Ramus, "Calibrating MBA Job Preferences for the 21st Century," Academy of Management Learning & Education (2011), 10(1), pp. 9–26.

3. G. Moran, "The Business of Better Benefits," Entrepreneur (May 2011), pp. 81–82.

4. J.C. Santora, "The Psychology of Defined-Benefits Pensions: When Do They Affect Employee Behavior," Academy of Management Perspectives (2010), 24(2), pp. 85–86.

5. G. Moran, "The Business of Better Benefits," Entrepreneur (May 2011), pp. 81–82.

6. R. Feintzeig, "Who Gets Free Lunch and Other Tech Perks," The Wall Street Journal (July 16, 2014), p. D2.

7. Ibid.

8. D. Blanchard, D. Hutson, E. Wills, The One Minute Entrepreneur (New York, NY: Currency, 2008).

9. J.C. Santora, "The Psychology of Defined-Benefits Pensions: When Do They Affect Employee Behavior," Academy of Management Perspectives (2010), 24(2), pp. 85–86.

10. http://www.businessweek.com/articles/2013-10-07/in-new-housing-complex-for-facebook-dogs-get-daycare-kids-dont/ (retrieved July 21, 2014).

11. http://fortune.com/2011/08/18/why-companies-are-cozying-up-to-napping-at-work/ (retrieved July 21, 2014).

12. D. Tobenkin, "Stay Well Together," HR Magazine (February 2013), pp. 63–66.

13. R.J. Grossman, "No Federal Regulatory Relief in Sight," HR Magazine (February 2013), pp. 22–27.

14. M. Collins, C. Hymowitz, "Who's Got the Best Retirement Plan?" Businessweek (July 28–August 3, 2014), pp. 36–38.

15. B. Leonard, "A Holistic Approach to an Onsite Health Clinic," HR Magazine (April 2013), p. 14.

16. http://www.whitehouse.gov/sites/default/files/omb/budget/fy2015/assets/tables.pdf (retrieved July 21, 2014).

17. http://www.whitehouse.gov/sites/default/files/omb/budget/fy2015/assets/tables.pdf (retrieved July 21, 2014).

18. http://www.ssa.gov/oact/cola/cbb.html (retrieved July 22, 2014).

19. https://faq.ssa.gov/ics/support/KBAnswer.asp?questionID=3829&hitOffset=140+133+126+121+117+106+105+84+74+58+48+35+29+7&docID=12620 (retrieved July 22, 2014).

20. http://www.socialsecurity.gov/dibplan/dqualify3.htm (retrieved July 22, 2014).

21. http://stats.oecd.org/Index.aspx?QueryId=29820 (retrieved July 22, 2014).

22. D. Blanchard, D. Hutson, E. Wills, The One Minute Entrepreneur (New York, NY: Currency, 2008).

23. http://www.socialsecurity.gov/pubs/retirechart.htm (retrieved July 22, 2014).

24. http://www.census.gov/popest/data/national/asrh/2009/tables/NC-EST2009-02.xls (retrieved July 22, 2014).

25. http://quickfacts.census.gov/qfd/states/00000.html (retrieved July 22, 2014).

26. http://www.socialsecurity.gov/oact/trsum/index.html (retrieved July 22, 2014).

27. Ibid.

28. http://www.socialsecurity.gov/survivorplan/survivors.htm (retrieved July 22, 2014).

29. http://www.socialsecurity.gov/pubs/EN-05-10043.pdf (retrieved July 22, 2014).

30. http://www.socialsecurity.gov/oact/trsum/index.html (retrieved July 22, 2014).

31. National Academy of Social Insurance, Workers' Compensation: Benefits, Coverage, and Costs, 2011, http://www.workcompcentral.com/pdf/2013/misc/nasiRptWkrsComp11v3b.pdf, p. 5 (retrieved September 28, 2014).

32. National Academy of Social Insurance, Workers' Compensation: Benefits, Coverage, and Costs, 2011, Washington, D.C. (August, 2013), p. 3

33. http://workforcesecurity.doleta.gov/unemploy/pdf/uilawcompar/2010/financing.pdf (retrieved July 22, 2014).

34. Ibid.

35. J. Rothstein, "Unemployment Insurance and Job Search in the Great

Recession (No. 17534)," National Bureau of Economic Research (2011).

36. http://www.dol.gov/whd/fmla/index.htm (retrieved July 2, 2011).

37. http://www.dol.gov/whd/fmla/fmlaAmended.htm#SEC_101_DEFINITIONS (retrieved July 22, 2014).

38. http://finduslaw.com/family_and_medical_leave_act_fmla_29_us_code_chapter_28/ (retrieved July 2, 2011).

39. http://www.shrm.org/legalissues/federalresources/pages/fmla-challenges.aspx (retrieved July 22, 2014).

40. R. Sutton, "How a Few Bad Apples Ruin Everything," *The Wall Street Journal* (2011), http://online.wsj.com/news/articles/SB10001424052970203499704576622550325233260/.

41. http://www.littler.com/publication-press/publication/employer-mandate-delay-beware-ignoring-aca/ (retrieved July 22, 2014).

42. MetLife [advertisement], "A Win-Win Solution," *Fortune* (July 1, 2013), p. 22.

43. HighRoads, *Fifth Annual Compliance Trends Survey Findings and Observations*, p. 6, http://www.highroads.com/compliance-trends2014/.

44. http://www.bls.gov/news.release/ecec.nr0.htm (retrieved July 22, 2014).

45. "What's News: Business and Finance," *The Wall Street Journal* (November 5, 2012), p. A1.

46. G. Colvin, "2013: The Year We Become the Health Care Nation," *Fortune* (January 14, 2013), p. 38.

47. http://www.smartmoney.com/plan/insurance/10-things-your-health-insurance-company-wont-say-1299280540906/ (retrieved July 23, 2014).

48. http://www.law.cornell.edu/uscode/html/uscode29/usc_sup_01_29_10_18_20_I_30_B_40_6.html (retrieved July 23, 2014).

49. http://www.hhs.gov/ocr/privacy/ (retrieved July 23, 2014).

50. http://www.hhs.gov/ocr/privacy/hipaa/understanding/coveredentities/index.html (retrieved July 23, 2014).

51. http://www.shrm.org/LegalIssues/FederalResources/Pages/BenefitPlanChanges.aspx (retrieved July 23, 2014).

52. http://www.pbgc.gov/wr/benefits/guaranteed-benefits.html (retrieved July 23, 2014).

53. Society for Human Resources Management, *Examining Paid Leave in the Workplace* (Alexandria, VA: SHRM, 2008), http://www.shrm.org/research/surveyfindings/articles/documents/09-0228_paid_leave_sr_fnl.pdf.

54. http://www.bls.gov/news.release/ecec.t01.htm (retrieved July 5, 2011).

55. Society for Human Resources Management, "2013 Employee Benefits," (Alexandria, VA: SHRM, 2013), p. 30, http://www.shrm.org/research/surveyfindings/articles/documents/13-0245%202013_empbenefits_fnl.pdf.

56. http://www.bls.gov/opub/ted/2013/ted_20130730.htm (retrieved July 23, 2014).

57. J. Bloom, S.A. Geurts, M.A. Kompier, "Effects of Short Vacations, Vacation Activities and Experiences on Employee Health and Well-Being," *Stress and Health* (2012), 28(4), pp. 305–318.

58. Society for Human Resources Management, "2013 Employee Benefits" (Alexandria, VA: SHRM, 2013), p. 31, http://www.shrm.org/research/surveyfindings/articles/documents/13-0245%202013_empbenefits_fnl.pdf.

59. http://hbr.org/2014/01/how-netflix-reinvented-hr/ar/1/ (retrieved July 24, 2014).

60. https://www.cms.gov/NationalHealthExpendData/downloads/tables.pdf (retrieved July 8, 2011).

61. http://www.bls.gov/ncs/ebs/benefits/2013/ownership/civilian/table06a.htm (retrieved July 23, 2014).

62. Costco, http://www.costco.com (retrieved August 4, 2014).

63. http://www.irs.gov/pub/irs-pdf/p969.pdf (retrieved July 23, 2014).

64. Society for Human Resources Management, "2013 Employee Benefits" (Alexandria, VA: SHRM, 2013), p. 64, http://www.shrm.org/research/surveyfindings/articles/documents/13-0245%202013_empbenefits_fnl.pdf.

65. http://www.bls.gov/ncs/ebs/benefits/2013/ownership/private/table02a.htm (retrieved July 23, 2014).

66. C. Santora, "The Psychology of Defined-Benefits Pensions: When Do They Affect Employee Behavior," *Academy of Management Perspectives* (2010), 24(2), pp. 85–86.

67. C. Rogers, "Chrysler to Freeze Workers' Pension," *The Wall Street Journal* (June 15–16, 2013), p. B3.

68. http://www.irs.gov/Retirement-Plans/Plan-Participant-Employee/Retirement-Topics-401k-and-Profit-Sharing-Plan-Contribution-Limits (retrieved July 23, 2014).

69. M. Collins, C. Hymowitz, "Who's Got the Best Retirement Plan?" *Businessweek* (July 28–August 3, 2014), pp. 36–38.

70. G. Jasen, "Your First Job? Think About Retirement," *The Wall Street Journal* (December 3, 2012), p. R9.

71. K. Blanchard, D. Hutson, E. Wills, *The One Minute Entrepreneur* (New York, NY: Currency, 2008).

72. http://www.irs.gov/Retirement-Plans/Plan-Participant-Employee/Retirement-Topics-IRA-Contribution-Limits (retrieved July 23, 2014).

73. http://www.dol.gov/ebsa/publications/sepplans.html (retrieved July 23, 2014).

74. http://www.bls.gov/ncs/ebs/benefits/2013/ownership/private/table12a.htm (retrieved July 24, 2014).

75. http://www.irs.gov/Government-Entities/Federal-State-&-Local-Governments/Group-Term-Life-Insurance (retrieved July 24, 2014).

76. N. Griswold, "The Death of Worksite Voluntary Benefits," *Employee Benefit Advisor* (2011), 9(2), pp. 26–28.

77. http://pueblo.gsa.gov/cic_text/employ/lt-disability/insurance.htm (retrieved July 24, 2014).

78. Ibid.

79. B. Shutan, "In View of Voluntary Value," *Employee Benefit Advisor* (2009), 7(12), pp. 26–29.

80. http://www.metlife.com/about/press-room/us-press-releases/2010/index.html?SCOPE=Metlife&MSHiC=65001&L=10&W=cancer%20insurance%20&Pre=%3CFONT%20STYLE%3D%22background%3A%23ffff00%22%3E&Post=%3C/FONT%3E&compID=24584 (retrieved July 23, 2014).

81. N. Griswold, "The Death of Worksite Voluntary Benefits," *Employee Benefit Advisor* (2011), 9(2), pp. 26–28.

82. B. Shutan, "In View of Voluntary Value," *Employee Benefit Advisor* (2009), 7(12), pp. 26–29.

83. Society for Human Resources Management, "2013 Employee Benefits" (Alexandria, VA: SHRM, 2013), p. 25, http://www.shrm.org/research/surveyfindings/articles/documents/13-0245%202013_empbenefits_fnl.pdf.

84. G. Moran, "The Business of Better Benefits," *Entrepreneur* (May 2011), pp. 81–82.

85. Ibid.

86. Bank of America Merrill Lynch, "Workplace Benefits Report," Bank of America (December 2013), p. A9.

87. http://www.shrm.org/hrdisciplines/benefits/articles/pages/domestic-partner-benefits.aspx (retrieved July 24, 2014).

88. http://www.shrm.org/hrdisciplines/benefits/articles/pages/transform-health-care.aspx (retrieved July 26, 2014).

89. Ibid.

90. http://www.shrm.org/hrdisciplines/benefits/articles/pages/hsas-hras-consumer-engagement.aspx (retrieved July 26, 2014).

91. http://www.bls.gov/ncs/ebs/benefits/2011/ownership/private/table02a.htm (retrieved September 30, 2011).

92. J. Broadbent, M. Palumbo, E. Woodman, *The Shift From Defined Benefit to Defined Contribution Pension Plans–Implications for Asset Allocation and Risk Management,* Federal Reserve Board working paper (December 2006), Washington, DC.

93. http://www.canadianbusiness.com/article/47197--royal-bank-joins-wave-by-

abandoning-defined-benefit-pensions-for-new-hires (retrieved September 30, 2011).

94. E. Smith, *Retirement Heist: How Companies Plunder and Profit From the Nest Eggs of American Workers* (New York: Penguin Group, 2011).

95. http://knowledgetoday.wharton.upenn.edu/2011/09/retirement-heist-pensions-past-and-present/ (retrieved September 30, 2011).

96. R. Leung, "Working the "Good Life," CBSNews. Retrieved from http://www.cbsnews.com/news/working-the-good-life/ (April 18, 2013).

97. M. Crowley," How SAS Became the World's Best Place to Work," *Fast Company & Inc.* Retrieved from http://www.fastcompany.com/3004953/how-sas-became-worlds-best-place-work/ (January 22, 2013).

98. M. Weitzner. "The Royal Treatment," *60 Minutes.* Retrieved from YouTube at https://www.youtube.com/watch?v=N-eblGpZIWI.

99. Ibid.

100. R. Leung, "Working the Good Life," CBSNews. Retrieved from http://www.cbsnews.com/news/working-the-good-life/.

101. Ibid.

102. Weitzner, M. "The Royal Treatment," *60 Minutes*," Retrieved from YouTube at https://www.youtube.com/watch?v=N-eblGpZIWI (September 15, 2007).

CHAPTER 14

1. K. Jiang, D.P. Lepak, J. Hu, J.C. Baer, "How Does Human Resource Management Influence Organizational Outcomes? A Meta-Analytic Investigation of Mediating Mechanisms," *Academy of Management Journal* (2012), 55(6), pp. 1264–1294.

2. R. Maurer, "Corporations Urged to Push Suppliers on Worker Safety," *HR Magazine* (February 2013), p. 15.

3. http://www.osha.gov (retrieved July 10, 2013).

4. S. Greenhouse, "BP to Pay Record Fine for Refinery," *The New York Times* (August 12, 2010), p. B1.

5. http://www.shrm.org/hrdisciplines/safetysecurity/articles/pages/contractor-murder-building-collapse.aspx (retrieved July 24, 2014).

6. http://www.shrm.org/hrdisciplines/safetysecurity/articles/pages/owner-prison-death-employee.aspx (retrieved July 26, 2014).

7. http://www.osha.gov/pls/oshaweb/owadisp.show_document?p_id=2743&p_table=OSHACT (retrieved July 20, 2011).

8. http://www.osha.gov/doc/outreachtraining/htmlfiles/introsha.html (retrieved July 20, 2011).

9. http://www.bls.gov/iif/oshwc/cfoi/cfoi_revised12.pdf (retrieved July 26, 2014).

10. http://www.bls.gov/news.release/osh.nr0.htm (retrieved July 26, 2014).

11. http://www.osha.gov/about.html (retrieved July 26, 2014).

12. http://www.osha.gov/Publications/3439at-a-glance.pdf (retrieved July 26, 2014).

13. http://www.shrm.org/legalissues/federalresources/pages/osha-inspectors.aspx (retrieved July 26, 2014).

14. http://www.shrm.org/legalissues/federalresources/pages/osha-inspectors.aspx (retrieved July 27, 2014).

15. https://www.osha.gov/Publications/3439at-a-glance.pdf (retrieved July 27, 2014).

16. https://www.osha.gov/FedReg_osha_pdf/FED20120326.pdf (retrieved July 27, 2014).

17. https://www.osha.gov/dsg/hazcom/hazcom-appendix-d.html (retrieved July 27, 2014).

18. http://www.osha.gov/Publications/osha3000.pdf (retrieved July 27, 2014).

19. http://cdc.gov/niosh/about.html (retrieved July 27, 2014).

20. http://www.cdc.gov/niosh/docs/strategic/ (retrieved July 27, 2014).

21. http://www.shrm.org/LegalIssues/StateandLocalResources/StateandLocalStatutesandRegulations/Documents/stateposting.pdf (retrieved July 27, 2014).

22. K. Stawarz, A.L. Cox, J. Bird, R. Benedyk, "I'd Sit at Home and Do Work Emails: How Tablets Affect the Work-Life Balance of Office Workers," In *CHI '13 Extended Abstracts on Human Factors in Computing Systems* (Paris, France: CHI, 2013), pp. 1383–1388.

23. B. Singh, T.T. Selvarajan, "Is It Spillover or Compensation? Effects of Community and Organizational Diversity Climates on Race Differentiated Employee Intent to Stay," *Journal of Business Ethics*, 115(2), pp. 259–269.

24. S.C. Paustian-Underdahl, J.R. Halbesleben, D.S. Carlson, K.M. Kacmar, "The Work-Family Interface and Promotability: Boundary Integration as a Double-Edged Sword," *Journal of Management* (2013), published online.

25. M. Conlin, "Work-Life Balance," *Businessweek* (December 7, 2009), p. 57.

26. "The Increasing Call for Work-Life Balance," *Businessweek* (March 27, 2009), http://www.businessweek.com/managing/content/mar2009/ca20090327_734197.htm.

27. V.C. Hahn, C. Dormann, "The Role of Partners and Children for Employees' Psychological Detachment From Work and Well-Being," *Journal of Applied Psychology* (2013), 98(1), p. 26.

28. L.M. Fiksenbaum, "Supportive Work-Family Environments: Implications for Work-Family Conflict and Well-Being," *The International Journal of Human Resource Management* (2014), 25(5), pp. 653–672.

29. D.A. Sharar, J. Pompe, R. Lennox, "Evaluating the Workplace Effects of EAP Counseling," *Journal of Health & Productivity* (2012), 6(12), pp. 5–14.

30. http://www.bls.gov/ncs/ebs/benefits/2010/ebbl0046.pdf (retrieved July 27, 2014).

31. G. Hargrave et al., EAP Treatment Impact on Presenteeism and Absenteeism: Implications for Return on Investment," *Journal of Workplace Behavioral Health* (2008), 23(3), pp. 283–293.

32. M. Attridge, P. Herlihy, P. Sharar, T. Amaral, T. McPherson, et al., "EAP Effectiveness and ROI," *EASNA Research Notes* (2009), 1(3).

33. M.E. Porter, M.R. Kramer, "Creating Shared Value," *Harvard Business Review*, 89(1/2), pp. 62–77.

34. L. Berry, A. Mirabito, W. Baun, "What's the Hard Return on Employee Wellness Programs?" *Harvard Business Review* (2010), 88(12), pp. 104–112.

35. Ibid.

36. http://www.cdc.gov/workplacehealthpromotion/evaluation/topics/disorders.html (retrieved July 27, 2014).

37. Ibid.

38. http://www.osha.gov/ergonomics/FAQs-external.html (retrieved July 29, 2014).

39. https://www.osha.gov/SLTC/ergonomics/index.html (retrieved July 29, 2014).

40. Ibid.

41. http://ehs.okstate.edu/kopykit/Office%20Ergonomics1.PDF (retrieved July 29, 2014).

42. http://ergo.human.cornell.edu (retrieved July 27, 2014).

43. http://www.forbes.com/sites/kathryndill/2014/04/18/survey-42-of-employees-have-changed-jobs-due-to-stress/ (retrieved July 27, 2014).

44. M.L. Marzec, A.F. Scibelli, D.W. Edington, "Examining Individual Factors According to Health Risk Appraisal Data as Determinants of Absenteeism Among US Utility Employees," *Journal of Occupational and Environmental Medicine* (2013), 55(7), pp. 732–740.

45. B.C. Deb, S.K. Biswas, "Stress Management: A Critical View," *European Journal of Business and Management* (2011), 3(4), pp. 205–212.

46. M.F. Marin, C. Lord, J. Andrews, R.P. Juster, S. Sindi, G. Arsenault-Lapierre, . . . S.J. Lupien, "Chronic Stress, Cognitive Functioning and Mental Health," *Neurobiology of Learning and Memory* (2011), 96(4), pp. 583–595.

47. C.R. Wanberg, J. Zhu, R. Kanfer, Z. Zhang, "After the Pink Slip: Applying Dynamic Motivation Frameworks to the Job Search Experience," *Academy of Management Journal* (2012), 55(2), pp. 261–284.

48. S. Shellenbarger, "Are You Hard-Wired to Boil Over From Stress?" *The Wall Street Journal* (February 13, 2013), p. D3.

49. C.R. Wanberg, J. Zhu, R. Kanfer, Z. Zhang, "After the Pink Slip: Applying Dynamic Motivation Frameworks to the Job Search Experience," *Academy of Management Journal* (2012), 55(2), pp. 261–284.

50. http://www.corporatewell nessmagazine.com/issue-24/worksite-wellness-issue-24/workplace-stress-strains-organizations-bottom-lines/ (retrieved July 27, 2014).

51. A.E. Nixon, J.J. Mazzola, J. Bauer, J.R. Krueger, P.E. Spector, "Can Work Make You Sick? A Meta-Analysis of the Relationships Between Job Stressors and Physical Symptoms," *Work & Stress* (2011), 25(1), pp. 1–22.

52. "Preserve Your Health Like Your Wealth," *Wall Street Journal* (April 15, 2009), pp. D5–D6.

53. L.S. Luscher, M.W. Lewis, "Organizational Change and Managerial Sensenmaking: Working Through Paradox," *Academy of Management Journal* (2008), 51(2), pp. 221–240.

54. M. Jokisaari, J.E. Nurmi, "Change in Newcomers' Supervisor Support and Socialization Outcomes After Organizational Entry," *Academy of Management Journal* (2009), 52(3), pp. 527–544.

55. J. Schramm, "Manage Stress, Improve the Bottom Line," *HR Magazine* (February 2013), p. 80.

56. E. Monsen, R.W. Boss, "The Impact of Strategic Entrepreneurship Inside the Organization: Examining Job Stress and Employee Retention," *Entrepreneurship Theory and Practice* (2009), 33(1), pp. 71–104.

57. K.E. Spaeder, "Time to De-stress," *Entrepreneur* (October 2008), p. 24.

58. L. Holloway, "Stress Case," *Entrepreneur* (August 2008), p. 35.

59. S.D. Sidle, "Workplace Stress Management Interventions: What Works Best?" *Academy of Management Perspective* (2008), 22(3), pp. 111–112.

60. "Preserve Your Health Like Your Wealth," *The Wall Street Journal* (April 15, 2009), pp. D5–D6.

61. Ibid.

62. Ibid.

63. S.D. Sidle, "Workplace Stress Management Interventions: What Works Best?" *Academy of Management Perspective* (2008), 22(3), pp. 111–112.

64. "Preserve Your Health Like Your Wealth," *The Wall Street Journal* (April 15, 2009), pp. D5–D6.

65. C.M Barnes, J.R. Hollenbeck, "Sleep Deprivation and Decision-Making Teams: Burning the Midnight Oil or Playing With Fire?" *Academy of Management Review* (2009), 34(1), pp. 56–66.

66. "Preserve Your Health Like Your Wealth," *The Wall Street Journal* (April 15, 2009), pp. D5–D6.

67. "When Sleep Leaves You Tired," *The Wall Street Journal* (June 9, 2009), p. D5.

68. Staff, "Over 34% of Americans," *The Wall Street Journal* (January 10–11, 2009), p. A1.

69. R. Tomsho, "Bulging Waist Carries Risk," *The Wall Street Journal* (November 13, 2008), p. D4.

70. C. Arnst, "Taxing the Rich—Food, That Is," *Businessweek* (February 23, 2009), p. 62.

71. "Preserve Your Health Like Your Wealth," *The Wall Street Journal* (April 15, 2009), pp. D5–D6.

72. S.D. Sidle, "Workplace Stress Management Interventions: What Works Best?" *Academy of Management Perspective* (2008), 22(3), pp. 111–112.

73. J. Welch, S. Welch, "Finding Your Inner Courage," *Businessweek* (February 23, 2009), p. 84.

74. "Preserve Your Health Like Your Wealth," *The Wall Street Journal* (April 15, 2009), pp. D5–D6.

75. S. Covy, "Time Management," *Fortune* (September 19, 2009), pp. 28–29.

76. S. Shellenbarger, "When Stress Is Good for You," *The Wall Street Journal* (January 24, 2012), pp. D1, D5.

77. "Top Security Threats and Management Issues Facing Corporate America: 2012 Survey of Fortune 1000 Companies," *Securitas Security Services USA* (2013), p. 6

78. http://www.cnn.com/2014/05/19/justice/china-hacking-charges/ (retrieved July 27, 2014).

79. http://www.shrm.org/hrdisciplines/safetysecurity/articles/pages/encrypt-company-laptops.aspx, (retrieved July 27, 2014).

80. R. Lussier, "Dealing With Anger and Preventing Workplace Violence," *Clinical Leadership & Management Review* (2004), 18(2), pp. 117–119.

81. R. Lussier, "Maintaining Civility in the Laboratory," *Clinical Leadership & Management Review* (2005), 19(62), pp. E 4–7.

82. D. Geddes, R.R. Callister, "Crossing the Lines: A Dual Threshold Model of Anger in Organizations," *Academy of Management Review* (2007), 32(3), pp. 721–746.

83. R. Lussier, "Dealing With Anger and Preventing Workplace Violence," *Clinical Leadership & Management Review* (2004), 18(2), pp. 117–119.

84. R. Lussier, "Maintaining Civility in the Laboratory," *Clinical Leadership & Management Review* (2005), 19(62), pp. E 4–7.

85. "How to Manage Anger," *TopHealth* (May 2007), p. 2.

86. R. Lussier, "Dealing With Anger and Preventing Workplace Violence," *Clinical Leadership & Management Review* (2004), 18(2), pp. 117–119.

87. Ibid.

88. Ibid.

89. http://www.dol.gov/elaws/asp/drugfree/drugs/screen92.asp.

90. http://www.shrm.org/hrdisciplines/safetysecurity/articles/pages/drugs-workplace-crisis.aspx (retrieved July 27, 2014).

91. http://www.shrm.org/templatestools/toolkits/pages/introsafetyandsecurity.aspx (retrieved July 27, 2014).

92. http://www.ojp.usdoj.gov/newsroom/pdfs/ojp_resource_guide_08.pdf (retrieved July 27, 2014).

93. http://www.cdc.gov/nchs/fastats/obesity-overweight.htm (retrieved July 28, 2014).

94. http://blogs.hbr.org/2013/01/sitting-is-the-smoking-of-our-generation/ (retrieved July 28, 2014).

95. N. Owen, G.N. Healy, C.E. Matthews, D.W. Dunstan, "Too Much Sitting: The Population-Health Science of Sedentary Behavior," *Exercise and Sport Sciences Reviews* (2010), 38(3), p. 105.

96. http://www.webmd.com/balance/news/20140106/workplace-wellness-programs-work/ (retrieved July 28, 2014).

97. J.P. Caloyeras, H. Liu, E. Exum, M. Broderick, S. Mattke, "Managing Manifest Diseases, but Not Health Risks, Saved PepsiCo Money Over Seven Years," *Health Affairs*, 33(1), pp. 124–131.

98. http://www.businessweek.com/articles/2013-05-06/employers-love-wellness-programs-dot-but-do-they-work (retrieved July 28, 2014).

99. S. Eder, K. Zernike, "Rutgers Leaders Are Faulted on Abusive Coach," *The New York Times* (April 4, 2013), p. A1.

100. http://www.si.com/nfl/audibles/2013/11/04/richie-incognito-done-miami-dolphins (retrieved July 29, 2014).

101. http://www.shrm.org/hrdisciplines/global/articles/pages/workplace-bullying-protections-differ-globally.aspx (retrieved July 29, 2014).

102. http://www.stopbullying.gov/laws/federal/index.html (retrieved July 29, 2014).

103. http://www.edocamerica.com/about/ (retrieved August 5, 2011).

104. S. Banjo, "Inside Nike's Struggle to Balance Cost and Worker Safety in Bangladesh," *The Wall Street Journal* (April 21, 2014). Retrieved from http://online.wsj.com/news/articles/SB10001424052702303873604579493502231397942/.

105. Hoover's Inc., *Nike, Inc.* [Hoover's company records: In-depth records] (June 23, 2014). Retrieved June 24, 2014, from Long Island University Academic Database.

106. S. Banjo, "Inside Nike's Struggle to Balance Cost and Worker Safety in Bangladesh," *The Wall Street Journal* (April 21, 2014). Retrieved from http://online.wsj.com/news/articles/SB10001424052702303873604579493502231397942/.

107. Ibid.

108. S. Cendrowski, "Can Outsourcing Be Improved?" *Fortune, 167*(8). Retrieved from http://scottcendrowski.com/can-outsourcing-be-improved/ (June 10, 2013).

109. S. Greenhouse, "Major Retailers Join Bangladesh Safety Plan," *The New York Times* (May 13, 2013). Retrieved from http://www.nytimes.com/2013/05/14/business/global/hm-agrees-to-bangladesh-safety-plan.html?_r=0.

110. S. Banjo, Nike CEO on Bangladesh: 'Is it a Perfect Situation? No.' [Interview with Mike Parker]. *The Wall Street Journal.* (April 22, 2014). Retrieved from http://blogs.wsj.com/corporate-intelligence/2014/04/22/nike-ceo-on-bangladesh-is-it-a-perfect-situation-no/.

111. S. Banjo," Inside Nike's Struggle to Balance Cost and Worker Safety in Bangladesh," *The Wall Street Journal* (April 21, 2014). Retrieved from http://online.wsj.com/news/articles/SB10001424052702303873604579493502231397942/.

CHAPTER 15

1. R.L. Hughes, R.C. Ginnett, G.J. Curphy, *Leadership: Enhancing the Lessons of Experience*, 7th ed. (Burr Ridge, IL: McGraw-Hill, 2011).

2. R. Murphree, "Visionary Leader: Gospel Is Key to Unlimited Success," *AFA Journal* (March 2013), p. 11.

3. C. Bonanos, "The Lies We Tell at Work," *Businessweek* (February 4–10, 2013), pp. 71–73.

4. P. Zak, *The Moral Molecule* (New York, NY: Penguin, 2012).

5. C. Downs, "Liar, Liar–Back's on Fire," *AARP Magazine* (October/November 2012), p. 22.

6. K. Leavitt, S.J. Reynolds, C.M. Barnes, P. Schilpzan, S.T. Hannah, "Different Hats, Different Obligations: Plural Occupational Identities and Situated Moral Judgments," *Academy of Management Journal* (2012), 55(6), pp. 1316–1333.

7. B.C. Gunia, L. Wang, L. Huang, J. Wang, J.K. Murnighan, "Contemplation and Conversation: Subtle Influences on Moral Decision Making," *Academy of Management Journal* (2012), 55(1), pp. 13–33.

8. D. Lange, N.T. Washburn, "Understanding Attributions of Corporate Social Irresponsibility," *Academy of Management Journal* (2012), 37(2), pp. 300–326.

9. N.M. Pless, T. Maak, D.A. Waldman, "Different Approaches Towards Doing the Right Thing: Mapping the Responsibility Orientations of Leaders," *Academy of Management Perspectives* (2012), 26(4), pp. 51–65.

10. A. Rasche, K.U. Gilbert, I. Schedel, "Cross-Disciplinary Ethics Education in MBA Programs: Rhetoric or Reality?" *Academy of Management Learning & Education* (2013), 12(1), pp. 71–85.

11. B.C. Gunia, L. Wang, L. Huang, J. Wang, J.K. Murnighan, "Contemplation and Conversation: Subtle Influences on Moral Decision Making," *Academy of Management Journal* (2012), 55(1), pp. 13–33.

12. C. Besio, A. Pronzini, "Morality, Ethics, and Values Outside and Inside Organizations: An Example of the Discourse on Climate Change," *Journal of Business Ethics* (2014), 119(3), pp. 287–300.

13. S. Robbins, M. Coulter, *Management* (Upper Saddle River, NJ: Pearson, 2014), p. 136.

14. R. Chandra, *Business Ethics* (Self-published, 2013).

15. C.A. Rusnak, "Are You Confusing People With Your Leadership Style?" *Costco Connection* (March 2012), p. 11.

16. J. Geisler, "Forgive? Forget? Not Likely," *Costco Connection* (December 2012), p. 10.

17. C. Bonanos, "The Lies We Tell at Work," *Businessweek* (February 4–10, 2013), pp. 71–73.

18. D. Ariely, "Why We Lie," *The Wall Street Journal* (May 26–27, 2012), pp. C1–C2.

19. M.K. Duffy, K.L. Scott, J.D. Shaw, B.J. Tepper, K. Aquino, "A Social Context Model of Envy and Social Undermining," *Academy of Management Journal* (2012), 55(3), pp. 643–666.

20. D.M. Mayer, K. Aquino, R.L. Greenbaum, M. Kuenzi, "Who Displays Ethical Leadership, and Why Does It Matter? An Examination of Antecedents and Consequences of Ethical Leadership," *Academy of Management Journal* (2011), 55(1), pp. 151–171.

21. B.C. Gunia, L. Wang, L. Huang, J. Wang, J.K. Murnighan, "Contemplation and Conversation: Subtle Influences on Moral Decision Making," *Academy of Management Journal* (2012), 55(1), pp. 13–33.

22. Ibid.

23. C. Bonanos, "The Lies We Tell at Work," *Businessweek* (February 4–10, 2013), pp. 71–73.

24. D. Ariely, "Why We Lie," *The Wall Street Journal* (May 26–27, 2012), pp. C1–C2.

25. Ibid.

26. Ibid.

27. S.D. Levitt, S.J. Dubner, "SuperFreakonomics: Global Cooling, Patriotic Prostitutes, and Why Suicide Bombers Should Buy Life Insurance," *Academy of Management Perspectives* (2011), 25(2), pp. 86–87.

28. D. Ariely, "Why We Lie," *The Wall Street Journal* (May 26–27, 2012), pp. C1–C2.

29. K. Leavitt, S.J. Reynolds, C.M. Barnes, P. Schilpzan, S.T. Hannah, "Different Hats, Different Obligations: Plural Occupational Identities and Situated Moral Judgments," *Academy of Management Journal* (2012), 55(6), pp. 1316–1333.

30. D. Ariely, "Why We Lie," *The Wall Street Journal* (May 26–27, 2012), pp. C1–C2.

31. P. Zak, *The Moral Molecule* (New York, NY: Penguin, 2012).

32. Ibid.

33. https://www.rotary.org/myrotary/en/learning-reference/about-rotary/history-rotary-international/ (retrieved August 5, 2014).

34. http://www.berkshirehathaway.com/govern/corpgov.pdf (retrieved August 5, 2014).

35. B.C. Gunia, L. Wang, L. Huang, J. Wang, J.K. Murnighan, "Contemplation and Conversation: Subtle Influences on Moral Decision Making," *Academy of Management Journal* (2012), 55(1), pp. 13–33.

36. D. Ariely, "Why We Lie," *The Wall Street Journal* (May 26–27, 2012), pp. C1–C2.

37. P. Zak, *The Moral Molecule* (New York, NY: Penguin, 2012).

38. http://smallbusiness.chron.com/key-components-code-ethics-business-244.html (retrieved August 1, 2014).

39. D. Meinert, "Creating an Ethical Culture," *HR Magazine* (April 2014), pp. 22–27.

40. J.R. Detert, M.C. Edmondson, "Implicit Voice Theories: Taken-for-Granted Rules of Self-Censorship at Work," *Academy of Management Journal* (2011), 54(3), pp. 461–488.

41. D. Ariely, "Why We Lie," *The Wall Street Journal* (May 26–27, 2012), pp. C1–C2.

42. C. Bonanos, "The Lies We Tell at Work," *Businessweek* (February 4–10, 2013), pp. 71–73.

43. P. Drucker, *Management* (New York, NY: Routledge, 2012).

44. http://dealbook.nytimes.com/2013/04/22/ralph-lauren-pays-1-6-million-to-resolve-bribery-case/ (retrieved August 2, 2014).

45. http://blog.thomsonreuters.com/index.php/judge-dismisses-class-discrimination-claims-against-wal-mart/ (retrieved August 5, 2014).

46. D. Lange, N.T. Washburn, "Understanding Attributions of Corporate Social Irresponsibility," *Academy of Management Journal* (2012), 37(2), pp. 300–326.

47. http://www.reuters.com/article/2014/06/30/us-gm-recall-idUSKBN0F52MS20140630/ (retrieved August 5, 2014).

48. http://www.reuters.com/article/2013/06/10/us-bofa-mbs-idUSBRE95916M20130610/ (retrieved August 2, 2014).

49. http://www.forbes.com/sites/nathanielparishflannery/2011/09/03/monsantos-pesticide-problems-raise-awareness-for-corporate-environmental-responsibility/ (retrieved August 2, 2014).

50. http://online.wsj.com/articles/furor-erupts-over-facebook-experiment-on-users-1404085840/ (retrieved August 5, 2014).

51. D. Lange, N.T. Washburn, "Understanding Attributions of Corporate Social Irresponsibility," *Academy of Management Journal* (2012), 37(2), pp. 300–326.

52. http://www.bloomberg.com/news/2014-03-26/wal-mart-says-bribery-probe-cost-439-million-in-past-two-years.html (retrieved August 5, 2014).

53. http://abcnews.go.com/US/lululemon-founder-chip-wilson-blames-womens-bodies-yoga/story?id=20815278 (retrieved August 5, 2014).

54. A.B. Carroll, K.M. Shabana, "The Business Case for Corporate Social Responsibility: A Review of Concepts, Research and Practice," *International Journal of Management Reviews* (2010), 12(1), pp. 85–105.

55. A.M. Grant, "Giving Time, Time After Time: Work Design and Sustained Employee Participation in Corporate Volunteering," *Academy of Management Review* (2012), 37(4), pp. 589–615.

56. A. Edmans, "The Link Between Job Satisfaction and Firm Value, With Implications for Corporate Social Responsibility," *Academy of Management Perspectives* (2012), 26(4), pp. 1–19.

57. "Master Class," *Businessweek* (May 6–12, 2013), p. 83.

58. D. Lange, N.T. Washburn, "Understanding Attributions of Corporate Social Irresponsibility," *Academy of Management Journal* (2012), 37(2), pp. 300–326.

59. R. Cohen, "Five Lessons From the Banana Man, *The Wall Street Journal* (June 2–3, 2012), p. C2.

60. http://money.cnn.com/2014/05/15/news/economy/fast-food-strike/ (retrieved August 5, 2014).

61. T. Donaldson, T.W. Dunfee, *Ties That Bind: A Social Contracts Approach to Business Ethics* (Boston, MA: Harvard Business School Press, 1999).

62. T.J. Donaldson, *Rights in the Global Market: The Ruffin Series in Business Ethics* (Oxford, UK: Oxford University Press, 1991), pp. 139–162.

63. E.L. Worsham, "Reflections and Insights on Teaching Social Entrepreneurship: An Interview With Greg Dees," *Academy of Management Learning & Education* (2012), 11(3), pp. 442–452.

64. B. Mycoskie, *Start Something That Matters* (New York, NY: Spiegel & Grau, 2012) p. 193.

65. http://www.usatoday.com/story/money/personalfinance/2013/01/13/older-workers-stay-working/1780291/ (retrieved August 2, 2014).

66. http://dealbook.nytimes.com/2013/04/02/why-so-few-women-reach-the-executive-rank/?_php=true&_type=blogs&_r=0 (retrieved August 5, 2014).

67. http://www.nolo.com/legal-encyclopedia/sexual-orientation-discrimination-rights-29541.html (retrieved August 2, 2014).

68. http://www.whitehouse.gov/the-press-office/2014/07/21/executive-order-further-amendments-executive-order-11478-equal-employment/ (retrieved August 3, 2014).

69. http://www.huffingtonpost.com/sally-steenland/americans-see-opportunity_b_4177762.html (retrieved August 2, 2014).

70. C. Dougherty, "New Faces of Childhood," *The Wall Street Journal* (April 6, 2011), p. A3.

71. M. Jordan, "Illegals Estimated to Account for 1 in 12 U.S. Births," *The Wall Street Journal* (August 12, 2010), pp. A1–A2.

72. "More White Americans Died," *The Wall Street Journal* (June 13, 2013), pp. A1, A8.

73. C. Dougherty, "U.S. Nears Racial Milestone," *The Wall Street Journal* (June 11, 2010), p. A3.

74. S. Reddy, "Latinos Fuel Growth in Decade," *The Wall Street Journal* (March 25, 2011), p. A2.

75. U.S. Census Bureau, reported in *The Wall Street Journal* (December 13, 2012), p. A3.

76. "Corporate Social Responsibility: Good Citizenship or Investor Rip-off?" *The Wall Street Journal* (January 9, 2006), p. R6.

77. D. Wakabayashi, "Tim Cook's Vision for His Apple Emerges," *The Wall Street Journal* (July 8, 2014), pp. B1, B5.

78. Bill & Melinda Gates Foundation, http://www.gatesfoundation.org (retrieved April 2, 2012).

79. P. Schreck, "Reviewing the Business Case for Corporate Social Responsibility: New Evidence and Analysis," *Journal of Business Ethics* (2011), 103(2), pp. 167–188.

80. J. Welch, S. Welch, "Giving in an Unforgiving Time," *Businessweek* (June 1, 2009), p. 80.

81. J. Morelli, "Environmental Sustainability: A Definition for Environmental Professionals," *Journal of Environmental Sustainability* (2013), 1(1), p. 2.

82. A. Nadim, R.N. Lussier, "Sustainability as a Small Business Competitive Strategy," *Journal of Small Strategy* (2012), 21(2), pp. 79–95.

83. S.B. Banerjee, "Embedding Sustainability Across the Organization: A Critical Perspective," *Academy of Management Learning & Education* (2011), 10(4), pp. 719–731.

84. H. Paulson, "Fortune Global Forum," *Fortune* (April 29, 2013), p. 20.

85. A. A. Marcus, A. R. Fremeth, "Green Management Matters Regardless," *Academy of Management Perspectives* (2009), 23(3), pp. 17–26.

86. K.K. Dhanda, P.J. Murphy, "The New Wild West Is Green: Carbon Offset Markets, Transactions, and Providers," *Academy of Management Perspectives* (2011), 25(4), pp. 37–49.

87. A. Nadim, R. N. Lussier, "Sustainability as a Small Business Competitive Strategy," *Journal of Small Strategy* (2012), 21(2), pp. 79–95.

88. N.M. Scarborough, *Essentials of Entrepreneurship and Small Business* (Upper Saddle River, NJ: Prentice Hall, 2011).

89. http://en.wikipedia.org/wiki/Chief_sustainability_officer/ (retrieved May 22, 2013).

90. "Who's the Greenest of Them All?" *Businessweek* (November 28–December 2, 2011), p. 59.

91. http://www.forbes.com/sites/jacquelynsmith/2014/01/22/the-worlds-most-sustainable-companies-of-2014/ (retrieved August 3, 2014).

92. B. Dumaine, "Google's Zero-Carbon Quest," *Fortune* (July 23, 2012), pp. 75–78.

93. http://www.walmart.com (retrieved May 22, 2013).

94. Briefs: Wal-Mart, *Businessweek* (February 13–19, 2012), p. 28.

95. K. Weise, "Sustainability: I'm With Wal-Mart," *Businessweek* (November 28–December 2, 2011), p. 60.

96. http://www.theguardian.com/sustainable-business/blog/best-practices-sustainability-us-corporations-ceres (retrieved August 3, 2014).

97. M. Porter, M. Kramer, "Strategy & Society: The Link Between Competitive Advantage and Corporate Social

Responsibility," *Harvard Business Review* (December 2006), 84(12), pp. 78–92.

98. O. Branzei, A. Nadkarni, "The Tata Way: Evolving and Executing Sustainable Business Strategies," *Ivey Business Journal* (March/April 2008), 72(2), pp. 1–8.

99. H. Haugh, A. Talwar, "How Do Corporations Embed Sustainability Across the Organization?" *Academy of Management Learning & Education* (2010), 9(3), pp. 384–396.

100. MIT Sloan Management Review, *Findings From the 2013 Sustainability & Innovation Global Executive Study and Research Project* (Boston, MA: MIT Sloan Management Review/Boston Consulting Group, 2013), p. 15.

101. http://www.environmentalleader .com/2014/04/23/spotlight-on-the-hows-and-whys-of-sustainable-products/ (retrieved August 5, 2014).

102. https://www.linkedin.com/ today/post/article/20140220123325-60894986-how-should-a-business-leader-understand-sustainability (retrieved August 5, 2014).

103. http://www.patagonia.com/us/ footprint/ (retrieved August 5, 2014).

104. http://www.chipotle.com/en-us/ fwi/fwi_facts/fwi_facts.aspx (retrieved August 4, 2014).

105. www3.weforum.org/.../WEF_ GAC_GovernanceSustainability_ GreenLight_January_Report_2014.pdf (retrieved August 4, 2014).

106. http://www.iso.org/iso/home/ standards/management-standards/ iso14000.htm (retrieved August 5, 2014).

107. http://www.unglobalcompact .org/AboutTheGC/TheTenPrinciples/index .html (retrieved August 5, 2014).

108. http://www.weforum.org (retrieved August 5, 2014).

109. http://www.csrwire.com/pages/ about_us (retrieved August 5, 2014).

110. N. Landrum, S. Edwards, *Sustainable Business: An Executive's Primer* (New York, NY: Business Expert Press, 2009), p. 32.

111. http://arkansasenergy.org/ industry/incentives-and-programs/ home-energy-assistance-loan-%28heal%29-program.aspx (retrieved July 28, 2011).

112. N. Landrum, S. Edwards, *Sustainable Business: An Executive's Primer* (New York, NY: Business Expert Press, 2009), p. 32.

113. A. Brief (Ed.), *Diversity at Work* (Cambridge, UK: Cambridge University Press, 2008), pp. 265–267.

114. R. Anand, M. Winters, "A Retrospective View of Corporate Diversity Training From 1964 to the Present,"

Academy of Management Learning & Education (2008), 7(3), pp. 356–372.

115. Ibid.

116. C. Holladay, M. Quinones, "The Influence of Training Focus and Trainer Characteristics on Diversity Training Eeffectiveness," *Academy of Management Learning & Education* (2008), 7(3), pp. 343–354.

117. Ibid.

118. H. Blodget, "In Case You Don't Appreciate How Fast the 'Windows Monopoly' Is Getting Destroyed...," *Business Insider*. Retrieved August 13, 2014, from http://www.businessinsider.com/windows-monopoly-is-getting-destroyed-2013-7

119. T. Worstall, "Microsoft's Market Share Drops From 97% to 20% in Just Over a Decade *Forbes*. Retrieved August 13, 2014 from http://www.forbes.com/sites/ timworstall/2012/12/13/microsofts-market-share-drops-from-97-to-20-in-just-over-a-decade/.

120. J. Yarow, "Chart of the Day: The Collapse of Microsoft's Monopoly," *Business Insider*. Retrieved August 13, 2014, from http://www.businessinsider.com/chart-of-the-day-consumer-compute-shift-2012-12?nr_email_referer=1&utm_ source=Triggermail&utm_ medium=email&utm_term=SAI%20 Chart%20Of%20The%20Day&utm_ campaign=SAI_COTD_120712

121. H. Leonard, "There Will Soon Be One Smartphone for every five people in the World *Business Insider*. Retrieved August 13, 2014, from http://www.businessinsider. com/15-billion-smartphones-in-the-world-22013-2.

122. J. Callaham, "The Top 10 Microsoft News Stories of 2013," *Neowin*. Retrieved August 13, 2014, from http:// www.neowin.net/news/the-top-10-microsoft-news-stories-of-2013.

123. "Nokia," in *Wikipedia*. Retrieved August 14, 2014, from http://en.wikipedia. org/wiki/Nokia.

124. J. Rossi, "Microsoft Layoffs Hit Finland Staff Hard," *Wall Street Journal*. Retrieved August 14, 2014, from http:// online.wsj.com/articles/microsoft-layoffs-hit-nokias-finland- 1405624498.

125. Ibid.

CHAPTER 16

1. M. Li, W.H. Mobley, A. Kelly, "When Do Global Leaders Learn Best to Develop Cultural Intelligence? An Investigation of the Moderating Role of Experiential Learning Styles," *Academy of Management Education & Learning* (2013), 12(1), pp. 32–50.

2. S.T. Hannah, B.J. Avolio, D.R. May, "Moral Maturation and Moral Conations: A Capacity Approach to Explaining Moral Thought and Action," *Academy of Management Review* (2011), 36(4), pp. 663–685.

3. http://www.fedex.com (retrieved May 16, 2013).

4. M. Li, W.H. Mobley, A. Kelly, "When Do Global Leaders Learn Best to Develop Cultural Intelligence? An Investigation of the Moderating Role of Experiential Learning Styles," *Academy of Management Education & Learning* (2013), 12(1), pp. 32–50.

5. J.H. Marler, "Strategic Human Resource Management in Context," *Academy of Management Perspectives* (2012), 26(2), pp. 6–11.

6. P. Ekins, S. Dresner, K. Dahlström, "The Four-Capital Method of Sustainable Development Evaluation," *European Environment* (2008), 18(2), pp. 63–80.

7. http://www.census.gov/popclock (retrieved August 25, 2014).

8. http://future.state.gov/when/ timeline/1921_timeline/smoot_tariff.html (retrieved August 24, 2014).

9. J.A. Finalyzson, M.W. Zacher, "The GATT and the Regulation of Trade Barrier: Regime Dynamics and Functions," *International Organization* (1981), 35(4), pp. 561–602.

10. http://www.wto.org/english/ thewto_e/whatis_e/wto_dg_stat_e.htm (retrieved August 12, 2014).

11. "Investing in America and American Jobs" [advertisement], *Fortune* (May 20, 2013), p. S1.

12. "Where Clothes Come From," *Fortune* (June 10, 2013), p. 17.

13. J.R. Hagerty, "'Made in America' Has Its Limits," *The Wall Street Journal* (November 23, 2012), p. B1.

14. http://www.imf.org/external/pubs/ ft/survey/so/2012/new083012a.htm (retrieved August 11, 2014).

15. N.J. Adler, S. Bartholomew, "Managing Globally Competent People," *The Executive* (1992), 6(3), pp. 52–65.

16. Ibid.

17. A. Molinsky, "The Psychological Processes of Cultural Retooling," *Academy of Management Journal* (2010).

18. M. Mendenhall, A. Arnardottir, G. Oddou, L. Burke, "Developing Cross-Cultural Competencies in Management Education Via Cognitive-Behavior Therapy," *Academy of Management Learning & Education* (2013).

19. http://digitalcommons.ilr.cornell .edu/cgi/viewcontent.cgi?article =1086&context=lawfirms/.

20. http://www.ecovis.com/focus-china/china-hr-21-asked-hr-questions-chinese-labor-law-part-22/ (retrieved August 13, 2014).

21. X. Liang, J. Marler, Z. Cui, "Strategic Human Resource Management in China: East Meets West," *The Academy of Management Perspectives* (2012).

22. http://www.globalemploymentlaw .com/2014/07/regions/north-america/ united-states/brazil-new-law-expands-the- maximum-term-for-engaging-temporary- workers/ (retrieved August 13, 2014).

23. http://thebrazilbusiness.com/ article/comparing-employment-law-in-usa- and-brazil/ (retrieved August 13, 2014).

24. D. Dowling, "Bringing Global Age Discrimination Provisions Into Compliance," http://www.shrm.org/hrdisciplines/global/ articles/pages/global-age-discrimination- compliance.aspx (retrieved August 13, 2014).

25. http://www.internationallaborlaw .com/2014/05/15/labor-and-employment- updates-from-around-the-world-germany/ (retrieved August 13, 2014).

26. http://www.eeoc.gov/facts/multi- employees.html (retrieved July 22, 2010).

27. Ibid.

28. J. Palazzolo, "Is It a Bribe . . . or Not?" *The Wall Street Journal* (July 22, 2013), p. R3.

29. http://geert-hofstede.com/national- culture.html (retrieved August 13, 2014).

30. http://geert-hofstede.com/ dimensions.html (retrieved August 13, 2014).

31. home.sandiego.edu/~dimon/ CulturalFrameworks.pdf

32. Adapted from M. Javidon, R.J. House, "Cultural Acumen for the Global Manager: Lessons From Project GLOBE," *Organizational Dynamics* (2001), 29(4), pp. 289–305.

33. T.J. Huang, S.C. Chi, J.J. Lawler, "The Relationship Between Expatriates' Personality Traits and Their Adjustment to International Assignments," *The International Journal of Human Resource Management* (2005), 16(9), pp. 1656–1670.

34. S. Mor, M. Morris, J. Joh, "Identifying and Training Adaptive Cross-Cultural Management Skills: The Crucial Role of Cultural Metacognition," *Academy of Management Learning & Education* (2013).

35. P.M. Caligiuri, "The Big Five Personality Characteristics as Predictors of Expatriate's Desire to Terminate the Assignment and Supervisor-Rated Performance," *Personnel Psychology* (2000), 53(1), pp. 67–88.

36. T.J. Huang, S.C. Chi, J.J. Lawler, "The Relationship Between Expatriates' Personality Traits and Their Adjustment to International Assignments," *The International Journal of Human Resource Management* (2005), 16(9), pp. 1656–1670.

37. F. van den Born, V. Peltokorpi, "Language Policies and Communication in Multinational Companies Alignment With Strategic Orientation and Human Resource Management Practices," *Journal of Business Communication* (2010), 47(2), pp. 97–118.

38. C. Dörrenbächer, J. Gammelgaard, F. McDonald, A. Stephan, H. Tüselmann, "Staffing Foreign Subsidiaries With Parent Country Nationals or Host Country Nationals? Insights From European Subsidiaries (No. 74)," Working Papers of the Institute of Management Berlin at the Berlin School of Economics and Law (HWR Berlin, 2013).

39. R. Maurer. "Emerging Markets Drive Global Talent Strategy Shift," http://www .shrm.org/hrdisciplines/global/articles/ pages/emerging-markets-global-talent- strategy.aspx) retrieved August 21, 2014).

40. N. Pisani, J.E. Ricart, "Offshoring and the Global Sourcing of Talent: Understanding the New Frontier of Internationalization," in *Proceedings of 2nd Annual Offshoring Research Network Conference and Workshop* (Philadelphia, PA: 2008).

41. http://www.numbeo.com/cost- of-living/city_result.jsp?country=Singapore &city=Singapore&displayCurrency= USD (retrieved August 23, 2014).

42. G.K. Stahl, M.Y. Brannen, "Building Cross-Cultural Leadership Competence: An Interview With Carlos Ghosn," *Academy of Management Learning & Education* (2013), 12(3), pp. 494–502.

43. http://www.shrm.org/education/ hreducation/documents/international_hrm_ presentation.pptx (retrieved August 23, 2014).

44. R.L. Minter, "Preparation of Expatriates for Global Assignments: Revisited," *Journal of Diversity Management* (2011), 3(2), pp. 37–42.

45. N. Cole, K. Nesbeth, "Why Do International Assignments Fail? The Expatriate Families Speak," *International Studies of Management and Organization* (2014), 44(3).

46. K. van der Zee, J.P. van Oudenhoven, "Culture Shock or Challenge? The Role of Personality as a Determinant of Intercultural Competence," *Journal of Cross- Cultural Psychology* (2013), 44(6), pp. 928–940.

47. http://www.shrm.org/education/ hreducation/documents/international_hrm_ presentation.pptx (retrieved August 23, 2014).

48. Society for Human Resource Management, "Repatriation: How Can My Company Best Retain Repatriated Employees?" http://www.shrm.org/ templatestools/hrqa/pages/ howcanmycompanybestretainrepa

triatedemployees.aspx (retrieved August 23, 2014).

49. C. Bailey, L. Dragoni, "Repatriation After Global Assignments: Current HR Practices and Suggestions for Ensuring Successful Repatriation," *People & Strategy Journal* (2013), 36(1), pp. 48–57.

50. T. Shelton, "Global Compensation Strategies: Managing and Administering Split Pay for an Expatriate Workforce," *Compensation and Benefits Review* (Jan/ Feb 2008), 40, pp. 56–60.

51. ORC Worldwide, *2006 Worldwide Survey of International Assignment Policies and Practices,* (New York, NY: ORC, 2007).

52. Society for Human Resource Management, "'Global: Expatriate': How Should We Compensate an Employee on a Foreign Assignment?" (December 11, 2012), http://www.shrm.org/templatestools/ hrqa/pages/howshould wecompensate anemployeeonaforeign assignment.aspx.

53. K.Y. Ng, L.V. Dyne, S. Ang, "From Experience to Experiential Learning: Cultural Intelligence as a Learning Capability for Global Leader Development," *Academy of Management Learning & Education* (2009), 8(1), pp. 511–526.

54. C. Rose, "Charlie Rose Talks to Mike Duke," *Businessweek* (December 2–6, 2010), p. 30.

55. "Work on Your Winning Strategy," *Global Management Consultancy Hay Group* (2010).

56. M. Segalla, D. Rouzies, M. Besson, B. Weitz, "A Cross-National Investigation of Incentive Sales Compensation," *International Journal of Research in Marketing* (2006), 23(4), pp. 419–433.

57. S. Fong, M. Shaffer, "The Dimensionality and Determinants of Pay Satisfaction: A Cross-Cultural Investigation of a Group Incentive Plan," *International Journal of Human Resource Management* (2003), 14(4), pp. 559–580.

58. http://www.metlife.com/assets/ institutional/services/insights-and-tools/ ebts/intl-ebts/intl-ebts.pdf (retrieved July 12, 2011).

59. Ibid.

60. Ibid.

61. http://www.forbes.com/sites/ johnkotter/2013/04/03/how-to-lead- through-business-disruption/ (retrieved August 24, 2014).

62. E. Kelly, *Business Trends 2014: Navigating the Next Wave of Globalization* (Westlake, TX: Deloitte University Press, 2014), p.6, http://dupress.com/periodical/ trends/business-trends-2014/?id=us: el:dc:bt14:awa.

63. Ibid. p. 3.

64. http://www.bcg.com/media/ pressreleasedetails.aspx?id=tcm:12-1449 44 (retrieved August 24, 2014).

65. C. Bailey, L. Dragoni, "Repatriation After Global Assignments: Current HR Practices and Suggestions for Ensuring Successful Repatriation," *People & Strategy Journal* (2013), 36(1), pp. 48–57.

66. http://www.wikipedia.com (retrieved May 19, 2011).

67. D. Roberts, "A New Labor Movement Is Born in China," *Businessweek* (June 14–20, 2010), pp. 7–8.

68. http://www.wharton.universia.net/index.cfm?fa=viewArticle&id=1349&language=english (retrieved May 11, 2011).

69. "Brazil: Labor Relations," *TozziniFriere Advogados* (2007), p. 1.

70. J. Almeida, *Brazil in Focus* (New York, NY: Nova Science, 2008), pp. 124–125.

71. "75% of Employers Expect Worse Labor Relations in 2011," *The Korea Times* (December 19, 2010), http://www.koreatimes.co.kr/www/news/nation/nation_view.asp?newsIdx=78249&categoryCode=113 Korea Times (retrieved May 11, 2011).

72. "Outlook for Industrial Relations After Allowing of Union Pluralism," *Labor in Focus* (February 7, 2011), p. 1.

73. http://www.eurofound.europa.eu/eiro/studies/tn0901028S/cz0901029q.htm (retrieved May 12, 2011).

74. Ibid.

75. A. Gregory, S. Milner, "Trade Unions and Work-Life Balance: Changing Times in France and the UK?" *British Journal of Industrial Relations* (March 2009), 47(1), pp. 122–146.

76. Hoover's Inc. *HSBC Holdings PLC* [Hoover's company records: In-depth records] (2014). Retrieved July 30, 2014, from Long Island University Academic Database.

77. The JobCrowd, *HSBC Bank PLC Job Reviews*. Retrieved August 4, 2014, from http://www.thejobcrowd.com/employer/hsbc-bank-plc/overview/.

78. PayScale, *Average Salary for HSBC Employees*. Retrieved August 4, 2014, from http://www.payscale.com/research/US/Employer=HSBC/Salary.

79. HSBC, *Benefits and Rewards*. Retrieved August 4, 2014, from http://www.us.hsbc.com/1/2/home/about/careers/benefits-rewards/.

80. ECA International, *Case Study: HSBC; Design and Implementation of a Custom Salary Management Programme*. Retrieved July 30, 2014, from http://www.eca-international.com/about_eca/our_clients/case_study__hsbc.

81. ECA International, *What We Do*. Retrieved July 30, 2014, from http://www.eca-international.com/about_eca/what_we_do.

82. ECA International, *Case Study: HSBC; Design and Implementation of a Custom Salary Management Programme*. Retrieved July 30, 2014, from http://www.eca-international.com/about_eca/our_clients/case_study__hsbc.

83. Marimari.com, *Singapore: General Information*. Retrieved August 4, 2014, from http://www.marimari.com/content/singapore/general_info/main.html.

84. Marimari.com, *Singapore: Shopping*. Retrieved August 4, 2014, from http://www.marimari.com/content/singapore/shopping/main.html.

85. Jurong Point, *Jurong Point Shopping Centre: Singapore's Largest Suburban Life Style Paradise!* Retrieved August 4, 2014, from http://www.jurongpoint.com.sg/corporate/.

86. S. V. Selvaretnam, *At Your Service*. Retrieved from http://www.hrmasia.com/case-studies/at-your-service/185525/.

··· Index

SAGE researchmethods

The essential online tool for researchers from the world's leading methods publisher

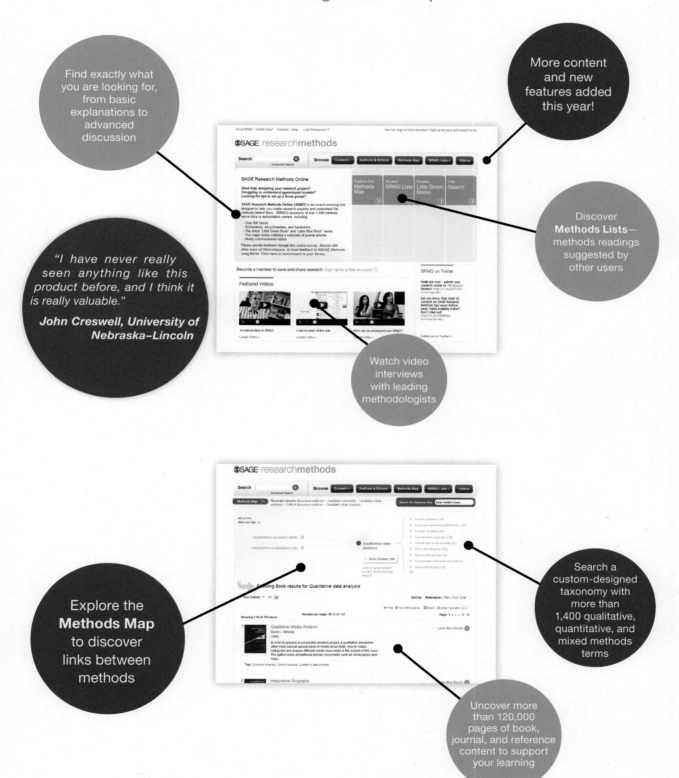

Find exactly what you are looking for, from basic explanations to advanced discussion

More content and new features added this year!

"I have never really seen anything like this product before, and I think it is really valuable."

John Creswell, University of Nebraska–Lincoln

Discover **Methods Lists**— methods readings suggested by other users

Watch video interviews with leading methodologists

Explore the **Methods Map** to discover links between methods

Search a custom-designed taxonomy with more than 1,400 qualitative, quantitative, and mixed methods terms

Uncover more than 120,000 pages of book, journal, and reference content to support your learning

Find out more at
www.sageresearchmethods.com